THE NATIONAL ROLL OF THE GREAT WAR.

The National Roll of the Great War

One of the most sought-after sets of reference books of the First World War is the *National Roll of the Great War*. The National Publishing Company attempted, shortly after hostilities ceased, to compile a brief biography of as many participants in the War as possible. The vast majority of entries refer to combatants who survived the Great War and the *National Roll* is often the only source of information available. Fourteen volumes were completed on a regional basis; **the Naval & Military Press has compiled a fifteenth volume which contains an alphabetic index to the fourteen now republished volumes**.

The National Roll - complete 15 vol. set	ISBN: 1 847340 33 4	£285.00
Section I - London	ISBN: 1 847340 34 2	£22.00
Section II - London	ISBN: 1 847340 35 0	£22.00
Section III - London	ISBN: 1 847340 36 9	£22.00
Section IV - Southampton	ISBN: 1 847340 37 7	£22.00
Section V - Luton	ISBN: 1 847340 38 5	£22.00
Section VI - Birmingham	ISBN: 1 847340 39 3	£22.00
Section VII - London	ISBN: 1 847340 40 7	£22.00
Section VIII - Leeds	ISBN: 1 847340 41 5	£22.00
Section IX - Bradford	ISBN: 1 847340 42 3	£22.00
Section X - Portsmouth	ISBN: 1 847340 43 1	£22.00
Section XI - Manchester	ISBN: 1 847340 44 X	£22.00
Section XII - Bedford & Northampton	ISBN: 1 847340 45 8	£22.00
Section XIII - London	ISBN: 1 847340 46 6	£22.00
Section XIV - Salford	ISBN: 1 847340 47 4	£22.00
Section XV - Index to all 14 volumes	ISBN: 1 847340 48 2	£22.00

The Naval & Military Press Ltd

Unit 10, Ridgewood Industrial Park, Uckfield,
East Sussex, TN22 5QE, England
Tel: 01825 749494   Fax: 01825 765701
www.naval-military-press.com
www.military-genealogy.com

THE NATIONAL ROLL
OF THE GREAT WAR
1914-1918

CONTAINED WITHIN
THE PAGES OF THIS
VOLUME WILL BE
FOUND THE NAMES
AND RECORDS OF
SERVICE OF THOSE
WHO HELPED TO
SECURE VICTORY FOR
THE EMPIRE DURING
THE GREAT WAR OF
1914-1918.

THE
NAVAL &
MILITARY
PRESS LTD
2006

Published by

The Naval & Military Press Ltd

Unit 10, Ridgewood Industrial Park,

Uckfield, East Sussex,

TN22 5QE England

Tel: +44 (0) 1825 749494

Fax: +44 (0) 1825 765701

www.naval–military-press.com

www.military-genealogy.com

© The Naval & Military Press Ltd 2006

FOREWORD

WHEN we quietly consider what the Great War, with its gains and losses, its cares and anxieties, has taught us, we are at once struck by the splendid heroism of all who took part in it. Many by reason of special qualities of mind or soul stand out more prominently than the rest ; but the names and deeds of others, who toiled no less meritoriously are officially left unsung.

Yet it is well, if only for purely personal and family reasons, that there should be some abiding record of the self-sacrificing services of all men and women who answered their Country's call in her hour of need, and who, whether on land or sea, or in the air, in hospital, or camp, or workshop, were ready to lay down life itself, if need be, that Britain might live and Right prevail over Might.

It is for this reason primarily that the present " National Roll of the Great War " was projected. In the pages of this and of succeeding volumes will be found records of devotion and patriotism of which the individual, the family, and the nation have every reason to be proud.

The National Roll makes no claim to being a complete book of reference—in fact no such record could be compiled—but it may safely claim to supply a wonderful memorial of splendid services, truly worthy of the thankful remembrance of a grateful Empire.

To all who by their Faith and Courage helped to bring Victory to our arms, we dedicate this book.

THE EDITOR.

1, York Place,
Baker Street,
London, W.1

SECTION. 1.

A

ABBEY, W., Pte., Middx. Regt. & Labour Corps.
He joined early in 1916, and from August of that year until February, 1918, served on the Western Front, taking part in the battles of the Somme, Ypres, Cambrai and Le Cateau. He was discharged in February, 1918, holding the General Service and Victory Medals.
9, Milford Road, W. Ealing.   10042A.

ABBEY, C. S., Pte., 4th Middlesex Regt.
He enlisted on September 8th, 1914, and served on the Western Front from August 1916. He took part in the battles of the Somme and Cambrai, and was wounded. Killed in action on October 12th, 1918, and buried between Briastre and Le Cateau.
He was entitled to the General Service and Victory Medals.
9, Milford Road, W. Ealing.   10042B.

ABBOTT, E., Corporal, R.G.A.
He joined in November, 1916, and in the following year was sent to France, where he served through battles at Ypres and Amiens, and many important engagements; was twice wounded and gassed.
He holds the General Service and Victory Medals.
24, Galena Road, W.6.   11806/A.

ABBOTT, E. (Mrs.) Special War Worker.
She was engaged on doping work at an aeroplane factory for 18 months, where she did important duties.
24, Galena Road, W.6.   11806/B.

ABBOTT, A. H., Pte., The Queen's (Royal West Surrey Regt.)
He joined in 1915 and went to France in 1917, taking part in several engagements, and on September 28th, 1917, was killed by a shell.
He was entitled to the General Service and Victory Medals.
5, Chalgrove Road, Tottenham.   X18974.

ABBOTT, L. A., Pte., Royal Fusiliers.
He joined in 1915 and served on the Western Front until he was discharged in August 1919. He took part in the battles of Loos (where he was twice wounded), Ypres, and the Retreat and Advance of 1918.
He holds the 1914-15 Star, General Service and Victory Medals.
52, Half Acre Road, Hanwell.   12378.

ABBOTT, G. J., Sergeant, Royal Field Artillery.
He joined in April, 1915, and in the same year was sent to the Western Front, where he took part in many of the big battles, including the Marne, the Somme, Ypres, Cambrai and Menin Road.
He was awarded the Croix de Guerre for bravery in the Field, holds the 1914-15 Star, General Service and Victory Medals, and was demobilised in May, 1919.
49, Goodhall Street, Willesden Junction.   12721.

ABBOTT, O. C., A.B., R.N., H.M.S. " Centaur " and " Curacoa."
He joined on August 4th, 1914, and served with the Harwich Squadron at the battles of Jutland and Heligoland. Suffered in consequence of being torpedoed and mined, and was treated in hospital for neurasthenia before being demobilised in 1919.
Holds the 1914-15 Star, General Service and Victory Medals.
44, Wilson's Road, Hammersmith.   15856A.

ABBOTT, A. (Miss), Special War Worker.
She was employed on the District Railway from January, 1916, until February, 1919, as ticket collector, to release a man for the Army, and did valuable work for the Company.
44, Wilson's Road, Hammersmith, W.6.   15856/B.

ABBOTT, C. (Mrs.), Special War Worker.
From 1915 until 1919 she was employed at the Filling Factories at Park Royal, doing dangerous work in the T.N.T. Department.
83, Barret's Green Road, Harlesden.   13561/A.

ABBOTT, A. E., Stoker, Royal Navy.
He joined in January, 1917, and did much valuable patrol work in the North Sea until the cessation of hostilities. Was on board H.M.S. " Canopus " when she was sunk, and after being rescued served on H.M.S. " Skilful."
He was demobilised in January, 1919, and holds the General Service and Victory Medals.
24, Moselle Street, Tottenham.   X18371.

ABBOTT, C. G., Gnr., 7th Div. R.H.A. (R. Bty.).
He joined on November 13th, 1914, served through many engagements on the Western Front, and was wounded in action on September 2nd, 1916, which resulted in his death the following day.
He holds the General Service and Victory Medals.
94, Barry Road, Stonebridge Park, Harlesden.   15663B.

ABBOTT, J. (Mrs.), Special War Worker.
For over 4 years during the war was engaged as a cartridge examiner at the Park Royal Munition Works, Willesden, where she did valuable work.
94, Barry Road, Stonebridge Park, Harlesden.   15663A.

ABBOTT, J. H., Pte., 4th Essex Regiment.
He joined in 1915, and in the following year was sent to France, where, after having been severely wounded in the head, he was taken prisoner. During his captivity he suffered great hardships.
Holds the General Service and Victory Medals, and was demobilised in 1919.
83, Barret's Green Road, Harlesden.   13561/B.

ABEL, H. S., Rifleman, 53rd Rifle Brigade.
He joined in 1918, and served with the Army of Occupation in Germany until 1920, when he was demobilised.
100, Ilex Road, Willesden.   15948/A.

ABEL, R. J., Pte., 5th Bat. Ryl. West Kent Regt.
He joined in 1915, went to Palestine in 1916, and served throughout the campaign in the East with General Allenby.
He holds the General Service and Victory Medals, and was demobilised in 1919.
100, Ilex Road, Willesden.   15948/B.

ABERDEIN, C. E., Pte., 2/10th Middlesex Regt.
He joined on June 2nd, 1915, and served in Egypt and Palestine. He was wounded in March, 1917, at Gaza, and was killed in action at Jerusalem on December 21st in the same year.
He is entitled to the 1915 Star, General Service and Victory Medals.
128, Ealing Road, Brentford.   9302A.

ABERDEIN, E. A., Gunner, 13th Bty. R.F.A.
He enlisted on October 2nd, 1914, and served on the Western Front for 4 years. He was in action on the Somme and at Cambrai and many other places.
He holds the 1915 Star, General Service and Victory Medals, and was demobilised on March 6th, 1919.
128, Ealing Road, Brentford.   9302B.

ABERY, W. W., Sapper, Royal Engineers.
During his service, which extended from June, 1916, until January, 1919, he was stationed on the searchlights at anti-aircraft depots on the coast of England and Scotland.
He holds the General Service Medal.
3, Pember Road, Kensal Rise.   X18191.

ABIGAIL, S. H., Rifleman, Royal Irish Rifles.
He joined in 1915, and in the following year was sent to France, where he remained until 1919, during which time he took part in engagements at Ypres, Cambrai, Vimy Ridge and other battles.
He was demobilised in 1919, and holds the Victory and General Service Medals.
36, Lateward Road, Brentford. 9764.

ABLITT, W., Pte., Royal Army Service Corps.
He joined in December, 1909, and in 1914 was sent to France, where he remained until 1918. He was present at the retreat from Mons and in action in 1915 at Ypres and Loos.
He holds the 1914 Star, General Service and Victory Medals, and was demobilised on December 11th, 1919.
37, St. Martin's Road, Edmonton. 12979.

ABRAHAM, J., Sergeant, R.F.A.
He joined in September 1914, and saw active service on the Eastern and Western Fronts. He took part in the capture of Jerusalem, and in the battles of Gaza, Beer Sheba, Vimy Ridge and the Somme.
He was mentioned in Despatches, and holds the 1914-15 Star, the General Service and Victory Medals. He was demobilised in June, 1919.
97, Lawrence Road, South Ealing. 7971.

ABRAHART, W. G., Rflmn., London Irish Rifles
He enlisted in August, 1914, served on the Western Front and took part in the battles of Loos, Ypres, Arras, the Somme and Cambrai.
He was demobilised in July, 1919, holding the 1915 Star, the General Service and Victory Medals.
11, Worlidge Street, Hammersmith. 12587.

ACASON, F. C., Sapper, Royal Engineers.
He joined in November, 1916, and saw service in Italy and afterwards in France and Belgium. He took part in the battle of Ypres, and was wounded on the Menin Road on October 8th, 1918. During his service he acted as a despatch rider.
He was demobilised in November, 1919, holding the General Service and Victory Medals.
52, Strafford Road, Barnet. 6735.

ACUTT, A. G., Pte., 2nd Border Regiment.
He joined on October 4th, 1915, and served on the Western, Front, taking part in many engagements in the Ypres sector. While in action at Menin Road he was killed on October 26th, 1917.
He was entitled to the General Service and Victory Medals.
158, Purves Road, Kensal Rise. X18255.

ACUTT, J. E., Rflmn., 1/18th Lond. Irish Rifles.
He joined in October, 1915, and went to the Western Front, serving there until the cessation of hostilities.
He was demobilised in February, 1919, holding the General Service and Victory Medals.
42, Hanwell Road, Fulham. 18074/A.

ADAMS, B. W., Pte., 1st Essex, and 44th Batt. Royal Fusiliers.
He joined on February 2nd, 1915, served at the Dardanelles, in Egypt and France. He was in action on the Somme and at Ypres, &c.
He was demobilised on February 24th, 1919, holding the General Service and Victory Medals.
66, St. Joseph's Road, Lower Edmonton. 11583.

ADAMS, C., Gunner, Royal Field Artillery.
Joining in March, 1917, he saw active service on the Western Front. Was at Arras and Cambrai and went into Germany with the Army of Occupation.
He was demobilised in September, 1919, and holds the General Service and Victory Medals.
10, Marlborough Road, Bowes Park. 5772

ADAMS, C. E., Sergeant, R.A.M.C.
He served from January, 1916, to September, 1919, chiefly on the Eastern Front, where he acted as Sanitary Inspector at Salonica. In 1917 he fought through the offensive in Macedonia and was present at the great Salonica air raid., and took part in the final offensive in 1918.
He holds the General Service and Victory Medals.
2, Ardilaun Road, Highbury. B2217.

ADAMS, C. J., Pte., Royal Army Service Corps.
He joined on June 5th, 1917, was sent to France and later to Italy, where he was stationed at Cremona.
He was demobilised in March, 1919, holding the General Service and Victory Medals.
136, Lincoln Road, Ponders End. 11235.

ADAMS, C. R., Sergeant, 4th Dragoon Guards.
He joined in August, 1914, and in the same year was sent out to France, where he remained until 1917. He took part in engagements at Mons, Ypres, Arras and Neuve Chapelle, and other important battles. He suffered from shell shock, and was discharged on March 18th, 1917.
He holds the Mons Star, General Service and Victory Medals.
37, Lawn Gardens, Hanwell. 12277.

ADAMS, E., Pte., 9th Seaforth Highlanders.
He joined in May, 1915, and saw active service in France. He took part in many engagements, and was killed at the Menin Gate on April 10th, 1917.
He was entitled to the General Service and Victory Medals.
12, Tintern Road, Wood Green. 7236.

ADAMS, W. J., Special War Worker.
From 1915 to 1917 he acted as a voluntary dispenser in the Hanworth Park Red Cross Hospital for Wounded Soldiers.
Woodcote, 37 Chiswick Lane, Chiswick. 5619/B.

ADAMS, E. F., C.Q.M.S.,5th Wilts.Regt.& M.G.C.
He joined in September, 1914, and saw much active service in the Dardanelles and in Mesopotamia.
He holds the 1914-15 Star, General Service and Victory Medals, and was demobilised in October, 1919.
15, Lefroy Road, W.12 8507A.

ADAMS, F. (Mrs.), Special War Worker.
During the war she was engaged upon important munition work at Messrs. Waring & Gillows, for which she was highly commended.
12, Percy Road, Shepherd's Bush, W. 9631A.

ADAMS, H. J. L., Special War Worker.
During the war he was engaged on the manufacture of aeroplanes at Messrs. Davidson's, Hammersmith Road, W., from whence he was transferred to the Aeronautical Inspection Department at Newcastle and later to Messrs. Blake's, Fulham, as Inspector of Aeroplanes.
12, Percy Road, Shepherd's Bush. 9631/B.

ADAMS, F. H., Lce.-Cpl., 8th The Queen's (Royal West Surrey Regiment).
He joined in May, 1916, and in the following year was sent to France, where he took part in several engagements. He was killed in action on March 26th, 1918, near Cambrai in the last Great Advance.
He was entitled to the General Service and Victory Medals.
71, Overstone Road, Hammersmith. 11173.

ADAMS, J. A., Driver, Royal Field Artillery.
He joined in February, 1916, and served in Italy, France and Germany.
He holds the General Service and Victory Medals, and was demobilised in September, 1919.
16, Olinda Road, N.16 7290A.

ADAMS, J. E., Pte., 4th Royal Fusiliers.
He joined on March 1st, 1917, and during his service in France took part in several battles, including Arras, where he was wounded.
He was discharged on November 8th, 1918, and holds the General Service and Victory Medals.
58, Lorenco Road, White Hart Lane, Tottenham. X18395.

ADAMS, T., Pte., Northampton Regiment and Labour Corps.
He joined in 1917, served on the Western Front, and took part in engagements on the Somme, Arras, Amiens, Lille and other places, including the final Advance of 1918.
He holds the Victory and General Service Medals, and was demobilised in 1919.
2, Gayford Road, Shepherd's Bush. 9106A.

ADAMS, J. (M.M.), Lce.-Cpl., 9th Batt. Ryl. Fus.
He enlisted in June, 1915, and served on the Western Front. He was reported missing on November 30th, 1917, after being wounded at the battle of Cambrai. He is supposed to have been taken prisoner, but has not been heard of since.
He was awarded Military Medal and is also entitled to the General Service and Victory Medals.
17, Pope's Lane, S. Ealing. 9040.

ADAMS, G. A., Corporal, Royal Engineers.
He joined on December 27th, 1916, and was demobilised on April 20th, 1919, during which period he saw active service in France.
He holds the General Service and Victory Medals.
36, Coleraine Road, Hornsey. 7136.

ADAMS, H. J., Sergeant-Observer, R.A.F.
He joined in December, 1917, and was engaged on special duties in England on coast patrol. He was in two aeroplane smashes.
He holds the General Service Medal, and was demobilised in February, 1920.
39, Glenhurst Road, Brentford. 8422A.

ADAMS, S. H., Pte., 23rd & 20th Middx. Regt.
He joined in December, 1915, and served long on the Western Front. He took part in many battles, and was wounded in September, 1916, in both thighs. He was taken prisoner on the Somme in April, 1918, and was again wounded in both thighs.
He holds the General Service and Victory Medals, and was demobilised in March, 1919.
39, Glenhurst Road, Brentford. 8422/B.

ADAMS, E. A. (Mrs.), Special War Worker.
From 1914 to 1918 she was President of the Chiswick Branch of Queen Mary's Needlework Guild and of the Chiswick branch of the Red Cross Society Central Work Rooms, which made bandages and garments entirely free of charge. Her sixty workers made 33,000 articles during the war.
Woodcote, 37, Chiswick Lane, Chiswick. 5619A.

ADAMS, A., Pte., London Scottish.
He joined in May, 1915, saw considerable active service in France, and was demobilised in September, 1917, holding the General Service and Victory Medals.
Lynton, Meadowcroft Road, Palmer's Green, N. 6495.

ADAMS, A. F. (Miss), Section Leader, W.R.A.F.
She joined in November, 1918, and served as Clerk and Typist at Earl's Court.
She was demobilised in November, 1919, and was highly commended for her work.
71, Garvan Road, Fulham. 14830B.

ADAMS, A. H., Pte., Coldstream Guards.
He joined in 1914 and served on the Western Front, taking part in the battles of Loos and Fleuris, and was wounded in 1916.
He returned home and was finally discharged in 1918, holding the 1914-15 Star, the General Service and Victory Medals.
96, Sheldon Road, Upper Edmonton. X17463.

ADAMS, D. J., Special War Worker
Was employed at Park Royal Munition Factory for 3 years, engaged in the examination of cartridges, &c., and duties of an important nature.
126, Barry Road, Stonebridge Park, Harlesden. 15664.

ADAMS, E., Gunner, Royal Garrison Artillery.
He joined in 1915, went to Salonica in the same year, and served there until February, 1919, when he was demobilised.
He holds the General Service and Victory Medals.
8, Sunnyside Road East, Lower Edmonton. 14561.

ADAMS, E. G., 1st Class Stoker, R.N., H.M.S. "Nonsuch."
He joined the Navy in January, 1916, and served with the Grand Fleet in the North Sea, was also engaged in Mine sweeping.
He was discharged in February, 1919 and holds the General Service and Victory Medals.
104, Sheldon Road, Upper Edmonton. X17450.

ADAMS, E. G., Pte., Suffolk Regiment.
Joined in 1915, and was sent to Salonica the following year. He received injuries whilst being conveyed to hospital with malaria fever, which necessitated his discharge in 1918.
Medals—General Service and Victory.
40, Maldon Road, Lower Edmonton. 15783B.

ADAMS, E. T., Pte., Royal Army Service Corps.
He joined in August, 1914, and served on the Western Front, taking part in the battles of Mons, the Somme, Ypres, Bullecourt and many other engagements. For 15 months he was engaged in the transport of rations and ammunition to the lines. He also served with the Royal Inniskilling Fusiliers. Was once wounded, and in January, 1919, was demobilised, holding the 1914 Star, General Service and Victory Medals.
123, Durban Road, Tottenham. X17962B.

ADAMS, F. J., Sergeant, 2/7th Middlesex Regt.
He joined on August 4th, 1914, served in Egypt during 1915, and later in France.
He was demobilised in March, 1919, and holds the 1915 Star, General Service and Victory Medals.
66, Somerset Road, Edmonton. 16859.

ADAMS, G. W., Pte., Royal Welsh Fusiliers.
He joined in February, 1916, and served in all engagements of his regiment in France until 1919, when he was demobilised.
He holds the General Service and Victory Medals.
37, Leamore Street, Hammersmith. 12611/A.

ADAMS, R. (Mrs.), Special War Worker.
For 2 years she was employed at Messrs. Gwynne's Foundry, Hammersmith, engaged in making pumping machinery for war ships, for which she was highly commended.
37, Leamore Street, Hammersmith. 12611/B.

ADAMS, J., Pte., Devonshire Regiment
He joined on November 1st, 1915, was sent to France in the following year, and was killed in action on the Somme on July 1st, 1916, having previously taken part in several other engagements.
Entitled to the General Service and Victory Medals.
54a, Deacon Road, Willesden. 16735.

ADAMS, J. T., Cpl., Royal Army Service Corps.
He was serving on the outbreak of hostilities, and went to the Western Front, where he took part in the retreat from Mons and the battles of Arras and Cambrai.
He holds the 1914 Star, General Service and Victory Medals, and was demobilised in March, 1919.
25, Leopold Road, Willesden. 14743.

ADAMS, J. T., Pte., Middlesex Regiment.
He joined in August, 1917, and served in all the engagements with his regiment on the Western Front, and was demobilised on October 22nd, 1919.
He holds the General Service and Victory Medals.
52, Raynham Avenue, Edmonton. (T)16482A.

ADAMS, J. W., Cpl., Notts. and Derby Regiment.
He joined in 1917, and during his service on the Western Front took part in the battles of the Somme, Armentieres, Ypres and Cambrai, and was 3 times wounded.
In 1919 he was demobilised, and holds the General Service and Victory Medals.
5, Lurgan Avenue, Hammersmith. 13447.

ADAMS, E. (Mrs.), Special War Worker.
During the war this lady did important munition work at Messrs. Waring & Gillow's factory at Shepherd's Bush, for which she was commended.
2, Gayford Road, Shepherd's Bush, W. 9106/C.

ADAMS, W., C.S.M., 1st London Regiment.
He joined in October, 1914, and served in France, taking part in many engagements and being wounded in the battle of Bullecourt.
He was discharged in January, 1918, and holds the General Service and Victory Medals.
8, Fotheringham Road, Enfield. 8735.

ADAMS, W. C., Sapper, Royal Engineers.
He enlisted in November, 1914, served on the Western Front from January 6th, 1915, until he was demobilised on November 20th, 1918, and took part in the battles of Ypres and Kemmel.
He holds the 1914-15 Star, General Service and Victory Medals.
34, Cardross Street, Hammersmith. 11516.

ADAMS, M. (Miss), Special War Worker.
During the war she was engaged on work of national importance at the Ministry of Food, Westminister, for which she was highly commended.
4, Humbolt Mansions, Lillie Road, Fulham. X18884.

ADAMS, W., Pte., Middlesex Regt. and R.E.
He joined in April, 1916, and in the following December went to Salonica, where he remained until 1919. He took part in many engagements, and holds the General Service and Victory Medals.
Discharged in July, 1919, suffering from malaria contracted on service.
13, Parkfield Road, Willesden. X17415.

ADAMS, W., 2nd Air Mechanic, Royal Air Force.
He joined in May, 1918, served on the Western Front, and was in action at Lille, Tournai and other places.
He was demobilised in November, 1919, and holds the General Service and Victory Medals.
183, Chapter Road, Willesden. X17207A.

ADAMS, W. T., Sapper, Royal Engineers.
He joined in July, 1915, and during his service on the Western Front was buried by a shell at Neuve Chapelle, and injured whilst being unearthed.
He was demobilised in January, 1919, and holds the 1914-15 Star, General Service and Victory Medals.
42, Brett Road, Harlesden. 15692.

ADAMSON, E. T. (Miss), Special War Worker.
Throughout the war this lady did good work in connection with the Soldiers' and Sailors' Families' Association. In connection with the Red Cross she made comforts for the soldiers in London and Scotland.
64, Durley Road, Stamford Hill. 5715/B.

ADAMSON, K. (Miss), Special War Worker.
During the war this lady, in connection with the Red Cross, made comforts of all kinds for the soldiers in London and Scotland.
64, Durley Road, Stamford Hill. 5715/A.

ADAMSON, S., A.B., R.N., H.M.S. "Weymouth."
He joined in March, 1913, and served with the Italian Fleet, taking part in the bombardment of Durazzo.
He holds the 1914 Star, General Service and Victory Medals, and was demobilised July 30th, 1919.
91, Olinda Road, Stamford Hill. 6821.

ADCOCK, B. J., Corporal, 12th London Regt. (The Rangers).
He joined in August, 1914, and served in France at Armentieres, the Somme, Etaples, Cambrai, Fricourt, Delville Wood and many other places.
He was wounded, holds the 1914-15 Star, General Service and Victory Medals, and was demobilised in January, 1919.
28b, Percy Road, Shepherd's Bush. 9633.

ADDISON, C., Lance-Corporal, Middlesex Regt.
He joined in August, 1914, and saw active service in France, where he was wounded twice.
He was demobilised in September, 1918, and holds the 1914-15 Star, the General Service and Victory Medals.
23, Cumberton Road, Tottenham, N. 7645.

ADEY, T., Stoker, R.N., H.M.S. "General Wolfe."
He joined in 1914, and during the war served with the Grand Fleet in the North Sea and off the Belgian coast.
He was demobilised in 1919, holding the 1914 Star, the General Service and Victory Medals.
114, Kimberley Road, Upper Edmonton. 16791A.

ADKINS, A.'V., Pte., 10th Battalion The Queen's (Royal West Surrey Regiment).
He joined in February, 1917, and after service in France and Belgium, where he was wounded, he was discharged in March, 1918, holding the General Service and Victory Medals.
1, Marlborough Road, Bowes Park. 5781.

ADKINS, E. R., A.B., R.N., H.M.S. "Yarmouth."
He joined in 1917, and was serving on the above boat when she torpedoed and sank the German liner "Marrominia." The "Yarmouth" was also instrumental in capturing several other enemy vessels.
He was demobilised in 1919, and holds the General Service and Victory Medals.
75, Hazelbury Road, Edmonton. X17581.

ADLAM, J., Stoker, R.N., H.M.S. "Inflexible."
He joined in August, 1914, and served in the North Sea Flotilla until February, 1919, when he was demobilised, holding the 1914-15 Star, General Service and Victory Medals.
86, Adeney Road, Fulham. 15161.

AFFLECK, W., Rflmn., Civil Service Rifles.
He joined on July 23rd, 1918, and served in France until he was demobilised in August, 1919. During his service overseas he was in hospital with septic poisoning.
He holds the General Service and Victory Medals.
8, Wellesley Avenue, Hammersmith. 11570.

AGATE, P. J., Pte., 17th Royal Fusiliers.
He joined on January 13th, 1916, and was sent to France, where he remained for 3 years, and took part in engagements at Cambrai, Somme, Vimy Ridge. He was wounded twice, and demobilised on February 1st, 1919.
Holds Victory and General Service Medals.
13, Gladesmore Road, S. Tottenham. 6521.

AGATE, S. W., Despatch Rider, Royal Air Force.
He joined in June, 1917, and was sent to France, where he took part in engagements at Arras, St. Quentin, Ypres and the Somme.
He was demobilised in January, 1919, and holds the General Service and Victory Medals.
31, Avondale Road, Palmer's Green. 6337.

AGATE, G. T., Corporal, 12th Middlesex Regt., and 2/2nd London Regt.
He joined on August 4th, 1914, at 17 years of age, and went to the Western Front the following year. He took part in many engagements, including those of the Somme, Arras, Ypres, and was killed in action in the great Retreat in 1918.
Entitled to the 1914-15 Star, General Service and Victory, Medals.
2, Mayo Road, Willesden. 15100.

AGATE, W., Sapper, Royal Engineers.
He joined on May 4th, 1917, and saw service in Egypt, Jerusalem, and other places. He was principally engaged on railway construction.
He holds the General Service and Victory Medals, and was demobilised in March, 1919.
10, Mayo Road, Willesden. 15098.

AGGUS, A., Corporal, 1st Middlesex Regiment.
He joined in October, 1916, was sent to France in the following January, and was twice wounded in 1917 (in the ankle at the battle of Arras, and in the right shoulder at Passchendaele).
He was demobilised in May, 1919, and holds the General Service and Victory Medals.
37, Bruce Castle Road, Tottenham. X18545.

AGONBAR, F. G., Corporal, King's Royal Rifles.
He joined in October, 1914, and was sent to France early in 1915, serving on many fronts. He was gassed twice, and was demobilised in January, 1919, holding the 1914-15 Star, the General Service and Victory Medals.
7, Reckitt Road, Chiswick. 5604.

AIERS, M. (Miss), Special War Worker.
This lady was employed at No. 7 Filling Factory at Hayes on important munition work from May, 1916, until December, 1918, for which she was highly commended.
2, Weston Road, Chiswick. 6019.

AINSWORTH, W. H., Pte., Northamptonshire Regiment.
He joined in 1915, and served for a considerable time on the Western Front, taking part in many engagements.
He obtained his discharge in February, 1918, and holds the General Service and Victory Medals.
15, St. Margaret's Road, Willesden. X17747.

AINSWORTH, E. W., Special War Worker.
He was employed for the duration of war at Waring & Gillows Aircraft Factory, Hammersmith, where he did valuable work on the output of war material.
58, Bradmore Park Road, Hammersmith. 10696A.

AINSWORTH, P. A., Pte., 2/10th Middx. Rgt.
He enlisted in 1915, served in Gallipoli and Palestine, and took part in the capture of Beer Sheba.
He was discharged as medically unfit in 1919, and holds the 1914-15 Star, General Service and Victory Medals.
58, Bradmore Park Road, Hammersmith. 10696B.

AIRD, W. J., Pte., 13th London Regiment (Kensington Battalion).
He joined in December, 1914, and served on the Western Front, Salonica, Egypt and Palestine. He took part in the battle of the Somme and the capture of Jerusalem.
He holds the General Service and Victory Medals, and was demobilised in June, 1919.
110, Shakespeare Road, Acton. 7198A.

AIRD, A. A., Gunner, Royal Field Artillery.
He joined in December, 1914, and saw much service on the Western Front. He took part in engagements at the Somme, Arras, Ypres, Bethune, St. Quentin, Vimy Ridge and Loos.
He holds the 1915 Star, General Service and Victory Medals, and was demobilised in June, 1919.
110, Shakespeare Road, Acton. 7198B.

AIRD, H. W., Pte., Royal West Kent Regiment.
He joined in September, 1914, and was sent to Mesopotamia in 1916. He contracted fever at Basra and died in May, 1916.
He was entitled to the General Service and Victory Medals.
110, Shakespeare Road, Acton. 7198C.

AIRS, A. J., Driver, Royal Field Artillery.
He joined in June, 1915, and during his service on the Western Front took part in the battles of Neuve Chapelle, Arras, Amiens, Armentieres, Ypres, and Bullecourt, and was twice wounded in action on the Somme.
He holds the 1914-15 Star, General Service and Victory Medals, and was demobilised in 1919.
48, Humbolt Road, Fulham. 15299.

AISH, W. (Mrs.), Special War Worker.
She was employed at Messrs. Napier's on Aircraft work
from 1915 till 1918, on the night shift, and was working at
very high pressure. She did very valuable work.
6, Bonheur Road, Chiswick, W. 7663.

AKAM, S. H., Pte., R.A.S.C. (M.T.).
He joined in 1916, and saw considerable active service in
Egypt.
He was demobilised in August, 1919, and holds the General
Service and Victory Medals.
85, Brooke Road, Stoke Newington, N. 7592B.

**AKERMAN, V. A., 1st Class Signaller, The Queen's
(Royal West Surrey Regiment).**
Joining in May, 1916, he put in over 3 years' active service in
France, where he took part in many engagements and was
twice wounded.
He was demobilised in November, 1919, and holds the General
Service and Victory Medals.
30, Evesham Road, New Southgate. 5153.

AKERMAN, W., Sergeant, Royal Field Artillery.
He joined in May, 1915, and served on the Western Front
from January of the following year, taking part in many
battles, including the Somme, Ypres and Cambrai.
He was demobilised in January, 1919, holding the General
Service and Victory Medals.
78, Franklyn Road, Willesden. 16322.

ALABASTER, J., Pte., R.A.S.C.
He joined in September, 1915, and saw active service in
France, from 1916 until 1918, when he was demobilised.
He holds the General Service and Victory Medals.
33, Gibson Gardens, N.16. 7724.

ALABASTER, W. P., Bombardier, R.F.A.
He joined on September 4th, 1914, and saw active service
in France, taking part in engagements at the Somme and
other battle fronts. He was wounded twice and gassed once,
and was demobilised on March 13th, 1919.
He holds the 1914-15 Star, General Service and Victory
Medals.
26, Wargrave Avenue, S. Tottenham. 6512.

ALABASTER, W. H., Gunner, R.F.A.
He joined on August 10th, 1915, and served on the Western
Front, taking part in the battles of Loos, the Somme, Messines,
Ypres, Croisilles, Epehy, Merville, Arras, La Bassée and
Tournai.
On May 6th, 1919, he was demobilised, and holds the 1915
Star, General Service and Victory Medals.
7, Mayo Road, Willesden. 15125.

ALAND, S. J., Corporal, Royal Air Force.
He joined in 1916, and was stationed at Dover, Wendover
and elsewhere, and was employed in the Repair Section of
the Aircraft Workshops.
He was demobilised in January, 1919, and holds the General
Service Medal.
9, Kilmaine Road, Fulham, S.W.6 TX18860/C.

**ALAND, A. W., Pte., 13th London Regt.
(Kensington Battalion).**
He joined on August 4th, 1914, and was sent to the Western
Front. He was killed in action at Neuve Chapelle on
March 14th, 1915, when only 16½ years of age.
He was entitled to the 1914-15 Star, General Service and
Victory Medals.
9, Kilmaine Road, Fulham, S.W.6 TX18860/B.

ALAND, J. D., Sergeant, Machine Gun Corps.
He was in the Territorials when war was declared, and was
mobilised on August 4th, 1914, and sent to the Western
Front. He served in many engagements in France, and
was invalided home. After treatment he returned to
France and served in the Labour Corps, and was demobilised
in January, 1919.
He holds the 1914-15 Star, General Service and Victory
Medals.
9, Kilmaine Road, Fulham, S.W.6 TX18860/A.

ALAWAY, C. F., Pte., 5th Royal Fusiliers.
He joined in January, 1916, and served on the Western Front.
Whilst on active service, near Beaumont Hamel, he contracted
nephritis, from which he died.
He was entitled to the General Service and Victory Medals.
18, Cowper Road, Acton. 7515B.

ALAWAY, R. A., Pte., 5th Royal Fusiliers.
He joined in January, 1916, and saw active service in France.
He took part in many important engagements and was
wounded on November 13th, 1916, at Beaumont Hamel.
He was demobilised in April, 1919, and holds the General
Service and Victory Medals.
18, Cowper Road, Acton. 7515A.

ALAWAY, C. E., Pte., Durham Light Infantry.
He joined in June, 1916, saw service in Salonica, and took
part in the Macedonian campaign.
He holds the General Service and Victory Medals, and was
demobilised in September, 1919.
134, Southfield Road, Bedford Park, W. 7544.

ALBERT, A. H., Driver, Royal Field Artillery.
He joined on August 7th, 1914, and was stationed at Salisbury and many other places in England.
He was demobilised in April, 1919.
142, Chapter Road, Willesden Green. X17368/A.

**ALBERT, A. H., Pte., Princess Patricia's Cana-
dian Light Infantry.**
He enlisted in 1914, served in France, taking part in many
engagements, including Ypres, the Somme and Vimy Ridge,
and was wounded four times. He was killed in action at
Passchendaele on November 10th, 1917.
Entitled to the 1914-15 Star, General Service and Victory
Medals.
142, Chapter Road, Willesden Green. X17368/B.

ALBERT, J. A., Gunner, Royal Field Artillery.
He enlisted in 1915, and whilst training at Shorncliffe was
killed during an air raid on August 29th, 1915.
142, Chapter Road, Willesden. X17368/C.

ALBERT, W. F., Gunner, Royal Field Artillery.
He joined in 1915, and was stationed at Shorncliffe, where
he was killed in the air raid on August 29th of the same
year.
142, Chapter Road, Willesden. X17368/D.

ALBERY, R. T., Pte., 8th East Lancs. Regt.
He joined on November 4th, 1914, and was on active service
in France from July, 1915. He took part in the battle of
the Somme and was mortally wounded there on July 15th,
1915, dying three days later.
He was entitled to the 1915 Star, General Service and Victory
Medals.
69, Fletcher Road, Acton Green. 6368.

ALBON, E., Gunner, Royal Field Artillery.
He joined in September, 1914, and during his five years' service
on the Western Front took part in the battles of Armentieres
and the Somme, and was twice wounded. He is now
demobilised.
Medals :—1914-15 Star, General Service and Victory.
15, Cedar Road, Edmonton. 14034.

ALBOROUGH, A. A., Pte., 22nd Manchester Rgt.
He joined on January 27th, 1917, was sent to the Western
Front in October, and served also in Italy, Austria and Egypt,
taking part in various engagements.
He was demobilised in January, 1920.
88, Churchill Road, Cricklewood. 16706/A.

ALBOROUGH, A. C., Staff-Sergeant, R.A.S.C.
He joined in January, 1915, was sent to France in January,
1916, took part in many engagements, and in 1917 was
invalided home suffering from throat trouble through
exposure.
He was demobilised in May, 1919, and holds the General
Service and Victory Medals.
88, Churchill Road, Cricklewood. 16706/B.

**ALBOROUGH, F. O., Corporal, The Buffs
(East Kent Regiment).**
He joined in 1916, served in France in the same year, and
was killed in action on the Somme in 1917.
Entitled to the General Service and Victory Medals.
3, Church Lane, Lower Edmonton. 15202.

ALBOROUGH, H. W., Gunner, R.F.A.
He joined in January, 1915, and in the following June was
sent to the Dardanelles. He also served in Egypt and
France, and was twice wounded in action.
He was demobilised in July, 1919, holding the General
Service and Victory Medals.
44, Beaconsfield Road, Willesden. 16328.

ALCORN, W. J., Private, Machine Gun Corps.
He joined in June, 1916, and fought in France in 1917-18
at Fleurbaix, Armentieres (where he was gassed), Passchendaele and Bailleul, where he was wounded.
He was demobilised in December, 1918, and holds the
General Service and Victory Medals.
12, Chase Road, Old Southgate. 5200.

ALDEN, H. G., Pte., R.A.S.C. (M.T.).
He joined in 1914, and was sent to France in November of
the same year, where he served over 4½ years. He was
engaged in all the battles on the Western Front till the
cessation of hostilities in 1918.
He was demobilised in May, 1919, and holds the 1914-15
Star, General Service and Victory Medals.
10, Holberton Gardens, College Park, Willesden, N.W.
X17558.

ALDEN, W. A., Gunner, Royal Field Artillery.
He joined in November, 1914, and died suddenly while training for service overseas on December 1st, 1915.
65, Hiley Road, Willesden, N.W.10   X18170.

ALDER, F., Sergeant, 13th London Regiment (Kensington Battalion).
He joined in 1914, and served on the Western Front for three years. During this period he took part in many important battles, including that of the Somme, was once wounded, and suffered from trench feet.
He holds the 1914–15 Star, General Service and Victory Medals, and was demobilised in February, 1919.
20, New Road, Brentford.   9742B.   9856.

ALDER, J. J., Sergeant-Major, Middlesex Regt.
After 21 years' service with the Military Police, he rejoined with the Middlesex Regiment in August, 1914. He was Sergeant-Major Instructor in physical training at Aldershot, and also in France, and whilst in the Service he died.
He was entitled to the General Service and Victory Medals.
5, Edinburgh Road, Hanwell.   1082/A.

ALDER, J., A.B., Royal Navy.
He joined in March, 1915, served on the "Hindustan" in the battle of Jutland, at the Dardanelles, and on H.M.S. "Furious" in the North Sea, India, Sierra Leone, and Italy. He holds the 1914–15 Star, General Service and Victory Medals. He also served on the destroyer H.M.S. "Sable."
5, Edinburgh Road, Hanwell.   10802/B.

ALDER, W., Gunner, Royal Field Artillery.
He joined on June 18th, 1915, was sent over to France on January 3rd, 1916, and was wounded by shrapnel at Bullecourt.
He was demobilised on February 21st, 1919, and holds the General Service and Victory Medals.
5, Travers Road, Old Southgate.   6714.

ALDER, F. H. (M.S.M.), R.S.M., King's Ryl. Rifles.
He joined on August 4th, 1914, went to France the same year, and took part in many battles, including those of Mons, Ypres and the Somme, and was wounded at Neuve Chapelle. He was awarded the Meritorious Service Medal for devotion to duty, holds the 1914 Star, General Service and Victory Medals, and was demobilised in February, 1919.
51, Guilsborough Road, Willesden.   15248.

ALDERMAN, E., Corporal, The Buffs (East Kent Regiment).
He joined on August 10th, 1914, and was on active service on the Western Front. He took part in battles at Mons and the Somme and was wounded twice.
He was discharged on December 9th, 1917, and holds the Mons Star, Victory and General Service Medals.
51, Kynaston Road, Enfield.   9187.

ALDERMAN, H., Gunner, R.G.A.
He joined in August, 1914, and during his service on the Western Front took part in the battles of Ypres (1915 and 1917) and that of Armentieres.
He holds the 1914–15 Star, General Service and Victory Medals, and was discharged in April, 1917.
52, Chauncey Street, Edmonton.   14261.

ALDERMAN, H. T., Driver, Royal Field Artillery.
He joined in January, 1916, saw active service in France on the Somme and at the battle of Ypres, and was wounded. He was demobilised in July, 1919, and holds the General Service and Victory Medals.
150, Durants Road, Ponders End.   10665.

ALDERMAN, W. T. G., Bombardier, R.F.A.
He joined on October 27th, 1914, went to France the same year, and was gassed at Loos on September 25th, 1915. He was discharged in April, 1916, holding the 1914–15 Star, General Service and Victory Medals.
72, Grosvenor Road, Edmonton.   12683.

ALDERTON, C., A.B., Royal Navy.
He joined on April 13th, 1915 and was on active service at sea until 1919, when he was demobilised.
He holds the Victory and General Service Medals.
41, Melina Road, W.12   10149.

ALDERTON, E., Rifleman, London Regt.
He joined on February 18th, 1915, and served on the Western Front, taking part in many engagements. On October 15th, 1916, he died from drinking poisoned water while on the Somme.
Entitled to the General Service and Victory Medals.
32, Deacon Road, Willesden.   16646.

ALDERTON, E., Gunner, Royal Marines.
He joined on February 6th, 1917, and was sent to France the same year. During his service he was on special duty at Zeebrugge and on the coast, and was present at several bombing raids.
He was demobilised in February, 1919, and holds the General Service and Victory Medals.
41, Barry Road, Stonebridge Park, Willesden.   14936.

ALDOUS, H. H., Lce.-Cpl., 6th Batt. M.G.C.
He enlisted in December, 1914, and served on the Western Front, where he took part in various engagements, including those of the Somme, Ypres and Cambrai; was wounded, and taken prisoner whilst conducting relief to his battalion. He was discharged in February, 1919, and holds the General Service and Victory Medals.
72, St. Dunstan's Road, Hammersmith.   13533.

ALDRIDGE, J. W., Corporal, 15th The Queen's (Royal West Surrey Regiment).
He joined in January, 1917, and served in France, where he took part in the engagements of Ypres, Arras, Lens, Loos, Bethune and Armentieres.
He was demobilised in November, 1919, and holds the General Service and Victory Medals.
5, Lavender Road, Enfield.   9560.

ALDRIDGE, K.M. (Miss), W.R.N.S. and W.R.A.F.
She joined on March 18th, 1918, and served as a 1st-class stewardess at Great Yarmouth, Dover and Kidbrooke. She was transferred from the W.R.N.S. to the W.R.A.F. on December 4th, 1918, and was discharged on December 4th, 1919.
5, Lavender Road, Enfield.   T10409.

ALDRIDGE, A. E., Pte., 5th Royal Sussex Regt.
He attested on October 7th, 1917, was called up for service on July 8th, 1918, and sent to the Italian front, where he took part in the fighting at Asiago Plateau and Trentino. He was demobilised on December 8th, 1919, and holds the General Service and Victory Medals.
5, Lavender Road, Enfield.   T10408.

ALDRIDGE, M. (Miss), Forewoman Women's Legion, and Q.M.A.A.C.
She joined in June, 1917, and served for 12 months in the Officers' Mess at Borden, at the end of which period she was promoted to non-commissioned rank. She then served as a forewoman clerk with the 4th Reserve Dragoons at Aldershot and later at Catterick.
She was discharged on October 12, 1919.   T10407.
5, Lavender Road, Enfield.

ALDRIDGE, D. (Miss), Forewoman, Women's Legion, and Q.M.A.A.C.
She joined in January, 1917, served at the Enteric Depot, Woldingham, Surrey, was sent to Rouen in June, 1917, where she served for two years with Q.M.A.A.C., and went to Boulogne in September, 1919, with the N.A.C.B.
She holds the General Service and Victory Medals.
5, Lavender Road, Enfield.   T10410.

ALDRIDGE, J. A., Gunner, R.G.A.
He joined in October, 1914, and served on the Western Front from January, 1915, taking part in the battles of Ypres and the Somme.
He was demobilised in February, 1919, and holds the 1914–15 Star, the General Service and Victory Medals.
16, Bridgman Road, Chiswick, W.   6267.

ALDRIDGE, W. F., Driver, R.A.S.C.
He joined on April 13th, 1916, and was retained on transport duty. He served in the R.A.S.C. for nearly three years, and was demobilised on February 28th, 1919.
178, Villiers Road, Willesden, N.W.   T.17328/A.

ALDRIDGE, R., Pte., 4th Middlesex Regiment.
He joined in March, 1912, was mobilised in August, 1914, and sent to the Western Front. He fought in the battle of Mons, where he was wounded and taken prisoner on August 23rd, 1914. He was in captivity in Germany for 4½ years, and after his release on the cessation of hostilities was discharged from the Army on April 29th, 1919.
He holds the 1914 Star, General Service and Victory Medals.
178, Villiers Road, Willesden, N.W.   T.17328/B.

ALEFOUNDER, J. W., Pte., Royal Fusiliers.
He joined in 1914, went to France in 1917, and took part in many engagements.
He holds the General Service and Victory Medals and was demobilised in 1919.
11, Durham Road, Lower Edmonton.   14874.

ALEXANDER, C., Pte., Dorset Regiment.
He joined in 1917, and served in France until 1919, when he
was demobilised. He took part in many engagements, and
holds the General Service and Victory Medals.
76, Rayleigh Road, W.14   12642/C.

ALEXANDER, W., Pte., Royal Fusiliers.
He joined in 1914, and served in France until 1917, when
he was killed in action at the battle of the Somme on
November 26th.
Entitled to the 1914–15 Star, General Service and Victory
Medals.
76, Rayleigh Road, W.14   12642/A.

ALEXANDER, A., Special War Worker.
He was engaged on work of National importance for 15
months, and was afterwards employed at one of the London
Military Hospitals as storekeeper.
76, Rayleigh Road, W.14   12642/B.

ALEXANDER, M., Corporal, Royal Air Force.
He joined in January, 1917, and served through the whole
war in the Photographic Section.
He was demobilised on March 3rd, 1919, and holds the
General Service Medal.
13, Graham Road, Chiswick.   6584.

ALEXANDER, F. C., Driver, R.F.A.
He joined in November, 1915, and served until March, 1920,
when he was demobilised.
32, Felixstowe Road, Edmonton.   15277.

**ALEXANDER, G., Corporal, Royal Air Force
(late Royal Naval Air Service).**
He joined on August 4th, 1914, and served on the Western
Front, being in action at Antwerp, Mons, Verdun and various
other places. During his campaign he was wounded once
and gassed. He had previously enlisted in 1909, and is
still serving.
He holds the 1914–15 Star, the General Service and Victory
Medals.
26, Everington Street, W.6   13973.

ALEXANDER, H., Gunner, R.F.A.
He joined in August, 1914, proceeded to France the same year,
and served at Mons, Arras and Cambrai, and was wounded
once.
He holds the Mons Star, General Service and Victory Medals,
and was demobilised in February, 1919.
6, Ascot Road, Edmonton.   15185.

ALEXANDER, J. L., Pte., Royal West Kent Regt.
He joined on May 17th, 1915, and died at Chatham on June
18th, 1918, from wounds received in action whilst in France.
Entitled to the General Service and Victory Medals.
1, Musard Road, Fulham.   15738.

ALEXANDER, P. F., Pte., Machine Gun Corps.
He was in the Army on the outbreak of hostilities and went
to France in 1914. He took part in the retreat from Mons.
In 1915 he was drafted to Salonica, where he remained until
his demobilisation in 1919. He took part in various engagements, and was wounded.
He holds the Mons Star, General Service and Victory Medals.
43, Felixstowe Road, Willesden, N.W.10   X17759.

ALEY, W. A., Pte., Royal Fusiliers.
He joined on March 20th, 1918, at the age of 18, served with
the army of occupation in Germany until demobilised in
March, 1920.
15, Rays Road, Lower Edmonton   15359.

ALFORD, A. O., Corporal, Grenadier Guards.
He joined in March, 1915, and served for two years on the
Western Front. After the taking of Fontaine Village he
was wounded, and reported missing at the battle of Cambrai
in 1917.
Entitled to the 1915 Star, General Service and Victory
Medals.
43, Berry Street, Willesden.   15410

ALLAN, D., Gunner, " J " Battery, R.H.A.
Regular soldier, served on the Western Front, 1914–19,
taking part in the following engagements :—Ypres, Passchendaele, Cambrai, Loos, Vimy Ridge, &c.
Holds the 1914–15 Star, General Service and Victory Medals,
and was demobilised in May, 1919.
25, Humbolt Road, Fulham   15156.

ALLAN, G. A., Pte., 17th Batt. Royal Fusiliers.
He joined on June 26th, 1918, at the age of 18, and saw active
service in France until the cessation of hostilities.
He holds the General Service and Victory Medals, and was
demobilised in April, 1920.
25, Humbolt Road, Fulham.   15157.

ALLAN, W., Corporal, R.A.S.C. (M.T.).
Joined 1915, and served at Salonica, where he was engaged
on transport work. Contracted malaria fever whilst serving
overseas.
Demobilised 1919. Medals :—General Service and Victory.
25, Humbolt Road, Fulham.   15140.

ALLAWAY, W. H., Sapper, Royal Engineers.
He was serving on the outbreak of hostilities, and was
discharged in 1914. He was re-enlisted in the R.E.'s and
served during many engagements on the Western Front.
He suffered from shell shock, and was discharged as medically
unfit on June 16th, 1916.
He holds the 1915 Star, General Service and Victory Medals.
15, Kilmaine Road, Fulham.   T.X18852.

ALLAWAY, A. R., Pte., 8th Royal Fusiliers.
He joined in July, 1916, and in the same year was sent to
France, where he took part in engagements at Arras and
Cambrai, and was wounded at the latter place on November
20th, 1917.
He holds the General Service and Victory Medals, and was
demobilised in February, 1919.
105, Harley Road, Harlesden.   13173.

**ALLBRIGHT, W. A., Pte., 18th Hussars and 1st
Hants. Regiment.**
He joined in August, and served on the Western Front
at Ypres, Arras, Dunkirk, Vimy Ridge, Passchendaele,
Armentieres, Amiens, Albert, Bullecourt, Cambrai, and
several other places.
He holds the 1914–15 Star, General Service and Victory
Medals, and was demobilised in February, 1919.
22, Montgomery Street, Hammersmith.   15880.

ALLBUTT, J. E. (M.M.), Sergeant, 3rd Lond.Rgt.
He joined on January 19th, 1915, and served on the Western
Front for four years, taking part in the battles of Loos,
Festubert, Givenchy, Ypres, Arras, the Somme, and many
other engagements. He was wounded and mentioned in
despatches. He was demobilised on March 26th, 1919, holding
the Military Medal awarded for bravery, the 1914–15 Star,
General Service and Victory Medals.
46, Mozart Street, Queen's Park, N.W.   X.18836.

ALLEN, C. S., Pte., 11th Essex Regiment.
He enlisted in June, 1915, and during his service in France
took part in many engagements, and was wounded once.
He holds the General Service and Victory Medals, and was
demobilised in October, 1919.
36, Aintree Street, Fulham.   X.18205/A.

ALLEN, L. W., Pte., 8th Norfolk Regiment.
He enlisted on August 5th, 1914, and served in France,
where he was killed in action on July 19th, 1916.
He was entitled to the 1914–15 Star, General Service and
Victory Medals.
36, Aintree Street, Fulham.   X.18205/B.

ALLEN, H. S., Rflmn., Post Office Rifles,
He joined in November, 1916, and served in France, where
he took part in many engagements, and was once wounded.
He holds the General Service and Victory Medals, and was
demobilised in February, 1919.
36, Aintree Street, Fulham.   X.18205/C.

ALLEN, E. (Mrs.), Special War Worker.
For 3½ years she was engaged as a post-woman in connection
with the West Brompton Post Office, and during her period
of service walked some thousands of miles, thus releasing a
man for service.
10, Lillie Mansions, Lillie Road, Fulham.   X.18459/B.

ALLEN, H., Lce.-Cpl., 1st Royal Berks Regt.
He joined in March, 1915, and was sent to the Western Front,
where he took part in engagements at the Somme, Ypres,
Armentieres, Arras and Festubert. He was badly wounded
in action at Loos, as a result of which he was invalided home
to hospital, where he remained for 14 months.
He was discharged medically unfit for further service in 1917,
and holds the 1914–15 Star, General Service and Victory
Medals.
10, Lillie Mansions, Lillie Road, Fulham.   X.18459/A.

ALLEN, V., Pte., 13th Middlesex Regiment.
He joined on August 8th, 1917, and served in France, where
he took part in many engagements, and was wounded once.
He holds the General Service and Victory Medals and was
demobilised in November, 1919.
36, Aintree Street, Fulham.   X.18205/D.

ALLEN, C., Pioneer, Royal Engineers.
He joined in March, 1915, and was sent to Salonica, taking part in many engagements on the Bulgarian Front. He suffered from malaria and was invalided to England in 1916, returning to Salonica, where he served until he was demobilised in June, 1919.
He holds the 1914/15 Star, General Service and Victory Medals.
22, Earlsmead Road, Kensal Rise. X.17777.

ALLEN, W. J., Pte., Royal Army Service Corps.
He joined on April 5th, 1915, and served in France. He went through many engagements, including Arras. Later he served at home at stations in Scotland, and was demobilised on February 13th, 1919.
He holds the General Service and Victory Medals.
15, Moselle Street, Tottenham. X.18369.

ALLEN, A. E., Lce.-Cpl., Duke of Cornwall's Light Infantry.
He enlisted in August, 1914, was sent to the Western Front in the following year, and was reported missing after the battle of Hill 60, in July, 1916.
Entitled to the 1914-15 Star, General Service and Victory Medals.
9, Oldfield Road, Willesden. T.16515.

ALLEN, C. A., Pte., 7th London Regt.
He joined on May 17th, 1915, and served in France until February 25th, 1919, during which time he was wounded once.
He holds the General Service and Victory Medals.
8, Delorme Street, Fulham. 14468.

ALLEN, E. J., Pte., 3rd London Regt.
He enlisted on August 6th, 1914, and did valuable work on the East Coast defences until demobilised in February, 1919.
23, Newlyn Road, Lower Tottenham. 16779.

ALLEN, E. J., Pte., 2nd Worcestershire Regt.
He was called up from the Reserve when war broke out and sent to France in August, 1914.
He was discharged in December, 1918, holding the 1914 Star, General Service and Victory Medals.
73, Shakespeare Avenue, Harlesden. 13705.

ALLEN, F., Pte., 7th Batt. The Queen's (Royal West Surrey Regiment).
He joined in December, 1915, and in the following year was sent to the Western Front, where he took part in the fighting at Ypres, Arras, St. Quentin, and the Somme. In 1918 he was invalided home with wounds, and was afterwards transferred to the Machine Gun Corps.
Demobilised January, 1919, holding the General Service and Victory Medals.
5, Ellerslie Road, Shepherd's Bush. 11930.

ALLEN, F. J., Pte., 53rd Battalion Australian Imperial Forces.
He joined on July 15th, 1915, and served on the Western Front. During the battle of the Somme he was taken prisoner. After suffering many hardships he was released. On October 25th, 1918, he was discharged, holding the General Service and Victory Medals.
9, Chaplin Road, Willesden. 16632.

ALLEN, F. S., 1st Air Mechanic, Royal Air Force.
He joined on the outbreak of hostilities, and did valuable work in the Royal Air Force, in Ireland and Farnborough, until demobilised in January, 1920. He holds the General Service Medal.
65, Denzil Road, Neasden. .15933.

ALLEN, F. W., Pte., 1st The Queen's (Royal West Surrey Regiment).
He joined in September, 1914, and in the same year was sent to France, where he remained until 1918. He took part in engagements including Mons, Ypres, and the Somme, and was twice wounded. He was discharged in October, 1918.
Holds the Mons Star, General Service and Victory Medals.
19, Brereton Road, Tottenham. X.18384.

ALLEN, H., Driver, Royal Field Artillery.
He enlisted in November, 1914, and during his service on the Western Front took part in various engagements, and was wounded.
He was demobilised on February 24th, 1919, holding the 1914-15 Star, General Service and Victory Medals.
43, Aintree Street, Fulham. X.18207/C.

ALLEN, S. G., Pte., 3rd London Regt.
He joined on November 27th, 1917, and served on the Western Front, where he was killed in action on August 24th, 1918, and buried near Albert.
Entitled to the General Service and Victory Medals.
79, Bramber Road, Fulham. 15720/A.

ALLEN, R. A., Driver, Royal Field Artillery.
He joined on July 19th, 1915, and served on the Western Front. He was invalided home suffering from shell shock, and on July 20th, 1916, was discharged as medically unfit.
He holds the General Service and Victory Medals.
79, Bramber Road, Fulham. 15720/B.

ALLEN, T. P., Pte., London Scottish.
He joined in February, 1916, and was sent to France, where he was killed in action in September, 1916.
Medals :—General Service and Victory.
39, Warwick Road, Edmonton. X17508.

ALLERTON, J. A., Pte., Royal Marines.
He joined in 1914, and went to the Dardanelles in the following year. In 1916 he was sent to France and served there until 1918, during which time he took part in many engagements, and was wounded twice.
He holds the 1915 Star, General Service and Victory Medals.
58, St. Mary's Road, Harlesden. 15112/A.

ALLERTON, J., 1st Mate, Mercantile Marine.
He joined in 1914, and saw service in Russia, India, China, Africa and Egypt. The s.s. " Glenstrae," on which he was serving, was torpedoed and sunk.
He holds the Mercantile Marine War Medal.
58a, St Mary's Road, Harlesden. 15112/B.

ALLEWAY, F. C., 1st Air Mechanic, R.A.F.
He joined in December, 1917, and did valuable work in repairing and testing aeroplanes at various places at home, until demobilised in 1919. He holds the General Service Medal.
30, Shelley Road, Harlesden. 13647.

ALLEY, F. (Miss), Special War Worker.
She volunteered for War Work and was employed from 1917 at Park Royal Filling Factory on dangerous work in connection with T.N.T. and C.E. powders.
29, Barret's Green Road, Harlesden. T.13630/A.

ALLINSON, G. F., Gunner, Royal Field Artillery.
He joined in August, 1914, and served for nearly five years on the Western Front, being in action at the retreat from Mons, the battles of Ypres, the Somme, Arras and Loos. He was wounded and also gassed.
He was demobilised in March, 1919, holding the 1914-15 Star, the General Service and Victory Medals.
48, Sheldon Road, Edmonton. X.17457A.

ALLINSON, H. W., Pte., Notts. and Derby Regt.
He joined in 1917 and served on the Western Front. On March 21st, 1918, whilst in action on the Somme, he was taken prisoner.
He was demobilised in October, 1919, and holds the General Service and Victory Medals.
48, Sheldon Road, Edmonton. X17457B.

ALLISON, E., Gunner, Royal Field Artillery.
He enlisted in December, 1913, was sent to Egypt in 1915, taken prisoner at Kut-el-Amara on April 29th, 1916, and died in captivity on July 22nd of the same year.
Entitled to the 1915 Star. General Service and Victory Medals. 14, Eldon Road, Edmonton. 13309.

ALLISON, T. J., Gunner, Royal Garrison Artillery.
He joined in April, 1918, went to France in the following September, and was killed in action on October 29th of the same year.
Entitled to the General Service and Victory Medals.
60, King's Road, Willesden Green. T.14975/14976A.

ALMAND, E., Pte., Royal Marine Light Infantry.
He was called up from the Reserve on the outbreak of war, landed in East Africa from H.M.S. " Challenger " in February, 1916, and remained there until invalided home in November, 1918.
He was demobilised in January, 1919, and holds the General Service and Victory Medals.
34, Buckingham Road, Harlesden. 12520.

ALSFORD, A. E., Pte., Ryl. Army Service Corps.
He joined in December, 1915, and was sent to German East Africa. He was on board the " Guildford Castle " when she was torpedoed.
He holds the General Service and Victory Medals.
21, Herbert Road, Edmonton. 12983.

ALSFORD, F., Lce.-Cpl., 10th Middlesex Regt.
He joined in April, 1916, and in the following year was sent to India, where he remained until demobilised in November, 1919.
He holds the General Service and Victory Medals.
26, Beresford Road, Edmonton. 14765

ALLSOP, J. G., Gunner, Royal Field Artillery.
He joined in September, 1914, and served on the Western Front, taking part in the battles of Passchendaele, Ypres, the Somme and Cambrai. He was invalided home suffering from shell shock, and in June, 1919, was demobilised.
He holds the 1914–15 Star, General Service and Victory Medals.
23, Linton Road, Edmonton. T.X17310A.

ALLSOP, W., Pte., 17th Middlesex Regiment.
He joined in June, 1915, served for nearly three years on the Western Front, being in action at Kemmel and on the Somme (three times wounded), at Ypres, Beaumont Hamel, and Cambrai.
In March, 1919, he was demobilised, holding the General Service and Victory Medals.
23, Linton Road, Edmonton. T.X17310B.

ALLSOPP, A. P., Pte., 2nd Middlesex Regiment.
He joined in October, 1916, and was sent to the Western Front, where he remained until 1919. In 1917 he took part in an engagement at Ypres and was gassed. After hospital treatment he returned to France and was taken prisoner during the retreat from Cambrai in May, 1918. He was released in the December.
He holds the General Service and Victory Medals and was demobilised in December, 1919.
6, Burns Road, Harlesden. 13138.

ALLUM, J., Sergt., 4th Batt. Royal Fusiliers.
He was serving on the outbreak of war and went to France, where he took part in engagements at Mons, the Aisne and the Marne, and was wounded.
He holds the 1914 Star, General Service and Victory Medals, and was discharged in 1916.
80, Willow Vale Road, Shepherd's Bush. 12056.

ALTUCCINI, A., Pte., Labour Corps.
He joined on June 8th, 1918, and served on the Western Front until his demobilisation on March 5th, 1919.
He holds the General Service and Victory Medals.
22, Aintree Street, Fulham. T.X18629.

AMBRIDGE, A. J., Rifleman, Rifle Brigade.
He joined on October 3rd, 1918, and served with the Army of Occupation in Germany until demobilised on March 2nd, 1920.
He holds the General Service and Victory Medals.
35, Delorme Street, Fulham. 13753.

AMBROSE, A. E., Pte., The Border Regiment.
He was recalled from the Reserve on August 4th, 1914, and during the whole war served on both Western and Eastern Fronts. He was in action at Mons, Ypres, Somme, Vimy Ridge, Cambrai, &c., and he also served in Italy for 18 months. He was wounded three times, and was demobilised on February 17th, 1919, after having served for 13 years.
He holds the Mons Star and the General Service and Victory Medals.
13, Charlton Road, Harlesden. 13100A.

AMES, A., A.B., Royal Navy.
He joined in 1915, served on H.M.S. " Comus " in the North Sea, and took part in several naval engagements.
He was demobilised in 1919, holding the General Service and Victory Medals.
88, Raynham Road, Edmonton. 16947.

AMEY, F., Bombardier, Royal Field Artillery.
He joined in September, 1914, served on the Western Front at Arras, Loos, the Somme and other places. He afterwards served for 12 months in Russia, and was demobilised in November, 1919. He holds the 1915 Star, General Service and Victory Medals.
66, West Street, Edmonton. T.14600.

AMOS, A. C., Corporal, Middlesex Regiment.
He enlisted in 1915, and served in France, taking part in many engagements, including the Somme, Loos, Ypres and Arras. He was wounded in 1916, and fought again at Ypres in 1917.
He holds the General Service and Victory Medals, and was demobilised in 1919.
64, St. Paul's Road, Tottenham. X18829/A.

AMOS, W. R. E., Corporal, The Buffs (East Kent Regiment).
He joined in September, 1914, and served in France, taking part in many engagements, including the Somme, Ypres and Loos, and was wounded three times.
He holds the 1914–15 Star, General Service and Victory Medals, and was demobilised in 1918.
64, St. Paul's Road, Tottenham. X.18829/B.

AMOS, J. R., Gunner, Royal Garrison Artillery.
He joined in 1918 and served at Gibraltar until 1919. He holds the General Service and Victory Medals.
64, St. Paul's Road, Tottenham. X.18829/C.

AMPLEFORD, G., Pte., Royal Fusiliers and " The Queen's."
He joined in 1915, went to France the same year, and took part in battles at Loos, the Somme, Cambrai, and Arras, afterwards being invalided home. In 1917 he returned to France, and was killed in action on the Somme in the Great Retreat on March 23rd, 1918. He was entitled to the 1914–15 Star, General Service and Victory Medals.
68, Purves Road, Willesden. X.18419/A.

AMPLEFORD, A. H., Stoker, Royal Navy.
He joined in 1914, and served in the North Sea, the Baltic and the Black Sea on patrol duty with the submarines. He was also employed as a diver.
He was demobilised in 1919, holding the 1914–15 Star, General Service and Victory Medals.
68, Purves Road, Willesden. X.18419/B.

AMSDEN, J., Gunner, Royal Field Artillery.
He joined in 1915, and served in many engagements in France.
He was demobilised in October, 1919. Medals :—General Service and Victory.
97, Winchester Road, Edmonton. 14959.

ANDERSON, C., Shoeing-smith, 11th Hussars.
He joined on August 4th, 1914, and went to France in the same month. He died of influenza and pneumonia, contracted through exposure.
Entitled to the 1914 Star, General Service and Victory Medals.
8, Nelson Road, Edmonton. 13286.

ANDERSON, F., Pte., 25th Middlesex Regiment.
He joined in August, 1916, and served in the Balkan campaign. He was invalided home with malaria, and on March 4th, 1919, was demobilised.
He holds the General Service and Victory Medals.
22, Westbury Road, Willesden. 15455B.

ANDERSON, J. F., A.B., R.N., H.M.S. "Thæsus," " Canopus," " Bulldog."
He joined in 1915, and served in the Dardanelles campaign, in Russia, and on patrol duty in the Mediterranean and other seas.
He holds the 1915 Star, the General Service and Victory Medals.
22, Westbury Road, Willesden. 15455A.

ANDERSON, G. E., Corporal, Royal Engineers.
He joined in 1916, and served at Dunkirk until 1919, being wounded in action during May, 1917.
He holds the General Service and Victory Medals.
101, Sheldon Road, Upper Edmonton. X17190.

ANDERSON, J., Pte., R.A.S.C. (attached M.G.C. Motors).
He joined on November 8th, 1915, and was sent to France, where he served until demobilised in September, 1919. During this period he was present at several engagements, including those of Arras, Cambrai and the Somme.
He holds the 1914–15 Star, General Service and Victory Medals.
52, Winchelsea Road, Harlesden. 13846.

ANDERSON, E. W., Lce.-Cpl., Northamptonshire Regiment.
He joined in 1916, and served at various stations. He was discharged in March, 1918, through ill health, having performed his duties in a very creditable manner throughout his service.
39, Kilmaine Road, Fulham. T.X18856.

ANDERSON, W., Pte., The Buffs (East Kent Regiment).
He joined in January, 1917, and in the same month was sent to India, where he served, taking part in the Afghan campaign, until demobilised in January, 1920. He was awarded the General Service and Victory Medals.
15, Burns Road, Harlesden. 14711.

ANDREWS, C., Pte., Royal Air Force.
He joined on July 7th, 1917, and was engaged on Home Defence duty. On October 24th, 1919, he died in Fulham Infirmary.
He held the South African Medal.
26, Aintree Street, Fulham. TX.18627.

ANDREWS, G. (jun.), Corporal, R.A.S.C.
He joined in 1914, and in the following year was sent to Egypt. He served previously with the American Expeditionary Force in Mexico.
In 1919 he was demobilised, and holds the 1914–15 Star, General Service and Victory Medals.
48, St. Mary's Road, Harlesden. 15117/15118B.

ANDREWS, G., Special War Worker.
Being rejected from the Army on medical grounds, he was employed on Munition Transport work for three years, from 1915 until 1918, at the Hendon and Hayes Munition Factories.
48, St. Mary's Road, Harlesden.   15117/15118A.

ANDREWS, G. (Mrs.), Special War Worker.
From 1916 to 1918 she was employed at Park Royal Munition Factory. Her work was of an unhealthy nature and she suffered in consequence. While thus engaged she experienced several enemy air raids.
48, St. Mary's Road, Harlesden.   15117/15118D.

ANDREWS, E., Pte., Royal Army Service Corps.
He joined in 1914, and saw active service in Egypt. Previous to this he was with the American Expeditionary Force in Mexico.
He was demobilised in 1919, and holds the 1915 Star, General Service and Victory Medals.
48, St. Mary's Road, Harlesden.   15117–15118C.

ANDREWS, E. J., Pte., 15th Hussars.
He was a Reservist on the outbreak of war, and immediately joined up, being sent in August, 1914, to the Western Front, where he served throughout the war. He was in action through all the engagements in France, and was wounded on three occasions. He was discharged suffering from shell shock in November, 1919.
He holds the 1914 Star, General Service and Victory Medals.
15, Holberton Gardens, College Park, Willesden, N.W.
                                                   X017555.

ANDREWS, G. W. (sen.), Pte., R.A.S.C.
He enlisted in November, 1914, and served on the Western Front on remount duty, taking horses up to the line and bringing back the wounded. He took part in the battles of Ypres, Bethune, Arras, St. Quentin and Cambrai, and was discharged in 1916, medically unfit for further service. He holds the 1914–15 Star, General Service and Victory Medals.
83, Rayleigh Road, Hammersmith.   12634/C.

ANDREWS, G. W. (jun.), Cpl., Ryl. Sussex Regt.
He enlisted in 1914, served in Palestine (taking part in the capture of Jerusalem) and in France, where he fought on the Somme, at Arras and Cambrai, and took part in the Advance of 1918.
He was demobilised in 1919, holding the General Service and Victory Medals.
83, Rayleigh Road, Hammersmith.   12634A.

ANDREWS, H., Pte., Cheshire Regiment.
He enlisted in August, 1914, and served for a year in France with a Red Cross Ambulance. He was then sent to Salonica, where he took part in the fighting.
He was demobilised in 1919, holding the General Service and Victory Medals.
83, Rayleigh Road, Hammersmith.   12634/B.

ANDREWS, H. J., Pte., 1/7th Middlesex Regt.
He joined in January, 1916, and was sent to France in 1917.
He was killed in action at Vimy Ridge on April 9th, 1917.
Medals :—General Service and Victory.
25, Westoe Road, Edmonton.   13114.

ANDREWS, J., Pte., 11th Middlesex Regiment.
He joined on August 28th, 1914, and served in France for four years, taking part in the battles of the Somme, Ypres and Arras.
He was demobilised in April, 1919, after being wounded five times. Medals :—1914 Star, General Service and Victory.
41, Cedar Road, Edmonton.   13947.

ANDREWS, J. J., Driver, R.A.S.C. (H.T.).
He joined in 1915, went to France the same year, and took part in many engagements. He was demobilised in June, 1919, holding the 1914–15 Star, General Service, and Victory Medals.
32, Star Road, W.14   .16686/A.

ANDREWS, W. F., Pte., 13th London Regiment ("Kensingtons").
He joined in 1915, went to France the same year, and took part in many engagements, including those of the Somme, Ypres and Arras. He was killed in action at Grandcourt in October, 1917.
Entitled to the 1914–15 Star, General Service and Victory Medals.
32, Star Road, W.14.   16686/B.

ANDREWS, W., Pte., R.A.S.C. (M.T.).
He was called up from the Reserve on May 28th, 1917, and served in France at Calais and Messines.
He was discharged in June, 1919, as medically unfit. Medals :—General Service and Victory.
6, Lamington Street, Hammersmith.   11100.

ANGLIN, A. V., Pte., Middlesex Regiment.
He joined in 1918, and was stationed on the coast on defence duties.
He was demobilised in 1920.
12, Kenninghall Road, Lower Edmonton.   16899.

ANGLISS, G. J. W., Gunner, Royal Field Artillery.
He joined in July, 1915, saw active service in France on the Somme and at Ypres, and was wounded.
He was discharged on April 20th, 1918. Awards :—General Service and Victory Medals.
6, Durham Road, Edmonton.   14693.

ANNAKIN, W., Pte., Middlesex Regiment.
He joined in October, 1916, served in France from the following year until 1919, and took part in many engagements.
He was demobilised in September, 1919, holding the General Service and Victory Medals.
80, Warwick Road, Edmonton.   X17906.

ANSELL, G. A., Pte., Royal Army Medical Corps.
He joined the Army in 1917, served in France until 1919, and was in action on the Somme and at Ypres.
He was demobilised in October, 1919, and holds the General Service and Victory Medals.
52, Newlyn Road, Tottenham.   X18506.

ANSELL, W., Pte., 4th Royal Fusiliers.
He joined on the outbreak of hostilities and went to France in August, 1914, and was wounded in the battle of the Aisne in September of the same year.
He was discharged in June, 1915, and holds the Mons Star, General Service and Victory Medals.
16, Denbigh Road, Willesden.   15532.

ANSTEAD, J., Pte., Royal Army Service Corps.
He joined in November, 1915, and served on the Eastern Front, in Mesopotamia, and Salonica. While there he contracted malaria fever.
In February, 1919, he was demobilised, holding the General Service and Victory Medals.
21, Everton Street, W.6   13967.

APPLEBY, T. H., Pte., Royal Air Force.
He joined on October 29th, 1915, and was sent to the Western Front. He was transferred to the Tank Corps during the period of his service.
He was discharged in May, 1919, holding the General Service and Victory Medals.
30, Colehill Lane, Fulham, S.W.6   X18908.

ARCHER, H. W., Pte., 17th Lancers.
He enlisted in August, 1914, was sent to France in the same year, took part in various engagements, including the battle of the Somme, and sustained a shrapnel wound on March 23rd, 1915.
He was demobilised in March, 1919, holding the 1914 Star, General Service and Victory Medals.
10, Alston Road, Lower Edmonton.   16505.

ARCHER, P. B., Pte., 4th Batt. Worcestershire Regiment.
He joined in May, 1915, served for a year in the Dardanelles, and contracted trench fever, as a result of which he was discharged on March 14th, 1916.
He holds the 1914–15 Star, General Service and Victory Medals.
51, Ancill Street, W.6   13750.

ARGENT, J., Corporal, R.A.S.C. (M.T.).
He joined in 1915, and served on the Western Front, taking part in many engagements, including the great Retreat and Advance in 1918. Later he served with the Army of Occupation in Germany, and was demobilised in 1919, holding the General Service and Victory Medals.
85, Berry Street, Willesden.   15419.

ARIENT, H., Special War Worker.
Throughout the war worked on munitions, first at Messrs. Whitehead's Small Arms Factory, Fulham, and later at Messrs. Blatchford's, making artificial limbs for soldiers.
32, Ancill Street, Hammersmith.   14101.

ARMITAGE, W., Quartermaster-Sergeant, The Queen's (Royal West Surrey Regiment).
He joined on August 8th, 1914, and was sent to France, where he took part in engagements at Mons, Loos, Arras, Ypres and the Somme.
He was demobilised in February, 1919, holding the Mons Star, General Service and Victory Medals.
92, St. Peter's Road, Lower Edmonton.   12327.

ARMITT, A., Pte., 21st Lancers.
He joined on August 4th, 1914, and served on the Western Front, taking part in many engagements. He is still serving, and is stationed in South Africa.
He had previously served in the South African War, and now holds the South African Medals, 1914–15 Star, and the General Service and Victory Medals.
1a, Werley Avenue, Fulham.   X17740A.

ARMITT, C., Sergeant, 5th Royal Fusiliers.
He joined on August 4th, 1914, and saw much service on the Western Front. While in action he was twice wounded in the leg and arm, and was in hospital in France.
He holds the 1914–15 Star, the General Service and Victory Medals.
1a, Werley Avenue, Fulham.   X17740C.

ARMITT, W., Sergeant, 18th Hussars.
He joined on August 4th, 1914, and served on the Western Front. During the battles of Ypres he was killed in action, in 1915.
He was entitled to the 1914–15 Star, the General Service and Victory Medals.
1a, Werley Avenue, Fulham.   X17740B.

ARMOUR, A. W., Gunner, Royal Garrison Arty.
He joined in November, 1916, and served three years at Gibraltar on Garrison duty.
He was discharged in November, 1919, and holds the General Service and Victory Medals.
128, Fifth Avenue, Paddington, W.10   X18588.

ARMSTRONG, G., Pte., Royal West Kent Regt. and Royal Army Service Corps.
He joined in 1915, went to France, and was wounded on the Somme in 1916, as a result of which he was invalided home.
He was discharged medically unfit in January, 1919, and holds the General Service and Victory Medals.
49, Greyhound Road, Willesden.   X17609.

ARNOLD, C. R., Pte., 5th Batt. Wiltshire Regt.
He joined in September, 1914, took part in the Dardanelles Campaign, saw service in Egypt and Palestine, and the Western Front, where he took part in the fighting at Arras, Messines Ridge, Ypres and the Somme, and was wounded.
He was demobilised in June, 1919, holding the 1914–15 Star, General Service and Victory Medals.
3, Preston Gardens, Willesden.   15980.

ARNOLD, F. C., Rifleman., King's Royal Rifle Corps.
He joined in October, 1916, went to France in the same year, and took part in many engagements, including those of Ypres and Armentieres.
He was demobilised in 1919, holding the General Service and Victory Medals.
82, Raynham Road, Edmonton.   16942.

ARNOLD, H., Pte., 11th West Yorkshire Regt.
He joined in June, 1916, and was sent out to France. Later he was transferred to Italy, where he was wounded by the explosion of a bomb. Afterwards he served at Cairo and Port Said.
Medals : General Service and Victory.
9, St. Peter's Road, Lower Edmonton.   12319.

ARNOLD, H. C., Pte., 7th London Regt.
He joined in 1915, and was demobilised in April, 1919. During this period he saw active service on the Western Front, in Salonica and in Egypt, where under General Allenby, he took part in engagements in Palestine, at Jaffa, Jericho, Beersheba and Jerusalem, and was wounded.
He holds the 1914–15 Star, General Service and Victory Medals.
30, Yeldham Road, Hammersmith.   12833.

ARNOLD, H. W., 1st-Cl. Stoker, R.N., H.M.S. "Renown."
He joined in 1917, serving with the Grand Fleet during the war.
He holds the General Service and Victory Medals.
5, Florence Road, Lower Edmonton.   16014.

ARNOLD, J. G., Driver, Royal Engineers.
He joined on September 16th, 1914, and served in France until 1917 with the 7th Division, taking part in many battles, including Neuve Chapelle, Festubert, Givenchy and Bullecourt. Later he went to Italy, and served there until 1919. He was twice wounded and gassed.
Demobilised on February 17th, 1919, holds the 1914–15 Star, General Service and Victory Medals.
2, Crefeld Road, W.6   14502.

ARNOLD, T., Driver, Royal Field Artillery.
He enlisted on September 4th, 1914, served on the Western Front from 1915 until 1918, and was wounded.
Was discharged as physically unfit through wounds on July 27th, 1918, and holds the 1914–15 Star, General Service and Victory Medals.
21, Wakefield Street, Edmonton.   16749.

ARNOLD, W. J., Pte., 1st Cambridgeshire Regt.
He joined in February, 1916, served in many engagements on the Western Front, and was wounded in action near Arras in August, 1917.
Was demobilised in March, 1919, holding the General Service and Victory Medals.
14, Corby Road, Harlesden.   14401.

ARNOLD, W., Pte., Middlesex Regiment.
He enlisted in October, 1914, and during his five years' service in France took part in many engagements, including Mons.
He was wounded, and was ultimately discharged in October, 1919, holding the Mons Star, General Service and Victory Medals.
44, Love Lane, Tottenham.   X18375.

ARNOLD, S. J. F., Pte., 4th Middlesex Regt.
He enlisted in February, 1916, and for three years did good service in France, where he took part in many engagements and was wounded and seriously gassed in 1917.
He was demobilised on September 6th, 1919, and holds the General Service and Victory Medals.
48, Church Road, Tottenham.   X18339.

ARNOLD, W. J., Driver, Royal Field Artillery.
He joined in September, 1914, and in the same year was sent to the Western Front, where he remained until 1919. He was in action at Loos, Ypres and Cambrai and in the Retreat in 1918, in which he was severely wounded, losing his leg.
He holds the 1914 Star, General Service and Victory Medals, and was demobilised in January, 1919.
47, Redfern Road, Harlesden.   13201.

ASCOTT, D., Pte., Royal Army Medical Corps.
He joined on November 4th, 1915, and served for a year on the Western Front in various hospitals.
On April 11th, 1918, he was discharged, being disabled and medically unfit, and now holds the General Service and Victory Medals.
14, The Grove, Crouch End, N.8   17595.

ASH, T. J. B., Pte., R.A.S.C. (M.T.).
He joined on October 15th, 1915, and was sent to the Western Front on March 17th, 1917, where he served two years. He was engaged with the Anti-Air Craft Section during the period of his service.
He was discharged on February 28th, 1919, and holds the General Service and Victory Medals.
16, Allington Lane, Kilburn Lane, N.W.10   X18779.

ASH, A., Pte., Royal Army Ordnance Corps.
He joined on February 7th, 1917, and was sent out to France and took part in engagements at Ypres, Neuve Chapelle, Arras and Cambrai.
Was demobilised on October 26th, 1919, holding the General Service and Victory Medals.
38, Studland Street, Hammersmith.   12426.

ASH, J., Sapper, Royal Engineers.
He joined in February, 1915, and served on the Eastern and Bulgarian Fronts. He was badly wounded and gassed. In June, 1916, was discharged as medically unfit, and now holds the 1914–15 Star, the General Service and Victory Medals.
48, Earlsmead Road, Kensal Rise.   X18037.

ASHBY, A. V., Pte., R.A.F. (late R.N.A.F.).
He joined on January 1st, 1918, and served at the Isle of Sheppey with the 58th Wing R.A.F.
He was demobilised on April 4th, 1919, and holds the General Service Medal.
91, Yeldham Road, W.6   13235/B.

ASHDOWN, W., Lce.-Cpl., Royal Engineers.
He joined in October, 1917, and went to the Western Front in March, 1918, taking part in the engagements at Cambrai, where he was wounded in the head. Later he served with the Army of Occupation in Germany, and was demobilised in 1919, holding the General Service and Victory Medals.
84, Franklyn Road, Willesden.   16323/B.

ASHDOWN, A., Rflmn., King's Royal Rifle Corps.
He joined in November, 1915, and went to the Western Front in March of the following year, taking part in the battles of the Somme and Ypres. He died on March 20th, 1917, of wounds received in action at Arras.
Entitled to the General Service and Victory Medals.
84, Franklyn Road, Willesden.   16323/A.

ASHDOWN, L. C., Gunner, R.G.A.

He joined in October, 1915, and went to Salonica in June of the following year, taking part in the Balkan campaign. He was sent home through ill-health in 1917. Later he was sent to the Western Front, and was taken prisoner at St. Quentin in March, 1918, and held captive in Germany until December of that year.
He was demobilised in January, 1919, holding the General Service and Victory Medals.
84, Franklyn Road, Willesden.   16323/C.

ASHFORD, J. P., Pte., Argyll and Sutherland Highlanders.

He joined in May, 1916, went to France the following year, and served until the cessation of hostilities, and was sent to Germany with the Army of Occupation.
He was demobilised in January, 1919, and holds the General Service and Victory Medals.
142, Winchester Road, Lower Edmonton.   1478.

ASHLEY, C., A.B. (Signaller), R.N., H.M.S. "Hercules."

He joined in May, 1915, and served in the North Sea. Took part in the battles of Jutland and Zeebrugge, and holds the 1914-15 Star, the General Service and Victory Medals.
7, Charlton Road, Harlesden.   13098A.

ASHLEY, J., Sapper, Royal Engineers.

He joined in October, 1915, and for nearly three years served on the Western Front and in Italy. He took part in the battles of the Somme, Ypres, and Vimy Ridge.
In February, 1919, he was demobilised, holding the General Service and Victory Medals.
7, Charlton Road, Harlesden.   13098B.

ASHLEY, J., Driver, Royal Field Artillery.

He joined on June 11th, 1915, and during his service on the Western Front contracted trench fever, and was also accidentally injured.
He holds the General Service and Victory Medals, and was demobilised on February 18th, 1919.
9, Hartopp Avenue, Fulham.   X17654.

ASHMAN, H. E. V., Machine Gunner, 4th Div. Machine Gun Corps.

He joined in 1916, and later served in many sectors of the Western Front.
He was demobilised in November, 1919, and holds the Victory and General Service Medals.
5, Railway Cottages, Sulgrave Road, W.6.   12095A.

ASHMAN, T. C., Rifleman, Queen Victoria's Rifles.

He joined in August, 1914, and served in France, taking part in many engagements, until April, 1919, when he was demobilised.
He holds the General Service and Victory Medals.
5, Railway Cottages, Sulgrave Road.   12095B.

ASHTON, W., Pte., K.O. Yorks. Lt. Infantry.

He joined in August, 1914, and went to France, taking part in the retreat from Mons. He was taken prisoner at Le Cateau on August 26th of the same year, and was sent to Sennelager Camp, suffering many hardships.
Demobilised in March, 1919, holding the Mons Star, General Service and Victory Medals.
40, Brousart Road, Fulham.   18897.

ASHWOOD, F., Bombardier, R.G.A.

He joined in June, 1916, and served on the Western Front, taking part in engagements of the Somme, Cambrai, Ypres, Arras, Bethune, &c. While in action at Beaumont Hamel he was gassed and wounded.
Discharged on December 9th, 1918, holding the General Service and Victory Medals.
38, Oldfield Road, Willesden.   15762.

ASKEY, M., Special War Worker.

During the war did clerical work for the Government in connection with the Health Insurance for the Army and Navy, thereby relieving a man for service.
32, Chesson Road, West Kensington.   X17234/A.

ASKEY, T. P., Pte., 1st Bedfordshire Regiment.

He enlisted in August, 1914, and served on the Western Front, taking part in many engagements, including the retreat from Mons. He was killed in action on July 27th, 1916. Entitled to the Mons Star, General Service and Victory Medals.
32, Chesson Road, West Kensington.   X17234/C.

ASKEY, C. (Miss), Special War Worker.

During the war she was employed on Munitions at Park Royal, Willesden, engaged on Shell Filling, and later in th Inspection Department. A work of great National importance.
32, Chesson Road, West Kensington.   X17234/B.

ASKEY, A. J., Cpl., Royal Berkshire Regiment.

He joined in September, 1914, and served in France, taking part in the battle of Loos, where he was wounded. On recovery he returned to France, where he took part in many engagements, and was killed in action on April 27th, 1917. He was entitled to the 1914 Star, General Service and Victory Medals.
32, Chesson Road, West Kensington.   X17234/D.

ASSER, D. G., Sapper, R.E. (Postal Section).

He joined in March, 1915, and went to France in the same year, serving there until the cessation of hostilities. Afterwards he was sent to Germany with the Army of Occupation.
He was demobilised in August, 1919, holding the 1914-15 Star, General Service and Victory Medals.
9, Wingmore Road, Tottenham.   X17976.

ASSER, G. A., Sergeant, Royal Berkshire Regt.

He joined in August, 1914, and saw active service in France, and was transferred from there to Salonica, where he was in action on the Dorian Front; he was again drafted to France and took part in the Cambrai battle in 1918.
He was demobilised in February, 1919, and holds the 1914 Star, the General Service and Victory Medals.
6, Laurel Terrace, Tottenham.   X18969.

ASSER, D. W., Corporal, Middlesex Regiment.

He joined in June, 1916, and served on the Western Front, taking part in many engagements, including the battles of Ypres, Arras, Bullecourt, Vimy Ridge, St. Quentin, Albert and others. He was demobilised in March, 1919, holding the General Service and Victory Medals.
93, Durban Road, Tottenham.   X17965.

ATKINS, A., Pte., The Queen's (Royal West Surrey Regiment).

He joined in 1917, went to France the same year, and served there until 1919, when he was demobilised.
Holds General Service and Victory Medals.
33, Hazelbury Road, Edmonton.   X17492.

ATKINS, C., Rifleman, 17th London Regiment and Pte., Middlesex Regt.

He joined on April 17th, 1915, and served on the Western Front, where he took part in the battles of the Somme, Cambrai, High Wood and Ypres.
On December 2nd, 1917, he was demobilised, and holds the General Service and Victory Medals.
105, Fortune Gate Road, Harlesden.   13467.

ATKINS, E. (Mrs.), Special War Worker.

From 1914 until 1918 she was employed in the T.N.T. shops at Messrs. Blake's Munition Works, and at the Perivale Filling Factory, Park Royal. The work upon which she was engaged was of a very dangerous nature, and affected her health. She was commended for her services.
34, Hilmer Street, W.14   16914B.

ATKINS, J. T., Sapper, Royal Engineers.

He joined in June, 1918, was drafted to France in the same year, and took part in the Great Advance.
He holds the General Service and Victory Medals, and was demobilised in March, 1919.
34, Hilmer Street, W.14   16914A.

ATKINS, F., Pte., Machine Gun Corps.

He enlisted in August, 1914, and during his service in France sustained a severe wound. He afterwards served with the Army of Occupation in Germany until demobilised in July, 1919.
Holds General Service and Victory Medals.
3, Short Street, Upper Edmonton.   X17087B.

ATKINS, R. J., Pte., Royal Army Service Corps.

He enlisted in August, 1914, served on the Western Front until demobilised in July, 1919, and took part in many engagements.
Holds the 1914-15 Star, General Service and Victory Medals.
3, Short Street, Upper Edmonton.   X17087A.

ATKINS, F. T., Shoeing-smith, R.F.A.

He joined on March 1st, 1915, and served on the Western Front, taking part in the battles of Ypres, the Somme and Cambrai. He was in hospital previous to being discharged in January, 1919, and holds the 1915 Star, General Service and Victory Medals.
29, Worlidge Street, Hammersmith.   12590A.

ATKINS, M. J. (Mrs.), Special War Worker.

She was employed from November, 1916, until August, 1919, making army beds and tarpaulin sheets, thus rendering very valuable service.
29, Worlidge Street, Hammersmith.   12590B.

ATKINS, R., A.B., Royal Navy.
He joined in August, 1914, and was engaged in the transport of troops to and from the various Fronts.
He holds the Mercantile Marine Medal, General Service and Victory Medals.
94, Ancill Street, W.6   13660.

ATKINSON, A., Pte., 3rd Middlesex Regiment.
He joined on November, 14th, 1914, served on the Western Front at Ypres, Dickebusch and St. Julien, and was wounded in action at St. Jean on May 8th, 1915.
He holds the 1914-15 Star, General Service and Victory Medals, and was discharged on July 14th, 1916.
41, Cooper Road, Willesden.   16298/A.

ATKINSON, A., Driver, Royal Field Artillery.
He enlisted on December 15th, 1914, and in July, 1915, was sent to Egypt and Palestine, where he was in action at Gaza and Jaffa. For two years he served in Salonica on the Dorian and Struma sectors, proceeding to Russia in 1918.
He was demobilised in June, 1919, and holds the 1914-15 Star, General Service and Victory Medals.
41, Cooper Road, Willesden.   16298/C.

ATKINSON, R., Pte., 12th Middlesex Regiment.
He joined on June 7th, 1915, served on the Western Front at Havincourt Wood and Givinchy, and was seriously wounded in action on the Somme. He died on July 23rd, 1916, and was buried at Etaples.
Entitled to the General Service and Victory Medals.
41, Cooper Road, Willesden.   16298/B.

ATTWOOD, A. E. G., Pte., Royal Fusiliers.
He joined in February, 1916, and served on the Western Front for two years, during which time he was wounded. As a result he was discharged in November, 1918, and holds the General Service and Victory Medals.
7, Oldfield Road, Willesden.   15758.

ATTWOOD, J., Lce.-Cpl., 10th London Regt.
He joined in August, 1918, and was in training until cessation of hostilities, after which he served at various Dispersal Stations.
He was demobilised in December, 1919.
35, Waldo Road, Willesden.   X17627/A.

ATTWOOD, W., Pte., Royal Scots Fusiliers.
He joined in August, 1916, and during his service on the Western Front took part in many engagements, including the Somme battles, and the great Retreat and Advance in 1918, and was wounded.
He holds the General Service and Victory Medals, and was demobilised in February, 1919.
35, Waldo Road, Willesden.   X17627/B.

AUBREY, F., Trooper, West Somerset Yeomanry.
He enlisted at the age of 18, on January 14th, 1918, and served until January 5th, 1920, when he was demobilised.
19, Hazelbury Road, Edmonton.   X17495.

AUCKLAND, F. (Mrs.), Special War Worker.
During the war she undertook special work, thus relieving a man for service.
Her services were highly commended.
63, Yeldham Road, Hammersmith.   14167A.

AUCKLAND, W., Pte., Machine Gun Corps.
He joined in March, 1915, and during his service in France took part in the battles of the Somme, Arras, Loos, Neuve Chapelle, Givenchy, Bullecourt, Armentieres, Lens, and was twice wounded.
He holds the 1914-15 Star, General Service and Victory Medals, and was demobilised in March, 1919.
63, Yeldham Road, Hammersmith.   14167B.

AUDEMARD, E. J., Sapper, Royal Engineers.
He joined in September, 1915, went to the Western Front in the following year, and served there until 1917. Afterwards he was sent to Italy, and whilst there took part in several engagements on the Piave.
He was demobilised in July, 1919. Holds General Service and Victory Medals.
9, Mortimer Road, Kensal Rise.   X17815.

AUGER, J., Rifleman, Rifle Brigade.
He joined on August 10th, 1914, and served on the Western Front. On December 19th, 1915, he died of wounds received in action, and was buried at Beauval.
Entitled to the 1914-15 Star, the General Service and Victory Medals.
53, Bramber Road, Fulham.   15716.

AUSTIN, A., Pte., Royal Army Medical Corps.
He joined in August, 1914, went to France and was present at many engagements, including those of Mons, Loos, Ypres, and the Somme. He suffered from neurasthenia, and after being for some time in hospital was discharged in 1918.
Holds the Mons Star, General Service and Victory Medals.
21, Raynham Avenue, Edmonton.   16891.

AUSTIN, C., Pte., 4th Batt., Royal Fusiliers.
He joined on August 4th, 1914, went to France the same year and fought in many battles, including those of Ypres, St. Eloi, the Somme, Messines Ridge and Passchendaele, and was wounded during the Great Retreat of April, 1918.
He holds the 1914 Star, General Service and Victory Medals. and was demobilised in February, 1919.
17, Guilsborough, Willesden.   15246.

AUSTIN, J. A., Trooper, Surrey Yeomanry.
He joined in April, 1917, and served in Ireland.
He was demobilised in April, 1919.
35, Oldfield Road, Willesden.   15745.

AUSTIN, S. G., 1st-Class Stoker, Royal Navy.
He was called up from the Reserve on the outbreak of war, served at the Dardanelles with H.M.S. "Kennet" and H.M.S. "Baslick" and was also on Mine-sweeping duty on board the "Monlocke."
He was demobilised in 1919, holding the 1914 Star, General Service and Victory Medals.
119, Durban Road, N.17   X18428.

AUSTIN, W., Pte., 4th Middlesex Regiment.
He joined on August 4th, 1914, and during his service on the Western Front took part in many battles, including those of Loos, Arras, Vimy Ridge, Cambrai and Ypres, and was wounded. In 1916 he returned to England and was discharged unfit for further service.
He holds the 1914-15 Star, General Service and Victory Medals.
63, Melville Road, Willesden.   15655.

AVERY, A., Pte., 15th Hussars.
He joined in March, 1918, and served on the Western Front. After the cessation of hostilities he was sent with the Army of Occupation to Germany, and thence to Holland. He was demobilised in November, 1919.
Holds the General Service and Victory Medals.
20, Alston Road, Lower Edmonton.   16502/B.

AVERY, C., Pte., Oxford and Bucks L.I.
He enlisted on August 4th, 1914, was sent to France in the same year, and after taking part in many engagements was killed in action on July, 31st, 1916.
Entitled to the 1914 Star, General Service and Victory Medals
20, Alston Road, Lower Edmonton.   16502/A.

AVERY, H., Pte., West Riding Regiment (Duke of Wellington's).
He enlisted in August, 1914, saw active service on the Western Front, and was also stationed in India. He was demobilised in December, 1919, and holds the General Service and Victory Medals.
68, Gilpin Road, Edmonton.   T16846.

AVERY, R. A., Pte., 17th Middlesex Regiment.
He joined in December, 1916, and served on the Western Front, taking part in many engagements, and was wounded. In November, 1917, he was taken prisoner, and held in captivity in Germany until January, 1919.
He was demobilised in June, 1919. General Service and Victory Medals.
38, Langhedge Lane, Edmonton.   X17265.

AVERY, W. E., Leading Seaman, R.N., H.M.S. "Juno."
He joined on August 4th, 1914, and served in the Persian Gulf for one year and nine months, for which he holds a special award. He was also with the forces that went to the relief of Kut, and was on board H.M.S. "Formidable" when she was torpedoed.
He holds the General Service and Victory Medals.
28, Moylan Road, Hammersmith.   015286.

AVIS, J. H., Bombardier, Royal Field Artillery.
He joined in August, 1914, went to the Western Front, and was killed in action on May 29th, 1916, during the battle of Ypres, and is buried at Zillebeke.
Entitled to the General Service and Victory Medals.
24, Denton Road, Harlesden.   14749.

AYLETT, C. E., Special War Worker.
He was employed on Air-craft work in the engineering department, and later assisted in the making of Tanks and Guns. He worked for the duration of the war.
33, Angel Road, Hammersmith.   12614/B.

AYLETT, R. A., Driver, R.A.S.C.
He joined in 1914, and served on the Western Front, taking part in engagements on the Somme and at Arras, Loos, Neuve Chapelle, Ypres, Amiens, St. Quentin, Armentieres, Albert and Cambrai.
He holds the 1914-15 Star, General Service and Victory Medals, and was demobilised in 1919.
33, Angel Road, Hammersmith.   12614/C.

AYLETT, V. W. (Miss), Special War Worker.
She was employed during the war in a munition factory, packing and dispatching shells.
Her services were very valuable and commendable.
33, Angel Road, Hammersmith.   12614/A.

AYLETT, R. (Mrs.), Special War Worker.
During the war she was employed at the Glendower Aircraft Co., Ltd., making wood-work parts for aeroplanes.
Her services were very valuable and highly commended.
25, Chesson Road, West Kensington.   X17171B.

AYLETT, W. A., Driver, R.A.S.C.
He joined in August, 1914, and served on the Western Front, where he took part in the Mons Retreat and the battles of Loos, Neuve Chapelle, Armentieres, Amiens, Ypres, Vimy Ridge and many other engagements.
He was demobilised in April, 1919, and holds the Mons Star, General Service and Victory Medals.
25, Chesson Road, West Kensington.   X017171A.

AYLOTT, E., Pte., 2nd Middlesex Regiment.
He joined in November, 1914, and while in action at St. Quentin was killed on August 7th, 1916.
Entitled to the General Service and Victory Medals.
58, Cornwalis Grove, Edmonton.   13325.

AYLWARD, H., Gunner, R.G.A.
He joined in October, 1916, and during his two years' service on the Western Front took part in the battles of Arras and Ypres, and the engagements on the Somme.
He was demobilised in April, 1919, and holds the General Service and Victory Medals.
29, Somerford Grove, Tottenham.   X18807.

AYTON, G., 1st-Class A.B., R.N., H.M.S. "Hampshire."
He joined in January, 1915, and served for a time with the North Sea Patrol. In June, 1916, whilst on board the H.M.S. "Hampshire" he was drowned with Lord Kitchener and his staff.
Entitled to the 1914-15 Star, General Service and Victory Medals.
115, Fortune Gate Road, Harlesden.   13468/A.

AYTON, W. C., 1st-Class Stoker, R.N., H.M.S. "Turbulent."
He joined in 1913, and after war broke out served in the Dardanelles and with the North Sea Patrol, took part in the battle of Jutland, in which he was killed on May 31st, 1916.
Entitled to the 1914-15 Star, the General Service and Victory Medals.
115, Fortune Gate Road, Harlesden.   13468/B.

B

BACK, Albert, Pte., Middlesex Regiment.
He joined in 1915, and served in France and Italy. He took part in the battles of the Somme, Ypres and other engagements, during which he was twice wounded. After being in hospital for some months he was demobilised.
Holds the General Service and Victory Medals.
115, Bulwer Road, Edmonton.   X17464.

BACK, Alfred, Pte., Middlesex Regiment.
He joined in 1916, and served on the Western Front for three years, during which time he took part in the battles of the Somme, Ypres and other engagements. After being in hospital for some months, suffering from ill-health, he was demobilised in 1919. Holds the General Service and Victory Medals.
115, Bulwer Road, Edmonton.   X17466.

BACKHOUSE, G., Rifleman, Rifle Brigade.
He joined in 1917, and served until he was demobilised in 1919, On January 10th of the same year he re-enlisted and was sent out to Mesopotamia.
He holds the General Service and Victory Medals.
19, Melville Road, Willesden, N.W.   14938/D.

BACKHOUSE, J., Pte., London Regiment.
He joined on August 10th, 1915, was sent to France in the following year, and later to Egypt, Palestine and Salonica.
He took part in many engagements whilst abroad, including the capture of Jerusalem, and was wounded.
He was demobilised on April 21st, 1919, and holds the General Service and Victory Medals.
19, Melville Road, Harlesden.   14938/A.

BACKHOUSE, E. C., Pte., 12th London Regiment.
He joined in March, 1915, and served on the Western Front until 1919, when he was demobilised. During this period he took part in the battle of Ypres and other engagements, and was twice wounded.
He holds the 1914-15 Star, General Service and Victory Medals.
19, Melville Road, Willesden.   14938/C.

BACKHOUSE, W., Pte., 13th London Regiment (Kensington Battalion).
He enlisted on August 4th, 1914, was sent to France in the same year, and took part in the battles of Mons, the Marne and the Aisne. In 1915 he was invalided home, and discharged, and later joined the British Red Cross Society, serving in Italy until June, 1919.
He holds the 1914 Star, General Service and Victory Medals.
19, Melville Road, Harlesden.   14938/B.

BACON, A., Stoker, R.N., H.M.S. "Plucky."
He was in the Navy at the outbreak of war, and served for five years in the North Sea, taking part in the battle of Jutland.
He was demobilised in April, 1919, holding the 1914 Star, the General Service and Victory Medals.
96, Carlyle Avenue, Harlesden.   14452.

BADENOCH, G. C., Lce.-Cpl., Royal Engineers.
He joined in April, 1915, served on the Western Front until demobilised on January 12th, 1919, and took part in the battles of Ypres, Cambrai, Vimy Ridge, Arras and many others.
He was awarded the 1914-15 Star, General Service and Victory Medals.
7, Melville Road, Willesden.   14627.

BADGER, E. A. (M.S.M.), Lce.-Cpl., R.E.
He joined in May, 1916, and in the following year went to the Western Front, where he served until October 1917, and was then drafted to Italy. In March, 1918, he returned to France and took part in several engagements, including those of the Somme, Ypres, Bethune and Bapaume.
He was awarded the Meritorious Service Medal for devotion to duty, and also holds the General Serivce and Victory Medals. He was demobilised in October, 1919.
29, Fourth Avenue, W.10   X18671.

BAGLEY, W. C. H., A.B., R.N., T.B.D. "Tactician."
He joined on August 4th, 1914, took part in the battle of Heligoland, and was on board H.M.S. "Hogue" when she was torpedoed. He was present on board H.M.S. "Tactician" when the German Fleet surrendered on November 21st, 1918, and was eventually discharged in March, 1919.
Holds the 1914 Star, General Service and Victory Medals.
6, Colville Road, Lower Edmonton.   12003.

BAILEY, A. J., Trooper, 1/1st Staffordshire Yeomanry.
He joined in 1917 and served on the Eastern Front in Palestine and Syria, taking part in the battles of Jaffa, Gaza and Homs.
He holds the General Service and Victory Medals, and was demobilised in 1920.
7, Colin Road, Willesden Green.   16293.

BAILEY, F. W., Sergt., Royal Horse Artillery.
He joined on August 5th, 1914, and served at the Dardanelles and on the Western Front. He was wounded, and holds the 1914 Star, General Service and Victory Medals.
58, Sherbrooke Road, Fulham.   18768/B.

BAILEY, C. H., Cpl., 10th Middlesex Regiment.
He joined on August 5th, 1914, and served in Mesopotamia, Egypt, and India.
He was demobilised in November, 1919, holding the 1914 Star, General Service and Victory Medals.
58, Sherbrooke Road, Fulham.   18768/A.

BAILEY, E. A. (M.M.), Pte., Machine Gun Corps.
He joined in September, 1914, and served in France, Russia and India. He was wounded, and was awarded the Military Medal for bravery in the field.
He also holds the General Service and Victory Medals.
58, Sherbrooke Road, Fulham.   18768/C.

BAILEY, W. J., Sergt., Royal Field Artillery.
He joined on December 1st, 1914, and served on the Western Front until 1916. He was then sent to the East, and saw service in Salonica, Egypt and Palestine.
He holds the 1915 Star, General Service and Victory Medals, and was demobilised in June, 1919.
32, West Ella Road, Harlesden. 15101/A.

BAILEY, H., Pte., R.A.S.C. (M.T.).
He joined on June 18th, 1915, and served on the Western Front from the following year until 1918, when he was sent home suffering from a fractured wrist. Later he went to India, and saw service there until August, 1919, when he was demobilised, holding the General Service and Victory Medals.
32, West Ella Road, Harlesden. 15101/B.

BAILEY, F., Cpl., Rifle Brigade.
He joined on July 1st, 1918, served on the Western Front, and later in Germany with the Army of Occupation on the Rhine.
He was demobilised in February, 1920, holding the General Service and Victory Medals.
32, West Ella Road, Harlesden. 15101/C.

BAILEY, H., Sergt., Royal Horse Artillery.
He joined on August 4th, 1914, went to France the same year, and took part in the battles of Mons, the Somme, Ypres, Cambrai, Arras and Neuve Chapelle, and was wounded in August, 1917.
He had previously been mentioned in despatches in July, 1917, for gallantry in the field, and holds the Mons Star, General Service and Victory Medals. Discharged May, 1918.
24, Guilsborough Road, Willesden. 15239.

BAILEY, J. W., Lce.-Cpl., King's Royal Rifles.
He joined in November, 1914, and was sent to the Western Front in 1915. At Delville Wood in 1916 he was severely wounded, and had to be discharged in consequence in 1917.
He holds the 1915 Star and the General Service and Victory Medals.
43, Monmouth Road, Lower Edmonton. 13024.

BAILEY, R., Pte., Lancashire Fusiliers.
He joined in August, 1914, went to the Western Front, and took part in the retreat from Mons, the battles of Loos, Neuve Chapelle, Armentieres, Amiens, Ypres, Vimy Ridge, and many others, including the Retreat, 1918. He was invalided home with trench fever, and was in hospital for three months. On recovery he returned to France, later going to Germany with the Army of Occupation.
He holds the Mons Star, General Service and Victory Medals, and was demobilised in 1919.
22, Chesson Road, West Kensington. X17152/A.

BAILEY, N. A. (Mrs.), Special War Worker.
During the war she worked at Woolwich Arsenal, making caps for bullets and cordite for the guns. Whilst there an explosion occurred, in which some lives were lost, and others injured, but she escaped unhurt. Later she was employed by Healey & Co., making bombs, also at Deacon Street, making shell cases.
22, Chesson Road, West Kensington. X17152/B.

BAILEY, W. N., Pte., A. & S. Highlanders.
He joined in April, 1915, was sent to France in the following year, and took part in the battles of the Somme, Passchendaele and St. Julien.
He was invalided home and discharged in February, 1919, holding the General Service and Victory Medals.
127, Felixstowe Road, Edmonton. 14546.

BAIN, R. G., Cpl., Royal Sussex Regiment.
He enlisted in 1914, went to India in the following year, and was stationed at Bangalor, where he died after seven months of fever on August 9th, 1915.
He was entitled to the 1914–15 Star, General Service and Victory Medals.
38, Milton Avenue, Harlesden. 15800.

BAINBOROUGH, E. J., Pte., West Yorks. Regt.
He enlisted in August, 1914, and served in France, taking part in many engagements, including the Somme, where he was wounded and lost his right arm.
He was discharged in April, 1917, and holds the 1914–15 Star, General Service and Victory Medals.
27, Hannell Road, Fulham. X18157.

BAINES, A. T., Lieut., Royal Air Force.
He joined in 1915, and after completing his training was detailed for special duties in France and elsewhere. In connection with these duties he was continuously employed, and was exposed to considerable risk.
He was eventually demobilised in 1919, holding the General Service and Victory Medals.
8, Kimberley Road, Upper Edmonton. 16456/A.

BAINES, A. S., Driver, Royal Horse Artillery.
He joined in 1916, and obtained his preliminary training in England. On completion he was unable to get transferred to an overseas unit, and was detained in this country for special duty in connection with the transport of cattle.
He was ultimately demobilised in 1919.
8, Kimberley Road, Upper Edmonton. 16456/B.

BAKER, A. (Miss), Special War Worker.
Throughout the war she was employed at Messrs. Llewellyn & Dent's Munition Factory at Shepherd's Bush on important work, for which she was highly commended.
69, Yeldham Road, Hammersmith. 13275/C.

BAKER, J. R., Pte., 10th West Yorkshire Regt.
He was one of the first to answer the call in August, 1914, and was eventually sent to France, where he took part in many engagements, and finally, during the battle of the Somme in July, 1916, he was killed.
He is entitled to the Victory and General Service Medals.
69, Yeldham Road, Hammersmith. 13275A

BAKER, E. E. (Miss), Special War Worker.
Throughout the war she was employed at Messrs. Waring & Gillows making important munitions, hospital tents and marquees. This work she continued in spite of frequent enemy air-raids until hostilities ceased, displaying devotion to duty throughout.
69, Yeldham Road, Hammersmith. 13275/B.

BAKER, J., Lce.-Cpl., Royal Engineers.
He joined in 1915, was sent to France in the same year, and then to Salonica, where he was wounded in action.
He was demobilised in February, 1919, holding the 1915 Star, General Service and Victory Medals.
80, Roseberry Road, Lower Edmonton. 14077/A.

BAKER, A. (M.M.), Sergt., 1st Herts. Regt.
He enlisted in 1914, served in France, and took part in the battles of Mons, the Somme, La Bassee, Arras and St. Julien, where he was wounded.
He was discharged in 1919, having been awarded the Military Medal for devotion to duty and conspicuous gallantry on the field, and holds the 1914 Star, General Service and Victory Medals.
80, Roseberry Road, Lower Edmonton. 14077/B.

BAKER, A. V., Lce.-Cpl., Middlesex Regiment.
He joined in November, 1914, and saw active service on the Western Front, being in action at Neuve Chapelle. He was also at Salonica, and in Russia with the Relief Forces.
He holds the 1915 Star, General Service and Victory Medals, and was demobilised in May, 1919.
35, Redfern Road, Harlesden. 13206B.

BAKER, C. R., Rifleman, K.R.R. Corps and Pte., R.A.M.C.
He joined in April, 1916, served on the Western Front during the following year, took part in various engagements, including the battle of Ypres, and was twice wounded and gassed.
He was demobilised on February 15th, 1920, holding the General Service and Victory Medals.
47, Mulgrave Road, S.W.6 16189.

BAKER, E. G., Pte., Royal Irish Fusiliers.
He joined on November 28th, 1917, and served on the Western Front, taking part in operations in the Ypres sector, where he was wounded.
In April, 1919, he was demobilised, holding the General Service and Victory Medals.
2, Field Road, Fulham. 15142.

BAKER, F., A.B., Royal Navy.
He joined in March, 1915, and served in various waters on board H.M.S. " Petard " and other vessels.
He was demobilised in 1919, holding the General Service and Victory Medals, and a Russian award.
2, Crefeld Road, W.6 T14501.

BAKER, F., Sergt., 7th Batt. Royal Fusiliers.
He joined in 1914, and while in action at Neuve Chapelle was killed on March 25th, 1915.
He was entitled to the 1915 Star, General Service and Victory Medals.
1, Winchester Road, Lower Edmonton. 14673.

BAKER, F. A., Cpl., Royal Engineers.
He joined in May, 1915, saw active service in Salonica and Egypt, and on other Fronts, and took part in operations in those theatres.
He holds the General Service and Victory Medals, and was demobilised in May, 1919.
25, Stanlake Road, Shepherd's Bush. 11837.

BAKER, F. J., Staff-Sergt., R.A.O.C.
Joining in June, 1916, he was subsequently drafted to India, where he was placed in charge of Government Ordnance. He remained two years in this theatre and was subsequently returned to England for discharge in 1919.
He holds the General Service and Victory Medals.
58, Hazelbury Road, Edmonton.   X17500.

BAKER, F. R., A.B., Royal Navy.
He joined in April, 1918, and served in Russia attached to H.M.S. "Glory" until demobilised in September, 1919, holding the General Service and Victory Medals.
47, Mulgrave Road, S.W.6   16188.

BAKER, G., Steward, Royal Navy.
He joined in 1916, and served with the Grand Fleet in the North Sea and in the Mediterranean. Whilst cruising off Weymouth the ship on which he was serving was torpedoed. He was demobilised in January, 1919, and holds the General Service and Victory Medals.
144, Town Road, Lower Edmonton.   13591.

BAKER, G. E., Pte., Middlesex Regiment.
He joined in October, 1915, went to France the same year, and was wounded in the right arm whilst in action on the Somme, in 1916.
He holds the 1915 Star, General Service and Victory Medals, and was discharged in June, 1918.
34, Maldon Road, Lower Edmonton.   15785.

BAKER, H. C., Gunner, Royal Horse Artillery.
He joined on December 12th, 1915, and served on the Western Front. He was in action on the Somme and at Arras, Fricourt and other sectors.
He was discharged in February, 1918, after seeing considerable service, and holds the General Service and Victory Medals.
70, Snells Park, Edmonton.   X17484.

BAKER, H. L., Pte., Royal Fusiliers.
He joined in 1918 and was sent to Ireland, where he was stationed at Carrickfergus and Armagh. Later he served at Clipstone Camp, Nottingham, before being demobilised in 1919. Previous to joining the Army he had been employed on Aircraft work in the machinery department of a factory at Fulham.
100, Archel Road, West Kensington.   16676.

BAKER, J. W., Lce.-Cpl., 1/9th Middlesex. Regt.
Joining in 1915, he was drafted to India and Mesopotamia, where he saw service in both theatres, taking part in operations on those Fronts.
In 1918 he was returned to England and demobilised, holding the General Service and Victory Medals.
2, Field Road, Fulham.   15141.

BAKER, J. W., Lce.-Cpl., 7th Middlesex Regt.
He joined in March, 1915, served on the Western Front until 1919, and took part in the battles of the Somme and Trones Wood, where he was wounded.
He was demobilised in May, 1919, and holds the General Service and Victory Medals.
107, Love Lane Tottenham.   X18523.

BAKER, T., Gunner, Royal Garrison Artillery.
He joined on April 8th, 1916, and was sent to France and Belgium on active service. Whilst overseas he took part in engagements at Ypres, the Somme, Arras and Cambrai, and eventually went into Germany with the Army of Occupation. He was demobilised in September, 1919, holding the General Service and Victory Medals.
34, Studland Street, Hammersmith.   12431.

BAKER, W., Pte., The Queen's (Royal West Surrey Regiment).
He joined in August, 1914, and served on the Western Front, taking part in the fighting at Loos, Ypres and the Somme. During his service he was gassed, and this affected his sight. He was demobilised in February, 1919, and holds the 1914-15 Star, the Victory and General Service Medals.
56, Laundry Road, Fulham.   15055.

BAKER, W., Royal Marine, H.M.S. "Carnarvon."
He joined in January, 1901, saw service on the West Coast of Africa and North and South America, and was present at the battle of the Falkland Islands.
He holds the Long Service and Good Conduct (R.N.) Medals, 1914 Star, General Service and Victory Medals.
30, Beryl Road, Fulham.   13356.

BAKER, W. B., Pte., The Queen's (Royal West Surrey Regiment).
He joined in September, 1916, went to the Western Front, and took part in many engagements, including those of Ypres, Arras, the Somme, and Cambrai, where he was wounded. Later he served with the Army of Occupation on the Rhine, and was demobilised in January, 1919, holding the General Service and Victory Medals.
14, Church Path, Hammersmith, W.6   16388/B.

BAKER, W. H., Pte., 5th London Regiment.
He joined in April, 1918, and served in Russia and Finland for nine months. During his service in Russia he was exposed to much danger and hardship.
He was demobilised in January, 1920, and is entitled to the Victory and General Service Medals.
14, Church Path, Hammersmith, W.6   16388/A.

BALDWIN, L, (Miss), Special War Worker.
Throughout the war she made comforts for wounded soldiers and all kinds of hospital necessities, which were sent to various military hospitals at home and abroad. Her efforts were greatly appreciated by the military authorities.
58, Averill Street, Hammersmith, W.6   13989A.

BALDWIN, A. (Miss), Special War Worker.
During the war she was employed in the land army on general farm work, in Essex and Sussex, near Brighton, doing a man's work with conspicuous competence and zeal.
58, Averill Street, Hammersmith, W.6   13989/B.

BALDWIN, A. C., Gunner, Royal Field Artillery.
He joined in 1914, and served on the Western Front. He was engaged at the battles of Armentieres, Ypres and the Somme, and remained at his post continuously for five years. He was finally demobilised in April, 1919, and holds the 1915 Star, General Service and Victory Medals.
38, Cornwallis Grove, Edmonton.   13322.

BALDWIN, H., Pte., Royal Fusiliers.
He enlisted in September, 1914, served in France, taking part in many engagements and being wounded in the arm. He was discharged from hospital in December, 1916, as medically unfit for further service owing to heart trouble, following on excessive strain. He holds the 1914-15 Star, General Service and Victory Medals.
20, Werley Avenue, Fulham.   X17872.

BALDWIN, W., Pte., Royal Berks. Rgt. & M.G.C.
Having joined the Colours in 1903, he was immediately sent to France in 1914, where he took part in the retreat from Mons, in which engagement he was wounded. He was again engaged at Neuve Chapelle, Loos (where he was again wounded), the Somme, and Arras (where he was gassed). Finally he took part in our last Big Advance in 1918, and was demobilised in February, 1919, holding the Mons Star and the General Service and Victory Medals.
11, Purves Road, Willesden.   H18021.

BALDWIN, W. E., Sergt., R.A.S.C.
He joined in January, 1915, and served in France from May of the same year until October, 1918. He was demobilised in April, 1919, and holds the 1915 Star, General Service and Victory Medals.
56, Harley Road, Harlesden.   13396.

BALDWIN, W. H., Special War Worker.
From 1914 until 1918 he was employed as a fitter at Pembroke Dockyard. He was engaged on testing and fitting submarine engines, and on several occasions whilst carrying out this important work his vessel was attacked by U-boats. His work was obviously of the greatest national importance and frequently involved considerable danger.
93, Barret's Green Road, Harlesden.   T13821.

BALL, A., Pte., Royal Army Service Corps.
He joined on March 17th, 1915, and was sent to the East in June the same year. There he saw service on various Fronts, in Egypt and Salonica, at Suez and Alexandria and on the Struma and at Dorian during the campaigns in those theatres. He was finally demobilised in March, 1919, and holds the 1915 Star, General Service and Victory Medals.
17, College Road, Kensal Rise.   X17183.

BALL, C. E., Pte., Connaught Rangers.
He joined on December 10th, 1915, and during his service in France took part in the battles of Ypres and Arras. He served also in Salonica and Palestine, and was demobilised in April, 1919. He holds the General Service and Victory Medals.
58, Millbrook Road, Lower Edmonton.   13958.

BALL, D., Special War Worker.
He was engaged on munition work at the important factory of the National Filling Station at Durham, and in particular on the work of reconstruction of that factory, following on the violent explosion which occurred there. His services were of great value.
18, Orbain Road, Fulham.   X18039/B.

BALL, W. D., Pte., R.A.O.C. and King's Own Royal Lancaster Regiment.
Joining in February, 1915, he served in the ammunition stores at Boulogne and Dunkirk, being exposed to no small risk from hostile bombing and long range gun fire. In October, 1918, he was transferred to the K.O.R.L. Regiment, and took part in our last Advance in 1918, when he was wounded and invalided home.
On leaving hospital he was demobilised in 1919, holding the 1915 Star, the General Service and Victory Medals.
18, Orbain Road, Fulham.   X18039/A.

BALL, G. E., Pte., Devonshire Regiment.
He joined in May, 1915, and was stationed at Devonport, Exeter and at Plymouth, where owing to injuries received in an accident he became deaf, resulting in his discharge in March of the following year.
17, Hartopp Avenue, Fulham. X17732.

BALL, H., 2nd Air Mechanic, Royal Air Force.
He joined on August 5th, 1914, and saw service in France until he was demobilised on November 8th, 1919.
He holds the General Service and Victory Medals.
99, Sherbrooke Road, Fulham. X18460.

BALL, J. F., Sergt., Middlesex Regiment.
He enlisted on November 14th, 1915, and served for two years in France, during which period he took part in many engagements and was badly gassed in the battle of Passchendaele. He gained his promotion for consistent good work throughout his service, and was finally demobilised in November, 1919, holding the General Service and Victory Medals.
12, Roundwood Road, Willesden. 16525.

BALLANCE, A., Pte., 11th Middlesex Regt. and Gunner, R.F.A.
He joined in August, 1914, and served on the Western Front till he was wounded at Loos in May, 1915. He then joined the R.F.A., from which he was discharged as medically unfit. Afterwards he rejoined the Colours, this time in the Navy, and served until his final discharge in May, 1916.
He holds the 1914–15 Star, the General Service and Victory Medals.
122, Carlyle Avenue, Harlesden. 14188A.

BALLANCE, T., Lce.-Cpl., Royal Engineers.
He joined in August, 1914, and went to the Western Front in the same year, taking part in the battles of Arras, Loos, the Somme, Ypres and many other engagements. He was severely wounded at Hulluch on July 4th, 1915, but is still serving.
He holds the 1914 Star, the General Service and Victory Medals.
122, Carlyle Avenue, Harlesden. 14188/B.

BALLARD, A. (Mrs.), Special War Worker.
During the war she was employed at Perivale Munition Factory, Park Royal, chiefly engaged on the inspection of fuses. In her duties there she was frequently exposed to considerable risk, but she remained at her post throughout this period.
90, Archel Road, West Kensington. 16675/A.

BALLARD, A. S., Air Mechanic, R.A.F.
He joined in May, 1916, and served with General Allenby's forces in Egypt and Palestine, taking part in the capture of Jerusalem.
He holds the General Service and Victory Medals, and was demobilised in 1919.
90, Archel Road, West Kensington. 16675/B.

BALLARD, J., Gunner, Royal Field Artillery.
He joined on January 26th, 1915, served on the Western Front from that year until 1919, and took part in the operations at Ypres, Cambrai, on the Somme, and went through the Retreat and Advance of 1918.
He was demobilised on June 21st, 1919, and holds the 1915 Star, General Service and Victory Medals.
59, Heron Road, Willesden. 15604/C.

BALLARD, G., Pte., Devonshire Regiment.
Enlisting at the outbreak of war, he was sent to France, where he took part in the retreat from Mons, the Marne and the Aisne. In 1915 he was drafted to Mesopotamia and thence to India. In this theatre he took part in local operations, and was admitted to hospital for a time suffering from dysentery and fever. He had been previously wounded in the arm.
In July, 1919, he was demobilised, holding the 1914 Star, General Service and Victory Medals.
29, Heron Road, Willesden. 15604/B.

BALLARD, T., 2nd Air Mechanic, R.A.F.
Joining up at the early age of 17 in April, 1917, he obtained his training in England, where he was retained for service. He has since signed on for a further period of two years, and holds the General Service Medal.
29, Heron Road, Willesden. 15604/A.

BALLARD, J., Gunner, Royal Field Artillery.
He joined in August, 1914, and went to the Eastern Front, where he saw active service in Egypt, Jericho, Palestine, Jaffa, Beer Sheba (where he was wounded), and at Jerusalem.
He holds the General Service and Victory Medals, and was demobilised in 1919.
41, Lurgan Avenue, Hammersmith. 13452.

BAMBRIDGE, M. (Mrs.), Special War Worker.
During the war she did very valuable work at the White City Factory, where she was employed in making soldiers' equipments, tents and other articles.
She was commended for her work.
14, Orbain Road, Fulham, S.W. X18046/A.

BAMBRIDGE, F. C., Bombardier, R.F.A.
He joined in 1915, and served on the Western Front, taking part in the engagements at the Somme, Loos, Arras, Armentieres, Amiens, Ypres, Vimy Ridge, Bullecourt and Lille, and the Advance of 1918. He then went to Germany with the Army of Occupation, and was demobilised in 1919, holding the 1915 Star, the General Service and Victory Medals.
14, Orbain Road, Fulham, S.W. X18046/B.

BANE, S., Pte., 7th London Regiment.
He was serving when war broke out, went to France in December, 1914, and took part in the battles of La Bassée and Festubert, where he was wounded in March, 1915.
He was discharged in April, 1916, and holds the 1914–15 Star, General Service and Victory Medals.
5, Manor Park Road, Harlesden. 13217.

BANGERT, F. G., Pte., Royal Fusiliers.
He joined in October, 1918, and served with the Army of Occupation in Germany from April, 1919, until March, 1920, when he was demobilised.
72, Villiers Road, Willesden. 16149.

BANGS, G. W., Pte., 13th Royal Fusiliers.
He joined on July, 25th, 1916, was sent to the Western Front in November and was reported missing on April 23rd, 1917. He was subsequently reported as lost in action.
He is entitled the General Service and Victory Medals.
33, Shakespeare Avenue, Harlesden. 13889.

BANGS, W., Pte., R.A.M.C. (1st Field Amb.).
He joined in August, 1914, and served in France until he was discharged on October 20th, 1915, suffering from chronic rheumatism.
He holds the 1914 Star, General Service and Victory Medals.
43, Haldane Road, Fulham. X17077.

BANKS, C., Pte., East Surrey Regiment.
He joined March, 1916, was sent to France in the same year, and took part in the battle of Cambrai, where he was wounded in 1917.
He was demobilised in 1919, holding the General Service and Victory Medals.
50, Shrubbery Road, Lower Edmonton. 14551.

BANKS, C. A., Pte., Royal Army Medical Corps.
He joined in October, 1916, and was sent to France in the same year, where he served two years. He was engaged in practically all the operations during that period and was demobilised in December, 1918.
He holds the General Service and Victory Medals.
33, Huddleston Road, Willesden. X17406.

BANKS, E. J., Pte., 7th London Regiment.
He joined on March 16th, 1915, served on the Western Front and took part in the battles of Ypres, the Somme, Arras and Cambrai. He was in hospital in France with influenza previous to being demobilised on March 17, 1919, holding the General Service and Victory Medals.
15, Everington Street, Fulham. 13964.

BANKS, H. P., A.B., R.N., H.M.S. " Canopus."
He joined in August, 1914, and served with the Grand Fleet in the Dardanelles. In 1918 he contracted influenza, of which he died in the same year.
He was entitled to the 1914 Star, General Service and Victory Medals.
12, Dyson's Road, Upper Edmonton. 16872A.

BANKS, L. A., A.B., R.N., H.M.S. " Douglas."
He joined in 1915 and served with the Grand Fleet, seeing service in the North Sea and elsewhere.
He holds the 1915 Star, General Service and Victory Medals, and is still in the Navy.
12, Dyson's Road, Upper Edmonton. 16872/B.

BANKS, J., Gunner, Royal Garrison Artillery.
He joined on March 6th, 1917, and served on the Western Front, taking part in many engagements, during which he was twice wounded. After being in hospital for six months, he went to Germany with the Army of Occupation, and served there until his demobilisation in November, 1919. He holds the General Service and Victory Medals.
2, Grove Street, Edmonton. X17643.

2

BANNING, A. W., Sergt., 2nd S. Lancs. Regt.
He joined in August, 1914, proceeded to the Western Front in 1915, and served at Ypres, Loos, Lens, the Somme, Arras and Cambrai. He was very severely wounded on the Somme, necessitating the amputation of his right leg.
He holds the King's and Queen's South African Medals, the 1914–15 Star, General Service and Victory Medals, and was discharged on July 27th, 1917.
54, Brownlow Road, Willesden.   15014.

BANNISTER, G. A. L., Pte., Machine Gun Corps.
He joined in February, 1918, and served with the Machine Gun Corps. He was unsuccessful in obtaining a transfer for service overseas, and was eventually demobilised in April, 1919.
22, Cobhold Road, Willesden.   10070.

BARB, F., Pte., 23rd Middlesex Regiment.
With three brothers already serving, he enlisted in April, 1915, but was prevented from going overseas owing to medical disabilities, and was finally discharged in October of the same year on medical grounds. During his service he was at Homebury Camp.
49, Ancill Street, W.6   13762.

BARBER, E. W., Driver, R.F.A., and 19th Baty. 7th London Brigade.
He was called up on August 4th, 1914, served on the Western Front from the following March until January, 1919, and took part in the fighting at Festubert, Loos, Ypres and elsewhere.
He was demobilised in February, 1919, holding the 1914–15 Star, General Service and Victory Medals.
7a, Vallier Road, College Park, Willesden.   X17673.

BARDEN, B., Pte., 19th Middlesex Regiment.
He enlisted in May, 1915, and was sent to the Western Front the following year, where he took part in many engagements, afterwards being drafted to Italy.
He was discharged suffering from shell shock on February 27th, 1919, and holds the General Service and Victory Medals.
39, Shakespeare Avenue, Harlesden.   13886.

BARDILL, H., Cpl., Royal Engineers.
He joined on March 3rd, 1915, served on the Western Front, taking part in the battle of Ypres, and was then sent to Salonica.
He was demobilised on March 4th, 1919, holding the General Service and Victory Medals.
51, Delorme Street, Fulham.   T13961.

BARGETON, S. M., Lieut., R.N.A.S. & Devon R.
He joined in March, 1915, served on the Western Front from July, 1916, until February, 1917, and from June until October, 1918, and took part in the fighting at Rheims, Vaulx-Vraucourt, Havrincourt, Flesquieres, Marcoing and Cambrai, being wounded. He was also stationed at Belfort with No. 3 Bombing Squadron, and acted as observer.
He received a commission in the Devon Regiment, and was demobilised in May, 1919, holding the General Service and Victory Medals.
81, Hawthorne Road, Willesden.   X17425C.

BARGETON, P. B. (M.M.), Sergt., Rifle Brigade (Prince Consort's Own).
He enlisted in August, 1914, was sent to France in the following January and wounded in the thigh at the battle of Neuve Chapelle. He was in hospital for a year, and after returning to the Western Front in March, 1916, was in action at Arras, Ypres, on the Somme and in the last Retreat and Advance.
He was awarded the Military Medal for devotion to duty and conspicuous gallantry, and he was mentioned for great bravery under fire. He is now serving in India.
He holds the 1914–15 Star, the General Service and Victory Medals in addition to the Military Medal.
81, Hawthorne Road, Willesden.   X17425B.

BARGETON, J. J., Pte., Australian M.G.C.
He reached England in February, 1917, and in the same month was sent to France, where he remained until September, 1918. He took part in various engagements, went through the Great Retreat of March, 1918, and was wounded.
He returned to Australia in October, 1918, and holds the General Service and Victory Medals.
81, Hawthorne Road, Willesden.   X17425A.

BARKER, A. G., Pte., 11th Royal Fusiliers.
He joined in September, 1914, and served through many engagements on the Western Front, including those of the Somme, Cambrai, Arras and Amiens, as despatch rider and runner.
He was mentioned in despatches, holds the 1914–15 Star, General Service and Victory Medals, and was demobilised in March, 1919.
24, Charlton Road, Harlesden.   13108/A.

BARKER, S. T. (M.M.), Lce.-Cpl., Middlesex Regiment and 2/2nd London Regt.
He joined in February, 1917, and was sent to the Western Front in July of the same year, where he took part in many engagments, including Messines, Vimy Ridge and Bullecourt. For gallantry and devotion to duty he was awarded the Military Medal. He was once wounded.
In addition to the Military Medal he holds the General Service and Victory Medals. Demobilised February, 1919.
24, Charlton Road, Harlesden.   13108/B.

BARKER, B. M. J., Sergt., Royal Fusiliers.
He joined for duty in August, 1914, but was not successful in his endeavours to get overseas, being retained on special duties at Southampton, Bury St. Edmund's and elsewhere, until he was demobilised in March, 1919.
3, Gowan Road, Willesden Green.   X17136.

BARKER, E., Gunner, Royal Field Artillery.
He joined on September 4th, 1914, and was sent to the Western Front the following year. He served four years in France, and took part in several engagements. He was in action on the Somme, at Ypres and La Bassée.
He was discharged in April, 1919, and holds the 1915 Star, General Service and Victory Medals.
10, Whitehall Street, Tottenham, N.17   X18129/A.

BARKER, F., Pte., Middlesex Regiment.
He enlisted in 1915, and was sent to France the following year. He took part in the heavy fighting on the Somme in August, 1916, where he was killed on the 18th day of that month.
He was entitled to the General Service and Victory Medals.
10, Whitehall Street, Tottenham, N.17   X18129C.

BARKER, W., Sergeant, Essex Regiment.
He joined in August, 1914, and was sent to France in the same year. He took part in many important engagements, including the battle of the Somme in 1916, and was killed in action on April 22nd, 1917.
He was entitled to the 1914 Star, General Service and Victory Medals.
10, Whitehall Street, Tottenham, N.17   X18129B.

BARKER, E. S., Driver, R.E. (57th Field Co.).
He enlisted on August 4th, 1914, and served in France, taking part in many engagements, including Mons, Ypres, the Somme and Armentieres. He was severely wounded in April, 1918, and lost his right leg in consequence.
He holds the 1914 Star, General Service and Victory Medals, and was discharged in 1919.
24, Love Lane, Tottenham.   X18376.

BARKER, E. W. (M.M.), Pte., Middlesex Regt.
He enlisted in November, 1914, and was sent to France in the following September. He took part in the battles of Loos, Ypres, Arras and the Somme, and was three times wounded and gassed.
He was mentioned in despatches, and awarded the Military Medal for conspicuous gallantry in the field near Arras, and holds also the 1914–15 Star and the General Service and Victory Medals. He was discharged in March, 1919.
5, Elthorne Avenue, Hanwell.   11066.

BARKER, F., Sergt., Royal Army Service Corps.
He enlisted on August 8th, 1914, and served on the Western Front, taking part in the battles of Mons, Loos, Neuve Chapelle and Ypres, where he was wounded in the left lung in 1916. He was admitted to the 4th London General Hospital, and was demobilised on March 31st, 1919, holding the 1914–15 Star, General Service and Victory Medals.
15, Worlidge Street, Hammersmith.   12588.

BARKER, W., Pte., 4th Middlesex Regiment.
He enlisted in August, 1914, was sent to France in the same month, and killed in action on August 23rd, 1914, at Mons. He was entitled to the 1914 Star, General Service and Victory Medals.
26, Oldfield Road, Willesden.   16112/A.

BARKER, J., Pte., 4th Middlesex Regiment.
He enlisted in August, 1914, was sent to France in the same month and took part in the battle of Mons. He was wounded, taken prisoner, and died of wounds on January 26, 1916, at Doberitz Camp, Germany.
He was entitled to the 1914 Star, General Service and Victory Medals.
26, Oldfield Road, Willesden.   16112/B.

BARKER, H., Rifleman, 9th Batt. London Regt.
He joined in 1916, and during his service on the Western Front was in action on the Somme, Cambrai, Bapaume and Ypres.
He was demobilised in 1919, and holds the General Service and Victory Medals.
26, Oldfield Road, Willesden.   16112/C

BARKER, G. (M.M.), Pte., 1st Middlesex Regt.
He joined in 1916, served on the Western Front, taking part
in the battles of Ypres and the Somme, was wounded, and
awarded the Military Medal for devotion to duty and
conspicuous gallantry on the field.
He holds also the General Service and Victory Medals, and
was demobilised in 1919.
26, Oldfield Road, Willesden. 16112/D.

BARKER, W., Pte., 1/19th London Regt.
He joined in March, 1915, and served for three years on the
Western Front, during which time he took part in the battles
of Cambrai and the Somme, being wounded in action at the
latter, and subsequently invalided home.
He was demobilised in December, 1919. He is entitled to
the General Service and Victory Medals.
19, Argyle Road, Lower Edmonton. 15264.

BARKER, P., Pte., Middlesex Regiment.
He joined in August, 1916, but was never allowed to proceed
overseas, being medically unfit, and was eventually discharged on medical grounds in February, 1917.
11, Bourke Road, Willesden, N.W.10. 15559B.

BARKER, J. W., Pte., 17th Middlesex Regt.
He enlisted in January, 1916, and was sent to the Western
Front in the following May. During severe fighting he was
killed on July 28th, 1916, at Delville Wood.
He was entitled to the General Service and Victory Medals.
11, Bourke Road, Willesden., N.W.10 15559A.

BARKER, L., Cpl., 2nd Batt. Royal Fusiliers.
At outbreak of war he was already in the Army, and was sent
to France in December, 1916. He took part in many engagements, and was killed during severe fighting at Passchendaele on October 26th, 1917.
He was entitled to the General Service and Victory Medals.
3, Gowan Road, Willesden Green. X17138.

BARLEY, W., Sergt., Middlesex Regiment.
He joined in September, 1914, but was not permitted to
proceed overseas owing to being over age. He served for
over four years on Home Defence. He was demobilised
in January, 1919.
103, Angel Road, Edmonton. 16581.

BARNARD, H., Cpl., 4/3rd Royal Fusiliers.
He joined in December, 1914, and was later sent to the
Western Front. He was wounded on September 23rd, 1917,
during the battle of Ypres, and was in consequence rendered
unfit for further overseas service.
He was demobilised in February, 1919, and holds the General
Service and Victory Medals.
37, First Avenue, Queen's Park, W. X18941.

BARNARD, W. C., Sapper, R.E. (R.O D.).
He joined in August, 1915, and proceeded to France shortly
afterwards, where he was engaged in active operations at
Ypres, the Somme, Arras, Cambrai and in several other
places.
He holds the 1915 Star, General Service and Victory Medals,
and was demobilised in February, 1919.
80, Oldfield Road, Willesden. 15765.

BARNES, A., Pte., East Surrey Regiment.
He joined in 1917, served on the Western Front until he was
demobilised in 1919. He took part in the fighting near
Mons, and elsewhere.
He holds the General Service and Victory Medals.
58, Pretoria Road, Upper Edmonton. X17026.

**BARNES, J. E., Pte., 13th London Regiment
(Kensington Battalion).**
He joined on August 5th, 1914, and served on the Western
Front in numerous engagements. He was awarded the
Croix-de-Guerre for bravery in the field at Verdun.
He holds the 1915 Star, General Service and Victory Medals,
and was discharged in January, 1916.
37, Wilson's Road, Hammersmith. 15855/A.

BARNES, A. H., Pte., Machine Gun Corps.
He joined in January, 1918, and during his service in France
was badly gassed, in consequence of which he was for some
time in hospital in France and England.
He holds the General Service and Victory Medals, and was
demobilised in 1919.
37, Wilson's Road, Hammersmith. 15855/B.

**BARNES, A. K., Pte., 6th London Regiment
and Machine Gun Corps.**
He joined on May 6th, 1915, and after training as a Machine
Gunner, went to France in June, 1918. He was killed in
action on August 21st in the same year, during the Great
Advance.
He was entitled to the General Service and Victory Medals.
114, Villiers Road, Willesden. 16724.

BARNES, B., Driver, Royal Field Artillery.
He joined in May, 1915, and went to the Western Front the
same year, taking part in many battles, including those of the
Somme, Ypres, Albert, Arras, St. Eloi, Cambrai and the
Great Retreat and Advance in 1918. He holds the 1914–15
Star, General Service and Victory Medals, and was demobi-
lised in May, 1919.
6, Ravensworth Road, Kensal Rise. X17621.

**BARNES, C. A., Pte., 3rd London Regt. (Royal
Fusiliers).**
He joined on January 12th, 1915, and went to the Western
Front in the following year. He took part in many engage-
ments including those of the Somme, Arras and Ypres, and
was wounded twice.
He was demobilised in March, 1919, holding the General
Service and Victory Medals, and died three months later
from an illness contracted whilst serving in the Army.
10, West Ella Road, Harlesden. 15105.

BARNES, E. (Mrs.), Special War Worker.
For nearly three years she was employed at Perivale Ammunition Works as an examiner in the Fuse Section. During
this period she was exposed to considerable danger, as several
bombing raids were made in the area.
She was commended for her work.
12, Winchelsea Road, Harlesden. 13716A.

**BARNES, G. E., Rifleman, K.R.R. Corps and
Sapper, R.E.**
He joined in February, 1915, and proceeded overseas in the
following August. For four years he was on the Western
Front, and took part in many engagements, including the
battles of Arras, Lens, Cambrai and Vimy Ridge.
He was discharged in February, 1919, suffering from a dis-
ablement contracted on service. He holds the 1915 Star,
General Service and Victory Medals.
12, Winchelsea Road, Harlesden. 13716B.

BARNES, E., Lce.-Corpl., 26th Middlesex Regt.
He joined in May, 1915, and served in Salonica for three years,
where he took part in all the local operations.
He was demobilised in March, 1919, holding the General
Service and Victory Medals.
77, Brett Road, Harlesden. 14521/A.

**BARNES, E., 1st-Class Boy, R.N., H.M.S.
"Tipperary."**
He joined in February, 1915, served in the North Sea, and
was killed during the battle of Jutland in May, 1916.
He was entitled to the General Service and Victory Medals.
77, Brett Road, Harlesden. 14521/B.

BARNES, G., S.M., 3rd Worcestershire Regt.
He joined in August, 1914, served on the Western Front,
in 1917 was sent to Italy, where he served for 12 months and
then returned to France. He took part in the battles of the
Somme, the Aisne and Valenciennes, being wounded at the
last two engagements.
He was discharged on June 18th, 1919, holding the 1914–15
Star, General Service and Victory Medals.
48, Minet Avenue, Willesden. 13910.

BARNES, G. W., Pte., 6th Wiltshire Regiment.
He joined in September, 1914, and during his service on the
Western Front took part in the battles of Loos, Arras, Ypres,
Cambrai and the Somme, and was for some time in hospital
in France and at home, suffering with neurasthenia.
He holds the 1914–15 Star, General Service and Victory
Medals and was demobilised in March, 1919.
37, Wilson's Road, Hammersmith. 15854A.

BARNES, J. W., Pte., R.A.M.C.
He joined in October, 1914, and during his service on the
Western Front took part in the battles of Loos, Arras, Ypres,
Cambrai and the Somme, was wounded and gassed,
in consequence of which he was for some time in hospital.
He holds the 1914–15 Star, General Service and Victory
Medals, and was demobilised in May, 1919.
37, Wilson's Road, Hammersmith. 15854B.

BARNES, P., Pte., Seaforth Highlanders.
He joined in May, 1916, and served in France, where he was
wounded in action at Arras, and invalided home.
He holds the General Service and Victory Medals and was
demobilised in January, 1920.
34, Yewfield Road, Willesden. 16370.

BARNES, V. W., Sergt., Oxford and Bucks. L.I.
He joined in 1915, served in Mesopotamia, where he contracted dysentery and sunstroke, and after being invalided
to India, died there in 1918 He was entitled to the General
Service and Victory Medals.
75, Burns Road, Harlesden. 13453/B.

BARNES, H., Sergt., 9th Middlesex Regiment.
He joined in November, 1915, and being medically unfit for active service, was engaged in a Record Office until his demobilisation in March, 1919.
75, Burns Road, Harlesden.   13453A.

BARNES, H. A., Rifleman, Rifle Brigade.
He joined in July, 1915, to France in the following February, and was killed in action on the Somme on July 1st, 1916.
He was entitled to the General Service and Victory Medals.
3, Minet Avenue, Willesden.   13905.

BARNES, J., Pte., Royal Fusiliers.
He joined in April, 1915, and served on the Western Front and in Egypt and Salonica. He was in action on the Somme and at Ypres, where he was wounded in 1917.
He was discharged in March, 1918, after being wounded four times, holding the 1915 Star, the General Service and Victory Medals.
46, Shakespeare Avenue, Harlesden.   13615.

BARNES, J., Cpl., 7th London Regiment.
He joined in 1915 and served with the City of London Regiment on important training duties until demobilised in 1918.
184, Blythe Road, Hammersmith.   12494.

BARNETT, A., Sergt., Norfolk Regiment.
He joined in June, 1911, and served from 1914 until 1916 at Mons, Ypres, Arras and elsewhere in France and Belgium. He then proceeded to Mesopotamia, where he was wounded, and was in hospital in India.
He holds the Somaliland Medal, Mons Star, General Service and Victory Medals, and was demobilised in March, 1919.
45, Brownlow Road, Harlesden.   15012.

BARNETT, A. S. H., A.B., R.N., H.M.S. "Ganges."
He was in the Navy at outbreak of hostilities, and served on escort duty to and from Canada, Africa and France.
He was demobilised in January, 1919, holding the 1914–15 Star, General Service and Victory Medals.
75, Villiers Road, Willesden.   16150.

BARNETT, C. W., Trumpeter, R.F.A.
He joined on August 16th, 1915, and served in France, where he took part in many engagements, including Loos, Arras, Ypres, the Somme and Cambrai. He was wounded at the Somme on April 16th, 1916.
He was demobilised on February 25th, 1919, holding the 1915 Star, General Service and Victory Medals.
11, Moselle Street, Tottenham.   X18363.

BARNETT, W. F., Pte., East Surrey Regiment.
He joined in February, 1915, was sent to France shortly afterwards and was killed in action at the battle of the Somme on July 31st, 1916. He is entitled to the 1915 Star, General Service and Victory Medals.
20, Bounces Road, Edmonton.   13954/B.

BARNETT, A. T., Pte., Royal Fusiliers.
He enlisted in August, 1914, served on the Western Front, and was killed in action on July 1st, 1916, on the Somme. He is entitled to the 1915 Star, General Service and Victory Medals.
20, Bounces Road, Edmonton.   13954/A.

BARNETT, J. H., Sergt., 9th Middlesex Regt.
He joined in August, 1914, served on the Western Front for two years and was in action at Ypres, Passchendaele, the Somme, Cambrai, Arras and St. Quentin, later being sent with the Army of Occupation to the Rhine.
He holds the General Service and Victory Medals, and was demobilised in February, 1919.
19, Corby Road, Willesden.   15768/A.

BARNETT, W. G., 3rd Air Mechanic, R.A.F.
He joined up in the Infantry in 1915, and served for two years on the Western Front, being present at the operations on the Somme (where he was twice wounded), La Bassée, Dickebusch and Kemmel. In 1915 he was transferred to the R.A.F. on medical grounds, where he served until demobilised the same year.
He holds the 1915 Star, General Service and Victory Medals.
19, Corby Road, Willesden.   15768/C.

BARNETT, E., Sapper, R.E. (R.O.D.).
He joined in 1916, and served with the R.O.D. on the Western Front on the Somme, the Marne, Ypres and in other sectors.
He holds the General Service and Victory Medals, and was demobilised in 1919.
19, Corby Road, Willesden.   15768/B.

BARNETT, J., 2nd Air Mechanic, R.A.F.
He joined on November 3rd, 1916, and served on the Western Front for six months on special duties with the Photographic Section.
He holds the General Service and Victory Medals, and was demobilised on March 29th, 1919.
6, Talbot Road, Willesden.   15971.

BARNS, J. S., Leading Seaman, Royal Navy.
He joined in August, 1914, and served with the Grand Fleet and in Africa.
He was demobilised in January, 1919, holding the 1914 Star, General Service and Victory Medals.
4, Lichfield Road, Lower Edmonton.   14670.

BARON, E. C., Cpl., Royal Berkshire Regiment.
He joined in September, 1914, and after seeing service in France was sent to Salonica, where he was killed in action on September 30th, 1916.
He was entitled to the 1915 Star, the General Service and Victory Medals.
51, Everington Street, W.6   13972.

BARR, H. G., A.B., R.N., H.M.S. "Walpole."
He joined on July 16th, 1911, and served in Egypt, at Alexandria and Cairo, and was wounded.
He holds the 1914 Star, General Service and Victory Medals, and is still serving.
25, Beaconsfield Road, Lower Edmonton.   14764/B.

BARR, J., Pte., Royal Defence Corps.
He served with the Royal Defence Corps from his enlistment in August, 1914, serving at Dover and elsewhere until discharged in June, 1917.
25, Beaconsfield Road, Lower Edmonton.   14764/A.

BARR, W., Pte., Royal Fusiliers.
He enlisted in August, 1914, and in the following year was sent to the Dardanelles, where he was wounded in action. Later he served in France from 1916 to 1918, took part in many engagements and was wounded at Ypres.
He holds the 1914–15 Star, General Service and Victory Medals, and was demobilised in May, 1919.
65, Pretoria Road, Upper Edmonton.   X17028.

BARRATT, A. E., Trooper, 4th Res. Regt Dragoons
He joined in December, 1914, and served first in Norfolk and at Aldershot. Later, having failed to secure his transfer overseas, he served at Brighton and London until finally demobilised in 1919.
5, Lintaine Grove, Fulham.   16814.

BARRATT, H., Pte., Royal Army Service Corps.
He joined in 1915, and acted as wheeler with the Army in France, Salonica and Egypt. He was invalided home from Malta unfit for further service in July, 1917.
He holds the 1915 Star, Victory and General Service Medals.
47, Redfern Road, Harlesden.   13200.

BARRATT, J. W., Sapper, Royal Engineers.
He joined in May, 1915, and served at the Dardanelles and in Egypt.
He was demobilised in March, 1919, and holds the General Service and Victory Medals.
13, Lichfield Road, Lower Edmonton.   14672.

BARRETT, W. H., Gunner, R.G.A.
He joined in August, 1917, and served in France and Germany.
He took part in engagements on the Somme, at Arras and Ypres, being gassed.
He holds the General Service and Victory Medals, and was demobilised in November, 1919.
61, Angel Road, Edmonton.   16493.

BARRETT, W., Pte., R.A.M.C.
He joined up in the Infantry in October, 1914, and served in France until 1919. He took part in the Somme battle, was wounded twice and subsequently transferred to the R.A.M.C.
Holds the 1914 Star, General Service and Victory Medals.
He was demobilised in 1919.
44, Church Road, Hammersmith.   11104/B.

BARRETT, T. J., Pte., Norfolk Regiment.
He joined in December, 1915, and was sent to the Western Front, where he was principally engaged on railway construction work during his 3½ years' service. He was wounded, and eventually discharged on May 11th, 1919.
He holds the General Service and Victory Medals.
24, Rosaline Road, Fulham, S.W.6   X18179.

BARRS, A. L., Bombardier, R.F.A. (" B " Battery, 82nd Brigade).
He joined in September, 1914, served in France, was in action on the Somme, where he was wounded in August, 1915, and later in March, 1916. He was discharged on December 16th, 1916, on account of wounds, and holds the 1915 Star, General Service and Victory Medals.
18, Disraeli Road, Harlesden. 14695.

BARRS, R. A., Pte., 1st Bedfordshire Regiment.
He joined in 1915, and was sent to France, where he took part in the last Advance of 1918. He was demobilised in 1919, and afterwards re-enlisted.
He holds the General Service and Victory Medals.
3, Orbain Road, Fulham. TX18638/A.

BARRS, J. A., Pte., Royal Fusiliers.
He joined in March, 1915, and was sent to the Dardanelles. He was invalided home, and after his recovery was sent to France, where he took part in the battles of Ypres, Arras, the Somme, Armentieres, Amiens, Messines, Bullecourt, St. Quentin, and others. He also acted as stretcher-bearer, and was twice wounded. He was demobilised in March, 1919.
He holds the 1915 Star, General Service and Victory Medals.
3, Orbain Road, Fulham. TX18638B.

BARRY, I. W., Pte., 4th Hussars and Sapper, R.E.
He was serving at the outbreak of war. Was sent to France in 1914, and took part in the Mons Retreat, the battles of the Aisne, the Marne, Ypres, and the Retreat and Advance of 1918.
He was discharged in April, 1919, holding the Mons Star, the General Service and Victory Medals.
5, St. Margaret's Road, Hanwell. 11053.

BARTER, A. W., Pte., 2nd East Surrey Regt.
He joined in February, 1915, and went to Salonica, serving there throughout the war.
He was demobilised in February, 1919, holding the General Service and Victory Medals.
34, Hanwell Road, Fulham. X18076.

BARTER, G., Pte., R.A.S.C. (M.T.).
He joined in December, 1915, and served with the Mechanical Transport Section in France until 1919, when he was demobilised.
He holds the General Service and Victory Medals.
25, St. Thomas Road, Fulham. X17231.

BARTER, H. F., Sergt., Northumberland Fus.
He enlisted in January, 1918, and was retained on duties in England for training purposes till the Armistice. He was then sent to Germany on escort duty with Germans repatriated from this country.
1, Gloucester Road, Edmonton. X17004.

BARTLETT, A. E., Pte., 11th Grenadier Guards.
He enlisted on August 4th, 1914, and served on the Western Front, where he took part in the battles of the Somme, Arras, Ypres and Cambrai, and was three times wounded, as a result of which he was discharged on December 14th, 1918.
He holds the 1914 Star, General Service and Victory Medals.
1, Lintaine Grove, Fulham. 16816.

BARTLETT, A. V., Pte., Middlesex Regiment.
He joined in September, 1914, and was sent to Egypt in the following year, later serving through many engagements with General Allenby in Palestine.
He was demobilised in 1920, holding the 1915 Star, General Service and Victory Medals.
20, Ambleside Road, Willesden. 16933/A.

BARTLETT, E., Pte., Middlesex Regiment.
He joined in 1914, went to Egypt the following year, and later was taken prisoner and interned in Turkey for over a year. He was demobilised in April, 1919, holding the 1915 Star, General Service and Victory Medals.
20, Ambleside Road, Willesden. 16933/B.

BARTLETT, G. C., Cpl., Royal Field Artillery.
He joined in August, 1914, went to the Western Front the following year, and took part in many battles, including those of the Somme, Ypres and Bullecourt, and was gassed in the Great Retreat of 1918.
He was demobilised in March, 1918, and holds the 1914-15 Star, General Service and Victory Medals.
20, Ambleside Road, Willesden. 16933/C.

BARTLETT, W. J., Rifleman, Rifle Brigade.
He joined in May, 1915, and whilst serving on the Western Front was wounded and taken prisoner, being in captivity for two years and two months.
He holds the General Service and Victory Medals, and was demobilised in February, 1919.
5, Cedar Road, Edmonton, 14036

BARTON, C. N., Pte., 2/10th Middlesex Regt.
He joined in June, 1916, and during his service on the Eastern Front, in Palestine and in Egypt, was in hospital three times, suffering from malarial fever.
He holds the General Service and Victory Medals, and was demobilised in December, 1919.
8, Laundry Road, Fulham. 15340/C.

BARTON, G. W., Pte., Royal Army Service Corps.
He joined on January 17, 1915, and during his service in France was present at the battles of Armentieres, the Somme, Arras, Ypres and Cambrai, and was badly gassed, as a result of which he was invalided home, and discharged on May 29th 1917.
He holds the 1914-15 Star and the General Service and Victory Medals.
8, Laundry Road, Fulham, W.6 15340A.

BARTON, G. W. (jun.), Lance-Corpl., 2/10th Middlesex Regiment.
He joined on January 10, 1915, and after having served on the Eastern Front, at the Dardanelles and in Egypt—where he was wounded—he died whilst a prisoner of war in Turkey in August, 1918.
He was entitled to the 1914-15 Star, General Service and Victory Medals.
8, Laundry Road, Fulham. 15340B.

BARTON, E. J., Sapper, Royal Engineers.
He joined in October, 1915, and served in France and Salonica, taking part in many engagements.
He was discharged on September 19, 1917, and holds the General Service and Victory Medals.
21, Aintree Street, Fulham. X18209.

BARTON, F., Pte., 1/2nd London Regiment.
He joined in January, 1915, and during his four years' service on the Western Front took part in the battles of the Somme, Ypres, Cambrai, Arras and Lens.
He was demobilised in March, 1919, holding the 1915 Star, the General Service and Victory Medals.
71, College Road, Kensal Rise. X18009,

BARTON, J., Pte., Royal Fusiliers.
He enlisted in February, 1915, and whilst serving he lost his eyesight in an accident.
He was discharged in June, 1919.
115, Felix Road, W. Ealing. 11018.

BARTON, G., Sapper, Royal Engineers.
He enlisted in December, 1914, was sent to France in 1916, and took part in various engagements, including the battles of Beaucourt, Arras and Albert.
He was demobilised in March, 1919, holding the General Service and Victory Medals.
27, Beaconsfield Road, Willesden. 16087.

BARTON, H. J., Bombardier, R.F.A.
He joined in 1914, served in France for four years, and took part in the battles of the Somme, Ypres, Arras, Loos, Armentieres, St. Quentin, Albert, Vimy Ridge, and the Great Retreat and Advance of 1918.
He was demobilised in June, 1919, holding the 1914-15 Star, General Service and Victory Medals.
74, Ancill Street, W.6 14004.

BARTON, W R., Sergt., R.E.
He was medically unfit for overseas service, and during his period in the Army, which extended from 1915 until 1919, acted as 1st-Class Certificated Master Cook at various places in England.
27, Letterstone Road, Fulham. X18443A.

BARTON, T., Special War Worker.
Being medically unfit for Army service, he was employed during the war on special work of national importance at a Fulham Munitions Factory.
27, Letterstone Road, Fulham. X18443B.

BARTON, T. H., Lce.-Corpl., Royal Sussex Regt.
He joined in 1915, served during the same year on the Western Front, taking part in the fighting at Zonnebeke, and was wounded in action in September, 1917.
He was demobilised in March, 1919, and holds the 1915 Star, General Service and Victory Medals.
78, Rosebery Road, Lower Edmonton. 14076/A

BARTON, W. J., Pte., Machine Gun Corps.
He joined in 1915, in the following year was sent to France, thence to Salonica, and later to Palestine and Egypt.
He was demobilised in August, 1919, and holds the General Service and Victory Medals.
78, Rosebery Road, Lower Edmonton. 14076/B.

BARWELL, C., Pte., The Buffs (East Kent Regt.).
He joined in May, 1916, and went to the Western Front in April of the following year, taking part in the battles of the Somme, Dickebusch, Ypres and many others, including the Great Retreat and Advance in 1918.
He was demobilised in November, 1919, holding the General Service and Victory Medals.
47, Waldo Road, Willesden.   X17632.

BARWICK, F. G. E., Pte., 10th Middlesex Regt.
He enlisted in October, 1914, at the age of 16, was sent to France and was killed in action on the Somme on August 31st, 1916.
He was entitled to the 1914-15 Star, General Service and Victory Medals.
27, Worlidge Street, Hammersmith.   12591.

BASHAM, F. J., Sergt., Notts. and Derby Regt.
He joined in 1916, and served in France for three years, during which time he took part in engagements on the Somme, at Cambrai, Arras, and at Ypres.
He holds the General Service and Victory Medals, and was demobilised in 1919.
27, Fourth Avenue, Paddington, W.   X18673.

BASING, W. H., Royal Navy, H.M.S. "Superb."
He joined in August, 1917, and served in the North Sea and Mediterranean, employed in issuing food and clothes to the men.
He is still with the Royal Navy, and holds the General Service and Victory Medals.
11, Dieppe Street, West Kensington.   16267.

BASSETT, C. W., Pte., D.L.I. and Y. & L. Regt.
He enlisted in June, 1917, and served on the Western Front.
Whilst in action at Ypres in July, 1918, he was killed.
He was entitled to the General Service and Victory Medals.
22, Mordaunt Road, Harlesden.   13732A.

BASSETT, E. A., Gunner, Royal Field Artillery.
He joined on April 13th, 1915, and served on the Western Front. While in action at the battle of Ypres on July 27th, 1916, he was killed.
He was entitled to the 1914-15 Star, the General Service and Victory Medals.
22, Mordaunt Road, Harlesden.   13732B.

BASSETT, P., A.B., R.N., H.M.S. "Renown."
He joined in April, 1916, and served with the Grand Fleet until August, 1917, when he was discharged unfit for further service owing to a nervous breakdown.
He holds the General Service and Victory Medals.
46, Pretoria Road, Upper Edmonton.   X17016.

BASSETT, W. E., Bombardier, R.G.A.
He joined in July, 1916, and in December was sent to Egypt, and thence to Salonica, where he remained until demobilised in November, 1919, being wounded and contracting malaria.
He holds the General Service and Victory Medals.
14, Mordaunt Road, Harlesden.   13631.

BASSETT, W. H., A.B., Royal Navy.
He joined in September, 1917, and served on board a "mystery" ship in the North Sea until he was demobilised in February, 1919.
He holds the General Service and Victory Medals.
26, Gloucester Road, Edmonton.   X17014.

BASTIN, A., Saddler, Royal Field Artillery.
He joined in December, 1915, and served in Salonica, where he contracted malaria. Later he went to France.
He was demobilised in June, 1919.
He holds the General Service and Victory Medals.
14, Nursery Street, Tottenham.   X18145.

BATCHELOR, C. W. F., Signaller, R.F.A.
He joined in 1915, and was wounded in action in France the following year.
He was demobilised in March, 1919, holding the General Service and Victory Medals.
21, Gowan Road, Willesden Green.   X16966/B.

BATCHELOR, S. R. N., Bombardier, R.F.A.
He joined in January, 1915, served throughout the Dardanelles campaign, and was later drafted to France, where he took part in many engagements. He was wounded during the Great Advance of 1918.
He was demobilised in March, 1919, and holds the General Service and Victory Medals.
21, Gowan Road, Willesden Green.   X16966/A.

BATCHELOR, E.W., 1st Air Mechanic, R.A.F.
He joined in 1915, and served in France from 1916 until 1919, when he was demobilised.
He holds the General Service and Victory Medals.
136, Montague Road, Edmonton.   15838.

BATEMAN, D. F., Rifleman, 6th Rifle Brigade.
He joined in October, 1914, served on the Western Front, and was engaged on transport work.
He holds the 1914-15 Star, General Service and Victory Medals, and was demobilised on February 28th, 1919.
22, Bayonne Road, Fulham.   14505.

BATEMAN, F., Sergt., R.A.S.C.
He joined in September, 1914, served on the Western Front and in East Africa, and took part in several engagements.
He was discharged medically unfit for further service in September, 1916, and holds the 1915 Star, General Service and Victory Medals.
38, Shrewsbury Road, Harlesden.   14127.

BATEMAN, W., Driver, R.A.S.C.
He re-enlisted in August, 1914, and served in France, where he died on April 8th, 1917.
He held the King's and Queen's South African Medals, and was entitled to the 1914 Star, General Service and Victory Medals.
125, Sherbrooke Road, Fulham.   X18681/B.

BATEMAN, W., Driver, R.A.S.C. (M.T.).
He joined in June, 1916, and being medically unfit for overseas service, served in Ireland and Scotland until he was demobilised in November, 1919.
125, Sherbrooke Road, Fulham.   X18681/A.

BATES, A. J., Bombardier, R.G.A.
He joined in September, 1915, was sent to France in the following year, and took part in the battles of Ypres, the Somme, Nieuport, Le Cateau, and in the Retreat and Advance of 1918.
He was demobilised in March, 1919, holding the General Service and Victory Medals.
35a, Drayton Road, Harlesden.   17993/A.

BATES, A. R., Pioneer, Royal Engineers.
He joined H.M. Forces in June, 1916, and embarked for France early in 1918. He saw active service in various sectors of the Western Front and took part in the Retreat and Advance of 1918. He was engaged on various special duties in France, until 1919, when he was demobilised.
He holds the General Service and Victory Medals.
16, Denbigh Road, Willesden.   15533.

BATES, A. S., Pte., Duke of Cornwall's L.I.
He joined on September 4th, 1914, went to the Western Front and fought in many battles, including those of Loos, Ypres and the Somme.
He was demobilised in April, 1919, holding the 1914-15 Star, General Service and Victory Medals.
2, Bayonne Road, Fulham.   14639.

BATES, E., Pte., 23rd Middlesex Regiment.
He joined in April, 1915, and served on the Western Front from September, 1915, until 1919. He was at Ypres, Arras, Cambrai, the Somme, Bethune and the Great Retreat and Advance in 1918, and was wounded. He also served with the Army of Occupation on the Rhine.
Was demobilised on March 24th, 1919, holding the 1914-15 Star, the General Service and Victory Medals.
79, Melville Road, Willesden.   14418.

BATES, E. J., Sapper, Royal Engineers.
He joined on November 5th, 1915, served on the Western Front for three years, and was in action at the Somme, Cambrai, Arras, Ypres, and in many other sectors.
He was demobilised on November 19th, 1919, holding the General Service and Victory Medals.
33, Shrewsbury Road, Harlesden.   14124.

BATES, J., Pte., 1st Northamptonshire Regt.
He joined in April, 1916, and served in France, where he was killed in action in the Great Advance in 1918. He was buried at Bertheaucourt Communal Cemetery.
Was entitled to the General Service and Victory Medals.
4, Honeywood Road, Harlesden.   12555/B.

BATES, J., Pte., "The Queen's" (Royal West Surrey Regiment).
He joined in March, 1917, and served on the Western Front, taking part in the Great Retreat and Advance in 1918.
He holds the General Service and Victory Medals, and was demobilised on September 15th, 1919.
4, Honeywood Road, Harlesden.   12555/A.

BATES, J. H., Pte., 2nd Loyal North Lancs. Regt.
He joined in August, 1914, and served on the Eastern Front, taking part in engagements in East Africa, India and Egypt. In April, 1917, he was discharged owing to injuries received in an accident in Egypt.
He holds the 1914-15 Star, the General Service and Victory Medals.
19, Hartopp Avenue, Fulham.   X17743.

BATH, G., Sapper, Royal Engineers.
He joined in August, 1916, but was not successful in his efforts to get overseas, being retained on special duties in Home Defence.
He was demobilised on January 14th, 1919.
29, Ancill Street, Hammersmith. 13736A.

BATH, J., Driver, 10th Field Ambulance.
He joined in August, 1914, and proceeded to the Western Front, where, attached to the 4th Division, he was present at many engagements, including those of Mons, Ypres, the Somme, Arras and Vimy Ridge, and was wounded.
He holds the 1914 Star, General Service and Victory Medals, and was demobilised in 1918.
152, Escourt Road, Fulham. 13736/C.

BATH, T., Driver, Royal Army Service Corps.
He joined in April, 1917, and was sent to the Western Front, where he was employed, often under heavy fire, conveying food and ammunition to forward dumps.
He was discharged in September, 1918, and holds the General Service and Victory Medals.
29, Ancill Street. Hammersmith, W.6 13736B.

BATH, P., Sapper, Royal Engineers.
During his period of service, from April, 1917, until he was demobilised in February, 1919, he was employed on special duties at Fort Matilda and Kilmarnock.
53, Delorme Street, Fulham Palace Road, Hammersmith. T13774B.

BATH, J., Sergeant, Labour Corps.
He joined on June 3rd, 1915, but was not successful in getting overseas, being retained on duties connected with Home Defence. He obtained his promotion for consistent good work.
55, Delorme Street, Fulham Palace Road, Hammersmith. T13774A.

BATHAM, A., Rifleman, K.R.R. Corps.
He joined on May 25th, 1918, and was shortly afterwards sent to France, where he was in action on the Somme and was wounded.
He was demobilised on September 17th, 1919, and holds the General Service and Victory Medals.
33, Brett Road, Harlesden. 14529.

BATHAM, G. E., Pte., R.A.S.C.
He joined on November 27th, 1915, and served in East Africa as baker to the regiment until March, 1919, when he was demobilised.
He holds the General Service and Victory Medals.
46, Carlyle Avenue, Harlesden. 14405/A.

BATHE, D. (D.C.M.), Cpl., 1/2nd Royal Fus.
He joined in January, 1915, and served in France until 1919, taking part in engagements at Ypres, the Somme and Arras.
Later in the Great Advance in 1918 he was awarded the D.C.M. for gallantry in carrying badly wounded men to safety under heavy hostile machine-gun fire.
He also holds the 1915 Star, General Service and Victory Medals, and was demobilised in March, 1919.
25, Ambleside Road, Willesden. 16118.

BATSTONE, W. J., Pte., Devonshire Regiment.
He joined in November, 1915, was sent to France in the following year, and in 1917 went to Egypt and Palestine, where he took part in several engagements, including the capture of Jerusalem. In 1918 he returned to the Western Front, where he was in action on the Somme.
He was demobilised in February, 1919, holding the General Service and Victory Medals.
54a, Deacon Road, Willesden. 16736.

BATT, G., Armourer, Royal Navy.
He joined in 1915, and served on Mine Sweepers. Was also engaged in dangerous work on the " Mystery " boats.
He was discharged in 1919, and holds the General Service and Victory Medals.
63, Monmouth Road, Lower Edmonton. 13019.

BATTAMS, J. T., Cpl., Labour Battalion.
He enlisted in September, 1915, and served in France from 1916 till the end of the war. He took part in most of the principal engagements during that time, and was finally demobilised in February, 1919, holding the General Service and Victory Medals.
44, Cardross Street, Hammersmith. 11138/A.

BATTAMS, G. W., Lce.-Cpl., 2nd Wiltshire Regt.
He joined in August, 1917, and served in France. He was in action at Ypres, where he was gassed in August, 1918.
He holds the General Service and Victory Medals, and was demobilised in November, 1919.
44, Cardross Street, Hammersmith. 11138/B

BATTER, C. J., Pte., 22nd London Regiment.
He joined in August, 1917, and served in France, taking part in many engagements. He was invalided home with pneumonia and gas poisoning, and was treated at Belmont Sanatorium, Sutton.
He was demobilised on January 28th, 1919, and holds the General Service and Victory Medals.
20, Werley Avenue, Fulham. X17873.

BATTY, C. H. W., 2nd-Class Aircraftsman, R.A.F.
He joined on September 29th, 1916, and from the following year, until the signing of the Armistice, was on duty at the aerodrome and landing station at Dunkirk. Afterwards he did repair work at various aerodromes on the Western Front.
He holds the General Service and Victory Medals, and was demobilised in October, 1919.
5, Bourke Road, Willesden. 15560.

BATUTE, G. J., Driver, Royal Field Artillery.
He joined in 1914, and served on the Western Front, taking part in the battles of the Somme, Arras, Loos, Neuve Chapelle Armentieres, Amiens, Ypres, Vimy Ridge, Lille, Bullecourt, St. Quentin, and various others, including the last Big Push.
He was demobilised in 1919, and holds the 1914-15 Star, General Service and Victory Medals.
20, Field Road, Fulham. 15031.

BAUGHAN, R. H., Pte., R.A.S.C
He joined in 1915, served at the Dardanelles and in Egypt in the same year, and in 1916 was sent to France. Took part in many important engagements up to the date of the Armistice, when he was sent to Germany with the Army of Occupation, where he was employed on transport work at Berlin.
He holds the 1915 Star, General Service and Victory Medals.
4, Crompton Terrace, Pretoria Road, Tottenham. X17933.

BAUMAN, G. (Mrs.), Special War Worker.
In order to release a man for active service she was employed by the General Omnibus Company as a conductress from September, 1916, till July 1919.
She was commended for her work.
22, Bathurst Gardens, Kensal Rise. X18416/B.

BAUMAN, C., Pte., Middlesex Regiment.
He joined in 1916, was sent to France in the following year, and took part in the battles of Ypres, Arras, Cambrai and Vimy Ridge. He also served as a telegraphist at General Headquarters and with the R.E. Signalling Section.
He was demobilised in 1919, holding the General Service and Victory Medals.
22, Bathurst Gardens, Kensal Rise. X18416/A.

BAVERSTOCK, C. J., Sapper, R.E.
He enlisted in April, 1915, and saw active service in Gallipoli and Mesopotamia. Was in hospital at Bombay and at Basra, suffering from malaria and dysentery.
He was finally demobilised on May 28th, 1919, after serving three years in the East, holding the 1914-15 Star, General Service and Victory Medals.
3, Bramber Road, Fulham. 16280.

BAXTER, W. G., Special War Worker.
Was employed from 1914 until 1920 at Woolwich Arsenal on the highly skilled and dangerous work connected with T.N.T. and C.E. Powders. This work caused much suffering amongst the workers.
She was highly commended for her work.
35, Ilex Road, Willesden. 16355/A.

BAXTER, A. G., A.B., R.N., H.M.S. "Abdiel."
He joined in 1914, and took part in the Dardanelles operations. From 1916 until 1918 he was employed in Mine Sweeping in the North Sea. In 1919 he was sent to the Baltic for duty.
He has been awarded the 1914 Star, General Service and Victory Medals.
35, Ilex Road, Willesden. 16355/B.

BAXTER, J., Rifleman, 1/5th London Rifle Brigade.
He enlisted on March 23rd, 1915, and served in France on the Somme Front and was reported missing on October 9th, 1916.
He was entitled to the General Service and Victory Medals.
36, Moselle Street, Tottenham. X18372.

BAYFORD, A., Pte., 1st Middlesex Regiment.
He joined in June, 1916, served on the Western Front from September 27th, until demobilised in March, 1919, and took part in the fighting on the Somme, at Ypres, Arras, Bullecourt, and in the last Advance of 1918, being twice wounded and slightly gassed.
He holds the General Service and Victory Medals.
58, Foyle Road, Tottenham. X18955.

BAYFORD, A., Driver, Royal Field Artillery.
He enlisted in August, 1914, and saw service the same year
in France. In 1917 he was drafted to Palestine, where he
took part in most of the engagements, until demobilised in
April, 1919.
He holds the 1914 Star, General Service and Victory Medals.
29, Maldon Road, Lower Edmonton.   14786/A.

BAYLEY, J., Sapper, Royal Engineers.
He joined in May, 1917, and being medically unfit for overseas, served until his demobilisation in February, 1919, at
Home stations.
2, Ely Place, White Hart Lane, Tottenham.   X18314.

**BAZELEY, J. A., Stoker, Royal Navy, H.M.S.
"Revenge."**
He joined the Navy in July, 1917, and was sent to the North
Sea, where he took part in several engagements. He was
also employed on escort duty to the surrendered German
Fleet.
He holds the General Service and Victory Medals.
124, Church Road, Tottenham, N.   X18136.

BEACH, J. W., Bombardier, R.F.A.
He joined in February, 1916, and served in France from 1917,
taking part in engagements at Cambrai, Arras and Armentieres, where he was severely gassed. He was in hospital in
France for four months, and afterwards sent to England as
physically unfit for further active service.
He holds the General Service and Victory Medals, and was
demobilised in November, 1919.
81, Rayleigh Road, W.14   12647.

BEADLE, L. G., Gunner, Royal Field Artillery.
He joined in October, 1914, served in Salonica and France,
and took part in many battles, including the Great Advance
of 1918.
He was demobilised on May 21st, 1919, holding the 1914-15
Star, General Service and Victory Medals.
28, Maybury Gardens, Willesden Green.   X17225.

BEAN, W. E., Pte., Middlesex Regiment.
He was already in the Army at the outbreak of war, and from
1914 to 1919 served on the Western Front. While in action
at the battle of Ypres he was wounded.
Was demobilised on March 11th, 1919, holding the 1914
Star, the General Service and Victory Medals.
66, Carlyle Avenue, Harlesden.   14413

BEANES, E. J., Pte., 7th Royal Fusiliers.
He joined in 1914 and served from 1915 on the Western
Front, and was in action at Dickebusch, Ypres and many
other sectors.
He was discharged in 1916, and holds the 1915 Star,
General Service and Victory Medals.
118, New Holly Lane, Willesden.   15390.

BEAR, W. A., Driver, Royal Field Artillery.
He enlisted in October, 1915, and served in England for some
time. He was sent to India in 1917, where he saw service
until demobilisation in February, 1919.
He holds the General Service and Victory Medals.
51, Wendover Road, Harlesden.   T12550A.

**BEAR, E., Rifleman, K.R.R. Corps and Rifle
Brigade.**
He joined in December, 1917, was sent to France in April,
1918, taken prisoner on April 22nd, and held captive for
seven months.
He was demobilised in September, 1919, holding the General
Service and Victory Medals.
51, Wendover Road, Harlesden.   T12550B.

**BEARD, H., Pte., 3/4th "The Queen's" (Royal
West Surrey Regiment).**
He joined in August, 1916, served in France, and was wounded
at Ypres in October of the following year, and invalided
home.
He holds the General Service and Victory Medals, and was
demobilised in January, 1919.
83, Ormiston Road, Shepherd's Bush.   11920A.

**BEARD, E. C., Air Mechanic, Royal Air Force
(late Royal Naval Air Service).**
He joined in October, 1915, and was killed whilst training
in England, preparatory to being drafted to Egypt.
83, Ormiston Road, Shepherd's Bush.   11920/B.

BEATTIE, C. J., C.S.M., Middlesex Regiment.
He enlisted in August, 1914, served on the Western Front
until 1919, and took part in the battles of Mons, the Somme,
Loos, the Marne, Neuve Chapelle, the Aisne, Cambrai and
Ypres, where he was wounded in the thigh.
He was demobilised in February, 1919, holding the 1914 Star,
General Service and Victory Medals.
34, Cobbold Road, Willesden.   16066.

BEAUCHAMP, Pte., West Yorkshire Regiment.
He joined in October, 1917, went to France in the following
year, and took part in the battles of Arras and Cambrai,
and the British Retreat and Advance of 1918.
He was wounded, and was discharged in October, 1919,
holding the General Service and Victory Medals.
136, Felix Road, W. Ealing.   11027.

**BEAVERSTOCK, H. W., Lce.-Cpl., Rifle Brigade
(attached Military Police).**
He enlisted in 1915, and was on service in England until 1916,
when he was discharged on medical grounds. He re-enlisted,
however, and served with the Military Police in London.
23, Grove Place, Ealing.   10847.

BECK, W. J., Gunner, Royal Field Artillery.
He joined in February, 1915, in the following year was sent
to France, where he took part in the battles of the Somme
and Cambrai, and in October, 1917, went to Italy. He returned to the Western Front, and was in action during the
Retreat of 1918, and at Ypres, Dickebusch, Kemmel Hill
and on the Somme. He served with the Army of Occupation
in Germany before being demobilised in April, 1919.
He was wounded, and holds the General Service and Victory
Medals.
18, Conley Road, Willesden.   15539.

BECKER, G. C., Sapper, Royal Engineers.
He enlisted in March, 1915, and owing to his special abilities
he was retained for service on the East Coast. He served
at Clacton-on-Sea on signalling duties until he was demobilised in 1919.
91, Archel Road, West Kensington.   16668.

BECKLEY, H. J., 1st Air Mechanic, R.A.F.
He joined in January, 1916, and was employed on special
mechanical work in connection with our air defences on the
East Coast, and the North of Scotland.
He was demobilised in March, 1919, and holds the General
Service Medal.
36, Brenthurst Road, Willesden.   16143.

BECKWITH, C. A., 3rd Air Mechanic, R.A.F.
He joined in October, 1918, and saw service on important
work in Scotland, until February, 1919, when he was demobilised.
He holds the General Service Medal.
106, Montague Road, Lower Edmonton.   16882/B.

BECKWITH, R. C., Lce.-Cpl., London Regt.
He joined in September, 1914, and during his service in
France took part in many battles. He was wounded in the
left eye in November, 1917, at Ypres, and also suffered from
trench fever.
Demobilised in February, 1919, holding the General Service
and Victory Medals.
106, Montague Road, Lower Edmonton.   16882/A.

BEDBOROUGH, F., Pte., 2nd Middlesex Regt.
He volunteered his services in November, 1914, and was despatched to France shortly afterwards. Saw active service
in various sectors, until he was killed in action at La Bassée
in June, 1916.
He was entitled to the 1915 Star, General Service and Victory
Medals.
7, Shakespeare Avenue, Harlesden.   13891/B.

BEDWELL, C. W. G., Sapper, Royal Engineers.
He joined in September, 1914, and saw active service in
various parts of France and Belgium, until December, 1919,
when he was demobilised, holding the 1914 Star, General
Service and Victory Medals.
7, Gastein Road, Fulham.   14818.

BEER, P. S., A.B., Royal Navy.
He was in the Navy at the outbreak of hostilities, and
afterwards served with the Grand Fleet in the North Sea, and
also on special duties in Chinese waters.
He holds the Persian Gulf special award, the 1914-15 Star,
General Service and Victory Medals, and served finally at
Chatham.
5, Talbot Road, Willesden.   15974/B.

BEER, G., Pte., D. of Cornwall's Light Infantry.
He joined in March, 1916, and served on the Western Front
from the following May. He was badly gassed, losing the
sight of both eyes, as a result of which he was discharged in
August of the same year.
He holds the General Service and Victory Medals.
5, Talbot Road, Willesden.   15974/A.

BEER, J., Pte., Middlesex Regiment.
He joined in December, 1915, and was sent to France, where
he took part in many battles, including that of the Somme,
and was wounded and taken prisoner at Arras in 1917.
He returned to England, was demobilised in August, 1919,
and holds the General Service and Victory Medals.
83, Shrewsbury Road, Harlesden.   13840.

BELL, H., Lce.-Cpl., Royal Fusiliers.
He enlisted in 1914, went to the Western Front later in the same year, and took part in engagements on the Somme, at Cambrai, Arras, Ypres, and at Armentieres.
He holds the 1914–15 Star, General Service and Victory Medals, and was demobilised in 1919.
57, Greyhound Road, Willesden.   X17605/A

BELLAMY, R. W., Pte., Royal West Kent Regt
He joined in May, 1918, and was sent to France, where he took part in the Great Advance of 1918.
He holds the General Service and Victory Medals, and was demobilised in March, 1920.
28, Letchford Gardens, College Park, Willesden. X17548/A.

BELLAMY, G., Pte., Middlesex Regiment.
He enlisted in June, 1915, and served on the Western Front, where he took part in many engagements, including the Somme, Mount Kemmel and the Great Retreat and Advance in 1918.
He holds the General Service and Victory Medals, and was demobilised in July, 1919.
28, Letchford Gardens, College Park, Willesden. X17548/B.

BELLEVUE DE SYLVA, A. A., Pte., 21st Middlesex Regiment.
He enlisted in February, 1916, and after a year's training was sent to France in January, 1917, and was in action at Arras, Gouzeaucourt and Cambrai.   He was wounded twice, first at Villiers Plough, then near Cambrai, November 23rd, 1917, and discharged in November, 1918.
He holds the General Service and Victory Medals.
7, Shakespeare Avenue, Harlesden.   13890/A.

BELLEVUE DE SYLVA, P. G., Pte., 1st ˙Batt. Middlesex Regiment.
He joined in February, 1916, and served in different parts of France and Belgium until September, 1919, when he was demobilised.
He holds the General Service and Victory Medals.
7, Shakespeare Avenue, Harlesden, N.W.   13890/B.

BELLWORTHY, E. L., Cpl., Royal Sussex Regt.
He joined in April, 1918, and after serving at home for a period, went out with the Army of Occupation to Germany.
He was demobilised in September, 1919.
3, Sandgate Road, Lower Edmonton.   15500A.

BELLWORTHY, A. W. H., Sapper, R.E.
He joined in March, 1917, and served on the Eastern, Egypt, and Western Fronts. While in action in France in 1918 he was badly wounded in the ankle, and was in hospital for six months.
He was demobilised on February 6th, 1920, holding the General Service and Victory Medals.
3, Sandgate Road, Lower Edmonton.   15500B.

BELTON, W. H., Pte., "The Queen's" (Royal West Surrey Regiment).
He joined on March 26th, 1917, went to France in 1918, and took part in several battles, principally those on the Somme.
He was demobilised on February 13th, 1919, holding the General Service and Victory Medals.
23, Cobbold Road, Willesden.   15944/B

BELTON, W. F., Pte., Middlesex Regiment.
He joined in May, 1915, and served for nearly four years on training duties.
He was demobilised in February, 1919.
23, Cobbald Road, Willesden.   15944/A.

BELVERSTON, E., Pte., Royal West Kent Regt.
He joined in August, 1916, and served in India with the Regimental and Garrison Police until his demobilisation on June 11th, 1919.
He holds the General Service and Victory Medals.
136, Bulwer Road, Edmonton.   X17199.

BENDER, E. G., Pte., 16th Middlesex Regiment.
He joined in 1915, saw active service on the Western Front at the Somme, and was killed on July 1st, 1916, in action at Beaumont Hamel.
He was entitled to the General Service and Victory Medals.
54, Oldfield Road, Willesden.   15776/B.

BENDLE, A. G., Pte., 11th "The Queen's" (Royal West Surrey Regiment).
He joined in June, 1917, and was sent to France in February, 1918. He went to Germany with the Army of Occupation, and was demobilised in March, 1920, holding the General Service and Victory Medals.
34, Bertie Road, Willesden Green.   X17395.

BENFORD, H. E., Pte., East Surrey Regiment.
He was in the Army when war broke out, was sent to France in August, 1914, and took part in the retreat from Mons, where he was taken prisoner. He was held in captivity, suffering many hardships, until May, 1919, when he was demobilised, holding the 1914 Star, the General Service and Victory Medals.
37, College Road, Kensal Rise.   X17808.

BENFORD, S. W., Pte., 137th Labour Corps.
He joined on March 15th, 1917, and served with the Labour Company on the Western Front, until his demobilisation in February, 1919.
He holds the General Service and Victory Medals.
33, Felixstowe Road, Willesden.   X17756.

BENNETT, C. W., Sergeant, Royal Engineers.
He joined in August, 1915, and went to the Western Front in the same year.
He was demobilised on January 19th, 1919, after a total service of 23 years. He holds the 1914–15 Star, General Service and Victory Medals.
9, Cornwallis Road, Edmonton.   13283.

BENNETT, F. A., Pte., 9th Middlesex Regiment.
He enlisted in August, 1914, went to the Dardanelles in the following year, and in 1916 to Egypt, where he remained for three years, and was wounded in the right elbow.
He was demobilised on April 15th, 1919, holding the 1915 Star, General Service and Victory Medals.
9, Hazeldean Road, Harlesden.   14905/B.

BENNETT, R. S., Cpl., 1/9th Middlesex Regt.
He enlisted in October, 1914, and served in India until 1918, when he went to Mesopotamia.
He was demobilised on April 8th, 1919. He holds the General Service and Victory Medals.
9, Hazeldean Road, Harlesden.   14905/C.

BENNETT, P. J., Lce.-Cpl., 9th Middlesex Regt.
He joined in May, 1915, went to France in August, 1916, and was killed in action on the Somme on April 18th, 1917.
He was entitled to the General Service and Victory Medals.
9, Hazeldean Road, Harlesden.   14905/A.

BENNETT, F. J., A.B., Royal Navy, H.M.S. "Conqueror."
He joined in 1916, and served with the Grand Fleet until he was demobilised in February, 1919.
He holds the General Service and Victory Medals.
33, Newlyn Road, Tottenham.   X18509.

BENNETT, H. H., Pte., 10th Batt. Royal Fusiliers.
Joining in August, 1914, he was drafted to France in 1915, where he took part in the battle of the Somme, was wounded, returned to the line and was killed at Vimy Ridge in October the same year.
He was entitled to the 1915 Star, the General Service and Victory Medals. He was commended for devotion to duty.
85, Felixstowe Road, Edmonton.   14852/A.

BENNETT, J. C., Lce.-Cpl., Military Mntd. Police.
He joined in March, 1917, and after six months' active service in France returned to England, where he remained until his demobilisation in July, 1919.
He holds the General Service and Victory Medals.
39, Guilsborough Road, Willesden.   15242.

BENNETT, W., Gunner, Royal Field Artillery.
He joined in February, 1915, and served for four years on the Western Front, taking part in the battles of Arras, Cambrai, La Bassée, the Somme, Neuve Chapelle and other engagements.
He was demobilised in June, 1919, and holds the 1914–15 Star, the General Service and Victory Medals.
29, Earlsmead Road, Kensal Rise.   X17831.

BENNETT, W P., Gunner, R.G.A.
He joined in March, 1917, and served in France nearly all the time, being in the Somme sector. After the Armistice he was sent into Germany with the Army of Occupation, until he was demobilised in October, 1919.
He holds the General Service and Victory Medals.
20, Winchester Road, Edmonton.   14685.

BENNETT, W. D. F., Torpedoman, R.N., H.M.S. "Daisy."
He joined in August, 1914, and served with the Navy on important patrol duty, &c., until demobilised in March, 1919.
He holds the 1914 Star, General Service and Victory Medals.
22, Church Road, Tottenham.   X18342.

BENNETT, W. E. (D.S.M.), A.B., R.N., H.M.S. "Natal."

He joined in August, 1914, and served with the Grand Fleet in the North Sea and Russian waters. He was principally engaged in operations against German submarines, serving with distinction and being awarded the Distinguished Service Medal in this connection.

He also holds the Mine-sweeping, 1914 Star, General Service and Victory Medals. He is still serving.

85, Felixstowe Road, Edmonton.   T14852.

BENNETT, W. F., Cpl., 9th Middlesex Regiment and R.A.S.C. (M.T.).

He joined in October, 1914, and served in France from 1917 until 1919, taking part in engagements in the Ypres sector, where he was wounded.

He was demobilised in August, 1919, and holds the General Service and Victory Medals.

40, Nightingale Road, Harlesden.   12512.

BENNETT, W. J., Bombardier, R.G.A.

He was in the R.G.A. Territorial Force when war broke out, was mobilised on August 4th, 1914, and served in German East Africa, from December, 1915, until June, 1918, when he contracted malaria.

He was discharged on February 7th, 1919, holding the 1914-15 Star, General Service and Victory Medals.

78, Holland's Road, Harlesden.   T12758.

BENSON, E. K., Riflmn., 6th London Rgt. (Rifles).

He enlisted in September, 1914, and served in France, taking part in many engagements, including Loos, where he was wounded.

He holds the 1914-15 Star, General Service and Victory Medals, and was discharged in September, 1918.

574, High Road, Tottenham.   X18142/B.

BENSON, B. T., Cadet, Royal Air Force.

He joined in August, 1918, and served at Hampstead, Reading and Cheltenham, training for the R.A.F.

He was demobilised in January, 1919.

1, Nursery Street, Tottenham.   X18142/A.

BENTLEY, A. J., Pte., 7th London Regt.

He joined in April, 1914, went to France the following year, and took part in an engagement at Festubert. He was taken ill and invalided to a hospital in London, and in April, 1916, was discharged, medically unfit.

He holds the 1914-15 Star, General Service and Victory Medals.

5, Mund Street, W.14   16907.

BENTLEY, S. A., Pte., 10th Middlesex Regt.

During his service, which extended from August 8th, 1914, until January 14th, 1920, he was stationed in India at Calcutta and Lucknow.

He holds the General Service and Victory Medals.

7, Delorme Street, Fulham.   T13773/A.

BENTLEY, F., Pte., 1st Essex Regiment.

He joined in November, 1916, served on the Eastern Front, took part in various engagements, including the capture of Jerusalem, and was twice wounded.

He holds the General Service and Victory Medals.

7, Delorme Street, Fulham.   T13773/B.

BERAET, C., Bombardier, R.G.A.; also Intelligence Corps.

He joined in 1915, and from that year served on the Western Front, taking part in the battles of Arras, Somme, Cambrai, Bullecourt, Passchendaele, and many other engagements.

He was demobilised in 1919, holding the 1915 Star and the General Service and Victory Medals.

15, Furness Road, Harlesden.   13094.

BERESFORD, F. G., Cpl., Royal Engineers.

He enlisted in August, 1914, and was sent immediately to the Western Front. He served five years in France, and was in action at Mons, the Somme, Ypres, Loos and many other engagements. He was wounded at the battle of the Somme in 1916.

He is still serving in the Army, and holds the 1914 Star, General Service and Victory Medals.

102, Sheldon Road, Upper Edmonton.   X17452A.

BERESFORD, W. E., Pte., Middlesex Regiment.

He joined in June, 1917, and was retained in England in the Training Corps and Labour Corps. He went to Germany with the Army of Occupation in 1919, and was discharged in February, 1920.

102, Sheldon Road, Upper Edmonton.   X17452B.

BERRILL, G., Pte., 2nd West Yorkshire Regt.

He joined in November, 1914, and was sent to the Western Front in April, 1916. He served during the two years he was in France in the Labour Battalion on Road and Defence works. He had previously been in the R.H.A. for seven years, from 1882-89.

He was discharged on February 17th, 1919, and holds the General Service and Victory Medals.

137, Villiers Road, Willesden, N.W.2   T17329.

BERRY, M. A. (Mrs.) (née BRETT), Special War Worker.

This lady, commencing in July, 1915, did important duties in connection with the manufacture of hand grenades. Later she accepted a position where she was employed in connection with the manufacture of fuses for shells and bombs.

She was highly commended for her work.

363a, Chapter Road, Willesden.   16719.

BERRY, A., Pte., 7th Royal Sussex Regiment.

He joined in April, 1917, proceeded to France in the same year, and was killed during the Great Retreat of April, 1918.

He was entitled to the General Service and Victory Medals.

105, Yeldham Road, W.6   13237/A.

BERRY, F. (Miss), Special War Worker.

For two years this lady was employed on important work in connection with the filling of shells at a munition works, for which work she was highly commended.

2, Welford Avenue, Fulham.   X18061/B.

BERRY, C., Pte., R.A.S.C. (M.T.).

He joined in 1916, and served in England, at Southampton, and Blackheath, where his arm was broken in an accident, necessitating his being in hospital for eight months.

He was demobilised in 1919.

2, Welford Terrace, Fulham.   X18061A.

BERRY, O. W. (M.M.), Sergt., Middlesex Regt. (Footballers' Battalion).

He enlisted in September, 1914, served on the Western Front from the following year until 1917, and took part in the fighting on the Somme and at Ypres. He was wounded twice and suffered from shell shock while abroad and was in hospital for many months.

He was awarded the Military Medal for conspicuous gallantry in the field at Vimy Ridge and holds also the 1914-15 Star, General Service and Victory Medals.

He was demobilised in May, 1919.

30, Durban Road, N.17   X18088/A.

BERRY, D. (Mrs.), Special War Worker.

This lady during the war was employed at an important munition factory on work connected with the supply of gas masks.

30, Durban Road, N.17   X18088/B.

BERRY, H., Pte., 2nd West Yorkshire Regt.

He joined in September, 1914, served in France, and was killed in action at the battle of the Somme on July 1st, 1916. Entitled to General Service and Victory Medals.

32, Rayleigh Road, Hammersmith.   12640.

BERRY, H. G., Pte., Middlesex Regiment.

He joined in April, 1915, and served in the Dardanelles, Egypt and Palestine. He took part in all the engagements with General Allenby in Palestine, and was wounded three times.

In April, 1919, he was demobilised, holding the General Service and Victory Medals.

102, Carlyle Avenue, Harlesden.   14453.

BERRY, H. R., Pte., Bedford Regiment.

He joined in April, 1918, and in March of the following year, was sent to Germany with the Army of Occupation. He was demobilised in April, 1920.

17, Guilsborough Road, Willesden.   15245.

BESSELL, H. G., Pte., 16th Warwickshire Regt.

He joined in January, 1915, and served on the Western and Italian Fronts. In France he took part in the battles of Ypres, the Somme, Bapaume, Arras, St. Quentin and several others. He went to Italy in January, 1918, and in March 1918 returned to France. During his service he was three times wounded.

He was demobilised in 1919, and holds the 1914-15 Star and the General Service and Victory Medals.

10, Conley Road, Willesden.   15522A.

BESSELL, F. J., Cpl., Middlesex Regiment.
He joined in April, 1915, and served on the Western Front, where he took part in the battles of Ypres, the Somme, Cambrai, and Bapaume. He was wounded at Cambrai, and in August, 1919, was discharged.
During his service he was awarded a medal for his good shooting. He holds the General Service and Victory Medals.
10, Conley Road, Willesden.   15522B.

BEST, A. E., Pte., Royal Fusiliers.
He joined in February, 1917, went to France in June, 1917, and was killed in action on September 27th, 1918. He had previously taken part in various engagements, including the Retreat of 1918.
He was entitled to the General Service and Victory Medals.
109, Rucklidge Avenue, Harlesden.   13157/A.

BEST, F. V., Rifleman, Irish Rifles.
He joined on November 6th, 1915, and served on the Western Front from 1916 until discharged on March 25th, 1919, on the clerical branch of the Headquarters Staff.
He holds the General Service and Victory Medals.
109, Rucklidge Avenue, Harlesden.   13157/B.

BEST, C., A.B., Royal Navy.
He joined in August, 1914, and saw service at the Dardanelles and took part in the battle of Jutland, being badly wounded in the leg and face at that engagement. He also served on H.M.S. " Vivid," " Ganges," " Leviathan," and " Warspite." Prior to the war he had served five years in the Navy.
He was demobilised in January, 1920, and holds the 1914–15 Star, the General Service and Victory Medals.
123, Winchester Road, Lower Edmonton.   14953/B.

BEST, G., Cpl., East Surrey Regiment.
He joined in 1915, and served in France, taking part in the battles of Neuve Chapelle (where he was wounded), and Cambrai (where he was again badly wounded), as a result of these wounds he spent 12 months in hospital in England.
He holds the 1915 Star, General Service and Victory Medals, and was demobilised in September, 1919.
123, Winchester Road, Lower Edmonton.   14953/A.

BEST, J., Bombardier, R.G.A.
He joined in August, 1914, and went to China the same year, serving there until 1915, when he went to France. He took part in many engagements, including the Somme, and was wounded twice during his service.
He was demobilised on July 16th, 1919, and holds the 1914–15 Star, General Service and Victory Medals.
9, Alston Road, Lower Edmonton.   16552.

BEST, T., Driver, R.A.S.C.
He enlisted in February, 1915, and in 1916 was sent to France, where he took part in engagements on the Somme, at Cambrai, Arras, Albert, Ypres, Armentieres and Bethune. Later, during 1917, he served in Italy, where he remained until April, 1919.
He holds the General Service and Victory Medals, and was demobilised on September 26th, 1919.
250, Chapter Road, Willesden Green.   X17128.

BESTIER, W. H., Leading Seaman, R.N., H.M.S. " Veteran."
He joined in August, 1914, and served with the Grand Fleet in the North Sea and at Scapa Flow until discharged on April 7th, 1920, as medically unfit for service.
He was awarded the 1914 Star, General Service and Victory Medals.
8, Swan Terrace, Pretoria Road, Tottenham.   X18121.

BESWICK, J. C., Pte., 10th London Regt.
He joined in September, 1914, and was retained for Home service, being certified medically unfit for service overseas. He was employed in guarding German prisoners of war at Alexandra Palace.
He was discharged in April, 1918, after 4½ years' service.
34, Waldo Road, Willesden, N.W.   X17564/B.

BESWICK, R. A., Pte., Bedford Regiment.
He joined in September, 1914, and was sent to the Western Front in March, 1915. He took part in several important engagements and was in action at the battles of Loos, Festubert and others. He was killed during the first advance on the Somme on July 1st, 1916.
He was entitled to the 1914–15 Star, General Service and Victory Medals.
34, Waldo Road, Willesden, N.W.   X17564/A.

BETTIS, W. G., Sapper, Royal Engineers.
He joined in 1916, and was sent to the Western Front, where he remained for two years, and was engaged on the railways during the Retreat in March, 1918, and the Big Push of the same year.
He holds the General Service and Victory Medals, and was demobilised in October, 1919.
51, Redfern Road, Harlesden.   13199.

BETTS, A. O., Gunner, R.G.A.
He joined in September, 1916, and was sent to France, taking part in engagements at Arras, Mons, and several other important battles. He was attached to the Army of Occupation in Germany, and demobilised in November, 1919, holding the General Service and Victory Medals.
29, St. Peter's Road, Lower Edmonton.   12321.

BETTS, F., Rifleman, 8th Rifle Brigade.
He joined in June, 1916, was sent to the Western Front, and took part in the battles of Arras and that of St. Quentin, in which he was wounded and taken prisoner.
He holds the General Service and Victory Medals, and was demobilised in January, 1920.
47, Delorme Street, Fulham.   T13777.

BEVAN, G., Pte., 13th Middlesex Regiment.
He joined in March, 1915, and on completing his training went to France, where he served for four years. On returning to England he was demobilised in January, 1919.
He is entitled to the 1915 Star, General Service and Victory Medals.
39, West Street, Edmonton.   14593.

BEVAN, T. W., Pte., Royal Fusiliers.
He joined in 1917, and served on the Western Front, until January, 1919, when he was demobilised.
He holds the General Service and Victory Medals.
115, Greyhound Road, Fulham.   15018.

BEVAN, W., Cpl., Royal Engineers.
He joined in 1917, after securing his release from railway work in England, and served at Slough, Dorset, until January 1919, when he was demobilised.
13, Linton Road, Edmonton.   X17473.

BEVERIDGE, D. T., Pte. 9th Lancers.
He joined in 1914, and in the same year went to the Western Front, where he took part in the retreat from Mons.
He holds the 1914 Star, General Service and Victory Medals, and was demobilised in 1919.
19, Bury Street, Edmonton.   13934.

BEW, F., Pte., Royal Army Medical Corps.
He joined in June, 1917, and was sent to the Eastern Front. He was stationed at Constantinople, where he served as First-class Orderly in various military hospitals, assisting at operations and performing other responsible duties.
He was discharged in April, 1920, and holds the General Service and Victory Medals.
83, Chesson Road, West Kensington.   X17687/A.

BEW, P. A. (Mrs.), Special War Worker.
She offered her services to her country and was employed, owing to her clerical capabilities, in the clerical department of the Army Pay Office at South Kensington, where she did valuable work.
83, Chesson Road, W. Kensington.   X17687/B.

BEXHELL, G., Gunner, R.F.A.
He joined in August, 1914, served on the Western Front, and whilst in action at the battle of Ypres was killed on February 16th, 1916.
He was entitled to the 1914–15 Star, General Service and Victory Medals.
73, Sheldon Road, Edmonton.   X17294.

BICKNELL, M., Sergt., 7th London Regt.
He volunteered his services in September, 1914, and was soon after sent to France, where he served for some time. He was employed in various sectors, until he was killed on April 7th, 1917.
He was entitled to the 1914–15 Star, the General Service and Victory Medals.
39, Rylston Road, S.W.6   16387.

BICKNELL, T. W., Pte., Highland Light Infantry.
He joined in March, 1917, and was stationed, amongst other places, in Ireland, where he was employed on Guard and other duties.
He was demobilised in October, 1919.
88, Durham Road, Tottenham, N.17   X17946.

BIDDLECOMBE, E. J., Chie fPetty Officer, R.N.
He was in the Navy, and after outbreak of hostilities served on H.M.S. " Iron Duke " in the North Sea, and took part in the battle of Jutland.
He holds the 1914–15 Star, General Service and Victory Medals, and was demobilised on August, 1919.
15, Essex Road, Willesden.   15938.

BIDDLES, E. (Mrs.), Special War Worker.
This lady was employed as a cartridge inspector at the munition factory at Park Royal, where she did valuable work. She attended to her duties on both day and night shifts.
34, Litchfield Gardens, Willesden Green.   X17438/A.

BIDDLES, G. (M.S.M.), Lce.-Cpl., Warwickshire Yeomanry.

He enlisted in August, 1914, and was sent to Egypt in 1915, where he took part in several engagements. Being a highly skilled man he was retained in England on return from Egypt on munitions till his discharge in June, 1919. He was on the "Wayfarer" when she was torpedoed, and for his gallantry at that time was awarded the M.S.M.
He holds in addition the 1914-15 Star, the General Service and Victory Medals.
34, Litchfield Road, Willesden Green.   X17438/B.

BIDWELL, T., Special War Worker.

For three years during the war he was employed at the Small Arms Factory at Enfield on work of great importance, and on this account he was prevented from doing military duty.
161, Bulwer Road, Edmonton.   X17193.

BIFIELD, W. J., Pte., Royal Sussex Regiment.

He joined in February, 1915, served in Egypt and Palestine, and was wounded during the capture of Jerusalem. Later he was drafted to France, where he was again wounded in action.
He is still with his regiment, and holds the General Service and Victory Medals.
50, Protheroe Road, Fulham.   16834.

BIGG, A. V., Lce.-Cpl., R.A.S.C. and 2nd King's Liverpool Regiment.

He joined in January, 1915, went to Salonica the following year, and served on the Doiran Front, Vardar and many other places.
He was demobilised on March 27th, 1919, holding the General Service and Victory Medals.
107, Oldfield Road, Willesden.   16054.

BIGGERSTAFF, G., Pte., The Buffs (East Kent Regiment).

He joined the Forces in December, 1916, and was sent to India, where he saw active service until the cessation of hostilities. He returned to England in 1919, and was demobilised.
He holds the General Service and Victory Medals.
59, Greyhound Road, Willesden.   X17605/B.

BIGGS, A. W., Cpl., 1/11th London Regiment.

He joined in September, 1914, and from May, 1915, until March, 1919, served on the Eastern Front at the Dardanelles, and in Egypt and Palestine, where he took part in the fighting with General Allenby's forces.
He holds the 1914/15 Star, General Service and Victory Medals, and was demobilised in March, 1919.
137, Roundwood Road, Willesden.   16723.

BIGGS, F., Special War Worker.

During the war was employed at Woolwich Arsenal on very dangerous and highly skilled munition work.
Was commended for the work done, and is retained there by the authorities.
34, Ilex Road, Willesden.   16089/B.

BIGGS, H. C., Pte., 14th Batt. Worcestershire R.

He joined in September, 1914, and served on the Western Front, taking part in the battles of Cambrai, Beaumont Hamel, Bullecourt and various others. He was twice wounded, while in action at Passchendaele and Bourlon Wood.
He was demobilised in February, 1919, and holds the 1914-15 Star, the General Service and Victory Medals.
137, Roundwood Road, Willesden.   16038.

BIGGS, W. E. (M.M.), Pte., 23rd Middlesex Regt.

He joined in 1916, and went to France the following year, taking part in actions on the Somme. Later he went to Italy, and returned to France in 1918. He was wounded once, and awarded the Military Medal for bravery in the field on the Somme on July 19th, 1918.
He also holds the General Service and Victory Medals and was demobilised in February, 1919.
70, Purves Road, Willesden.   X18403/A.

BIGNALL, A., Sapper, Royal Engineers.

He offered his services in October, 1915, and soon after, in 1916, he was despatched to France. Here he saw active service up till June, 1919, when he was sent home.
He holds the General Service and Victory Medals.
123, Victor Road, Willesden.   X17535.

BIGNELL, F. J., Driver, R.A.S.C. (M.T.).

He enlisted in April, 1916, and was later despatched to France and was at first stationed at Rouen, afterwards he was in action at Ypres and also at Arras. He served in various sectors until he was demobilised on January 16th, 1919.
He holds the General Service and Victory Medals.
34, Leamore Street, Hammersmith.   12581.

BIGWELL, E. P., Sergt., R.A.S.C. (M.T.).

He joined in September, 1914, and served in Egypt on special duties, and in charge of stores. Later he went to France and took part in the battles of the Somme and the Great Retreat and Advance in 1918.
He holds the 1914-15 Star, General Service and Victory Medals, and was demobilised on July 3rd, 1919.
429, Chapter Road, Willesden Green, N.W.   16311.

BILBEE, H., Rifleman, Rifle Brigade, and Gunner, R.F.A.

He enlisted in August, 1914, served in France until discharged in 1918, took part in the battles of the Somme, Ypres, Vimy Ridge, Arras and Cambrai, and was wounded on four different occasions. He has since rejoined in the R.F.A., and holds the 1914-15 Star, General Service and Victory Medals.
20, Humbolt Road, Fulham, W.6   15147/C.

BILLERS, J., A.B., Royal Navy.

He volunteered in August, 1914, and was posted to H.M.S. "Abercrombie," on which ship he served through the Dardanelles campaign, he was afloat on active service until September, 1918.
He holds the 1914-15 Star, the General Service and Victory Medals.
54, Oldfield Road, Willesden.   15776/A.

BILLETT, L. J., Pte., Middlesex Regiment.

He enlisted for service in April, 1915, and after two years' extensive training in England, was sent to Salonica in 1917, where he remained for two years, until his demobilisation in February, 1919.
He holds the General Service and Victory Medals.
14, Town Road, Edmonton.   13565A.

BILLING, A. E., Sergt., 2/13th London Regt.

He joined in June, 1916, and served in France, Salonica and with the Egyptian Expeditionary Force. During this time he was wounded, and on August 28th, 1919. was demobilised.
He holds the General Service and Victory Medals.
13, Chaldon Road, Fulham.   X17646.

BILLING, F., Machine Gunner, London Regt.

He joined in September, 1914, and served on the Western Front, at the Dardanelles, and in Egypt. He was invalided home from the Dardanelles in 1916 and in 1917 was sent out to Egypt.
He was demobilised in January, 1919, and holds the 1914-15 Star, the General Service and Victory Medals.
8, Purves Road, Willesden.   X18017.

BILLSON, M. A., Special War Worker.

This lady was employed during the war on important work at the Park Royal Filling Factory. Her duties, working with the T.N.T. and C.E. powders, were dangerous, and she was commended for her work.
34, Steele Road, Harlesden.   14137/A.

BILLSON, G. A., Sapper, Royal Engineers.

He joined in 1916, and in the same year was sent to France, where he was on despatch and other important duties.
He was demobilised in 1919, holding the General Service and Victory Medals.
34, Steele Road, Harlesden.   14137/B.

BINGHAM, A. F., Pte., Royal Fusiliers.

He offered his services in February, 1915, and was shortly afterwards despatched to France. He saw active service on the French Front continuously until the cessation of hostilities.
He was demobilised in March, 1919, and holds the 1915 Star, General Service and Victory Medals.
2, Beryl Road, Fulham.   13353/B.

BINGHAM, H. E., Lce.-Cpl., Royal Fusiliers.

He joined in January, 1916, and did important duties of a clerical nature at Shoreham Camp and other places.
He was demobilised in January, 1919.
53, Chester Road, Lower Edmonton.   12710.

BINNING, W. J., Pte., 10th Durham Light Infty.

He joined in June, 1916, and served for two years on the Western Front. He was on active service at Cambrai, St. Quentin and La Fère. On March 21st, 1918, he was taken prisoner, but was eventually demobilised in April, 1919.
He holds the General Service and Victory Medals.
40, Tasso Road, W.6   14651.

BIRCH, W. J., Pte., R.A.S.C. (M.T.).

He enlisted in October, 1914, was sent to France in the same year, and took part in the battles of Ypres, the Somme, Loos, La Bassée and Arras.
He was demobilised in May, 1919, holding the 1914 Star, General Service and Victory Medals.
35, Marryat Street, Hammersmith.   12508.

BIRCH, J. F., Sergt., 11th Hussars and R.A.M.C.
He joined in August, 1914, and served on the Western Front and in Italy. In France he took part in the battles of Loos, Arras, the Somme and Ypres, and in Italy was engaged on the Piave. He returned to France and took part in the last Advance in 1918.
In May, 1919, he was demobilised, holding the 1914-15 Star, the General Service and Victory Medals.
51, College Road, Kensal Rise.   X18015.

BIRCH, W., Pte., 3rd Labour Corps.
He joined in 1915, went to France the same year, being engaged on various duties of a strenuous kind.
He was demobilised in 1919, holding the 1915 Star, General Service and Victory Medals.
18, New Holly Lane, Willesden.   15580/B.

BIRCH, W. J., Cpl., Royal Army Medical Corps.
He joined in 1917 and served on important hospital duties at various places.
He was demobilised in 1919.
1, Wingmore Road, Tottenham.   X17977.

BIRD, E. W., Pte., 7th London Regiment.
He joined in May, 1915, and was sent to the Western Front. He was in action on several occasions in France, and was wounded at Vimy Ridge on May 23rd, 1916. He was sent to hospital in France, invalided home, and finally discharged as unfit in January, 1919.
He holds the Victory and General Service Medals.
16, Hartopp Avenue, Fulham, S.W.6   X17683.

BIRD, F. G. N., Pte., Royal Army Medical Corps.
He joined in June, 1915, and was sent to France the same year, where he remained until he was demobilised in January, 1919. His chief duties where in connection with sanitation and water supply.
He holds the 1915 Star, General Service and Victory Medals.
145, Harley Road, Harlesden.   13171.

BIRD, J., Pte., Machine Gun Corps.
He enlisted in December, 1915, and later was sent to France, where he took part in several engagements. He was wounded, and finally discharged in February, 1919.
He holds the General Service and Victory Medals.
2, Marryat Street, Hammersmith.   12504.

BIRKETT, R. D., Staff-Sergt., 7th East Surrey Regiment and R.A.S.C.
He joined in March, 1916, and was sent to the Western Front, where he took part in several engagements. He was twice wounded during the battle of Arras in April, 1917. In July, 1918, after leaving hospital he was drafted to Mesopotamia, where he served until he was demobilised in December, 1919.
He holds the General Service and Victory Medals.
21, Snell's Park, Upper Edmonton.   X17485.

BIRKS, F., Pte., Kent Cyclist Battalion.
He joined in February, 1917, but was not successful in being drafted overseas owing to medical disabilities. He was later transferred to the Labour Corps and was finally demobilised in February, 1919.
75, Carlyle Avenue, Harlesden.   13811.

BIRMINGHAM, T., Cpl., Duke of Cornwall's L.I.
He joined in August, 1914, went to France and took part in the retreat from Mons, the battles of the Marne, Ypres, the Aisne, and was wounded at Ypres in December of the same year.
He holds the Mons Star, General Service and Victory Medals, and was discharged in January, 1917.
22, Essex Road, Willesden.   15590.

BISHOP, A. S., Hydrophone Operator, R.N., H.M.S. " Queen."
He joined in January, 1918, and served in the Adriatic Sea until he was demobilised in February, 1919.
He holds the General Service and Victory Medals.
3, Guilsborough Road, Willesden.   15238/B.

BISHOP, C. V., Pte., 2/10th Middlesex Regt.
He joined in February, 1915, served at the Dardanelles, and later took part in the capture of Jerusalem, during which fighting he was wounded.
He was demobilised in May, 1919, and holds the General Service and Victory Medals.
3, Guilsborough Road, Willesden.   15238/A.

BISHOP, D., Pte., 3rd Bedfordshire Regiment.
He joined in December, 1917, but being under age was not allowed to proceed overseas.
He served on Home Defence until November, 1919, when he was demobilised.
18, Montague Street, Hammersmith.   16402B.

BISHOP, E. A., Pte., Royal Fusiliers.
He joined in July, 1916, served on the Western Front from the following year, until 1919, and took part in the battles of Ypres, Arras, Cambrai, Amiens, the Somme and Vimy Ridge, where he was wounded.
He was demobilised on April 28th, 1919, holding the General Service and Victory Medals.
127, Mayo Road, Willesden.   15431.

BISHOP, E. B., Pte., 1st Devonshire Regiment.
He joined in September, 1914, and served with the Expeditionary Force in Egypt and was wounded.
He holds the General Service and Victory Medals, and was demobilised on June 5th, 1919.
49, Beryl Road, Fulham.   13349A.

BISHOP, H. G., Bombardier, R.G.A.
He enlisted on August 4th, 1914, was demobilised in June, 1919, and holds the 1914-15 Star, General Service and Victory Medals. During his service on the Western Front he was for a time with the Balloon Section. He took part in the battles of Ypres, Arras, and the Somme, and was twice wounded.
16, Everington Street, Fulham.   14311/A.

BISHOP, N. J., Royal Air Force.
He joined in September, 1918, and was immediately sent to the Italian Front, where he served until he was demobilised in January, 1919.
He holds the General Service and Victory Medals.
18, Montague Street, Hammersmith.   16402A.

BISHOP, W., Sapper, Royal Engineers.
He joined in March, 1918. and was sent on a special Army Cookery Course, which he passed successfully and was afterwards retained as Cook, until he was demobilised in February, 1919.
16, Everington Street, Hammersmith, W.6   14311B.

BISS, F. E., Pte., 1/8th Middlesex Regiment.
He joined in August, 1914, and served on the Western Front. He was killed whilst in action on September 25th, 1915, at the battle of Loos, and was entitled to the 1914 Star, General Service and Victory Medals.
25, Werley Avenue, Fulham.   X17744A.

BISS, G., Pte., Bedfordshire Regiment.
He joined in February, 1918, but was not successful in being sent overseas as he was retained for special guard duties connected with Home Defence.
He was demobilised in December, 1919.
25, Werley Road, Fulham.   X17744B.

BISSELL, F. C., Lce.-Sergt., 17th Middlesex Rgt.
He joined in April, 1915, and during his service on the Western Front was in action at Vimy Ridge, on the Somme, and at Cambrai, and was twice wounded.
He was demobilised on April, 19th, 1919, and holds the 1914-15 Star, General Service and Victory Medals.
6, Kilmaine Road, Fulham.   X18761.

BLACK, C., Pte., R.A.S.C. (M.T.).
He joined in August, 1915, and was sent to the Western Front the same year, where he was engaged in conveying ammunition and supplies to the forward dumps.
He was demobilised in July, 1919, and holds the 1915 Star, General Service and Victory Medals.
3, Mooltan Street, West Kensington.   X17144.

BLACK, C. F., Pte., Essex Regiment.
He enlisted in 1914, served for four years on the Western Front, and was taken prisoner at Albert. After suffering great hardships whilst in captivity he was eventually released, and in 1919 was discharged, holding the 1915 Star, General Service and Victory Medals.
69, Raynham Road, Edmonton.   16747/B.

BLACK, L. H., Pte., Tank Corps.
He joined in 1916, served on the Western Front until demobilised in 1919, and saw service with the Tanks on various sectors.
He was awarded the General Service and Victory Medals.
69, Raynham Road, Edmonton.   16747/A.

BLACK, T., Special War Worker.
He was employed on important engineering work at Woolwich Arsenal from 1916-19, during which time he was frequently exposed to great danger from hostile air raids.
27, Stracey Road, Harlesden.   15673.

BLACKBURN, F. G., Driver, R.A.S.C. (M.T.).
He joined in January, 1917, and, attached to the Ammunition Column, served in many sectors of the Western Front, including the Somme, Ypres and Arras.
He was demobilised in January, 1920, holding the General Service and Victory Medals.
70, Burn's Road, Harlesden.   13462.

BLACKBURN, F. J., Pte., R.A.V.C.
He enlisted in 1917, proceeded to France later and was employed on important duties in attending on wounded and disabled horses.
He was demobilised in November, 1919, and holds the General Service and Victory Medals.
2, Lanfrey Place, West Kensington, W.14   15699/A.

BLACKBURN, W. F., Pioneer, K.R.R. Corps.
He joined in April, 1915, and proceeded to France in the same year. Saw active service on various sectors, during which time he was gassed He was killed in action on June 27th, 1917, and was entitled to the 1915 Star, General Service and Victory Medals.
2, Lanfrey Place, W.14   15699/B.

BLACKHAM, F., Pte., R.A.S.C. (M.T.).
He joined in April, 1917, and during his service in France was wounded at Monchy in August, 1918.
He holds the General Service and Victory Medals.
55, Lorenco Road, White Hart Lane, Tottenham.   X18394.

BLACKHAM, F. C., Bombardier, R.F.A.
He joined in October, 1914, and served on the Western Front from 1915 until 1919, being in action at Loos, La Bassee, Ypres, on the Somme and at Armentieres.
He was demobilised in 1919, and holds the 1915 Star, General Service and Victory Medals.
25, Florence Road, Lower Edmonton, N.18   16018.

BLACKMAN, T., Pte., 3rd Bedford and Hertfordshire Regiment.
He joined in August, 1918, was in action on the Western Front, and later served with the Army of Occupation on the Rhine.
He was demobilised in March, 1920, and holds the General Service and Victory Medals.
93, Sherbrooke Road, Fulham.   X18471.

BLACKMORE, A., Stoker, Royal Naval Division.
He joined in 1914, served at Antwerp in the same year, and was wounded in action at the Dardanelles in June, 1915.
He holds the 1914 Star, General Service and Victory Medals, and was invalided out of the Navy in January, 1919.
124, Kimberley Road, Upper Edmonton.   16865.

BLACKSHAW, T. W. A., Gunner, R.G.A.
He joined in August, 1914, was sent to France in the same month, and took part in the retreat from Mons, the battles of Arras, Loos, the Somme, Ypres, Cambrai and others.
He was demobilised in March, 1919, holding the Mons Star, General Service and Victory Medals.
53, Carlyle Avenue, Harlesden.   14197.

BLAKE, A., A.B., Royal Navy.
He joined in July, 1916, and was posted to H.M.S. "Verdun" with the Grand Fleet in the North Sea.
He is entitled to the General Service and Victory Medals, and is still serving.
90, Sheldon Road, Edmonton.   X17460.

BLAKE, B. R., Sergt., Middlesex Regiment.
He joined in 1915, and served for three years on the Western Front, taking part in the battles of the Somme, Ypres and Loos.
He was demobilised in 1919, and holds the 1915 Star, General Service and Victory Medals.
88, Sheldon Road, Edmonton.   X17459A.

BLAKE, C. N., Gunner, Royal Field Artillery.
He joined in 1915, and served on the Western Front, taking part in the engagements at Dickebusch, the Somme, Ypres, Bullecourt and many other places.
He was invalided home in 1919, and holds the 1915 Star, General Service and Victory Medals.
5, Everington Street, Fulham.   14472.

BLAKE, F. J., Pte., Middlesex Regiment.
He joined in 1918, served at Aldershot and Norwich, and afterwards was sent to France, and thence with the Army of Occupation to Germany.
He was demobilised in 1920, holding the General Service and Victory Medal.
56, Averill Street, Fulham.   14183.

BLAKE, A. G., Special War Worker.
During the war he was retained by the Ministry of Food in one of their factories for distribution of food to the Army. His special mechanical knowledge rendered his services indispensable.
56, Averill Street, Fulham.   14177.

BLAKE, A. A., Rifleman, Post Office Rifles.
He joined in February, 1916, served on the Western Front, and was in action at Arras, Vimy Ridge, Amiens and Cambrai, and in the Retreat and Advance of 1918.
He was demobilised in 1919, holding the General Service and Victory Medals.
56, Averill Street, Fulham.   14182.

BLAKE, I. (Miss), Special War Worker.
This lady was engaged during the war upon important work at Messrs. Waring & Gillow's factory for munitions and articles of Army equipment. She was commended for her work.
56, Averill Street, Fulham.   14180.

BLAKE, G., Lce.-Cpl., Royal Fusiliers.
He volunteered for service in July, 1915, and was soon after sent to France, where he took part in operations until he was killed on September 15th, 1916.
He was entitled to the 1915 Star, General Service and Victory Medals.
39, Waldo Road, Willesden.   X17631.

BLAKE, W. J., Pte., "The Queen's" (Royal West Surrey Regiment).
He joined in July, 1915, and went to the Western Front the same year, taking part in many engagements, including those of Arras, Ypres and Somme. He was taken prisoner in March, 1918, and on returning to England was transferred to the R.A.M.C., and served with them until August, 1919, when he was demobilised.
He holds the 1914-15 Star, General Service and Victory Medals.
13, Heron Road, Willesden.   15596.

BLAND, F. M., Pte., Royal Fusiliers.
He joined in June, 1916, and was sent to the Western Front. He was severely gassed in 1916, and was sent home to a hospital, where he was treated. He is still suffering from the effects of gas poisoning. From time to time he was called up for service, but was finally discharged in June, 1919.
He holds the General Service and Victory Medals.
18, Langhedge Lane, Edmonton.   X17483.

BLAND, P., Pte., Oxford & Bucks Light Infantry.
He joined in 1916, and was sent to the Western Front, in 1917. He took part in numerous engagements, and was fighting on the Somme, at Arras and Cambrai. He was also serving in the last big advance in 1918. He went to the Rhine with the Army of Occupation in 1918, and is now serving in Ireland.
He holds the General Service and Victory Medals.
34, Dudden Hill Lane, Willesden Green, N.W.   X17393.

BLANDFORD, E., Pte., 1st Batt. Royal Fusiliers.
He was called up from the Reserve on August 4, 1914, and served in France from 1914 to January 16, 1916, when he was killed in action at Ypres. He had previously taken part in several important engagements.
He was entitled to the Mons Star, General Service and Victory Medals.
122, Felix Road, W. Ealing.   11030B

BLANEY, G., Corporal, R.A.O.C.
He joined in June, 1915, and was engaged on gun repairs during his service on the Western Front, being attached to No. 2 Mobile Workshops.
He was demobilised in July, 1919, and holds the 1914-15 Star, General Service and Victory Medals.
19, Church Lane, Willesden.   16028.

BLAVER, S., Pte., East Surrey Regiment.
He joined in February, 1916, and after two years' active service in France, during which time he took part in several engagements, including that of Albert, he was killed in action at Cambrai on August 4, 1918.
He was entitled to the General Service and Victory Medals.
85, Barry Road, Willesden.   14933A.

BLAVER, A. G., Cpl., Royal Field Artillery.
He joined in September, 1914, and during his service on the East Coast was on special defence duty, and also acted as Cook.
He was demobilised in June, 1919.
85, Barry Road, Willesden.   14933B.

BLAVER, A. (Miss), Special War Worker.
This lady was engaged on special war work as a cartridge examiner at the Park Royal Munition Factory, and was also engaged at the Bowden Wire Works, making aeroplane fittings.
85, Barry Road, Willesden.   14933/C.

BLAYNEY, J. H., Sergt., 1st Middlesex Regt.
He was serving at the outbreak of hostilities, and was sent to the Western Front, where he took part in the retreat from Mons, and was wounded. Later he served in India and Egypt.
He holds the Mons Star, General Service and Victory Medals.
85, Drayton Road, Harlesden, N.W.10   15252B.

BLAZEY, A. G., Pte., 7th Royal West Kent Regt.
He joined in July, 1918, and served on the Western and Eastern Fronts, in the Cambrai sector, in Palestine and Egypt. He was demobilised in December, 1919, holding the General Service and Victory Medals.
16, Bayonne Road, Fulham.   14515.

BLETSO, F., Stoker, R.N., H.M.S. " Roxburgh."
He joined in 1917, and was on important patrol and escort duty in the North Sea and Atlantic, until discharged in 1919.
He holds the General Service and Victory Medals.
1, Steele Road, Harlesden.   15681/B.

BLETSO, H., Gunner, Royal Garrison Artillery.
He joined in 1916, was sent to France in the same year, and took part in actions at Loos, Arras and the Somme.
He was discharged in 1918, suffering from shell-shock, and holds the General Service and Victory Medals.
1, Steele Road, Harlesden.   15681/A.

BLETSO, J., Cpl., Machine Gun Corps.
He joined in 1917, served on the Western Front until demobilised in 1919, and took part in the battles of the Somme, Ypres, Cambrai, and other engagements.
He holds the General Service and Victory Medals.
1, Steele Road, Harlesden.   15681/C.

BLIGH, R. G., Pte., R.A.S.C. (M.T.).
He joined in January, 1916, and served on the Western Front, taking part in the battles of the Somme, Passchendaele, Ypres, St. Quentin, Armentieres, Amiens, Le Cateau, Bullecourt, Vimy Ridge, Festubert and many other engagements, with the 66th Division.
In August, 1919, he was demobilised, holding the General Service and Victory Medals.
93, Archel Road, West Kensington.   16670A.

BLIGH, E. E., 1st Air Mechanic, R.A.F.
He joined in 1917, and served with the R.A.F. at Farnborough and elsewhere.
He was demobilised in 1919, and holds the General Service Medal.
93, Archel Road, West Kensington.   16670B.

BLIGHT, R., Pte., R.A.S.C. (M.T.).
He enlisted in November, 1914, and served on the Western Front until 1919, being engaged in the transport of ammunition, food and wounded.
He was demobilised in April, 1919, holding the 1914–15 Star, General Service and Victory Medals.
24, Ashford Road, Tottenham, N.17.   X18210.

BLIZZARD, W., Pte., 6th Middlesex Regt. and 17th Batt. Machine Gun Corps.
He joined in February, 1915, was sent to the Western Front in the following year, and was in action at Ypres, Armentieres, on the Somme (in July, 1916), at Cambrai, High Wood, Delville Wood and elsewhere.
He was demobilised in March, 1916, and holds the General and Victory Medals.
15, Hawkshead Road, Willesden.   16057.

BLOOM, F. H., Pte., 7th Norfolk Regiment.
He joined on October 28th, 1914, and served in France, taking part in engagements round Arras.
He was killed in action at Ypres on July 17th, 1915, and was entitled to the 1914-15 Star, the General Service and Victory Medals.
14, Faroe Road, West Kensington.   12651.

BLOSS, A. E., Stoker, R.N., H.M.S. " Pembroke."
He joined in June, 1917, and owing to injuries received during his service, was engaged later on special duties at Chatham.
He holds the General Service and Victory Medals.
13, Lowdon Road, Lower Edmonton.   12852.

BLOW, A. W., Pte., 19th Middlesex Regiment.
He enlisted in January, 1916, and went to France in the same year. In 1917 he went to Italy, and served there for some time.
He was demobilised on March 27th, 1919, and holds the General Service and Victory Medals.
14, Alston Road, Lower Edmonton.   16504A.

BLOW, A. A., Pte., Northumberland Fusiliers.
He joined in June, 1917, and served in France, where he was wounded in the leg during an engagement on the Aisne on May 27th, 1918, and taken prisoner on the same day. He was released on December 27th, 1918, and demobilised on December 11th, 1919.
He holds the General Service and Victory Medals.
14, Alston Road, Lower Edmonton.   16504/B.

BLOWES, E. W., Pte., Royal Army Service Corps.
He enlisted in August, 1914, and was on active service in France until December, 1919, when he was demobilised.
He holds the 1914 Star, General Service and Victory Medals.
23, Lorenco Road, Tottenham.   X17989.

BLOWS, A. (Mrs.), Special War Worker.
This lady offered her services, and was engaged during the war on important inspection duties in connection with the supply of cartridges and fuses at both Park Royal and Perivale.
431A, Chapter Road, Willesden.   16310/B.

BLOWS, H. A., Pte., Royal Fusiliers.
He joined in July, 1916, went to the Western Front and took part in many battles, including Arras, Ypres, Vimy Ridge, Menin Road, and in the Great Retreat and Advance in 1918. He was wounded five times during his service.
He holds the General Service and Victory Medals, and was demobilised in February, 1919.
431A, Chapter Road, Willesden.   16310/A.

BLUETT, F., 2nd Air Mechanic, R.A.F. (late R.N.A.S.).
He joined in May, 1916, and served in England. During his service he was stationed in Yorkshire on workshop duty.
He was demobilised in May, 1919, holding the General Service Medal.
24, Brenthurst Road, Willesden.   16385/B.

BLUNDELL, C., Pte., 5th Royal Berkshire Regt.
He joined in September, 1914, proceeded to France in 1915, and served at the battles of Loos, 1915; the Somme, 1916; Arras and Cambrai, 1917; and Amiens, 1918.
He was demobilised in January, 1919, holding the 1915 Star, General Service and Victory Medals.
65, Barbot Street, Lower Edmonton.   14581.

BLUNDEN, F. J., Sapper, Royal Engineers.
He enlisted in August, 1914, and from 1914 to 1919 was in France, where he took part in several engagements, and served on various special duties in the telegraph and telephone service. He was discharged on October 20th, 1919.
He holds the 1914–15 Star, General Service and Victory Medals.
98, Felix Road, W. Ealing.   11022:

BLYTH, T. F. W., A.B., Royal Navy.
He was serving, and after the outbreak of war cruised in the North Sea, and in Russian waters on board H.M.S. " Engadine," and was wounded.
He holds the 1914 Star, General Service and Victory Medals.
85, Drayton Road, Harlesden.   15252A.

BOARD, D., Pte., Machine Gun Corps.
He joined in August, 1914, and in the following year was drafted to the Western Front, where he took part in several engagements, and in May, 1917, was wounded in action near La Bassee. For two years he served in Italy, where he was continuously in the firing-line.
He holds the 1914–15 Star, the General Service and Victory Medals, and was demobilised in June, 1919.
42, Lancefield Street, Paddington.   X18570.

BOATMAN, N. M. (Mrs.), Special War Worker.
This lady was engaged at a shell-filling factory in the T.N.T. department, where she did important work. Later she was engaged at Messrs. Handley Page's aeroplane factory, and also did duty at the Y.W.C.A. canteen at Kensington.
102, Yeldham Road, Hammersmith.   13278/C.

BOATMAN, W. J., Pte., Worcester & Essex Regts.
He joined in 1914, and saw service in the Gallipoli campaign and in Egypt. Later he went to France, where he was in action on the Somme, and at Bapaume, Bertincourt, Beaumont Hamel and Cambrai, and took part in the last Advance. He was wounded on several occasions.
He holds the General Service and Victory Medals, also the 1914–15 Star, and was demobilised in 1919.
102, Yeldham Road, Hammersmith.   13278/A.

BOBBINS, H., Pte., 1st Middlesex Regiment.
He joined on August 5th, 1914, went to the Western Front the same month, and took part in many engagements, including those of Mons, the Marne and the Aisne, and was killed in action on January 12th, 1915.
He was entitled to the Mons Star, General Service and Victory Medals.
18, Mayo Road, Willesden.   15099.

BOCCIUS, F. C., Cpl., 3rd Middlesex Regiment.
He enlisted in 1906, and on the outbreak of war was sent to the Western Front, where he was killed in action at the battle of Ypres on February 10th, 1915.
He was entitled to the 1914 Star, General Service and Victory Medals.
39, Ilex Road, Willesden.   T16354/B.

BOCCIUS, F. (Miss), Special War Worker.
For two years during the war she did important work as an examiner of cartridges at the Park Royal Munition Works. She worked on alternate day and night shifts, often being on duty whilst air raids were in progress.
39, Ilex Road, Willesden, N.W.10   T16354C.

BOCCIUS, Pte., Royal Army Medical Corps.
He enlisted in 1907, and was stationed at Devonport, where he contracted consumption while on hospital duties.
He was discharged unfit for further service in 1914, and died on April 21st, 1916.
39, Ilex Road, Willesden.   T16354A.

BODIMEADE, E. E., Lce.-Cpl., 9th Middx. Regt.
He joined in August, 1914, and served in Mesopotamia, where he took part in several engagements, and was wounded. He holds the 1914-15 Star, General Service and Victory Medals, and was discharged in June, 1919.
23, Cobbold Road, Willesden.   15943.

BOLT, J., Cpl., Middlesex Regiment.
He volunteered for duty in September, 1914, and was employed on important guard duties at a large munition factory. He was invalided out of the service in 1918, on account of heart trouble.
21, Kimberley Road, Edmonton.   16587.

BOLTON, A. J., Pte., 63rd Batt. (Hood) R.N.D.
He joined in January, 1916, went to the Western Front in May of the same year, and took part in several engagements, including those of Arras, Ypres and Cambrai. He was so badly wounded on December 27th, 1917, as to necessitate the amputation of his left leg, and was discharged as a result in December of the following year.
He holds the General Service and Victory Medals.
17, Leopold Road, Willesden.   14742.

BOLTON, B. C. (M.M.), Cpl., 16th Battalion Australian Imperial Forces.
He joined on January 23rd, 1915, and from June 1st until the following September served at the Dardanelles. Afterwards he was drafted to Egypt, and on January 1st, 1917, to France, where he took part in the battles of Bullecourt, Hamel, Messines, Passchendaele, Villers Bretonneux and Hebuterne. On August 29th, 1918, he was awarded the Military Medal for gallantry in the field and devotion to duty. He was twice wounded, returned to England in December, 1918, and was demobilised in November, 1919, holding the 1914-15 Star, the General Service and Victory Medals.
29, Milton Avenue, Harlesden.   15797.

BOLTON, E. E., Cpl., 1/9th Middx. R. and R.E.
He enlisted in August, 1914, and served in India, taking part in the fighting on the North-Western Frontier. He was also on garrison duty before being sent to Mesopotamia in 1916 with the R.E.
He was demobilised in June, 1919, holding the 1914 Star, the Frontier, General Service and Victory Medals.
13, Waldo Road, Willesden.   X18187C.

BOLTON, J. G., Sergt., 1/9th Middlesex Regiment.
He offered his services in August, 1914, and owing to his ability as an instructor was retained in order to train recruits on signalling duties. He also acted as drill instructor, and was demobilised in February, 1919.
13, Waldo Road, Willesden.   X18187A.

BOLTON, J. R., Lce.-Cpl., 1/9th Middx. R. & R.E.
He enlisted in August, 1914, and served on the North-Western Frontier and on garrison duty in India, until 1916, when he was sent to Mesopotamia with the R.E.'s.
He was demobilised in March, 1919, and holds the 1914-15 Star, the Frontier, General Service and Victory Medals.
13, Waldo Road, Willesden.   X18187B.

BOLWELL, J. H., Rifleman, 8th K.R.R.C.
He joined in August, 1914, and went to the Western Front, where he fought in many battles and was killed in action on May 3rd, 1917.
He was entitled to the 1914-15 Star, General Service and Victory Medals.
59, Chaldon Road, Fulham.   X17727.

BOND, B. G., Rflmn., 18th London Regiment.
He joined in 1916, and served from 1916 to 1918 in France, taking part in many engagements, including Messines and Arras. He was twice severely gassed, and sent home and died in hospital at Brighton on October, 19th, 1918.
He was entitled to the General Service and Victory Medals.
10, Denmark Street, N.17   X18797/A.

BOND, C. E. (Miss), Special War Worker.
For two years during the war this lady was engaged on important work at a munition factory, producing flares and other war appliances, where she did valuable work.
15, Hartopp Avenue, Fulham.   X17734.

BOND, J. F., Pte., 3rd Middlesex Regiment (Territorial Force).
He enlisted in 1915, in 1917 went to France and thence in the following year to Italy, Greece and Salonica. He took part in actions at Loos, the Somme, the Marne, Cambrai and Bullecourt, and was discharged in 1919, holding the General Service and Victory Medals.
135, Framfield, Road, Hanwell.   10884A.

BOND, G. R. (M.M.), Trooper, Fort Garry Horse.
He joined in 1916, went to France in the same year, and took part in the battles of Neuve Chapelle, Hill 60, Bourlon Wood, the Marne and Cambrai. He was demobilised in 1919.
Was awarded the Military Medal for gallantry in the Field and holds the General Service and Victory Medals.
135, Framfield Road, Hanwell.   10884/B.

BOND, T. D., Ldg. Stoker, R.N., H.M.S. "Weymouth."
He joined in 1914, served off East Africa, and from 1916 off Italy. He was also on duty at Portsmouth in connection with captured German vessels.
He was discharged in 1919, holding the 1914-15 Star and the General Service and Victory Medals.
135, Framfield Road, Hanwell.   10884C.

BOND, J. W., Pte., 19th London Regiment.
He enlisted in April, 1915, and served from 1916 to 1918 in Egypt and Palestine. He was severely wounded and was in hospital for two years.
He holds the General Service and Victory Medals, and was demobilised in July, 1919.
10, Denmark Street, N.7   X18797/B.

BOND, H., Pte., 7th London Regiment.
He joined in April, 1915, served on the Western Front at Ypres and Cambrai, and was severely wounded in action on the Somme on August 10th, 1916, losing his right eye. He was in hospital in France and England, and went to Germany with the Army of Occupation.
He holds the General Service and Victory Medals, and was demobilised on May 2nd, 1919.
32, Bayonne Road, Fulham, W.6   14509.

BONDFIELD, R., Pte., R.A.S.C.
He joined in May, 1915, and served on the Western Front. He returned home in June, 1917, and died in hospital. He had been in the Army previous to joining in 1915, and was entitled to the General Service and Victory Medals.
2a, Lorenco Road, Tottenham, N.   X17998/B.

BONDFIELD, R. J., Stoker, R.N., H.M.S. "Fermoy."
He joined the Navy in June, 1914, and served at the Dardanelles, and later in South African waters. He was badly wounded in June, 1917.
He holds the 1914 Star, General Service and Victory Medals.
2a, Lorenco Road, Tottenham, N.   17998A.

BONE, A. S., Gunner, Royal Field Artillery.
He joined in January, 1915, went to the Western Front in March of the same year, and took part in many engagements, including those of the Somme, Ypres, Vimy Ridge, Arras, Albert and Amiens.
He was demobilised on May 27th, 1919, holding the 1914-15 Star, General Service and Victory Medals.
34, Meyrick Road, Willesden, N.W.10   16340/A.

BONE, E. J. (Miss), Special War Worker.
This lady was in the first place engaged in the manufacture of small munitions at Messrs. Rotax, but later joined Messrs. Berwick's Aeroplane Works, where she was engaged for about nine months on work connected with the covering of aeroplane wings.
26, Napier Road, College Park, Willesden.   17528/B.

BONE, L. E. (Miss), Special War Worker.
This lady was engaged for about three years at the Rotax Munition Works. She later joined the staff at Messrs. Berwick's Aeroplane Works, where she was employed chiefly on work connected with aeroplane wings.
26, Napier Road, College Park, Willesden.   17528/A.

BONE, F. W., Rifleman, 17th London Regt.
He joined in January, 1918, and was sent to France the same year. He was in action during the Great Advance of 1918, from August to November, and took part in several engagements during that period. He was once wounded, and was finally discharged in September, 1919, holding the General Service and Victory Medals.
26, Napier Road, Willesden, N.W.   X17525/B.

BONE, H. J., Pte., 23rd Middlesex Regiment.
He joined in March, 1915, and was sent to France in the same year. He served four years in France and took part in many engagements. He was present at Ypres, Arras, Cambrai, and the Somme, and was also fighting through the German Offensive in March, 1918, and was again in the last Big Push in September, 1918. During his service he was twice wounded, and once gassed. He was discharged in June, 1919, and holds the 1914-15 Star, General Service and Victory Medals.
26, Napier Road, Willesden, N.W.   X17525/A.

BONFIELD, W., A.B., Royal Navy.
He joined in August, 1914, and was employed on Hospital Ships and in carrying troops and foodstuffs to many places abroad.
He holds the Mercantile Marine, the General Service and Victory Medals, and was demobilised on March 21st, 1919.
20, Oxford Road, Edmonton.   13121.

BONNER, A., Pte., Middlesex Regiment.
He was serving at the outbreak of war and was sent to France in 1914. He fought at Mons, and was killed in action on July 1st, 1915.
He was entitled to the 1914 Star, General Service and Victory Medals.
14, Ambleside Road, Willesden.   16128.

BONNER, C. F., Rifleman, Rifle Brigade & Pte., R.A.S.C.
He joined in 1918 and went to the Rhine with the Army of Occupation in the following year. He was transferred from the Rifle Brigade to the R.A.S.C., and was engaged on transport duties while abroad.
He was demobilised in December, 1919.
16, Greyhound Road, Willesden, N.W.   X17804/A.

BONNER, F., Pte., R.A.S.C. (M.T.).
He joined in 1915 and in 1916 was sent to the Western Front, where he remained for two years. He was engaged on transport duties while abroad, conveying ammunition to the firing line, and was in action on the Somme, on the Marne, at Ypres and other places.
He was wounded, and was discharged in 1919, holding the General Service and Victory Medals.
16, Greyhound Road, Willesden, N.W.   X17804/B.

BONNER, G., Pte., Oxford and Bucks L.I.
He was serving in India when war broke out, and in 1914 was sent to Mesopotamia, where he remained until 1919, being once wounded.
He was demobilised in March, 1919, holding the 1914 Star, General Service and Victory Medals.
29, Hilmer Street, W.14   15695/A.

BOOKER, W. H., Pte., 19th Hussars.
He joined in November, 1914, and was employed on transport duties between England and France.
He was discharged in March, 1915, holding the 1915 Star, General Service and Victory Medals.
53, Southerton Road, Hammersmith.   11146.

BOORMAN, S., Pte., East Surrey and Essex Regt.
He joined in September, 1914, and went to the Western Front in 1915. There he fought at Ypres, Loos and several other places, afterwards going to Servia, where he was employed as a sniper. He went back to France in time for the Retreat and Advance in 1918, and was wounded.
He holds the 1914-15 Star, General Service and Victory Medals, and was demobilised in February, 1919.
77, Berry Street, Willesden.   15416.

BOOTH, A., Sergt., Welsh Regt. & Army C.C.
He joined in August, 1909, and at the outbreak of war proceeded from India to the Western Front, where he took part in the battles of Loos and Ypres. Later he was sent to Salonica, where he contracted malaria, was invalided home in August, 1918, and after being for some time in hospital was discharged, unfit for further service in March, 1919.
He holds the 1914-15 Star, General Service and Victory Medals.
70, Mordaunt Road, Harlesden.   13857/B.

BOOTH, W. A., Pte., Duke of Cornwall's L.I.
He joined in April, 1917, and after taking part in many battles died in June, 1918, as a result of wounds received in action near Ypres.
He was entitled to the General Service and Victory Medals.
70, Mordaunt Road, Harlesden.   13857/A.

BOOTH, E., Pte., 12th Middx. & Royal Fusiliers.
He joined in August, 1914, served on the Western Front, at Arras, Loos, Neuve Chapelle, Armentieres, Amiens, Ypres, Vimy Ridge, Bullecourt and Cambrai, and in the Great Retreat and Advance of 1918. He was wounded twice on the Somme, and at Arras.
He holds the 1914-15 Star, General Service and Victory Medals, and was demobilised in 1919.
20, Field Road, Fulham.   15045.

BOOTMAN, A. E., Pte., Sherwood Foresters.
He joined in August, 1914, served in France at Armentieres, Ypres and Kemmel, and was wounded six times.
He holds the 1914-15 Star, General Service and Victory Medals, and was discharged on July 6th, 1916.
131, Greyhound Road, Fulham.   14823.

BOREHAM, H., Pte., Labour Corps.
He enlisted in June, 1917, and owing to the fact that he was medically unfit for General service, he was retained for Home service, and attached to the Royal Engineers.
He was demobilised in February, 1919.
105, Burn's Road, Harlesden.   13455.

BOREHAM, H. J., Pte., Royal Sussex Regiment.
He joined in 1915 and served with our troops in India until 1919, when he was demobilised.
He holds the General Service and Victory Medals.
17, Durham Road, Lower Edmonton.   14872.

BORLEY, R. S. (M.M.), Sergt., Highland L.I.
He joined in August, 1914, and served in France for over three years, taking part in many engagements. He was awarded the Military Medal for conspicuous bravery in the field and was also mentioned in despatches. Later he was in Germany with the Army of Occupation, and was demobilised in December, 1919.
He also holds the 1914 Star, General Service and Victory Medals.
134, Blythe Road, Hammersmith.   12418/A.

BORLEY, J. E., Pte., Royal Defence Corps.
He joined in August, 1914, and served on important Home Defence duties until February, 1919, when he was demobilised.
134, Blythe Road, Hammersmith.   12418/B.

BORMAN, H., Pte., Bedfordshire Regiment.
He joined in September, 1914, was sent to the Western Front, and after taking part in the battle of Loos, was wounded by the explosion of a mine. He was taken prisoner at Ypres in April, 1916.
He holds the 1914-15 Star, General Service and Victory Medals, and was demobilised in May, 1919.
17, Humbolt Road, Fulham.   15304.

BORRETT, A. L., Cpl., R.A.S.C.
He joined in August, 1914, went to the Western Front, and was in action with the 22nd Royal Fusiliers. He was wounded in the head, as a result of which he was in hospital for some time.
He holds the 1914-15 Star, General Service and Victory Medals, and is still serving.
52, Lintaine Grove, Fulham.   X16955.

BOSTON, C., Gunner, Royal Garrison Artillery.
He joined on August 4th, 1914, having previously served in the Territorial Force, and saw service on both Western and Eastern Fronts. He is at present serving in Egypt, and holds the 1914-15 Star, the General Service and Victory Medals.
35, Bramber Road, Fulham.   15712A.

BOSTON, W., Gunner, Royal Garrison Artillery.
He joined in 1916, and served on the Western Front, and later with the Army of Occupation in Germany.
He was demobilised in 1919, and holds the General Service and Victory Medals.
35, Bramber Road, Fulham.   15712B.

BOUDIER, J., Pte., Black Watch.
He joined in 1916, and during his service in France took part in many important engagements, including those of Ypres, and Messines, and was badly gassed.
He holds the General Service and Victory Medals, and was discharged suffering from shell shock in 1918.
27, Newlyn Road, Tottenham, N.17   X18510A.

BOUDIER, W. C., Pte., Manchester Regiment.
He joined in August, 1914, and was on active service in France until 1919. During this period he took part in engagements at Mons, Loos, Ypres, and the Somme, and suffered from shell shock.
He holds the 1914 Star, General Service and Victory Medals, and was demobilised in January, 1920.
27, Newlyn Road, Tottenham, N.17   X18510/B.

BOUGHEN, F. C., Pte., 21st Middlesex Regt.
He enlisted on October 6th, 1916, and was despatched to France, where he saw active service on several sectors, and fought in the battle of the Somme.
He was discharged on November 13th, 1917, holding the General Service and Victory Medals.
9, Strode Road, Willesden.   X17093.

BOUGHEN, R. G., Driver, R.F.A.

He joined in November, 1914, served on the Western Front
from April, 1915, until 1919, and was in action at Loos,
Arras, Givenchy, on the Somme, at Ypres, and Cambrai.
He holds the 1914-15 Star, General Service and Victory
Medals, and was demobilised in June, 1919.
109a, Deacon Road, Willesden.   16609.

BOULD, A. S. V., Cpl., Lancashire Regiment.

He joined in November, 1914, and served on the Western
Front for five years, during which period he took part in the
battles of Ypres, Cambrai and Arras, and in the Great Retreat
and Advance of 1918.
He was taken prisoner and was demobilised on January 6th,
1919, holding the 1914-15 Star, General Service and Victory
Medals.
15, Shrewsbury Road, Harlesden.   14128.

BOULD, L. A. (Mrs.), Special War Worker.

This lady offered her services in October, 1917, in order to
release a man for military service. She was employed as
a post-woman until 1919, and was commended for her work.
Westgate, 4, Roundwood Road, Willesden.   16307.

BOUSTRED, C. F., Driver, R.F.A.

He joined in November, 1914, and served for some time on
the Western Front, later being transferred to the Egyptian
Expeditionary Force. He served at Salonica and was
twice wounded.
He was demobilised in February, 1919, holding the General
Service and Victory Medals.
5 Durham Road, Edmonton.   14682.

BOVINGDON, W., Sergt., Norfolk Regiment.

He joined in November, 1916, and a year later was sent to
Mesopotamia. In this theatre he saw considerable service,
and was eventually demobilised in April, 1920.
He holds the General Service and Victory Medals.
5a, Sunnyside Road South, Lower Edmonton. N.9   14342/A.

BOWDEN, E. G., Driver, Royal Engineers.

He joined in May, 1915, served on the Western Front, and
took part in operations on all sectors, including the Somme,
Ypres and Arras. In the course of the fighting he was
gassed twice.
He was demobilised in March, 1919, holding the 1914-15
Star, General Service and Victory Medals.
138, Estcourt Road, Fulham.   16231.

BOWDEN, J., Pte., 1/9th Middlesex Regiment.

He joined in August, 1914, and saw service at Aden and in
India, where he remained for a considerable period.
He holds the General Service and Victory Medals, and was
demobilised on December 27th, 1919.
317, Chapter Road, Willesden Green.   16717.

BOWDEN, J. J., Cpl., 6th London Regt.

He joined in May, 1915, and served on the Western Front,
being engaged in the battles of Vimy Ridge, Bullecourt, the
Somme and Ypres, during which he was gassed, and suffered
from shell shock. On April 27th, 1919, he was demobilised,
and holds the 1914-15 Star, General Service and Victory
Medals.
25a, Cooper Road, Willesden.   16638.

BOWEN, F., Lce.-Cpl., 1st Royal West Kent Regt.

He joined in 1913, and in August, 1914, was sent to France,
where he took part in the battles of Mons, Ypres, the Somme
and many other engagements. He was twice wounded at
Armentieres, and on April 14th, 1920, was demobilised,
holding the 1914 Star, General Service and Victory Medals.
58, Durban Road. Tottenham.   X17953.

BOWEN, J., Cpl., The Queen's (24th London R.).

He joined in August, 1914, and served on both the Eastern
and Western Fronts, being at Salonica and in Egypt and
France. He saw much fighting in all these theatres.
He holds the 1915 Star, General Service and Victory Medals,
and was demobilised in June, 1919.
22, Estcourt Road, Fulham, S.W.   16649.

BOWEN, R., Cook, R.N., H.M.S. " Egmont."

He joined up in August, 1914, and saw service in all waters as
a Mine-sweeper. He was invalided home from Malta and
demobilised in February, 1919.
He holds the 1914 Star, the General Service and Victory
Medals.
22, Estcourt Road, Fulham, S.W.   17084.

BOWERMAN, G. E., Driver, R.E.

He enlisted in September, 1914, served on the Western Front
until 1919, and took part in the battles of Arras, Cambrai,
Ypres, Armentieres, the Somme and in the Retreat and
Advance of 1918, being wounded. He then served with the
Army of Occupation in Germany until demobilised in May,
1919, holding the 1914-15 Star, General Service and Victory
Medals.
39, Earlsmead Road, Kensal Rise.   X17834B.

BOWERMAN, B. H., Sergt., Bedfordshire Regt.

He joined in January, 1916, served on the Western Front until
1919, and took part in the fighting at Arras, Cambrai, on the
Somme, at Ypres, La Bassée and elsewhere, being gassed.
He also acted as bayonet instructor, and obtained his pro-
motion for consistent good work in the field.
He was demobilised in November, 1919, holding the General
Service and Victory Medals.
39, Earlsmead Road, Kensal Rise.   X17834A.

BOWERMAN, T. F. (M.M.), Sergt., 10th Middx.R.

He enlisted in August, 1914, was sent to France in the same
year and took part in the battles of Arras, Cambrai, La
Bassée, Loos and the Somme. He was awarded the Military
Medal for conspicuous gallantry in the field at Trones Wood,
and holds also the 1914-15 Star, General Service and Victory
Medals.
He was discharged in November, 1918.   X17834C.
39, Earlsmead Road, Kensal Rise.

BOWERS, H. A., Pte., R.A.S.C. (M.T.).

He joined in July, 1915, and was sent to the Western Front,
where he was employed in conveying rations and ammunition
to and from the firing line.
He holds the 1915 Star, General Service and Victory Medals,
and was demobilised in June, 1919.
47, Sherbrooke Road, Fulham.   X18479.

BOWLD, E., Driver, Royal Field Artillery.

He joined in 1915, and served for four years in Mesopotamia,
and while there contracted dysentery.
In April, 1919, he was discharged, holding the 1914-15 Star,
General Service and Victory Medals.
16, Winchelsea Road, Harlesden.   13808.

BOWLING, T., A.B., R.N., H.M.S. " Lion."

He joined in November, 1917, and served in the North Sea
engagements on the above named vessel.
He holds the General Service and Victory Medals, and is
still in the Navy.
107, Angel Road, Edmonton.   16578.

BOWLTING, A., Lce.-Cpl., 2nd Welsh Regiment.

He enlisted in January, 1915, served on the Western Front,
and during a night attack received wounds which caused him
to lose the sight of one eye.
He was demobilised in January, 1920, holding the General
Service and Victory Medals.
28, Estcourt Road, Fulham.   16648.

BOWRON, J. C., Sergt., Royal Fusiliers and Dorset Regiment.

He joined in August, 1914, and served for a year at Malta and
for two years on the Western Front. He took part in the
battles of Ypres, Loos—where he was wounded—Neuve
Chapelle, Festubert, the Somme, Cambrai and Arras. He
was returned to England in 1917 on account of wounds, and
was demobilised in February, 1919.
He holds the 1915 Star, General Service and Victory Medals.
20, Kenmont Gardens, Willesden.   X17574.

BOWYER, W., Cpl., 8th Battalion The Buffs (East Kent Regiment).

He joined in September, 1914, and served on the Western
Front from August, 1915, until September 26th of the same
year, when he was killed in action at Loos.
He is entitled to the 1915 Star, General Service and Victory
Medals.
27, Albert Terrace, Milton Avenue, Stonebridge Park, N.W.10
                    14333.

BOWYER, W., Pte., 7th London Regt.

He joined in August, 1914, and served in England, at Salisbury, until 1916, when he was discharged, having failed to
secure his transfer overseas.
121A, Greyhound Road, Fulham.   15021.

BOXELL, H., Pte., Norfolk Regiment.

He joined in May, 1916, and served in India until the cessation
of hostilities.
He was demobilised in May, 1919, and holds the General
Service and Victory Medals.
29, Moselle Street, Tottenham.   X18399.

BOYALL, H., 1st-Cl. Stoker, R.N., H.M.S. " Duncan."

Joining in 1914, he saw service in many waters, chiefly on
patrol duty and as escort for food transports.
He holds the 1914-15 Star, General Service and Victory
Medals, and is still serving.
17, Yeldham Road, W.6   12810.

BOYCE, J., Pte., Royal Marines.

He joined in April, 1900, and in 1914 was sent to Antwerp,
where he took part in all the fighting at that critical period.
In 1915 he went to the Dardanelles.
He was demobilised in March, 1919, and holds the 1914 Star,
General Service and Victory Medals.
77, Lopen Road, Upper Edmonton.   TX17591.

BOYNTON, V., Pte., Royal Fusiliers.

He joined in August, 1914, and served in France from 1915 to 1917, taking part in the operations on the Somme and at Cambrai, and was twice wounded.
He holds the 1915 Star, General Service and Victory Medals. He was discharged in November, 1917.
85, Rayleigh Road, W.14   12649.

BRABROOK, G. E., Pte., 10th Lincoln Regt.

He joined in July, 1916, and served during 1917–18 on the Western Front, where he was in action at Peronne and Bullecourt. He was reported missing, and last heard of at the battle of Bullecourt in March, 1918.
He holds the General Service and Victory Medals.
85, Denzil Road, Neasden Lane, N.W.   15932.

BRACE, G., Pte., Essex Regiment.

He joined in June, 1916, and having completed his training in England served in Egypt and Palestine until he was demobilised in October, 1919.
He holds the General Service and Victory Medals.
27, Chichester Road, Edmonton.   14854.

BRACE, J. F., Pte., Argyll and Sutherland Hldrs.

He enlisted in March, 1915, was stationed for a while in Scotland, and later was drafted to Egypt, and thence to Mesopotamia. In June, 1918, he returned to England, and ten days later died from pneumonia.
He was entitled to the General Service and Victory Medals.
34, Gilpin Grove, Edmonton.   16802B.

BRACE, P. G., Pte., R.A.S.C.

He joined in April, 1915, was stationed at Romsey, and afterwards served in Egypt, where he took part in all local operations.
He was demobilised on March 1st, 1919, holding the General Service and Victory Medals.
34, Gilpin Grove, Edmonton.   16802A.

BRACE, S. T., R.F.A. and R.E.

He joined on June 30, 1915, and during his service on the Western Front took part in the battles of Ypres, Cambrai, and the Somme, and was also employed with the Royal Engineers on railway work in Belgium.
For some time he was in hospital in France, suffering from dysentery and trench fever.
He holds the General Service and Victory Medals, and was demobilised in April, 1919.
9, Garvan Road, W.6   14638.

BRACKLEY, J., Pte., Oxford & Bucks L.I.

He joined in January, 1915, and was sent to the Western Front, where he took part in the battles of Ypres, Armentieres and Givenchy, where, on September 24th, 1915, he was so badly wounded as to necessitate the amputation of both legs, and on October of the same year was discharged unfit for further service.
He holds the 1914–15 Star, the General Service and Victory Medals.
54, Hazel Road, Willesden.   X17780.

BRADBURY, H. G., A.B., Royal Navy.

He joined in August, 1914, served on H.M.S. " Repulse," and also on mine-sweeping boats in the North Sea and other places for five years.
He was demobilised in 1919, holding the 1914–15 Star, General Service and Victory Medals.
104, Ancill Street, W.6   13663/A.

BRADBY, R. J., Pte., Argyll & Suth. Highldrs.

He joined in June, 1916, went to the Western Front in the following year, and took part in several engagements, including those of Arras and Cambrai.
He was demobilised in September, 1919, holding the General Service and Victory Medals.
9, Heron Road, Willesden.   15597.

BRADE, A. E., Pte., The Queen's (Royal West Surrey Regiment).

He joined in December, 1915, was sent to France in February of the following year, and after taking part in the fighting at Ypres and the Somme, was killed in action at Cambrai in May, 1917.
Entitled to the General Service and Victory Medals.
10, Goodson Road, Harlesden.   14929.

BRADLEY, C., Pioneer, R.E. (Railway Section).

He joined in August, 1915, and served at Salonica for a year, was sent home in 1916, having contracted illness there. In 1917 he was discharged as medically unfit for further military service.
He holds the 1914–15 Star, General Service and Victory Medals.
19, Kenmont Gardens, College Park, Willesden, N.W.   X17570A.

BRADLEY, H. B., Pte., R.A.S.C.

He joined in November, 1916, and saw service at various stations with the Mechanical Transport section of the R.A.S.C. He was demobilised in 1919.
19, Kenmont Gardens, College Park, Willesden.   X17570B.

BRADLEY, E. H., Pte., 3rd London Regiment.

He joined in September, 1914, and served at the Dardanelles, in Egypt, Malta, and the Soudan. Later he went to France, and took part in engagements at Bullecourt (where he was wounded), at Arras, and in the Great Retreat and Advance of 1918.
He holds the 1915 Star, General Service and Victory Medals, and was demobilised in January, 1919.
287, Chapter Road, Willesden Green.   X17120/A.

BRADLEY, J., A.B., R.N., H.M.S. " Leonidas."

He joined in 1916, and served in the North Sea, where his ship was engaged in dangerous work in scouting and attacking submarines.
He holds the General Service and Victory Medals, and was demobilised in February, 1919.
287, Chapter Road, Willesden Green.   X17120/B.

BRADLEY, F., Pte., 19th Batt., London Regt.

He enlisted at the outbreak of war, but was not successful in being sent overseas, as he was retained on escort and special guard duties until April, 1918, when he was discharged on medical grounds.
76, Milton Avenue, Harlesden.   14319.

BRADSHAW, A., Pte., Royal Irish Fusiliers.

He enlisted in August, 1914, and was later sent to Egypt and Mesopotamia, where he served until he returned to England, and was discharged in August, 1917.
He holds the General Service and Victory Medals.
49, Hannell Road, Fulham.   X18154B.

BRADSHAW, W. A., A.B., R.N., H.M. Minesweeper " Widnes."

He joined in August, 1914, and served in the East. His ship was torpedoed, and he was for many hours in the water before being picked up.
He was discharged in November, 1919, holding the General Service and Victory Medals.
28, Garvan Road, Fulham.   15062/C.

BRADSHAW, C. J., Rifleman, London Irish Rifles.

He joined in 1916, served on the Western Front with the Royal Engineers, and was severely wounded on July 23rd, 1917.
He was discharged physically unfit on account of wounds on May 27th, 1918, and holds the General Service and Victory Medals.
28, Garvan Road, Fulham.   15062/B.

BRADSHAW, V., Pte., Australian Imperial Force.

He joined in 1916, and during his service on the Western Front was gassed and severely wounded at Bullecourt.
He was discharged in December, 1918, and holds the General Service and Victory Medals.
28, Garvan Road, Fulham.   15062A.

BRADSHAW. E. B., Cpl., Rifle Brigade.

He joined in 1916, and served for two years in France, taking part in the battle of Vimy Ridge, where he was taken prisoner, in October, 1916, and kept for 18 months in Germany.
He holds the General Service and Victory Medals.
3, Tasso Road, W.6   14648C.

BRADSHAW, E. T., Sergt., 2nd Bedford Regt.

He joined in November, 1916, and was sent to India. While there he contracted malarial fever and was admitted to hospital.
He holds the General Service and Victory Medals.
3, Tasso Road, W.6   14648A.

BRADSHAW, S. R., Rifleman, Rifle Brigade.

He joined in May, 1918, and served in France and in Germany with the Army of Occupation, and was afterwards sent to India.
He holds the General Service and Victory Medals.
3, Tasso Road, W.6   14648B.

BRADSHAW, G., Pte., Royal Fusiliers.

He enlisted in August, 1914, and served on the Western Front, taking part in various engagements. After a short period of Home service he was then sent to Germany with the Army of Occupation, remaining there until demobilised in March, 1919.
He was awarded the 1914–15 Star, General Service and Victory Medals.
28, Church Path, Hammersmith.   16398.

BRADY, F., Cpl., Royal Field Artillery.
He joined in August, 1914, and during his three years' service on the Western Front took part in the battles of Mons, Ypres, the Somme, Loos, Bullecourt and Vimy Ridge, where he was wounded and gassed.
He was discharged medically unfit in November, 1917, and holds the Mons Star, the General Service and Victory Medals.
62, Foyle Road, Tottenham.   X18954.

BRADY, J., Driver, Royal Field Artillery.
He re-enlisted on February 21st, 1915 (having previously served 12 years in the R.F.A., and seven years in the 3rd Battalion Royal West Kents), and was sent to France in July, 1915, remaining for six months. He served on the Western Front also from December 16th, 1916, until his discharge on April 6th, 1919.
He holds the 1915 Star, General Service and Victory Medals.
6, Grove Place, Ealing.   10839.

BRAGG, G. J. H., Cpl., Royal West Kent Regt.
He joined in 1914, went to the Western Front in 1915, took part in many engagements, and was wounded at Cambrai, later being taken prisoner in the Great Retreat in 1918. He was a captive for nine months, afterwards serving with the Army of Occupation.
He holds the 1915 Star, the General Service and Victory Medals.
5, Berry Street, Willesden.   15407.

BRAGGER, S. E., Pte., Middlesex Regiment.
He joined in November, 1914, and was sent to Egypt in the following June. He served four years in Egypt, and was engaged in observation work in the desert.
He was discharged in July, 1919, and holds the 1915 Star, General Service and Victory Medals.
42, Waldo Road, Willesden, N.W.   X17561/B.

BRAGGER, W. E., Pte., Middlesex Regiment.
He joined in November, 1915, and was sent to the Western Front, where he took part in many important engagements. He was in action on the Somme and at Ypres, where he was wounded. During his service he was gassed and buried.
He was discharged in July, 1919, and holds the General Service and Victory Medals.
42, Waldo Road, Willesden, N.W.   X17561/A.

BRAHANY, J. E., Gunner, R.F.A.
He joined on March 26th, 1918, having previously been employed making munitions of war, and served in France, taking part in the battle of Cambrai.
He was demobilised in May, 1919. holding the General Service and Victory Medals.
87, Winchester Road, Lower Edmonton.   14752.

BRANCH, A. H., Pte., Northamptonshire Regt.
He joined in 1916, served on the Western Front until demobilised in 1919, and was twice wounded.
He was awarded the General Service and Victory Medals.
4, Pretoria Road, Upper Edmonton.   X17019A.

BRANCH, C. W., Trooper, 4th Royal Irish Dragoon Guards.
He enlisted in 1914, served on the Western Front, and took part in the retreat from Mons. He was also stationed at Rouen, and was wounded in action on May 24th, 1915. He died of wounds on June 4th, 1915, and was entitled to the 1914 Star, General Service and Victory Medals.
4, Pretoria Road, Upper Edmonton.   X17019B.

BRANCH, F. G., Sergt., Northamptonshire Regt.
He joined in 1917, served on the Western Front until demobilised in 1919, and took part in the fighting on the Somme and elsewhere.
He was awarded the General Service and Victory Medals.
4, Pretoria Road, Upper Edmonton.   X17019C.

BRANCH, E. C., Pte., Labour Corps.
He joined in September, 1915, was sent to the Western Front in the same year, and served in many engagements, being in action on the Somme in 1916, at Cambrai, Arras, Ypres, also at Armentieres and Poperinghe. He took part in the last big Advance in 1918, and was demobilised in February, 1919, holding the 1915 Star, General Service and Victory Medals.
24, Greyhound Road, Willesden, N.W.   X17791A.

BRANCH, F. A., Gunner, Royal Field Artillery.
He joined in 1915, and in the following year was sent to the Western Front, where he served for two years, and took part in numerous battles, including that of the Somme in 1916, Cambrai, Arras and Bapaume. He was twice wounded and gassed, and in February, 1919, was discharged, holding the General Service and Victory Medals.
24, Greyhound Road, Willesden, N.W.   X17794/B.

BRANDOM, L., Sergt., 1st Bedfordshire Regt.
He enlisted in August, 1914, and during his service on the Western Front took part in the battles of Mons, Loos, Arras, Ypres, the Somme, and Cambrai, being severely wounded four times.
He was discharged on April 16th, 1919, holding the 1914 Star, General Service and Victory Medals.
70, Bramber Road, Fulham, W.6   16229.

BRANDON, E., Lce.-Cpl.. 2/15th London Regt.
He joined in June, 1918, and was attached to the military police at Armentieres, Aix, Etaples, Abbeville, Dunkirk, St. Pol, and many other places.
He was demobilised on May 1st, 1920, and holds the General Service and Victory Medals.
55, Durban Road, Tottenham.   X18283.

BRANDON, H. E., Air Mechanic, R.A.F.
He joined in 1916, and was engaged in testing and repairing aero engines in France.
He was demobilised in November, 1919, and holds the General Service and Victory Medals.
55, Durban Road, Tottenham.   X18282.

BRANDON, W., Drummer, 1st Manchester Regt.
He joined in August, 1914, and went to the Western Front in September of the same year, taking part in several engagements, and was killed in action at La Bassée in the battle of Givenchy, on December 21st, 1914.
He was entitled to the 1914 Star, General Service and Victory Medals.
59, Waldo Road, Willesden.   X17634.

BRANSON, G., Driver, Royal Horse Artillery.
He enlisted in August, 1914, was sent to France in the same year, took part in the battles of Mons, the Somme, Ypres, Loos, St. Quentin and Bullecourt, and was three times wounded.   Later he served with the Army of Occupation in Germany until demobilised in 1919.
He holds the 1914 Star, General Service and Victory Medals.
30, Aspenlea Road, W.6   14291/B.

BRANSON, W. E., Pte., The Queen's (Royal West Surrey Regt.).
He joined in November, 1917, and served in India, takiug part in operations there.
He holds the General Service and Victory Medals.
30, Aspenlea Road, W.6   14291/C.

BRANTOM, H. M., Pte., 1/9th Middlesex Regt.
He joined in September, 1915, and was sent to India in the following May, and to Mesopotamia in November, 1917. While abroad he acted as a Lewis gunner.
He was demobilised in February, 1919, and holds the General Service and Victory Medals.
3, Beaconsfield Road, Willesden.   16083.

BRATTON, T., Sergt., R.A.S.C. (M.T.).
He joined in February, 1915, went to Egypt in April, and thence to the Dardanelles, where, in spite of ill-health, he served on transport duty with the R.A.S.C. and the New Zealand transport service.
He was discharged in February, 1919, holding the 1914-15 Star, the General Service and Victory Medals.
115, Rucklidge Avenue, Harlesden.   13155.

BRAY, F., Driver, R.A.S.C.
He joined in July, 1915, and in the same year went to France, where he remained until 1919.
He holds the 1915 Star, General Service and Victory Medals.
55, Wendover Road, Harlesden.   12552.

BRAY, W. H., Lce.-Cpl., Bedfordshire Regt.
He was recalled from the Reserve on August 4th, 1914, proceeded to the Western Front the same month, and served at Mons, Loos, Festubert, Neuve Chapelle, La Bassée, Givenchy, Ypres, Cambrai, and many other places, and was killed in action in October, 1917.
He was entitled to the Mons Star, General Service and Victory Medals.
20, Milton Road, Harlesden.   15638.

BRAZIER, H. N., Fitter, R.F.A.
He joined in January, 1915, served in France until demobilised in April, 1919, and took part in several engagements.
He holds the 1914-15 Star, General Service and Victory Medals.
32, Alric Avenue, Harlesden.   14435.

BRAZIER, J. W., Sapper, Royal Engineers.
He joined in February, 1915, and served from August, 1915, to November, 1915, on the Western Front, and from then to November, 1918, in the Balkans.
He was demobilised in January, 1919, and holds the 1914-15 Star, the General Service and Victory Medals.
39, Hiley Road, Willesden.   X18236.

BRAZIER, T. H., Pte., 13th Middlesex Regt.
He joined on April 27th, 1915, and went to France in September of the same year. He took part in the battles of Loos and Ypres, was wounded in action on the Somme in August, 1916, and was eventually discharged as medically unfit in the following year.
He holds the 1915 Star, General Service and Victory Medals.
48, Essex Road, Willesden. 15594.

BRECKLEY, H. G., Pte., 13th Middlesex Regt.
He joined in July, 1916, was sent to the Western Front in November, and was killed in action at Ypres on August 24th, 1917.
He was entitled to the General Service and Victory Medals.
107, Villiers Road, Willesden. 16519.

BREED, E., Pte., Royal Army Ordnance Corps.
He joined in August, 1917, and saw active service in France, and was afterwards sent to Bagdad.
He holds the General Service and Victory Medals.
39, Felixstowe Road, Willesden. X17758.

BREEZE, W., Cpl., Labour Corps (attached to the Black Watch).
He joined in March, 1917, and was for some time engaged on special duties on the Western Front.
He holds the General Service and Victory Medals, and was demobilised in March, 1919.
3, Westgate, Roundwood Road, Willesden. 16301/A.

BRETT, K. A., Special War Worker.
During the war this lady did work of an important nature in connection with the manufacture of munitions at a factory in London. The work was very strenuous, and she attended both day and night duties.
363a, Chapter Road, Willesden Green. 16720.

BRETT, A. L. (Miss), Special War Worker.
From 1914 to 1919 this lady was engaged in the manufacture of war munitions, and also on inspection duties in connection with the making of cartridges, &c. She performed work of great importance, and continued her duty during many air raids.
363a, Chapter Road, Willesden Green. 16718.

BRETT, C., Driver, Royal Field Artillery.
He joined in August, 1914, and served for five years in Salonica, taking part in various engagements.
He was demobilised in 1919 and holds the 1914-15 Star, and the General Service and Victory Medals.
29, Linton Road, Edmonton. X17476C.

BRETT, W. G., Lce.-Cpl., 32nd Royal Fusiliers.
He joined in August, 1914, and served on the Western Front and in Egypt. He took part in the battles of Mons and the Somme, and was twice wounded.
In 1919 he was demobilised, holding the Mons Star, the General Service and Victory Medals.
29, Linton Road, Edmonton. X17476A.

BRETT, R., Lce.-Cpl., 4th Middlesex Regiment.
He joined in August, 1914, and served for nearly four years on the Western Front. During that time he took part in the battles of Mons, the Somme, Ypres, and other engagements.
In March, 1918, during the last Advance, he was first reported missing, and afterwards killed.
He was entitled to the Mons Star, the General Service and Victory Medals.
59, Linton Road, Edmonton. X17476B.

BRETT, H., Pte., Border Regiment.
He enlisted in 1914, at the age of 16. He saw much service, first in France, where he had trench fever, later in Salonica, where he suffered badly from malaria, and finally in Italy.
He holds the 1914-15 Star, the General Service and Victory Medals.
19, Church Road, Tottenham. X18344.

BRETT, S. G., A.B., Royal Navy.
He enlisted in 1914, served in the North Sea, taking part in many engagements, and was also stationed at Chatham.
He holds the General Service and Victory Medals, and was demobilised in February, 1919.
116, Angel Road, Edmonton. 16576.

BRETT, W., Pte., 1/9th Middlesex Regiment.
He joined in August, 1916, and served in Mesopotamia and Kurdistan until April, 1920, when he was demobilised.
He holds the General Service and Victory Medals.
1, Jervis Road, Fulham. X17151.

BRETT, W. J., Pte., Royal West Kent Regiment.
He travelled from South America to join in 1918, and served with the Royal West Kent Regiment until demobilised in 1919.
363a, Chapter Road, Willesden Green. 16168/A.

BREW, C. W., Pte., 6th Middlesex Regiment.
He joined in 1916, and served on the Western Front until he was demobilised in 1919. He took part in the fighting on various sectors, and was awarded the General Service and Victory Medals.
102, Kimberley Road, Upper Edmonton. 16785.

BREWER, H., Pte., 13th Batt. London Regiment.
He enlisted in 1914, and served in France as a despatch-rider in engagements on the Somme, at Arras, Loos, Neuve Chapelle, Armentieres, Ypres, Vimy Ridge, Bullecourt, St. Quentin, Cambrai and the Retreat and Advance in 1918.
He holds the 1914-15 Star, General Service and Victory Medals, and was demobilised in 1919.
238, Lillie Road, Fulham. X18790.

BREWER, J. T., Stoker, Royal Navy.
He joined in October, 1914, and served in the North Sea. He took part in the battle of Jutland, and on H.M.S. "Taurus" in the raid on Zeebrugge and the destruction of the Mole.
He was demobilised in November, 1919, holding the 1914-15 Star, General Service and Victory Medals.
72, Franklyn Road, Willesden. 16321.

BREWER, T., Driver, Royal Army Service Corps.
He enlisted in 1914, and served throughout in France. He took part in many engagements, including the Somme, Ypres, Arras, Armentieres, Loos, Vimy Ridge, Neuve Chapelle, Amiens, St. Quentin and the advance at Cambrai.
He holds the 1914-15 Star, General Service and Victory Medals, and was demobilised in 1919.
238, Lillie Road, Fulham. X18789.

BRIANT, C. W., Pte., Royal Fusiliers.
He enlisted in 1914, served on the Western Front, and took part in the battles of the Somme, St. Eloi, Loos, Neuve Chapelle, Albert, Vimy Ridge, Ypres, Armentieres, Amiens and Bullecourt, and was wounded.
He was discharged in 1918, holding the 1914-15 Star, General Service and Victory Medals.
53, Tasso Road, Fulham. 14633/A.

BRIANT, C. W. (jun.), Driver, R.A.S.C.
He joined in 1916, and was retained at home in various camps for duty with the R.A.S.C. On account of ill-health, he was discharged in 1918.
53, Tasso Road, Fulham. 14633/B

BRICKNELL, E. (M.M.), Driver, Royal Field Artillery.
He joined in February, 1915, and went to France in July of the same year, serving there until the cessation of hostilities.
He was awarded the Military Medal for great bravery, remaining at his post whilst in great danger, and also holds the 1915 Star, General Service and Victory Medals. He was demobilised in April, 1919.
24, St. Margaret's Road, Willesden. X17818/B.

BRICKNELL, W., Pte., The Queen's (Royal West Surrey Regiment).
He joined in March, 1916, went to France in the following June, and served at Cambrai and other places. He was killed in action on the Somme on November 18th of the same year.
He is entitled to the General Service and Victory Medals.
24, St. Margaret's Road, Willesden. X17818/A.

BRIDGE, A. E., Sergt., East Yorkshire Regt.
He joined in August, 1914, and from 1916 until 1919 saw active service in France, being wounded.
He was demobilised in January, 1919, holding the General Service and Victory Medals.
148, Town Road, Edmonton. 13589.

BRIDGEMAN, J., Cpl., 16th Warwickshire Rgt.
He joined in August, 1916, was sent to the Western Front in the following year, and took part in the fighting at Gommecourt, and during the Retreat and Advance of 1918. Later he served in Italy and in Turkey, and was demobilised in November, 1919, holding the General Service and Victory Medals.
9, Eli Street, West Kensington. 16435/A.

BRIDGES, A. (Miss), Special War Worker.
This lady was engaged during the war at Messrs. Blake's, Hammersmith, and at Perivale munition factories. Her work was frequently of a dangerous nature.
64, Lurgan Avenue, Hammersmith. 13801.

BRIDGES, A. V., Pte., 13th London Regiment (Kensington Battalion).
During his service, which extended from May, 1915, until April, 1917, he was retained for training duties at Tadmouth, near Epsom, and at Winchester.
92, Ancill Street, Hammersmith. 13759/B

BRIDGES, E. (Mrs.), Special War Worker.
During the war this lady was engaged on very dangerous work at Messrs. Blake's factory at Hammersmith. Her duties included shell-filling, and she was commended for her work.
92, Ancill Street, Hammersmith.   13759/A.

BRIDGES, E. E. (Mrs.), Special War Worker.
Throughout the war this lady was engaged in the T.N.T. shop at Messrs. Blake's munition factory and at the Park Royal works. Her work was of an arduous and dangerous nature.
56, Lurgan Avenue, Hammersmith.   13451/A.

BRIDGES, R. G., Pte., Middlesex Regiment.
He joined in September, 1914, served in Egypt for two years, and in 1916 was sent to the Western Front. During the battle of the Somme he was wounded, and in March, 1919, was demobilised.
He holds the 1914-15 Star, the General Service and Victory Medals.
4, Ashford Road, Tottenham.   X18355B.

BRIDGES, J. M., Rifleman, 8th Rifle Brigade.
He joined in December, 1914, and served on the Western Front, taking part in many engagements, including the battle of Ypres.
He was demobilised in February, 1919, holding the 1914-15 Star, the General Service and Victory Medals.
4, Ashford Road, Tottenham.   X18355A.

BRIDGES, N. S., Pte., 12th Royal Fusiliers and 13th London Regiment (Kensington).
He enlisted in September, 1914, and was stationed at Shoreham, with the Royal Fusiliers, and at Winchester, with the 13th London Regiment, until discharged physically unfit for further service in April, 1916.
92, Ancill Street, Hammersmith.   13760.

BRIDGES, W. W., Pte., 3rd Batt. E. Surrey Regt.
He joined in 1915, was stationed at Dover and Newhaven, and failing to secure his transfer abroad, formed part of the Home Defence Force, in which capacity he performed good work until demobilised.
56, Lurgan Avenue, Hammersmith.   13451/B.

BRIDGES, W. J., Pte., Suffolk Regiment.
He joined in 1915, and during his service, which lasted until 1919, was stationed at various places, including Norfolk, Whitby Camp, Aldershot, Sevenoaks and Tunbridge Wells, where he did good and useful work.
64, Lurgan Avenue, Hammersmith.   13802.

BRIDGLAND, G., Bombardier, R.F.A.
He joined in May, 1915, and during his service on the Western Front took part in the battles of Armentieres and St. Quentin, and other engagements.
He was demobilised in May, 1919, and holds the General Service and Victory Medals.
43, Delorme Street, Fulham.   T13776.

BRIDGMAN, A. H., Stoker Petty Officer, R.N., H.M.S. " Shannon."
He joined the Navy in July, 1911, and during his war service took part in the battle of Jutland, and was present at Scapa Flow at the surrender of the German Fleet.
He was discharged in November, 1919, and holds the 1914 Star, General Service and Victory Medals.
14, Cumberland Road, Lower Edmonton.   12998.

BRIDLE, E., Signaller, Middx. Regt. and R.A.F.
He joined in November, 1915, and the following year was sent to the Western Front, where he remained until 1919. He was wounded at Beaumont Hamel, and was later transferred to the R.A.F. motor transport, where he served till demobilised in March, 1919.
He holds the General Service and Victory Medals.
24, Fifth Avenue, Queen's Park.   X18433/B.

BRIDLE, A. W. H., Pte., 9th Suffolk Regiment.
He joined in August, 1914, and went to the Western Front. He took part in engagements at Loos and Arras, and was wounded on the Ancre in 1915, and the following year on the Somme. He was then sent back to England, and there served with the Labour Corps.
He holds the 1915 Star, Victory and General Service Medals, and was demobilised in January, 1919.
24, Fifth Avenue, Queen's Park.   X18433/A.

BRIEN, G. A., Pte., 8th Norfolk Regiment.
He joined in June, 1915, and was sent to France on December 26th, 1915. He was in action on the French and Belgian fronts. His regiment was cut off for four days in Delville Wood in July, 1916. He served later as a Lewis gunner, and took part in several engagements. He was severely wounded, and died of his wounds on November 11th, 1917, and is entitled to the General Service and Victory Medals.
26, Stowe Road, Shepherd's Bush.   T10331.

BRIGHTWELL, F., Pte., Royal West Kent Regt.
He enlisted in August, 1914, and served on the Western Front, where he took part in many engagements, was twice wounded, and was for some time in hospital suffering from frost-bite.
He was discharged in November, 1918, medically unfit for further service, and holds the 1914-15 Star, General Service and Victory Medals.
22, Lintaine Grove, Fulham.   X17081.

BRIMFIELD, F., Pte., Highland Light Infantry.
He joined in June, 1915, and was drafted to Salonica, where he took part in many engagements.
He was discharged in October, 1918, holding the 1915 Star, General Service and Victory Medals.
14, Gilpin Grove, Edmonton.   16808.

BRIMMICOMBE, C., Sapper, Royal Engineers.
He enlisted in 1914, and in the same year was sent to France, where he took part in many engagements.
He was demobilised in 1919, holding the 1914-15 Star, General Service and Victory Medals.
48, Roseberry Road, Lower Edmonton.   14352.

BRINKLEY, G. W., Sapper, Royal Engineers.
He joined in June, 1915, and served in France from 1916 until he was demobilised in 1918.
He holds the General Service and Victory Medals.
57, Guilsborough Road, Willesden.   15247.

BRINKMAN, G., Pte., Suffolk Regiment.
He joined in August, 1915, proceeded to France in 1916, and in the same year received serious accidental injuries.
He was discharged on April 23rd, 1918, as medically unfit for further service, and holds the General Service and Victory Medals.
1, Ray's Road, Lower Edmonton.   15348.

BRINN, F. W. F., Pte., 1st Buffs (East Kent Rgt.).
He joined in June, 1916, and went to the Western Front the same year. He took part in several important engagements, and was killed near Bethune on March 4th, 1917.
He was entitled to the General Service and Victory Medals.
121, Rucklidge Avenue, Harlesden.   13150.

BRINSON, H., Cpl., Royal Irish Regiment.
He enlisted in August, 1914, went to France in the same year, was reported missing after the fighting near Loos in 1916, and later reported killed in action.
He was entitled to the 1914 Star, Victory and General Service Medals.
110, Shakespeare Avenue, Harlesden.   14203/B.

BRISCOE, E. Gunner, R.F.A.
He joined in January, 1915, and served on the Western Front, taking part in many engagements while there.
In February, 1919, he was demobilised, holding the General Service and Victory Medals.
49, Disraeli Road, Harlesden.   14150.

BRISCOE, G. J., Pte., Royal Fusiliers.
He joined in 1917, and served in France in the final Offensive of 1918.
On October 27th, 1919, he was demobilised, and holds the General Service and Victory Medals.
54, Dimsdale Road, S.W.   16448A.

BRISCOE, W., Gunner, Royal Field Artillery.
He joined in July, 1915, and the following year went to the Western Front, where, after taking part in the battles of the Somme, Ypres, Loos and Bullecourt, he was taken prisoner in the German advance in March, 1918. During the time he was in captivity he suffered great hardships, including that of being forced to work in the salt mines.
He was eventually demobilised in April, 1919, and holds the General Service and Victory Medals.
91, Coomer Road, Fulham, S.W.6   16448/B.

BRISCOE, T., Sapper, Royal Engineers.
He joined in August, 1914, and served for five years on the Western Front. He took part in the battles of Mons, Ypres, the Somme and Cambrai, and many other engagements, during which he was gassed.
He was demobilised in October, 1919, and holds the 1914 Star, the General Service and Victory Medals.
91, Coomer Road, Fulham, S.W.6   16449.

BRISTOW, G., Pte., 2nd Coldstream Guards.
He joined in August, 1914, and served on the Western Front, where he fought in the battles of Mons, Loos, Arras, Ypres, the Somme and Cambrai. During his service he was three times wounded. In March, 1919, he was demobilised, and holds the Mons Star, the General Service and Victory Medals.
72, Bramber Road, Fulham.   16220.

BROADBENT, W., Sergeant, Royal Air Force.
He joined in July, 1916, and did duty as instructor at the R.A.F. Central Flying School on Salisbury Plain, incurring in his work great risks.
He was demobilised in May, 1919, and holds the General Service Medal.
67, Alston Road, Lower Edmonton. 16549.

BROADBRIDGE, H., Pte., East Surrey Regt.
He joined in 1914, and served in France the same year, taking part in the retreat from Mons, at the Marne, La Bassée, Ypres and Hill 60, where he was taken prisoner. He was kept in captivity for three years and eight months, and was demobilised in 1919.
He holds the Mons Star, General Service and Victory Medals.
42, Ranelagh Road, Harlesden. 12563/C.

BROADBRIDGE, W., Gunner, R.F.A.
He joined in March, 1915, and served on many sectors of the Western Front, and was wounded at Guichy Wood.
He was demobilised in April, 1919, holding the 1915 Star, General Service and Victory Medals.
51, Greyhound Road, Hammersmith. 15016.

BROADHURST, J., Corporal, R.F.A.
He joined in August, 1914, proceeded to the Western Front the following year, and took part in many engagements, including Ypres, Arras, Armentieres and the Somme. He was wounded, mentioned in despatches for bravery on the field at Ypres, and demobilised in March, 1919.
He holds the 1915 Star, General Service and Victory Medals.
48, Milton Avenue, Harlesden. 14323A.

BROADLEY, A. C., Pte., R.A.S.C. (M.T.).
He joined in May, 1915, and later was sent to the Western Front, where he was employed in conveying supplies and ammunition to forward dumps. He was wounded in 1916, and after he was discharged from hospital took part in the Retreat and Advance of 1918.
He was demobilised in August, 1919, and holds the 1915 Star, General Service and Victory Medals.
59, Carlyle Avenue, Harlesden. 14417.

BROCKLEHURST, W. E., Pte., 27th Middlesex.
He enlisted in April, 1916, and later was sent to Salonica. He also served in Rumania and Egypt.
He was demobilised in November, 1919, and holds the General Service and Victory Medals.
49, Leopold Road, Willesden. 14910.

BRODIE, G. H., Pte., 9th Middlesex Regiment.
Although only sixteen years of age, he enlisted in August, 1914, and was sent to Egypt the same year, where he served until he was demobilised in June, 1919, having been through the Palestine campaign under General Allenby.
He holds the 1914 Star, General Service and Victory Medals.
4, Ambleside Road, Willesden. 15551.

BROOKER, F., Sgt.-Instr., East Surrey Regt.
He enlisted on October 6th, 1915, and served on the Eastern Front at Salonica, and later at Constantinople on special duties. He was transferred to the Royal Welsh Fusiliers in 1919, and was discharged on January 8th, 1920, holding the General Service and Victory Medals.
124, Felix Road, W. Ealing. 11021.

BROOKER, H., Cpl., Duke of Cornwall's L.I.
He was serving on the outbreak of hostilities, and came from India (where he was stationed) to France, taking part in many engagements, including those of Arras, Vimy Ridge, and Ypres. He was wounded twice, and discharged in 1918, holding the 1914-15 Star, General Service and Victory Medals.
6, West Ella Road, Harlesden. 15106.

BROOKS, A. E., Rifleman, 1/21st London Regt.
He joined in February, 1916, served through various engagements on the Western Front, and was killed in action on September 15th of the same year.
He was entitled to the General Service and Victory Medals.
39, Melville Road, Willesden. 15659B.

BROOKS, A. E., Pte., 1st Middlesex Regiment.
He served on the Western Front from his enlistment in 1916 until he was demobilised in 1919. He took part in engagements at Ypres, Cambrai, the Somme, and the Retreat and Advance of 1918. He was twice wounded, and holds the General Service and Victory Medals.
155, Rucklidge Avenue, Harlesden. T12926B.

BROOKS, D. H., Pte., The King's Liverpool Regt.
He joined in 1915, and was eventually sent to the Western Front. He took part in several engagements, and was killed in action on March 23rd, 1916.
He was entitled to the General Service and Victory Medals.
155, Rucklidge Avenue, Harlesden. T12926C.

BROOKS, E., Pte., 40th Labour Corps.
He joined in 1916, and was sent to the Western Front, where he took part in engagements at various places.
He was demobilised in 1919, and holds the General Service and Victory Medals.
5, Colbin Street, Hammersmith. 14979.

BROOKS, E., Pte., Royal Army Service Corps.
He joined in August, 1914, and was later sent to Salonica. He also saw service in Mesopotamia and Russia.
In 1918 he was discharged, and holds the 1915 Star, General Service and Victory Medals.
41, West Street, Edmonton. 14594B.

BROOKS, E. J., 2nd Air Mechanic, R.A.F.
He enlisted in August, 1914, serving with the Territorials on the outbreak of war. He was sent to the Western Front, and was in action at Doullens, Marieux, Rouen and St. Omer. He was accidentally wounded at Marieux, and in consequence had his right leg amputated.
He was discharged as disabled in February, 1917, and holds the 1915 Star, the General Service, Victory and Territorial Medals.
82, Chesson Road, W. Kensington. X17693/A.

BROOKS, F. E., Sub-Lieut., R.N.V.R.
He joined in September, 1915, served on the Western Front, and was killed in action at Ypres on November 9, 1918, after having previously taken part in many other engagements. He was entitled to the 1914-15 Star, General Service and Victory Medals.
3, Varna Road, Fulham. X18757.

BROOKS, G., Rifleman, King's Royal Rifle Corps.
He joined in August, 1916, but was not successful in getting his transfer overseas, being retained for duties connected with Home Defence. He was demobilised in August, 1919.
41, West Street, Edmonton. 14594C.

BROOKS, H. A., Sapper, Royal Engineers.
He joined in November, 1915, and was drafted to the Western Front, where he served for three years on special work.
He was demobilised in January, 1919, and holds the General Service and Victory Medals.
3, Hartington Road, Lower Edmonton. 14238.

BROOKS, J. J., Pte., 73rd Labour Corps.
He joined in June, 1916, and served on the Western Front in connection with the despatch of ammunition to the forward dumps. He was present at the battles of Ypres, Vimy Ridge and the Somme.
He was demobilised in February, 1919, and holds the General Service and Victory Medals.
47, Bayonne Road, Fulham. 14656.

BROOKS, L. (Mrs.), Special War Worker.
During the war this lady was employed in the fitting shop of an aircraft factory, where she did valuable work, and thereby released a man for service.
82, Chesson Road, W. Kensington, W. X17693B.

BROOKS, T. W., Pte., Bedfordshire Regiment.
He joined in May, 1915, and was later sent to the Western Front, where he took part in several engagements, being twice wounded at the battle of the Somme.
He was demobilised in March, 1919, and holds the General Service and Victory Medals.
3, Montague Road, Edmonton. 13088.

BROOKS, W., Sapper, Royal Engineers.
He joined in August, 1914, and upon completion of training was sent to the Western Front, where he served at Arras, Ypres, on the Somme and elsewhere, until he was discharged in March, 1918.
He holds the General Service and Victory Medals.
41, West Street, Lower Edmonton. 14594A.

BROOKS, W. T., Sapper, Royal Engineers.
He joined in May, 1917, and was sent in the same month to the Western Front, where he was employed on railway and defence work in various sectors. He was engaged at Messines, Arras, and other places, and was wounded while in action. After the Armistice he was sent to Germany with the Army of Occupation, remaining until he was demobilised in October, 1919.
He holds the General Service and Victory Medals.
61, Villiers Road, Willesden, N.W.10 T17325.

BROOM, J. H., Pte., R.A.S.C. (M.T.).
He joined in August, 1914, and served on the Western Front until 1919, conveying stores and ammunition to the forward dumps.
He was demobilised on June 28th, 1919, and holds the 1914 Star, General Service and Victory Medals.
34, Deacon Road, Willesden. 16644.

BROOM, P. S., Pte., 9th London Regiment.
He joined in July, 1916, and served on the Western Front, taking part in the battle of the Somme and many other engagements. He later went to Germany with the Army of Occupation.
On October 24th, 1919, he was demobilised, and holds the General Service and Victory Medals.
300, Chapter Road, Willesden.   16703.

BROOME, J. W., 1st Air Mechanic, R.A.F.
During his service,which extended from 1916 until November, 1919, he was stationed at the R.A.F. workshops at Farnborough, the principal station of the R.A.F. He holds the General Service Medal.
16, Carlyle Avenue, Harlesden.   14205.

BROTHERSTON, A. W., Driver, R.F.A.
He joined in February, 1915, and the same year was sent to the Western Front, where he took part in many engagements, including Arras, Loos, Ypres and the Somme, being twice wounded during the latter engagement. He also served in Italy before being demobilised in March, 1919.
He holds the 1915 Star, General Service and Victory Medals.
55, Tasso Road, Fulham.   B146,1.

BROTHERSTON, E. (Mrs.), Special War Worker.
In order to release a man for war service this lady volunteered her services, and was engaged in the manufacture of shell boxes.
55, Tasso Road, Fulham.   14631/A.

BROTHERTON, J. W., Pte., Middlesex Regt.
He rejoined in September, 1914, was sent to the Western Front in the following year, and took part in the battles of Loos, Ypres, Albert, Arras, Amiens and the Somme. He was reported missing and believed to have been killed in action in October, 1916.
He held the Queen's South African Medal with three bars, and was entitled to the 1915 Star, General Service and Victory Medals.
47, Hiley Road, Willesden.   X18173B.

BROWELL, R., Sergt., 4th Middlesex Regiment.
He enlisted in 1915 and served in France, taking part in many engagements, including Arras, Cambrai and Ypres, and was wounded.
He holds the 1915 Star, General Service and Victory Medals, and was demobilised in 1919.
68, Litchfield Gardens, Willesden Green.   X17431.

BROWN, A., Sapper, Royal Engineers.
He joined in July, 1918, and served with the R.E. until February, 1919. Due to the cessation of hostilities, he was not successful in being sent overseas.
56, Winchester Road, Edmonton.   14867/B.

BROWN, A., Pte., 7th London Regiment.
He joined in June, 1915, went to France in January, 1917, and took part in the battles of Ypres, and Villers Bretonneux. He holds the General Service and Victory Medals, and was demobilised in March, 1919.
23, Alexandra Road, West Kensington.   12089.

BROWN, A. E., Sergeant, 17th London Regt.
He joined in March, 1915, and served for three years on the Western Front, taking part in the battles of Ypres, Cambrai, Arras, the Somme, Loos and many other engagements, during which he was three times wounded.
In February, 1919, he was demobilised, holding the 1915 Star, General Service and Victory Medals.
51, Melville Road, Willesden.   15649.

BROWN, A. E., Lce.-Cpl., Lincolnshire Regt. (Labour Corps).
He joined in June, 1916, and was engaged on various special duties at Lincoln, Melton Mowbray and other stations. He was demobilised in February, 1919, after three years' continuous service.
4, Welford Terrace, Fulham.   X18059.

BROWN, A. E., Sapper, R.E. (105th Field Coy.).
He joined in January, 1915, served on the Western Front, and was wounded in action at Albert in 1916.
He was demobilised in February, 1919, holding the General Service and Victory Medals.
33, Shakespeare Avenue, Harlesden.   13888.

BROWN, A. G., Gunner, Royal Field Artillery.
He joined in February, 1915, and served in France, Salonica and Egypt. While in France he took part in the battles of Arras, the Somme and Albert.
He was demobilised in August, 1919, holding the General Service and Victory Medals.
44, Tasso Road, Fulham, W.6   14650.

BROWN, A. G., Driver, Royal Field Artillery.
He joined in August, 1915, at the age of 15, and served until April, 1916, when he was discharged in consequence of his age being discovered.
56, Winchester Road, Edmonton.   14867/A.

BROWN, A. G., Pte , Machine Gun Corps.
He joined in August, 1914, went to the Western Front the same year, and took part in many engagements, including the Retreat and Advance of 1918.
He holds the 1914 Star, General Service and Victory Medals, and was demobilised in 1919.
54, Carlyle Avenue, Harlesden.   14412/C.

BROWN, A. J., Pte., Middlesex Regiment.
He rejoined in August, 1914, and in the same year went to the Western Front, where he took part in many engagements, including the battle of Arras and the Retreat and Advance of 1918, and was twice wounded.
He holds the King's and Queen's South African Medals, the 1914 Star, General Service and Victory Medals, and was demobilised in January, 1920.
54, Carlyle Avenue, Harlesden.   14412.1B.

BROWN, C., Driver, R.F.A.
He joined in October, 1914, and in the following year went to France, where he took part in many engagements, including those of the Somme, La Bassée and Ypres.
He was demobilised in April, 1919, holding the 1915 Star, General Service and Victory Medals.
58, Kenninghall Road, Edmonton.   16896.

BROWN, C. E., Pte., R.A.S.C. and R.A.F. (83rd Training Reserve).
He enlisted in September, 1914, and in the same year was sent to France. He saw fighting on all sectors of the Allied line until 1918, when he returned to England and was demobilised.
He holds the 1914 Star, General Service and Victory Medals.
14, Ray's Road, Edmonton.   15493.

BROWN, C. H., Lce.-Cpl., 8th Devonshire Regt.
He joined in June, 1915, and during his service on the Western Front took part in many battles, including Loos, Arras, Ypres, Festubert, Givenchy and the Somme. He was wounded twice.
He holds the 1915 Star, General Service and Victory Medals.
13, Welford Terrace, Fulham.   X18073.

BROWN, E., Pte., 1st Batt. The Buffs (East Kent Regt.)
He enlisted in August, 1914, was sent to France in the same year, and was severely wounded at the battle of the Somme in July, 1916.
He was discharged in 1917, holding the 1914 Star, the General Service and Victory Medals.
54, Carlyle Avenue, Harlesden.   14404/B.

BROWN, E. E., Rifleman, King's Royal Rifles.
He joined in 1915, and served at various stations, performing important duties, until April, 1919, when he was demobilised, after four years' continuous service.
91, Angel Road, Edmonton.   16569.

BROWN, E. R., Pte., R.A.S.C. (M.T.).
He joined in August, 1914, served on the Western Front, being present at the battles of Mons, the Marne, the Aisne, Arras, Cambrai, Ypres, the Somme and at other engagements. While abroad he was on special duties with the motor ambulances.
On March 9th, 1919, he was demobilised, holding the Mons Star, General Service and Victory Medals.
46, Deacon Road, Willesden.   17354.

BROWN, E. T., Petty Officer, R.N., H.M.S. " Humber."
He rejoined in August, 1914, having previously served for 20 years, and was on patrol duty off the Belgian coast until 1915, when he took part in the landing at the Dardanelles. He served also in Egyptian waters, and was in many engagements with enemy submarines. He was also on board H.M.S. " Pembroke," " Lion " and " Repulse " before being discharged in 1919, and holds the 1914–15 Star, General Service, Victory and Somaliland Medals.
21, Milton Avenue, Harlesden.   13875.

BROWN, F., Pte., 1st Batt. Coldstream Guards.
He joined on September 9th, 1914, was sent to the Western Front in February, 1915, and took part in the battles of the Somme and Arras, where he was wounded on March 26th, 1918.
He was demobilised on April 5th, 1919, and holds the 1915 Star, General Service and Victory Medals.
18, Disbrowe Road, Hammersmith.   15919.

BROWN, F., Pte., 5th Wiltshire Regiment.
He joined on May 26th, 1916, served in Mesopotamia until August, 1918, when he was sent to India, where he remained until May, 1919.
He was demobilised in February, 1920, holding the General Service and Victory Medals.
24, Alric Avenue, Harlesden. 14438.

BROWN, F. J., Sergt., Hampshire Regiment.
He enlisted in March, 1915, and served in France, Belgium, on the Servian Front, and with the Army of Occupation on the Rhine.
He was discharged in March, 1919, holding the 1914-15 Star, the General Service and Victory Medals.
36, Grove Road, Ealing. 10846.

BROWN, F. J., Driver, R.A.S.C. (M.T.).
He joined in 1916, and served for three years on the Western Front, engaged in carrying supplies to the lines.
He was demobilised in 1919, and holds the General Service and Victory Medals.
378, High Road, Willesden. 16622A.

BROWN, F. O. (M.M.), Cpl., R.F.A.
He joined in September, 1914, went to France the following year, and took part in many engagements, being gassed twice during his service.
He was awarded the Military Medal for gallantry in the field and, in addition, holds the 1915 Star, General Service and Victory Medals, and was discharged in February, 1919.
71, Warwick Road, Edmonton. X17514.

BROWN, F. T., Bombardier, R.G.A.
He joined in February, 1916, went to the Western Front the following year, and was killed in action in April, 1917, having previously taken part in actions at Arras, Ypres and Cambrai.
He was entitled to the General Service and Victory Medals.
90, Deacon Road, Willesden, N.W. X17110.

BROWN, G., Shoeing Smith, R.F.A.
He enlisted in October, 1914, served on the Western Front from September, 1915, until 1919, and took part in the battles of Ypres, Amiens, Neuve Chapelle, the Somme, Cambrai and Arras.
He was demobilised in September, 1919, and awarded the 1914-15 Star, General Service and Victory Medals.
11, Gilpin Crescent, Edmonton. T16857.

BROWN, G. A., Gunner, R.F.A.
He joined in March, 1917, and for two years served on the Eastern Front in Palestine and Syria, taking part in the capture of Jaffa.
He was demobilised in March, 1919, holding the General Service and Victory Medals.
6, Shelley Road, Harlesden. 13880/B.

BROWN, H., Pte., 9th Devonshire Regiment.
He was called up in August, 1914, was sent to France, and killed in action on the Somme in July, 1916.
He was entitled to the 1914-15 Star, General Service and Victory Medals.
97, Ancill Street, W.6 13664/B.

BROWN, H., Sergt., 47th Canadian Regiment.
He joined in 1915, went to France the following year and took part in numerous engagements, including those of the Somme, Ypres, Loos and the Big Advance of 1918. He was severely wounded at Vimy Ridge, which resulted in the loss of an eye.
He was demobilised in March, 1919, holding the General Service and Victory Medals.
13, Estcourt Road, S.W.6 16692.

BROWN, H., Pte., Suffolk Regiment.
He joined in April, 1915, and in the same year was sent to France, where he was severely wounded.
He was discharged in September, 1917, as the result of his wounds. He holds the 1915 Star, General Service and Victory Medals.
36, Marsden Road, Edmonton. 13074.

BROWN, H., Sapper, Royal Engineers.
He joined in August, 1915, and served in France, where he took part in many important engagements, including those of Cambrai, Ypres, the Somme and Albert. Later he was with the Army of Occupation in Germany, and was demobilised in April, 1919.
He holds the General Service and Victory Medals.
10, Lamington Street, Hammersmith. 11099.

BROWN, H. A., Gunner, R.F.A.
He enlisted in 1915, and was drafted to France, where he took part in many engagements, including those of the Somme, Ypres and La Bassée.
He holds the General Service and Victory Medals, and was demobilised in 1919.
22, Kenninghall Road, Edmonton. 16902/B.

BROWN, H. W., Gunner, R.F.A.
He joined in 1914, and during his service on the Western Front was wounded. He took part in the battles of Arras, the Somme, Neuve Chapelle and Cambrai.
In 1919 he was demobilised, holding the 1914-15 Star, the General Service and Victory Medals.
378, High Road, Willesden. 16622B.

BROWN, J., Pte., Middlesex Regiment.
He joined in August, 1914, and in the same year was sent to France, where he took part in the retreat from Mons. In 1915 he was transferred to Egypt, where he remained until 1919, and was wounded.
He holds the 1914 Star, General Service and Victory Medals, and was demobilised in May, 1919.
51, Westminster Road, Edmonton. T12697.

BROWN, J., Pte., Northumberland Fusiliers.
He joined in 1914, and in the following year was sent to the Western Front, where he was engaged in various sectors, taking part in the battles of the Somme, the Marne, Cambrai and Bapaume. He was wounded at the latter place in March, 1918, and died of wounds on the same day.
He was entitled to the 1914-15 Star, General Service and Victory Medals.
2, Steward Road, West Kilburn. X17797/B.

BROWN, J. B., Pte., 11th Batt. Royal Sussex R.
He joined in June, 1915, and in the same year was sent to the Western Front, where he took part in the battles of Ypres and the Somme, and was wounded at the latter place in September, 1916.
He holds the 1915 Star, General Service and Victory Medals, and was discharged in January, 1917.
97, Ancill Street, Hammersmith. 13664/A.

BROWN, J. H., Pte., The Queen's (Royal West Surrey Regiment).
He joined in November, 1915, and was sent to France, and later to Italy. He was in action at Ypres, where he was wounded, and at Messines, where he was again wounded. After the Armistice he went to the Rhine with the Army of Occupation, and was discharged in February, 1919.
He holds the General Service and Victory Medals.
1, Brereton Road, Tottenham, N. X18104.

BROWN, N. E. (Mrs.), Special War Worker.
This lady was engaged in the manufacture of important war supplies during the war, and her work was frequently of a dangerous nature.
63, Yeldham Road, Hammersmith. 14165/B.

BROWN, P., Pte., 1st Batt. Yorkshire Regt.
He joined in August, 1914, after having previously served in the Army for 14 years, and was sent to the Western Front, where he was killed in action in September, 1914.
He was entitled to the 1914 Star, General Service and Victory Medals.
65, Grove Street, Edmonton. X17888/A.

BROWN, P. G., Rifleman, K.R.R. Corps.
He joined in July, 1916, and served on the Western Front, where he was taken prisoner. He died in captivity in Germany in February, 1917.
He was entitled to the General Service and Victory Medals.
24, Haldane Road, Fulham. X17380/A.

BROWN, R. (Miss), Special War Worker.
This lady was engaged during the war on work connected with the manufacture and inspection of cartridges at the Park Royal Works.
She was commended for her work.
26, Disraeli Road, Harlesden. 14391.

BROWN, S. (M.M.), Pte., 9th Battalion Royal Fusiliers.
He joined in June, 1916, proceeded to France in the same year, served at Messines Ridge, Cambrai, in the Great Retreat and Advance of 1918, and in many other engagements, and lost his left leg whilst in action in August, 1918.
He won the Military Medal for conspicuous bravery in the field, and also holds the General Service and Victory Medals.
53, Brett Road, Harlesden. 14520

BROWN, S., Gunner, Royal Field Artillery.
He joined in August, 1914, served on the Western Front in the same year, and was wounded in the battle of the Somme in 1917 as a result of which he was discharged as unfit for further service
He holds the 1914 Star, General Service and Victory Medals.
54, Carlyle Avenue, Harlesden 14411/C

BROWN, S. B., Sergt., Suffolk Regiment.
He joined in August, 1915, served in France until 1919, and took part in the battles of Ypres and Tower Hamlets, where he was wounded in September, 1917.
He was demobilised in February, 1919, holding the General Service and Victory Medals.
48, Fairfield Road, Edmonton.   15618.

BROWN, W., Pte., 4th Bedford Regiment.
He joined in 1917, went to the Western Front the following year, and took part in the Great Retreat and Advance of 1918. He died from influenza in November, 1919, and is buried in a Belgian cemetery.
He was entitled to the General Service and Victory Medals.
54, Carlyle Avenue, Harlesden.   14412/AB

BROWN, W., Sergt., Rifle Brigade.
He joined in August, 1914, and from 1916 served on the Western Front. In July, 1916, he was severely wounded at Trones Wood.
He holds the General Service and Victory Medals.
102, Burn's Road, Harlesden.   13137A.

BROWN, W. A., Gunner, R.F.A.
He joined in 1915, served on the Western Front from the following year until demobilised in 1919, and saw service on the Somme and at Ypres, and also took part in several other engagements.
He holds the General Service and Victory Medals.
110, Kimberley Road, Upper Edmonton.   16792/A.

BROWN, W. C., Pte., Machine Gun Corps.
He joined in April, 1915, and served on the Western Front, where he took part in the battles of the Somme, Ypres, Vimy Ridge and several other engagements, and was once gassed. From 1917 until his demobilisation in February, 1919, he served at home, being medically unfit for further overseas duties, owing to disabilities caused in action.
He holds the 1914-15 Star, General Service and Victory Medals.
12, Goodson Road, Harlesden.   14926.

BROWN, W. G., Pte., R.A.S.C. (M.T.).
He joined in March, 1915, went to the Western Front, and took part in the engagements at Cambrai, Arras, Ypres, the Somme and Bethune. In 1917 he was sent to Italy, and served there until 1919, when he was demobilised.
He holds the 1914-15 Star, General Service, Victory and Italian Medals.
10, Oldfield Road, Willesden.   16106/A.

BROWN, W. J., Lce.-Cpl., 7th Royal Fusiliers.
He joined in August, 1914, went to the Western Front the following year, and took part in the engagements at Ypres, Loos, Vimy Ridge, Messines, Cambrai, the Somme, Bapaume and Armentieres, and was wounded twice.
He holds the 1914-15 Star, General Service and Victory Medals, and was demobilised in February, 1920.
10, Oldfield Road, Willesden.   16106/B.

BROWN, W. J., A.B., R.N., H.M.S. " Benbow."
He joined in August, 1914, served in the North Sea and at Scapa Flow, and took part in the battle of Jutland.
He holds the 1914-15 Star, General Service and Victory Medals, and was discharged as the result of wounds received in an accident in 1917.
63, Yeldham Road, Hammersmith.   14165A.

BROWN, W. W., Gunner, Royal Field Artillery.
He enlisted in August, 1917, and served in France in many engagements, being demobilised in June, 1919.
He holds the General Service and Victory Medals.
24, Haldane Road, Fulham.   X17380/B.

BROWNING, E. (Mrs.), Special War Worker.
This lady was engaged during the war at the important munition factories at Perivale and Neasden, chiefly in the inspection departments. She did arduous and valuable work.
2, Chapman Park, Willesden.   16626.

BROWNING, W. J., Gunner, R.F.A.
He joined in September, 1915, and served throughout in France. He took part in many engagements, including Arras, Ypres and the Somme.
He was demobilised in May, 1919, and holds the General Service and Victory Medals.
17, Moselle Street, Tottenham.   X18368.

BRUCE, H., Cpl., Royal Army Service Corps.
He enlisted in March, 1915, and served in France for four years, during which period he took part in many engagements, including those of the Somme, Ypres, Arras and Bapaume. He holds the 1914-15 Star, General Service and Victory Medals, and was demobilised in May, 1919.
82, Dyson's Road, Edmonton.   16870.

BRUTON, J., Sapper, Royal Engineers.
He enlisted in 1914, served at the Dardanelles in the following year, in Egypt in 1916, France 1917, and in East Africa in 1918.
He was demobilised in 1919, and holds the 1914-15 Star, General Service and Victory Medals.
23, Sebastopol Road, Lower Edmonton.   14550.

BRYAN, L. W., 2nd Air Mechanic, R.A.F.
He enlisted in August, 1916, and in September was sent to France, where he was engaged in the engine repair shops until April, 1919, when he was demobilised.
He holds the General Service and Victory Medals.
52, Sandringham Road, Willesden Green.   16712/A.

BRYAN, P. J., Pte., 9th Middlesex Regiment.
He enlisted in April, 1915, and served in France. He took part in engagements on the Somme, and was wounded in October, 1916.
He holds the General Service and Victory Medals, and was demobilised on May 9th, 1919.
52, Sandringham Road, Willesden Green.   16712/B.

BRYANT, A. H., Cpl., Essex Yeomanry and Suffolk Regiment.
He joined in 1916, served on the Western Front from the following year until 1919, and took part in various engagements, including operations on the Somme, at Armentieres, Bethune and Ypres, being once gassed. He was demobilised in November, 1919, and holds the General Service and Victory Medals.
70, Oldfield Road, Willesden.   15543/A.

BRYANT, A. W., Saddler, R.A.S.C. (Remount Section).
He enlisted in October, 1914, and served in France until 1919, being stationed at the Remount Depots at Le Havre, Abbeville and Etaples.
He was demobilised in April, 1919, holding the 1914-15 Star, General Service and Victory Medals.
70, Oldfield Road, Willesden.   15543/B.

BRYANT, C., Pte., R.A.S.C. (M.T.).
He joined in November, 1915, and served for nearly four years on the Western Front, during which time he took part in the battles of the Somme, Ypres, the Marne and the Aisne. In July, 1919, he was demobilised, holding the 1914-15 Star, the General Service and Victory Medals.
193, Chapter Road, Willesden.   X17204.

BRYANT, E. J., Pte., 7th East Surrey Regiment.
He joined in August, 1914, went to France, and was killed in action in October, 1916.
He was entitled to the General Service and Victory Medals.
26, Sandilands Road, Fulham.   14278.

BRYANT, F. A., Pte., 14th Essex Regiment.
He joined in 1916, and in the same year went to France, where he died as the result of exposure.
He was entitled to the General Service and Victory Medals.
166, Croyland Road, Edmonton.   13925.

BRYANT, H., Bandsman, 1st Middlesex Regt.
In 1914 at the outbreak of war, being a Regular, he was sent to the Western Front with the first Expeditionary Force and took part in the early engagements. He was taken prisoner, and during his captivity made three attempts to escape, but was unsuccessful.
He was demobilised in March, 1919, and holds the Mons Star, General Service and Victory Medals.
82, Shakespeare Avenue, Harlesden.   13625.

BRYANT, J. (M.M.), Cpl., R.F.A.
He joined in October, 1915, served on the Western Front at Ypres, the Somme, Albert, Cambrai, Arras and other places, and was awarded the Military Medal at Verdun in 1917 for great bravery on the field. He was wounded four times during his service. After the Armistice he served with the Army of Occupation on the Rhine until May, 1919, when he was demobilised, holding the Military Medal, 1914-15 Star, General Service and Victory Medals.
48, Milton Avenue, Harlesden.   14323/B.

BRYANT, T. W., Pte., R.A.S.C.
He joined in January, 1915, and served on the Western Front, until demobilised in January, 1919. During this period he was stationed at Paris and Rouen, and was also present at several engagements, one of which was the battle of Arras.
He was awarded the 1914-15 Star, General Service and Victory Medals.
12, Drayton Road, Harlesden.   14396.

BRYON, S., Lce.-Cpl., 2/1st Norfolk Yeomanry.
He joined in April, 1916, and was chiefly engaged on guard duty in Ireland.
He was demobilised in August, 1919.
16, Mulgrave Road, S.W.6   16688.

BRYSON, H., Pte., 3rd Hussars.
He joined in 1914, and was stationed in Ireland at Remount Depots training remounts for overseas from 1915 till 1918. He was demobilised in January, 1918.
3, Kenninghall Road, Lower Edmonton, N.18   16469.

BUCHANAN, G. G., Pte., 12th Cheshire Regt.
He joined in February, 1916, and served in Salonica on the Struma Front until 1918, when he was sent to France. During this time he took part in several engagements, including those of Vimy Ridge and Bullecourt, and whilst in the East contracted malaria fever and also suffered from shell shock in France.
He holds the General Service and Victory Medals, and was demobilised in August, 1919.
16, Steele Road, Harlesden.   13833/B.

BUCHANAN, Mary A., Special War Worker.
During the war this lady was engaged at the Park Royal Munition Factory. She was employed on preparing fuses, &c., and also on clerical duties. Her work was of great importance.
16, Steele Road, Harlesden.   13833/A.

BUCK, Annie, Special War Worker.
During the war this lady was engaged at the Park Royal Munition Factory on important work, chiefly on the manufacture of shells.
She was commended for her work.
373, Chapter Road, Willesden.   16164/A.

BUCK, A. (Miss), Special War Worker.
This lady was engaged during the war on work connected with the manufacture of special articles for trench warfare at an important Willesden factory.
373, Chapter Road, Willesden.   16164/B.

BUCK, C., Pte., Middlesex Regiment.
He joined in November, 1915, was sent to the Western Front in the same year, and took part in the battles of Ypres and the Somme, where he was slightly wounded, and also suffered from trench feet.
In 1918 he was discharged, and holds the 1914-15 Star, General Service and Victory Medals.
50, Raynham Road, Edmonton.   16941.

BUCK, C. (Mrs.), Special War Worker.
During the war this lady was engaged in the inspection department of the Perivale Munition Works. This work entailed very exacting and arduous duties, which she successfully performed.
14, Berry Street, Willesden.   15549.

BUCKERIDGE, G., Driver, R.A.S.C.
He rejoined in August, 1914, having previously served through the South African campaign, and went to the Western Front, where he remained until his demobilisation in February, 1919. He took part in several important engagements, including those of Mons, Ypres, La Bassée and the Somme, and holds the King's and Queen's South African, 1914 Star, General Service and Victory Medals.
4, Cranbrook Road, Tottenham.   X18692.

BUCKERIDGE, H., Gunner, R.F.A.
He was mobilised in August, 1914, served on the Western Front until 1919, and was in action at Arras, La Bassée, Cambrai, Vimy Ridge and elsewhere. He was twice wounded and suffered from shell shock.
He was demobilised in May, 1919, and holds the 1914-15 Star, General Service and Victory Medals.
8, St. John's Buildings, Kilburn Lane, N.W.   X18659.

BUCKINGHAM, G. R., Royal Engineers and Labour Corps.
He joined in August, 1917, and was engaged until his demobilisation in October, 1919, on important duties in connection with the construction of the coast defences.
90, Burn's Road, Harlesden.   13146.

BUCKINGHAM, R. J., Rifleman, London Rifle Brigade.
He joined in 1916, and served on the Western Front, taking part in the battles of Ypres, Cambrai, Somme and various other engagements. He was wounded while in action near Arras in October, 1918, and was discharged as the result of his wounds the same year.
He holds the General Service and Victory Medals.
38, Litchfield Gardens, Willesden Green.   X17448A.

BUCKINGHAM, T., S.M., 1st South African Infantry Regt. (The Springboks).
He joined in 1915, saw service in East Africa and on the Western Front, where he was wounded and taken prisoner during the Great Retreat of 1918. He suffered great hardships and ill-treatment while in captivity.
He holds the German East African Medal, 1915 Star, General Service and Victory Medals and was demobilised in March, 1919.
91, Drayton Road, Harlesden.   15256.

BUCKLAND, J., Pte., Middlesex Regiment.
During his service, which extended from 1914 to 1919, he was employed with the Volunteers on important work in connection with the construction of our defences.
130, Shakespeare Avenue, Harlesden.   13897.

BUCKLE, W. M. L. (Mrs.), Special War Worker.
She was employed during the war on dangerous work in the T.N.T. mixing room at Messrs. Blake's Shell Filling Factory at Hurlingham.
Her work was very valuable and highly commended.
52, Shorrolds Road, Walham Green.   X17703.

BUCKLEY, A. E., Pte., R.A.S.C.
He joined in April, 1916, and saw active service in Egypt and Salonica. He contracted malaria fever at the latter place, and was discharged medically unfit in September, 1919.
He holds the General Service and Victory Medals.
12, Barbot Street, Edmonton.   14580/A.

BUCKLEY, E., Gunner, Royal Field Artillery.
He joined in August, 1915, served in France for four years, taking part in many engagements, including the battle of the Somme, and was wounded.
He was demobilised in June, 1919, and is entitled to the 1914-15 Star, General Service and Victory Medals.
12, Barbot Street, Edmonton.   14580/B.

BUCKLEY, J., Gunner, Royal Field Artillery.
He joined in January, 1915, and was sent to the Western Front. He served at Loos, the Somme, Arras and at Ypres, where he was first wounded. On recovery from his wounds he was sent to Cambrai, where he was again wounded. He was also at the Marne and in the last Big Advance in 1918. He was seven months in hospital.
He was demobilised in November, 1919, and holds the 1914-15 Star, General Service and Victory Medals.
40, Star Road, W.14   T17061.

BUCKLEY, W., Trooper, Cavalry M.G.C.
He enlisted in September, 1914, and was sent to France in 1916, where he served three years. He took part in various engagements, including the Somme and Arras.
He was discharged on April 5th, 1919, and holds the General Service and Victory Medals.
40, Star Road, W.14   T17063.

BUDD, E. (Miss), Special War Worker.
This lady was engaged during the whole period of the war at a National Box Factory. Her work entailed long hours and arduous duties.
20, Steele Road, Harlesden.   13835/B.

BUDD, M. (Miss), Special War Worker.
During the war this lady was engaged at the Park Royal Small Arms Factory upon work of great national importance. She successfully performed her duties often under the most trying conditions
20, Steele Road, Harlesden.   13835/A.

BUDD, T. J., Pte., 1st Middlesex Regiment.
He joined in 1915, was sent to France and was killed in action at the battle of Loos in September, 1915.
He was entitled to the 1914-15 Star, General Service and Victory Medals.
20, Steele Road, Harlesden.   13835/D.

BUDGE, F. C., Acting Bombardier, R.F.A.
He joined in 1916, went to France the same year, and took part in many engagements. He was taken prisoner by the Germans and kept in captivity for 18 months.
He holds the General Service and Victory Medals, and was demobilised in 1919.
3, Ilex Road, Willesden.   16097/A.

BUGG, R. E., Lce.-Cpl., 8th Royal Sussex Regt.
He joined in September, 1914, was sent to France in 1915, where he served through many engagements and was wounded twice.
He was demobilised in March, 1919, and holds the 1915 Star, General Service and Victory Medals.
33, Nelson Road, Edmonton.   13583.

BULL, A. A., Pte., Middlesex Regiment.
He joined in August, 1914, and served for five years on the Western Front, taking part in numerous engagements.
He was demobilised in January, 1919, holding the 1914 Star, General Service and Victory Medals.
33, Hartington Road, Lower Edmonton.   14241B.

BULL, C., Driver, Royal Field Artillery.
He joined in September, 1915, served on the Western Front, and was wounded in action in 1916.
He was demobilised in February, 1919, holding the 1914-15 Star, General Service and Victory Medals.
33, Hartington Road, Lower Edmonton.   14241A.

BULL, E., Rifleman, 18th London Regt. (London Irish Rifles).
He joined in May, 1917, served on the French Front, taking part in numerous engagements, and was wounded twice in action.
He holds the General Service and Victory Medals, and was demobilised in January, 1919.
53, Purcell Crescent, Fulham.   15158.

BULL, F. W. (D.S.M.), A.B., R.N., H.M.S. "Thistle."
He joined in August, 1914, and served on the East Coast of Africa, where he won the D.S.M. for gallant conduct in carrying despatches through the lines.
He was demobilised in 1919, and also holds the 1914 Star, General Service and Victory Medals.
9, Archel Road, W. Kensington.   T16198.

BULL, W. G., Sergt., Northamptonshire Regt.
He joined in February, 1916, and served for four years on the Western Front, taking part in numerous engagements.
He was demobilised in February, 1920, and holds the General Service and Victory Medals.
17, Hartington Road, Lower Edmonton.   14245.

BULLEN, J., Special War Worker.
He was employed from 1914 until 1919 at Messrs. Blake's Munition Factory, Fulham, building powder huts and also on work that necessitated the handling of the powder.
On leaving he was given a certificate of appreciation of his services.
29, Field Road, Fulham.   15150/A.

BULLEN, J. H., Pte., Middlesex Regiment and Royal Fusiliers.
He joined in 1918, served in France, and took part in the last Retreat and Advance of 1918, when he was gassed.
He was demobilised in 1919, holding the General Service and Victory Medals.
29, Field Road, Fulham.   15150/D.

BULLEN, M. (Miss), Special War Worker.
This lady was engaged for 18 months making hand-grenades at an important munition factory in Fulham, where she was highly commended for her work.
29, Field Road, Fulham.   15150/C.

BULLEN, M. L. (Mrs.), Special War Worker.
During the war this lady was engaged at the Hurlingham Munition Factory in the T.N.T. shop. This was often work of an extremely dangerous nature, which she performed successfully.
29, Field Road, Fulham.   15150/B.

BULLER, T. H., Pte., Middlesex Regiment.
He joined in August, 1914, and served for two years on the Western Front. He was in the retreat from Mons, and was also at various other engagements.
He was discharged in 1917, holding the 1914 Star, General Service and Victory Medals.
16, Monmouth Road, Edmonton.   13319.

BULLEY, C. T., Driver, Royal Field Artillery.
He joined in September, 1915, went to France the same year, and took part in the battles of the Somme, Loos and Cambrai.
He was demobilised in March, 1919, holding the 1915 Star, General Service and Victory Medals.
48, Felixstowe Road, Edmonton.   15275.

BULLEY, G., Pte., The Buffs (East Kent Regt.).
He joined in July, 1916, was sent to France the same year, and was wounded at the battle of Arras.
He was discharged as the result of his wound in January, 1918, and holds the General Service and Victory Medals.
24, Raynham Road, Edmonton.   16487.

BULLOCK, A. E., Driver, Royal Field Artillery.
He joined in 1915, went to Mesopotamia in the same year, and was taken prisoner at Kut-el-Amara.
He was demobilised in 1919, holding the 1914-15 Star, General Service and Victory Medals.
45, Church Lane, Lower Edmonton.   15206A.

BULLOCK, G. E., Gunner, R.G.A.
He joined in November, 1914, and served in the Dardanelles and Egypt from 1915 to 1919. He took part in engagements in the Dardanelles and later was with General Allenby through the Egyptian campaign. He died in March, 1920, through illness contracted whilst on active service.
He was entitled to the 1914-15 Star, General Service and Victory Medals.
25, Ambleside Road, Willesden.   16117.

BULLOCK, R. L., Bombardier, R.H.A.
He enlisted in August, 1914, and in the same year took part in the retreat from Mons, during which he was wounded.
He was discharged unfit for further service as the result of his wounds in 1915, and holds the 1914 Star, General Service and Victory Medals.
45, Church Lane, Lower Edmonton.   15206/B.

BULPIN, F. A., Rifleman, K.R.R. Corps.
He joined in August, 1918, and served in France and with the Army of Occupation at Cologne from the cessation of hostilities until his demobilisation in November, 1919.
355, Chapter Road, Willesden Green.   T17344.

BULPIT, C., Cpl., Middlesex Regiment.
He joined in February, 1915, and served in France, being wounded at Ypres in 1915. Later he was sent to India, where he remained until 1919, when he was demobilised.
He holds the 1914-15 Star, General Service and Victory Medals.
18, Oldfield Road, Willesden.   16109/B.

BULPIT, J., Mechanic, Royal Air Force.
He joined in 1917, and during his duty with the Royal Air Force was stationed, among other places, at Sheffield on work connected with the repair of aeroplanes.
He was demobilised in 1919, and holds the General Service Medal.
18, Oldfield Road, Willesden.   16109/C.

BUNKER, A., Pte., 1st North Staffordshire Regt.
He joined in February, 1916, served in France and was wounded and taken prisoner at St. Quentin in March, 1918, and detained at a camp in Germany until November of the same year.
He was demobilised in March, 1919, and holds the King's Certificate, General Service and Victory Medals.
5, Cannon Terrace, Hammersmith.   13795.

BUNKER, F. J., Pte., 12th Batt. Suffolk Regt.
He joined in 1915, served in France and Egypt, and was twice wounded. He was captured and held prisoner of war in Germany from March, 1918, until November of the same year.
He holds the General Service and Victory Medals, and was demobilised in December, 1919.
5, Cannon Terrace, Ship Lane, Hammersmith.   13796.

BUNKER, H., Sergt., Queen's Westminster Rifles.
He joined in August, 1914, and served in France for two years, during which time he took part in many engagements, including those of the Somme, Ypres and the Great Advance of 1918, in which he was wounded.
He holds the 1914-15 Star, General Service and Victory Medals, and was demobilised in December, 1918.
101, Deacon Road, Willesden.   16606.

BUNKER, W. E., Rifleman, London Rifle Brigade.
He joined in May, 1915, was sent to France in August, 1917, and was wounded at Bourlon Wood, having previously taken part in other engagements. He was invalided home as the result of his wounds in December, 1917, and remained on Home defence until discharged in April, 1918.
He holds the General Service and Victory Medals.
63, Carlyle Avenue, Harlesden.   14192.

BUNTON, A., A.B., R.N., H.M.S. "Resolution."
He joined in November, 1915, served in the North Sea and at Scapa Flow, and took part in the naval engagement at Heligoland.
He was demobilised in November, 1919, holding the General Service and Victory Medals.
15, Cedar Road, Edmonton.   14033.

BURBAGE, A. G., Pte., Royal West Kent Regt.
He joined in May, 1917, and served in England at the London Command, also at Chatham on special duties.
He was demobilised in June, 1919
2, West Ella Road, Harlesden.   15107/A.

BURBIDGE, H., Pte., London Regiment.
He joined in April, 1915, and served for two years in France. He took part in many engagements, including that of Vimy Ridge. He was killed in action in September, 1917.
He was entitled to the 1914-15 Star, General Service and Victory Medals.
46, Love Lane, Tottenham.   TX18374.

BURBRIDGE, E., Pte., Beds. and Lancs. Regts.
He joined in 1918, and after one month's active service on the Western Front at Passchendaele, died from the effects of mustard gas poisoning in the same year.
He was entitled to the General Service and Victory Medals.
89, Tubbs Road, Willesden Junction.   12877A.

BURBRIDGE, W. J., Sapper, Royal Engineers.
He joined in August, 1914, went to France in the same year, and took part in the battles at Mons, Ypres, Loos, the Somme, Arras, Cambrai, Bullecourt, Hill 60, Passchendaele and others.
He holds the 1914 Star, General Service and Victory Medals, and was demobilised in April, 1919.
89, Tubbs Road, Willesden Junction.   12877B.

BURCH, W. (M.C.), Lieut., 12th Royal Fusiliers.
He joined in July, 1915, and was promoted to his present rank. He took part in many engagements, and was wounded during his service.
He was awarded the M.C. for great bravery in the field, and also holds the General Service and Victory Medals.
He had previously served in the Coldstream Guards and R.A.F., and was demobilised in 1919.
11, Fabian Road, Fulham.   X18060.

BURDETT, R. A., Bombardier, R.F.A.
He joined in March, 1916. He did duty for three years in Mesopotamia and Palestine, where he served with General Allenby's forces. He contracted malaria during this service.
He holds the General Service and Victory Medals, and was demobilised in February, 1920.
70, Star Road, W. Kensington.   T.17060.

BURGESS, A. S., Pte., Royal Fusiliers.
He joined in March, 1917, and served for two years on the Western Front. While in action at the battle of Cambrai he was gassed, and in the Great Advance, October, 1918, was wounded.
He was demobilised in November, 1919, and holds the General Service and Victory Medals.
14, Selwyn Road, Harlesden.   14616.

BURGESS, E. (Miss), Special War Worker.
This lady, during the whole period of the war, was engaged in the manufacture of important war supplies at a London factory, where she did valuable work.
25, Aldensley Road, Hammersmith.   11095.

BURGESS, E F., Lce.-Cpl., Grenadier Guards.
He joined in August, 1914, and was sent to the Western Front, where he took part in several engagements. He was wounded on September 25th, 1916, during the battle of the Somme, as a result of which he died in hospital the following day.
He was entitled to the 1915 Star, General Service and Victory Medals.
7, Ancill Street, W.6   13740.

BURGESS, H., Pte., The Queen's (Royal West Surrey Regiment).
He joined in March, 1918, and was drafted to France, where he took part in many engagements during the latter stages of hostilities.
He was demobilised in 1919, and holds the General Service and Victory Medals.
175, Winchester Road, Lower Edmonton.   15198/A.

BURGESS, H. R., Gunner, R.F.A.
He joined in February, 1915, and served on the Western Front in the battles of Ypres and other engagements. Later he went to Salonica and Egypt, where he saw much service.
He holds the General Service and Victory Medals and was demobilised in July, 1919.
25, Aldensley Road, Hammersmith.   11096.

BURGESS, J. H., Pte., 2nd Border Regiment.
He enlisted in August, 1914, was sent to France in September, and after taking part in several engagements was killed in action on November 12th of the same year.
He was entitled to the 1914 Star, the General Service and Victory Medals.
30, Dyson's Road, Edmonton.   16850.

BURGESS, P. T., Pte., 1st Hertfordshire Regt.
He enlisted in September, 1914, was sent to France in the following year, and was killed in action at Villers-Bretonneux on April 22nd, 1918.
He was entitled to the 1914-15 Star, General Service and Victory Medals.
27, Nightingale Road, Harlesden.   12515.

BURGESS, S. T., Pte., Machine Gun Corps.
He joined in August, 1914, went to France in 1916, and died on July 27th of the same year, from wounds received in action near Albert.
He was entitled to the General Service and Victory Medals.
175, Winchester Road, Lower Edmonton.   15198/B.

BURGESS, S. W., Pte., 13th London Regiment (Kensingtons).
He joined in 1915, was sent to France, and took part in the battles of Vimy Ridge and the Somme. He was severely wounded in September, 1916, and was in hospital in England until discharged on March 4th, 1919,
He holds the General Service and Victory Medals.
21, Worlidge Street, Hammersmith.   12589.

BURGESS, T., Bandsman, Royal Fusiliers.
He rejoined in May, 1914, having previously completed 12 years' service. He was retained in this country on training duties, &c., until his discharge in 1916.
24, Balfour Road, Edmonton.   T14050/B.

BURGESS, W. J., Pte., Machine Gun Corps.
He enlisted in August, 1914, and during his service in France took part in the battles of Arras and Albert, and was twice wounded.
He was discharged in February, 1919, holding the General Service and Victory Medals.
24, Balfour Road, Edmonton.   T14050/A.

BURGIE, C., Sergt., 7th London Regiment.
He served for many years in the Volunteers and Territorials, and for 12 years in the 1st Middlesex Regiment, before being transferred to the 7th Battn., London Regiment. He was sent to France at the age of 55, and took part in the battles of Loos, the Somme, and that of Albert, in which he received 12 wounds in the leg on September 15th, 1916, resulting in his death at Guildford hospital on October 5th of the same year. He held the Long Service Medal, and was entitled to the 1914-15 Star, General Service and Victory Medals.
82, Milton Avenue, Harlesden.   14313.

BURN, A. S., Driver, Royal Horse Artillery.
He joined in August, 1914, went to France in the same year, and took part in several engagements, and in 1916 was invalided home. After his recovery he was drafted to India, where he remained until he was demobilised in 1919.
He holds the Mons Star, the General Service and Victory Medals.
52, Dyson's Road, Edmonton.   16772.

BURNETT, H. W., Pte., 1st Middlesex Regiment.
He joined in November, 1914, and saw five years' service on the Western Front, during which time he took part in many important engagements, including those of Ypres and the Somme.
He was demobilised in January, 1919, and holds the 1915 Star, General Service and Victory Medals.
13, Cedar Road, Edmonton.   14038.

BURNETT, J. G., Sergt., Royal Welsh Fusiliers.
Joining in November, 1914, he served throughout on the Western Front. He was in action in many important engagements, and was wounded at Mametz Wood in July, 1916. After hospital treatment in France and England, he was discharged in December, 1916.
He holds the 1915 Star, General Service and Victory Medals.
5, Sandgate Road, Lower Edmonton.   15499.

BURNS, D F. W., Pte., Somerset Light Infantry.
He joined in February, 1917, and served in France and Egypt. He was killed on September 2nd, 1918, whilst in action at Cambrai.
He was entitled to the General Service and Victory Medals.
36, Crefeld Road, W.6   14494A.

BURNS, E. H., Pte., Middlesex Regiment.
He joined in October, 1917, and served for two years on the Western Front, taking part in the battle of the Somme and the Last Advance of 1918.
He was demobilised in 1919, holding the General Service and Victory Medals.
36, Crefeld Road, W.6   14494B.

BURNS, H. P., Pte., 2/9th Middlesex Regiment.
He joined in December, 1914, and served on the Eastern Front for four years. He was first sent to Gallipoli in 1915, where he was wounded. Later he went to Palestine and was in action at Gaza and Beersheba.
He was discharged on April 11th, 1919, and holds the 1915 Star, General Service and Victory Medals.
49, Victor Road, Willesden.   X17534.

BURNS, P. C., Pte., 18th Middlesex Regiment.
He joined in July, 1916, and served on the Western Front during 1916 and 1917, taking part in the battles of Ypres, the Somme, Messines and Passchendaele Ridge.
He was demobilised in February, 1919, and holds the General Service and Victory Medals.
40, Woolmer Road, Edmonton.   16479.

BURNS, R., Cpl., 2nd South Lancashire Regt.
He joined in November, 1914, went to France on the 23rd
of the same month, and was reported wounded and missing
on September 25th of the same year.
He was entitled to the 1914-15 Star, General Service and
Victory Medals.
46, Hartington Road, Lower Edmonton.   14057.

BURR, A. E., Driver, Royal Engineers.
He joined in January, 1915, and served in France, taking
part in the battle of the Somme, in which he was wounded.
He was invalided home and was for some time in hospital.
Later he went to Mesopotamia.
He holds the 1915 Star, the General Service and Victory
Medals, and was demobilised in May, 1919.
61, Everington Street, Fulham.   13974/A.

BURR, A. E., Bombardier, R.G.A.
He was sent to Egypt in the follow-
ing year, and in 1916 to France. He was killed in action at
St. Quentin on May 10th, 1918, and was entitled to the 1915
Star, General Service and Victory Medals.
49, Bruce Road, Harlesden.   14444.

BURR, M. A. (Mrs.), Special War Worker.
For six months this lady was engaged at Fulham on the
heavy work of filling shells. She also held important and
responsible positions in the Wood Lane and Hurlingham
Explosive Factories, and whilst performing dangerous duties
suffered from poisoning caused by the fumes of chemicals
on which she was working. She was commended for her work.
61, Everington Street, Fulham.   13974/B.

BURRELL, F., Gunner, Royal Field Artillery.
He joined in September, 1914, served in Mesopotamia and
Russia, and while abroad contracted malaria.
He was demobilised in May, 1919, and holds the General
Service and Victory Medals.
29, Raynham Road, Edmonton.   16001B.

BURRELLS, A. A., Pte., Royal Irish Fusiliers.
He joined in September, 1917, and served on the Western
Front, taking part in many engagements. He was killed in
September, 1918, whilst in action.
He was entitled to the General Service and Victory Medals.
20, Osman Road, Edmonton.   14537/A.

BURRELLS, C. S., Driver, R.A.S.C.
He joined in July, 1915, and served on the Western Front,
taking part in many engagements.
He was demobilised in January, 1919, and holds the General
Service and Victory Medals.
20, Osman Road, Edmonton.   14537/B.

BURRIDGE, G. W., Pte., 1/7th Middlesex Regt.
He joined in 1915, went to France the same year, and was
wounded during the battle of the Somme in October, 1916.
He was demobilised in 1918, holding the 1915 Star, General
Service and Victory Medals.
41, Maldon Road, Lower Edmonton.   14789/B.

BURRIDGE, J. J., Signaller, Royal Fusiliers.
He joined in February, 1917, went to France the same year,
and was killed in action at Cambrai in March, 1918.
He was entitled to the General Service and Victory Medals.
41, Maldon Road, Lower Edmonton.   14789/A.

**BURROUGH, S. J., A.B., R.N., H.M.S.
"Agamemnon."**
He joined in February, 1917, served on patrol duty in the
Mediterranean, Dardanelles and the Black Sea, and was
engaged in the sinking of the "Breslau" and the capture of
the "Goeben."
He was demobilised in February, 1919, holding the General
Service and Victory Medals.
84, Burn's Road, Harlesden.   13460.

**BURROWS, G. W., Pte., Middlesex Regt. & East
Kent Regt.**
He joined in 1916, and was stationed on garrison duty at
Northampton, Sevenoaks, Folkestone and Dover.
He also served for four months at the dispersal station at
the Crystal Palace before being demobilised in October, 1919.
226, Chapter Road, Willesden Green.   X17126.

BURROWS, I. B. (Miss), Special War Worker.
This lady was engaged at the Park Royal Munition Factory
in the Small Arms Inspection Department for three years and
six months, performing very necessary and valuable services.
39, Melville Road, Willesden.   15659/A.

BURROWS, M. (Miss), Special War Worker.
During the war this lady was engaged at Messrs. Blake's
Munition Factory in connection with the manufacture of
hand-grenades. She was also for some time in the service of
the G.P.O., and performed valuable duties.
11, Humbolt Road, Fulham.   15300.

BURROWS, W. J., Pte., R.A.S.C.
He joined in August, 1914, and in the same month was sent to
the Western Front, where he took part in the retreat from
Mons and numerous other engagements.
He holds the 1914 Star, the King's and Queen's South
African Medals, and the General Service and Victory Medals,
and was discharged in April, 1917.
20, Hiley Road, Willesden.   X18654A. X18698A.

BURT, H. T., Pte., 19th Middlesex Regiment.
He joined in June, 1915, in the following year was sent to the
Western Front, where he took part in the battles of Ypres,
Cambrai and Arras, and in 1917 went to Italy. He returned
to France in 1918, and was taken prisoner in March of that
year during the retirement, having been twice wounded.
He was demobilised in March, 1919, holding the General
Service and Victory Medals, and an Italian Award.
51, Heron Road, Willesden.   15611.

BURTON, A. F., Petty Officer, R.N.
He joined in October, 1915, and on H.M.S. "Assistance"
served in the North Sea, took part in the battle of Jutland,
and was present at the surrender of the German Fleet at
Scapa Flow.
He was demobilised in July, 1919, holding the 1915 Star,
General Service and Victory Medals.
23, Colville Road, Lower Edmonton.   11998.

BURTON, C., A.B., R.N., H.M.S. "Courageous."
He joined the Navy in August, 1914, and served both in the
North Sea and at the Dardanelles. After 5 years of strenuous service in the Navy he was discharged in December, 1919,
and holds the General Service and Victory Medals, and the
1914 Star.
16, Charles Street, Tottenham, N.   X18296.

**BURTON, C. F., Pte., The Queen's (Royal West
Surrey Regiment).**
He enlisted in May, 1917, and served in France, where he took
part in many engagements and was once wounded.
He holds the General Service and Victory Medals, and was
demobilised in March, 1920.
28, Aintree Street, Fulham.   X18466.

**BURTON, H., Pte., The Queen's (Royal West
Surrey Regiment).**
He joined in February, 1917, and was sent to France in the
same year. He was reported missing in September, 1917, and
is believed to have been killed in action.
He was entitled to the General Service and Victory Medals.
33, Linton Road, Edmonton.   TX17251/C.

BURTON, W., Pte., 22nd Royal Fusiliers.
He joined in February, 1916, was sent to France in the same
year, and was killed in action at the battle of the Somme
in August, 1916.
He was entitled to the Victory and General Service Medals.
33, Linton Road, Upper Edmonton.   TX17251/B.

BURTON, W., Pte., Hampshire Regiment.
He joined in July, 1916, and was sent to the Eastern Front
in the same year. He was serving in Salonica in November,
1916, and was in action on the Struma and at Doiran. He
contracted malaria while abroad, and was discharged in May,
1919, holding the Victory and General Service Medals.
33, Linton Road, Upper Edmonton.   TX17251/A.

BURTON, W., Pte., 6th Middlesex Regiment.
He joined in October, 1915, and served on the Eastern
defences until May, 1916, when he was discharged on
medical grounds.
45, Kimberley Road, Edmonton.   16584.

BURTON, W. F., Pte., Tank Corps.
He joined in December, 1916, went to the Western Front,
and was in action on the Somme, at Ypres, Cambrai and at
Arras.
He was demobilised in February, 1920, holding the General
Service and Victory Medals.
60, Barbot Street, Lower Edmonton.   14221.

BURTON, W. J. G., Pte., 3rd East Surrey Regt.
He joined in May, 1916, was sent to France in the following
year, and in August of the same year was very dangerously
wounded.
He was discharged from hospital in July, 1918, and from the
Army in March, 1919, holding the General Service and Victory
Medals.
15, Colville Road, Lower Edmonton.   T12000.

**BURTON, W. R., Steward, R.N., H.M.S.
"Defence."**
He joined in May, 1915, served in the North Sea, and was
killed in action at the battle of Jutland in May, 1916.
He was entitled to the 1915 Star, General Service and
Victory Medals.
84, Warwick Road, Edmonton.   X17905.

BUSBY, F. G., Sergt., 13th East Surrey Regt.
He joined in August, 1914, served on the Western Front from 1917 until 1919—on the Somme, at Bullecourt and in the Retreat and Advance of 1918. He was wounded three times. He holds the General Service and Victory Medals, and was demobilised in February, 1919.
22, Brownlow Road, Willesden. 15006/A.

BUSBY, W. C., Driver, R.A.S.C. (M.T.).
He joined the Middlesex Regiment in June, 1915, in January of the following year was sent to the Western Front, and was wounded in action at Arras. In June, 1916, he was invalided home, and after his recovery was transferred to the Royal Army Service Corps for duty in England.
He was demobilised in April, 1919, and holds the General Service and Victory Medals.
12, Brownlow Road, Harlesden. 14920.

BUSBY, W. G., Pte., Cameron Highlanders.
He joined in February, 1918, and served on the Western Front with the Labour Corps, at Vimy Ridge, Arras and Cambrai. Afterwards he went to Germany with the Army of Occupation, and served there until his demobilisation in November, 1919.
He holds the General Service and Victory Medals.
3, Earlsmead Road, Kensal Rise. X18027.

BUSH, A. A., Merchant Seaman, H.M.T. " Minanha."
He joined in August, 1914, and served in the Suez Canal, North Sea and Mediterranean until demobilised in 1919.
He holds the 1914 Star, General Service and Victory Medals, and also the Mercantile Marine Award.
8, Alston Road, Lower Edmonton. 16506.

BUSH, A. A., A.B., Mercantile Marine.
He joined in August, 1914, and served with the Mercantile Marine until his demobilisation in October, 1919.
He holds the 1914 Star, the Merchant Service and Victory Medals.
37, Balfour Road, Edmonton. 14041.

BUSH, C. M., Pte., Royal Fusiliers.
He joined in July, 1918, and although anxious to serve overseas, was unable to pass the necessary medical examination, and was discharged on medical grounds in December of the same year.
19, Felixstowe Road, Willesden, N.W.10 X17766B.

BUSH, J., Pte., 1/7th Middlesex Regiment.
He joined in March, 1915, and in the same year went to France, where he was severely wounded, losing his left leg at the battle of the Somme.
He was discharged in 1918, and holds the 1915 Star, General Service and Victory Medals.
14, Maldon Road, Lower Edmonton. 14096/B.

BUSH, T. H., Pte., 1/3rd Royal West Kent Regt.
He joined in June, 1916, proceeded to India in the same year, and afterwards served in Mesopotamia, where he was wounded in action in October, 1918. He died in hospital at Bagdad in December, 1918, and was entitled to the General Service and Victory Medals.
4, Belton Road, Willesden. 16600.

BUSH, W., Rifleman, King's Royal Rifle Corps.
He joined in July, 1917, and during his service on the Western Front was wounded at Albert in July, 1918. He was in hospital for 10 days in France and for over four weeks in Chichester.
In October, 1919, he was demobilised, holding the General Service and Victory Medals.
1, Short Street, Upper Edmonton. X17088.

BUSH, W. H., Pte., 1st Middlesex Regiment.
He enlisted in March, 1915, and was sent to France, where he was killed at the battle of the Somme in July, 1916.
He was entitled to the General Service and Victory Medals.
19, Felixstowe Road, Willesden. X17766/A.

BUSHNELL, F., 1st-Class Stoker, R.N., H.M.S. " Chameleon."
He joined in April, 1916, and served in the Dardanelles, patrolling the coasts of Turkey, Greece, and Italy.
He was demobilised in April, 1919, holding the General Service and Victory Medals.
25, Ashwell Grove, Edmonton. X17479.

BUSS, R. E., Pte., Royal Sussex Regiment.
He joined in April, 1915, and served in France from 1917 until February, 1919, taking part in several engagements.
He holds the General Service and Victory Medals.
144, Winchester Road, Lower Edmonton. 14782.

BUSSY, A. L., Pte., Norfolk Regiment.
He joined in September, 1914, went to France the following year, and was killed in action on the Somme in July, 1916.
He took part in all operations prior to his death.
He was entitled to the 1915 Star, General Service and Victory Medals.
27, Maldon Road, Lower Edmonton. 14785/B.

BUSSY, G. H., Driver, R.A.S.C. (M.T.).
He joined in May, 1917, and was sent to East Africa the same year. During his service there he contracted malaria.
He was ultimately demobilised in December, 1919, holding the General Service and Victory Medals.
27, Maldon Road, Lower Edmonton. 14785/A.

BUTCHER, G., Pte., Royal Defence Corps.
He joined in November, 1914, and served as military guard on the railways, at aerodromes, munition works and elsewhere.
He was demobilised in February, 1919, after over four years' service, having performed necessary and important duties throughout this period.
99, Victor Road, Willesden, N.W. X17536.

BUTCHER, H., Sergt., Royal Field Artillery.
As a regular soldier, he went with the first Expeditionary Force to France, and was wounded in the retreat from Mons. He served on the Dardanelles Front in 1915, and on the Russian Front, returning again to the Western Front, where he took part in several engagements.
He was recommended for the M.M. and D.C.M., holds the 1914 Star, General Service and Victory Medals, and recommendations for good service.
4, Averill Street, W.6 13995.

BUTCHER, H. E., Gunner, Royal Field Artillery.
He joined in April, 1916, served on the Western Front and was wounded at the battle of Ypres. After being in hospital in France and England, he was sent to Germany with the Army of Occupation, and was demobilised in September, 1919, holding the General Service and Victory Medals.
7, Mooltan Street, Fulham. X17143.

BUTCHER, W., A.B., R.N., H.M.S. " Vindictive."
He joined in January, 1918, and served in Russia, seeing considerable service in that theatre.
He holds the General Service and Victory Medals.
20, Chamberlain Road, Edmonton. 14223.

BUTCHER, W., Pte., R.A.S.C.
He joined in April, 1916, and was sent to the Western Front. He took part in many engagements, and was principally employed in taking up rations and ammunition to the front lines. He saw active service on all sectors.
He holds the General Service and Victory Medals.
23, Felixstowe Road, Willesden. X17755.

BUTLER, C., Pte., 2nd Black Watch.
He enlisted in August, 1914, was sent to France, and took part in the battles of Mons (where he was wounded), Ypres, Vimy Ridge, Loos, the Somme, the Marne and Arras, and was again wounded.
In January, 1918, he went to Mesopotamia, and thence to Egypt, where he remained until discharged in September, 1919, holding the 1914 Star, General Service and Victory Medals.
31, Tubbs Road, Harlesden, N.W.10 12892.

BUTLER, C. F., Rifleman, Rifle Brigade.
He joined in December, 1915, saw active service in France at Ypres and on the Somme, and was wounded three times. He holds the General Service and Victory Medals, and was demobilised in March, 1919.
127, Greyhound Road, Fulham. 14821.

BUTLER, C. H., Pte., Royal Army Service Corps.
He joined in August, 1915, and served continuously in France until March, 1919, when he was demobilised. He was present at all the operations on the Western Front throughout his service overseas, and on discharge became entitled to the General Service and Victory Medals.
2, Beryl Road, Fulham. 13353/A.

BUTLER, E. G., Cpl., King's Own Yorks L.I.
Having previously served in the Boer war, he rejoined the Colours in August, 1914, and served for three years on the Western Front, taking part in the battles of Ypres, the Somme, Armentieres, Loos, Arras and many others. While in action on the Somme he was very severely wounded and buried, and was detained in hospital in France and England for six months.
He was eventually demobilised in March, 1919, holding the King's and Queen's South African Medals, the 1915 Star, the General Service and Victory Medals.
15, Fane Street, W. Kensington, W.14 15926.

BUTLER, F. M. (Mrs.), Special War Worker.
This lady was engaged during the war at Perivale Munition Factory, where her duties, among others, consisted in the inspection of shells of all calibres, and in working generally in the C.I.W. powder shop. Her duties were strenuous, and she was commended for her work.
35a, Drayton Road, Harlesden. 14993/B.

BUTLER, H. J., Pte., 7th Royal Fusiliers.
Joining in March, 1916, he was almost immediately sent to France, where he was continuously in action until very severely wounded towards the end of the year.
As a result of his wounds he was discharged from the Service on medical grounds in May, 1917, holding the General Service and Victory Medals.
18, Love Lane, Tottenham. X18386.

BUTLER, J. W., Gunner, R.F.A.
He joined in August, 1914, and during his service in France, which lasted four years, took part in the battles of Cambrai, Ypres and the Somme, and was for some months in hospital, having been seriously wounded and gassed.
He holds the 1915 Star, General Service and Victory Medals, and was demobilised in February, 1919.
70, Ancill Street, W.6 14092.

BUTLER, W. H., Driver, R.A.S.C.
Having served prior to the war, he re-enlisted in August, 1914, and saw service throughout the campaign on practically every sector of the Western Front. In spite of being engaged in every operation of any importance he escaped unhurt, and remained with the forces until fighting ceased.
He holds the 1915 Star, General Service and Victory Medals.
11, Kimberley Road, Edmonton. 16588.

BUTLER, W. J., Gunner, R.F.A.
He joined in November, 1914, and served overseas for nearly five years. He was first sent to France, and thence drafted to Salonica, where he fought in the Balkans. Later he was sent to Palestine, and took part in many engagements under General Allenby. He fought at Jericho and Beersheba and marched with the victorious armies into Jerusalem. He served at one period in Egypt, and was finally sent back to France, and was in action in the last Advance of 1918 at St. Quentin and Cambrai. He terminated his service in Belgium, where he was demobilised.
He holds the 1915 Star, General Service and Victory Medals.
11, Mirabel Road, Walham Green. X17712.

BUTT, C., Rifleman, King's Royal Rifle Corps.
He joined in August, 1914, and served on the Western Front, taking part in the battles of the Somme, Loos, Neuve Chapelle and other engagements. During this period he was wounded and gassed, and in 1915 was discharged, having lost his left eye.
He holds the 1914 Star, General Service and Victory Medals.
39, Archel Road, W. Kensington. 16202.

BUTTON, P., Gunner, Royal Garrison Artillery.
He joined early in the war, and was sent to France in 1916. During his service he took part in several engagements, and in 1918 gave his blood for transfusion to save the life of a comrade.
He holds the General Service and Victory Medals, and was demobilised in February, 1919.
57, Roseberry Road, Lower Edmonton. 14350.

BUXTON, L., 1st-Class Stoker, R.N., H.M.S. "Ettrick."
He first joined in 1908, and was called up from the Reserve in August, 1914. He was on service with the Destroyer Squadron until July, 1917, when he was torpedoed and drowned at sea.
He was entitled to the 1915 Star, General Service and Victory Medals.
58, Sheldon Road, Upper Edmonton. TX17293.

BUXTON, V. E., Gunner, R.G.A.
He joined in 1915, went to the Western Front the following year, where he took part in many important engagements. He served continuously on this front until his demobilisation in 1919.
He holds the General Service and Victory Medals.
7, Tedworth Road, Tottenham. X18117.

BUY, P. W., 1st-Class Petty Officer, R.N., H.M.S. "Gaillardia."
He joined in August, 1914, and served in the North Sea on board the submarines "C.12," "H.10," and "C.18," until March, 1918, when the minesweeper, H.M.S. "Gaillardia," on which he was then serving, was struck by a floating mine, and he lost his life, together with 64 men and two officers.
He was entitled to the 1915 Star, General Service and Victory Medals.
52, Maldon Road, Edmonton. 15788.

BYATT, A. W., Pte., Royal Marines.
Joining at the outbreak of war, in August, 1914, he was practically continuously afloat, seeing service chiefly in the North Sea. In May, 1916, he had the distinction of serving on board H.M.S. "Queen Mary" at the battle of Jutland, and lost his life in that action when his ship went down, with practically all hands.
He was entitled to the 1914 Star, General Service and Victory Medals.
40, Archel Road, West Kensington. 16421/A.

BYATT, G. T., Gunner, Royal Field Artillery.
He joined in 1915, and served in France, taking part in many engagements, including the battles of the Somme, Arras, Loos, Neuve Chapelle, Armentieres, Amiens, Ypres, Vimy Ridge, Lille, St. Quentin, Bullecourt, Cambrai, and the Retreat and Advance of 1918.
He holds the 1915 Star, General Service and Victory Medals, and was demobilised in 1919.
40, Archel Road, West Kensington, W.14 16421/B.

BYATT, R. (Miss), Special War Worker.
Throughout the war this lady was continuously employed in making all kinds of comforts for the troops, giving up her leisure and recreation for this purpose, and continuing in her work with untiring energy and devotion.
40, Archel Road, West Kensington. 16432.

BYFIELD, A. C. (D.C.M.), R.S.M., 17th Middx. Regiment.
He enlisted in August, 1914, was sent to France in the same year, and took part in the battles of Mons, the Somme, Cambrai, Delville Wood, Ypres and Oppy Wood. He was severely wounded and was awarded the Distinguished Conduct Medal for conspicuous gallantry on the field.
He holds also the 1914 Star, General Service and Victory Medals, and was discharged in March, 1919.
32, Hartington Road, Lower Edmonton. 14052.

C

CADMAN, H., 1st Air Mechanic, R.A.F.
Joining in November, 1915, he was trained as an Air Mechanic in England. On completion of his training he was unsuccessful in obtaining a transfer overseas, and was retained in England on special duty.
On the cessation of hostilities he remained in the Service, and holds the General Service Medal.
150, Church Road, Tottenham, N. X18143.

CAHALARNE, H., Special War Worker.
During the war this lady was engaged at an important London munition factory in connection with the manufacture of cases for ammunition, &c. Her work was of an arduous nature, and she was commended for her assistance.
49, Orbain Road, Fulham. X18439.

CAHALARNE, J., Pte., West Kent Regiment.
Joining in 1917, he completed his training, and afterwards served in various parts, including Dublin and Galway. He was demobilised in September, 1919.
49, Orbain Road, Fulham. X18440.

CAHALARNE, J., Pte., R.A.S.C.
He joined in June, 1915, and during his service on the Western Front took part in many battles, including those of the Somme, Arras, Loos, Neuve Chapelle, Armentieres, Ypres, Vimy Ridge, Amiens, St. Quentin and Cambrai.
He holds the 1915 Star, General Service and Victory Medals, and was demobilised on April 14th, 1919.
49, Orbain Road, Fulham. X18438.

CAHALARNE, J. T., Cpl., King's Own (Royal Lancaster Regiment).
He joined in August, 1915, and during his service on the Western Front took part in the battles of the Somme, Armentieres and La Bassée, where he was wounded, afterwards being invalided home. Later he served in England, and was demobilised in 1919, holding the General Service and Victory Medals.
49, Orbain Road, Fulham. X18437.

CAHILL, H. (Miss), Q.M.A.A.C.
Joining in 1917, this lady was attached to the 3rd King's Shropshire Light Infantry, and was stationed in Ireland. Later she was sent to France, and served at Albert, Dieppe and Le Havre.
She was demobilised in July, 1919, and holds the General Service and Victory Medals.
101, Osterley Park, View Road, Hanwell. 12346/A.

CAHILL, T., Pte., 1st Royal Irish Fusiliers.
He joined in August, 1914, and was sent to the Dardanelles, where he was badly wounded, and in consequence invalided home. In 1916 he was drafted to the Western Front, where he took part in the battles of the Somme, Arras, St. Quentin, Passchendaele, Vimy Ridge, Loos and Bapaume, and in March, 1918, was again wounded and taken prisoner.
He holds the 1914-15 Star, General Service and Victory Medals, and was demobilised in March, 1919.
101, Osterley Park, View Road, Hanwell.   12346/B.

CAIRNS, G. H., C.S.M., Royal Inniskilling Fus.
He joined in September, 1914, and served in Ireland on training and other duties until he was discharged medically unfit in 1916.
26, Leopold Road, Willesden.   14912.

CAIRNS, J. A., Pte., Bedfordshire Regiment.
He joined in July, 1918, and after training in England served with the Army of Occupation in Germany. Whilst on the Rhine he was attached to the R.E. Signals as despatch rider. He was demobilised in September, 1919.
274, Chapter Road, Willesden Green.   X17389.

CAKEBREAD, R., Pte., 8th Leicestershire Regt.
He joined in January, 1916, served on the Western Front for eight months, and was killed in action at Gueudecourt in September, 1916.
He was entitled to the General Service and Victory Medals.
45, Ilex Road, Willesden.   16358.

CALLAGHAN, G., C.S.M., Royal Fusiliers.
He enlisted in September, 1914, and served on the Eastern Front from January until December, 1915, when he was sent to France. He was killed in action on the Somme on September, 1916.
He was entitled to the 1914-15 Star, General Service and Victory Medals.
33, Villiers Road, Willesden.   16730/B.

CALLINGHAM, A. V., A.B., R.N., H.M.S. " Lord Nelson."
He joined the Navy in 1914, saw active service at the Dardanelles, taking part in many engagements, and was wounded.
He holds the 1914-15 Star, General Service and Victory Medals.
28, Nursery Street, Tottenham.   X18148.

CALLOW, S. J., Armourer, R.N., H.M.S. " Prince George."
He joined in May, 1918, and was engaged on the repairing of guns while stationed at Chatham and Sheerness.
Was demobilised in February, 1919, and holds the General Service and Victory Medals.
20, Talbot Road, Willesden.   16036.

CALLOW, T. S., Pte., 1st Middlesex Regiment.
He joined in October, 1914, and in January, 1915, went to France, where he took part in the fighting on the Somme, Ypres, Bullecourt and Arras. He was severely gassed during the latter engagement, and was discharged in consequence in March, 1919.
He holds the 1915 Star, General Service and Victory Medals, and also holds a valuable letter from his C.O., commending him for his service.
123, Durban Road, Tottenham.   X17962/A.

CALLOW, W. H., Sergt., 33rd Middlesex Regt.
He was serving in August, 1914, and during his service on the Western Front took part in the battles of Mons, the Somme, Ypres and Neuve Chapelle, and was wounded. Also served in Italy, where he was again wounded. In October, 1918, he died in hospital from ptomaine poisoning.
He was entitled to the 1914 Star, General Service and Victory Medals.
127, Durban Road, Tottenham.   X17961.

CALVER, R. E., Rifleman, Rifle Brigade.
He joined in June, 1916, and went to the Western Front in September of that year, taking part in several engagements, including Ypres, where he was killed in action in August, 1917.
He was entitled to the General Service and Victory Medals.
37, Waldo Road, Willesden.   X17630.

CAME, E., Pte., Duke of Cornwall's L.I.
He joined in August, 1915, and served in France. Took part in many engagements, including Arras, and was killed in action near Guillemont in August, 1916.
He was entitled to the General Service and Victory Medals.
207a, Kilburn Lane, W.10   X18715/C.

CAME, H., Pte., Dorset Regiment.
He was in the Regular Army when war broke out, and served on the Eastern Front from 1914 to 1919. During his service in Mesopotamia he took part in numerous engagements, and was wounded twice, near Kut.
He was demobilised in June, 1919, and holds the 1914-15 Star, General Service and Victory Medals.
207a, Kilburn Lane, W.10   X17815/B.

CAME, W., Pte., Duke of Cornwall's L.I.
He joined in 1915, and from 1916 to 1919 saw much service in many engagements on the Bulgarian Front. While there he suffered from malaria. In 1920 he was in Ireland for a time previous to being demobilised in April of that year.
He holds the General Service and Victory Medals.
207a, Kilburn Lane, W.10   X18715/A.

CAMERON, D., Gunner, Royal Field Artillery.
He joined in March, 1917, and served with our Armies in India until May, 1919, when he was demobilised.
He holds the General Service and Victory Medals.
47, Somerset Road, Edmonton.   X17030.

CAMERON, G. P., Pte., Seaforth Highlanders.
He joined in December, 1915, but was discharged in May, 1916, on medical grounds, having suffered the loss of an eye.
24, Whitehall Road, Tottenham, N.17.   X18130.

CAMERON, J., Pte., 1st Middlesex Regiment.
He joined in August, 1914, and served on the Western Front, taking part in the battles of the Somme, Ypres and Cambrai. During this time he was wounded, and lost the sight of his left eye.
In January, 1919, he was demobilised, and holds the 1915 Star, the General Service and Victory Medals.
20, Westbury Road, Willesden.   15456.

CAMERON, R. F., Pte., R.A.S.C. (M.T.).
He joined in April, 1915, having previously served in the Merchant Service, and in the same year was sent to France, where he was in action at Armentieres, Cambrai, Arras and on the Somme. From 1917 until 1919 he served in Salonica, at Doiran, and on the Struma Plains, on transport duties.
He was demobilised in May, 1919, holding the 1915 Star, General Service and Victory Medals. Also awarded the Merchant Service Torpedo Badge.
61, Brownlow Road, Harlesden.   14720.

CAMM, A., Pte., 23rd Middlesex Regiment.
He enlisted in October, 1914, was sent to France in the following year, and was killed in action in June, 1917.
He was entitled to the 1915 Star, General Service and Victory Medals.
65, Cobbold Road, Willesden.   16072/B.

CAMM, J., Pte., 9th Middlesex Regiment.
He enlisted in December, 1914, and served in Egypt from the following year until he was demobilised in April, 1919.
He holds the 1915 Star, General Service and Victory Medals.
65, Cobbold Road, Willesden.   16072/A.

CAMP, J., Gunner, Royal Garrison Artillery.
He joined in October, 1917, served as a gun-layer in Italy until demobilised in February, 1919, and on two occasions was commended for good work.
He holds the General Service and Victory Medals.
1, Jervis Road, Fulham.   X17665A.

CAMPBELL, E., Cpl., R.A.M.C.
He joined in January, 1915, and did important medical duties at various stations. He was demobilised in November, 1918.
57, Chaplin Road, Willesden.   16628A.

CAMPBELL, J. E., Driver, R.A.S.C.
He joined in August, 1914, and served in Salonica for four years, where he took part in all the operations on that front. In May, 1919, he was demobilised, and holds the 1915 Star, General Service and Victory Medals.
57, Chaplin Road, Willesden.   16628B.

CAMPBELL, R., Lce.-Cpl., 47th Batt. Royal Fusiliers.
He joined in May, 1916, and served on the Western Front, taking part in many engagements, during which he was gassed.
In February, 1920, he was demobilised, and holds the General Service and Victory Medals.
57, Chaplin Road, Willesden.   16628C.

CAMPBELL, W. S., Pte., 7th London Regt.
He joined in April, 1915, went to the Western Front in the following November, and was killed in action in April, 1916, having previously taken part in other engagements.
He was entitled to the 1915 Star, General Service and Victory Medals.
139, Kilburn Lane, Willesden, N.W.   X18572.

4

CAMPION, C., Pte., R.A.M.C.
He enlisted in January, 1915, and served in France, at Aire and Merville, on important medical duties in the military hospitals.
He holds the 1915 Star, General Service and Victory Medals, and was demobilised in February, 1919.
194, Lillie Road, Fulham. X18793/B.

CAMPION, E. (Miss), Special War Worker.
- During the war this lady devoted her time, and did most useful work, in connection with the Kensington Hospital Supply Depot, making large numbers of bandages, swabs, &c., for wounded soldiers in various hospitals.
194, Lillie Road, Fulham. X18793/A.

CANDLER, H. C., Rifleman, Queen Victoria Rifles.
He enlisted in September, 1914, served on the Western Front, and was known to have been wounded at the battle of the Somme in 1916. He was conveyed to a dressing station which was subsequently destroyed by shell-fire, and he was never heard of since. He was reported " missing, believed killed," and was entitled to the General Service and Victory Medals.
24, St. Margaret's Mansions, Lillie Road, Fulham. X18871/A.

CANDLER, J., Cpl. (Signaller), Queen Victoria Rifles.
He joined in August, 1914, and during his service on the Western Front took part in many battles, including those of the Somme, Albert, Loos, Neuve Chapelle and Armentieres. He was demobilised in 1919, holding the 1915 Star, the General Service and Victory Medals.
24, St. Margaret's Mansions, Lillie Road, Fulham. X18871/B.

CANHAN, D., Pte., East Surrey Regiment.
He joined in 1917, and was sent to France in the same year. He was in action at Arras, where he was wounded, and also took part in the last Advance in 1918.
He was discharged in 1918, and holds the General Service and Victory Medals.
7, Durban Road, Tottenham, N.17 X18101.

CANHAN, H., Rifleman, Rifle Brigade.
He joined in 1918, and was sent to Germany in 1919, with the Army of Occupation.
He was discharged in February, 1920.
7, Durban Road, Tottenham, N.17 X18102.

CANHAN, T., Gunner, Royal Garrison Artillery.
He joined in September, 1916, served on the Western Front during 1917 and 1918, and was in action at Hill 70 and Lens. He was demobilised in 1919, and holds the General Service and Victory Medals.
8, Wimborne Road, Lower Edmonton. 15210.

CANN, G. R., Signaller, H.A.C.
He joined in May, 1918, and obtained his training at Blackheath and Caterham. He did duty at various stations, and was demobilised in January, 1919.
7, Vicarage Road, Willesden. 15744/A.

CANN, H., Driver, Royal Engineers.
He joined in April, 1915, was sent to France in the same year, and took part in the battles of Ypres, the Somme, Hill 60, Bullecourt, Arras, Vimy Ridge, St. Quentin and Albert. He received injuries while overseas, and was demobilised in 1919, holding the 1915 Star, General Service and Victory Medals.
20, Humbolt Road, Fulham. 15147/B.

CANN, J. P., Pte., 1st East Surrey Regiment.
He joined in February, 1917, and served in France from May until October of the same year, when he was killed near Poperinghe.
He was entitled to the General Service and Victory Medals.
7, Vicarage Road, Willesden. 15744/B.

CANNAFORD, A. S., Pte., Middlesex Regiment.
He joined in 1915, went to the Western Front, taking part in the battles of the Somme, Arras, Loos, Neuve Chapelle, Armentieres, Ypres, Bullecourt, and the final Advance of 1918. He was wounded during his service.
He holds the 1915 Star, General Service and Victory Medals, and was demobilised in 1919.
23, Dieppe Street, West Kensington. 16255.

CANNELL, S., Saddler, Royal Field Artillery.
He joined in December, 1915, and was shortly afterwards sent abroad, where he served four years. He was engaged on the Western Front, and took part in many engagements, including Arras, Ypres, the Somme, the Ancre and Verdun, and was wounded.
He was discharged in May, 1919, and holds the General Service and Victory Medals.
15, Napier Road, College Park, Willesden, N.W. X17519.

CANNING, A. W., Pte., R.A.S.C.
He joined in March, 1918, and in November went to France with the Labour Corps, where he took part in operations then pending.
He holds the General Service and Victory Medals.
113a, Deacon Road, Willesden. 16611.

CANNON, A. J. W., Pte., 4/8th Middlesex Regt.
He enlisted in January, 1915, and served for eight months. He was discharged on medical grounds in August of the same year, and died shortly afterwards.
72, St. Margaret's Road, Hanwell. 11059.

CANNON, F. (M.M.), Battery S.M., R.F.A.
A serving soldier, he went to France in August, 1914, where he served until August, 1919, when he was demobilised. During this period he was in action at Mons, Ypres, Lille and many other places, and was awarded the Military Medal for conspicuous gallantry and devotion to duty in the field, in March, 1918. In addition, he holds the King's and Queen's South African Medals, the Mons Star, the General Service, Victory, Long Service and Good Conduct Medals. He had completed 21 years' service.
17, Charlton Road, Harlesden. 13107.

CANNON, G. S. (Mrs.), W.R.A.F.
This lady joined in May, 1918, and was stationed at Melton, with the Royal Air Force. She was demobilised in September, 1919, after having rendered important and valuable services.
31, Waldo Road, Willesden. X18193/A.

CANNON, S. H., Pioneer, Royal Engineers.
He joined in 1916, served on the Western Front, took part in the battles of the Somme and Ypres, and later was stationed at Dunkirk on work connected with the railways.
He was demobilised in April, 1919, and holds the General Service and Victory Medals.
31, Waldo Road, Willesden. X18193B.

CANNON, T., Pte., 1st Royal West Kent Regt.
He joined in November, 1916, and during his service in France took part in the battles of Ypres, Cambrai and Bapaume; he was wounded in May, 1918, and again in August of the same year.
He holds the General Service and Victory Medals.
17, Disraeli Road, Harlesden. 14157.

CAPELL, A., Pte., 3rd Middlesex Regiment.
He joined in March, 1915, and served on the Western Front for three months. In September, 1915, he was killed during the fighting near Nieuport.
He was entitled to the 1915 Star, the General Service and Victory Medals.
97, Carlyle Avenue, Harlesden. 13819.

CAPELL, O., Sapper, Royal Engineers.
He joined in November, 1914, and served for four years on the Western Front, taking part in the battles of Ypres, the Somme, Verdun, Arras, and many other engagements. In January, 1919, he was demobilised, holding the 1915 Star, the General Service and Victory Medals.
97, Carlyle Avenue, Harlesden. 13820B.

CAPELL, R., Pte., The Queen's (Royal West Surrey Regiment).
He joined in April, 1916, and served on the Western Front. While in action at Messines in 1917 he was badly wounded, and was discharged in consequence in May, 1919.
He holds the General Service and Victory Medals.
97, Carlyle Avenue, Harlesden. 13820A.

CAPES, H. C., Machine Gunner, 1st Battalion Royal West Kent Regiment.
He joined in January, 1915, and served on the Western Front, taking part in the battles of Ypres, Arras, Albert and the Somme. He was wounded at Arras, and again at St. Eloi. After being in hospital in France and England for four months he was demobilised in February, 1919.
He holds the 1915 Star, General Service and Victory Medals.
23, Snell's Park, Edmonton. X17642.

CAPON, A., Bombardier, Royal Field Artillery.
He enlisted in October, 1914, served on the Western Front from the following year until 1919, and took part in the fighting on the Somme, at Ypres, Arras, Vimy Ridge, Bullecourt, Cambrai, Albert and in the last Advance of 1918. He was demobilised in February, 1919, and holds the 1915 Star, General Service and Victory Medals.
1, Bridport Road, Upper Edmonton. X17894.

CAPON, G., Pte., Royal Fusiliers.
He joined in 1918, and served with the transport section on duty at Newmarket and other stations until demobilised in March, 1919.
1, Bridport Road, Upper Edmonton. X17893.

CAPON, H., Sergt., 1/8th London Regiment.
He joined in August, 1914, and served on the Western Front, taking part in the battles of the Somme, Ypres, Arras, Loos and the last Advance in 1918. He was twice wounded.
He was demobilised in March, 1919, holding the 1915 Star, the General Service and Victory Medals.
44, Purves Road, Willesden. X18024,

CAPON, H. G., C.Q.M.S., R.A.S.C. (M.T.).
He joined on February, 1915, served on the Western Front, and was mentioned in despatches for good work in April, 1918.
He was demobilised in March, 1919, and holds the General Service and Victory Medals.
51, Station Road, Hanwell. 12384/A.

CAPON, H. T., Pte., 8th Royal West Kent Regt.
He joined in August, 1916, and in the following January was sent to the Western Front, where he took part in the fighting on all sectors.
He holds the General Service and Victory Medals.
51, Station Road, Hanwell. 12384/B.

CAPON, R., Driver, R.F.A.
He joined in September, 1915, and for some time he served in the Remount Depot in India, subsequently being transferred to battery duty. He afterwards contracted malaria and was admitted to hospital.
He holds the General Service and Victory Medals.
1, Bridport Road, Upper Edmonton. TX17590.

CARDEW, E. S., Pte., 7th London Regiment (transferred to Royal Irish Rifles).
He joined in May, 1915, and was sent to France, where he took part in engagements at Ypres, Arras, Nieuport and Cambrai. He was twice wounded at Ypres, and demobilised in February, 1919.
He holds the General Service and Victory Medals.
49, Faroe Road, W. Kensington. 12434.

CARDEW, F. T., Petty Officer (1st Class), R.N., H.M.S. "Dominion."
He joined in August, 1914, and was for two years on the Northern Patrol. He also served with the mystery ships ("Q" boats), for two years in the Atlantic.
He holds the 1914 Star, General Service and Victory Medals.
49, Faroe Road, W. Kensington. 12432.

CARDEW, S., Cpl., R.A.S.C. (M.T.).
He joined in May, 1916, and was sent to France, and later to Belgium, where he took part in engagements at Ypres, Arras, Cambrai, St. Quentin and the Somme.
He was demobilised in February, 1919, and holds the General Service and Victory Medals.
49, Faroe Road, W. Kensington. 12433,

CARESWELL, E. F., Rifleman, 15th Royal Irish Rifles.
He enlisted in 1916 and served in France in the same year, took part in engagements on the Somme, and was killed in action near Cambrai in November, 1917.
He was entitled to the General Service and Victory Medals.
250, Chapter Road, Willesden. X17129.

CARESWELL, F. J., Pte., Middx. R. and M.G.C.
He joined in March, 1916, served in France until demobilised in January, 1919, and took part in the battles of the Somme, Bapaume, Ypres, Arras, Albert and Loos, being twice invalided home with dysentery and trench fever.
He holds the General Service and Victory Medals.
24, Yuletide Road, Willesden. 15080.

CARESWELL, G. W., Pte., Machine Gun Corps.
He joined in August, 1914, served in France from 1914 until 1919, and took part in the battles of the Somme, Ypres, Neuve Chapelle, Cambrai, and St. Quentin, and was badly gassed.
He holds the 1914 Star, General Service and Victory Medals, and was demobilised in February, 1919.
30, Bridge Road, Willesden. 15461/B.

CARESWELL, H., Pte., Royal Army Vet. Corps.
He joined in July, 1917, and served with the Veterinary Corps for 10 months. Being unfortunately medically unfit at the time, he was discharged on these grounds, after having given valuable service.
30, Bridge Road, Willesden. 15461/A.

CARESWELL, R. W. (M.M.), Cpl., R.E.
He joined in November, 1915, saw active service in France from 1915 until 1917, and was awarded the Military Medal for bravery in the field. He died at Arras in November, 1917, from wounds received in action.
He was entitled to the 1915 Star, General Service and Victory Medals.
30, Bridge Road, Willesden. 15461/C.

CAREY, E. W., Pte., East Surrey Regiment.
He joined in November, 1915, and in 1916–17 served on the Western Front, taking part in actions at Loos, the Somme, Cambrai and St. Quentin. He was wounded in 1917, and discharged in May, 1918, holding the General Service and Victory Medals.
61, Monmouth Road, N.9 13022.

CAREY, R., Pte., Essex Regiment.
He joined in 1916, and served with the Essex Regiment until discharged in 1917. He performed useful services, and was discharged on medical grounds, being certified unfit for further military service.
5, Wimborne Road, Lower Edmonton. 15213.

CARLSON, C., 1st-Class Stoker, Mercantile Marine.
He joined the Navy in 1914, and served four years on merchant transports, including the "Montebelle." He was torpedoed several times during his service, the last time in June, 1918, when he was drowned.
He was entitled to the 1914 Star, General Service and Victory Medals, and also the Mecantile Marine Medal.
32, Durban Road, Tottenham, N.17 X18083/B.

CARLTON, F., Bombardier, R.F.A.
He joined in October, 1915, was sent to France in the following May, took part in the battles of Ypres, Arras, Passchendaele and Armentieres, and was wounded in action near Ypres in September, 1917, and at Nieppe Forest in May, 1918. He then served with the Army of Occupation in Germany until demobilised in August, 1919.
He holds the General Service and Victory Medals.
167, Purves Road, Willesden. X18408.

CARMAN, D. A. A., Rifleman, Civil Service Rifles.
He joined in June, 1918, and served on the Western Front in the same year. Due to the cessation of hostilities, he was demobilised in October, 1919.
He holds the General Service and Victory Medals.
182, Croyland Road, Lower Edmonton. 13924.

CARMICHAEL, T., Driver, R.A.S.C.
He rejoined in August, 1914, having seen several years' previous service with the Colours, and served at the Dardanelles, in Salonica, Egypt, Palestine and France.
He holds the 1915 Star, General Service and Victory Medals.
53, Chamberlain Road, Lower Edmonton. 14026.

CARPENTER, H. E., Gunner, R.F.A.
He enlisted in August, 1914, and during his service in France took part in the battles of Mons, Loos, Ypres, Armentieres and the Somme, where he was wounded. He was in hospital in France and England previous to being discharged in February, 1918, on medical grounds.
He holds the 1914 Star, General Service and Victory Medals.
23, Eldon Road, Lower Edmonton. 13058.

CARPENTER, W. H. T., Pte., 11th Battalion The Queen's (Royal West Surrey Regt.).
He joined in August, 1918, and served at Cologne for eleven months with the Army of Occupation as a qualified signaller. He was demobilised in April, 1920, and holds the General Service and Victory Medals.
158, Estcourt Road, Fulham. 16247.

CARPENTER, W. J., Pte., R.A.O.C.
He joined in October, 1916, went to France the following year, and was badly wounded at the battle of Ypres in September, 1917, and was subsequently invalided to England. Later he was employed on Home service duties, until demobilised in February, 1919.
He holds the General Service and Victory Medals.
79, Raynham Road, Upper Edmonton. 16950.

CARR, A. (Mrs.), Special War Worker.
This lady was engaged during the war in connection with the manufacture of equipment for the Admiralty at a West London works. Her duties were of a strenuous nature, and she did valuable work for the country.
57, Tasso Road, Fulham. 14629A.

CARR, C. C., Sergt., 26th Canadian Regiment.
He enlisted in August, 1914, and served in France and Belgium, and then with the Army of Occupation in Germany until his demobilisation in May, 1919. He holds the 1914 Star, the General Service and Victory Medals.
3, Eldon Road, Lower Edmonton. 13059/A.

CARR, D., Cpl., R.A.S.C. (M.T.).
He joined in 1916, and during his service on the Western Front was present at actions on the Somme, and in the Arras, Loos, Neuve Chapelle, Armentieres, Amiens, Bullecourt, Ypres, Vimy Ridge and Cambrai sectors, and at the final Advance of 1918.
He was demobilised in 1919, holding the General Service and Victory Medals.
57, Tasso Road, Fulham. 14629/B.

CARR, E. W., Special War Worker.
He was employed on work of great importance, forging shells at the Ponder's End Shell Works. This work was of a very arduous nature, and called for great skill and endurance, and was of vital national importance. He was fully exempt from military service.
78, Durban Road, Tottenham. X17949.

CARR, H. A., Pte., Oxford and Bucks L.I.
He rejoined from the Reserve in August, 1914, and served in France. He took part in the battles of Mons, Loos, Arras and Ypres, and was killed in action on the Somme in August, 1916.
He was entitled to the Mons Star, the General Service and Victory Medals.
3, Eldon Road, Lower Edmonton. 13059B.

CARR, J., Q.M.S., Scots Guards.
He joined in August, 1914, and during his service on the Western Front took part in the fighting at Arras, Cambrai and Ypres, and in the Retreat and Advance of 1918. Later he went with the Army of Occupation to Cologne.
He holds the General Service and Victory Medals, and was demobilised in March, 1919.
45, Barry Road, Stonebridge Park. 14935.

CARR, W. S., Gunner, R.F.A.
He enlisted in August, 1914, and served in France, where he was twice wounded. He took part in the battles of Mons, Ypres, Loos, Arras and the Somme. He served also in Mesopotamia and Russia, and was demobilised in May, 1919.
He holds the 1914 Star, General Service and Victory Medals.
3, Eldon Road, Lower Edmonton. 13059/C.

CARRINGTON, E. J., Pte., 11th Middlesex Regt.
He joined in September, 1915, and during his service on the Western Front took part in the battles of Arras, Loos, Ypres and the Somme, and was in hospital for over two months, suffering from the effects of gas.
He was demobilised in March 1919. He holds the 1915 Star, the General Service and Victory Medals.
5, St. James' Place, Tottenham. X18542.

CARSWELL, C. G., Sergt., R.A.V.C.
He joined in 1915, and served on the Western Front on important duties with the R.A.V.C. until demobilised in March, 1919, having gained his promotion for consistent good work.
He holds the 1915 Star, General Service and Victory Medals.
8, Lion Road, Lower Edmonton. 15200/B.

CARSWELL, W. J. D., Pte., Royal Sussex Regt.
Joining in February, 1915, he was engaged on training and Home Defence duties at various stations with his regiment.
He was demobilised in April, 1920.
8, Lion Road, Lower Edmonton. 15200/A.

CARTER, A. J., Pte., Middlesex Regiment.
He enlisted in 1914, served on the Western Front until 1916, when he was sent to Salonica, where he remained until demobilised in 1919. While abroad he took part in many engagements, including the battle of Neuve Chapelle, and was wounded.
He holds the 1914 Star, the General Service and Victory Medals. 39, Florence Road, Lower Edmonton. 16019A.

CARTER, A. R., Air Mechanic, Royal Air Force.
He joined in 1917, and served in France during 1918 and 1919, taking part in the last Retreat and Advance of 1918. He finally went to Germany with the Army of Occupation, where he remained until demobilised in 1919.
He holds the General Service and Victory Medals.
283, Chapter Road, Willesden Green. X17122/C.

CARTER, A. R. T., Sapper, Royal Engineers.
He joined in March, 1915, and was sent to France in November of the same year, being present during many engagements. He was discharged in January, 1917, being unfit for further service owing to shell-shock.
He holds the 1915 Star, General Service and Victory Medals.
45, Westminster Road, Edmonton. T12708/C.

CARTER, D. J., Pte., 3/9th Middlesex Regiment.
He joined in December, 1914, and for four years served on the Western Front. He was afterwards transferred to the Labour Corps.
In February, 1919, he was demobilised, and holds the 1915 Star, the General Service and Victory Medals.
2, West Block, Garnet Mansions, Garnet Road, Willesden. 15967B.

CARTER, E. (D.S.M.), Leading Stoker, R.N., H.M.S. "Bacchante."
He joined in August, 1914, and served with the Grand Fleet in the North Sea, and later in German East Africa.
He was awarded the D.S.M. for great gallantry, and was wounded four times. He holds the 1914 Star, General Service and Victory Medals, and was demobilised in April, 1919.
48, Shakespeare Avenue, Harlesden. 13616.

CARTER, E., Lce.-Cpl. (Signaller), K.R.R. Corps.
He joined in November, 1914, and served on the Western Front, being in action at Arras, Ypres and Cambrai. On two occasions he was severely gassed, and was also in hospital in France on account of injuries sustained.
He was demobilised in December, 1919, and holds the 1915 Star, General Service and Victory Medals.
35, Bramber Road, Fulham. 15713.

CARTER, E. H. A., Pte., The Queen's (Royal West Surrey Regiment).
He joined in September, 1914, and in the following year was sent to France, where he took part in several engagements. He was wounded at Loos in 1915.
He holds the 1915 Star, General Service and Victory Medals, and was demobilised in March, 1919.
45, Westminster Road, Edmonton. T12708/B.

CARTER, F., Pte., Machine Gun Corps.
He joined in 1915, and served on the Western Front, being in action at the battles of the Somme, Ypres, Loos, Arras and St. Quentin. During this time he was gassed twice.
He was demobilised in June, 1919, and holds the 1915 Star, the General Service and Victory Medals.
10, Fane Place, W.14 15696.

CARTER, F. W., 1st Air Mechanic, R.A.F.
He joined in August, 1916, and was sent to France the same year, where he served with the R.A.F. until after the Armistice.
He was demobilised in April, 1919, and holds the General Service and Victory Medals.
45, Westminster Road, Edmonton. T12708/A.

CARTER, G., Gunner, Royal Field Artillery.
He joined in March, 1915, and served for two years with the R.F.A. in Salonica.
He was demobilised in April, 1919, and holds the General Service and Victory Medals.
24, Ascot Road, Edmonton. T15176.

CARTER, G. C., Pte., 16th Middlesex Regiment.
He joined in June, 1917, and after taking part in several engagements, he was killed at Messines Ridge in 1918, whilst carrying wounded from the field.
He had previously served in the Volunteers, and was entitled to the General Service and Victory Medals.
91a, Ormiston Road, Shepherd's Bush. 11922.

CARTER, G. E., Cpl., Royal Air Force.
During his service, which extended from July, 1915, until March, 1919, he was employed on important clerical duties with the R.A.F. at various stations.
He holds the General Service Medal.
8, Cornwall Road, Edmonton. 15620.

CARTER, G. W., Pte., Machine Gun Corps.
He was serving at the outbreak of war, and in 1915 went to the Dardanelles, where he was wounded. Later, on the Western Front, he was in action during the Retreat and Advance of 1918, at Ypres, on the Somme, and at Arras.
He holds the 1915 Star, General Service and Victory Medals, and was demobilised in May, 1919.
283, Chapter Road, Willesden Green. X17122/A.

CARTER, H., Gunner, Royal Field Artillery.
He joined in January, 1917, at the age of 18, and the same year saw active service in France, where he remained until 1918, when he was transferred to the Army of Occupation on the Rhine.
He was demobilised in May, 1919. He holds the General Service and Victory Medals.
47, Chester Road, Lower Edmonton. 12709.

CARTER, J., Cpl., 2nd The Queen's (Royal West Surrey Regiment).
He joined in August, 1914, and during his service on the Western Front was severely wounded. He was discharged in January, 1916, on medical grounds, and holds the 1915 Star, General Service and Victory Medals.
13, Welford Terrace, Fulham. X18058.

CARTER, J. J., Driver, R.A.S.C.
He joined in 1916, and served on the Western Front, taking part in many engagements. Later he went with the Army of Occupation to Germany, and in January, 1920, was demobilised, holding the General Service and Victory Medals.
39, Florence Road, Lower Edmonton. 16019B.

CARTER, T. G., Pte., 1st Royal West Kent Regt.
He joined in December, 1917, was sent to France in June, 1918, and took part in the final Advance of that year.
He holds the General Service and Victory Medals.
81, Shakespeare Avenue, Harlesden. 13702/A.

CARTER, J. S., Pte., 8th Devonshire Regiment.
He joined in April, 1915, and saw service on the Western Front, where he was killed in action on July 1st, 1916.
He was entitled to the General Service and Victory Medals.
30, Aintree Street, Fulham. X18182.

CARTER, W. C., Cpl., R.A.F.
He joined in May, 1915, was attached to the Dover Patrol until May, 1916, and afterwards served with the Grand Fleet, and was present at the surrender of the German Fleet at Scapa Flow.
He holds the General Service and Victory Medals, and was demobilised in March, 1919.
50, Glynfield Road, Harlesden. 14738.

CARTER, W. E., Pte., Royal Warwickshire Regt.
He enlisted in 1914, and in 1916 was sent to France, where he took part in many engagements. He died in November, 1917, of wounds received in action, and was buried at Rouen.
He was entitled to the General Service and Victory Medals.
283, Chapter Road, Willesden Green. X17122/B.

CARTER, W. W., Pte., Queen's Own Oxfordshire Hussars.
He joined in October, 1915, was sent to France in the following March—where he took part in many engagements—and thence to Egypt, where he also saw much service.
He was demobilised in April, 1919, holding the General Service and Victory Medals.
81, Shakespeare Avenue, Harlesden. 13702/B.

CARY, S. C., Lce.-Cpl., 8th London Regt.
He joined in April, 1917, and was sent to France the following year, where he took part in several engagements, and was killed in action on August 26th, 1918, at Delville Wood.
He was entitled to the General Service and Victory Medals.
88, Minet Avenue, Harlesden. 13641.

CASE, A., Pte., 4th Middlesex Regiment.
He joined in August, 1914, and served on the Western Front, taking part in the battles of Arras, the Somme, Cambrai, Ypres and other engagements. While in action he was killed, on April 24th, 1917.
He was entitled to the General Service and Victory Medals.
6, Litchfield Gardens, Willesden Green. X17435.

CASELY, W., Cpl., 18th Rifle Brigade.
He joined in September, 1914, and was later sent to India, where he served at various stations.
He was demobilised in December, 1919, and holds the 1915 Star, General Service and Victory Medals.
80, Winchester Road, Lower Edmonton. T14759.

CASH, F., Sergt., Irish Guards.
He joined in 1915, and during his service on the Western Front took part in the battles of Loos, Ypres, Armentieres and Neuve Chapelle, where he was severely wounded. After being six months in hospital in France, he was invalided home, and died in Clapham Hospital in November, 1919.
He was entitled to the 1914-15 Star, General Service and Victory Medals
63, Guinness's Buildings, Hammersmith. X17700A.

CASSELDEN, F., Gunner, R.M.A.
He joined in January, 1915, and during his service on the Western Front took part in the battles of Ypres, Messines and the Somme.
He was demobilised in April, 1919, and holds the 1915 Star, General Service and Victory Medals.
247a, Kilburn Lane, N.W.10 X18740.

CASSELL, H., Driver, Royal Field Artillery.
He joined immediately on the outbreak of war, and was later sent to the Eastern Front. He served in Egypt, Salonica and Bulgaria, and was in the Serbian Retreat.
He was demobilised in April, 1919, and holds the 1914-15 Star, General Service and Victory Medals.
54, Guinness's Buildings, Hammersmith. X17927.

CASTLE, E., Sergt., 18th Middlesex Regiment.
He enlisted in March, 1915, and the same year was sent to the Western Front, where he took part in several engagements, including those at the Somme, Arras, Vimy Ridge and Loos.
He holds the 1915 Star, General Service and Victory Medals, and was demobilised in February, 1919.
7, Tasso Road, Fulham. 14636A.

CASTLE, G., Pte., R.A.V.C.
He joined in April, 1915, and during his service in France took part in the fighting at Loos, Arras, the Somme and Cambrai, and as a result of having been badly gassed, he was invalided home, and was ultimately discharged as unfit for further service on March 4th, 1919.
He holds the 1915 Star, the General Service and Victory Medals. 14, Laundry Road, Fulham. 15338.

CASTLE, G. E., Cpl., Middlesex Regiment.
He enlisted in September, 1914, served in France, and was in action on the Somme, at Ypres, and at Cambrai. He was wounded and invalided home, and on October 15th, 1918, was discharged medically unfit for further service.
He holds the General Service and Victory Medals.
26, Vallier Road, College Park, Willesden. X17676.

CASTLE, J. E., 1st-Class Gunner, R.M.A.
He joined in 1914, and on H.M.S. " Barham " served in the North Sea, took part in the battle of Jutland, and was present at the surrender of the German Fleet at Scapa Flow.
He holds the 1914-15 Star, General Service and Victory Medals.
7, Tasso Road, Fulham. 14636C.

CASTLE, T. J., Pte., Highland Light Infantry.
He joined in 1915, and later was sent to the Western Front, where he took part in many engagements, and was killed in action near Arras on July 7th, 1918. He is buried in the military cemetery at Bienvillers, and was entitled to the General Service and Victory Medals.
7, Tasso Road, Fulham. 14636B.

CASWELL, H., Pte., Royal Army Service Corps.
He joined in August, 1915, and later was sent to the Western Front, where he was twice wounded in action, and as a result was discharged in December, 1918.
He holds the General Service and Victory Medals.
53, Lintaine Grove, Fulham. 16829.

CASWELL, W. G., Lce.-Cpl., East Surrey Regt.
He joined in December, 1915, and after completing his training was sent to the Eastern Front. He there contracted malaria, and was eventually discharged medically unfit in January, 1918.
He holds the General Service and Victory Medals.
7, Kilmaine Road, Fulham. TX18859/A.

CATER, J. W., Gunner, Royal Field Artillery.
He was mobilised in August, 1914, and afterwards went to the Western Front, where he took part in many engagements, and was badly gassed.
He was demobilised in 1919, having served for sixteen years, and holds the General Service and Victory Medals.
21, Hartopp Avenue, Fulham. X17746.

CATER, W., Pte., Royal Sussex Regiment.
He joined in August, 1914, and was sent to France, where, after taking part in many battles, he was killed in action in November, 1917.
He was entitled to the 1914-15 Star, General Service and Victory Medals.
16, Ranelagh Road, Harlesden. 12746/A.

CATES, W. S., Pte., 3rd London Regiment.
He was in the Territorials before the war, was mobilised on August 4th, 1914, went to Egypt in the following year, and served there until 1917, when he was sent to the Western Front. He took part in many engagements, remaining in France until the cessation of hostilities.
He holds the 1915 Star, General Service and Victory Medals.
18, St. Margaret's Road, Kensal Rise. X17827.

CATLIN, A. S., Pte., 1/4th Lincolnshire Regt.
He joined at the outbreak of war in August, 1914, and the same year was sent to the Western Front, where he took part in several engagements, and was killed in action at St. Julien on July 31st, 1917. He was buried in the military cemetery near Vermelles, and was entitled to the 1914-15 Star, General Service and Victory Medals.
60, Carlyle Avenue, Harlesden. 14415.

CATTERMOLE, W. G., Gunner, Australian Field Artillery.
He joined in February, 1916, and was later drafted to the Western Front, where he took part in many engagements. He holds the General Service and Victory Medals, and was demobilised in 1919.
46, Town Road, Edmonton. 13569B.

CATTERMOLE, W. T., Sapper, R.E.
He joined in June, 1916, and the same year was sent to the Western Front, where he was specially employed on field telephones. Owing to his knowledge of the German language he was later employed as interpreter for the prisoners of war.
He holds the General Service and Victory Medals.
30, Waldo Road, Willesden. X17568.

CAUDERY, G. H., Pte., 3rd Middlesex Regt.
He enlisted in September, 1914, and the following year was
sent to France, where he took part in several engagements,
and was killed in action at Loos on September 3rd, 1915.
He was entitled to the 1915 Star, General Service and Victory
Medals.
31, Rucklidge Avenue, Harlesden.   12735.

**CAUDERY, N. (Miss), (now Mrs. STAPLES),
Special War Worker.**
This lady was employed from September, 1915, until August,
1919, as chief examiner of small arms ammunition in the
national arms department at Park Royal munition factory,
where she did excellent work for which she was commended.
31, Rucklidge Avenue, Harlesden.   T12756A.

CAUDLE, C., Lce.-Cpl., Royal Fusiliers.
He was mobilised in August, 1914, and later sent to the
Western Front, where he served during the whole of the war.
He was demobilised in March, 1919, but re-enlisted shortly
afterwards, and is still serving, having previously completed
15 years in the Army.
He holds the 1914-15 Star, the General Service and Victory
Medals.
36, Hartopp Avenue, Fulham.   X17741A.

CAULDWELL, F., Pte., 11th Hampshire Regt.
He enlisted in September, 1914, and received his training at
Winchester. He was later sent to Ireland, but was not
successful in being transferred to the war zone, and was
finally discharged in 1915 on medical grounds.
13, Butterswick Cottages, Great Church Lane, Hammersmith.   X19131.

CAVELL, C. B., Rifleman, King's Royal Rifles.
He joined in 1915, and during his service in France—which
lasted until the cessation of hostilities—he took part in many
engagements, and was badly gassed.
He holds the 1914-15 Star, General Service and Victory
Medals, and was demobilised in 1920.
40, Furness Road, Harlesden.   13364/C.

CAVELL, S. H., Mechanic, R.A.F. (late R.N.A.S.).
He joined in 1915, and during his service in France—where
he was engaged in preparing machines for flight—he
was badly gassed, and suffered from shock.
He holds the 1914-15 Star, General Service and Victory
Medals, and was demobilised in 1919.
40, Furness Road, Harlesden.   13364/B.

CAVILL, C. B., Pte., 8th Royal Irish Regiment.
He joined in 1916, and in the same year was sent to France,
where he took part in the battles of Ypres, Armentieres,
Messines and Arras, in the Retreat and Advance of 1918,
and was among the first to enter Lille after its capture by
the British. He also served in Egypt, Syria and Palestine
before being demobilised in March, 1920, and holds the
General Service and Victory Medals.
110, Shakespeare Avenue, Harlesden.   13901.

CESSARE, A., Special War Worker.
During the war he was engaged on special work on the construction of aeroplanes, having been rejected as medically
unfit for military service. His work was of the greatest
importance.
26, Disraeli Road, Harlesden.   14392A.

CESSARE, J. (Mrs.), Special War Worker.
During the war this lady was engaged on important work in
connection with the construction of aeroplanes at a London
factory.
26, Disraeli Road, Harlesden.   14392/C.

CESSARE, W. (Miss), Special War Worker.
This lady was employed at the Rotax Works for three years
during the war on important work in the construction of
aeroplanes.
26, Disraeli Road, Harlesden.   14392/B.

CHALK, A., Pte., 8th Duke of Cornwall's L.I.
Joining in September, 1914, he served the whole of his time
on the French Front, except for eighteen months, when he was
in Salonica. He took part in many engagements, and was
wounded.
He was discharged on Jan. 22nd, 1918, and holds the 1914-15
Star and the General Service and Victory Medals.
45, Chaldon Road, Fulham.   X17651/A.

CHALK, E. T. (M.S.M.), Sergt., R.G.A.
He joined in August, 1914, and saw service in France, Palestine and Italy. He took part in many engagements, including those of Vimy Ridge, Cambrai, Ypres, Arras, Armentieres
and the final Advance, and was awarded the Meritorious
Service Medal for bravery and good work in the field. He
also holds the General Service and Victory Medals, and was
demobilised in May, 1919.
19, Tasso Road, Fulham.   14814.

CHALK, E. V. (Miss), Special War Worker.
During the war this lady was engaged in making and preparing parts for aeroplanes at the Glendower Aircraft Co., Ltd.,
South Kensington. Her work was of great value.
28, Chesson Road, W. Kensington.   X17169.

CHALK, F. E., Air Mechanic, Royal Air Force.
He joined in 1916, and until his demobilisation in 1919 did
duty at various stations with the R.A.F. He was medically
unfit for overseas duty, and holds the General Service Medal.
28, Chesson Road, W. Kensington.   X17165.

CHALK, G. A., Rifleman, King's Royal Rifles.
He joined in 1917, and in 1918 served with the Army of
Occupation in Germany until his demobilisation in 1920.
13, Winchester Road, Lower Edmonton.   14678B.

CHALK, G. H., Lce.-Cpl., Royal Engineers.
He joined in February, 1917, and served on important duties
in the shipyard at Sandwich, and other stations. He was
demobilised in 1919.
66, Hawthorn Road, Edmonton.   X17048/A.

CHALK, H. W., Pte., R.A.M.C.
Joining in 1917, he served overseas, and was at No. 8 Station-
ary Hospital in France, on important medical duties.
He was demobilised in 1919, and holds the General Service
and Victory Medals.
66, Hawthorn Road, Edmonton.   X17048/B.

CHALK, J. A., Guardsman, Grenadier Guards.
He joined in April, 1915, and served at various stations until
his demobilisation in 1919. Due to being unfit, he was not
successful in being posted overseas.
28, Chesson Road, W. Kensington.   X17166.

CHALK, N., Gunner, 26th Siege Battery, R.G.A.
He joined in July, 1916, and served on the Western Front,
where he took part in many important engagements, prior
to his demobilisation in December, 1918.
He holds the General Service and Victory Medals.
45, Chaldon Road, Fulham.   X17651/B.

CHALK, T. A., Shoeing smith, R.A.V.C.
He joined in 1914, and served on the Western Front and in
Italy, on important duties with the R.A.V.C.
He was demobilised in 1919, and holds the General Service
and Victory Medals.
13, Winchester Road, Lower Edmonton.   14678A.

CHALK, W., Pte., Lancashire Fusiliers.
He joined in August, 1914, and went to France, and later to
Salonica, where he served for three years. Afterwards, in
July, 1918, he again saw service in France, where he remained
until demobilised in February, 1919.
He holds the 1914 Star, the General Service and Victory
Medals.
161, Estcourt Road, Fulham.   16652.

CHALK, W. G., Cpl., Royal Engineers.
He joined in August, 1915, and went to France the same year.
He was engaged chiefly on bridge construction at Amiens,
and work in connection with lock gates, often coming under
heavy enemy shell-fire.
He holds the 1915 Star, General Service and Victory
Medals, and was demobilised in May, 1919.
3, May Street, W.14.   15700.

CHALKLEY, P. G., Pte., East Lancashire Regt.
He joined in 1917, and served on the Western Front, taking
part in the battles of the Somme and Ypres
He was demobilised in February, 1919, and holds the General
Service and Victory Medals.
90, Sheldon Road, Edmonton.   X17462.

CHAMBERLAIN, A., Pte., Suffolk Regiment.
He enlisted in September, 1915, and served four years in
France. He was a Lewis gunner, and was twice wounded,
and gassed.
He was discharged on March 3rd, 1919, and holds the 1915
Star, the General Service and Victory Medals.
36, Star Road, W.14.   T17062.

CHAMBERLAIN, C., Sapper, Royal Engineers.
He joined in 1915, and was sent to France, where he remained
for six months, being in action on the Somme. He then
served in Salonica, Egypt and Palestine, where he took part
in the engagements at Jerusalem, Beersheba, Jericho and
Jaffa, with General Allenby's forces.
He was demobilised in 1919, holding the General Service and
Victory Medals.
100, Archel Road, W. Kensington.   16672.

CHAMBERLAIN, H., Special War Worker.
He attempted to enlist, but was rejected on medical grounds,
and in consequence took up war work. He was employed in
the manufacture of shells for three years, only giving up this
employment when the Armistice was signed.
6, Linton Road, Edmonton, N.18   T.X.17281.

CHAMBERLIN, T. A., Bombardier, R.G.A.

He joined in 1915, and served for two years on the Western Front, taking part in the battles of the Somme, Arras and Messines Ridge. He was wounded in the latter engagement, and was discharged in November, 1917.

He holds the 1915 Star, the General Service and Victory Medals.

31a, Drayton Road, Harlesden. 14992.

CHAMBERS, E. A., Driver, R.E.

He joined in May, 1915, served for three and a half years in Mesopotamia, and was wounded.

On September 19th, 1919, he was demobilised, holding the 1915 Star, General Service and Victory Medals.

21, Ascot Road, Edmonton. 15172.

CHAMBERS, G. V., Sergt., Rifle Brigade.

He was recalled from the Army Reserve on the day of the declaration of war, and was sent immediately to the Western Front. He took part at Mons, and was in action at Loos, Ypres, Amiens, Albert and Arras. He was severely wounded at Arras, and again at Ploegsteert Wood in March, 1917.

He was discharged in October, 1917, holding the Mons Star, General Service, and Victory Medals.

33, Hazel Road, Willesden, N.W.10 X18164/A.

CHAMBERS, J. A., Cpl., R.A.V.C.

He enlisted in 1915, and served for four years on the Western Front, at Le Havre and elsewhere, on veterinary duties.

He was demobilised in March, 1919, holding the 1915 Star, General Service and Victory Medals.

9, Winchelsea Road, Harlesden. 13713/B.

CHAMBERS, S. (Mrs.), Special War Worker.

This lady was employed during the war in the canteen at the National Filling Factory, Park Royal; later as a packer of fuses at Perivale Ammunition Works, and also as a policewoman at the filling factory. Her work was highly commended.

9, Winchelsea Road, Harlesden. 13713/A.

CHAMBERS, T. W., Gunner, R.G.A. (153rd Siege Battery).

He joined in November, 1915, was sent to France in the following January, and took part in various engagements, including the battles of Ypres and Arras.

He was demobilised in April, 1919, and holds the General Service and Victory Medals.

57, Denbigh Road, Willesden. 15091/B.

CHAMBERS, V. S. (Miss), Special War Worker.

This lady was employed at Woolwich Arsenal on the examination of shells from March, 1918, until January, 1919. Her work was of an important nature, and she was commended for her services.

57, Denbigh Road, Willesden. 15091/A.

CHAMBERS, W. A., Air Mechanic, R.A.F.

He joined in March, 1916, and being medically unfit for service overseas, did duty with the R.A.F. in England. He was engaged as storekeeper during his three years in the Air Force, and was demobilised in May, 1919, holding the General Service Medal.

33, Hazel Road, Willesden. X18164/B.

CHAMP, A. H. W., Stoker Petty Officer, R.N., H.M.S. "Renown."

He joined the Navy in April, 1893, and was serving at the outbreak of war. He served with the Grand Fleet, and acted as P.O. Stoker. He was on H.M.S. "Renown" in the North Sea, and also at Scapa Flow.

He was discharged in February, 1919, and holds the Long Service, 1914 Star, General Service and Victory Medals.

27, Napier Road, College Park, N.W. X17521.

CHAMPION, A. D. (M.M.), Pte., Royal Suffolk R.

He joined in March, 1915, served on the Western Front, taking part in the battle of Arras and other engagements, and was awarded the Military Medal for great gallantry and devotion to duty in the field. On March 20th, 1917, he was killed in action.

He was also entitled to the General Service and Victory Medals.

5, Mayo Road, Willesden. 15126.

CHAMPION, W. G., Pte., R.A.V.C.

He joined on May 31st, 1917, and served on the Western Front from that year until February, 1919, when he contracted pneumonia and died.

He was entitled to the General Service and Victory Medals.

84, Brownlow Road, Harlesden. 14731.

CHAMPNEY, G. E., Chief Petty Officer, R.N.

He joined in 1914, and served on H.M.S. "Renown" in the North Sea, and was present at the engagement off Heligoland. He was also engaged on "decoy" work at Skagger Rack.

He holds the 1914 Star, General Service and Victory Medals, and was demobilised in 1919.

7, Ilex Road, Willesden. 16132.

CHAMPNEY, R. W. (sen.), Sapper, R.E.

Joining in 1914, he saw service in France with the Royal Engineers, and was twice wounded. As a result of his service his health is now impaired.

He holds the 1914-15 Star, the General Service and Victory Medals, and was demobilised in 1919.

7, Ilex Road, Willesden. 16098/A

CHAMPNEY, R. W. (jun.), Gunner, R.F.A.

He joined in 1914, and during his service on the Western Front took part in many important engagements, including those of Mons, Arras, Loos, Verdun, Ypres, Cambrai and Grandcourt. He was twice wounded and gassed.

He holds the 1914-15 Star, the General Service and Victory Medals, and was demobilised in 1919.

7, Ilex Road, Willesden. 16098B.

CHANDLER, A. B., Pte., R.A.S.C.

He joined in April, 1915, went to France in the same year, and was engaged in the transportation of ammunition and food to the Western Front.

He holds the 1915 Star, the General Service and Victory Medals, and was demobilised in February, 1919.

4, Helton Road, W.6 15170.

CHANDLER, F. A., Pte., 4th Middlesex Regt.

He joined in 1912, and re-enlisted in 1914, going to the Western Front the same year. He took part in many engagements, including the retreat from Mons, the battles of Ypres, Loos, Vimy Ridge and the Somme. He was wounded twice, and taken prisoner in March, 1918, and returned to England in December of that year.

He holds the Mons Star, General Service and Victory Medals, and was demobilised in March, 1919.

29, Holly Lane, Willesden. 15528/C.

CHANDLER, F. J., Rifleman, King's Royal Rifles.

He joined in 1916, served on the Western Front, and was killed in action near Bapaume on August 21st, 1918.

He was entitled to the General Service and Victory Medals.

10, Dieppe Street, West Kensington. 16254/B.

CHANDLER, G. A., Bombardier, R.F.A.

He joined in January, 1915, and was sent to the Western Front in 1916, when he was in action at the battles of the Somme and Ypres. Later he was sent to the Eastern Front, and fought at Salonica. He contracted malaria, and died from the effects after being demobilised.

He was entitled to the General Service and Victory Medals.

4, Ravensworth Road, Kensal Rise. X17622/A.

CHANDLER, G. A., Pte., Royal Welsh Fusiliers

He joined in June, 1916, and served at Salonica for three years, during which period he took part in several engagements, and afterwards went to Constantinople.

He was demobilised in October, 1919, and holds the General Service and Victory Medals.

97, Kimberley Road, Edmonton. 16804.

CHANDLER, H. W., 1st A.B., Royal Navy.

He was serving at the outbreak of hostilites, and saw service on H.M.S. "Black Prince" in the North Sea and the Mediterranean. He took part in several engagements, and was killed in action at the battle of Jutland on May 31st, 1916.

He was entitled to the 1914 Star, General Service and Victory Medals.

29, Holly Lane, Willesden. 15528/A.

CHANDLER, J. G., Guardsman, 1st Grenadier Guards.

He joined in October, 1916, and served on the Western Front in 1917-18. He was present at the battles of the Somme and Ypres, and at other engagements. During his service he was wounded twice.

After a long period of hospital treatment he was demobilised in November, 1919, holding the General Service and Victory Medals. He was also mentioned in despatches for gallant conduct.

16, Charlton Road, Harlesden, N.W.10 13106.

CHANDLER, J. J., Gunner, R.F.A.

He enlisted in October, 1914, was sent to France in the following July, and took part in the offensive of July, 1916, the battles of Ypres, Passchendaele, the Somme and Cambrai, and the last Retreat and Advance of 1918.

He was demobilised in January, 1919, holding the 1914-15 Star, the General Service and Victory Medals.

30, Hiley Road, Willesden. X18424.

CHANDLER, T., Gunner, R.F.A.

He joined in July, 1915, and served on the Western and Italian Fronts. In France he took part in the battles of the Somme, Cambrai, St. Quentin, Ypres and Armentières.

He went to Italy in 1917, and in March, 1918, returned to France.

During his service he was wounded, and in February, 1919, was demobilised, holding the General Service and Victory Medals.

20, Kenmont Gardens, Willesden. X17575.

CHANDLER, T., Cpl., 1/9th Middlesex Regiment.

He joined in September, 1914, and served in Mesopotamia and India. He took part in many engagements in Mesopotamia, including the battle of Mosul. In India he served on garrison duty.

He was demobilised in April, 1919, holding the 1914–15 Star, General Service and Victory Medals.

56, Carlyle Avenue, Harlesden.   14456.

CHANDLER, W.A., R.F.C. and R.A.F.

Joining in 1917, he went to the Italian Front in the same year, being attached to a bombing squadron at Toranto. He did much flying during his service, and took part in the flight from Kenley (Surrey) to Paris during the Peace Conference.

He holds the General Service and Victory Medals.

29, Holly Lane, Willesden.   15528/B.

CHANDLER, W. L., Sapper, Royal Engineers.

He joined on February 7, 1916, and during his service on the Western Front took part in the battles of Ypres, Arras, Cambrai and Vimy Ridge ; was wounded and gassed, and was for a time attached to the R.O.D.

He holds the General Service and Victory Medals, and was demobilised on May 6, 1919.

45, Melville Road, Willesden.   15651A.

CHANNELL, W. H., Telegraphist, R.N.

He joined the Navy in 1916, and served for four years. He was employed as a telegraphist and served in the following ships : H.M.S. " Intrepid," " Ganges," " Powerful," " Pembroke," " Leviathan," " Highflyer," " Iris," " Cricket " and " Fox."

He was demobilised in 1920, and holds the General Service and Victory Medals.

13, Durban Road, Tottenham, N.   X18099.

CHANNER, E. (Miss), Special War Worker.

This lady was engaged for a long period during the war as a checker of fuses at Harling Munition Factory. Her work was of a very important and skilful nature.

30, Crefeld Road, W.6   14498/C.

CHANNER, H., Cpl., R.A.V.C.

He joined in 1916, went to France the same year, and was principally engaged in tending sick and wounded horses. During his service he suffered from shell-shock. He holds the General Service and Victory Medals, and was demobilised in March, 1919.

30, Crefeld Road, Fulham.   14498/B.

CHANNER, H., Gunner, R.F.A.

He joined in September, 1914, went to France in 1916, and took part in many battles, including the final Advance in 1918. He holds the General Service and Victory Medals, and was demobilised in 1919.

30, Crefeld Road, W.6   14498/A.

CHANNING, H. C., Gunner, R.G.A.

He was serving at a China station when war was declared, and in November, 1914, was sent to France, where he took part in the battles of Ypres, Vimy Ridge, Loos, Arras, Cambrai and the Somme. He was wounded, and was later transferred to the R.A.F.

He holds the 1914 Star, General Service and Victory Medals.

145, Rucklidge Avenue, Harlesden.   13160.

CHAPLIN, J., Acting Cpl., 2nd Middlesex Regt.

He was mobilised in August, 1914, and served at home for a short period. He was sent to France in December, 1914, and was killed in action at Neuve Chapelle on March 14th, 1915. He was entitled to the 1914 Star and the General Service and Victory Medals.

13, Charles Street, White Hart Lane, Tottenham, N.   X18294.

CHAPLIN, R., Special War Worker.

He was engaged on important work in connection with the construction of munition factories at Salisbury and elsewhere, and was retained on this duty during the whole period of the war.

25, Steele Road, Harlesden.   14374/B.

CHAPLIN, W. J. (Miss), Special War Worker.

This lady was employed at Messrs. Fellows' Magneto Co. making magnetos for aircraft use, for four years. Her work required special skill, and was of an arduous nature.

25, Steele Road, Harlesden.   14374A.

CHAPMAN, A. H., Pte., R.A.M.C.

He enlisted in August, 1914, was sent to France in the same year, and was reported missing after the battle of Mons. He was entitled to the 1914 Star, General Service and Victory Medals.

25, Osborne Road, Willesden.   XT17403A.

CHAPMAN, C., Pte., 2nd Royal Fusiliers.

He joined in November, 1915, and during his service on the Western Front fought in many battles, including Bullecourt, Ypres and the Somme. He was twice wounded.

He was demobilised in September, 1919, holding the General Service and Victory Medals.

83, Orbain Road, Fulham.   X18069.

CHAPMAN, C. W., Pte., R.A.S.C. (M.T.).

He joined in August, 1914, and whilst serving on the Western Front, took part in the engagements on the Somme, at Arras, Neuve Chapelle, Lille, Bullecourt, Vimy Ridge, Amiens, Ypres, Armentieres and Loos, and was twice wounded during the last Advance of 1918.

He holds the 1914 Star, the General Service and Victory Medals, and was demobilised in 1919.

114, Bronsart Road, Fulham.   X19005.

CHAPMAN, E., Drummer, Royal Fusiliers.

He enlisted in August, 1914, served on the Western Front, and took part in the battles of Mons, Neuve Chapelle, the Somme and Amiens. He was wounded at Mons, and again at Amiens. He served also at the Dardanelles, and was discharged in February, 1919, holding the 1914 Star, the Genera Service and Victory Medals.

10, Findon Road, Lower Edmonton.   12673.

CHAPMAN, F., Pte., R.M.L.I.

He enlisted in 1914, and during that year served in East Africa and Zanzibar. During the following two years he was on home duties, and then served in various waters on board escort ships.

He was demobilised in 1919, holding the 1914 Star, General Service and Victory Medals.

397, High Road, Tottenham.   16741.

CHAPMAN, F. E., Special Constable, Metropolitan Special Constabulary.

Throughout the war this gentleman served as a special constable in the Metropolitan Special Constabulary, rendering valuable services. He was on duty in all air raids and also did guard duty at Fulham.

He was awarded the Long Service Medal.

136, Bronsart Road, Fulham, S.W.6   X19011.

CHAPMAN, G. (M.M.), Sergt., R.F.A.

He enlisted in August, 1914, served in France, and took part in the battles of the Somme, Ypres and Arras.

He was awarded the Military Medal for devotion to duty and conspicuous gallantry, and holds also the 1914 Star, General Service and Victory Medals. He was demobilised in April, 1919.

16, Chapel Street, Hammersmith.   12501/A.

CHAPMAN, G. E., Lce.-Cpl., Royal Engineers.

He joined in August, 1914, and served during 1915–18 on the Western Front, taking part in the battles of Neuve Chapelle, the Somme, Ypres and many other engagements. In 1918 he was sent to German East Africa, and in January, 1919, was demobilised.

He holds the 1915 Star, the General Service and Victory Medals.

28, Franklyn Road, Willesden.   16021–16022A.

CHAPMAN, G. F., Cpl., R.A.S.C. (M.T.).

He joined on April 27th, 1917, and went to France the following year, serving there with a Guards' Regimental M.T. section.

He was demobilised in November, 1919, and holds the General Service and Victory Medals.

31, Guilsborough Road, Willesden.   15240.

CHAPMAN, G. H., Sergt., R.F.A.

He joined in August, 1914, and during his service on the Western Front took part in many battles, including those of Mons, Arras, the Somme, Loos, Amiens, Armentieres, Neuve Chapelle, Bullecourt, and the last Advance.

He holds the Mons Star, General Service and Victory Medals.

114, Bronsart Road, Fulham.   X19004.

CHAPMAN, H., Cpl., Royal Field Artillery.

He joined in November, 1914, went to France the following year, and was wounded during the battle of Armentieres in 1917. Later he served in Germany with the Army of Occupation until he was demobilised in June, 1919.

He holds the 1914–15 Star, General Service and Victory Medals.

102, Montague Road, Lower Edmonton.   16881.

CHAPMAN, J. (M.M.), Pte., Royal Welsh Fusiliers.

He joined in 1915, went to France in the following year, and served as a stretcher-bearer in several engagements, including Ypres. On June 8, 1918, he was killed in action.

He had been awarded the Military Medal for conspicuous gallantry in the field, and was entitled in addition to the General Service and Victory Medals.

5, Shotley Street, Fulham.   14800A.

CHAPMAN, J., Pte., Royal Fusiliers.
During his service, which lasted from April, 1915, to January, 1919, he took part in the fighting on various sectors of the Western Front, and was wounded.
He holds the General Service and Victory Medals.
16, Chapel Street, Hammersmith. 12501 /B.

CHAPMAN, R. E., Cpl., R.A.O.C.
He joined in November, 1915, served in Salonica until 1919, and took part in many engagements whilst abroad.
He was demobilised in December, 1919, holding the 1914-15 Star, General Service and Victory Medals.
25, Osborne Road, Willesden. XT17403/B.

CHAPMAN, S. J., Pte., Royal Army Service Corps.
He enlisted in November, 1915, and served for four years in France, where he took part in many important engagements.
He was demobilised in April, 1919, and holds the 1915 Star, General Service and Victory Medals.
25, Osborne Road, Willesden, N.W. X17404.

CHAPMAN, S. J., Pte., Royal Army Service Corps.
He joined in October, 1915, and in the same month was sent to France, where he served on the Somme with the Indian Veterinary Corps, being twice wounded.
He was demobilised in April, 1919, and holds the 1915 Star, General Service and Victory Medals.
25, Osborne Road, Willesden Green. XT17403C.

CHAPMAN, W. G., Pte., 10th Lincoln Regiment.
He joined in November, 1916, and was sent to the Western Front, where he took part in several engagements, and was wounded and taken prisoner whilst in action on the Somme. In September, 1918, he was released, and discharged in October of the same year.
He holds the General Service and Victory Medals.
55, Greyhound Road, Willesden. X17607.

CHAPMAN, W. F., Sapper, Royal Engineers.
He joined the Army in May, 1918, but while taking a gas course during his training was unfortunately badly poisoned. In consequence he was invalided out of the Service in May, 1919.
28, Franklyn Road, Willesden. 16021-16022B.

CHAPPELL, E. G., Pte., The Queen's (Royal West Surrey Regiment).
He joined in August, 1915, and during his service in Mesopotamia and Egypt saw much of the heavy fighting, and was in hospital on several occasions for medical treatment.
He holds the 1915 Star, General Service and Victory Medals, and was demobilised in April, 1919.
22, Lintaine Grove, Fulham. X17080.

CHAPPELL, W. E., Pte., 3rd King's (Liverpool R.).
He joined in December, 1916, and saw service in the Balkans, on the Struma Front, and in Bulgaria and Turkey. He was wounded, and suffered from malaria.
He holds the General Service and Victory Medals, and was demobilised in July, 1919.
13, Everington Street, Fulham. 13975/A.

CHAPPLE, A. E., Pte., The Buffs (East Kent R.).
He enlisted in August, 1914, served for two months on the Western Front, and was killed in action on October 26, 1914, during the retreat from Mons.
He was entitled to the 1914 Star, General Service and Victory Medals.
46, Winchelsea Road, Harlesden. 13487/B.

CHARKER, T., Pte., 2nd East Surrey Regiment.
He joined in 1915, and served on the Western Front from the following year until 1918, taking part in various engagements. He was then sent with the Army of Occupation to Germany.
He holds the General Service and Victory Medals.
22, Byam Street, Fulham. 16180A.

CHARLETT, J. T., Pte., 8th Essex Regiment.
He joined in October, 1916, and was retained for duty at various stations until his demobilisation in February, 1919.
7, Cobbold Road, Willesden. 16057/B.

CHARLTON, A. J., Lce.-Cpl., Royal Engineers.
He joined in August, 1915, served on the Western Front from the following March until discharged in February, 1918. He took part in the fighting at Ploegsteert Wood and Vimy Ridge, and was gassed in March, 1917.
He holds the General Service and Victory Medals.
3, Marker Terrace, Taylor's Lane, Willesden. 15135/B.

CHARTER, H. J., Pte., R.A.S.C.
He joined in October, 1915, and served in France on transport duties with the R.A.S.C. from the following year until April, 1919, when he was demobilised.
He holds the General Service and Victory Medals.
55, Guilsborough Road, Willesden. 15250.

CHASE, A., Cpl., Middlesex Regiment.
He enlisted in August, 1914, and was sent to France the same year, taking part in the retreat from Mons and the battles of the Somme and Arras. In 1916 he was transferred to Italy, where he remained until he was demobilised in 1919.
He holds the 1914 Star, General Service and Victory Medals.
4, Cranbrook Road, Tottenham. X18561.

CHATER, R., Rifleman, King's Royal Rifles.
He joined in 1917, and did duty at various stations until his demobilisation in 1919. During the whole of this period he was retained on the staff as a chauffeur.
81, Purves Road, Willesden. X18199.

CHATHAM, G., Pte., 13th London Regiment.
He joined in April, 1915, and served in France in several engagements until discharged in October, 1917, suffering from the effects of gas.
He holds the 1915 Star, General Service and Victory Medals.
16, Garvan Road, Fulham. 14658.

CHATTERTON, H. F., Pte., 7th Buffs (East Kent Regiment).
He joined in September, 1914, was sent to France, and killed in action on November 18th, 1916, on the Somme.
He was entitled to the 1915 Star, the General Service and Victory Medals.
64, St. Peter's Road, Lower Edmonton. 12326.

CHATTERTON, W., Pte., 3rd London Regt. (Royal Fusiliers).
He joined in June, 1915, was sent to France, and took part in engagements at Ypres, Arras, Loos and the Somme.
He was demobilised in February, 1919, and holds the 1915 Star, General Service and Victory Medals.
64, St. Peter's Road, Lower Edmonton. 12325.

CHEATER, A. A. C., Pte., 1st Wiltshire Regt.
He joined in March, 1917, served in France, and was taken prisoner on April 10th, 1918. He died on October 25th, 1918, from pneumonia, caused by exposure and starvation.
He was entitled to the General Service and Victory Medals.
149, Estcourt Road, Fulham. 16240.

CHELSOM, J. R., Sergt., 7th London Regiment.
He enlisted in October, 1914, served in France, and took part in engagements at Bapaume and on the Somme.
He holds the General Service and Victory Medals, and was demobilised in June, 1919.
33, Gloucester Road, Edmonton. X17177.

CHENERY, M. (Miss), Special War Worker.
This lady was engaged during the war in important duties at a munition factory in North West London. Her duties were very arduous, and she was highly commended for her work.
80, Barry Road, Harlesden. 14977.

CHERRY, W. H., Sapper, Royal Engineers.
He joined in July, 1915, and in the same year was sent to Salonica, where he contracted malaria and dysentery.
He was discharged in January, 1919, and holds the 1915 Star, General Service and Victory Medals.
48, Cedar Road, Edmonton. 14355.

CHICK, A. J., Lce.-Cpl., Rifle Brigade.
He joined in August, 1914, and during his service in France took part in the battle of the Somme, in which he was wounded and lost the sight of his right eye.
He holds the 1915 Star, General Service and Victory Medals, and was demobilised in April, 1919.
5, Felixstowe Road, Edmonton. 15382.

CHILD, H., Gunner, Royal Field Artillery.
He enlisted in September, 1914, and served in France, taking part in many engagements, including the battles of the Somme and Ypres.
He holds the 1915 Star, General Service and Victory Medals. and was demobilised in January, 1919.
43, Gloucester Road, Edmonton. X17178.

CHILDS, P. E., Pte., 9th Middlesex Regiment and R.A.S.C. (M.T.).
He joined in 1915 at the age of 16, but in the same year was discharged when his age was discovered.
After the Armistice he rejoined in the R.A.S.C. (M.T.), and is now serving.
50, Mozart Street, Queen's Park, W. X18834/A.

CHILDS, R. B., Sergt., Middlesex Regiment.
He was mobilised in August, 1914, and was sent to Salonica, where he took part in the Balkan campaign. He contracted malaria there, and was sent home, being demobilised in May, 1919.
He holds the South African, General Service and Victory Medals, and the 1914-15 Star.
50, Mozart Street, Queen's Park, W. X18834/B.

CHILD, J. R. W., Rifleman, 9th London Regiment.
He enlisted in May, 1915, and was sent to the Western Front in the following March. During the battle of Gommecourt he was taken prisoner, and was released in November, 1918. He was discharged in March, 1919, and holds the General Service and Victory Medals.
16a, Allington Road, Kilburn Lane, N.W. X18608.

CHILD, L. (D.C.M.), Sergt., 5th E. Surrey Regt.
He joined in August, 1914, and went to France the same year, where he took part in most of the important engagements, including the Somme. He was wounded twice, and awarded the D.C.M. for devotion to duty and conspicuous gallantry in the field. In addition he holds the 1914 Star, the General Service and Victory Medals.
58, Winchester Road, Edmonton. 14864.

CHILDS, B. H., Cpl., Royal Engineers.
He joined in August, 1914, and was sent to France, where he took part in many important engagements. He was awarded the Belgian Croix de Guerre for conspicuous bravery in the field. Although he himself had been wounded, he brought in wounded under very heavy fire. He also holds the 1914-15 Star, General Service and Victory Medals.
50, Mozart Street, Queen's Park, W. X18834/C.

CHILDS, F. (Miss), Special War Worker,
During the course of the war this lady was engaged at an important munition factory on work connected with the manufacture of fuses. She carried out her duties to great satisfaction.
14, Holly Lane, Willesden. 15582/A.

CHILDS, F. W., Sapper, R.E. (Railway Troops).
He joined in March, 1917, and was until 1919 engaged on transport duty at Ypres, Armentieres, Bethune, the Somme, Cambrai and other places on the Western Front. During this time he was gassed, and in November, 1919, was demobilised. He holds the General Service and Victory Medals.
6, Conley Road, Willesden. 15524.

CHILDS, H., Pte., R.A.S.C.
He enlisted in 1915, and served in France, taking part in many important engagements. He was invalided home and discharged in 1917, holding the 1915 Star, General Service and Victory Medals.
14, Holly Lane, Willesden. 15582/B.

CHILDS, W., 1st-Class P.O. Stoker, R.N.
He was serving on H.M.S. "Hawkins" on the outbreak of hostilities, and took part in the operations at the Dardanelles. He was also on patrol and escort duty in the Mediterranean and Chinese waters, and has 14 years' service to his credit. He holds the 1914 Star, General Service and Victory Medals.
28, Heron Road, Willesden. 15567.

CHILDS, W. H., Pte., Royal Marines.
He joined in 1917, served at Deal, Portsmouth and in Scotland, and was also engaged in mine duty in the Baltic Sea, on H.M.S. "Malaya," "Margaret" and "Neptune."
He holds the General Service and Victory Medals.
14, Holly Lane, Willesden. 15582/C.

CHILLINGWORTH, C. H., Pte., E. Surrey Regt.
He joined in December, 1914, served on the Western Front, taking part in the battles of the Somme and Ypres, and was wounded in action in 1916. He was demobilised in February, 1919, and holds the 1915 Star, the General Service and Victory Medals.
13, Raynham Road, Edmonton. 16002.

CHINNERY, W. R., Special War Worker.
He had previously served in the Royal Navy, and during the recent war held a responsible and important position with the London United Tramways, on which work he was retained.
83, Sherbrooke Road, Fulham, S.W. X18463.

CHIPPERTON, J. F. D., Pte., 23rd Middx. Regt.
He joined on November 8th, 1915, and served on the Western Front, and in Italy. He took part in the battles of the Somme, Ypres, Bullecourt, Arras, St. Quentin and others. He was wounded and gassed, and discharged on March 27th, 1918.
He holds the General Service and Victory Medals.
9, Eli Street, W. Kensington. 16435C.

CHIPPERTON, W. J., Lce.-Cpl., 12th West Yorkshire Regiment.
He joined in January, 1914, and during 1915 and 1916 served at the Dardanelles and on the Western Front. He was killed in action at Ypres on May 4th, 1916.
He was entitled to the 1914-15 Star, the General Service and Victory Medals.
9, Eli Street, W. Kensington. 16435B.

CHISNALL, H. E., Mechanic, Royal Air Force.
He joined in July, 1917, and in the same year proceeded to France, where he remained until 1919, doing duty at Dunkirk and Paris.
He was awarded the French Croix de Guerre for conspicuous gallantry, and also holds the General Service and Victory Medals.
66, Oxford Road, Edmonton. 12963.

CHITTY, F. J., Lce.-Cpl., Middlesex Regiment.
He was serving in India on the outbreak of war, went to France in 1914, and took part in the battle of La Bassée, and was killed on April 21st, 1915.
He was entitled to the 1914 Star, General Service and Victory Medals.
1b, Vallier Road, College Park, Willesden. X17675/B.

CHITTY, T., Pte., The Queen's (Royal West Surrey Regiment).
He joined in April, 1917, and served on the Western Front until he was sent to India in July, 1919. During this period he took part in several engagements, including the last Great Retreat and Advance, and was badly gassed.
He holds the General Service and Victory Medals.
1b, Vallier Road, College Park, Willesden. X17675A.

CHITTY, H., Driver, Royal Engineers.
He enlisted in May, 1915, and was sent to France, where he took part in many engagements, including Loos, Ypres and the Somme.
He was demobilised on January 17th, 1919, and holds the General Service and Victory Medals.
8, Stanley Grove, White Hart Lane, Tottenham. X18302.

CHITTY, W. C., 16th Lancers and Inniskilling Dragoons.
He joined in August, 1915, and served in France, where he took part in many engagements, .
He was demobilised in February, 1919, and holds the General Service and Victory Medals.
1b, Vallier Road, College Park, Willesden, X17675/C.

CHIVERTON, F. C., Pte., 10th Battalion Royal Fusiliers.
He joined in 1916, was sent to France in the same year, and served with the Labour Corps (attached to the Royal Fusiliers) at Vimy Ridge, Arras and Cambrai. He was gassed, and was demobilised in 1919, holding the General Service and Victory Medals.
7, Steele Road, Harlesden. 14366/C.

CHIVERTON, J. I., Driver, R.A.S.C.
He joined in 1915, and in the following year was sent to Salonica, where he did transport duty. He contracted malaria and dysentery, and was discharged in 1919, holding the General Service and Victory Medals.
7, Steele Road, Harlesden. 14366/A.

CHIVERTON, J. W., 2nd Air Mechanic, R.A.F.
He joined in July, 1916, and was killed on November 25th, 1916, whilst in action on the Western Front. He is buried at Etaples, and was entitled to the General Service and Victory Medals.
14, Kinnoul Road, Hammersmith. 15282.

CHOWNS, G. N., Lce.-Cpl., Machine Gun Corps.
He joined in February, 1917, and saw active service in France and Italy, taking part in many engagements.
He was demobilised in February, 1919, and holds the General Service and Victory Medals.
93, Bruce Castle Road, Tottenham. X18316.

CHRISTIE, D., Pte., 17th Middlesex Regiment.
He joined in January, 1915, and served at various stations. Being classified as medically unfit for overseas service at the time, he was retained on special duties in this country.
64, Greyhound Road, Willesden. X17601/B.

CHRISTIE, E. G., A.B., R.N., H.M.S. "Revenge."
He joined in April, 1915, and during his service took part in the battle of Jutland and other naval engagements.
He holds the 1915 Star, General Service and Victory Medals.
67, Garvan Road, Fulham. 14831C.

CHRISTIE, J., Sergt., Welch Regiment.
He joined in August, 1914, went to the Western Front, and died in November, 1917, from wounds received in action at Ypres.
He was entitled to the 1914 Star, General Service and Victory Medals.
138, Estcourt Road, Fulham. 16249.

CHRISTIE, W. D. A., Pte., 3rd London Regt. (Royal Fusiliers).
He joined in 1916, and served for two years on the Western Front, taking part in the operations on the Somme, at Cambrai, Albert, Arras, Ypres, Loos and many other places. He was wounded and gassed, and was demobilised in January, 1919, holding the General Service and Victory Medals.
64, Greyhound Road, Willesden. X17601A.

CHRISTY, A., Pte., 3rd Batt. The Buffs (East Kent Regiment).
He joined in 1916, went to France the same year, and took part in many engagements. He was wounded three times and badly gassed once.
He holds the General Service and Victory Medals, and was demobilised in 1919.
92, Ilex Road, Willesden. 15950/B.

CHRISTY, N., Special War Worker.
From 1916 until 1918 this lady was engaged at Park Royal Munitions Factory on inspection duties in connection with the manufacture of fuses. Her duties were of an arduous nature, and she performed her work in an exemplary manner.
92, Ilex Road, Willesden. 15950/A.

CHURCH, C. W., Pte., Machine Gun Corps.
He joined in April, 1917, was sent to France in the same year, took part in the fighting on the Somme, and was taken prisoner during the Retreat of March, 1918. He was finally released after the cessation of hostilities, having suffered many hardships whilst in captivity.
In October, 1919, he was demobilised, holding the General Service and Victory Medals.
30, Brereton Road, Tottenham. X18114.

CHURCH, R. T., Cpl., R.E., and Hampshire Regt. (Works Coy.).
He joined in March, 1916, and was stationed on duty at various depots. In Ireland he took part in the suppression of the Sinn Fein riots.
He was demobilised on November 1, 1919.
28, Brereton Road, Tottenham. X18113.

CHURCH, W., A.B., R.N., H.M.S. "Furious."
He rejoined on August 8th, 1914, having previously served for six years, and during the war was in action at the Dardanelles and in other waters.
He holds the 1914 Star, General Service and Victory Medals.
80, Langhedge Lane, Upper Edmonton. X17090.

CHURCHILL, J., Pte., 11th Welch Guards.
He joined in May, 1916, went to Salonica in the same year, and was wounded on February 18th, 1918. After six months in hospital at Malta, he was invalided home, and there discharged in 1919.
He holds the General Service and Victory Medals.
42, Aspenlea Road, W.6. 14289/B.

CHURCHLEY, Pte., R.A.S.C.
He joined in 1917, and served in various Remount Depots, breaking in mules and horses for overseas. His health failed on account of overwork, and he was discharged in consequence in 1917.
50, Orbain Road, Fulham. X18221.

CHURCHLEY, W., Pte., 53rd Royal Sussex Regt.
He joined in 1918, and was stationed at various places. He afterwards went to Germany with the Army of Occupation. He was demobilised in 1919.
50, Orbain Road, Fulham. X18222.

CHURCHMAN, J. W., Driver, Royal Engineers.
He joined in March, 1915, saw active service on the Western Front at Arras, the Somme, Beaumont Hamel and Cambrai, and was in hospital for some time owing to an accident which occurred whilst in action on the Somme.
He holds the General Service and Victory Medals, and was demobilised in March, 1919.
20, Laundry Road, Fulham. 15346/A.

CHURCHYARD, W. M., Rifleman, 16th Rifle Brigade.
He joined in March, 1915, served on the Western Front from February of the following year, and took part in many engagements, including those of the Somme, Ypres, Messines Ridge and Arras, and the final Advance of 1918.
He was demobilised in February, 1919, holding the General Service and Victory Medals.
56, Roundwood Road, Willesden. 15977.

CLARIDGE, T., Pte., 1st Welch Regiment.
He joined in August, 1914, and served during the early operations on the Western Front. He was killed in action in March, 1915, and was entitled to the 1914 Star, the General Service and Victory Medals.
2, Disbrowe Road, Hammersmth. 15918.

CLARK, A. (Miss), Special War Worker.
This lady volunteered and was engaged at Park Royal Munition Factory on shell-box making and other munition work for three years. This work entailed long hours and hard work, and was of great importance.
24, Steele Road, Willesden. 13837A.

CLARK, A. (Mrs.), Special War Worker.
During the war this lady was engaged at an important munition factory in connection with the manufacture of bombs and shells, and their despatch to the front. She was commended for her work, which was of an arduous nature.
4, Field Road, Fulham. 15034/A.

CLARK, A., Pte., The Queen's (Royal West Surrey Regiment).
He joined in February, 1917, was sent to France in the same year, and served with a Labour Battalion for two years.
He was demobilised in October, 1919, and holds the General Service and Victory Medals.
22, Huddlestone Road, Willesden. X17409.

CLARK, A, Pte., 2nd Norfolk Regiment.
He was in the Army when war broke out, having enlisted in January, 1911. He went out to the Eastern Front, and saw much service in Mesopotamia. On December 12th, 1915, he was wounded in action, and was for a very long period in hospital.
He was discharged in March, 1917, and holds the 1915 Star, General Service and Victory Medals.
4, Charles Street, Tottenham. X18304.

CLARK, A., Pte., 4th Middlesex Regiment.
He joined in July, 1913, and in August, 1914, was sent to France, where he took part in the battle of Mons. In 1915 he was wounded at Ypres, and was in hospital for 15 months.
He was discharged on November 19th, 1917, and now holds the Mons Star, General Service and Victory Medals.
62, Durban Road, Tottenham. X17952.

CLARK, A. E., Sergt., Machine Gun Corps.
He joined in March, 1916, and during his service in France, which commenced in the following year, took part in the battle of Vimy Ridge and in the Retirement of 1918. After the signing of the Armistice he served with the Army of Occupation in Germany until his demobilisation in October, 1919.
He holds the General Service and Victory Medals.
15, Dyson's Road, Edmonton. T16854A.

CLARK, A. G., Driver, Royal Engineers.
He joined in March, 1915, and served on the Western Front until 1918. He was in action at Vimy Ridge, Arras and Ypres.
On March 19th, 1919, he was demobilised, holding the General Service and Victory Medals.
57, Monmouth Road, N.9 13028.

CLARK, A. T., Driver, Royal Field Artillery.
He joined in January, 1915, served in France for three years, and took part in the fighting on the Somme, at Arras and elsewhere.
He was demobilised in July, 1919, holding the 1914-15 Star, General Service and Victory Medals.
15, Dyson's Road, Edmonton. T16854/B.

CLARK, C., Rifleman, K.R.R. Corps.
Joining in 1914, he served at various stations. As he was medically unfit at the time, he was not successful in being drafted overseas.
4, Field Road, Fulham. 15034/B.

CLARK, C. C., Pte., East Surrey Regiment.
He joined in 1917, and served on the Western Front, taking part in many engagements, including the battles of Ypres and Armentieres. He was subsequently wounded at Bailleul and after treatment in hospital was invalided home. He then did Home duties until demobilised in March, 1919.
He holds the General Service and Victory Medals.
22, Lillie Mansions, Fulham, S.W. X18785.

CLARK, E. H., Driver, Royal Field Artillery.
He joined in November, 1914, and served on the Western Front from that year until June, 1919, when he was demobilised. He took part in many engagements, including the Great Retreat and Advance in 1918, and holds the 1914 Star, General Service and Victory Medals.
61, Berry Street, Willesden. 15423/B.

CLARK, F. B. (Mrs.), Special War Worker.
During the war this lady volunteered her services and was engaged at an important London munition factory, in the Cartridge Inspection Department. Her duties were of a responsible nature.
68, Humbolt Road, Fulham. 15307A.

CLARK, F. E., Driver, R.A.S.C. (M.T.).
He served in France from his enlistment in May, 1916, and took part in the battles of Ypres, Vimy Ridge, the Somme, Arras and Cambrai. He was then sent to Germany with the Army of Occupation and remained there until he was demobilised in July, 1919.
He holds the General Service and Victory Medals.
64, Nightingale Road, Harlesden.   12517.

CLARK, F. G., Pte., Middlesex Regiment.
He joined in October, 1915, went to the Western Front in the following year, and was killed in action on October 4th, 1916, in the battle of the Somme.
He was entitled to the General Service and Victory Medals.
105, Berry Street, Willesden.   T15422.

CLARK, G. C., Pte., 7th Warwickshire Regiment.
He joined in March, 1915, and in the capacity of First-class Lewis Gunner, saw active service on the Western Front at Arras, Loos, Ypres, the Somme and Cambrai; and was severely wounded.
He holds the 1914–15 Star, General Service and Victory Medals, and was demobilised in March, 1919.
67, Stroud Road, Fulham.   15333.

CLARK, G. E., Pte., Labour Corps.
He joined in May, 1917, and was employed at various stations till 1919, when he was sent to Germany with the Army of Occupation, where he remained until he was demobilised in November, 1919.
26, Yewfield Road, Willesden.   16363B.

CLARK, G. W., Pte., 9th Middlesex Regiment.
He enlisted in February, 1916, and served in France for three years, during which time he took part in many engagements, including those of Ypres, Vimy Ridge and Guillemont.
He holds the General Service and Victory Medals, and was demobilised in October, 1919.
26, Yewfield Road, Willesden.   16363A.

CLARK, H. (Mrs.), Special War Worker.
This lady was engaged throughout the period of the war at two London munition factories. Her duties consisted of the examination of cartridges, &c., and other responsible work.
27, Leopold Road, Willesden.   14741.

CLARK, H., Pte., Royal Marines.
He joined in August, 1914, served in the North Sea, and helped to sink an enemy submarine near Scapa Flow. He was on board H.M.S. "Natal" when she was blown up whilst in harbour in the North of Scotland. Afterwards he was transferred to H.M.S. "Lancaster," on which he was engaged in patrolling the Pacific.
He holds the General Service and Victory Medals.
68, Humbolt Road, Fulham.   15307B.

CLARK, H. G. J., Pte., R.A.S.C.
He joined in August, 1915, was sent to the Eastern Front, and during his service in Mesopotamia contracted malaria fever, of which he died on March 24th, 1918.
He was entitled to the 1914–15 Star, General Service and Victory Medals, and his relatives hold a letter of condolence from H.M. the King.
2, Bayonne Road, Fulham.   14640.

CLARK, J., C.S.M., Northumberland Fusiliers.
He joined in 1915, was sent to France in the following year, where he took part in many engagements, and served in Italy from 1917 until he was demobilised in 1919.
He holds the General Service and Victory Medals.
67, Pretoria Road, Upper Edmonton.   X17018.

CLARK, J., Pte., 3rd Middlesex Regiment.
He joined in August, 1914, and served in France for five years. He took part in the battles of Mons, Ypres and the Somme, and was wounded.
He is entitled to the 1914–15 Star, General Service and Victory Medals.
131, Bounces Road, Edmonton.   13014.

CLARK, J., Cpl., Royal Field Artillery.
He enlisted in 1910, and served in India until 1918, when he was transferred to France, where he took part in the last Advance and was killed in action in November, 1918.
He was entitled to the 1915 Star, General Service and Victory Medals.
25, Tenterden Road, Tottenham, N.17   X18278A.

CLARK, J. A., Sapper, Royal Engineers.
He joined in November, 1914, and saw service on the Western Front, taking part in the battles of the Somme, Ypres, and the Great Retreat and Advance in 1918.
He holds the 1914 Star, General Service and Victory Medals, and was demobilised in April, 1919.
61, Berry Street, Willesden.   15423A.

CLARK, J. A., Sergt., Royal Field Artillery.
He joined in 1914, went to France in the same year, and took part in the retreat from Mons, the battles of the Somme, Ypres and many other engagements.
He holds the 1914 Star, General Service and Victory Medals.
3, William Terrace, Albany Road, Upper Edmonton.   16464.

CLARK, M. (Mrs.), Special War Worker.
This lady was engaged at Park Royal National Filling Factory, as an inspector of fuses, &c., for four years. She commenced this important work early in 1915 and only retired on the conclusion of hostilities.
24, Steele Road, Willesden.   13837B.

CLARK, R., Pte., Middlesex Regiment.
He joined in August, 1914, and served on the Western Front, taking part in many engagements. During the severe winter he contracted trench feet in a very severe form.
He is entitled to the 1914–15 Star, General Service and Victory Medals. He was demobilised in April, 1919.
26, Bounces Road, Edmonton.   13943.

CLARK, R., Cpl., 17th Middlesex Regiment.
He joined on August 8th, 1914, and was sent to the Western Front, where he took part in many engagements. He was wounded on this Front and died from the effects on November 10th, 1916.
He is entitled to the 1915 Star, General Service and Victory Medals.
28, Eastbourne Avenue, Edmonton.   13580B.

CLARK, W., Pte., 10th Batt. Royal Fusiliers.
He joined in 1915, was sent to France the following year, took part in the battles of Ypres, the Somme and Hill 60, and was three times wounded. In 1919 he was sent to England, and a few days after his arrival died from effects of exposure.
He was entitled to the General Service and Victory Medals.
7, Steele Road, Harlesden.   14366B.

CLARK, W., Pte., 13th Middlesex Regiment.
He joined in 1914, and served on the Western Front, taking part in the battles of Mons, Loos, Arras, the Somme, Neuve Chapelle, Hill 60 and Ypres. During his service he was twice wounded, and gassed, and ultimately discharged in 1918, holding the 1914–15 Star, the General Service and Victory Medals. 24, Steele Road, Willesden.   13837C.

CLARK, W., Pte., West Yorkshire Regiment.
He joined in 1914, served during many engagements on the Western Front, and was killed in the local fighting near Locs on July 5th, 1916.
He was entitled to the General Service and Victory Medals.
4, Field Road, Fulham.   15034C.

CLARK, W. A. (M.M.), Sergt., Middlesex Regt.
He enlisted in August, 1914, served on the Western Front until 1919, and took part in the fighting at Ypres, Cambrai, on the Somme and elsewhere.
He was awarded the Military Medal for conspicuous bravery in the field near Arras, and holds also the 1914–15 Star, General Service and Victory Medals, and was demobilised on June 9th, 1919.
49, Earlsmead Road, Kensal Rise.   X17833.

CLARK, W. F., Cpl., 5th Rifle Brigade.
He joined in December, 1915, and served on the Western Front, taking part in engagements on the Somme and at Cambrai and Ypres. He was wounded at Mount Kemmel in August, 1916, and was also badly gassed.
He was discharged in January, 1918, holding the General Service and Victory Medals.
5, Lochaline Street, Fulham.   13347.

CLARK, W. H., Driver, R.A.S.C. (H.T.).
He joined in August, 1914, and during his service on the Western Front was engaged in conveying ammunition and food to the lines, and was wounded.
He holds the 1914–15 Star, General Service and Victory Medals. 9, Ancill Street, W.6   13743.

CLARK, W. J., Pte., Middlesex Regiment.
He joined in 1918, and served at various stations with his Regiment.
He was eventually demobilised in January, 1919.
19, Hilmer Street, W.14   15707.

CLARKE, A. T., Pte., 7th Middlesex Regiment.
He joined in 1916, and served in France, where he took part in many engagements, and was killed in action at Ypres in April, 1918.
He is entitled to the General Service and Victory Medals.
24, York Road, Lower Edmonton.   16780A.

CLARKE, C. E., Pte., The Queen's (Royal West Surrey Regiment.
He joined in November, 1917, at the age of 18, and served in France for one year, taking part in several engagements.
He was demobilised in September, 1919, holding the General Service and Victory Medals.
22, Leopold Road, Willesden.   14914.

CLARKE, C. F., Pte., 1st Wiltshire Regiment.
He joined in October, 1914, went to the Western Front in 1918, and was wounded and taken prisoner during the Retreat in May of the same year. He was released in the following December, and in January, 1919, was demobilised, holding the General Service and Victory Medals.
32, Gowan Road, Willesden. X16964C.

CLARKE, C. G. T., Acting Sergt., R.A.M.C.
He joined in August, 1914, was sent to France, and was present at engagements at Mons, Loos, Arras, Ypres, the Somme and many other places. He was attached to No. 1 Ambulance Train.
He holds the Mons Star, General Service and Victory Medals, and was demobilised on January 20th, 1919.
30, St. Peter's Road, Lower Edmonton. 12322.

CLARKE, C. H., Pte., Duke of Cornwall's L.I.
He joined in August, 1914, and has seen service in China and France, and later in Salonica. While in France he took part in many battles, including those of the Somme, La Bassée and Arras.
He was demobilised in 1919, holding the 1914 Star, General Service and Victory Medals.
66, Seymour Avenue, Tottenham, N.17 X19161.

CLARKE, E., Sergt., Bedfordshire Regiment.
He joined in June, 1916, and in 1917 went to India as reinforcement for the Mesopotamian Front.
He holds the General Service and Victory Medals.
32, Gowan Road, Willesden. X16964B.

CLARKE, E., Pte., 9th Middlesex Regiment (Labour Corps).
He joined in 1916, served on the Western Front, and was wounded in action in August, 1916, at Delville Wood, and afterwards invalided home to England, where he was stationed on special duty at Chatham, until 1919.
He holds the General Service and Victory Medals, and was demobilised in February, 1919.
20, Shelley Road, Harlesden. 13645/A.

CLARKE, E. R., Lce.-Cpl., The Queen's (Royal West Surrey Regiment).
He volunteered in August, 1914, and served with the Queen's on duty at various stations.
In June, 1918, he was discharged as physically unfit for further service for his country.
41, Huddlestone Road, Willesden. X17408.

CLARKE, G., C.S.M., Devonshire Regiment.
He enlisted in September, 1914, and during his service on the Western Front was gassed whilst on duty at Dunkirk. He took part in several engagements in the Somme sector.
He holds the 1914-15 Star, General Service and Victory Medals, and was demobilised in January, 1919.
29, Cedar Road, Edmonton. 14030.

CLARKE, G. E., S.M., London Yeomanry.
He joined in August, 1914, served at Gallipoli, and for nearly four years in Egypt, during which time he was mentioned in despatches for his consistent good work.
He holds the 1914-15 Star, and the General Service and Victory Medals, and was demobilised in May, 1919.
32, Gowan Road, Willesden. X16964A.

CLARKE, G. H., Pte., Royal Suffolk Regiment.
He joined in June, 1916, and was sent to France in the following year. He took part in many engagements, including the battles of the Somme and Ypres, and was twice wounded and once gassed during his service. He was in action through the last Advance in 1918, and was discharged in August, 1919.
He holds the General Service and Victory Medals.
1, Durban Road, Tottenham. X18097/B.

CLARKE, G. W., Sapper, Royal Engineers.
He joined in November, 1915, and in 1917 went to France, where he served at Dunkirk and Dieppe, and took part in many battles, including the last Advance. During his service he was gassed.
He was demobilised in January, 1919, and holds the General Service and Victory Medals.
5, Eli Street, W. Kensington. 16440.

CLARKE, H., Sergt., Royal Fusiliers.
He joined in August, 1914, and served for nearly five years on the Western Front, during which time he took part in the battles of Ypres, Arras, Cambrai, Loos, La Bassée, Messines and Vimy Ridge. He suffered from shell-shock while abroad, and in June, 1919, was demobilised, holding the 1914-15 Star, General Service and Victory Medals.
100, Deacon Road, Willesden. X17312.

CLARKE, H. E., Pte., Welch Fusiliers.
Having served two years in the Territorials previous to the outbreak of war, he did duty in August, 1914, and was sent to Egypt, where he remained.
He holds the General Service and Victory Medals.
24, Church Path, W.6 16393.

CLARKE, J. T., Rifleman, 1/12th London R.
He joined in September, 1914, and served in France during 1915 and 1916, and was killed in action at Givenchy on September 9th, 1916.
He was entitled to the 1914-15 Star, General Service and Victory Medals.
52, Sandringham Road, Willesden Green. 16712/C.

CLARKE, L. E. (Mrs.), Special War Worker.
This lady volunteered and was engaged during the war at two important munition factories, where she did arduous duties.
She was commended for her work.
1, Durban Road, Tottenham. X18097/A.

CLARKE, L. L., Pte., 2nd Middlesex Regiment.
He enlisted in August, 1914, and served in France, where he took part in many engagements, and was wounded in the head during the battle of Cambrai.
He was demobilised in 1918, and holds the Mons Star, General Service and Victory Medals.
12, York Road, Lower Edmonton. 16782/C.

CLARKE, L. S., Flying Officer, Royal Air Force.
He joined in February, 1916, and after completing his training saw active service on the Western Front in 1918. He took part in operations generally and sustained injuries while flying during this period of his service.
He was demobilised in June, 1919, and holds the General Service and Victory Medals.
6, Napier Road, College Park, Willesden. X17526.

CLARKE, P. (M.M.), Pte., R.A.M.C.
He joined in August, 1914, and served for four years on the Western Front as a stretcher-bearer. He was many times mentioned in despatches, and in September, 1918, was awarded the Military Medal for great bravery. He was once gassed, and in February, 1919, was demobilised, holding the 1914-15 Star, the General Service and Victory Medals.
54, Waldo Road, Willesden. X17641.

CLARKE, R., Pte., Royal Fusiliers and R.E.
He joined in 1915, and was engaged on special duties on the Western Front and in India and Burma. He had previously served in the Tibet Expedition in 1903-4.
He was demobilised in February, 1920, and holds the Tibet Expedition Medal, the 1914-15 Star, the General Service and Victory Medals.
21, Berry Street, Willesden. 15408.

CLARKE, R. H., Driver, R.A.S.C.
He enlisted in August, 1914, went to the Western Front, and was badly wounded in three places during the Retreat from Mons. Afterwards he took part in the battles of Loos, Ypres, Cambrai and the Somme, and went with the Army of Occupation to Germany.
He was demobilised in February, 1919, and holds the 1914 Star, General Service and Victory Medals.
11, Chancellor's Road, Hammersmith. 12820.

CLARKE, S. J., Engine-Room Artificer, R.N.
He joined in February, 1917, and served with his ship on important and dangerous patrol duties.
He was demobilised in February, 1919, and holds the General Service and Victory Medals.
24, York Road, Lower Edmonton. 16780/B.

CLARKE, T., Pte., Royal Fusiliers.
He joined in 1918, and at the close of his training was drafted to Egypt, where he did much useful work.
He was demobilised in 1919, and holds the General Service and Victory Medals.
333, Brettenham Road East, Upper Edmonton, N.18 15625.

CLARKE, T., Pte., Royal Fusiliers.
He joined the Army in 1917. and was sent to the Egyptian Expeditionary Force, with which he saw service.
He was demobilised in February, 1920, and holds the General Service and Victory Medals.
12, York Road, Edmonton, N.18 16782/A.

CLARKE, W., Trooper, 2nd Dragoon Guards.
He joined in August, 1914, went to France in 1915, and took part in many engagements. In 1920 he was sent to Egypt and Palestine.
He holds the 1914-15 Star, General Service and Victory Medals.
12, York Road, Lower Edmonton. 16782/B.

CLARKE, W. E., Pte., Seaforth Highlanders.
He joined in 1915, and was sent to France in 1917. He was killed in action at Armentieres in April, 1917.
For his service he was entitled to the General Service and Victory Medals.
104, Bulwer Road, N.18   X17517.

CLARKE, W. H., Pte., 26th Royal Fusiliers.
He joined in 1916, and during his service on the Western Front was severely wounded. After his recovery he was sent to Italy, and later, until his demobilisation in April, 1919, served with the Army of Occupation in Germany.
He holds the General Service and Victory Medals.
24, Church Path, Hammersmith.   16397.

CLARKSON, C. E., Pte., 11th Border Regiment.
He joined in 1916, and was sent to the Western Front, taking part in several engagements, and was finally at Nieuport, where he fell in action on June 28th, 1917.
He was entitled to the General Service and Victory Medals.
11, Chesson Road, W. Kensington, W.   X16983/A.

CLARKSON, F. R., Pte., Royal Warwickshire R.
He joined in 1917, and was sent to the Western Front, where he took part in several engagements. He was wounded on April 14th, 1918, and was serving in the last Great Advance, when he was killed in action on June 29th, 1918.
He was entitled to the General Service and Victory Medals.
11, Chesson Road, W. Kensington, W.   X16983/B.

CLAYDEN, W., Gunner, R.G.A.
He joined in October, 1916, and during his service on the Western Front took part in many battles, including that of Ypres, and the last Retreat and Advance.
He holds the General Service and Victory Medals, and was demobilised in February, 1919.
43, Deacon Road, Willesden.   X17211.

CLAYDON, W. W., Pte., Middlesex Regiment.
He enlisted in August, 1914, and during his service in France, which lasted five years, took part in many battles, including that of the Somme, and was wounded.
He holds the 1914 Star, General Service and Victory Medals, and was demobilised in 1919.
34, Kenninghall Road, Lower Edmonton.   16898.

CLAYTON, F. W. A., Pte., Middlesex and Devonshire Regiments.
He joined in September, 1916, and did duty at various stations. He was attached to the Royal Army Service Corps in connection with the supply of forage.
He was demobilised in November, 1918.
38, Gilpin Grove, Edmonton.   T16844.

CLAYTON, T. S., Sergt., 2nd London Regiment.
He enlisted in August, 1914, served on the Western Front, and took part in the battles of Ypres, Gommecourt, Cambrai, Hooge, Mons and the last Retreat and Advance of 1918.
He was demobilised in April, 1919, and holds the 1914 Star, General Service and Victory Medals.
Whitstable, 2, Roundwood Road, Willesden. 16303.

CLEAVER, J. T., Sapper, Royal Engineers.
He joined in 1916, and was engaged on the Western Front until 1919 on the construction of railways connecting up the various sectors.
He was demobilised in 1919, and holds the General Service and Victory Medals.
10, Ilex Road, Willesden.   16093C.

CLEAVER, L. (Mrs.), Special War Worker.
This lady volunteered and was engaged during the war at a London munition factory. She was appointed as a final examiner of cartridges, and was commended for her work.
10, Ilex Road, Willesden.   16093A.

CLEAVER, W. H., Pte., R.A.S.C. (M.T.).
He joined in 1915, and served from 1916 to 1919 on the Western Front, on dangerous and arduous transport duties.
He was demobilised in 1919, and holds the General Service and Victory Medals.
10, Ilex Road, Willesden.   16093B.

CLEMAS, E., Sapper, Royal Engineers.
He joined in 1917, served on the Western Front, and took part in the last Retreat and Advance, and was wounded.
He holds the General Service and Victory Medals, and was demobilised in 1918.
27, Denton Road, Harlesden.   14973.

CLEMENT, G. H., Cpl., R.A.S.C.
He joined in August, 1914, and served in England until December, 1917, when he was sent to Salonica, remaining there until his demobilisation in March, 1919.
He holds the 1914-15 Star, General Service and Victory Medals.
49, Raynham Avenue, Edmonton.   16889.

CLEMENTS, A. J., A.B., Royal Navy.
He joined in September, 1916, and served on board H.M.S. "Resolution" with the Grand Fleet on dangerous duties.
He was demobilised in February, 1919, and holds the General Service and Victory Medals.
22, Ashford Road, Tottenham.   X18352/B.

CLEMENTS, E., Pte., West Riding Regiment.
He joined in January, 1917, served on the Western Front from the following December until October, 1918, and took part in the fighting in the Arras sector.
He was demobilised in February, 1919, and holds the General Service and Victory Medals.
245a, Kilburn Lane, W.10   X18943.

CLEMENTS, F. (Miss), Member, W.R.A.F.
This lady offered her services, and joined the W.R.A.F. in 1918, and did duty in London.
She was demobilised in 1919.
22, Ashford Road, Tottenham.   X18352/D.

CLEMENTS, F. W., Stoker, R.N., H.M.S. "Argus."
He joined in June, 1916, and served with the Grand Fleet, and later with the Baltic Squadron, on H.M.S. "Volunteer."
He holds the General Service and Victory Medals.
22, Ashford Road, Tottenham.   X18352C.

CLEMENTS, G., Special War Worker.
During the war this lady was engaged at Messrs. Richardson's, Vauxhall Bridge Road, in connection with the manufacture of water-purifying machinery for the Army. This work was of the greatest importance.
100, Chesson Road, W. Kensington.   X17238.

CLEMENTS, G. H., Gunner, R.G.A.
He joined in November, 1914, and served on the Western Front, taking part in several engagements, including the battle of Ypres, where he was wounded on April 22nd, 1915.
He was demobilised on March 3rd, 1919, and holds the 1914-15 Star, the General Service and Victory Medals.
22, Ashford Road, Tottenham.   X18352A.

CLEMENTS, H. A., Lce.-Cpl., Royal Irish Rifles.
He joined in April, 1916, and was sent to the Western Front in that year. He contracted trench fever on the Somme, and was invalided home. In 1918 he was drafted to Ireland, and later went to Brockton Camp to guard German prisoners of war.
He was discharged in August, 1919, and holds the General Service and Victory Medals.
124, Sheldon Road, Upper Edmonton.   X17451.

CLEMENTS, H. H., Sergt., R.A.O.C.
He joined in April, 1917, and served in Mesopotamia and India, engaged as regimental clerk to the Commanding Officer of his unit.
He was demobilised on March 25th, 1920, and holds the General Service and Victory Medals.
110, Claxton Grove, Fulham, W.6   13439.

CLEMENTS, J. (D.C.M.), Gunner, R.F.A.
He joined in January, 1915, and served on the Western and Italian Fronts, being in action at Loos, Ypres, Arras and Cambrai, and was awarded the Distinguished Conduct Medal for gallantry and distinguished conduct on the field. He was subsequently very severely gassed.
He also holds the 1914-15 Star, General Service and Victory Medals, and was demobilised in March, 1919.
71, Garvan Road, Fulham.   14826.

CLEMENTS, N. H. R., Cpl., Duke of Cornwall's Light Infantry.
He enlisted in September, 1914, and served in France, taking part in many engagements, and was killed in action on March 7th, 1917.
He was entitled to the 1914-15 Star, General Service and Victory Medals.
39, Hannell Road, Fulham.   X18156.

CLEWLEY, F. W. J., Rifleman, Rifle Brigade.
He joined in September, 1914, proceeded to France in 1915, and was killed in action in September of the same year at the battle of Loos.
He was entitled to the 1914-15 Star, General Service and Victory Medals.
12, Wakefield Street, Edmonton.   15812.

CLIFFE, S. O., Sergeant, R.A.O.C.
He joined in January, 1915, and served at various stations on important ordnance duties until his demobilisation in May, 1919. He gained his promotion for consistent good work.
31, Star Road, W. Kensington, W.14   16176.

CLIFFORD, O. V. O., Pte., 24th London Regiment (Queen's).
He joined in December, 1915, went to the Western Front, and took part in many battles, including High Wood, where he was severely wounded, and in consequence of which he lost a leg. He was discharged in June, 1917, and holds the General Service and Victory Medals.
11, Varna Road, Fulham. X18771.

CLIFFORD, T. E., Pte., 11th Middlesex Regt.
He joined in August, 1914, was sent to France in the following year, and was killed by a hand-grenade at Loos on February 13th, 1916.
He was entitled to the 1914-15 Star, General Service and Victory Medals.
68, Chester Road, Lower Edmonton. 12287.

CLIFT, G. W., Warrant Officer, R.N., H.M., T.B.D. " Minos."
He rejoined in August, 1914, served in various waters, and took part in the battle of Heligoland, being three times wounded. He was discharged on February 18th, 1915. He had previously served for over 23 years, during the Boer War, the Boxer Risings and with the Benin Expeditionary Force.
He holds the King's and Queen's South African Medals, with three bars, Medals awarded for his Chinese service, Benin Expeditionary Force, Long Service, General Service and Victory Medals and the 1914 Star.
72, Greyhound Road, Hammersmith. 15027.

CLIGGETT, D., Pte., Royal Fusiliers.
He joined in August, 1914, went to the Western Front, and took part in many battles, including those of Mons, Bullecourt, Arras, the Somme, and the last Retreat and Advance, and after the Armistice served for four months with the Army of Occupation in Germany.
He was demobilised in April, 1919, holding the 1914 Star and the General Service and Victory Medals.
67, Humbolt Road, Fulham, W.6 15317B.

CLIGGETT, N. (Mrs.), Special War Worker.
This lady volunteered, and was engaged for two years during the war at a London munition factory on dangerous and highly important work.
67, Humbolt Road, Fulham, W.6 15317/A.

CLIMO, J. B., Pte., Machine Gun Corps.
He joined in 1917, and served on the Western Front, taking part in the battles of Ypres and Passchendaele and many other engagements. Afterwards, until his demobilisation in January, 1920, he served with the Army of Occupation in Germany.
He holds the General Service and Victory Medals.
82, Shakespeare Avenue, Harlesden. 13624.

CLOUGH, H. G., Rifleman, London Rifle Brigade.
He joined in February, 1916, was sent to France in the same year, and took part in the fighting on the Somme, where he was wounded in action. He was invalided home in 1917, and discharged unfit for further service in June, 1918.
He holds the General Service and Victory Medals.
72, Deacon Road, Willesden. 17359A.

CLOUGH, J. B., Lce.-Cpl., Notts and Derby Regt.
He enlisted in November, 1914, served on the Western Front from the following year until 1918, and took part in various engagements, including the battles of Cambrai, the Somme and St. Quentin, where he was wounded in action.
He was mentioned in despatches for conspicuous bravery late in 1916, and holds the 1914-15 Star, General Service and Victory Medals, and was demobilised in March, 1919.
72, Deacon Road, Willesden. 17359B.

CLOVER, I. W., Pte., Royal Suffolk Regiment.
He joined in May, 1917, and was sent to India, where he served at various stations with his regiment.
He was demobilised in November, 1919, and holds the General Service and Victory Medals.
15, Charles Street, Tottenham, N. X18295.

CLOW, C., Shoeing smith, R.F.A.
He joined in October, 1914, went to the Western Front in 1915, and later to the Eastern Front, at Salonica. He served 3½ years, and was employed as shoeing-smith during that time.
He was demobilised in March, 1919, holding the 1914-15 Star, General Service and Victory Medals.
57, Hiley Road, Willesden, N.W.10 X18168.

CLOWES, A., Driver, Royal Field Artillery.
He enlisted in November, 1914, and during his service on the Western Front, took part in many engagements, including the battles of Ypres and Messines.
He was demobilised on April 3rd, 1919, and holds the 1914-15 Star, General Service and Victory Medals.
3, Delorme Street, Fulham. T13779.

COAKER, W., Driver, Royal Field Artillery.
He enlisted in December, 1914, was sent to France in the following September, and took part in the battles of Loos, the Somme, La Bassée and Ypres.
He was demobilised in April, 1919, holding the 1914-15 Star, General Service and Victory Medals.
22, South Street, Hammersmith. 12510.

COAN, P. O., Rifleman, King's Royal Rifles.
He joined in November, 1915, served on the Western Front and in Italy, taking part in several engagements.
He was demobilised on February 14th, 1919, and holds the General Service and Victory Medals.
7, Ancill Street, W.6 13739.

COATES, A. C., Pte., 1st Buffs (East Kent Regt.).
He joined in August, 1916, and served in France. where he took part in many engagements, including those near Ypres, the Somme, Loos and Cambrai. He was wounded three times and was also gassed.
He holds the General Service and Victory Medals, and was demobilised on February 4th, 1919.
11, Napier Road, College Park, Willesden. X17770/A.

COATES, J. W., Lce.-Cpl., 1st Middlesex Regt.
He joined in March, 1915, went to the Western Front in the same year, and was reported missing, but is believed to have been killed in the battle of Ypres on October 4th, 1917. He had previously taken part in many other engagements, including those of Arras, Cambrai, and the Somme, and was entitled to the 1915 Star, General Service and Victory Medals.
11, Napier Road, College Park, Willesden, N.W.10 X17770B.

COATES, L. A. (Miss), Special War Worker.
During the war this lady was engaged as an operator on the automatic weighing and gauging machines, and for two years as an examiner of small arms ammunition, working on alternate day and night shifts, and often being on duty for very long periods.
11, Napier Road, College Park, Willesden, N.W.10 X17770C.

COBB, F. E., Leading Seaman, R.N., H.M.S. " Royal Oak."
He joined in June, 1915, served with the Grand Fleet, and took part in the battle of Jutland.
He holds the 1914 Star, General Service and Victory Medals.
40, Brett Road, Harlesden. 15690A.

COBB, M. L. (Mrs.), Special War Worker.
During the war this lady gave her time for the troops, making for them all kinds of comforts and garments, and forwarding them overseas. Her work was of a very patriotic nature.
89, Mirabel Road, Walham Green. X17862/A.

COBB, W., Air Mechanic, R.A.F.
He joined in 1916, and was sent to the Western Front, where he was employed in the Photographic Section. He was in action at Arras, Bapaume, Amiens, Neuve Chapelle and other places. He was also in the Advance of 1918.
He was demobilised in 1919, holding the General Service and Victory Medals.
89, Mirabel Road, Walham Green. X17862/B.

COBB, W. E., Pte., 1st Middlesex Regt.
He joined on May 1st, 1915, was sent to France in the following July, and killed in action on the Somme in June, 1916.
He was entitled to the 1914-15 Star, General Service and Victory Medals.
40, Brett Road, Harlesden. 15690B.

COBBOLD, A. W., Driver, M.G.C.
He joined in January, 1916, and served in France, taking part in many engagements, including those near Loos, Arras, Ypres and the Somme.
He was demobilised in January, 1919. He holds the General Service and Victory Medals.
2, Shakespeare Road, Edmonton. X17183.

COCK, D., Sergt., 2nd Bn. Middlesex Regt.
He joined in August, 1914, served on the Western Front at Arras, Neuve Chapelle, the Somme, Givenchy, Amiens, Armentieres, Ypres and Bullecourt, and was wounded three times.
He was demobilised in 1919, and holds the 1914-15 Star, General Service and Victory Medals.
81, Ancill Street, Fulham. 13804.

COCK, E. (Mrs.), Special War Worker.
This lady volunteered for war work, and was engaged at a London rubber works in connection with the manufacture of rubber parts for our aeroplanes. Her work was of the greatest importance.
81, Ancill Street, Fulham. 13652/B.

COCK, G. (M.M.), S.M., 17th Middlesex Regt.
He joined in 1915, served on the Western Front at Amiens, Arras, Ypres, Cambrai and Festubert, and was wounded at Delville Wood.
He was awarded the Military Medal for great bravery in the field, holds the 1915 Star, General Service and Victory Medals, and was demobilised in 1919.
81, Ancill Street, Fulham. 13805.

COCK, H., A.B., R.N., H.M.S. "Lowestoft."
He joined in 1918, and served on important duties at sea and at Devonport. He afterwards served on H.M.S. "New Zealand," Lord Jellicoe's flagship.
He holds the General Service and Victory Medals.
81, Ancill Street, Fulham. 13652A.

COCK, P., Gunner, R.F.A.
He joined in 1915, served on the Western Front at Arras, Loos, Neuve Chapelle, Ypres, Festubert, Vimy Ridge and St. Quentin, was wounded and gassed.
He was discharged in 1918, and holds the 1915 Star, General Service and Victory Medals.
81, Ancill Street, Fulham. 13806.

COCKS, A. J. C., Pte., 3/10th Middlesex Regt.
He joined in January, 1915, and during his service on the Western Front took part in the battles of Bullecourt, Monchy, Armentieres, St. Quentin, Hill 60 and Gommecourt. He was wounded in action at Ypres, and again on the Somme, so badly as to necessitate the amputation of his left leg. Whilst in hospital at Etaples he was again wounded during an air raid in 1918.
He holds the General Service and Victory Medals, and was demobilised in 1919.
57, Chesson Road, West Kensington, W.14 X17156.

COCKS, W. T., Pte., R.A.S.C.
He joined in 1915, and served through the Dardanelles campaign, later going to Egypt and Salonica, where he took part in many engagements. He contracted malarial fever, and was sent to Malta.
He was discharged through wounds received in action in 1917, and holds the 1914-15 Star, General Service and Victory Medals.
57, Chesson Road, W. Kensington. X17157.

COCUP, C., Sapper, Royal Engineers.
He joined in June, 1918, and served on important duties with the Royal Engineers at various stations.
He was demobilised in March, 1919.
61, Stroud Road, Fulham. 15336.

CODLING, A., Pte., 3rd East Lancashire Regt.
He joined in March, 1915, served on the Western Front from the following July until July, 1916, and took part in the battles of Loos, Ypres, the Somme and Beaumont Hamel, where he was severely wounded.
He was demobilised in April, 1919, and holds the 1915 Star, General Service and Victory Medals.
36, Hazel Road, Willesden. X17787B.

CODLING, A., Pte., Royal Fusiliers.
He joined in August, 1914, and was sent to Malta and thence to France in the same year. He took part in fighting on the Somme, and was severely wounded in May, 1915, being subsequently invalided home, and discharged in 1916.
He holds the 1914 Star, General Service and Victory Medals.
77, Asplin Road, Tottenham, N.17 X19079.

CODLING, G., Cpl., 6th Middlesex Regt.
He re-enlisted in October, 1914, having previously served with the 3rd Suffolk Regt., and being over age for overseas service, was stationed at Chatham on important duties until demobilised in February, 1919.
36, Hazel Road, Willesden. X17787A.

COE, R. W., Sapper, Royal Engineers.
He joined in 1917, and served with the Royal Engineers on important duties until his demobilisation in 1920.
33, Estcourt Road, S.W.6 16692A.

COE, R. W. M., Sapper, Royal Engineers.
He joined in September, 1914, went to France in 1917, and was chiefly engaged in connection with the transporting of ammunition to the lines. He was gassed during his service abroad.
He holds the General Service and Victory Medals, and was demobilised in December, 1919.
33, Estcourt Road, S.W.6 16692B.

COFFIN, F. W., Driver, R.A.S.C.
He joined in April, 1917, and did duty with the Mechanical Transport Section at various stations. In 1919 he was transferred to Malta.
61, Hartington Road, Tottenham, N.17 X19143.

COGAN, E., Driver, R.F.A.
He joined in April, 1915, and served first on the French Front, then in Salonika, and later with the Expeditionary Force in Egypt.
He was discharged on June 19th, 1919, holding the General Service and Victory Medals.
29, Haldane Road, Fulham. TX17074A.

COGAN, F. T., Pte., 2nd Loyal North Lancs. R.
He enlisted in the Regular Army in June, 1907. He served during the war in Egypt, where he died of fever in June 1916.
He was entitled to the 1914-15 Star, the General Service and Victory Medals.
29, Haldane Road, Fulham. TX017074B.

COGAN, H., Pte., 22nd Royal Fusiliers.
He enlisted in October, 1914, and was sent to the Western Front, where he served till the end of the war.
After much service, he was demobilised in April, 1919, and holds the 1914-15 Star, General Service and Victory Medals.
29, Haldane Road, Fulham. TX17074C.

COGGINS, H., Pte., Royal Fusiliers.
He joined in 1915 and in the same year was sent to France, where he acted as a bomber. He was killed in action at Loos in 1915, and was entitled to the 1914-15 Star, General Service and Victory Medals.
346, High Road, Willesden. 16746A.

COGHILL, A. S., 1st-Class Stoker, R.N., H.M.S. "Ruby."
He joined in August, 1914, and served with the Grand Fleet in various waters and on dangerous duties until his demobilisation in 1919.
He holds the 1914-15 Star, the General Service and Victory Medals.
88, Sheldon Road, Edmonton. X17459B.

COKER, P., Pte., 9th Durham Light Infantry.
He joined in July, 1915, and served at Salonica, on the Doiran and Varda Fronts, where he was on special guard duties.
He was demobilised in March, 1919, holding the 1914-15 Star, General Service and Victory Medals.
92, Milton Avenue, Harlesden. 14212B.

COKER, P. J., Pte., 12th Suffolk Regt.
He joined in 1917, and in the same year went to the Western Front, where, three weeks after landing in France, he was taken prisoner on the Somme, and held captive for ten months.
He holds the General Service and Victory Medals, and was demobilised in 1919.
92, Milton Avenue, Harlesden. 14212C.

COLBETT, M. (Mrs.), Special War Worker.
From 1915 until 1918 this lady was engaged on inspection work at Perivale Munition Works, Park Royal. This work was of an arduous nature, entailing long hours, and she was commended for her work.
82, Holly Lane, Willesden. 15393—15392A.

COLE, A., Cpl., Norfolk and Middlesex Regts.
He joined in August, 1914, went to Mesopotamia the following year, and took part in the engagements at Kut, San-i-Yat, and many other places. During his service he was wounded three times.
He was demobilised in 1919, holding the 1914-15 Star, General Service and Victory Medals.
119, Oldfield Road, Willesden. 16104.

COLE, A., Gunner, R.F.A.
He joined in October, 1915, and served for nearly three years on the Western Front, taking part in the battles of Albert, the Somme, Ypres, Cambrai, Arras and St. Quentin. He was demobilised in March, 1919, holding the General Service and Victory Medals.
18, Sandringham Road, Willesden. T17320.

COLE, A. (Mrs.), Special War Worker.
During the war this lady volunteered her services, and was engaged at the Fulham Military Hospital, where she did valuable work for our soldiers.
6, Shotley Street, Fulham. 14811B.

COLE, E. R., Cpl., Tank Corps.
He joined in 1918, served in many sectors of the Western Front, taking part in several engagements, and was gassed.
He holds the General Service and Victory Medals, and was demobilised in 1919.
75, Tubb's Road, Willesden Junction. 12881.

COLE, E. T., Sergt., R.A.M.C.
He was mobilised on August 4th, 1914, and served on hospital trains from Southampton to London until January, 1917. He then went to the Western Front and served at the 63rd Clearing Station, and at Lille, Messines, Cambrai, Ypres and the Somme.
He was demobilised in February, 1919, holding the General Service and Victory Medals.
22, Heron Road, Willesden. 15566A.

COLE, F., 1st Air Mechanic, R.A.F.
He enlisted in August, 1914, and saw active service in Russia, Egypt and France.
He was demobilised on June 23rd, 1919, holding the General Service and Victory Medals.
26, Rayleigh Road, Hammersmith. 12637.

COLE, F. G., Air Mechanic, R.A.F.
He joined in November, 1917, went to France the following year, and was principally engaged with the Kite Balloon Section at Ypres.
He was demobilised in March, 1919. He holds the General Service and Victory Medals.
7, Colville Road, Lower Edmonton. 11996.

COLE, F. J., Special War Worker.
During two years of the war he was employed on important duties in the Boot Department of the Royal Army Clothing Depot, Marylebone. From 1889 to 1901 he had served in the Army and fought through the South African War, the medals for which he holds.
7, Varna Road, Fulham, W.6 X18765.

COLE, H. R., Pte., Bedfordshire Regt.
He joined in August, 1914, and in the same year was sent to the Dardanelles. In 1917 he was transferred to France, and in April was killed during the battle of Arras.
He was entitled to the 1914-15 Star, the General Service and Victory Medals.
23, Felixstowe Road, Willesden. X17792.

COLE, J., Pte., 18th Middlesex Regt.
He joined in June, 1916, served on the Western Front from January, 1917, until January, 1919, took part in the battles of Arras, Amiens, Vimy Ridge, Messines and the last Advance in 1918. He holds the General Service and Victory Medals, and was demobilised in January, 1919.
67, Mayo Road, Willesden. 15472.

COLE, J., Pte., 30th Middlesex Regt.
He joined in June, 1916, and served in France from August, 1917, until discharged in March, 1919. He was attached for some time to a Labour Battalion.
He holds the General Service and Victory Medals.
28, Elthorne Park Road, Hanwell. 11077.

COLE, R. S., Pte., 22nd London Regt. (Queen's).
He joined in 1915, served on the Western Front, on the Somme, at Arras, Ypres, St. Quentin, Armentieres, Loos, in the Retreat and Advance of 1918. Later he served with the Army of Occupation in Germany.
He holds the 1915 Star, General Service and Victory Medals, and was demobilised in 1919.
6, Shotley Street, Fulham. 14811A.

COLE, R., Pte., Royal Fusiliers.
He volunteered in October, 1914, proceeded to France in 1915, and took part in operations on practically all sectors during his four years' service on the Western Front.
He was demobilised in February, 1919, and holds the 1915 Star, General Service and Victory Medals.
15, Pottery Road, Brentford. 9418.

COLE, W. F., Sergt., R.A.S.C.
He was mobilised on August 4th, 1914, having previously served in the Territorials, and was sent to the Western Front, taking part in many engagements. He was wounded once and suffered from shell-shock, and after being in hospital in France and England, was demobilised in March, 1919.
He holds the 1914-15 Star, the General Service, Victory and Territorial Medals.
7, Varna Road, Fulham. X18749.

COLE, W. H., Sergt., 3rd East Surrey Regt.
He joined in September, 1914, went to France in 1915, and was wounded and taken prisoner at Ypres the same year. He was demobilised in May, 1919, holding the 1915 Star, General Service and Victory Medals.
39, Aspenlea Road, W.6 14298.

COLE, W. J., Pte., 2/13th London Regt. (Kensingtons).
He joined in August, 1918, and during his service on the Eastern Front was stationed at Adana and Alexandria. He also helped to quell the riots in Cairo.
He was demobilised in March, 1920, and holds the General Service and Victory Medals.
112, Villiers Road, Willesden, N.W.2 T16156.

5

COLE, W. S., Pte., 3rd Middlesex Regt.
He was called from the Reserve on August 5th, 1914, and drafted to France, where he served for five years. During this period he took part in many battles, including those of Mons, the Somme, Ypres, St. Quentin, Albert, Bullecourt and Arras, was once wounded and contracted malarial fever.
He was demobilised in March, 1919, holding the 1914 Star, General Service and Victory Medals.
4, Shotley Street, Fulham. 14795.

COLEMAN, A., Pioneer, R.E.
He joined in 1915, was sent to France in the same year, and took part in the battles of Arras, Ypres and Armentieres and in the Retreat and Advance of 1918.
He was discharged in July, 1918, holding the 1914-15 Star, General Service and Victory Medals.
130, Shakespeare Avenue, Harlesden. T13898A.

COLEMAN, A. (Mrs.), Special War Worker.
This lady was engaged during the war in the catering department for the workers at the Park Royal Munition Factory, where she performed very much appreciated duties.
130, Shakespeare Avenue, Harlesden. T13898C.

COLEMAN, A. E., Pte., 7th Middlesex Regt.
He enlisted in January, 1915, and served on the Western Front, taking part in many engagements, including the Somme, Ypres, Arras and Cambrai, being gassed twice and wounded. Later, in March, 1920, he went to Germany with the Army of Occupation.
He holds the General Service and Victory Medals.
52, Dudden Hill Lane, Willesden. X17390.

COLEMAN, A. L., Air Mechanic, R.A.F.
He joined in September, 1918, and was stationed with the R.A.F. at the Grahame-White Aerodrome, Hendon, where the manufacture and testing of aeroplanes was conducted on a very large scale.
He was demobilised in January, 1919.
Deal House, Roundwood Road, Willesden. 16936.

COLEMAN, A. W. (jun.), Pte., M.G.C.
He joined in 1915, and after a period of training, proceeded to India for duty with the Machine Gun Corps.
He holds the General Service and Victory Medals.
130, Shakespeare Avenue, Harlesden. T13898B.

COLEMAN, C. T., Cpl., M.G.C.
He joined in February, 1916, and was drafted to France, where he took part in many engagements, including those of Arras, Cambrai and the Somme.
He was demobilised in August, 1919, and holds the General Service and Victory Medals.
40, Napier Road, College Park, Willesden, N.W.10 X17773.

COLEMAN, E., Sapper, R.E.
He enlisted in February, 1916, and served in Salonica, where he took part in many engagements, and was specially employed on the railways.
He holds the General Service and Victory Medals, and was demobilised in March, 1919.
16, Victor Road, College Park, Willesden. X17769.

COLEMAN, H. B., Air Mechanic, R.A.F. (late D.L.I.)
He joined in August, 1916, and although most anxious to see active service, was unable to pass the necessary medical examination, owing to his defective sight. He served at various stations with his regiment, and after being transferred to the Royal Air Force, was stationed at Farnborough and elsewhere, until he was demobilised in February, 1919.
65, Ilex Road, Willesden. T16362B.

COLEMAN, H. G., Pte., 8th Middlesex Regt.
He was serving at the outbreak of war, went to Gibraltar in 1914, and in the following year to the Western Front, where he took part in the battles of Ypres, Arras, Cambrai and Vimy Ridge, and was very badly gassed.
He holds the 1914-15 Star, General Service, Long Service and Victory Medals, and was demobilised in September, 1918.
19, Talbot Road, Willesden. 15964.

COLEMAN, J., Mechanic, R.A.F.
He enlisted in 1917, and after a period of training, served in Egypt during 1918 and 1919.
He holds the General Service and Victory Medals, and was demobilised in February, 1919.
139, Bulwer Road, Edmonton. X17195B.

COLEMAN, J., Gunner, R.F.A.
He joined in July, 1915, served in France from May until December, 1916, and took part in the battle of Vimy Ridge and in the fighting on the Somme and at Ypres, where he was wounded.
He was discharged in November, 1917, holding the General Service and Victory Medals.
35, Alric Avenue, Harlesden. 14445.

COLEMAN, M., Pte., Royal Marine Light Infty.
He was recalled from the Reserve on August 2nd, 1914, and in October was sent to the Western Front, where he was in the retreat from Antwerp. He also served in North Russia, and was present during the bombardment of Lowestoft.
He was demobilised in August, 1919, holding the 1914-15 Star, General Service and Victory Medals and an award for service during the Boxer Risings.
22, Hazel, Road, Willesden. X17790.

COLEMAN, S. T., Lce.-Cpl., Royal Fusiliers.
He joined in 1917, and served in France, taking part in the Advance of 1918, when he was wounded, and invalided to England.
He holds the General Service and Victory Medals, and was demobilised in February, 1919.
139, Bulwer Road, Edmonton. X17195A.

COLEMAN, W. H., Cpl., R.A.S.C. (M.T.).
He joined in March, 1915, and was for four years engaged with the Mechanical Transport in carrying stores and ammunition to the various depots and sectors in France.
He was demobilised in June, 1919, and holds the 1914-15 Star and the General Service and Victory Medals.
14a, Deacon Road, Willesden. 16142.

COLES, G. L., Sapper, R.E.
He enlisted in July, 1916, and in the same year was sent to East Africa, where he served until 1919 as a telegraphist.
He suffered from malaria whilst on active service, and was demobilised in April, 1919, holding the General Service and Victory Medals.
12, Hawthorn Road, Upper Edmonton. X17046.

COLES, T., Pioneer, R.E., 1st Labour Batt.
He joined early in August, 1915, was sent to France almost immediately, and took part in the fighting in several sectors.
He holds the 1914-15 Star, General Service and Victory Medals, and was demobilised in February, 1919.
123, Shakespeare Avenue, Harlesden. 13694.

COLESHILL, J., Sergt., Queen's Own Oxfordshire Hussars.
He joined in October, 1914, and served on the Western Front, taking part in many battles, including those of the Somme, Loos, Neuve Chapelle, Armentieres, Arras, Ypres, Vimy Ridge and St. Quentin. He was wounded during his service, and died from pneumonia in November, 1918.
He was entitled to the 1914-15 Star and the General Service and Victory Medals.
99, Archel Road, W. Kensington. 16673B.

COLESHILL, R., Sergt., R.F.A.
He joined in 1914, and served in Salonica, Egypt, and Palestine, where he was present at the fall of Jerusalem with General Allenby. Later he went to France and took part in the final Advance at Cambrai.
He was demobilised in 1919, holding the 1915 Star, General Service and Victory Medals.
99, Archel Road, W. Kensington. 16673A.

COLESHILL, R., Driver, Royal Engineers.
He joined in 1915, and served for a time at Aldershot, engaged on important duties in connection with the care of horses.
He was discharged in 1916 through ill-health.
99, Archel Road, W. Kensington. 16673C.

COLESHILL, W. E., Driver, R.A.S.C. (M.T.).
He joined in 1917, was taken ill on duty whilst stationed at Grove Park, and died in hospital at Woolwich on October 29th, 1918, whilst serving his country.
51, Humbolt Road, Fulham. 15311.

COLLARD, F. E., Cpl., Northumberland Fus. (M.G.C.).
He joined in July, 1907, and was serving in India at the outbreak of war. He went to France in January, 1915, took part in several engagements, including those of Ypres, the Somme and Festubert, and was wounded three times. Later he served in England, being unfit for further service overseas, until he was demobilised in April, 1919.
He holds the Delhi Durbar Medal, 1915 Star, General Service and Victory Medals.
32, Preston Gardens, Willesden. 15978.

COLLARD, F. W. J., Sergt., 13th Middlesex Regt.
He enlisted in November, 1914, and served in France from the following year until 1919. He took part in many engagements, and was wounded in 1915.
He holds the 1914-15 Star, General Service and Victory Medals, and was demobilised in 1919.
109, Sheldon Road, Upper Edmonton. X17186.

COLLIER, A. E., Bandsman, Royal Marines.
He joined the Marines in July, 1915, and served on H.M.S. "Cornwall" and H.M.S. "Hercules," on dangerous duties with the Atlantic Patrol.
He holds the 1914-15 Star, General Service and Victory Medals.
7, Pellant Road, Fulham, S.W. X17849.

COLLIER, C., Bandsman, Royal Marines.
He joined on March 3rd, 1912, and served on H.M.S. "Orion," on patrol and other duties in the North Sea and elsewhere.
He was demobilised in December, 1919, holding the 1914-15 Star, the General Service and Victory Medals.
7, Pellant Road, Fulham. X17848.

COLLIER, G. H., Pte., R.A.S.C. and Labour Corps.
He joined in October, 1918, and served at various stations with the Mechanical Transport Section. He was not allowed to proceed overseas on account of his being under age. He is still serving his country.
10, Hiley Road, Willesden. X18330.

COLLINGWOOD, A. R. C., Pte., 15th Middlesex Regt.
He joined in August, 1915, and after training went to Egypt in January of the following year, serving there until his demobilisation in April, 1919. Whilst on service in Egypt he was wounded in action.
He holds the General Service and Victory Medals.
49, St. Margaret's Road, Willesden. X17820

COLLINS, A., Pte., Royal Sussex Regt.
He joined in February, 1916, and was sent to France in the same year, taking part in several engagements. He went to Egypt in 1919, and holds the General Service and Victory Medals.
5, Marsden Road, Lower Edmonton. 13066.

COLLINS, A. J., Pte., Middlesex Regt.
He enlisted in October, 1914, served on the Italian Front, in Egypt and in France, and was wounded during the Retreat of March, 1918, and again at Lens.
He was discharged in January, 1919, after three years' active service, and holds the General Service and Victory Medals.
76, Mordaunt Road, Harlesden. 14201.

COLLINS, B., Pte., 6th Royal Warwickshire Regt.
He enlisted in November, 1914, and saw active service in France, taking part in engagements at Ypres, Arras, Armentieres, Ploegsteert, the Somme and La Bassée.
He was discharged medically unfit, through loss of sight from wounds received at the battle of La Bassée, in February, 1917.
He holds the 1914-15 Star, General Service and Victory Medals.
39, Mablethorpe Road, Fulham. X19223.

COLLINS, C. E., Officers' Steward, R.N., H.M.S. "Alexander."
He joined in January, 1915, and served in the North Sea, Baltic, Black Sea, Red Sea and the Atlantic. His ship was torpedoed three times.
He was demobilised in July, 1919, holding the 1915 Star, General Service and Victory Medals.
44, Chester Road, Lower Edmonton. 12286.

COLLINS, F., 2nd Air Mechanic, R.A.F. (Kite Balloon Section).
He joined in May, 1917 and served on the Western Front, at Ypres, Passchendaele and elsewhere, and also with the Army of Occupation in Germany.
He holds the General Service and Victory Medals, and was demobilised in May, 1919.
25, Villiers Road, Willesden. 16725.

COLLINS, F., Q.M.S., 17th Middlesex Regt.
He joined in July, 1915, went to France in 1918, and was gassed during the Advance in August of that year.
He was demobilised in April, 1919, having taken part in many engagements, holding the General Service and Victory Medals.
43, Guilsborough Road, Willesden. 15243.

COLLINS, G. E. C., Lce.-Cpl., Middlesex Regt.
He joined in August, 1915, and after training was retained in England as an instructor, until he was sent to France in 1917. Here he took part in many important engagements, including those at Arras, Ypres and Vimy Ridge, and was wounded.
He was discharged in June, 1918, and holds the General Service and Victory Medals.
211a, Kilburn Lane, W.10 X18716.

COLLINS, J. E., Pte., 2nd Middlesex Regt.
He enlisted in August, 1914, and served in France, where he
was wounded in an engagement at Neuve Chapelle in May,
1915, in consequence of which he lost a leg.
He was discharged in February, 1916, unfit for further service.
He holds the 1914 Star, General Service and Victory Medals.
17, Lorenco Road, Tottenham. X17990B.

COLLINS, J. H., Pte., Notts and Derby Regt.
He joined in November, 1916, and in the following year was
sent to France, where he took part in several engagements,
including the battle of Cambrai. He was badly gassed while
on active service.
He holds the Victory and General Service Medals, and was
demobilised in February, 1920.
11, Brereton Road, Tottenham. X18381.

COLLINS, M., Rifleman, Rifle Brigade and Driver, R.A.S.C.
He joined in January, 1916, was sent to France in March,
and took part in the battles of Arras, Albert, Bapaume and
Ypres, where he was gassed. He was invalided home early
in 1918, and, after being discharged from hospital, was driving
in the R.A.S.C. until demobilised in January, 1919.
He holds the General Service and Victory Medals.
11, Carlyle Avenue, Harlesden. 13691.

COLLINS, T., Pte., Royal West Kent Regt.
He enlisted in September, 1914, was sent to France in
the following year, and was severely wounded in the battle
of the Somme in 1916.
He died of wounds on October 30th, 1916, and was entitled
to the 1914-15 Star, General Service and Victory Medals.
10, Sandringham Road, Willesden. T17346.

COLLINS, T., Sergt., R.F.A.
He joined in October, 1915, went to France in the same year,
took part in several battles, and lost his left arm and leg as
the result of shell fire at Cambrai in December, 1917.
He was discharged in October, 1918, and holds the 1914-15
Star, General Service and Victory Medals.
1, Tebworth Road Tottenham. X18119.

COLLINS, T. W., Pte., Royal Fusiliers.
He enlisted in October, 1915, and served in France for two
and a half years, taking part in all important engagements
on the Somme Front and elsewhere.
He was discharged in February, 1919, holding the General
Service and Victory Medals.
30, Western Road, Ealing. 10851.

COLLINS, W., Pte., South Wales Borderers.
He enlisted in August, 1914, and served at the Dardanelles
and in China. He was discharged in June, 1916, having been
rendered medically unfit through contracting malaria whilst
on service.
He holds the 1914-15 Star, General Service and Victory
Medals.
90, Angel Road, Edmonton. 16580.

COLLINS, W., Pte., Royal Fusiliers.
He joined in July, 1916, went to France in the same year,
to Italy in 1917, and to France again in 1918. He took part
in various engagements, including the battles of Hill 60
and Kemmel Hill; he was gassed and thrice wounded.
He was discharged in February, 1919, holding the General
Service and Victory Medals.
58, St. Margaret's Road, Hanwell. 11056.

COLLINS, W. J., Pte., 29th Labour Battalion.
He joined in October, 1917, and went to the Western Front
in November of the same year, taking part in numerous
engagements, until demobilised in January, 1919.
He holds the General Service and Victory Medals.
59, Waldo Road, Willesden. X17635.

COLLINSON, W. H., Pte., 7th London Regiment.
He joined in August, 1914, and saw active service in France,
and was killed at the battle of Cambrai on March 22nd, 1918.
He was entitled to the Victory and General Service Medals.
123, Harley Road, Harlesden. 13179.

COLLISON, J. E., Pte., Royal Scots Fusiliers and Seaforth Highlanders
He rejoined in November, 1915. but owing to an old wound
received during the South African Campaign, he was rejected
for service overseas. On making a special application,
however, his wish was gratified, and he was sent to the
Western Front, where he served from 1918 until he was
demobilised in January of the following year.
He holds the King's South African Medal with two clasps,
the Queen's South African Medal with seven clasps, and the
General Service and Victory Medals.
7, West Street, Lower Edmonton. 14232.

COLLS, C. C., Gunner, Trench Mortar Battery.
He joined in September, 1917, was sent to the Western
Front and took part in engagements at Ypres, Passchendaele,
Kemmel, Vimy, Messines and in the 1918 Advance. Later
he served with the Army of Occupation in Germany.
He holds the General Service and Victory Medals, and was
demobilised in 1919.
9, Lillie Mansions, Lillie Road, Fulham. X18458.

COLWELL, D. (Miss), Special War Worker.
This lady was engaged in the early part of the war in the
important work of aeroplane construction, and latterly was
employed in connection with life-saving devices at sea, a
work of very great national importance during the submarine
campaign. She only quitted the arduous work on the
Armistice being declared.
86, Chesson Road, W. Kensington. X17692.

COLWELL, D., Lce.-Cpl., Rifle Brigade.
He joined in August, 1914, and during his service on the
Western Front took part in many battles, including Neuve
Chapelle, La Bassée, Armentieres, and Sailly. He was
wounded and taken prisoner at Fromelles in May, 1915, and
escaped in November, 1916, being recaptured two days later,
but finally escaped six months previous to the Armistice.
He was demobilised in November, 1919, holding the 1915
Star, General Service and Victory Medals.
86, Chesson Road, West Kensington. 17239A.

COLWELL, F., Pte., Devonshire Regt.
He joined in 1915, and during his service on the Western
Front was wounded at the battle of Loos. After being in
hospital some time, he was invalided home. His ship,
however, was torpedoed in the Channel and he was drowned
with many others.
He was entitled to the 1914-15 Star, General Service and
Victory Medals.
86, Chesson Road, West Kensington. X17239B.

COLWELL, J. (M.M.), Pte., 2nd Batt. Royal Fusiliers.
He joined in August, 1914, and saw service in India, later
going to the Dardanelles, where he won the Military Medal
for conspicuous bravery in the field. He suffered from
trench feet, and was discharged in 1916, holding the 1914-15
Star, General Service and Victory Medals.
86, Chesson Road, West Kensington, W.14 X17240.

COLWELL, W. C., Gunner, R.G.A.
He joined in June, 1916, and served on the Western Front,
where he took part in many engagements. He was in hospital for 12 months on account of illness contracted on active
service.
On September 5th, 1919, he was demobilised, holding the
General Service and Victory Medals.
1, Lintaine Grove, Fulham. 16815.

COMBER, J., Gunner, R.F.A.
He was called up in August, 1914, and proceeded to France,
where he took part in the battles of Mons, the Somme, Vimy
Ridge, Arras, Albert, St Quentin and many others. For
seven months he was in hospital, having been invalided home,
and also underwent two operations as a result of an illness
caused through exposure whilst overseas.
He was demobilised in April, 1919, holding the 1914 Star,
General Service and Victory Medals.
8, Mund Street, W.14 16927.

CONDON, R., Pte., Royal Fusiliers and Labour Corps.
He joined in September, 1915, and during his service on the
Western Front took part in the fighting at the Somme,
Ypres, Armentieres, Amiens, Vimy Ridge and in the last
Advance, and later was sent down to the base, where he held
an important post.
He holds the General Service and Victory Medals, and was
demobilised in January, 1919.
16, Butterswick Cottages, Great Church Lane, Hammersmith.
15878B.

CONDON, W., Pte., Worcestershire Regt.
He joined in 1916, and during his service in India helped to
quell a rising that occurred, and afterwards was stationed at
Poona, Bombay, engaged on clerical work in the Accounts
Department.
He holds the General Service and Victory Medals, and was
demobilised in 1919.
16, Butterswick Cottages, Great Church Lane, Hammersmith.
15878A.

CONNELL, G. E., Pte., 7th London Regiment.
He joined in July, 1915, and served on duty at various stations
with his unit until discharged in the same year as medically
unfit for further service for his country.
32, Humbolt Road, W.6 15146B.

CONNELL, H. P., Sapper, R.E.
He joined in March, 1915, and served on the Western Front, taking part in many engagements. He was invalided home and discharged in September, 1918, suffering from shell-shock. He holds the General Service and Victory Medals.
6, Protheroe Road, Fulham.   16833.

CONNELL, J., Cpl., 3/9th Middlesex Regt. (attached Labour Corps).
He joined the Middlesex Regiment in 1914, and was later transferred to the Labour Corps and sent to France. He served on the Western Front for some time, and was demobilised in 1918.
He holds the General Service and Victory Medals.
98, Holly Lane, Willesden.   15395.

CONNELL, J. M., Pte., 11th Royal Fusiliers.
He joined in October, 1914, and went out to the Western Front almost immediately. He saw a great deal of active service, taking part in numerous engagements, till he was eventually killed in an engagement at Armentieres in August, 1916.
He was entitled to the 1914-15 Star, General Service and Victory Medals.
89, Bounces Road, Edmonton.   13076.

CONNELLY, M. C., Sergt., R.H.A. and Royal Defence Corps.
He rejoined in August, 1914, having previously served for 12 years, and was stationed at various places with his unit, on important guard duties.
He holds the King's and Queen's South African Medals, and was demobilised in June, 1919.
27, Greyhound Road, Willesden.   X17611.

CONNIRE, M., Pte., R.A.S.C.
He enlisted in 1914, was sent to France in the same year, and took part in the battles of Mons, Ypres, Loos, Arras, the Somme, Bullecourt, Passchendaele, Neuve Chapelle and Hill 60.
He was demobilised in 1919, and holds the 1914 Star, General Service and Victory Medals.
35, Barret's Green Road, Harlesden.   13783C.

CONNON, W. B., Pte., R.A.S.C.
He joined in 1915, and served for four years on the Western Front. As a driver he was attached to a field ambulance during the Great Retreat and Advance in 1918.
In 1919 he was demobilised, holding the 1915 Star, the General Service and Victory Medals.
19, Denton Road, Harlesden.   14705.

CONNOR, J., Pte., R.A.S.C.
He joined in May, 1915, and later was drafted to the Western Front, where he was engaged with the food transport, and was present during engagements at Ypres, Loos, Neuve Chapelle, Armentieres, Vimy Ridge, Bullecourt, Messines and Amiens, and in the final Advance of 1918. Afterwards he was employed on graves' registration in France.
He holds the 1915 Star, General Service and Victory Medals, and was demobilised in January, 1919.
56, Orbain Road, Fulham.   X18684.

CONROY, E. A., Cpl., 2/10th Middlesex Regt.
He joined in March, 1915, and went to the Dardanelles in November of the same year. Later he was drafted to Egypt. During his service he was wounded three times. He was demobilised in August, 1919, holding the 1915 Star, General Service and Victory Medals.
114, Gresham Road, Neasden.   15742.

CONROY, E. W., Pte., 2/7th Middlesex Regt.
He enlisted in 1914, was sent to Egypt in the same year, and in 1916 to France. He was severely wounded while in action on the Somme, after taking part in other engagements, and in February, 1917, was discharged unfit for further service.
He holds the 1914 Star, General Service and Victory Medals.
118, Kimberley Road, Upper Edmonton.   16790.

CONSTABLE, C., Pte., R.A.S.C.
He joined in January, 1915, served in France, where he took part in many engagements, and later was sent to Russia. He was demobilised in August, 1919, holding the General Service and Victory Medals.
95, Kimberley Road, Edmonton.   16803.

CONSTABLE, W. H., Pte., Middlesex Regt. and R.A.S.C.
He joined in July, 1915, served on the Western Front from March until September, 1916, and from April to September, 1917, and took part in the battles of Ypres, Arras, Amiens, Albert, Messines, where he was wounded in August, 1916, and the Somme, where he was again wounded in the following year.
He was demobilised on February 27th, 1919, holding the General Service and Victory Medals.
12, Rigeley Road, College Park, Willesden.   X17672.

CONWAY, C. W., Driver, R.F.A.
He joined in October, 1915, served on the Western Front for three years, and took part in the fighting at Arras, Messines, Ypres, Passchendaele, Cambrai, and in the Retreat and Advance of 1918.
He was demobilised in August, 1919, holding the General Service and Victory Medals.
62, Dyson's Road, Edmonton.   T16849.

COOK, A. A., Driver, R.F.A.
He joined in August 1914, saw active service in France, at Ypres and on the Somme, and was gassed whilst in action. He holds the 1914 Star, the General Service and Victory Medals, and was discharged in July, 1916.
2, Winchester Road, Edmonton.   14689B.

COOK, A. A., Rifleman, King's Royal Rifle Corps.
He joined in 1915, and served in France until 1918, during which period he took part in various engagements, and was wounded in action in April, 1917.
He was demobilised in 1919, and holds the 1915 Star, General Service and Victory Medals.
19, Winchester Road, Lower Edmonton.   14877.

COOK, A. E., Pte., Royal Fusiliers.
He joined in August, 1918, and after training was sent out to the East to serve with the Army of Occupation in Mesopotamia.
28, Berry Street, Willesden.   15414B.

COOK, A. E., Driver, R.F.A.
He enlisted in September, 1914, served on the Western Front from June, 1915, until he was demobilised in March, 1919, and took part in the battles of Loos, the Somme, Armentieres, Arras, Amiens, Albert and Cambrai.
He was awarded the 1914-15 Star, General Service and Victory Medals.
92, Strode Road, Willesden.   X17314.

COOK, A. E., Pte., 3rd London Regt.
He joined in November, 1915, was sent to France in the following year, and took part in the third battle of Ypres, the battle of Arras, and the Retreat and Advance of 1918, serving with the trench mortars.
He was demobilised in August, 1919, holding the General Service and Victory Medals.
18, Shakespeare Avenue, Harlesden.   14200.

COOK, A. T., Gunner, R.G.A.
He joined in December, 1915, and served in France for two years, during which time he was in action at Ypres, Passchendaele, St. Quentin, Amiens, Peronne, St. Julien and other places.
He was demobilised in March, 1919, holding the General Service and Victory Medals.
123, Felixstowe Road, Edmonton.   14097A.

COOK, A. T., Sapper, Royal Engineers.
He joined in January, 1915, and served in France, taking part in the battles of the Somme, Ypres and Arras.
He was demobilised in December, 1918, holding the General Service and Victory Medals.
1, Chancellor's Street, Hammersmith.   13268.

COOK, C., Pte., Northumberland Fusiliers.
He joined in September, 1914, and went to the Western Front in 1915, taking part in the battles of Ypres, Loos, Armentieres, Rheims, Amiens and the Great Retreat and Advance in 1918.
He had previously fought in the Boer War, and served at Khartoum and in the Soudan, and holds the Medals for those campaigns, also the 1915 Star, General Service and Victory Medals.
He was demobilised in February, 1919.
89, Berry Street, Willesden.   15420.

COOK, C., Pte., R.A.S.C. (M.T.).
He joined in December, 1915, and served on the Western Front, engaged on the transport of food and ammunition. He was present at the battles of Ypres, the Somme, Arras, Cambrai, Bullecourt, Albert, St. Quentin and many others, and was gassed.
On February 27th, 1919, he was demobilised, and holds the General Service and Victory Medals.
23, Mulgrave Road, Fulham.   16177.

COOK, C. G., Pte., 21st Middlesex Regt.
He joined in June, 1915, and did duty at various stations. He was discharged in the same year, being unable to render his country further service in the Army, due to being medically unfit.
123, Felixstowe Road, Edmonton.   14097B.

COOK, C. W., Gunner, R.F.A.
He joined in August, 1916, and served on the Western Front, being in action at Ypres and Cambrai. During his service he was in hospital for a time, suffering with neuritis.
In June, 1919, he was demobilised, and holds the General Service and Victory Medals.
18, Bramber Road, Fulham.   16263.

COOK, C. W. G., Gunner, Royal Garrison Artillery.
He joined the R.A.M.C. in October, 1914, and was on active service in France, Salonica and Egypt; he was also with General Allenby at the victorious entry into Jerusalem, having transferred to the Artillery while in Egypt. He was wounded and suffered from malaria.
He holds the General Service and Victory Medals, and was demobilised in February, 1919.
97, Yeldham Road, W.6   13241.

COOK, E., Lce.-Cpl., 7th London Regiment.
He joined in April, 1915, served on the Western Front, and took part in the battles of Ypres, Arras, Bourlon Wood, Cambrai, High Wood, Hill 60, Messines and Villers-Bretonneux, where he was badly gassed.
He was demobilised in March, 1919, holding the General Service and Victory Medals.
79, Archel Road, W. Kensington.   16665A.

COOK, E. F., Pte., 2/3rd Royal Fusiliers.
He joined in May, 1915, went to the Western Front in 1917, and died on May 8th of the same year, from wounds received in action during the battle of Ypres, and is buried at the cemetery at Achiet le Grand.
He was entitled to the General Service and Victory Medals.
25, Denton Road, Harlesden.   14704A.

COOK, E. N., Pte., 2nd Royal Berkshire Regt.
He enlisted in 1908, left India for France on the outbreak of war, and took part in the retreat from Mons and the battles of Ypres and Loos, where he was wounded in September, 1915.
He was discharged unfit for further service in June, 1916, and holds the Mons Star, General Service and Victory Medals.
103, Oldfield Road, Willesden.   16059A.

COOK, E. R. (jun.), Lce.-Cpl., 9th East Surrey Regt.
He joined in April, 1917, and served on the Western Front, taking part in the last Advance in 1918, during which he was wounded.
Before his demobilisation in October, 1919, he served for a short period in Germany. He holds the General Service and Victory Medals.
3, Hetton Street, W.6   15137.B.

COOK, E. R., Sapper, Royal Engineers.
He enlisted in August, 1915, and was sent to the Western Front the same year, being stationed for most of his service in France at No. 5 Labour Park.
On October 16th, 1917, he was discharged, and holds the 1915 Star, General Service and Victory Medals.
3, Hetton Street, W.6   15137A.

COOK, F., P.O., R.N., H.M.S. " Bacchante."
He joined in August, 1914, and served in the Dardanelles, Gallipoli and the North Sea, taking part in the battle of Heligoland and the defence of the Suez Canal. He was once wounded.
He was discharged in May, 1919, holding the 1914 Star, General Service and Victory Medals.
22, Delorme Street, Fulham.   14088.

COOK, F. A., Signalman, R.N., H.M.S. " Castor."
He joined in January, 1915, and served with the Grand Fleet in the North Sea and at Scapa Flow. He took part in the battle of Jutland, where he lost his leg.
He was discharged on November 2nd, 1916, holding the 1915 Star, the General Service and Victory Medals.
56, St. Margaret's Road, Hanwell.   11057.

COOK, F. J., Sergt., 2nd Durham Light Infantry.
He enlisted in September, 1916, and was sent to France, where he saw active service for some time. Later he went to Russia, and remained there with his battalion.
He holds the General Service and Victory Medals.
12, Osman Road, Edmonton.   15779.

COOK, G. C., Pte., Wiltshire Regt.
He joined in March, 1917, and saw service on the Western Front. In the German Advance in April, 1918, he was captured, and was kept a prisoner for nine months. Whilst in Germany he suffered greatly from lack of proper food, and was admitted to hospital in consequence.
After repatriation he was demobilised in January, 1920, holding the General Service and Victory Medals.
50, Rosaline Road, Fulham.   X18196.

COOK, G. H., Signaller, R.F.A.
He enlisted in April, 1916, and was drafted to France in December of the same year. He was in action at Ypres, Cambrai, Lille and numerous other sectors, and was demobilised in March, 1919, holding the General Service and Victory Medals.
51, Leopold Road, Willesden.   14911.

COOK, I. (Mrs.), Special War Worker.
This lady volunteered her services for war work at the time of national danger, and was engaged on work of no small importance in a food store room, where her duties were of an arduous nature. 79, Archel Road, W. Kensington.   16665B.

COOK, L. W., Gunner, R.G.A.
He joined in January, 1917, and was sent to France in December of the same year. He was in action at Ypres, the Somme, Arras, Amiens and Vimy Ridge. He was gassed and subsequently discharged in December, 1918.
He holds the General Service and Victory Medals.
63, Villiers Road, Willesden.   T17326.

COOK, P., Sergt., Royal West Kent Regt.
He enlisted in 1916, was sent to the East in the same year, and took part in operations in India until 1919, when he was demobilised.
He holds the General Service and Victory Medals.
103, Sheldon Road, Upper Edmonton.   X17189.

COOK, T., Pte., Middlesex Regt.
He joined in November, 1915, and in the same year was sent out to Salonica, where he took part in many engagements and was wounded in the leg.
He was demobilised in January, 1920, and holds the 1915 Star, General Service and Victory Medals.
43, Eastbourne Avenue, Lower Edmonton.   13301.

COOK, T., Pte., Royal Fusiliers.
He enlisted in August, 1914, and was sent out to France, where he saw active service in various sectors. Whilst in France he met with a serious accident, and died from the effects in Chichester Military Hospital.
He was entitled to the 1914 Star, General Service and Victory Medals.
16, Aintree Street, Fulham.   TX18634.

COOK, V. G., Pte., Middlesex Regt.
He joined in June, 1918, and after a period of training served with the Army of Occupation in Germany.
He was subsequently demobilised in March, 1920.
25, Denton Road, Harlesden.   14704B.

COOK, V. J., Pte., 3rd London Regt.
He joined in 1916, and in the same year was drafted to France. He took part in several engagements, and was wounded at Passchendaele Ridge. For a period he was placed in charge of German prisoners.
He was demobilised in January, 1918, and holds the General Service and Vitctory Medals.
18, Shakespeare Avenue, Harlesden.   14199.

COOK, W. G., Lce.-Cpl., R.A.S.C.
He enlisted in March, 1915, and was stationed for two years on duty in Ireland. In 1917 he was sent to France, where he is still serving.
He holds the General Service and Victory Medals.
16, Gilpin Grove, Edmonton.   16809.

COOK, W. J., Cpl., Royal Defence Corps.
He volunteered in January, 1915, and was employed on important guard and garrison duties until he was demobilised in February, 1919. He had previously served his country for over 20 years in the Navy.
16, College Road, Willesden.   X18004.

COOK, W. W., Petty Officer Stoker, R.N., H.M.S. " Hussar."
He joined in August, 1914, and was engaged in highly dangerous mine-sweeping and patrol duties in the Irish and Mediterranean Sea, and in the Atlantic. After being demobilised in January, 1919, he volunteered for Russia and, with the Mercantile Marine, served there from May, 1919, until the following November.
He holds the 1915 Star, General Service and Victory Medals.
79, Burn's Road, Harlesden, N.W.10   13458.

COOKE, W. H., Special War Worker.
Being exempted from military service, he was engaged on work of the greatest national importance at Messrs. Brown's Aircraft Works at Hammersmith, in connection with the construction of aeroplanes for the Royal Air Force. His work was of great value.
25, Mablethorpe Road, Fulham.   X19226/C.

COOLE, L., Lce.-Cpl., Royal Army Ordnance Corps.
He volunteered for service in 1915, and did duty at various stations, but was discharged in 1917 as being medically unfit for further service. He, however, re-enlisted in September, 1919, and was sent to Russia until March, 1920.
40, Shelley Road, Harlesden.   13648

COOMBER, A., Pte., 1st Royal West Kent Regt
He joined in August, 1914, went to France, and was killed in action at Hill 60 on April 18th, 1915.
He was entitled to the Mons Star, the General Service and Victory Medals.
63, Greyhound Road, Fulham.   15281.

COOMBES, A. J., Gunner, R.F.A.
He was serving at the outbreak of war and in October, 1914, proceeded to France, afterwards being sent to Egypt and Salonica.
He was demobilised in June, 1919, having taken part in numerous engagements, and holds the 1914 Star, the General Service and Victory Medals.
15, Corby Road, Harlesden.   14402.

COOMBES, C. A., Pte., Royal Scottish, and The Queen's (Royal West Surrey) Regts.
He joined in October, 1915, and was sent to the Western Front in March, 1918. He was in action in France during the last Great Retreat, and again in the final Advance in September, 1918.
He was discharged in April, 1919, and holds the General Service and Victory Medals.
40, Waldo Road, Willesden, N.W.   X17562.

COOMBS, G. D., Pte., Essex Regt. and 11th Middlesex Regt.
He joined in December, 1914, and was sent to the Western Front, where he took part in engagements at Loos, Ypres and elsewhere. He was twice severely wounded, and was in hospital in France and England.
He was discharged in January, 1919, and holds the 1915 Star, General Service and Victory Medals.
71, Reporton Road, Fulham, S.W.   X18917.

COOPER, A., Pte., 11th Essex Regt.
He joined in November, 1914, and in the following year went to the Western Front, where he fought on the Somme. On December 19th, 1915, he was killed at Loos, being buried by the collapse of a dug-out.
He was entitled to the 1914-15 Star, the General Service and Victory Medals.
87, Durban Road, N.17   X17968.

COOPER, A. E., Pte., O.T.C. (Inns of Court).
He volunteered in September,1914, and saw service at various stations. Being unfit for foreign service at the time he was retained for duties with the Officers' Training Corps at Berkhampstead and elsewhere until May, 1919, when he was demobilised.
50, Bramber Road, Fulham.   16269.

COOPER, A. V., Pte., Norfolk and Border Regt.
He joined in May, 1915, and served in Egypt for 10 months, and afterwards he was sent to France, where he took part in many engagements, including Ypres, Loos, the Somme, Cambrai and Arras, being killed in action on September 27th, 1916.
He was entitled to the 1914-15 Star, General Service and Victory Medals.
18, Oldfield Road, Willesden.   16109A.

COOPER, A. M. (Miss), Special War Worker.
This lady volunteered for service during the war, and was engaged in the T.N.T. shop at the Park Royal National Filling Factory. Her duties were of an arduous and dangerous nature.
19, Steele Road, Harlesden.   14372A.

COOPER, C., Gunner, R.F.A.
He joined in 1914, and served on the Western Front, taking part in the battles of Ypres, Dickebusch and Neuve Chapelle. He was badly gassed, and invalided out of the Army as medically unfit for further service in 1915.
He holds the 1914-15 Star, General Service and Victory Medals. 19, Steele Road, Harlesden.   14372C.

COOPER, C. A., Pte., R.A.S.C. and Labour Corps.
He enlisted in March,1915, and served in France and Belgium with the R.A.S.C. and Labour Corps, taking part in many engagements, until he was demobilised in January, 1919.
He holds the General Service and Victory Medals.
4, Lorenco Road, Tottenham.   X17997A.

COOPER, C. A. (jun.), Air Mechanic, R.A.F.
He joined in March, 1917, and after a period of training saw service with the Royal Air Force at various stations. He was later drafted for duty to the East, and was demobilised in November, 1919.
He holds the General Service and Victory Medals.
4, Lorenco Road, Tottenham.   X17997B.

COOPER, C. H., Pte., Middlesex Regt.
He joined in 1917, was sent to France in the same year, and took part in the fighting on the Somme and at Ypres, and was once severely wounded.
He was demobilised in March, 1919, and holds the General Service and Victory Medals.
26, Gloucester Road, Edmonton.   X17013.

COOPER, D. R. (Mrs.), R.A.S.C.
This lady volunteered her services and served with the Forage Corps in various parts of the country, her assistance being of the greatest importance.
6, Eli Street, West Kensington.   16918B.

COOPER, D. V. (Miss), Q.M.A.A.C.
This lady joined the Q.M.A.A.C. in 1917, and served in France at Abbeville.
At the time of her service Abbeville was subjected to very severe night bombing raids by the enemy, and she was subjected to considerable danger.
She was demobilised in 1919, holding the General Service and Victory Medals.
19, Steele Road, Harlesden.   14372B.

COOPER, E., Pte., R.A.S.C.
He joined in 1915, and served on the Western Front. He was in hospital with bronchitis in France and Portsmouth, and was finally discharged unfit for further service in May, 1918.
He was awarded the 1914-15 Star, General Service and Victory Medals.
66, Bramber Road, Fulham.   16227A.

COOPER, E. H., Leading Stoker, Royal Navy, H.M.S. " Queen."
He was in the Navy at the outbreak of war, and since 1914 saw much service in the North Sea, the Dardanelles and Adriatic.
He was demobilised in March, 1920. Entitled to 1914-15 Star, General Service and Victory Medals.
27, Manor Park Road, Harlesden.   13224B.

COOPER, E. T., Rifleman, The Rifle Brigade.
He joined in March, 1917, was sent to France, and taken prisoner in March, 1918, at St. Quentin. He was in captivity for nine months, returned home and then went to Egypt, where he served until demobilised in April, 1920.
He holds the General Service and Victory Medals.
66, Bramber Road, Fulham.   16227B.

COOPER, F. M. (Mrs.), Special War Worker.
From 1916 until the Armistice this lady was engaged on work of the greatest national importance at a London munition factory on the inspection of fuses and other munitions. She was commended for her work.
90, Ilex Road, Willesden.   15946A.

COOPER, G., Air Mechanic, R.A.F.
He joined in May, 1918, and being at the time medically unfit for overseas service, was stationed at the Royal Gun Factory at Waltham Cross. Whilst on duty he met with a serious accident.
He holds the General Service Medal, and was demobilised in 1919.
115, Durban Road, Tottenham.   X17956.

COOPER, G. W., Sergt., 5th Royal Fusiliers.
He joined in September, 1914, and served for two years on the Western Front. During this period he took part in the battles of the Somme, Ypres, Cambrai, Vimy Ridge, St. Quentin and many other engagements. He was twice wounded, and gassed. From April, 1917, until his demobilisation in April, 1920, he served at home, being then medically unfit for further service overseas.
He holds the 1914-15 Star, General Service and Victory Medals.
13, Brownlow Road, Harlesden, N.W.10   14931.

COOPER, H., Lce.-Cpl., 20th Middlesex Regt.
He joined in August, 1914, and served for three years on the Western Front, taking part in the battles of Arras, Cambrai, Vimy Ridge, Somme, Ypres and other engagements.
He was demobilised in June, 1919, and holds the General Service and Victory Medals.
46, Purves Road, Kensal Rise, N.W.10   X18038.

COOPER, H. F., Acting-Sergt., R.A.S.C. (M.T.).
He joined in June, 1915, and served on the Western Front. In 1916 he was discharged as medically unfit, but in 1918 re-enlisted in the Army Pay Corps. He had previously served ten years in the R.M.L.I.
He was demobilised in June, 1919, and is entitled to the 1915 Star, General Service and Victory Medals.
27, Manor Park Road, Harlesden.   13224A.

COOPER, L. J., Pte., Bedfordshire Regt.
He joined in July, 1918, and after his period of training served in Germany with the Army of Occupation until April 20th, 1920, when he was demobilised.
14, Cranbrook Road, Tottenham, N.17   X18560A.

COOPER, R. F., Pte., 2nd Essex Regt. and 22nd London Regt.
He joined in April, 1917, and during his service on the Western Front took part in the battle of Arras and the last Advance, was gassed, and suffered from shell shock. Later he was drafted to Egypt, where he remained until his demobilisation in March, 1920.
He holds the General Service and Victory Medals.
9, Eric Road, Willesden, N.W.10   15979.

COOPER, W., Pte., 7th Royal Sussex Regt.

He joined in September, 1915, and served for a time on the Western Front, after a long period of service in various places in England, taking part in the last Advance in 1918. He was demobilised in February, 1919, and holds the General Service and Victory Medals.
6, Eli Street, W. Kensington. 16918A.

COOPER, W., Gunner, R.F.A.

He enlisted in August, 1914, served on the Western Front, and was in action at Loos, Arras, Ypres, Cambrai and on the Somme. He was awarded the Belgian Military Medal for conspicuous gallantry on the field during the fighting at Poelcappelle on September 28th and 29th, 1918, and also has a letter from the General Officer commanding the 15th Army Corps, commending him for his excellent work. He was demobilised in June, 1919, holding the 1914-15 Star, General Service and Victory Medals.
68, Bramber Road, Fulham. 16228.

COOPER, W., Rifleman, King's Royal Rifle Corps.

He enlisted in August, 1914, and served on the Western Front. He was reported missing, and later was reported to have been killed in action at Cambrai on November 21st, 1917.
Mrs. Cooper in due course received from his C.O. a letter of condolence.
He was entitled to the 1914-15 Star, General Service and Victory Medals.
19, Montagu Street, Hammersmith. 16404.

COOPER, W., Sergt., R.A.S.C.

He enlisted in 1914, was sent to Egypt in the following year, and in 1916 to France, where he was employed on important office duties until he was demobilised in 1919.
He holds the 1914-15 Star, General Service and Victory Medals.
90, Ilex Road, Willesden. 15946B.

COOPER, W. G. (D.C.M.), Sergt., Royal Engineers.

He joined in September, 1914, and after taking part in the Dardanelles campaign, was sent to Egypt. Later he was drafted to France, thence to Italy, and after a while back again to the Western Front, where he took part in the battle of the Somme, and was awarded the Distinguished Conduct Medal and a Belgian Award for conspicuous bravery and gallantry on the field.
He holds also the 1914-15 Star, General Service and Victory Medals, and was demobilised in March, 1919.
16, Laundry Road, Fulham. 15339.

COOPER, W. T. F. (M.M.), Sergt., Duke of Wellington's (West Riding Regt.).

He joined in February, 1915, and served in France, taking part in many engagements. He was awarded the Military Medal for conspicuous gallantry in the field, and was mentioned in despatches for distinguished conduct and devotion to duty at Valenciennes. He was also in action on the Cambrai Front in the last big Advance, and was demobilised in February, 1919.
He also holds the General Service and Victory Medals.
30, Purves Road, Kensal Rise, N.W.10 X18243.

COOTE, A. C., Pte., Royal Welch Fusiliers.

He joined in July, 1916, went to France the following year, and served in many sectors of the Western Front and at many engagements.
He holds the General Service and Victory Medals, and was demobilised in October, 1919.
11, Sunnyside Road South, Lower Edmonton. 14344.

COOTE, C. J., Rifleman, London Rifle Brigade.

He joined in May, 1915, and in June, 1916, was discharged on medical grounds. The strain of military service impaired his constitution, and he died shortly afterwards.
51, Love Lane, Tottenham. X18308.

COOTE, C. S., Pte., 2nd Manchester Regt.

He re-enlisted in August, 1914, having previously served for six years, and while on the Western Front took part in the battles of Mons, Loos, Arras, Ypres and the Somme. He was wounded in action in the right leg, and injured in both feet by an accident, and was detained in hospital for some months in consequence.
He was demobilised in January, 1919, holding the Mons Star, General Service and Victory Medals.
10, King's Road, Tottenham. X18543.

COPE, A. E., Pte., The Queen's (Royal West Surrey Regt.).

He joined in 1916, and the same year was sent to France, where he took part in engagements on the Somme, and was killed in December, 1916.
He was entitled to the General Service and Victory Medals.
67, St. Paul's Road, Tottenham. X18823B.

COPE, A. L., Pte., Royal Fusiliers.

He joined in 1917, and the same year was sent to France, where he took part in engagements on the Somme. He was killed in action in October, 1918, and was entitled to the General Service and Victory Medals.
67, St. Paul's Road, Tottenham. X18823C.

COPE, C. W., Pte., Royal Defence Corps.

He volunteered for service in September, 1914, and served until January, 1918, when he was discharged medically unfit, as a result of rheumatism contracted whilst in the Service.
11, Gloucester Road, Edmonton. X17172.

COPE, F. W., Pte., Connaught Rangers.

He joined in 1914, and the following year was sent out to France, where he was present in engagements on the Somme. From 1916 he saw much service in Mesopotamia and Palestine.
He holds the 1915 Star, General Service and Victory Medals, and was demobilised in January, 1919.
67, St. Paul's Road, Tottenham. X18823A.

COPE, H. A., Gunner, Canadian R.F.A.

He joined in 1915, and served on the Western Front, being in action on the Somme, at Armentieres, Ypres and other places, and was wounded.
In 1918 he was discharged as medically unfit, owing to wounds, and holds the 1914-15 Star, General Service and Victory Medals.
39, Archel Road, W. Kensington, W.14 16201C.

COPPERWHEAT, W. G., Driver, R.F.A.

He joined in April, 1915, and in the same year went to the Western Front, where he took part in the battle of Ypres. In December, 1915, he was drafted to Salonica, and for nearly three years served on the Doiran Front. Whilst overseas he was wounded three times, and twice gassed, in consequence of which he was discharged unfit for further service in March, 1919.
He holds the 1915 Star and the General Service and Victory Medals.
31, Droop Street, Queen's Park, W.10 X18581B.

CORBETT, B. L. (Mrs.), Special War Worker.

This lady was engaged at Park Royal in the I.S.A.A. Department as overseer in the ammunition section for four years. She went through several air raids while on duty, and holds the Kitchener certificate. Her work was of the greatest importance.
97, Rucklidge Avenue, Harlesden. 13154A.

CORBETT, J. J., Stoker, R.N., H.M.S. " Cornwall."

He joined in March, 1916, and was engaged on highly dangerous convoy duties, taking part in several submarine engagements.
He holds the General Service and Victory Medals, and was demobilised in March, 1919.
97, Rucklidge Avenue, Harlesden. 13154B.

CORBOULD, A., Pte., Military Police and Sapper, R.E. (Postal Service).

He joined in 1917, and in the following year was sent out to the Western Front, where he took part in the last Advance in 1918. He was then transferred to the Army of Occupation on the Rhine, and is still serving at Cologne, being attached to the 1st Brigade, Rhine Army Signals.
He holds the General Service and Victory Medals.
118, Fortune Gate Road, Harlesden. 13189.

CORBY, H., Pte., 9th Middlesex Regt.

He joined in March, 1916, and in the same year went out to the Western Front, where he remained until 1919. He took part in engagements at Ypres, Arras, Cambrai, Bullecourt and many other important battles, including the German offensive in 1918. He was twice wounded, once very severely, and was discharged as unfit for further service in December, 1919.
He holds the General Service and Victory Medals.
121, Rucklidge Avenue, Harlesden. 13149B.

CORBY, S., Pte., R.A.S.C.

He joined in September, 1916, and went to the Western Front the same year, where he remained until 1919. He was engaged on special duties until he was demobilised on October 18th, 1919.
He holds the General Service and Victory Medals.
121, Rucklidge Avenue, Harlesden. 13149A.

CORDING, A., Driver, Middlesex Regt. and R.E.

He enlisted in 1914, and served in France from 1915 to 1919, taking part in many engagements.
He holds the 1914-15 Star, General Service and Victory Medals, and was demobilised in February, 1919.
73, Somerset Road, Edmonton. X17041B.

CORDON, G. R., Signaller, 18th Rifle Brigade.
He joined in October, 1914, and served for four years in India and Burma on detachment duty. He had formerly served in the Boer War with the City Imperial Volunteers. On December 31st, 1919, he was demobilised, holding the General Service and Victory Medals. He also holds the South African Medals.
92, Carlyle Avenue, Harlesden. 14451.

CORDWENT, G. A., Driver, R.F.A.
He joined in April, 1915, served on the Western Front from December, 1915, until July, 1919, taking part in the battles of the Somme, Ypres, Ancre, Arras, Nieuport and Meteren, and was wounded.
He was demobilised in July, 1919, holding the 1915 Star, General Service and Victory Medals.
74, Mordaunt Road, Harlesden. 13858.

CORIO, P. W., Rifleman, King's Royal Rifle Corps.
He enlisted in August, 1914, was sent to France, and killed in action at Neuve Chapelle on March 10th, 1915.
He was entitled to the 1914 Star, General Service and Victory Medals.
1, Chapel Street, Hammersmith. 12502.

CORNELL, G., Pte., The Queen's (Royal West Surrey Regt.).
He enlisted in 1915 and served in France, taking part in many engagements, and was killed in action, and buried at Arles, on the Somme, on February 27th, 1917.
He was entitled to the General Service and Victory Medals.
38, Nursery Street, Tottenham. X18150.

CORNELL, H., Sapper, Royal Engineers.
He joined in February, 1915, and went to the Western Front in the September following. He served through many engagements in France, at Amiens and Mericourt, and was later transferred to the Eastern Front, where he took part in battles on the Struma and Doiran Fronts in the Balkan campaign, and the advance on the Turkish frontier.
He was discharged in May, 1919, and holds the 1915 Star, the General Service and Victory Medals.
20, Hiley Road, Willesden, N.W.10 X18650.

CORNELL, H. F., Pte., Machine Gun Corps.
He joined in June, 1915, and served in Egypt and Palestine as an officer's servant until 1920. He was wounded at the battle of Gaza on May 5th, 1917, and was in hospital at El-Arish.
Entitled to General Service and Victory Medals.
125, Raynham Avenue, Edmonton. 15832.

CORNELL, J. H., Gunner, R.F.A.
He joined in June, 1915, and served on the Western Front for four years, taking part in the battles of Arras, Loos, the Somme and other engagements.
He was demobilised in June, 1919, holding the 1915 Star, General Service and Victory Medals.
125, Raynham Avenue, Edmonton. 15833.

CORNISH, W. W., Sapper, R.E. (Railway Troops).
He joined in 1916, served on the Western Front, and took part in the fighting at Ypres, Dickebusch, Hazebrouck, St. Jean, and Roulers.
He was demobilised in January, 1919, and holds the General Service and Victory Medals.
46, Oldfield Road, Willesden. 16061.

CORNWELL, C. G., Driver, R.G.A.
He enlisted in May, 1916, and proceeded to France in the same year, where he saw service in various sectors. He remained in France until 1919, and was demobilised in September of the same year, holding the General Service and Victory Medals.
34, Lopen Road, Upper Edmonton. X17902.

CORNWELL, J., Cpl., Middlesex Regt.
He volunteered in August, 1914, and served in France, taking part in the battle of Mons. Here he was made prisoner of war, and was in captivity, suffering many hardships, until he eventually escaped in November, 1918.
He holds the Mons Star and General Service and Victory Medals, and was demobilised in May, 1920.
47, Church Road, Tottenham. X18346.

CORRIE, W. R., Pte., 13th Middlesex Regt.
He joined in September, 1914, and was sent to the Western Front in September of the following year. He was engaged at Loos, Armentieres, and in several battles in the Ypres sector.
He was discharged in December, 1917, and holds the 1914-15 Star, General Service and Victory Medals.
73, Deacon Road, Willesden, N.W. T17331A.

CORRIE, W. R., 1st Air Mechanic, R.A.F.
He joined in January, 1918, and after his period of training did duty at an important bombing school. He was engaged in repairing and tending aero engines, a duty calling for considerable technical skill.
73, Deacon Road, Willesden. T17331B.

COSTEN, J. E., Pte., Royal Army Vet. Corps.
He joined in July, 1915, and served in France for one year, and later in Italy for three years. He is now suffering from a fractured toe, the result of an injury received while on service.
He was demobilised in April, 1919, holding the General Service and Victory Medals and 1915 Star.
90, Angel Road, Lower Edmonton. 16568.

COSTON, T. W., Pte., 9th Middlesex Regt.
He joined in May, 1915, served on the Western Front from October until December, 1915, and in Salonica from the following year until 1918, when he was again sent to France. He took part in many engagements whilst abroad, was demobilised in March, 1919, and holds the 1915 Star, General Service and Victory Medals.
34, Sandringham Road, Willesden. 17350.

COTCHING, H., Lce.-Cpl., 57th Gordon Highlanders, Royal Fusiliers, and 2/4th Black Watch.
He joined in May, 1916, and was retained on special duties as an orderly to a medical officer.
He was demobilised in January, 1919.
59, Harley Road, Harlesden. 13178.

COTTAM, C., Sapper, Royal Engineers.
He joined in 1916, and after training in various parts of England, was sent to France, where he stayed until October, 1919, doing duty in various sectors.
He was then demobilised, and holds the General Service and Victory Mdeals.
10, Gilpin Grove, Edmonton. 16807.

COTTINGHAM, H., Rifleman, King's Royal Rifles.
He joined in June, 1915, and during his service on the Western Front took part in the battles of the Somme and Ypres, and was twice wounded.
He was demobilised in August, 1919, holding the General Service and Victory Medals.
25, Lowdon Road, Edmonton. 12850.

COTTON, F. J., Mechanic, R.A.F.
He joined in June, 1917, and saw service with the Royal Air Force and the Labour Corps at various stations. He was demobilised in March, 1919.
15, Werley Avenue, Fulham. X17737.

COTTRELL, A. E. (Mrs.), Special War Worker.
For three years during the war this lady was engaged on work of the greatest national importance, filling shells at the Filling Station, Stevenage Road, Fulham. Her duties were dangerous and very arduous, and she was commended for her work.
2, Averill Street, Fulham. 13998B.

COTTRELL, S. M., Airman, R.N.A.S. and R.A.F.
Joining originally the Royal Naval Air Service in 1917, he was later transferred to the Royal Air Force. His duties carried him to an important air-shed in Scotland, where he did good work in connection with the Air Ships.
He was demobilised in March, 1919.
2, Averill Street, Fulham. 13998A.

COUCH, J., Pte., Northumberland Fusiliers.
He joined in May, 1917, was sent to France in the same year, taking part in many engagements, and was wounded in action in 1918.
He was discharged in 1919, holding the General Service and Victory Medals.
20, South Street, Hammersmith. 12509.

COUCHMAN, T., Bombardier, R.F.A.
He joined in August, 1915, and was sent to the Western Front, where he was in action at Ypres, Arras, on the Somme, and at Cambrai with No. 177 Battery.
He was discharged in April, 1919, and holds the 1915 Star, General Service and Victory Medals.
65, Reporton Road, Fulham. X18913.

COULTER, A. M., Pte., R.A.M.C.
He volunteered in November, 1914, was sent to France in November, 1915, and in the following year to Greece, where he did important duty in a field ambulance.
He was discharged in November, 1917, and holds the 1915 Star, General Service and Victory Medals.
3, Beaconsfield Road, Willesden. 16084.

COULTON, J., Pte., 5th Buffs (East Kent Regt.).
He joined in March, 1917, and in the same year was sent to Mesopotamia, where he remained until 1919, taking part in the operations in that theatre.
He holds the General Service and Victory Medals, and was demobilised in October, 1919.
17, Newlyn Road, Tottenham. X18512.

COUNTER, J. H., Pte., Grenadier Guards.
He enlisted in 1915, served in France from 1916 to 1917, taking part in many engagements, and was badly wounded at the battle of the Somme.
He holds the General Service and Victory Medals, and was discharged in 1917, unfit for further service.
43, Star Road, W.14 16685.

COURT, F., Cpl., Middlesex Regt.
He joined in 1914, and saw much service on the Western Front up to 1916, when he was killed in action.
He was entitled to the 1914-15 Star, the General Service and Victory Medals.
22, Holly Lane, Willesden. 15570C.

COUSINS, A. E., Pte., 2nd Border Regt.
He enlisted in November, 1916, and served in France, taking part in many engagements.
He was sent to hospital for some time, was demobilised in March, 1919, and holds the General Service and Victory Medals.
24, Kingwood Road, Fulham, S.W.6 X19021.

COUSINS, E. H., Pte., R.A.M.C.
He joined in January, 1915, went to France the same year, and was present at many battles, including those of the Somme, Arras and La Bassée.
He holds the 1915 Star, General Service and Victory Medals, and was demobilised in 1919.
7, Sunnyside Park South, Lower Edmonton. 14343B.

COUSINS, H. A., Pte., 6th Dorset Regt.
He joined in April, 1917, served in France, and was killed in action on October 20th, 1917.
He was entitled to the General Service and Victory Medals.
84, Claybrook Road, Fulham. 13677A.

COUSINS, H. E., Trooper, Suffolk Yeomanry.
He volunteered in 1915, and was sent to Egypt in the same year. During his long service abroad he suffered very severely from malaria. He secured his demobilisation in August, 1919, holding the 1914-15 Star, the General Service and Victory Medals.
32, Lion Road, Lower Edmonton. 15192B.

COUSINS, H. G., Pte., R.A.M.C.
He joined in January, 1915, went to France the same year, and was present at the battles of the Somme, Ypres, Arras, La Bassée and Cambrai.
He holds the 1915 Star, General Service and Victory Medals, and was demobilised in June, 1919.
7, Sunnyside Road South, Lower Edmonton. 14343A.

COUSINS, M. H., Lce.-Cpl., R.A.M.C.
He joined in April, 1917, and served in France and with the Army of Occupation on the Rhine on important medical duties until demobilised in June, 1919.
He holds the General Service and Victory Medals.
84, Claybrook Road, Fulham. 13677B.

COVENTRY, R. M., Lce.-Cpl., 5th Middlesex Regiment.
He joined in February, 1916, and served with the Middlesex Regiment at various stations.
He was discharged in July, 1917, on account of ill-health.
79, Wendover Road, Harlesden. 12547.

COVENTRY, W. C., Driver, Royal Field Artillery.
He joined in August, 1914, served on the Western Front, at the battles of the Somme, Arras, Loos, Neuve Chapelle, Lille, Armentieres, Ypres, Bullecourt and in the last Advance at Cambrai, and was twice wounded.
He holds the 1914-15 Star, General Service and Victory Medals, and was demobilised in May, 1919.
64, Humbolt Road, Fulham. 15295.

COWARD, A. S., Steward, Transport Ship "Teelin Head."
He joined in August, 1914, and served in the North Sea on dangerous duties, where he was drowned on January 21st, 1918.
He was entitled to the Mercantile Marine, General Service and Victory Medals.
11, Lawn Gardens, Hanwell. 12283B.

COWARD, H. G., Driver, R.A.S.C. (M.T.).
He joined in January, 1916, and served on the Western Front until 1919, when he was demobilised. He was engaged on transport work in many parts of France with the Mechanical Section, and holds the General Service and Victory Medals.
11, Lawn Gardens, Hanwell. 12283A.

COWARD, W. N., Sergt., Northumberland Fus.
He joined in November, 1916, and was drafted to the Western Front, where he took part in the battles of Arras, Loos, Ypres, the Somme and other engagements, and was wounded. Later he served with the Army of Occupation in Germany, until he was demobilised in November, 1919.
He holds the General Service and Victory Medals.
54, Chamberlain Road, Edmonton. 14224.

COWDREY, T. W., Driver, R.A.S.C., attached 64th Field Ambulance.
He enlisted in September, 1914, was sent to France in the following November, and served on important transport duties in various sectors.
He was demobilised in May, 1919, holding the 1914 Star, the General Service and Victory Medals.
5, Corby Road, Harlesden. 14398.

COWELL, A., Gunner, Royal Garrison Artillery.
He volunteered in November, 1915, and saw service with the R.G.A. at various stations. Being at the time unfit for duty abroad, he was unsuccessful in being drafted overseas.
He was demobilised in 1917.
42, Ranelagh Road, Harlesden. 12563A.

COWELL, F.W., Gunner, Royal Garrison Artillery.
He joined in November, 1915, and served in France, being killed in action during the Advance on October 14th, 1918.
He was buried in the British Cemetery at Poperinghe, and was entitled to the General Service and Victory Medals.
42, Ranelagh Road, Harlesden. 12563B.

COWLAND, S., Pte., 1st Middlesex Regiment.
He joined in 1918 and went to France the same year. He took part in the engagements at Cambrai, on the Somme and at Ypres.
He was demobilised in February, 1919, and holds the General Service and Victory Medals.
27, Whitehall Street, Tottenham. X18348.

COWNE, A., Pte., Royal Berkshire Regiment.
He joined in August, 1914, and served on the Western Front, taking part in the battles of Ypres, the Marne, the Aisne and Arras, where he was wounded in 1916.
He was discharged in April, 1917, and holds the 1914-15 Star, General Service and Victory Medals.
359, Chapter Road, Willesden Green. T17322.

COWPER, W. H., Pte., Royal Fusiliers.
He enlisted in August, 1914, served on the Western Front, and took part in the battles of Cambrai, Arras and Loos, and was blown up and buried by enemy shell-fire during the Somme Advance in July, 1916.
He was demobilised in February, 1919, holding the 1915 Star, General Service and Victory Medals.
5, Church Path, Hammersmith. 15900.

COX, A., Gunner, Canadian Field Artillery.
He joined in 1915 and served in France, taking part in engagements at Vimy Ridge, St. Quentin, Arras, Armentieres, Lille and in the final Advance of 1918. He was gassed at Vimy Ridge, and was in hospital at Etaples.
He was demobilised in 1919, and holds the General Service and Victory Medals.
8, Humbolt Mansions, Lillie Road, Fulham. TX18886C.

COX, A. E. (Mrs.), Driver, W.R.A.F.
This lady volunteered for service, and in July, 1917, joined the W.R.A.F. and did duty at No. 1 S.A.R.D., Farnborough. Her duties were of an arduous nature, but she did not give up her post until August, 1919.
7, Church Lane, Willesden. 16031C.

COX, A. J., Lieut., Royal Air Force.
He joined the Middlesex Regiment in August, 1914, and also served in the Royal Inniskilling Fusiliers, and finally was transferred to the R.A.F. as an observer. In December, 1915, he was sent out to the Balkans, and remained there for two years, during which time he took part in many engagements. Later he went to India and took part in the Afghanistan campaign, in which he greatly distinguished himself, and was mentioned in despatches and recommended for a decoration.
He holds the 1915 Star, General Service, Victory and Afghan Medals.
88, Mordaunt Road, Harlesden. 13859.

COX, C., Pte., Royal Marines and Labour Corps.

He joined in 1915, and was sent to France at the latter end of the same year. He served from 1915 to 1918 in France, and was discharged as medically unfit, due to the strain of active service, in March, 1919.
He holds the 1914–15 Star, General Service and Victory Medals.
21, Holberton Gardens, College Park, Willesden, N.W.
X17553.

COX, C. F., Bombardier, Royal Field Artillery.

He volunteered in 1914, and served in France, taking part in engagements at Loos and the Somme. Later he went to Palestine, where he took part in local operations.
He was demobilised in 1919, and holds the Territorial, General Service and Victory Medals.
74, Tubb's Road, Harlesden, N.W.   12560A.

COX, F., Lce.-Cpl., 4th Irish Dragoon Guards.

He enlisted in 1914, and served in France, taking part in many engagements, including those of the Somme, Loos, Neuve Chapelle, Armentieres, Amiens, Vimy Ridge, Ypres, Bullecourt, St. Quentin and the Advance of 1918, and was wounded. Finally he went with the Army of Occupation, and was demobilised in 1919, holding the 1915 Star, General Service and Victory Medals.
8, Humbolt Mansions, Lillie Road, Fulham.   X18886B.

COX, F., 1st Air Mechanic, Royal Air Force.

He joined in 1918, and served in Germany with the Army of Occupation on important duties with the R.A.F. until his demobilisation in March, 1920.
74, Tubb's Road, Harlesden.   12560B.

COX, F., Sapper, Royal Engineers.

He joined in 1916, and was sent to France after a few months' training, serving for some time as driver on the Military Railways operating from Boulogne. He was transferred from this duty and took part in the fighting during the German Offensive and British Advance of 1918.
He was demobilised in 1919, and holds the General Service and Victory Medals.
65, Berry Street, Willesden.   15412.

COX, F. G., Gunner, Royal Garrison Artillery.

He joined in October, 1915, and served on the Western Front, taking part in the battles of Ypres, Cambrai, Loos, La Bassée, the Somme and other engagements, and in the Retreat and Advance of 1918 did important duty as a despatch carrier.
He was demobilised in March, 1919, and holds the 1915 Star, General Service and Victory Medals.
7, Church Lane, Willesden.   16031A.

COX, F. J., 1st Air Mechanic, Royal Air Force.

He volunteered in January, 1916, and was engaged at various stations with the R.A.F. (including Ireland and Farnborough) in overhauling the machines, a work calling for a high degree of skill.
He holds the General Service Medal.
7, Church Lane, Willesden.   16031B.

COX, F. T., Lce.-Cpl., Middlesex Regiment and Machine Gun Corps.

He joined in June, 1915, and the following year was sent to France, where he remained until he was demobilised in June, 1919. During this period he took part in engagements at Ypres and the Somme, was wounded in action at Cambrai in November, 1917, and also took part in the last Advance of 1918.
He holds the General Service and Victory Medals.
27, Hiley Road, Willesden.   TX18185.

COX, G., Rifleman, King's Royal Rifles.

He joined in May, 1915, served on the Western Front, and was taken prisoner in the German Advance of March, 1918, and not released until December, 1919. He suffered many hardships during the period of his captivity.
He holds the 1915 Star, General Service and Victory Medals.
48, Millbrook Road, Lower Edmonton.   13959.

COX, G. B., Gunner, Royal Field Artillery.

He volunteered in 1914, and was killed in action at Cambrai in 1917, having previously taken part in the retreat from Mons, the battles of Ypres, Loos, Arras and the Somme.
He was entitled to the 1914 Star, General Service and Victory Medals.
110, Ilex Road, Willesden.   16364A.

COX, G. H. S., Pte., 2/7th Middlesex Regiment.

He joined in September, 1914, and served in Egypt and France during 1916. He was killed in action on October 15th of that year, and is entitled to the General Service and Victory Medals.
7, Wingmore Road, Tottenham.   X17975.

COX, H., Gunner, Royal Field Artillery.

He volunteered in August, 1914, served on the Western and Eastern Fronts, in France, Salonica, Egypt and Palestine, taking part in many engagements.
He holds the 1914–15 Star, General Service and Victory Medals, and was demobilised in May, 1919.
He had previously served for over thirteen years in the Royal Navy.
22, Bayonne Road, Hammersmith.   14504.

COX, H. J. G., Cpl., 10th Hampshire Regiment.

He joined in September, 1914, and served on the Eastern Front, where he was killed in action in the Balkans on December 7th, 1915.
He was entitled to the 1915 Star, General Service and Victory Medals.
22, Haldane Road, Fulham.   17381.

COX, J., Pte., 3rd Middlesex Regiment.

He joined in 1914 and went to France in that year, where he took part in engagements at Mons, Loos, and the Marne, and was killed in action near Neuve Chapelle in 1916.
He was entitled to the 1914 Star, General Service and Victory Medals.
110, Ilex Road, Willesden.   16364C.

COX, J., Sergt., Middlesex Regiment.

He joined in 1914, and served until 1919 at various stations with the 6th Battalion and with the 338 Works Company. Was engaged on important engineering work and other duties.
110, Ilex Road, Willesden.   16364B.

COX, J., Mechanic, Royal Air Force.

Enlisting in the infantry (Devonshire Regiment), in 1915, he obtained his training in England, being stationed at Plymouth and Oxford. Subsequently he was transferred to the R.A.F., where he served on important duties until demobilisation in 1919.
He holds the General Service Medal.
6, York Road, Lower Edmonton.   16783C.

COX, J. G., Driver, Royal Army Service Corps.

He volunteered in September, 1914, served on the Western Front, and was in action at Loos, Arras, Ypres and the Somme. He was thrown from his horse and was in hospital at Rouen until May, 1918, when he was discharged unfit for further service.
He holds the 1914–15 Star, General Service and Victory Medals.
46, Bayonne Road, Fulham.   14512.

COX, J. J., Pte., Middlesex Regiment.

He joined in June, 1915, and was sent to the Western Front in November of the same year. He took part in many engagements, including the third battle of Ypres, the Somme battles, Cambrai and others. He was in action during the German Offensive in March, 1918, and was wounded and taken prisoner. He was released under the terms of the Armistice, and demobilised in March, 1919, holding the 1914–15 Star, General Service and Victory Medals.
6, Hiley Road, Willesden, N.W.10   X18653.

COX, N. (Miss), Special War Worker.

During the war this lady did valuable service as a van driver at a food supply depot, thereby releasing a man for active service.
8, Humbolt Mansions, Lillie Road, Fulham.   X18869B.

COX, R. W., Pte., 13th Middlesex Regiment.

He joined in 1916 and served on the Western Front, taking part in operations in numerous sectors. He was killed in action on April 4th, 1917, at Vimy Ridge.
He was entitled to the General Service and Victory Medals.
49, Archel Road, West Kensington, W.14   16209.

COX, S., A.B., R.N., H.M.S. " Opportune."

He joined in August, 1914, and was on dangerous convoy and patrol duties in the North Sea. He also took part in the battle of Jutland, and was present at the surrender of the German Fleet at Scapa Flow.
He holds the 1914–15 Star, General Service and Victory Medals.
8, Humbolt Mansions, Lillie Road, Fulham.   TX18886A.

COX, S. (Miss), Special War Worker.

This lady was engaged during the war as a van driver at an important food depot in London. Her work was of great value as she released a man for service at the Front.
8, Humbolt Mansions, Lillie Road, Fulham.   X18869A.

COX, W. G., Pte., Durham Light Infantry.

He joined in August, 1916, and in the same year was sent to France and took part in several engagements, including the battle of St. Quentin, where he was badly gassed, and also suffered from shell-shock.
He was discharged in September, 1917, medically unfit for further military service. He holds the General Service and Victory Medals.
19, Chalgrove Road, Tottenham, N.17   X18971.

COX, W. H. (sen.), Pte., Middlesex Regiment.
During his service, for which he volunteered in the national emergency, and which extended from October, 1915, until January, 1919, he formed part of the East Coast Defence Forces, being over age for foreign service.
27, Hiley Road, Willesden. X18429.

COX, W. H. (jun.), Sergt., Royal Field Artillery.
He joined in August, 1912, and in August, 1914, was sent to France, where he took part in the battles of Mons, Festubert, Loos, Ypres, the Somme, and other engagements. He was in France for four years, and was wounded.
He was demobilised in February, 1920, holding the Mons Star, the General Service and Victory Medals.
27, Hiley Road, Willesden. X18244.

COX, E. E., Pte., 2/22nd London Regiment and Royal Fusiliers.
He joined in May, 1918, and was eventually sent to Egypt, where he served on important duties with his regiment for twelve months.
On April 28th, 1920, he was demobilised, and holds the General Service and Victory Medals.
80, Victoria Road, Willesden Junction, N.W.10 T12530.

COZENS, W. G , Pte., Hampshire Regiment.
He volunteered in September, 1914, and whilst on duty at the Isle of Wight met with a serious accident, owing to which he was discharged in December of the same year, being unfit for further service.
29, Haldane Road, Fulham, S.W. TX17073.

CRABB, F. J., Sergt., Middlesex Regt.
He volunteered in August, 1914, served on the Western Front until 1916, and took part in the battles of Mons, Ypres and the Somme. While abroad he suffered from frost-bite and was wounded in action. He was invalided home, and in hospital for five months in England. On his recovery he was sent to India.
He holds the 1914 Star, General Service and Victory Medals.
19, Chalgrove Road, Tottenham. X18958.

CRABTREE, H., Driver, R.A.S.C.
He joined in September, 1914, and served for three and a half years on the Western Front. He was engaged on transport duties on the Somme, at Ypres, Cambrai, Arras and Loos.
In March, 1919, he was demobilised, and holds the 1915 Star, the General Service and Victory Medals.
43, Westbury Road, Willesden. 15452.

CRACKNELL, A. A., Driver, R.F.A.
He joined in March, 1915, and served on the Western Front in practically all sectors, taking part in many engagements.
He was demobilised in April, 1919, and holds the 1914–15 Star, General Service and Victory Medals.
36, Montague Road, Lower Edmonton. 16510.

CRADDOCK, J. J., Mechanic, Royal Air Force.
He joined in June, 1917, and served with the R.A.F. at various stations on important duties until he was demobilised in June, 1919.
He holds the General Service Medal.
13, Raynham Terrace, Edmonton. 16473B.

CRADDOCK, T. H., Cpl., Royal Field Artillery.
He joined in September, 1914, and was stationed in Scotland and Ireland until he went to Mesopotamia, where he was wounded in September, 1916, and sent to hospital at Mudros. From 1917 he served in France until he was demobilised in May, 1919.
He holds the General Service and Victory Medals.
13, Raynham Terrace, Edmonton. 16473A.

CRADOCK, C. E., 1st Air Mechanic, Royal Naval Air Service and Royal Air Force.
He joined on February 17th, 1917, and served in the North Sea on H.M.S. " Valiant III." as an airman.
He was discharged on March 1st, 1919, after having rendered valuable service, and holds the General Service and Victory Medals.
10, Pellant Road, Fulham, S.W. X17870.

CRAIG, A., Special War Worker.
During the war he did valuable work at Woolwich Arsenal in the shell department, and was commended for his work. This gentleman's two sisters also assisted the country by work of national importance.
55, Orbain Road, Fulham. X18449.

CRAIG, A. E. (Miss), Special War Worker.
This lady volunteered for duty during the war, and was engaged at a London munition factory in connection with the manufacture of hand-grenades and other munitions, her work being of great value.
55, Orbain Road, Fulham. X18448.

CRAIG, F. A. M. (Miss), Special War Worker.
During the war this lady was engaged on important munition work, filling shells and making flares and star lights at a London munition works. She continued in these duties throughout the war, performing valuable services.
55, Orbain Road, Fulham. X18450.

CRAKANTHORP, R., Mechanic, Royal Air Force.
He joined in 1916, and saw service on important duties with the R.A.F. at various stations.
He was demobilised in August, 1919, and holds the General Service Medal.
6, Forest Gardens, Bruce Grove, Tottenham. X18532.

CRAKER, J., 2nd Cpl., Royal Engineers.
He joined in February, 1915, and proceeded to the Western Front the same year, where he took part in many engagements, including Festubert, Arras, Albert and Ypres. He was wounded.
He holds the 1915 Star, General Service and Victory Medals.
Demobilised February, 1919.
63, Oldfield Road, Willesden. 15984.

CRAMB, C., Pte., 1/10th Middlesex Regiment.
He joined in October, 1915, and served in India on garrison duty until December, 1919, when he was demobilised.
He holds the General Service and Victory Medals.
42, Carlyle Avenue, Harlesden. 14407C.

CRAMB, G. W., Gunner, Royal Field Artillery.
He joined in 1914, went to the Western Front the same year, and took part in many engagements, including the Retreat and Advance in 1918, when he contracted influenza, and died on November 10th, 1918.
He was entitled to the 1914 Star, General Service and Victory Medals.
42, Carlyle Avenue, Harlesden. 14407A.

CRAMB, J. (M.M.), Pte., Royal Fusiliers.
He joined in July, 1915, and saw service on the Western Front and in Italy. He took part in many engagements, including the Somme, Ypres and the Advance in 1918, where he was wounded. He was awarded the Military Medal for great bravery in the field, holds also the 1915 Star, General Service and Victory Medals, and was demobilised in July, 1919.
42, Carlyle Avenue, Harlesden. 14407B.

CRAMMOND, T. C., Air Mechanic, Royal Air Force (late Royal Naval Air Service).
He joined in 1915, and for twelve months was engaged as bombing instructor at Uxbridge and Eastchurch. Later he was employed on air defence at various depots until he was demobilised in January, 1919.
He holds the General Service Medal.
3, Greyhound Road, Willesden, N.W.10 X17803A.

CRAMOND, W. D., Gunner, R.G.A.
He joined in November, 1915, and went to the Western Front in May of the following year, taking part in the battles at Arras, the Somme, Vimy Ridge, and Messines, where he was wounded in both legs in June, 1917.
He was discharged in January, 1918, and holds the General Service and Victory Medals.
41, Strode Road, Willesden. 17218A.

CRANE, C. W., Carpenter, R.N., H.M.S. " King George."
He volunteered in July, 1915, and served in the North Sea, being engaged on dangerous duties until he was demobilised in February, 1919.
He holds the 1915 Star, General Service and Victory Medals.
49, Gloucester Road, Edmonton. X17274.

CRANE, E., Pte., South Wales Borderers.
He volunteered in February, 1916, was sent to Salonica in the same year, and took part in many important engagements before being taken prisoner in September, 1918.
He was demobilised in November, 1919, holding the General Service and Victory Medals.
53, Barry Road, Willesden. 14945.

CRANE, J., Special War Worker.
During the war he did valuable work as a heavy motor driver with the British Emaillite Co., being also engaged on work of national importance making rope and propellers for the same firm.
75, Drayton Road, Harlesden. 14997.

CRANMER, A. V., Cpl., 12th and 20th Royal Fusiliers.
He volunteered in September, 1914, and during his service on the Western Front took part in many important battles, including that of Loos, in which he was wounded.
He holds the 1915 Star, General Service and Victory Medals, and was demobilised in April, 1919.
68, Rayleigh Road, W.14 T12068.

CRANN, J. A., Pte., 24th London Regiment (Queen's).
He volunteered in September, 1914, and fought in France, where he was wounded in action at Richebourg in 1915 and at Vimy Ridge in 1916. In 1917 he served in Egypt and Palestine, taking part in important engagements on the Jordan and at Jerusalem and Beersheba. He returned to the Western Front in 1918, where he remained until the Armistice.
He was demobilised in 1919, and holds the 1915 Star, General Service and Victory Medals.
19, Bertie Road, Willesden Green.   X18687.

CRANSHAW, F. A., Pte., Sherwood Foresters.
He volunteered in 1916, and went to France the same year. He took part in many important battles, including the Somme and Ypres.
He holds the General Service and Victory Medals, and was demobilised in 1919.
5, Manor Road, Tottenham, N.17   X18815.

CRANSTON, G. A., Gunner, R.G.A.
He joined in February, 1917, and was sent to Italy, where he rendered valuable services with the Siege Artillery in many important engagements.
He was demobilised in April, 1919, and holds the General Service and Victory Medals.
27, Hilmer Street, W.14   15702.

CRAWFORD, J., Pte., Argyll and Sutherland Highlanders.
He volunteered in August, 1914, and served in France, taking part in engagements at Festubert, Neuve Chapelle, Arras, the Somme, Ypres, Vimy Ridge, Bullecourt, Armentieres, Lille and elsewhere. He was wounded in 1915, gassed on the Somme in the following year, and severely wounded again at Ypres, being invalided home and discharged in 1918, owing to his wounds.
He holds the 1915 Star, General Service and Victory Medals.
74, Chesson Road, West Kensington.   X17696B.

CRAWFORD, M. (Mrs.), Special War Worker.
During the war this lady did valuable work at Messrs. Vickers' Aircraft Works, where for two years she made parts for aeroplanes. She was then engaged on the manufacture of machine guns until the Armistice, and rendered valuable services throughout the war.
74, Chesson Road, West Kensington.   X17696A.

CRAWLEY, A., Pte., 1st Middlesex Regiment.
He volunteered in June, 1916, and served on the Western Front, where he took part in the battle of Cambrai. On April 17th, 1918, he was killed in action, and was buried at the Military Cemetery near Poperinghe.
He was entitled to the General Service and Victory Medals.
100, St. Peter's Road, Lower Edmonton.   12328.

CRAWLEY, A. A., Driver, Tank Corps.
He joined in February, 1917, and went to France the same year, where he took part in important engagements at La Bassée, Arras, Amiens and in the Advance of 1918, when he was gassed while in action.
He was demobilised in November, 1919, and holds the General Service and Victory Medals.
33, Villiers Road, Willesden.   16729.

CRAWLEY, A. J., Pte., Machine Gun Corps.
He volunteered in August, 1916, and during his three years' service on the Western Front took part in engagements at Ypres, Passchendaele, the Somme, Nieuport, La Bassée, Cambrai, St. Quentin and many others. He was wounded and gassed.
In September, 1919, he was demobilised, holding the General Service and Victory Medals.
40, Earlsmead Road, Kensal Rise.   X18034.

CRAWSHAW, E. T., Lce.-Cpl., The Queen's (3rd Royal West Surrey Regiment).
He volunteered in April, 1915, and on being sent to the Western Front, took part in many important engagements. He remained in France until his demobilisation in May, 1919.
He holds the General Service and Victory Medals.
22, Hazelbury Road, Edmonton.   X17499.

CRAYMER, F. G., Driver, R.A.S.C. (M.T.).
He volunteered in June, 1915, and in the same year went to France, where he rendered valuable services until July, 1919. He took part in operations generally throughout his service in France.
He holds the 1915 Star, Victory and General Service Medals, and was demobilised in July, 1919.
123, Harley Road, Harlesden.   13180.

CREASY, D. M. R., Special War Worker.
During the war this lady did valuable work for five years at Park Royal Munition Works, where she was engaged as an examiner of cartridges. This work, requiring great skill, has unfortunately injured her eyes owing to the strain.
40, Furness Road, Harlesden, N.W.   13364A.

CRESSEY, W. E., Pte., R.A.S.C. (M.T.).
He joined in October, 1916, and was sent to the Western Front. He was engaged in transport duties of an arduous nature with the Machine Gun Corps, and was wounded during the second battle of the Somme in 1918.
In 1919 he was discharged as unfit for further service. He holds the General Service and Victory Medals.
16, Waldo Road, Willesden, N.W.   X17569.

CRESSWELL, R., Sapper, Royal Engineers.
He volunteered in July, 1915, and in the same year was sent to France, where he remained until 1919. While abroad he took part in many important engagements, including the battle of the Somme.
He holds the 1915 Star, Victory and General Service Medals, and was demobilised in May, 1919.
5, Brereton Road, Tottenham.   X18379.

CRICK, E. M. (Miss), Special War Worker.
For two years during the war this lady rendered valuable services in the manufacture of shell boxes at a large munition works in Tottenham. She was commended for her work.
15, Durban Road, Tottenham, N.17   X18289B.

CRICK, H., Pte., 6th Essex Regiment.
He volunteered in July, 1916, and served with his regiment at various stations on important and special duties in connection with food supply and agriculture.
He was demobilised in September, 1919, after performing valuable services.
9, Orbain Road, Fulham.   TX18639.

CRIDDLE, J., Pte., Middlesex Regiment.
He volunteered in February, 1915, was sent to the Western Front the same year, and was killed in action at the battle of Loos on September 30th, 1915.
He was entitled to the 1915 Star, General Service and Victory Medals.
8, Raynham Road, Edmonton.   16492.

CRIGHTON, D., Machine Gunner, 33rd Batt. M.G.C.
He joined in 1917, and was sent to France in the following year, where he took part in the 1918 Advance.
He holds the General Service and Victory Medals, and was demobilised in April, 1920.
87, Rylston Road, S.W.6   16185B.

CRIGHTON, G., Lce.-Cpl., R.A.S.C. (M.T.)
He volunteered in 1915, and the same year went to Mesopotamia, where he was engaged on important duties in connection with the transportation of food and ammunition.
He holds the 1915 Star, General Service and Victory Medals, and was demobilised in 1918.
87, Rylston Road, S.W.6   16185A.

CRIPPS, A. R., Staff-Sergt., Army Canteen Board.
He volunteered in December, 1915, and during his service in France, which lasted nearly four years, rendered valuable services whilst engaged on canteen work and with the Army Pay Corps.
He holds the General Service and Victory Medals, and was demobilised on May 3rd, 1919.
40, Dyson's Road, Edmonton.   16774.

CRIPPS, J. T., Pte., Scots Guards.
He was serving at the outbreak of hostilities, and went to the Western Front in the following year. He took part in many engagements, including those of Ypres, Arras, Cambrai and Vimy Ridge, and was wounded. He was killed in action on October 15th, 1918.
He was entitled to the 1914-15 Star, General Service and Victory Medals.
25, Heron Road, Willesden.   15601.

CRIPPS, T., Gunner, Royal Garrison Artillery.
He joined in July, 1916, and was sent to India in the same year. He was wounded whilst taking part in important frontier engagements, and was invalided home and discharged in June, 1917, as a result of his wounds.
He holds the General Service and Victory Medals.
34, Lower Mall, Hammersmith.   12496.

CRISELL, P. H., Rifleman, Rifle Brigade.
He volunteered in September, 1914, and saw service in France and Salonica. He was wounded at La Bassée in 1915, and whilst in the East suffered from malarial fever.
He holds the 1914-15 Star, General Service and Victory Medals, and was demobilised in February, 1919.
42, Warwick Road, Edmonton.   X17516.

CROCKER, H. W., Gunner, R.F.A.
He volunteered in February, 1915, and was sent to France, where he was in several important engagements, being eventually transferred to Italy, where he rendered other valuable services.
He was demobilised in April, 1919, and holds the General Service and Victory Medals.
284, Lillie Road, Fulham. 15290.

CROCKER, W. H., Pte., R.N.D. and R.A.S.C. (M.T.).
He served in 1914 with the Royal Naval Division at Antwerp, remaining with that unit six months, and in May, 1915, transferred to the R.A.S.C. He was sent to the Western Front in June of the same year, and in November, 1917, was gassed near Ypres, as a result of which he was invalided home.
He was discharged in June, 1918, holding the 1914 Star, General Service and Victory Medals.
19, Gowan Road, Willesden Green, N.W.10 X16968.

CROCKETT, C., Pte., Royal Army Service Corps.
He volunteered in May, 1915, and was employed at various stations with his unit on important duties.
In May, 1918, owing to his being over military age, he was discharged, whereupon he rendered valuable services in a munition factory.
86, Archel Road, West Kensington. 16657A.

CROCKETT, C., Rifleman, King's Royal Rifles.
At the outbreak of war he was under age. On reaching military age in 1918 he joined the Army and was employed on important duties with his unit at various stations. He later proceeded to Germany with the Army of Occupation, and was demobilised in March, 1920.
86, Archel Road, West Kensington. 16657B.

CROCKFORD, W. B., Cpl., 13th London Regt. and R.E. (R.O.D.).
He joined in February, 1917, and rendered valuable services in Egypt with the Railway Operative Division. He also took part in the Palestine campaign with General Allenby's forces.
He was demobilised in March, 1920, holding the General Service and Victory Medals.
83, Oldfield Road, Willesden. 16025.

CROFT, A. W., Sapper, Royal Engineers.
He joined in April, 1918, and took part in the Advance of 1918 on the Western Front. He went with the Army of Occupation to the Rhine, and was demobilised in September, 1919.
He holds the General Service and Victory Medals.
7, Sandgate Road, Lower Edmonton. 15498A.

CROFT, W., Pte., Middlesex Regiment.
He volunteered in August, 1914, and served in important engagements in France and Salonika, where he contracted malarial fever.
He was discharged in April, 1919, and holds the Mons Star, General Service and Victory Medals.
40, Cedar Road, Edmonton. 14218.

CROKER, C. G., Pte., 19th London Regt., Dorset Regt. and Cameron Highlanders.
He volunteered in April, 1915, and served with distinction in Mesopotamia until he was demobilised in 1919. While abroad he took part in several engagements, suffered from malaria and, as a result, lost the hearing of one ear.
He holds the General Service and Victory Medals.
49, Ilex Road, Willesden. 16520B.

CROKER, H. F., Sergt., 4th and 17th Middlesex Regiment.
He volunteered in 1914, was sent to France in the same year and took part in the battles of Mons, Arras and the Somme. He was killed in action on November 13th, 1916, having previously been wounded and suffered from shell-shock.
He was entitled to the 1914 Star, General Service and Victory Medals.
49, Ilex Road, Willesden. 16520A.

CROKER, J. W., Cpl., Royal Engineers.
He volunteered in 1915 and served in France on important transport and railway engineering duties until demobilised in 1919. He was present during the battle of the Somme and other engagements, and holds the 1914-15 Star, General Service and Victory Medals.
49, Ilex Road, Willesden. 16520C.

CROKER, R., Pte., Royal Army Service Corps.
He volunteered in August, 1915, and after serving in many important engagements on the Western Front, was invalided home and discharged in 1917, suffering with neuritis.
He is entitled to the General Service and Victory Medals.
45, Greyhound Road, Hammersmith. 15481.

CROLEY, H. C., Sergt., Herts. Yeomanry.
He volunteered in 1914, and was sent out to Egypt. In 1915 he was transferred to Gallipoli, where he took part in much severe fighting. On the evacuation of the Peninsula, he returned to Egypt. During his service he suffered from typhoid and dysentery.
He was demobilised in 1919, and holds the 1914-15 Star, General Service and Victory Medals.
57, Furness Road, Harlesden. 13360.

CRONE, A., 1st Class Stoker, R.N., H.M.S. "St. George."
He enlisted in June, 1914, and after the outbreak of war served for three and a half years in Salonica. After taking part in many important engagements, he was wounded, and was discharged in January, 1919, holding the General Service and Victory Medals.
15, Aintree Street, Fulham. X18208.

CRONK, B., Pte., 2nd Contingent Canadian Forces.
He volunteered in 1916, and took part in many important engagements on the Western Front. He returned to Canada in 1919, after rendering valuable services to the Empire.
He holds the General Service and Victory Medals.
9, Meyrick Road, Willesden. 16343B.

CRONK, G., Pte., Oxford and Bucks. Light Infty.
He joined in November, 1916, proceeded to the Western Front in June, 1917, and took part in many engagements in the Offensive of that year. He was killed in action on August 3rd, 1917, and was entitled to the General Service and Victory Medals.
9, Meyrick Road, Willesden. 16343C.

CRONK, J., Sergt., 1st Contingent Canadian Forces.
He volunteered in August, 1914, and from March, 1915, until May, 1918, served in many important engagements on the Western Front, and was wounded.
He holds the King's and Queen's South African Medals, the 1914-15 Star, General Service and Victory Medals.
He returned to Canada in May, 1918, where he is now serving as Sergeant-at-Arms in British Columbia.
9, Meyrick Road, Willesden. 16343A.

CRONK, W., Rifleman, 7th King's Royal Rifles.
He volunteered in 1915 and served in many important engagements on the Western Front until discharged in 1918. He took part in the battles of Loos, Ypres, Passchendaele, Armentieres and Arras. He was twice wounded, and as a result of his wounds he was discharged as medically unfit.
He holds the 1914-15 Star, General Service and Victory Medals.
16, Yuletide Road, Willesden. 15081.

CROOK, A., Pte., R.A.S.C. (M.T.).
He volunteered in December, 1914, and during his service on the Western Front took part in the severe fighting at Loos, Arras, Ypres, Albert and the Somme. He was for a time employed at G.H.Q.
He holds the 1915 Star, General Service and Victory Medals, and was demobilised in March, 1918.
27, Wilson's Road, Hammersmith. 15861.

CROOK, E. (D.C.M.), Cpl., 17th Middlesex Regt.
He volunteered in June, 1916, and during his service on the Western Front took part in many engagements. He was awarded the Distinguished Conduct Medal for conspicuous bravery in the field at Cambrai, where he was also wounded on December 1st, 1917.
He was discharged in October of the following year, unfit for further service as a result of his wounds. He holds the General Service and Victory Medals.
26, Gresham Road, Neasden. 15740.

CROPLEY, J. H., Pte., 9th Middlesex Regiment.
He volunteered in 1915, and later in the same year was sent to the Western Front, where he took part in numerous engagements, including those of Ypres and the Somme and in the Advance of 1918. In 1918 he was invalided to England suffering from shell-shock, from the effects of which he died.
He was entitled to the 1915 Star, the General Service and Victory Medals.
39, Fourth Avenue, Paddington, W.10 X18675.

CROPP, C. T., Pte., 7th London Regt.
He joined in June, 1917, served in many engagements on the Western Front, including those of Ypres and Arras, was wounded and gassed. After being for some time in hospital in France, he was invalided to Leicester, where he was again in hospital.
He was demobilised in January, 1919, holding the General Service and Victory Medals.
4, Laundry Road, Fulham. 15341.

CROSBY, W. J., Mechanic, Royal Air Force.
He enlisted in August, 1916, and served for nearly three years in France on important work with the R.A.F. in many sectors, and was demobilised in January, 1919, holding the General Service and Victory Medals.
152, Estcourt Road, Fulham.   16248.

CROSS, A., Driver, Royal Army Service Corps.
He volunteered in August, 1914, and served on both Western and Eastern Fronts. While in France in 1915 he took part in the fighting near Bethune, and in the battle of Festubert, where he was wounded. After being invalided home, he was sent to Salonica and again wounded.
In 1919 he was demobilised, holding the 1914-15 Star, General Service and Victory Medals.
88, Archel Road, West Kensington.   16663.

CROSS, C. J., Wireman, R.N., H.M.S. "Onslow."
He volunteered in May, 1915, and served on dangerous duties with the North Sea Flotilla. He also served at Malta and at Scapa Flow.
He holds the General Service and Victory Medals, and was demobilised in December, 1918.
18, Purcell Crescent, Fulham.   15165A.

CROSS, E. T., Cpl., Royal Engineers.
He volunteered in March, 1915, and went to France the same year. He was in action on the Somme, where he was severely wounded.
He died of his wounds in April, 1917, and was entitled to the 1915 Star, General Service and Victory Medals.
42, Whitehall Street, Tottenham, N.17   X18122.

CROSS, E. T., Flight-Sergt., Royal Air Force.
He volunteered in June, 1915, and served with his squadron in the Egyptian Expeditionary Force, doing valuable duty until April, 1919, when he was demobilised, holding the General Service and Victory Medals.
18, Purcell Crescent, Fulham.   15165B.

CROSS, G. J., Pte., 14th Suffolk Regiment.
He volunteered in June, 1916, and did duty with his regiment at various stations, including those of the East Coast defences.
He was demobilised in April, 1919.
427, Chapter Road, Willesden Green.   16157.

CROSS, S., Lce.-Cpl., R.A.S.C. (M.T.).
He volunteered in August, 1914, was sent to France in the following month and took part in the battles of Mons, Ypres, Neuve Chapelle, the Somme, Loos, Arras, Nieuport and in the last Advance of 1918. He was once wounded. He was demobilised in April, 1919, holding the 1914 Star, General Service and Victory Medals.
69a, Deacon Road, Willesden.   17362.

CROSS, S., Lce.-Cpl., 2nd Sherwood Foresters.
He joined in 1916, and served with distinction on the Western Front. While in action at the battle of the Somme in 1918 he was killed.
He was entitled to the General Service and Victory Medals.
26, Steele Road, Harlesden.   13838A.

CROSS, W. E., Q.M.S., Labour Corps.
He volunteered in April, 1916, and performed important duties as Quartermaster-Sergeant at various stations. His duties were of a most responsible nature.
He secured his demobilisation in March, 1919.
18, Purcell Crescent, Fulham.   15165C.

CROSS, W. J., Pte., Suffolk Regiment.
He joined in September, 1916, and shortly afterwards was sent to the Western Front, where he took part in the fighting at Ypres, Cambrai and in the Great Advance of 1918, when he was wounded.
He was demobilised in January, 1919, and holds the General Service and Victory Medals.
3, Felixstowe Road, Edmonton.   15383.

CROSSMAN, W. F., Sergt., Coldstream Guards.
He volunteered in August, 1914, and served on the Western Front, taking part in the battles of Mons, the Marne, the Aisne, Neuve Chapelle, Ypres, the Somme, Vimy Ridge and many others. He was twice wounded, at the battles of the Aisne and the Somme, and in 1918, on account of his wounds, was discharged unfit for further service.
He holds the Mons Star, General Service and Victory Medals.
79, Archel Road, West Kensington.   16664.

CROTON, G. (sen.), Pte., 9th Norfolk Regt.
He volunteered in January, 1915, and served in France, where he took part in many engagements with distinction. He suffered from shell-shock, of which he died in November, 1919.
He was entitled to the 1914-15 Star, General Service and Victory Medals.
127, Sherbrooke Road, Fulham.   X18682B.

CROTON, G. (jun.), Band-Cpl., West Yorks. Regt.
He volunteered in September, 1914, and served on the North-West Frontier of India until he was demobilised in November, 1919.
He holds the General Service and Victory Medals.
127, Sherbrooke Road, Fulham.   X18682C.

CROTON, J., Pte., West Yorkshire Regiment.
He volunteered in September, 1914, and served in France for a considerable time.
He was ultimately discharged, holding the 1914 Star, General Service and Victory Medals.
127, Sherbrooke Road, Fulham.   X18682A.

CROWDY, C. G., Leading Stoker, R.N., H.M.S. "Commonwealth."
At the outbreak of war he was already in the Service, and during hostilities was with his ship at the Dardanelles, China, and the North Sea on dangerous duties.
He is still serving, and holds the 1914 Star, General Service and Victory Medals.
19, Gowan Road, Willesden, N.W.10   X16967.

CROWE, A. H., Sergt., 13th London Regiment (Kensington Battalion).
He joined in 1916, went to Salonica and was wounded in action. On recovery he was sent to Egypt, later serving under General Allenby throughout the Palestine campaign.
He was demobilised in November, 1919, holding the General Service and Victory Medals.
17, Orbain Road, Fulham.   X18441.

CROWHURST, J., Pte., R.A.O.C.
He joined in May, 1917, went to Egypt with the Expeditionary Force, where he saw much service, and was demobilised in March, 1920.
He holds the General Service and Victory Medals.
26, Beryl Road, Fulham.   13355.

CROWTHER, A., Carpenter, Merchant Service.
He volunteered in 1914, and served on board the S.S. "Cuirassier," on the dangerous duty of conveying munitions from English to French ports.
He was discharged in 1919, holding the 1914-15 Star, General Service, Victory and Mercantile Marine Medals.
25, Mozart Street, Queen's Park.   X18931.

CROXFORD, C., Staff-Sergt., R.A.O.C.
He joined in January, 1915, and went to France in the same year, where he served in various sectors. His work was of a most responsible nature.
He was demobilised in June, 1919, holding the 1915 Star, the General Service and Victory Medals.
25, Cooper Road, Willesden.   16637.

CRUCEFIX, R. J., Pte., 23rd London Regiment.
He volunteered in August, 1914, and served in France from February, 1915, until December, 1916, during which time he took part in many engagements. He was wounded and gassed at Loos, and was discharged in February, 1917, on account of his wounds.
He holds the 1914-15 Star, General Service and Victory Medals.
33, Alric Avenue, Harlesden.   14440.

CRUICKSHANKS, G., Pte., Notts. & Derby Regt.
He volunteered in August, 1914, and during his service on the Western Front was badly wounded and gassed, as a result of which he was for some time in hospital in France and England.
He holds the 1914-15 Star, General Service and Victory Medals, and was demobilised in January, 1919.
6, Hartopp Avenue, Fulham.   X17733.

CRUNDEN, J. A., Pte., R.A.S.C.
He volunteered in April, 1915, and in April of the following year was sent to the Eastern Front, where he took part in many engagements. He served on the Struma and Doiran Fronts in the Balkans, and assisted in putting down the riots in Athens.
He was demobilised in February, 1919, and holds the General Service and Victory Medals.
1, Hiley Road, Willesden.   X18333.

CRUST, C. (Mrs.), Special War Worker.
For a period of four years during the war this lady was engaged on valuable work in a small arms and shell-filling factory. During this period her work was often of a dangerous nature, and she was commended for her services.
12, Melville Road, Willesden.   14429A.

CRUST, E. H., Sapper, Royal Engineers (R.O.D.)
He joined in August, 1917, served on the Western Front from 1918 until demobilised in November, 1919, and was on special duties with the Railway Operative Division, carrying troops and stores.
He holds the General Service and Victory Medals.
12, Melville Road, Willesden.   14429B.

CRUTCHFIELD, W. J., Mechanic, Royal Air Force.
He joined in 1916, and was engaged on important work at various aerodromes with the R.A.F. until his demobilisation in 1919.
He holds the General Service Medal.
54, Newlyn Road, Tottenham, N.17   X18507.

CULLEN, E. A., Gunner, R.G.A.
He volunteered in 1915, went to France in the following year, and took part in engagements on the Somme, at Cambrai, Arras, Albert, Bapaume, Ypres, and Armentieres.
He holds the General Service and Victory Medals, and was demobilised in 1919.
41, Greyhound Road, Willesden.   X17603.

CULLEY, H. P., Pte., Machine Gun Corps.
He joined in August, 1916, proceeded to the Western Front in March, 1917, and saw much service on the Somme and at Cambrai, Albert, Loos, Armentieres, St. Quentin and Ypres.
He was wounded in action in the Advance of 1918.
He holds the General Service and Victory Medals, and was discharged in January, 1919.
46, Brownlow Road, Harlesden.   15011.

CUMMINGS, G., Pte., 3/9th Middlesex Regt.
He volunteered in May, 1915, served in Egypt and throughout the Palestine campaign, and was wounded at the battle of Gaza in April, 1917.
He was demobilised in July, 1919, holding the General Service and Victory Medals.
21, Oldfield Road, Willesden.   15750.

CUNNINGHAM, J. F., Pte., 17th Royal Fusiliers.
He joined in February, 1916, and served on the Western Front, taking part in engagements at Ypres, Arras, Cambrai and elsewhere. He was gassed, invalided home, and on June 21st, 1919, demobilised.
He holds the General Service and Victory Medals.
30, Deacon Road, Willesden.   16645.

CURL, J., Rifleman, 9th London Regiment.
He joined in 1917 and served on the Western Front, where he took part in the battles of the Somme, Albert, Arras and other engagements. After the Armistice he was employed on graves registration work.
He holds the General Service and Victory Medals, and was demobilised in 1919.
10, Shotley Street, Fulham.   14806.

CURL, T. H., Gunner, Royal Field Artillery.
He joined in January, 1918, and served in France, taking part in engagements at Arras (where he was wounded), Albert, and the Somme, where he was again wounded.
He was in hospital for five months, and was demobilised in March, 1919, holding the General Service and Victory Medals.
47, Lorenco Road, Tottenham.   X17986.

CURNOW, H. G., Pte., 2nd Northamptonshire Regiment.
He volunteered in November, 1915, and was stationed at Yarmouth for 14 months. He afterwards went to France, where he took part in many important battles, and was wounded at Bourlon Wood in October, 1917.
He holds the General Service and Victory Medals, and was demobilised in November, 1918.
19, Siddons Road, Tottenham, N.17   X19154.

CURRIE, J., Gunner, Royal Garrison Artillery.
He volunteered in 1915, and was sent to France in the same year. Later he was drafted to Salonica, where he contracted malaria. On recovery he went again to the Western Front, where he took part in the battle of the Somme.
He was demobilised in February, 1919, holding the 1914–15 Star, General Service and Victory Medals.
2, Steele Road, Harlesden.   13827B.

CURRIN, M., Bombardier, R.F.A.
He volunteered in May, 1915, and in the same year was sent to France. In 1916 he was transferred to Palestine, where he saw much service until his return in 1918.
He holds the 1915 Star, General Service and Victory Medals, and was demobilised on May 17th, 1919.
122, Minet Avenue, Harlesden.   13402.

CURTIS, A. T., Pte., R.A.S.C. (M.T.).
He volunteered in October, 1914, and went to France soon afterwards. During his service overseas he was in engagements at Arras, Loos, Neuve Chapelle, Armentieres, Amiens, Bullecourt, Festubert, St. Quentin, Lille and the last Advance of 1918.
He was demobilised in April, 1919, and holds the 1914 Star, General Service and Victory Medals.
3, Mablethorpe Road, Fulham.   X19224.

CURTIS, B. Rifleman, Civil Service Rifles.
He joined in February, 1917, and whilst in France took part in many engagements until 1919, when he was demobilised. He was once seriously wounded, and holds the General Service and Victory Medals.
8, Hartham Road, Fulham.   X18518.

CURTIS, G. B., Gunner, Royal Field Artillery.
He volunteered in November, 1915, and in April, 1916, went to France, where he took part in various engagements, including the battles of the Somme, Ypres, Cambrai and Vimy Ridge, and was wounded.
He was discharged on account of wounds in August, 1918, holding the General Service and Victory Medals.
17, Elthorne Avenue, Hanwell.   11070.

CURTIS, G. E., Wireman, R.N.
He volunteered in August, 1914, and was on board the "Blenheim" and "Onslow." Whilst with these ships he was engaged on arduous and dangerous patrol and mine-sweeping duties in the North Sea.
He holds the 1914 Star, General Service and Victory Medals.
35, Oldfield Road, Willesden.   15746.

CURTIS, G. T. A., Cpl., Highland Light Infantry.
He rejoined from the Reserve in August, 1914, and was sent to France, where he fought in the retreat from Mons and most of the big battles until his discharge in December, 1918.
For a time he was attached to the Machine Gun Corps. While in France he was blinded by a Verey light, and has since died of pneumonia.
Entitled to Mons Star, General Service and Victory Medals.
46, Ascot Road, Edmonton.   T15178.

CURTIS, H. A., Pte., Highland Light Infantry.
He volunteered in August, 1914, and saw much service in France, until September, 1917, on which date he was killed in action.
He was entitled to the 1914 Star, the General Service and Victory Medals.
130, Montague Road, Edmonton.   15847.

CURTIS, H. C., Pte., Grenadier Guards.
He joined in 1916, served in several engagements on the Western Front, and was killed in action at Vimy Ridge in April of the same year.
He was entitled to the General Service and Victory Medals.
22, Fane Street, West Kensington.   15892A.

CURTIS, J., Pte., Royal Inniskilling Fusiliers.
He volunteered in 1915, went to the Western Front the same year, and took part in many engagements, including the battle of the Somme and the Retreat and Advance in 1918.
He was wounded twice and demobilised in 1919, holding the 1915 Star, General Service and Victory Medals.
39, Ravensworth Road, Kensal Rise.   X17615.

CURTIS, J. M. (Miss), Special War Worker.
During the war this lady was engaged on valuable work at a London food supply depot, thereby releasing a man for active service.
She was commended for her services.
22, Fane Street, West Kensington.   15892C.

CURTIS, W., Sergt., Royal Air Force.
He volunteered in December, 1915, and did valuable work in the R.A.F. workshops in various stations until his demobilisation in March, 1919. His duties called for a high degree of mechanical skill.
He holds the General Service Medal.
2, Chester Road, Lower Edmonton.   12711.

CURTIS, W. E., Pte., 13th London Regiment (Kensington Battalion).
He volunteered in 1915, and during his service on the Western Front took part in the fighting on the Somme and at Neuve Chapelle, Armentieres, Amiens, Ypres, Vimy Ridge, St. Quentin and in the last Advance of 1918.
He holds the 1914–15 Star, General Service and Victory Medals, and was demobilised in 1919.
22, Fane Street, West Kensington.   15892B.

CUSICK, F. A., Pte., Royal Marine Light Infty.
He volunteered in 1915, and in the same year was sent to Canada on special duty in connection with the war.
He holds the General Service and Victory Medals.
12, Durham Road, Edmonton.   14870A.

CUSICK, J., Trooper, 2nd Dragoon Guards.
He volunteered in 1914, proceeded to France the same year, and took part in many important engagements.
He holds the 1914 Star, General Service and Victory Medals, and was demobilised in 1919.
12, Durham Road, Edmonton.   14870C.

CUSICK, J. A. T. (M.S.M.), Leading Seaman, R.N.
He volunteered in 1914 and was engaged on arduous and dangerous duties with the Grand Fleet in different waters, until 1919, when he was demobilised.
He served continuously for five years, and was finally awarded the Meritorious Service Medal for gallant conduct and consistent good work. He holds in addition the 1914 Star, General Service and Victory Medals.
12, Durham Road, Edmonton.   14870B.

CUTTEN, H., Mechanic, Royal Air Force.
He joined in October, 1918, at the age of 18 years, and served in Turkey on important aircraft work until his demobilisation in November, 1919.
He holds the General Service Medal.
17, Warwick Road, Edmonton.   X17907.

CUTTER, W. A., Pte., Royal Army Service Corps.
He volunteered in October, 1915, and served in Gallipoli, and later in France. He took part in several engagements, and was wounded.
He was discharged in February, 1918 (after hospital treatment), unfit for further service owing to his wounds, and holds the General Service and Victory Medals.
11, Wycombe Road, Tottenham.   X19070.

CUTTING, C. F., Pte., 93rd Labour Company.
He joined in June, 1916, and served in France, being engaged on special duty until his demobilisation in October, 1919.
He holds the General Service and Victory Medals.
42, Bloemfontein Road, Shepherd's Bush.   12054.

CROUCHER, C., Stoker, R.N., H.M.S. "Conqueror."
He joined in May, 1916, and was engaged in arduous and dangerous work with the Grand Fleet in the North Sea.
He was demobilised in May, 1919, and holds the General Service and Victory Medals.
68, Harley Road, Harlesden.   13400.

CUTTS, E. G., Sapper, Royal Engineers, 28th Light Railway Tractor Repairing Company.
He joined in September, 1916, and served overseas from April, 1917, to October, 1919. He was engaged on important duties throughout his service with a Light Railway unit.
He was demobilised in November, 1919, holding the General Service and Victory Medals.
296, Chapter Road, Willesden, N.W.   TX17843B.

CUTTS, F. J., Sergt., Royal Warwickshire Regt.
He volunteered in September, 1914, and served on the Western Front, taking part in engagements on the Somme, at Ypres, Arras, Albert, St. Quentin, Loos, Lens, and Cambrai. Later he was sent to Italy, where he was wounded in action.
He was demobilised in February, 1919, and holds the 1914 Star, General Service and Victory Medals.
23, Mozart Street, Queen's Park, W.   X18929.

CUTTS, J. F., Pte., 1st London Regiment (Royal Fusiliers).
He was serving at the outbreak of war, was sent to the Western Front in August, 1914, and took part in the retreat from Mons. He was killed in action at Fleurbaix in November, 1914, and was entitled to the Mons Star, General Service and Victory Medals.
296, Chapter Road, Willesden.   TX17843A.

CYSTER, A. E., Sergt., Royal Air Force.
He joined in 1916, and saw much service on the Western Front and in Egypt, taking part in all engagements with General Allenby in Palestine.
He was demobilised in February, 1919, holding the General Service and Victory Medals.
9, Ravensworth Road, College Park, Willesden.   X17614.

D

DAKER, A. S., Sergt., Duke of Cornwall's L.I.
He volunteered in August, 1914, served on the Western Front, and was killed in action on September 6th, 1916.
He was entitled to the 1914 Star, General Service and Victory Medals.
43, Church Path, Hammersmith.   15908.

DALE, C. F., Rifleman, 11th Rifle Brigade.
He volunteered in 1915, and served on all sectors in France, being twice wounded and invalided to hospital in Scotland for three months.
He was demobilised in April, 1920, holding the General Service and Victory Medals.
6, Raynham Terrace, Edmonton.   16472A.

DALE, E. E., Rifleman, London Rifle Brigade.
He joined in May, 1916, and was engaged on important duties with his unit at various stations until he was sent to France. He took part in many engagements, and was eventually demobilised in March, 1919, holding the General Service and Victory Medals.
6, Raynham Terrace, Edmonton.   16472C.

DALE, G., Pioneer, Royal Engineers.
He volunteered in August, 1915, and served in many engagements on the Western Front, where he contracted pneumonia after the battle of Arras. He died at Rouen on October 17th, 1917.
He was entitled to the General Service and Victory Medals.
18, Osman Road, Lower Edmonton.   15778.

DALE, G. A., Sergt., Royal Field Artillery.
He volunteered in December, 1914, went to France the following year, and took part in practically all operations, including the Somme and Arras.
He was demobilised in February, 1919, holding the 1914–15 Star, the General Service and Victory Medals.
71, Angel Road, Edmonton.   16571.

DALE, W. G., Pte., Royal Welch Fusiliers.
He volunteered in November, 1914, served in France, where he took part in many engagements, was wounded, and finally reported " missing."
He was entitled to the 1914–15 Star, the General Service and Victory Medals.
6, Raynham Terrace, Upper Edmonton.   16472B.

DALEY, F. C., Sergt., R.A.F. (late R.N.A.S.).
He volunteered in 1915, and in the same year was sent to the Western Front, where he was engaged on the Field Wireless work at Ypres and Dixmude for three and a half months. In 1916 he served in Italy, and after five months went to Malta, where he remained until 1919, acting as Chief Petty Officer in charge of the Maintenance and Repair Depot.
He was demobilised in April, 1919, and holds the 1915 Star, General Service and Victory Medals.
31, Cranbrook Road, Tottenham, N.17   X18563.

DALEY, W. H. (M.M.), Signaller, R.E.
He joined in March, 1914, and in the following year went to the Western Front, where he took part in many engagements, including those of the Somme, Ypres, Arras, Cambrai and the Retreat and Advance of 1918.
He was awarded the Military Medal for great bravery in the field, holds the 1914–15 Star, General Service and Victory Medals, and was demobilised in November, 1919.
291, Chapter Road, Willesden Green.   X17119.

DALLIMER, F. W., Pte., Royal Fusiliers.
He volunteered in September, 1914, went to France and took part in the battles of the Somme, Ypres, Arras, Albert, Loos, and others. Later he went to Salonica, and served in the Balkan campaign. During his service he was wounded three times, being discharged as a result of wounds in August, 1917.
He holds the 1915 Star, General Service and Victory Medals.
12, Ambleside Road, Willesden.   16125.

DALOTTO, F., Pte., 3rd Royal Berkshire Regt.
He volunteered in August, 1914, and during his service in France took part in the retreat from Mons, the battles of the Somme, Loos, Ypres, and was wounded.
He was demobilised in February, 1919, and holds the 1914 Star, General Service and Victory Medals.
15, Welford Terrace, Fulham.   X18068.

DALTON, R. C., Cpl., 19th London Regiment.
He joined in November, 1916, went to France in the same year, was gassed and taken prisoner at Bourlon Wood in 1917. He was released under the terms of the Armistice after enduring many hardships, and was demobilised in 1919, holding the General Service and Victory Medals.
190, Winchester Road, Lower Edmonton.   14886.

DALWOOD, C., Gunner, Royal Horse Artillery.
He volunteered in November, 1914, and was sent to the Western Front. Through illness he was in hospital for a considerable time, and was sent home. He returned to France later, when he took part in several engagements. Prior to his demobilisation in 1919 he went to the Rhine with the Army of Occupation. He holds the 1915 Star, General Service and Victory Medals.
30, Colehill Lane, Fulham, S.W.6   X18909.

DAMERELL, G. (M.M.), Sergt., R.F.A.
He was called up from the Reserve in August, 1914, was sent to France in the same year, and acted as gunnery instructor there. He was in action at Ypres and Vimy Ridge, where he was wounded and gassed.
He won the Military Medal for great bravery in the field, and also holds the 1914 Star, General Service and Victory Medals. He was discharged in 1918.
52, Averill Street, Hammersmith.   13993D.

DAMERELL, H., Sapper, Royal Engineers.

He volunteered in September, 1914, and in the following year went to France, where he took part in the engagements at Ypres, Loos, and the Somme. He was wounded twice and gassed, and also suffered from shell-shock.
He holds the 1914–15 Star, the General Service and Victory Medals, and was discharged in 1917 as a result of his wounds.
52, Averill Street, Hammersmith. 13993C.

DAMERELL, J., Cpl., Royal Sussex Regiment.

He was called up in August, 1914, was sent to France in the following February, and was killed in action at Festubert on May 9th, 1915.
He was entitled to the 1914–15 Star, the General Service and Victory Medals.
52, Averill Street, Hammersmith. 13993A.

DAMERELL, R., Gunner, R.F.A.

He volunteered in August, 1914, proceeded to France in 1915, and was wounded near Albert on the Somme in 1916. Later he went to Salonica.
He was demobilised in April, 1919, holding the 1914–15 Star, the General Service and Victory Medals.
52, Averill Street, Hammersmith. 13993B.

DAMSELL, J. W. C., Pte., 24th London Regt. (Queen's), and Royal Fusiliers.

He volunteered in May, 1915, served in German East Africa from later in the same year until 1916, and on the Western Front until 1917, being wounded at Arras in August of that year.
He holds the Legion of Frontiersmen's Badge, the 1915 Star, General Service and Victory Medals, and was demobilised in February, 1919.
47, Westbury Road, Willesden. 15450.

DANIELLS, G., Pte., 2nd Border Regiment.

He volunteered in August, 1914, proceeded to France in January, 1915, and was killed in action at Neuve Chapelle on March 12th, 1915.
He was entitled to the 1914–15 Star, General Service and Victory Medals.
64, Milton Avenue, Harlesden. 14315B.

DANIELS, A., Pte., Royal Warwickshire Regt.

He volunteered in August, 1914, and during his service on the Western Front took part in the battle of the Somme, where he was badly wounded, and was discharged as a result in March, 1916.
He holds the 1914 Star, General Service and Victory Medals.
31, Felixstowe Road, Edmonton. 15384B.

DANIELS, E., Pte., 8th Devonshire Regiment.

He volunteered in April, 1915, and served on the Western Front, taking part in the battles of Loos, the Somme and Passchendaele. He later went to Italy.
In March, 1919, he was demobilised, holding the 1915 Star, General Service and Victory Medals.
7, Fane Street, West Kensington. 15925B.

DANIELS, F., Pte., Middlesex Regiment.

He joined in 1916, and in the same year was sent to Egypt, where he took part in many engagements. While in action in March, 1917, he was killed.
He was entitled to the General Service and Victory Medals.
14, Tilson Road, Tottenham, N.17 X19094A.

DANIELS, F. A., Pte., 20th London Regiment.

He joined in 1917, went to France in the following year, and took part in the second battle of the Somme. Later he served in Germany with the Army of Occupation until he was demobilised in 1919, holding the General Service and Victory Medals.
20, Beaufoy Road, Tottenham. X17940B.

DANIELS, H., Pte., 17th Lancers.

He volunteered in August, 1914, went to India, and then to France in October of the same year. He took part in many engagements, including those of the Somme, Ypres and La Bassée.
He was demobilisd in February, 1919, holding the 1914 Star, General Service and Victory Medals.
16, Beaufoy Road, Tottenham. X17940A.

DANIELS, R. J., Pte., 13th Middlesex Regiment.

He volunteered in 1915, and served with distinction on the Western Front. He was killed in action at the battle of the Somme on August 18th, 1916.
He was entitled to the General Service and Victory Medals.
29, Eldon Road, Lower Edmonton. 13050.

DANIELS, T. G., Pte., The Queen's (Royal West Surrey Regt.)

He joined in 1916, and in the same year, after a short training, went to France, where he was killed in action on the Somme after a brief period.
He was entitled to the General Service and Victory Medals.
14, Tilson Road, Tottenham, N.17 X19094B.

DANIELS, W. G., Pte., 6th East Surrey Regt.

He volunteered in November, 1914, and served on the Western Front, taking part in the battles of Loos, the Somme and Ypres.
He was demobilised in April, 1919, holding the 1914–15 Star, General Service and Victory Medals.
12, Montague Road, Hammersmith. 16410.

DANN, W. G., Pte., Army Cyclist Corps.

He volunteered in May, 1915, and served in Salonica until 1918, taking part in many engagements. He was then sent to Russia.
He holds the 1914–15 Star, General Service and Victory Medals, and was demobilised in November, 1919.
107, Sheldon Road, Upper Edmonton. X17187.

DARE, J. J., Pte., Middlesex Regiment.

He volunteered in November, 1915, was sent to France in the following April, and was killed in action in September, 1916, after having been previously twice wounded.
He was entitled to the General Service and Victory Medals.
34, Hiley Road, Willesden. X18426A.

DARLING, W. (M.M.), Rifleman, King's Royal Rifle Corps.

He volunteered in April, 1915, and in the same year was sent to the Western Front, where he remained until 1919, during which period he took part in numerous engagements, including the Retreat and Advance of 1918. He was wounded at Delville Wood in 1916, and again in 1918, and was awarded the Military Medal for conspicuous bravery and devotion to duty in the field.
He also holds the 1915 Star, General Service and Victory Medals, and was demobilised in May, 1919.
6, Portnall Road, Maida Hill, W.9 X19369B.

DARNELL, H. W., Pte., West Yorkshire Regt.

He volunteered in April, 1915, and saw active service on the Western Front, where he was severely wounded.
He was discharged in 1917, as the result of his wounds, being found medically unfit for further service. He holds the General Service and Victory Medals.
24, Sherbrooke Road, Fulham. X18473.

DARTON, H. A., Lce.-Cpl., Suffolk Regiment.

He volunteered in December, 1915, and served on the Western Front, being in action on the Somme and at Kemmel Hill. He was gassed at both these places, but continued to serve until he was demobilised in 1919, holding the General Service and Victory Medals.
30, Ashford Road, Tottenham. X18358.

DAVEY, E. (Mrs.), Special War Worker.

During the war this lady was engaged on important work at a shell-filling factory. She rendered most valuable services.
35, Steele Road, Harlesden. 14376A.

DAVEY, W., Pte., 2/10th Middlesex Regiment.

He joined in 1916, served in Egypt and Palestine, and took part in many engagements, including the capture of Jerusalem. He was sent to France in 1918, and demobilised in the following year, holding the General Service and Victory Medals.
35, Steele Road, Harlesden. 14376B.

DAVIDSON, A., Pte., Middlesex Regiment.

He volunteered in October, 1915, served on the Western Front from 1916 until January, 1919, and took part in various engagements, including the fighting at Loos, Lens and Lille.
He was demobilised in April, 1919, and holds the General Service and Victory Medals.
84, Drayton Road, Harlesden. 15071.

DAVIDSON, A. J., Pte., Duke of Wellington's Regiment.

He volunteered in January, 1915, and served on Home stations, being medically unfit for overseas service owing to a disablement received while in India.
He was demobilised in February, 1919.
145, Felixstowe Road, Edmonton. 14545.

DAVIE, J. E., Rifleman, King's Royal Rifle Corps.

He volunteered in December, 1915, and served in Salonica, where he took part in many engagements. He was awarded the Medaille d'Honneur for conspicuous bravery in the field, and also holds the General Service and Victory Medals. He was demobilised in March, 1919.
4, Felixstowe Road, Willesden. X17764.

DAVIES, Ada (Miss), Special War Worker.

During the war this lady was engaged for five years on valuable work in the manufacture of wire entanglements. This was very arduous work, for which she was highly commended for her untiring efforts.
99, Barret's Green Road, Harlesden. 13826D.

6

DAVIES, A., Observer, Royal Air Force.

He joined in December, 1917, and served as an observer until his demobilisation in March, 1919. He carried out these difficult and dangerous duties with considerable ability and courage.

36, Selwyn Road, Harlesden. 14617B.

DAVIES, A. S., Pte., 7th London Regiment.

He was mobilised in 1914, and served on the Western Front, where he took an active part in the fighting near Loos and in other sectors. He was badly gassed on two occasions, and was demobilised in 1919, holding the General Service and Victory Medals.

99, Barret's Green Road, Harlesden. 13826A.

DAVIES, E. T., Gunner, Machine Gun Corps.

He was retained on munition work previous to joining in April, 1918, from which date, until his demobilisation in January, 1919, he was doing important duty at various stations.

25, Field Road, Fulham. 15149B.

DAVIES, F. J., Pte., Royal Fusiliers.

He joined in 1917, and served during many engagements on the Western Front.

He was demobilised in 1919, and holds the General Service and Victory Medals.

110, Kimberley Road, Upper Edmonton. 16792B.

DAVIES, J. L., Lce.-Cpl., East Surrey Regiment and Hants. Regiment.

He volunteered in October, 1914, and was sent to the Western Front, where he took part in several engagements, and was gassed during the fighting at Ypres. Later he went to the East, and whilst there contracted malarial fever. He holds the 1914-15 Star, General Service and Victory Medals, and was discharged unfit for further service on November 14th, 1917.

22, Albert Terrace, Milton Avenue, Stonebridge Park, N.W.22 14331.

DAVIES, J. M., Pte., 4th Essex Regiment.

He volunteered in June, 1915, and was stationed on the East Coast Defences until September, 1918, when he was sent to France. He took part in the engagements on the Somme, and was demobilised on March 4th, 1919, holding the General Service and Victory Medals.

39, Raynham Avenue, Edmonton. 16471.

DAVIES, L. L. (Mrs.), Special War Worker.

For two years this lady did most useful and skilful work at the Fulham Munition Factory, in connection with the manufacture of hand-grenades, for which she was highly commended.

25, Field Road, Fulham. 15149A.

DAVIES, L. S., Cpl. 1st Air Mechanic, R.A.F.

He joined in February, 1918, at the age of 18, and, volunteering for the Russian Expeditionary Force, he embarked for Russia in 1919, where he rendered good services.

13, Colville Road, Lower Edmonton. 11997.

DAVIES, P. S., Driver, Royal Field Artillery.

He volunteered in August, 1914, and served in France until 1919, taking part in many engagements, including Mons, the Somme, Ypres, Bullecourt, Arras and the Advance of 1918.

He holds the 1914 Star, General Service and Victory Medals, and was demobilised in January, 1919.

8, Mund Street, W.14 15192.

DAVIES, R. (Miss), Special War Worker.

This lady was engaged for four years making wire entanglements, and also on various other important duties at the National Filling Factory, Park Royal. Her services were very valuable, and she was highly commended for her work.

99, Barret's Green Road, Harlesden. 13826C.

DAVIES, R. W. N., Lieut., Artists' Rifles, Northumberland Fusiliers and R.A.F.

He joined in September, 1914, and in 1916 was transferred to the Royal Air Force. After being stationed at Dover for a few months, he went to France, and on April 6th, 1917, was killed near Arras.

He was entitled to the General Service and Victory Medals.

191, Chapter Road, Willesden. X17205.

DAVIES, S. A., Pte., 7th Duke of Cornwall's L.I.

He joined in March, 1916, and served on the Western Front for two years. He was in action at Arras, Cambrai, Ypres, Lens, Neuve Chapelle and elsewhere, and was severely wounded at Arras.

He was discharged as a result of his wounds in October, 1918, holding the General Service and Victory Medals.

88, Minet Avenue, Harlesden. 13639.

DAVIES, W., 1st Air Mechanic, Royal Air Force.

He joined in December, 1916, and was engaged on important duties in France for a year, acting as driver to the Officer Commanding.

He was demobilised in February, 1919, holding the General Service and Victory Medals.

36, Selwyn Road, Harlesden. 14617A.

DAVIES, W. J., Bandsman, 2nd South Lancashire Regiment.

He volunteered in August, 1914, and served on the Western Front, taking part in the retreat from Mons (as a stretcher-bearer) and many other engagements. He was wounded twice during his service.

He holds the 1914 Star, General Service and Victory Medals, and was demobilised in February, 1919.

164, Estcourt Road, Fulham. 16245.

DAVIS, A., Gunner, Royal Garrison Artillery.

He volunteered in April, 1915, and served in France until 1919, during which time he took part in many engagements. He holds the 1914-15 Star, General Service and Victory Medals, and was demobilised in January, 1919.

2, Somerset Road, Edmonton. X17034A.

DAVIS, A. E., Pte., The Queen's (Royal West Surrey Regiment).

He joined in 1916, and served on the Western Front, taking part in numerous engagements. He contracted pneumonia and was invalided home. During his return voyage the ship on which he sailed was sunk, and he was in the water for many hours before being picked up.

He was demobilised in 1919, and holds the General Service and Victory Medals.

198, Church Road, Willesden. 16742—16743A.

DAVIS, A. T., Lce.-Cpl., 2nd East Surrey Regt.

At the outbreak of war he was serving in India, and was immediately sent to the Western Front, where he took part in many engagements. He was badly wounded, and as a result was discharged unfit for further military service in April, 1917.

He holds the 1914 Star, the General Service and Victory Medals.

32, Church Path, Hammersmith. 16396.

DAVIS, C., Driver, Royal Field Artillery.

He joined in 1917, and served with distinction on the Western Front in the Retreat and Advance of 1918. He holds the General Service and Victory Medals, and was demobilised in 1919.

4, Denton Road, Harlesden. 14697.

DAVIS, C. T. (M.M.), Pte., 10th Middlesex Regt.

He volunteered in November, 1914, and served at the Dardanelles, Egypt and Palestine, and took part in the capture of Jerusalem. He was mentioned in despatches and awarded the Military Medal for conspicuous gallantry and devotion to duty in the field.

He also holds the 1915 Star, the General Service and Victory Medals, and was demobilised in July, 1919.

26, Faroe Road, West Kensington. T12655.

DAVIS, C. W., Gunner, Royal Garrison Artillery.

He joined in 1916, and served at the Dardanelles, afterwards going to the Western Front, where he took part in many engagements, including the Somme and Ypres.

He was demobilised in 1919, holding the General Service and Victory Medals.

68, Purves Road, Willesden. 18419C.

DAVIS, E. M., Sergt., 19th Middlesex Regiment.

He volunteered in August, 1915, and was sent to France in April, 1916, where he served for four years, taking part in many engagements. He was at Arras, Cambrai, Vimy Ridge and on the Somme.

He was discharged in 1919, holding the General Service and Victory Medals.

19, Napier Road, College Park, Willesden, N.W. X17520.

DAVIS, F., Pte., Honourable Artillery Company,

He joined in 1918, was sent to France in the same year, and took part in several engagements. After the Armistice he served with the Army of Occupation in Germany until he was demobilised in March, 1920.

He holds the General Service and Victory Medals.

2, Somerset Road, Edmonton. X17034B.

DAVIS, G., Sergt., 10th Middlesex Regiment.

He volunteered in August, 1914, and was engaged on important training duties. He went to France in 1917, and saw active service on the Ypres Front and at Cambrai. He also acted as a gas instructor in France.

He was demobilised in April, 1919, and holds the General Service and Victory Medals.

89, Fifth Avenue, Queen's Park, W.10 X18738.

DAVIS, G. J., 1st-Class Stoker, Royal Navy.
He joined in 1917, and carried out arduous duties on H.M.S. "Temeraire" with the Grand Fleet in the North Sea.
He was demobilised in 1919, holding the General Service and Victory Medals.
38, Ladysmith Road, Upper Edmonton. 16465.

DAVIS, H. E., Pte., 3rd Middlesex Regiment.
He joined in August, 1914, went to France the following year, and was discharged as medically unfit for further service in June, 1916, in consequence of wounds received in action.
He holds the 1914-15 Star, General Service and Victory Medals.
94, Barry Road, Harlesden. T14978.

DAVIS, J., Cpl., Royal Engineers (Railways).
He joined in 1916, and was engaged on very important duties in France until 1919, doing splendid work on the light railways in connection with several important engagements.
He was demobilised in 1919, holding the General Service and Victory Medals.
107, Framfield Road, Hanwell. 10885.

DAVIS, M. (Mrs.), Special War Worker.
During the war this lady rendered valuable services as a munition worker in the Admiralty Munition Works. Her duties, which were in connection with the examination of fuses, were arduous, and she was commended for her untiring energy.
198, Church Road, Willesden. 16742—16743B.

DAVIS, T., Sergt., 23rd Middlesex Regiment.
He volunteered in August, 1915, and served on the Western Front, and was in action at Ypres, the Somme, and Cambrai. He was wounded, and also suffered from trench feet.
He holds the General Service and Victory Medals, and was demobilised in March, 1919.
42, Bayonne Road, Fulham. 14513A.

DAVIS, T. G., Cpl., The Buffs (East Kent Regt.).
He joined in March, 1916, and after serving in several engagements on the Western Front, was killed in action in October, 1918.
He was entitled to the General Service and Victory Medals.
42, Bayonne Road, Fulham. 14513B.

DAVIS, W. L., Gunner, Royal Garrison Artillery.
He joined in August, 1917, and being medically unfit for General service, he was employed on special duties with his unit until demobilised in March, 1919.
79, Coomer Road, Fulham. 16447.

DAVISON, E. G., 1st Air Mechanic, R.A.F.
He joined in August, 1915, and during his long service overseas served with his squadron at Dunkirk and elsewhere. His duties called for a high degree of mechanical skill.
He secured his demobilisation in February, 1919, and holds the General Service and Victory Medals.
11, Shrewsbury Road, Harlesden. 14131.

DAVISON, G., Pte., East Surrey Regiment.
He volunteered in 1914, and being medically unfit, was engaged on duties of importance at various stations.
He was eventually discharged, through ill-health, in March, 1916.
10, May Street, West Kensington. 15887A.

DAW, S. H. (M.C.), Capt., London Regiment.
He volunteered in October, 1914, and joined the Royal Field Artillery. He rendered valuable work as assistant to the Veterinary Officer at a large Remount Depot. Commissioned into the London Regiment, he went to the Western Front and took part in numerous engagements. He was awarded the Military Cross for conspicuous gallantry under fire, and also holds the General Service and Victory Medals.
He secured his demobilisation shortly after the cessation of hostilities.
21, Abbey Gardens, St. John's Wood. TX20127.

DAWE, E., 23rd Red Cross, Middlesex Detachment.
He joined in 1918, and during his service tended and looked after the general welfare of wounded soldiers returning from the various Fronts. His work was greatly appreciated and of great value.
1, Stracey Road, Harlesden. 15669.

DAWES, G. H., Pte., 26th Middlesex Regiment.
He volunteered in December, 1915, and served on the Salonica Front, where he contracted malaria. He was invalided home in consequence in 1919, and was demobilised later in the same year.
He holds the General Service and Victory Medals.
9a, Lorenco Road, Tottenham. X17994.

DAWKINS, H. W. C., Sergt., Northumberland Fusiliers.
He joined in May, 1916, served in France until 1919, and took part in many engagements, being severely gassed in March, 1918.
He was demobilised in September, 1919, and holds the General Service and Victory Medals.
75, Somerset Road, Edmonton. X17040.

DAWSON, A., Pte., King's Own (Royal Lancs. Regiment).
He volunteered in August, 1914, and served on the Western Front, where he took part in the retreat from Mons, the battles of the Somme and Loos, and on one occasion was reported missing. He was returned to England for medical treatment, and was eventually discharged as unfit for further service.
He holds the 1914 Star, General Service and Victory Medals.
34, Bramber Road, Fulham. 16270.

DAWSON, J., Cpl., East Surrey Regiment.
He enlisted in March, 1914, and on the outbreak of hostilities was drafted to the Western Front. He was in action at Ypres, La Bassée and Poperinghe, and was wounded. He also served in Egypt and Salonica, and after hospital treatment at Malta, was discharged in July, 1916, as unfit for further service.
He holds the 1914 Star, General Service and Victory Medals.
27, Humbolt Road, Fulham. 15040.

DAWSON, J. H., Pte., Royal Fusiliers.
He volunteered in 1915 and was sent to the Western Front in the same year, where he saw considerable service in many sectors for four years.
He was demobilised in 1919, holding the 1915 Star, General Service and Victory Medals.
21, Ray's Avenue, Edmonton. 15485.

DAWSON, W. H., Special War Worker.
Was employed during the war on especially important duties in connection with the construction of aeroplanes, and thus rendered valuable assistance to his country.
18, Crefeld Road, Fulham. 14500A.

DAWSON, W. J., Rifleman, 1/5th London Rifle Brigade.
He joined in August, 1916, went to France and was killed in action on January 27th, 1917, after being in many engagements.
He was entitled to the General Service and Victory Medals.
89, Adeney Road, Fulham. 15324.

DAY, A., Driver, R.A.S.C. (M.T.).
He volunteered in October, 1914, and in the same year was sent out to the Western Front, where he served until 1919. He was in action in the Great Advance, and was gassed while carrying ammunition and food to the troops in the line.
He holds the 1914 Star, General Service and Victory Medals, and was demobilised in April, 1919.
9, Portnall Road, Maida Hill, W.9 X19301.

DAY, A., Gunner, Royal Garrison Artillery.
He joined in 1916, and during his service on the Western Front took part in many battles, including those of Ypres, Arras and our final Advance in 1918, and was gassed.
He was demobilised in 1919, holding the General Service and Victory Medals.
59, Hartington Road, Tottenham, N.17 X19142.

DAY, C., Sergt., Northumberland Fusiliers.
He joined in 1916, and was eventually sent to France, where he took part in many engagements, including the battle of Ypres. He was wounded, and finally demobilised in November, 1919, holding the General Service and Victory Medals.
79, Rayleigh Road, Hammersmith. 12632A.

DAY, C. F., Pte., Norfolk Regiment.
He volunteered in August, 1914, and was employed on various and important duties with his unit at a number of stations.
He was demobilised in April, 1919.
16, Ranelagh Road, Harlesden. 12746B.

DAY, E. (Miss), Special War Worker.
Being anxious to assist her country, this lady volunteered, and during the war rendered very valuable services as a land worker in different parts of the country. Her duties were of an arduous nature.
79, Rayleigh Road, Hammersmith. 12632B.

DAY, E., Sapper, Royal Engineers.
He joined in November, 1916, and in the following year was sent to the Western Front, where he was engaged on special duties on the light railways. He took part in the last Retreat and Advance, and in December, 1918, was demobilised.
He holds the General Service and Victory Medals.
94, Portnall Road, Maida Hill, W.9   X19539.

DAY, G. F., Driver, Royal Field Artillery.
He volunteered in August, 1914, and served on the Western Front, taking part in the battles of Loos, Arras, Ypres, the Somme and Cambrai, during which time he was wounded and gassed.
He was demobilised in February, 1919, and holds the 1915 Star, the General Service and Victory Medals.
34, Bramber Road, Fulham.   16271.

DAY, H., Gunner, Royal Field Artillery.
He volunteered in 1915, went to the Dardanelles, and took part in the bitter fighting during the Suvla Bay landing. Later he served in France and was killed in action on the Somme in October, 1916.
He was entitled to the 1915 Star, General Service and Victory Medals.
88, Holly Lane, Willesden.   15406A.

DAY, H. J., Pte., Middlesex Regt. and M.G.C.
He volunteered in June, 1915, and transferred to the Machine Gun Corps in September, 1916. He was sent to Salonica, where he remained for three years, taking part in several engagements. Afterwards he went to Egypt and was stationed in Cairo and Alexandria until his demobilisation in August, 1919.
He is in receipt of a pension for illness contracted through malaria fever, and holds the General Service and Victory Medals.
10, Lyndhurst Road, Edmonton.   T15515.

DAY, R., Gunner, Royal Garrison Artillery.
He joined in March, 1918, and took part in many engagements on the Western Front as a signaller. He was invalided home, and in March, 1919, was discharged as unfit for further service.
He holds the General Service and Victory Medals.
77, Bramber Road, Fulham.   16275.

DAY, W. E. C., Pte., 2nd and 4th York and Lancaster Regiment.
He volunteered in November, 1915, and served on the Western Front, taking part in the battles of the Somme, Arras, Gommecourt, Bourlon Wood, Cambrai and the Marne. He was twice wounded, and was taken prisoner in July, 1918. He was demobilised in November, 1919, holding the General Service and Victory Medals.
79, Rayleigh Road, Hammersmith.   12632C.

DAYKIN, A. R., A.B., Royal Navy.
He volunteered in March, 1915, and met his death on board H.M.S. "Begona," which was lost at sea in September, 1917.
He was entitled to the General Service and Victory Medals.
59, Lintaine Grove, W.14   16830B.

DAYKIN, F. C., Pte., East Surrey Regiment.
He volunteered in August, 1915, and served on the Western Front in many engagements until March, 1918, when he was discharged.
He holds the General Service and Victory Medals.
59, Lintaine Grove, W.14   16830A.

DAYKIN, H. J., Pte., 7th London Regiment.
He volunteered in January, 1915, went to France, and was killed in action in March of the following year.
He was entitled to the General Service and Victory Medals.
59, Lintaine Grove, Fulham.   16830C.

DAYKIN, H. J., Pte., 1/7th London Regiment.
He volunteered in April, 1915, went to France in the same year, took part in the fighting on the Somme, and was killed in action at Loos in February, 1916.
He was entitled to the 1915 Star, General Service and Victory Medals.
34, Hilmer Street, W.14   16923.

DE BANK, W. L., Lce.-Cpl., M.G.C.
He volunteered in April, 1915, saw varied service in Gallipoli, Mesopotamia and the North of India, and was twice wounded in action.
He was demobilised in December, 1919, and holds the 1915 Star and the General Service and Victory Medals.
22, Fernhead Road, Maida Hill, W.4   X19390.

DE-GRUSSA, A. W., Cpl., King's Royal Rifle Corps.
He volunteered in 1914, and served for three years in France, taking part in the battles of Ypres and the Somme, and many other engagements. From 1918 till his demobilisation in 1919 he served with the Army of Occupation in Germany.
He holds the 1914-15 Star, General Service and Victory Medals.
51, Sheldon Road, Edmonton.   X17301.

DE ROSA, A., Pte., Northamptonshire Regt.
He joined in March, 1918, went to France, and was killed in the final Advance on August 30th, 1918.
He was entitled to the General Service and Victory Medals.
40, Durban Road, N.17.   X18079.

DEACON, A., Pte., R.A.M.C.
He volunteered in 1915, and was sent to France in the following year. He served with the East Surreys on the Western Front, and was present in many engagements, including the battles of the Somme, Ypres and the last Advance in 1918. He was in hospital for some months, and was demobilised in August, 1919.
He holds the General Service and Victory Medals.
34a, Durban Road, Tottenham, N.17   X18080.

DEACON, A. R., Driver, Royal Field Artillery.
He volunteered in August, 1915, and was sent to France in the same year. Later he served at Salonica with distinction.
He was demobilised in April, 1919, and holds the 1915 Star, General Service and Victory Medals.
6, York Road, Lower Edmonton.   16783B.

DEACON, E. R. (Mrs.), Special War Worker.
During the war this lady was engaged in connection with the manufacture of important war supplies at a London factory. She rendered good services and was commended for her work.
52, Ancill Street, Hammersmith.   13754B.

DEACON, T. J. E., Pte., R. West Kent Regt.
He volunteered in September, 1914, and served in France, taking part in many engagements, including Delville Wood, where he was seriously wounded. He was in hospital in England two years, and was discharged owing to his wounds in March, 1919.
He holds the 1914-15 Star, General Service and Victory Medals.
17, Tenterden Road, N.17   X18277.

DEACON, W. O., Driver, R.F.A.
He volunteered in August, 1914, and during his service on the Western Front was in action on the Somme, at Loos, Vimy Ridge, Ypres and in the Advance of 1918.
He holds the 1914-15 Star, General Service and Victory Medals.
52, Ancill Street, Hammersmith.   13754A.

DEADMAN, J. W., Driver, Machine Gun Corps.
He joined in 1918, and remained with his unit, which was employed on many important duties, until demobilised in the following year, after the cessation of hostilities.
27, Crefeld Road, Hammersmith.   14480.

DEAKINS, A., Pte., 7th London Regiment.
He volunteered in August, 1914, and served on the Western Front with distinction, taking part in the battles of Loos, Ypres, the Somme and Lille, and was slightly wounded. He was demobilised in February, 1919, holding the 1914 Star, General Service and Victory Medals.
57, Everington Street, W.6   13973.

DEAN, A., Special War Worker.
During two years of the war he was engaged on work of national importance at the Perivale Munition Factory, Park Royal, and was employed in the laborious and dangerous duties of loading shells for transport overseas. His services were greatly commended.
305, Shirland Road, Maida Hill, W.9   X19567B.

DEAN, A. W., Sergt., Royal Engineers.
He volunteered in October, 1915, and was sent to France in the same year, where he took part in the battle of the Somme, and was wounded. He subsequently fought at Ypres, Lens, Arras, and was present at the Retreat and Advance of 1918. He was also engaged in mine operations, and was demobilised in May, 1919, holding the 1914-15 Star and the General Service and Victory Medals.
14, Ambleside Road, Willesden.   16127.

DEAN, C., Bombardier, Royal Field Artillery.
He volunteered in August, 1914, and served in France during many engagements until he was demobilised in December, 1918. He was wounded, and holds the 1914-15 Star, General Service and Victory Medals.
25, Leamore Road, Hammersmith.   12613B

DEAN, F. A., Sergt., 1/9th Middlesex Regiment.

He was in the Territorials before the war, was mobilised in August, 1914, and served in India until 1917, when he went to Mesopotamia, where he took part in many engagements. He holds the Territorial Efficiency Medal, General Service and Victory Medals, and was demobilised in February, 1919.
60, St. Margaret's Road, Willesden. X17819.

DEAN, G., Cpl., Royal Fusiliers.

He joined in 1917, saw service in East Africa and on the Western Front, where he took part in many engagements, including the Retreat and Advance of 1918.
He holds the General Service and Victory Medals, and was demobilised in 1919.
54, Carlyle Avenue, Harlesden. 14411B.

DEAN, H. D., Pte., Middlesex Regiment.

He joined in July, 1917, on reaching military age, and went to the Western Front the following April. Two months later he was killed in action by shell fire.
He was entitled to the General Service and Victory Medals.
305, Shirland Road, Maida Hill. X19568A.

DEAN, H. J., Pte., Middlesex Regiment.

He volunteered in October, 1914, and saw much service on the Western Front. He received two severe wounds in August, 1916, as a result of which he was discharged unfit for further service in April, 1917.
He holds the 1915 Star, General Service and Victory Medals.
20, West Street, Edmonton. 14231.

DEAN, H. J., Mechanic, Royal Air Force.

He joined in May, 1916, and served in France from March, 1917, until April, 1918. He broke his leg during the last Retreat, and was discharged physically unfit in consequence in November, 1918.
He holds the General Service and Victory Medals.
12, Rigeley Road, College Park, Willesden. X17671.

DEAN, J. W., Pte., The Buffs (East Kent Regt.).

He volunteered in September, 1914, and from the following year until 1917, when he was invalided home, served on the Western Front. During this period he took part in many of the principal engagements, including those at Albert and Trones Wood, where he was wounded. On recovery, he did important work until his demobilisation in January, 1919. He holds the 1915 Star and the General Service and Victory Medals.
305, Shirland Road, Maida Hill, W.9 X19568B.

DEAN, R. J., Pioneer, Royal Engineers.

He volunteered in 1915, served on the Western Front in the same year, and took part in many engagements, including the Retreat and Advance of 1918. He had previously served in the South African War, and holds the King's and Queen's South African Medals, 1914–15 Star, General Service and Victory Medals.
He was demobilised in March, 1919.
54, Carlyle Avenue, Harlesden. 14411A.

DEAN, T., Pte., 17th Middlesex Regiment.

He volunteered in 1915, and served on the Western Front until he was demobilised in 1919. He took part in many engagements, and holds the 1915 Star, General Service and Victory Medals.
25, Leamore Street, Hammersmith. 12613C.

DEAN, V. J., Special War Worker.

During the war he carried out arduous and trying work in the sheet-metal department of a Hendon aircraft manufacturing company, thereby rendering services of a most valuable nature.
305, Shirland Road, Maida Hill, W.9 X19567A.

DEAN, W., Cpl., 2nd Dragoon Guards (Queen's Bays).

He volunteered in September, 1914, and served in France, where he took active part in many engagements until he was demobilised in April, 1919.
He holds the 1914–15 Star, General Service and Victory Medals.
25, Leamore Street, Hammersmith. 12613A.

DEANUS, W., Driver, R.A.S.C. (M.T.).

He volunteered in April, 1915, served with distinction in France and Mesopotamia, and was wounded.
He holds the 1915 Star, General Service and Victory Medals, and was demobilised in March, 1919.
84, Adeney Road, Hammersmith. 14464.

DEAR, E. H., Mechanic, Royal Air Force.

He joined in May, 1918, and was retained with his unit performing important duties at various stations until his demobilisation in February, 1919.
14, Maldon Road, Edmonton. 14096A.

DEAR, W. C., Pte., Royal Fusiliers.

He volunteered in February, 1916, served on the Western Front, taking part in the battles of Loos, Arras, Ypres and the Somme, and was wounded on two occasions. He was operated upon whilst in France, and was in hospital for many months.
He was demobilised in January, 1919, and holds the General Service and Victory Medals.
6, Moselle Street, Tottenham. X18206B.

DEARING, C. A., Lce.-Cpl., Duke of Cornwall's Light Infantry.

He was called up as a Reservist at the outbreak of war, and proceeded to the Western Front, where he took part in the retreat from Mons, the battles of Ypres, the Somme and other engagements. He also fought in the 1918 battles and was taken prisoner. Whilst overseas he was twice wounded and gassed.
He was demobilised in April, 1919, holding the 1914 Star, General Service and Victory Medals.
31, Hartington Road, Tottenham, N.17 X19138.

DEARING, G., Gunner, Royal Field Artillery.

He volunteered in June, 1915, and served on the Western Front, taking part in the battles of the Somme, Ypres, Arras, and Bullecourt. While in action at Messines he was wounded, and was in hospital in France for some months.
He was demobilised in February, 1920, and holds the General Service and Victory Medals.
7, Eli Street, West Kensington. 16434.

DEARING, J. A., Cpl., R.A.S.C. (Supply).

He joined in 1916, and served on the Western Front, being engaged in important canteen work.
He holds the General Service and Victory Medals, and was demobilised in 1920.
27, Fourth Avenue, Paddington, W.10 X18674.

DEARING, T., Lce.-Cpl., Royal Fusiliers.

He joined in May, 1918, and was employed with his regiment on duty at various stations until his demobilisation in 1919. Previous to joining he was actively employed on important Government work with the Police Force.
123a, Deacon Road, Willesden. 16613.

DEARLOVE, A. E. J., Pte., The Queen's (Royal West Surrey Regiment).

He volunteered in February, 1916, served in Italy and with the Egyptian Expeditionary Force in many engagements, and was wounded.
He holds the General Service and Victory Medals, being demobilised in September, 1919.
95, Adeney Road, Fulham. 15323B.

DEARMAN, C. W., Sapper, Royal Engineers.

He volunteered in May, 1915, went to France the same year, and was wounded on the Somme in October, 1916. The following year he was sent to Mesopotamia, and later to India.
He holds the 1914–15 Star, General Service and Victory Medals, and was demobilised in September, 1919.
27, Hazelbury Road, Edmonton. 17494.

DEARMAN, E. F., Sapper, Royal Engineers.

He volunteered in June, 1915, and being medically unfit, he was employed on important duty at various stations. He died in hospital in December, 1915.
2, Linton Road, N.18 X17279.

DEATH, E. (M.M.), Sergt., Royal Engineers.

He volunteered in September, 1914, and was sent to France in 1916. He took part in the Somme engagements of that year, was awarded the Military Medal for conspicuous gallantry and devotion to duty in the field, and continued to serve on that Front for the following two years.
He also holds the General Service and Victory Medals, and was demobilised in December, 1918.
48, Tilson Road, Tottenham, N.17 X19088.

DEATH, W., Sapper, Royal Engineers.

He joined in June, 1916, and saw much important service in Salonica. He suffered from malarial fever, and was demobilised in February, 1920, holding the General Service and Victory Medals.
22, Felixstowe Road, Edmonton. 15279.

DEBLEY, A. E., Cpl., 1st East Surrey Regiment.

He was in the Army at the outbreak of war, and served on the Western Front. He took part in the battles of Mons and the Marne, where he was wounded in September, 1914. He was rendered unfit for further service, and was discharged in July, 1916, holding the 1914 Star, the General Service and Victory Medals.
72, Shakespeare Avenue, Harlesden. 13621.

DEBLEY, R. J., Sapper, Royal Engineers.
He joined in February, 1917, and served on the Western Front from May, 1917, till November, 1919. He was employed as an operator on the light railways at Armentieres and Ypres.
He was demobilised in November, 1919, holding the General Service and Victory Medals.
42, Mordaunt Road, Harlesden.   13728.

DEERING, E., Pte., R.A.S.C.
He joined in February, 1918, and served on the Western Front, being employed on important duties in connection with the supply of rations to the troops.
He was demobilised in July, 1919, holding the General Service and Victory Medals.
167, Portnall Road, Maida Hill, W.9   X19577.

DEETMAN, A., Pte., Bedfordshire Regiment.
He joined in February, 1917, and served with his unit, performing various and important duties, until he was demobilised in September, 1919.
65, Monmouth Road, Lower Edmonton, N.9   13018.

DEIGHTON, A. H., Pte., 23rd Middlesex Regt.
He volunteered in November, 1915, was sent to France, and was killed in an engagement on the Somme in October, 1916.
He was entitled to the Victory and General Service Medals.
2, Kilmaine Road, Fulham, S.W.6   XT18879.

DELANEY, A. (Mrs.), Special War Worker.
This lady was engaged during the war at the Park Royal Filling Factory, where she performed skilful and valuable work in connection with the output of shells and other ammunition.
57, Shrewsbury Road, Harlesden.   14125C.

DELANEY, A. A., Gunner, Royal Field Artillery.
He was serving at the outbreak of war, and in 1914 went to the Western Front, where he took part in the fighting at Mons, the Marne, the Aisne and in many other sectors. In 1915 he was drafted to the East, took part in the Palestine campaign, and was twice wounded in Mesopotamia, having taken part in the fighting at Kut.
He holds the 1914 Star, the General Service and Victory Medals, and was demobilised in May, 1919.
57, Shrewsbury Road, Harlesden.   14125A.

DELANEY, B. E., Pte., 8th Middlesex Regiment.
He volunteered in August, 1914, served on the Western Front and took part in engagements at Cambrai, Arras, Ypres, the Somme, and other sectors.
He was demobilised in June, 1919, holding the 1914-15 Star, General Service and Victory Medals.
57, Shrewsbury Road, Harlesden.   14125B.

DELASALLE, A. E., 1st Air Mechanic, Royal Air Force.
He volunteered in January, 1916, and after doing duty in England, went to Russia with the Expeditionary Force, where he was wounded in action.
He holds the General Service and Victory Medals.
122, Dyson's Road, Edmonton.   16514.

DELASALLE, H. F., Pte., R.A.S.C. (M.T.).
He volunteered in August, 1914, and was sent to the Western Front, where he served continuously for two years. He was present at numerous important engagements, and took part in the battles of Ypres (1914), Soissons (1914), Dickebusch, Armentieres, Loos, the Somme, Albert, Arras, Bapaume, and elsewhere.
He was discharged in May, 1916, and holds the 1914 Star, General Service and Victory Medals.
40, Dudden Hill Lane, Willesden.   T17338.

DELDERFIELD, E., Pte., Royal West Kent Regiment.
He volunteered in January, 1915, served on the Western Front, and was killed in action on the Somme on November 11th, 1916.
He was entitled to the General Service and Victory Medals.
130, Carlyle Avenue, Harlesden.   14187A.

DELDERFIELD, L. A. (Miss), Special War Worker.
This lady was engaged during the war in shell filling for thirteen months at Perivale Filling Factory, and for nine months as an examiner of small-arms ammunition at Park Royal Munition Works. She performed her duties skilfully and diligently, and was highly commended for her services.
130, Carlyle Avenue, Harlesden.   14187/B.

DELLAR, A. J., Special War Worker.
During the war he was engaged for three and a half years on the dangerous work of sand-blasting. By this means services of a most valuable nature were rendered and gained high commendation.
53, Durban Road, Tottenham.   X18284.

DELLOW, A. J., A.B., R.N., H.M.S. " Renown."
He was serving on the outbreak of hostilities, and during the war took part in the dangerous and trying operations at the Dardanelles, and in all the big engagements in the North Sea.
He holds the 1914 Star, General Service and Victory Medals.
39, Denbigh Road, Willesden.   15093A.

DELLOW, F. M. (Miss), Special War Worker.
During the war this lady was engaged on work of national importance at the J.A.P. Munition Factory, Tottenham, where she operated very successfully a lathe for turning shells. Her work required much skill, and she was highly commended.
57, Sutherland Road, Tottenham, N.17   X18803C.

DELLOW, J. A., Pte., Royal Scots Fusiliers.
He volunteered in August, 1914, and served on the Western Front. During the battle of Mons he was taken prisoner and was employed in the coal mines in Germany, where he suffered great hardships and ill-treatment.
He was demobilised in August, 1919, and holds the 1914 Star, General Service and Victory Medals.
57, Sutherland Road, Tottenham, N.17   X18803B.

DELLOW, S. P., Cpl., R.A.M.C.
He volunteered in August, 1914, and took part in the campaign in Egypt and Palestine from the following January until he was demobilised in May, 1919.
He holds the 1915 Star, General Service and Victory Medals.
39, Denbigh Road, Willesden.   15093B.

DELLOW, W. T., Pte., The Queen's (Royal West Surrey Regiment).
He volunteered in February, 1915, and served on the Western Front. He took part in the battles of the Somme, Ypres, Arras and Bullecourt, and was wounded at Arras.
He was demobilised in January, 1919, and holds the 1915 Star, the General Service and Victory Medals.
57, Sutherland Road, Tottenham, N.17   X18803A.

DENCHFIELD, W., Pte., 3rd Middlesex Regt.
He volunteered in 1915, served in France from the following year until demobilised in January, 1919. He took part in the battles of the Somme, Albert, Ypres and Loos, was wounded and gassed, and was mentioned in despatches for conspicuous gallantry on the field.
He holds the General Service and Victory Medals.
7, Oak Road, Willesden.   15086.

DENGEL, H. F. J., Pte., Royal Defence Corps.
He joined in September, 1914, and during his service was stationed with his unit at various places on important defence duties.
He was discharged in March, 1918, owing to blindness caused through shock received during his service.
40, Herries Street, North Kensington, W.10   X18726B.

DENGEL, J., Pte., Royal Defence Corps.
He joined in December, 1917, at a very early age, and served with the Volunteers on the defence of the East Coast. He rendered valuable and important services with his regiment at various stations until his demobilisation in 1919.
40, Herries Street, North Kensington, W.10   X18726A.

DENMAN, F. E., Pte., R.A.S.C.
He joined in November, 1916, and served on the Western Front, where he was engaged on important duties. He received severe injuries, and was in hospital for a considerable time, being eventually demobilised in November, 1918.
He holds the General Service and Victory Medals.
26, Mulgrave Road, Fulham.   16172.

DENNIS, A. E., Pte., 9th Royal Welsh Fusiliers,
He volunteered in September, 1914, and was at first unfit for foreign service. He went to France in 1918 and, after the cessation of hostilities, to Germany with the Army of Occupation, remaining until he was demobilised in June, 1919.
He holds the General Service and Victory Medals.
87, Sandringham Road, Willesden Green.   17131A.

DENNIS, E., A.B., R.N., H.M.S. " Vulcan."
He volunteered in August, 1914, and was on board H.M.S. " Vulcan " during the war, in the North Sea, where he had many dangerous and varied experiences.
He was demobilised in February, 1919, and holds the 1914 Star, the General Service and Victory Medals.
57, Cobbold Road, Willesden.   16076.

DENNIS, J., Pte., The Queen's (Royal West Surrey Regiment).
He volunteered in August, 1914, and was sent to the Western Front in the following year. He took part in numerous engagements, including Ypres, Loos, Cambrai, Arras and the Somme, and was twice wounded.
He was discharged in consequence of his wounds in April, 1917, and holds the 1915 Star, General Service and Victory Medals.   66, Kilburn Lane, W.10   X18604.

DENISON, G. F., Pte., Grenadier Guards.
He volunteered in August, 1914, went to the Western Front and took part in the battles of the Somme, Ypres and Arras. Later he served in Salonica and Egypt, taking part in many engagements, and remaining there until he was demobilised in 1918. He was wounded twice, and holds the 1914 Star, General Service and Victory Medals.
119, Estcourt Road, Fulham. 16235.

DENNIS, W., Shoeing-smith, R.F.A.
He volunteered in June, 1915, and served on many sectors of the Western Front. He was wounded and gassed, suffered from trench fever, and was demobilised in March, 1919, holding the General Service and Victory Medals.
9, Hartopp Avenue, Fulham. X17655.

DENNISON, F., Pte., Royal Sussex Regiment and Middlesex Regiment.
He joined in 1916, was sent to France in the following year, and took part in the fighting at Ypres, Cambrai, Arras, on the Somme and during the Retreat of 1918. He was severely wounded twice, and was demobilised in 1919, holding the General Service and Victory Medals.
56, Deacon Road, Willesden. 16737B.

DENTON, A. W., Pte., Royal Sussex Regiment.
He joined in 1917, and served on the Western Front, taking part in the Retreat of 1918. He was wounded during these operations, and was demobilised in December, 1918, holding the General Service and Victory Medals.
78, Willow Vale Road, Shepherd's Bush. 12055B.

DENTON, E. J., Signaller, 9th Royal Fusiliers.
He volunteered in 1915, and was drafted to the Western Front, where he took part in important engagements on the Somme, at Arras and Cambrai. He was wounded and discharged in consequence in 1919.
He holds the General Service and Victory Medals.
60, St. Mary's Road, Harlesden. 15111.

DENTON, H. G., Sergt., 1/8th Hampshire Regt.
He volunteered in December, 1915, and the following month was sent to India. Later he saw active service with the Egyptian Expeditionary Force. He was then transferred to the Mesopotamian seat of war, and was present at the capture of Bagdad.
He was demobilised in January, 1920, holding the General Service and Victory Medals.
38, Denbigh Road, Willesden. 15537B.

DENTON, J. H., Cpl., 3rd Middlesex Regiment.
He joined in October, 1916, and went to Salonica in January of the following year, later going to Constantinople and serving there until he was demobilised in November, 1919. He holds the General Service and Victory Medals.
38, Denbigh Road, Willesden. 15537A.

DENTON, T. H., Leading Seaman, R.N., H.M.S. "Arlanza."
He was serving at the outbreak of war, and was engaged with the North Sea Patrol on the dangerous duties of escorting troops to the Front.
He holds the Mercantile Marine, General Service and Victory Medals, and was demobilised in February, 1919.
78, Willow Vale Road, Shepherd's Bush. 12055C.

DENTRY, H., Pte., Royal Scots.
He joined in 1916, and served in France until 1919, taking part in engagements on the Somme, &c. He was wounded, and holds the General Service and Victory Medals, being demobilised in 1919.
68, Kimberley Road, Upper Edmonton. 16539.

DENYER, G., Sapper, Royal Engineers.
He volunteered in February, 1915, and served with distinction on the Western Front. He was later selected for special building and construction work, and in this capacity was employed at various strategic points.
He was demobilised in March, 1919, and holds the General Service and Victory Medals.
39, Chesson Road, West Kensington. TX17067.

DERRY, E. R., Pte., 1st Bedford Regiment.
He joined in August, 1914, and in the same year went to France, where he took part in the retreat from Mons, the battles of the Somme, Hill 60, Loos and Ypres, and many others.
He was demobilised on March 28th, 1919, holding the 1914 Star, General Service and Victory Medals.
45, Sandringham Road, Willesden. X17099.

DESBOROUGH, W., Sergt., Royal Fusiliers and Labour Corps.
He joined in June, 1916, and in July was sent to France, where he was employed throughout his service on important railway and defensive works.
He was demobilised in September, 1919, and holds the General Service and Victory Medals.
19, Elthorne Avenue, Hanwell. 11069.

DETTMER, G. A., Leading Seaman, R.N.
He was serving on H.M.S. "Emperor of India" at the outbreak of hostilities, and almost immediately left Home waters for German East Africa, where he took part in the important operations off that coast, remaining there until the cessation of the war.
He holds the 1914 Star, General Service and Victory Medals.
13, Lyndhurst Road, Edmonton. 15510.

DEVILLE, G., Rifleman, 2nd Rifle Brigade.
He volunteered in September, 1914, served on the Western Front, at the Somme, Arras, Loos, Neuve Chapelle, Ypres and elsewhere, and was wounded five times.
He holds the 1914-15 Star, General Service and Victory Medals, and was demobilised in 1919.
5, Francis Street, Fulham. 14813.

DEVILLE, J. G., Pte., Durham Light Infantry.
He joined in 1916, and served in France. He took part in many important engagements, including the Somme, Ypres, Arras, Armentieres, Amiens, Vimy Ridge, Hill 60 and the last Advance in 1918, and was wounded.
He was demobilised in 1919, holding the General Service and Victory Medals.
220, Lillie Road, Fulham. X18795.

DEVINE, J., Driver, Royal Field Artillery.
He joined in 1914, and in the same year was sent to the Western Front, where he remained until 1919. He took part in the engagement at Mons, the Somme and Arras, where he was wounded.
He holds the 1914 Star and the General Service and Victory Medals, being eventually demobilised in January, 1919.
80, Ancill Street, Hammersmith. 13656.

DEVINE, J., Pte., Connaught Rangers.
He volunteered in August, 1914, and during his service on the Western Front took part in the retreat from Mons and many other important engagements. He was wounded twice, and holds the 1915 Star, General Service and Victory Medals.
32, Lowden Road, Edmonton. 11962.

DEVONSHIRE, A. E., Sergt., 7th London Regiment and Lancashire Fusiliers.
He joined in 1917, and served on the Western Front, taking part in the battle of Ypres. During this engagement he was buried during a heavy enemy bombardment, and was invalided home in consequence, with shell-shock. After his recovery, he served with the Lancashire Fusiliers in Belgium, and in Germany with the Army of Occupation.
He was demobilised in November, 1919, holding the General Service and Victory Medals.
46, Humbolt Road, Fulham. 15297.

DEVONSHIRE, E. G., Pte., Middlesex Regt.
He volunteered in 1915, and saw much service in France. He took part in many engagements, including the Somme, Ypres and the last Advance in 1918, and was wounded twice.
He was demobilised in 1919, holding the 1915 Star, General Service and Victory Medals.
16, Headcorn Road, N.17 X18489.

DEVONSHIRE, E. V., Rifleman, 21st London Regiment.
He joined in August, 1917, served on the Western Front at Lille, Albert, Tournai and elsewhere, and took part in the last Advance of 1918.
He holds the General Service and Victory Medals, and was demobilised in March, 1919.
46, Humbolt Road, Fulham. 15294.

DEWEY, G. W. A., Gunner, R.G.A.
He joined in May, 1917, and served in France, where he contracted nephritis through exposure, and was discharged in April, 1919. He died from his disability on November 19th of the same year.
He is entitled to the General Service and Victory Medals.
16, Grosvenor Road, Edmonton. 12121.

DEWSALL, W., Cpl., R.A.S.C. (M.T.).
He volunteered in 1915, having previously served through the South African Campaign, and in April of the same year was sent to France, where he was engaged on various duties.
He holds the 1915 Star, General Service and Victory Medals, and the South African Awards. He was demobilised in June, 1919.
10, Montgomery Street, Hammersmith. 15877.

DIAMOND, A. F. T., Lce.-Cpl., R.E.
He volunteered in January, 1916, and during his service on the Western Front took part in several important engagements, including that of St. Quentin. He was badly wounded in August, 1918, as a result of which he was for some time in hospital.
He holds the General Service and Victory Medals.
33, Raynham Avenue, Edmonton. 16892B.

DIAMOND, A. T., Sergt., 3rd (King's Own) Hussars.
He volunteered in August, 1914, having previously served for twenty-three years. In 1917 he was drafted to the Western Front, and after the signing of the Armistice went with the Army of Occupation to Cologne.
He was demobilised in 1919, and holds the General Service and Victory Medals.
33, Raynham Avenue, Edmonton. 16892A.

DIBBLE, S. A., Cpl., Royal Engineers.
He joined in January, 1916, and was engaged on important duties with his regiment at various stations.
He was demobilised in February, 1919.
55, Musard Road, Fulham. 15728.

DIGGINS, F., Mechanic, Royal Air Force.
He joined in September, 1918, and whilst engaged with the Royal Air Force rendered valuable services in many places, calling for a high degree of mechanical skill.
He was demobilised in March, 1919, and holds the General Service Medal.
63, Sherbrooke Road, Fulham. X18467.

DILBECK, A. H. V., Sapper, Royal Engineers.
He volunteered in April, 1915, and in the same year was sent to the Eastern Front, and was in action with the 11th Division Signal Company at the Dardanelles. Later he was transferred to the Western Front and took part in several engagements, including Ypres, the Ancre and the Somme.
He holds the 1915 Star, General Service and Victory Medals, and was demobilised in May, 1919.
247, Shirland Road, Maida Hill, W.9 X19530.

DILLEY, S. A., Pte., 12th East Surrey Regt.
He joined in March, 1916, served in Italy and on the Western Front, where he took part in many engagements, including those of Ypres, Arras, Cambrai and the Somme. Later he went to Germany with the Army of Occupation.
He was demobilised in June, 1919, holding the General Service and Victory Medals.
84a, Deacon Road, Willesden. X17112.

DILLOW, E. (Miss), 58th Middlesex V.A.D.
During the war this lady rendered valuable services at Dollis Hill House Hospital until March, 1918. She was then transferred as a nurse to the 58th Middlesex V.A.D., where she also did splendid work, being commended for her services.
1, Ashmore Road, Maida Hill, W.9 X19463A.

DILLOW, G., Special War Worker.
He was a senior member of the Church Lads' Brigade, and throughout the war did much service of a most useful character. He was on duty at railway stations and other important points during air raids, and organised and controlled the crowds seeking shelter at those places.
1, Ashmore Road, Maida Hill, W.9 X19463C.

DILLOW, N. (Miss), Nurse, V.A.D.
This lady volunteered in August, 1914, as a nurse, and did valuable work in St. Mary's Hospital, Harlesden, and at Dollis Hill House Hospital until March, 1919. She was complimented for her excellent work.
1, Ashmore Road, Maida Hill, W.9 X19463B.

DILTHEY, C. (D.C.M.), Pte., R.A.M.C. (2/1st City of London Field Ambulance).
He volunteered in September, 1914, and proceeded to France in the following year. Though himself wounded during the battle of the Somme in 1917, he continued to attend to the wounded in the field, and for his gallantry and devotion to duty on this occasion was awarded the D.C.M. He also holds the 1915 Star, the General Service and Victory Medals.
26, Lion Road, Edmonton. 15188.

DIMBLEBY, G. A., Gunner, Royal Field Artillery.
He volunteered in August, 1915, and during his service on the Western Front, which lasted three years, was in action at Verdun, the Somme, Ypres, Cambrai, Loos, Vimy Ridge, Passchendaele and on many other sectors.
He was demobilised in April, 1919, holding the General Service and Victory Medals.
34, Mordaunt Road, Harlesden. 14119.

DIMMOCK, J. W., Sergt., Royal Irish Regiment.
He was serving with the Forces on the outbreak of the war, and went to France in November, 1914, where he took part in numerous engagements. He was later ordered to Salonica and Egypt, and was demobilised in August, 1919.
He holds the 1914 Star, General Service and Victory Medals.
93, Manor Park Road, Harlesden. 13226.

DINES, A. T., Pte., Middlesex Regiment.
He volunteered in August, 1914, and served on the Western Front, where he took part in the battle of Ypres and the Retreat and Advance in 1918, and was wounded in action. Later he went to Russia with the Relief Force.
He holds the 1915 Star, General Service and Victory Medals.
22, Portnall Road, Maida Hill, W.9 X19374B.

DINES, F., Pte., 9th Middlesex Regiment.
He volunteered in October, 1914, and was engaged on important duties with his regiment until February, 1916, when he was discharged medically unfit for further service.
He holds the Territorial Efficiency Medal.
37, Deacon Road, Willesden. X16972.

DINES, W. H., Pte., Machine Gun Corps.
He crossed from America in 1916 in order to join the Army, and in the same year was sent to the Western Front, where he took part in the Retreat and Advance of 1918.
In May, 1919, he was demobilised, holding the General Service and Victory Medals. He had previously served with the American Army during the unrest on the Mexican border.
22, Portnall Road, Maida Hill, W.9 X19374C.

DISDALE, R. W., Pte., East Surrey Regiment and Labour Corps.
He joined in July, 1916, and being medically unfit for duty overseas, served at various stations on important duties until his discharge in February, 1919.
29, Albert Terrace, Milton Avenue, N.W.10 14336.

DITCH, C., Sapper, Royal Engineers (R.O.D.).
He volunteered in November, 1914, served with distinction on the Western Front from the following January until demobilised in February, 1919, and saw service at Ypres, Arras, on the Somme and elsewhere.
He holds the 1915 Star, General Service and Victory Medals.
68a, Sandringham Road, Willesden. T17349.

DITCH, F., Pte., 6th Leicestershire Regiment.
He joined in 1916, and during his service on the Western Front was wounded in action. He was in hospital in France and England, and also suffered from neurasthenia.
In October, 1919, he was discharged physically unfit, holding the General Service and Victory Medals.
3, Reporton Road, Fulham. X18862.

DIXON, G. R., A.B., R.N., H.M.S. " Superb."
He volunteered in August, 1914, and served in the North Sea and the Atlantic. He took part in the battles of Jutland and Zeebrugge, and was also engaged in the dangerous duties of convoying troops and food from America, for which he received the special decoration awarded by the American Government.
He holds the General Service and Victory Medals, and was demobilised in 1919.
74, Archel Road, West Kensington. 16677.

DIXON, R. H. G., Rifleman, 9th London Regiment (Queen Victoria's Rifles).
He volunteered in March, 1915, and in November of the same year was drafted to the Western Front, where he served until October, 1916. He took part in the Offensive of July, 1916, Bullecourt and Ypres. He was killed in action in an engagement on the Somme in October, 1916.
He was entitled to the 1915 Star, General Service and Victory Medals.
26, Bravington Road, Paddington, W. X19194.

DIXON, W. E., Rifleman, 9th London Regiment (Queen Victoria's Rifles).
He volunteered in October, 1915, and the same year was sent to the Western Front, where he served with distinction until 1918. He took part in several engagements, including the Offensive in July, 1916, Ypres and Bullecourt, and was wounded.
He holds the 1914-15 Star, General Service and Victory Medals, and was demobilised in February, 1919.
26, Bravington Road, Paddington. X19194B.

DOBINSON, H. E., Pte., Northumberland Fus.
He joined in September, 1916, and from the following June was in France until November, 1917. He was then sent to Italy until 1919, when he was demobilised.
He holds the General Service and Victory Medals.
34, Herries Street, Queen's Park. X18724B.

DOBINSON, J. R., Pte., 2nd Bedford Regiment.
He joined in February, 1918, and in June the same year was sent to France. In September, 1918, he was wounded near Albert.
He was demobilised in February, 1919, and holds the General Service and Victory Medals.
34, Herries Street, Queen's Park, W. X18724A.

DOBSON, A. E., Driver, Royal Field Artillery.
He volunteered in August, 1914, served in France from the following year until 1916, and took part in the fighting on the Somme. Later he was drafted to Salonica, and thence to Palestine, where he took part in General Allenby's campaign.
He holds the 1914-15 Star, General Service and Victory Medals, and was demobilised in May, 1919.
42, Shrewsbury Road, Harlesden. 14008A.

DOBSON, F. J., Pte., R.A.S.C. (M.T.).
He volunteered in February, 1916, was drafted to France in the same year, and employed on transport work with the motor lorries. He was in action during the battle of the Somme and was wounded.
He holds the General Service and Victory Medals, and was demobilised in March, 1919.
23, Beaufoy Road, Tottenham. X17942.

DOBSON, H. E. V., Signaller, R.F.A.
He volunteered in October, 1915, and served on the Western Front for three years, during which time he took part in the battles of Mons, Arras, Cambrai, Ypres, Neuve Chapelle and many other engagements, and was wounded.
He was demobilised in June, 1919, holding the General Service and Victory Medals.
42, Shrewsbury Road, Harlesden. 14008B.

DOCKER, C., Lce.-Cpl., Northumberland Fus.
He volunteered in November, 1915, and served with distinction in India and Mesopotamia from February, 1916, until December, 1919.
He was demobilised in January, 1920, and holds the General Service and Victory Medals.
5b, Vallier Road, College Park, Willesden. X17681.

DOCKRELL, G. D., Sergt., Labour Corps.
He joined in August, 1916, served on the Western Front from the following year until 1919, and took part in engagements at Arras and on the Somme, being gassed while in action.
He was demobilised in August, 1919, holding the General Service and Victory Medals.
16, Brereton Road, Edmonton. X18115.

DOCWRA, S. J., Driver, R.A.S.C. (M.T.).
He volunteered in August, 1914, and served in France, where he took part in many engagements, and was wounded. He died on April 27th, 1919, from the effects of wounds received in action.
He was entitled to the 1914 Star, the General Service and Victory Medals. He also held the South African Medal with five bars, and the Chitral Expedition Medal with one bar.
75, Sherbrooke Road, Fulham. X18468.

DODD, J. A., Pte., 7th Middlesex Regiment.
He volunteered in 1914, was sent to France in 1916, and served with distinction on the Somme. He was killed in action at Arras in 1917, and was entitled to the General Service and Victory Medals.
17, Beamish Road, Edmonton. 13939.

DODDS, R. (M.S.M.), Staff Q.M.S., R.A.S.C.
He volunteered in August, 1914, and served on the Western Front, at Salonica, and also with General Denikin's Army in Russia.
He was awarded the 2nd Class Order of St. Stanislaus for conspicuous gallantry whilst serving in Russia, was twice mentioned in despatches, and awarded the M.S.M. for distinguished conduct and devotion to duty. In addition, he holds the 1914 Star, the General Service and Victory Medals. He was demobilised in December, 1919.
16, Chancellor Street, Hammersmith. 13263.

DOE, R. H., Rifleman, 8th London Regiment.
He joined in February, 1918, and was attached to the R.A.S.C. He carried out various important duties whilst serving with his unit, and was eventually demobilised in June, 1919.
27, Heron Road, Willesden. 15602.

DOGGETT, W. A., Pte., 5th Middlesex Regiment.
He volunteered in September, 1915, and served until April, 1916, at various stations on important work, when he was discharged as medically unfit.
27, Mordaunt Road, Harlesden. 13865.

DOHERTY, W., Pte., Middlesex Regiment.
He joined in October, 1916, served on the Western Front, where he contracted bronchial pneumonia through exposure, and died in hospital at Etaples in February, 1917.
He was entitled to the General Service and Victory Medals.
33, Mordaunt Road, Harlesden. 13864B.

DOIG, P., Rifleman, King's Royal Rifle Corps.
He volunteered in 1915, and during his service on the Western Front took part in many engagements, including those on the Somme, Ypres, Arras, Verdun, Cambrai and in the Advance of 1918. He was wounded and gassed, and was demobilised in December, 1919, holding the General Service and Victory Medals.
83, Mirabel Road, Walham Green. X17863B.

DOLPHIN, A., Cpl., Gloucestershire Regiment.
He joined in December, 1916, and during the following three years saw much varied service in India, Mesopotamia and Russia. In Mesopotamia he was in action on numerous occasions, and in Russia he was engaged on special duties on the railways.
He was demobilised in November, 1919, and holds the General Service and Victory Medals.
20, Portnall Road, Maida Hill, W.9 X19372.

DOLPHIN, F., Pte., 1st Middlesex Regiment.
He joined in October, 1916, and served on the Western Front, taking part in the battles of Arras, Ypres, the Somme, Nieuport and Bailleul, where he was wounded in April, 1918.
He was demobilised in February, 1919, holding the General Service and Victory Medals.
61, Carlyle Avenue, Harlesden. 14190.

DOLTON, A. C. (M.S.M.), Pte., 4th Royal Fus.
After previous service in the Territorial Force, he was mobilised in August, 1914, and quickly sent to France. Soon afterwards he was taken prisoner, and was in German hands for four years. During this time he suffered harsh treatment, and was demobilised in December, 1918, after his return from Germany.
He holds the Meritorious Service Medal, which he won by his gallantry and devotion to duty, the 1914 Star, and the General Service and Victory Medals.
39, Rosaline Road, Fulham, S.W.6 TX18622A.

DOLTON, H., Pte., 13th Hussars.
After over four years' service in India before the war, he came to Europe and served on all parts of the Western Front. He was severely gassed while he was in France, and after long treatment in hospital abroad and at home, was discharged in 1919 as medically unfit for further service.
He holds the 1915 Star and the General Service and Victory Medals.
39, Rosaline Road, Fulham, S.W.6 TX18622B.

DOLTON, E. F., Bandsman, 2nd King's Own (Yorkshire Light Infantry).
He volunteered in August, 1914, served on the Western Front, where, whilst acting as stretcher bearer, he was killed in 1915.
He was entitled to the 1915 Star, the General Service and Victory Medals.
39, Rosaline Road, Fulham, S.W.6 TX18622C.

DOMONEY, W., Cpl., Royal Engineers.
He volunteered in March, 1915, and in the same year was sent to France, where he served during many engagements until demobilised in January, 1919.
He holds the 1915 Star, the General Service and Victory Medals.
48, Montague Road, Lower Edmonton. 16509.

DONALD, L. J., Gunner, Machine Gun Corps.
He joined in May, 1918, and owing to his age, was retained with his unit at various stations, doing important duties until he was demobilised in 1920.
59, Ancill Street, Fulham. 13867.

DONKIN, W., Rifleman, King's Royal Rifle Corps, and Pte., Royal Army Ordnance Corps.
He volunteered in February, 1915, and served for three years on the Western Front, where he took part in the battles of Loos, the Somme and Messines Ridge. He was wounded at Loos, and again during an air raid at Calais. Being unfit for further service overseas, he was returned home and served on home stations until demobilised in March, 1919.
He holds the 1914-15 Star, the General Service and Victory Medals.
36, Mordaunt Road, Harlesden. 13730.

DONMALL, H. R., Cpl., 15th Hampshire Regt.
He volunteered in September, 1914, and was sent to the Western Front. He was severely wounded, and died from the effects in February, 1919.
He was entitled to the General Service and Victory Medals.
5, Kilmaine Road, Fulham, S.W.6 XT18877.

DONNE, C. (Mrs.), Special War Worker.
This lady was for three years at Perivale Munition Factory, where she was engaged in the T.N.T. and C.E. shops. She served in this dangerous and arduous occupation untiringly for this period, and her services were very valuable and commendable. 20, New Holly Lane, Willesden. 15570A.

DONNE, V., Pte., The Queen's (Royal West Surrey Regiment).

Joining in 1917, he served for two years on the Western Front. He took part in many engagements with distinction, and while in action at Cambrai was badly wounded.
He was demobilised in 1919, and holds the General Service and Victory Medals.
20, New Holly Lane, Willesden.   15579C.

DONNE, W. E., B.S.M., 51st R.F.A.

He volunteered in 1914, and served throughout on the Western Front. He took part in the battles of Mons, Loos, Arras, the Somme, Bullecourt, Neuve Chapelle, Hill 60, Ypres and Cambrai. During his service he was wounded and gassed, and suffered temporarily from loss of speech.
He was demobilised in 1920, and holds the 1914 Star, the General Service and Victory Medals.
20, New Holly Lane, Willesden.   15579B.

DONOVAN, A. G., Special War Worker and Border Regiment.

At the outbreak of war he was engaged on important aeroplane work, but later he joined the Border Regiment. During his service with this regiment he was engaged at various stations and on dangerous duties in Ireland.
11, Lillie Mansions, Lillie Road, Fulham.   X18455.

DONOVAN, A. J., Driver, R.A.S.C. (M.T.).

He was called from the Reserve in August, 1914, was sent to France in the same year, and was present at the battles of Mons, Ypres, the Somme, Loos, Neuve Chapelle and in the last Advance of 1918. He then served in Germany with the Army of Occupation until he was demobilised in May, 1919, holding the 1914 Star, General Service and Victory Medals. 26, Durban Road, N.17   X18091.

DONOVAN, H., Pte., East Surrey Regiment.

He joined in 1917, and was for a time engaged on important work at various stations. Later he went to France, where he was engaged on transport duties.
He was demobilised in 1919, and holds the General Service and Victory Medals.
11, Lillie Mansions, Lillie Road, Fulham, S.W.6   X18456.

DORE, A., Pte., Royal Fusiliers.

He volunteered in 1915, was drafted to France in the following year, and on February 17th, 1916, was killed in action on the Somme.
He was entitled to the General Service and Victory Medals.
38, Rowallan Road, Fulham, S.W.6   X19342.

DOREY, J. S., Pioneer, Royal Engineers.

He joined in 1916, and did much useful work at various places before proceeding to the Western Front. During his service in France he was engaged in many sectors, being specially employed on wireless telegraphy. After the Armistice he went to Cologne with the Army of Occupation. He was demobilised in November, 1919, and holds the General Service and Victory Medals.
56, Kilburn Lane, N.W.10   X18605.

DORKINS, C. R., Gunner, R.G.A.

He volunteered in November, 1915, and during his service on the Western Front took part, with distinction, in many battles, including those of the Somme, Ypres, St. Quentin and Beaumont Hamel.
He was demobilised in January, 1919, and holds the General Service and Victory Medals.
25, Farm Lane, Walham Green, S.W.6   X19493.

DORMAN, R., Gunner, Royal Garrison Artillery.

He joined in June, 1916, and in the following September went to France, where he took part in the battles of Arras and the Somme and many other engagements.
He holds the General Service and Victory Medals, and was demobilised in January, 1919.
32, Allestree Road, Fulham, S.W.6   TX19205.

DORMER, C. A., Pte., 3rd Royal Fusiliers.

He volunteered in November, 1914, and in May, 1916, was sent to France, where he took part in the battle of the Somme, being killed in action in October, 1916.
He was entitled to the General Service and Victory Medals.
23, Alfred Road, Paddington.   16954B.

DORMER, E. C., Pte., Royal Fusiliers.

He joined in May, 1916, and in the same year was sent to France and took part in engagements at Bullecourt and in the Arras sector. He was killed in action in May, 1917, and was entitled to the General Service and Victory Medals.
65, Chester Road, Lower Edmonton.   12718.

DORMER, H. H., Pte., 9th Lancers.

He volunteered in September, 1914, and was employed with his unit on various important duties until he was discharged through ill-health in January, 1918.
111, Victor Road, Willesden, N.W.   X17533.

DORMER, R., Gunner, Royal Garrison Artillery.

He volunteered in August, 1914, and served on the Western Front from the following year until 1919, when he was demobilised. During this period he took part in many important battles, including those of the Somme, Ypres and Loos, and on November 8th, 1918, was mentioned in despatches for distinguished services and gallantry in the field.
He holds the 1915 Star, the General Service and Victory Medals.
9, Cobbold Road, Willesden.   16954A.

DORRELL, A. E., Cpl., Royal Engineers.

He enlisted in December, 1914, and was sent to France in May, 1915, and served with the 81st Infantry Brigade (27th Division) at Armentieres, on the Somme and at Arras. In November, 1915, he went to Salonica with the 27th Division, and was on the Doiran Front at Karosouli, Savamali and on the Struma until March, 1918, when he was invalided home suffering from malaria.
He was finally discharged in May, 1919, holding the 1915 Star, General Service and Victory Medals.
71, Ashmore Road, Paddington, W.9   TX20152.

DORRELL, M. E. (Mrs.), Special War Worker.

During the war this lady rendered valuable services at the Filling Factory at Park Royal, where she was engaged on work, which besides being of a dangerous nature, demanded the greatest care and accuracy.
71, Ashmore Road, Harrow Road. W.9   X19808B.

DORRELL, G. T. (V.C.), Capt., R.F.A.

He originally joined the Service in 1895, and in the first month of the war went to France as sergeant-major of the famous " L," Battery, R.H.A., fighting at the retreat from Mons. He was awarded the Victoria Cross for his great gallantry on September 1st, 1914, at Nervy, and was also promoted to commissioned rank for his service in the field. He commanded in France " A " Battery, 119th Brigade (afterwards 122nd Brigade), and " B " Battery, 190th Brigade, R.F.A., and was twice mentioned in despatches. He took part in a great number of engagements, including the battles of the Somme and Ypres. On returning to England in 1917 he commanded " C " Battery, 321st Brigade, and 52nd Battery, 3rd Brigade, R.F.A. This officer holds in addition the King's and Queen's South African Medals with eight bars, the 1914 Star, General Service, Victory, and the Long Service and Good Conduct Medals.
He was born in London (Paddington), and at the present time is Adjutant at the R.F.A. (T.F.) Barracks at Handel Street, London.
Artillery House, Handel Street, W.C.1   TX20153.

DORSETT, J. A., Pte., Royal Marines.

He volunteered in August, 1914, and served as a machine gunner in Gallipoli in 1915. Later he was drafted to the Western Front. He was reported missing after the fighting at Beaumont Hamel in November, 1916, but is now believed to have been killed in that engagement.
He was entitled to the 1914–15 Star, General Service and Victory Medals.
91, Yeldham Road, W.6   13235A.

DOUBLE, H., Mechanic, Royal Air Force.

He joined in January, 1918, and was sent to France in the same year. He took part and rendered good service with the R.A.F. in the Retreat and Advance of 1918.
He was demobilised in February, 1919, and holds the General Service and Victory Medals.
4, Ravensworth Road, Kensal Rise.   X17622B.

DOUGLAS, G. H., Pte., Leicestershire Regiment.

He joined in 1916 and served on important duties with his unit in Yorkshire and at various stations.
He secured his demobilisation in 1919.
38, Ancill Street, Hammersmith, W.6   13985A.

DOUGLAS, M. (Mrs.), Special War Worker.

During the war this lady was engaged on valuable work in connection with the despatch overseas of shells and other munitions. Her work was difficult and of an arduous nature, but she successfully performed her duties.
38, Ancill Street, Hammersmith, W.6.   13985B.

DOUST, A. W., Pte., 13th London Regiment (Kensington Battalion).

He joined in May, 1916, served with distinction on the Western Front, and was twice wounded in action at Bourlon Wood.
He was discharged as a result of his wounds in June, 1918, and holds the General Service and Victory Medals.
40, Moylan Road, Fulham, S.W.6   15292.

DOVE, B., Pte., Royal Army Service Corps.
He volunteered in October, 1915, and saw service at the Dardanelles and in Egypt. Later he went to France, and served there in many engagements.
He was discharged in February, 1918, holding the 1914-15 Star, General Service and Victory Medals.
156, Estcourt Road, Fulham.   16246.

DOVE, W. F., Sapper, Royal Engineers.
He volunteered in December, 1914. In the following year he was sent to France, where he took part in many engagements. During one of these he was severely gassed, and sent home in 1919.
He was demobilised in March of that year, and holds the 1914-15 Star, the General Service and Victory Medals.
34, Hartington Road, Lower Edmonton.   14054.

DOVE, W. H., Cpl., Royal Sussex Regiment.
He volunteered in 1915, served on the Western Front from the following year until demobilised in 1919, taking part in various engagements, including the battles of the Somme and Ypres.
He holds the General Service and Victory Medals.
42, Kimberley Road, Upper Edmonton.   16535.

DOVER, H., Cpl., Royal Air Force.
He joined in June, 1916, and served with distinction in France with the Royal Air Force, from January, 1917, until he was demobilised in 1919.
He holds the General Service and Victory Medals.
67, Leghorn Road, Harlesden.   12953B.

DOVER, H. A., Pte., Royal Army Service Corps.
He joined in 1916, and saw active service in France with the R.A.S.C. on the Somme and on other sectors, where he did important duties.
He was demobilised in 1919, holding the General Service and Victory Medals.
33, Beamish Road, Edmonton.   13942.

DOVEY, S. T., Pte., 4th Royal Fusiliers.
He was in the Army at the outbreak of hostilities, and was sent to the Western Front, where he was killed in action at La Bassée in October, 1914.
He was entitled to the 1914 Star, the General Service and Victory Medals.
15a, Kilburn Lane, Willesden.   X18571A.

DOVEY, W. H., Bugler, 52nd King's Royal Rifles.
He joined in October, 1917, at an early age and rendered valuable services at various stations. On account of his youth he was retained for Home Service, and carried out his duties at all times in a conscientious and soldierly manner.
He was demobilised in February, 1919.
151a, Kilburn Lane, Willesden.   X18571B.

DOWLE, R. H. D., Sergt., Oxford and Bucks. Light Infantry.
He volunteered in September, 1914, and crossed to France the following year. He was in action in many engagements, and lost his arm at the Somme in 1916.
In consequence of this, he was discharged in October, 1917, and holds the 1915 Star, the General Service and Victory Medals.
35, Shorrolds Road, Walham Green, S.W.6   X19491.

DOWLING, C. F., Gunner, R.G.A.
He volunteered in December, 1915, and went to the Western Front the following year, taking part in the battles of the Somme, Cambrai, Arras, Ypres, Vimy Ridge and the final Advance in 1918. He was twice wounded, and was demobilised in March, 1919, holding the General Service and Victory Medals.
10, Purves Road, Willesden.   X18403B.

DOWLING, E., 1st Petty Officer, R.N., H.M.S. "Royal Sovereign."
He was mobilised in August, 1914, and served with the Grand Fleet during the principal engagements in the North Sea and elsewhere.
He holds the 1914-15 Star, General Service and Victory Medals, and was demobilised in July, 1919.
He had previously served 14 years in H.M. Navy.
41, Rednall Terrace, Hammersmith.   16211.

DOWLING, H., Pte., 9th East Surrey Regiment.
He volunteered in November, 1914, served on the Western Front, and was killed in action on the Somme in August, 1916. He had previously taken part in many engagements, including that of Hill 60.
He was entitled to the 1914-15 Star, the General Service and Victory Medals.
77, Oldfield Road, Willesden.   16026.

DOWNING, A. J., Cpl., 1/9th Middlesex Regt.
He volunteered in August, 1914, and served with distinction in Mesopotamia, taking part in many important engagements. He was demobilised in 1919, and holds the General Service and Victory Medals. 55, Wendover Road, Harlesden. 12553

DOWNS, C. H., 1st-Class Stoker, R.N., H.M.S. "Aquarius."
He volunteered in 1915 and served in the North Sea, taking part in many engagements, including the battle of Jutland. He was present during the surrender of the German Fleet at Scapa Flow, and was demobilised in August, 1919, holding the 1915 Star, General Service and Victory Medals.
8, Hewish Road, Upper Edmonton, N.18   X17909A.

DOWNS, C. W., Pte., 14th London Regt. (London Scottish.)
He volunteered in December, 1915, and saw active service in France, was reported missing on July 1st, 1916, and is presumed to have been killed in action.
He was entitled to the General Service and Victory Medals.
37, Purcell Crescent, Fulham, S.W.6   15168B.

DOWNS, E., 2nd Air Mechanic, R.A.F.
During his service, which extended from 1916 until November, 1919, he was employed at various stations, where he carried out skilful duties as an airship mechanic.
8, Hewish Road, Upper Edmonton.   X17909B.

DOWNS, F., Pte., East Yorkshire Regiment.
He volunteered in 1915, and served on the Western Front. He took part in many engagements, and was wounded twice, being eventually killed in action by a sniper on August 24th, 1917.
He was entitled to the General Service and Victory Medals.
37, Farrant Street, W.10   X19062B.

DOWNS, G., Pte., Royal Marines.
He re-enlisted in August, 1914, served on board H.M.S. "Revenge," cruising off the Belgian coast, and in 1915 left Dunkirk with H.M.S. "Perth" for the Persian Gulf. He served also at the Dardanelles, and in Baltic and Egyptian waters.
He was discharged on March 13th, 1919, having served for 20 years in the Royal Marines. He holds the 1914 Star, the General Service and Victory Medals. He was recommended during his service for great gallantry at sea.
39, Milton Avenue, Harlesden.   15793B.

DOWNS, W., Signaller, 1/4th East Yorks. Regt.
He volunteered in November, 1915, and served on the Western Front. He took part in many engagements, including Ypres, Arras, and Cambrai, and was wounded. He was demobilised in February, 1919, and holds the General Service and Victory Medals.
37, Farrant Street, W.10   X19062A.

DOWSETT, W. H., Driver, R.F.A.
He volunteered in August, 1915, and was discharged in the following November as medically unfit. He, however, joined again in November, 1916, was drafted to France, and was finally discharged in November, 1917. He holds the General Service and Victory Medals.
154, Montague Road, Edmonton.   15835.

DOWSON, S., Bombardier, Royal Horse Artillery.
He volunteered in August, 1914, and served on the Western Front, where he took part in the battles of Mons, the Marne, the Aisne, Arras, Cambrai and Vimy Ridge.
He was wounded and subsequently discharged in August, 1918, holding the 1914 Star, General Service and Victory Medals.
69, Dudden Hill Lane, N.W.10   X17108.

DOWZALL, A. E., Pte., 13th London Regiment (Kensington Battalion).
He volunteered in April, 1915, and after serving for a time in France, was sent to Salonica, where he took part in the local fighting, and was wounded. Later he was drafted to Palestine, and was again badly wounded, in consequence of which he was invalided home.
He holds the General Service and Victory Medals, and was discharged in December, 1918.
49, Lochaline Street, Fulham, S.W.6   13253.

DOYLE, A. J., Pte., R.A.S.C. (M.T.).
He volunteered in August, 1914, and served on both Western and Eastern Fronts. In France he was engaged on the transport of stores and ammunition to the trenches, and in Salonica drove a Staff car. He was invalided home on account of ill-health, and discharged in May, 1916.
He holds the 1914 Star, General Service and Victory Medals.
43, Brenthurst Road, Willesden, N.W.10   16370.

DOYLE, J., Trooper, Surrey Yeomanry.
He joined in 1916 and served at various stations, being engaged with his unit on duties of importance. He carried out his duties with keenness and despatch.
He was demobilised in January, 1919.
17, Glynfield Road, Harlesden.   14722.

DRAKE, F. A., Pte., 1st Border Regiment.
He volunteered in April, 1915, and served from October, 1915, on the Western Front, in the battles of Ypres, Somme, Arras, Loos, Vimy Ridge, Passchendaele and other important engagements. During his war service he was wounded three times, and later served with the Army of Occupation. He holds the 1915 Star, General Service and Victory Medals.
108, Rucklidge Avenue, Harlesden.   12939A.

DRAKE, F. E., Pte., Machine Gun Corps.
He joined in February, 1918, and served on the Western Front. Whilst in action at Cambrai he was buried in débris after the explosion of a shell, and sustained injuries. On his return from France he did duty with the Armoured Car Section in Ireland, and was demobilised in March, 1920, holding the General Service and Victory Medals.
108, Rucklidge Avenue, Harlesden.   12939B.

DRAKE, H., Pte., 1st Yorkshire Regiment.
He was serving his country at the outbreak of war, and saw service at various important centres in India.
He eventually secured his demobilisation in 1919, after having served continuously in the Eastern theatre for 5 years.
54, Gowan Road, Willesden, N.W.10   X16963A.

DRAKE, J., Pte., Norfolk Regt.
He joined in June, 1916, and being at the time medically unfit for overseas service, was retained on important duties at various stations with his unit, where he did valuable work. He was discharged on account of ill-health in 1917.
102, Portnall Road, Maida Hll, W.9   X19533B.

DRAKE, J., Pte., 8th Norfolk Regiment.
He joined in July, 1917, and served for over a year on the Western Front, taking part with distinction in several engagements, including the battles of Ypres and the Retreat and Advance of 1918.
He was demobilised in January, 1919, and holds the General Service and Victory Medals.
46, College Road, Kensal Rise.   X18008.

DRAKE, P., Pte., Royal Fusiliers.
He joined in March, 1918, and was engaged on important duties at various stations with his regiment until his demobilisation in January, 1919.
54, Gowan Road, Willesden.   X16963B.

DRAKE, T. G., Cpl., 17th Middlesex Regiment.
He volunteered in January, 1915, went to France later in the same year, and took part in the battles of Cambrai, Messines, Loos, Ypres and the Somme.
He was demobilised in June, 1919, holding the 1915 Star, General Service and Victory Medals.
27, Halford Road, Walham Green, S.W.6   X19472.

DRAPER, C., 1st Air Mechanic, Royal Air Force.
He enlisted in 1915, and was drafted to the Western Front, where he took part in many engagements, including those of the Somme and Amiens.
He was demobilised in January, 1919, and holds the General Service and Victory Medals.
59, Greyhound Road, Willesden.   X17606.

DRAPER, F., Sergt., 16th Middlesex Regt.
He volunteered in April, 1915, and during his service on the Western Front took part in the battles of Ypres, the Somme, Cambrai, Loos, Arras, Armentieres, Bethune and St. Quentin, and was taken prisoner in April, 1918.
He was mentioned in despatches for gallantry and devotion to duty, holds the 1914-15 Star, General Service and Victory Medals, and was demobilised in February, 1919.
25, Glynfield Road, Harlesden.   14726.

DRAPER, H., Gunner, Royal Garrison Artillery.
Volunteering in January, 1916, he was drafted to India, where he served at various stations with his unit on important duties.
He eventually secured his demobilisation in 1919, after having rendered valuable service for his country.
21a, Lorenco Road, Tottenham.   X17999.

DRAPER, H., Pte., 7th Middlesex Regiment.
He volunteered in 1914, went to France the following year, and took part with distinction in many battles, including Ypres and the Somme.
He was demobilised in June, 1919, holding the 1915 Star, General Service and Victory Medals.
26, Ladysmith Road, Upper Edmonton.   16463.

DRAWATER, F. H., Rifleman, King's Royal Rifle Corps.
He joined in May, 1918, and during his service was stationed at various places with his unit, where he gave valuable services.
He was demobilised in February, 1919, when danger of hostilities being renewed had passed.
39, Faroe Road, West Kensington.   12438.

DRAY, E. T. E., Cpl., Queen Victoria's Rifles.
He was in the Army on the outbreak of hostilities, and from 1916 served on the Western Front, where he took part in the battles of Havrincourt Wood, Ypres, Bullecourt, Beaumont Hamel, Arras and Albert, and was present during the Retreat and Advance of 1918, being attached for special duty to H.Q. Staff.
He was demobilised in March, 1919, holding the General Service, Victory and Territorial Efficiency Medals.
4, Sandwich House, Roundwood Road, Willesden.   16937.

DRAYTON, G., Pte., Labour Corps.
He volunteered in October, 1915, and was engaged for three years in Salonica, where he saw much service.
In February, 1918, he was discharged, and holds the 1915 Star, the General Service and Victory Medals.
5, Osman Road, Edmonton.   14540A.

DRAYTON, H. S., Pte., 4th London Regiment.
He volunteered in August, 1914, and served on the Western Front, taking part in the battles of Ypres, Neuve Chapelle and the Somme, where he was killed in action in September, 1916. He was entitled to the 1914-15 Star, the General Service and Victory Medals.
5, Osman Road, Edmonton, N.9   14540B.

DREDGE, H. A., Pte., R.A.S.C. (M.T.).
He joined in February, 1915, and the same year saw service on the Western Front, where he was engaged in conveying stores, ammunition and troops to different sectors. Whilst acting as a despatch-rider he was blown off his motor-cycle, and as a result was detained for some time in hospital. He was also gassed on one occasion during his four years' service in France.
He was demobilised in March, 1919, and holds the 1915 Star, General Service and Victory Medals.
11, Talbot Road, Willesden.   15961.

DREW, H., Pte., 2nd East Surrey Regiment.
He volunteered in September, 1914, served on the Western Front, and took part in the battles of Ypres, St. Eloi, Messines, Loos, Neuve Chapelle, Givenchy and Festubert. He was invalided home, having been injured through the trench being blown in by a shell, and was in hospital for five months.
He was demobilised in April, 1919, holding the 1914 Star, the General Service and Victory Medals.
75, Orbain Road, Fulham.   X18447B.

DREW, H., Special War Worker.
He was over military age at the outbreak of war, and served his country by rendering valuable services in an important munition factory. His duties were both arduous and exacting, but he resolutely continued at his work and was commended for his services.
45, Orbain Road, Fulham.   X18447A.

DREWREY, T. W., Driver, R.A.S.C. (M.T.).
He volunteered in June, 1915, and was engaged with the M.T. section on the transport of rations and ammunition on the Somme, at Ypres and Cambrai, and other places on the Western Front.
In June, 1919, he was demobilised, and holds the 1915 Star, the General Service and Victory Medals.
69, Waldo Road, Willesden.   X17637.

DRINKWATER, G. A., Pte., Lincolnshire Regt.
He joined in January, 1917, served on the Western Front from February of the following year until demobilised in February, 1919. He took part in the Retreat and Advance of 1918, and was wounded.
He holds the General Service and Victory Medals.
36 Brett Road, Harlesden.   15694B.

DRINKWATER, J., R.E. and Labour Corps.
He volunteered in August, 1915, and served with the Labour Corps in France until discharged in November, 1916, on medical grounds. He re-enlisted in June, 1919, and served until the following December.
He holds the 1915 Star, General Service and Victory Medals.
36, Brett Road, Harlesden.   15694C.

DRINKWATER, J. W., Pte., Middlesex Regt. and Somerset Light Infantry.
He volunteered in May, 1915, and served in India for four years, taking part in the Afghan Campaign. During that time he contracted malaria, and in April, 1919, was demobilised, holding the 1915 Star, the Afghan, General Service and Victory Medals.
12, Goodson Road, Harlesden.   14927A.

DRINKWATER, W., Driver, R.F.A.
He volunteered in August, 1914, was sent to France in the following year, and took part in various engagements, being wounded in action on the Somme in March, 1916. He was then drafted to India, where he remained until demobilised in April, 1919.
He holds the 1915 Star, the General Service and Victory Medals. 36, Brett Road, Harlesden.   15694A.

DRISCOLL, G., Lce.-Cpl., 1st Duke of Cornwall's Light Infantry.
He volunteered in August, 1914, and served in France, taking part in engagements at Mons, the Marne, Ypres, the Somme, Passchendaele and elsewhere. He was wounded in July, 1916, and was mentioned in despatches and recommended for the D.C.M. for gallantry.
He holds the Mons Star, General Service and Victory Medals, and was demobilised in February, 1919.
49, Nasmyth Road, Hammersmith. 11150.

DUBERY, A. V., Pte., 1st Prince of Wales's Leinster Regiment.
He was serving at the outbreak of war, was sent to France in 1915, where he took part in several engagements, and was reported missing in February, 1918, in the Ypres sector.
He was entitled to the 1915 Star, the General Service and Victory Medals.
45, Denzil Road, N.W.10 16953B.

DUBERY, R. J., Pte., 9th Middlesex Regiment.
He volunteered in August, 1914, and later served in India. He was afterwards sent to Mesopotamia, where he saw considerable service and remained until 1919, in November of which year he was demobilised.
He holds the 1914–15 Star, General Service and Victory Medals. 21, Essex Road, Willesden. 16953A.

DUCK, W. C., Cpl., Middlesex Regiment.
He joined in June, 1916, served in Salonica and in France, where he took part in the battles of the Somme and Loos, and was wounded.
He was demobilised in September, 1919, holding the General Service and Victory Medals.
51, Raynham Avenue, Edmonton. 15824.

DUDLEY, E. M. (Mrs.), Special War Worker.
This lady took up work of national importance at the commencement of hostilities in the manufacture of life-saving devices for those at sea. She worked throughout the period of the war, and was commended for her services.
45, Averill Street, Fulham. 14168A.

DUDLEY, F., Rifleman, King's Royal Rifles.
He joined in 1916, and was engaged on important duties with his regiment at various stations until he was discharged as medically unfit in 1917.
45, Averill Street, Fulham. 14168B.

DUDLEY, W., Pte., R.A.V.C.
Volunteering in August, 1915, he saw service at various stations on veterinary work. Being at the time medically unfit for further service, he was discharged in December, 1918. 80, Bramber Road, Fulham. 16216.

DUDLEY, W. J., 1st Air Mechanic, R.A.F.
Joining in 1917, he went through a period of training, and later served with his unit at various stations, including the large and important aerodrome at Cranwell. His work required considerable technical skill.
He secured his demobilisation in 1919.
22, Werley Avenue, Fulham, S.W.6 X17867B.

DUDMAN, A. V., Pte., 3/9th Middlesex Regt.
He volunteered in December, 1915, served in France with distinction, and was reported missing after the battle of the Somme in October, 1916.
He was entitled to the General Service and Victory Medals.
58, Felixstowe Road, Willesden. X17767.

DUFFIELD, S. N., A.B., R.N., H.M.S. "Canterbury."
He joined in 1916, and served with the Grand Fleet at the battle of Jutland and in the Baltic, where he gave valuable service.
He was demobilised in May, 1919, and holds the General Service and Victory Medals.
115, Bulwer Road, Edmonton. X17465.

DUFFY, J. E., Pte., King's Own Royal Lancaster Regiment.
He volunteered in July, 1915, and served on the Western Front for four years, taking part in the battles of Arras, Ypres, Cambrai, Vimy Ridge and other engagements. He was wounded, and in June, 1919, was demobilised, holding the 1915 Star, the General Service and Victory Medals.
29, Earlsmead Road, Kensal Rise. X17830.

DUFFY, W. P., Pte., 17th Royal Fusiliers.
He joined in February, 1917, served in France during 1918 and 1919, and took part with distinction in several engagements, including the Retreat and Advance of 1918, when he was gassed.
He was demobilised in June, 1919, holding the General Service and Victory Medals.
68, Mayo Road, Willesden. 15438.

DUFOUR, A. H., Driver, R.A.S.C. (M.T.).
He joined in May, 1917, and during his service on the Western Front was present at the battles of the Somme, Arras, Armentieres, Ypres, Vimy Ridge, Bullecourt, Monchy, Givenchy, St. Quentin, Passchendaele and the Advance of 1918.
He was demobilised in February, 1920, holding the General Service and Victory Medals.
47, Ongar Road, Fulham, S.W.6 X19627.

DUFOUR, S. L., Gunner, R.G.A.
He joined in 1916, and saw active service in Salonica, where he contracted malaria. He was also stationed on important duties at Constantinople for a time.
He was demobilised in February, 1920, and holds the General Service and Victory Medals.
47, Ongar Road, Fulham, S.W.6 X19625.

DUGGAN, J. (M.M.), Cpl., 2nd Royal Dublin Fus.
He volunteered in August, 1914, was sent to France in the following year, and took part in the battles of Ypres, Armentieres, Loos, Lens, Arras, Cambrai, St. Quentin and Bapaume. He was awarded the Military Medal for conspicuous bravery and devotion to duty whilst in action on the Somme.
He was demobilised in August, 1919, holding the King's and Queen's South African Medals, the 1914–15 Star, and the General Service and Victory Medals, in addition to the Military Medal. 28, Fortune Gate Road, Harlesden. 14724.

DUKE, F. W., Sapper, Royal Engineers.
He volunteered in August, 1914, and served on the Western Front, taking part in the battle of Mons and many other engagements.
He is still serving, and holds the 1914 Star, the General Service and Victory Medals.
18, Roseberry Road, Lower Edmonton. 14066.

DUKES, A. L., Pte., Seaforth Highlanders and Labour Corps.
He volunteered in February, 1915, served in France from the following June until January, 1919, and took part in many engagements, including the second battle of Ypres and the battle of the Somme, in which he was twice wounded.
He was in hospital for five months prior to being discharged in June, 1919, and holds the 1915 Star, General Service and Victory Medals.
30, Mordaunt Road, Harlesden. 14117.

DULEY, R., Cpl., Royal Air Force.
He volunteered in August, 1915, and in the following year was sent to Egypt, and thence to Arabia and Palestine, where he took part in the capture of Jerusalem and other engagements with General Allenby's forces. He also served in Salonica, where he contracted malaria.
He was demobilised in June, 1919, holding the General Service and Victory Medals and a decoration awarded for his excellent service in Arabia.
36, Litchfield Gardens, Willesden Green. X17437.

DULSON, T., Driver, R.A.S.C. (M.T.).
He volunteered in April, 1915, and served on the Western Front. He was employed in an ammunition column, and was present at the battles of Cambrai, Arras, St. Quentin and various other engagements, being badly wounded.
In July, 1917, he was discharged, and holds the 1915 Star, the General Service and Victory Medals.
21, West Ella Road, Willesden, N.W.10 15128.

DUMMER, A., Sergt.-Major, R.A.S.C.
He volunteered in August, 1914, and served throughout the war on the Western Front, where he took part in the battles of Mons, the Marne, Aisne, Arras, Lens, Passchendaele and other engagements, and was badly wounded in the eyes.
In June, 1919, he was demobilised, and holds the 1914 Star and the General Service and Victory Medals.
10a, Deacon Road, Willesden. 16145B.

DUMMER, A. G. W., Pte., London Regiment.
He volunteered in September, 1914, and served in many engagements on the Eastern Front, in Egypt and Mesopotamia. He suffered badly from frost-bite, and in 1916 was discharged for that reason as unfit for further service.
He holds the 1914–15 Star, and the General Service and Victory Medals. 10a, Deacon Road, Willesden. 16145.

DUNCAN, A. T., Driver, R.A.S.C.
He volunteered in September, 1914, and during his service on the Western Front was present at several important engagements, including those of Loos, Givenchy, Vimy Ridge, Amiens, St. Quentin, Arras, Bullecourt and Festubert. Whilst in France he was accidentally injured, and in consequence was invalided home, and in June, 1918, was discharged unfit for further service.
He holds the 1914–15 Star and the General Service and Victory Medals.
73, Orbain Road, Fulham, S.W.6 X18643A.

DUNCAN, E. (Mrs.), Special War Worker.
During the war this lady rendered valuable services in a munition factory. Later she was employed on very heavy work in connection with the stacking of shell boxes at the docks, but carried out her onerous duties with great fortitude. She was commended for her services.
73, Orbain Road, Fulham, S.W.6   X18643B.

DUNCAN, J. (Miss), Special War Worker.
At the commencement of the war this lady rendered valuable services in the difficult and dangerous work of manufacturing hand-grenades. Later she joined the Land Army, and whilst thus engaged rendered extremely valuable help on important farms. Her work throughout was highly commended.
73, Orbain Road, Fulham, S.W.6   X18644.

DUNCAN, J. T., Pte., Labour Corps.
He joined in March, 1917, and served in various sectors on the Western Front, where he rendered very valuable services. He was eventually demobilised in October, 1919, and holds the General Service and Victory Medals.
2, Cuba Cottages, Upton Road, Lower Edmonton.   16476.

DUNCAN, P., Cpl., Royal Canadian Regiment.
When war broke out he was already serving, and in 1914 was sent out to France, where he took part in the battles of Ypres, Arras, the Somme, Vimy Ridge and several other engagements, and was gassed while at Ypres.
He holds the 1914 Star and the General Service and Victory Medals.
4, Garnet Road, Willesden.   15973B.

DUNCAN, R. H. H., Pte., 8th Queen's (Royal West Surrey Regiment).
He joined in January, 1917, and in the same year was sent to the Western Front, where he stayed until September, 1918, taking part in numerous engagements. He was very badly wounded at Holleheke, near Ypres, in July, 1917 and was discharged in September, 1918.
He holds the General Service and Victory Medals.
106, Burn's Road, Harlesden.   13143A.

DUNHAM, A. C. (Mrs.), Special War Worker.
From 1917 until 1919 this lady was engaged on important duties as a munitions examiner at Park Royal, chiefly on fuses. During her services, which were of a very valuable nature, she worked untiringly, and was highly commended.
22, Stracey Road, Harlesden, N.W.   15677B.

DUNHAM, C. S., Wireless Operator, Mercantile Marine.
He served on various ships as a wireless operator from December, 1917, until December, 1918. His duties were of a very exacting and trying nature, necessitating his being on duty for extremely long periods. His steadfastness during critical periods were highly commended.
He is entitled to the Mercantile Marine Medal.
15, Carlyle Avenue, Harlesden.   13602.

DUNHAM, D. A. (Miss), Special War Worker.
This lady rendered services of a valuable nature from 1917 to 1919, during which period she was engaged in a munition factory. She carried out her arduous duties in a skilful manner, and was commended for her untiring efforts.
22, Stracey Road, Harlesden.   15677A.

DUNK, B., Driver, Royal Field Artillery.
He was in the Territorials at the outbreak of war, and was immediately mobilised and quickly sent to France. He served throughout the war on the Western Front, and was present at all the principal engagements.
He was demobilised in June, 1919, holding the 1914-15 Star, General Service and Victory Medals.
21, Bertie Road, Willesden Green, N.W.   X17398.

DUNLOP, R. M., Lce.-Cpl., King's Royal Rifle Corps.
He volunteered in August, 1914, and was sent to the Western Front. He took part in several engagements, including Armentieres, Dickebusch and Chapelle-d'Armentieres, at which battle he was severely wounded. He was invalided home and discharged on account of his wounds as unfit for further service in February, 1916.
He holds the 1914 Star, General Service and Victory Medals.
75, Chesson Road, West Kensington, W.   X17690.

DUNMOW, J., Pte., 1st Essex Regiment.
He volunteered in 1915, and served with distinction in Gallipoli, where he was wounded in action. In May, 1916, he was sent to France, and was reported missing in October, 1916.
He was entitled to the 1915 Star, General Service and Victory Medals.
405, High Road, Willesden Green.   17351A.

DUNN, J. H., Pte., 10th London Regiment.
He volunteered in August, 1916, went to France the same year, and took part in many important battles, including the Somme and Ypres, where he was wounded.
He was demobilised in 1919, after having rendered valuable service, holding the General Service and Victory Medals.
86, Angel Road, Edmonton   16570.

DUNN, W., Pte., Machine Gun Corps.
He joined in May, 1916, served on the Western Front, and was severely wounded in action. After six months in hospital, he returned to his unit, and was discharged in May, 1918, physically unfit for further service.
He holds the General Service and Victory Medals.
125, Claxton Grove, Fulham.   13670.

DUNN, W. J. (D.C.M., M.M.), Sergt., 23rd London Regiment.
He volunteered in September, 1914, and was sent to the Western Front, where he took part in the battles of the Somme, Arras, Ypres, Loos, Neuve Chapelle, Festubert, Bullecourt, Vimy Ridge, Givenchy, Cambrai and the last Advance of 1918. He was awarded the Distinguished Conduct Medal for conspicuous bravery and gallant conduct at High Wood, where he was badly wounded. On returning to his unit he again displayed the utmost courage under fire and was awarded the Military Medal for his gallantry in consequence.
He was demobilised in February, 1919, and holds in addition the 1915 Star, General Service and Victory Medals. His military career was of a most distinguished character.
14, May Street, West Kensington, W.14   15886.

DUNNETT, H. J. S., 1st Air Mechanic, R.A.F.
He volunteered in April, 1915, and went to the Western Front in the following month, where he served nearly three and a half years. He took part in the engagements on the Somme, Ypres and Arras, and was employed as wireless operator, being attached to a Heavy Battery R.G.A. He died in Belgium in October, 1918, and was entitled to the 1915 Star, General Service and Victory Medals
20, First Avenue, Queen's Park, W.10   X18840.

DUNNING, S., Stoker Petty Officer, R.N., H.M.S. "Falcon."
He volunteered in August, 1914, served in the English Channel until 1918, and off Italy in the following year. He was also in action off the Belgian coast and in the Adriatic. He was discharged in December, 1919, holding the 1914-15 Star, General Service and Victory Medals. Throughout the war his duties were of a most dangerous nature.
69, Tubb's Road, Willesden Junction, N.W.10   T12889.

DUNSDON, E., Air Mechanic, Royal Air Force.
He volunteered in December, 1915, and went to France in the following year. He was engaged on work which required skill and technical knowledge of a high degree, and was continuously serving until the cessation of hostilities He was demobilised in March, 1919, holding the General Service and Victory Medals.
57, Warwick Road, Edmonton.   X17511.

DUNTON, J., Gunner, Royal Field Artillery.
He volunteered in August, 1915, went to France in the following year, and took part in the battles of Loos and the Somme, where he was wounded. On his recovery he was sent to India, and served there for nine months, afterwards returning to France in July, 1918, and taking part in the final Advance of 1918. Later he was sent to Germany with the Army of Occupation. Whilst there he met with a serious accident, which caused him to be invalided home and finally discharged as medically unfit in May, 1919.
He holds the General Service and Victory Medals.
43, Chalgrove Road, Tottenham, N.17   X18962.

DURACK, F. C., Pte., Royal Fusiliers.
He was serving in India when war broke out, returned to England in 1915, and was sent from there to the Dardanelles, where he was killed in action in April, 1915, at the first landing. He was entitled to the 1915 Star, General Service and Victory Medals. 118, Deacon Road, Willesden.   X16975.

DURBIN, L. A. (Mrs.), Special War Worker.
During the war this lady rendered valuable services in connection with the manufacture of aeroplanes. Her work required great skill, and she was commended for her zeal and energy. 28, Chesson Road, West Kensington. X17167.

DURRANT, C., Pte., Royal Fusiliers.
He volunteered in November, 1915, and was sent in the following year to the Western Front. He took part in many important engagements in Belgium and France, including the battles of the Somme, Cambrai, Lens, Ypres, Loos, Albert and Arras. In 1916 he was sent to Salonica, where he was severely wounded, and discharged as medically unfit for further service in January, 1918.
He holds the General Service and Victory Medals.
5, Dudden Hill Lane, N.W.10   T17335.

DURRANT, C. A., Gunner, R.F.A.
He volunteered in September, 1914, served in France from
1915 until 1919. During this period he saw much fighting,
on the Somme in 1916, and at Cambrai in 1918.
He was demobilised in January, 1919, holding the 1915 Star,
General Service and Victory Medals.
234, Town Road, Edmonton. 13578.

DURRANT, E., Mechanic, Royal Air Force.
He joined in October, 1916, and was engaged with his unit
at various stations on work of great importance. He was
at the time physically unfit for duty overseas, and was
demobilised in March, 1919.
59, Mulgrave Road, S.W.6 16186B.

**DURRANT, G. T., Pte., The Buffs (2/5th East
Kent Regiment).**
He joined for duty in August, 1916, and during his military
service contracted pneumonia. He died from heart failure,
as a result, in May of the following year, and was buried
with military honours in England.
140, Bronsart Road, Fulham, S.W.6 X19012.

DURRANT, R., Driver, Royal Field Artillery.
He volunteered in April, 1915, and served with distinction
in France, where he took part in many engagements, including the Somme, Arras, Ypres, Cambrai, Loos, Lens,
Kemmel, Passchendaele, Festubert, Albert and Mons.
He holds the 1915 Star, General Service and Victory Medals,
and was demobilised in March, 1919.
15, Farrant Street, Queen's Park, W.10 X19061.

**DURRANT, S., Pte., Norfolk Regiment (T.F.),
and R.A.S.C. (M.T.)**
He was mobilised in August, 1914, and in December of the
same year was discharged as medically unfit. He rejoined
in the R.A.S.C. in December, 1915, and served for three
years on the Western Front, where he saw much active
service at the Somme and Ypres while employed with an
ammunition column.
He was demobilised in May, 1919, holding the General
Service and Victory Medals.
43, Charlton Road, Harlesden, N.W.10 13104B.

DYALL, T. H., 2nd Air Mechanic, R.A.F.
During his service, which extended from April, 1915, until
February, 1919, he was engaged on duties requiring skill and
technical knowledge at various important flying centres with
the Royal Air Force. He holds the General Service Medal.
29, Felixstowe Road, Willesden. TX18689.

DYER, A. G., Pte., Royal Fusiliers.
He joined in May, 1916, and served in France until 1919,
during which time he took part in the battle of Cambrai,
and was in hospital for a time through illness contracted in
the trenches He was demobilised in January, 1919, holding
the General Service and Victory Medals.
76, Felixstowe Road, Edmonton. 15379.

**DYER, J., Sergt., 9th Middlesex and 1st East
Lancashire Regiments.**
He volunteered in August, 1914, and served with distinction
on the Western Front, taking part in the battles of Ypres,
Passchendaele and Arras. In 1917 he was invalided home,
after being badly gassed, and until his demobilisation in
February, 1919, was engaged on special duties.
He holds the General Service and Victory Medals.
131, Fortune Gate Road, Harlesden. 15003.

DYMOCK, A. T. J., Cpl., Royal Engineers.
He joined in July, 1916, and after his training, served on
the Western Front till 1919. He took part in the Retreat
and Advance of 1918, and was engaged chiefly on important
railway work.
He was demobilised in October, 1919, holding the General
Service and Victory Medals.
9, Ravensworth Road, College Park, Willesden. X17613.

E

**EADE, A., Rifleman, 1/18th London Regiment
(Irish Rifles).**
He joined in March, 1916, and in the same year went to
the Western Front, where he took part in manv engagements, including those of the Somme and Ypres. He was
killed in action in November, 1917, and was entitled to the
General Service and Victory Medals.
42, Lydford Road, Maida Hill, W.9 X19434.

EADE, J., Pte., Royal Fusiliers.
He volunteered in May, 1915, and in the following year
was drafted to the Western Front, where he took part in
many engagements, including those of Ypres and the
Somme, and was wounded.
He holds the General Service and Victory Medals, and was
demobilised in May, 1919.
77, Barnsdale Road, Maida Hill, W.9 X19544B.

EADE, M. (Mrs.) (née Wood), Special War Worker.
During the war this lady was engaged at an aeroplane
factory at Kensington and at Messrs. Barry's Shell Factory.
She held responsible and important positions at both places,
and was highly commended for her valuable services.
77, Barnsdale Road, Maida Hill, W.9 X19544A.

EALEY, J., Pte., Welch Regt. and Lancs. Regt.
He joined in February, 1916, and in the following year was
sent to France, where he remained until 1919. He took
part in engagements at Ypres, Arras and Cambrai, and was
wounded.
He holds the General Service and Victory Medals, and was
demobilised in March, 1919.
237, Kilburn Lane, W.10 X18719.

EAMES, E. (Miss), Special War Worker.
This lady was engaged for five years during the war on
munition work. During this period she rendered extremely
valuable services, carrying out her arduous duties with the
greatest skill. She was highly commended for her untiring
energy.
7, Chapman's Cottages, High Road, Willesden. 16616A.

EAMES, G., Cpl., 11th Middlesex Regiment.
He joined in 1915 and proceeded to France the same year,
where he took part in many engagements, including the
battles of Arras, the Somme, Ypres and Armentieres. He
was severely wounded and gassed in 1916, and invalided
home.
He holds the 1914-15 Star, General Service and Victory
Medals, and was demobilised in 1919.
7, Chapman's Cottages, High Road, Willesden. 16616B.

EAMES, J., Pte., 2/9th Middlesex Regiment.
Although of indifferent health, he nevertheless volunteered
for duty, and joined in May, 1915. During his training,
however, his health broke down, and he was discharged as
unfit for further military service.
32, Westbury Road, Willesden. 15446.

EAST, J. C. (M.M.), Rifleman, 2nd Rifle Brigade.
He joined in April, 1917, and went to the Western Front in
June of the same year. He took part in numerous engagements, including the fighting around Arras and at Passchendaele Ridge. For conspicuous gallantry and devotion to
duty he was awarded the Military Medal at Passchendaele.
He was subsequently severely wounded during the fighting
in this sector.
In addition to the Military Medal, he holds the General
Service and Victory Medals.
16, Hiley Road, Willesden. X18649.

EAST, J. W., Driver, Royal Field Artillery.
He volunteered in January, 1915, went to the Western Front
in June of the same year, and took part in many engage-
ments, including those of Armentieres, Arras, Ypres, Vimy
Ridge, Loos, the Somme and Passchendaele.
He was demobilised in March, 1919, holding the 1915 Star,
General Service and Victory Medals.
31, Oldfield Road, Willesden. 15748.

EAST, N. (Mrs.), Special War Worker.
During the war this lady was engaged in valuable services
with Messrs. Whitley's. Her work, which was in connection
with St. George's and St. Mary's Hospitals, was of a very
arduous nature, but her energy was untiring.
30, Averill Street, Fulham, S.W.6 14170B.

EAST, T. R., Pte., 4th Middlesex Regiment.
He joined in April, 1915, and at the conclusion of his training
served in France, where he took part in many engagements
and was badly gassed.
He was discharged as a consequence in September, 1916, as
unfit for further service, and holds the General Service and
Victory Medals.
83, Portnall Road, Maida Hill, W.9 X19509.

EAST, W. G., Stoker, R.N., H.M.S. " Revenge."
He volunteered for the Royal Navy in October, 1915, and
served with the Grand Fleet in the North Sea, taking part
in the battle of Jutland. He also served on H.M.S. " Revenge " in the Dardanelles, where he saw much fighting.
In 1919 he was demobilised, and holds the 1915 Star, General
Service and Victory Medals.
30, Averill Street, Fulham. 14170A.

**EASTAFF, T., Chief Petty Officer, R.N., H.M.S.
" Lightfoot " and " Conquest."**
He joined in 1914, and during the war saw much
service of a dangerous nature in the North Sea. While
chasing German raiders he had many exciting adventures
and surprising escapes. On one occasion the " Conquest "
was badly damaged.
He was demobilised in 1919, and holds the 1914 Star, the
General Service and Victory Medals.
26, Holly Lane, Willesden. 15572A.

EASTER, A. H., Cpl., Middlesex Regiment.

He volunteered in 1914, served with his unit on the Western Front from 1915 until 1918, and took part in the battles of the Somme, Ypres and Loos.
He was demobilised in 1919, and holds the 1915 Star, the General Service and Victory Medals.
224, Brettenham Road East, Edmonton, N.18   15216.

EASTER, S. A., Cpl., Royal Field Artillery.

He volunteered in September, 1914, and was sent a year later to Egypt. At the end of 1915 he was sent to France, where he served with distinction, and was killed in April, 1917, at Arras.
He was entitled to the General Service and Victory Medals and the 1914-15 Star.
3, Alma Place, Kensal Green, N.W.10   X18248.

EASTWELL, F., Pte., 2nd Dorset Regiment.

He volunteered in 1914, and served in India and at the Dardanelles, being present at the landing at Suvla Bay, where he was wounded. He has been wounded twice. While abroad he suffered from fever, and was generally incapacitated for further active service.
He was demobilised in 1919, and holds the 1914 Star, General Service and Victory Medals.
52, St. Mary's Road, Harlesden, N.W.10   15114B.

EASTWELL, J., Pte., 2nd Dorset Regiment.

He volunteered in 1914, and served with distinction in Mesopotamia in 1915, and on the Western Front. Whilst in action in France he sustained a wound necessitating the amputation of his leg, and was discharged in 1917.
He holds the 1914-15 Star, General Service and Victory Medals.
52, St. Mary's Road, Harlesden.   15114A.

EASTWOOD, J., Sergt., 2nd East Surrey Regt.

He volunteered in September, 1914, was sent to France in the same year, took part in the fighting at Mons, Ypres, on the Somme, at Arras, Bullecourt and elsewhere, and later served in Salonica, where he contracted malaria. Whilst abroad he was eight times wounded.
He was discharged in February, 1919, holding the Mons Star, General Service and Victory Medals.
8, Bridport Road, Edmonton, N.18   X17896.

EASTWOOD, W., Staff-Sergt., R.A.S.C.

He volunteered in April, 1915, went to Salonica in November of the same year, and served on the Balkan Front on important duties for the whole period of his service.
He holds the 1914-15 Star, General Service and Victory Medals, and was demobilised in January, 1919.
10, Milton Avenue, Harlesden, N.W.10   14338.

EATON, C. E., Pte., Royal Fusiliers and Sapper, R.E.

He volunteered in August, 1914, and served in India, France, Egypt, Salonica and Italy. In France he took part in the battle of Ypres, and from 1918 till 1919 he served with the R.E. in Italy.
He was demobilised in February, 1919, and holds the 1915 Star, the General Service and Victory Medals.
34, Sheldon Road, Edmonton.   X17454.

EATON, R. T., C.S.M., R.E. (Traffic Section).

He volunteered in May, 1916, and owing to his special abilities was employed in connection with traffic duties for three years, and rendered good services.
He was demobilised in February, 1919.
84, Fortune Gate Road, Harlesden.   13187.

EBBS, R. (Mrs.), Special War Worker.

For the duration of the war this lady offered her services, and was employed on work of national importance, for which she was commended. By her patriotic action she released a man for military service.
25, Chesson Road, West Kensington, W.14   X17163B.

EBBS, W., Sergt., The Rifle Brigade.

He volunteered in August, 1914, and was sent to France, where he took part in the retreat from Mons and the battles of Neuve Chapelle, Loos, Armentieres, Amiens, Arras, St. Quentin, Bullecourt, Ypres, Vimy Ridge and the retreat from Cambrai. He was wounded three times, and was invalided home with shell-shock. Later he was sent to Ireland on important duties.
He was demobilised in 1920, and holds the 1914 Star, General Service and Victory Medals.
25, Chesson Road, West Kensington, W.14   X17163A.

ECKETT, W. C., Rifleman, King's Royal Rifle Corps.

He volunteered in October, 1914, and served on the Western Front, taking part in many important engagements, including the battles of the Somme, Armentieres, Ypres, and Bullecourt. Later he was sent to Salonica, where he contracted malaria, and was invalided to Malta. On recovery he was ordered to France, and took part in the fighting at Cambrai during the final Advance, and was wounded four times.
He was demobilised in January, 1919, and holds the 1914 Star, General Service and Victory Medals.
60, Orbain Road, Fulham.   X18230.

ECUYER, A., Pte., 2nd Middlesex Regiment.

He volunteered in October, 1915, and after a few months' training was sent to France, where for three years he saw much service on all parts of the Front, taking part in many important engagements.
He was demobilised in 1919, and holds the General Service and Victory Medals.
11, Ray's Avenue, Edmonton.   15489.

EDDEN, J. H., Sergt., King's Royal Rifle Corps.

He volunteered in September, 1914, went to France the following year, and took part in several engagements, including Cambrai, where he was wounded. He was wounded three times during the war, and was demobilised in February, 1919, holding the 1915 Star, General Service and Victory Medals.
64, Alston Road, Edmonton, N.18   16548B.

EDDEN, J. V., Pte., Middlesex Regiment.

He joined in 1916, went to France the same year, and took part in many engagements, serving there until March, 1919, when he was demobilised. During his service abroad he suffered badly from trench feet, &c.
He holds the General Service and Victory Medals.
64, Alston Road, Edmonton, N.18   16548A.

EDDINGTON, E., Pte., R.A.M.C.

He was mobilised in August, 1914, and during his important service on the Western Front was engaged in attending the wounded, for which he holds a first-class certificate.
In June, 1916, he was discharged, suffering from shell-shock.
He holds the 1914-15 Star, General Service and Victory Medals.
51, Aspenlea Road, Hammersmith, W.6   14299.

EDE, G. F., Cpl., Bedfordshire Regiment.

He joined in February, 1916, and went to France a few months later and took part in the battle of the Somme. During the severe fighting around Albert he was killed on October 31st, 1916.
He was entitled to the General Service and Victory Medals.
38a, Denzil Road, Neasden Lane, N.W.10   16081B.

EDE, H. A., 2nd Lieut., 1/9th Middlesex Regt. (Territorials).

He was serving at the outbreak of war, and was sent to India in October, 1914, for garrison duty. Later he went to Mesopotamia, and took part in many engagements on that Front with distinction until 1919.
He was demobilised in May, 1919, and holds the 1914-15 Star, General Service and Victory Medals.
38a, Denzil Road, Neasden.   16081A.

EDEN, G. H., Driver, Royal Horse Artillery.

He joined in October, 1916, served on the Western Front, and took part in the battles of the Somme, Arras, Neuve Chapelle, Ypres and Cambrai.
In March, 1919, he was demobilised, holding the General Service and Victory Medals.
56, Averill Street, Hammersmith.   T13990A.

EDEN, J., Leading Stoker, R.N., H.M.S. "Hogue."

He volunteered in August, 1914, and while in action in the North Sea was killed in September of the same year. His wife received a letter of condolence from the Admiralty.
He was entitled to the 1914 Star, the General Service and Victory Medals.
10, Wilson's Road, Hammersmith.   16415.

EDEN, P. L. (Mrs.), Special War Worker.

During the war this lady offered her services, in order to release a man for military duty, and did valuable work, assisting in an important business house. She was commended for her good work.
56, Averill Street, Hammersmith.   T13990B.

EDEN, S. W., Leading Stoker, R.N., H.M.S. "Alictor."

He was mobilised in August, 1914, and served with the Grand Fleet for four and a half years. After useful and varied service of a dangerous and trying nature, he was discharged in February, 1919, and holds the 1914 Star, the General Service and Victory Medals.
19, Whitehall Street, Tottenham.   X18125

EDEY, J., Pte., Royal West Kent Regiment.

He joined in July, 1916, and was sent to France in November of the same year. He was wounded and taken prisoner during the battle of Arras in May, 1917, having served in several engagements previously with distinction.
He was discharged in December, 1918, and holds the General Service and Victory Medals.
47, Carlyle Avenue, Harlesden. 14195.

EDGE, B. G., Sergt., R.A.V.C.

At the outbreak of war he offered himself as a special constable, but in September, 1915, he joined the Army, and the same year saw service on the Western Front as veterinary sergeant. Owing to his professional knowledge he was able to render valuable services until his demobilisation in April, 1919.
He holds the 1915 Star, General Service and Victory Medals.
2, Chesson Road, West Kensington. 16436.

EDGE, C., 1st Air Mechanic, Royal Air Force.

He volunteered in 1914, and went to Egypt with the Middlesex Regiment, later being transferred to the R.A.F. He saw much service during the war, and holds the 1914 Star, General Service and Victory Medals.
118, Purves Road, Willesden. X18186C.

EDGE, J. H., Pte., The Queen's (Royal West Surrey Regiment).

He joined in 1916, and went to Italy the following year, taking part in many battles. He was killed in action on October 29th, 1918, and was buried in Zebe Cemetery, Italy.
He was entitled to the General Service and Victory Medals.
118, Purves Road, Willesden. X18186A.

EDGE, T., Pte., Royal Fusiliers, and Driver, R.A.S.C.

He joined in 1917, and served with his unit on duties of importance for some time. Later he went to Germany, transferred to the R.A.S.C., with the Army of Occupation, and was eventually demobilised in 1919.
118, Purves Road, Willesden. X18186B.

EDINBOROUGH, E., Pte., Royal Marines.

He volunteered in August, 1914, was sent to the Western Front in the same year, and took part in the battles of Ypres and Cambrai. He was also in action in Gallipoli and in the battle of Jutland.
He was demobilised in May, 1919, and holds the 1914 Star, General Service and Victory Medals.
25, St. John's Buildings, Kilburn Lane, N.W. X18665.

EDKINS, F., Rifleman, King's Royal Rifle Corps.

He volunteered in January, 1915, and served on the Western Front in the same year, taking part in several engagements. He was severely wounded at Lille, and as a result, remained in hospital some considerable time.
He was demobilised in January, 1919, and holds the 1915 Star, General Service and Victory Medals.
6, Welford Terrace, Fulham. X18063.

EDMEADES, D., Driver, Royal Field Artillery.

He volunteered in March, 1915, and was sent to France the same year, where he took part in several engagements, including the battle of Loos. He was later drafted to Salonica, where he remained until after the Armistice.
He was demobilised in 1919, and holds the 1915 Star, General Service and Victory Medals.
19, Monmouth Road, Lower Edmonton, N.9 12991A.

EDMEADES, J., Cpl., R.A.M.C.

He volunteered in October, 1914, and later saw service in France, where he took part in the battle of the Somme, the fighting around La Bassée, and several other engagements, giving important medical services.
He was demobilised in 1919, and holds the General Service and Victory Medals.
19, Monmouth Road, Lower Edmonton, N.9 12991B.

EDMEADES, W. T., Pte., R.A.S.C.

He served in France from his enlistment in September, 1914, until demobilised in 1919. He was present during many engagements, including the battles of La Bassée and Arras.
He holds the 1914 Star, the General Service and Victory Medals.
19, Monmouth Road, Lower Edmonton, N.9 12991C.

EDMONDS, A. J., Lce.-Cpl., The Queen's (Royal West Surrey Regiment).

He joined in October, 1916, and the same year was sent to France, where he remained until 1919. He took part in many engagements, including Ypres and the battle of the Somme.
He holds the General Service and Victory Medals, and was demobilised in March, 1919.
9, Asplin Road, Tottenham, N.17 X18820A.

EDMONDS, C. A., Sapper, Royal Engineers.

He volunteered in August, 1915, served with distinction on the Western Front from January, 1917, until he was demobilised in July, 1919. He was in action at Ypres, on the Somme, at Amiens, Arras and during the last Advance of 1918.
He holds the General Service and Victory Medals.
28, Hiley Road, Willesden. X18425.

EDMONDS, F., Pte., Middlesex Regiment.

He joined in May, 1916, and served in France from that year until 1918. While there he was in action in many engagements, including those at Ypres and the Somme, and was badly gassed. After the Armistice he went to Germany with the Army of Occupation.
He holds the General Service and Victory Medals.
9, Asplin Road, Tottenham. X18820B.

EDMONDS, G. E., Pte., R.A.S.C.

He joined in June, 1917, and in the same year went to France, where he served until September, 1919. He was demobilised in the following November. Previous to joining the Colours, he had been engaged on work of national importance connected with the output of munitions.
He holds the General Service and Victory Medals.
14, Herbert Road, Edmonton, N.9 13042D.

EDMONDS, H., Pte., 12th Middlesex Regiment.

He volunteered in January, 1916, and went to France in the following April. He was killed in action in October, 1916, and was entitled to the General Service and Victory Medals.
14, Herbert Road, Edmonton, N.9 13042C.

EDMONDS, T. J., Sapper, Royal Engineers.

During his service, which lasted from June, 1916, until April, 1917, he was on important duty with his unit in France.
He holds the General Service and Victory Medals, and was discharged through ill-health contracted during his service to the country.
14, Herbert Road, Edmonton. 13042A.

EDMONDS, W. J., Pte., 2nd-Bn. The Buffs (East Kent Regiment).

He joined in March, 1916, and in August of the same year was sent to Salonica, where he saw considerable service until he was invalided home suffering from malaria. He later served with the Military Police in Ireland until he was demobilised in August, 1919.
He holds the General Service and Victory Medals.
14, Herbert Road, Edmonton. 13042B.

EDWARDS, A. G., S.M., 3rd Middlesex Regiment.

He volunteered in August, 1914, took part with distinction in the battle of Mons, and after being wounded in France, was in 1916 sent to Salonica. In March, 1919, he returned and served with the Army of Occupation in Germany.
He holds the 1914 Star, the General Service and Victory Medals.
102, Brett Road, Harlesden. 14381.

EDWARDS, C. W., Gunner, R.F.A.

He volunteered in August, 1914, and served in France, taking part in many engagements. He suffered from shell-shock, and was, as a consequence, discharged in July, 1916.
He holds the 1914 Star, General Service and Victory Medals.
35, Belton Road, Willesden. 16592.

EDWARDS, E. E., 2nd Stoker Petty Officer, R.N., H.M.S. M.L. " K.54."

He volunteered in August, 1914, and saw active service in Salonica and the Mediterranean.
He was demobilised in May, 1919, and in July of the same year died in the 1st London General Hospital of sickness contracted whilst in the Service.
He was entitled to the General Service and Victory Medals.
85, Winchester Road, Edmonton, N.9 14751.

EDWARDS, G., A.B., R.N., H.M.S. " Europa."

He was in the Navy at the outbreak of war, and was engaged on dangerous mine-sweeping duties.
He holds the 1914 Star, General Service and Victory Medals, and was demobilised in February, 1920.
96, Churchill Road, Willesden. 16707.

EDWARDS, G., Driver, R.A.S.C. (H.T.).

He volunteered in September, 1914, and served on the Western Front for five years. During this period he was present at many engagements, including those of Peronne, Beaumont Hamel, Albert, Armentieres, Gommecourt and Nieuport.
He was demobilised in January, 1919, holding the 1914 Star and the General Service and Victory Medals.
130, Fortune Gate Road, Harlesden. 14186.

7

EDWARDS, F. W., Gunner, R.G.A.
He joined in 1916, and served with distinction on the Western Front for two years, taking part in the battles of St. Quentin, Bullecourt, the Somme and many others. He was invalided home, suffering from myalgia, and was demobilised in 1919, holding the General Service and Victory Medals.
405, High Road, Willesden.   17351B.

EDWARDS, G., Pte., East Surrey Regiment.
He joined in 1916, and in the following year was sent out to France, and in October was reported killed at the battle of Ypres.
He was entitled to the Victory and General Service Medals.
29, Leghorn Road, Harlesden.   13363B.

EDWARDS, G. H., Gunner, R.F.A.
He volunteered in December, 1915, and on completing his training was sent to France, where he took part with distinction in several engagements, being afterwards sent to Italy. He there contracted malaria, and was in hospital for some time.
He was demobilised in March, 1919, and holds the General Service and Victory Medals.
40, Bruce Castle Road, Tottenham.   X18549.

EDWARDS, J. F. G., Pte., Royal Sussex Regt.
He volunteered in September, 1914, went to France in the following year and took part in many battles, including those of the Somme, Ypres and Arras.
He was demobilised in February, 1919, holding the 1915 Star, General Service and Victory Medals.
50, Beaconsfield Road, Edmonton.   14564.

EDWARDS, J. W., Sapper, Royal Engineers.
He joined in August, 1917, and served with his unit on extremely important duties at many places, being commended for his good work and conduct by his Commanding Officer. He underwent an operation at Newport Hospital, and was discharged as a result in September, 1918, having performed his duties with great credit.
35, Bayonne Road, Fulham.   14510.

EDWARDS, M. (Mrs.), Special War Worker.
During the war this lady held a responsible post in the clerical department of the Navy and Army Canteen Board, and performed her duties, which were of a very valuable nature, to great satisfaction.
142, Bronsart Road, Fulham, S.W.6   X18991A.

EDWARDS, P. J., Lce.-Cpl., 8th Middlesex Regt.
He joined in June, 1916, and during his service on the Western Front took part in the battles of Ypres and Arras, where he was wounded. He was mentioned in despatches in 1918 for distinguished conduct in the field during the Offensive at Cambrai, where he was temporarily blinded by gas. He was discharged in March, 1918, and holds the General Service and Victory Medals.
32, Fifth Avenue, Queen's Park, W.10   X18320.

EDWARDS, R., Pte., 2nd Royal Fusiliers.
He was serving in the Army on the outbreak of war, having enlisted in 1910. He was sent to the Eastern Front in April, 1915, and took part in operations at the Dardanelles, where he was wounded in action. In February, 1917, he was transferred to the Western Front, and was present at the battle of the Somme and other engagements. He was twice wounded in action and died of his wounds in October of the same year.
He was entitled to the 1915 Star, General Service and Victory Medals.
40, Hiley Road, Willesden, N.W.10   X18163.

EDWARDS, W., Sergt., 9th and 12th Middlesex Regiment.
He enlisted in 1917, and served on the Western Front, and was wounded at the battle of Armentières, as a result of which he was in hospital for 18 months. He was in action afterwards on the Somme, at Arras and Loos.
He was demobilised in November, 1919, holding the South African, General Service and Victory Medals.
26, Yuletide Road, Willesden.   15079.

EDWARDS, W. H., Petty Officer, R.N., H.M.S. "Iphigenia."
He was already serving at the outbreak of war, and in 1914 saw active service in the North Sea. He took part in the battle of Jutland, the bombardment of Zeebrugge and the battle of Heligoland. During his service he was blown up at Dunkirk and wounded.
He was demobilised in December, 1919, and holds the 1914 Star, the General Service and Victory Medals.
11, Denton Road, Harlesden.   14708.

EDWARDS, W. J., Sergt., East Surrey Rifles.
He volunteered in October, 1915, and during his service on the Western Front took part in the battles of the Somme, Ypres, Cambrai, St. Quentin and others, and was thrice wounded.
He was demobilised in January, 1919, holding the General Service and Victory Medals.
37, Biscay Road, Hammersmith, W.6   T13043.

EDWARDS, W. L., Sapper, Royal Engineers.
He joined in January, 1917, and during his service on the Western Front took part in the battles of St. Quentin, Arras, Ypres and many other engagements, including the 1918 Advance. Later he went with the Army of Occupation to Germany.
He was demobilised in September, 1919, and holds the General Service and Victory Medals.
142, Bronsart Road, Fulham, S.W.6   X18991B.

EDWARDS, W. S. T., Gunner, R.G.A.
He joined in June, 1917, and served with the Royal Garrison Artillery at Portsmouth and other stations on important training and other duties.
He secured his demobilisation in February, 1919.
32, Leeds Street, Edmonton.   15814.

EELES, W. J., Driver, R.A.S.C. (M.T.).
He volunteered in January, 1915, and served on the Western Front, being engaged in the important work of transporting food and ammunition to the Front.
He was demobilised in April, 1919, and holds the 1915 Star, the General Service and Victory Medals.
95a, Deacon Road, Willesden.   16604A.

EGGLETON, F. T., Lce.-Cpl., 2nd West Riding Regiment.
He volunteered in August, 1914, and shortly afterwards was sent to the Western Front, where he took part in the severe fighting at Hill 60 with distinction, being reported missing after the battle. He was later reported killed.
He was entitled to the 1914-15 Star, General Service and Victory Medals.
31, Lorenco Road, Tottenham.   X18404.

EGGLETON, H., Cpl., 4th Middlesex Regiment.
He volunteered in August, 1914, and served in France from that year until 1916, when he was sent to Egypt. During his service he was wounded three times in action.
He holds the 1914 Star, General Service and Victory Medals.
146, Winchester Road, Lower Edmonton.   14781.

EGGLETON. W. A., Pte., Royal Fusiliers.
He volunteered in January, 1915, and during his service on the Western Front was in action at Arras and Ypres and on the Somme. He was sent to hospital at Rouen, having been seriously gassed.
He was demobilised in October, 1919, holding the 1915 Star, General Service and Victory Medals.
19, Everington Street, Fulham.   13965B.

EKE, A., Rifleman, 2/11th London Regiment.
He volunteered in November, 1915, went to France and took part in many battles.
He was killed in action in September, 1917, and was entitled to the General Service and Victory Medals.
50, Kilmaine Road, Fulham.   X18775A.

EKE, W., Gunner, Royal Field Artillery.
He volunteered in January, 1915, and served on the Western Front from the same year until the cessation of hostilities, taking part in many severe engagements.
He holds the 1915 Star, General Service and Victory Medals, and is still in the Army.
50, Kilmaine Road, Fulham.   X18775B.

ELBRA, J. J., Pte., Royal Army Ordnance Corps.
Volunteering in November, 1915, he was drafted to the East, and for three years gave important services in Mesopotamia. Later he was transferred to France, where he remained until 1919.
He holds the General Service and Victory Medals, and was demobilised in 1919.
95, Angel Road, Edmonton.   16575.

ELBROW, J. F., Rifleman, Rifle Brigade.
He joined in April, 1918, and was engaged on training and other duties until a year later, when he joined the Army of Occupation in Germany.
He secured his demobilisation in September, 1919.
145, Park Terrace, Stonebridge Park.   15802A.

ELBROW, W. T., Pte., Machine Gun Corps.
He joined in April, 1916, served on the Western Front until March, 1919, took part in several engagements, including the battles of Ypres and Arras, and was twice wounded.
He holds the General Service and Victory Medals, and lately has been serving in the M.G.C. School.
145, Park Terrace, Stonebridge Park.   15802B.

ELCOCK, W. J., Stoker, R.N., H.M.S. "Newcastle."

Although he had previously given 15 years' service to the country, he rejoined in August, 1914, and almost immediately went to sea. He was on duty with his ship in the East, and also did service in the North Sea on dangerous and important missions.
He holds the 1914 Star, the General Service and Victory Medals, and was demobilised in February, 1919.
29, Chauncey Street, N.9   14267.

ELDERFIELD, T. D., Driver, R.F.A.

He joined in September, 1917, and was stationed with his unit at various places on important duties, including Ireland. As the result of a serious accident which occurred whilst on service, he was discharged in April, 1918.
17, Disraeli Road, Harlesden.   14158.

ELDERFIELD, W. F., Pte., Suffolk Regiment and Lincolnshire Regiment.

He volunteered in December, 1915, and served on the Western Front from January, 1918, until demobilised in February, 1919. He was in action with his unit at Arras and Cambrai, during which service he met with an accident, sustaining severe injuries.
He holds the General Service and Victory Medals.
41, Mordaunt Road, Harlesden.   13863.

ELDRED, H., Petty Officer, R.N., and M.G.C.

He joined the Royal Navy in June, 1915, and later transferred to the Machine Gun Corps. During his service he took part with distinction in several engagements on the Western Front, in Italy, Mesopotamia and Russia.
He holds the 1915 Star, General Service and Victory Medals, and was demobilised in March, 1919.
44, Tubb's Road, Harlesden.   12739.

ELDRET, E., Driver, R.A.S.C.

He volunteered in November 1915, and served on the Western Front, being in action at the battle of Hill 60, where he sustained a severe shrapnel wound.
In March, 1918, he was discharged, having contracted rheumatism in a severe form while abroad.
He holds the General Service and Victory Medals.
23, Raynham Road, Edmonton.   16000.

ELDRIDGE, A., Cpl., Welch Regiment.

He volunteered in September, 1914, served throughout the Dardanelles campaign, and later in Mesopotamia.
He holds the 1914-15 Star, General Service and Victory Medals, and was demobilised in October, 1919. During his services overseas he was present at many important engagements.
53a, Ormiston Road, Shepherd's Bush.   11925A.

ELDRIDGE, C. J., Sergt., Royal Field Artillery.

He joined in 1916 and went to France in the same year. Owing to his special abilities, he was attached to General Headquarters for two and a half years.
He was demobilised in May, 1919, and holds the General Service and Victory Medals.
64, Purves Road, Willesden.   X18421B.

ELDRIDGE, P. A. C. (M.M.), Bombardier, R.F.A.

He volunteered in 1914, was sent to France in the following year, and took part in various engagements, including the battles of Ypres, Passchendaele, Loos, the Somme, Cambrai and Arras. He was awarded the Military Medal for conspicuous gallantry in the field, and holds also the 1915 Star, General Service and Victory Medals.
He was demobilised in 1919.
64, Purves Road, Willesden, N.W.10   X18421A.

ELEY, H., Pte., R.A.S.C. (M.T.).

He joined in November, 1917, and was sent to France in the following month. He served in France till the Armistice, and then accompanied the Army of Occupation to Germany, where he was employed at Cologne. He died from pneumonia in January, 1920, whilst serving his country at Cologne. He is entitled to the General Service and Victory Medals.
27, Holberton Gardens, Willesden, N.W.   X17552.

ELGOOD, L., Bombardier, 37th Div., R.F.A.

He joined in May, 1916, and was sent to France in the same year, where he took part in many engagements. He was twice wounded and was reported "missing, believed killed," at Ypres on May 19th, 1918.
He was entitled to the General Service and Victory Medals.
21, Bolton Avenue, Lincoln.   16954C.

ELKIN, G. F., Rifleman, Rifle Brigade.

He joined in May, 1916, went to the Western Front, where he saw much fighting, serving with distinction, and was severely wounded in October of the same year.
He was discharged in June, 1917, on account of wounds, being unfit for further service. He holds the General Service and Victory Medals.
45, Wilson's Road, Hammersmith.   15850.

ELLEDGE, N. H., Pte., 7th London Regiment.

He volunteered in September, 1915, and in the following year was sent to the Western Front, where he took part in the fighting at Ypres, Arras and Cambrai. He was reported missing in December, 1917.
He was entitled to the General Service and Victory Medals.
56, Fordingley Road, Maida Hill, W.9   X19669.

ELLIFF, A. W., Lce.-Cpl., 33rd Royal Fusiliers.

He volunteered in October, 1915, and during his service on the Western Front took part in the battles of the Somme, Arras, Vimy Ridge, La Bassée and in the last Advance of 1918.
He was demobilised in June, 1919, and holds the 1915 Star, General Service and Victory Medals.
120, Bronsart Road, Hammersmith.   13756.

ELLIFF, F. G., Pte., Norfolk Regiment.

He volunteered in August, 1914, and later was sent to the Western Front, where he saw considerable fighting, being present during the engagements at Ypres, Loos, the Somme, Arras, Passchendaele and elsewhere. He was wounded on three occasions, and as a result was discharged in March, 1918, as unfit for further military service.
He holds the 1914-15 Star, General Service and Victory Medals.
2, Ancill Street, Hammersmith.   13757.

ELLIFF, J. E., Rifleman, 10th Rifle Brigade.

He joined in November, 1916, served on the Western Front, where he took part with distinction in many engagements, including the battles of Arras, Albert, Cambrai and the fighting on the Somme. He was twice wounded, and was demobilised in October, 1919, holding the General Service and Victory Medals.
2, Ancill Street, Hammersmith.   13758.

ELLIOTT, A. A. J., Cpl., 2nd South Lancs. Regt.

He volunteered in August, 1914, and during his service on the Western Front was in action at Mons and Le Cateau, where he was taken prisoner in August, 1914. He was in captivity at Doberitz Camp and elsewhere, and suffered much from ill-treatment.
He was finally released, and in March, 1919, was demobilised, holding the Mons Star, General Service and Victory Medals.
74, Bronsart Road, Fulham, S.W.6   X18893A.

ELLIOT, A. E., Sergt., R.A.M.C.

He joined in July, 1917, and took part in many engagements in France until the cessation of hostilities, later going to Germany, on important medical duties, with the Army of Occupation.
He was demobilised in December, 1919, holding the General Service and Victory Medals.
42, Warwick Road, Edmonton.   X17515.

ELLIOTT, E., Cpl., East Surrey Regiment.

He volunteered in February, 1915, and the same year served on the Western Front, where he took part with distinction in many engagements, including the battles of St. Eloi, Loos, Arras and the fighting around Kemmel.
In February, 1919, he was demobilised, and holds the 1915 Star, General Service and Victory Medals.
73, Carlyle Avenue, Harlesden.   13916.

ELLIOTT, F., Sergt., R.A.S.C. (M.T.).

He volunteered in 1914, and was killed in France, near Arras, in April, 1918.
He was entitled to the 1914-15 Star and the General Service and Victory Medals.
Sergt. Elliott's father has received letters of condolence from officers, who mention the gallantry of his actions throughout his service.
55, Archel Road, West Kensington.   16210B.

ELLIOTT, F. J., Special War Worker.

For the duration of war he was employed at Woolwich Dockyard as supervisor of military accoutrements. His services were of a responsible and valuable nature, he having under his supervision many hundreds of workers.
55, Archel Road, West Kensington.   16210A.

ELLIOTT, F. G., Pte., Royal West Sussex Regt.

He joined for duty in 1916, and, being medically unfit for overseas service, served with his unit for three years at many important stations. He was discharged in February, 1919, having performed his duties throughout with zeal and energy.
8, Durban Road, N.17   X18096.

ELLIOTT, F. G., Special War Worker.

During the war he was employed at Woolwich Arsenal on work of vital importance connected with the manufacture of S.A.A. Owing to his energy and good work, he was promoted to examiner, in which capacity his services were particularly valuable.
55, Archel Road, West Kensington.   16210C.

ELLIOTT, H. M., Sapper, Royal Engineers.
He volunteered for service in June, 1915, and served on important and dangerous duties in France for three years. He later went to Italy, and remained there 12 months. He holds the General Service and Victory Medals, and was demobilised in April, 1920.
31, Ascot Road, Edmonton. 15365.

ELLIOTT, M. (Mrs.), Special War Worker.
Throughout the war this lady was engaged on valuable work in connection with the output of munitions. At Park Royal she was employed in shell filling, and from there was transferred to Willesden, and finally to Hayes, where she was occupied with work of a very dangerous nature. Her services were highly commended.
74, Bronsart Road, Fulham, S.W.6. X18893B.

ELLIOTT, P. R., Special War Worker.
During the war he was employed at Woolwich Arsenal on important duties. Later he joined the Army and Navy Canteen Board, and served on H.M.S. "Victorious" and H.M.S. "London," and was manager of the canteen on H.M.S. "Dublin."
55, Archel Road, West Kensington. 16210D.

ELLIOTT, S. H., Q.M.S., R.A.S.C. (M.T.).
He volunteered in August, 1914, and served in France with distinction on many sectors of the Front, being engaged on important transport duties. Later he was drafted to Mesopotamia with the armoured cars.
He holds the 1914-15 Star, General Service and Victory Medals, and was demobilised in July, 1919.
32, Parkfield Road, Willesden. X17420.

ELLIS, A. J., Rifleman, 11th London Regiment.
He volunteered in August, 1914, and served at the Dardanelles from August, 1915, until the evacuation, taking part with distinction in several engagements.
He was demobilised in February, 1919, and holds the 1915 Star, General Service and Victory Medals.
7, Ashwell Grove, Edmonton. X17589.

ELLIS, E. A., Pte., Royal West Kent Regiment.
He volunteered in September, 1914, and served on the Western Front. He was in action in many great battles, and was killed in October, 1918, when hostilities were almost at an end.
He was entitled to the 1915 Star, General Service and Victory Medals. 7, Sandgate Road, Edmonton N.18 15498B.

ELLIS, G., Special War Worker.
Owing to his age he was unable to enlist for military duty, but rendered important service with the British Thompson Houston Co. in the manufacture of shells and other munitions. His work required skill and high technical knowledge, and he rendered valuable services. 27, Ilex Road, Willesden. 16102B.

ELLIS, P. J., Sergt., 3rd London Regiment.
He volunteered in August, 1914, and was sent to Malta, where he served until January, 1915. He then transferred to France, and was engaged in much of the important fighting.
He was demobilised in June, 1916, holding the 1915 Star, General Service and Victory Medals.
54, Minet Avenue, Harlesden. 13912.

ELLIS, R. P., Rifleman, The London Regiment, (Queen's Westminster Rifles.)
He volunteered in September, 1914, and served with distinction in France, Egypt, Salonica and Palestine, in which places he took part in many engagements.
He was demobilised in January, 1919, and holds the 1915 Star, General Service and Victory Medals.
6, Folkestone Road, Edmonton. 15362.

ELLIS, T., Cpl., Middlesex Regiment and East Lancashire Regiment.
He volunteered in January, 1915, and went to France in September, 1917. During his service he took part in the engagements at Ypres, Arras, Armentieres, Bullecourt and Kemmel Hill, and was wounded.
He holds the General Service and Victory Medals, and was demobilised in March, 1919.
18, Heron Road, Willesden. 15565.

ELLIS, W., Driver, Royal Army Service Corps.
He volunteered in December, 1915, and served on all parts of the Western Front for three and a half years, where he rendered valuable services.
He holds the General Service and Victory Medals, and was demobilised in June, 1919.
30, Hawley Crescent, Camden Town, N.W.1 15866.

ELLIS, W., Pte., R.A.S.C. (M.T.).
He volunteered in August, 1914, and during his service on the Western Front was chiefly engaged in conveying stores and ammunition to the line. He met with a serious accident, and was discharged as medically unfit in May, 1918.
He holds the 1915 Star, General Service and Victory Medals.
12, Bathurst Gardens, Kensal Rise. X18203.

ELLNER, P. G., Lce.-Cpl., 2/9th Middlesex Regiment and 3rd Lahore Division.
He volunteered in May, 1915, and served till 1919 in France, the Dardanelles and Egypt. He was in action at Suvla Bay, Gallipoli, Kantara and elsewhere, and was twice wounded.
He was demobilised on April 18th, 1919, and holds the 1915 Star, the General Service and Victory Medals.
74, Holly Lane, Willesden, N.W.10 15391A.

ELLSMORE, R., Rifleman, King's Royal Rifle Corps.
He volunteered in 1914, was sent to France and taken prisoner whilst in action in September of the same year. He was finally released after suffering many hardships in captivity, and in 1919 was demobilised, holding the Mons Star, General Service and Victory Medals.
114, Kimberley Road, Upper Edmonton. 16791B.

ELMORE, H., Chief Steward, R.N., "Prince Adelbert."
He volunteered in June, 1915, and was engaged on exceedingly dangerous work in the mine-sweeping service for 12 months, and also served on a ship supplying oil to the Grand Fleet. He has also served at Gibraltar and in the Baltic.
He was demobilised in March, 1919, and holds the 1915 Star, General Service, Victory and Mercantile Marine War Medals. 17, Spezzia Road, Harlesden. T12951B.

ELMORE, H. E., Pte., Royal Fusiliers.
He volunteered in 1914, and in 1915 was sent to the Dardanelles, and later transferred to Salonica. In these theatres of war he saw much service. In 1916, after having been in England a short time, he went to the Western Front, where he was killed in May, 1917, on the Somme.
He was entitled to the 1915 Star, General Service and Victory Medals. 17, Spezzia Road, Harlesden, N.W.10 T12951C.

ELMSLIE, G., Pte., East Surrey Regiment.
He volunteered in September, 1914, and was sent to France in the following year. He served on the Western Front for 12 months, taking part in the fighting at Ypres, Hill 60 and on the Somme. He was wounded during his service, being demobilised in March, 1919, holding the 1915 Star and the General Service and Victory Medals.
4, Durban Road, Tottenham, N.17 X18098B.

ELMSLIE, L. (Miss), Special War Worker.
During the war this lady volunteered for duty, and was engaged in the manufacture of small arms ammunition. Her work was of a most valuable nature, and she was commended for her energy and zeal.
4, Durban Road, Tottenham, N.17 X18098A.

ELSEY, A., Pte., North Staffordshire Regt.
He volunteered in August, 1915, and served on the Western Front, taking part in the battles of Ypres, Arras, Cambrai, Bullecourt, the Somme and other engagements. He was wounded whilst in action near Ypres, and in March, 1920, was demobilised, holding the General Service and Victory Medals. 18, Church Lane, Willesden. 16029.

ELSIP, A., Sergt., Royal Army Service Corps.
He volunteered in September, 1914, and later was sent to Salonica, where he served with distinction. He was present during the fighting on the Doiran Front, taking part in the big advance.
In January, 1919, he was demobilised, and holds the General Service and Victory Medals.
19, Third Avenue, Queen's Park, W.10 X18936.

ELSTON, A. W., Pte., Royal Fusiliers.
He joined in 1916, went to France the same year, and took part in many battles, including the Somme, Ypres and the Advance of 1918. He was wounded twice and gassed, and after being in hospital some months, was discharged as medically unfit, as a result of his service, in January, 1919.
He holds the General Service and Victory Medals. 94, Bulwer Road, N.18 X17286.

ELSTON, E. G., Pte., York and Lancaster Regt.
He joined in June, 1917, and later was sent to the Western Front, where he took part in several engagements, and was in action during the great Advance of 1918. He afterwards served with the Army of Occupation in Germany on important guard duties.
He was demobilised in February, 1920, and holds the General Service and Victory Medals.
94, Bulwer Road, N.18 X17288.

ELTON, T., Gunner, Royal Field Artillery.
He enlisted in 1911, and was sent to France when war was declared. He took part in many engagements, including the battles of Ypres, Somme, Marne and the last Advance of 1918, and was wounded. Later he was sent with the Army of Occupation to Germany, where he remained till discharged in March, 1919.
He holds the 1914 Star, General Service and Victory Medals.
60, Milton Avenue, Harlesden. 14314B.

ELVEY, W. J., 1st-Class Stoker, R.N.
He volunteered in November, 1915, and saw considerable service on H.M.S. " Lancaster " in Chinese waters and the Pacific Ocean.
He was discharged in April, 1919, after having given valuable service, as unfit for further duty. He holds the General Service and Victory Medals.
20, Denbigh Road, Willesden. 15529.

ELVIN, A. E., Pte., R.A.S.C. (M.T.).
He volunteered in August, 1914, and was sent to the Western Front in the same year, where he saw considerable service with the Mechanical Transport Section, being present during many engagements in various sectors.
He holds the Mons Star, General Service and Victory Medals, and was demobilised in May, 1919.
44, Delorme Street, Fulham. T14081A.

ELVIN, E. J., A.B., R.N., H.M.S. " Hood."
He joined in September, 1916, and served for some considerable time on H.M.S. " Vanoc," engaged in the dangerous duties of mine-laying. He was later transferred to H.M.S. " Hood," on which ship he continued to serve.
He holds the General Service and Victory Medals.
44, Delorme Street, Fulham. T14081C.

ELVIN, H., Driver, Royal Field Artillery.
He volunteered in June, 1915, and was sent to France, where he took part in many important engagements with his battery.
He was demobilised in March, 1919, and holds the General Service and Victory Medals.
44, Delorme Street, Fulham. T14081B.

EMBLETON, F. O. (D.C.M., M.S.M.), Sergt., Royal Engineers.
He joined in August, 1914, and during his service on the Western Front took part in many of the principal engagements, including the retreat from Mons, the battles of the Somme, Loos, Arras, Vimy Ridge and Armentieres and the Great Advance of 1918. He was wounded, and was awarded the Distinguished Conduct Medal for conspicuous bravery displayed in bringing in wounded under heavy shell-fire.
He also holds the Meritorious Service Medal for efficient and gallant work in the field, the Mons Star and the General Service and Victory Medals.
28, Mablethorpe Road, Fulham, S.W.6 X19255.

EMBLETON, F. W., Pte., 4th Royal Fusiliers.
He joined the Royal Fusiliers in November, 1916, and served with the 4th Battalion in France, taking part in many engagements. He was wounded during the battle of Arras in April, 1917, and again in September during the fighting at Zonnebeke on the Passchendaele Ridge. In the Great Advance of 1918 he was wounded for the third time at Bullecourt.
He holds the General Service and Victory Medals, and was demobilised in July, 1919.
24, Burlington Road, Tottenham, N.17 X19104.

EMBURY, A., Pte., Oxford and Bucks. Light Infantry.
At the outbreak of war he was already serving in India, having enlisted in 1902. In 1915 he went to Mesopotamia, where he took part with distinction in many engagements in the advance to Kut-el-Amara. He also saw service with the R.A.F.
He was discharged in January, 1919, and holds the 1914-15 Star, General Service and Victory Medals.
65, Milton Avenue, Harlesden. 14106A.

EMBURY, S. G., Gunner, R.G.A.
He volunteered for service in 1915, and saw service with his unit at various stations. Being, however, medically unfit for further military duty at the time, he was discharged in the following year
65, Milton Avenue, Harlesden. 14106C.

EMBURY, S. W., Driver, Royal Field Artillery.
He joined in 1915, and served for three years on the Eastern Front, taking part in the fighting in Macedonia, where he was wounded.
He was demobilised in January, 1919, and holds the 1915 Star, General Service and Victory Medals.
65, Milton Avenue, Harlesden. 14106B.

EMBURY, T. W., Bombardier, R.F.A.
He volunteered in November, 1914, served on the Western Front at Ypres, Cambrai and Arras, and was wounded in action on the Somme in 1916. In 1917 he was sent to Mesopotamia, where he served until demobilised in May, 1919.
He holds the 1914 Star, General Service and Victory Medals.
73, Milton Avenue, Harlesden. 14104

EMERY, E., Gunner, Royal Horse Artillery.
At the outbreak of war he was sent to France, having already completed six years' service in Egypt. He took part in several engagements on the Western Front, and was killed in action at the opening of the battle of Loos on September 25th, 1915.
He was entitled to the 1914 Star, General Service and Victory Medals.
131, Claxton Grove, Hammersmith. 13668

EMERY, E. J., Pte., 13th London Regiment.
He joined in April, 1916, and was sent to the Western Front, where he took part in several engagements, contracting rheumatic fever. He was finally invalided home and demobilised in January, 1919, holding the General Service and Victory Medals.
131, Claxton Grove, Hammersmith. 13667.

EMERY, F. E. (D.C.M.), Pte., 13th London Regt.
He volunteered in August, 1914, and was later sent to the Western Front, where he remained until the cessation of hostilities. During his service he took part in much of the heavy fighting, and was badly wounded. He was awarded the Distinguished Conduct Medal for conspicuous gallantry in the field at Armentieres.
He also holds the 1914 Star, General Service and Victory Medals.
15, Delorme Street, Fulham. 13752—13751C.

EMERY, H. (Miss), Special War Worker.
For twelve months this lady was engaged on very dangerous work in connection with the manufacture of hand-grenades at a munition factory in Acton. Her services were greatly appreciated, and she was commended for her work.
5, Ancill Street, W.6 13866A.

EMERY, J. F., Mechanic, Royal Air Force.
He joined in December, 1917, and during his service on the Western Front took part with distinction in various engagements, including the battle of Cambrai, and was wounded. He was demobilised in September, 1919, and holds the General Service and Victory Medals.
15, Delorme Street, Fulham. 13752—13751B.

EMERY, W., Bombardier, Royal Field Artillery.
He volunteered in August, 1914, and was sent to France the same year, where he took part in many engagements in various sectors. In February, 1916, he was killed in action at Ypres.
He was entitled to the 1914 Star, General Service and Victory Medals.
15, Delorme Street, Fulham. 13752—13751A.

EMERY, W. H., Pte., Lancashire Fusiliers.
He joined in May, 1916, and gave valuable service on the Western Front, taking part in the battle of the Somme. He also served in Egypt, where he remained until he was demobilised in June, 1919.
He holds the General Service and Victory Medals.
5, Ancill Street, W.6 13866B.

EMMS, A. V., Pte., 25th London Regiment.
He volunteered in August, 1914, and later was sent to India, where he was engaged on important duties with his unit at various points.
He holds the General Service and Victory Medals, and was demobilised in November, 1919.
50, Haldane Road, Fulham. X17377A.

EMMS, A. W., Pte., East Surrey Regiment.
He joined in February, 1918, and was sent to the Western Front, where he took part in the Great Advance, and was killed in action in October of the same year.
He was entitled to the General Service and Victory Medals.
50, Haldane Road, Fulham. X17377C.

EMMS, J. W., Pte., Royal Fusiliers.
He joined in 1917, and after his training served at various stations on important duties with his unit. He gave valuable services, but was not successful in obtaining his transfer overseas before the cessation of hostilities.
He was demobilised in 1919.
32, Letchford Gardens, Willesden, N.W.10 X17549.

EMMS, T., Driver, Royal Horse Artillery.
He joined in July, 1916, and served with his unit at various stations on duties of importance.
He secured his demobilisation in January, 1919.
50, Haldane Road, Fulham. X17377B.

ENDACOTT, F., A.B., Royal Navy.
He volunteered at the outbreak of war, and was at sea from 1914 until 1918, during which period he took part in several engagements. As a result of his service he was discharged as unfit in 1918, and is still suffering from the disabilities caused by his service for the country.
He holds the 1914 Star, and the General Service and Victory Medals.
12, Britannia Court, W.6 15875B.

ENGLAND, W., Gunner, Royal Field Artillery.
He volunteered in November, 1914, and served in France, taking part with distinction in many important engagements. He was wounded at Ypres in October, 1917, and was demobilised in April, 1919, holding the 1915 Star, General Service and Victory Medals.
82, St. Mary's Road, Lower Edmonton.   T11980.

ENGLAND, W. T., Pte., Middlesex Regiment.
He joined in June, 1917, and after undergoing training in various parts of England, was sent to the Western Front, where he took part in many engagements.
He was demobilised in January, 1919, and holds the General Service and Victory Medals.
29, Herbert Road, Edmonton, N.9   13034.

ENGLEMAN, W., Pte., Middlesex Regiment.
He joined in June, 1916, went to the Western Front in 1918, and took part in numerous engagements, including those of the Somme, Canal-du-Nord and the Great Advance of that year. Later he served with the Army of Occupation in Germany until his demobilisation in January, 1920.
He holds the General Service and Victory Medals.
114, Bravington Road, Maida Hill, W.9   X19467.

ENGLISH, G., Gunner, R.F.A., and Sapper, R.E.
He volunteered in November, 1914, and went to the Western Front the following year, taking part in the battles of the Somme and Ypres. In 1915 he was sent to Egypt on H.M.S. "Aragon," which was torpedoed. He served in Egypt for twelve months, afterwards returning to France.
He holds the 1915 Star, General Service and Victory Medals, and was demobilised in May, 1919.
19, Hawkshead Road, Willesden, N.W.10   16058B.

ENGLISH, M., Bombardier, R.G.A.
He was mobilised on August 4th, 1914, and served on the Western Front, taking part in the battles of Mons, Loos, Neuve Chapelle, Ypres and the Somme. During this time he was twice wounded, and after being in hospital in France and England, was discharged on September 8th, 1917. Altogether he has served for seventeen and a half years.
He holds the 1914 Star, the General Service, Victory and Long Service Medals.
31, Werley Avenue, Fulham, S.W.6   X17745.

ENGLISH, W., Wireless Operator, Royal Navy.
He volunteered for service in 1916, and served in the following countries :—Hungary, Russia, the West Indies and Serbia. He is now serving at Budapest, and holds the General Service and Victory Medals. His duties were of a most important nature, calling for great skill and endurance.
19, Hawkshead Road, Willesden, N.W.10   16058A.

ENGWELL, C. H., Pte., Middlesex Regiment and 1/4th Hertfordshire Regiment.
He joined in April, 1916, and was in training and engaged on other duties with his unit until January, 1917, when, owing to ill-health, he was discharged as medically unfit for further service.
99, Carlyle Avenue, Harlesden.   13817A.

ENSTONE, F., Pte., Royal West Kent Regiment.
He was serving at the outbreak of war, and was sent to Mesopotamia and India, where he was engaged on important duties. He contracted malarial fever whilst on service.
He holds the 1914 Star, General Service and Victory Medals, and was demobilised in August, 1919.
29, Barry Road, Stonebridge Park.   14937B.

EPHRAIM, C., Armourer, Royal Navy.
He joined in July, 1917, and served on H.M.S. "Pembroke" with the Grand Fleet, taking part with distinction in the naval raid on Zeebrugge.
He secured his demobilisation in February, 1919, holding the General Service and Victory Medals.
27, Ashwell Grove, N.18   X17480.

ERWOOD, E. J., Pte., Essex Regiment.
He enlisted in 1916 and, after his period of training, served in France until 1919, taking part in many important engagements on the Western Front.
He was discharged in February, 1919, suffering from ill-health. He holds the General Service and Victory Medals.
69, Somerset Road, N.18   X17042.

ESSEX, H., Pte., Middlesex and Norfolk Regts.
He volunteered in November, 1914, and served in India and Baluchistan from 1915 until 1919, being stationed at Karachi, Quetta and elsewhere. Whilst in India he was employed on the railways and important guard duties.
He was demobilised in December, 1919, and holds the 1915 Star, General Service and Victory Medals.
16, Oak Road, Willesden.   15085.

ESSEX, J., Pte., Duke of Cornwall's Light Infty.
He volunteered in April, 1915, and served on the Western Front the same year. He took part in many engagements, and was wounded at Delville Wood during the battle of the Somme in 1916, and also gassed. He later served through the Retreat and Advance of 1918, and remained on the Western Front after the Armistice.
He holds the 1915 Star, General Service and Victory Medals.
6, Portnall Road, Maida Hill, W.9   X19369C.

ESSEX, J. E., Sapper, Royal Engineers.
He joined in January, 1917, and shortly afterwards served on the Western Front, taking part in the battle of Arras the same year and in the offensive at Cambrai. He later took part in the Retreat and Advance of 1918.
In November, 1919, he was demobilised, and holds the General Service and Victory Medals.
168, Wandsworth Bridge Road, Fulham, S.W.6   X19850B.

ESWORTHY, G. W., Lieut., 9th Middlesex Regt.
He volunteered in August, 1914, and was sent to France the following year. He took part with distinction in the battles of Ypres, the Somme, Cambrai, Loos, Arras and Armentieres. In 1917 he was severely wounded and invalided home.
He was demobilised in February, 1920, and holds the 1915 Star, General Service and Victory Medals.
67, Brownlow Road, Harlesden.   14721.

ETESON, C. H., Sergt., Royal Fusiliers.
He had been serving five years in the Territorial Force when war was declared, and was mobilised in September, 1914, and sent to the Western Front. He took part in several engagements in France, including Neuve Chapelle, where he was wounded. He was later in action on the Somme, and again wounded. In June, 1917, he returned to England and served as instructor during the remainder of his service.
He was demobilised in February, 1919, and holds the 1914-15 Star, General Service and Victory Medals.
45, Hiley Road, Willesden.   X18238.

ETESON, J., Sapper, Royal Engineers.
He volunteered in January, 1915, and was sent to the Western Front shortly afterwards. He served there until November, 1915, when he was drafted to the Balkans. He saw considerable service in Macedonia, taking part in the actions on the Struma. He returned to England in March, 1919, and was demobilised, holding the 1915 Star, General Service and Victory Medals.
39, Hiley Road, Willesden, N.W.10   X18237B.

ETESON, J. W., Pte., The Queen's (Royal West Surrey Regiment).
He joined in October, 1916, and was sent to France the following year, where he took part in the severe fighting at the battle of Arras. During that engagement he received a dangerous head wound, as a result of which he was discharged some months later, being unfit for further military service.
He holds the General Service and Victory Medals.
39, Hiley Road, Willesden, N.W.10   X18237A.

ETHRIDGE, J., Gunner, R.G.A.
He joined in April, 1917, and after a period of training was sent to Egypt and Palestine. He took part in many engagements whilst with General Allenby's forces, being demobilised in July, 1919.
He holds the General Service and Victory Medals.
105, Deacon Road, N.W.2   16608D.

ETOE, G. W., Lce.-Cpl., 2nd Royal Berks. Regt.
He volunteered in November, 1915, and served on the Western Front. He took part with distinction in many engagements, including the battle of the Somme, and while in action at Messines in October, 1917, he was killed.
He was entitled to the General Service and Victory Medals.
4, Franklyn Road, Willesden.   16023.

EVANS, A. H., Pte., 10th Middlesex Regiment.
He volunteered for service in 1914, and was on duty at various stations with his unit. On account of his defective eyesight, and against his wish, he was not allowed to proceed on active service.
He secured his demobilisation in 1919.
34, Ilex Road, Willesden.   16089A.

EVANS, A. L., Rifleman, 16th K.R.R.C.
He joined in September, 1917, and the following year was sent to France, where he remained until demobilised in 1920. During his service he was in several engagements, and in the severe fighting at Lens was wounded and gassed.
He holds the General Service and Victory Medals.
32, King's Road, Tottenham.   X18555A.

EVANS, A. S., 2nd Lieut., Royal Air Force.
He joined at the age of 18 in May, 1918, and was successful in passing the necessary examinations to obtain his commission. He saw service at various stations with his unit, and performed his duties throughout with zeal and energy.
He secured his demobilisation in April, 1919.
53, Maldon Road, N.9   15791A.

EVANS, C. (M.S.M.), Q.M.S., 2nd Suffolk Regt.
He volunteered in December, 1914, and three months later was sent to France, where he took part in several engagements, including those on the Somme, at Ypres, Amiens and Cambrai. He was wounded, and was awarded the M.S.M. for great gallantry and devotion to duty, and also holds the 1915 Star and the General Service and Victory Medals He was demobilised in March, 1919.
14, Gowan Road, Willesden. X17105.

EVANS, C. R., Cpl., 19th Middlesex Regiment.
He joined in November, 1916, and served in France, where he was slightly wounded in the same year. He then went to Italy, where he took part in the battle of the Piave, and in 1918 returned to France for the Allied Advance. He was demobilised in September, 1919, after serving with the Army of Occupation. He holds the General Service and Victory Medals.
15, Carlyle Avenue, Harlesden. 13688.

EVANS, C. T., Gunner, Royal Field Artillery.
He volunteered in August, 1914, and was sent to France, serving on several sectors of the Western Front. He was sent to hospital at Rouen in a serious state of health, and was discharged in April, 1918, as being medically unfit to render his country further service.
He holds the 1915 Star and the General Service and Victory Medals.
5, Welford Terrace, Fulham. X18062.

EVANS, E. B. J., Cpl., Royal Air Force.
Offering his services in 1916, he was, due to his special abilities, retained by the authorities on important work at the Air Ministry in London, where he gave valuable service.
45, Archel Road, West Kensington. 16203.

EVANS, E. J., Pte., Machine Gun Corps.
He volunteered in February, 1915, was sent to France in the following year, and received severe bullet wounds at the battle of the Somme in September, 1916.
He was demobilised in February, 1919, and holds the General Service and Victory Medals.
53, Maldon Road, Lower Edmonton. 15791B.

EVANS, G., Sergt., 2nd Middlesex Regiment.
He volunteered in 1915, went to the Western Front in the same year and took part in many battles, including those of Ypres, Loos and the Somme, where he was wounded. He was invalided to England, but on his recovery returned to France, fought in the 1918 Advance, and was again wounded. He was twice mentioned in despatches for bravery and devotion to duty on the field, and holds the 1915 Star and the General Service and Victory Medals.
86, Third Avenue, Queen's Park, W.10 X19289.

EVANS, G. E., Cpl., 1st Middlesex Regiment.
He joined in February, 1916, and the same year went to France, taking part in engagements at Ypres, Bailleul and on the Somme, and was wounded in April, 1918.
He holds the General Service and Victory Medals, and was demobilised in August, 1919.
32, King's Road, Tottenham. X18555B.

EVANS, H. A., Pte., Royal Marines, H.M.S. "Ajax."
He volunteered in August, 1914, and served with his ship in the North Sea, being engaged in the battle of Jutland and at Zeebrugge, where he served with distinction.
He was demobilised in 1919, holding the 1914 Star, the General Service and Victory Medals.
82, Yeldham Road, Hammersmith, W.6 13279.

EVANS, J. H., Sapper, Royal Engineers.
He volunteered for service and joined for duty in February, 1916. He was on duty with his unit at various stations on important defence work with the searchlights. In 1918, however, he was admitted to hospital and was eventually discharged in April, 1919, being unfit for further service.
91, Birkbeck Road, Tottenham, N.17 18557B.

EVANS, K. (Miss), Special War Worker.
This lady rendered valuable services to the country during the war, being engaged at an important munition works in a responsible position as an inspector of cartridges. She performed her duties to great satisfaction.
27, Barret's Green Road, N.W.10 13559.

EVANS, L., Sapper, Royal Engineers.
He volunteered in 1915, served for three months in France, and in the same year was sent to Mesopotamia, where he was engaged on most important work in connection with bridge construction. While abroad he contracted malaria, from which he still suffers.
He was demobilised in 1919, holding the 1915 Star, General Service and Victory Medals.
59, Ilex Road, Willesden. 16361A.

EVANS, M. (Mrs.), Special War Worker.
This lady rendered valuable services during the war at a large munition factory Her work of examining fuses was of an arduous nature, and required much care and skill. She was commended for her services.
34, Ilex Road, Willesden. 16089C

EVANS, P. E., Cpl., King's Royal Rifle Corps.
He volunteered in August, 1914, and the following year was sent to the Western Front, where he took part with distinction in several engagements In 1917 he was invalided home and discharged on medical grounds unfit for further military service.
He holds the 1915 Star, General Service and Victory Medals.
91, Birkbeck Road, Tottenham. X15557A.

EVANS, R. W., Special War Worker.
During the whole period of the war he was engaged at Messrs. Beardmore's works at Glasgow on extremely important and technical work in connection with the sights for howitzers. He rendered valuable services.
21, Bertie Road, Willesden, N.W.10 X17399.

EVANS, S. T., Pte., Welch Regiment.
He volunteered in May, 1915, and was sent to the Western Front in that year. He took part in the battle of the Somme, was wounded, being sent home to hospital at Netley. On his recovery he was sent back to France and taken prisoner. He suffered many privations during his imprisonment in Germany, and was released at the Armistice. He was discharged in November, 1918, and holds the 1915 Star, General Service and Victory Medals.
35, Mozart Street, Queen's Park, W.10 X18837.

EVANS, W., Rifleman, 18th London Regt. (London Irish Rifles).
He volunteered in May, 1915, and served in France. At the battle of the Somme he was reported missing, and later, in September, 1916, to have been killed.
He was entitled to the General Service and Victory Medals.
77, Coomer Road, Fulham, S.W.6. 16445.

EVENETT, A. (D.C.M.), Cpl., Oxfordshire and Buckinghamshire Light Infantry.
He volunteered in 1914, and took part in the Dardanelles campaign. Later he served under General Townsend, was taken prisoner at Kut, and in 1916 died of starvation. He was awarded the D.C.M. for conspicuous bravery in the field, was entitled to the 1915 Star, General Service and Victory Medals.
10, Durham Road, Lower Edmonton, N.9 14868A.

EVENETT, W., Driver, Royal Field Artillery.
He volunteered for service in 1914, and was sent to Salonica in 1915, where he served until 1918. He was then transferred to the Western Front, where he saw much fighting. Here he remained until demobilised in 1919.
He holds the 1915 Star, General Service and Victory Medals.
172, Brettenham Road East, N.9 15225C.

EVENETT, W. H., Pte., Royal Fusiliers.
He volunteered in 1914, went to France in 1917, and took part in several battles with distinction. He was wounded, and holds the General Service and Victory Medals, being demobilised in 1919, after having rendered valuable services.
10, Durham Road, N.9 14868B.

EVERARD, C., Cpl., Royal Field Artillery.
He volunteered in September, 1914, served for a time on the Western Front, and later in Salonica, where he contracted malarial fever, and in consequence was invalided home. He holds the 1915 Star, General Service and Victory Medals, and was discharged, as a consequence of his service, unfit for further duties in February, 1919.
59, Garvan Road, Fulham. 14832B.

EVERARD, H., Gunner, Royal Field Artillery.
He volunteered in October, 1914, and served on both the Western and Eastern Fronts. Whilst in Salonica he contracted malarial fever, and was in hospital for some time. He was demobilised in May, 1919, holding the 1914-15 Star and the General Service and Victory Medals.
67, Garvan Road, Fulham, W.6 14831A.

EVERARD, J. W. (M.M.), Cpl., M.G.C.
He joined in February, 1916, and served on the Western Front until his demobilisation in October, 1919. During this period he took part in engagements at Ypres, Arras, Cambrai and the Somme.
He was awarded the Military Medal for conspicuous bravery in the field at Passchendaele, and also holds the General Service and Victory Medals.
67, Garvan Road, Fulham. 14831B.

EVERARD, T., Gunner, Royal Field Artillery.
He volunteered in April, 1915, and served on the Western
Front, taking part in the battles of Loos, the Somme, Arras,
Neuve Chapelle, Ypres and Cambrai. He afterwards went
with the Army of Occupation to Germany.
He was demobilised in March, 1919, and holds the 1914-15
Star, the General Service and Victory Medals.
59, Garvan Road, Fulham.   14833.

EVEREST, H., Pte., Royal Army Service Corps.
He joined in December, 1916, and was later drafted to the
Western Front, where he served in most important engage-
ments.
He was demobilised in February, 1920, holding the General
Service and Victory Medals.
31, Musard Road, W.6   15734B.

EVEREST, R. C., Rifleman, Rifle Brigade.
He joined in August, 1917, and shortly afterwards served on
the Western Front, where he took part in several engagements, and was eventually killed in action on November 6th,
1918.
He was entitled to the General Service and Victory Medals.
31, Musard Road, W.6   15734A.

EVERETT, A. E., Driver, Royal Field Artillery.
He volunteered in March, 1915, and was sent to the Western
Front in September of the same year. He took part in
many engagements, and was badly gassed, being eventually
discharged as unfit for further military service in June, 1917,
as a result.
He holds the 1915 Star, General Service and Victory Medals.
55, Shakespeare Avenue, Harlesden.   13883.

EVERETT, E. J. (Mrs.), Special War Worker.
During the war this lady was engaged on very heavy work
in the Royal Army Clothing Department at the White City,
packing clothes for our prisoners of war and for military
purposes. Her work was greatly appreciated.
9a, Guinness's Buildings, Hammersmith, W.6   14473B.

EVERETT, L., Acting Sergt., R.G.A.
He volunteered in November, 1915, and during his service
on the Western Front took part with distinction in the
fighting on the Somme, at Dixmude, Vimy Ridge, Messines,
Amiens and elsewhere.
He was demobilised in July, 1919, holding the General
Service and Victory Medals.
8, Osman Road, Edmonton.   16512.

EVERETT, R. E., Pte., Royal Marine Light Infty.
He volunteered in August, 1914, and served on H.M.S.
"Ceres." Whilst returning from Russia his ship was torpedoed and many lives were lost. He himself was very
severely wounded, but was fortunately picked up and brought
to safety.
He holds the 1914-15 Star, General Service and Victory
Medals, and was demobilised in April, 1919.
9a, Guinness's Buildings, Hammersmith, W.6   14473A.

EVERETT, W., Pte., R.A.S.C. (M.T.).
He volunteered in May, 1915, and saw service on the Western
Front, taking part in many engagements, including Arras,
the Somme, St. Quentin, Armentieres and the Advance of
1918. He was attached to the caterpillar tractors drawing
big guns.
He holds the General Service and Victory Medals, and was
demobilised in May, 1919.
53, Angel Road, Hammersmith.   12617.

EVERITT, H., Gunner, Royal Field Artillery.
He enlisted in 1913 was sent to France in August, 1914,
and took part in the battles of Mons, the Aisne, the Marne,
Ypres, Arras. the Somme and in the Retreat and Advance
of 1918. He also served at the Dardanelles, in Gallipoli
and in Egypt before being demobilised in October, 1919,
holding the Mons Star, General Service and Victory Medals.
4, Broadstairs, Roundwood Road, Willesden.   16518.

**EVERITT, H., Driver, 9th Battery Royal Field
Artillery (Ammunition Column).**
He was in the Army at the outbreak of hostilities, went to
France in August, 1914. and took part in the retreat from
Mons and the battles of the Marne, Ypres and Neuve Chapelle.
Later he served at the Dardanelles and in Egypt.
He was demobilised in November, 1919, holding the Mons
Star, General Service and Victory Medals.
28, Gresham Road, Neasden.   15739.

EVERITT, M. (Mrs.), Special War Worker.
This lady rendered war-work services of a most valuable and
arduous nature, being engaged in the manufacture of tents
at the White City during the whole of the war. Her
energy was untiring, and she was commended for her
patriotism.
411, High Road, Willesden Green.   T17341—17340A.

EVERITT, R., Rifleman, Rifle Brigade.
He joined in November, 1916, and was sent to France, where
he took part in several important engagements, including
the battle of Passchendaele. He was wounded very severely
in the face, and permanently injured. He was taken
prisoner in 1917, and suffered greatly in captivity.
He was discharged in December, 1918, and holds the Victory
and General Service Medals.
411, High Road, Willesden Green.   T17340—17341B.

EVERSON, T., Lce.-Cpl., 1st Middlesex Regt.
He volunteered in August, 1914, served on the Western
Front until 1919, and was demobilised in February of the
same year. He took part in the retreat from Mons, the
battles of the Somme, Ypres and Cambrai, where he was
wounded in 1918.
He holds the 1914 Star, General Service and Victory Medals.
3, Newlyn Road, Tottenham, N.17   X18517.

EVES, E. (Mrs.), Special War Worker.
Throughout the Great War this lady was employed at the
dangerous work of shell and bomb filling at the works of
Messrs. Blake, Fulham, and holds a certificate given her by
the firm in recognition of her valuable services and good
conduct. 19, Werley Avenue, Fulham.   X17735B.

EVES, J., Driver, Royal Field Artillery.
He volunteered in August 1914, and during his service on
the Western Front took part in the retreat from Mons and
the battles of Loos, Arras, Ypres and the Somme. After
being for some time in hospital in France suffering from shell-
shock, he was invalided home, and in 1919 was discharged
as medically unfit.
He holds the 1914 Star, the General Service and Victory
Medals. 19, Werley Avenue, Fulham, S.W.6   X17735A.

EWER, A. J., 2nd Lieut., 3rd Machine Gun Coy.
He volunteered in the Wiltshire Regiment in September,
1914, and went to France the following year. In 1917 he
obtained his commission in the M.G.C. for valuable
services, and took part with distinction in several engagements. He was gassed in May, 1918, invalided home, and
demobilised in April, 1919.
He holds the 1915 Star, General Service and Victory Medals.
165, Purves Road, Kensal Rise.   X18407.

EWER, F. S., Gunner, Royal Field Artillery.
He joined in March, 1916, served in France from December
of the same year, and took part in many engagements,
including those of Ypres and Cambrai.
He was demobilised in July, 1919, and holds the General
Service and Victory Medals.
27, St. John's Avenue, Harlesden, N.W.10   14746.

**EWER, H., Signaller, 13th King's Royal Rifle
Corps.**
He joined in April, 1918, as soon as he was of age for military
service, and in March of the following year was sent with
the Army of Occupation to Germany, where he served until
demobilised in February, 1920.
22, Ashmore Road, Maida Hill, W.9   X19466.

EWINGS, M. E. (Mrs.), Special War Worker.
For over four years this lady was engaged on valuable and
dangerous work, requiring much care and skill, at a large
munition factory. Her work, though arduous, was carried
out with untiring energy and zeal, and she was highly
commended.
19, Winchelsea Road, Harlesden.   13722B.

EWINGS, W. H., Gunner, Royal Field Artillery.
He volunteered in August, 1914, and served for five years
on the Western Front. He took part in the battles of Mons,
Arras, Cambrai, Vimy Ridge, the Somme and other engagements. He was wounded, and in December, 1918, died from
influenza.
He was entitled to the 1914 Star, General Service and
Victory Medals.
19, Winchelsea Road, Harlesden.   13722A.

EXCELL, C. W., Pte., Royal Defence Corps.
Having previously seen service in the South African campaign, he re-enlisted in October, 1914, and for a time was
engaged in guarding prisoners of war at various stations.
He was also in Ireland during the Sinn Fein risings, which
he took part in suppressing.
He holds the King's and Queen's South African Medals, and
was demobilised in January, 1919.
27, Portnall Road, Maida Hill, W.9   X19310.

EXWORTH, H., A.B., R.N., H.M.S. "Cardiff."
He had served in the Royal Navy for over six years when
war broke out, and afterwards did duty with the North Sea
and Dover Patrols, and took part in the engagement at
Heligoland.
He holds the 1914 Star, General Service and Victory Medals,
and was demobilised in November, 1919, after having
rendered very valuable services.
42, Charlton Road, Harlesden.   13113.

EYDMANN, S. C., Pte., R.A.M.C.

He rejoined in August, 1914, and whilst serving on the Western Front was blown up by an explosion at Ypres, as a result of which he was discharged in June, 1915, suffering from shell-shock. For four years and three months afterwards he was unable to speak.

He holds the Queen's South African Medal and Clasps, 1914-15 Star, General Service and Victory Medals.
31, Haldane Road, Fulham.   TX17075.

EYLES, J. H., Pte., 5th Middlesex Regiment.

He volunteered in August, 1914, served on the Western Front, and fought in the battles of the Somme, Arras, Loos, Neuve Chapelle, Armentieres, Amiens, Albert and the Advance of 1918, and was wounded three times. Later he served with the Army of Occupation in Germany.

He was demobilised in March, 1919, holding the 1914-15 Star, General Service and Victory Medals.
48, Averill Street, W.6   14179A.

EYLES, R. (Mrs.), Special War Worker.

During the war this lady was engaged on most important and arduous work at a National Filling Factory, making flares and cordite rings for shell charges. She carried out her duties in a patriotic manner, and was highly praised for her work.
48, Averill Street, W.6   14179B.

F

FACEY, E. H., Rifleman, King's Royal Rifle Corps.

He joined in May, 1917, and after a period of duty on transport work, was sent to France, where he gave very valuable services in various sectors of the line.

He was demobilised in October, 1919, and holds the General Service and Victory Medals.
22, Milton Avenue, Harlesden, N.W.10   15642.

FAGG, A., Pte., 6th Leicester Regiment.

He volunteered in February, 1915, and later was sent to the Western Front, where he took part in several engagements, and was finally killed in action at Cambrai in March, 1918.

He was entitled to the General Service and Victory Medals.
16, Montpelier Road, Hammersmith, W.6   13274B.

FAGG, W., Pte., 13th Middlesex Regiment.

He volunteered in August, 1914, and after a period of training, was sent to France, where he saw considerable fighting, being killed in action during the Somme offensive of 1916.

He was buried at Albert, and was entitled to the 1914-15 Star, General Service and Victory Medals.
16, Montpelier Road, Hammersmith, W.6   13265B.

FAIRBANK, W. R., A.B., Royal Navy.

He volunteered in August, 1915, and on H.M.S. "Cumberland" and other ships saw service in the North Sea, the Baltic and other waters, engaged on highly dangerous missions.

He holds the 1914-15 Star, the General Service and Victory Medals, and is now on board H.M.S. "Shamrock."
41, Fortune Gate Road, N.W.10   14734.

FAIRBRASS, J. W., Pte., 14th London Regt. (London Scottish).

He volunteered for service in December, 1915, having previously been in the Royal Navy, was sent to the Western Front in the following year, and took part in the fighting at Vimy Ridge. In the same year he served in Salonica on the Doiran Front until June, 1917, when he was sent to Egypt and Palestine, where he was in action at Beersheba, the Jordan and elsewhere. In June, 1918, he returned to France, took part in the last Advance of the Allies, and was wounded.

He was discharged as medically unfit for further service in March, 1919, after a serious illness, and holds the General Service and Victory Medals.
26, Farrant Street, Queen's Park, W.10   X19176.

FAIRHURST, A. W., Pte., 1st Middlesex Regt.

He volunteered in October, 1914, and was eventually sent to the Western Front, where he saw considerable fighting, and was killed in action on July 19th, 1915.

He was entitled to the 1914-15 Star, General Service and Victory Medals.
52, Cornwallis Grove, Edmonton.   13328.

FAIRHURST, H. G., Pte., 1st Middlesex Regt.

He volunteered in 1914, and was sent to France in the same year. During his overseas service, which lasted until 1919, he took part in many important engagements, including the retreat from Mons and the battles of Ypres and the Somme.

He was demobilised in 1919, and holds the Mons Star, General Service and Victory Medals.
1, Newlyn Road, Tottenham, N.17   X18504.

FAIRMAN, W. F., Pte., R.A.S.C.

He joined in 1916, and served on the Western Front, taking part in engagements at the Somme, Arras, Loos and the Advance of 1918, his duties being in connection with the transport of food and ammunition to the forward dumps.

He was demobilised in 1919, and holds the General Service and Victory Medals.
49, Averill Street, W.6   14176.

FAIRWEATHER, W. J., Driver, R.A.S.C.

He volunteered in November, 1915, served on the Eastern Front, at Gaza, Jaffa, Kantara and Jerusalem.

He was demobilised in April, 1919, holding the General Service and Victory Medals.
98, Milton Avenue, Harlesden.   14109.

FALCONER, G. F., Driver, R.A.S.C.

He volunteered in March, 1915, and the same year was sent to the Eastern Front, where he served at Salonica and elsewhere, rendering most important services.

He holds the 1915 Star, General Service and Victory Medals.
42, Chauncey Street, N.9   T14259A.

FALCONER, R., Cpl., The Black Watch.

He volunteered in May, 1915, served in India and Mesopotamia, and was present at the capture of Baghdad under General Maude. For bravery in that action he was recommended for a decoration by the Colonel of the regiment.

He was demobilised in July, 1919, and holds the General Service and Victory Medals.
42, Chauncey Street, Edmonton, N.9   T14259B.

FANE, A. J., 1st-Class Stoker, R.N., H.M.S. "Lion."

Having previously served in the Royal Navy, he joined for duty on the outbreak of war, and saw service at the Dardanelles and in the North Sea. He took part in the battle of Jutland and was wounded in action.

He was demobilised in December, 1919, and holds the 1914 Star, General Service and Victory Medals.
18, Chameleon Road, Tottenham, N.17   X18963.

FARLEY, W., Pte., 3rd Middlesex Regiment.

He was serving at the outbreak of war, and was sent to the Western Front in 1914, where he took part in several engagements, including the first and second battles of Ypres and the battle of Loos. While in France he was wounded in action, but later served in Egypt and also in Bulgaria, where he was in action during the big offensive, being finally sent to Constantinople.

He holds the 1914 Star, General Service and Victory Medals.
17, Hawthorn Road, Willesden, N.W.10   X17446.

FARMER, E. J., Rifleman, 6th Bn. The London Regt.

He volunteered in August, 1915, and in the following year was sent to France, where he took part in engagements at Loos, the Somme and Ypres and in other important battles. He received a severe bullet wound at the battle of Cambrai in November, 1918, and was demobilised in February, 1919.

He holds the General Service and Victory Medals.
4, Chester Road, Lower Edmonton, N.9   12712.

FARMER, M. (Mrs.), Special War Worker.

During the war this lady rendered valuable services at the White City in the making of Army equipment. She was employed in making gas masks and tent material. She carried out her duties in a painstaking and thorough manner, and received high commendation.
80, Third Avenue, Queen's Park, W.10   X19295B.

FARMER, R. L. N., Pte., 3rd London Regiment (Royal Fusiliers).

He was mobilised in August, 1914, and the same year was sent to Malta. While abroad he was taken seriously ill, invalided home, and discharged in 1915 as unfit for further military service.

He holds the 1914 Star, General Service and Victory Medals.
80, Third Avenue, Queen's Park, W.10   X19295A.

FARNSWORTH, G. A., Sapper, R.E.

He volunteered in June, 1915, and later went to the Western Front, where he was present during many engagements. He was killed in action in the Ypres salient on January 1st, 1917.

He was entitled to the General Service and Victory Medals.
65, Brettenham Road, Lower Edmonton.   15234B.

FARNSWORTH, W., Pte., 21st Middlesex Regt.

He volunteered in June, 1915, and during his service on the Western Front took part in many important engagements, and was three times wounded. Later he served with the Army of Occupation in Germany until his demobilisation in March, 1920.

He holds the General Service and Victory Medals.
65, Brettenham Road, Lower Edmonton.   15234A.

FARR, T. J., Special War Worker and Special Constabulary.

During the war he was employed on important work in connection with the construction of aircraft. He also volunteered as a special constable, and was on duty during all air raids. His work throughout was of a valuable and patriotic nature.

40, Sherbrooke Road, Fulham. X18770.

FARRANCE, C. E., Sergt., Royal Field Artillery.

He volunteered in August, 1914, and in the following June was sent to France. Here he took part in several engagements, including the battles of Ypres, Arras and the Somme. He was promoted sergeant as a result of consistent good work and attention to duty.

He was demobilised in March, 1919, holding the 1915 Star, General Service and Victory Medals.

110, St. Margaret's Road, Hanwell. 11058.

FARRELL, W., Rifleman, The Cameronians (Scottish Rifles).

He joined in April, 1917, and was engaged with his unit on important duties at various stations, where he rendered valuable services. He was discharged in June, 1918.

2a, William Street, White Hart Lane, Tottenham, N.17 X18297.

FARRER, A. B., Gunner, Royal Field Artillery.

He volunteered in March, 1915, and saw service the same year in France. He was later transferred to Salonica, and from there to Serbia and Egypt. In these parts he suffered severely from malaria, and was for a long period in hospital in consequence. In 1918 he again went to Salonica, and from there to Turkey and Bulgaria. He saw considerable fighting and was wounded. In 1919 he was finally discharged, suffering from ill-health and medically unfit for further service.

He holds the 1915 Star, General Service and Victory Medals.

18, Headcorn Road, Tottenham, N.17 X18487.

FARRINGTON, W., Lce.-Cpl., 3rd Royal Sussex Regiment.

He joined in 1917, and the same year saw much service in France, where in August, 1918, he was wounded. He later saw service in Egypt, and holds the General Service and Victory Medals.

152, Winchester Road, Lower Edmonton. 14779.

FARTHING, C. H., Pte., Machine Gun Corps.

He joined in January, 1915, and served at the Dardanelles, taking part in the landing at Suvla Bay and Cape Hellas. Later he went to France and took part in engagements in the Bethune sector, at Albert, Peronne, Delville Wood, Bourlon Wood, St. Eloi and Cambrai.

He was demobilised in February, 1920, holding the 1915 Star, General Service and Victory Medals.

6, Ravensworth Road, N.W.10 X17623.

FATHERS, F., Sergt., Royal Engineers.

He volunteered in September, 1914, and on completion of training was sent to Russia, where he saw service, enduring considerable hardships and suffering from the intense cold. He was demobilised in 1919, and holds the General Service and Victory Medals.

61, Steele Road, Harlesden, N.W.10 14145—14146C.

FATHERS, J. A., Pte., 17th Middlesex Regiment.

He joined early in 1916, and the same year was sent to France. During the battle of the Somme he was killed in action, and was entitled to the General Service and Victory Medals.

61, Steele Road, Harlesden. 14145—14146B.

FAULDER, R. A., 2nd Air Mechanic, R.A.F.

He joined in June, 1918, and was stationed with the R.A.F. at various important depots. His duties required a high degree of technical skill.

He was eventually discharged, suffering from ill-health, in 1919.

99, Rucklidge Avenue, Harlesden. 13151.

FAULKNER, J. H., Pte., Durham Light Infty.

He joined in June, 1916, went to the Western Front, and was wounded in action on the Somme in 1917. He took part in the Retreat and Advance of 1918, later serving with the Army of Occupation in Germany.

He holds the General Service and Victory Medals, and was demobilised in March, 1920.

4, Abbotsbury, Ambleside Road, N.W.10 16135.

FAULKNER, S. J. T., Driver, R.F.A.

He enlisted in March, 1915, and served on the Western and Eastern Fronts from May of the same year until June, 1919, when he was demobilised. He took part in the fighting at Ypres, and also on the Doiran Front, being wounded on one occasion. He also contracted malaria.

Holds the 1914-15 Star, General Service and Victory Medals.

8, Albert Terrace, Milton Avenue, N.W.10 14110.

FAWCETT, E. W., Sergt., Royal Engineers.

He volunteered in March, 1915, and from June of the following year until May, 1919, when he was demobilised, served at Salonica. He was attached to the Railway Troops, and for a considerable time was employed as clerk at Divisional H.Q.

He was mentioned in despatches for excellent work, and holds the General Service and Victory Medals.

23, Mordaunt Road, Harlesden, N.W.10 14120.

FEAKINS, P. J., Pte., Durham Light Infantry.

He volunteered in November, 1915, and was stationed with his unit at various stations. He was employed on important duties during the whole of his service.

He was demobilised in October, 1919.

149, Croyland Road, N.9 13927.

FEAR, A. E., Pte., Middlesex Regiment.

He volunteered in November, 1915, and the following year was sent to France, where he took part in the severe fighting on the Somme, being killed in action there on September 16th, 1916.

He was entitled to the General Service and Victory Medals.

159, Bulwer Road, Edmonton, N.18 X17194.

FEAREY, G. H., Pte., 8th Black Watch.

He volunteered in 1914, and was sent to France in the same year. He took part in several engagements, and was killed in action on October 12th, 1917.

He was entitled to the 1914 Star, General Service and Victory Medals.

180, Brettenham Road East, Edmonton, N.18 15221.

FEAST, G., Driver, Royal Field Artillery.

He volunteered in July, 1915, served in Egypt from January of the following year until 1919, and was wounded twice. He took part in many important engagements, and was demobilised in July, 1919.

He holds the General Service and Victory Medals.

183, Winchester Road, Lower Edmonton. 15199.

FEATHERS, W. N., Sapper, Royal Engineers.

He joined in May, 1916, and during his service in France was engaged with the searchlights, took part in the battles of Ypres and Cambrai, and was for some time in hospital at Rouen, suffering from fever.

He holds the General Service and Victory Medals, and was demobilised in September, 1919.

121, Claxton Grove, Fulham, W.6 13809.

FEAVER, E., Pte., 14th London Regiment (London Scottish).

He joined in November, 1916, and was later sent to the Western Front, where he took part in several engagements and was wounded.

He was discharged in October, 1918, and holds the General Service and Victory Medals.

40, Chaldon Road, Fulham, S.W.6 X17725.

FELIX, W. A. (sen.), 1st Air Mechanic, R.A.F.

He joined in April, 1918, and later saw service on the Western Front, being stationed in many places with the R.A.F. on important duties.

He was demobilised in 1919, and holds the General Service and Victory Medals.

68, Humbolt Road, Fulham, S.W.6 T15771B.

FELIX, W. A. (jun.), Pte., Bedfordshire Regt.

He joined in January, 1917, and after a period of training, was sent to the Western Front, where he took part in the second battle of the Somme, and was killed in his first action at Albert on April 14th, 1918.

He was entitled to the General Service and Victory Medals.

68, Humbolt Road, Fulham, S.W.6 T15771A.

FELL, F. H., Pte., Royal Fusiliers.

He volunteered in December, 1915, and went to the Western Front in the following year. He took part in the severe fighting near Ypres and in the battle of the Somme, where he was killed in action in 1916.

He was entitled to the General Service and Victory Medals.

92, Portnall Road, Maida Hill, W.9 X19540A.

FELSTEAD, F., Pte., Middlesex Regiment.

He joined in May, 1916, saw service in France and Belgium, and was a prisoner of war in Germany for 17 months. During this time he endured many hardships.

He was demobilised in October, 1919, and holds the General Service and Victory Medals.

78, Durant Road, Ponders End. 10923.

FELTS, C. E., Driver, Royal Army Service Corps.

He volunteered in August, 1914, and was sent to the Western Front the same year, where he saw considerable service and was present during many engagements on all sectors. Four times he was wounded, and finally discharged as a result in August, 1918.

He holds the Mons Star, General Service and Victory Medals.

3, Elric Street, Hammersmith. 15862.

FENNELL, J. W., Driver, Welsh Mule Transport Corps.
He volunteered in April, 1915, and later was sent to the Western Front, where he saw considerable service in many sectors.
He holds the General Service and Victory Medals, and was demobilised in January, 1919.
68, Adeney Road, Fulham. 14665A.

FENNELL, R. J., Rifleman, The Rifle Brigade.
He joined in October, 1918, and was stationed with his unit at various places, during which time he carried out many important duties.
He was demobilised in November, 1919.
17, Werley Avenue, Fulham. X17736.

FENNELL, S. W., Gunner, Royal Field Artillery.
He volunteered in January, 1915, served in France from the following September until he was demobilised in May, 1919.
He took part in the battles of Loos, the Somme, Arras, Neuve Chapelle, Bullecourt and Cambrai. He was wounded, and holds the 1915 Star, General Service and Victory Medals.
34, Wendover Road, Harlesden. 12957.

FENNELL, W., Pte., Royal Army Service Corps.
He volunteered in April, 1915, was drafted to the Western Front and took part in all the operations in that theatre during the next three years.
He was eventually demobilised in February, 1919, and holds the 1915 Star, General Service and Victory Medals.
68, Adeney Road, Fulham. 14665B.

FENNEMORE, A. E., Gunner, R.G.A.
He joined in March, 1916, and the same year saw service in France, where he took part in the fighting on the Somme.
He later was sent to Turkey, where he remained until October, 1919, being demobilised the following month.
He holds the General Service and Victory Medals.
83, Macfarlane Road, Shepherd's Bush, W.12 10798B.

FENNEMORE, A. L., 2nd Air Mechanic, 23rd Kite Balloon Section, Royal Air Force.
He joined in April, 1918, and later was sent to the Western Front, where he served on important observation duties with the Balloon Section. After the Armistice he went with the Army of Occupation into Germany, being finally demobilised in August, 1919.
He holds the General Service and Victory Medals.
83, Macfarlane Road, Shepherd's Bush, W.12 10798C.

FENNEMORE, R., Sapper, Royal Engineers.
He volunteered in May, 1915, and during his four years' service in France took part in engagements at Arras, the Somme and at Ypres, and in the Retreat and Advance of 1918.
He holds the 1915 Star, General Service and Victory Medals, and was demobilised in August, 1919.
83, Birkbeck Road, Tottenham. X18556.

FENNEMORE, W. J., Gunner, R.G.A.
He volunteered in May, 1915, and on completion of training was sent to the Western Front. During the severe fighting in the Ypres sector he was badly wounded, and afterwards invalided home. He later served with the anti-aircraft guns until he was demobilised in 1918.
He holds the General Service and Victory Medals.
24, Framfield Road, Hanwell, W.7. 10798A.

FENNEYMORE, H., Pte., Middlesex Regiment.
He volunteered in March, 1915, went to France the same year, took part in several battles, including those of the Somme and Arras, and was wounded twice.
He was demobilised in March, 1919, entitled to the 1915 Star, General Service and Victory Medals.
18, Felixstowe Road, Edmonton. 15280.

FEREADY, C. V., Gunner, R.H.A.
He volunteered in October, 1914, and was sent to France in May, 1915. He served in numerous sectors during his three years' service in France, and was wounded in action at the battle of the Ancre.
He was discharged in June, 1918, and holds the 1915 Star, General Service and Victory Medals.
27, Bertie Road, Willesden Green, N.W. X17400.

FERGUSON, G., Pte., 7th Gloucestershire Regt.
He volunteered in September, 1914, and was sent to the Western Front, where he remained for a year, taking part in several engagements. Later he was drafted to Mesopotamia, where he contracted malaria.
He holds the 1915 Star, General Service and Victory Medals, and was demobilised in May, 1919.
417, High Road, Willesden. T17339A.

FERGUSON, G., Pte., 5th King's Own Shropshire Light Infantry.
He joined in March, 1916, and served on the Western Front, taking part in the battles of the Somme and Ypres. While in action on the Somme, he was wounded in September, 1916, and in December, 1917, was invalided home with trench fever.
He was demobilised in February, 1919, and holds the General Service and Victory Medals.
36, Bridge Avenue, Hammersmith, W.6 15033.

FERN, S. T., Pte., 1st East Surrey Regiment.
He volunteered in August, 1914, served in France, where he was wounded in action at Mons in 1914, and afterwards took part in many engagements on the French Front.
He holds the 1914-15 Star, General Service and Victory Medals, and was demobilised in 1919.
5, St. Alban's Terrace, Fulham, S.W.6 14817.

FEVER, H., Rifleman, 4th Rifle Brigade.
He volunteered in 1914, went to France in the same year, and took part in the battles of Ypres and Loos. In 1916 he went to Salonica, where he took part in several engagements and contracted malaria.
He was demobilised in 1919, holding the 1914 Star, General Service and Victory Medals.
26, Furness Road, Harlesden, N.W.10 13166B.

FEVER, J., Mechanic, R.A.F. (late R.N.A.S.).
He volunteered in December, 1914, was sent to France in the following year, where he rendered important duties. He lost the drum of his ear as the result of a bombing raid on Dunkirk.
He was demobilised in April, 1919, holding the 1915 Star, General Service and Victory Medals.
26, Furness Road, Harlesden. 13166A.

FEVER, W., Rifleman, 3rd Rifle Brigade.
He volunteered in August, 1914, went to France the same year, and took part in the retreat of Mons, battles of Ypres, Loos and Arras. He was killed in action on the Somme in August, 1916.
He was entitled to the Mons Star and General Service and Victory Medals.
26, Furness Road, Harlesden. 13166C.

FEWSTER, C. R., Sergt., R.A.S.C. (M.T.).
He volunteered in September, 1914, and served throughout the war on the Western Front, during which time he rendered valuable and responsible duties.
He was demobilised in April, 1919, holding the 1915 Star, the General Service and Victory Medals.
49, Pellant Road, Fulham, S.W.6 X17871.

FICE, P. A., Pte., 1/9th Middlesex Regt.
He volunteered in August, 1914, and was sent to India in October, 1914, where he did garrison duty until sent to Mesopotamia. Here he served until April, 1919, when he was demobilised.
He holds the General Service and Victory Medals.
21, Shakespeare Avenue, Harlesden. 13881A.

FICE, S. T., Rifleman, 17th London Regiment (Poplar and Stepney Rifles).
He volunteered in June, 1915, and went to France in August of the following year. On October 1st, 1916, he was reported missing, and later killed, in his 19th year.
He was entitled to the General Service and Victory Medals.
21, Shakespeare Avenue, Harlesden, N.W.10 13881B.

FIELD, A., Stoker, R.N., H.M.S. " Lilac " and " Diligence."
He volunteered in 1915, and served on board H.M.S. "Lilac" on mine-laying duty until she was blown up. He was then transferred to the repair ship " Diligence," and saw further service of a very dangerous character in many waters.
He was demobilised in 1920, holding the 1915 Star, General Service and Victory Medals.
37, Ilex Road, Willesden, N.W.10 16353A.

FIELD, B., Sergt., Royal Engineers.
He enlisted in the Regular Army in 1913, and at the outbreak of war was sent to France, where he fought in the retreat from Mons. While in action at the battle of the Somme he was killed on July 20th, 1916, and was buried near Albert.
He was entitled to the Mons Star, the General Service and Victory Medals.
100, Carlyle Avenue, N.W.10 14454.

FIELD, F., R.E. and Oxford and Bucks L.I.
He volunteered in 1915, and was stationed with his regiment at various places whilst carrying out important duties. He was later sent to Egypt, and there saw much service.
He was demobilised in 1920, holding the General Service and Victory Medals.
37, Ilex Road, Willesden. 16353C.

FIELD, H. P., Pte., 3rd Bedfordshire Regiment.
He joined in 1916, and was employed on duties of great importance with his unit for three years at various stations. He was at the time declared medically unfit, and secured his discharge in 1919.
37, Ilex Road, Willesden.   16353B.

FIELD, J., Q.M.S., 1st Middlesex Regiment.
He volunteered in August, 1914, served with distinction on the Western Front until 1919, taking part in the battles of Mons, Ypres and the Somme, and was wounded whilst in action.
In May, 1919, he was demobilised, holding the 1914 Star, General Service and Victory Medals.
3, Raynham Road, Edmonton.   15996.

FIELD, R. W., Gunner, Royal Garrison Artillery.
He joined in July, 1917, and was sent to France, where he took part in the battles of the Somme. After the Armistice he was sent to Germany with the Army of Occupation, where he remained until demobilised in October, 1919.
He holds the General Service and Victory Medals.
33, Love Lane, Tottenham.   X18377.

FIELDER, A. H., Cpl., R.A.S.C.
He joined in January, 1917, went to France the same year, and was engaged on special and responsible duties. He was demobilised in October, 1919, holding the General Service and Victory Medals.
8, West Ella Road, N.W.10   15108.

FIELDING, A. W., Bombardier, R.G.A.
He volunteered in 1914, and served on the Western Front, taking part in the battles of the Somme, Ypres, Arras and La Bassée, during which time he was twice wounded. He is still serving with the Forces, and holds the 1915 Star, the General Service and Victory Medals.
15, Winchester Road, Lower Edmonton.   14680.

FINBOW, A. E., C.Q.M.S., 16th London Regiment (Queen's Westminster Rifles).
He volunteered in 1914, and in the same year was sent to France, where he remained until 1919. While abroad he took part in engagements at Loos, Arras, the Somme and Ypres.
He holds the 1914 Star, General Service and Victory Medals, and was demobilised in 1919.
58, St. Paul's Road, Tottenham, N.17   X18825.

FINBOW, H. G., Pte., 6th Suffolk Regiment.
He volunteered for duty in September, 1914, and after receiving training at Skegness, was drafted to the Western Front, where he was engaged on special guard duties. He saw fighting on the Somme, at Albert, Amiens and other engagements in the Great Retreat and Advance of 1918. He holds the General Service and Victory Medals, and was demobilised in April, 1919.
241, Portnall Road, Maida Hill, W.9   X19829.

FINCH, C., Sapper, Royal Engineers.
He joined in June, 1917, and served for a considerable time in Egypt, where he rendered valuable service with the R.E. He was demobilised in 1920, holding the General Service and Victory Medals.
28, Waterloo Street, Hammersmith, W.6   12585.

FINCH, E. W., Pte., Essex Regiment.
He volunteered in 1915, and served in the Dardanelles and Egypt. He was killed in action at Gaza on March 27th, 1917.
He was entitled to the 1915 Star, General Service and Victory Medals.
10, Town Road, Lower Edmonton, N.9   13564B.

FINCH, F., Pte., Bedfordshire Regiment and Suffolk Regiment.
He joined in June, 1918, and was retained for important duties at various Anti-Aircraft Stations. He secured his demobilisation in January, 1919.
41, Leamore Street, W.6   12583.

FINCH, R. F., Cpl., Royal Field Artillery.
He volunteered in October, 1914, and was sent to France the same year, where he fought in many engagements until he was wounded at Arras in March, 1918. He was finally demobilised in July, 1919. He holds the 1914-15 Star, General Service and Victory Medals.
53, Oxford Road, N.9   12966B.

FINCH, R. T., Cpl., Royal Engineers.
He volunteered in June, 1915, and was sent to France in the same year, where he remained until 1919. During this time he was employed on many important and responsible duties.
He was demobilised in May, 1919, and holds the 1915 Star, General Service and Victory Medals.
53, Oxford Road, N.9   12966A.

FINDON, T., Battery Sergt. Major, R.F.A
He volunteered in August, 1914, and was sent to the Eastern Front in June, 1915, serving in Egypt, Serbia, Bulgaria, Roumania and Salonica.
He was mentioned in despatches for devotion to duty, and holds the 1915 Star, General Service and Victory Medals, being demobilised in June, 1919.
67, Willow Vale, Shepherd's Bush, W.12   11918.

FINN, F. T. (sen.), Staff-Sergt., Military Police.
Having previously completed 21 years' service, he answered the call at the outbreak of war, and until he was demobilised in August, 1919, rendered valuable services in many places on the staff of the Provost-Marshal.
During his military career he served in the South African Campaign, the medals for which he holds.
159a, Kilburn Lane, Willesden.   X18568A.

FINN, F. T. (jun.), Rifleman, King's Royal Rifle Corps.
He volunteered in February, 1918, being then 18 years of age, and went for training to Northampton and Colchester. He afterwards served at various stations until his demobilisation in February, 1920, having rendered good service for the country.
159a, Kilburn Lane, Willesden.   X18568B.

FINNERTY, L. F. (Mrs.), Special War Worker.
During the war this lady was engaged at the White City on special work in connection with the making of munitions. Her services were of a most valuable nature, and she was commended for her work.
34, Ancill Street, W.6   13987D.

FINNERTY, W. A., Driver, R.F.A.
He joined in October, 1916, and later served on the Eastern Front and in India. He was with the Forces of General Allenby in Palestine, taking part in the capture of Jericho and Jerusalem and in other engagements during the offensive of 1918 in that theatre.
He holds the General Service and Victory Medals, and was demobilised in 1919.
34, Ancill Street, W.6   13987C.

FINUCANE, H. T., Cpl., 3rd (K.O.) Hussars.
He volunteered in March, 1915, and later served on the Eastern Front in Egypt and Palestine, taking part in the capture of Jericho and the entry into Jerusalem with General Allenby.
He was demobilised in February, 1919, and holds the General Service and Victory Medals.
11, Humbolt Road, Fulham.   15309.

FIRMAN, S. H., Driver, R.A.S.C.
He volunteered in 1915, and the following year served on the Western Front, taking part in many operations, including the battle of the Somme and the third battle of Ypres in 1917, later serving with the Army of Occupation in Germany.
He was demobilised in 1919, and holds the General Service and Victory Medals.
5, Sebastopol Road, Lower Edmonton.   14548B.

FISH, A. R., Sergt., Royal Fusiliers.
He volunteered in September, 1914, and shortly after was sent to the Western Front, where he took part in numerous engagements, including the battle of the Somme. He was wounded and afterwards transferred to the Chinese Labour Corps. For consistent good work and devotion to duty he gained rapid promotion to the rank of sergeant, being finally demobilised in June, 1919, holding the 1914-15 Star, General Service and Victory Medals.
54, St. Margaret's Road, Hanwell.   11055A.

FISH, J., Pte., Royal Fusiliers.
He volunteered in September, 1914, and the following year was sent to Egypt, where he remained until 1916, in which year he was sent to France. He there took part in several engagements, and was killed in action at the battle of the Somme on July 1st, 1916.
He was entitled to the 1914-15 Star, General Service and Victory Medals.
54, St. Margaret's Road, Hanwell.   11055B.

FISH, W., Pte., Royal Army Medical Corps.
He volunteered in November, 1915, and shortly afterwards was sent to France, where he took part in several engagements, afterwards being drafted to Salonica, where he was again in heavy fighting. and died of wounds received in action on May 24th, 1917.
He was entitled to the General Service and Victory Medals.
54, St. Margaret's Road, Hanwell.   11055C.

FISHER, D., Cpl., R.A.S.C. (M.T.).
He volunteered in 1914, and during his service on the Western Front was actively employed during the engagements on the Somme and at Loos, Armentieres, Neuve Chapelle, Ypres, St. Quentin and the final Advance of 1918.
He was demobilised in 1919, holding the 1915 Star, General Service and Victory Medals.
8, Humbolt Mansions, Lillie Road, Fulham. X18869C.

FISHER, E. M. (Mrs.), Special War Worker.
During the war this lady was engaged on very dangerous work at Messrs. Blake's Munition Factory, Fulham, shell-filling and making hand-grenades. Her services were of a most valuable nature, and she was specially commended.
13, Humbolt Road, Fulham. 15301B.

FISHER, F., Driver, Royal Army Service Corps.
He joined in June, 1918, and was engaged on important duties with the R.A.S.C. at various stations.
He secured his demobilisation in March, 1920, after having rendered valuable services.
87, Woodheyes Road, N.W.10 15459B.

FISHER, G. H. A., Rifleman, Rifle Brigade.
He volunteered in August, 1914, and the following year saw service on the Western Front, where he took part in many engagements, and was wounded in the fighting at Ypres. During 1916 he was again in action, and was seriously wounded at Mailly-Mailly in July, as a result of which he was discharged on account of wounds in April, 1918.
He holds the 1914–15 Star, General Service and Victory Medals.
102, Burn's Road, Harlesden. 13137B.

FISHER, H., 3rd Air Mechanic, R.A.F.
He joined in October, 1916, and served with the R.A.F. on important and valuable duties until February, 1917, when he was discharged unfit for further service, through illness contracted whilst in the Service.
42, Gloucester Road, Edmonton. X17007.

FISHER, J., Rifleman, 2/6th London Regiment.
He joined in November, 1917, and was sent to the Western Front, where he served in various sectors. He was reported missing after the fighting at Bullecourt in May, 1918, since when no further news of him has been received.
He was entitled to the General Service and Victory Medals.
1, Jervis Road, Fulham. X17665B.

FISHER, J. H., Pte., 3rd Hampshire Regiment.
He joined in May, 1918, and was sent to France the same year, taking part in the Advance of 1918. After the Armistice he was stationed in France until his demobilisation in January, 1919.
He holds the General Service and Victory Medals.
87, Woodheyes Road, Willesden. 15459C.

FISHER, W., Lce.-Cpl., R.A.S.C.
He volunteered in August, 1915, and was sent to France in September of the same year. Here he saw service until, as a result of an accident, he was rendered unfit for further military duty.
He was discharged in 1916 in consequence, and holds the 1915 Star, General Service and Victory Medals.
45, Denzil Road, Neasden. 15930.

FISHER, W., Pte., 4th Royal Fusiliers.
He was mobilised in August, 1914, having previously served in the Army, and was first sent to India and then transferred to France, where he saw considerable fighting, being later drafted to Salonica.
He holds the 1914–15 Star, General Service and Victory Medals.
8, Laurel Terrace, Tottenham, N.17 X18964.

FISHER, W., Pte., Honourable Artillery Coy.
He joined in 1916, and was sent to France, taking part in many engagements, including Ypres, where he was wounded. Later he fought in the Retreat and Advance of 1918, and was demobilised in 1919.
He holds the General Service and Victory Medals.
33, Letchford Gardens, Willesden. X17543B.

FISHER, W. F., Driver, Royal Field Artillery.
He joined in 1917, and during his service on the Western Front took part in many engagements, including those of Bapaume, the Somme, Havrincourt Wood and Cambrai. In June, 1918, he was invalided home, suffering from pneumonia and shell shock, and was demobilised in the following year.
He holds the General Service and Victory Medals.
12, Humbolt Road, Fulham. 15301A.

FISHLOCK, W. R., Pte., R.A.M.C.
He volunteered in June, 1915, served in Egypt during the same year, and in 1916 was sent to the Western Front, where he acted as stretcher-bearer. He was present at the fighting at Ypres and the Somme (where he was wounded), and in the 1918 Retreat and Advance, being again wounded. In January, 1919, he was demobilised, holding the 1915 Star, General Service and Victory Medals.
84, Portnall Road, Maida Hill, W.9 X19542A.

FITCH, A. J., Gunner, Royal Garrison Artillery.
He volunteered in November, 1915, and served until 1917 in France. Here he took part in many important engagements, including those at the Somme, Ypres and Albert. He was twice wounded, and was killed in action on November 3rd, 1917.
He was entitled to the 1915 Star, General Service and Victory Medals.
9, Denmark Street, Tottenham. X18796A.

FITCH, E. W., Pte., Royal Fusiliers and M.G.C.
He volunteered in January, 1916, served on the Western Front from the following December until May, 1917, and from June until September, 1918, and took part in the engagements at Ypres, the Somme, Vimy Ridge and Arras, where he was wounded in May, 1917.
He was demobilised in January, 1919, holding the General Service and Victory Medals.
50, Hawthorn Road, Willesden. X17421.

FITCH, W. J., Pte., Suffolk Regiment.
He joined in 1916, and served in Salonica the same year, where he remained until he was demobilised in 1919. He took part in all operations on this Front and contracted malaria while on service.
He holds the General Service and Victory Medals.
9, Denmark Street, N.17 X18796C.

FITZGERALD, A., C.Q.M.S., The Queen's (Royal West Surrey Regt.)
He volunteered in December, 1915, and was sent to France, where he saw much service and was wounded. He later served with the Army of Occupation in Germany.
He holds the General Service and Victory Medals, and was demobilised in April, 1920.
8, St. Thomas's Road, Fulham, S.W.6 X17232.

FITZGERALD, J., Pte., Royal Fusiliers.
He volunteered in May, 1915, and served on the Western Front in the same year, taking part in many operations on various sectors.
He holds the 1914–15 Star, General Service and Victory Medals.
67, Musard Road, Fulham. X15330.

FITZGERALD, J. P., Sergt., R.F.A.
He volunteered in 1914 and was sent to France in the following year, and was attached to the 86th Brigade R.F.A. He took part in many engagements, including those of Loos, the Somme, Ancre, Arras, Messines, Passchendaele and Le Cateau.
He holds the 1915 Star, General Service and Victory Medals, and was demobilised in March, 1919.
69, Ancill Street, W.6 14000.

FITZGIBBON, J., Cpl., Royal Field Artillery.
He volunteered in August, 1914, went to France the same year, and took part with distinction in the battles of Mons, Loos and other engagements, and was wounded.
He was discharged in 1916 unfit for further service, and holds the 1914 Star, General Service and Victory Medals.
27, Alexandra Road, West Kensington. 12090A.

FITZHUGH, A., Bombardier, R.F.A.
He volunteered in April, 1915, and during his service on the Western Front took part in the fighting at Arras, Loos, Ypres and the Somme, and was twice wounded.
He was demobilised in February, 1919, and holds the General Service and Victory Medals.
3, Kennet Road, Maida Hill, W.9 X19392.

FLANAGAN, H., Sergt., R.A.S.C.
He joined in 1916, and for the whole period of his service held a responsible position, and was in charge of large ration stores in important camps on the Western Front.
He holds the General Service and Victory Medals, and was demobilised in April, 1919.
39, Sherbrooke Road, Fulham, S.W.6 X18474.

FLATT, G. (M.M.), Pte., 1st Middlesex Regt.
He volunteered in August, 1914, and during his five years' service in France was twice wounded and gassed, and also suffered from shell shock.
He was awarded the Military Medal for conspicuous bravery and devotion to duty, holds the 1914 Star, General Service and Victory Medals, and was demobilised in March, 1919.
130, Montague Road, Edmonton. 15846.

FLATT, G. H., Sapper, Royal Engineers.
He joined in June, 1918, and after his training was retained with the Royal Engineers, performing very important duties at various stations until he was demobilised in December, 1918.
10, Bridport Road, Upper Edmonton, N.18 X17897A.

FLATT, H. J., Gunner, Royal Field Artillery.
He volunteered in September, 1915, and was sent the same year to France, where he took part in many engagements during 1916.
He was demobilised in February, 1920, and holds the 1915 Star, General Service and Victory Medals.
140, Church Road, Tottenham, N.17 X18137.

FLATT, H. J., Pte., 19th Middlesex Regiment.
He volunteered in September, 1914, and served for three years on the Western Front, where he took part in the fighting at Ypres, Albert, the Somme, Fricourt, Delville Wood and High Wood.
He was demobilised in January, 1919, holding the General Service and Victory Medals.
121, Durban Road, Tottenham, N.17 X17960.

FLATT, T. F., Gunner, Royal Field Artillery.
He was in the Police Force prior to his enlistment in May, 1917, and on the completion of his training was sent to France, where he took part in the battle of Cambrai in 1918. He was wounded and gassed, and later was transferred for duties with the Military Mounted Police.
In November, 1919, he was demobilised, holding the General Service and Victory Medals.
14, Bridport Road, Upper Edmonton, N.18 X17582A.

FLAVILL, H. (M.M.), Sergt., Welch Regiment.
He volunteered in August, 1914, and served for five years on the Western Front, taking part in the fighting at Mons, the Somme, Ypres and Arras. He was twice wounded and gassed, and after being in hospital for some months was demobilised in September, 1919.
He was awarded the Military Medal for conspicuous gallantry and devotion to duty in the field, and also holds the 1914 Star, the General Service and Victory Medals.
70, Durban Road, Tottenham, N.17 X17951.

FLEMING, A., Pte., Somerset Light Infantry.
He volunteered in February, 1915, and served on the Western Front. While in action near Elverdinghe he was killed on June 15th, 1915.
He was entitled to the 1915 Star, General Service and Victory Medals.
37, Hartington Road, Lower Edmonton, N.9 13917A.

FLEMING, A. E. V., Pte., 13th London Regt. (Kensington).
He joined in January, 1916, and served with distinction on the Western Front, taking part in many important engagements.
He was demobilised in February, 1919, holding the General Service and Victory Medals.
27, Kinnoul Road, Hammersmith, W.6 14458.

FLEMING, A., Lce.-Cpl., R.E., 222nd Field Coy.
He volunteered in May, 1915, and served with distinction on the Western Front for over a year.
He was discharged in June, 1917, holding the 1915 Star and the General Service and Victory Medals.
37, Hartington Road, Lower Edmonton, N.9 13917C.

FLEMING, R., Pte., Somerset Light Infantry.
He volunteered in February, 1915, and shortly after was sent to France, where he took part in several engagements. While fighting in the battle of the Somme in 1916, he sustained severe wounds, from which, on October 30th, he died. He was entitled to the 1915 Star and the General Service and Victory Medals.
37, Hartington Road, Lower Edmonton, N.9 13917B.

FLEMING, R., Pte., R.A.S.C. (M.T.)
He volunteered in October, 1914, and during his service, which lasted over four and a half years, was employed as a fitter. He served in France until his demobilisation in February, 1919, and holds the 1914 Star and the General Service and Victory Medals.
81, Minet Avenue, Willesden, N.W.10 13642A.

FLEMING, T. F., Pte., 754th Co. Labour Corps.
He joined in March, 1916, and was sent to France, where he rendered valuable services. He was taken prisoner on the Somme in March, 1917, and later released, and was demobilised in September, 1918, holding the General Service and Victory Medals.
81, Minet Avenue, Willesden, N.W.10 13642B.

FLETCHER, A. C., Pte., Lancashire Fusiliers.
He volunteered in June, 1915, and served for nearly four years on the Western Front, where he was in action on the Somme, and was wounded.
He was demobilised in November, 1919, holding the 1915 Star, General Service and Victory Medals.
124, Bounces Road, Lower Edmonton, N.9 13011.

FLETCHER, A. T., Pte., East Surrey Regiment.
He volunteered in September, 1915, and served on the Western Front, where he took part in engagements at Neuve Chapelle, Loos, Arras, Ypres, the Somme, Vimy Ridge and St. Quentin.
He holds the 1915 Star and the General Service and Victory Medals, and was discharged in September, 1918, on account of ill-health, due to his service.
23, Chesson Road, West Kensington, W.14 TX17066A.

FLETCHER, E. (Miss), Special War Worker.
During the war this lady was engaged on dangerous work in a large munition factory, where she was working in a T.N.T. powder room. Her work throughout was of a most valuable and patriotic nature.
23, Chesson Road, West Kensington, W.14 X16980B.

FLETCHER, E. K. (Miss), Special War Worker.
This lady immediately undertook work in a munition factory at the outbreak of war. Her duties were of a very arduous and dangerous nature, and she received praise for her energy and patriotism.
23, Chesson Road, West Kensington, W.14 X16980A.

FLETCHER, G., Sergt., King's Own Yorkshire Light Infantry.
He volunteered in May, 1915, and served on the Western Front, taking part with distinction in many engagements.
He was demobilised in February, 1919, and holds the General Service and Victory Medals.
6, Kimberley Road, Upper Edmonton, N.18 16455.

FLETCHER, G. H., Gunner, R.G.A.
He volunteered in 1914 and served on the Western Front, where he took part in many engagements, including the battles of Neuve Chapelle, the Somme, Loos, Ypres, St. Quentin and Cambrai.
In 1919 he was demobilised, holding the 1915 Star, General Service and Victory Medals.
23, Chesson Road, West Kensington, W.14 TX17059A

FLETCHER, J. H., Pte., Royal Fusiliers.
He volunteered at the outbreak of war in August, 1914, and was sent to the Western Front, where he took part in many engagements. He was killed in action in Belgium on January 20th, 1915, and was entitled to the General Service and Victory Medals.
23, Chesson Road, West Kensington, W.14 X16980D.

FLETCHER, J. W., Pte., R.A.S.C.
He volunteered in October, 1915, and was sent to East Africa, where he saw service until 1919. He was in action through the German East African Campaign, and suffered acutely from malaria.
He was demobilised in March, 1919, and holds the General Service, the Victory and East African War Medals.
20, Milton Avenue, Willesden, N.W.10 15639.

FLETCHER, R. E. E. (Mrs.), Special War Worker.
Throughout the war this lady was engaged at Messrs. Blake's Munition Factory, Shepherd's Bush, where she held an important and responsible position, and was employed on work of a very dangerous nature in the T.N.T. room. Her valuable services were highly commended.
23, Chesson Road, West Kensington, W.14 TX17066B.

FLETCHER, S., Special War Worker.
He was employed from 1915 until 1918 on heavy and continuous work at a Government contractor's at Wembley, breaking in Army horses. This work required much skill and patience, and was of great value to the country.
15, Steele Road, Harlesden. 14368.

FLETCHER, S. M. (Miss), Special War Worker.
This lady worked on munitions for the duration of the war, and was first employed at Blake's Shell-filling Factory, Fulham, in the danger zone. While thus employed an explosion took place. Later she went to Hayes and was engaged in the T.N.T. powder-room. Her valuable services were highly commended.
23, Chesson Road, West Kensington, W.14 X16980C.

FLETCHER, W. (Mrs.), Special War Worker.
During the war this lady rendered valuable services in an important munition factory, and was also employed making parts for motor lorries, this being work which required much care and skill. She rendered valuable services, for which she was complimented.
23, Chesson Road, West Kensington. TX17059B.

FLETCHER, W., Sapper, Royal Engineers.
During his service, which lasted from 1918 till March, 1919, he was engaged on board vessels running to and from France.
He holds the General Service and Victory Medals. His duties were frequently of a very dangerous nature.
34, Shakespeare Avenue, Harlesden. 13611.

FLETCHER, W. F., Cpl., Herts Regiment and Royal Defence Corps.
He joined in 1916 and was stationed at many places of importance. Later, owing to being medically unfit for overseas Service, he was transferred to the Royal Defence Corps, where he rendered splendid service until he was discharged in 1919.
32, Archel Road, West Kensington, W.14 X16981.

FLINT, W. A., Stoker, R.N., M.S. " Erin's Isle."
He joined in November, 1916, served with H.M.S. "Adventure" at Gibraltar, and with the mine-sweeper " Erin's Isle " on dangerous work in the North Sea and elsewhere, before she was mined in the mouth of the Thames off Sheerness.
He was discharged in May, 1919, holding the General Service and Victory Medals.
35, Barry Road, N.W.10 14941.

FLOWER, A. E., Pte., 4th (Queen's Own) Hussars.
He volunteered in August, 1914, and during his service on the Western Front was in action at Loos, Vimy, Arras, Cambrai and on the Somme. He was severely wounded at Cambrai in November, 1917, and as a result was discharged in 1918, holding the 1914 Star, General Service and Victory Medals.
33, Garvan Road, Fulham, W.6 14646A.

FLOWERS, E. H., Gunner, Royal Field Artillery.
He volunteered in September, 1914, served on the Western Front, and took part in the battles of Loos, Arras, Ypres, the Somme and Cambrai, and later went to Germany with the Army of Occupation.
He was demobilised in May, 1919, holding the 1915 Star, General Service and Victory Medals.
33, Garvan Road, Fulham. 14646B.

FLOWERS, G. A., Cpl., Royal Field Artillery.
He volunteered in August, 1914, and served on the Western Front throughout the war. He was in action at Mons, on the Somme and at Ypres, where he was severely wounded in March, 1916, as a result of which he was in hospital for several months.
He was demobilised in April, 1919, and holds the 1914 Star, General Service and Victory Medals. He had previous to the war served two years with the Colours.
24, Garvan Road, Fulham, W.6 13442.

FLOWERS, J. E. (M.M. and Bar), Sapper, R.E.
He was serving at the outbreak of war, and in 1914 went to France, where he remained until 1919. He took part in engagements at Mons, the Aisne and the Great Retreat and Advance in 1918, and was with the Army of Occupation in Germany.
He was mentioned in despatches for gallantry in the field, and was awarded the Military Medal and bar for conspicuous bravery and devotion to duty under very heavy enemy fire. He also holds the 1914 Star, General Service and Victory Medals, and was demobilised in January 1919.
41, Ranelagh Road, Harlesden 12559

FLOYD, A. T., Cpl., 4th Middlesex Regiment.
He volunteered in September, 1914, and from December, 1914, served on the Western Front. He took part in the battles of Neuve Chapelle, Ypres, the Somme, Hill 60 and Bullecourt. While in action on the Somme he was killed in July, 1916, and buried near Fricourt.
He was entitled to the 1914 Star and the General Service and Victory Medals.
103, Villiers Road, Cricklewood, N.W.2 16147.

FLOYD, C. E., Cpl., Royal Engineers.
He volunteered in April, 1915, and served in France with the 172nd Tunnelling Company at the battles of the Somme, Arras, Ypres, Messines, Kemmel, St. Eloi, Vimy Ridge, Holnon, the Scarpe, Villers Bretonneux and Valenciennes, where his work was always of a dangerous nature.
He holds the 1915 Star, General Service and Victory Medals, and was demobilised in 1919.
70, Orbain Road, Fulham. X18232.

FLOYD, C. J., Boy (1st Class), R.N., H.M.S. " Glatton."
He joined in 1918 and saw service in the North Sea and English Channel. On September 16th, 1918, just before the " Glatton " was sailing out to bombard the German defences on the Belgian coast, an explosion occurred and he was badly injured, while many of his comrades were killed or drowned.
He was demobilised in 1919, and holds the General Service and Victory Medals.
70, Orbain Road, Fulham. X18231.

FLYNN, H., Sapper, Royal Engineers (I.W.T.).
He joined in March, 1917, and served on the Western Front from the same year until 1919. He was stationed at Dunkirk, Calais, St. Omer and elsewhere on the Front on important transportation duties.
He was demobilised in November, 1919, and holds the General Service and Victory Medals.
47, Denzil Road, N.W.10 16129.

FOGG, R. J., Pte., The Queen's (Royal West Surrey Regiment).
He joined in February, 1917, and was stationed with his unit at various places. During this time he was employed on important duties, but owing to his being medically unfit at the time, he was discharged in October, 1918.
5, Church Path, Hammersmith, W.6 15871.

FOLEY, M., Pte., 5th (Royal Irish) Lancers.
He was mobilised in 1914, and in the same year was sent to France, where he took part in the retreat from Mons and the battles of Ypres and the Somme. In 1916 he was, as a result of his service, discharged as unfit for further military duties, but later he volunteered, and was engaged at Woolwich Arsenal on important munition work.
He holds the 1914 Star, General Service and Victory Medals.
50, Third Avenue, Queen's Park, W.10 X19291A.

FOLEY, R. F. (Mrs.), Special War Worker.
For a considerable period this lady rendered valuable services as an examiner of shells in the Inspection Department of a large munition works. The work required care and skill, and her duties throughout were carried out in a thoroughly efficient and commendable manner.
50, Third Avenue, Queen's Park Estate, W.10 X19291B.

FOLKES, C., Sapper, Royal Engineers.
He volunteered in August, 1914, and in the same year was sent to France, where he remained until 1918. While abroad he took part in engagements at Mons and Ypres, and was killed in action in April, 1918.
He was entitled to the 1914 Star, General Service and Victory Medals.
34, Love Lane, Tottenham. 18387.

FONTANA, A., Interpreter and Steward, Mercantile Marine.
He volunteered in 1914, and was engaged on dangerous convoy work in the North Sea. He was subjected to much strain and many arduous duties during his services.
He is still serving, and holds the 1915 Star, the Mercantile Marine, General Service and Victory Medals.
419, High Road, Willesden. 16627B.

FOOKS, C., Gunner, Royal Garrison Artillery.
He volunteered in November, 1914, served on the Western Front from April, 1915, until November, 1917, and took part in the battles of Loos, Neuve Chapelle, Cambrai, the Somme, Arras and Ypres. He suffered greatly from chronic rheumatism and was discharged in March, 1918, holding the 1915 Star, General Service and Victory Medals.
23, Barry Road, Willesden. T14943.

FOOT, A. S., Rifleman, Rifle Brigade.
He volunteered in 1914 and was sent to France in January, 1915, where he served two years. He took part in several important engagements, including Loos, Arras, Cambrai, La Bassée and the Somme. During these campaigns he was severely wounded, and was sent home disabled and unfit for further military service.
He was discharged in April, 1917, and holds the 1915 Star, General Service and Victory Medals.
13, Napier Road, N.W.10 X17518A.

FOOT, K. (Mrs.), Special War Worker.
This lady was employed throughout the first part of the war as munition worker in an important munition factory. She was promoted for her valuable services. Later she became a conductress in the London Omnibus Company's service. She did splendid work throughout
13, Napier Road, N.W.10 X17518B.

FOOTE, E. J., Rifleman, 16th London Regiment (Queen's Westminster Rifles).
He joined in September, 1917, was sent to France in the following year, where he served with distinction. He was wounded at St. Quentin in April, 1918.
He was discharged unfit for further service in August, 1918, and holds the General Service and Victory Medals.
66, Drayton Road, Harlesden. 15074.

FORBES, J. H., Pte., 8th East Surrey Regiment.
He volunteered in August, 1914, and served on the Western Front, taking part in many engagements, and was twice wounded, losing a finger. He was also severely gassed, and was in hospital in France and Bristol.
He has served 13 years in the Army, and was demobilised in March, 1919, holding the 1915 Star, General Service and Victory Medals.
12, Werley Avenue, Fulham, S.W.6 X17877.

FORD, A. H., Cpl., London Rifle Brigade.

He volunteered in 1915, and in January, 1917, whilst on his way to Egypt on board the " Ivernia," the ship was torpedoed. During his service in the East he was stationed at the headquarters at Kantara, and was mentioned in despatches for his good work in June, 1918.

He was demobilised in July, 1919, and holds the General Service and Victory Medals.

12, Parkfield Road, Willesden, N.W.10   X17414.

FORD, A. W., Rifleman, King's Royal Rifle Corps.

He volunteered in November, 1915, and served with the King's Royal Rifle Corps on important duties at various stations until January, 1917, when he was discharged as physically unfit for further service.

18, Meyrick Road, Willesden, N.W.10   16350.

FORD, B., A.B., Royal Naval Division.

He joined in 1916, and served at sea and in France, where he was wounded by shell fire, and died on February 4th, 1917.

He was entitled to the General Service and Victory Medals.

33, Rylston Road, Fulham.   16182A.

FORD, C. J., Pte., R.A.S.C. (M.T.)

He volunteered in November, 1915, and served on the Western Front at Arras, Ypres, Cambrai and the Somme. He was chiefly engaged in conveying ammunition to the lines and transporting wounded.

He holds the 1915 Star and the General Service and Victory Medals, and was demobilised in February, 1919.

81, Bramber Road, W.14   15723A.

FORD, D. J., Sergt., 23rd Middlesex Regiment.

He volunteered in January, 1915, and while in France took part in the battles of the Somme, Ypres, Arras and many other engagements. In 1917 he was sent to Italy, and in March, 1919, was demobilised, holding the General Service and Victory Medals.

33, Rylston Road, Fulham.   16182B.

FORD, E. J., Driver, Royal Field Artillery.

He joined in May, 1916, and after a period of training, was drafted to India. During his two years' service there he was engaged with his unit on important garrison duties at various stations.

In November, 1919, he obtained his demobilisation, and holds the General Service and Victory Medals.

44, Greyhound Road, College Park, N.W.10   X17600C.

FORD, F. W., Sergt., 13th London Regiment (Kensington).

He volunteered in August, 1914, and served on the Western Front, where he took part in engagements at Loos, the Somme, Ypres and Cambrai. He was in hospital in France and England, suffering from frost-bite, and in March, 1919, was demobilised, holding the 1915 Star and the General Service and Victory Medals.

14, Wilson's Road, Hammersmith, W.6   16414.

FORD, F. W., Sergt., R.A.V.C.

He volunteered in August, 1914, and served on the Western Front for over four years, taking part in all operations during that period. His duties were in connection with the care and treatment of wounded horses.

He was demobilised in February, 1919, and holds the 1915 Star, General Service and Victory Medals.

3, Westbury Road, Willesden, N.W.10   15070.

FORD, G., Pte., Royal Army Service Corps.

He joined in November, 1916, and on the completion of his training was employed as butcher at an R.A.S.C. Depot. He was unsuccessful in his efforts to obtain a transfer overseas, owing to ill-health, and was demobilised in December, 1919.   51, Hiley Road, Willesden, N.W.10   X18234B.

FORD, G. F., Pte., 14th Middlesex Regiment.

He volunteered in November, 1915, and served in Salonica and Egypt. During his service abroad he contracted malaria, and was demobilised in March, 1919, holding the General Service and Victory Medals.

7, Chichester Road, Lower Edmonton, N.9   14986.

FORD, H., Lce.-Cpl., Middlesex Regiment.

He volunteered in 1914, and after his period of training was stationed for three years in Egypt and Malta, where he was engaged in important duties.

In 1920 he was demobilised, holding the 1915 Star and the General Service and Victory Medals.

3, Wimborne Road, Lower Edmonton, N.9   15208.

FORD, J., Driver, R.A.S.C. (M.T.)

He joined in February, 1916, and served on various sectors of the Western Front for nearly four years, being chiefly engaged in transporting ammunition and rations to the fighting line.

He was demobilised in November, 1919, and holds the General Service and Victory Medals.

542, Fulham Road, Fulham, S.W.6   X20219.

FORD, K. (Mrs.), Special War Worker.

During the war this lady was engaged on very arduous work at Messrs. Blake's, Fulham, making 18-pounder shell and smoke-bomb boxes ; and also at Messrs. Edgar's, Hammersmith, where she worked as checker in the hand-grenade department. Her valuable services were greatly appreciated.

81, Orbain Road, Fulham, S.W.6   X18259B.

FORD, R. P., Gunner, Royal Field Artillery.

He joined in December, 1916, and served on the Western Front, where he was wounded and gassed. He latterly served with the Army of Occupation in Germany, and was demobilised in October, 1919, holding the General Service and Victory Medals.

81, Bramber Road, West Kensington, W.14   15723B.

FORD, S., Sapper, Royal Engineers.

He joined in February, 1917, and served on the Western Front, taking part with distinction in the last Advance of 1918.

He was demobilised in January, 1920, holding the General Service and Victory Medals.

51, Hiley Road, Willesden, N.W.10   X18234A.

FORD, S., Driver, Royal Field Artillery.

He volunteered in June, 1915, and during his service on the Western Front took part in numerous engagements, including those at Ypres, Loos, the Somme, Arras, Vimy Ridge, Bullecourt, Albert, Verdun, and the final Advance. He was wounded at Ypres in July, 1917, and was demobilised in July, 1919, holding the General Service and Victory Medals.

81, Orbain Road, Fulham, S.W.6   X18259A.

FORD, T., Pte., 1st King's (Liverpool Regt.)

He enlisted in September, 1904, and immediately on the outbreak of hostilities was sent to the Western Front, where he took part in the retreat from Mons and the battles of Arras, Ypres and the Somme.

He was discharged in July, 1916, suffering from severe shell-shock, and holds the Mons Star and the General Service and Victory Medals.

69, Chauncey Street, Lower Edmonton, N.9   T14263.

FORD, W. A., Mechanic, Royal Air Force.

He joined in June, 1917, and on completion of his training, served at various aerodromes and training centres, where he did valuable work. Despite his efforts, he was unable to obtain his transfer overseas, being retained for duty with the R.A.F. at Home.

45, College Road, Kensal Rise, N.W.   X18014A.

FORD, W. R., Driver, Royal Field Artillery.

He volunteered in September, 1915, and during his service on the Western Front took part in engagements at Arras, Vimy Ridge, Messines, Ypres, Passchendaele (where he was wounded), and Cambrai. Later he was sent to Italy, but returned to France in time to take part in the Advance of 1918. After the Armistice he was stationed at Cologne with the Army of Occupation until his demobilisation in September, 1919.

He holds the General Service and Victory Medals.

2, Lillie Mansions, Lillie Road, Fulham, S.W.6   X18451.

FORDER, G. A., Pte., 8th East Surrey Regt.

He volunteered in July, 1915, and served in France, where he took part in several engagements and was wounded, and suffered severely from shell-shock. After being in hospital for some time, he was discharged in July, 1919, as unfit for further military service.

He holds the 1915 Star and the General Service and Victory Medals.

16, Kingwood Road, Fulham, S.W.6   X19022.

FORDHAM, A. J., Pte., 1st Middlesex Regiment.

He volunteered early in August, 1914, and was sent almost at once to France, where he took part in the battle of and retreat from Mons, and the battles of the Marne, Aisne, Ypres, Loos, and the Somme   While in action at the battle of the Somme he was severely wounded near Albert on July 14th, 1916, and died the next day.

He was entitled to the Mons Star and the General Service and Victory Medals.

39, Milton Avenue, Willesden, N.W.10   15793A.

FORDHAM, C. W., Pte., 2/13th London Regt. (Kensington).

He volunteered in August, 1914, and served in France during 1915, taking part in several engagements. Later he was transferred to the Eastern Front, and saw service in Salonica and Palestine, where he was present at the fall of Jerusalem. During his service he was wounded and suffered from shell-shock

In March, 1919, he was demobilised, holding the 1915 Star and the General Service and Victory Medals.

10, Francis Street, Hammersmith, W.6   15154B.

FORDHAM, C. W., Pte., R.A.V.C.

He joined in April, 1916, and served for three years with distinction on the Western Front, where he was employed with the Mobile Section of the Royal Army Veterinary Corps. In June, 1919, he was demobilised, and holds the General Service and Victory Medals.
21, Hiley Road, Willesden, N.W.10   X18165A.

FORDHAM, H., Pte., 1st Bedfordshire Regt.

He volunteered in August, 1915, and on the completion of his training was sent to India, where he remained for four years, being stationed at various places on garrison duty. He was demobilised in January, 1920, and holds the General Service and Victory Medals.
20, Milton Road, Upper Edmonton, N.18   X17256.

FORDHAM, H. (jun.), Shoeing-smith, R.F.A.

He re-enlisted in August, 1914, having already seen service prior to the outbreak of war, and was sent to France, where he took part with distinction in several engagements.
After four and a half years' service during the war he was demobilised, holding the 1914 Star, General Service and Victory Medals.
20, Milton Road, Upper Edmonton, N.18   X17257.

FORDHAM, J. W., Shoeing-smith, 3rd (King's Own) Hussars.

He volunteered in August, 1914, and served in France, taking part in the retreat from Mons and the battles of Ypres, Neuve Chapelle, the Somme and Arras, and the Advance of 1918.
He was demobilised in 1919, and holds the Mons Star, General Service and Victory Medals.
6, Headcorn Road, Tottenham, N.17   X18486,

FORDHAM, W., Pte., Royal West Kent Regt.

He volunteered in 1915, and during the four following years served on both the Western and Eastern Fronts. He took part in many engagements in France, Salonica and Serbia, and was wounded.
He was demobilised in April, 1919, and holds the 1915 Star, and the General Service and Victory Medals.
21, Hiley Road, Willesden, N.W.10   X18165B.

FORDHAM, W. C., Driver, R.A.S.C. (H.T.).

He volunteered in April, 1915, and was sent to the Eastern Front, where he served in Egypt and at Salonica. During the Salonica Campaign he was actively employed on the Struma, and suffered severely from shell-shock and malaria.
He was demobilised in March, 1919, and holds the 1915 Star, General Service and Victory Medals.
10, Francis Street, Hammersmith, W.6   15154A.

FORDHAM, W. J., Pte., Middlesex Regiment.

He volunteered in 1915, and later in the same year was sent to France, where he was present at several engagements. While at Guillemont in 1916 he was wounded, and on May 15th, 1917, he was killed in action at Dickebusch.
He was entitled to the 1915 Star and the General Service and Victory Medals.
52, Carlyle Avenue, Willesden, N.W.10   14410A.

FORREST, F., Gunner, Royal Field Artillery.

He joined in 1916, and served in India until 1917, when he was drafted to France, where he took part with distinction in many engagements.
He holds the General Service and Victory Medals, and was demobilised in 1919.
28, Kenninghall Road, Upper Edmonton, N.18   16904B.

FORREST, G. H., 1st-Class Stoker, Royal Navy.

He joined in 1917, and served in H.M.S. "Sviatogor" with the Grand Fleet, and also in the White Sea on ice-breaking and other important duties.
He was demobilised in 1919, holding the General Service and Victory Medals.
28, Kenninghall Road, Upper Edmonton, N.18   16904A.

FORRESTER, A. W., Pte., Machine Gun Corps.

He volunteered in January, 1915, and during his three years' service in India acted in a responsible position as staff clerk. He was for some time in hospital suffering from malaria. He holds the General Service and Victory Medals, and was demobilised in November, 1919.
16, Durban Road, Tottenham, N.17   X18095.

FOSTER, C., Pte., Labour Corps.

He joined in 1917 and was sent to France in September of the following year. He was employed at various places behind the lines on special duties until his demobilisation in July, 1919.
He holds the General Service and Victory Medals.
2, Fourth Avenue, Queen's Park Estate, W.10   X18402B.

FOSTER, C. C., Pte., Coldstream Guards.

He was mobilised in August, 1914, and served on the Western Front, where he took part in several engagements. Whilst at La Bassée in January, 1915, he was taken prisoner and sent to Germany, where he suffered great hardships.
On his release after the Armistice he was demobilised in 1919, and holds the 1914 Star and the General Service and Victory Medals.
94, Bronsart Road, Munster Road, S.W.6   X18996.

FOSTER, E. M. (Miss), Special War Worker.

During the war this lady was engaged at the War Office, Whitehall, as a messenger, and carried out her duties with energy and diligence.
98, Bronsart Road, Munster Road, S.W.6   X19001.

FOSTER, E. W. (M.M.), Pte., 11th (Pioneer Batt.) Hampshire Regiment.

He volunteered in March, 1915, and went to the Western Front in July of that year. He took part in many engagements, and was wounded on the Somme in July, 1916.
He was awarded the Military Medal for conspicuous bravery and devotion to duty in the field in August, 1917. He also holds the 1915 Star and the General Service and Victory Medals, and was demobilised in February, 1919.
24, Brett Road, N.W.10   15684.

FOSTER, G. H., Pte., Royal Irish Regiment.

He joined in June, 1916, and was sent to Salonica and thence to Egypt. With the Egyptian Expeditionary Force he went through the Palestine Campaign, and saw fighting at Jericho, Jaffa, Beersheba and Jerusalem. Later he was drafted to France, and after taking part in the last Advance, went with the Army of Occupation to Cologne.
He holds the General Service and Victory Medals, and was demobilised in September, 1919.
126, Bronsart Road, Fulham, S.W.6   X18992.

FOSTER, H. L., Pte., Somerset Light Infantry and Oxfordshire and Buckinghamshire L.I.

He joined in 1916 and served for some time in Egypt, where he was wounded. He remained in hospital for six months, and afterwards served in France, and later was again sent to Egypt.
He was demobilised in February, 1920, holding the General Service and Victory Medals.
41, Lopen Road, Upper Edmonton, N.18   TX17592.

FOSTER, J. G., 1st Air Mechanic, R.A.F.

He joined in April, 1916, and on the completion of his training served with the R.A.F. at various stations. He contracted tuberculosis while on service, and died in January, 1919.
He was entitled to the General Service Medal.
46, Minet Avenue, Willesden, N.W.10   13909

FOSTER, J. H., Pte., 13th Middlesex Regiment.

He volunteered in January, 1915, and was sent to France in the following April, where he took part in several engagements, being killed in action at Guillemont on August 18th, 1916.
He was entitled to the 1915 Star, the General Service, and Victory Medals.
33, Alric Avenue, N.W.10   14441.

FOSTER, J. H., Petty Officer, R.N., H.M.S. "Diadem."

He volunteered in August, 1914, and was posted to the "Diadem" He served on board this ship with the Grand Fleet in the North Sea, and was in action at the battle of Jutland.
He is still serving with the Royal Navy, and holds the 1914 Star and the General Service and Victory Medals.
29, Hartington Road, Lower Edmonton, N.9   14240.

FOSTER, L. H., Rifleman, Rifle Brigade.

He volunteered in March, 1915, and shortly after went to France. He was killed at Poperinghe, when a troop train going to the trenches was bombed by the enemy on September 20th, 1915.
He was entitled to the 1915 Star and the General Service and Victory Medals.
94, Bronsart Road, Fulham, S.W.6   X18995.

FOSTER, L. O., Pte., 2nd Lincolnshire Regiment, and Driver, R.A.S.C.

Having enlisted in March, 1910, he was sent to France when war broke out in 1914, and was attached as driver to the Gordon Highlanders, London Rifle Brigade and East Yorkshire Regiment at Mons, the Marne, the Aisne, the first and second battles of Ypres, the Ancre, the Somme and Cambrai.
During his service he was wounded, and was discharged in October, 1918, holding the Mons Star and the General Service and Victory Medals.
51, Burnthwaite Road, Walham Green, S.W.6   X20301.

S

FOSTER, R. S., Cpl., Royal Engineers.
He volunteered in April, 1915, and during his service on the Western Front took part in several engagements, including those of the Somme, Hill 60, Arras, Ypres and the Advance of 1918.
He was demobilised in January, 1919, holding the 1915 Star, General Service and Victory Medals.
90, Bronsart Road, Fulham, S.W.6   X18997.

FOSTER, S. J., Pte., Royal West Kent Regt.
He volunteered in 1914, and two years later was sent to Mesopotamia, where he served with distinction. During his service he saw much fighting, and in 1919 was demobilised, holding the General Service and Victory Medals.
19, Sunnyside Road North, Lower Edmonton, N.9   14559.

FOSTER, W. E., Cpl., Royal Engineers.
He volunteered in February, 1915, and proceeded to France, where he saw much service until April, 1916, when he was wounded. On his recovery he was sent to Egypt, where he remained until he was demobilised in June, 1919.
He holds the General Service and Victory Medals.
42, Fernhead Road, Maida Hill, W.9   X19391.

FOSTER, W. H., Pte., Duke of Cornwall's L.I.
He volunteered in August, 1914, and was sent to France, where he took part in the battles of Mons, Loos and Arras, and was taken prisoner at La Bassée in October, 1914. He was in captivity for over four years, during which time he suffered much privation, and was demobilised in January, 1919, holding the Mons Star, General Service and Victory Medals.
25, Bayonne Road, Hammersmith, W.6   14309.

FOULGER, R. A., Pte., 21st Middlesex Regt.
He joined in November, 1916, proceeded to the Western Front in 1917, and served through several engagements, including the battle of Cambrai. In November, 1917, he was reported missing, but has since been reported killed in action.
He was entitled to the General Service and Victory Medals.
35, Talbot Road, Willesden, N.W.10   15963.

FOUNTAIN, C., Cpl., Royal Air Force.
He joined the Royal Air Force in August, 1917, and after completing his training was stationed at various places with his squadron. He was unable to obtain a transfer overseas, being retained on special defence duties until he was demobilised in October, 1919, holding the General Service Medal.
55, Ancill Street, Hammersmith, W.6   13735.

FOUNTAIN, C. E., Q.M.S., Royal Engineers.
He volunteered in September, 1914, and the following year was sent to the Western Front, where he saw considerable service and was employed on important duties.
He holds the 1914-15 Star, General Service and Victory Medals, and was demobilised in June, 1919.
55, Rednall Terrace, Hammersmith, W.6   16214.

FOUNTAIN, C. J., Mechanic, Royal Air Force.
He joined in October, 1917, and was stationed with his unit at many important places. He rendered services of an important character, although unfit for overseas service.
He was demobilised in October, 1919, and holds the General Service Medal.
1, Hannell Road, Fulham, S.W.6   X17868C.

FOUNTAIN, W., Pte., 3rd Middlesex Regiment.
He joined in July, 1918, and was stationed with his unit at various places, where he carried out many important duties. Despite his efforts, he was unable to obtain a transfer overseas.
He was demobilised in February, 1919.
1, Hannell Road, Fulham, S.W.6   X17868A.

FOUNTAIN, W. H., Cpl., Army Cyclist Corps and Middlesex Regiment.
He volunteered in February, 1915, and the same year saw service in France, where he took part with distinction in numerous engagements and was wounded.
In April, 1919, he was demobilised, and holds the 1914-15 Star, General Service and Victory Medals.
2, Chaldon Road, S.W.6   X17718.

FOUNTAIN, W. J., Signalman, R.N., H.M.S. "Falmouth."
He joined in August, 1914, and served with the Grand Fleet in the North Sea, taking part in the engagement at Dogger Bank and in the battle of Jutland. He was badly wounded when his ship was torpedoed, but was rescued and is still serving.
He holds the 1914 Star, General Service and Victory Medals.
1, Hannell Road, S.W.6   X17868B.

FOWLER, A., Pte., 2nd Wiltshire Regiment.
He volunteered in August, 1914, and the following November went to France, where he took part in many important engagements up to and including the Retreat in March, 1918, when he was taken prisoner. He suffered many hardships whilst in captivity.
After the Armistice he was released and demobilised in February, 1919, holding the 1914 Star, General Service and Victory Medals.
51, St. Margaret's Road, Willesden, N.W.10   X17822.

FOWLER, A. G., Pte., Middlesex Regiment.
He volunteered at the outbreak of war in 1914, and the following year was sent to the Dardanelles, when he took part with distinction in the operations at Suvla Bay and in Gallipoli.
As a result of his service he was discharged as medically unfit in August, 1917, and holds the 1914-15 Star, General Service and Victory Medals.
107, Carlyle Avenue, Willesden, N.W.10   13681.

FOWLER, R. C., Cpl., 1st London Regiment (Royal Fusiliers).
He volunteered in March, 1915, and was sent to France in the same year, where he took part in many engagements in various sectors until 1919. During his service he was wounded, and was demobilised in June, 1919, holding the 1915 Star, General Service and Victory Medals.
172, Victoria Road, Lower Edmonton, N.9   14591.

FOX, A., Air Mechanic, Royal Air Force.
He volunteered in August, 1915, and served on various stations. During his service he made many flights overseas in airships, chiefly with the giant airship R.31.
He holds the 1915 Star, General Service and Victory Medals, and was demobilised in February, 1920.
11, Linton Road, Upper Edmonton, N.18   X17474.

FOX, A. G., Pte., Royal Fusiliers.
He joined in June, 1916, and the following year was sent to France, where he took part in several engagements and was twice wounded. In 1918 he went with the Army of Occupation to Germany, serving there until he was demobilised in May, 1919, holding the General Service and Victory Medals.
44, Linton Road, Upper Edmonton, N.18   TX17250A.

FOX, A. L. (Miss), Special War Worker.
This lady volunteered and rendered most valuable services of a dangerous nature in a large munition factory. Her work was of a very trying description, and she was commended for her untiring efforts.
42, Holyport Road, Crabtree Lane, Fulham, S.W.6   14178.

FOX, E., Stoker, R.N., H.M.S. "Tiger."
He joined the Navy in November, 1916, and was engaged in many arduous duties during operations in the North Sea and elsewhere, running great danger.
He is still serving, and holds the General Service and Victory Medals.
44, Linton Road, Upper Edmonton, N.18   TX17250B.

FOX, G., Pte., R.A.S.C. (M.T.).
He volunteered in November, 1914, and later was sent to the Western Front, where he took part in the operations at Loos, Ypres, the Somme and Cambrai. Owing to his technical knowledge he was also employed on special duties in the repair shops.
He was demobilised in May, 1919, and holds the 1914-15 Star, General Service and Victory Medals.
26, Kingwood Road, Fulham, S.W.6   X19020.

FOX, G., Pte., 9th Lancers.
He enlisted in July, 1900, and at the outbreak of hostilities was sent to the Western Front, where he served for three years. During this period he took part with distinction in many of the principal engagements, including the retreat from Mons, the battles of Ypres, the Somme, Loos and Passchendaele, and was wounded five times.
He holds the Mons Star and the General Service and Victory Medals, and was discharged in February, 1919.
184, Shirland Road, Maida Hill, W.9   X19600.

FOX, G. H., 1st Air Mechanic, R.N.D. and R.A.F.
He volunteered in October, 1914, and in the following year took part in the landing at Gallipoli, and later in the evacuation. From the Dardanelles he was drafted to Egypt, and thence to Salonica, where he served for some months. Afterwards he went to France and took part in the Advance of 1918. During his service overseas, which lasted over four years, he was wounded.
He holds the 1915 Star, General Service and Victory Medals, and was demobilised in January, 1919.
49, Droop Street, Queen's Park Estate, W.10   X18574.

FOX, J. (D.C.M.), Cpl., East Surrey Regiment.
He volunteered in October, 1914, and served on the Western Front, taking part in the battles of Neuve Chapelle, the Somme, Ypres and Messines. He was awarded the Distinguished Conduct Medal for conspicuous gallantry and devotion to duty, and in his last engagement was badly gassed. He also holds the 1915 Star, the General Service and Victory Medals, and was demobilised in March, 1919.
62, Coomer Road, Fulham, S.W.14   16442.

FOX, J., Special War Worker.
During the war he was engaged on duties which were of a very dangerous nature. His duties consisted of filling bombs and mines, and required much care and skill. He was highly commended for his valuable services.
42, Holyport Road, Crabtree Lane, Fulham, S.W.6   14517A.

FOX, R. T., Gunner, Royal Field Artillery.
He volunteered in 1914, and served for some time at various stations with his unit. Whilst under training he severely strained himself and was invalided out of the Army in 1915 as unfit for further military service.
162, Brettenham Road, Upper Edmonton, N.18   15388.

FOX, W., Pte., 2/3rd Royal Fusiliers.
He joined in March, 1916, and was drafted to France, where he served in various sectors. On March 7th in the following year he was killed in action near Vimy Ridge.
He was entitled to the General Service and Victory Medals.
42, Holyport Road, Crabtree Lane, Fulham, S.W.6 14517B.

FOX, W. D. (D.C.M.), Sergt., 1st Middlesex Regt.
He rejoined in August, 1914, and during his service on the Western Front took part with distinction in several battles. Later he was drafted to Russia, where he was awarded the Distinguished Conduct Medal for conspicuous gallantry. He also holds the 1914 Star, General Service and Victory Medals, and was discharged in January, 1919. He has completed 20 years' service with the Colours, and during this period took part in the South African Campaign, the Medals for which he also holds.
50, Lintaine Grove, West Kensington, W.14   X16994.

FOY, W. (M.M.), Sergt., Royal Fusiliers.
He volunteered in August, 1914, and saw service in France and at Salonica, where he suffered severely from malaria. He was awarded the Military Medal for conspicuous gallantry and holds, in addition, the 1915 Star and the General Service and Victory Medals.
During his service he was twice wounded, being discharged in January, 1919. He later re-enlisted and took part in the Russian Campaign.
48, Lintaine Grove, West Kensington, W.14   15725.

FOYLE, G. W., Pte., R.A.S.C. (M.T.).
He joined in February, 1917, and served on the Western Front from August, 1918, until demobilised in October, 1919. While abroad he was engaged on important duties with the supply columns at Arras, Cambrai and Amiens.
He holds the General Service and Victory Medals.
56, Bravington Road, Maida Hill, W.9   X19185.

FOYLE, T., Sergt. Mechanic, Royal Air Force.
He volunteered in August, 1914, and served with distinction in Italy from 1916 until October, 1918, when he died from pneumonia, and was buried in the British Cemetery in Italy.
He was entitled to the General Service and Victory Medals.
7, Honeywood Road, Harlesden.   12556.

FRANCIS, A. E., Pte., 27th Royal Fusiliers.
He joined in May, 1916, and during his service on the Western Front took part in the battle of the Somme, and was on two occasions invalided home suffering from trench fever and sent to hospital.
He was demobilised in February, 1919, and holds the General Service and Victory Medals.
12, Lochaline Street, Fulham, W.6   13443.

FRANCIS, F., Pte., 17th Middlesex Regiment.
He volunteered in November, 1915, and during his service in France took part with distinction in many battles, including those of Loos, Arras, Ypres, Cambrai, the Somme and Armentieres.
He was discharged as unfit for further service in February, 1918, and holds the General Service and Victory Medals.
15, Forest Gardens, Bruce Grove, Tottenham, N.17 X18531.

FRANCIS, F. H., Pte., 8th Bedfordshire Regt.
He volunteered in September, 1914, and during his service on the Western Front took part in the fighting on the Somme, at Loos, Ypres, Armentieres, Delville Wood, Bullecourt and elsewhere. While in action at High Wood he sustained a wound which necessitated the amputation of his right arm. He was in hospital at Rouen and at Birmingham before being discharged physically unfit for further service in May, 1917, and holds the 1915 Star, the General Service and Victory Medals. 198, Lillie Road, Fulham.   X18898

FRANCIS, G., Pte., 1st Royal Fusiliers.
He volunteered for duty in August, 1914, and was soon drafted to the Western Front, where, after taking part in several engagements, he was killed in action on the Ypres Front on August 18th, 1915.
He was entitled to the 1914 Star, General Service and Victory Medals.
32, Rock Avenue, Fulham Road, S.W.6   X20081.

FRANCIS, G. F., Rifleman, The Rifle Brigade.
He volunteered in September, 1914, and served on the Western Front, taking part in many engagements. He was reported missing and afterwards "killed in action" on September 18th, 1916
He was entitled to the 1915 Star and the General Service and Victory Medals.
6, Werley Avenue, Fulham.   X17879.

FRANCIS, G. F., Rifleman, Rifle Brigade.
He volunteered in September, 1914, and was very soon sent to France, where he saw active service in various sectors He was killed in action on the Somme in September, 1916, and was entitled to the 1914 Star, the General Service and Victory Medals.
17, Gastein Road, Fulham, W.6   14825A.

FRANCIS, H. C., Driver, Royal Field Artillery.
He volunteered in April, 1915, and was sent to France. Here he served with distinction on various sectors, afterwards being drafted to Salonica, and finally to Egypt.
He was demobilised in August, 1919, holding the General Service and Victory Medals.
17, Gastein Road, Fulham, W.6   14825B.

FRANCIS, H. E., Leading Signalman, R.N., H.M.S. "Tiger."
He volunteered in August, 1914, and saw service on important and dangerous missions with the Grand Fleet, rendering most important duties.
He holds the 1914 Star, the General Service and Victory Medals, and remained with his ship after the cessation of hostilities. 38, Pretoria Road, Upper Edmonton. X17023.

FRANCIS, H. J., Rifleman, 1/11th London Rifle Brigade.
He volunteered in August, 1915, and served in Egypt and Palestine. He took part in various engagements, and was severely wounded at Gaza in February, 1918.
He was discharged in July, 1919, and holds the 1915 Star, General Service and Victory Medals.
10, Kilmaine Road, Fulham.   X18762.

FRANCIS, J., Sergt., R.F.A. and R.G.A.
Volunteering in October, 1914, he was engaged on highly responsible duties in the Anti-Aircraft Service at various points. He was afterwards transferred from the R.F.A. to the R.G.A. for East Coast defence duties.
On account of his general ill-health, he was discharged the year previous to the cessation of hostilities, holding the General Service Medal.
18, Lillie Mansions, Lillie Road, Fulham.   X18791.

FRANCIS, J., Pte., Northamptonshire Regt.
He joined in March, 1917, and after his period of training was drafted to the Western Front, where he served in various sectors. After having rendered valuable services, he was demobilised in March, 1919, holding the General Service and Victory Medals. 27, Purcell Crescent, S.W.6   15163.

FRANCIS, J. P., Cpl., 7th London Regiment.
He volunteered in 1915 and joined the London Regiment. Due to his special knowledge and abilities, and due to the fact that at the time he was medically unfit for overseas service, he was engaged on farm work in Suffolk, where his duties were of the greatest value to the country.
He was demobilised in March, 1919.
72, Ancill Street, W.6   14002B.

FRANCIS, S., Rifleman, King's Royal Rifles.
He volunteered in November, 1915, and saw much service on the Eastern Front. Returning to England, he was engaged on important railway work, and was for a time in hospital owing to an accident.
He was demobilised in March, 1920, and holds the General Service and Victory Medals.
54, Rosaline Road, Fulham.   X18195.

FRANCIS, T., Pte., Middlesex Regiment.
He joined in 1917 and was drafted to India, where for a short time he was on garrison duties, being sent later to Salonica, and from there to Egypt, where he took part in many engagements, including the final Advance under General Allenby.
He was demobilised in 1919, and holds the General Service and Victory Medals.
81, Berry Street, Willesden, N.W.10   15417.

FRANCIS, W. C., Rflm., 6th London Regiment.
He volunteered in 1915 and was sent to the Western Front, where he took part in many engagements, including those of the Somme, Loos, Neuve Chapelle, Armentieres, Ypres, Bullecourt, St. Quentin and the last Advance of 1918. He was once wounded and severely gassed at Hill 60.
He was discharged in 1919, and holds the General Service and Victory Medals.
264, Lillie Road, Fulham, S.W.6   X18783.

FRANCKE, F. W., Lce.-Cpl., 1st Coldstream Gds.
He was mobilised in August, 1914, was sent to France and killed in action during the retreat from Mons in the same month.
He was entitled to the Mons Star, General Service and Victory Medals.
16, Bramber Road, Fulham.   16285.

FRANKCOM, C. V., Driver, R.A.S.C. (Horse T.).
He volunteered in November, 1915, and served in France, taking part with distinction in many important engagements in various sectors.
He was demobilised in March, 1919, and holds the General Service and Victory Medals.
56, Claybrook Road, Fulham.   13769.

FRANKLIN, A., Pte., Machine Gun Corps.
He enlisted in 1909, and at the outbreak of war was sent to India, and from there to Mesopotamia, where he took part in numerous operations during the Advance to Kut-el-Amara.
In April, 1919, he was demobilised, and holds the 1914 Star, General Service and Victory Medals.
51a, Drayton Road, Harlesden.   14995A.

FRANKLIN, A. J., Rifleman, 8th London Regiment and A.B., Royal Navy.
He was mobilised in August, 1914, and saw service first in the Army. In January, 1917 he was transferred to the Navy, and thenceforward saw service in H.M.S. "Lord Nelson" with the North Sea 3rd Battle Squadron and the Eastern Mediterranean Squadron, taking part in many operations until demobilised in July, 1919.
He holds the General Service and Victory Medals.
29a, Allington Road, W.10   X18011.

FRANKLIN, A. J. F., Pte., 1st Royal Scots Fus.
He joined in August, 1914, and the same year saw service on the Western Front, taking part in the battle of Mons, where he was taken prisoner. During his captivity he endured considerable hardship.
In 1919 he was demobilised, and holds the Mons Star, General Service and Victory Medals.
63, Westminster Road, Lower Edmonton, N.9   T12696.

FRANKLIN, F. E., Bombardier, R.F.A.
He joined in October, 1916, was sent to France in 1918 and took part with distinction in the 1918 Retreat and Advance.
He was demobilised in April, 1919, and holds the General Service and Victory Medals.
51a, Drayton Road, Harlesden.   14995B.

FRANKLIN, G., Pte., Middlesex Regiment.
He volunteered in 1915, and the same year was sent to France, where he remained until demobilised in 1919. During this period he took part in engagements at Ypres, Somme and many other battles of importance.
He holds the 1915 Star, General Service and Victory Medals.
25, Newlyn Road, Tottenham.   X18511.

FRANKLIN, J., Pte., The Queen's (Royal West Surrey Regiment).
He joined in March, 1916, was sent to France in July of the same year, and took part in the advance on the Somme, where he was killed in action in October, 1916.
He was entitled to the General Service and Victory Medals.
16, Meyrick Road, Willesden.   16347A.

FRANKLIN, S., Lce.-Cpl., Suffolk Regiment.
During his service, which extended from April, 1917, until March, 1919, he was employed with his unit at various important stations. Due to his abilities and knowledge, he was engaged as a machine gunnery instructor, and rendered valuable services.
51a, Drayton Road, Harlesden.   14995C.

FRANKLIN, S. J., A.B., R.N., H.M.S. "Pyramus."
He volunteered in October, 1914, and served with his ship in the Mediterranean and elsewhere on very dangerous mine-sweeping and escort duties.
He was discharged in May, 1919, holding the 1914-15 Star and the General Service and Victory Medals.
6, Cornwall Road, N.18   15619.

FRANKLIN, T., Pte., Middlesex Regiment and 16th Worcestershire Regiment.
He volunteered in June, 1915, was sent to the Western Front in September, 1916, and after taking part in engagements on the Somme and elsewhere, was wounded in action at Ypres in January, 1917. He was invalided home and in March, 1919, was demobilised, holding the General Service and Victory Medals.
16, Meyrick Road, Willesden.   16347B.

FRANKUM, C. J., Gunner, R.G.A.
He volunteered in November, 1915, and served in England on training duties for 18 months, afterwards proceeding to France, where he served for two years.
He was demobilised in March, 1919, holding the General Service and Victory Medals.
2, Stanley Grove, White Hart Lane, Tottenham. X18405.

FRASER, W. J., Pioneer, Royal Engineers.
He joined in May, 1917, and in the same year went to the Western Front, where he served during the Great Retreat. He died of wounds received in action at St. Quentin on March 28th, 1918.
He was entitled to the General Service and Victory Medals.
20, Novello Street, Parsons Green, S.W.6   X19951.

FRATER, C. A., Leading Seaman, R.N., Torpedo Boat No. 2.
He volunteered in August, 1914, served in many parts of the world, and took part with distinction in the Cuxhaven Raid.
He was demobilised in December, 1918, holding the 1914 Star, General Service and Victory Medals. The duties on this class of craft were most arduous and dangerous.
28, Moylan Road, Fulham.   15287.

FREE, C. T., Pte., The Queen's (Royal West Surrey Regiment).
He joined in February, 1917, and the same year was sent to the Western Front, where he took part in numerous engagements.
He was demobilised in October, 1919, and holds the General Service and Victory Medals.
14, Ray's Road, Upper Edmonton, N.18   15492.

FREE, H., Pte., 13th Middlesex Regiment.
He joined in July, 1916, and was sent to the Western Front the same year, where he took part in several engagements until he was drafted to Egypt. He saw considerable service in Palestine, and holds the General Service and Victory Medals, being demobilised in August, 1919.
44, Church Road, Tottenham, N.17   X18341.

FREEBAIRN, A., Gunner, Royal Field Artillery.
He volunteered in August, 1914, went to France the same year and took part in the retreat from Mons and several other engagements, including the Somme and Ypres.
He holds the Mons Star and the General Service and Victory Medals, and was demobilised in May, 1919.
78, Angel Road, Upper Edmonton, N.18   16572.

FREEBORN, F., Pte., Royal Army Medical Corps.
He volunteered in December, 1914, and was immediately sent to the Western Front, where he served for four years in the Royal Army Medical Corps After the Armistice he went with the Army of Occupation to Germany, where he remained until his return to England for demobilisation in May, 1919.
He holds the 1914-15 Star, General Service and Victory Medals.
8, Marryat Street, Hammersmith, W.6   .   12503.

FREEMAN, A., Pte., Machine Gun Corps.
He volunteered in September, 1914, and served for nearly three years in Mesopotamia as a machine gunner, where he took part in the engagements at Kut and Baghdad.
In May, 1919, he was demobilised, and holds the General Service and Victory Medals.
85, Deacon Road, Cricklewood, N.W.2   16701.

FREEMAN, A., Pte., 1st Gloucester Regiment.
He joined in March, 1917, and proceeded to France in the same year, where he took part in many engagements.
He was demobilised in November, 1919, holding the General Service and Victory Medals.
234, Winchester Road, Lower Edmonton, N.9   14880.

FREEMAN, A. (Mrs.), Special War Worker.
This lady volunteered immediately at the outbreak of war, and rendered most valuable services in a large munition factory Her work was of a skilful and arduous nature, for which she received high commendation.
45, Steele Road, Willesden, N.W.10   14148C.

FREEMAN, E., Pte., Worcestershire Regiment.
He volunteered in August, 1914, and was immediately sent to the Western Front, where he took part in the retreat from Mons. A serious injury, received at Ypres in 1914, necessitated his being invalided to England, where he was employed as an ambulance orderly until his discharge in March, 1918.
He holds the Mons Star and the General Service and Victory Medals.
30, Fifth Avenue, Queen's Park Estate, W.10   X18321.

FREEMAN, G. H., Driver, R.F.A.
He volunteered in October, 1915, and was sent to the Western Front a year later. From France he was transferred to Italy, where he saw much service and took part in many engagements.
He was demobilised in March, 1919, and holds the General Service and Victory Medals.
36, Maldon Road, Lower Edmonton, N.9   15784

FREEMAN, J., Driver, Royal Field Artillery.
He volunteered in 1915, and was sent to the Western Front in the same year, where he took part in many engagements, including the battle of the Somme.
He holds the 1914-15 Star, General Service and Victory Medals, and was demobilised in 1919.
45, Steele Road, Willesden, N.W.10   14148A.

FREEMAN, J., Pte., 1st Royal Fusiliers.
He volunteered in 1914 and served on the Western Front, where he took part in engagements at Loos, Verdun, the Somme, Arras, Ypres and Cambrai, and was four times wounded.
He holds the 1915 Star and the General Service and Victory Medals.
45, Steele Road, Willesden, N.W.10   14148B.

FREEMAN, J., Driver, R.A.S.C.
He volunteered in September, 1914, and was sent to France, taking part in several engagements. Later he served in the Dardanelles, where he was wounded.
He holds the 1915 Star and the General Service and Victory Medals, and was demobilised in June, 1919.
21, Maybury Gardens, Willesden, N.W.10   X17367B.

FREMONT, L. G., Pte., 1/6th Black Watch.
He joined in June, 1916, was sent to France the same year, and took part in the battles of the Somme, Ypres, Cambrai and the Marne He went to Germany with the Army of Occupation in 1918, and was demobilised in August, 1919, holding the General Service and Victory Medals. He fought throughout with the 52nd Division.
24, Goodhall Street, Harlesden, N.W.10   T12724.

FRENCH, A., Sapper, Royal Engineers.
He joined in August, 1916, and the following year was sent to Mesopotamia, where he saw considerable service, taking part with distinction in the operations at Kut and Baghdad. He was demobilised in September, 1919, and holds the General Service and Victory Medals.
34, Gowan Road, Willesden, N.W.10   X16961

FRENCH, W. Henry, Rifleman, Rifle Brigade.
He volunteered in November, 1914, and later served on the Western Front, where he took part in many engagements and was killed in action on May 10th, 1915.
He was entitled to the 1915 Star, General Service and Victory Medals.
4, Purcell Crescent, Fulham, S.W.6   14849A.

FRENCH, W. Harold, Pte., Devonshire Regt.
He volunteered in September, 1914, and served on the Western Front, where he took part in many engagements in various sectors and was twice wounded.
In November, 1919, he was demobilised, holding the General Service and Victory Medals.
4, Purcell Crescent, Fulham, S.W.6   14849B.

FREWIN, J. S., Rifleman, The Rifle Brigade.
He joined in April, 1917, served on the Western Front in several engagements, and was badly gassed. He was in hospital at Boulogne, and in February, 1919, was demobilised, holding the General Service and Victory Medals.
117, Sherbrooke Road, Fulham, S.W.6   X18619.

FREWING, F., Special War Worker.
He was employed by the National Projectile Co., making shells and other essential munitions, and was afterwards employed in the manufacture of aeroplanes at Hayes, Middlesex, being in the engineers' department. His work required great care and skill, and was carried out in an efficient manner.
87, Mirabel Road, Fulham, S.W.6   X17852.

FRIBBINS, A. W., Cpl., 20th King's Royal Rifle Corps.
He joined in July, 1918, and served on the Western Front, where he was principally engaged on important guard duties. After the Armstice he was sent to Germany with the Army of Occupation.
He holds the General Service and Victory Medals, and was demobilised in March, 1920.
28, Wilson's Road, Hammersmith, W.6   15860.

FRIBBINS, T. N., Pte., 2nd Royal Fusiliers.
He volunteered in May, 1915, and was drafted to the Western Front, where he took part in many engagements, including those of the Somme, Ypres and Cambrai, and was twice wounded.
He holds the 1915 Star, General Service and Victory Medals, and was demobilised in March, 1919.
28, Wilson's Road, Hammersmith, W.6   15859.

FRIDAY, T. C., Driver, Royal Field Artillery.
He volunteered in August, 1914, and in the following March was sent to the Western Front, where he took part in several important engagements, including Loos. Unfortunately he contracted typhoid fever, and was invalided home as unfit. In September, 1915, he died from the effects.
He was entitled to the 1915 Star and the General Service and Victory Medals.
16, Fifth Avenue, Queen's Park Estate, W.10   X18323.

FRIEND, A. C., Sapper, Royal Engineers.
He volunteered in 1915, and the same year was sent to the Western Front, where he took part in several engagements. He was later transfererd to Salonica, and there contracted malaria. After his recovery he served at Malta. During his service he was wounded and gassed.
He holds the 1915 Star, General Service and Victory Medals, and was demobilised in 1919.
90, Hartington Road, Tottenham, N.17   X19117.

FRIEND, A. R., Lce.-Cpl., 1st Middlesex Regt.
He volunteered in August, 1914, went to the Western Front, and was killed in action at Loos on September 25th, 1915, having previously taken part in the fighting at Ypres.
He was entitled to the 1914-15 Star, General Service and Victory Medals.
48, Oldfield Road, Willesden, N.W.10   16105B.

FRIEND, A. R., Pte., Royal Fusiliers.
He volunteered in 1915, went to France in the same year, and took part in the battle of the Somme in July, 1916. He returned to England suffering from shell-shock, and was later drafted to Italy, where he served for twelve months. In 1919 he was demobilised, holding the 1915 Star, General Service and Victory Medals.
48, Oldfield Road, Willesden, N.W.10   16105C.

FRIEND, F. C., Cpl., 2/9th Middlesex Regiment.
He volunteered in 1915, was sent to the Western Front in 1917, and took part in the battles of the Somme and Cambrai, being killed in action at the latter place in November of the same year.
He was entitled to the General Service and Victory Medals.
48, Oldfield Road, Willesden, N.W.10   16105A.

FRINDLE, A., Sergt., Norfolk Regiment.
He volunteered in August, 1914, and the following year was sent to France, where he saw considerable service, and was on one occasion buried by a shell.
He holds the 1914-15 Star, General Service and Victory Medals.
29, Maldon Road, Lower Edmonton, N.9   14786B.

FRITH, W., Pte., Royal Fusiliers.
He joined in April, 1918, and after completing his training, served with the Army of Occupation in Germany, where he rendered valuable services.
He was demobilised in March, 1920.
137a, Deacon Road, Cricklewood, N.W.2   15317.

FRITH, W., Pte., Army Cyclist Corps.
He joined in March, 1918, and after his period of training, was sent to Germany with the Army of Occupation, and served at Duren, near Cologne, until demobilised in November, 1919.
74, Carlyle Avenue, Willesden, N.W.10   14446.

FROMBERG, L., Gunner, R.G.A.
He joined in August, 1916, and having completed his training, served at various stations with his battery. Despite his efforts, his ill-health prevented him from obtaining a transfer overseas.
He was demobilised in February, 1919.
24. Brereton Road, Tottenham, N.17   X18112

FROST, A., Pte., Royal Army Service Corps.
He volunteered in April, 1915, and during his four years on the Western Front, served at Loos, Ypres, Cambrai and the Somme with the supply and ambulance columns. In 1918 he got shell-shock at Villers Bretonneux, and was demobilised in April, 1919, holding the 1915 Star and the General Service and Victory Medals
124, Farm Lane, Walham Green, S.W.6   X19634.

FROST, F. J., 1st-Class Stoker, Royal Navy.
He joined in January, 1918, and served with the Grand Fleet in the North Sea, being with his ship on various important and dangerous missions.
He secured his demobilisation in September, 1919, holding the General Service and Victory Medals.
14, Town Road, Lower Edmonton, N.9   13565C.

FROST, H. C., Driver, Royal Army Service Corps.
He volunteered in August, 1914, and in that year went to France, where he remained throughout the war. During his long service he was engaged on various sectors of the Front.
He was demobilised in March, 1919, and holds the 1914 Star and the General Service and Victory Medals.
38, Herries Street, North Kensington, W.10   X18725.

FROST, W., Air Mechanic, Royal Air Force.
He joined in 1917, and after the completion of his training, served at various stations with the Royal Air Force on important duties. His work called for a high degree of technical skill.
He secured his demobilisation in 1919.
123, Sheldon Road, Upper Edmonton, N.18   X17296.

FROST, W. H., Pte., Middlesex Regiment.
He volunteered in June, 1915, and served with distinction on the Western Front, where he was killed in March, 1918, at the second battle of the Somme.
He was entitled to the General Service and Victory Medals.
14, Town Road, Lower Edmonton, N.9   13565B.

FROSTICK, J., Cpl., R.A.S.C. (M.T.).
Volunteering in 1915, he saw service on the Western Front on important transport duties with the Mechanical Transport Section, being principally engaged on the Somme and in the Ypres, Arras and Loos sectors.
He was demobilised in July, 1919, and holds the 1915 Star and the General Service and Victory Medals.
157, Fifth Avenue, W.10   X18734.

FRY, A. E., Canteen Manager, H.M.S. "Canada."
He joined in 1914, and throughout the war served in the H.M.S. "Canada" in the North Sea and Home waters. His duties often took him into great danger in the submarine and mined areas.
He holds the General Service and Victory Medals.
32, Stracey Road, Stonebridge Park, N.W.10   15679B.

FRY, A. O., Lce.-Cpl., 12th Middlesex Regt.
He volunteered in 1914, and during his service on the Western Front took part in several engagements. He received in September, 1916, such severe wounds while in action that he was discharged in the following year.
He holds the 1915 Star and the General Service and Victory Medals.
30, Stracey Road, Stonebridge Park, N.W.10   15679C.

FRY, B. R., Sergt., Royal Marines.
He volunteered in 1914 and served in H.M.S. "Malaya" in the North Sea with the Grand Fleet. In May, 1916, he took part in the battle of Jutland, and was demobilised in 1919, holding the 1914-15 Star and the General Service and Victory Medals.
30, Stracey Road, Stonebridge Park, N.W.10   15679A.

FRY, G. C., Pte., 9th Middlesex Regiment and Sapper, Royal Engineers.
He volunteered in 1914 and served in India, where he was stationed at Karachi and Rawal-Pindi. Later he was sent to Mesopotamia, where he saw fighting against the Turks. In 1919 he was sent home and demobilised, holding the General Service and Victory Medals.
34, Cooper Road, Stonebridge Park, N.W.10   16641.

FRY, J., Sergt., 1/9th Middlesex Regiment.
He volunteered in August, 1914, and served with distinction in India and in Mesopotamia, where he took part in several engagements. In 1919 he served in the Afghan campaign.
He holds the 1914-15 Star, General Service and Victory Medals, and was demobilised in November, 1919, after five years' active service. He is also entitled to the Afghan award.
38, Dudden Hill Lane, Willesden, N.W.10   X17391.

FRY, P. G., Sergt., Royal Army Service Corps.
He volunteered in 1915, was engaged on important transport duties in France, and in 1917 was drafted to East Africa, where during his service he contracted malaria.
He holds the 1915 Star, General Service and Victory Medals, and was demobilised in 1919 on his return to England.
32, Stracey Road, Stonebridge Park, N.W.10   15679D.

FRYER, J., Pte., 3rd Wiltshire Regiment.
He volunteered in March, 1915, and during his service on the Western Front took part in engagements at Ypres, Cambrai and Arras. While in the lines near High Wood he was severely wounded, and on his recovery was sent to Salonica, where he saw active service against the Bulgarians.
He was sent home and demobilised in 1919, holding the 1915 Star and the General Service and Victory Medals
10, Melville Road, Stonebridge Park, N.W.10   14426.

FRYETT, J. W., Pte., 17th Essex Regiment.
He joined in 1917, and for a year served on the Western Front. He was chiefly employed guarding prisoners of war, but took part in the Retreat and Advance of 1918, during which period he was wounded.
He was demobilised in March, 1919, and holds the General Service and Victory Medals.
36, Shakespeare Avenue, Willesden, N.W.10   13612.

FUELLING, G. W., Stoker, R.N., H.M.S. "Grampus" and "Yarmouth."
Volunteering in December, 1915, he served from 1916 to 1918 in the Mediterranean, and from 1918 to 1919 with the North Sea Fleet on important and dangerous missions.
He secured his demobilisation in March, 1919, holding the General Service and Victory Medals.
115, Felixstowe Road, Lower Edmonton, N.9   14542.

FUGGLE, H., Pte., Middlesex Regiment.
He volunteered in August, 1914, and was sent to France, where he served on various sectors, including the Somme and Ypres. He was wounded twice at Ypres, and was discharged in August, 1918, holding the General Service and Victory Medals.
52, Barbot Street, Lower Edmonton, N.9   14222.

FULLBROOK, F. S., A.B., R.N.V.R.
He volunteered in September, 1915, and served on the Belgian coast. He was recommended for the Croix-de-Guerre at Nieuport, for distinguished service in manning the battery under a heavy gas-shell and high explosive bombardment, and assisted in bringing an effective fire to bear on hostile batteries in reply. The loss in officers and men on this occasion was considerable.
He holds the 1915 Star, General Service and Victory Medals, and was demobilised in February, 1919.
26, Hilmer Street, West Kensington, W.14   16262.

FULLER, A. V., Cpl., 3/7th Middlesex Regt.
He volunteered in 1915 and served on the Western Front from 1916 to 1919, taking part in the battles of the Somme and Vimy Ridge.
He was demobilised in February, 1919, holding the General Service and Victory Medals.
26, Town Road, Lower Edmonton, N.9   13563A.

FULLER, C., Pte., 18th Middlesex Regiment.
He volunteered in July, 1916, and during his service in France took part in the battles of the Somme, Arras and Ypres.
He holds the General Service and Victory Medals, and was demobilised in 1919.
256, Brettenham Road East, Upper Edmonton, N.18   15629B.

FULLER, E. J., Pte., Middlesex Regiment.
He volunteered in August, 1914, was sent to France in the same year, and was wounded at La Bassée. He died of wounds in February, 1915, and was entitled to the 1914 Star, General Service and Victory Medals.
256, Brettenham Road East, Upper Edmonton, N. 1815629A.

FULLER, G. A. (Miss), Special War Worker.
From August, 1916, until January, 1917, this lady was engaged on important work as an examiner in the fuse inspection department of Park Royal Munition Factory, after which she worked in the clerical department until October, 1917, when she returned to her former duties. In September, 1918, she resigned, having rendered valuable services during the two years she was engaged on war work.
101, Ashmore Road, Harrow Road, W.9   X19648.

FULLER, G. G., Pte., 5th Royal Irish Regt.
Volunteering in October, 1915, he was drafted to Salonica in 1916. He also saw service in the Palestine campaign until 1918, when he was sent to France.
He was demobilised in March, 1919, holding the General Service and Victory Medals.
26, Town Road, Lower Edmonton, N.9   13563B.

FULLER, H. A., Sapper, Royal Engineers, and Pte., 24th Manchester Regiment.
He volunteered in February, 1915, and was sent overseas in 1917. During his service he was employed on transport duties on both Western and Eastern Fronts.
In January, 1919, he returned to England and was demobilised, holding the General Service and Victory Medals.
3, Albert Terrace, Harlesden, N.W.10   15635A.

FULLER, H. T., Lce.-Cpl., 9th Middlesex Regt. and North Staffordshire Regiment.
He volunteered in August, 1914, was sent to France in 1916, and took part in the battles of the Somme, Arras, Vimy Ridge, Ypres, Passchendaele and Cambrai. He was wounded while overseas, and was discharged in February 1919, holding the General Service and Victory Medals.
40, Nightingale Road, Harlesden, N.W.10   12514.

FULLER, J. J., Cpl., 9th Middlesex Regiment and Royal West Kent Regiment.
He volunteered in August, 1914, and in the following year went to France, where he took part in several engagements. In January, 1918, he was invalided out through ill-health, caused by active service, and has since died.
He was entitled to the 1915 Star and the General Service and Victory Medals.
40, Nightingale Road, Harlesden, N.W.10   12513.

FULLER, L. (Mrs.), Special War Worker.
This lady volunteered and rendered valuable services as a post woman throughout the war. Her duties, which were of a tiring nature, were carried out in a most efficient manner, and she was very highly commended for her work.
3, Albert Terrace, Milton Avenue, Willesden, N.W.10
                                                 15635B.

FULLER, L. A., Rough Rider, R.A.S.C.
He volunteered in September, 1914, and served on various sectors of the Western Front during the whole period of his service.
He was demobilised in November, 1919, and holds the 1915 Star, General Service and Victory Medals.
51, Lintaine Grove, West Kensington, W.14   16823A.

FULLER, S. G., Lce.-Cpl., The London Regt. (Royal Fusiliers).
He volunteered in July, 1915, and was sent to Egypt. A year later he served in France, taking part with distinction in several engagements, and was wounded at Hebuterne in May of the same year.
He was discharged medically unfit in May, 1917, and holds the General Service and Victory Medals.
52, Windsor Road, Cricklewood, N.W.2   X17388.

FULLER, W. T., Pte., 2nd Northamptonshire Regiment.
He joined in August, 1916, and during nearly two years service on the Western Front took part in engagements at the Somme, Vimy Ridge, Lens, St. Quentin, Cambrai, Ypres, Bapaume and Bullecourt. He was killed in action on September 1st, 1918, near Arras, and was buried at the military cemetery at Aux Rietz.
He was entitled to the General Service and Victory Medals.
25, Milton Avenue, Willesden, N.W.10   13874B.

FULLICK, J., Pte., Duke of Cornwall's Light Infantry.
He volunteered in 1915 and served on the Western Front. While in action near St. Jean he received a severe wound, was retained in hospital for a considerable period, and was eventually discharged in 1916.
He holds the General Service and Victory Medals.
20, Protheroe Road, Fulham, S.W.6   16837.

FULLICK, E. T., Driver, Royal Field Artillery.
He volunteered in November, 1914, and was sent to the Western Front, where he served through many important engagements. He took part in fighting at the Somme, Arras, Neuve Chapelle, Amiens, Loos and Cambrai. He was also in action during the last Advance at Cambrai in 1918, and was twice wounded and gassed.
He was discharged in 1918, holding the 1915 Star and the General Service and Victory Medals.
28, Orbain Road, Fulham, S.W.6   X18217.

FUNNELL, A., Pte., 24th London Regiment.
He volunteered for service in September, 1914, and was drafted overseas. He took part in various engagements on the Western Front, including the fighting in the Loos, Arras, and Ypres sectors. He was severely wounded in action in May, 1915, and in consequence was discharged as medically unfit for further service in November, 1915.
He holds the 1915 Star, General Service and Victory Medals.
19, Wilson's Road, Hammersmith, W.6   16412.

FURMEDGE, A. J. W., Cpl., R.A.S.C. (M.T.).
He volunteered in August, 1914, went to the Western Front the same year, and was chiefly engaged in conveying stores and ammunition to the forward lines.
He holds the 1914 Star, General Service and Victory Medals, and was demobilised in June, 1919.
22, West Ella Road, Willesden, N.W.10   15102.

FURNELL, H., Sergt., West Yorkshire Regiment.
He volunteered in September, 1914, and during his service on the Western Front took part in engagements on the Somme, at Arras, Loos, Neuve Chapelle, Festubert and Ypres.
He was discharged in 1917, suffering from the effects of gas poisoning and trench feet, and holds the 1915 Star and the General Service and Victory Medals.
17, Lurgan Avenue, Hammersmith, W.6   13443.

FURNELL, H. T., Gunner, R.G.A.
He volunteered in 1915, served in France from that year until 1919, and took part in engagements on the Somme, at Ypres, Bullecourt, Messines and in the Advance of 1918.
He was demobilised in April, 1919, holding the 1915 Star, General Service and Victory Medals
35, Aspenlea Road, Hammersmith, W.6   14296B.

FURNELL, L. (Mrs.), Special War Worker.
This lady rendered services of a most valuable character during the war, when she was employed in a large munition works. She carried out her arduous work with painstaking diligence, and was highly commended.
35, Aspenlea Road, Hammersmith, W.6   14296A.

FURNESS, H., Lce.-Cpl., 13th Essex Regiment.
He volunteered in 1915, and during his service on the Western Front took part in engagements on the Somme, Ypres, Bullecourt and Arras. He was gassed and twice wounded and, while in the Advance of 1918, was killed in September.
He was entitled to the 1915 Star and the General Service and Victory Medals.
4, Durban Road, Tottenham, N.17   X18098D.

FURNESS, J., Gunner, Royal Marine Artillery.
Being on the Reserve when war was declared, he was called up in August, 1914, and sent to France in the same month. He also served in Egypt, and later on mine-sweeping . While in a merchant ship he was torpedoed in 1918 at the Firth of Forth, and was discharged in March, 1919, holding the 1914 Star and the General Service and Victory Medals.
14, St. Margaret's Road, Willesden, N.W.10   X17828.

FURNESS, J., Pte., Royal Scots.
He volunteered in 1915, and was sent in the following year to France, where he served for three years and took part in many engagements, including the battles of the Somme and Ypres. He was also in action through the Advance of 1918, and was discharged in April, 1919, holding the General Service and Victory Medals.
4, Durban Road, Tottenham, N.17   X18098C.

FURNISH, W. H., Pte., The Queen's (Royal West Surrey Regiment).
He joined in July, 1916, and served on the Western Front, and later in Italy. In 1918 he was invalided home, owing to ill-health, and after being in a sanatorium for a short time, was discharged in January, 1919.
He holds the General Service and Victory Medals.
6, Moselle Street, Tottenham, N.17   X18206A

FUSSEL, W. A., Pte., Wiltshire Regiment.
He was in the Army at the outbreak of war, and immediately crossed to France, where he went through the retreat from Mons and the battles of Ypres, Loos and the Somme. During his service he was wounded, gassed and suffered from shell-shock, and after a long stay in hospital was discharged in May, 1917, as medically unfit for further service.
He holds the Mons Star and the General Service and Victory Medals.   16, Kennet Road, Maida Hill, W.9   X19376.

G

GADD, J., Pte., Royal Army Service Corps.
He volunteered in August, 1914, and was sent to the Western Front, where he was employed on important duties on the railways. He remained overseas until June, 1919, when he was demobilised, holding the General Service and Victory Medals.
38, Church Path, Hammersmith, W.6   16395.

GAGE, G., Gunner, Royal Field Artillery.
He volunteered in February, 1915, and was sent to France, where he rendered services with his Battery throughout the war.
In June, 1919, he was demobilised, holding the General Service and Victory Medals.
16, Worlidge Street, Hammersmith, W.6   13267.

GAINEY, R. A., Pte., 3rd Royal Fusiliers.
Having previously served in the Army, he was mobilised in August, 1914, and was later sent to the Western Front, where he took part in several engagements, including the battles of Ypres and Loos. He was afterwards drafted to Salonica, and while there contracted malaria, being finally discharged in November, 1917.
He holds the 1914-15 Star, General Service and Victory Medals.
39, Bramber Road, West Kensington, W.14   15715.

GAINSBURY, C. (Mrs.), Special War Worker.
During the war this lady was engaged on important duties in connection with the construction of aeroplanes, doing valuable work of an essential nature.
11, Humbolt Road, Hammersmith, W.6   15306B.

GAINSBURY, V., Driver, Royal Field Artillery.
He volunteered in January, 1915, and later was sent to the Eastern Front, where he saw considerable service. He was finally invalided home, suffering from malaria, and demobilised in February, 1919.
He holds the General Service and Victory Medals.
11, Humbolt Road, Hammersmith, W.6   15306A.

GALE, A., Cpl., Royal Fusiliers.
He volunteered in September, 1914, and served on the Western Front from June, 1915, to August, 1916. He fought on the Somme and at Ypres, and in many other engagements, and was killed at Fricourt.
He was entitled to the 1915 Star, the General Service and Victory Medals.
43, Charlton Road, Harlesden, N.W.10   13104A.

GALE, A. V., Cpl., 9th London Regt. and R.A.F.
He volunteered in September, 1914, and was engaged on the Western Front, where he saw much fighting. He was afterwards transferred to the Royal Air Force, and is still serving.
He holds the 1914 Star and the General Service and Victory Medals.
9, Chaldon Road, Fulham, S.W.6   X17645.

GALE, J. H., Pte.., Royal Fusiliers and Machine Gun Corps.
He volunteered in April, 1915, and was sent to Salonica in 1916. Ten months later he went to Egypt and afterwards to Palestine, where he was present at the battles of Gaza and Jerusalem. Whilst in Egypt he contracted malaria and returned to England, being demobilised in August, 1919.
He holds the General Service and Victory Medals.
34, Goodhall Street, Harlesden, N.W.10   T12725B.

GALE, J. W., Lce.-Cpl., R.A.S.C.
He volunteered in August, 1914, and was sent to France a year later. He took part in the battles of Ypres (1915), the Somme (1916), Cambrai (1917), Arras, Loos, Albert, Bapaume and Maricourt, and was at Lille in the Final Advance of 1918.
He was demobilised in April, 1919, holding the 1915 Star and the General Service and Victory Medals.
34, Goodhall Street, Harlesden, N.W.10   T12725A.

GALE, W., Pte., The Queen's (Royal West Surrey Regiment) and Middlesex Regiment.
He joined in June, 1916, and after he had completed his training, served at various stations with his unit, carrying out important duties. He was unable to obtain a transfer overseas before the cessation of hostilities, and was demobilised in January, 1919.
43, Charlton Road, Harlesden, N.W.10   13104C.

GALE, W., Pte., 5th Middlesex Regiment.
He joined in 1916, served on the Western Front, and took part in several engagements, including those at Ypres, Cambrai, Lens and Arras. He was severely wounded at Monchy, and was discharged medically unfit for further service in March, 1918, holding the General Service and Victory Medals.
68, Brownlow Road, Willesden, N.W.10   14719.

GALL, J., Cpl., Scots Guards.
He volunteered in 1914 and fought at Mons. Later he was wounded and taken prisoner at the first battle of Ypres, and was interned for four years in Germany at Wittenberg Camp, where he suffered great privations.
He was discharged as medically unfit in 1918, after his release, and holds the Mons Star and the General Service and Victory Medals.
41, Milton Avenue, Willesden, N.W.10   14108.

GALLAGHER, B. (Mrs.), Special War Worker.
During the war this lady rendered services of a very valuable character. At first she was employed in a large munition factory, and later served as a canteen steward. Her work at all times was deserving of every praise, her duties being carried out in a thoroughly efficient manner.
37, Redfern Road, Willesden, N.W.10   13205B.

GALLAGHER, J., Pte., 1/9th Middlesex Regt.
He volunteered in December, 1914, and was sent to the Western Front, where he took part in the Retreat and Advance of 1918.
He holds the General Service and Victory Medals, and was demobilised in March, 1919.
37, Redfern Road, Willesden, N.W.10   13205A.

GALLIERS, H., Gunner, Royal Garrison Artillery.
He volunteered in November, 1915, and during his service on the Western Front took part in the fighting near Loos. In June, 1916, he was so badly wounded in action at Vimy Ridge on the 9th that it was necessary to amputate both legs. He was discharged in July, 1917, and holds the General Service and Victory Medals.
3, First Avenue, Queen's Park Estate, W.10   X19040.

GALLIERS, M. J., Pte., Royal Fusiliers.
He volunteered in December, 1915, and in January, 1917, was sent to the Western Front, where he was in action at Arras, Vimy Ridge and Bullecourt, and was twice wounded. He holds the General Service and Victory Medals, and was discharged in September, 1917.
229, Shirland Road, Maida Hill, W.9   X19524.

GALTON, H. V., Pte., R.A.S.C. (M.T.).
He joined in April, 1916, and was engaged on special duties at various sections with his unit. He rendered valuable services, but was unsuccessful in obtaining his transfer overseas before the cessation of hostilities.
He was demobilised in September, 1919.
63, Harley Road, Willesden, N.W.10   13176.

GALVIN, A., Pte., Royal Army Service Corps.
He joined in May, 1917, and served with his unit at various stations. His duties were of great importance, and he was retained on transport work until he secured his demobilisation in October, 1919.
18, Orbain Road, Fulham, S.W.6   X18044B.

GALVIN, A. (Mrs.), Special War Worker.
For the duration of the war this lady was employed on essential work in the packing and box-making department of a large munition factory. She carried out her duties in a skilful and efficient manner, and was presented with a certificate for her valuable work from the firm with which she was employed.
18, Orbain Road, Fulham, S.W.6   X18044A.

GALVIN, E. (Mrs.), Special War Worker.
Throughout the war this lady was engaged at a London filling station. She was chiefly engaged in shell-filling and flare-packing. This work, which was of an arduous nature, she carried out with skill and energy, to the satisfaction of her employers.
40, Orbain Road, Fulham, S.W.6   X18227

GALVIN, J., Pte., 12th Suffolk Regiment.
He volunteered in August, 1915, and served on the Western Front, taking part with distinction in several engagements. He was demobilised in March, 1919, and holds the General Service and Victory Medals.
47, Aintree Street, Dawes Road, S.W.6   X18212A.

GALVIN, J. W., Pte., 3rd Bedfordshire Regiment.
He joined in May, 1918, and after he had completed his training, served at various stations on important duties with his unit. He was unable to obtain a transfer overseas before the end of the war, and was demobilised in January, 1920.
47, Aintree Street, Dawes Road, S.W.6   X18212B.

GAME, A. G., Pte., Royal Army Service Corps.
He joined in February, 1917, and saw service on important transportation duties on the Western Front, and later with the Army of Occupation in Germany.
He was demobilised in October, 1919, and holds the General Service and Victory Medals.
54, Lyndhurst Road, Upper Edmonton, N.18   15507.

GAMESTER, S., Sergt., 2nd Royal Warwickshire Regiment.
He volunteered in 1915, took part in the Dardanelles Campaign, and in 1917 went to France, where he served for two years. During his service he took part in many important engagements, and holds the 1915 Star, General Service and Victory Medals.
25, Belton Road, Cricklewood, N.W.2   16593B.

GAMMOND, R., Pte., R.A.S.C. (H.T.).
He volunteered in 1914, and during his service was engaged in the important duty of conveying horses to France and in taking those that were wounded back to England.
He was discharged owing to ill-health in 1916, and holds the 1915 Star and the General Service and Victory Medals.
16, Hilmer Street, West Kensington, W.14   16264.

GANDER, R., Driver, Royal Army Service Corps.
He volunteered in August, 1914, and during his service in France was employed in the Somme, Loos and Cambrai sectors, and was wounded three times.
He was demobilised in March, 1919, and holds the 1914 Star and the General Service and Victory Medals.
14, Beaconsfield Road, Lower Edmonton, N.9   T14767B.

GANNON, A. E., Pte., Royal Army Service Corps.
He volunteered in February, 1915, and served on the French Front. In April, 1916, he was badly wounded, and after hospital treatment in France and England for several months, was discharged as medically unfit for further service.
He holds the General Service and Victory Medals.
11, Moselle Street, Tottenham, N.17   X18366.

GARDEN, J. C., Sapper, Royal Engineers.
He volunteered in July, 1915, and served on many sectors of the Western Front, engaged on bridge-building and other duties.
He was discharged through ill-health in February, 1917, and holds the 1915 Star, General Service and Victory Medals.
3a, Barclay Road, Walham Green, S.W.6   X19708.

GARDEN, L. E., Pte., 20th London Regt.
He joined in March, 1917, and saw service on both Western and Eastern Fronts While in the East he took part in the advance through Palestine, seeing much fighting.
He died on December 7th, 1917, and was entitled to the General Service and Victory Medals.
17, First Avenue, Queen's Park Estate, W.10   X18944.

GARDENER, J. A. A., Rifleman, 8th London Regiment (Post Office Rifles).
He volunteered in August, 1914, and served in France, where he took part with distinction in several engagements, and was twice wounded.
He was demobilised in February, 1919, and holds the 1914 Star and the General Service and Victory Medals.
44, Haldane Road, Walham Green, S.W.6   X17378.

GARDINER, B., Pte., Royal Marine Light Infantry.
He enlisted in January, 1914, and saw service in France, the Dardanelles, Russia and the North Sea. He took part in many engagements, including the battle of Jutland, and was wounded. He is still serving, and holds the 1915 Star and the General Service and Victory Medals.
150, Bounces Road, Lower Edmonton, N.9   13012.

GARDINER, E., Pte., The London Regiment.
He volunteered his services in 1915, and after completing his training, was stationed at various places with his unit. He seriously injured his spine through an accident, and was discharged in 1916, but died later from his injuries.
22, Werley Avenue, Dawes Road, S.W.6   X17867A.

GARDINER, F. J., Mechanic, Royal Air Force.
He volunteered in 1915, and was stationed with the R.A.F. at various places. His duties called for a high degree of mechanical skill, and he rendered valuable services until he secured his demobilisation in 1919.
35, Barret's Green Road, Willesden, N.W.10   13628B.

GARDINER, F. R. (Mrs.), Special War Worker.
Throughout the war this lady was engaged in a large munition factory, where she rendered services of a most valuable character. Her duties were essential to the country, and she was commended for her patriotism.
35, Barret's Green Road, Willesden, N.W 10   13628A.

GARDINER, H. E., Pte., Royal Irish Regiment.
He volunteered in September, 1914, and during his service on the Western Front took part in many engagements, was gassed twice and wounded. He was in hospital in France and England before being demobilised in March, 1919, and holds the 1915 Star, General Service and Victory Medals.
22, Werley Avenue, Dawes Road, S.W.6   X17869.

GARDINER, L. C., Lce.-Cpl., Royal Engineers (Signalling Section).
He joined in July, 1917, and was sent to France. While on the Western Front he fought in several battles, including those at the Somme, Cambrai, Arras, Bapaume and Ypres. In 1918 he was sent to Germany with the Army of Occupation, and was demobilised in November, 1919, holding the General Service and Victory Medals.
19, Cooper Road, Dudden Hill, N.W.10   16643B.

GARDINER, R. A., Pte., Labour Corps.
He joined in January, 1917, and served on the Western Front till 1919. Among other places, he was at the Somme, Ypres and Cambrai, and was demobilised in January, 1920, holding the General Service and Victory Medals.
19, Cooper Road, Dudden Hill, N.W.10   16643C.

GARDINER, W., Pte., West Kent (Queen's Own) Hussars.
He joined in February, 1916, and served with distinction on the Western Front, taking part in many engagements, including the fighting near Hill 60, and on other sectors.
He was demobilised in February, 1919, and holds the General Service and Victory Medals.
40, Sheldon Road, Upper Edmonton, N.18   X17456.

GARDNER, A., Pte., Middlesex Regiment.
He volunteered in 1914, was sent to France in 1915, and took part in many engagements, including the battles of the Somme and Ypres. He was wounded and taken prisoner in 1916, and suffered many hardships whilst in captivity. He holds the 1915 Star, General Service and Victory Medals, and was demobilised in 1919.
22, Star Road, West Kensington, W.14   16681A.

GARDNER, A. R., Pte., 9th Middlesex Regiment and 2nd Air Mechanic, Royal Air Force.
He volunteered in May, 1915, and was stationed with his unit at several places for over a year. He was then discharged as medically unfit, but in March, 1918, he re-enlisted in the R.A.F. and rendered valuable services. He was unsuccessful in his efforts to proceed overseas, and was finally demobilised in November, 1919.
14, Holly Lane, Willesden, N.W.10   15525.

GARDNER, C., Pte., Army Cyclist Corps.
He volunteered in 1915, and after he had completed his training was sent to Salonica, where he took part in several engagements during his three years' service.
He was demobilised in November, 1919, and holds the General Service and Victory Medals.
14, Sheldon Road, Upper Edmonton, N.18   X17304.

GARDNER, F. J., Gunner, Royal Field Artillery and Pte., Royal Army Medical Corps.
In August, 1914, he volunteered in the R.F.A. and took part in the Dardanelles Campaign, where he was wounded. He was later drafted to Egypt and again wounded, being in hospital some time. In 1917 he was transferred to the R.A.M.C., and remained with them until demobilised in February, 1919.
He holds the 1914 Star and the General Service and Victory Medals.
52, Raynham Avenue, Upper Edmonton, N.18   T16482B.

GARDNER, F. J., Pte., Royal Army Medical Corps and Gunner, Royal Field Artillery.
He volunteered in 1914 and was sent to Egypt, where, during his four years' service, he was in action on numerous occasions.
He was demobilised in March, 1919, and holds the 1914-15 Star and the General Service and Victory Medals.
104, Kimberley Road, Upper Edmonton, N.18   16784B.

GARDNER, G., Mechanic, Royal Air Force.
He volunteered in September, 1915, and served on the Western Front, where he was occupied on very important duties. Later he went to Germany with the Army of Occupation. While there he was sent to hospital, and in March, 1919, was demobilised, holding the General Service and Victory Medals.
17, Montagu Street, Hammersmith, W.6   16401.

GARDNER, H., Gunner, Royal Field Artillery.
He was serving at the outbreak of war, and was sent to France in 1915, where he took part in several engagements, and was wounded at Festubert. In 1917 he was sent to Italy, and served there until his demobilisation in March, 1919.
He holds the 1915 Star and the General Service and Victory Medals.
31, Sandringham Road, N.W.2   X17102.

GARDNER, H. W., Pte., Royal Fusiliers.
He joined in 1918, and after his training served at various stations on important duties with his unit. He was unable to obtain a transfer overseas before the cessation of hostilities.
He was demobilised in 1919.
104, Kimberley Road, Upper Edmonton, N.18   16784A.

GARDNER, I. (Mrs.), Special War Worker.
During the war this lady was engaged on war work of a very arduous nature. At first she was at a small-arms factory, and later undertook the duties of a night operator at a large telephone exchange in order to release a man for active service. Her valuable work was highly commendable.
27, Ilex Road, Willesden, N.W.10   16102A.

GARDNER, J., Pte., Labour Corps.
He joined in 1916 and served on the Western Front, rendering important service at Bapaume, Cambrai and elsewhere.
He was demobilised in February, 1919, holding the General Service and Victory Medals.
6, Bayonne Road, W.6   14643.

GARDNER, S. W., Pte., 6th West Yorkshire Regt.

He joined in July, 1916, and served in France, taking part in many engagements, including the Retreat and Advance of 1918. He did duty as a stretcher-bearer.
He holds the General Service and Victory Medals, and was demobilised in October, 1919.
18, Letchford Gardens, Willesden, N.W.10   X17544.

GARDNER, T., Pte., 2nd Essex Regiment.

He joined in June, 1917, and in the same year was sent to France, where he took part with distinction in several engagements, being wounded.
He holds the General Service and Victory Medals, and is now serving abroad.
39, St. Martin's Road, Lower Edmonton, N.9   T12980.

GARDNER, T. W., Pte., Machine Gun Corps.

He joined in May, 1917, and during his service on the Western Front took part in engagements near Albert and Arras.
He was demobilised in November, 1919, and holds the General Service and Victory Medals.
67, Brett Road, N.W.10   14524.

GARFORD, T., 1st-Class Petty Officer, R.N.

He was called up from the Reserve when war broke out, and was engaged in the dangerous work of escorting transports, and also saw service in the Dardanelles. He took part in the battle of Heligoland, and was in H.M.S. " Lorenzo " when she was sunk in the North Sea. He also served in H.M.S. "Newmarket," and was demobilised in April, 1919, having completed 29 years' service.
He holds the China Medal, the 1914 Star, the General Service, Victory, Long Service and Good Conduct Medals.
42a, Eynham Road, Shepherd's Bush, W.12   12399.

GARLICK, E., Sergt., 6th Cheshire Regiment.

He volunteered in August, 1914, and served on the Western Front, where he took part in the retreat from Mons and the battles of the Marne, the Aisne and Ypres, and was wounded. During the latter part of the war he acted as an instructor, and was demobilised in 1919, holding the Mons Star and the General Service and Victory Medals.
363a, Chapter Road, N.W.2   16168B.

GARLICK, F. M., Driver, Royal Field Artillery.

He volunteered in November, 1915, and was sent to France, where he served on the Somme, at Bethune, Beaumont-Hamel, Tournai and during the Advance of 1918.
He was demobilised in January, 1919, holding the General Service and Victory Medals.
44, Ancill Street, Hammersmith, W.6   13984.

GARMAN, B. C., Staff-Sergt., Royal Engineers.

He joined in May, 1916, and later was sent to the Western Front, where he was engaged on important and responsible duties in connection with the searchlights.
He holds the General Service and Victory Medals, and was demobilised in October, 1919.
111, Harley Road, N.W.10   13182.

GARNER, A., Special War Worker.

Throughout the war he was employed at Woolwich Arsenal, where he rendered valuable and indispensable services on work of vital importance.
88, Bronsart Road, S.W.6   X18998

GARNER, F. C., Driver, R.A.S.C.

He volunteered in November, 1914, and served as a despatch-rider on many sectors of the Western Front, including the Somme, Ypres and Cambrai. He was attached to H.Q. Staff, and also did transport work.
He holds the 1915 Star, the General Service and Victory Medals, and was demobilised in October, 1919.
15, Waldo Road, N.W.10   X17625.

GARNER, G., Sapper, Royal Engineers.

Volunteering in January, 1915, he served on the Western Front, taking part in the fighting around Bapaume, La Bassée, Ypres and Poperinghe. He was chiefly engaged on expert work in connection with railway construction.
He holds the Victory and General Service Medals, and was demobilised in February, 1919.
31, Archel Road, West Kensington, W.14   16206.

GARNER, W. A., Pte., Royal Irish Fusiliers.

He volunteered in June, 1915, and was drafted to the Western Front, where he took part in the battles of the Somme and Ypres, and was wounded in action at Messines in 1917. After being in hospital at Boulogne and in England for six months, he was stationed in Ireland until he was demobilised in March, 1919.
He holds the General Service and Victory Medals.
16, Bronsart Road, S.W.6   TX18987.

GARNHAM, G., Cpl., R.A.F. (Balloon Section).

He volunteered in January, 1916, and on completion of training was sent to the Western Front, and later served in Greece (Corfu) and Russia on important observation duties.
He was demobilised in August, 1919, and holds the General Service and Victory Medals.
23, Ashwell Grove, Upper Edmonton. N.18   X17890.

GARRARD, F. G., Petty Officer, Royal Navy.

He joined in August, 1914, and served in the Dardanelles during 1915, and was also present at the battle of Heligoland and Jutland.
He holds the 1914 Star and the General Service and Victory Medals.
18, Hartington Road, Lower Edmonton, N.9   14249A.

GARRETT, A., Rifleman, 2nd King's Royal Rifle Corps.

He joined in September, 1917, and during his service was engaged on important duties at various stations with his unit. He was unsuccessful in obtaining his transfer overseas before the end of the war, and was demobilised in November, 1919.
7, Hartington Road, Lower Edmonton, N.9   14239.

GARRETT, A. G., Cpl., 9th Middlesex Regiment.

He was mobilised in August, 1914, and served throughout the war in India, where he took part in the Afghanistan Campaign in 1919. On his return to England he was demobilised in November, 1919, and holds the 1914-15 Star and the General Service and Victory Medals, and the India General Service Medal with clasp—Afghanistan, North West Frontier, 1919.
111, Roundwood Road, Willesden, N.W.10   16049A.

GARRETT, F., Pte., Middlesex Regiment.

He volunteered in October, 1914, and after completing his training, served at various internment camps, guarding German prisoners. Owing to his being over age, he could not obtain his transfer overseas, and was discharged in April, 1916. Previous to the Great War he had served in the Egyptian Campaign of 1882, and holds the Egyptian Medal and Star.
111, Roundwood Road, Willesden, N.W.10   16049B.

GARRETT, H., Drummer, 13th London Regt.

He joined in February, 1917, and served in Egypt, Palestine and Syria, taking part in the capture of Jerusalem.
He was demobilised in April, 1920, holding the General Service and Victory Medals.
113a, Hill Side, Stonebridge Park, N.W.10   14605B.

GARRETT, J., Lce.-Cpl., Machine Gun Corps.

He volunteered in August, 1915, and the following year was sent to the Western Front, where he took part with distinction in engagements on the Somme, the Ancre, at Arras and Ypres.
He was discharged in April, 1919, and holds the General Service and Victory Medals.
17, Mozart Street, North Kensington, W.10   X18926.

GARRETT, W., Sapper, Royal Engineers and Pte., Middlesex Regiment.

He volunteered in 1915, and served on the Western Front from 1916 to 1919, taking part in engagements at the Somme, Ypres, Hill 60, Vimy Ridge, Cambrai, Arras, Loos and Bethune. He was gassed and twice wounded, and on his return to England was demobilised in 1919, holding the General Service and Victory Medals.
113a, Hill Side, Stonebridge Park, N.W.10   14605A.

GARROD, W., Sapper, Royal Engineers.

He volunteered in September, 1914, and in the following year was sent to Gallipoli, where he took part in the landing at Suvla Bay. In 1916 he served at Salonica, being in action in various engagements, including the Serbian Retreat. He was demobilised in March, 1919, on his return home, holding the 1915 Star, General Service and Victory Medals.
83, Barry Road, N.W.10   14944.

GARRUD, A., Sergt., Royal Garrison Artillery.

He was serving at the outbreak of war, and was sent to France immediately, taking part in the retreat from Mons. He was also in action at Ypres, the Somme, Armentieres and Cambrai, and was killed in action on April 9th, 1917.
He was entitled to the Mons Star and the General Service and Victory Medals.
34, Glynfield Road, N.W.10   15131A—16521.

GARRUD, G., Pte., 4th Middlesex Regiment.

He joined in April, 1916, served on the Western Front from the following January until October, 1919, and took part in various engagements during that period, including the battles of the Somme, Arras and Amiens.
He was serving in Gibraltar in 1920, and holds the General Service and Victory Medals.
34, Glynfield Road, N.W.10   15131B—16521.

GARVEY, E. E., Pte., The Queen's (Royal West Surrey Regiment).
He joined in August, 1916, and a few months later was sent to the Western Front, where he took part in engagements at Ypres, Arras and Cambrai. His active service greatly affected his health, and he was invalided home and discharged in February, 1919, holding the General Service and Victory Medals. 9, Fordingley Road, W.9 X19679.

GARVEY, M. J. W., Pte., Royal Dublin Fusiliers.
He volunteered in August, 1914, and the following year was sent to the Western Front, where in April, 1915, he received, at St. Julien, a severe wound, which necessitated the amputation of his leg.
He was discharged in August, 1917, and holds the 1915 Star and the General Service and Victory Medals.
31, Ray's Road, Upper Edmonton, N.18 15357.

GATE, W. R., Pte., Royal Army Service Corps.
He volunteered in September, 1914, and during his service on the Western Front, which lasted four years, was present at the battles of Loos, Cambrai, Arras, Ypres, the Somme and the Advance of 1918.
He holds the 1915 Star, General Service and Victory Medals, and was demobilised in May, 1919, on his return to England.
36, Halford Road, Walham Green, S.W.6 X19475.

GATES, A. T., Pte., 1/7th London Regiment.
He volunteered in July, 1915, and served for two and a half years on the Western Front, where he was four times wounded, at Menin Road, High Wood, the Somme and Albert, and twice gassed, at Bourlon Wood and again at Albert.
On his return home he was demobilised in February, 1919, and holds the 1915 Star and the General Service and Victory Medals. 28, Somerset Place, Hammersmith, W.6 13790.

GATES, H. W., Special War Worker.
Throughout the war he did very valuable work as a rifle finisher at the Royal Small Arms Factory, Enfield Lock. Prior to the outbreak of hostilities he had served for five years in the East Surrey Regiment. His work at Enfield was of a highly skilled nature.
26, Hiley Road, Willesden, N.W.10 X18652.

GATTY, T., Cpl., M.G.C. and Scottish Rifles.
He volunteered in January, 1915, and was sent out to France, where he took part with distinction in many important engagements, including the battles of Loos, Arras and the Somme. He was wounded and gassed, and was taken prisoner at St. Quentin, being kept in Germany for eight months.
On his release he was demobilised in April, 1919, and holds the 1915 Star, General Service and Victory Medals.
27, Rosaline Road, Fulham, S.W.6 TX18625.

GAVARON, C., Pte., Suffolk Regiment.
He joined in June, 1916, and was almost immediately sent to Salonica, where he took part in many important engagements.
On his return he was demobilised in August, 1919, and holds the General Service and Victory Medals.
8, Gilpin Grove, Upper Edmonton, N.18 16806C.

GAVARON, J., Pte., Royal Fusiliers.
He volunteered for service in January, 1916, and after his training was drafted overseas. He took part in many engagements on the Western Front, being employed as a signaller, and was reported missing and afterwards killed in action at Epéhy on September 21st, 1918.
He was entitled to the General Service and Victory Medals.
8, Gilpin Grove, Upper Edmonton, N.18 16806A.

GAVARON, W., Pte., 2nd Manchester Regiment.
He joined in December, 1916, went to the Western Front, where he took part in several engagements and was wounded in March, 1918, and again in October of the same year. He was in hospital for eight months, and in March, 1919, was demobilised.
He holds the General Service and Victory Medals.
8, Gilpin Grove, Upper Edmonton, N.18 16806B.

GAY, F. A., Sergt., Royal Engineers.
He was in the Army at the outbreak of war, and was sent to Mesopotamia, where he took part in many engagements, and was with General Townshend in Kut.
He holds the 1914 Star, General Service, Territorial and Victory Medals.
On his return to England he was demobilised in March, 1919.
22a, Deacon Road, N.W.2 16139B.

GAY, J., Pte., Royal Army Service Corps (M.T.).
He volunteered for service in April, 1915, and at the conclusion of his training was drafted overseas to Salonica, where he was engaged on transport duties in various sectors of the Balkan Front, and was wounded.
He holds the General Service and Victory Medals, and was demobilised in October, 1919.
92, Adeney Road, Hammersmith, W.6 14467.

GAY, R. E., Rifleman, Rifle Brigade.
He volunteered in October, 1915, and served on the Western Front from 1916 to 1919, taking part in several engagements, including the battles of Ypres, Arras and the Somme. He was transferred to the Machine Gun Corps and was sent to Russia and later to India, where he is still serving. During his service he was twice wounded, and was awarded a Russian decoration for gallantry, and holds, in addition, the General Service and Victory Medals.
22a, Deacon Road, Cricklewood, N.W.2 16139A.

GEALL, A., 2nd Air Mechanic, Royal Air Force.
He joined up for service in August, 1917, and after his training was drafted overseas, where he was engaged on important duties at aerodromes on the Western Front. He remained in France until after the cessation of hostilities, when he returned to England and was demobilised in January, 1920.
He holds the General Service and Victory Medals.
64a, Sandringham Road, Cricklewood, N.W.2 16711C.

GEALL, F., Pte., 5th Middlesex Regiment.
He volunteered in August, 1914, and served in France in 1915, taking part in engagements on the Somme. He was taken prisoner in April, 1918, and suffered many hardships whilst in captivity.
He holds the 1915 Star, General Service and Victory Medals, and on his release was demobilised in 1919.
64a, Sandringham Road, Cricklewood, N.W.2 16711B.

GEALL, W., Cpl., 1/9th Middlesex Regiment.
He volunteered in August, 1914, and was sent to India, where he served until 1917. He was then transferred to Mesopotamia, remaining there for two years and seeing much service. He was sent back home in June, 1919, was demobilised, holding the 1914-15 Star and the General Service and Victory Medals.
64a, Sandringham Road, Cricklewood, N.W.2 16711A.

GEARD, S. A. (M.M.), Cpl., 2nd Leinster Regt.
He volunteered in August, 1914, and saw active service in the Dardanelles, France, Egypt and Salonica, and was twice wounded. He was mentioned in despatches and was awarded the Military Medal for conspicuous gallantry in saving life under heavy shell-fire.
He was sent home and demobilised in April, 1919, holding, in addition to the Military Medal, the 1915 Star and the General Service and Victory Medals.
41, Masbro' Road, West Kensington, W.14 12025.

GEARING, A. M. (Mrs.), Special War Worker.
During the war this lady was engaged in a large Army equipment factory, where she rendered most valuable services. Her work was of the greatest importance.
2, Mablethorpe Road, Fulham, S.W.6 X19249B.

GEARING, M. P., Lce.-Cpl., Rifle Brigade.
He volunteered in August, 1914, served on the Western Front and took part in engagements at Loos, Arras, Neuve Chapelle, Amiens, Bullecourt, Festubert, Ginchy, Ypres, Vimy Ridge and the Advance of 1918.
He was sent home and demobilised in 1919, holding the 1914 Star, General Service and Victory Medals.
2, Mablethorpe Road, Fulham, S.W.6 X19249A.

GEARING, W., Gunner, Royal Garrison Artillery.
He volunteered in November, 1915, and served on the Western Front, taking part in engagements at Arras, Loos, Neuve Chapelle, Ypres, Vimy Ridge, Hill 60 and the Somme. He also fought in the Advance of 1918, and after his return was demobilised in February, 1919, holding the General Service and Victory Medals.
20, Francis Street, Hammersmith, W.6 15035.

GEDGE, C. F., Cpl., Royal Field Artillery.
He volunteered in August, 1915, was sent to the Western Front in the following year, and took part in several engagements, including the battles of the Somme and Ypres. He was wounded in September, 1917, and after his return demobilised in March, 1919, holding the General Service and Victory Medals.
25, Melville Road, Stonebridge Park, N.W.10 14624.

GEDGE, R. G., Pte., 23rd Middlesex Regiment.
He volunteered in June, 1915, and served on the Western Front and in Italy. He took part in the battles of Ypres, Arras, Cambrai and Vimy Ridge, and was killed in action during the fighting at Ypres on April 30th, 1917.
He was entitled to the 1915 Star and the General Service and Victory Medals.
55, Melville Road, Stonebridge Park, N.W.10 15648.

GEERING, A. (Mrs.), Special War Worker.
During 1917 and 1918 this lady rendered valuable services on important and dangerous work at No. 3 Filling Factory, Park Royal, and gave great satisfaction by her care and thoroughness.
56, Barnsdale Road, Maida Hill, W.9 X19682B.

GEERING, H. G. W., Lce.-Cpl., Border Regiment.

He enlisted in October, 1910, and at the outbreak of war went to the Western Front, where he took part in the retreat from Mons, the battles of Ypres, the Somme and Bullecourt, and was wounded and gassed. Later he was sent to Gallipoli and served in the Dardanelles campaign, where he was again wounded. On his recovery he was stationed in England as an instructor until discharged in February, 1919.
He holds the Mons Star and the General Service and Victory Medals.
56, Barnsdale Road, Maida Hill, W.9   X19682A.

GEEVES, C., A.B., Royal Navy.

He joined the Navy in February, 1917, and served in H.M.S. "Avoca" in the Mediterranean. While near the Dardanelles he was badly wounded, but soon came back to duty. On his return to England he was demobilised in December, 1919, and holds the General Service and Victory Medals.
46, Gloucester Road, Upper Edmonton, N.18   X17005.

GEEVES, F. C., Sergt., R.A.S.C. (M.T.).

He joined in November, 1916, and after his training was drafted to India, where he was engaged at various stations on important duties with his unit. He rendered important and responsible duties, and returned to England, where he was demobilised in January, 1920.
He holds the General Service and Victory Medals.
150, Town Road, Lower Edmonton, N.9   13587.

GEEVES, J. H., Rifleman, 1st King's Royal Rifle Corps.

He joined in March, 1917, and in the following January was sent to France, where he took part in the battle of Cambrai. In March, 1918, he was badly gassed, and seven months later was wounded. He was sent back to England, and was demobilised in October, 1919, holding the General Service and Victory Medals.
12, Chester Road, Lower Edmonton, N.9   12714.

GENTRY, G. F., Sapper, Royal Engineers.

He joined in June, 1916, and served in France, taking part in several engagements, including those at Amiens, Ypres and the Somme. He was wounded, and was demobilised in February, 1919, holding the General Service and Victory Medals.
29, Warwick Road, Upper Edmonton, N.18   X17505.

GEORGE, A., Sergt., Northumberland Fusiliers.

He volunteered for service in 1915, and at the conclusion of his training was drafted to Mesopotamia, where he took part with distinction in many engagements He remained in this theatre of war until 1919, when he returned to England for demobilisation.
He holds the General Service and Victory Medals.
108, Montague Road, Lower Edmonton, N.9   16883.

GEORGE, A. F. A. (Miss), Special War Worker.

During the war this lady was engaged at Messrs. Waring & Gillows' Factory at Hammersmith, on work of great importance in connection with the manufacture of aeroplanes. She afterwards released a man for military service by taking his place as a van-driver at a large London food supply depot, where she gave valuable service.
5, Mablethorpe Road, Fulham, S.W.6   X19121.

GEORGE, A. P., Rifleman, 6th London Regiment (Rifles).

He joined in June, 1916, and during his service on the Western Front was severely wounded while in action on the Somme. On February 21st, 1917, he died of wounds. He was entitled to the General Service and Victory Medals.
72, Bramber Road, West Kensington, W.14   16221.

GEORGE, E., Pte., Labour Corps.

He joined in 1917 and was engaged on duties of an important nature at various stations with his unit. He rendered valuable services, but was unsuccessful in obtaining his transfer overseas before hostilities ceased.
He was demobilised in 1919.
401, High Road, Willesden, N.W.10   16738B.

GEORGE, G., Pte., R.A.S.C. (M.T.).

He joined in 1915, and during his service on the Western Front took part in the fighting at the Somme, Arras, Loos, Neuve Chapelle, Armentieres, Amiens, Bullecourt, Festubert, St. Quentin, Ypres, Vimy Ridge, Cambrai and the last Advance of 1918.
He was demobilised in 1919, and holds the 1915 Star, General Service and Victory Medals.
5, Mablethorpe Road, Fulham, S.W.6   X19123.

GEORGE, G.E., A.B., R.N., H.M.S. "Orpheus."

He joined in 1916, served with the Grand Fleet in the North Sea on dangerous convoy and patrol duties, and was present at the surrender of the German Fleet at Scapa Flow.
He holds the General Service and Victory Medals, and was demobilised in 1919.
5, Mablethorpe Road, Munster Road, S.W.6   X19122.

GEORGE, L. (Mrs.), Special War Worker.

During the war this lady was engaged on arduous work at Perivale Munition Factory, and throughout rendered services of a valuable nature, for which she was highly commended.
401, High Road, Willesden, N.W.10   16738A.

GERAHTY, P., Lce.-Cpl., North Staffordshire Regiment.

He volunteered in August, 1914, and served on the Western Front, where he took part in the battles of Ypres and the Somme. He was so severely wounded that he was sent to England and invalided out of the Army in September, 1917.
He holds the 1914-15 Star and the General Service and Victory Medals.
327, Brettenham Road East, Upper Edmonton, N.18
15622.

GERCKEN, C. E. W., Pte., 6th Middlesex Regt.

He joined in April, 1916, and was engaged throughout on duties of a special nature at important dockyards. He gave valuable services, but was not successful in obtaining his transfer overseas before the fighting ceased, and was demobilised in 1919.
351, Chapter Road, Cricklewood, N.W.2   T17345.

GERRELLI, J., Pte., 13th Middlesex Regiment.

He joined in June, 1916, and two months later was sent to France, where he took part in the battle of the Somme, and died of wounds received in action on September 16th, 1916.
He was entitled to the General Service and Victory Medals.
80, Chaplin Road, Cricklewood, N.W.2   16631.

GIBBARD, W., Rifleman, Rifle Brigade.

After twelve years' previous service he rejoined in August, 1914, and was quickly sent to the Western Front. He took part in many important engagements, including the retreat from Mons and the battles of the Somme, Ypres and Cambrai. He was wounded twice, and was discharged on account of wounds in May, 1918, as medically unfit for further service.
He holds the Mons Star and the General Service and Victory Medals.
2, Armadale Road, Walham Green, S.W.6   X19424.

GIBBENS, S., 1st-Class Petty Officer, Royal Naval Air Service and Royal Air Force.

He volunteered in November, 1914, and after completing his training, was engaged on important and responsible duties at various stations with the Anti-Aircraft Section
He was demobilised in January, 1919, and holds the General Service Medal.
8, Rosaline Road, Munster Road, S.W.6   X18174.

GIBBINS, J., Bombardier, 32nd Siege Battery, Royal Garrison Artillery.

He joined in June, 1916, and later was sent to France, where he took part in several engagements. During the battle of Cambrai in November, 1917, he was taken prisoner, and during his captivity suffered considerable hardship.
He was released after the Armistice, and demobilised in August, 1919, holding the General Service and Victory Medals.
17, Bertie Road, Willesden, N.W.10   X17397.

GIBBONS, B., Gunner, Royal Garrison Artillery.

He volunteered in August, 1914, and was sent to France a year later, where he took part in the battles of the Somme, Arras, Cambrai, Ypres and the Retreat and Advance of 1918. He was gassed during his service, and was demobilised in June, 1919, holding the 1914-15 Star and the General Service and Victory Medals.
73, Barry Road, Stonebridge Park, N.W.10   14934A.

GIBBONS, C. H., Driver, Royal Field Artillery.

He volunteered in November, 1914, and the following year was sent to the Western Front, where he took part in many engagements, including the battles of the Somme, Arras, Vimy Ridge and the Retreat and Advance of 1918.
He holds the 1914-15 Star, General Service and Victory Medals, and was demobilised in June, 1919.
73, Barry Road, Stonebridge Park, N.W.10   14934B.

GIBBONS, J., Pte., Royal Army Service Corps.

He volunteered early in 1916, and after a period of training was sent to France in the same year, where he was engaged in the transportation of supplies. He later rendered valuable services in connection with the evacuation of the wounded. In 1919 he was demobilised, and holds the General Service and Victory Medals.
3, Ilex Road, Willesden, N.W.10   16097C.

GIBBONS, J., jun., Pte., Northumberland Fus.
He joined in 1917, and after completing his training, was engaged with his unit on special duties at various stations. He gave valuable services, but was not successful in obtaining his transfer overseas before the cessation of hostilities. He was demobilised in 1919.
3, Ilex Road, Willesden, N.W.10   16097B.

GIBBS, A., Pte., Royal Army Medical Corps.
He volunteered in September, 1914, and served for three years on the Western Front, during which time he was engaged on important medical duties, and gave valuable services
He was demobilised in 1919, holding the General Service and Victory Medals.
21, Chaldon Road, S.W.6   X17648.

GIBBS, E. J., Rifleman, Rifle Brigade.
He joined in 1916, and after a period of training, was engaged on special duties with his unit at various places. He was later attached to the Royal Air Force and gave valuable services, but was unsuccessful in obtaining his transfer overseas before the signing of the Armistice. He was demobilised in January, 1919
22, Hannell Road, S W.6   X17866.

GIBBS, G. T., Pte., 3rd Suffolk Regiment.
He volunteered in August. 1914, and after the completion of his training, was engaged on important work at various stations. Despite his efforts, his ill-health prevented him from obtaining a transfer overseas, and he was discharged in July, 1916.
74, Queen Street, Hammersmith, W.6   13269.

GIBBS, G. W., Pte., Canadian Infantry.
He joined in 1916, and was immediately sent to the Western Front where, after taking part in many engagements, he was killed on April 11th, 1917.
He was entitled to the General Service and Victory Medals.
77, Bruce Castle Road, Tottenham, N.17   X18317.

GIBBS, H., Pte., R.A.S.C. (M.T.).
He joined in 1918, and was engaged on important duties with the Motor Transport Section of the R A.S.C He was drafted to Ireland, and during the trouble in that country rendered valuable services as a dispatch rider. He was demobilised in 1920.
40, Hilmer Street, West Kensington, W.14   16266B.

GIBBS, J. A., Cpl., 2nd Middlesex Regiment.
He volunteered in August, 1914, and was sent to the Western Front, where, after seeing much hard fighting, he was killed on February 26th, 1917, whilst in action on the Somme. He was entitled to the General Service and Victory Medals.
9, Walbrook Road, Lower Edmonton, N.9   13081.

GIBBS, W. H., Pte., Labour Corps.
He volunteered in September, 1915, and served on the Western Front, taking part in the engagements at the Somme, Amiens and Bullecourt.
He was demobilised in February, 1919, and holds the 1915 Star, General Service and Victory Medals.
40, Hilmer Street, West Kensington, W.14   16266A.

GIBSON, A., Bombardier, R.F.A.
He volunteered in November, 1915, and served in France, where he took part in many engagements, including the battle of the Somme, and was severely wounded. On his return to England he was demobilised in May, 1919, and holds the 1915 Star and the General Service and Victory Medals.
17, Chamberlain Road, Lower Edmonton, N 9   14022.

GIBSON, A. G., Cpl., Royal Engineers.
He volunteered in May, 1915, and during his service on the Western Front took part in several engagements. At one period his health broke down and he was kept in hospital for some time in France and England.
On his return he was demobilised in April, 1919, and holds the General Service and Victory Medals.
38, Rosaline Road, Fulham, S.W.6   X18180.

GIBSON, C. E., 2nd Air Mechanic, R.A.F.
He joined in October, 1916, and after completing his training, served as an observer at various aerodromes. Later he also acted as an armourer with No. 117 Squadron and rendered valuable services.
He was demobilised in February, 1919.
190, Portnall Road, Maida Hill, W.9   X19659.

GIBSON, D. J., Driver, 104th Brigade, R.F.A.
He volunteered in July, 1915, and in the following October was sent to the Western Front, where he took part in the battles of Arras, Cambrai and the Somme, and was twice wounded.
On his return to England, he was demobilised in April, 1917, and holds the 1915 Star and the General Service and Victory Medals.
7, Corby Road, Willesden, N.W.10   14399.

GIBSON, E. R. (M.M.), Cpl., 1st Middlesex Regt.
He volunteered in August, 1914, was sent to the Western Front the same year, and was wounded at La Bassée. On his recovery he was transferred to Salonica and later to Egypt. He was awarded the Military Medal for conspicuous gallantry in the field, and on his return to England was demobilised in February, 1919.
He holds, in addition, the 1914 Star and the General Service and Victory Medals.
42, Maldon Road, Lower Edmonton, N.9   15782.

GIBSON, E. R., Pte., 5th Middlesex Regiment.
He volunteered in 1915, and after completing his training, was stationed with his unit at several important stations. In 1916, owing to ill-health, he was discharged as being medically unfit for further military service.
164, Winchester Road, Lower Edmonton, N.9   14783C.

GIBSON, G. T., Pte., The Queen's (Royal West Surrey Regt.).
He volunteered in 1915, and was sent to France the same year, where he took part in several engagements, including those of the Somme, Cambrai, Ypres and Arras. He was wounded three times, and is still serving in the Army in India, and holds the 1915 Star and the General Service and Victory Medals.
164, Winchester Road, Lower Edmonton, N.9   14783B.

GIBSON, H., Pte., Royal Army Service Corps.
On reaching military age in October, 1918, he joined the Army and, having completed his training, was stationed at various places with his unit, being chiefly employed in the transport of supplies. He was unable to obtain his transfer overseas before the Armistice, and was demobilised in November, 1919.
31, Chauncey Street, Lower Edmonton, N 9   T14269

GIFFEN, E. F., Lce.-Cpl., 1st Bedfordshire Regt.
He was serving at the outbreak of war, having enlisted in July, 1913, and was sent to the Western Front, where he saw much fighting, and was twice wounded. He was invalided home, and in November, 1917, was discharged as unfit.
He holds the 1914 Star and the General Service and Victory Medals. 2, Purcell Crescent, Fulham, S.W.6   14850.

GIGG, A. F., Gunner, Royal Field Artillery
He volunteered in May, 1915, and served on the Western Front in several engagements, including Ypres, the Somme and the Marne. Whilst employed with the trench mortars he was killed in action on August 26th, 1917, and entitled to the 1915 Star and the General Service and Victory Medals. 18, Shelley Road, Willesden, N.W.10   13644.

GILBERT, A. J., Cpl., Middlesex, Suffolk and Bedfordshire Regiments.
He volunteered in November, 1915, and on completing his training was employed on special duties with his unit. In July, 1918, he was successful in obtaining his transfer overseas, and was sent to the Western Front, where he took part in engagements at Albert and Arras. While in action at Combles he was killed.
He was entitled to the General Service and Victory Medals.
35, Shelley Road, Willesden, N.W.10   13606B.

GILBERT, F., Lieut., Royal Engineers.
He volunteered in September, 1914, and was quickly sent to the Western Front, where he rendered valuable and highly responsible services at the Military Forwarding Office on all sectors
In June, 1919, he was demobilised, and holds the 1914 Star and the General Service and Victory Medals.
51, Lime Grove, Shepherd's Bush, W.12   12096.

GILBERT, G. H., Bombardier, R.G.A.
He joined in July, 1917, and in the following December was sent to the Western Front, where he took part in the battle of Ypres and several important engagements.
He was sent home and demobilised in February, 1919, and holds the General Service and Victory Medals.
6, Goodson Road, Willesden, N.W.10   14928.

GILBERT, H., Captain, Royal Engineers.
He volunteered in September, 1914, and served in France and Italy. He was decorated by the Italian Government for conspicuous gallantry and devotion to duty, and in addition holds the 1914 Star and the General Service and Victory Medals.
He was demobilised in April, 1919.
2, Railway Cottages, Sulgrave Road, W.6   12097.

GILBERT, R. W., Pte., 13th London Regt.
He volunteered in September, 1914, was sent to France, and killed in action at Aubers Ridge on May 9th, 1915, having previously taken part in the battle of Neuve Chapelle.
He was entitled to the 1914–15 Star, General Service and Victory Medals.
35, Shelley Road, Willesden, N.W.10   13606A.

GILDERSON, W. C., Pte., Royal Warwickshire Regiment.

He volunteered in August, 1914, on the outbreak of war, and was sent to the Western Front the following year. After taking part in several engagements, he was killed in action on June 18th, 1915.
He was entitled to the 1915 Star and the General Service and Victory Medals.
11, Nelson Road, Lower Edmonton, N.9   13288.

GILDON, S. H., Pte., Middlesex Regiment.

He volunteered in August, 1914, and served on the Western Front, where he took part with distinction in several important engagements and was wounded, and suffered greatly from trench feet.
On his return to England he was demobilised in February, 1919, and holds the 1914–15 Star, General Service and Victory Medals.
3, Eley Place, White Hart Lane, Tottenham, N.17   X18312.

GILES, B. W., Cpl., Rifle Brigade.

He joined in September, 1918, on attaining military age, and served from March, 1919, in France, Belgium, and with the Army of Occupation in Germany.
He returned to England, and was demobilised in March, 1920, having attained his stripes for his smart and efficient work.
5, Disraeli Road, N.W.10   14160B.

GILES, E. E., Pte., Royal Army Medical Corps.

He volunteered in August, 1914, and was sent to the Western Front, where he took part in engagements at Delville Wood (during the battle of the Somme), Arras and Vimy Ridge. He was wounded at Delville Wood and was taken prisoner near Cambrai in March, 1918.
On his release he was demobilised in January, 1919, holding the 1915 Star and the General Service and Victory Medals.
21, Archel Road, West Kensington, W.14   16196A.

GILES, E. M. (Mrs.), Special War Worker.

During the war this lady rendered valuable services at a large munition factory, where she was engaged in filling shells. This work required great care and skill, and she was complimented for her services.
21, Archel Road, West Kensington, W.14   16196B.

GILES, F., Special War Worker.

For a period of four and a half years during the war this lady was engaged on important work in connection with the supply of hospital equipment. Her services, which were of a valuable nature, were greatly appreciated and she received high commendation.
38, Brett Road, N.W.10   15693B.

GILES, M., Special War Worker.

At the beginning of the war this lady was engaged on important work at Perivale Munition Factory. Her duties, which were in connection with the making of fuzes, were often of a dangerous nature, and at all times needed great care and skill. Later, she was engaged on arduous work at an Army equipment stores. Throughout she rendered services of a very valuable nature to her country.
38, Brett Road, N.W.10   15693A.

GILES, W., Pte., 8th Gloucestershire Regiment.

He joined in May, 1916, and during his service, which extended from October, 1916, till 1918, took part in several engagements, including those at Arras and Cambrai, where he was wounded.
He was demobilised in November, 1918, holding the General Service and Victory Medals.
5, Disraeli Road, N.W.10   14160A.

GILL, A. H., Rifleman, King's Royal Rifle Corps.

He volunteered in August, 1914, and after a period of training, was sent to Salonica. He was later transferred to the Western Front, where, in October, 1918, he was killed in action.
He was entitled to the 1914–15 Star, General Service and Victory Medals.
31, Felixstowe Road, Lower Edmonton, N.9   15384A.

GILL, F., Sergt., Royal Field Artillery.

He volunteered in August, 1914, and the same year was sent to the Western Front, where he took part in many engagements, and in August, 1917, was killed in action.
He was entitled to the 1914 Star, the General Service and Victory Medals.
13, Chapman Cottages, High Road, Willesden, N.W.10   16625C.

GILL, G., Pte., Middlesex Regiment.

He volunteered in August, 1914, and served from 1915 till 1919 on the Western Front, where he took part in many engagements.
He was demobilised in 1919, holding the 1915 Star, General Service and Victory Medals.
157a, Kilburn Lane, North Kensington, W.10   X18569A.

GILL, J. V. H., Driver, Royal Field Artillery.

He volunteered in October, 1914, and was sent to the Western Front in 1915, where he took part with distinction in many engagements, including the battles of Ypres and the Somme. He was wounded in 1916.
He holds the 1914–15 Star, General Service and Victory Medals, being demobilised in April, 1919.
112, Sheldon Road, Upper Edmonton, N.18   X17583.

GILL, O., Special War Worker.

He volunteered but was rejected for military service, and was engaged on work of supreme national importance in connection with the manufacture of aeroplane parts. This work required great care and skill, and his services were highly appreciated.
20, Tenterden Road, Tottenham, N.17   X18495.

GILL, R. (Miss), Special War Worker.

For a considerable period of the war this lady rendered valuable services as an examiner of cartridges at Park Royal Munition Works. After two and a half years she took up work at an Army equipment factory, where her services were highly commended.
157a, Kilburn Lane, North Kensington, W.10   X18569B.

GILL, V., Cook, Royal Navy.

He volunteered in 1915, and during the same year served at Archangel. The next year he was at Gibraltar. He served in H.M. Ships "Intrepid" and "Laggan," on dangerous convoy work with merchant and food ships.
He was still serving in 1920, and holds the 1915 Star and the General Service and Victory Medals.
13, Chapman Cottages, High Road, Willesden, N.W.10   16625B.

GILLAM, P., Pte., Queen's Own (R. W. K. Regt.).

He volunteered in August, 1914, and during his service on the Western Front, took part in the battle of Loos, where he was twice wounded. After six months in hospital in France and England, he returned to duty, and in November, 1919, was demobilised, holding the 1914–15 Star and the General Service and Victory Medals.
92, Winchester Road, Lower Edmonton, N 9   14762B.

GILLAM, W. G., Pte., Middlesex Regiment.

He joined in May, 1916, and was drafted to India. Whilst there he was stationed on duty with his unit at many important places until his return to England for demobilisation in December, 1919.
He holds the General Service and Victory Medals.
92, Winchester Road, Lower Edmonton, N.9   14762A.

GILLAM, W. H., Pte., Middlesex Regiment.

He volunteered in October, 1915, and served on the Western Front, taking part in the battle of the Somme. He was invalided home after over two years' service overseas, and in March, 1919, was demobilised, holding the General Service and Victory Medals.
49, Raynham Road, Upper Edmonton, N.18   15994.

GILLAN, E. J., Driver, Royal Engineers.

He volunteered in November, 1915, and the following year was sent to Egypt, where he served for a period in the Mechanical Transport, and later took part in the Big Offensive under General Allenby in the Palestine Campaign.
On his return to England he was demobilised in September, 1919, and holds the General Service and Victory Medals.
40, Portnall Road, Maida Hill, W.9   X19452.

GILLARD, S. V., Driver, R.A.S.C. (M.T.).

He volunteered in August, 1914, and was quickly sent to the Western Front. During his four and a half years' service overseas he was engaged on important transport work with an ammunition column.
He was sent to England and demobilised in March, 1919, holding the 1914–15 Star, the General Service and Victory Medals.
15, Osborne Road, Cricklewood, N.W.2   X17402.

GILLETT, A., Special War Worker.

For over three years during the war this lady was engaged at the Park Royal Munition Factory. Her work was of a dangerous character, as she was employed in the T.N.T. and high explosive departments. Her valuable services were highly commendable.
29, Barret's Green Road, Willesden, N.W.10   T13630B.

GILLETT, H. C., Pte., Royal West Kent Regt. and the London Regiment.

He volunteered in May, 1915, and in the following year proceeded to Egypt. Later he was attached to the Egyptian Expeditionary Force and served in Palestine and Syria, taking part in the fighting on the Jordan, at Jericho, Jerusalem and Damascus.
On his return to England he was demobilised in March, 1919, holding the General Service and Victory Medals.
7, Dudden Hill Lane, N.W.10   T17333.

GILLHAM, G. E. C., Gunner, R.F.A.
He volunteered in August, 1915, and five months later was sent to the Western Front, where he served with distinction through several engagements.
In July, 1917, he was invalided home and discharged on account of ill-health as physically unfit for further service. He holds the General Service and Victory Medals.
67, Reporton Road, Munster Road, S.W.6　　TX18914.

GILLHAM, J. A., Pte., 10th Middlesex Regiment.
He volunteered for service in August, 1914, and later was sent to France. While in action he was taken prisoner and held in captivity for two years in Germany, where he received much ill-treatment.
On his release he was demobilised in December, 1919, holding the General Service and Victory Medals.
80, Adeney Road, Hammersmith, W.6　　14460

GILLING, E. W., Pte., Royal Army Service Corps.
He joined in August, 1916, and after a period of training was sent to Italy, where he took part in several engagements, and was wounded. He remained in Italy until he was sent home for demobilisation in January, 1919.
He holds the General Service and Victory Medals.
117, Winchester Road, Lower Edmonton, N.9　　14955.

GILLINGS, A. E. (sen.), Pte., 18th Middlesex Regiment.
He volunteered in February, 1915, and the following year was sent to the Western Front, where he took part in the battles of the Somme, Arras and Ypres. In 1918 he was severely gassed and was invalided home and discharged in April, 1918.
He holds the General Service and Victory Medals.
10, Roundwood Road, Willesden, N.W.10　　16344B.

GILLINGS, A. E. (jun.), Cpl., R.A.M.C.
He volunteered in August, 1914, and in the February following was sent to the Western Front. During his service he was present at engagements at Ypres, the Somme, Arras, Vimy Ridge, Messines and Albert.
On his being sent home to England, he was demobilised in June, 1919, holding the 1914-15 Star, and the General Service and Victory Medals.
10, Roundwood Road, Willesden, N.W.10　　16344A.

GILLINGS, R. J., Pte., Royal Sussex Regiment.
He joined in June, 1918, on attaining military age, and after his training was engaged on important duties at various stations with his unit. He gave valuable services, but was not successful in obtaining his transfer overseas before hostilities ceased. He, however, went to Germany with the Army of Occupation, and remained there until sent home for demobilisation in September, 1919.
26, Alric Avenue, Stonebridge Park, N.W.10　　14437.

GILLINGWATER, A., Cook, R.N., H.M.S. "Dragon."
He joined early in 1918 and saw service on important and dangerous duties in the North Sea with the Grand Fleet. He was still serving in 1920 in H.M.S. "Dragon," and holds the General Service and Victory Medals.
16, Cranbrook Road, Tottenham, N.17　　X18559B.

GILLINGWATER, A. J., A.B., R.N., H.M.S. "Digby."
He volunteered in November, 1914, and saw much service of a dangerous nature with the Grand Fleet in the North Sea.
He holds the 1914 Star, General Service and Victory Medals, and was demobilised in August, 1919.
16, Cranbrook Road, Tottenham, N.17　　X18559A.

GILLINGWATER, E. A., A.B., Royal Navy.
He volunteered in November, 1914, and served with the Dover Patrol and in dangerous mine-sweeping duties in the North Sea and English Channel. During his four and a half years at sea he gave valuable services, and in March, 1919, was demobilised.
He holds the 1914-15 Star and the General Service and Victory Medals.
97, Roundwood Road, Willesden, N.W.10　　16039.

GILLINGWATER, H. W., Cook, Merchant Service.
He volunteered in 1915 and served on one of the White Star Line vessels engaged in the important work of conveying troops from Australia to the various theatres of war.
In 1916 he was discharged as medically unfit for further service. He holds the 1914-15 Star, General Service, Victory and the Merchant Service War Medals.
33, Ambleside Road, Willesden, N.W.10　　16121A.

GILLINGWATER, S. L. (Mrs.), Special War Worker.
During the war this lady was engaged on important work at the Park Royal Munition Factory. She held a responsible position while at this factory, and carried out her duties in an efficient manner: Her services were very valuable, and she received high commendation,
33, Ambleside Road, Willesden, N.W.10　　16121B.

GILLMAN, J. W., Pte., 10th Middlesex Regiment and 2/19th London Regiment.
He volunteered in October, 1914, and after completing his training, was sent to France, where he was in action on several occasions. Later he was transferred in turn to Salonica, Egypt and Palestine, and served in the London Regiment. While overseas he contracted pneumonia, and died on December 7th, 1918, at Alexandria.
He was entitled to the 1914-15 Star and the General Service and Victory Medals.
21, Montagu Street, Hammersmith, W.6　　16408.

GILLON, J. A., Sergt., Royal Horse Artillery.
He volunteered in August, 1914, and served with distinction in France and Gallipoli, where he was amongst the first of our troops to land. On 15th July, 1915, he was severely wounded, and as a result has lost the sight of his left eye. He was demobilised in 1920, and holds the 1915 Star, General Service and Victory Medals.
69, Dieppe Street, West Kensington, W.14　　T16428.

GILROY, G. F., Gunner, Royal Garrison Artillery.
He joined in April, 1916, and during his service on the Western Front, which lasted two years, took part in many of the principal engagements, and was severely gassed.
He was demobilised in January, 1919, holding the General Service and Victory Medals.
7, Stanley Road, King's Road, S.W.6　　X19870

GILTROW, A. E., Pte., Middlesex Regiment.
He volunteered in 1914, and after his training was sent to France in the following year. While on this Front he served in many engagements, and was killed in action on July 15th, 1916.
He was entitled to the 1914-15 Star and the General Service and Victory Medals.
28, Eldon Road, Lower Edmonton, N.9　　13053B

GILTROW, C. A., Driver, Royal Engineers.
He volunteered in 1915, and in the same year was sent to the Western Front, where he took part in many important engagements, and was killed in action on June 24th, 1916.
He was entitled to the 1914-15 Star and the General Service and Victory Medals.
28, Eldon Road, Lower Edmonton, N.9　　13053A.

GILTROW, W. A., Pte., R.A.M.C.
He joined in June, 1917, and after completing his training was sent to Italy, where he served for a considerable time, and took part in the campaign against the Austrians. He was still serving in 1920, and holds the General Service and Victory Medals.
28, Eldon Road, Lower Edmonton, N.9　　13053C.

GINGELL, T. E., Driver, Royal Field Artillery.
He volunteered in January, 1915, and was retained for some time on important duties at various stations with his unit.
In 1918 he was drafted to France, where he took part in the Retreat and Advance of that year, and was killed in action on September 2nd, 1918.
He was entitled to the General Service and Victory Medals.
79, Melville Road, Stonebridge Park, N.W.10　　14419.

GIRDLESTON, E., Pte., Middlesex Regiment.
He joined in August, 1916, and after his training, was drafted to India, where he was engaged on important duties at various stations with his unit.
He returned to England and was demobilised in November, 1919, holding the General Service and Victory Medals
65, Gloucester Road, Upper Edmonton, N.18　　X17271.

GLADMAN, F., Sergt., 9th London Regt. (Queen Victoria's Rifles).
He was mobilised in August, 1914, and was sent to the Western Front in November of the same year. During his four years' service in this theatre of war he took part with distinction in many engagements, including those of Hill 60, Ypres and the Somme.
On his return home he was demobilised in February, 1919, and holds the 1914 Star and the General Service and Victory Medals.
30, Caird Street, Queen's Park Estate, W.10　　X18946

GLAFIELD, A., Pte., Royal Army Medical Corps (103rd Field Ambulance).
He volunteered in September, 1915, and served on the Western Front as stretcher-bearer at Ypres, Armentieres, Loos, Arras and on the Somme He was killed on July 14th, 1916, at Albert during the Somme Offensive, and was entitled to the General Service and Victory Medals.
139, Fortune Gate Road, Harlesden, N.W.10   13470.

GLANFIELD, W. J., Lce.-Cpl., Bedfordshire Regiment.
He joined in 1918, and after his training was engaged on important duties at various stations with his unit. He gave valuable services, but was unsuccessful in obtaining his transfer overseas before the signing of the Armistice. He was then drafted to France and went to Germany with the Army of Occupation.
He was sent home and demobilised in 1920.
6, Ancill Street, Hammersmith, W.6   13755B.

GLANVILLE, J., Pte., Middlesex Regiment.
He volunteered in 1915, and after his training was engaged on important duties with his unit at various stations. He gave valuable services, but was not able to secure his transfer overseas owing to ill-health, and was discharged in January, 1917, as being medically unfit for further military service.
167, Estcourt Road, Fulham, S.W.6   T17071.

GLASS, E. T., Pte., 14th London Regiment (London Scottish).
He joined in 1917, and served for two years in France, during which period he took part in the battles of Arras and Cambrai, and was in hospital for some time.
On his return from overseas he was demobilised in January, 1919, and holds the General Service and Victory Medals.
26, Third Avenue, Queen's Park Estate, W.10   X19284.

GLAZEBROOK, G., Sapper, Royal Engineers.
He volunteered in November, 1915, and during nearly three years' service in France and Flanders, took part in the battle of the Somme and several important engagements. After the Armistice he was sent to Germany with the Army of Occupation, and remained there for over a year.
In 1919 he was sent back to England and demobilised in April, holding the General Service and Victory Medals.
174, Brettenham Road, Upper Edmonton, N.18   15224A.

GLAZEBROOK, R., Sapper, Royal Engineers.
He volunteered in November, 1915, and was sent to France in the following year. While on this Front he took part in many operations, including those in connection with the battle of the Somme.
In 1919 he was sent to England and demobilised in June, holding the General Service and Victory Medals.
174, Brettenham Road, Upper Edmonton, N.18   15224B.

GLAZEBROOK, W., Driver, Royal Engineers.
He volunteered in 1914, and during his service on the Western Front took part in the battle of the Somme. Later he was sent to Egypt, and took part in the Palestine campaign.
He holds the General Service and Victory Medals, and was demobilised in 1919, after his return.
174, Brettenham Road, Upper Edmonton, N.18   15224C.

GLEDHILL, H., Pte., 5th Middlesex Regiment.
He joined in 1916, went to France the same year, and took part in engagements at Arras, Ypres, Cambrai and the Somme. He was wounded three times, and after his return to England was demobilised in 1920, holding the General Service and Victory Medals.
164, Winchester Road, Lower Edmonton, N.9   14783A.

GLENDENEN, R. D., 2nd Air Mechanic, R.A.F.
He joined in November, 1916, at the age of 17, and whilst flying in England, received a severe injury in an aeroplane crash. On recovery he was sent to France, where he was gassed and suffered from shell-shock.
In 1919 he was sent home and demobilised in January, holding the General Service and Victory Medals.
58, Maldon Road, Lower Edmonton, N.9   15790.

GLENDENNING, W. C., Cpl., Middlesex Regt. and Royal Air Force.
He volunteered in March, 1915, and during three years' service on the Western Front took part in engagements at Ypres and the Somme, and was also in the Retreat of 1918.
On his return to England he was demobilised in March, 1919, holding the 1914-15 Star and the General Service and Victory Medals.
77, Hawthorn Road, Willesden, N.W.10   X17424.

GLENISTER, A. T., Pte., Middlesex Regiment and Lancashire Fusiliers.
He volunteered in November, 1915, and during three years' service on the Western Front took part in the battles of the Somme, Ypres and Arras. He returned to England and was demobilised in February, 1919, but seven months later he re-enlisted, and is now serving with the Army of Occupation in Germany.
He holds the General Service and Victory Medals.
59, Brownlow Road, Willesden, N.W.10   14728B.

GLENISTER, E. E., Sapper, Royal Engineers.
He volunteered in April, 1915, and in the following July was sent to the Western Front, where he took part in the battles of Ypres and the Somme. He was twice wounded, and in 1916 was invalided to England, where he was engaged on special duty until his demobilisation in January, 1919. Four months later he re-enlisted, and was still serving in 1920.
He holds the 1914-15 Star and the General Service and Victory Medals.
59, Brownlow Road, Willesden, N.W.10   14728A.

GLENN, C., Pte., 10th Essex Regiment.
He volunteered for duty in 1915 and after the close of his training served on the Western Front, where he was killed in action at the battle of the Somme on September, 28th, 1916.
He was entitled to the General Service and Victory Medals.
26, Rock Avenue, Fulham Road, S.W.6   X20079.

GLIBBERY, A., Lce.-Cpl., 1st Middlesex Regt.
He volunteered in February, 1915, and served for three years on the Western Front, during which period he took part in several engagements and was twice wounded, once at Arras and again at Cambrai.
After his return, he was demobilised in January, 1919, and holds the General Service and Victory Medals.
6, Maldon Road, Lower Edmonton, N.9   14237.

GLOVER, G. A. (D.C.M.), Sergt., R.E.
He was mobilised in 1914, and in the same year was sent to France, where he served until 1919. During this time he took part in engagements at Mons, Ypres, Arras, the Somme, Bullecourt, Vimy Ridge and the 1918 Advance.
He was awarded the Distinguished Conduct Medal for conspicuous gallantry and devotion to duty in the field, and was wounded and gassed.
He also holds the 1914 Star, the General Service and Victory Medals.
98, Third Avenue, Queen's Park Estate, W.10   X19288.

GODDARD, F. (Mrs., _née_ Till), Special War Worker.
For 3½ years during the war this lady was engaged on important work at a large Army equipment factory.
Her services were very valuable and she received the highest commendation.
142, Third Avenue, Queen's Park Estate, W.10   X19382B.

GODDARD, J., Rifleman, Rifle Brigade.
He volunteered in 1915 and saw service in France, where he took part in many engagements and was severely wounded in 1917. After long hospital treatment he was discharged in that year as medically unfit for further service.
He holds the General Service and Victory Medals.
142, Third Avenue, Queen's Park Estate, W.10   X19382A.

GODDARD, W., Driver, R.A.S.C.
He volunteered in December, 1914, and was sent later in the same year to France, where he served on many sectors of the Western Front. In 1918 he was sent to Germany with the Army of Occupation, and in June, 1919, was returned to England and demobilised, holding the 1914-15 Star and the General Service and Victory Medals.
99, Winchester Road, Lower Edmonton, N.9   14958.

GODDEN, R. H., Pte., Royal Army Service Corps.
He volunteered in April, 1915, and was sent to the Western Front later in the same year. While in this theatre of war he was engaged on important transport duties with his unit, until he was sent home in February, 1919, to be demobilised.
He holds the 1914-15 Star and the General Service and Victory Medals.
10, South Street Cottages, Hammersmith, W.6   12507

GODDIN, W. J., Pte., R.M.L.I.
He volunteered in August, 1914, and served on various duties with the Grand Fleet. On two occasions during his service his ship was torpedoed and he was in the water several hours before being picked up, and he was also wounded.
He is still serving, and holds the 1914 Star and the General Service and Victory Medals.
172, Winchester Road, Lower Edmonton, N.9   14889.

GODFREY, E., Cpl., East Surrey Regiment.

He volunteered in 1914, and after his training was engaged on special duties for two years at various stations with his unit. In 1916 he was drafted to France, where he took part in many important engagements. On his return he was demobilised in January, 1919, and holds the General Service and Victory Medals.

7, Florence Road, Upper Edmonton, N.18   16012

GODFREY, J. E., Cpl., Middlesex Regiment.

He volunteered in August, 1914, and later in the same year was sent to France, where he took part in many important engagements, including those at Ypres and Neuve Chapelle (where he was wounded).

In June, 1919, he was sent home and demobilised, holding the 1914 Star and the General Service and Victory Medals.

14, Cedars Road, Lower Edmonton, N.9   14359.

GODFREY, W. P., Staff-Sergt., R.E.

He volunteered in February, 1915, was sent to the Dardanelles in the same year, and took part with distinction in the landing at Suvla Bay. He was later drafted to Salonica, where he served until sent home and demobilised in August, 1919.

He holds the 1914-15 Star and the General Service and Victory Medals.

103, Carlyle Avenue, Willesden, N.W.10   13682.

GODIER, C., Sergt., Royal Garrison Artillery.

He was serving at the outbreak of war, and was in France from 1914 until 1916, when his time expired. During this period he took part in engagements on the Marne and Aisne, and at Vimy Ridge and Cambrai. In 1917 he re-enlisted and returned to the Front, where he remained until sent home for demobilisation in June, 1919.

He was awarded the Croix de Guerre for conspicuous bravery, and in addition holds the 1914 Star and the General Service and Victory Medals.

7, Melville Road, Willesden, N.W.10   14703.

GODMAN, W., Pte., Royal West Kent Regiment and Royal Army Medical Corps.

He volunteered in January, 1916, and served on the Western Front, where he took part in the battles of Ypres, Arras and Cambrai, and was wounded. He was invalided to England and transferred to the R.A.M.C., with which he served until his demobilisation in April, 1919.

He holds the General Service and Victory Medals.

4, Winchelsea Road, Willesden, N.W.10   13714.

GODWIN, H., Pte., 2nd Royal Sussex Regiment.

He volunteered in August, 1914, and served on the Western Front, where he was severely wounded at La Bassée in January, 1915. Shortly afterwards he died of his wounds in hospital in London.

He was entitled to the 1914 Star and the General Service and Victory Medals.

2, Chancellor's Street, Hammersmith, W.6   13262.

GOEBECK, E., Pte., 4th Middlesex Regiment.

He volunteered in August, 1914, and was engaged on duties of an important nature until 1916. He was certified unfit for active service overseas, and was finally discharged in July, 1916, on medical grounds.

35, Aspenlea Road, Hammersmith, W.6   14295B.

GOGGIN, J. E., Pte., 24th Training Reserve Battn.

He volunteered in August, 1918, on attaining military age, and was in training until the following November, when, owing to heart trouble, he was discharged as being medically unfit for further military service.

111, Deacon Road, Cricklewood, N.W.2   TX17208C.

GOGGIN, J. M., Pioneer, Royal Engineers.

He joined in August, 1918, and volunteered for overseas, but was retained on construction work at various important centres, until he was demobilised in March of the following year.

111, Deacon Road, Cricklewood, N.W.2   TX17208B.

GOGGIN, M. (Miss), Section Leader, W.R.A.F.

This lady joined the W.R.A.F. in the early part of 1918, and rendered services of a valuable nature as a telephone operator in the Royal Air Force. Her duties were of an arduous nature, and she was specially commended for her work.

She was demobilised in September, 1919.

111, Deacon Road, Cricklewood, N.W.2   TX17208A.

GOLD, A. J., Pte., Machine Gun Corps.

He joined in June, 1916, served in France, where he took part in many engagements, and was wounded twice at St. Quentin in March, 1918. He was taken prisoner at the time, and after being interned in Germany, was released from Switzerland. After hospital treatment abroad and at home for nine months, he was demobilised in January, 1919.

He holds the General Service and Victory Medals.

21, Moselle Street, Tottenham, N.17   X18367.

GOLD, C. (M.M.), Sergt., Royal Field Artillery.

He enlisted in May, 1908, and at the outbreak of war was serving in India. In 1914 he was drafted to the Western Front, where he took part in the retreat from Mons and many more of the principal engagements, including the battles of Ypres, Loos, Vimy Ridge, Passchendaele and the Great Retreat and Advance of 1918.

He was twice wounded and gassed, and was awarded the Military Medal for conspicuous bravery in the field and devotion to duty.

He also holds the Mons Star, General Service and Victory Medals, and was demobilised in May, 1920.

149, Ashmore Road, Harrow Road, W.9   X19745A.

GOLD, M. E. (Mrs., née Purvor), Women's Royal Air Force.

This lady joined in August, 1918, and during her service did excellent work as a clerk at No. 2 Depot, Regent's Park, in the dispatching department.

She was demobilised in August, 1919.

149, Ashmore Road, Harrow Road, W.9   X19745B.

GOLDING, G. W. P., Pte., Labour Corps.

He joined in June, 1918, and, after completing his training, was engaged on duties of an important nature at various places until his demobilisation in 1919. He gave valuable services while with his unit, but was unable to obtain his transfer overseas, due to being unfit at the time.

19, Oldfield Road, Willesden, N.W.10   15752/B.

GOLDING, J. T., Pte., R.A.S.C.

He volunteered in March, 1915, and was engaged on important duties in connection with the transportation of horses to France. In 1916 he went to Egypt, and served at the Remount Depot, training horses.

He holds the General Service and Victory Medals, and was demobilised in February, 1919, on his return to England.

19, Oldfield Road, Willesden, N.W.10   15752A.

GOLDING, J. T., Pte., 8th Royal West Kent Regt.

He joined up for service in February, 1917, and was drafted overseas two months later. He took part in various engagements on the Western Front, including the battle of the Somme, where he was wounded.

He holds the General Service and Victory Medals, and was demobilised in March, 1919, on his return from overseas.

36, Disraeli Road, Acton Lane, N.W.10   14396A.

GOLDING, R. (Mrs.), Special War Worker.

During the war this lady rendered services of a very valuable nature as an examiner of fuses at Perivale Munition Factory. She carried out these duties in a very efficient manner, and received high praise for her work.

36, Disraeli Road, Acton Lane, N.W.10   14396B.

GOLDING, R., Pte., Middlesex Regiment.

He volunteered in 1915, and served with distinction on the Western Front, where he was killed in action at the battle of the Somme in 1916.

He was entitled to the General Service and Victory Medals.

132, Shakespeare Avenue, Willesden, N.W.10   13894.

GOLDING, W. J., Pte., Royal Fusiliers.

He joined in September, 1916, and after being engaged on special duties was sent to the Western Front, where he served until 1919. He took part in engagements at Ypres and Cambrai, and the Retreat and Advance of 1918.

He holds the General Service and Victory Medals, and was demobilised in February, 1919, after his return from overseas.

156, Portnall Road, Maida Hill, W.9   X19664.

GOLDSMITH, A. L. (Mrs.), Special War Worker.

For a period of two years during the war this lady was engaged on work of an important nature at Woolwich Arsenal. Her work required great skill and care, and was carried out in an efficient manner.

She rendered valuable services and was highly commended.

12, Headcorn Road, Tottenham, N.17   X18494.

GOLDSMITH, C., Gunner, Royal Field Artillery.

He volunteered in January, 1915, and in the same year was sent to France, where he remained for four years. While abroad he took part in engagements at Ypres, Arras, Bullecourt and the Somme, also in the Advance of 1918.

He holds the 1915 Star, General Service and Victory Medals, and was sent home and demobilised in June, 1919.

12, Headcorn Road, Tottenham, N.17   X18494A.

GOLDTHORPE, S. C., Cpl., Royal Fusiliers.

He volunteered in June, 1915, and was sent to the Western Front, where he took part in engagements at Ypres, Arras and the Somme. In March, 1919, he was demobilised, holding the General Service and Victory Medals.

9, Church Path, Hammersmith, W.6   15872.

GOMMON, G., Sapper, R.E. (Railway Troops).
He joined in February, 1917, and was sent to the Western
Front in the same year. He served through many important
engagements, and was in action at Ypres, Passchendaele,
Cambrai, Arras and the Somme. After the Armistice he went
with the Army of Occupation to the Rhine, where he re-
mained until sent home for demobilisation in November, 1919.
He holds the General Service and Victory Medals.
19, Kenmont Gardens, College Park, Willesden, N.W.10.
X17570C.

GONDOUIN, C. F., Cpl., Royal Air Force.
He volunteered in July, 1915, and during his two years'
service on the Western Front took part in engagements on the
Somme and at Albert and Loos. During the last period of
his service he was engaged on special duties at various
stations until he was demobilised in January, 1919.
He holds the 1914–15 Star and the General Service and
Victory Medals.
62, Farrant Street, Queen's Park Estate, W.10   X19064A.

GOOCH, A. C. M., Trimmer, Merchant Service.
He joined in 1917, and served on H.M.S. " Usend," being
engaged in transporting troops and food to Russia and in
bringing back prisoners.
He is still serving in the Merchant Service, and holds the
General Service, Victory and Mercantile Marine War Medals.
98, Chesson Road, West Kensington, W14   X17243.

GOOCH, H. M. (Miss), Special War Worker.
During the war this lady rendered valuable services in an
important motor factory. Her work was of an arduous
nature, but she showed great energy and skill, and was
commended for her services.
98, Chesson Road, West Kensington, W.14   X17245.

GOOCH, J. H. J., Stoker, Royal Navy.
He volunteered in August, and served in the North Sea and
also off the coast of Zanzibar. Whilst
in H.M.S. " Weymouth " in the Mediterranean, he took
part in the pursuit of the German crusiers " Goeben " and
" Breslau " during their rush for Turkish waters. He was
in H.M.S. " Terror " when she was struck and severely
damaged by a torpedo. Fortunately she was run aground
before she sank.
He was demobilised in 1919, and holds the 1914–15 Star and
the General Service and Victory Medals.
96, Chesson Road, West Kensington, W.14   17244.

GOOCH, L. M. (Miss), Special War Worker.
For a considerable period during the war this lady was
engaged on services of a special nature at a large motor works,
thereby releasing a man for military service.
She was specially commended for her services.
98, Chesson Road, West Kensington, W.14   X17247.

GOOCH, T. F. A., Pte., Royal Fusiliers.
He joined in 1917, and during his service on the Western
Front took part in engagements at Arras, Bullecourt, Amiens,
Ypres, Vimy Ridge and Cambrai, and was wounded at
Armentieres.
He was demobilised in 1919, holding the General Service
and Victory Medals.
98, Chesson Road, West Kensington, W.14.   X17242.

GOODACRE, A. F., Pte., East Surrey Regt.
He volunteered in 1915 and was sent out to the Western
Front, where he took part in engagements at Arras, Loos,
the Somme, Cambrai and Bullecourt. He was invalided
home and sent to hospital at Mitcham, where he remained
for some months. After his recovery he was transferred to
the R.A.S.C., where he was engaged on special duties until
his demobilisation in 1919.
He holds the 1915 Star, General Service and Victory Medals.
38, Orbain Road, Fulham, S.W.6   X18223B.

GOODACRE, E., Pte., East Surrey Regiment.
He joined up for service in February, 1917, and three months
later was drafted to France. He was afterwards sent to
Italy and was in action on various sectors of the Fronts.
In 1918 he returned to the Western Front, where he took
part with distinction in the Retreat of 1918, and was killed
in action on May 24th, 1918.
He was entitled to the General Service and Victory Medals.
166, Church Road, Tottenham, N.17   X18133.

GOODACRE, E. (Mrs.), Special War Worker.
During the war this lady was engaged on work of a dangerous
nature in connection with the making of bombs and shells.
She was later transferred to a large Army equipment stores,
and throughout rendered services of a valuable character.
38, Orbain Road, Fulham, S.W.6   X18223A.

GOODALL, B. (Mrs.), Special War Worker.
For a considerable period during the war this lady was
engaged at the Park Royal Munition Factory, where she was
working on the manufacture of small-arms ammunition. She
rendered services of a valuable nature, and earned high praise
for her useful work.   35, Disraeli Road, N.W.10   14155.

GOODALL, J. A., Pte., 7th London Regiment.
He volunteered in April, 1915, and whilst serving on the
Western Front was wounded and taken prisoner. Later he
died of wounds whilst still in captivity.
He was entitled to the General Service and Victory Medals.
13, Bayonne Road, Hammersmith, W.6   14306.

GOODALL, J. T., Pte., 8th Bedfordshire Regt.
He joined in February, 1916, and in the following November
went to the Western Front, where he took part in many
engagements, and was wounded at Cambrai in 1918.
He holds the General Service and Victory Medals, and is
still serving.
32, Disraeli Road, Acton Lane, N.W.10   14394.

**GOODALL, J. T., Pte., 16th York and Lancaster
Regiment.**
He joined in March, 1916, and was engaged on work of a
special nature. At the end of the year he met with a serious
accident, and was in hospital for a considerable period.
He was eventually demobilised in 1919, having been unsuccessful in obtaining his transfer overseas before hostilities
ceased.
8, Wilson's Road, Hammersmith, W.6   16416.

GOODCHILD, A. J., Pte., 2/9th Middlesex Regt.
He volunteered in August, 1914, and a year later was sent
to the Dardanelles, where he took part in the landing. After
the evacuation he was sent to Egypt, and was later transferred to Palestine, where he was in action at Gaza, Jerusalem
and Jaffa. Whilst in Egypt he was mentioned in despatches
for gallantry in action, and in 1919 was sent to England and
demobilised in March.
He holds the 1914–15 Star and the General Service and
Victory Medals.
13, Kenmont Gardens, College Park, N.W.10.   X17572.

GOODCHILD, A. L., 2nd Air Mechanic, R.A.F.
He joined in 1918 on attaining military age, and after a period
of training was sent to Egypt in the same year. He was
there engaged on important duties with his unit at various
stations, and contracted malaria.
In 1919 he was sent home and demobilised, and holds the
General Service and Victory Medals.
27, Leghorn Road, Harlesden, N.W.10   13163B.

GOODCHILD, J., Pte., 7th Bedfordshire Regt.
He joined in 1916, and was drafted to the Western Front,
where he served until 1919, and was demobilised in December
of the same year. While overseas he took part in several
important battles, including those of Ypres and the Somme,
and holds the General Service and Victory Medals.
50, Newlyn Road, Tottenham, N.17   X18505.

GOODCHILD, J. I., Lce.-Cpl., Royal Engineers.
He volunteered in 1915, and at the conclusion of his training
was drafted overseas. He took part in many engagements
on the Western Front, including the battles of Ypres, Arras
and the Somme.
He returned to England after the cessation of hostilities,
and was demobilised in 1919. He holds the 1914–15 Star,
General Service and Victory Medals.
27, Leghorn Road, Harlesden, N.W.10   13163A.

GOODCHILD, O. E., Sergt. R.A.S.C. (M.T.).
He joined in 1917, and gained his promotion for consistent
good work. He was engaged on special duties with his unit,
but was not successful in obtaining his transfer overseas
before hostilities ceased. He was still serving in 1920.
27, Leghorn Road, Harlesden, N.W.10   13613C.

GOODCHILD, R., Rifleman, Rifle Brigade.
He volunteered in September, 1914, and was sent to France
in the same year. He served in various sectors of the
Western Front, and was killed in action at Ypres in July,1915.
He was entitled to the 1914–15 Star and the General
Service and Victory Medals.
45, Felixstowe Road, Lower Edmonton, N.9   15387.

GOODES, A., Pte., Royal Fusiliers.
He volunteered in 1914, and was sent the following year to
the Western Front, where he served on many sectors, and
was in action on the Somme and at Loos, Ypres, Arras and
Cambrai. During his service he was twice wounded, and in
1918 he was killed.
He was entitled to the 1914–15 Star and the General Service
and Victory Medals.
21, Dudden Hill Lane, N.W.10   T17332B.

GOODES, G., Pte., East Surrey Regiment.
He joined in June, 1918, and after his training was engaged
on important duties with his unit at various stations. He
gave valuable services, but was not successful in obtaining
his transfer overseas prior to the cessation of the fighting.
He was demobilised in September, 1919.
21, Dudden Hill Lane, N.W.10   T17332A.

GOODES, H. E., Pte., 2/9th Middlesex Regiment.
He volunteered for service in June, 1915, and was drafted overseas during the same year. He took part with distinction in many engagements on the Western Front, including the battles of the Somme and Ypres, and was gassed. He returned to England and was demobilised in March, 1919, holding the 1914–15 Star, General Service and Victory Medals.
16, Gowan Road, Willesden, N.W.10   X17106.

GOODFELLOW, H. G., Sergt., Royal Engineers.
He volunteered in November, 1915, and was sent to Egypt. He was later drafted to Palestine, where, owing to special qualifications and ability, he was engaged on important duties on the lines of communication.
He returned home, and in December, 1919, was demobilised, holding the General Service and Victory Medals.
12, North Road, Lower Edmonton, N.9   11958A.

GOODALL, C. D., Pte., R.A.V.C.
He volunteered in September, 1915, and being over military age for service in the front line, served on the Western Front in the Veterinary Corps, and was engaged in duties of a special nature in connection with the treatment of sick and wounded horses.
In February, 1919 he was demobilised, holding the General Service and Victory Medals.
17, Parkfield Road, Willesden, N.W.10   X17416.

GOODMAN, A., Sapper, Royal Engineers.
He volunteered in 1914, and after his training was retained on special duties with his unit at various stations until 1918. He was then drafted to France, and took part in the engagements of that year, being employed on the railways in the forward areas during the Advance.
He was demobilised in 1919, and holds the General Service and Victory Medals.
53, Ilex Road, Willesden, N.W.10.   16357A.

GOODMAN, F., Pte., 1st Middlesex Regiment.
He volunteered in 1915, and in the following year went to the Western Front, where he took part in many engagements, including those of the Somme, Ypres, Cambrai and Arras. Whilst in action in the Advance of 1918 he was killed on September 29th.
He was entitled to the General Service and Victory Medals.
3, Hawkshead Road, Willesden, N.W.10.   16053.

GOODMAN, H., Rifleman, Rifle Brigade.
He joined in 1918, and on the completion of his training was engaged on important duties at various stations with his unit. He gave valuable services, but was unsuccessful in obtaining his transfer overseas before hostilities ceased.
In 1919 he was demobilised.
53, Ilex Road, Willesden, N.W.10   16357B.

GOODMAN, H., Sergt., 3/9th Middlesex Regt.
He volunteered in 1915, was sent to France in the same year, and took part with distinction in the battles of Loos, the Somme, Arras, Vimy Ridge and Cambrai. He was twice wounded, and in 1919 he was demobilised, holding the 1914–15 Star and the General Service and Victory Medals.
53, Ilex Road, Willesden, N.W.10   16357C.

GOODRIDGE, J. W., Gunner, R.F.A.
He volunteered in September, 1914, and was sent to France in the same year. He took part in many engagements on the Western Front, until 1916, when he was drafted to the East, where he remained for over two years.
In 1919 he was sent home and was demobilised, holding the 1914–15 Star and the General Service and Victory Medals.
6, York Road, Upper Edmonton, N.18   16783A.

GOODWAY, D. (Mrs.), Special War Worker.
During the war this lady was engaged on important duties at Messrs. Blake's Munition Factory, Fulham. Her work was of an arduous nature and was carried out with energy and efficiency.
She rendered valuable services and was commended for her work. 77, Orbain Road, Fulham, S.W.6   TX18637B.

GOODWAY, W. J. E., Pte., East Surrey Regt.
He volunteered for service in 1914, and, after his training, was drafted overseas. where he saw much fighting on the Western Front. He took part in the battles of Neuve Chapelle, Loos, the Somme, Arras and Cambrai. He was wounded three times, and in consequence was discharged in 1918 as medically unfit for further service.
He holds the 1914–15 Star, General Service and Victory Medals. 77, Orbain Road, Fulham, S.W.6   TX18637A.

GOODWIN, G. F., Pte., Sherwood Foresters.
He joined in May, 1916, and served in France, taking part in many engagements on the Western Front, including the battles of the Somme, Ypres and Arras.
He holds the General Service and Victory Medals, and was demobilised in October, 1919.
39, Mozart Street, North Kensington, W.10   X18833B.

GOODWIN, H. E., Stoker, Royal Navy.
Joining in January, 1917, he was posted to H.M.S. " Stour," and served with the fleet in the North Sea. being chiefly engaged on dangerous patrol and convoy duties.
He was demobilised in March, 1919, and holds the General Service and Victory Medals.
46, Goodwin Road, Lower Edmonton, N.9.   13001A.

GOODWIN, H. W., Sick Berth Orderly, R.N.
He volunteered for service in August, 1914, and was engaged on special duty at the Naval Hospital, Chatham, and on hospital ships crossing the Channel. He did good work and rendered every assistance to the sick and wounded.
He holds the General Service and Victory Medals, and was demobilised in May 1919.
39, Mozart Street, North Kensington, W.10   X18833A.

GOODWIN, J. A., Pte., Worcestershire Regt.
He joined up in April, 1917, and shortly afterwards was drafted overseas. He was actively engaged in various sectors of the Western Front and was killed in action on October 9th, 1917.
He was entitled to the General Service and Victory Medals.
46, Goodwin Road, Lower Edmonton, N.9   13001B.

GOODWIN, M. (Miss), Special War Worker.
In the early part of the war this lady gave her services at a large munition factory, where she was engaged on work of a very arduous nature.
She continued throughout the war, rendering valuable services and was commended for her work.
30, Dawlish Street, Wilcox Road, S.W.8   15394B.

GOODYEAR, P., Rifleman, 18th London Regt. (London Irish Rifles).
He volunteered in May, 1915, at the age of 15, and after his training was drafted overseas. He took part in many engagements on the Western Front, and was severely wounded in action in June, 1916.
He holds the 1914–15 Star, General Service and Victory Medals, and was demobilised in February, 1919.
4a, Effie Place, Walham Green, S.W.6   X19704.

GORMAN, E., Rifleman, King's Royal Rifle Corps.
He volunteered for service in August, 1914, and was shortly afterwards drafted overseas. He saw much fighting in France and took part in many engagements, including the battle of La Bassée, where he was severely wounded.
He was discharged in March, 1916, as medically unfit for further service in consequence of his wounds, and holds the 1914 Star, General Service and Victory Medals.
141, Estcourt Road, Fulham, S.W.6   16237.

GORRINGE, W. T., Pte., Middlesex Regiment.
He volunteered for service in October, 1915, was sent to the Western Front in the following year, and took part in the fighting at the Somme, Arras, Ypres, and at other engagements. He died in January, 1918, of illness brought on by his Army service.
He was entitled to the General Service and Victory Medals, and his relatives received the King's Scroll.
30, Farrant Street, Queen's Park, W.10   X19180.

GOSDBN, J. W., Tpr., 3rd County of London Yeomanry and Bombardier, R.F.A.
He volunteered in 1915 and served with his unit at various stations on important duties. He was later transferred to the R.F.A. and was promoted to Bombardier in charge of signallers. He was sent to France in 1917, and was in action on the Menin Road and at Zonnebeke.
In 1919 he was demobilised, and holds the General Service and Victory Medals.
2, Lichfield Road, Lower Edmonton, N.9   14669.

GOSSON, O. G., Rifleman, 16th London Regt. (Queen's Westminster Rifles).
He volunteered in 1914, at the age of 16, and in the following February was sent to Egypt. Later he was drafted to the Western Front, where he took part in several engagements, and was killed in action in the Ypres sector on October 1st, 1916.
He was entitled to the 1914–15 Star and the General Service and Victory Medals.
23, Westbury Road, Willesden, N.W.10   15065A.

GOSSON, W. F. (M.M.), Lce.-Cpl., Middlesex Regiment.
He volunteered in April, 1915, and during his three years' service on the Western Front took part in various engagements, and was awarded the Military Medal for conspicuous gallantry in the field during the advance of April, 1917.
He also holds the General Service and Victory Medals, and was demobilised in March, 1919.
23, Westbury Road, Willesden, N.W.10   15065B.

GOSTLING, W. A., Pte., The London Regiment.
He volunteered for service in August, 1914, and at the conclusion of his training was drafted overseas. He saw active service in various sectors of the Western Front, and in March, 1917, he was wounded and taken prisoner.
Upon his release he returned to England, and was demobilised after the Armistice, holding the General Service and Victory Medals. 202, Montague Road, Lower Edmonton, N.9 15843.

GOTZ, J., Pte., Middlesex Regiment.
He joined in 1917, and during his service was engaged on important duties with his regiment at various stations. Early in 1918 he met with an accident, and was instantly killed as a result.
He had rendered valuable services for his country.
9, Humbolt Mansions, Lillie Road, Fulham, S.W.6 X18870A.

GOUDIE, C. H., Cpl., 18th London Regiment (London Irish Rifles).
He volunteered in August, 1914, having previously served with the Territorials, went to France in the following year, and took part in many battles, including those of Ypres, Neuve Chapelle, Cambrai and Arras.
He was demobilised in May, 1919, holding the 1914-15 Star and the General Service and Victory Medals.
32, Crefold Road, Hammersmith, W.6.   T14102B.

GOUGH, A. G., Sapper, Royal Engineers.
He volunteered in January, 1915, and after his training was retained on important duties at various stations with his unit.
He gave valuable services, but was unable to secure his transfer overseas before the cessation of hostilities. He was demobilised in 1919
39, Brett Road, Stonebridge Park, N.W.10.   14519B.

GOUGH, G., Leading Aircraftsman, R.A.F.
He volunteered in June, 1915, and in the following year was sent to the Western Front. While there he served in various sectors with his squadron, and rendered valuable services. His duties called for a high degree of technical skill. In November, 1919, he was demobilised, and holds the General Service and Victory Medals.
39, Brett Road, Stonebridge Park, N.W.10.   14519A.

GOUGH, L. (Mrs.), Special War Worker.
At the outbreak of war this lady rendered valuable services at a large munition factory. Her duties called for great care and long hours, but she worked with energy and efficiency and was highly complimented for her splendid work.
11, Station Road, Hanwell, W.7   12389B.

GOUGH, W. T. J., Rifleman, King's Royal Rifle Corps.
Volunteering in November, 1915, he was sent to France in the following May, seeing much fighting. He was wounded in action at Pozières and again at Havrincourt Wood. He was later drafted to Italy. He did valuable duty as a signaller during his service.
His demobilisation was secured in February, 1919, and he holds the General Service and Victory Medals.
11, Station Road, Hanwell, W.7   12389A.

GOULD, A. J., Pte., Sherwood Foresters and South Staffordshire Regiment.
He volunteered in 1915, and served on the Western Front for three years, during which period he took part in the fighting on the Somme, at Lens and Cambrai, and was wounded and slightly gassed.
He holds the General Service and Victory Medals, and was demobilised in September, 1919.
111, Felixstowe Road, Lower Edmonton, N.9   15780.

GOULDING, B., Pte., 20th London Regt.
He joined in March, 1916, and during his service on the Western Front took part in many battles, including those of Ypres, the Somme, Cambrai, and Albert, where he was wounded in March, 1917.
He holds the General Service and Victory Medals, and was demobilised in April, 1919.
1, Effie Road, Walham Green, S.W.6   X19705.

GOVEN, W. A., 1st-Class Stoker, Royal Navy.
He volunteered in 1915, and served in the North Sea with the Grand Fleet, where his duties were of a hazardous and important nature. He was discharged in 1917 as medically unfit for further service, owing to ill health.
He holds the 1914-15 Star, the General Service and Victory Medals.
7, Bury Street, Lower Edmonton, N.9   13932.

GOVER, J., Pte., Middlesex Regiment.
He volunteered in December, 1914, and after his training was engaged on important duties at many stations. He gave valuable services, but was unsuccessful in obtaining his transfer overseas before hostilities ceased.
He was demobilised in March, 1919.
2, Durban Road, Tottenham, N.17   X18100B.

GOVER, J., Stoker, R.N., H.M.S. "Revenge."
He volunteered in 1915, and was posted to H.M.S. "Revenge." He served on this ship for three years, during which time he was engaged on dangerous duties.
He is still serving, and holds the 1914-15 Star, the General Service and Victory Medals.
2, Durban Road, Tottenham, N.17   X18100C.

GOVER, J. (jun.), Lce.-Cpl., 7th Middlesex Regt.
He was in the Army Reserve when war was declared, and was mobilised in August, 1914. He went to the Western Front in 1915, and was in action at Ypres, Arras, Neuve Chapelle and the Somme, where he was wounded. He was invalided home, and was in hospital for some months, suffering from shell-shock.
He was finally discharged in July, 1917, being medically unfit for further service. He holds the 1914-15 Star, General Service and Victory Medals.
2, Durban Road, Tottenham, N.17.   X18100D.

GOVER, J. W., Sergt., King's Royal Rifle Corps.
He volunteered in January, 1915, and was sent to France early in the following year. He took part in many engagements, and was wounded at Delville Wood in 1917.
In January, 1919, he was demobilised, holding the General Service and Victory Medals.
4, Marsden Road, Lower Edmonton, N.9   13068A.

GOVER, T. G., Sergt., R.A.S.C. (H.T.).
He volunteered for duty in September, 1914, and during his service was engaged on important and responsible duties with his unit, being in charge of valuable stores.
He was demobilised in March, 1920.
211, Portnall Road, Maida Hill, W.9   X19827.

GOVER, W., Lce.-Cpl., 11th Middlesex Regt.
He volunteered in 1914, and was sent in the following year to the Western Front, where, while in action at the battle of Loos, he was killed on October 15th, 1915. He was buried near Vermelles, and was entitled to the 1914-15 Star, the General Service and Victory Medals.
2, Durban Road, Tottenham, N.17   X18100A.

GOVER, W. A., Ship's Printer, Royal Navy.
He volunteered in May, 1915, and was posted to H.M.S. "Zealander." During his service he spent a large portion of his time with North Sea squadrons, and took part in the battle of Jutland. He was severely wounded when his ship struck a mine, and was discharged in January, 1918.
He was entitled to the 1914-15 Star and General Service, and Victory Medals.
4, Marsden Road, Lower Edmonton, N.9   13068B.

GOVIER, H. T., Pte., 26th Middlesex Regiment.
He joined in March, 1916, and was sent to Salonica the following July, where he took part in many operations, and while on service contracted malaria, from which he died on September, 15th, 1918.
He was entitled to the General Service and Victory Medals.
49, Denzil Road, Neasden Lane, N.W.10   15927.

GOWER, E. W., Pte., East Surrey Regiment.
He joined in July, 1918, and served on the Western Front, where he took part in the Advance of 1918. After the Armistice he served with the Army of Occupation at Cologne. He was demobilised in October, 1919, holding the General Service and Victory Medals.
18, Mordaunt Road, N.W.10   13733.

GRACE, F. W., Bombardier, R.F.A.
He volunteered in October, 1914, and was sent to the Western Front, where he took part with distinction in actions at Neuve Chapelle, Ypres, the Somme and other engagements, being wounded at Ploegsteert and Vimy Ridge.
He holds the 1914-15 Star, General Service and Victory Medals, and was demobilised in March, 1919.
4, Stanley Grove, Tottenham, N.17   TX18292.

GRACE, W., Cpl., Royal Engineers.
He volunteered in October, 1914, was sent to the Dardanelles, and later to Egypt. Afterwards he went to the Western Front, where he took part in the fighting at Arras, and was twice wounded at Ypres.
He holds the 1914-15 Star, General Service and Victory Medals, and was demobilised in September, 1919.
54, Yeldham Road, Hammersmith, W.6   12832.

GRACO, A. G., Lce.-Cpl., 6th Middlesex Regt.
He enlisted in July, 1916, having previously been employed on important Government work, and served at various stations on special duties as a qualified Hotchkiss Gun Instructor, having passed the necessary examinations and holding the official certificate for that post.
He was demobilised in October, 1919.
23, Hiley Road, Willesden, N.W.10   X18171B.

GRACO, H. A., Pte., 4th Middlesex Regiment.

He was serving when war broke out, went to France in 1914, and was taken prisoner during the retreat from Mons. After suffering great privation whilst in captivity, he was released in December, 1918, and was demobilised in October of the following year.
He holds the Mons Star, the General Service and Victory Medals.
53, Felixstowe Road, Willesden, N.W.10   X17763A.

GRACO, W. T., Rifleman, Rifle Brigade.

He joined in July, 1918, on attaining military age, and after his training was engaged on important duties at various stations with his unit. He was unsuccessful in obtaining his transfer overseas owing to the early cessation of hostilities after his joining the Army.
He was demobilised in November, 1919.
53, Felixstowe Road, Willesden, N.W.10   X17763B.

GRAHAM, F., Pte., West Riding Regiment.

He enlisted in March, 1917, and later in the same year was drafted to France, where he took part with distinction in engagements at Ypres and other sectors, and was wounded. He was demobilised in April, 1919, holding the General Service and Victory Medals.
37, Croxley Road, Maida Hill, W.9   X19972.

GRAHAM, F., Pte., 2/7th Northumberland Fus.

He volunteered in March, 1915, and on the completion of his training served with his unit at various stations on important duties. Despite his efforts, his physical unfitness prevented his transfer overseas, and he was discharged in December, 1917, after rendering valuable services.
2, Herries Street, N. Kensington, W.10   X18721.

GRAHAM, R., Cpl., 3rd Canadian Regiment.

He volunteered in August, 1914, and served in France, taking part in engagements at Loos, Arras, Ypres, the Somme, Givenchy, Festubert, Ploegsteert, and Vimy Ridge. He was wounded twice and was in hospital in France and England.
He holds the 1914-15 Star, General Service and Victory Medals, and was demobilised in August, 1919.
25, Lintaine Grove, West Kensington, W.14   16653.

GRAINGER, J., 2nd Air Mechanic, R.A.F.

He joined in May, 1918, and after his training was engaged on special duties at various stations with his unit. He gave valuable services, and his duties called for a high degree of technical skill, but he was unsuccessful in obtaining his transfer overseas prior to the cessation of hostilities.
He was demobilised in May, 1919, and holds the General Service Medal.
132, Minet Avenue, N.W.10   13395.

GRANGE, C., Pte., 1st Middlesex Regiment.

He joined in 1916, and served for two years on the Western Front, taking part in the fighting in the Arras, Loos, Somme, Ypres and Armentieres sectors, and was wounded. In 1920 he was demobilised, and holds the General Service and Victory Medals.
28, Holly Lane, Willesden, N.W.10   15573.

GRANGE, E., Trooper, 1st Life Guards.

He volunteered in August, 1914, served on the Western Front from August, 1915, until 1917, and was in action at Ypres, Laventie, Arras and on the Somme. He was wounded, and was discharged on account of wounds in October, 1917, being medically unfit for further service.
He holds the 1914-15 Star, General Service and Victory Medals.
129, Mayo Road, Willesden, N.W.10   15432.

GRANT, F. (Miss), Special War Worker.

During the war this lady was engaged on work of a very important nature in several large munition factories in connection with the manufacture of aircraft and hand-grenades. Her work was of a dangerous nature and called for great skill.
1, Lundy Street, W.6   14804.

GRANT, F. S., Trooper, 5th Dragoon Guards.

He volunteered for service in September, 1914, and, after completing his training was engaged on work of an important nature with his unit until 1915, when owing to being medically unfit for further services, he was discharged, after having rendered valuable services.
1, Lundy Street, Hammersmith, W.6   14812A.

GRANT, H. R., Stoker, Royal Navy.

He joined in August, 1917, and was posted to H.M.S. " Flying Fish." During his service he was engaged on dangerous patrol duties in the North Sea and other waters for a period of two years.
In March, 1919, he was demobilised and holds the General Service and Victory Medals.
48, Yuletide Road, Willesden, N.W.10   15076.

GRANT, L., Pte., 13th London Regiment, (Kensingtons).

He volunteered in August, 1914, and in the following month was sent to the Western Front. During his five years' service in France he took part with distinction in many of the principal engagements.
In 1919 he returned to England and was demobilised, holding the 1914 Star, General Service and Victory Medals.
131, Kilburn Lane, North Kensington, W.10   X18573.

GRANT, M. (Mrs.), Special War Worker.

For a period of over 4 years during the war this lady rendered services of a valuable character at Messrs. Blake's Munition Factory, Putney. Her work, which was in connection with fuses and in the T.N.T. departments, was of a dangerous nature, but she worked with untiring energy, and was given a certificate of appreciation for her splendid work.
25, Hilmer Street, West Kensington, W.14   15704.

GRANT, M. E. (Mrs.), Special War Worker.

During the war this lady rendered valuable services at Park Royal Munition Factory, where she was engaged in box-making. Her duties were heavy and of a trying nature, but she performed her work to great satisfaction.
41, Steele Road, Willesden, N.W.10.   14534A.

GRANT, P. H., Rifleman, 6th London Regiment (Rifles).

He joined in March, 1916, and was sent to the Western Front, where he was engaged in the fighting at Arras, Bourlon Wood, Bullecourt, Oppy Wood, Monchy, Cambrai and the Retreat and Advance of 1918. During his service he was wounded twice.
He holds the General Service and Victory Medals, and was demobilised in February, 1919.
1, Lundy Street, Hammersmith, W.6   14809.

GRANT, W. F., Driver, Royal Field Artillery.

He volunteered in September, 1914, and saw active service on the Western Front, where he took part in the fighting at Neuve Chapelle, Loos, the Somme, Arras, Armentieres, Ypres and the Retreat and Advance of 1918. After the cessation of hostilities he served with the Army of Occupation on the Rhine. He returned to England for his demobilisation in April, 1919, and holds the 1914-15 Star, General Service and Victory Medals.   1, Lundy Street, Hammersmith, W 6   14812B.

GRANT, W. J., Pte., The Queen's (Royal West Surrey Regiment).

He joined in 1917, and after his training was drafted overseas to India, where he was engaged on special duties at various stations with his unit.
He returned to England in 1919, and was demobilised, holding the General Service and Victory Medals.
41, Steele Road, Willesden, N.W.10   14534B.

GRANTHAM, G., Driver, Royal Field Artillery.

He volunteered in December, 1914, and served in France until December, 1915, when he was sent to the Balkans, where he took part in the fighting on the Struma. After the Armistice he served in Russia for a few months.
He returned to England and was demobilised in May, 1919, holding the 1914-15 Star, General Service and Victory Medals. 23, Villiers Road, Cricklewood, N.W.2   16722.

GRAVES, A., Gunner, Royal Field Artillery.

He joined in April, 1917, and after his training was sent to France early in 1918. While on the Western Front he took part in much of the important fighting, and was wounded in action.
In April, 1919, he was demobilised, holding the General Service and Victory Medals.
8, Cobbold Road, Willesden, N.W.10   16069.

GRAVES, A. F., Pte., 2/10th London Regt.

He joined in February, 1916, and at the conclusion of his training was drafted overseas. He took part in the fighting on practically all sectors of the Western Front, and was wounded in action.
He holds the General Service and Victory Medals, and was demobilised in 1919.
32, Chaldon Road, Fulham, S.W.6   X17724.

GRAVESTOCK, J., Pte., East Surrey Regiment.

He volunteered for duty in February, 1915, and served at various stations on important duties with the Labour Battalion, the Royal Air Force, and the East Surrey Regiment. He was demobilised in March, 1919, after having rendered valuable services.
30, Avalon Road, New King's Road, S.W.6   X19775A.

GRAVESTOCK, J. H. (jun.), Driver, R.F.A.

He volunteered for service in April, 1915, and during his service on the Western Front took part in many of the principal engagements.
He was demobilised in July, 1919, and holds the 1915 Star, the General Service and Victory Medals.
30, Avalon Road New King's Road, S.W.6   X19775B.

GRAY, A., Rifleman, 13th King's Royal Rifle Corps.
He joined in November, 1917, and was sent to France shortly afterwards. He took part in many engagements on the Western Front, and was wounded in action at Albert. He was demobilised in January, 1920, and holds the General Service and Victory Medals.
31, Ashford Road, Tottenham, N.17 X18351B.

GRAY, C., Driver, Royal Field Artillery.
He volunteered in 1915, went to France the same year, and took part in many engagements, including those of the Somme, Arras and Ypres.
He holds the 1914-15 Star, the General Service and Victory Medals, and was demobilised in July, 1919.
60, Kenninghall Road, Upper Edmonton, N.18 16895.

GRAY, C. W., Pte., 1st Cyclist Corps.
He volunteered in August, 1914, and in 1915 was sent to Gallipoli, where he took part in the heavy fighting, and afterwards saw service in France. He was killed in action at Loos, on the 25th of November, 1916.
He was entitled to the 1914-15 Star, the General Service and Victory Medals.
31, Ashford Road, Tottenham, N.17 X18351D.

GRAY, D. C., A.B., R.N., H.M.S. " Hampshire."
He was mobilised in August, 1914, and was engaged on hazardous duties with the Grand Fleet in the North Sea. He took part in many engagements, including the battle of the Dogger Bank. In December, 1915, he was discharged as medically unfit for further service.
He holds the 1914-15 Star, General Service and Victory Medals. 9, Somerford Grove, Tottenham, N.17 X18804.

GRAY, E., Pte., King's Own (Yorkshire Light Infantry).
He joined up in May, 1916, and after his training was drafted to France, where he took part in many engagements on the Western Front, and was wounded in action at Cambrai.
He holds the General Service and Victory Medals, and was demobilised in February, 1919.
31, Ashford Road, Tottenham, N.17 X18351A.

GRAY, G. F., Sapper, Royal Engineers.
He volunteered in August, 1914, and was sent to the Western Front, where he was engaged on special duties, and served with distinction at the battles of Loos, Ypres and Arras.
In December, 1917, he was discharged as medically unfit for further service, and holds the 1914-15 Star, General Service and Victory Medals.
80, Fernhead Road, Maida Hill, W.9 X19462.

GRAY, J., Sergt., 10th Argyll and Sutherland Highlanders.
He rejoined in August, 1914, after having previously served in the Army, and was sent to the Western Front, where he gained quick promotion and took part in many engagements.
He was killed in action in June, 1916, after a total of 21 years' service.
He was entitled to the 1914-15 Star, the General Service and Victory Medals.
49, Allestree Road, Munster Road, S.W.6 X19261.

GRAY, S., 1st Air Mechanic, Royal Air Force.
He joined in April, 1916, and served in France. He was on board H.M.S. " Arragon " when she was torpedoed on her passage from France to Egypt, and was drowned on 30th December, 1917.
He was entitled to the General Service and Victory Medals.
31, Ashford Road, Tottenham, N.17 X18351C.

GRAY, W. R., Pte., 13th Royal Fusiliers.
He joined in July, 1916, and in the same year was sent to the Western Front, where he took part in many engagements. He is believed to have been killed in action near Arras on April 10th, 1917.
He was entitled to the General Service and Victory Medals.
48, Portnall Road, Maida Hill, W.9 X19453.

GREEN, A., Air Mechanic, Royal Air Force.
He joined in 1918, and was engaged on duties of a special nature. His work required a high degree of technical skill. Owing to the loss of an eye he was unable to obtain his transfer overseas, and was demobilised in 1919.
23, Manor Road, Tottenham, N.17 X18980.

GREEN, A., Pte., Royal Army Service Corps.
Having previously served in the South African War, he was mobilised in August, 1914, and served on important duties on the Western Front
In February, 1915, he was discharged as unfit for further service, and holds the 1914-15 Star, the General Service and Victory Medals.
26, Laundry Road, Hammersmith, W.6 15050.

GREEN, A. J., Pte., 16th Middlesex Regiment.
He joined in March, 1916, and served on the Western Front, taking part in many engagements, including the battles of the Somme. He was killed in action on the Ypres Front on May 30th, 1916, and was entitled to the General Service and Victory Medals.
32, Parkfield Road, Willesden, N.W.10 X17419A.

GREEN, A. J., Driver, R.F.A.
He volunteered in August, 1914, and went to France in the following year. He served with distinction in many engagements on the Western Front, and was wounded three times. He was demobilised in April, 1919, and holds the 1914-15 Star, General Service and Victory Medals.
172, Winchester Road, Lower Edmonton, N.9 14884.

GREEN, A. T., Sapper, Royal Engineers.
He volunteered in August, 1915, and went out to France, where he saw active service and was in engagements at Ypres, Arras, Albert and Cambrai.
In October, 1917, he was discharged as medically unfit for further service, and holds the General Service and Victory Medals.
3, Dover House, Roundwood Road, Willesden, N.W.10.
16935A.

GREEN, A. T. (jun.), Stoker, R.N., H.M.S. " Kendal."
He joined in 1918, and was engaged on dangerous mine-sweeping duties in the North Sea. On two occasions the vessels on which he was serving were blown up and he narrowly escaped drowning.
He was demobilised in 1919, and holds the General Service and Victory Medals.
3, Dover House, Roundwood Road, Willesden, N.W.10.
16935B.

GREEN, A. T., Pte., 7th Middlesex Regiment.
He volunteered in September, 1914, and during his service in France took part in the battles of Mons, Loos, Arras, Ypres and the Somme.
He was demobilised in January, 1919, and holds the Mons Star, General Service and Victory Medals.
27, Eldon Road, Lower Edmonton, N.9 13060.

GREEN, E., Pte., The Buffs (East Kent Regt.) and Middlesex Regiment.
He volunteered in 1914, served in France and took part in the fighting at Ypres and Loos.
He was twice wounded, and was demobilised in 1919, holding the General Service and Victory Medals.
95, Monmouth Road, Lower Edmonton, N.9 13016A.

GREEN, F., Pte., Honourable Artillery Company.
He joined iu May 1918, and during his service was engaged on duties of a special nature at important stations. He was unsuccessful in securing his transfer overseas before hostilities ceased, and after rendering valuable services was demobilised in February, 1919.
4, Cobbold Road, Church End, N.W.10 16067A.

GREEN, F., Pte., The Queen's (Royal West Surrey Regiment).
He volunteered for service in August, 1914, and in the same year went to France, where he took part in engagements at Ypres, Loos, Albert, the Somme, Arras and Cambrai, and was wounded three times in action.
He was demobilised in August, 1919, holding the 1915 Star, General Service and Victory Medals.
13, Rectory Road, Parsons Green, S.W.6 X20014.

GREEN, F. C., Pte., 1st Border Regiment.
He volunteered in February, 1915, and went to France the same year. He took part in many engagements, and was reported missing during the battle of the Somme, and presumed killed in July, 1916.
He was entitled to the 1914-15 Star, General Service and Victory Medals.
51, Oldfield Road, Willesden, N.W.10. 15989.

GREEN, G., Cpl., Royal Field Artillery.
He volunteered in August, 1914, and went to France in the following year. During his period of active service he took part in many engagements, and was promoted for good work.
He was demobilised in 1919, and holds the 1914-15 Star, the General Service and Victory Medals.
95, Monmouth Road, Lower Edmonton, N.9. 13016B.

GREEN, G. (M.S.M.), Cpl., Royal Air Force.
He joined in November, 1916, served in Egypt, and was later sent to South Russia He was awarded the Meritorious Service Medal for his continuous good work and gallant service abroad, and was also mentioned in despatches in October, 1919.
He was demobilised in April, 1920, holding the General Service and Victory Medals.
14, Mirabel Road, Fulham, S.W.6. X17861.

GREEN, G., Pte., 5th Royal Berkshire Regt.
He volunteered in May, 1915, and was sent to France the same year. He took part in many engagements, including Ypres and Givenchy, where he was severely wounded. He was discharged as medically unfit for further service, as the result of his wounds, in August, 1916, and holds the 1914-15 Star, General Service and Victory Medals.
33, Cooper Road, Dudden Hill, N.W.10   16642.

GREEN, G., Sapper, Royal Engineers.
He joined in April, 1916, and was sent to Salonica in December of the same year, where he served throughout the Balkan campaign, being engaged on important engineering work. He was demobilised in September, 1919, and holds the General Service and Victory Medals.
32, Parkfield Road, Willesden, N.W.10   X17419B.

GREEN, G. F., Pte., Gloucestershire Regiment.
He joined in September, 1916, and was sent in the following year to France, where he took part in the battles of Ypres, the Somme and Cambrai, and was gassed. He went to India in October, 1919, and is still serving.
He holds the General Service and Victory Medals.
30, Charlton Road, Harlesden, N.W.10   13110.

GREEN, H., Rifleman, King's Royal Rifle Corps.
He joined in January, 1918, and was sent to France, where, on account of his age, he was employed on special duties. He, however, took part in the Advance of 1918, and later served with the Army of Occupation in Germany. He was demobilised in December, 1919, and holds the General Service and Victory Medals.
107, Felix Road, West Ealing, W.13   11028.

GREEN, H., Pte., 18th Middlesex Regiment.
He volunteered in March, 1915, and saw active service in France. He took part in many engagements, including those at Ypres, Verdun and Arras.
He was demobilised in March, 1919, and holds the 1915 Star, General Service and Victory Medals.
35, Beaconsfield Road, Willesden, N.W.10   16332.

GREEN, H. P., Pte., East Yorkshire Regiment, attached Royal Army Service Corps (M.T.).
He joined in 1917, and went to France the same year, where he was engaged on important transport work. He was invalided home owing to ill-health, and eventually discharged in 1919, as medically unfit for further service.
He holds the General Service and Victory Medals.
17, Ilex Road, Willesden, N.W.10   16099A.

GREEN, H. T., Pte., 5th Royal Fusiliers.
He joined in September, 1917, and after completing his training served at various stations with his unit. He tried to obtain his transfer overseas, but this was prevented by his ill-health. After rendering valuable services he was demobilised in August, 1919.
65, Redfern Road, Harlesden, N.W.10   13197.

GREEN, J., Gunner, Royal Field Artillery.
He volunteered in August, 1914, and served for four years in France, where he took part in engagements on the Somme, Ypres, Arras, and in the Advance of 1918. He was wounded three times, and was demobilised in February, 1919, holding the 1914-15 Star, General Service and Victory Medals.
9, Denmark Street, Tottenham, N.17   X18796B.

GREEN, J., Pte., Royal Army Service Corps.
He volunteered in February, 1915, and was sent to the Western Front the same year. While in this theatre of war he was engaged on duties of an important nature in many engagements.
He was demobilised in June, 1919, holding the 1914-15 Star, the General Service and Victory Medals.
38, Hannell Road, Munster Road, Fulham, S W.6   X18075.

GREEN, J., Driver, Royal Field Artillery.
He volunteered in June, 1915, and during his service on the Western Front took part in the battles of Ypres and the Somme, where he was wounded, being awarded the Croix de Guerre for conspicuous gallantry in the field. He was demobilised in May, 1919, holding the General Service and Victory Medals.
13, Cedars Road, Edmonton, N.9   14037.

GREEN, J. D., Lce.-Cpl., 11th Middlesex Regt.
He volunteered in October, 1914, went to the Western Front, and was killed in action at Vimy Ridge on October 18th, 1915, having previously taken part in other engagements. He was entitled to the 1914-15 Star, the General Service and Victory Medals.
75, Durban Road, Tottenham, N.17   X18280.

GREEN, O. G., Gunner, Royal Garrison Artillery.
He was serving at the outbreak of war, and was sent to France in August, 1914, where he took part in the battles of Mons, the Somme, Ypres, Cambrai and Arras, being wounded and gassed.
He was demobilised in February, 1920, holding the Mons Star, General Service and Victory Medals.
4, Cobbold Road, Church End, N.W.10   16068.

GREEN, P., Pte., Highland Light Infantry.
He was mobilised in August, 1914, and immediately went to France, where he took part in many engagements on the Western Front.
He was discharged in January, 1919, having completed 21 years' service, and holds the 1914 Star, General Service and Victory Medals.
61, Chauncey Street, Lower Edmonton, N.9   14265.

GREEN, P. A., Rifleman, The London Regiment.
He joined in September, 1917, and was sent to the Western Front, where he took part in many engagements. After the Armistice he went with the Army of Occupation to Germany, and in September, 1919, was demobilised, holding the General Service and Victory Medals.
25, Oldfield Road, Willesden, N.W.10   16024A

GREEN, R., Sapper, Royal Engineers.
He enlisted in June, 1915, and in the same year went to France, where he was engaged on important duties. He was demobilised in 1919, and holds the 1914-15 Star, the General Service and Victory Medals.
17, Ilex Road, Willesden, N.W.10   16099B.

GREEN, T. W., Pte., Royal Fusiliers.
He volunteered in September, 1914, and served on the Western Front, taking part in many engagements, including the battle of the Somme. While in action at Ypres he was killed on August 13th, 1917.
He was entitled to the 1914-15 Star, General Service and Victory Medals.
14, Goodson Road, Willesden, N.W.10   15132.

GREEN, V. W., Pte., R.A.S.C. (M.T.).
He volunteered in November, 1915, and in the same year went to the Western Front, where he was engaged in transport work during the battles of the Somme, Ypres and Arras. He was demobilised in July, 1919, and holds the 1914-15 Star, the General Service and Victory Medals.
3, Asplin Road, Tottenham, N.17   X18816.

GREEN, W. C., Driver, Royal Horse Artillery.
He joined in January, 1917, proceeded to the Western Front in the same year, and took part in the engagements, and in the great Advance of that year. After the signing of the Armistice he went to Germany with the Army of Occupation, serving there till his demobilisation in August, 1919.
He holds the General Service and Victory Medals.
49, Bulow Road, Fulham, S.W.6   X20800.

GREEN, W. E., Driver, Royal Army Service Corps.
He volunteered in November, 1915, and was sent to Salonica, where he took part in important operations during the Balkan campaign. He contracted malaria, was invalided home, and demobilised in February, 1919.
He holds the General Service and Victory Medals.
32, Parkfield Road, Willesden, N.W.10   X17419C.

GREEN, W. H., Pte., Suffolk Regiment and Gloucestershire Regiment.
He joined in June, 1916, and during his service on the Western Front took part in many engagements, including those of Ypres and the Somme, being wounded. He was taken prisoner in April, 1918, and kept in Germany until December of that year, when he was released. He holds the General Service and Victory Medals, and was demobilised in January, 1919.
55, Fernhead Road, Maida Hill, W.9   X19456.

GREEN, W. J., Pte., Royal Army Service Corps.
He joined in July, 1917, and was drafted to the Western Front, where he was engaged on duties of a special nature, holding a responsible position in the E.F.C. He was demobilised in March, 1919, and holds the General Service and Victory Medals.
32, Rayleigh Road, West Kensington, W.14   12641/B.

GREEN, W. S., Pte., 1st London Regiment (Royal Fusiliers).
He volunteered in 1914, and went to Malta the same year on garrison duty. In 1915 he was sent to France, and took part in many engagements on the Western Front, being killed in action in June, 1916, during the preparation for the battle of the Somme.
He was entitled to the 1914-15 Star, General Service and Victory Medals.
17, Ilex Road, Willesden, N.W.10   16099C.

GREENAWAY, C. F., Pte., Royal Welch Fus.

He volunteered in 1915, and in the following year was sent to France, where he took part in the battles of the Somme and Ypres. He was in hospital for a considerable period, owing to a severe illness contracted whilst on service.
In February, 1919, he was demobilised, and holds the General Service and Victory Medals.
19, Francis Street, Hammersmith, W.6   15153.

GREENAWAY, G. A., Pte., Royal Fusiliers.

He joined in May, 1917, and was stationed in Ireland on important duties with his unit. He gave valuable services but was not successful in obtaining his transfer overseas, being medically unfit for Foreign service, and was demobilised in April, 1919.
14, Raynham Road, Upper Edmonton, N.18.   16491.

GREENAWAY, J. H., Gunner, R.G.A.

He joined in June, 1916, and was engaged on important anti-aircraft duties on the coast. He brought down a hostile aeroplane and received a message of congratulation from H.M. the King.
He was demobilised in August, 1919, and holds the General Service Medal.
101A, Deacon Road, Cricklewood, N.W.2   16607.

GREENAWAY, R., A.B., R.N., H.M.S. " Dublin."

He volunteered in November, 1915, and was engaged on dangerous duties with the Fleet in Russian waters and also in the North Sea with his ship.
He was demobilised in January, 1919, and holds the General Service and Victory Medals.
16, Montpelier Road, Hammersmith, W.6   13265A.

GREENFIELD, L. (Mrs.), Special War Worker.

For a considerable period of the war this lady was engaged on arduous duties at Messrs. Darracq's Munition Works. She rendered valuable services throughout, and received high praise for her important work.
13, Hilmer Street, West Kensington, W.14   15924B.

GREENFIELD, W., Rifleman, 5th London Regt. (London Rifle Brigade).

He joined in December, 1915, and during his 2½ years' service on the Western Front was in action at Ypres, Cambrai and Arras, where he was severely gassed in March, 1918.
In February, 1919, he was demobilised, holding the General Service and Victory Medals.
48, Fermoy Road, Maida Hill, W.9   X19584.

GREENFIELD, W. J., Sapper, Royal Engineers.

He joined in 1916, and was sent to Egypt, where he was engaged at important stations as a signaller. Whilst in the East he suffered from malaria.
He was demobilised in September, 1919, and holds the General Service and Victory Medals.
13, Hilmer Street, West Kensington, W.14   15924A.

GREENHILL, J., Driver, R.F.A.

He volunteered in 1914, and later was sent to the Western Front, where he took part in many engagements, including the battles of Ypres and the Somme.
He holds the 1914-15 Star, General Service and Victory Medals.
15, Winchester Road, Lower Edmonton, N.9   14681.

GREENING, J. W. (D.C.M.), Sergt., Royal Fus.

He volunteered in 1914, and was sent to the Western Front in the following year, where he took part in much heavy fighting and was awarded the Distinguished Conduct Medal for conspicuous gallantry and devotion to duty in the field.
He also holds the 1914-15 Star, the General Service and Victory Medals, and was demobilised in April, 1919.
39, Sherbrooke Road, Fulham, S.W.6   T18475.

GREENLAND, H., Pte., Royal Fusiliers.

He volunteered in July, 1915, and was sent to France the following year, where he took part in many important engagements.
He was killed in action on April 23rd, 1916, and was entitled to the General Service and Victory Medals.
22, Milton Avenue, Willesden, N.W.10   15643.

GREENROD, T. E., Pte., Middlesex Regiment.

He volunteered in September, 1914, and the same year was sent to the Western Front, where he took part with distinction in many important engagements, and was killed in action in January, 1917.
He was entitled to the 1914-1915 Star, General Service Victory Medals.
60, Hawthorn Road, Upper Edmonton, N.18   X17365.

GREENSHIELDS, T. G., Pte., Royal Dublin Fus.

He volunteered in August, 1914, and the same year was sent to the Western Front, where he took part in many important engagements, being killed in action on August 17th, 1917.
He was entitled to the 1914 Star, General Service and Victory Medals
28, St. Thomas's Road, Fulham, S.W.6   X17230.

GREENWAY, W. A., Pte., Middlesex Regt.

He volunteered in November, 1915, and was almost immediately sent out to France, where he took part in the fighting on several sectors.
He was killed in action in July, 1916, and was entitled to the General Service and Victory Medals.
106, Angel Road, Upper Edmonton, N.18   16579

GREENWOOD, G. G., Air Mechanic, R.A.F.

He joined in January, 1915, the 9th Middlesex Regiment, and was later transferred to the Royal Air Force. During his three years' service on the Western Front he was engaged on special duties in various sectors, including the battle areas of Arras, Cambrai and Ypres.
He was afterwards attached to a balloon section, where he did valuable work. After the Armistice he went with the Army of Occupation to Germany, and returned to England for his demobilisation in February, 1919.
He holds the 1914-15 Star, General Service and Victory Medals.
88, Deacon Road, Cricklewood, N.W.2   X17115.

GREENWOOD, J., Pte., Royal Fusiliers.

He volunteered in April, 1915, and was sent to the Western Front, where he took part in many engagements, including those at Loos, the Somme and Ypres.
During his service he was three times wounded, and in March, 1919, he was demobilised, holding the 1915 Star, General Service and Victory Medals.
42, Church Path, Hammersmith, W.6   16392.

GREENWOOD, W. F. (M.M.), Sapper, R.E.

He volunteered in October, 1914, served on the Western Front from the following year until 1919, and took part in the battles of the Somme, Ypres, Loos, Bullecourt and Arras, and in the Advance of 1918. He also acted as signaller and telegraphist on the Headquarters Staff.
He was awarded the Military Medal for devotion to duty and conspicuous gallantry in carrying despatches under heavy fire. He also holds the 1914-15 Star, General Service and Victory Medals, and was demobilised in February, 1919.
50, Durban Road, Tottenham, N.17   X18092.

GREER, A. J., Pte., 1st Royal Fusiliers.

In August, 1914, he was recalled from the Army Reserve, and the same month was sent to France. He took part in the battle of and the retreat from Mons, and also in the battles of La Bassée, Ypres and the Somme.
On September 30th, 1917, he was killed in action in the Ypres sector, and was entitled to the Mons Star, General Service and Victory Medals.
16, Beethoven Street, North Kensington, W.10   X18744.

GREGORY, D., Pte., Essex Regiment.

He joined in January, 1917, and was sent to France in the following year, where he took part in the fighting at Arras, Bethune, Cambrai, and the Retreat and Advance of 1918.
He was demobilised in September, 1919, holding the General Service and Victory Medals.
2, Waldo Road, Willesden, N.W.10   X18188.

GREGORY, E., Cpl., Royal Fusiliers.

He volunteered in August, 1914, and during his service on the Western Front took part in many engagements, including those of the Somme and Ypres. He was severely wounded at the latter place, and in consequence had his right arm amputated.
After a long period in hospital he was discharged in 1916 as medically unfit for further service. He holds the 1914 Star, General Service and Victory Medals.
139, Poynton Road, Tottenham, N.17   X18950.

GREGORY, E., Pte., 5th Middlesex Regiment and R.A.M.C.

He volunteered in April, 1915, and after being engaged on special duty, was sent to Egypt in July of the following year. He was at Alexandria and Kantara, and was later sent to Asia Minor.
In October, 1918, he was discharged as medically unfit for further service, and holds the General Service and Victory Medals.
22, Shakespeare Road, Upper Edmonton, N.18   X17263.

GREGORY, G., Pte., 3rd Royal Fusiliers.
Having previously served in the Army, he joined for duty in August, 1914, and was immediately sent to Malta. The following year he went to the Western Front, where he took part in numerous engagements, including the second battle of Ypres, Loos, Armentieres, the Somme, Arras and Albert. In addition to the South African Medals, he holds the 1914-15 Star, General Service and Victory Medals, and was demobilised in February, 1919.
5, Dudden Hill Lane, N.W.10   T17334

GREGORY, G. (sen.), Special War Worker.
Being over age for military duties, he offered his services at the Park Royal Munitions Factory, where he was engaged on work of an important and dangerous nature, and was at work when the great explosion occurred in this factory. He performed his duties to entire satisfaction, and rendered valuable services.
16, Steele Road, Willesden, N.W.10   13832A.

GREGORY, H., Cpl., 7th Middlesex Regiment.
He volunteered in August, 1914, and was sent to France. While on this front he took part in many engagements, and during the battle of the Somme in 1916 was severely wounded. As a result, he lost the sight of both eyes, and subsequently died on November 1st, 1916.
He was entitled to the General Service and Victory Medals.
21, Elric Street, Hammersmith, W.6   15864.

GREGORY, W., Pte., Cambridgeshire Regt.
He volunteered in December, 1915, and served on the Western Front for nearly three years. During this period he took part in many battles, including those of the Somme, Ypres, Arras and Cambrai, and was wounded, and on another occasion was temporarily blinded by the explosion of a shell, and buried.
He was demobilised in January, 1919, and holds the General Service and Victory Medals.
5, Westbury Road, Willesden, N.W.10   15069.

GRENESKI, G., Sapper, Royal Engineers.
He joined in May, 1915, and after training was sent to the Western Front. During his service there he took part in important operations, and was on active service overseas until his return to England for demobilisation in April, 1919.
He holds the General Service and Victory Medals.
29, Ray's Road, Upper Edmonton, N.18   15349.

GRETTON, F. M. (Mrs.), Special War Worker.
During the first portion of the war this lady rendered valuable services at a large munition factory, where her work was of an important nature. Later she joined the V.A.D., and served in a military hospital. Her services throughout received high commendation.
21, Mirabel Road, Fulham, S.W.6   X17921B.

GRETTON, J. H., Leading Seaman, R.N., H.M.S. "Kilclare."
He volunteered in August, 1914, and was engaged on duties of a hazardous nature with one of His Majesty's "mystery" ships in the North Sea. During his period of service the vessel was blown up by a mine. Later he went to the Mediterranean on special convoy duties, and remained there until his return to England for demobilisation in February 1919. He holds the 1914-15 Star, General Service and Victory Medals.
21, Mirabel Road, Fulham, S.W.6   X17921A.

GREY, R., Cpl., 18th London Regt. (London Irish Rifles).
He volunteered in 1914, and was sent to France early in the following year, where he took part in the battles of Neuve Chapelle, Festubert and Arras In 1918, owing to a severe illness, he was discharged as being medically unfit for further service.
He holds the 1914-15 Star, the General Service and Victory Medals.
13, Furness Road, Harlesden, N.W.10   13093B.

GREYGOOSE, A. (Miss), Special War Worker.
During the war this lady was engaged on duties of a dangerous nature at a large munition factory, where she worked on detonators for use in hand-grenades and aeroplane bombs. Her services were very valuable, and she received high commendation for her work.
52, Distillery Road. Brentford.   9734—9735C.

GRIDLEY, F. A., Cpl., 3/10th Middlesex Regt.
He volunteered for service in September, 1914, but owing to a severe injury was certified as physically unfit for service overseas. He was employed on duties of a special nature until January, 1916, when he was discharged to take up other duties of national importance.
10, Everington Street, Hammersmith, W.6   14518,

GRIEVE, B., Leading Aircraftsman, R.A.F.
He joined in 1916, and was sent to the Western Front, where his duties were of a special nature, and required great skill and care. After the Armistice he went to Germany with the Army of Occupation, and remained there until his return to England for demobilization in August, 1919.
He holds the General Service and Victory Medals.
7, Garvan Road, Hammersmith, W.6   14645B.

GRIEVE, M., Pte., 13th London Regiment (Kensingtons).
He volunteered in August, 1914, served on the Western Front, and took part in the retreat from Mons and the battle of Neuve Chapelle. He suffered from frost-bite, and was invalided out of the Army in 1916 as unfit for further service. He holds the Mons Star, the General Service and Victory Medals. 7, Garvan Road, Hammersmith, W.6   14645A.

GRIEVSON, S. J. (M.M.), Lce.-Cpl., K.R.R.
He volunteered in January, 1915, and served on both Eastern and Western Fronts. During his stay in Egypt he was kept in hospital with fever for some time, and while in France was so seriously wounded that he lost his leg.
He was awarded the Military Medal for conspicuous gallantry and devotion to duty, and holds in addition the 1914-15 Star and the General Service and Victory Medals.
31, Mooltan Street, West Kensington, W.14   X17141.

GRIFFIN, A. G., Gunner, R.F.A.
He volunteered for service in August, 1914, and was shortly afterwards drafted overseas, where he took part in many important engagements on the Western Front. He remained in France until after the cessation of hostilities, when he returned to England, and was demobilised in March, 1919.
He holds the 1914 Star, General Service and Victory Medals.
27, Marsden Road, Lower Edmonton, N.9   13062.

GRIFFIN, C. W., Driver, R.F.A.
He volunteered in January, 1915, and served in France, where he took part in many engagements. He was taken prisoner and kept in captivity for a considerable period in Germany, where he suffered many hardships.
He holds the 1914-15 Star, General Service and Victory Medals, and was demobilised in January, 1919.
8, Colehill Lane, Fulham, S.W.6   X18923.

GRIFFIN, E. (Mrs.), Special War Worker.
During the war this lady rendered valuable services in a large munition factory, where her work was connected with the making of fuses and was of a dangerous character. She was later promoted to the position of inspector, and received high praise for her work.
8, Corby Road, Willesden, N.W.10   14365A.

GRIFFIN, F. C., Pte., Labour Corps.
He joined in March, 1917, and was employed on important duties in connection with the roads and railways in France from 1918 until demobilised in January, 1919.
He holds the General Service and Victory Medals.
37, Westbury Road, Willesden, N.W.10   15063.

GRIFFIN, G., Pte., 10th Loyal North Lancashire Regiment.
He volunteered for service in July, 1915, and was drafted to France the same year.
He took part in various engagements on the Western Front, and was killed in action on the Somme in March, 1918.
He was entitled to the 1914-15 Star, General Service and Victory Medals.
3, Marker Terrace, Taylor's Lane, Willesden, N.W.10   T15135A.

GRIFFIN, G. T., Cpl., Royal Engineers.
He volunteered for service in July, 1915, and at the conclusion of his training was drafted overseas. He was engaged on various duties in battle areas of the Western Front, and was killed in action at Arras on January 29th, 1916.
He was entitled to the General Service and Victory Medals.
37, Banim Street, Hammersmith, W.6   13229A.

GRIFFIN, H., Rifleman, 12th London Regiment (Rangers).
He volunteered in April, 1915, went to France in the following year, and was killed in action at the battle of Arras in April, 1917, having previously taken part in many other engagements.
He was entitled to the General Service and Victory Medals.
8, Corby Road, Willesden, N.W.10   14365B.

GRIFFIN, J. W., Pte., 15th Royal Warwick Regt.
He volunteered in August, 1914, and saw service on the Western Front, where he took part in engagements on the Somme and at Bullecourt and Ypres. He was killed in action at Passchendaele Ridge on October 26th, 1917, and was entitled to the 1914-15 Star, General Service and Victory Medals. 37, Banim Street, Hammersmith, W.6   13229B

GRIFFITH, A., Special War Worker, British Red Cross Society.
Being unfit for military duty, he volunteered his services with the British Red Cross Society, and went over to France early in 1918. He served with his detachment at Boulogne and elsewhere as a fitter in the workshops, and returned to England in December, 1918, after doing much valuable work.
10, Knivet Road, Walham Green, S.W.6 X19405.

GRIFFITHS, A., Air Mechanic, R.A.F.
He joined in June, 1917, and owing to his special qualifications, was engaged on duties of an important nature in connection with aeroplane engines. Previous to his joining the Royal Air Force he was engaged on Government work for two years.
He was demobilised in April, 1919.
3, Hiley Road, Willesden, N.W.10 X18246.

GRIFFITHS, A., Cpl., R.A.S.C. (M.T.).
Joining in 1916, he went to France in the same year, and was engaged on the important duties of transporting ammunition to the forward areas during the actions on the Somme and at Ypres, Albert and Cambrai..
In 1919 he was demobilised, holding the General Service and Victory Medals.
17, Halford Road, Walham Green, S.W.6 X19470.

GRIFFITHS, J., Pte., 1st Suffolk Regiment.
He volunteered for service in December, 1914, and after his training was drafted to France in April, 1915. The following month he was severely wounded and taken prisoner during the fighting at St. Julien. After nearly four years' captivity in Germany, during which time he suffered many privations, he was released and returned to England for his demobilisation in May, 1919.
He holds the 1914–15 Star, General Service and Victory Medals.
31, Sandringham Road, Cricklewood, N.W.2 X17101.

GRIMMETT, A. (sen.), Pte., R.A.V.C.
He volunteered in October, 1915, and was engaged on special duties in connection with the medical treatment of horses. In 1916 he was in hospital for some time, and was afterwards temporarily released from military service for agricultural work. He rendered valuable services throughout, and was demobilised in January, 1919.
99, Carlyle Avenue, Willesden, N.W.10 13818A.

GRIMMETT, A., Rifleman, 17th London Regt.
Volunteering in April, 1915, he was sent to France in the following year, and took part in engagements at Ypres, on the Somme and at Cambrai, where he was wounded and taken prisoner. During his captivity he suffered many hardships, and was released in December, 1918.
In April of the following year he was demobilised, holding the General Service and Victory Medals.
99, Carlyle Avenue, N.W.10 13818B.

GRIMSDALE, H., Rifleman, 5th London Regt. (London Rifle Brigade).
He volunteered in August, 1914, and was sent to India, where he was engaged on important duties at various stations. In October, 1916, owing to ill-health, he was discharged as medically unfit for further service.
He holds the 1914–15 Star, General Service and Victory Medals.
18, Eldon Road, Lower Edmonton, N.9 13054.

GRIMSON, T. H., Driver, R.F.A.
He volunteered in November, 1914, and was sent to the Western Front in the following year. He took part in the fighting at Ypres, on the Somme, at Bullecourt, Arras, Amiens and Albert, and was wounded. He died of pneumonia at Le Havre on May 26th, 1918, and was entitled to the 1914–15 Star, the General Service and Victory Medals.
32, Hazel Road, Willesden, N.W.10 17788A.

GRIMWADE, N. V. E., Pte., R.A.M.C.
He volunteered in August, 1914, and after being engaged on special duties at various stations was sent to Salonica in 1917, where he was engaged in the care and transportation of the wounded.
In April, 1919, he was demobilised, and holds the General Service and Victory Medals.
13, St. Thomas Road, Craven Park Road, N.W.10 14723.

GRINYER, A. F., Cpl., R.A.S.C.
He volunteered in May, 1915, and went to the Western Front, where he was engaged on transport duties in connection with the actions on the Somme, at Arras, Vimy Ridge, Bullecourt, and in the Retreat and Advance of 1918. He later went to Germany with the Army of Occupation, and was demobilised in April, 1919.
He holds the General Service and Victory Medals.
256, Lillie Road, Fulham. S.W.6 X18784B.

GRINYER, E. M. (Mrs.), Special War Worker.
Throughout the war this lady was employed on work of great responsibility in the clerical department of the Army Pay Office in Regent Street and later at the Imperial Institute, South Kensington. Her duties were accomplished in an able manner and she received high commendation for her work. 256, Lillie Road, Fulham, S.W.6. X18784A.

GRISWOOD, J. W. (sen), Pioneer, R.E. (R.O.D.).
He volunteered in October, 1915, and owing to his special qualifications was sent to Salonica on important duties. He remained there for three years, and was then transferred to France. He was discharged in February, 1919, as medically unfit for further service.
He holds the General Service and Victory Medals.
96, Gresham Road, Neasden, N.W.10 15741A.

GRISWOOD, J. W. (jun.), Cpl., R.E. (R.O.D.).
He volunteered in March, 1915, and was sent to France the following year, where he was engaged on special transport work in connection with the operations on the Somme.
In March, 1919, he was demobilised, and holds the General Service and Victory Medals.
96, Gresham Road, Neasden, N.W.10 15741B.

GROVE, A. H., Cpl., R.A.S.C. (M.T.).
He volunteered in November, 1915, and was sent to France, where he was engaged on duties in connection with the transport of supplies. Later he went with the Army of Occupation to Germany, and on his return to England was demobilised in May, 1919.
He holds the General Service and Victory Medals.
2, Colville Road, Lower Edmonton, N.9 12002.

GROVE, G. J. H., Cpl., Royal Engineers.
He volunteered in January, 1915, and during his service on the Western Front took part in the fighting at Ypres, the Somme, Arras, Cambrai, and Loos, being wounded and gassed.
He was demobilised in January, 1919, and holds the 1914–15 Star, General Service and Victory Medals.
30, Winchelsea Road, Willesden, N.W.10 13851.

GROVE, W. H., Driver, Royal Field Artillery.
He volunteered in August, 1914, and after his training was engaged on important duties at various stations with his unit. Owing to his defective eyesight, he was not eligible at the time for foreign duty, but gave valuable services throughout the war, and was demobilised in April, 1919.
107, Angel Road, Upper Edmonton, N.18 16577.

GROVER, B. J., Pte., Royal Welch Fusiliers.
Joining in June, 1916, he was sent to the Western Front, where he served at Ypres, the Somme and Cambrai, and was wounded in July, 1917. After being in hospital for some time in England he returned to the Front.
He holds the General Service and Victory Medals, and was demobilised in September, 1919.
32, Laundry Road, W.6 15048.

GROVER, F., Pte., R.A.M.C.
He volunteered in January, 1915, and was engaged in a field ambulance section during the operations at Arras, Cambrai, Vimy Ridge and Bullecourt. He suffered from shell-shock and trench fever, and in June, 1919, was demobilised, holding the General Service and Victory Medals.
22, Bathurst Gardens, Kensal Rise, N.W.10 X18415.

GROVER, H. F., Rifleman, The Rifle Brigade.
He joined up for service in May, 1916, and two months later was drafted overseas, where he took part in many engagements on the Western Front.
He was killed in action near Zonnebeke in August, 1917, and was entitled to the General Service and Victory Medals.
33, Villiers Road, Cricklewood, N.W.2 16731A.

GROVES, H., Pte., R.A.S.C. (M.T.).
He was serving at the outbreak of war, and proceeded to France in 1914, where he took part in many engagements. He was discharged in 1918, and on December 28 of the following year died of illness contracted whilst on active service. He had formerly taken part in the South African campaign, for which he held the King's and Queen's South African Medals.
He was entitled to the 1914–15 Star, and the General Service and Victory Medals.
28, Ambleside Road, Willesden, N.W.10 16929.

GROWNS, A. W., Pte., 13th London Regiment (Kensingtons).
He volunteered in 1915, and in the same year was sent out to France. He took part in engagements at Ypres, Loos, the Somme and the Marne, and was wounded at Loos.
He holds the 1914–15 Star and the General Service and Victory Medals, and was demobilised in 1919.
70, St. Mary's Road, Craven Park. N.W.10 13367C.

GROWNS, C., Rifleman, K.R.R.
He volunteered in 1915, and was drafted overseas shortly afterwards. He took part in various engagements on the Western Front, and was killed in action on October 24th during the Advance of 1918.
He was entitled to the 1914–15 Star, General Service and Victory Medals.
70, St. Mary's Road, Craven Park, N.W.10   13367B.

GROWNS, F. T., Pte., 13th London Regiment (Kensingtons).
He volunteered in 1915, and in the following year was sent to France, where he saw much fighting. He was later transferred to Salonica, and from there to Egypt, and took part in the Palestine campaign.
In 1919 he was demobilised, and holds the General Service and Victory Medals.
70, St. Mary's Road, Craven Park, N.W.10   13367A.

GRUNDON, F., Pte., R.A.S.C.
When war broke out he was working for a firm of builders in France, and was able to render valuable service before returning to England in 1916. In September of the same year he joined the Royal Army Service Corps, and in the following October was sent to the Western Front. He served for three years, and during this time saw action in various sectors, attached to ammunition and supply columns.
He was demobilised in May, 1919, holding the General Service and Victory Medals.
15, Beethoven Street, North Kensington, W.10   X19039.

GRUNDON, G., Driver, Royal Field Artillery.
He volunteered in November, 1914, and served in France for nearly 3¼ years, during which period he was in action on the Somme, at Ypres, Neuve Chapelle, Vimy Ridge and Cambrai. He returned to England, and was demobilised in February, 1919, and holds the 1914–15 Star, the General Service and Victory Medals.
80, Harley Road, Willesden, N.W.10   13398.

GRUNDON, G., Gunner, Royal Field Artillery.
He volunteered for service in October, 1914, and in the following year at the conclusion of his training was drafted to the Western Front. While there he took part in many important engagements, including the battles of Ypres, the Somme, Arras and Cambrai, and was demobilised in January, 1919, holding the 1914–15 Star, General Service and Victory Medals.
367a, Chapter Road, Cricklewood, N.W.2   16167B.

GRUNDON, T., Cpl., R.A.S.C. (M.T.).
He volunteered for service in October, 1914, and was shortly afterwards drafted overseas, where he was engaged on transport duties in various sectors of the Western Front. In 1916 he was sent to Italy, and was in action on the Piave. He returned to France the following year and took part in the Advance of 1918.
He holds the 1914 Star, General Service and Victory Medals, and was demobilised in February, 1919.
367a, Chapter Road, Cricklewood, N.W.2   16167C.

GRUNDON, W., Cpl., Middlesex Regiment.
He volunteered for service in September, 1914, and fought on both Western and Eastern Fronts. During 1917 and 1918 he was with the Expeditionary Force under General Allenby in the Palestine campaign.
In February, 1919, he was demobilised, and holds the General Service and Victory Medals.
367a, Chapter Road, Cricklewood, N.W.2   16167A.

GUBB, E., Sapper, Royal Engineers.
Volunteering in 1914, he was quickly sent to France, where he was employed with the Royal Engineers. The following year he was drafted to India, and took part in the fighting on the North-West Frontier, and was severely wounded. After over two years' service in India he was transferred to the Egyptian Expeditionary Force, and took part in General Allenby's victorious advance through Palestine and Syria. He suffered badly from malaria and dysentery.
He returned to England and was demobilised in 1920, holding the 1914–15 Star, General Service and Victory Medals.
419, High Road, Willesden, N.W.10   16627A.

GUBBY, G. W., Stoker, Royal Navy.
He joined in November, 1916, and served on H.M.S. " Gossamer," being engaged on dangerous mine-sweeping duties in the North Sea.
In June, 1919, he was demobilised, and holds the General Service and Victory Medals.
45, Raynham Avenue, Upper Edmonton, N.18   15823.

GUDGEON, A. E., Lce.-Cpl., 4th Middlesex Regt.
He was serving in the Regular Army on the outbreak of hostilities, and in August, 1914, was drafted to the Western Front, where he served until 1918. During this period he took part in the retreat from Mons, the battle of Ypres, and many other engagements. After the cessation of hostilities he was sent to Gibraltar.
He holds the Mons Star, the General Service and Victory Medals. 6, Tenterden Road, Tottenham, N.17   X18273A.

GUDGEON, A. E. (Mrs.), Special War Worker.
This lady for 2¼ years during the war was engaged on very important work in connection with the manufacture of boxes for ammunition, at Tottenham, and was highly commended for her services.
6, Tenterden Road, Tottenham, N.17   X18273B.

GUDGEON, C. W., Pte., Royal Fusiliers.
He volunteered in 1914, went to France the following year, and took part in the battles of the Somme, Ypres and Loos. During his service he was severely wounded.
He was demobilised in 1919, holding the 1914–15 Star, the General Service and Victory Medals.
9, Kenninghall Road, Lower Edmonton, N.18   16468B.

GUDGEON, T., Pte., Royal Fusiliers.
He volunteered in 1914, and was shortly afterwards drafted overseas, where he served on the Western Front until 1915, when he was sent to Salonica. He was in action in various sectors of the Balkan Front, and returned to France in time to take part in the Retreat and Advance of 1918.
He holds the 1914 Star, General Service and Victory Medals.
9, Kenninghall Road, Lower Edmonton, N.18   16468A.

GULLIVER, C. O., Pte., 6th Wiltshire Regt.
He volunteered in 1914, and in the following year was drafted overseas. He took part in many engagements on the Western Front, and was severely wounded in action, in consequence of which he was invalided home and discharged as medically unfit for further service in 1916.
He holds the 1914–15 Star, General Service and Victory Medals.
60, Ilex Road, Willesden, N.W.10   15956B.

GULLIVER, R. S., Petty Officer, R.N., H.M.S. " Chester."
He volunteered in 1914, served with the North Sea Fleet on patrol and other duties, and took part in the battle of Jutland. He holds the 1914–15 Star, General Service and Victory Medals, and was demobilised in 1919.
60, Ilex Road, Willesden, N.W.10   15956A.

GULVIN, E. A., Pte., 2nd Dorset Regiment.
He joined in May, 1916, and went to Salonica in the following November. Later he served in France, where he took part in many engagements, and was wounded at Le Cateau in October, 1918.
He is still with his regiment, and holds the General Service and Victory Medals.
21, Colville Road, Lower Edmonton, N.9   12001A.

GULVIN, F. W., Pte., 6th Northamptonshire Regt.
He joined up for service in March, 1917, and was drafted to France in the same year. He took part in various engagements on the Western Front, including the battle of Ypres, and remained in this theatre of war until the cessation of hostilities, when he returned to England and was demobilised in November, 1919.
He holds the General Service and Victory Medals.
21, Colville Road, Lower Edmonton, N.9   12001B.

GUMM, F. W., Lce.-Cpl., 2nd Btn. K.R.R.
He joined in August, 1915, served with distinction on the Western Front, and was killed in action on July 23rd, 1916, in the battle of the Somme. He was entitled to the 1915 Star, General Service and Victory Medals.
24, Shorrolds Road, Walham Green, S.W.6   X19356.

GUNDRY, F. A., Pte., R.A.S.C.
He volunteered for service in 1915, and after his training was employed on special duties until 1917, when he was drafted to France. He was in action for a short time on the Western Front, and then went to Italy, where he was engaged on important transport duties with his unit.
He was demobilised in 1919, holding the General Service and Victory Medals.
71, Roseberry Road, Lower Edmonton, N.9   14075.

GUNN, A., Pte., Oxfordshire and Buckinghamshire Light Infantry and Dorset Regt.
He volunteered in 1914, and during his service on the Western Front took part in the fighting at Mons, Ypres, Loos and the Somme.
He was badly wounded at Festubert in 1915 and was discharged as medically unfit for further service in May, 1918, holding the Mons Star, the General Service and Victory Medals. 11, Purves Road, Kensal Rise, N.W.10   TX18020.

GUNN, H., Pte., 3rd Middlesex Regiment.
He volunteered in July, 1915, and was sent to Salonica.
While in the Balkans he took part with distinction in many
important engagements. In April, 1919, he was demobilised,
and holds the General Service and Victory Medals.
1, Orchard Place, White Hart Lane, Tottenham, N.17.
X18533.

GUNTRIP, A. G., Pte., 19th Middlesex Regt.
He volunteered in May, 1915, served on the Western Front,
and took part in the battle of the Somme and other engagements.
He was demobilised in January, 1919, but re-enlisted in July
of the same year, and is now serving in the Royal Engineers.
He holds the General Service and Victory Medals.
41, Disraeli Road, Acton Lane, N.W.10   14153.

GURDEN, E. H., Pte., R.A.S.C.
He volunteered in August, 1915, and during his service on
the Western Front was engaged on important duties in connection with the transportation of supplies to the forward
areas.
In November, 1917, owing to ill-health, he was discharged as
medically unfit for further service, and holds the 1914-15
Star, the General Service and Victory Medals.
74, Strode Road, Willesden, N.W.10   X17217.

GURDEN, T. W. E., 1st Air Mechanic, R.A.F.
He volunteered in September, 1915, and was sent to the
Western Front, where he remained for 3½ years. During his
service overseas he was engaged on important duties in
connection with the battles of the Somme, Arras and Cambrai.
In February, 1919 he was demobilised, and holds the 1914-15
Star, General Service and Victory Medals.
61, Dudden Hill Lane, N.W.10   X17216.

GURLING, F. J., Pte., Essex Regiment.
He volunteered for service in 1915, and went to France the
following year. He took part in many engagements on the
Western Front, including the battles of the Somme, Ypres
and the Advance of 1918. He was wounded and suffered
from dysentery during his service overseas.
He holds the General Service and Victory Medals, and was
demobilised in February, 1919.
23, Headcorn Road, Tottenham, N.17.   X18268.

GURNEY, A. H., Pioneer, Royal Engineers.
He volunteered for duty in September, 1914, and during his
service on the Western Front, which lasted three years,
took part with distinction in many of the principal engagements, and was wounded in action at Loos and on one other
occasion.
He holds the 1915 Star, General Service and Victory Medals,
and was discharged unfit for further service in November,
1918. 35, Croxley Road, Maida Hill, W.9   X19969.

**GURNEY, A. G. V., Sergt., 8th London Regt.
(P.O. Rifles).**
He volunteered in September, 1914, and served on the
Western Front. He took part in the fighting on the Somme,
at Arras, Ypres, Festubert and Cambrai. He gave valuable
services as a bombing instructor.
He was demobilised in March, 1919, and holds the 1914-15
Star, General Service and Victory Medals.
11, Oldfield Road, Willesden, N.W.10   15755B.

GURNEY, C. W., Pte., 3rd Royal Dublin Fus.
He volunteered in December, 1914, and was drafted to
Salonica. During his service on the Balkan Front he was
wounded and taken prisoner. He suffered many hardships,
and after nearly three years' captivity was released, and returned to England for demobilisation in January, 1919.
He holds the 1914-15 Star, General Service and Victory
Medals.
5, Armadale Road, Wallham Green, S.W.6   X19421.

GURNEY, P. W., 1st-Class Petty Officer, R.N.
He was serving at the outbreak of war, and was engaged
with H.M.S. "Hecla" in the north sea and the Adriatic.
His duties were of a very trying and dangerous nature, and
he took part in several of the important naval engagements.
He completed in 1920 over 21 years' service in the Navy,
and holds the 1914 Star, the General Service and Victory
Medals. 1, Galloway Road, Shepherd's Bush, W.12   11937.

**GURNEY, W. H., Lce.-Cpl., 11th and 4th Middle-
sex Regiment.**
He volunteered for service in August, 1914, and was drafted
overseas shortly afterwards. He took part in many engagements on the Western Front, and was wounded in action at
Festubert in February, 1916. He was invalided home, and
upon his recovery was again sent to France, where he was
wounded a second time in April, 1918.
He holds the 1914 Star, General Service and Victory Medals,
and was discharged in November, 1918.
11, Oldfield Road, Willesden, N.W.10   15755A.

GUY, A. W., Driver, Royal Field Artillery.
He volunteered in August, 1914, and served on the Western
Front, taking part in many important engagements, until
November, 1917, when he was invalided home.
He was demobilised in March, 1919, and holds the 1914-15
Star, the General Service and Victory Medals.
162, Blythe Road, West Kensington, W.14   12623A.

GUY, G. A., Driver, Royal Field Artillery.
He volunteered for service in 1915, and was drafted overseas.
He took part in many important engagements on the Western
Front, including the battles of the Somme and Ypres, where
he had two horses shot under him, and he was also severely
wounded.
He holds the General Service and Victory Medals, and was
demobilised in January, 1919.
6, Dieppe Street, West Kensington, W.14   15709B.

GUY, S., Air Mechanic, R.A.F.
He joined in 1916, and was engaged on special duties in
connection with the repair of aeroplane engines. His work
required a high degree of technical skill. He was unsuccessful in obtaining his transfer overseas before hostilities ceased,
and was demobilised in 1919 after rendering valuable services
to his country.
6, Dieppe Street, West Kensington, W.14   15709C.

GUY, T., Sergt., Royal Field Artillery.
He volunteered in November, 1914, and was sent to France,
where he took part with distinction in many important
engagements.
In February, 1918, he was discharged owing to ill-health as
medically unfit for further service, and holds the King's
Certificate, the General Service and Victory Medals.
162, Blythe Road, West Kensington, W.14   12623B.

GUY, W. H., Special War Worker.
During the war he was engaged on work of a very important
nature at large aerodromes, for which he held special
qualifications. His work was carried out in a very able and
efficient manner, and was of the greatest value.
6, Dieppe Street, West Kensington, W.14   15709A.

GUYATT, E. E. H., Pte., 1st Essex Regiment.
He volunteered in August, 1914, was sent to France in the
same year, and invalided home early in 1915. He was then
sent to the Dardanelles, where he was wounded in action in
August, 1915, and in the following year returned to the
Western Front. He was reported missing during the battle
of the Somme, but was subsequently reported killed in action
on October 12th, 1916.
He was entitled to the 1914 Star, General Service and Victory
Medals.
28, Sheldon Road, Upper Edmonton, N.18   X17309A.

GUYATT, W. J., Sapper, Royal Engineers.
He volunteered for service in 1915, and after his training was
drafted overseas, where he remained until 1919. He was
engaged on various duties in battle areas on the Western
Front, and was wounded in action at the battle of the
Somme. He was demobilised in September, 1919, holding
the 1914-15 Star, General Service and Victory Medals.
28, Sheldon Road, Upper Edmonton, N.18   X17309B.

GUYVER, P. G., Pte., 13th Bedfordshire Regt.
He joined in April, 1917, and owing to his being unfit at the
time for overseas service was engaged with his unit on
special duties of an important nature.
He was demobilised in May, 1919, having rendered valuable
services. 113, Durban Road, Tottenham, N.17   X17955.

GUYVER, S. G., 2nd Air Mechanic, R.A.F.
He joined in September, 1917, and was engaged for a time
on special duties until sent in 1919 to the Western Front,
where he was employed on important work at various aerodromes.
He afterwards went to Germany with the Army of Occupation
and was eventually demobilised in November, 1919, holding
the General Service and Victory Medals.
113, Durban Road, Tottenham, N.17   X17955A.

GYER, F., Driver, Royal Field Artillery.
He volunteered in January, 1915, and was sent to Salonica.
Whilst in this theatre of war he saw much fighting, and
suffered from malaria and dysentery. On his recovery he
was sent to Egypt, and in March, 1919, was sent home and
demobilised.
He holds the General Service and Victory Medals.
30, Cornwallis Grove, Lower Edmonton, N.9   13332.

GYPPS, F., Pte., 1/5th Royal West Kent Regt.
He joined in April, 1917, and in the same year was sent to
India, where he was engaged on important duties with his
unit at various stations. He was later drafted to Mesopo-
tamia, and took part in the fighting.
He was demobilised in March, 1920, and holds the General
Service and Victory Medals.
59, King Edward's Road, Ponder's End.   T11259.

H

HACKETT, T. J., Driver, Royal Engineers.
Joining in December, 1916, he was sent to Salonica in 1917, and while on the Balkan Front was engaged on important transport work. Later he was drafted to Russia, where he served for nearly a year and was then sent to Constantinople. In 1919 he returned home and was demobilised in September of the same year. He holds the General Service and Victory Medals.
116, Milton Avenue, Willesden, N.W.10   14215.

HACKETT, W., Cpl., Royal Engineers.
He volunteered in July, 1915, and in the same year went to Salonica, where, after being engaged on work of an important nature, he contracted severe illness and was invalided home. On recovery he was sent to France and took part in the fighting around Cambrai, Arras and the Somme.
In March, 1919, he was demobilised, and holds the 1914–15 Star, General Service and Victory Medals.
112, Milton Avenue, Willesden, N.W.10   14213.

HADDON, C., Cpl., R.E. (Signal Section).
He volunteered in May, 1915, and went to France in the following year. He was there engaged on important duties at special signalling stations for two years, and later took part in actions at Arras, Bailleul, Armentières, and the Somme, doing excellent work on advanced communications. In May, 1919, he was demobilised, and holds the General Service and Victory Medals.
11, Hawkshead Road, Willesden, N.W.10   16056.

HADWELL, T. F., A.B., Royal Navy.
He volunteered in November, 1914, and was posted to H.M.S. " Hollyhock," in which ship he was engaged on important duties in the North Sea with the Grand Fleet, and took part in many of the engagements in those waters. He went to the Dardanelles in 1915 and took part in the naval operations during the Gallipoli campaign.
He is still serving and holds the 1914–15 Star, the General Service and Victory Medals.
28, Warwick Road, Upper Edmonton, N.18   X17504.

HAGGER, W. J., Driver, R.A.S.C.
He joined in 1916, and was sent to the Western Front, where he was engaged on transport duties of an important nature in connection with the supply of rations to the forward areas.
He returned to England for his demobilisation in August, 1919, and holds the General Service and Victory Medals.
15, Westbury Road, Willesden, N.W.10   15066B.

HAGGERTY, E. (Miss), Special War Worker.
For a period of over three years during the war this lady rendered valuable services with the Land Army. She was engaged on several large and important farms, and carried out her duties in a thorough manner.
23, Hannell Road, Munster Road, S.W.6   X18161B.

HAGGERTY, W. (sen.), Pte., Middlesex Regt.
He volunteered in August, 1914, and after completing his training was sent to France in the following year. While on the Western Front he took part in important engagements until January, 1916, when he was discharged as medically unfit for further service.
He holds the 1914–15 Star, the General Service and Victory Medals, and having previously served during the South African war, he also holds the Queen's and King's Medals for that Campaign.
23, Hannell Road, Munster Road, S.W.6   X18161A.

HAGREEN, F. (Mrs.), Special War Worker.
During the war this lady was engaged on important duties at the Army Pay Office, where she held the responsible position of Lady Superintendent of the Clerical Department, and carried out her duties in a very capable manner.
She received high commendation for her valuable services.
83, Chesson Road, West Kensington, W.14   X17667B.

HAGREEN, W. C., Pte., R.A.S.C.
He joined in April, 1917, and was sent to the Western Front, where he was engaged on special duties in connection with the fighting on the Somme, at Arras, and during the Retreat and Advance of 1918.
He was demobilised in February, 1920, and holds the General Service and Victory Medals.
83, Chesson Road, West Kensington, W.14   X17667A.

HAHNER, E., Pte., 2nd Border Regiment.
Volunteering in August, 1914, he was sent to the Western Front in February, 1915, and while in this theatre of war took part in many important engagements.
On May 16th, 1915, he was killed in action at Festubert, and was entitled to the 1914–15 Star, General Service and Victory Medals.
18, Disraeli Road, Acton Lane, N.W.10   14403.

HAHNER, H., Cpl., Royal Berkshire Regiment.
He volunteered in August, 1914, and was sent to France the same year. He took part in the fighting at Mons, on the Marne and Aisne, and at Ypres in 1914. In the following year he fought at Neuve Chapelle and Festubert, and was severely wounded. In consequence of his wounds he was discharged as medically unfit for further service in April, 1916. He holds the Mons Star, the General Service and Victory Medals.
85, Carlyle Avenue, Willesden, N.W.10   13814.

HAIG, H., Pte., R.A.S.C. (M.T.).
He volunteered in October, 1914, and in the same year was sent to the Western Front, where he was engaged on important transport duties in connection with operations at Ypres and on the Somme. While conveying supplies to the forward areas he was twice wounded. He was demobilised in February, 1919, holding the Mons Star and the General Service and Victory Medals.
35, Fourth Avenue, Queen's Park Estate, W.10   X18672.

HAILEY, J., Pioneer, Royal Engineers.
He volunteered in 1915, and was sent to the Western Front, where he was engaged on important duties with his unit in connection with many of the big operations. After the Armistice he went with the Army of Occupation to Germany, and remained there until his return to England for demobilisation in April, 1919.
He holds the General Service and Victory Medals.
7, Grove Street, Upper Edmonton, N.18   X17481.

HAINES, M. H., Pte., Middlesex Regiment.
He volunteered in July, 1915, and after his period of training was sent to the Western Front in the following year. While in this theatre of war he was engaged on important duties at Army Headquarters until April, 1919.
In May, 1919, he was demobilised, and holds the General Service and Victory Medals.
52, Minet Avenue, Willesden, N.W.10   13911.

HALE, A. E., Gunner, Royal Field Artillery.
Joining in April, 1916, he was engaged on important duties in connection with training horses for overseas, and early in 1918 was sent to the Western Front. While overseas he was in action near La Bassée, and took part in the Retreat and Advance of 1918.
In January, 1919, he was demobilised, and holds the General Service and Victory Medals.
27, Gowan Road, Willesden, N.W.10   X16965

HALE, B. W., Sapper, Royal Engineers.
He volunteered in April, 1915, and was sent to France in the same year, where he was engaged on important duties with his unit. For a considerable period he was in hospital with pneumonia, contracted whilst on service.
He was demobilised in January, 1919, and holds the 1914–15 Star, General Service and Victory Medals.
38, Rosaline Road, Munster Road, S.W.6   X18197.

HALE, F. R. B., Pte., 123rd Labour Company.
He volunteered in February, 1915, and was drafted to the Western Front early in 1917. During his service overseas he was engaged in digging trenches and building bridges to expedite the advances on the Somme in 1917, and in the final engagements in 1918.
In April, 1919, he was demobilised, and holds the General Service and Victory Medals.
427a, Chapter Road, Cricklewood, N.W.2   16312.

HALE, H. G., Special War Worker.
During the whole period of the war he was engaged on important work at the British Thomson-Houston Munition Factory at Neasden. His work, which was in connection with the manufacture of shells, was of a highly important nature, and required great care and skill. He rendered very valuable services.
47, Denzil Road, Neasden Lane, N.W.10.   15928.

HALES, H., Sapper, Royal Engineers.
He volunteered in 1915, and was drafted to the Western Front in the following year. While in this theatre of war he was engaged on special duties in connection with many important engagements, including those on the Somme and at Ypres.
In 1919 he was demobilised, and holds the General Service and Victory Medals.
33, Winchester Road, Lower Edmonton, N.9.   14876.

HALES, H. A., Pte., R.A.M.C.
He joined in 1916, and after completing his training was retained on important medical duties at large military hospitals. He gave valuable services, but was unsuccessful in obtaining his transfer overseas. In 1918, owing to ill-health, he was discharged as being medically unfit for further service.
100, Archel Road, West Kensington, W.14   16674.

HALFORD, J., Pte., Middlesex Regiment.

He joined in June, 1916, and was drafted to the Western Front in the same year. While in this theatre of war he took part with distinction in many engagements, including those on the Somme, and was wounded and gassed at Maurepas in 1916.
In August, 1919, he was demobilised, and holds the General Service and Victory Medals.
7a, Allington Road, North Kensington, W.10   X18697.

HALL, A., Pte., Royal Fusiliers.

He joined for service in June, 1917, and was shortly afterwards drafted overseas, where he took part in the battles of the Somme and Ypres. Suffering from trench fever, he was invalided to hospital in England, and remained there for some time before being demobilised in February, 1919.
He holds the General Service and Victory Medals.
81, Felixstowe Road, Lower Edmonton, N.9   15616.

HALL, C., Pte., Bedfordshire Regiment.

Volunteering in October, 1915, he was drafted to Egypt, and after serving there for a time he was engaged in escorting Turkish prisoners to India. While carrying out these duties he had to cross seas rendered dangerous by the presence of mines and enemy submarines.
He gave valuable services throughout, and was demobilised in November, 1919, holding the General Service and Victory Medals.
39, Reporton Road, Munster Road, S.W.6   X18868.

HALL, D., Gunner, Royal Field Artillery.

He volunteered in November, 1914, and after his training was engaged on important duties at various stations with his unit. He gave valuable services, but in March of the following year was discharged as being medically unfit for further service on account of ill-health.
9, Oldfield Road, Willesden, N.W.10   15756A.

HALL, E. T. L., A.B., Royal Navy.

He joined as a first-class boy in 1916, and served on H.M.S. " Princess Royal " while on patrol duties in the North Sea. On qualifying as an A.B., he took part in several engagements, and was present at the surrender of the German High Seas Fleet at Scapa Flow. He was later transferred to H.M.S. " Renown," and served on this ship when she conveyed H.R.H. the Prince of Wales to Canada and Australia.
He holds the General Service and Victory Medals.
95, Archel Road, West Kensington, W.14   16671.

HALL, F. M., Pte., Middlesex Regiment, Lancashire Fusiliers and Cheshire Regiment.

Joining in February, 1916, he was sent a year later to the Western Front, and engaged in heavy fighting at the battles of the Somme and Ypres. While taking part in the operations on Passchendaele Ridge in October, 1917, he was severely wounded and invalided home.
In January, 1919, he was demobilised, and holds the General Service and Victory Medals.
5, Windsor Place, Maida Hill, W.9   X20685A.

HALL, F. W., Pte., Royal Fusiliers.

He joined in December, 1916, and in the following year was drafted to the Western Front, where he took part in many engagements, including the battle of Cambrai and the operations during the Advance of 1918.
In February, 1919, he was demobilised, and holds the General Service and Victory Medals.
106, Churchill Road, Cricklewood, N.W.2   16708.

HALL, G., Sapper, Royal Engineers.

He joined in November, 1916, and after his training served at various stations on important duties with his unit. He gave valuable services, but on account of ill-health was unable to obtain a transfer overseas before the termination of the war.
He was demobilised in December, 1918.
13, De Morgan Road, Townmead Road, Fulham, S.W.6
          X20844.

HALL, G. H., Pte., Royal Fusiliers.

He volunteered in August, 1915, and later in that year was sent to France, where he took part in many engagements, including those on the Somme and at Ypres, Loos and Arras. He holds the 1914-15 Star, the General Service and Victory Medals, and was demobilised in February, 1919.
50, St. Paul's Road, Tottenham, N.17   X18827.

HALL, H., Driver, Royal Field Artillery.

Joining in April, 1916, he was sent to the Western Front in the following July. He took part in many of the principal engagements during his service, and after the cessation of hostilities went with the Army of Occupation to Germany, where he remained until 1919, when he returned to England and was demobilised.
He holds the General Service and Victory Medals.
2, Edenham Street, North Kensington, W.10   X20190.

HALL, H., Sergt., Middlesex Regiment.

He volunteered in August, 1914, and was sent to Gibraltar in the same year, where he was engaged on important garrison duties. He was later drafted to France, and while on this Front took part in many engagements, and gained promotion for valuable work. In 1917 he was invalided home, after being seriously wounded at Arras, and on recovery was retained on important duties until his demobilisation in February, 1919.
He holds the 1914 Star, General Service and Victory Medals.
50, Newlyn Road, Tottenham, N.17   X18503.

HALL, H., Pte., 9th Black Watch.

He joined in June, 1916, and after his training was drafted to France in the following September. While on the Western Front he took part in many important engagements, and on March 25th, 1918, was seriously wounded. He died as a result of these wounds later in the same day.
He was entitled to the General Service and Victory Medals.
43, Shakespeare Avenue, Willesden, N.W.10   13884.

HALL, H. H. (M.M.), Staff-Sergt. Fitter, R.A.O.C. (attached 175th Brigade R.F.A.).

He volunteered in August, 1914, and was sent to France in the following year. While on this Front he served with distinction in many engagements, including those at Loos, the Somme and Messines Ridge. For conspicuous bravery and devotion to duty at Messines he was awarded the Military Medal. Later he was drafted to Italy, and after taking a prominent part in engagements there, returned to the Western Front, and served throughout the Retreat and Advance of 1918.
He also holds the 1914-15 Star, the General Service and Victory Medals, and was demobilised in February, 1919.
51, Garvan Road. Hammersmith, W.6   14839.

HALL, I. R., 1st Air Mechanic, R.A.F.

He joined in March, 1916, and was posted to one of His Majesty's seaplane carriers. While on this vessel he was engaged on important duties in the North Sea., particularly in the vicinity of Heligoland. He was later sent to South Russia, where he took part in the fighting.
He obtained his demobilisation in February, 1919, and holds the General Service and Victory Medals.
50, Bathurst Gardens, Kensal Rise, N.W.10   X18418.

HALL, J., Bombardier, Royal Field Artillery.

He volunteered in July, 1915, and the following year was sent to the Western Front. He took part in several engagements, and was wounded during the battle of the Somme in September, 1916. On his recovery he was again in action in France, and was gassed at the battle of Ypres in 1917. The following year he took part in the Final Advance, and was present at the battle of Cambrai in September 1918.
He was demobilised in March, 1919, and holds the General Service and Victory Medals.
40, Lorenco Road, Tottenham, N.17   X18392.

HALL, J., Driver, Royal Field Artillery.

He joined in November, 1917, and on the completion of his training was drafted to the Eastern theatre of war. While on this Front he was engaged on important transport duties with the R.A.S.C. during General Allenby's advance through Palestine.
In May, 1920, he was demobilised, and holds the General Service and Victory Medals.
28, Loveridge Road, Kilburn, N.W.6   15564.

HALL, J. H., Driver, Royal Field Artillery.

He volunteered in July, 1915, and after a period of training was sent to the Western Front, where he took part in many important engagements, and was wounded four times. He was in hospital for a considerable time in France and England, and in March, 1919, he was demobilised, holding the General Service and Victory Medals.
1, Hartopp Avenue, Dawes Road, S.W.6   X17660.

HALL, R., Cpl., Rifle Brigade.

He volunteered in August, 1914, and during the same year served on the Western Front, taking part in the retreat from Mons and the battle of Ypres, where he was wounded. He later took part in the Advance of 1918, and was again wounded in the fighting at Bapaume.
He holds the Mons Star, General Service and Victory Medals, and was demobilised in February, 1919.
110, Dyson's Road, Upper Edmonton, N.18   16776.

HALL, W. G., 1st Air Mechanic, Royal Air Force.

He volunteered in August, 1915, and was drafted to the Eastern Front, in the same year. While there he took part in the heavy fighting at the Dardanelles, and was wounded. On recovery he was sent to Egypt, and there took part in many engagements.
He holds the 1914-15 Star, General Service and Victory Medals, and was still serving in the East in 1920.
21, Albert Terrace, Milton Avenue, Willesden, N.W.10
          15644.

HALL, W. H., Special Constable, " B " Division.

He volunteered as a Special Constable in August, 1914, and was on duty at many important points in London. He devoted the whole of his available time to this responsible work, and was called out during many air raids.
He gave valuable services to his country, and holds the Long Service Badge and War Service Medal.
234, Lillie Road, Fulham, S.W.6   X18786.

HALL, W. J., Pte., Royal Defence Corps and Middlesex Regiment.

Volunteering for duty in January, 1915, he completed his training in England, and performed duties of an important nature. His services were particularly valuable, as they were connected with defensive measures against enemy aircraft at several stations. Owing to his age, he was prevented from being sent overseas, and was discharged in August, 1918.
5, Windsor Place, Maida Hill, W.9   X20685B.

HALL, W. T., Cpl., 13th London Regiment and Coldstream Guards.

He was mobilised in August, 1914, and was sent to the Western Front in the following month. During his four years' service in France he took part in engagements at Mons, Festubert, Givenchy, Ypres and on the Aisne, Marne and Somme.
In 1918 he was wounded, and in January of the following year was demobilised, holding the Mons Star, General Service and Victory Medals.
35, Lancefield Street, North Kensington, W.10   X18846.

HALLÉ, C. R. F., Pte., Royal Air Force.

He joined in 1918, and after his training was engaged on important duties with his unit at various stations. He gave valuable services, but was not successful in obtaining his transfer overseas before hostilities ceased.
He was demobilised in January, 1919.
16, Town Road, Lower Edmonton, N.9   13567.

HALLETT, A. W., Pte., Gloucestershire Regt.

He volunteered in 1915, and after a short period of training was drafted to Egypt later in the same year. After being engaged on important duties there he was sent to Palestine, where he took part in many engagements. While in action in December, 1916, he was killed.
He was entitled to the 1914–15 Star, General Service and Victory Medals.
33, Winchelsea Road, Willesden, N.W.10   13708A.

HALLETT, W. J. P., Pte., Royal West Kent Regiment and Royal Fusiliers, and Sapper, Royal Engineers.

He joined in December, 1916, and first saw active service on the Western Front, where he took an active part in many important engagements, including those at Messines Ridge and Ypres in 1917. In March, 1918, he was wounded while in action on the Somme, and on his recovery was sent to North Russia, and engaged on important duties there until August, 1919, when he was sent home and demobilised.
He holds the General Service and Victory Medals.
70, Mordaunt Road, Willesden, N.W.10   13856.

HALLS, H., Gunner, Royal Garrison Artillery.

He volunteered in March, 1915, was sent to France in the following year, and took part in the battles of Ypres, Arras, Cambrai, Loos, the Somme and in the Retreat and Advance of 1918. He then served with the Army of Occupation in Cologne until demobilised in June, 1919
He holds the General Service and Victory Medals.
58, Deacon Road, Cricklewood, N.W.2   17356B.

HALSEY, A., Pte., Royal Army Medical Corps.

He volunteered in September, 1915, and was sent to the Western Front in the following year. He took part in the fighting on the Somme, at Vimy Ridge, Cambrai and in the Retreat and Advance of 1918. He carried out the important duties of a stretcher-bearer, and was wounded.
He was demobilised in March, 1919, and holds the General Service and Victory Medals.
6, Melville Road, Stonebridge Park, N.W.10   14425.

HALSEY, A. J., Pte., The Queen's (Royal West Surrey Regiment).

He joined in March, 1916, and during his service on the Western Front took part in many engagements, including the Advance of 1918, where he was wounded whilst acting as stretcher-bearer.
He holds the General Service and Victory Medals, and was demobilised in January, 1919.
28, Letchford Gardens, Willesden, N.W.10   X17547.

HAMBIDGE, I. (Miss), Special War Worker.

This lady rendered valuable services during the war at a large joinery works, where she was engaged on the manufacture of munition boxes. Her duties, which were of an arduous nature, were carried out with great care.
28, Dieppe Street, West Kensington, W.14   16193B.

HAMBIDGE, J. L., Sapper, Royal Engineers.

He joined in 1916, and was engaged on important duties at various stations with his unit. He gave valuable services, but was unsuccessful in obtaining his transfer overseas before hostilities ceased.
He was demobilised in 1919.
28, Dieppe Street, West Kensington, W.14   16193A.

HAMBROOK, W. H. R., Rifleman, 8th London Regiment (P.O. Rifles).

He joined in February, 1918, and after his training was engaged on duties of an important nature with his unit at various stations. He gave valuable services, but was unsuccessful in obtaining his transfer overseas before the cessation of hostilities.
He was demobilised in February, 1919.
8, Conley Road, Willesden, N.W.10   15521.

HAMER, F. J., Sergt., 1/7th Middlesex Regt.

He volunteered in August, 1914, and was drafted to France in the following year. He gained early promotion and took part in much of the fighting on the Western Front. Owing to deafness contracted on active service he was discharged as medically unfit in April, 1916, and holds the 1914–15 Star, the General Service and Victory Medals.
14, Dyson's Road, Upper Edmonton, N.18   T16848.

HAMILTON, F. T., Sergt., R.A.S.C.

He was serving on the outbreak of war, and was immediately sent to the Western Front, where he was engaged on the important work of conveying food and ammunition up to the front lines during important engagements. On one occasion his lorry was blown up while passing through a heavily shelled area, but he escaped injury.
In 1919 he was demobilised, and holds the 1914 Star, the General Service and Victory Medals.
20, Maybury Gardens, Willesden, N.W.10   X16959A.

HAMILTON, J., Pioneer, Royal Engineers.

He volunteered in 1915, and was sent to the Western Front, where he took part in the battle of Ypres. Later in the same year he was drafted to Gallipoli and saw heavy fighting there, and was severely wounded. He was invalided home, and on his recovery volunteered for the Russian Relief Force. In October, 1919, he was again sent to England and discharged in 1920. He holds the 1914–15 Star, the General Service and Victory Medals.
6, Colvin Street, Hammersmith, W.6   14477.

HAMLET, C., Trimmer, Royal Navy.

He joined in 1917, and did valuable and highly dangerous duties in the North Sea on board a mine-sweeper.
He was demobilised in 1919, and holds the Merchant Service War Medal, the General Service and Victory Medals.
22, Portnall Road, Maida Hill, W.9   TX19810.

HAMLET, J., Q.M.S., Royal Garrison Artillery.

He was serving when war broke out, and was drafted to the Western Front, where he took part in much of the heavy fighting in various sectors In 1916 he was killed in action during an advance on the Somme.
He was entitled to the 1914 Star, the General Service and Victory Medals.
22, Portnall Road, Maida Hill, W.9   TX19373.

HAMLET, J. A., Q.M.S., Royal Marine Artillery.

He volunteered for service in 1914, and was drafted to the Western Front, where he took part in the defence of Antwerp. Later he saw fighting in Gallipoli and Egypt, and, with General Allenby's Forces, went through the Palestine campaign. He then returned to France and took part in the Retreat and Advance of 1918. For one period of the war he was engaged on special work at Coventry in connection with the production of big guns.
He holds the 1914 Star, the General Service and Victory Medals, and was demobilised in December, 1919.
22, Portnall Road, Maida Hill, W.9.   TX19811.

HAMLYN, W. P., Pte., 14th London Regiment (London Scottish).

He joined in February, 1917, and served on the Western Front, taking part in many engagements, including the battles of the Somme, Cambrai and Arras. During this time he was three times wounded and once gassed.
In September, 1919, he was demobilised, and holds the General Service and Victory Medals.
20, Earlsmead Road, College Park, N.W.10   X18031.

HAMM, E. C. W., Sergt., 1/7th Middlesex Regt.

He volunteered in August, 1914, and the same year was sent to France, where he served in many important engagements on the Western Front, and quickly gained promotion. In December, 1918, he died from an illness contracted while on service, and was buried in France.
He was entitled to the 1914 Star, General Service and Victory Medals.
39, Salisbury Road, Lower Edmonton, N.9   13957A.

HAMMENSON, A. L. H., Pte., R.A.O.C.

He volunteered for service in September, 1914. Later in January, 1917, whilst *en route* for Egypt, his ship, the " Ivernia," was torpedoed, but he was rescued by a trawler, and continued his voyage. Sharing in much of the heavy fighting with General Allenby's Forces during the Palestine campaign, he was present at the capture of Jerusalem, and was wounded.
He holds the General Service and Victory Medals, and was demobilised in May, 1919.
241, Portnall Road, Maida Hill, W.9   X19828.

HAMMETT, W. W., Rifleman, 2nd K.R.R.

He volunteered for service in April, 1915, and in the following July was drafted to the Western Front, where he was wounded in action near Loos in December of the same year. He also took part in the fighting on various other sectors, including Ypres and Cambrai. His service overseas lasted until 1919, when he returned to England and was demobilised.
He holds the 1914-15 Star, the General Service and Victory Medals.
4, Edenham Street, North Kensington, W.10   X20192.

HAMMOND, A. J., Cpl., R.A.S.C.

He volunteered in August, 1914, and was sent to France in the following year. He was there for four years and was engaged on special duties during many of the important engagements.
In February, 1919, he was demobilised, and holds the 1914-15 Star, the General Service and Victory Medals.
81, Winchester Road, Lower Edmonton, N.9   14755.

HAMMOND, A. J., 2nd Air Mechanic, R.A.F.

He joined in February, 1917, and during his service on the Western Front was engaged on special duties in the Royal Air Force workshops.
In January, 1920, he returned to England, and in the following month was demobilised, holding the General Service and Victory Medals.
72, Clarendon Street, Paddington, W.2   X20358C.

HAMMOND, A. W., Sergt., Royal Sussex Regt.

He joined in April, 1918, and after his training was engaged on important duties with his unit at various stations. He gave valuable services and gained rapid promotion. He was unsuccessful in obtaining his transfer overseas before hostilities ceased, but was later sent to Germany with the Army of Occupation, where he remained until demobilised, in March, 1920.
4, Mooltan Street, West Kensington, W.14   X17146.

HAMMOND, D. C., Sergt., 8th London Regiment (Post Office Rifles).

He volunteered in January, 1915, and served with distinction on the Western Front for nearly three years, taking part in many important engagements. During the German Offensive in March, 1918, he was wounded, and in April, 1919, was demobilised.
He holds the General Service and Victory Medals.
33, St. Margaret's Road, Willesden, N.W.10   X17754.

HAMMOND, E. C., 1st-Class Stoker, Royal Navy.

He joined in 1917, and served on H.M.S. " Repulse," on which ship he was engaged on dangerous duties with the Grand Fleet in the North Sea. He took part in the actions with the Fleet off the Belgian coast, and in April, 1919, was demobilised, holding the General Service and Victory Medals.
129, Winchester Road, Lower Edmonton, N.9   14952.

HAMMOND, F. (Mrs.), Special War Worker.

During the war this lady was engaged at the Park Royal Munition Factory. Her work was of a dangerous nature, as she was employed in the C.E. powder rooms. She carried out her duties until 1918, when she was injured while at work. She was highly praised for valuable services.
34, Steele Road, Willesden, N.W.10   14138.

HAMMOND, P. J., Rifleman, 13th K.R.R.

He volunteered in September, 1914, and after completing his training was drafted to the Western Front, where he took part in many engagements and was wounded. In 1917 he was sent to Italy and took part in much of the fighting, and was again wounded in action on the Piave. As a result of his wounds he was discharged in July, 1918, as medically unfit for further service.
He holds the General Service and Victory Medals.
6, Jervis Road, Fulham, S.W.6   TX17374.

HAMMOND, R. G., Trooper, 1st Life Guards.

He joined in February, 1917, and having completed his training, served at various stations on special duties with his unit. He was not successful in being drafted overseas before the cessation of hostilities, but rendered valuable services until his demobilisation in March, 1919.
72, Clarendon Street, Paddington, W.2   X20358A.

HAMMOND, R. W. J., Pte., 4th Royal Sussex Regiment.

He joined in February, 1916, and in the following year was drafted to Egypt. He went through the Palestine campaign with General Allenby's Forces, and in 1918 was sent to the Western Front, where during the last Advance he was wounded at Soissons.
In 1919 he returned to England, and in May of the same year was demobilised, holding the General Service and Victory Medals.
72, Clarendon Street. Paddington, W.2   X20358B.

HAMPTON, H. W., Pte., Middlesex Regiment.

He joined in March, 1916, and after his training was drafted to the Western Front. While there he took part in many engagements, and was wounded three times.
As a result of his wounds he was for a considerable period in hospital, and was invalided home. Upon his recovery, he was demobilised in March, 1919, and holds the General Service and Victory Medals
8, Lancaster Road, Upper Edmonton, N.18   X17056.

HANCOCK, A. E. (Mrs.), Special War Worker.

During the war this lady rendered valuable services in the employ of the General Post Office, and thereby released a man for military service. Her duties were carried out in an efficient manner, and she was commended for her patriotic work.
94, Bronsart Road, Munster Road, S.W.6   X19014B.

HANCOCK, E. T., Bombardier, R.G.A.

He joined in October, 1916, and was sent to the Western Front. He took part in many important engagements while in this theatre of war, including those at Arras, Messines Ridge, Passchendaele and Vimy Ridge. In March, 1918, during the German Offensive, he was wounded, invalided to England, and in June of the same year was discharged medically unfit for further service owing to his wounds.
He holds the General Service and Victory Medals.
94, Bronsart Road, Munster Road, S.W.6   T19014A.

HANCOCK, G., Driver, R.A.S.C. (H.T.).

He volunteered in August, 1914, and after his training was sent to the Western Front in the same year. While in France he took an active part in many important operations, during which he was engaged on transport duties.
In April, 1919, he obtained his demobilisation, and holds the 1914 Star, General Service and Victory Medals.
51, Aintree Street, Dawes Road, S.W.6   X18213.

HANCOCK, R. E. G., Pte., Royal Sussex Regt.

He joined in May, 1917, and after completing his training was drafted to India. During his two years' foreign service he was engaged on special duties at many important stations with his unit in North-west India.
In December, 1919, after rendering valuable services, he was demobilised, holding the General Service and Victory Medals.
48, Aberdeen Road, Upper Edmonton, N.18   16589.

HANDFORD, E. J., Air Mechanic, R.A.F.

He joined in 1917, and after his training was engaged on important work at a large aerodrome. His duties called for a high degree of technical skill, and he gave valuable services, but was unsuccessful in obtaining his transfer overseas, and in 1918, owing to ill-health, was discharged as medically unfit for further service.
52, Humbolt Road, Hammersmith, W.6   15347.

HANDLEY, C., Royal Field Artillery.

He joined in February, 1916, and after his training was engaged on important duties with his unit at various stations. He gave valuable services, but was unsuccessful in obtaining his transfer overseas before hostilities ceased. In 1918 he was discharged, but in December of the same year rejoined the Army, and was sent to Russia. He was still serving in India in 1920.
78, Langhedge Lane, Upper Edmonton, N.18   X17089.

HANDS, A., Sapper, Royal Engineers.

He volunteered in November, 1915, and after his training was retained on important duties at various stations with his unit until March, 1917. He was then drafted to France, and was engaged on special railway work in the forward areas during many important engagements.
In October, 1919, he was demobilised, and holds the General Service and Victory Medals.
28, Guilsborough Road, Willesden, N.W.10   15244.

HANDS, W. T., Pte., The Buffs (East Kent Regt.).

He volunteered in September, 1914, and early in the following year was drafted to the Western Front. While in this theatre of war he took part in many of the important engagements of 1915-16
On August 8th, 1916, he was killed in action, and was entitled to the 1914-15 Star, General Service and Victory Medals
37, Gloucester Road, Upper Edmonton, N.18   X17370.

HANDY, R., Rifleman, King's Royal Rifles.

He joined in April, 1917, at the early age of 16½ years, and after completing his training was sent to France, and served in several engagements until October, 1919, when he was sent home to be demobilised.
Later he re-enlisted for 12 years.
He holds the General Service and Victory Medals.
7, Bayonne Road, Hammersmith, W.6   14304.

HANKS, J. C. E. G. (M.M.), Rifleman, The Rifle Brigade.

He volunteered in March, 1915, and was sent a year later to France, where he took part in the battles of Ypres, the Somme, Lens, Passchendaele, Neuve Chapelle and St. Quentin. In November, 1917, he was awarded the Military Medal for conspicuous gallantry in the field at Cambrai. He was twice wounded, and was demobilised in February, 1919, holding the Military Medal and General Service and Victory Medals.
120, Shakespeare Avenue, Willesden, N.W.10   T13902B.

HANKS, T. H., Pte., 1st Middlesex Regiment.

He volunteered in August, 1914, and was sent to India, where he was engaged on special duties at various garrison outposts. Later he was transferred to Mesopotamia, where he took part in many of the important engagements.
In August, 1919, he was demobilised, and holds the 1914-15 Star, General Service and Victory Medals.
120, Shakespeare Avenue, Willesden, N.W.10   T13902A.

HANLAN, W., Driver, Royal Field Artillery.

He volunteered in April, 1915, and was sent in the following December to France, where he took part in the fighting at Bethune, the Somme, Arras, St. Quentin and Ypres.
He was demobilised, in February, 1919, and holds the 1914-15 Star, General Service and Victory Medals.
58, Denbigh Road, Willesden, N.W.10   15389.

HANNABUSS, F. C., Driver, R.A.S.C. (Remount Section).

Serving in the Army at the outbreak of war, he was sent to France in the same year. Later he was engaged on the important duties of transporting remounts across the Channel. In 1915 he was sent to Salonica, and was engaged on responsible duties during the Balkan campaign.
In June, 1918, he was discharged as medically unfit for further service, owing to ill-health, and holds the 1914 Star, General Service and Victory Medals.
23, Mozart Street, North Kensington, W.10   X18928.

HANNAFORD, A. E., Pte., Middlesex Regiment.

He volunteered in August, 1914, and the same year was sent to the Western Front, where he was severely wounded in 1915. On recovery, he was sent in the following year to Salonica, and there contracted malaria.
On his return he was demobilised in May, 1919, and holds the 1914 Star, General Service and Victory Medals.
100, Montague Road, Lower Edmonton, N.9   16880.

HANNAFORD, J. F., Pte., R.A.S.C.

He joined in April, 1916, and after his training was sent to France in the same year. While on the Western Front he took part in many engagements, including the battle of the Somme (where he was wounded), and was later sent to Mesopotamia, and served throughout the Advance in that country.
In December, 1919, he was demobilised, and holds the General Service and Victory Medals.
12, Walbrook Road, Lower Edmonton, N.9   13083.

HANNAH, W. J., Pte., 20th (Reserve) Canadian Regiment.

He volunteered in February, 1915, was sent to France in the following year, and took part in the battles of the Somme, Ypres, and Vimy Ridge, where he was severely wounded in 1917.
He was demobilised in July, 1919, holding the General Service and Victory Medals.
22, College Road, Willesden, N.W.10   X18183B.

HANNAY, H. T., 2nd Lieut., 1/4th London Regt. (Royal Fusiliers).

He volunteered in 1914 in the ranks, and in the following year was sent to Gallipoli, where he served throughout the campaign. For distinguished services in the field he was granted a commission. On the evacuation of the Peninsula he was sent to Egypt, and after serving with distinction there for two years, was again drafted to France, where he was killed in action in 1918.
He was entitled to the 1914-15 Star, General Service and Victory Medals.
60, Goldstone Road, Hove, Sussex.   13365A.

HANNELL, H., Cpl., Royal Field Artillery.

He volunteered in August, 1914, and after being engaged on important duties at various stations, was sent to France in the following May. While on the Western Front he took part in many engagements until July 11th, 1916, when he was killed in action during the battle of the Somme. He was entitled to the 1914-15 Star, General Service and Victory Medals.
122, Minet Avenue, Willesden, N.W.10   14184.

HANSCOMBE, H. A. W., Sergt., Essex Regiment.

He volunteered in January, 1916, and after a short period of training was sent to France in the same year. He remained on this Front for three years, and for consistent good work and devotion to duty was promoted to the rank of sergeant. He took a prominent part in many important engagements, and was wounded in October, 1918.
He was demobilised in January, 1919, and holds the General Service and Victory Medals.
7, Newlyn Road, Tottenham, N.17   X18514.

HANSELL, W. J., Gunner, R.F.A.

He volunteered in July, 1915, and in the following year was sent to France, where after taking part in many engagements, he was badly gassed. He was in hospital for a considerable period, and on his recovery was drafted to Mesopotamia. Here he served for a time, but was invalided home owing to the ill-effects of gas poisoning received in France. He died as a result on June 23rd, 1919.
He was entitled to the General Service and Victory Medals.
51, Sherbrooke Road, Fulham, S.W.6   X18482.

HANSEN, E., Pte., Royal Army Medical Corps.

He volunteered in February, 1915, and after being engaged for a period on special duties, was sent to Salonica. While there he served on the Bulgarian Front in many important engagements.
Later he suffered from malaria, and in March, 1919, was demobilised, holding the General Service and Victory Medals.
26, Melville Road, Stonebridge Park, N.W.10   14432.

HANSON, A., Pte., M.G.C. and Tank Corps.

He volunteered in 1914, and early in the following year was sent to the Western Front, where he took part in many important engagements, and was wounded in 1916 during the battle of the Somme. He was later transferred to the Tank Corps, with which he took part in much of the fighting during the last two years of the war.
He was demobilised at the end of 1918, and holds the General Service and Victory Medals.
113, Sheldon Road, Upper Edmonton, N.18   X17185.

HANSON, W. R., Sergt., King's Royal Rifles.

He volunteered in September, 1914, and was sent to France in the following year. While on this Front he served with distinction in many important engagements, including the battles of Loos, Arras, Ypres and the Somme. He was wounded and badly gassed.
In February, 1919, he was demobilised, and holds the 1914-15 Star, General Service and Victory Medals.
16, Brettenham Road, Upper Edmonton, N.18   15236.

HARBOUR, W. D., Driver, R.A.S.C. (M.T.).

He volunteered in 1915, and was sent to the Western Front, where he was employed on important duties in connection with the engagements at Loos, Neuve Chapelle, the Somme, Arras, Vimy Ridge, Ypres, Cambrai, and the Retreat and Advance of 1918. He then went with the Army of Occupation, and remained in Germany until demobilised in 1919.
He holds the 1914-15 Star, the General Service and Victory Medals.
17, Crefold Road, Hammersmith, W.6   14452.

HARBRIDGE, R. C., Pte., Royal Sussex Regt.

He volunteered in December, 1915, and was sent to the Western Front in the following August. While overseas he took part in many important engagements, including those at Ypres, the Somme and Albert (where he was wounded).
In November, 1918, he was discharged as medically unfit for further service, and holds the General Service and Victory Medals.
44, Brett Road, Stonebridge Park, N.W.10   15689.

HARBUTT, L., Pte., 8th (King's Royal Irish) Hussars.

He volunteered in 1914, and was drafted to the Western Front. While in this theatre of war he took part in the Retreat from Mons and in the battles of La Bassée, Loos and the Somme.
In 1919 he was demobilised, and holds the Mons Star, General Service and Victory Medals.
40, Ladysmith Road, Upper Edmonton, N.18   16460.

HARDCASTLE, G. L. (Mrs.), Nurse, V.A.D.

During the war this lady was engaged as a nurse at the Denton Military Hospital. She carried out her duties with great care and skill, and was awarded a medal for her services. She was demobilised in June, 1919.
16, Alston Road, Upper Edmonton, N.18.   16503B.

HARDCASTLE, J. F., Cpl., Royal Air Force.

He volunteered for service in August, 1914, and was drafted overseas in the same year. Whilst on the Western Front he was engaged on various duties with his squadron, and during his service was seriously injured when swinging the propeller of an aeroplane. He remained in France until after the cessation of hostilities and then returned to England, and was demobilised in April, 1919.
He holds the 1914 Star, General Service and Victory Medals.
16, Alston Road, Upper Edmonton, N.18   16503A.

HARDEE, H., Pte., Royal Fusiliers.

He joined in 1916, and was sent to the Western Front after a short period of training. While in this theatre of war he took part in many engagements, including the battle of the Somme. Early in 1918, owing to illness contracted in France, he was discharged as medically unfit for further service, and holds the General Service and Victory Medals.
102, Lopen Road, Upper Edmonton, N.18   X17914.

HARDESTY, R. W., Pte., Middlesex Regt.

He volunteered in April, 1915, and was drafted to France in the following year. While on the Western Front he took part in many engagements, and was wounded during the battle of the Somme in 1916. He was later sent on important duties to Singapore, and from there was drafted to Russia, where he took part in the campaign.
He remained in Russia until his return to England for demobilisation in May, 1919, holding the General Service and Victory Medals.
18, Argyle Road, Upper Edmonton, N.18   15261A.

HARDIMENT, A. B., Cpl., Royal Air Force.

He joined in July, 1916, and during exactly three years in the Air Force, performed the duties of pay-clerk and recruiting corporal. Early in his service he was sent to Canada, and was stationed at Victoria and Vancouver, in British Columbia, and at Winnipeg, in Manitoba. While overseas he sustained a severe injury, and on his return to England was demobilised in February, 1919.
35, Lochaline Street, Hammersmith, W.6   13257.

HARDING, A., Sapper, Royal Engineers.

He volunteered in 1915, and was sent to the Western Front, where he was engaged on important duties in connection with the operations at Ypres, on the Somme, at Arras and Cambrai, and was gassed. Later he served in Germany with the Army of Occupation until his demobilisation in March, 1919.
He holds the General Service and Victory Medals.
73, Garvan Road, Hammersmith, W.6   14829.

HARDING, E. J., Sergt., R.E. (R.O.D.).

He joined in 1917, and in the same year went to France, where he was engaged on important transport work. Later he held a responsible position in the Traffic Control Department, and quickly gained promotion.
In 1919 he was demobilised, and holds the General Service and Victory Medals.
83, Ilex Road, Willesden, N.W.10   16352.

HARDING, G. F., Pte., Royal Army Service Corps.

He joined in August, 1916, and served with the Army Remounts. He was specially employed on convoy duties, rendering valuable services in connection with the transport of animals overseas
He was demobilised in November, 1919, and holds the General Service and Victory Medals.
46, Chauncey Street, Lower Edmonton, N.9   T14256.

HARDING, J., Gunner, Royal Field Artillery.

Volunteering in November, 1914, he was sent to the Western Front in the following year, and took part in many of the more important engagements. He was killed in action at Ypres on December, 2nd, 1917.
He was entitled to the 1914-15 Star, General Service and Victory Medals.
4, Kenneth Road, West Kensington, W.14   X17150.

HARDING, T. W., Sergt., R.A.M.C.

He volunteered in September, 1914, and was engaged on special duties until 1916, when he was sent to Salonica. While there he served with an advanced field ambulance, and was promoted sergeant for consistent good work, and later transferred to an ambulance train which conveyed the wounded from the forward areas.
In May, 1919, he was demobilised, and holds the General Service and Victory Medals.
1, Elmtree Villas, Brett Road, Stonebridge Park, N.W.10.   14389.

HARDING, W., Pte., Royal Fusiliers.

He had previously served for 19 years, and rejoined in September, 1914. After taking part in several engagements on the Western Front, including those at Loos, Ypres and Cambrai, he was sent to Salonica, where he saw further fighting, and was wounded.
He holds the 1914-15 Star, General Service and Victory Medals, and was demobilised in March, 1919.
108, St. Dunstan's Road, Hammersmith, W.6   13232.

HARDING, W. A., Lce.-Cpl., Royal Welch Fus.

He volunteered in April, 1915, and was sent to France in the same year. After taking part in many of the important engagements, he was killed in action during the severe fighting on the Somme in July, 1916. He was entitled to the 1914-15 Star, General Service and Victory Medals.
15, Ancill Street, Hammersmith, W.6   13872B.

HARDY, T. C., A.B., Royal Navy.

He was mobilised in August, 1914, having served previously with the Royal Navy for 18 years. He was posted to H.M.S. " Actæon " and whilst in this vessel was engaged on patrol duties of an important nature.
In January, 1918, owing to ill-health contracted on service, he was discharged as medically unfit for further service. He holds the 1914 Star, and the General Service and Victory Medals.
24, Raynham Avenue, Upper Edmonton, N.18.   16762.

HARDY, W., 1st-Class Stoker, Royal Navy.

He volunteered in June, 1915, and after a period of training was posted to H.M.S. " Albcore." While with this ship he was engaged on important and dangerous duties with the Grand Fleet in the North Sea, and took a prominent part in the battle of Jutland.
He was demobilised in February, 1919, and holds the General Service and Victory Medals.
1a, Lorenco Road, Tottenham, N.17   TX17996.

HARE, A. H., Cpl., Oxfordshire and Buckinghamshire Light Infantry.

He volunteered in October, 1914, and in the following year was sent to the Western Front, where he took part in the battles of the Somme, Ypres, Arras, Bullecourt and Vimy Ridge. He was wounded in 1916, and was in hospital for some months before he was discharged as medically unfit for further service.
He holds the 1914-15 Star and the General Service and Victory Medals.
29, Hilmer Street, West Kensington, W.14   15695B.

HARE, R., Pte., The Middlesex Regiment.

He volunteered in August, 1914, and was almost immediately sent to the Western Front, where he served until 1919. He took part in many of the important engagements on this Front, including the battles of the Somme and Armentières, and was wounded.
In March, 1919, he was demobilised, holding the 1914 Star and the General Service and Victory Medals.
15, Chichester Road, Lower Edmonton, N.9   15272.

HARE, T., Pte., Royal Fusiliers.

Having previously taken part in the South African War, he was sent in August, 1914, to the Western Front. He took part in the retreat from Mons, where he was wounded, and the battles of the Aisne, Ypres and the Somme. Towards the close of the War he served in the Retreat and Advance of 1918.
In the following year he was demobilised, and holds the Queen's and King's South African Medals, the Mons Star, and the General Service and Victory Medals.
30, Ambleside Road, Willesden, N.W.10   16932C.

HARMAN, E., Sapper, 106th Field Company, R.E.

He joined in January, 1915, and in the same year was sent to the Western Front, where he remained until 1918. He was in action on the Somme and at Albert, Messines, Dickebusch, Ploegsteert, St. Eloi, Armentières and Vimy Ridge, and was demobilised in March, 1919.
He holds the 1915 Star and the General Service and Victory Medals.
12, Francis Street, Hammersmith, W.6   T15773A.

HARMAN, V. (Miss), Special War Worker.
During the war this lady held a responsible position at the Metropolitan Joinery Co.'s Works, Fulham Road, where she was engaged on important work in connection with the manufacture of boxes for munitions. Her services proved of the greatest value.
12, Francis Street, Hammersmith, W.6   T15773B.

HARMAN, W. H., Armourer Petty Officer, R.N., H.M.S. "Royal Oak."
He volunteered in August 1914, and was engaged on important duties with the Grand Fleet in the North Sea. He took a prominent part in the raid on Zeebrugge, and later suffered shell-shock whilst in action off Dunkirk.
He holds the 1914 Star, the General Service and Victory Medals.
28, Somerset Road, Upper Edmonton, N.18   16863.

HARMAN, W. T., Pte., Machine Gun Corps.
Volunteering in August, 1914, he was drafted to India after a period of training, and for two years served at various stations. He was then sent to Mesopotamia, and later to Egypt, where he took part in many engagements, being later transferred to the Western Front, and taking part in the fighting at Messines and in the Retreat and Advance of 1918.
He holds the 1914-15 Star, General Service and Victory Medals, and was demobilised in February, 1919.
26, Glynfield Road, Willesden, N.W.10   14919.

HARMER, T. H., Pte., Norfolk Regiment.
He joined in November, 1916, and after his training was engaged on important duties at various stations with his unit. Owing to heart trouble, he was not successful in obtaining his transfer overseas.
He gave valuable services, but in 1917 was demobilised as medically unfit for further service.
25, Garvan Road, Hammersmith, W.6   14837.

HARMER, T. J., Sapper, Royal Engineers.
He volunteered in February, 1915, and was sent to France, where he took part in important operations. He was later transferred to Salonica, and while there contracted malaria, and was in hospital for some time.
In March 1919, he was demobilised, holding the 1914-15 Star and the General Service and Victory Medals.
1, Mirabel Road, Fulham, S.W.6   TX17707.

HARMER, W., Sergt., Royal Engineers.
He joined in 1916, and later was sent to Mesopotamia, where he took part in many important operations, and was promoted. Whilst in the East he contracted malaria and was in hospital for a considerable time in Bombay.
In 1919 he was demobilised, and holds the General Service and Victory Medals.
204, Lillie Road, Fulham, S.W.6   X18792.

HARNETTY, E. E. (Mrs.), Special War Worker.
During the war this lady gave very valuable services. At first she was engaged on important work at a large Aeroplane Factory in Fulham, where her duties required great care. She later went to Blake's Filling Station, Fulham, where she was engaged in the filling of cartridges. She carried out her duties in a particularly satisfactory manner.
4, Orbain Road, Fulham, S.W.6   X18052.

HARNETTY, E. J., Sergt., M.G.C.
He volunteered in March, 1914, and in December of the same year was sent to the Western Front. He remained in this theatre of war until June, 1915, when he was transferred to Salonica, where he took part in many important engagements and was wounded in action.
He holds the 1914-15 Star and the General Service and Victory Medals, and is still serving.
8, Aintree Street, Dawes Road, S.W.6   TX18630.

HARNETTY, J., Special War Worker.
At the outbreak of war he was over age for military duties. He offered his services for special work at a large London Food Supply Depot, thereby releasing a younger man for the Army. He rendered valuable services throughout, and received high commendation for his excellent work.
4, Orbain Road, Dawes Road, S.W.6   X18052A.

HARNETTY, T. C., Air Mechanic, R.A.F.
On attaining military age in 1918, he joined the R.A.F., and on completing his training, was engaged at important Aerodromes on important duties, which called for a high degree of technical skill. His services were very valuable, but he was not successful in obtaining his transfer overseas before hostilities ceased.
He was demobilised in 1919.
4, Orbain Road, Dawes Road, S.W.6   X18052B.

HAROLD, C. E., Pte., 8th Middlesex Regiment.
Volunteering in June, 1915, he was soon sent to Egypt, but was later transferred to France. While on the Western Front he took part in engagements on the Somme and at Cambrai, and was three times wounded.
He returned home, and in February, 1919, was demobilised, holding the 1914-15 Star and the General Service and Victory Medals. 28, Netley Road, Brentford.   T16513C.

HARPER, A. V., Lce.-Cpl., Devonshire Regt.
He volunteered in 1915, and in the same year was sent to France. While on the Western Front he took part in many engagements, and was severely wounded at the battle of the Somme in 1916. Being then transferred to Mesopotamia, he took part in the fighting throughout that campaign, and also suffered from malaria.
In 1919, he was sent home and demobilised, holding the 1914-15 Star and the General Service and Victory Medals.
14, Ilex Road, Willesden, N.W.10   16091A.

HARPER, D., Pte., Royal Sussex Regiment.
He joined in July, 1918, and served on the Western Front, where he took part in the final Advance. Later he went to Germany with the Army of Occupation, and remained there until he returned to England for his demobilisation in March, 1920.
He holds the General Service and Victory Medals.
58, Hawthorn Road, Upper Edmonton, N.18   X17050A.

HARPER, E., 1st-Class Stoker, R.N.
Volunteering at the outbreak of War, he served on hazardous and trying duties in the North Sea, until he was transferred to the Mediterranean, where he took part in the landing and evacuation of the Gallipoli Peninsula. On the conclusion of the Dardanelles campaign, he returned to the North Sea, taking part in the engagement in Heligoland Bight.
He was demobilised in 1919, and holds the 1914 Star and the General Service and Victory Medals.
59, Roseberry Road, Lower Edmonton, N.9   14347A.

HARPER, E., 1st-Class Stoker, R.N., H.M.S. "Indomitable."
Called up from the Reserve on the mobilisation of the Fleet in the early days of August, 1914, he served in the North Sea, taking part in the engagement of Heligoland Bight. Later he served during the Dardanelles campaign, and shortly after his return to the North Sea fought in the battle of Jutland.
He holds the 1914 Star and the General Service and Victory Medals, and was demobilised in February, 1919.
69, Durban Road, Tottenham, N.17   X18290A.

HARPER, E. (Mrs.), Special War Worker.
For four years during the war this lady was engaged on work of national importance at the Shell Factory, Ponder's End, and at Messrs. Klinger's and Messrs. Eley's Works. Her ability soon won her promotion, and before she left she was appointed to the responsible post of examiner of gas masks.
69, Durban Road, Tottenham, N.17   X18290B.

HARPER, H. R., Pte., 1/5th East Surrey Regt.
He volunteered in April, 1915, and was shortly afterwards sent to India, where he was engaged on special duties at several important garrison stations. He was later transferred to Mesopotamia, taking part in much of the fighting on that Front.
In February, 1919, he was sent home and demobilised, holding the 1914-15 Star and the General Service and Victory Medals.
95, Osterley Park View Road, Hanwell. W.7   T11896.

HARPER, J. A. (M.M.), Lce.-Cpl., 2nd M.G.C.
He joined in April, 1916, and in the following year was sent to the Western Front, where he participated in the battles of the Somme, Arras, Cambrai, and the Retreat and Advance of 1918, and was wounded. He was awarded the Military Medal for conspicuous gallantry in the field, and holds in addition the General Service and Victory Medals.
He was demobilised in November, 1919.
31, Winchelsea Road, Willesden, N.W.10   13709.

HARPER, M. E. (Mrs.), Special War Worker.
During the war this lady was engaged on important work at a large Munition Factory in London. She was employed in the T.N.T. room, where her duties were of an arduous and dangerous nature, and she received high praise for her valuable services.
14, Ilex Road, Willesden, N.W.10   16091B.

HARPER, W., Pte., East Surrey Regiment.
He volunteered in 1915, and in the following year was sent to France, where he took an active part in many important engagements, including those of the Somme, Arras and La Bassée. During his services overseas he was wounded, and in 1919 was demobilised, holding the General Service and Victory Medals.
59, Roseberry Road, Lower Edmonton, N.9   14347B.

HARPER, W. E., Rifleman, 8th London Regt. (Post Office Rifles).

He joined in 1917, and, after completing his training, was engaged on important duties at various stations with his unit. He rendered valuable services, but was unsuccessful in securing his transfer overseas before the cessation of hostilities. He was demobilised in 1918.
62, Ilex Road, Willesden, N.W.10   15952.

HARPER, W. G., Cpl., Royal Field Artillery.

He volunteered in September, 1914, and first saw active service when drafted to the Dardanelles in the following year. While there he took a prominent part in the Gallipoli campaign, and after the evacuation of the Peninsula was sent to France, where he served through many engagements. In March, 1919, he was demobilised, and holds the 1914-15 Star and the General Service and Victory Medals.
13, Holberton Gardens, Willesden, N.W.10   X17554.

HARPER, W. S., Flight-Sergt., R.A.F.

He volunteered for service in 1915, and at the conclusion of of his training served at various aerodromes on important duties with his squadron. In 1917 he was drafted overseas, where he was actively engaged at aerodromes on the Western Front. He occupied a responsible position and displayed high technical skill.
He holds the General Service and Victory Medals.
58, Hawthorn Road, Upper Edmonton, N.18   X17050B.

HARRINGTON, A. F., Sergt., R.F.A.

He volunteered in August, 1914, and after being engaged on important duties until 1916, was sent to the Western Front, where he served through several engagements, and was wounded.
He was demobilised in July, 1919, holding the General Service and Victory Medals.
232, Winchester Road, Lower Edmonton, N.9   14881.

HARRINGTON, C., Pte., Northumberland Fus.

Joining in September, 1916, he was sent a year later to the Western Front, where he took part in engagements on the Somme and at Ypres, and was wounded in September, 1917. At the end of that year he was drafted to Italy, and served there for about nine months. He returned, however, to France in time to take part in the Advance of 1918, and remained on the Western Front till 1919.
He holds the General Service and Victory Medals, and was demobilised in October, 1919.
11, Broughton Road, Fulham, S.W.6   X20919.

HARRINGTON, J. T., Pte., Royal Sussex Regt.

He volunteered in September, 1914, and was sent to the Western Front, where, after taking part in various engagements, he was severely wounded. Having been in hospital for some time, he was discharged in June, 1916, as medically unfit for further service in consequence of his wounds
He holds the 1914-15 Star and the General Service and Victory Medals.
34, Kilmaine Road, Munster Road, S.W.6   X18759.

HARRIS, A. F., Pte., 13th London Regiment.

He volunteered in January, 1915, and served on various sectors of the Western Front, and in Salonica and Egypt. He was sent to hospital both in France and in Alexandria owing to illness contracted on active service, and was demobilised in January, 1919, holding the 1914-15 Star and the General Service and Victory Medals
74, Bramber Road, West Kensington, W.14   16219.

HARRIS, A. T. (M.M.), C.S.M., 13th Royal Fus

He volunteered in September, 1914, and in the following July was sent to the Western Front, where he took part in engagements on the Somme, at Cambrai, Arras, and Beaumont Hamel. He was awarded the Military Medal for conspicuous gallantry at Arras, and was killed on October 4th, 1917. He was entitled to the 1914-15 Star and the General Service and Victory Medals.
38, Charlton Road, Harlesden, N.W.10   13112B.

HARRIS, A. W. (D.C.M.), Pte., M.G.C.

He rejoined in August, 1914, having previously served in the Army in the 4th Hussars, and was sent to the Western Front, where he took part in the retreat from Mons and in the battle of Ypres, Festubert, Loos, the Somme, Arras and Cambrai. For conspicuous gallantry in action at Mons he was awarded the D.C.M., and was mentioned in despatches in November, 1914, for devotion to duty at Ypres. He was later transferred to Russia, where he again served with distinction.
He also holds the Mons Star, General Service and Victory Medals.
3, Knivet Road, Walham Green, S.W.6   X19423.

HARRIS, A. W., Lce.-Cpl., 2nd Royal Fusiliers

Having volunteered for service in 1914, he was drafted overseas in the same year and took part in the retreat from Mons. After being in action on further occasions, he was severely wounded and discharged in consequence in 1916.
He holds the Mons Star and the General Service and Victory Medals.
2, Ely Place, White Hart Lane, Tottenham, W.17   X18313.

HARRIS, A. W., Pte., Royal West Kent Regt.

He volunteered in December, 1915, and was sent to the Western Front, where he took part in much of the heavy fighting at St. Eloi and in the Ypres salient. In 1917 he was in hospital for a considerable period with shell-shock, which resulted in his discharge in October of the same year.
He holds the General Service and Victory Medals.
56, Winchester Road, Lower Edmonton, N.9   14863.

HARRIS, C., Gunner, Royal Garrison Artillery.

He joined in October, 1917, having previously rendered valuable services on special war work, and after his training was drafted overseas in June, 1918. He took part in various engagements during the Retreat and Advance of 1918, and remained in France until after the cessation of hostilities, when he returned to England and was demobilised in September, 1919.
He holds the General Service and Victory Medals.
69, Milton Avenue, Willesden, N.W.10   14105

HARRIS, C. H., Sapper, Royal Engineers.

He joined in June, 1916, but during his training contracted a serious illness. He was taken to hospital, where, after undergoing treatment for several months, he died on May 27th, 1917.
41, Essex Road, Willesden, N.W.10   15940.

HARRIS, C. H., Sapper, Royal Engineers.

He volunteered in 1915, and was engaged on special engineering duties at various important stations until April, 1917, when he was drafted to France. While on the Western Front he did useful work in connection with telephonic communication in the field. After the signing of the Armistice he went to Germany with the Army of Occupation and remained there until his demobilisation in December, 1918.
He holds the General Service and Victory Medals.
4, Ilex Road, Willesden, N.W.10   16351.

HARRIS, C. J., Pte., Suffolk Regiment and 4th Royal Fusiliers

He joined in April, 1917, and in the following year was sent to the Western Front, where he took part in the battle of the Somme. He was invalided home, but shortly after was sent out again and took part in the fighting at Cambrai, Albert, and Arras. He was killed in action on August 31st, 1918, at Bapaume, and was buried there.
He was entitled to the General Service and Victory Medals.
30, Glynfield Road, Willesden, N.W.10   15004.

HARRIS, C. W., Cpl., 2/10th Middlesex Regt.

He volunteered in September, 1914, and was sent to the Dardanelles in the following July, where he took part in much of the severe fighting. Later he was transferred to the Egyptian Expeditionary Force in Palestine and was killed at the second battle of Gaza on April 19th, 1917.
He was entitled to the 1914-15 Star and the General Service and Victory Medals.
38, Charlton Road, Harlesden, N.W.10   13112A.

HARRIS, D., Gunner, Royal Field Artillery.

He volunteered in August, 1914, and was sent to the Western Front, where he took part in many important engagements, including the battles of Ypres and Cambrai. He was wounded and gassed, but on recovery was drafted to Italy, where he was engaged on special duties.
In February, 1919, he was demobilised, and holds the 1914-15 Star, General Service and Victory Medals.
42, Aspenlea Road, Hammersmith, W.6   14289A.

HARRIS, E. A., Sergt., Royal Field Artillery.

He joined in August, 1916, and during his service on the Western Front took part in the battles of the Somme, Ypres and Cambrai. Later, he served with the Army of Occupation in Germany, and was demobilised in 1919, holding the General Service and Victory Medals.
3, Hartopp Avenue, Dawes Road, S.W.6   X17659.

HARRIS, E. E., King's (Liverpool Regiment).

He joined for service in 1917, and after a short period of training, was drafted to the Western Front, where he took part in many engagements. While acting as a stretcher-bearer during severe fighting in August, 1917, he was killed. He was entitled to the General Service and Victory Medals.
65, Hartington Road, Tottenham, N.17   TX19233B.

HARRIS, E. W., Sapper, Royal Engineers.

Joining in May, 1917, he was sent to Salonica, where he took part in many of the important engagements on the Struma Front. After serving through the Balkan campaign, he returned to England and was demobilised in February, 1919. He holds the General Service and Victory Medals.

9, Third Avenue, Queen's Park Estate, W.10 X18933.

HARRIS, F., Pte., King's Own (Royal Lancaster Regiment).

He volunteered for service in November, 1915, and in the following year was sent to the Western Front, where he took part in several engagements, and served throughout the Retreat and Advance of 1918.

In November, 1919, he was demobilised, and holds the General Service and Victory Medals.

47, Woodchester Street, Paddington, W.2 X20657B.

HARRIS, F. J., Gunner, Royal Field Artillery.

He volunteered in January, 1915, and in the following year was sent to Salonica. While there he took part in numerous engagements against the Bulgarians and served throughout the Balkan campaign.

In 1919 he was sent back to England, and was demobilised in May, holding the General Service and Victory Medals.

42, Maybury Gardens, Willesden, N.W.10 X17223.

HARRIS, G., Pioneer, Royal Engineers.

He volunteered in October, 1915, and was sent to Salonica a month later. During a period which extended for over three years, he took part in many important operations connected with the Balkan campaign and gave valuable services.

He returned home in 1919, and in March was demobilised, holding the 1914-15 Star and the General Service and Victory Medals.

161, Purves Road, Kensal Rise, N.W.10 X18400.

HARRIS, G., Rifleman, King's Royal Rifle Corps.

He volunteered for service in February, 1915, and in the same year was sent to the Western Front, where he took part in the Battle of Ypres and several other engagements. In 1916 he was drafted to Salonica, and served there for three years. During this period he contracted malaria, owing to which he was invalided out of the Service in December, 1919.

He holds the 1914-15 Star and the General Service and Victory Medals.

47, Woodchester Street, Paddington, W.2 X20654A.

HARRIS, G. R., Cpl., Royal Fusiliers and The Queen's (Royal West Surrey Regiment).

He joined in 1916, and during his service on the Western Front, took part in the battles of Ypres, where he was wounded, Albert, the Somme and Arras.

He was discharged as medically unfit for further service owing to his wound, in March, 1919, and holds the General Service and Victory Medals.

30, Glynfield Road, Willesden, N.W.10 14894.

HARRIS, G. T., Pioneer, Royal Engineers.

He volunteered in November, 1914, and was sent to France in the following year, where he took part in many of the important engagements, and was severely wounded. Having spent a considerable period in hospital he was sent to the Balkan Front, and after serving for some time, was again wounded. He was invalided to England, and in March, 1919, he was demobilised.

He holds the 1914-15 Star and the General Service and Victory Medals.

3, Hartopp Avenue, Dawes Road, S.W.6 X17658.

HARRIS, G. W., Pte., 5th Grenadier Guards.

Volunteering in November, 1914, he was sent to France in the following month. During his service in this theatre of war, he took part in several severe engagements on the Western Front, including those at Ypres, the Somme and Arras.

He was demobilised in February, 1919, and holds the 1914-15 Star and the General Service and Victory Medals.

38, Hernes Street, North Kensington, W.10 X18732.

HARRIS, H. G., Cpl., Royal Artillery (Trench Mortar Battery).

He volunteered in August, 1914, and in the same year was sent to France, where he took part in many engagements. He was later transferred to Gallipoli and afterwards to Palestine. While there he took part in much of the severe fighting, and during his service overseas was wounded.

In February, 1919, he was demobilised, and holds the 1914 Star and the General Service and Victory Medals.

10, Sherbrooke Road, Fulham, S.W.6 X18464.

HARRIS, J., Sergt., Machine Gun Corps.

Volunteering in August, 1914, he was sent to France early in the following year and served at Ypres, and Hill 60. In the latter engagement he was severely wounded and was invalided home. After a long time in hospital he was drafted to the Italian Front and served in the Piave sector, where he was again wounded.

In February, 1919, he was demobilised, holding the 1914-15 Star and the General Service and Victory Medals.

40, Wilson's Road, Hammersmith, W.6 15851.

HARRIS, J., Driver, R.A.S.C. (M.T.).

Volunteering in June, 1915, he was engaged in duties of a special nature, until drafted to the Western Front in 1916. While in this theatre of war he rendered valuable services in connection with the transport of ammunition and supplies to the firing line.

After the cessation of hostilities he returned to England and was demobilised in September, 1919.

He holds the General Service and Victory Medals.

13, Purcell Crescent, Fulham, S.W.6 15164.

HARRIS, M., Pte., R.A.F. (late R.N.A.S.).

Joining for service in June, 1916, he was drafted overseas in the same year and was engaged on various duties at aerodromes on the Western Front until 1917. He then returned to England, and was sent to the Shetland Isles, where he remained with his squadron until after the signing of the Armistice.

His duties called for high technical skill, and he was demobilised in April, 1919, holding the General Service and Victory Medals.

38, Town Road, Lower Edmonton, N.9 13570.

HARRIS, M. A. (Mrs.), Special War Worker.

During the whole period of the war, this lady was engaged on important work at large military equipment factories in London. Her duties, which were of a responsible nature, were carried out with great care and efficiency, and she received high commendation for her valuable services.

71, Durban Road, Tottenham, N.17 X18291C.

HARRIS, S. F., Pte., 11th The Queen's (Royal West Surrey Regiment).

He joined in 1917, and served for two years on the Western Front, where he took part in the battles of Ypres, Cambrai, Vimy Ridge, the Somme and the Retreat and Advance of 1918.

During his service he was wounded, and in October, 1919, was demobilised, holding the General Service and Victory Medals.

6a, Deacon Road, Cricklewood, N.W.2 16144.

HARRIS, T. W., Lce.-Cpl., R.M.L.I.

He volunteered in August, 1914, and served in several ships, including H.M. Ships, " Lion " " Cornwall," " Gibraltar," and " Havelock." He served with the Grand Fleet for nearly five years, and was engaged on duties of a dangerous nature until invalided home owing to a severe illness.

In May, 1919, he was demobilised, holding the 1914-15 Star, General Service and Victory Medals.

71, Durban Road, Tottenham, N.17 X18291A.

HARRIS, W. C., Cpl., 1st London Regiment (Royal Fusiliers).

At the outbreak of war he was serving in Malta, and was shortly after sent to France. While in this theatre of war, he took part in many engagements, including that of Neuve Chapelle, where he was wounded. On recovery he took part in the battle of the Somme, and was killed in September, 1916.

He was entitled to the 1914 Star, General Service and Victory Medals.

2, Bridge Road, Willesden, N.W.10 15464.

HARRIS, W. J., Pte., Middlesex Regiment.

He volunteered for service in 1915, and after completing his training was drafted overseas in the following year. He took part in many engagements on the Western Front, and was severely wounded in action at the battle of Arras in May, 1917. In March, 1918, he was discharged as medically unfit for further service owing to his wounds, and holds the General Service and Victory Medals.

341, Brettenham Road East, Upper Edmonton, N.18 15623.

HARRISON, A. E., Pte., East Surrey Regiment and The Queen's (Royal West Surrey Regt.).

He joined in May, 1916, and was sent overseas in the same year, taking part in many engagements on the Western Front, including the battles of the Somme, Ypres and Passchendaele.

He was wounded during his service, and was demobilised in March, 1919, holding the General Service and Victory Medals.

53, Westminster Road, Lower Edmonton, N.9 T12707.

HARRISON, C., Driver, Royal Field Artillery.

He volunteered in 1914, and was sent to the Western Front in the following year. While in France he took part in severe fighting at Loos, Armentieres and the Somme, and was later sent to Salonica, whence, after serving in important engagements, he was drafted back to France. On his return to this theatre of war he took part in the fighting at Arras, Cambrai, and the Advance of 1918.
A year later he was demobilised, and holds the 1914-15 Star and the General Service and Victory Medals.
88, Rayleigh Road, West Kensington, W.14   12633A.

HARRISON, H., 1st Air Mechanic, R.A.F.

He volunteered for service in December, 1915, and in the following year was drafted to the Western Front, where for three years he was engaged in repairing aeroplanes. In this capacity he saw service in many sectors, and was also present during the last Retreat and Advance.
He holds the General Service and Victory Medals, and was demobilised in April, 1919.
55, Warlock Road, Maida Hill, W 9   X19825B.

HARRISON, J., Pte., 7th London Regiment.

He volunteered for service in April, 1915, and after completing his training was drafted overseas in the following year. He took part in many engagements on the Western Front, and was severely wounded in action. He was invalided home and discharged, owing to his wounds, as medically unfit for further service, in September, 1916.
He holds the General Service and Victory Medals.
5, Wilson's Road, Hammersmith, W.6   16417B.

HARRISON, J., Pte., Middlesex Regiment.

He joined in 1915, and in the same year was sent to the Western Front, where he took part in several engagements. While in action at the battle of the Somme, in 1916, he was killed, and was entitled to the 1914-15 Star and the General Service and Victory Medals.
55, Warlock Road, Maida Hill, W.9   X19825C.

HARRISON, J. A., Pte., Royal Fusiliers.

Having enlisted in 1910, he was sent two years later to India, where he remained until 1915. While there he suffered from Malaria, and also met with a serious accident which caused him to be invalided to England. On his recovery, he was retained on special duties in this country until March, 1919, when, after rendering valuable services, he was demobilised.
He holds the 1914 Star and the General Service and Victory Medals.
65, Hartington Road, Tottenham, N.17   TX9233A.

HARRISON, J. H., Steward, Merchant Service.

He joined in January, 1917, and was posted to the "Rimkuate." While on this vessel he was engaged on important duties in Australian, South African, Chinese and Russian waters, and was wounded.
In April, 1919, he was demobilised, and holds the Mercantile Marine, General Service and Victory Medals.
79, Claybrook Road, Hammersmith, W.6   13810.

HARRISON, M., Pte., Royal Fusiliers.

He joined in January, 1918, and after completing his training was stationed at various places on important duties. He gave valuable services, but was unable to obtain a transfer overseas before the cessation of hostilities, and was demobilised in December, 1918.
55, Warlock Road, Maida Hill, W.9   X19825A.

HARRISON, W., Cpl., 18th Canadian Regiment.

He volunteered his services in November, 1914, and after a period of training, was sent to the Western Front in the following year. While in this theatre of war he took part in many of the important engagements and was seriously wounded.
He was demobilised in July, 1919, and holds the 1914-15 Star and the General Service and Victory Medals.
5, Wilson's Road, Hammersmith, W.6   16417C.

HARRISON, W. G., Bombardier, R.G.A.

He enlisted in the Army in 1908, and at the outbreak of war was retained on special duties at important stations. Early in 1915, he was drafted to the Eastern Front, where he took part in the heavy fighting on the Gallipoli Peninsula and in the evacuation. He was then transferred to the Western Front, and served with distinction on the Somme, at Albert, Cambrai and Ypres. During his services he was twice wounded, and after the signing of the Armistice, was sent to Ireland.
He holds the 1914-15 Star and the General Service and Victory Medals.
57, Lancefield Street, North Kensington, W.10   X18841.

HARRISON, W. J., Rifleman, Royal Irish Rifles.

He was in the Army when war broke out, and until 1916, when he was drafted to the Western Front, was engaged on special duties. His service overseas lasted for three years, during which time he saw fighting in various sectors of the Front, including Ypres, Messines, and Cambrai, where he was severely wounded.
In 1919 he was invalided home, and in June of the same year was discharged physically unfit owing to his wound. He holds the General Service and Victory Medals.
90, Clarendon Street, Paddington, W.2   X20368.

HARROWELL, H. E., Pte., Gloucestershire Regt.

He joined in May, 1916, and after a period of training, was sent to the Western Front early in the following year. After taking part in many important engagements, he was killed in action during the Advance of 1918, and was buried at Arras.
He was entitled to the General Service and Victory Medals.
21, Maybury Gardens, Willesden, N.W.10   X16959B.

HARROWELL, M., Rifleman, 17th London Regt.

He volunteered in August, 1914, and for a short time was engaged on important duties in England. He was then drafted to the Western Front, where he saw service in many engagements until he was wounded in the battle of the Somme. On recovery, he again served in France, and took part in the Advance of 1918, when he was again wounded. He was demobilised in March, 1919, and holds the General Service and Victory Medals.
21, Maybury Gardens, Willesden, N.W.10   X17367A.

HARROWELL, W. J., Sergt., 13th Middlesex Regt.

He volunteered in September, 1914, and was sent overseas in the same year. During his service on the Western Front he took part in many important engagements, and was killed in action in the Somme sector on May 4th, 1916. He was buried near Armentieres, and was entitled to the 1914-15 Star and the General Service and Victory Medals.
21, Maybury Gardens, Willesden, N.W.10   X16959C.

HARSTON, C. A., Rifleman, 18th London Regt. (London Irish Rifles).

He joined in November, 1917, and after his training was engaged on important duties at various stations with his regiment. He gave valuable services, but was not successful in obtaining his transfer overseas before hostilities ceased. After the signing of the Armistice he was sent to Germany with the Army of Occupation, and remained there until his demobilisation in March, 1920.
55, Lancaster Road, Upper Edmonton, N.18.   X17058.

HART, A. H., Pte., The Black Watch (Royal Highlanders).

He joined for service in May, 1916, and was drafted to the Western Front shortly afterwards. While in this theatre of war, he served in many important engagements, and was severely wounded. As a result of his wounds he obtained his discharge in 1918, being medically unfit for further service.
He holds the General Service and Victory Medals.
25, Barbot Street, Lower Edmonton, N.9   14589

HART, F. W., Driver, Royal Field Artillery.

He volunteered for service in 1915, and was retained on special duties of an important nature until 1917, when he was sent to France. While serving on the Western Front he took part in many important engagements, including the battles of Ypres in 1917, and the Somme in 1918.
He was demobilised in May, 1919, holding the General Service and Victory Medals.
12, Kimberley Road, Upper Edmonton, N.18   16458.

HART, G. H., Pte., Northamptonshire Regt.

He volunteered for service in September, 1914, and in the same year was drafted to the Western Front, where he took part in several engagements, including the battle of the Somme, and was wounded. Later he went to Salonica, and saw service during the Balkan campaign.
He was sent home, and demobilised in March, 1920, holding the 1914-15 Star, General Service and Victory Medals.
37, Heckfield Place, Fulham Road, S.W.6   X20344.

HART, H., Gunner, Royal Garrison Artillery.

He volunteered in August, 1914, and after a period of training was retained at home on special duties, until March, 1916, when he was drafted to the Western Front. After taking part in engagements on the Somme, at Arras and Ypres, and during the Retreat and Advance of 1918, he was demobilised in December, 1918, and holds the General Service and Victory Medals.
26a, Drayton Road, Harlesden, N.W.10   14895.

HART, J., Pte., Royal Warwickshire Regiment.
He volunteered in August, 1914, and in the same year was
sent to the Western Front, where he took part in many important engagements. Later he was transferred to Italy
and fought on the Piave.
In October, 1919, he was sent home and demobilised, holding
the 1914 Star, General Service and Victory Medals.
74, Protheroe Road, Fulham, S.W.6   16832.

**HART, J. E., Pte., Essex Regiment and Here-
fordshire Regiment).**
He joined in June, 1916, and after a short period of training
was sent to France. During his two years' service on the
Western Front he took part in many important engagements,
and during the Advance of 1918, was reported missing and
presumed killed on September 2nd.
He was entitled to the General Service and Victory Medals.
11, Dyson's Road, Upper Edmonton, N.18   T16794.

HART, J. W., Pte., Royal Naval Division.
Joining in February, 1916, he was sent to the East on the
completion of his training. While in Egypt he saw much
service, but was sent to hospital with a severe wound. Later
he was invalided to England, but died of his wound in
December, 1917
He was entitled to the General Service and Victory Medals.
4, Kilburn Lane, North Kensington, W.10   X18778.

HART, S. G. (M.M.), Sapper, Royal Engineers.
He volunteered at the outbreak of war, and was sent to
France in January, 1915. While in this theatre of war he
took part in many important engagements, including the
battles of Ypres, Arras and Cambrai, and was awarded the
Military Medal for conspicuous gallantry and devotion to duty
whilst laying telephone wires in a gas attack
In March, 1919, he was demobilised, and also holds the 1914-15
Star, General Service and Victory Medals.
2, Beaconsfield Road, Church End, N.W.10   16335.

HART, W. G., Pte., Royal Fusiliers.
He volunteered in October, 1914, but owing to an old wound
received in the South African War, he was medically unfit for
service overseas. He was, therefore, retained on important
duties of a special nature at various stations, until in April,
1919, after rendering valuable services, he was demobilised.
He holds the Queen's and King's South African Medals.
15, Hartington Road, Lower Edmonton, N.9   14244.

HARTFORD, W. L. H., Pte., 10th Royal Fus.
He volunteered in May, 1915, and was sent to France in the
same year. During his service overseas he took part in
many important engagements, and was wounded on the
Somme in October, 1916. He was invalided to England,
and after his recovery retained on special duties with the
Machine Gun Corps, until he was discharged in January,
1918, as medically unfit for further service in consequence
of his wounds.
He holds the 1914-15 Star, General Service and Victory
Medals.   13, Willow Vale, Shepherd's Bush, W.12   11914.

HARTILL, W. J., Pte., Middlesex Regiment.
He volunteered in December, 1915, and after completing his
training, was sent to the Western Front in the following
year. After only a short time on active service, he was
killed in action on July 1st, 1916, during the battle of the
Somme.
He was entitled to the General Service and Victory Medals.
26, Huddlestone Road, Cricklewood, N.W.2   X17410.

HARTWELL, C. A., A.B., Royal Navy.
He volunteered in October, 1915, and was engaged on dan-
gerous patrol and convoy duty in the North, Black, Arctic
and Mediterranean Seas. While serving in H.M. Trawler
" James Fennell," his ship was wrecked in the Channel.
In January, 1920, he was demobilised, holding the Order of
St. George (4th-class), the 1914-15 Star, General Service and
Victory Medals.
61, College Road, Willesden, N.W.10   X18012.

HARTWELL, F., Pte., East Surrey Regiment.
He joined for service in July, 1917, and after his training
was sent to the Western Front, where he took part in many
engagements, including the battles of Arras and Ypres.
During the German Advance of March, 1918, he was taken
prisoner, and was kept in captivity until the cessation of
hostilities, when he returned to England, and was demobilised in December, 1919.
He holds the General Service and Victory Medals.
23, Lopen Road, Upper Edmonton, N.18   X17580.

HARTWELL, S. J., Cpl., Royal Defence Corps.
He volunteered in September, 1914, and being unable to
join the fighting forces, was engaged on important duties of
a special nature with the Royal Defence Corps.
For four years he rendered valuable services, and was
discharged in March, 1918, owing to his failing health.
61, College Road, Willesden, N.W.10   X18011.

HARVEY, A., Cpl., R.A.M.C.
He volunteered in January, 1915, and after his training
was engaged on important duties with his unit. He gave
valuable service, but owing to his ill-health was unable to
obtain his transfer overseas, and in November of the following
year was consequently discharged as medically unfit for
further military duty.
12, Chaldon Road, Dawes Wood, S.W.6   X17720.

HARVEY, E. F. (Mrs.), Special War Worker.
For a considerable period during the war, this lady
rendered valuable services as an employée of the Post Office,
thus releasing a man for military service. Her work, which
was of an arduous nature, was carried out with efficiency and
care, and she received high praise for her services.
4, Westgate, Roundwood Road, Willesden, N.10   16308B.

**HARVEY, F., Pte., The Queen's (Royal West
Surrey Regiment).**
He volunteered in August, 1914, and was sent in the same
year to the Western Front, where he took part in practically
all operations, and in particular in the battles of Passchendaele
(1917) and the Somme (1918), where he was wounded on
both occasions.
He was demobilised in February, 1919, holding the 1914-15
Star, General Service, and Victory Medals.
62, Angel Road, Upper Edmonton, N.18   16495.

HARVEY, F., Pte., Royal Fusiliers.
He volunteered in October, 1915, and after being engaged on
special duties, was sent to the Western Front, where he took
part in many engagements and was taken prisoner.
During his captivity he suffered many hardships, and on his
release returned to England, and was demobilised in December, 1919, holding the General Service and Victory Medals.
25, Chichester Road, Lower Edmonton, N.9   14855.

HARVEY, G. F., Pte., 7th Royal Fusiliers.
He joined in July, 1916, and later in the same year was sent
to the Western Front, where he took part in engagements
at Cambrai, Peronne and the Advance of 1918.
After rendering valuable services, he was demobilised in
September, 1919, and holds the General Service and Victory
Medals.
5, Osborne Road, Cricklewood, N.W.2   X17407.

HARVEY, G. W., Sergt. Major, R.G.A.
He volunteered in October, 1914, and in the same year
was sent to France, where he served until 1916 as Battery-
Sergeant-Major. While on active service he contracted
chest trouble and was discharged in June, 1917, but died
eighteen months later, on December 24th, 1918, from the
effects of his illness.
He was entitled to the 1914-15 Star, General Service and
Victory Medals.
75, Raynham Road, Upper Edmonton, N.18   16951.

**HARVEY, H. H., A.B., R.N.V.R. (Royal Naval
Division).**
He volunteered in November, 1915, and was sent to the
Western Front in October of the following year. While
there he took part in many important engagements, including those on the Somme and at Arras. After the capture
of Gavrelle, on the Hindenburg Line, he was one of the
garrison who stoutly held out against nine counter attacks
in two and a half days, being without food and water during
the whole time   Shortly afterwards he was wounded, and as
a result was discharged as medically unfit for further service
in September, 1918.
He holds the General Service and Victory Medals.
37, Alexandra Road, Southfield Road, Chiswick, W.4 T14090.

HARVEY, H. W. H., Bombardier, R.F.A.
Volunteering in August, 1914, he was sent to the Western
Front and took part in the retreat from Mons and the battles
of the Marne, the Aisne, Ypres, Arras and Cambrai.
Being seriously wounded in 1918, he was discharged, and
holds the Mons Star, the General Service and Victory Medals.
4, Westgate, Roundwood Road, Willesden, N.W.10 16308A.

**HARVEY, J., Sergt., Scots Guards and 24th
London Regiment.**
Enlisting originally in November, 1902, he was sent to the
Western Front at the outbreak of war, and took part in the
retreat from Mons, and the battles of the Marne and Ypres.
Three years later he was transferred to Salonica, and shortly
afterwards to Egypt. Having been attached to the Egyptian
Expeditionary Force, he was sent to Palestine, and was
present at the capture of Jerusalem, and took part in several
engagements on the banks of the Jordan. Towards the close
of the war he was again drafted to France, taking part in
fighting near Epéhy, Cambrai and Lille.
During his service he was twice wounded, and in February,
1919, was demobilised, holding the Mons Star, General Service
and Victory Medals.
100, Fortune Gate Road, Harlesden, N.W.10   13193.

HARVEY, S. D., R.Q.M.S., 18th London Regt. (London Irish Rifles) and M.G.C.
He volunteered in 1914, and was drafted to the Western Front, where he took a distinguished part in the battles of Neuve Chapelle, Ypres, Loos, Vimy Ridge, the Somme, Arras and Cambrai.
He was wounded at Loos and Cambrai, and in 1919 was demobilised, holding the 1914-15 Star, the General Service and Victory Medals..
272, Lillie Road, Fulham, S.W.6   X18372.

HARVEY, S. J., Cpl., 5th Middlesex Regiment.
He joined in 1916, and in the following year was sent to the Western Front where he saw much severe fighting, and was present at the battles of Rheims, Ypres and Cambrai. During most of his service he acted as a stretcher-bearer.
He was demobilised in November 1919, holding the General Service and Victory Medals.
14, Napier Road, Kensal Green, N.W.10   X17775.

HARWOOD, F., Cpl., The Middlesex Regiment.
He volunteered in September, 1914, and was sent to the Eastern Front in January, 1916. He served with the Egyptian Expeditionary Force in Palestine and fought at the battles of Gaza and Beersheba, and the capture of Jerusalem.
He was sent home in March, 1919, and demobilised a month later, holding the General Service and Victory Medals.
50, Shakespeare Avenue, Willesden, N.W.10   13617.

HARWOOD, F. A., Bombardier, R.F.A.
He volunteered for service in September, 1914, and early in the following year was drafted to France, where he took part in many important engagements, including those at Ypres, Loos, the Somme, Arras and La Bassée.
He was demobilised in June, 1919, and holds the 1914-15 Star and the General Service and Victory Medals.
24, Tilson Road, Tottenham, N.17   X19096B.

HARWOOD, F. C., Cpl., 2/10th Middlesex Regt.
He volunteered for service in August, 1914, and after his training was sent to the Dardanelles, where he took part in much fighting. He was subsequently drafted to Egypt, and later to Palestine, where he was killed in action at Gaza, in March, 1917.
He was entitled to the 1914-15 Star, General Service and Victory Medals.
2, Disbrowe Road, Hammersmith, W.6   15915.

HARWOOD, R. I., A.B., R.N., H.M.S. "Indefatigable."
He volunteered in August, 1914, and served with the Grand Fleet in the North Sea, where he was engaged on important duties. He took part in the battle of Jutland on May 31st, 1916, and was drowned when his vessel was sunk.
He was entitled to the 1914 Star and the General Service and Victory Medals.
61, Tilson Road, Tottenham, N.17   X19096A.

HASLER, T. J., Pte., The Queen's (Royal West Surrey Regiment).
He joined for service in June, 1916, and after a period of training, was sent to France later in the same year. While on the Western Front he served in many important engagements, and was demobilised in March, 1919, holding the General Service and Victory Medals.
61, Raynham Road, Upper Edmonton, N.18   15992.

HASLETT, H., Pte., Royal Fusiliers.
He volunteered in August, 1914, and in the following year was drafted to the Dardanelles, where he served throughout the whole of the campaign, taking part in much heavy fighting. After the evacuation of the Peninsula he was drafted to India, and was there employed on important duties at various stations.
He holds the 1914-15 Star, General Service and Victory Medals.
14, Raynham Terrace, Upper Edmonton, N.18   16474.

HASLETT, T., Cpl., Royal Fusiliers.
He joined in March, 1918, and was sent to the Western Front, where he took part in the Retreat and Advance of that year. He remained in this theatre of war for nearly a year and was then drafted to India, where he was employed on important duties at various stations.
He holds the General Service and Victory Medals.
14, Raynham Terrace, Upper Edmonton, N.18   16475.

HATHAWAY, F. G., Pte., 18th Middlesex Regt.
He volunteered in February, 1915, and served on the Western Front, taking part in the battles of the Somme, Arras and Ypres. During his service overseas he was gassed, and in August, 1919, he died from the effects.
He was entitled to the 1914-15 Star and the General Service and Victory Medals.
24, Florence Road, Upper Edmonton, N.18   16009.

HATHAWAY, J. G., Gunner, R.G.A.
He volunteered in 1915, and after his training was engaged on important duties with his unit at various stations. He rendered valuable services, but was unsuccessful in obtaining his transfer overseas before the cessation of hostilities.
In 1919 he was demobilised.
6, Fane Street, West Kensington, W.14   15882.

HAUPT, H., Trooper, Royal Buckinghamshire Hussars and Pte., 4th (Queen's Own) Hussars.
Volunteering in November, 1915, he was sent to Egypt on completing his training, and spent his whole service on the Eastern Front, seeing fighting in the Sinai Peninsula and taking part in the battle of Beersheba and the capture of Jerusalem. During his service he was wounded, and towards the close of the war was at Damascus.
On his return to England in June, 1919, he was demobilised, and holds the General Service and Victory Medals.
3, Carlyle Avenue, Willesden, N.W.10   13689.

HAVILL, M., Pte., Middlesex Regt. and M.G.C.
He volunteered in August, 1914, and after a period of training was sent to the Western Front in the following year, where he was in action at the battles of Ypres, the Somme, Arras and Cambrai.
In March, 1919, he was demobilised, and holds the 1914-15 Star, General Service and Victory Medals.
96, Deacon Road, Cricklewood, N.W.2   X17313.

HAWES, A. J., Wireless Operator, R.N.
He joined for service in November, 1917, and was engaged on the important duties of a wireless operator on vessels of the Grand Fleet, operating in the North Sea.
While carrying out his duties he was wounded, and in February, 1919, was demobilised, holding the General Service and Victory Medals
37, Warwick Road, Upper Edmonton, N.18   X17507.

HAWES, B. W. E., Rifleman, 12th London Regt. (Rangers).
Joining in March, 1916, he was sent in the following August to the Western Front, taking part in the battle of the Somme. He was killed on the first day of the battle of Arras, on April 9th, 1917, and was entitled to the General Service and Victory Medals.
36, Heron Road, Willesden, N.W.10   15568.

HAWES, C., Pte., Royal Marine Light Infantry.
He joined in 1916, and after a short training was sent to the Western Front in the following August. While in this theatre of war he took part in many important engagements, and during the Advance of 1918 was taken prisoner. In consequence of ill-treatment he received in Germany he died whilst in captivity.
He was entitled to the General Service and Victory Medals.
Manor Farm, Oakley Brill, Bucks.   15574A.

HAWES, J. S., Pte., The Queen's (Royal West Surrey Regiment).
He joined in 1916, and saw service in Salonica, Russia and Constantinople. He fought in many engagements on the Bulgarian Front, and suffered greatly from malaria. In 1919 he was sent to England and demobilised, holding the General Service and Victory Medals.
28, Holly Lane, Willesden, N.W.10   15574B.

HAWKES, W. H., Rifleman, King's Royal Rifles.
He volunteered in September, 1914, and served on the Western Front, taking part in the battles of Neuve Chapelle, Loos, the Somme, Albert, Arras, Bullecourt, Armentieres, Ypres and Vimy Ridge. He was three times wounded and was discharged as medically unfit for further service in 1917, suffering from shell-shock.
He holds the 1914-15 Star, General Service and Victory Medals. 54, Archel Road, West Kensington, W.14   16191.

HAWKINS, A. T., Driver, Royal Engineers.
Volunteering in August, 1914, he was soon sent to the Western Front, where he took part in the retreat from Mons and the battle of the Marne. Later he played an active part in the battles of Neuve Chapelle, Vimy Ridge and Cambrai.
In 1919, he was demobilised, holding the Mons Star, General Service and Victory Medals.
32, Melville Road, Stonebridge Park, N.W.10   14421.

HAWKINS, C. A., Pte., West Yorkshire Regt.
He was called up from the Reserve in August, 1914, and at once sent to France. He took part in the desperate struggle in the opening stages of the war, fought at Mons and was wounded at Ypres. After long hospital treatment he was exempted from further overseas service owing to his wounds, and was employed on important duties at various places until his discharge in February, 1919.
He holds the Mons Star, General Service and Victory Medals.
21, Hilmer Street, West Kensington, W.14   T15706C

HAWKINS, D., Pte., Royal Army Service Corps.
He volunteered in April, 1915, and was sent to the Western
Front, where he was engaged on special duties in connection
with the making of roads through devastated areas, thereby
rendering valuable services.
He was demobilised in February, 1919, and holds the 1914-15
Star, General Service and Victory Medals.
20, Barbot Street, Lower Edmonton, N.9   14579.

**HAWKINS, E., Cpl. (Acting Sergt.), 2nd South
Wales Borderers.**
He first enlisted in September, 1907, and for the two years
prior to the war was stationed in North China.   In 1915
he was sent to the Dardanelles, taking part in heavy fighting
there until the evacuation of the Peninsula.   In the following
year he was transferred to the Western Front, and took part
in the battle of the Somme, where he was severely wounded.
After being in hospital for over a year, he was discharged
owing to his wounds in April, 1918, and holds the 1914-15
Star, General Service and Victory Medals.
18, Mulgrave Road, Fulham, S.W.6   16174.

**HAWKINS, F. A., Pte., The Queen's (Royal West
Surrey Regiment).**
He volunteered in November, 1915, and after his training
was retained on important duties with his unit at various
stations until March, 1917.   He was then sent to France,
where he took part in many important engagements, and
during the fighting at Ypres in that year suffered from shell-
shock.   He was discharged in consequence in May, 1918, as
medically unfit for further services, and holds the General
Service and Victory Medals.
60, Strode Road, Willesden, N.W.10   X17215.

HAWKINS, F. G., Pte., Royal Warwickshire Regt.
He volunteered for service in 1915, and was drafted overseas
in the same year.   He took part in the battles of the
Somme and Arras, where he was wounded, and in 1916 was
sent to Italy, taking part in the heavy fighting on the Piave.
After the Armistice he returned to England, and was
demobilised in February, 1919.
He holds the 1914-15 Star, General Service and Victory
Medals.
231, Mund Street, West Kensington, W.14   16926B.

**HAWKINS, F. L., Lieut., 25th Lon. Regt. (Cyclists),
9th Middlesex Regiment and 36th Sikhs.**
He volunteered for service in August, 1914, and was sent to
India, where he served at various stations on important duties
with his unit.   He was later drafted to Mesopotamia, and
served there with distinction, taking part in many important
engagements.   He was granted a commission in the 9th
Middlesex Regiment for conspicuous bravery in the field, and
was afterwards transferred to the 36th Sikhs, with which
unit he remained until after the cessation of hostilities.
He was wounded during his service overseas, and holds the
General Service and Victory Medals, being demobilised in
October, 1919.
18, West Ella Road, Willesden, N.W.10   15103A.

HAWKINS, H. T., Pte., Middlesex Regiment.
He volunteered in August, 1914, and after completing his
training was sent to the Western Front in the following
year.   While in this theatre of war, he took part in many
engagements, and was killed in action on April 30th, 1916.
He was entitled to the 1914-15 Star, General Service and
Victory Medals.
14, Hartopp Avenue, Dawes Road, S.W.6   X17684A.

HAWKINS, H. W., Pte., 13th Middlesex Regt.
Volunteering in March, 1915, he was sent in the same year
to the Western Front, and took part in the fighting at Loos,
Cambrai, Amiens and Armentieres, where he was severely
wounded and lost an eye.
He was demobilised in May, 1919, and holds the 1914-15
Star, General Service and Victory Medals.
18, West Ella Road, Willesden, N.W.10   15103B.

HAWKINS, H. W. S., Lce.-Cpl., Royal Fusiliers.
He volunteered in March, 1915, and in the following year
was sent to the Western Front.   While there he took an active
part in the fighting, and was engaged for a considerable
period on important work in connection with the construction
and repair of roads.
He was demobilised in February, 1919, and holds the 1914-15
Star and the General Service and Victory Medals.
16, Mulgrave Road, Fulham, S.W.6   16175B.

HAWKINS, J., Driver, Royal Field Artillery.
He volunteered in October, 1914, and early in the following
year was sent to France, where he took part in several engagements, including those at Ypres and Arras.   On January 29th,
1916, he was killed in action whilst taking ammunition to
the guns.
He was entitled to the 1914-15 Star, General Service and
Victory Medals.
4, Melville Road, Stonebridge Park, N.W.10   14424.

HAWKINS, J., Pte., Royal Fusiliers.
He joined in 1918, and after his training served at various
stations on important duties with his unit.   He gave valuable
services, but was not successful in obtaining his transfer
overseas before the cessation of hostilities.
He was demobilised in 1919.
52, Carlyle Avenue, Willesden, N.W.10   14410B.

HAWKINS, L. M. (Mrs.), Special War Worker.
For a considerable period of the war this lady rendered
valuable services at a large munition factory, where she was
engaged on duties of an arduous nature.   She carried out her
work in a highly satisfactory manner.
231, Mund Street, West Kensington, W.14   16926A.

HAWKINS, M. G., Special War Worker.
During the war he rendered valuable services at a large factory
where he was engaged on special work in connection with
the manufacture of aeroplanes.   He carried out his duties
in an efficient and skilful manner
16, Mulgrave Road, Fulham, S.W.6   16175A.

HAWKINS, S. W., Driver, R.A.S.C. (H.T.).
He volunteered in December, 1914, and after a period of
training was sent to Salonica in the following year.   While
on this Front he was engaged on the important duties of
transporting rations and munitions to the forward areas.
During his service he suffered from malaria, and in April,
1919, was demobilised, holding the 1914-15 Star, General
Service and Victory Medals.
25, Hilmer Street, West Kensington, W.14   15705.

HAWKINS, W., Sergt., 17th Middlesex Regiment.
He volunteered in April, 1915, and was sent to the Western
Front in the same year.   While there he took a prominent
part in many engagements, and was wounded at Cambrai
during the advance in November, 1918.
In March, 1919, he was demobilised, and holds the 1914-15
Star, General Service and Victory Medals.
56, Hartington Road, Lower Edmonton, N.9   14062.

**HAWKINS, W. H., Pte., Duke of Wellington's
(West Riding Regiment).**
After pre-war service in India, he was drafted to France in
1914, and was on active service there from the early struggles
on the Aisne, and the Somme and Ypres, right through to
the concluding Retreat and Advance of 1918.   He was
wounded three times, once in the battle of Ypres, 1914, and
was demobilised in June, 1919, holding the 1914 Star and
the General Service and Victory Medals
64, Portnall Road, Maida Hill, W.9   X19448

HAWTHORN, F. T., 1st Air Mechanic, R.A.F.
He joined in October, 1916, and after his training was engaged
at various stations on important duties, which called for a
high degree of technical skill.
He gave valuable services, but was not successsful in securing
his transfer overseas before the cessation of hostilities.
He was demobilised in 1919.
19, Chaldon Road, Dawes Road, S.W.6   X17647.

HAWTHORN, W. T., Pte., 2nd Middlesex Regt.
Volunteering at the outbreak of war, he was sent to the
Western Front, and took part in the battles of Neuve Chapelle
(where he was wounded) and the Somme.   Later he was
drafted to Salonica, and served in the Balkan campaign.
In 1919 he returned to England, and was demobilised in
April, holding the 1914 Star and the General Service and
Victory Medals.
109, Felixstowe Road, Lower Edmonton, N.9   14538.

HAYCOCK, G. H., Pte., 2/10th London Regt.
He volunteered for service in January, 1915, and after his
training was drafted overseas in February, 1916.   He took
part in many important engagements on the Western Front,
including the Retreat and Advance of 1918, and was killed
in action in the Ypres sector on August 17th, 1918.
He was entitled to the General Service and Victory Medals.
10, Caird Street, Queen's Park Estate, W.10   X18942.

**HAYDAY, C. L. W., Pte., Bedfordshire Regt.
and M.F.P.**
In August, 1917, he joined the Bedfordshire Regiment, and
after a period of training was transferred to the Military
Police, with which unit he was engaged on special duties.
He gave valuable services, but was unsuccessful in obtaining
his transfer overseas before hostilities ceased   In May, 1919,
he was demobilised.
16, Cedars Road, Lower Edmonton, N.9   14358.

HAYDEN, C., Cpl., 17th Lancashire Fusiliers.
He volunteered for service in January, 1915, and was drafted
to the Western Front in the following year.   He was in action
in the principal engagements on the Somme Front in 1916,
and in those which followed, until he was wounded at Ypres
in 1918.
He was demobilised in November, 1919, and holds the
General Service and Victory Medals.
38, Southam Street, North Kensington, W.10   X20566

HAYDEN, E., Pte., Middlesex Regiment.

He volunteered in February, 1915, and was drafted overseas in the same year. He was wounded in action at the battle of the Somme in 1916, and he also took part in many other engagements on the Western Front, including those of Ypres and La Bassée.
He holds the 1914–15 Star, General Service and Victory Medals, and was demobilised in 1919.
111, Asplin Road, Tottenham, N.17   X19085.

HAYDEN, F. H. (M.M.), Sergt., Royal Fusiliers.

Volunteering at the outbreak of the war, he was sent to the Western Front in the following year, taking part in several engagements, including the battles of Ypres, Loos, the Somme and Arras. During his service he was taken to hospital suffering from a severe illness, but returned to duty shortly after.
For conspicuous gallantry in the field he was awarded the Military Medal, and holds also the 1914–15 Star, General Service and Victory Medals, and was still serving in 1920.
121, Portnall Road, Maida Hill, W.9   X19518.

HAYDON, B. L., Pte., Royal West Kent Regt.

He volunteered in 1914, and in the following year was drafted to the Western Front. While in this theatre of war, he served in many important engagements, including those at Loos (where he was wounded) and Messines. Later in the same year he was discharged as medically unfit owing to his wound, and holds the 1914–15 Star, General Service and Victory Medals.
2, Wimborne Road, Lower Edmonton, N.9   14879C.

HAYDON, E. E., Cpl., 2nd Canadian Infantry.

He volunteered in 1914, and in the same year was drafted to the Western Front, where he took part in many important engagements, and was killed in action at the battle of Ypres in 1915.
He was entitled to the 1914 Star, the General Service and Victory Medals.
2, Wimborne Road, Lower Edmonton, N.9   14879A.

HAYDON, G. W., Sergt., 2nd County of London Yeomanry (Westminster Dragoons).

He volunteered in 1914, and early in the following year was drafted to Egypt, where he took part in many encounters with the Turks. During his service in this theatre of war he was wounded, and in 1918 was transferred to the Western Front, taking part in the Advance of that year.
He was killed in action in 1918, and was entitled to the 1914–15 Star, General Service and Victory Medals.
2, Wimborne Road, Lower Edmonton, N.9   14879B.

HAYES, A. F. (M.M.), Lce.-Cpl., 11th Middx. Regt.

He volunteered in November, 1915, and in the following year was sent to France, where he took part in many of the important engagements, and was wounded. At the battle of Arras, in April, 1917, he was awarded the Military Medal for conspicuous bravery and devotion to duty.
In November, 1918, he was demobilised, and in addition to the Military Medal, holds the General Service and Victory Medals.
5, Lowdon Road, Lower Edmonton, N.9   12853.

HAYES, F., Pte., Royal West Kent Regiment.

He joined in March, 1916, and after his training was drafted overseas two months later. Whilst in action at the battle of the Somme in July, 1916, he was severely wounded, and invalided home to hospital, where he remained until March, 1918, when he was discharged as medically unfit for further military service.
He holds the General Service and Victory Medals.
5, Alric Avenue, Stonebridge Park, N.W.10   14618

HAYES, G., Cpl., Royal Engineers.

Volunteering in April, 1915, he was soon sent to the Western Front, where he took part in engagements at Ypres, St. Julien, Hill 60, Arras and the Somme. During his service he contracted a serious illness, but recovered.
In February, 1919, he was demobilised, holding the 1914–15 Star, General Service and Victory Medals.
17, Rucklidge Avenue, Harlesden, N.W.10   12917

HAYES, G. W., Rifleman, Rifle Brigade.

He joined in 1918, on attaining military age, and after a short period of training was drafted to France, taking part in the Advance of that year, and being wounded in September. He was in hospital for a long period, and was eventually demobilised in 1919, holding the General Service and Victory Medals.
19, Winchester Road, Lower Edmonton, N.9   14875.

HAYES, J., Pte., Hampshire Regiment.

He volunteered in August, 1914, and in the following year was sent to the Western Front, where he took part in many important engagements, and was severely wounded at Hill 60. He was later drafted to the Balkan Front, and was killed in action in the same year.
He was entitled to the 1914–15 Star, General Service and Victory Medals.
11, Aintree Street, Dawes Road, S.W.6   TX18635.

HAYES, W., Driver, R.A.S.C. (H.T.).

He volunteered for service in June, 1915, and later in the same year was drafted to the Western Front, where he was engaged in conveying food and ammunition to the various sectors. From 1917 until 1919 he served in the same capacity in Italy, and on both Fronts did excellent work.
He holds the 1914-15 Star, General Service and Victory Medals.
53, Clarendon Street, Paddington, W.2   X20391.

HAYES, W., A., Pte. 4th Middlesex Regiment.

He enlisted in 1913, and shortly after the outbreak of war was drafted to the Western Front, taking part in the retreat from Mons and the fighting at La Bassée, where he was severely wounded. After being invalided home, and being in hospital until the following year, he returned to France and took part in the second battle of Ypres, but was again wounded and gassed. This confined him to hospital again for nearly a month, but on his recovery he rejoined his unit, with which he fought at the battle of Loos. Later he was transferred to Salonica, and took part in the Balkan campaign, but contracted malaria. In 1919 he was sent with the relief force to Russia, and after being there for six months was returned home and demobilised in April, 1920, holding the Mons Star, General Service and Victory Medals.
53, Clarendon Street, Paddington, W.2   X20389.

HAYHOE, E., 1st Air Mechanic, R.A.F.

He volunteered in January, 1915, and after qualifying as an air mechanic, was sent to the Western Front in the same year. During his four years' service overseas he was engaged in the important operations at Ypres, the Somme, Arras, Armentieres, St. Quentin and Lille, and was wounded four times.
In March, 1919, for giving services which called for high technical skill, he was demobilised, and holds the 1914–15 Star, General Service and Victory Medals.
22, Lydford Road, Maida Hill, W.9   X19439.

HAYLOCK, G. (M.M.)., Bombardier, R.F.A.

Volunteering at the outbreak of war, he was sent to the Dardanelles in 1915, and took part in the landing in April. After the evacuation of the Peninsula he was drafted to the Western Front, where he was in action on the Somme and at Cambrai during the Retreat and Advance of 1918.
He was awarded the Military Medal for conspicuous gallantry in bringing in a wounded officer under heavy fire, and holds in addition the 1914-15 Star, General Service and Victory Medals. He was demobilised in January, 1919.
19, Mozart Street, North Kensington, W.10   X18927.

HAYNES, A., Pte., Bedfordshire Regiment.

He volunteered in June, 1915, and from the following year until 1919 served in India, taking part in the fighting during the risings on the North-Western Frontier and the Amritsar Riots.
He was demobilised in July, 1919, holding the General Service and Victory Medals, and the Indian General Service Medal with the Afghanistan clasp—N.W. Frontier, 1919.
28, Westbury Road, Willesden, N.W.10   15443.

HAYNES, C., Pte., King's Shropshire L.I.

He joined for service in February, 1917, and was sent to France 13 months later. While on this Front he took part in the Retreat of 1918, when he was wounded and taken prisoner in March.
After his release he returned to England, and was demobilised in November, 1919, holding the General Service and Victory Medals.
105, Roundwood Road, Willesden, N.W.10   16047.

HAYNES, C., C.S.M., Royal Fusiliers.

He volunteered in August, 1914, and was at first retained at various stations on duties of an important nature. In October, 1917, he was drafted to the Western Front, and after taking a distinguished part in some of the heavy fighting was wounded two months later.
He was demobilised in March, 1919, and holds the General Service and Victory Medals.
88, Burn's Road, Harlesden, N.W.10   13459.

HAYNES, C. A. E., Sapper, Royal Engineers.

He volunteered in November, 1914, and in the following year was sent to France, where he took part in engagements at Ypres, Loos, Lens and the Somme, with a field-company. In July, 1916, after taking part in the battle of the Somme, he suffered from shell-shock, and was invalided home, being discharged in consequence as medically unfit for further service. He holds the 1914–15 Star, General Service and Victory Medals.
68, Oldfield Road, Willesden, N.W.10   15544.

HAYNES, E. (Mrs.), Special War Worker.

This lady was employed during the war on the staff of the Post Office, and rendered very valuable services until the cessation of hostilities. She received high commendation for her useful work.
23a, Guinness's Buildings, Fulham Palace Road, Hammersmith, W.6   14474A.

HAYNES, E., Rifleman, The Cameronians (Scottish Rifles).
He joined in April, 1917, and after his period of training was engaged on special duties at various stations with his unit. He rendered valuable services, but was not successful in obtaining his transfer overseas before hostilities ceased. He was demobilised in November, 1919.
61, Chaplin Road, Cricklewood, N.W.2   16629.

HAYNES, H. J., Pte., Middlesex Regiment.
He volunteered in April, 1915, and after completing his training was engaged on important duties at various stations with his unit. He rendered valuable services, but was not successful in obtaining his transfer overseas owing to his being rejected as medically unfit. He was demobilised in April, 1919.
5, Beetham Street, North Kensington, W.10   X18615A.

HAYNES, J., Gunner, Royal Garrison Artillery.
Joining in November, 1916, he completed his training, and was engaged on special duties at several stations. Owing to a fractured arm, which he sustained during his training, he was unable to pass the medical examination which was necessary before proceeding overseas, but gave valuable services before he was discharged through his injury in December, 1918.
34, Kingwood Road, Fulham, S.W.6   X19015.

HAYNES, L., Pte., Royal Marine Light Infantry.
He volunteered in August, 1914, and in the following year was sent to the Dardanelles. After taking part in the landing at Gallipoli, he was killed in action at Kritlia in May, 1915, about a fortnight after landing on the Peninsula. He was entitled to the 1914–15 Star, General Service and Victory Medals.
23a, Guinness's Buildings, Fulham Palace Road, Hammersmith, W.6   14474B.

HAYNES, W. C. H., Pte., Buffs (East Kent Regt.)
He joined in January, 1917, and after a short period of training was sent out to France in the following March. While on this Front he took part in many engagements, but during the German Offensive of 1918 was killed in action on March 23rd.
He was entitled to the General Service and Victory Medals.
5, Beethoven Street, North Kensington, W.10   X18615B.

HAYSMAN, S., Pte., Machine Gun Corps.
Volunteering in August, 1914, he was sent a year later to the Western Front, and took part in several engagements, including those at Ypres, Passchendaele, Arras and the Somme. During the Advance of 1918 he was severely wounded, and in March, 1919, was demobilised, holding the 1914-15 Star, General Service and Victory Medals
3, Bridport Road, Upper Edmonton, N.18   TX17588.

HAYWARD, E. J., Cook, Royal Navy.
Volunteering in 1914, he served with the Grand Fleet in the North Sea. He was in H.M.S. " Lawford " at the battle of Heligoland, and was later transferred to H.M.S. " Lowestoft." He rendered valuable services throughout, and holds the 1914 Star, General Service and Victory Medals He is still serving.
14, Beaufoy Road, Tottenham, N.17   17939B.

HAYWARD, F., Gunner Petty Officer, R.N.
He volunteered in August, 1914, and was in charge of the guns on board a trawler attached to H.M.S. " Wildfire." Throughout the war he remained with the Northern Patrol on dangerous duties in mine-strewn waters, and in February, 1919, was demobilised.
He holds the 1914 Star, General Service and Victory Medals.
5, Faroe Road, West Kensington, W.14   12436.

HAYWARD, F. W., Driver, R.A.S.C.
He volunteered in 1914, and the same year was sent to France where he was engaged on various duties in the forward areas. He was wounded in March, 1917, while in action on the Somme, and was demobilised in 1919, holding the 1914-15 Star, General Service and Victory Medals.
14, Beaufoy Road, Tottenham, N.17   X17939A.

HAYWARD, P. J., Pte., Middlesex Regiment.
He volunteered in September, 1914, and was sent overseas the following year. He was actively engaged in much of the fighting on the Western Front until 1916, when he was drafted to Salonica, where he took part in many engagements on the Balkan Front.
He returned to England after the cessation of hostilities, and was demobilised in January, 1919, holding the 1914–15 Star, General Service and Victory Medals.
52, Essex Road, Willesden, N.W.10   15595.

HAZELWOOD, A., Pte., Middlesex Regiment.
He volunteered in April, 1915, and in the following year was sent to the Western Front. During his two years' service in this theatre of war he took part in many engagements, including those at Ypres, the Somme, and Albert. After the cessation of hostilities he was admitted to hospital, where he remained for some time until discharged owing to ill-health in August, 1919.
He holds the General Service and Victory Medals.
127, Durban Road, Tottenham, N.17   X17959C.

HAZELWOOD, E. V., Pte., Middlesex Regiment.
Volunteering in 1915, he was sent a year later to France, and served on the Western Front for two years, during which time he took part in many important engagements, including the battles of Ypres and the Somme. He was wounded and gassed while in action, and was in hospital for over twelve months, when he was discharged owing to his wounds in 1918.
He holds the General Service and Victory Medals.
127, Durban Road, Tottenham, N.17   X17959B.

HAZELWOOD, W., C.S.M., Middlesex Regiment.
He volunteered in August, 1914, and was soon sent to France, where he took part in the retreat from Mons and the battle of the Somme. While in action at Ypres, in 1917, he was taken prisoner, and during his captivity, which lasted till after the Armistice, suffered many hardships.
On his release in 1919 he was demobilised, and holds the Mons Star, the General Service and Victory Medals.
127, Durban Road, Tottenham, N.17   X17959A.

HAZELWOOD, W. V. (D.C.M.), C.S.M., 2nd Middlesex Regiment.
He volunteered in 1914, and was drafted to France in the following year. While on the Western Front he took a prominent part in many important engagements, and was twice wounded. For conspicuous bravery and devotion to duty he was awarded the Distinguished Conduct Medal and also two Divisional parchment certificates for continuous good work.
In April, 1919, he was demobilised, and also holds the 1914–15 Star, General Service and Victory Medals.
27, Cedars Road, Lower Edmonton, N.9   14031.

HEAD, A. A., Driver, Royal Field Artillery.
He volunteered in September, 1914, and in the next year was sent to the Western Front. During his service in this theatre of war he took part in many important engagements, including those at Loos, the Somme, Arras and Ypres, where he was badly gassed and suffered from shell-shock. He was in hospital for nearly a year, and was demobilised in January, 1919, holding the 1914–15 Star, General Service and Victory Medals.
29, Siddons Road, Tottenham, N.17   X19153.

HEAD, J., Pte., Middlesex Regiment.
He volunteered for service in August, 1914, and was shortly afterwards sent overseas, where he took part in much of the early fighting on the Western Front, including the retreat from Mons, the battles of La Bassée, Ypres, Loos and the Somme.
After the cessation of hostilities he returned to England, and was demobilised in 1919. He holds the Mons Star, General Service and Victory Medals.
106, Kimberley Road, Upper Edmonton, N.18   16789.

HEAD, W. H., Cpl., Royal Army Ordnance Corps.
He volunteered for service in January, 1915, and after his training was drafted overseas to the Dardanelles, where he was engaged on special duties until the evacuation of the Peninsula. He was afterwards sent to Egypt, and served at various stations on important duties with his unit.
He holds the 1914–15 Star, General Service and Victory Medals.
72, Adeney Road, Hammersmith, W.6   14664.

HEADING, A., Pte., 2nd Royal Fusiliers.
He was serving at the outbreak of war, and was sent to the Dardanelles, where he served throughout the campaign. On the evacuation of the Peninsula he was transferred to this country, where he was retained on important duties.
He was discharged, owing to ill-health, in March, 1918, and holds the 1914–15 Star, General Service and Victory Medals.
35, Denbigh Road, Willesden, N.W.10   15088.

HEAFORD, H. J., Cpl., Middlesex Regiment and Machine Gun Corps.
He joined in February, 1917, and in the same year was sent to the Western Front, where he took part in the battle of Cambrai and in the fighting around Loos and Lille during the Advance of 1918.
In February, 1919, he was demobilised, holding the General Service and Victory Medals.
78, Drayton Road, Harlesden, N.W.10   15072.

HEALY, G., Rifleman, Rifle Brigade.

He joined in 1916, and in the same year was sent to France, where he was wounded at the battle of the Somme. On his recovery he was drafted to Salonica, serving there against the Bulgarians, and later was transferred to the Russian Front, where he was employed on the lines of communication between Batum and Kars. During his service in Armenia he contracted malaria, and was invalided home and demobilised in 1919, holding the General Service and Victory Medals.

42, Dieppe Street, West Kensington, W.14   16422.

HEALEY, G. E., Sergt., R.A.S.C.

He volunteered in August, 1914, and served with his unit on important mechanical transport duties. He was placed in charge of an important depot, and gave valuable services, for which he was recommended for a decoration, but was not successful in obtaining his transfer overseas before the cessation of hostilities.

He was demobilised in February, 1919.

31, Cornwallis Road, Lower Edmonton, N.9   13408A.

HEALEY, H., Pte., 15th Essex Regiment.

He joined for service in September, 1916, and on completion of his training was sent overseas, taking part in many engagements on the Western Front, including those at Arras, Armentieres and La Bassée.

He was demobilised in October, 1919, and holds the General Service and Victory Medals.

31, Cornwallis Road, Lower Edmonton, N.9   13408B.

HEALEY, H., A.B., Merchant Service.

He joined in 1918, and during the latter part of the war was in the " Huntsend," conveying troops to the Murmansk coast, through the North Sea. Later he was sent to South Africa, and holds the General Service and Mercantile Marine War Medals.

62, Carlyle Avenue, Willesden, N.W.10   14416B.

HEARD, A., Pte., Middlesex Regiment.

He volunteered in 1915, and was sent to the Western Front almost immediately. While in France he took part in important engagements in the Ypres and Lens sectors, and was killed in action at Loos in 1915.

He was entitled to the 1914-15 Star, General Service and Victory Medals.

11, Church Path, Hammersmith, W.6   15870.

HEARD, E. J., Cpl., Royal Engineers.

He joined in 1916, and in October, 1917, was sent to the Western Front, where he served with distinction in many important engagements, including those at Arras, Lille and Valenciennes. Previous to the Great War he had served in South Africa, and holds the King's and Queen's South African Medals with four clasps, in addition the General Service and Victory Medals. He was demobilised in 1920.

26, Hiley Road, Willesden, N.W.10   X18651.

HEARN, A., Lce.-Cpl., Royal Fusiliers

He volunteered in October, 1916, and was drafted to the Western Front in the following year, serving in many of the principal engagements, and being severely wounded. On recovery he again took part in heavy fighting, and on April 30th, 1917, was killed in action.

He was entitled to the 1914-15 Star, General Service and Victory Medals.

21, Halford Road, Walham Green, S.W.6   X19481.

HEARN, R. H., Lce.-Cpl., R.A.M.C.

He joined for service in October, 1916, and after a period of training was drafted to the Western Front, where he was employed in many of the important engagements, including those of Arras and Cambrai.

He was demobilised in November, 1919, and holds the General Service and Victory Medals.

57, Wendover Road, Harlesden, N.W.10   12545.

HEASMAN, W. J., Driver, R.F.A. and Gunner, R.G.A.

He volunteered in January, 1915, and in the following June was sent to the Western Front. During his service there he took part in many important engagements, including those at Ypres, Hill 60 (where he was gassed) and the Somme. He was subsequently sent to the Balkans, where he again took part in heavy fighting.

In May, 1919, he was sent to England and demobilised, and holds the 1914-15 Star, General Service and Victory Medals.

9, Beethoven Street, North Kensington, W.10   X18746.

HEATH, E. E. (Mrs.), Special War Worker.

During the war this lady was engaged for nearly two years at No. 3 Filling Factory, Perivale, Park Royal, working on alternate day and night shifts. On several occasions she was on duty during air raids, but remained at her work all the time. She carried out her duties in a very satisfactory manner, and was highly commended.

37, Melville Road, Stonebridge Park, N.W.10   15647B.

HEATH, G., Cpl., Royal Engineers.

He joined in February, 1916, and in the same year was drafted to Salonica, where he was engaged on important transport duties, but was invalided home suffering from malaria, and was in hospital for a considerable period. On his recovery he was sent to France, and took part in many important operations during the Advance of 1918.

He was demobilised in March, 1919, and holds the General Service and Victory Medals.

37, Melville Road, Stonebridge Park, N.W.10   15647A.

HEATH, G. F., Signaller, Royal Navy.

He joined in 1916, and after completing his training in H.M.S. " Warspite," was posted to H.M.S. " Atlanta." While on this ship he was engaged on important patrol duties off the coasts of Spain and Italy, and in the Atlantic Ocean and North Sea. He rendered valuable services as a signaller, and in 1919 was demobilised, holding the General Service and Victory Medals.

112, Fortune Gate Road, Harlesden, N.W.10   T13188.

HEATH, H. J., Gunner, Royal Garrison Artillery.

He volunteered in December, 1915, and on completing his training was retained on important duties with his unit until April, 1918, when he was drafted to France. While on this Front he took part in the severe fighting in the Retreat and Advance of 1918, particularly that around Albert and St. Quentin.

In June, 1919, he was demobilised, and holds the General Service and Victory Medals.

99, Minet Road, Willesden, N.W.10   13640.

HEATH, W. J., Pte., Royal Marine Light Infty.

He volunteered in January, 1915, at the age of 15, and in the same year was sent to the Dardanelles, where he served throughout the campaign. After the evacuation of the Peninsula he was sent to France, and later to India. During his service he was wounded and gassed, and in July, 1919, was demobilised, holding the 1914-15 Star, General Service and Victory Medals.

21, Kilmaine Road, Munster Road, S.W.6   TX18881.

HEATHER, A. D., Gunner, Royal Field Artillery.

He volunteered in September, 1914, and was sent to the Western Front early in the following year, being in action at Ypres, Loos, the Somme, Arras and Cambrai. During his service he was severely wounded in action, and was in hospital for a long period.

He was demobilised in March, 1919, holding the 1914-15 Star, General Service and Victory Medals.

1, Bramber Road, West Kensington, W.14   16281.

HEATHER, J. S., Sergt., 23rd Middlesex Regt.

He volunteered for service in 1915, and at the conclusion of his training was drafted overseas. He took part in many important engagements on the Western Front, including the battles of Ypres, Bullecourt, Vimy Ridge and Cambrai, and during his service was wounded and gassed.

He was demobilised in January, 1919, and holds the General Service and Victory Medals.

12, Mund Street, West Kensington, W.14   16910.

HEAVENS, G. W., Driver, Royal Field Artillery.

He volunteered in May, 1915, and after completing his training was drafted to the Western Front, where he took part in many important operations. After rendering valuable services he was killed in action on September, 26th, 1917, and was entitled to the General Service and Victory Medals.

49, Sherbrooke Road, Fulham, S.W.6   X18481.

HEATHFIELD, W., Steward, Royal Navy.

He volunteered in August, 1914, and was engaged on important duties in the North Sea. He took part in the battle of Jutland, where his ship was engaged on scout duties.

In November, 1919, after five years' service, he was demobilised, and holds the 1914-15 Star, General Service and Victory Medals.

32, Crefeld Road, Hammersmith, W.6   T14102A.

HEBBS, M. (Mrs.), Special War Worker.

During the war this lady was engaged on work of national importance at the Perivale National Filling Factory, Willesden. Her duties were of an arduous nature, and were carried out with great care. She rendered valuable services throughout, and was highly commended.

40, Disraeli Road, Acton Lane, N.W.10   14397

HEDGES, E. A., 1st Air Mechanic, R.A.F. (late R.N.A.S.).

He joined in June, 1916, and owing to his high technical abilities, was engaged on important duties at the Aeronautical Inspection Department, in connection with the testing of aero engines. In September of the following year he was released from military duties in order to take up the responsible position of an inspector of engines at the Air Ministry. He rendered valuable services throughout.

26, Vallier Road, College Park, N.W.10   X17674

HEDGES, F. A., Pte., Highland Light Infantry.

He volunteered in August, 1915, and after a period of training was sent to the Western Front in the following year. He was on active service for nearly three years, and during this time took part in many important engagements, including those at St. Quentin and Passchendaele in 1917.
In January, 1919, he was demobilised, and holds the General Service and Victory Medals.
47, Brett Road, Stonebridge Park, N.W.10   14526.

HEDGES, J. B. (Mr.), Special War Worker.

For a period of nearly four years during the war he was engaged on responsible duties of an important nature at Messrs. Smith & Son's works at Cricklewood. He carried out his duties with care and efficiency, and rendered valuable services throughout.
2, Beaconsfield Road, Church End, N.W.10   16334.

HEDGES, J. W., Pte., R.A.S.C. (M.T.).

He joined in July, 1917, and owing to his skill as a fitter and turner, was engaged on special duties at various stations. He gave valuable services, but was not successful in obtaining his transfer overseas before hostilities ceased.
He was demobilised in November, 1919.
22, Bravington Road, Maida Hill, W.9   X19191.

HEIER, J. F., Driver, R.A.S.C.

He joined up for service in June, 1916, and after his training was drafted overseas. He was engaged on work in connection with the repair of motor transport in various parts of the Western Front, particularly at Ypres, Vimy Ridge, Armentieres, St. Quentin, Hazebrouck and Cambrai.
He was demobilised in 1919, and holds the General Service and Victory Medals.
76, Chesson Road, West Kensington, W.14   X17691B.

HEIGHTON, W. G., Gunner, R.G.A. (163rd Siege Battery).

Volunteering in November, 1915, he was sent to the Western Front in November, 1917, and was in action at Ypres and during the Retreat of 1918. He brought down an enemy aeroplane with a Lewis gun at Tilley Wood in March, 1918, and a few days later was taken prisoner at Monchy.
He was released after the Armistice, and in March, 1919, was demobilised, holding the General Service and Victory Medals.
39, Bravington Road, Maida Hill, W.9   X19321.

HEITMAN, C., Sapper, Royal Engineers.

He volunteered in September, 1915, and was sent to the Western Front in the following year, where he was engaged on important duties in the forward areas. During his service overseas he was twice wounded, and was in hospital for a long period. On his recovery he went to Germany with the Army of Occupation, and remained there until his return to England for demobilisation in August, 1919.
He holds the General Service and Victory Medals.
77, Sherbrooke Road, Fulham, S.W.6   X18483.

HEITMAN, H. C. W., Pte., H.A.C., Royal Fusiliers and Sapper, Royal Engineers.

He joined in May, 1918, and at the close of his training volunteered for service in Russia, being sent there in May, 1919. He returned to England in the following October, and was demobilised ten months later, but shortly afterwards he re-enlisted in the Royal Engineers.
44, Shorrolds Road, Walham Green, S.W.6   X19363.

HEMBREY, H., Cpl., Royal Welch Fusiliers.

He volunteered in February, 1915, and was sent to France in the same year. During his service on the Western Front he took part in many important engagements, including those at Ypres and Vimy Ridge, and was gassed.
In January, 1919, he was demobilised, and holds the 1914-15 Star, General Service and Victory Medals.
67, Leghorn Road, Harlesden, N.W.10   12958A.

HEMBROUGH, H., Gunner, R.F.A. (transferred as Sapper to R.E.).

He was serving at the outbreak of war, and was immediately sent to the Western Front, where he took part in the battles of Mons, Ypres, the Somme, Vimy Ridge, Cambrai, Messines Ridge and Givenchy.
In March, 1919, he was demobilised, after serving for seven years with the Colours. He holds the Mons Star, the General Service and Victory Medals.
34, Glynfield Road, Willesden, N.W.10   16521—15131C.

HEMMING, A. G., A.B., Royal Navy, H.M.S. "Blanche."

Having volunteered for duty in August, 1915, he served with the Grand Fleet in the North Sea on dangerous missions, and took part in several naval engagements, including that in the Heligoland Bight.
He was demobilised in June, 1919, and holds the 1914-15 Star, General Service and Victory Medals.
41, Clarendon Street, Paddington, W.2   X20636.

HEMMINGS, A., A.B., Royal Navy.

He volunteered in August, 1914, and served on H.M.S. "President" with the Grand Fleet in the North Sea. In 1915 he was invalided home through ill-health, and on his recovery was attached to an anti-aircraft battery, with which he was engaged on important defence duties.
In 1919 he was demobilised, and holds the 1914 Star, General Service and Victory Medals.
131, Sandringham Road, Cricklewood, N.W.2   T17317.

HEMMINGS, C. J., Pte., Middlesex Regiment.

He joined in December, 1916, and after his training was sent to the Western Front in the following May. During his service he took part in many important engagements, including those at Arras, Ypres and Cambrai, and was wounded while in action at Ypres.
Upon his return from France he was demobilised in November, 1919, and holds the General Service and Victory Medals.
41, Hazeldene Road, Stonebridge Park, N.W.10   14615A.

HEMMINGS, H. W., Sergt., Royal Berkshire Regt.

He volunteered in August, 1914, and being sent to France immediately afterwards, took part in the retreat from Mons and several important engagements. In 1916, while in action, he was severely wounded, and was invalided home. After a considerable period in hospital he was discharged in May, 1918, as medically unfit for further military service owing to his wound.
He holds the Mons Star, General Service and Victory Medals.
15, Wingmore Road, Tottenham, N.17   X17978A.

HEMMINGS, J. G., Pte., Norfolk Regiment.

He joined in March, 1918, on attaining military age, and after a short period of training, was sent to the Western Front, where he took part in many important engagements during the advance of 1918, and was wounded in action near St. Quentin.
In February, 1919, he was demobilised, and holds the General Service and Victory Medals.
41, Hazeldene Road, Stonebridge Park, N.W.10   14615B.

HENBERY, A. Cpl., 15th Worcestershire Regt., 13th London Regt. (Kensington) and Y. & L. Regt.

Volunteering for service in October, 1915, he met with a bad accident during his training, and consequently was unable to pass the medical examination for service overseas. However, he gave valuable services at various stations, and was demobilised in March, 1919.
22, Novello Street, Parson's Green, S.W.6   X19933.

HENDERSON, E. A., Pte., Gordon Highlanders.

He joined in August, 1918, but after his training was unsuccessful in obtaining his transfer overseas to the battle areas before the cessation of hostilities. However, he was sent to Germany with the Army of Occupation, and served there until he returned to England for his demobilisation in March, 1920.
25, Milton Avenue, Willesden, N.W.10   13874A.

HENDY, F. J., Pte., Middlesex Regiment.

He volunteered in November, 1914, and during his training met with a serious accident, owing to which he was retained on important duties at various stations with his unit. He gave valuable services, but was unsuccessful in obtaining his transfer overseas because of his injury.
In November, 1918, he was discharged as medically unfit for further service.
25, Haldane Road, Walham Green, S.W.6   TX17072.

HENNESSEY, A. J., Rifleman, Royal Irish Rifles.

Having previously served in the Army, he rejoined in October 1914, and was retained on special duties of an important nature with his unit.
He contracted a serious illness while in the Service, from the effects of which he died on April 29th, 1917.
He held the King's and Queen's South African and the India General Service Medals.
26, Archel Road, West Kensington, W.14   18773A.

HENNESSEY, J. (Mrs.), Nurse, St. John Ambulance Corps.

For the whole period of the war this lady was engaged on various nursing duties with the 28th Division of the St. John's Ambulance Corps. Throughout she gave very valuable services in tending the sick and wounded, and her work was worthy of high praise.
7, Clyde Flats, Rylston Road, Fulham, S.W.6   18773B.

HENNESSEY, S. J. C., Sergt., Royal Fusiliers.

He was recalled from the Reserve in August, 1914, having enlisted originally in 1903. Owing to his qualifications he was retained on special duties of an important nature for some time, but in 1915 was sent to Salonica, where he took part in the Balkan campaign. On May 17th, 1917, he was killed in action.
He was entitled to the 1914-15 Star, the General Service and Victory Medals.
6, Mooltan Street, West Kensington, W.14   X17147

HENNING, C., Pte., R.A.S.C.

He joined for service in January, 1917, and after his period of training was sent to France, where he took part in operations near Loos, La Bassée, Ypres, and the Somme.
In May, 1920, he was demobilised, and holds the General Service and Victory Medals.
4, Rowallan Road, Munster Road, S.W.6   X19271.

HENSON, A. G., Pte., 11th Hampshire Regiment.

He volunteered in September, 1914, and during his service in France took part in the fighting at Ypres, Bullecourt, the Somme, Arras, St. Quentin and Albert, and was wounded twice and gassed. He was in hospital for some time, suffering from his wounds, and in March, 1919, was demobilised, holding the 1914-15 Star, General Service and Victory Medals.
9, Shotley Street, Hammersmith, W.6   14798.

HENSON, C., Pte., 9th (Queen's Royal) Lancers.

He enlisted in 1912, and from 1914 until 1918 saw service on the Western Front. During this period he took part in the retreat from Mons, the battles of Ypres, the Somme, Albert and St. Quentin, and was wounded and gassed.
He holds the Mons Star, General Service and Victory Medals, and was demobilised in July, 1919.
59, Humbolt Road, Hammersmith, W.6   T15310A.

HENSON, E., Rifleman, 5th London Regiment (L.R.B.).

He volunteered for service in June, 1915, and was sent to Gibraltar, on garrison duty. He later served with his unit in Egypt and afterwards in France, where he was severely wounded in action on the Somme in October, 1916.
He holds the General Service and Victory Medals and was demobilised in November, 1919.
59, Brettenham Road, Upper Edmonton, N.18   15232B.

HENSON, H. W. (M.M.), Q.M.S., 1st Royal Warwickshire Regiment.

He was mobilised in August, 1914, and in the same year was drafted to the Western Front, where he remained until 1918.
He took part in many of the principal engagements, including the retreat from Mons, and the battles of Ypres, Hill 60 and Arras. On two occasions he was badly wounded, once in action at Armentieres, and was also gassed.
He was awarded the Military Medal for conspicuous bravery in the field, and also holds the Mons Star, General Service and Victory Medals.
59, Humbolt Road, Hammersmith, W.6   T15310B.

HERAUD, C. P., Rifleman, Rifle Brigade.

He volunteered in August, 1914, and shortly afterwards was drafted overseas, where he took part in many important engagements on the Western Front.
He was killed in action on August 16th,1916, and was entitled to the 1914 Star, General Service and Victory Medals.
70, Fairfield Road, Upper Edmonton, N.18   15775B.

HERAUD, J. A., Rifleman, Rifle Brigade.

He volunteered in November, 1915, and after his training was drafted to the Western Front, where he took part in many important engagements and was wounded on the Somme.
In February, 1919, he was demobilised, and holds the General Service and Victory Medals.
70, Fairfield Road, Upper Edmonton, N.18   15775A.

HERBERT, E., Pte., R.A.S.C. (M.T.).

He joined in August, 1917, and was almost immediately sent to the Western Front, where, owing to his special qualifications, he was engaged as a driver of a staff car.
He gave very valuable services, and in November, 1919, was demobilised, holding the General Service and Victory Medals.
84, Deacon Road, Cricklewood, N.W.2   X17116A.

HERBERT, E. R., Sergt., Gloucestershire Regt.

He volunteered in September, 1914, and was sent to the Western Front in the following year. While there he took a prominent part in many important engagements, including those at Hill 60, Ypres, Cambrai and Albert, and was wounded.
After the signing of the Armistice he proceeded to Germany with the Army of Occupation, and remained there until he returned to England for his demobilisation in November, 1919.
He holds the 1914-15 Star, General Service and Victory Medals.
81, Rayleigh Road, West Kensington, W.14   12645.

HERBERT, G. A., Rifleman, 6th London Regt. (Rifles).

He volunteered for service in December, 1915, and after his training served at various stations on important duties with his unit. He gave valuable services, but was not successful in obtaining his transfer overseas, owing to ill-health, and he was discharged in consequence in September, 1916.
17, Rosaline Road, Munster Road, S.W.6   TX18695.

HERBERT, J. E., Pte., Middlesex Regiment.

He joined in 1916, and after a short period of training was drafted to the Western Front. While in action at the battle of the Somme, on July 1st, 1916, he was killed.
He was entitled to the General Service and Victory Medals.
75, Pretoria Road, Upper Edmonton, N.18   X17029.

HERDSMAN, A. E., Pte., The Queen's (Royal West Surrey Regiment).

Joining in February, 1916, he was drafted to the Western Front, where he took part in engagements at Ypres, Arras, Cambrai and the Somme. During his service he was severely wounded and gassed, and in September, 1919, was demobilised, holding the General Service and Victory Medals.
88, Clarendon Street, Paddington, W.2   X20370.

HERMAN, H., Cpl., Middlesex Regiment.

He joined in 1916, and after completing his training was sent to France. While on the Western Front he took part in engagements at Ypres, Loos and La Bassée.
In 1919 he was demobilised, and holds the General Service and Victory Medals.
25, Shorrolds Road, Walham Green, S.W.6   X19399C.

HERMAN, P., Pte., R.A.S.C.

He volunteered in 1915, and in the same year was sent to the Western Front, where he took an active part in several important engagements, including those at Loos, La Bassée, the Somme and Ypres.
He was demobilised in 1919, holding the 1914-15 Star, the General Service and Victory Medals.
25, Shorrolds Road, Walham Green, S.W.6   X19399A.

HERMAN, W. E., Cpl., Middlesex Regiment.

He joined for service in 1916, and after his training was drafted overseas in the same year, taking part in many engagements on the Western Front, including the battles of the Somme and Ypres.
He was demobilised in 1919, and holds the General Service and Victory Medals.
25, Shorrolds Road, Walham Green, S.W.6   X19399B.

HERNING, A. V., Cpl., R.F.A.

He volunteered in September, 1914, and was sent to France, where he took part in the battles of Loos and the Somme. Later he was drafted to Italy in October, 1917, and was in action on the Piave. In March, 1918, he returned to France, and was engaged in the Retreat and Advance of that year.
During his service he was wounded, and holds the 1914-15 Star and the General Service and Victory Medals, being demobilised in January, 1919.
167, Chapter Road, Cricklewood, N.W.2   X17369B.

HERNING, J., Pte., Royal Irish Fusiliers.

He volunteered for service in November, 1915, and in the following year was drafted overseas to France, where he took part in the battle of the Somme. On April 13th, 1918, he died at Poperinghe of wounds received in action near Ypres during the German Offensive.
He was entitled to the General Service and Victory Medals.
167, Chapter Road, Cricklewood, N.W.2   X17369A.

HERRINGTON, E. W., Pte., Middlesex Regiment.

He volunteered in 1915, and after his period of training was engaged on important duties at various stations with his unit. He gave valuable services, but owing to ill-health was not successful in obtaining his transfer overseas, and in 1918 was discharged as medically unfit for further service.
32, Caird Street, Queen's Park Estate, W.10   T18948A.

HERRINGTON, W. A., Pte., 13th London Regt. (Kensington).

He was mobilised in August, 1914, and was immediately sent to the Western Front, where he took part in many engagements including those at La Bassée and Festubert. In November, 1914, he was wounded while in action, and was discharged owing to his wounds in August 1916 as medically unfit for further service.
He holds the 1914 Star, the General Service and Victory Medals.
32, Caird Street, Queen's Park, Estate, W.10   X18948B.

HERSEY, C., Pte., Royal Army Medical Corps.

He volunteered in January, 1916, and being physically unfit for service overseas, was retained on special duties at a large military hospital.
In June, 1916, he was discharged, owing to ill-health, as medically unfit for further military service.
89, Ancill Street, Hammersmith, W.6   13800A.

HERSEY, M. (Mrs.), Special War Worker.

During the war this lady gave valuable services on the Metropolitan Railway, thus releasing a man for military service. Her work, which was often of an arduous nature, was carried out in a very able and willing manner, and she received high praise for her services.
89, Ancill Street, Hammersmith, W 6   13800C.

HERSEY, W., Gunner, Royal Field Artillery.

He volunteered in 1915, and was sent to France in the same year. During his service in this theatre of war he took part in many important engagements, including those at Neuve Chapelle, Loos, Ypres, the Somme and Vimy Ridge. He was later invalided home through illness contracted while on service. On his recovery he was transferred to the Tank Corps, and was engaged on special duties with that Corps.

In 1919 he was demobilised, and holds the 1914–15 Star, General Service and Victory Medals.

89, Ancill Street, Hammersmith, W.6   13800B.

HESSING, R. H., Special War Worker.

For a period of five years during the war he was engaged on important duties at a large machine equipment works in London. He was retained for this work owing to his skill as a fitter and turner, and throughout gave satisfaction for the efficient manner in which he carried out his duties.

32, Westoe Road, Lower Edmonton, N.9   13125.

HEWETT, G., Pte., The Queen's (Royal West Surrey Regiment).

He volunteered in January, 1916, and was sent to France in the following June. During his three years' active service he took part in many important engagements, including those on the Somme, at Cambrai, Armentieres, Albert, Bethune, St. Quentin and Ypres, and was wounded.

In March, 1919, he was demobilised, and holds the General Service and Victory Medals.

17, Oak Road, Willesden, N.W.10   15075.

HEWITT, A. V., Rifleman, K.R.R.

He volunteered at first in 1914, in the Middlesex Regiment, but being under military age, was discharged. In August of the following year, on attaining the required age, he volunteered again in the King's Royal Rifle Corps, and was accepted. After a period of training he was sent to France, where he was killed in action on January 8th, 1916, and is buried at Arras.

He was entitled to the 1914–15 Star, the General Service and Victory Medals.

36, Hartopp Avenue, Dawes Road, S.W.6   X17731B.

HEWITT, C., Pte., 13th London Regiment (Kensingtons).

He volunteered in September, 1914, and was sent to France in the following February. While in this theatre of war he took part in important engagements around Neuve Chapelle, and was killed there on April 26th, 1915.

He was entitled to the 1914–15 Star, the General Service and Victory Medals.

22, Elthorne Park Road, Hanwell, W.7   11076.

HEWITT, G., Cpl., Rifle Brigade.

He volunteered in September, 1914, and in the following year was sent to the Western Front, where he took part in engagements at Arras and Ypres. He was badly gassed and contracted bronchitis, as a result of which he was invalided home and was discharged as medically unfit for further service in August, 1917.

He holds the 1914–15 Star, the General Service and Victory Medals.

14, Vallier Road, College Park, N.W.10   X17678.

HEWITT, J., Pte., Lancashire Fusiliers.

He volunteered in October, 1915, and in the following year was drafted to France, where he took part in many engagements, including the battles of the Somme, Arras, Ypres and Cambrai. During his active service he was wounded three times, and was in hospital a considerable period in France and in England.

In February, 1919, he was demobilised, and holds the General Service and Victory Medals.

36, Hartopp Avenue, Dawes Road, S.W.6   X17731A.

HEWITT, J. W., Pte., Royal Fusiliers.

He volunteered in August, 1914, and went to the Western Front in April of the following year, taking part in several engagements.

He was killed in action near Loos on September 29th, 1915, and was entitled to the 1914–15 Star, the General Service and Victory Medals.

22, Heron Road, Willesden, N.W.10   15566B.

HEWKIN, E. T., Pte., Royal Irish Fusiliers.

He volunteered in August, 1914, and after his training was drafted to France, where he took part in many important battles, and was wounded at Neuve Chapelle in March, 1915. In the following November he was sent to Salonica, and served in several engagements until September 17th, 1916, when he was killed in action.

He was entitled to the 1914 Star, General Service and Victory Medals.

13, Church Path, Hammersmith, W.6   15898.

HEWLETT, G., Gunner, Royal Field Artillery.

At the outbreak of war he was employed at a large munition factory, where he rendered valuable services until August, 1915, when he volunteered in the Royal Field Artillery. After a period of training he was drafted to the Western Front, and served for over two years, during which period he took part in many important engagements, including the Retreat and Advance of 1918.

He was demobilised in July, 1919, and holds the General Service and Victory Medals.

16, Winchelsea Road, Willesden, N.W.10   13718C.

HEWLETT, H., Sapper, Royal Engineers.

He volunteered in December, 1914, and was sent to France in the following year. During his four years' service on the Western Front he took part in the engagements at Loos, Pozières, La Bassée and Arras, and was wounded.

He was still serving in 1920, and holds the 1914–15 Star, the General Service and Victory Medals.

16, Winchelsea Road, Willesden, N.W.10   13718A.

HEWLETT, H. G., Stoker, R.N., H.M.S. "Blenheim."

He volunteered in May, 1915, and was present with his ship during the operations in the Dardanelles. He was afterwards engaged for four years on important convoy duties in the Mediterranean Sea, where the vessel had many encounters with submarines.

In May, 1919, he was demobilised, and holds the 1914–15 Star, General Service and Victory Medals.

87, Shrewsbury Road, Stonebridge Park, N.W.10   13843A.

HEWLETT, J., Pte., Machine Gun Corps.

Joining in June, 1916, he was soon drafted to the Western Front, where he served in many important engagements, including the Retreat and Advance of 1918, when he was wounded.

In February, 1919, he was demobilised, and holds the General Service and Victory Medals.

16, Winchelsea Road, Willesden, N.W.10   13718B.

HEWLETT, M. (Mrs.), Special War Worker.

For more than three years during the war this lady rendered services of a valuable nature at Park Royal Munition Factory as an inspector of small arms ammunition. Her duties were carried out in an efficient manner and she received high commendation for her work.

87, Shrewsbury Road, Stonebridge Park, N.W.10   13843B.

HEYDON, W. C., Gunner, Royal Field Artillery.

He volunteered for service in September, 1914, and was sent to France in the same year. After taking part in many engagements, including the battles of Ypres and Neuve Chapelle, where he was wounded. He was later in action and was killed near Cambrai on October 15th, 1917.

He was entitled to the 1914 Star, General Service and Victory Medals.

118, Villiers Road, Cricklewood, N.W.2   16151.

HICKFORD, C. H., Pte., Sherwood Foresters.

He joined in 1917, and after his training served at various stations on important duties with his unit. He rendered valuable services, but was unsuccessful in obtaining his transfer to the fighting areas before the cessation of hostilities.

In January, 1919, he was demobilised.

27, Cranbrook Road, Tottenham, N.17   X18558B.

HICKFORD, E. T., Pte., 19th London Regiment.

He volunteered in May, 1915, and having completed his period of training was retained on important duties with his unit. He gave valuable services, but was unable to secure his transfer overseas before hostilities ceased, and was demobilised in December, 1919.

27, Cranbrook Road, Tottenham, N.17   X18558A.

HICKMAN, A. S., Trooper, Leicestershire Yeomanry.

Volunteering in August, 1915, he was sent a year later to the Western Front, where he took part in several engagements, including the Retreat and Advance of 1918. During the latter he was severely wounded near Mons on the day before the Armistice was signed, and was in hospital for some time.

In August, 1919, he was demobilised, holding the General Service and Victory Medals.

53, Somerset Road, Upper Edmonton, N.18   X17031.

HICKMAN, E. H., 1st Air Mechanic, R.A.F.

He joined for service in February, 1916, and after his training was drafted overseas, where he was actively engaged with his squadron at Marquise. He was later employed on special duties at the aerodrome near St. Omer, where owing to frequent air-raids, he suffered from shell-shock. His duties called for a high degree of technical skill.

He holds the General Service and Victory Medals, and was demobilised in May, 1919.

7, Lundy Street, Hammersmith, W.6   14794.

HICKS, A., Pte., Hampshire Regiment.

He volunteered in March, 1915, and in the same year was sent to the Dardanelles, where he took part in the landing at Suvla Bay, and served through the Gallipoli campaign. On the evacuation of the Peninsula he was sent to Egypt, where he remained for nearly a year, and was then drafted to France, taking part in the battles of the Somme (1916), Arras and Ypres (1917), and being badly wounded and gassed. Consequently he was invalided home and discharged in September, 1917, as medically unfit for further service.
He holds the 1914–15 Star, General Service and Victory Medals.
15, St. John's Building, Kilburn Lane, N. Kensington, W.10
X18663.

HICKS, F., Pte., Middlesex Regiment.

Volunteering in August, 1914, he was drafted to France in the following July. During his three and a half years' service overseas he participated in many important engagements, and was wounded three times.
In February, 1919, he was demobilised, holding the 1914–15 Star, General Service and Victory Medals.
40, Ponsard Road, College Park, N.W.10   X17750.

HICKS, F. C., Pte., The Queen's (Royal West Surrey Regiment).

He joined in November, 1917, and was soon sent to France, where he took part in important engagements around Ypres and Passchendaele during the Retreat and Advance of 1918.
In December, 1919, he was discharged as medically unfit for further service owing to heart trouble, and holds the General Service and Victory Medals.
337, " K " Block, Guinness's Buildings, Hammersmith, W.6
13230.

HICKS, L. V., Pte., 4th Royal Fusiliers.

He joined early in 1918, and after his training served at various stations with his unit on important duties. He was unable to obtain his transfer overseas before the cessation of hostilities, but immediately after the signing of the Armistice was sent to Mesopotamia, where he was still serving in 1920.
He is entitled to the Victory Medal.
19, Archel Road, West Kensington, W.14   16197.

HIGGINS, G. A., Pte., 1st Wiltshire Regiment.

He joined in March, 1917, and after a year's training was sent to the Western Front. A month later he went into action near Ploegsteert, but on April 12th was reported missing.
He was entitled to the General Service and Victory Medals.
24, Ilex Road, Willesden, N.W.10   15957A.

HIGGINS, H. F., Pte., The Queen's (Royal West Surrey Regiment).

He joined in 1917, and after a short period of training, was sent to France in the same year. During his service in this theatre of war he took part in many engagements, and was severely wounded at Passchendaele.
In 1919 he was demobilised, and holds the General Service and Victory Medals.
54, Ilex Road, Willesden, N.W.10   15957B.

HIGGINS, H. J., Driver, Royal Field Artillery.

He volunteered in August, 1914, and was sent to France in the following year. During his service on this Front he took part in engagements at Ypres, Loos, the Somme (1916), Bullecourt (1917), and during the Retreat and Advance of 1918. He was invalided home with trench feet and was in hospital in England for some time, and in 1920 was demobilised, holding the 1914–15 Star, General Service and Victory Medals.
20, Mulgrave Road, Fulham, S.W.6   16173.

HIGGINS, W. Pte., Middlesex Regiment.

He volunteered in August, 1914, and in the following year was sent to the Western Front, where he took part in important engagements at Ypres, the Somme, Vimy Ridge and Cambrai. He also served throughout the Retreat and Advance of 1918, and in February of the following year was demobilised, holding the 1914–15 Star, General Service and Victory Medals.
45, Heron Road, Willesden, N.W.10   15608.

HIGGS, D. C., Pte., Royal Army Service Corps.

He volunteered in April, 1915, and after a period of training was drafted to Egypt, where he remained until March, 1918. During this period he was engaged on important operations in that theatre of war and was then sent to the Western Front, serving there throughout the Retreat and Advance of 1918.
In June, 1919, he was demobilised, and holds the General Service and Victory Medals.
2, William Street, Tottenham, N.17   X18303.

HIGGS, H. A., Pte., 7th London Regiment.

Volunteering in August, 1914, he was sent to France in the same year, and during his four years' service in this theatre of war took part in many important engagements. While in action at Vimy Ridge, in 1918, he was seriously wounded and died as a result in November of the same year. He was entitled to the 1914 Star, General Service and Victory Medals.
32, Aintree Street, Dawes Road, S.W.6   X18204C.

HIGGS, J. T., Driver, Royal Engineers.

He volunteered in September, 1914, and after a period of training was sent to Egypt, where he took part in the operation against the Senussi and the Turks. After the signing of the Armistice he went to Germany with the Army of Occupation, and was still serving there in 1920.
He holds the General Service and Victory Medals.
32, Aintree Street, Dawes Road, S.W.6   X18204B.

HIGGS, J. W., Pte., 13th Hussars.

He volunteered in October, 1915, and after completing his training was sent to Mesopotamia, where he took part in several important engagements against the Turks.
In December, 1919, he was sent home for demobilisation, and holds the General Service and Victory Medals.
32, Aintree Street, Dawes Road, S.W.6   X18204A.

HIGINBOTTOM, A. G., Pte., R.M.L.I.

Joining in 1917, he was engaged on important duties with the Grand Fleet in the North and Mediterranean Seas. While thus employed his vessel often encountered enemy submarines and passed through mine-strewn areas.
He holds the General Service and Victory Medals.
14, Marsden Road, Lower Edmonton, N.9   13069B.

HIGINBOTTOM, G., Sergt., 8th Royal Fusiliers.

He volunteered in August, 1914, and in the same year was sent to France, where he served with distinction in many important engagements, including those at Mons, Cambrai, and the Somme.
He holds the Mons Star, General Service and Victory Medals, and was demobilised in January, 1919.
14, Marsden Road, Lower Edmonton, N.9   13069A.

HIGINBOTTOM, J. C., Pte., M.G.C.

He enlisted in July, 1919, on attaining military age, and after his period of training, was sent to Ireland on special duties with his unit.
14, Marsden Road, Lower Edmonton, N.9   13069C.

HIGINBOTTOM, W. J., Sergt., Middlesex Regt.

He was mobilised in August, 1914, having previously been in the Army and was soon sent to France, where he served with distinction throughout, taking part in many important engagements. During his service he was wounded four times (at Vermelles, Givenchy, Festubert and Monchy), and holds the 1914 Star and General Service and Victory Medals.
13, Millbrook Road, Lower Edmonton, N.9   13960.

HILES, J. (M.M.), Sergt., 7th London Regiment.

He volunteered for service in May, 1915, and was drafted to the Western Front, where he took part in the engagements at Loos, Ypres, the Somme, Festubert, Givenchy and Cambrai, and was wounded in action four times. He was awarded the Military Medal for conspicuous bravery and devotion to duty in the field at High Wood.
He also holds the 1914–15 Star, General Service and Victory Medals, and was demobilised in February, 1919.
5, Bayonne Road, Hammersmith, W.6   14301.

HILL, A., Pte., Middlesex Regiment and Inniskilling Fusiliers.

Volunteering in March, 1915, he was sent to France in the same year. During his service on the Western Front he took part in engagements at Ypres, Loos, the Somme, Arras, Albert and Lille.
In January, 1919, he was demobilised. He holds the 1914–15 Star, General Service and Victory Medals.
296, Chapter Road, Cricklewood, N.W.2   16727.

HILL, A. A., Sergt., 3rd London Regiment (Royal Fusiliers).

Volunteering in September, 1914, he was employed on important duties in England on the completion of his training, but was, however, successful in obtaining his transfer in 1916 to the Western Front, where he took part in several engagements and was severely wounded. He was invalided home, being retained in hospital for a considerable period, and on his recovery remained at home on special duties until December, 1919, when he was demobilised, holding the General Service and Victory Medals.
8, Fermoy Road, Maida Hill, W.9   X19583.

HILL, A. C., Lce.-Cpl., Royal Fusiliers.

He volunteered in September 1914, and was retained on important duties with his unit until 1916, when he was sent to France. During his service he was actively engaged in various battle areas of the Western Front, and was killed in action on the Somme on July 14th 1916.
He was entitled to the General Service and Victory Medals.
100, Kimberley Road, Upper Edmonton, N.18   16786B.

HILL, A. E. (M.M.), C.S.M., 10th Sherwood Foresters.

He volunteered in August 1914, and was sent to Gallipoli, where he took a prominent part in the severe fighting on the Peninsula and was severely wounded. He was invalided home, being for a long period in hospital, but on his recovery was drafted to the Western Front, and saw much fighting, being again wounded.
For conspicuous bravery and devotion to duty in the field he was awarded the Military Medal, and, in addition, holds the 1914-15 Star, General Service and Victory Medals, being demobilised in February 1919.
34, Disbrowe Road, Hammersmith, W.6   15907.

HILL, A. J. W., Pte., Hampshire Regiment.

He volunteered in 1915, and after his training was engaged on important duties on the East Coast with an Anti-aircraft Section. He rendered valuable services during enemy air-raids, but was not successful in obtaining his transfer overseas owing to being medically unfit for foreign service, and was demobilised in September 1919, holding the General Service Medal.
100, Kimberley Road, Upper Edmonton, N.18   16786A.

HILL, A. W., Pte., 18th Australian Light Infty.

He volunteered in 1915, and in the same year was sent to Gallipoli, where he served through the campaign. On the evacuation of the Peninsula he was sent to France early in 1916, and, after taking part in many important engagements, died of wounds received in action at Bapaume in May 1917.
He was entitled to the 1914-15 Star, General Service and Victory Medals.
9, Rowallan Road, Munster Road, S.W.6   X19343B.

HILL, D. (Mrs.), Special War Worker.

During the war this lady rendered valuable services at Messrs. Eley Brother's, Edmonton, where she was engaged in connection with the output of munitions. Her work was of an arduous and responsible character, and she fulfilled her duties satisfactorily.
22, Westoe Road, Lower Edmonton, N.9   13126B.

HILL, E., Sergt., Middlesex Regiment.

He volunteered for service in 1914, and owing to special qualifications was retained on special duties with his unit until 1918, when he was drafted overseas. He was killed in action near Cambrai during the Advance of 1918, four weeks after landing in France.
He was entitled to the General Service and Victory Medals.
40, Ilex Road, Willesden, N.W.10   16740A.

HILL, E., Petty Officer, Royal Navy.

He was mobilised in August 1914, and served with the Grand Fleet in the North Sea. During his service he was in H.M. Ships " St. George," " Swiftsure " and " Bonaventure," and rendered distinguished services.
In March 1919, he was demobilised, and holds the 1914 Star, General Service, Victory, Coronation and Good Conduct Medals.
31, Monmouth Road, Lower Edmonton, N.9   13023.

HILL, E. C., Driver, Royal Field Artillery.

He volunteered in 1915, and was sent to France the same year. During his service on this Front he was in action at Ypres, Loos and the Somme, was wounded, and later suffered from shell-shock. In 1918, in consequence of his wounds, he was discharged as medically unfit for further service. He holds the 1914-15 Star, General Service and Victory Medals. 9, Rowallan Road, Munster Road, S.W.6 X19343A.

HILL, F., Gunner, Royal Field Artillery.

He volunteered in October 1915, and, after his training, was sent to the Western Front, where he took part in many important engagements in various sectors.
He was demobilised in March 1919, and holds the General Service and Victory Medals.
86, Adeney Road, Hammersmith, W.6   14465.

HILL, F., Pte., Royal Fusiliers.

He volunteered in August 1914, and on completion of his training was sent to France, where he was wounded during the fighting in 1916. He was invalided home, and upon his recovery was again drafted to the Western Front, but was killed in action on April 23rd, 1917.
He was entitled to the 1914-15 Star, General Service and Victory Medals.
13, Knivet Road, Walham Green, S.W.6   X19430A.

11

HILL, F. W., Pte., Royal Fusiliers and Royal Dublin Fusiliers.

He volunteered in 1915, and was sent to the Western Front, where, during his two years' service overseas he took part in many important engagements, and was wounded.
In March 1919, he was demobilised, but in February, 1920, he rejoined the Army in the Royal Dublin Fusiliers. He holds the General Service and Victory Medals.
13, Conley Road, Willesden, N.W.10.   15523.

HILL, G. H., Pte., R.A.S.C. (M.T.).

He volunteered in August 1915, and after a short period of training, was drafted to the Western Front. Throughout his service overseas he did excellent work with the Mechanical Transport Section in various battle areas, including Hill 60, Ypres, Loos and the Somme, and in 1918 was severely wounded at Cambrai.
He returned to England, and in November of the same year was invalided out of the Service owing to his wounds. He holds the 1914-15 Star, General Service and Victory Medals.
114, Chippenham Road, Maida Hill, W.9   X20775.

HILL, G. R., Pte., R.A.S.C. and 1st Wiltshire Regt.

He joined for service in 1916 in the R.A.S.C., and after his training was retained on important duties with his unit. He was later transferred to the Wiltshire Regiment, and sent to France in 1918, taking an active part in the fighting during the Retreat and Advance of that year. He was buried by shell-fire, and in consequence suffered from shell-shock. He was demobilised in 1919, and holds the General Service and Victory Medals.
32, Stracey Road, Stonebridge Park, N.W.10   15680B.

HILL, H., Pte., R.A.S.C. (M.T.), and Labour Corps.

He joined in April 1916, and in the following June was drafted to the Eastern Front. During his two years' service he was engaged in the operations on the Salonica Front, remaining there until December 1918. He was then sent home, and was employed on special duties until his demobilisation in April 1920.
He holds the General Service and Victory Medals.
20, Hiley Road, Willesden, N.W.10   X18698—X18654B.

HILL, H. R., Rifleman, 28th London Regiment (Artists' Rifles).

He volunteered in September 1914, and was drafted to the Western Front in the following year. During his service in this theatre of war he took part in many engagements, including those at Ypres and on the Somme. He was gassed while in action at Bullecourt, and in March 1919, was demobilised, holding the 1914-15 Star, General Service and Victory Medals.
85, Love Lane, Tottenham, N.17   X18311

HILL, H. T., Pte., 3rd Worcestershire Regiment.

He joined in July 1917, and having received training at various stations in England, was drafted to the Western Front, where he was killed in action during the Retreat in April 1918.
He was entitled to the General Service and Victory Medals.
22, Walham Avenue, Fulham Road, S.W.6   X20236.

HILL, J., Cpl., 1st (King's) Dragoon Guards.

He volunteered in August 1914, and during his service on the Western Front was in action at Loos, Neuve Chapelle, Armentières, Amiens, Ypres, Arras and Cambrai.
Owing to ill-health he was discharged in November 1915, and holds the 1914 Star, General Service and Victory Medals.
2, Mablethorpe Road, Munster Road, S.W.6   X19250.

HILL, J. F., Pte., R.A.S.C. (M.T.).

He volunteered for duty in September 1915, and was sent to the Western Front, where he took part in several engagements. During his service he contracted septic poisoning, and was invalided home. On his recovery he returned to France, remaining there till his demobilisation in August 1919.
He holds the 1915 Star, General Service and Victory Medals.
5, Rock Avenue, Fulham Road, S.W.6   X20222.

HILL, K. (Mrs.), Special War Worker.

During the war this lady offered her services at the Park Royal Munition Factory. While there she was engaged on dangerous work in the powder room, and as a result suffered from poisoning, and was in hospital several months.
She was worthy of the highest commendation for her valuable services.
63, Rayleigh Road, Hammersmith, W.6   12635.

HILL, L. (Miss), Special War Worker.

During the war this lady gave up her time voluntarily to knitting garments and comforts for soldiers on active service. She also gave valuable assistance to many war charities. Her patriotic services and work were very highly appreciated.
55, Berry Street, Willesden, N.W.10   14630A.

HILL, M. A., Cpl., 3rd (King's Own) Hussars.

He volunteered in August 1914, and was sent to the Western Front in the same year. During his service overseas, he took part in many important engagements, but while in action at Ypres he was killed on April 28th, 1917. He was entitled to the 1914 Star, General Service and Victory Medals.
95, Berry Street, Willesden, N.W.10   15545B.

HILL, P., S.M., R.G.A. and New Zealand Forces.

He was serving in the Royal Garrison Artillery at the outbreak of war, and after being retained on special duties at important stations, was transferred to the New Zealand Forces, and sent to Gallipoli in June 1915. After short, but gallant services there, he was killed in action on August 9th of the same year, and was entitled to the 1914-15 Star, General Service and Victory Medals.
39, Merville Road, Stonebridge Park, N.W.10   15661A.

HILL, R. V., Pte., Duke of Cornwall's L.I.

He volunteered for service in August 1914, and whilst in training preparatory to being drafted overseas, died of fever at Wareham on January 31st, 1916.
37, Bravington Road, Maida Hill, W.9   X19322A.

HILL, T., Pte., 6th Buffs (East Kent Regiment).

He joined for service in February 1917, and was drafted to the Western Front, where he took part in many important engagements, including the battles of the Somme, Ypres and Bullecourt. After being in action he suffered from shell-shock, and was in hospital for a time.
He holds the General Service and Victory Medals, and was demobilised in 1919.
55, Chesson Road, West Kensington, W.14   X17158.

HILL, T. H., Rifleman, Rifle Brigade.

He joined in 1916, and after his training was sent to France in the same year. During his service on the Western Front he took part in engagements on the Somme and at Vimy Ridge, Arras, Cambrai and St. Quentin, and was wounded in action at Vimy Ridge.
In December 1919 he was demobilised, and holds the General Service and Victory Medals.
22, Tasso Road, Hammersmith, W.6   14649.

HILL, W., Special War Worker.

For a period of four years during the war, he rendered valuable services as a charge hand at the munition works of Messrs. Eley Brother's, Edmonton. He carried out his duties throughout in a thorough and capable manner.
22, Westoe Road, Lower Edmonton, N.9   13126A.

HILL, W., Pte., 7th London Regiment.

He volunteered in 1915, and after completing his training was sent to the Western Front, where he took part in many important engagements, and was killed in action on June 3rd, 1917.
He was entitled to the General Service and Victory Medals.
13, Knivet Road, Walham, Green, S.W.6   X19430B.

HILL, W. F., 1st-Class Stoker, Royal Navy.

He was already in the Navy at the outbreak of war, and served with his ship in the North Sea. He was in H.M.S. "Queen Mary," at the battle of Jutland, and was drowned when his vessel was sunk by the German High Seas Fleet. He had served for six years in the Navy, and was entitled to the 1914 Star, General Service and Victory Medals.
20, Hiley Road, Willesden, N.W.10   X18698--X18654C.

HILL, W. H. G., Pte., Royal Fusiliers.

He enlisted in May 1914, and was sent to France a few months after the outbreak of the war. While on the Western Front he took part in the battles of Neuve Chapelle, Hill 60, Ypres, Loos, the Somme, Arras, Vimy Ridge, Bullecourt, and in the engagements during the Retreat and Advance of 1918. During his services he was wounded, and in 1919 was demobilised, holding the 1914-15 Star, General Service and Victory Medals.   77, Queen's Street, Hammersmith, W.6   14630C.

HILL, W. J., Cpl., Royal Engineers.

He was serving when war broke out and was at once drafted to the Western Front, where he remained for nearly five years. During this period he took part in the retreat from Mons, the battles of Neuve Chapelle, Loos, Arras, St. Quentin, Ypres and the Somme, and was severely wounded.
He holds the Mons Star, General Service and Victory Medals, and was demobilised in March 1919.
37, Bravington Road, Maida Hill, W.9   X19322B.

HILL, W. T., Sapper, Royal Engineers.

He joined in 1916, and after his training was sent to France in the following year. During his service on this Front he took part in several important operations and was employed on special duties.
In 1919 he was demobilised, and holds the General Service and Victory Medals.
40, Ilex Road, Willesden, N.W.10   16740B.

HILLIER, C., Driver, Royal Field Artillery.

He joined in September 1916, and in the following year was sent to France, where he took part in many important engagements, including the battle of Cambrai.
He was demobilised in January 1919, and holds the General Service and Victory Medals.
21, Aspenlea Road, Hammersmith, W.6   14293B.

HILLIER, C. J., Pte., Canadian Expeditionary Force.

He volunteered in 1914, and after being engaged on special duties at various stations, was sent to the Western Front in 1916, where he served in many engagements in different battle areas.
In 1919 he was demobilised, and holds the General Service and Victory Medals.
22, Ladysmith Road, Upper Edmonton, N.18.   16461B.

HILLIER, G. W., Cpl., Royal Field Artillery.

Being on the Reserve, he was mobilised at the outbreak of the war and sent to France, where he took part in the retreat from Mons and the battles of Ypres, the Somme, Arras, Vimy Ridge, Cambrai and Bullecourt.
He was wounded, and in January 1919 was demobilised, holding the General Service and Victory Medals.
25, Aspenlea Road, Hammersmith, W.6   14293A.

HILLIER, R., Cpl., Royal Field Artillery.

He enlisted in January 1914, and on the outbreak of war was sent to France. During his five years service he took part in the battles of Mons, Ypres, the Somme, Arras, Bullecourt and Cambrai, and in the engagements during the Advance of 1918.
In February 1920 he was demobilised, and holds the Mons Star, the General Service and Victory Medals.
21, Aspenlea Road, Hammersmith, W.6   14293C.

HILLIER, W. H., Pte., Middlesex Regiment.

He volunteered in 1914, and in the following year was drafted to India, where he served for four years, and was engaged on important duties at various stations. He was also in action on the N.W. Frontier.
He was demobilised in 1919, and holds the 1914-15 Star, General Service and Victory Medals, and the Indian General Service Medal with the Afghan (N.W. Frontier, 1919) clasp.
22, Ladysmith Road, Upper Edmonton, N.18   16461A.

HILLMAN, A., Sapper, Royal Engineers.

He volunteered in May 1915 in the 9th Middlesex Regiment, but was transferred to the Royal Defence Corps, and afterwards to the Royal Engineers. He was sent to France, taking part in engagements at Arras, Amiens and the Somme, and was later drafted to the East, where he served at Alexandria, Mustapha, Kantara, Ismailia and in Palestine.
Owing to ill-health, he was discharged as medically unfit for further service in July 1918, and holds the General Service and Victory Medals.
34, Leamore Street, Hammersmith, W.6   12580.

HILLS, G. W., Pte., Royal Army Service Corps.

He volunteered in February 1915, and in the same year was sent to the Western Front. While in this theatre of war he took part in many of the important engagements and was severely wounded in 1916. He was invalided home and was in hospital for a considerable period.
He was demobilised in February 1919, and holds the 1914-15 Star, General Service and Victory Medals.
31, Kennet Road, Maida Hill, W.9   X19458.

HILLS, H., Cpl., Wiltshire Regiment.

He joined in March 1917, and after a period of training was sent to the Western Front a year later. He took part in the Retreat of 1918, and was severely wounded in action at Messines.
He was invalided home, and eventually demobilised in September 1919, holding the General Service and Victory Medals.
64, Hawthorn Road, Willesden, N.W.10   X17422.

HILLS, J. B., Trooper, 1st Life Guards.

He volunteered in August 1914, and was sent to the Western Front in the following year. While in this theatre of war he served in the battles of Ypres, the Somme, Vimy Ridge and Cambrai, and was badly wounded and gassed. He was invalided home and was for a long period in hospital.
In March 1919 he was demobilised, and holds the 1914-15 Star, General Service and Victory Medals.
13, Ranelagh Road, Harlesden, N.W.10   12745.

HILLS, W. R., Pte., Royal Fusiliers.

He volunteered in August 1915, and in the following year was drafted to France, where he took part in many engagements, including the battles of the Somme and Ypres. He was taken prisoner at Ypres, and during his captivity suffered many privations.
On his release he was returned to England, and was demobilised in March 1919, and holds the General Service and Victory Medals.
2, Fane Place, West Kensington, W.14   15699.

HILTON, F. J., Pte., Middlesex Regiment.

He volunteered in September 1914, and in the following year was sent to India. He remained there for nearly three years, and during this time was engaged on special duties at various important stations. He was then sent to Mesopotamia, where he took part in many engagements during the Turkish retreat. He returned to England and was demobilised in March 1919, holding the 1914-15 Star, General Service and Victory Medals.

6, Bridge Road, Willesden, N.W.10   15465A.

HINCE, A. S., Cpl., Devonshire Regiment.

He joined in 1916, and after completing his training was sent to the Western Front. During his service there he took a prominent part in engagements at Albert, the Somme, Montdidier, Arras, Armentières, Ypres, and during the Advance of 1918.

He returned to England after the signing of the Armistice, and was demobilised in 1919, holding the General Service and Victory Medals.

64, Bronsart Road, Fulham, S.W.6   X18895B.

HINCE, E. M. (Mrs.), Special War Worker.

During the early part of the war this lady was engaged on work of national importance in connection with the manufacture of cartridges at Messrs. Eley Brothers' Munition Factory, at Edmonton. She later went to work at a large military equipment factory. Throughout her services she did very useful work and carried out her duties with great care.

64, Bronsart Road, Fulham, S.W.6   X18895A.

HINCKLEY, H. F., Cpl., Northamptonshire Regt.

He joined in 1916, and after a period of training was sent to France later in the same year. During his three years overseas he gave valuable services with the Labour Corps, and was engaged in the battle of the Somme and in the Ypres sector. In March 1919 he returned to England, and was retained on special duty at various stations until his demobilisation in August.

He holds the General Service and Victory Medals.

19, Purves Road, Kensal Rise, N.W.10   X18018.

HINDMARSH, A. G., 1st Air Mechanic, R.A.F. (late R.N.A.S.)

He joined in June 1917, and after his period of training was retained on special duties in connection with the building of seaplane stations. His services were of a highly technical nature, but he was not successful in obtaining his transfer overseas before the cessation of hostilities.

He was demobilised in February 1919.

7, Nelson Road, Lower Edmonton, N.9   13290A.

HINE, J. F. C., Driver, Royal Field Artillery.

He volunteered in October 1914, and in the following year was sent to France, where he served in many important engagements, including the battles of Ypres and Loos. He remained in France until his return to England for demobilisation in June 1919, and holds the 1914-15 Star, General Service and Victory Medals

91, Sandringham Road, Cricklewood, N.W.2   X17135.

HINKINS, A. J., Pte., Middlesex Regiment.

He joined in February 1916, and later in the same year was sent to Salonica. During his services in this theatre of war he took a prominent part in many important engagements on the Balkan Fronts.

He was sent home for demobilisation in October 1919, and holds the General Service and Victory Medals.

21, Ray's Road, Upper Edmonton, N.18   15360.

HINTON, J., Special War Worker.

At the outbreak of war he was 65 years of age, but he offered his services at the Park Royal Munition Works, and was there engaged on responsible work in the inspection department, where he carried out his arduous duties with great energy and care.

59, Chesson Road, West Kensington, W.14   X17154.

HITCHCOCK, W., Cpl., R.A.S.C.

He joined in April 1916, and after completing his training was drafted overseas. He was engaged on important duties in various sectors of the Western Front, and after the signing of the Armistice went to Germany with the Army of Occupation, remaining there until his demobilisation in October 1919.

He holds the General Service and Victory Medals.

62, Grosvenor Road, Lower Edmonton, N.9   11993.

HITCHCOX, A. E., Pte., 7th London Regiment.

He joined in December 1916, and during his service in France, to which front he was drafted in the following year, took part in heavy fighting at Neuve Chapelle, Loos, Vimy Ridge, Amiens and St. Quentin.

He holds the General Service and Victory Medals, and was demobilised in February 1919.

18, Musard Road, Hammersmith, W.6   15315.

HITCHINER, H. W., 2nd Officer, Mercantile Fleet Auxiliary.

Volunteering in August 1914, he saw much service in the North Sea with the Grand Fleet. He also took part in the battle of the Falkland Isles and the raid on Zeebrugge, rendering distinguished services. In March 1919 he was demobilised, holding the 1914 Star, General Service and Victory Medals.

33, Cedars Road, Lower Edmonton, N.9   T14028.

HITCHING, A. C., Driver, Royal Field Artillery.

He volunteered in December 1914, and during his training met with a serious accident. While at work he was crushed by his horse against a wall, and after several months in hospital was discharged in July of the following year as medically unfit for further military service.

21, Westbury Road, Willesden, N.W.10   15067B.

HITCHING, J., Gunner, Royal Field Artillery.

He volunteered in 1914, and was sent to the Western Front in the following February. During his four years' service there he took part in many important engagements, including those at Loos, Ypres, the Somme and Cambrai, and received a severe wound.

In January 1919 he was sent home for demobilisation, and holds the 1914-15 Star, General Service and Victory Medals.

21, Westbury Road, Willesden, N.W.10   15067A.

HITCHMAN, G. L., Pte., Machine Gun Corps.

He joined in 1916, and after a short period of training was sent to France later in the same year. During his service on this front he took part in many engagements, but in November 1918, a few days before the Armistice, he died from wounds received in action.

He was entitled to the General Service and Victory Medals.

43, Roseberry Road, Lower Edmonton, N.9   14069C.

HITCHMAN, G. V. E., Pte., R.A.S.C. (M.T.)

He joined up in July 1916, and during his service was employed on special duties with the Mechanical Transport at various stations.

He did good work, but was unable to secure his transfer overseas before the signing of the Armistice, and was demobilised in December 1919.

17, Portnall Road, Maida Hill, W.9   X19306.

HITCHMAN, W., Pte., Yorkshire Regiment.

He volunteered in 1915, and later in the same year was sent to the Western Front, where he took part in many important engagements, and was killed in action on September 15th, 1918, during the advance in the La Bassée sector.

He was entitled to the 1914-15 Star, General Service and Victory Medals.

43, Roseberry Road, Lower Edmonton, N.9   14069B.

HITT, C. E., Cpl., R.A.M.C. and R.A.S.C.

Having served in the Army prior to the war, he volunteered for service immediately on the outbreak of hostilities, and was sent to the Western Front, where he took part in the retreat from Mons and the battles of Ypres, Loos, Arras and Cambrai. He was later transferred to the R.A.S.C., and was employed on special duties of an important nature with that unit until the signing of the Armistice.

In February 1919 he was demobilised, and holds the Mons Star, General Service and Victory Medals.

25, Bramber Road, West Kensington, W.14   16277.

HIXSON, A., A.B., Merchant Service.

He volunteered in May 1915, and was engaged on important coastal patrol work and submarine chasing in the Mediterranean. He was later drafted to Egypt to the Canal Defence Flotilla, and while there took part in several actions against the Turks. He was also engaged on dangerous mine-laying duties.

In 1919 he was demobilised, and holds the Mercantile Marine, General Service and Victory Medals.

5, Ravensworth Road, College Park, N.W.10   X17616.

HOAR, S. A. (Mrs.), Special War Worker.

During the war this lady was engaged on work of national importance in the T.N.T. shop at the Park Royal Munition Factory. Her duties, which were of a dangerous nature, were carried out with efficiency, and she was promoted to the responsible position of charge hand for her splendid work.

92, Bronsart Road, Fulham, S.W.6   X19002.

HOARE, A. M. (Miss), Special War Worker.

In order to release a man for military service this lady offered her services as a ticket-collector on the London Electric Railway and did useful work. She later went to the Park Royal Munition Factory, where she was engaged on important duties in the bullet inspection department. During her time there she contracted an illness from which she died in July 1918, after rendering valuable services.

14, Berry Street, Willesden, N.W.10   15548C.

HOARE, F., Petty Officer, R.N.A.S.

He volunteered in October 1915, and was sent to Northern Russia with the armoured car section in the following month. He served there for a period and was then sent to Roumania, where, after taking a prominent part in the operations on that Front, was killed in action in April 1917.
He was entitled to the 1914-15 Star, General Service and Victory Medals.
43, Strode Road, Willesden, N.W.10   17218B.

HOARE, G., Special War Worker.

During the war he held a responsible position at the Park Royal Munition Works, where he was engaged in the packing department.
His duties were carried out in a very capable manner and he rendered valuable services.
14, Berry Street, Willesden, N.W.10   15548A.

HOARE, L. (Mrs.), Special War Worker.

During the earlier part of the war this lady was engaged on important duties at the Park Royal National Filling Factory, where she worked in the shell and fuse-filling departments. After doing valuable work there she went to a large Willesden garage and held the responsible position of a forewomen. She carried out her duties in a very capable manner and received commendation for her useful services.
14, Berry Street, Willesden, N.W.10   15548B.

HOBBIS, C., Pte., West Yorkshire Regiment and Middlesex Regiment.

He joined in June 1917, and later in the same year was sent to the Italian Front, where he took part in the operations on the Piave. He was then drafted to Gibraltar, and was engaged on important garrison duties.
He holds the General Service and Victory Medals.
32, Yuletide Road, Willesden, N.W.10   15077A.

HOBBIS, C., Pte., 18th Middlesex Regiment.

He volunteered in March 1915, and was sent in the same year to the Western Front, where, during his four years' service, he fought at Ypres, Loos, Arras, the Somme, Cambrai and St. Quentin.
In January 1919 he was demobilised, and holds the 1914-15 Star, General Service and Victory Medals.
32, Yuletide Road, Willesden, N.W.10   15077B.

HOBBS, L. H., Pte., 4th Royal Fusiliers.

He joined in March 1918 on attaining military age, and after his training served with his unit at various stations on important duties. He was not successful in obtaining his transfer overseas before the cessation of hostilities, but in September, 1919, was sent to Mesopotamia.
1, Essex Road, Willesden, N.W.10   15936.

HOBBS, N., Pte., Royal Gloucestershire Hussars.

He joined in April 1917, and was drafted to the Western Front, where he took part in many important engagements. He was later sent to the Eastern theatre of war, and served in the Palestine campaign. He suffered from malaria, and died at Damascus on October 16th, 1918.
He was entitled to the General Service and Victory Medals.
14, Purcell Crescent, Fulham, S.W.6   14844.

HOCKIN, S., Lce.-Cpl., R.A.S.C.

He volunteered in 1914, and in the following year was sent to France. After serving there for a time he was drafted to Salonica, where he took part in important operations throughout the campaign in the Balkans and was wounded. He remained in this theatre of war until January 1919, when he was sent home for demobilisation.
He holds the 1914-15 Star, General Service and Victory Medals.
44, Mozart Street, North Kensington, W.10   X18830.

HOCKLEY, A. J., Pte., Royal Berkshire Regiment.

He volunteered in 1915, and in the same year was sent to the Western Front, where he was severely wounded in action at the battle of Loos. He was invalided home, and after continuous hospital treatment in England and Ireland, during which time he had five operations, he was discharged in 1917 as medically unfit for further service.
He holds the 1914-15 Star, General Service and Victory Medals.
51, Chesson Road, West Kensington, W 14   X17159.

HOCKLEY, G., Armourers' Crew Warrant Officer, Royal Navy.

Volunteering in June 1915, he served in H.M.S. " Warrior," and took part in the battle of Jutland. While in H.M.S. " Fearless " in the North Sea his ship was damaged in a collision with a submarine during a fog.
In January 1919 he was demobilised, and holds the 1914-15 Star, General Service and Victory Medals.
108, Sherbrooke Road, Fulham, S.W.6   18757.

HOCKRIDGE, A. J., Pte., Royal Fusiliers.

He joined in August 1917, and after his training was sent overseas to the Western Front at the beginning of the German offensive in March 1918. He served throughout the Retreat and Advance of that year and was wounded.
He was demobilised in November 1919 and holds the General Service and Victory Medals.
6, Milton Avenue, Stonebridge Park, N.W.10   14112B.

HOCKRIDGE, J., Cpl., Royal Engineers.

He volunteered in November 1915, and was sent to the Western Front in the same month. While there he was engaged on important duties with a Tunnelling Company and gave valuable services.
In February 1919 he was demobilised, and holds the 1914-15 Star, General Service and Victory Medals.
6, Milton Avenue, Stonebridge Park, N.W.10   14112A.

HOCKRIDGE, W., A.B., Royal Navy.

He was serving when the war broke out, and went with his ship to the North Sea. He was with H.M.S. " Hampshire " prior to her being sunk with Lord Kitchener on board. He took part in the battle of Jutland and also saw much service in the Mediterranean Sea. Later he served in Indian waters in submarine " L.5," and holds the 1914 Star, General Service and Victory Medals.
He has ten years' service in the Navy.
6, Milton Avenue, Stonebridge Park, N.W.10   14112C.

HODDER, A. E., Pte., East Surrey Regiment.

He volunteered in 1914, and in the following year was sent to France, where he took part in many important engagements. In 1916 he was invalided home with severe illness, and was in hospital for some time.
In 1918 he was discharged as medically unfit for further service owing to ill-health, and holds the 1914-15 Star, General Service and Victory Medals.
54, Holly Lane, Willesden, N.W.10   15403A.

HODDER, R., Pte., Middlesex Regiment.

He volunteered in 1914, and later in the same year was sent to the Western Front. During his service overseas he took part in many important engagements, and was twice in hospital suffering from shell-shock.
In 1919 he was demobilised, and holds the 1914 Star, General Service and Victory Medals.
54, Holly Lane, Willesden, N.W.10   15403B.

HODDLE, R. J., A.B., Royal Navy, H.M.S. " Temeraire."

He joined in 1917, and served with his ship in the North Sea on important patrol duties. He was also engaged on dangerous convoy work with ships crossing the English Channel, carrying supplies, munitions and troops.
He holds the General Service and Victory Medals.
83, Barret's Green Road, Willesden, N.W.10   13562.

HODGES, A. J., Sergt., Royal Horse Artillery.

Having enlisted in 1908, he remained in India, where he was already serving at the outbreak of war, until 1915, when he was sent to France. While on the Western Front he took part in several important engagements, including the battles of the Somme, Ypres and Loos.
In January, 1919, he was discharged after ten years' service, and holds the 1914 Star, General Service and Victory Medals.
43, Shorrolds Road, Walham Green, S.W.6.   X19346.

HODGES, C. W., Pte., Middlesex Regiment.

He volunteered in 1914, and after his training was sent to Egypt in the following year. He served in operations there for nearly 12 months, and was then sent to Salonica, where he took part in many important engagements against the Bulgarians. He remained in the Balkans for three years, and was then invalided home.
In September 1919 he was demobilised, and holds the 1914-15 Star, General Service and Victory Medals.
25, Sheldon Road, Upper Edmonton, N.18   X17306.

HODGES, J. R., Cpl., Royal Fusiliers and R.A.F.

In August 1914 he was mobilised with the Royal Fusiliers, and was sent to the Western Front in the following January. He took part in the battle of Neuve Chapelle in March 1915, and was severely wounded. After a long period in hospital he was invalided home, and on recovery was attached to the R.A.F., and having been certified medically unfit for service overseas, was retained at various aerodromes, where his duties called for a high degree of technical skill.
In February 1919 he was demobilised, and holds the 1914-15 Star, General Service and Victory Medals.
61, Hiley Road, Willesden, N.W.10   X18169.

HODGETTS, J. E., Lce.-Cpl., R.A.S.C. (M.T.)

He volunteered in April 1915, and in the same year was sent to the Western Front, where he took part in operations at Ypres, Loos, Vimy Ridge, the Somme, Amiens and St. Quentin. During his service he was badly gassed and invalided home, but on his recovery he was again drafted to the Western Front, remaining there until his demobilisation in February 1919.
He holds the 1914-15 Star, General Service and Victory Medals.
31a, Bronsart Road, Fulham, S.W.6   X19008.

HODGKINSON, S. C., Pte., Royal Fusiliers.

In February 1916 he joined for service, and after his period of training was sent to France in the following year. During his service on the Western Front he fought at Vimy Ridge and Cambrai, but during an engagement at Arras he was taken prisoner and suffered many hardships while in captivity. After his release he returned to England and was demobilised in March 1919.
He holds the General Service and Victory Medals.
15, Barry Road, Stonebridge Park, N.W.10   14621.

HODGSON, J. E., Bombardier, R.F.A.

He volunteered in August 1914, and in the same year was drafted to the Western Front. He took part in numerous engagements, including those at Ypres, Arras, Albert, Vimy Ridge and Armentières, and during his service was wounded three times.
In June 1919 he was demobilised, and holds the 1914 Star, General Service and Victory Medals.
41, Clarendon Street, Paddington, W.2   X20638.

HODSALL, F., Sapper, Royal Engineers.

He volunteered in August 1914, and early in the following year was sent to France, where he took part in important operations on the Somme, at Ypres, Arras, Armentières and during the Retreat and Advance of 1918.
He was demobilised in February 1917, holding the 1914-15 Star, General Service and Victory Medals.
8, Meyrick Road, Willesden, N.W.10   16348.

HODSON, J., 2nd Air Mechanic, R.A.F.

He joined in August 1916, and after completing his training as a mechanic was retained on special duties at a large aeroplane factory. He gave valuable services but was unsuccessful in obtaining his transfer overseas before the cessation of hostilities.
His duties required high technical skill, and he was demobilised in February 1919.
40, Brownlow Road, Willesden, N.W.10   15009.

HODSON, J. F., Driver, R.F.A.

Volunteering in May 1915, he served on the Western Front from the following September until 1919, and took part in many engagements. He was awarded the French Croix de Guerre for conspicuous gallantry in rescuing a gun and ammunition under heavy fire, and holds the 1914-15 Star, General Service and Victory Medals, being demobilised in June 1919.
13, Gowan Road, Willesden Green, N.W.10   X16970A.

HODSON, R. W., Cpl., 2nd West York. Regt.

He joined in July 1917, and was drafted to the Western Front in the following April. While in this theatre of war he took part in the heavy fighting during the Retreat and Advance of 1918, and in January 1920 was demobilised, holding the General Service and Victory Medals.
13, Gowan Road, Willesden, N.W.10   X16970B.

HOGAN, D. A., Gunner, Royal Garrison Artillery.

Joining in November 1917, he was soon sent to the Western Front, where he took part in several engagements, and contracted a serious illness which caused him to be sent to hospital. On his recovery he was drafted to Gibraltar and was employed on garrison duty.
Having met with an accident, he was again sent to hospital, and in February 1919 was demobilised on his return to England, holding the General Service and Victory Medals.
84, Sherbrooke Road, Fulham, S.W.6   X18752.

HOGGAR, A. W., Pte., Grenadier Guards.

He joined in November 1916, and was sent to France in the same year. During his three years on the Western Front he took part in many important engagements, and was three times wounded. He spent a long period in hospital in France and was then invalided to England. On recovery he again went to France, where he remained until his demobilisation in January 1919.
Shortly after he re-enlisted in the R.A.F., and holds the General Service and Victory Medals.
27, Argyle Road, Upper Edmonton, N.18   15266.

HOLDEN, H. W., Pte., Middlesex Regiment.

He volunteered in 1915, and after his training was retained on important duties with his unit at various stations. He gave valuable services, but was unsuccessful in obtaining his transfer overseas before hostilities ceased.
He was demobilised in 1919.
15, Monmouth Road, Lower Edmonton, N.9   12988.

HOLDER, F., Pte., Middlesex Regiment.

He volunteered in September 1914, and after his training was retained on important duties with his unit at various stations. He gave valuable services but was unsuccessful in obtaining his transfer overseas.
He contracted an illness while on duty and died from the effects in November 1915.
89, Deacon Road, Cricklewood, N.W.2   16702A.

HOLDER, J., Driver, R.A.S.C. (M.T.)

He volunteered in January 1915, and after his period of training was sent to India in the following year, but was later sent to Mesopotamia, where during his services he was engaged on transport duties in several operations on that Front.
In April 1919 he was demobilised, and holds the General Service and Victory Medals.
43, Hazel Road, Willesden, N.W.10   X17598A.

HOLDER, L. J., Cpl., Middlesex Regiment.

He volunteered in January 1916, and after his training was retained on important duties on the coast with his unit. He gave valuable services, but was unsuccessful in obtaining his transfer overseas owing to heart trouble.
He was demobilised in January 1919.
89, Deacon Road, Cricklewood, N.W.2   16702B.

HOLDFORD, T., Pte., Middlesex Regiment.

He volunteered in April 1915, and in the following September was sent to France, where during his three years' service he took part in engagements at La Bassée, Ypres, the Somme, Arras and Cambrai, and was twice wounded. He also served in Italy for a short time, but was soon sent back to the Western Front.
He holds the 1914-15 Star, General Service and Victory Medals, and was demobilised in March 1919.
30, Hazel Road, Willesden, N.W.10   X17789.

HOLDWAY, H., Pte., Devonshire Regiment.

He volunteered in May 1915, and after his training was sent in the same year to the Western Front, where he took part in many important engagements, and was killed in action on March 23rd, 1916. He is buried at Becordel Military Cemetery, near Albert, and was entitled to the 1914-15 Star, General Service and Victory Medals.
12, Bayonne Road, Hammersmith, W.6   T14989.

HOLE, H. (D.C.M.), C.S.M., King's Royal Rifles.

He volunteered in 1915, and early in the following year was sent to the Western Front, where he took part in many important engagements, including the battle of the Somme. In September 1917 he was awarded the Distinguished Conduct Medal for conspicuous gallantry and devotion to duty at Bucquoy, but was killed in action at the beginning of the German Offensive on March 21st, 1918.
He was also entitled to the General Service and Victory Medals. 29, Beaufoy Road, Tottenham, N.17   X18003.

HOLLAND, A., Pte., R.A.S.C. (M.T.)

He joined in March 1917, and owing to his special qualifications as a fitter, was retained on important duties with his unit at various stations. He was unsuccessful in obtaining his transfer overseas before the signing of the Armistice, but early in 1919 he was sent to France on special duties, and remained there until demobilised in November of that year.
8, Harlesden Road, N.W.10   X17429.

HOLLAND, G. W., Pte., 13th London Regiment (Kensingtons).

He volunteered in May 1915, and later in the same year was drafted to the Western Front, where he took part in many engagements, including those at Loos, the Somme, Neuve Chapelle and St. Quentin. Later he was transferred to Salonica, and was actively engaged in the operations on the Balkan Front, and was wounded in action. Upon his recovery he was sent to Palestine, and entered Jerusalem with General Allenby's forces. While in Palestine he contracted malaria, and on his return to England was demobilised in 1919, holding the 1914-15 Star, General Service and Victory Medals.
67, Dieppe Street, West Kensington, W.14   16423B.

HOLLAND, H. J., Driver, R.F.A.

He volunteered in March 1915, and in the following October was drafted to France. After a short period there he was sent to the Balkans, and took part in many important engagements, remaining on this Front until 1919.
He was then sent home and demobilised in July, holding the 1914-15 Star, General Service and Victory Medals.
32, Yewfield Road, Willesden, N.W.10   T16367.

HOLLAND, J., Pte., 19th London Regiment.

Volunteering in September 1914, he was sent to the Western Front in the following March, taking part in the battle of Loos in September 1915, and being badly wounded. On recovery he was drafted to Salonica, where he fought in the Balkans. From there he was sent in 1917 to Egypt, where he was engaged with General Allenby's forces against the Turks, and was present at the capture of Jerusalem.
In July 1919 he was demobilised, and holds the 1914-15 Star, General Service and Victory Medals.
26, Tubb's Road, Harlesden, N.W.10   12737.

HOLLAND, J. C. B., Cpl., Royal Engineers.

He joined in September 1916, and after his period of training was engaged on duties of an important nature at various stations with his unit. He gave valuable services, but was unsuccessful in obtaining his transfer overseas. During his service he carried out special duties in connection with submarines on trial trips.
He was demobilised in June 1919.
161, Purves Road, Kensal Rise, N.W.10   X18431.

HOLLAND, J. T., Pte., R.A.M.C.

Joining in August 1916, he was engaged on important duties with his unit at various stations, but was not successful in obtaining his transfer overseas before the cessation of hostilities.
After rendering valuable services, he was demobilised in May 1919.
150, Ilbert Street, Queen's Park Estate, W.10   X18676.

HOLLAND, J. W., Pte., Royal Fusiliers.

He volunteered in August 1914, and in the same year was sent to France, where he took part in the retreat from Mons and in the fighting around Armentières and Ypres. During his service he was twice wounded, and in January 1919 was demobilised, holding the Mons Star, General Service and Victory Medals.
47, Monmouth Road, Lower Edmonton, N.9   13089.

HOLLAND, S., Pte., Royal Fusiliers and Labour Corps.

He volunteered in May 1915, and after his training was sent to the Western Front, where he took part in many important engagements, and was wounded and gassed while in action in the battle of the Somme.
He was demobilised in April 1919, and holds the General Service and Victory Medals.
50, Bounces Road, Lower Edmonton, N.9   13946.

HOLLAND, V. (Miss), Special War Worker.

During the war this lady was engaged on responsible duties in the clerical department of the Australian Headquarters in London. She carried out her work very efficiently, and was commended for her useful services.
67, Dieppe Street, West Kensington, W.14   16423A.

HOLLAND, W. A., Pte., Middlesex Regiment.

He volunteered in August 1914, and on completing his training was sent to the Dardanelles in the following year. He served throughout the Gallipoli campaign, and after the evacuation of the Peninsula was drafted to Egypt, where he remained until 1918.
He holds the 1914-15 Star, General Service and Victory Medals.
115, Winchester Road, Lower Edmonton, N.9   14960.

HOLLAND, W. G., Pte., Bedfordshire Regiment.

He joined in 1918 on attaining military age, and after his period of training was retained on important duties with his unit at various stations. He gave valuable services, but was unsuccessful in obtaining his transfer overseas prior to the Armistice. On the cessation of hostilities he went to Germany with the Army of Occupation, and remained there until January 1920, when he was demobilised.
42, Shelley Road, Willesden, N.W.10   13650A.

HOLLAND, W. H., Gunner, R.G.A.

He joined in August 1916, and after completing his training served with his unit on important duties at various stations. He rendered valuable services, but was unsuccessful in obtaining his transfer overseas before hostilities ceased, and was demobilised in January 1919.
42, Shelley Road, Willesden, N.W.10   13650B.

HOLLELY, E. W., Rifleman, K.R.R.

He volunteered in 1915, and served on the Western Front, where he took part in the battles of Arras and Cambrai and in fighting around Ypres. He was severely wounded at Cambrai, and was invalided home, where he was in hospital for a long time. He was also gassed during his service overseas.
In February 1919 he was demobilised, holding the General Service and Victory Medals.
10, Bayonne Road, Hammersmith, W.6   T14990

HOLLEY, J., Air Mechanic, R.A.F.

He joined in 1918 on reaching military age, and after completing his training he served at various stations on important duties, which called for a high degree of technical skill. He gave valuable services, but was unable to obtain his transfer overseas before the signing of the Armistice.
He was demobilised in 1919.
12, Pretoria Road, Upper Edmonton, N.18   X17020.

HOLLINGSWORTH, A. W., Pte., Essex Regt.

He volunteered in August 1914, and was sent to France in the following year. During his service on this Front he took part in important engagements near Armentières, Ypres (where he was gassed), and on the Somme, where he was badly wounded in July 1916. He was invalided home, and after a long period in hospital was discharged as medically unfit for further service owing to his wounds.
He holds the 1914-15 Star, General Service and Victory Medals.
40, Leamore Street, Hammersmith, W.6   12582.

HOLLIS, T. W., Cpl., Royal Engineers.

He volunteered in June 1915, and in the following September was drafted to the Western Front. During his four years' service in this theatre of war he was engaged on important railway and defence works during the operations in the Ypres, Somme and Arras sectors.
He was demobilised in April 1919, and holds the 1914-15 Star, General Service and Victory Medals.
6, Vallier Road, College Park, N.W.10   X17682.

HOLLISS, J. H., Driver, Royal Field Artillery.

He volunteered in 1914, and was sent to the Western Front early in the following year. While on service there his health broke down, and he was invalided home and discharged as medically unfit for further service in 1915.
He holds the 1914-15 Star, General Service and Victory Medals.
65, Redfern Road, Willesden, N.W.10   13196.

HOLLISTER, C. E., Gunner, R.G.A.

He volunteered in January 1915, and in the following August was sent to France, where he took part in important engagements on the Somme. He was then drafted to Egypt, but after a short time there returned to France, and was badly wounded in the battle of Ypres in 1917.
He was invalided home and discharged as medically unfit for further service in May 1918 owing to his wound.
He holds the 1914-15 Star, General Service and Victory Medals.
59, Carlyle Avenue, Willesden, N.W.10   14191.

HOLLOWAY, B., Cpl., Middlesex Regiment.

He volunteered in August 1914, and in the same year was sent to India, where he served on the North-Western Frontier. He was later transferred to Mesopotamia, and took part in several important engagements there, including the attempted relief of Kut.
In 1919 he was sent home and demobilised in February, holding the 1914 Star, General Service and Victory Medals.
6, Brett Road, Stonebridge Park, N.W.10   14384B.

HOLLOWAY, E. W., Lce.-Cpl., Norfolk Regt.

He volunteered in August 1914, and in November of the same year was sent to the North Western Frontier of India, where he took part in local operations. He was later sent to Mesopotamia, and served during important operations there, and was killed in action at Kut-el-Amara on December 1st, 1915.
He was entitled to the 1914 Star, General Service and Victory Medals.
6, Brett Road, Stonebridge Park, N.W.10   14384A.

HOLLOWAY, F. S. (Mrs.), Special War Worker.

During the war this lady offered her services to the Post Office Authorities in order to release a man for military service. She held a responsible position at the Earl's Court Road Post Office, and carried out her work in a capable manner.
47, Mulgrave Road, Fulham, S.W.6   16187B.

HOLLOWAY, F. W., Pte., The Queen's (Royal West Surrey Regiment).

He volunteered in October 1914, and in the following year was sent to France, where he fought in the battle of Loos in September. He was taken prisoner in this engagement and was in captivity in Germany and Russia, suffering many hardships.
Upon his release in January 1919 he returned to England and was demobilised, and holds the 1914-15 Star, General Service and Victory Medals.
47, Mulgrave Road, Fulham, S.W.6   16187A.

HOLLOWAY, J. E., Pte., Middlesex Regiment.

He joined in March 1916 at the age of 18, and after his training served with his unit on important duties at various stations until February of the following year. He was then released from military service, owing to his special qualifications, in order to take up work of national importance at Woolwich Arsenal, where for the remainder of the war he rendered valuable services.

6, Brett Road, Stonebridge Park, N.W.10   14384C.

HOLLOWAY, T., Leading Seaman, Royal Navy.

Volunteering in 1914 he saw service afloat, and was stationed at Bermuda. Subsequently he was engaged in transporting munitions of war to the fighting areas. During the war he served in H.M. Ships "East Wales" and "Clan Ranald." While in the former his vessel was torpedoed and sunk, but he was saved. He was demobilised in 1919, and holds the 1914–15 Star, General Service and Victory Medals.

61, Steele Road, Willesden, N.W.10   14145—14146A.

HOLMAN, J. W., Pte., Wiltshire Regiment.

He volunteered in February 1915 and was drafted overseas in the same year. He took part in many engagements on the Western Front and was killed in action at Hooge on September 26th, 1915.

He was entitled to the 1914–15 Star, General Service and Victory Medals.

67a, Drayton Road, Harlesden, N.W.10   14998.

HOLMES, A. C., Pte., Essex Regiment.

Volunteering in July 1915 he was sent in the following December to Egypt, where during four years' service he took part in many important engagements and was twice wounded. In November 1919 he was demobilised, and holds the 1914–15 Star, General Service and Victory Medals.

91, Manor Park Road, Harlesden, N.W.10   13216.

HOLMES, C. A., Cpl., Machine Gun Corps.

He joined in 1916, and in the same year was sent to France, where he took a prominent part in many important engagements, including those at Ypres and Cambrai, and was twice wounded.

In 1919 he was demobilised, and holds the General Service and Victory Medals.

43, Shorrolds Road, Walham Green, S.W.6   X19348.

HOLMES, C. W., Sapper, Royal Engineers.

He joined in March 1917, and later in the same year was sent to the Western Front. During his service in this theatre of war he took part in many important engagements, including the Retreat and Advance of 1918.

He remained in France until June 1919, when he was sent home for demobilisation. He holds the General Service and Victory Medals.

29, Hawthorn Road, Upper Edmonton, N.18   X17052.

HOLMES, D., Pte., Duke of Wellington's (West Riding Regiment).

Called up from the Reserve at the outbreak of war, he was sent to France, where he took part in the retreat from Mons. At the battle of Ypres he was so severely wounded that he was invalided to England, and discharged in August 1915, after being for some months in hospital.

He holds the Mons Star, General Service and Victory Medals.

3, Linton Road, Upper Edmonton, N.18   TX17280.

HOLMES, F. G., Pte., R.A.S.C. (M.T.)

Volunteering in August 1914 on the outbreak of war, he was engaged on special duties with his unit, after completing his training, until March 1915. He was then discharged owing to ill-health, being medically unfit for further service. After his demobilisation he was engaged on important work at a large aeroplane factory, and rendered valuable services.

20, Kingwood Road, Fulham, S.W.6   X19030.

HOLMES, J. S., Rifleman, 16th London Regt. (Queen's Westminster Rifles).

Volunteering in May 1915, he was engaged on important duties with his regiment at various stations on the completion of his training. He rendered valuable services, but owing to heart trouble was unable to secure his transfer overseas, and in 1917 was discharged as medically unfit.

14, Gloucester Road, Upper Edmonton, N.18   X17003.

HOLT, H., Cpl., Essex Yeomanry.

He volunteered in 1914, and after completing his training was drafted to France in the following year. He remained on this Front for four years, taking part during this time in many important operations.

In 1919 he was sent home for demobilisation, and holds the 1914–15 Star, General Service and Victory Medals.

31, Droop Street, Queen's Park Estate, W.10   X18581A.

HOLT, J., Special War Worker.

From the beginning of the war he was engaged as a skilled mechanic at Messrs. Cleaver & Berwick's aircraft factory, owing to his special capabilities. He rendered valuable services, carrying out his duties in a capable and efficient manner. Whilst at his work he met with a serious accident, and lost two of his fingers.

28, Steele Road, Willesden, N.W.10   14135B.

HOLT, M. (Mrs.), Special War Worker.

During the war this lady was employed in the canteen at the Park Royal Munition Factory, where she rendered very useful services. She was employed at this factory for about a year, and gave every satisfaction.

28, Steele Road, Willesden, N.W.10   14135A.

HOLTON, G. F., Pte., 2nd London Regiment (Royal Fusiliers).

He volunteered in September 1914, and was sent to Malta on garrison duty, where he stayed three months. He was then sent to France, taking part in engagements on the Somme, at Loos, Neuve Chapelle, Armentières, Amiens, Ypres, Vimy Ridge, Lille, and in the Advance of 1918. He was twice wounded during his service, and holds the 1915 Star, General Service and Victory Medals. He was demobilised in 1919.

3, Mirabel Road, Fulham, S.W.6   X17710.

HOLTON, R. C., 1st Air Mechanic, R.A.F.

Joining in May 1916, he completed his training in England, and was employed with his unit, where his high technical skill was particularly valuable. He was unable to obtain his transfer overseas before the cessation of hostilities, and was demobilised in January 1919.

234, Chapter Road, Cricklewood, N.W.2   X17127.

HOLTON, S. J. (Miss), Special War Worker.

During the war this lady was engaged as a ward-maid at the American Red Cross Military Hospital in London She carried out her duties in a painstaking and efficient manner, and received high commendation for her services.

3, Mirabel Road, Fulham, S.W.6   X17711.

HOLTON, W. W., Cpl., Royal Fusiliers.

He volunteered in June 1915, and was drafted to France later in the same year. During his four years' service overseas he took part in many important engagements, and was present at the battles of Cambrai and Ypres, and was badly gassed In September 1919 he was demobilised, and holds the 1914–15 Star, General Service and Victory Medals.

18, Cedars Road, Lower Edmonton, N.9   14356.

HOLYMAN, A. F. G., Pte., Hampshire Regt.

He volunteered in December 1914, and in the following year was sent to the Western Front, where he took part in many important engagements. On March 28th, 1918, he was killed in action at Arras.

He was entitled to the 1914–15 Star, General Service and Victory Medals.

40, Shakespeare Avenue, Willesden, N.W.10   13782.

HOMEWOOD, A., Special War Worker.

During the war this lady rendered valuable service of national importance at the factory of Messrs. Klingers, Tottenham, where she was employed in the manufacture of gas masks for eight months. She carried out her duties in a skilful manner, and received high commendation for her work.

34, Elsdon Road, Tottenham, N.17   18498B.

HOMEWOOD, L., 1st-Class Stoker, Royal Navy.

Called up from the Reserve in August 1914, he was sent to sea and served on H.M.S. "Recoon." Later he was transferred to H.M.S. "Warpole," with which ship he was serving in 1920. He saw considerable service, and holds the 1914 Star, General Service and Victory Medals.

34, Elsdon Road, Tottenham, N.17   X18498A.

HONE, C. T., Sergt., R.A.S.C. (M.T.)

He volunteered in 1915, and after a period of training was sent to the Western Front in the following year. During his service overseas he was engaged on important transport duties during the engagements at Ypres, the Somme, Arras, Cambrai and the Marne during the Retreat of 1918.

In March 1919 he was demobilised, and holds the General Service and Victory Medals.

6, Shelley Road, Willesden, N.W.10   13880A.

HONE, C. W., Pte., Middlesex Regiment.

He volunteered in August 1914, and was sent to France the same year, where he took part in the battles of Ypres and Neuve Chapelle. He was wounded at Ypres in 1915, and in consequence was invalided home. In 1918 he was again drafted to France, and took part in important engagements on the Somme, at Albert and Cambrai.

In 1919 he was demobilised, holding the 1914 Star, General Service and Victory Medals.

24, Brownlow Road, Willesden, N.W.10   15007A.

HONE, F. A., Rifleman, 13th King's Royal Rifles.

He volunteered in August 1914, and was sent to France in the same year. While on this Front he took part in engagements at Ypres, Neuve Chapelle, Loos, the Somme, Albert, St. Quentin and Le Cateau, and was wounded.
In January 1919 he was demobilised, and holds the 1914 Star, General Service and Victory Medals
24, Brownlow Road, Willesden, N.W.10   15007B.

HONE, H. (M.M.), Pte., R.A.M.C.

He volunteered in August 1914, and was drafted to France in the same year. While on this Front he served at Ypres, Lens, Loos, the Somme, Albert and Arras. In 1918 he was sent to Italy, and during the heavy fighting there, was awarded the Military Medal for conspicuous bravery and devotion to duty in the field.
He holds in addition the 1914 Star, General Service and Victory Medals, and was demobilised in December 1919.
24, Brownlow Road, Willesden, N.W.10   15007C.

HONEY, A., Pte., Royal Fusiliers.

He volunteered in December 1914, and was sent to France in the following year. He served on this Front until the cessation of hostilities, and during this time took part in many engagements.
In March 1919 he was demobilised, and holds the 1914–15 Star, General Service and Victory Medals.
53, Lintaine Grove, West Kensington, W.14   16824.

HONEYBUN, A., Cpl., East Lancashire Regt.

He volunteered in September 1914, and after his period of training was engaged on special duties until February 1916, when he was drafted to France. While on this Front he took part in the engagements at Albert, St. Quentin and Cambrai.
In March 1919 he was demobilised, and holds the General Service and Victory Medals.
35, Leopold Road, Willesden, N.W.10   14739.

HONNOR, A. T., Sapper, Royal Engineers.

He joined in August 1916, and was sent to the Western Front early in the following year. While in France he took part in important operations with his unit, particularly in the Somme and Ypres sectors.
In March 1919 he was demobilised, and holds the General Service and Victory Medals.
155, Sheldon Road, Upper Edmonton, N.18   X17192.

HONNOR, C. H., Pte., Wiltshire Regiment.

He volunteered in August 1914, and in the following year was sent to the Dardanelles, where he took part in the Gallipoli campaign. On the evacuation of the Peninsula, he was drafted to Mesopotamia, and served in important operations on that Front. He was later sent to Russia, remaining there until 1919. He was wounded during his service, and was still serving in 1920.
He holds the 1914–15 Star, General Service and Victory Medals.
40, Bath Road, Lower Edmonton, N.9   13133.

HOOK, W., Stoker, Royal Navy.

Volunteering in June 1915, he served on board H.M.S. " Rother " on the important work of conveying troops from this country to France His vessel was also engaged on patrol duties
He was demobilised in January 1920, and holds the 1914–15 Star, General Service and Victory Medals.
57, Adeney Road, Hammersmith, W.6   15159.

HOOKER, A. H., Sergt., Canadian Railway Troops Battalions.

He volunteered in 1915, and in the same year was sent to France, where he was engaged with his unit on important duties on the lines of communication in the fighting areas. He served with distinction during the Advance of 1918, and in May 1919 was demobilised.
He holds the 1914–15 Star, General Service and Victory Medals, and has now returned to Canada.
106, Shakespeare Avenue, Willesden, N.W.10   13899C.

HOOKER, A. J., Cpl., Royal Air Force.

He volunteered in 1915, and later in the same year was sent to the Western Front. He was there engaged on important duties, which required a high technical skill, with his unit on important sectors of the Front. He remained in this theatre of war until 1919, when he returned to England for his demobilisation.
He holds the 1914–15 Star, General Service and Victory Medals.
106, Shakespeare Avenue, Willesden, N.W.10   13899B.

HOOKER, W. A., Rifleman, King's Royal Rifles.

In April 1915 he volunteered for duty, and in the following August was sent to the Western Front, where he took part in engagements at Ypres, Arras and Cambrai. On March 29, 1916, he died from wounds received in action.
He was entitled to the 1914–15 Star, General Service and Victory Medals.
51, Melville Road, Stonebridge Park, N.W.10   15660.

HOOKHAM, H. C., A.B., Royal Navy.

He was mobilised from the Reserve in August 1914, and served on H.M.S. " Good Hope " off Nova Scotia and in American waters. He was killed in action in the engagement off Coronel on November 1st, 1914.
He was entitled to the 1914 Star, General Service and Victory Medals.
10, Denbigh Road, Willesden, N.W.10   15531.

HOOKHAM, W., Pte., 13th Middlesex Regt. and R.A.O.C.

He volunteered in July 1915, and was sent to France in the same year. He took part in many engagements on the Western Front, including Ypres, Loos, Lens, Vimy Ridge, the Somme, Bullecourt, Arras and Cambrai, and was afterward transferred to the Royal Army Ordnance Corps, with which he was engaged on important duties at Dieppe.
He was demobilised in June 1919, holding the 1914–15 Star, General Service and Victory Medals.
He has since died from illness contracted on active service.
85, Milton Avenue, Willesden, N.W.10   14216A.

HOOKHAM, W. G. R., Lce.-Cpl., The Queen's (Royal West Surrey Regiment) and Royal Sussex Regiment.

He joined in March 1917, and was drafted to the Western Front, where he took part in engagements on the Somme, at Ypres, Albert, Arras, Bapaume, and during the operations in the Retreat and Advance of 1918. During his service he was twice wounded, and mentioned in despatches on two occasions for conspicuous services in the field.
He was demobilised in March 1919, and holds the General Service and Victory Medals.
85, Milton Avenue, Willesden, N.W.10   14216B.

HOOPER, H., Rifleman, Rifle Brigade.

He volunteered in August 1914, and was drafted overseas shortly afterwards. He took part in several engagements, and was wounded in action at Hooge in August 1915. After suffering from shell-shock, he was discharged as medically unfit for further military service in September 1916.
He holds the 1914 Star, General Service and Victory Medals.
56, Beaufoy Road, Tottenham, N.17   X17971.

HOPE, H. E., Cpl., Royal Field Artillery.

He volunteered in 1914, and after completing his training was sent to France in the following year. He took part in many engagements, including those on the Somme, at Ypres (1917), and was wounded in October 1918, during the Allied Advance. Owing to his wound, he was discharged as medically unfit for further service, and holds the 1914–15 Star, General Service and Victory Medals.
5, Sebastopol Road, Lower Edmonton, N.9   14548A.

HOPGOOD, E., Rifleman, King's Royal Rifles.

He joined in 1917, and after his training served at various stations on important duties with his unit. He gave valuable services, but was not successful in obtaining his transfer overseas before the cessation of hostilities.
He was demobilised in April 1919.
95, Greyhound Road, Hammersmith, W.6   15024.

HOPKINS, A. W., Sergt., Royal Fusiliers.

He volunteered in September 1914, and early in the following year was drafted to the Western Front, where he took part in important engagements at Loos, Ypres, the Somme, Arras, Cambrai, St. Quentin, Béthune, Albert and Armentières. During his service he was twice wounded, and in February 1917 he was demobilised, holding the 1914–15 Star, General Service and Victory Medals.
121, Hill Side, Stonebridge Park, N.W.10   15794.

HOPKINS, E., Pte., Durham Light Infantry.

He volunteered in July 1915, and after completing his training was sent to Salonica in the following year. He was engaged on duties of great importance throughout the Balkan campaign, and rendered valuable services.
He was demobilised in February 1919, and holds the General Service and Victory Medals
65, Waldo Road, College Park, N.W.10   X17636.

HOPKINS, E. (Miss), Special War Worker.

For a considerable period during the war this lady was engaged in making boxes at the Park Royal Munition Factory. Her duties, which were of an arduous nature, were carried out in a very capable manner.

35, Barret's Green Road, Willesden, N.W.10   13783A.

HOPKINS, F. J., Gunner, R.F.A.

Volunteering in 1915, he was sent a year later to France, where he took part in the battles of the Somme, Cambrai, Arras and Albert. In the following year he was drafted to Italy, but returned after four months to the Western Front, taking part in engagements at Bapaume, Kemmel Hill, Dickebusch and the Somme. Later he served with the Army of Occupation in Germany until March 1919, when he was returned to England and demobilised.

He holds the General Service and Victory Medals.

121, Hill Side, Stonebridge Park, N.W.10   15795.

HOPKINS, R. D., Sapper, Royal Engineers.

Volunteering in November 1914, he was drafted to France in the following year. Later he was transferred to the Italian Front, and took part in the important operations there. During his service overseas he was wounded.

In October 1919, he obtained his demobilisation, and holds the 1914–15 Star, General Service and Victory Medals.

52, Haldane Road, Walham Green, S.W.6   X17376.

HOPKINS, W. H., Pte., West Yorkshire Regt.

He joined in 1917, and after a short period of training was sent to the Western Front later in the same year. He there took part in many engagements, and during the Allied Advance in 1918 was killed in action at Cambrai.

He was entitled to the General Service and Victory Medals.

35, Barret's Green Road, Willesden, N.W.10   13783B.

HOPPER, D. W., Pte., R.A.S.C.

He volunteered in January 1915, and later in the same year was sent to Salonica. During his three years' service in this seat of war he was engaged on important transport duties throughout the engagements of the Balkan campaign.

In 1918 he returned to England, and was demobilised in March of the following year. He holds the 1914–15 Star, General Service and Victory Medals.

4, Beaconsfield Road, Church End, N.W.10   16325.

HOPPER, H., Pte., Queen's Own (Royal West Kent Regiment).

He joined in December 1916, and in the same year was sent to India, where he was engaged on important garrison duties. He was later transferred to the Mesopotamia theatre of operations, and served in many notable engagements. While crossing the river Tigris in an attack, he was drowned on November 1st, 1918.

He was entitled to the General Service and Victory Medals.

78, Carlyle Avenue, Willesden, N.W.10   14448.

HOPPING, A., Pte., Middlesex Regiment.

He volunteered in 1915, and after completing his training was retained on important duties with his unit until 1917. He was then drafted to Egypt and took part in heavy fighting in that theatre of operations.

He was demobilised in 1919, and holds the General Service and Victory Medals.

10, Durham Road, Lower Edmonton, N.9.   14869B.

HOPPING, A. A., Rifleman, The Cameronians (Scottish Rifles).

Entering the Army in February 1915, he was sent later in the same year to the Western Front. He served with a Trench Mortar Battery and took part in important operations on the Somme and at Ypres. There he was wounded, and subsequently he was killed in action at Arras on March 29th, 1917.

He was entitled to the 1914–15 Star, General Service and Victory Medals.

9, Linton Road, Upper Edmonton, N.18   X17478A.

HOPPING, E. A., Driver, R.A.S.C. (M.T.).

He joined in 1916, and after completing his training was retained on important transport duties in Ireland. He rendered valuable service, but was unable to obtain his transfer overseas prior to the cessation of hostilities. He was demobilised in 1919.

9, Linton Road, Upper Edmonton, N.18   X17478B.

HOPPING, J., Pte., Royal Fusiliers.

He joined in 1917, and after his period of training, was sent to France in the following year at the beginning of the German Offensive. He served throughout the Retreat and Advance of the Allied Armies during 1918. After the signing of the Armistice he was sent home and was demobilised in 1919.

He holds the General Service and Victory Medals.

10, Durban Road, Lower Edmonton, N.9   14869A.

HORLOCK, A. E., Staff-Sergt., R.A.M.C.

He volunteered in 1914, and in the same year was sent to the Western Front, where he took part in the retreat from Mons. He was later engaged on important duties at various stations in France, where he did work of a highly responsible character. In May 1919 he was demobilised.

He holds the Mons Star, General Service and Victory Medals.

44, Pretoria Road, Upper Edmonton, N.18   X17024.

HORNE, H. R., 1st-Class Stoker, R.N., H.M.S. "Tiger."

He joined in 1916, and was posted to H.M.S. "Tiger," in which ship he took a prominent part in all the important engagements of the Grand Fleet in the North Sea He was in action several times against the German Fleet.

In 1919, he obtained his demobilisation, and holds the General Service and Victory Medals.

1, Manor Road, Tottenham, N.17   X18817.

HORNIBROOK, A., Special War Worker.

Owing to his qualification and skill as a builder, he was engaged on work of military importance at several stations in France, in connection with the erection of buildings for use by the British Army. He gave valuable services to his Country, and carried out his work in a very capable manner.

82, Yeldham Road, Hammersmith, W.6   13280A.

HORNIBROOK, T. A., Pte., The Queen's (Royal West Surrey Regiment).

He volunteered in February 1915, and in the same year was sent to France. While on the Western Front he took part in engagements at Ypres, the Somme (where he was wounded), Arras, Vimy Ridge, Armentières, Bullecourt, Cambrai and in the Advance of 1918 He was also gassed while in action at Dickebusch.

In January 1919 he obtained his demobilisation, and holds the 1914–15 Star, General Service and Victory Medals.

82, Yeldham Road, Hammersmith, W.6   13167.

HOROBIN, H. J., Sergt., Yorkshire Regiment.

He volunteered on the outbreak of war in August 1914, and after training was retained on important duties with his unit at various stations. He gave valuable services and gained the rank of sergeant for continuous good work.

Owing to ill-health he was unsuccessful in obtaining his transfer overseas, and in July 1916, was discharged as medically unfit for further service.

7, Humbolt Mansions, Lillie Road, Fulham, S.W.6   TX18885.

HORSEY, T. H., Gunner, R.F.A.

He volunteered in November 1914, and was sent to the Western Front after completing his training. He took part in important operations at Arras and on the Somme. Later he served in the Balkans until the close of the campaign He was then drafted to Palestine, being present at the fall of Jerusalem. While in this theatre of operations he contracted malaria.

In February 1919 he obtained his demobilisation, and holds the 1914–15 Star, General Service and Victory Medals.

44, Studland Street, Hammersmith, W.6   12427.

HORSLEY, C., Cpl., King's Royal Rifle Corps.

He volunteered in September 1914, and in the following year was sent to the Western Front. While there he took part in many engagements, and in 1916 was badly wounded. In September 1917, he was again severely wounded, and was taken prisoner. He was for a considerable period in hospital in Germany.

In February 1919 he obtained his demobilisation, and holds the 1914–15 Star, General Service and Victory Medals.

16, Colville Road, Lower Edmonton, N.9   11909.

HORT, E. C., Pte., Royal Fusiliers.

Volunteering in August 1914, he was sent in the same year to France. He took part in the retreat from Mons and was severely wounded. On recovery he was sent to the Dardanelles. After the evacuation of the Peninsula, he was engaged on special duties at Malta. During his service overseas he was twice wounded, and in October 1918, was discharged as being medically unfit for further service.

He holds the Mons Star, General Service and Victory Medals.

61, Adeney Road, Hammersmith, W.6   15328.

HORTON, A., Pte., Middlesex Regiment.

He joined in 1916, and later in the same year was drafted overseas. During his two years' service on the Western Front he took part in important engagements on the Somme, at Ypres and in the Retreat and Advance of the Allied Armies. He was twice wounded, and in August 1918, was discharged as medically unfit for further service in consequence of his wounds.

He holds the General Service and Victory Medals.

31, Whitehall Street, Tottenham, N.17   X18350D.

HORTON, H. (M.S.M.), Sergt., R.A.M.C. (M.T.).

He volunteered in February 1915, and in the same year was sent to France. He was there attached to a heavy howitzer brigade of artillery, and took part in many engagements, including those at Ypres, Loos, the Somme, Cambrai, Béthune, Amiens, and Courtrai. He was awarded the Meritorious Service Medal for great gallantry and devotion to duty, and in addition holds the 1914–15 Star, General Service and Victory Medals.
He was demobilised in March 1919.
108, Fortune Gate Road, Harlesden, N.W.10   13191.

HORTON, H. G., Pte., Suffolk Regiment.

He joined in August 1917, and was sent to the Western Front in the same year. While in this theatre of war he took part in many engagements, and was wounded while in action on the Somme in 1918. In November of the following year he was demobilised.
He holds the General Service and Victory Medals.
31, Whitehall Street, Tottenham, N.17   X18350C.

HORTON, J. T., Pte., Royal Defence Corps.

He volunteered in 1915, and owing to indifferent health was retained on important defence duties on the East Coast. He rendered excellent services while in this corps.
In 1917 he was discharged as medically unfit for further military service.
31, Whitehall Street, Tottenham, N.17   X18350A.

HORTON, T. G., Pte., Middlesex Regiment.

He joined in October 1916, and later in the same year was sent to the Western Front. While in this theatre of war he took part in many engagements, the most important of which were at Ypres, La Bassée and on the Somme. In June 1918, he was discharged as medically unfit for further service due to his military duties overseas.
He holds the General Service and Victory Medals.
31, Whitehall Street, Tottenham, N.17   X18350B.

HORWITZ, D., Pioneer, Royal Engineers.

He volunteered in January 1915, and after completing his training, was sent in the same year to the Eastern theatre of war. He took part in important operations on the Balkan Front, and served through the great Serbian retreat. After arduous service in Russia, he was drafted to Constantinople were he contracted malaria, being in hospital for a considerable period.
He was demobilised in May 1919, and holds the 1914–15 Star, General Service and Victory Medals.
30, Chesson Road, West Kensington, W.14   X17170.

HORWOOD, A. E., Sapper, R.E. (R.O.D.).

He joined in March 1917, and was sent to the Western Front. While there he was engaged on important work on the lines of communication, and took an active part in the operations at Passchendaele, Cambrai and the Retreat and Advance of 1918. In April 1919, he was demobilised.
He holds the General Service and Victory Medals.
6, Drayton Road, Harlesden, N.W.10   14898.

HORWOOD, H. A., Farrier, R.A.V.C.

Volunteering in January 1915, he was sent to the Western Front in the same year. While there he was engaged on important work in connection with the treatment of sick and wounded horses where his technical knowledge and skill were of great value.
In January 1919 he was demobilised, holding the 1914–15 Star, General Service and Victory Medals.
73, Melville Road, Stonebridge Park, N.W.10   15657.

HOSKEN, L. C., Sapper, Royal Engineers.

He enlisted in August 1913, and on the outbreak of war was immediately sent to the Western Front. He took part in the operations of that year in Belgium and was taken prisoner at Antwerp. During the earlier portion of his captivity he suffered many hardships but was later interned in Holland. Upon his release he returned to England and was discharged in August 1919.
He holds the 1914 Star, General Service and Victory Medals.
59, Rylston Road, Fulham, S.W.6   16181.

HOULSTON, G. W., C.Q.M.S., West Yorks. Regt.

He was serving at the outbreak of war and was sent to France later in the same year. He fought in the first and second battles of Ypres, and was recommended for a decoration for meritorious services and devotion to duty. Later he was drafted to East Africa and served with distinction in the campaign there. In 1920 he was still serving with the King's African Rifles.
He holds the 1914 Star, General Service and Victory Medals.
75, Woodheyes Road, Neasden, N.W.10   15458A.

HOULSTON, H. E., Lce.-Cpl., R.E.

He volunteered in May 1915, and was sent overseas in the same year. He took part in operations in various sectors of the Western Front and was mentioned in despatches for conspicuous bravery at Loos in February 1916.
He obtained his demobilisation in April 1919, and holds the 1914–15 Star, General Service and Victory Medals.
75, Woodheyes Road, Neasden, N.W.10   15458B.

HOULSTON, J. A., 2nd Air Mechanic, R.A.F.

He joined in April 1918, and was almost immediately sent to the Italian seat of war, where he was engaged on important duties at various aerodromes in connection with the extensive operations on the Asiago Plateau and the Piave River.
In April 1919 he obtained his demobilisation and holds the General Service and Victory Medals.
75, Woodheyes Road, Neasden, N.W.10   15458C.

HOUNSELL, F. J., Pte., R.A.O.C.

He volunteered in May 1915, and in the same year was sent to Salonica. While there, he was engaged on special duties at large ammunition depots. After rendering valuable services he was demobilised in April 1919.
He holds the 1914–15 Star, General Service and Victory Medals.
23, Winchelsea Road, Willesden, N.W.10   13845.

HOUNSLOW, A., Pte., Norfolk Regiment.

He was called up from the reserve in August 1914, and early in the following year was sent to Mesopotamia. After taking part in the first engagements in the Kut-el-Amara advance, he was engaged on important convoy duties to and from the firing line.
He was serving in 1920, and holds the 1914–15 Star, General Service and Victory Medals.
45, Star Road, West Kensington, W.14   16694.

HOUNSLOW, G., Gunner, Royal Field Artillery.

This gunner volunteered in September 1914, and after completing his training, was sent to France in the following year. During his four years' service in this theatre of war, he took part in the battles of Ypres, the Somme, Arras and many other engagements.
In February 1919, he was demobilised and holds the 1914–15 Star, General Service and Victory Medals.
74, Ancill Street, Hammersmith, W.6   13999.

HOW, F. W., Sapper, Royal Engineers.

He volunteered in October 1914, and was engaged on special duties at various stations with his unit, until 1916, when he was sent to France. While there he was attached to the R.O.D., and took an active part in the operations during the Retreat and Advance of 1918.
He was demobilised in March 1919, and holds the General Service and Victory Medals.
63, Redfern Road, Willesden, N.W.10.   13198.

HOWARD, A. D., Special War Worker.

On leaving school at the age of 14 years, this youth, desirous of helping his Country, offered his services at the munition works of Messrs. Lyon and Wrench where he was engaged on dangerous work in connection with the manufacture of fuses. He worked well, and was highly commended.
8, Ilex Road, Willesden, N.W.10   16094A.

HOWARD, A. E., Lce.-Cpl., East Surrey Regt.

He volunteered in September 1914, and was sent to France early in the following year where he took part in many important engagements. On June 13th 1916, he was killed in action at Fricourt, near Albert.
He was entitled to the 1914–15 Star, General Service and Victory Medals.
108, Purves Road, Kensal Rise, N.W.10   X18423.

HOWARD, A. R., Sapper, Royal Engineers.

He joined in April 1918, and was sent to France the same year, where he was engaged on important railway transport. He was demobilised in December 1919, after rendering valuable services.
He holds the General Service and Victory Medals.
65, Carlyle Avenue, Willesden, N.W.10   14198.

HOWARD, E. (Mrs.), Special War Worker.

During the war this lady was engaged on important work a Messrs. Vandenplas Aircraft Factory in connection with the manufacture of aeroplane parts. She carried out her responsible duties with great care and skill, and was highly praised for her splendid work.
58, Averill Street, Hammersmith, W.6   13991A.

HOWARD, G. P., Sapper, Royal Engineers.
He volunteered in June 1915, and was sent to France in the same year. While on the Western Front he took part in many of the important engagements, including those on the Somme and at Ypres, and was twice wounded.
He was in France for nearly four years, and in April 1919 obtained his demobilisation, holding the 1914–15 Star, General Service and Victory Medals.
107, Sheldon Road, Upper Edmonton, N. 18   X17188.

HOWARD, H. (Mrs.), Special War Worker.
For a period of two years during the war this lady was engaged on very arduous duties of a special nature at the Perivale Munition Factory. She carried out her work with great care and efficiency and rendered very valuable services to her Country.
8, Ilex Road, Willesden, N.W.10   16094B.

HOWARD, H., Gunner, R.G.A.
He volunteered in November 1915, and on completion of his training was sent to France. He took part in many important engagements on the Western Front, including the battles of Ypres and Cambrai.
He was demobilised in January 1919, and holds the General Service and Victory Medals
37, Shakespeare Avenue, Willesden, N.W.10   13887.

HOWARD, H. J., Cpl., Royal Engineers.
He joined in 1917, and on completion of his training was sent to France later in the same year. During his service on the Western Front he took part in many important operations and was in action during the Retreat and Advance of 1918.
He was demobilised in 1919, and holds the General Service and Victory Medals.
9, Kenninghall Road, Upper Edmonton, N.18   16468C.

HOWARD, T., Sapper, Royal Engineers.
He volunteered in October 1915, and on completion of his training was sent to the seat of operations at Salonica. He was there engaged on important duties during the severe fighting on the Balkan Front.
In May 1919 he obtained his demobilisation, and holds the General Service and Victory Medals.
58, Averill Street, Hammersmith, W.6   13991B.

HOWARD, W., Cpl., Essex Regiment.
He joined in March 1917, and later in the same year was drafted to the Western Front. He took part in the operations on the Somme in 1917, and also fought in the battle of Arras, where he was wounded.
He was demobilised in April 1919, and holds the General Service and Victory Medals.
34, Warwick Road, Upper Edmonton, N.18   X17266.

HOWARD-SPINK, B., Cpl., R.G.A.
He volunteered in September 1915, and in the following December was sent to Egypt. After a short period there, he was transferred to the Western Front where he took part in heavy fighting on the Somme, and at St. Quentin, Mametz Wood and Cambrai. During his service he was twice wounded
He was demobilised in May 1919, and holds the 1914–15 Star, General Service and Victory Medals.
113, Carlyle Avenue, Willesden, N.W.10   13780.

HOWARTH, H. E., Pte., The Buffs (East Kent Regiment).
He volunteered in August 1914, and was sent to France early in the following year. While on the Western Front he took part in many engagements until he was killed in action on November 21st, 1915, at the battle of Loos.
He was entitled to the 1914–15 Star, General Service and Victory Medals.
84, Brownlow Road, Willesden, N.W.10   15123.

HOWARTH, W. J., Driver, R.F.A.
He volunteered in October 1914, and in the following year was sent to the Dardanelles where he fought throughout the whole of the Gallipoli Campaign. After the evacuation of the Peninsula he was sent to the Western Front where he took part in many engagements, including the battles of the Somme, and Cambrai, being twice wounded.
He holds the 1914–15 Star, General Service and Victory Medals, and was still serving in 1920.
76, Brownlow Road, Willesden, N.W.10   14729.

HOWE, A. J., Pte., Machine Gun Corps.
He joined in February 1916, and after his period of training was sent to the Western Front. He took part in many important operations during the Retreat and Advance of the Allied Armies in 1918.
He was demobilised in January 1919, and holds the General Service and Victory Medals.
64, Claybrook Road, Hammersmith, W.6   13767A.

HOWE, F. G., Cook, Royal Navy, H.M.S. " Sir Thomas Picton."
He volunteered in 1915 and served with his ship, " H.M.S. " Sir Thomas Picton," on submarine chasing duties. His vessel was also engaged on dangerous mine-sweeping operations in the Mediterranean Sea, and later took part in the bombardment of Zeebrugge in May 1917.
In 1919 he was demobilised, and holds the 1914–15 Star, General Service and Victory Medals.
8, Redfern Road, Willesden, N.W.10   T13489.

HOWE, G. H., Driver, Royal Field Artillery.
He was called up from the Reserve in August 1914, and was sent to France in 1916. While in this theatre of war he took part in many engagements including those at Ypres, the Somme, Arras, Bullecourt, and in the Advance of 1918.
He was discharged in November 1919, and holds the General Service and Victory Medals.
30, Chalgrove Road, Tottenham, N.17   TX18960.

HOWE, J., Sergt., Royal Welch Fusiliers.
He volunteered in August 1914, and in the same year was sent to the Western Front. During his service in this theatre of war he took a prominent part in many operations in various sectors, and was wounded in action.
In January 1919 he was demobilised, and holds the 1914 Star, General Service and Victory Medals.
3, Gastein Road, Hammersmith, W.6   14816.

HOWE, T. G., Staff-Sergt., Royal Engineers.
Volunteering in August 1914 he was drafted to the Western Front in the following year. During his long service overseas he was engaged on special duties of an important nature until after the cessation of hostilities.
He was demobilised in May 1919, and holds the 1914–15 Star, General Service and Victory Medals.
178, Winchester Road, Lower Edmonton, N.9   14888.

HOWELL, W. J. N., Sergt., 8th London Regt. (Post Office Rifles).
He volunteered in September 1914, and was sent to France in March of the following year. While in this theatre of war he took part in the engagements at Festubert, Loos, Vimy Ridge, High Wood, and Butte de Warlencourt. He was twice wounded. Later he was promoted to the rank of sergeant, and owing to his special qualifications acted as a musketry instructor.
In February 1919 he obtained his demobilisation, and holds the 1914–15 Star, General Service and Victory Medals.
66, Mordaunt Road, Willesden, N.W.10   14116.

HOWES, B., Pte., 12th Middlesex Regiment.
He volunteered in September 1914, and after his training was engaged on important duties with his unit at various stations. He gave valuable services, but owing to indifferent health was not successful in obtaining his transfer overseas.
In November 1917 he was discharged as being medically unfit for further military service
2, West Block, Garnet Mansions, Garnet Road, Willesden. N.W.10   15967A.

HOWES, W. H., Rifleman, 18th The London Regt. (London Irish Rifles).
Joining in June 1917, he was sent to the Western Front on completion of his training. During his services overseas he took an active part in many of the important operations during the Allied Retreat and Advance of 1918.
He was demobilised in November of the following year, and holds the General Service and Victory Medals.
22, Purcell Crescent, Fulham, S.W.6   14842

HOWLETT, A. G., Pte., 4th Middlesex Regiment.
He volunteered in June 1915, and after completing his training was sent to France the following year. He took part in many important engagements on the Western Front, including the battles of the Somme and Cambrai. He was wounded twice, and holds the General Service and Victory Medals.
He was still serving in 1920.
47, Maldon Road, Lower Edmonton, N.9   15792.

HOWLETT, A. T., Rifleman, 6th London Regt. (Rifles).
He volunteered in November 1915, and after his training served at various stations on important duties, until January 1917, when he was drafted overseas. He took part in the fighting on the Somme, at Bullecourt, Passchendaele, Bourlon Wood, Amiens and Villers-Bretonneux where he was severely wounded. He was invalided to England, and discharged as medically unfit for further service in 1918.
He holds the General Service and Victory Medals.
1086, Harrow Road, Willesden, N.W.10   X17593.

HOWLETT, F. J. A., Gunner, R.G.A.

He volunteered in 1915, and after a period of training was sent to France in the following year. He took part in engagements on the Somme, at the Vimy Ridge, Ypres and St Quentin. In the last named engagement he was taken prisoner, and during his captivity suffered many hardships. He was released after the armistice and returned to England for demobilisation in February 1919.
He holds the General Service and Victory Medals.
10, Vallier Road, College Park, N.W.10   17679C.

HOWLETT, M. (Miss), Special War Worker.

At the outbreak of war this lady was engaged on work of national importance at Woolwich Arsenal where her duties were often of a dangerous nature. She later transferred to the land army, and was employed on important forestry work. Throughout the war she rendered valuable services, and holds a certificate for excellent work from the Ministry of Agriculture.
10, Vallier Road, College Park, N.W.10   17679D.

HOWLETT, R. W. (M.M.), Pte., Royal Sussex Regt.

He joined in April 1917, and after completing his training was sent overseas. He took part in many important engagements on the Western Front, and was awarded the Military Medal for conspicuous gallantry and devotion to duty in the field. He was subsequently killed in action in the Advance, on October 24th, 1918, and was buried at Ferme-de-Etonoile, near Catillon. He was also entitled to the General Service and Victory Medals.
10, Vallier Road, College Park, N.W.10   X17679A.

HOWLETT, W., Pte., 6th Middlesex Regiment.

He joined in October 1916, and served on the Western Front for two years, during which time he took part in engagements at Arras, Ypres, and the Somme. He was twice wounded, and also suffered from shell-shock.
He holds the General Service and Victory Medals, and was demobilised in February 1919.
80, Harley Road, Willesden, N.W.10   13399.

HOWLETT, W. J., A.B., Royal Navy.

He joined in July 1917, and served on board H.M.S "Revenge," patrolling the North Sea and Russian waters. In November 1917 he took part in the battle of the Kattegat. He was serving in 1920 on H.M.S. "Clio."
He holds the General Service and Victory Medals.
24, Grove Place, Ealing, W.5   10848.

HOWORTH, F. H., Pte., Royal Fusiliers.

He volunteered in August 1914, and shortly after was sent to France, where, among many other engagements, he fought in the retreat from Mons. He took part later in the Gallipoli Campaign, and on the evacuation of the Peninsula returned to the Western Front, where he fought at Ypres and in the final battles of 1918.
He was twice wounded during his service, and in February 1919 obtained his demobilisation.
He holds the Mons Star, General Service and Victory Medals.
39, Monmouth Road, Lower Edmonton, N.9   12984.

HUBBLE, A. G., Sergt., Machine Gun Corps.

Volunteering in April 1915, he was sent to the Eastern theatre of war on completion of his training. He was present at the capture of Baghdad and the battle of Ramadieh. Later he was drafted to India, and owing to his special qualifications, was appointed as signalling instructor at the M.G.C. Depot. In November 1919 he returned from India for demobilisation, and holds the General Service and Victory Medals.
139, Rucklidge Avenue, Harlesden, N.W.10   13161A.

HUBBLE, A. V., Pte., R.A.S.C. (M.T.).

Volunteering in March 1915, he was retained for a time on important duties with his unit. In 1917 he was drafted to France, and after three months' service was wounded and invalided home. On recovery he was sent to German East Africa and thence to Egypt. While in the last named theatre of war he took part in many important engagements. In March 1919 he was sent home for demobilisation.
He holds the General Service and Victory Medals.
139, Rucklidge Avenue, Harlesden, N.W.10   13161B.

HUBBLE, H. E., Pte., Machine Gun Corps.

He volunteered in September 1915, and after his training was retained on important duties with his unit until March 1917 when he was sent to France. While there he took part in engagements on the Somme, and at Ypres, Arras and Cambrai. He suffered severely from trench fever and was for a time in hospital.
In April 1919 he obtained his demobilisation, and holds the General Service and Victory Medals.
139, Rucklidge Avenue, Harlesden, N.W.10   13161C.

HUBER, J. H., Gunner, Royal Field Artillery.

Volunteering in May 1915, this Gunner was sent to the Western Front in the same year. He took part in the battles of the Somme, Arras and Ypres (1917). On one occasion, while acting as a driver, he picked up a live bomb in the endeavour to save his horses. The bomb exploded, and he received serious injuries to his hand, losing a finger and thumb. During his services he was thrice wounded.
In March 1919 he was demobilised and holds the 1914-15 Star, General Service and Victory Medals.
34, Dieppe Street, West Kensington, W.14   16252.

HUBER, R. A., Pte., 7th Middlesex Regiment.

He joined in March 1918, and after a short period of training was sent to France. In this theatre of operations he took part in engagements at Ypres, Kemmel Hill, Armentières and on the Somme in the final Advance of the Allied Armies. He was demobilised in October 1919, and holds the General Service and Victory Medals.
34, Dieppe Street, West Kensington, W.14   16258.

HUDSON, A. O. F., Pte., Bedfordshire Regt.

He joined in May 1918, although over military age and medically unfit for services overseas. He was therefore retained on important duties at various stations with his unit, rendering valuable services until his demobilisation in January 1919,
117, Deacon Road, Cricklewood, N.W.2   16612.

HUDSON, C. (M.M.), Pte., Middlesex Regiment.

He volunteered in 1915 and was sent to the Western Front in the following year. He took part in many important engagements, and during the Advance of 1917 was awarded the Military Medal for conspicious gallantry and devotion to duty in the field. Shortly after he was severely wounded and invalided home, and later in the same year was discharged as medically unfit for further service.
He also holds the General Service and Victory Medals.
36a, Chapter Road, Cricklewood, N.W.2   16166.

HUDSON, E. L., Pte., 1st Gordon Highlanders.

Volunteering in July 1915 he was sent to France early in the following year. While on this front he took part in engagements at Montauban and Albert. After the action of November 13th, 1917, he was missing and was later reported as killed on that date.
He was entitled to the General Service and Victory Medals.
No. 4, Estella House, 296, Chapter Road, Cricklewood, N.W.2   T17323.

HUDSON, K. (Miss), Special War Worker.

During the war this lady was engaged at Messrs. Becton's Factory as a lathe worker. Her duties, which were of an arduous nature, required much skill and were performed with efficiency. She rendered valuable services to her Country and was commended for her work.
31, Ancill Street, Hammersmith, W.6   13744A.

HUDSON, P. A., Gunner, Royal Field Artillery.

During the first two years of the war he was engaged at the Park Royal Munition Factory, but in 1916, on attaining the age of eighteen, he joined the Army. He was sent to Egypt, and later to Palestine. While in this theatre of war he took part with General Allenby's Forces in the operations at Jerusalem, Jericho and Jaffa.
In 1918 he was demobilised and holds the General Service and Victory Medals.
3, Fane Place, West Kensington, W.14   15895.

HUFFEY, W. J., Sergt., Royal Irish Regiment.

He volunteered in October 1915, and after his training served with his unit at various stations on important duties. He rendered valuable service but was unsuccessful in obtaining his transfer overseas.
He was in hospital a considerable time through injuries received in an accident, and in August 1919 was demobilised.
5, Wilsons Road, Hammersmith, W.6   16417A.

HUGGINS, E. H., Sergt., Gloucestershire Regt.

Volunteering in August 1914 he was sent to France in the following year where he served with distinction in many important engagements. He fought in the battles of Ypres and the Somme. He was thrice wounded. In June 1917, after a long period in hospital, he was discharged as medically unfit for further service owing to wounds.
He holds the 1914-15 Star, General Service and Victory Medals.
30, Gowan Road, Willesden, N.W.10   X16962.

HUGHES, A. J., Pte., Middlesex Regiment.

Volunteering in August 1914 he was quickly sent to the Western Front where he took part in the retreat from Mons. After subsequent fighting on the Somme, he was in action during the battle of Loos, where he was killed on September 29th, 1915.
He was entitled to the Mons Star, General Service and Victory Medals.   65, Durban Road, Tottenham, N.17   X18288.

HUGHES, C. R. G., Sapper, Royal Engineers.

He volunteered in August 1914, and was sent in the following year to the Western Front, where he was engaged in the dangerous duties of laying mines in the trenches. Later he took part in the fighting on the Somme, and at Ypres, Arras and Cambrai. In February 1919 he was demobilised. He holds the 1914-15 Star, General Service and Victory Medals.
9, Pember Road, Willesden, N.W.10   X18192.

HUGHES, E., Cpl., Middlesex Regiment.

Having previously served in the Territorial Force, he volunteered in August 1914, and early in 1915 was sent to India. While there he took part in fighting on the North West Frontier. Later he was transferred to the Mesopotamian seat of war and fought there throughout the Campaign. In March 1919 he was demobilised.
He holds the General Service and Victory Medals, the Indian General Service Medal, with clasp (Afghanistan, N.W. Frontier, 1919), and the Territorial Efficiency Medal.
94, Fortune Gate Road, Harlesden, N.W.10   13185.

HUGHES, H., Rifleman, Rifle Brigade.

He volunteered in March 1915 and in the following year was sent to France. During his service on the Western Front he took part in many important engagements, and in February 1917 was severely wounded. After a considerable period spent in hospital, he was discharged in August 1918, as medically unfit for further service owing to wounds.
He holds the General Service and Victory Medals.
92, Burn's Road, Harlesden, N.W.10   13141.

HUGHES, J. D., 2nd Air Mechanic, R.A.F.

He joined in March 1918 on reaching military age, and on passing the necessary tests for a skilled mechanic, was retained on important duties with his unit at various aerodromes. He gave valuable services, but was not successful in obtaining his transfer overseas before hostilities ceased.
He was demobilised in October 1919.
20, Inman Road, Craven Park, N.W.10   14903.

HUGHES, J. F., Cpl., Royal Engineers.

Volunteering in August 1914, he was quickly sent to the Western Front, where he joined in the retreat from Mons. He took part in battles at Ypres, the Somme and St. Julien. After being badly gassed he was invalided home. Following a long course of treatment in hospital, he was demobilised in June 1919.
He holds the Mons Star, General Service and Victory Medals.
134, Kimberley Road, Upper Edmonton, N.18   T16855

HUGHES, N. W., Sergt., Middlesex Regiment.

He volunteered in November 1915, and after his training was drafted to the Western Front. He served with distinction in the battles of Ypres, Cambrai and the Somme, where he was killed in action on January 3rd, 1918.
He was entitled to the General Service and Victory Medals.
46, King's Road, Tottenham, N.17   X18537.

HUGHES, T. A., Sapper, Royal Engineers.

He volunteered in May 1915 and was sent to France in the same year. While on this Front he took an active part in many engagements, including those of the Somme and at Ypres and La Bassée.
In December 1919 he was demobilised, holding the 1914-15 Star, General Service and Victory Medals.
1, Florence Road, Upper Edmonton, N.18   16015.

HULCOOP, W. S., Pte., 1/8th Hampshire Regt.

He joined in June 1916, and on completion of his training was drafted to Egypt in the following year. After taking part in several engagements he was killed in action at the battle of Gaza on April 20th, 1917.
He was entitled to the General Service and Victory Medals.
94, Dyson's Road, Upper Edmonton, N.18   16778.

HULKS, G. A., Pte., 2nd Queen's (Royal West Surrey Regiment).

He joined in September 1917, and after finishing his training was sent to France early in the following year, where he took an active part in the Retreat and Advance of the Allied Armies.
He was later sent to India, where he was still serving in 1920, and holds the General Service and Victory Medals.
17, Marsden Road, Lower Edmonton, N.9   13063A.

HULKS, J. J., Pte., Middlesex Regiment.

He joined in October 1916, and on completion of his training went to France in the same year. While in this theatre of war he took part in many engagements, including the Retreat and Advance of the Allies in 1918.
In October 1919 he obtained his demobilisation and holds the General Service and Victory Medals.
17, Marsden Road, Lower Edmonton, N.9   13063B.

HULL, A. W., Driver, Royal Field Artillery.

This driver volunteered in 1915 and was drafted to France in the same year. After taking part in important engagements on this front he was transferred to Mesopotamia, where he served under General Townshend throughout the Kut campaign and was severely wounded.
He holds the 1914-15 Star, General Service and Victory Medals   He was demobilised in 1919.
61, Barret's Green Road, Willesden, N.W.10   13554B.

HULL, M. (Mrs.), Special War Worker.

Throughout the war this lady (who is a widow with four children) was engaged on important duties at the Perivale and Park Royal Munition Works. Her work, which was in connection with the inspection of fuses and small arms ammunition, was of a responsible nature, and was carried out with great care and efficiency. She rendered very valuable services to her Country.
61, Barret's Green Road, Willesden, N.W.10   13554A.

HULL, W., Gunner, Royal Garrison Artillery.

Re-enlisting in April 1915, having previously served for 12 years with the colours, this gunner was sent to France in the following month. He took part in several engagements on the Western Front, including the battle of Loos. On account of shell-shock, he was invalided to hospital in England, and in July 1916 was discharged as medically unfit.
He holds the Queen's South African Medal, the 1914-15 Star, General Service and Victory Medals.
1, Rigsley Road, Willesden, N.W.10   X17791.

HULLEY, P., Cpl., Rifle Brigade.

He volunteered in August 1914, and, as he was unfit for transfer overseas owing to indifferent health, was retained on duties of an important nature at various stations with his unit. For consistent good work he was promoted corporal, but in September 1917 he was discharged as being medically unfit for further service.
128, Blythe Road, West Kensington, W.14   12627.

HULLIS, A. G., Petty Officer, Royal Navy.

He enlisted in the Navy in 1908, and at the outbreak of war proceeded with his ship to the North Sea, where he took a prominent part in the actions at Heligoland and the Dogger Bank. He also served through the Naval operations at the Dardanelles and in connection with the Mesopotamia and Salonica campaigns. Later he did duty with his ship in Egyptian and Italian waters, and in November 1919 was discharged, holding the 1914 Star, General Service and Victory Medals.
21, Tasso Road, Hammersmith, W.6   14647.

HUMBLESTONE, W. H., Pte., Middlesex Regt. and Imperial Camel Corps.

He was in the Army at the outbreak of war, and in 1915 was sent to the Dardanelles, where he served throughout the Gallipoli Campaign. After the evacuation of the Peninsula he was sent to Egypt and thence to Palestine, where he took part in the capture of Jerusalem and several other engagements with General Allenby's Forces.
He was demobilised in May 1919, and holds the 1914-15 Star, General Service and Victory Medals.
31, Deacon Road, Cricklewood, N.W.2   X16971.

HUMPHREY, A. L., Pte., Middlesex Regiment.

He volunteered in October 1915, and in April of the following year was drafted to the Western Front, where he took part in many of the principal engagements, including those of Ypres and the Somme, and was twice wounded. He was killed in action on April 14th, 1918, during the Retreat.
He was entitled to the General Service and Victory Medals
234, Shirland Road, Maida Hill, W.9   X19607.

HUMPHREY, C., Driver, Royal Field Artillery.

He volunteered in July 1915, and on completing his training was engaged on important duties at various stations with his unit. He gave valuable services, but was unsuccessful in obtaining his transfer overseas before the signing of the Armistice.
He was still serving in 1920.
43, Aintree Street, Dawes Road, S.W.6   X18207A.

HUMPHREY, C. S., Rifleman, Royal Irish Rifles.

He volunteered in November 1914 and was sent to France in the following April. While in action at Dickebusch he was severely wounded and was invalided home. In June 1916, as a result of his wounds, he was discharged as medically unfit for further service.
He holds the 1914-15 Star, General Service and Victory Medals.   38, Disraeli Road, Acton Lane, N.W.10   14395.

HUMPHREY, H., Lce.-Cpl., Royal Fusiliers.

He joined in June 1917, and after his training was sent to the Western Front. While there he took part in the fighting at Cambrai and Arras and in the Retreat and Advance of 1918. He was twice wounded.
In January 1919 he secured his demobilisation, and holds the General Service and Victory Medals.
39, Guilsborough Road, Willesden, N.W.10   15241.

HUMPHREY, I. G., Pte., R.A.S.C.

He volunteered in 1915, and in the same year was sent to the East. He took part in many engagements in Egypt and was later drafted to Salonika. He was there engaged on important duties in connection with the operations around Lake Doiran and elsewhere in the Balkans.
In 1919 he was demobilised, and holds the 1914–15 Star, General Service and Victory Medals.
8, Mirabel Road, Fulham, S.W.6　　　　X17857.

HUMPHREY, W., Lce.-Cpl., 18th London Regt. (London Irish Rifles).

Volunteering in August 1914, he was sent to the Western Front in the following year. During his service in this seat of operations he took an active part in many important engagements and was wounded.
He holds the 1914–15 Star, General Service and Victory Medals, and was still serving in 1920.
43, Aintree Street, Dawes Road, S.W.6　　　　X18207B.

HUMPHREY, W. L., 1st-Class Petty Officer (Engineer Fitter), Royal Navy.

He volunteered in December 1914, and owing to his special qualifications was promoted to petty officer's rank. He served with H.M.S. "President" on important duties in South American Waters, and took part in the Naval battle off the Falkland Islands. In August 1915 he was discharged as medically unfit for further Service, and holds the 1914–15 Star, General Service and Victory Medals.
11, Ranelagh Road, Harlesden, N.W.10　　　　12743.

HUMPHREYS, H., Pte., 2nd Queen's (Royal West Surrey Regiment).

Volunteering in 1916 he was drafted to the Western Front later in the same year. During his service there, he took part in many important engagements. He was in action at the battles of Vimy Ridge, Arras, Bullecourt and Ypres.
In 1919 he obtained his demobilisation, and holds the General Service and Victory Medals.
12, Chapman Park, Church End, N.W.10　　　　16617.

HUMPHREYS, H. C., Sapper, Royal Engineers.

He volunteered in May 1915 and was drafted to France in the same year. While on this front he took part in many important operations, and while in action near Arras was killed on February 12th, 1917.
He was entitled to the 1914–15 Star, General Service and Victory Medals.
56, Florence Road, Upper Edmonton, N.18　　　　16011B.

HUMPHREYS, H. S., Bombardier, R.F.A.

He volunteered in August 1915, and after his training was drafted to the Western Front. While in this theatre of war he took part in many engagements, including those on the Somme, at Cambrai and Armentières.
In June 1919 he obtained his demobilisation, and holds the General Service and Victory Medals.
56, Florence Road, Upper Edmonton, N.18　　　　16011A.

HUMPHREYS, R. A., 2nd-Class Aircraftsman, Royal Air Force.

He joined in February 1918 on attaining military age, and was sent to France the following month. While there he took an active part in the Retreat and Advance of the Allied Armies. After the Armistice he went to Germany with the Army of Occupation.
He was still serving in 1920, and he holds the General Service and Victory Medals.
21, Fortune Gate Road, Harlesden, N.W.10　　　　14737A.

HUMPHREYS, W. G., Cpl., Royal Fusiliers.

Volunteering in June 1915 he was sent to the Western Front in the following November. He took part in important engagements until June 1916 when he was severely wounded at Vimy Ridge. He was invalided home and upon recovery was declared medically unfit for further service overseas. He was retained and given important duties at various stations until his demobilisation in March 1919.
He holds the 1914–15 Star, General Service and Victory Medals.
21, Fortune Gate Road, Harlesden, N.W.10　　　　14737B.

HUMPHREYS, W. H., Pte., Northamptonshire Regiment.

He joined in March 1917, and during his service on the Western Front took part in several battles, including those of Ypres and Passchendaele, and was for some time attached for special duty to a Labour Company of the 25th Division. After the Armistice he went with the Army of Occupation to Germany, where he served at the 2nd Corps Headquarters.
He holds the General Service and Victory Medals and was demobilised in December 1919.
60, Protheroe Road, Fulham, S.W.6　　　　16831.

HUMPHRIES, E. J., Pte., Labour Corps.

He joined in May 1916, and was drafted to the Salonika theatre of war, where he was engaged on important duties of a special nature at various stations. He gave valuable services during his service on this front.
In September 1919 he returned to England for demobilisation, and holds the General Service and Victory Medals.
1, Myrtle Cottages, Penn Street, Lower Edmonton, N.9 14964.

HUMPHRY, C., Lce.-Cpl., Royal Defence Corps.

Having served previously for 6 years in the Guernsey Militia, he volunteered in February 1915 and was retained on special guard duties at various important stations with his unit. During his four years' service he rendered valuable services to his country, and was demobilised in March 1919.
6, Harlesden Road, Willesden, N.W.10　　　　X17426.

HUMPHRYES, W., Pte., Middlesex Regiment.

He volunteered in 1915, and owing to physical unfitness, was retained on important duties with his unit at various places on the East Coast Defences. He rendered valuable service but was unable to secure his transfer overseas before the cessation of hostilities.
He was demobilised in 1919.
20, Kimberley Road, Upper Edmonton, N.18　　　　16531.

HUNT, A. B., Pte., Royal Fusiliers.

He volunteered in September 1914, and after a period of training was retained on special duty in a large London military hospital. He rendered excellent service but was discharged later in the year as medically unfit for further military service.
120, Lopen Road, Upper Edmonton, N.18　　　　TX17920.

HUNT, A. P., Gunner, Royal Garrison Artillery.

He volunteered in January 1915, and later in the same year was sent to France. During his four years there he took part in many of the important engagements. In November 1917 he was badly gassed.
He holds the 1914–15 Star, General Service and Victory Medals, and was demobilised in April 1919.
150, Montague Road, Lower Edmonton, N.9　　　　15836.

HUNT, C. H., Bombardier, R.G.A.

Volunteering at the outbreak of war he was immediately sent to France where he took part in the retreat from Mons and at the battles of Ypres, La Bassée, the Somme and Arras. He served in this theatre of operations throughout the war, and returned to England for demobilisation in 1919. He holds the Mons Star, General Service and Victory Medals.
15, Lichfield Road, Lower Edmonton, N.9　　　　14671.

HUNT, F., Gunner, Royal Field Artillery.

He volunteered in 1914 and was sent to France in the following year. There he took part in many important engagements, including those on the Somme and at Ypres. In February 1919 he was demobilised.
He holds the 1914–15 Star, General Service and Victory Medals.
96, Ancill Street, Hammersmith, W.6　　　　13661.

HUNT, H. R., Rifleman, 6th London Regiment (Rifles).

He volunteered in September 1914, and was sent to France in the following March. He was actively engaged in many battles on the Western Front, including those of Loos and Neuve Chapelle. During his service he suffered from shell-shock and was for some time in hospital. He holds the 1914–15 Star, General Service and Victory Medals.
He was discharged as medically unfit for further service in July 1917.
78, Harley Road, Willesden, N.W.10　　　　13397.

HUNT, J., Gunner, Royal Field Artillery.

Volunteering in March 1915, this gunner was drafted to the Western Front in the following December. During his service there he took part in many engagements. He was in action during the battle of the Somme in 1916, and was killed at the battle of Arras on May 2nd, 1917.
He was entitled to the 1914–15 Star, General Service and Victory Medals.
19, Alric Avenue, Stonebridge Park, N.W.10　　　　14442B.

HUNT, S., Gunner, Royal Garrison Artillery.

He volunteered in March 1915 and was sent to France in the following year. During his strenuous two years service he took part in many engagements. In 1918, after the signing of the Armistice, he went to Germany with the Army of Occupation, being demobilised in May 1919.
He holds the General Service and Victory Medals.
48, Wingmore Road, Tottenham, N.17　　　　X17970.

HUNT, W. J., Pte., R.M.L.I.

He volunteered in August 1914, and served with his ship on important duties with the Grand Fleet in the North Sea. On March 28th, 1916, he was drowned whilst serving on board H.M.S. "Conquest."
He was entitled to the 1914 Star, General Service and Victory Medals.
79, Brett Road, Stonebridge Park, N.W.10   14522.

HUNTER, C. A., Sergt., Canadian Infantry.

He volunteered in 1915, and was sent to the Western Front the same year. He took part in many important engagements, and died of wounds received in action in August 1916.
He was entitled to the 1914–15 Star, General Service and Victory Medals.
60, Bruce Castle Road, Tottenham, N.17   X18548B.

HUNTER, P., Pte., 2/24th Queen's (Royal West Surrey Regiment).

He volunteered in April 1915. Twelve months later he was sent to Salonica, where he took part in important operations on the Balkan Front. In 1917 he was transferred to Egypt, and saw service there until the following year, when he was drafted to France and fought throughout the Allies' Retreat and Advance. During his service he suffered from enteric fever and dysentry and was in hospital some time.
In January 1919 he obtained his demobilisation, and holds the General Service and Victory Medals.
47, Beaconsfield Road, Church End, N.W.10   16330.

HURLOCK, E., Pte., 1/4th York and Lancaster Regiment.

Joining in November 1917 he was sent to France in the following year and was in action at Cambrai, Arras, Ypres and during the Retreat and Advance of the Allies in 1918. During his service he was wounded.
He was demobilised in March 1919 and holds the General Service and Victory Medals.
131, Sheldon Road, Upper Edmonton, N.18   X17297A.

HURLOCK, W., Sapper, R.E., and Gunner, Royal Garrison Artillery.

He volunteered in August 1914 and went to France immediately, where he took part in the retreat from Mons. He also fought in the battles of the Somme, Ypres, Arras and in the engagements during the Retreat and Advance of 1918. He served overseas for five years, and in 1919 returned to England for demobilisation, holding the Mons Star, General Service and Victory Medals.
131, Sheldon Road, Upper Edmonton, N.18   X17297B.

HURREN, F., Pte., Northumberland Fusiliers.

He volunteered in August 1914 and was sent overseas shortly afterwards. He took part in many important engagements on the Western Front, including the fighting at Armentières and Bullecourt. He was both wounded and gassed.
He holds the 1914 Star, General Service and Victory Medals. and was demobilised in March 1919.
35, Church Path, Hammersmith, W.6   15910.

HURST, C. J., Pte., 12th Royal Fusiliers.

He volunteered in September 1914 and was drafted to France during the following year. Whilst engaged on the Western Front he took part in many important battles and was wounded twice. The second wound deprived him of the sight of his right eye. He was discharged in January 1916 as medically unfit for further service.
He holds the 1914–15 Star, General Service and Victory Medals.
37, Hazelbury Road, Lower Edmonton, N.9   X17491A.

HURST, H. J., Driver, Royal Field Artillery.

He volunteered in September 1914 and in the following year was drafted to the Western Front. After taking part in many engagements there he was sent to Salonica, where he again saw much fighting. During his overseas service he was wounded.
In April 1917 he was demobilised, and holds the 1914–15 Star, General Service and Victory Medals.
20, Ascot Road, Upper Edmonton, N.18   15179.

HURST, L., Signaller, Royal Navy.

He joined in 1917 and served on board H.M.S. "Cleopatra." This vessel was engaged on very important and hazardous duties as convoy to American transports, bringing troops across the Atlantic to England and the Western Front. In 1918 he was sent with his ship to the Baltic in connection with the Russian campaign.
He holds the General Service and Victory Medals, and was still serving in 1920.
37, Hazelbury Road, N.9   X17491B.

HUTCHINGS, H. (sen.), Pte., R.D.C.

He volunteered in February 1915, and owing to indifferent health was retained on important duties in connection with the guarding of German prisoners. He gave valuable services, and in October 1916 was discharged as being medically unfit for further military services.
64, Ormiston Road, Shepherd's Bush, W.12   11921A.

HUTCHINGS, H. J., Acting S.M., Royal Fus. and Royal Air Force.

He volunteered in August 1914, and in the following month went to France. He fought with distinction in the battles of the Marne and the Aisne and was badly wounded near Ypres in July 1915. He was in hospital for a considerable period, and on recovery was transferred to the Royal Air Force, with which unit he remained on important duties in this country until his demobilisation in March 1919.
He holds the 1914 Star, General Service and Victory Medals.
64, Ormiston Road, Shepherd's Bush, W.12   11921B.

HUTCHINGS, R. S., Pte., R.M.L.I.

He was serving at the outbreak of war and was posted to H.M.S. "Good Hope." This vessel cruised principally in South American waters. He lost his life.when she was torpedoed and sunk off the coast of Chile on November 1st, 1914.
He was entitled to the 1914 Star, General Service and Victory Medals.
64, Ormiston Road, Shepherd's Bush, W.12   11921.

HUTCHINGS, W. G., Ldg. Seaman, Royal Navy.

He enlisted in the Royal Navy in 1912, and on the outbreak of war left home waters for the Mediterranean. While there he served on board H.M. Mine Sweeper "Burbress," and was engaged on dangerous mine-sweeping duties in the Mediterranean Sea. He also saw service in Eastern Waters. He holds the 1914 Star, General Service and Victory Medals, and was still serving in 1920.
23, Seymour Road, Lower Edmonton, N.9   13335A.

HUTCHINS, A. (Miss), Special War Worker.

During the war, for a period of more than two years, this lady was engaged on important aircraft work at Messrs. Fellow's Magneto Works, Park Royal. Her position was one of great responsibility, and she carried out her duties in a very efficient and capable manner.
50, Holly Lane, Willesden, N.W.10   15402B.

HUTCHINS, A. (Miss), Special War Worker.

During the war this lady was engaged on work of national importance at the Park Royal Munition Factory, Willesden. Her work, which was in connection with the manufacture of fuses, was of a dangerous nature and was carried out with great skill and efficiency. She rendered valuable services and was worthy of the highest commendation.
62, Buckingham Road, Harlesden, N.W.10   12519.

HUTCHINS, E. E., Pte. (Lewis Gunner), Middlesex Regiment.

He volunteered in September 1914, and in the following August went to the Dardanelles, where he took part in the landing at Suvla Bay. In September of the same year he was wounded in action and invalided to hospital. On recovery he was transferred to Egypt, and from there to Palestine. He served under General Allenby, and was twice wounded near Jerusalem. He was sent later to the Western Front where he served throughout the Allied Advance in 1918.
In 1919 he was demobilised, and holds the 1914–15 Star, General Service and Victory Medals.
67, Denbigh Road, Willesden, N.W.10   15092.

HUTCHINS, G., Driver, Royal Engineers.

He joined in 1917, and on completion of his training was drafted to France. While there he took part in the Retreat and Advance of 1918 and did valuable work of a special nature in the Arras, Cambrai and Belgian sectors of the Western Front.
He was demobilised in 1919, and holds the General Service and Victory Medals.
50, Holly Lane, Willesden, N.W.10   15402A.

HUTCHINS, J. H., Pte., 4th Middlesex Regiment.

He volunteered in April 1915 was sent to the Western Front in July, and took part in heavy fighting at Ypres, Cambrai, the Somme, Loos and in the Retreat and Advance of 1918.
He was killed in action on August 25th, 1918, and was entitled to the 1914–15 Star, General Service and Victory Medals.
84, Mayo Road, Willesden, N.W.10   15435.

HUTCHINS, L. (Mrs.), Special War Worker.

During the war this lady was engaged on work of national importance at the Munition Factory of Messrs. Smith, at Cricklewood. Her work required great care and skill, and was carried out in a very able manner. By her patriotic action she rendered valuable services to her country.
50, Holly Lane, Willesden, N.W.10   15402C.

HUTCHINGS, R. A., Pte., 9th Gloucestershire Regt.

He joined in February 1917, and after completing his training was sent to France in the following year. While in this theatre of war he took part in the Allied Retreat and Advance, and fought in the second battle of Cambrai in 1918.
In November 1919 he was demobilised, and holds the General Service and Victory Medals.
23, Seymour Road, Lower Edmonton, N.9   13335B.

HUTTON, A. F., Pte., Middlesex Regiment.

He joined in October 1916, and on completion of his training was sent to India. He was later drafted to Mesopotamia, where he took part in many engagements during the advance from Baghdad. In April 1919 he obtained his demobilisation, and holds the General Service and Victory Medals.
84, Felixstowe Road, Lower Edmonton, N.9   15380.

HUTTON, A. G., Gunner, Royal Field Artillery.

He volunteered in January 1916, and was later sent to the Western Front. While in this theatre of war he took part in the battles of Ypres and Cambrai in 1917, and in engagements at St. Quentin, Albert and Villers-Bretonneux (where he was wounded).
He was demobilised in June 1919, and holds the General Service and Victory Medals.
12, Agate Road, Hammersmith, W.6   11148.

HUYTON, W., Lce.-Cpl., R.A.M.C.

He volunteered in October 1915, and in the following year was sent to France. During his three years' service on this front he was engaged on important duties during the battle of Arras, and in the operations during the Allied Retreat and Advance. In March 1919 he returned home for demobilisation, and holds the General Service and Victory Medals.
67a, Drayton Road, Harlesden, N.W.10   14999.

HYNE, Pte., Royal Army Veterinary Corps.

He joined in September 1916, and owing to his qualifications was engaged on special duties in connection with the treatment of horses. He gave valuable service but was not successful in securing his transfer overseas before hostilities ceased.
He was demobilised in December 1919.
178, Blythe Road, West Kensington, W.14   12492.

I

IBBOTT, H., Sapper, Royal Engineers.

Volunteering in August 1915, he served on the Western Front for four years, taking part in the battles of Arras, the Somme and Cambrai. During his service he was gassed, and in February 1919 he was demobilised, holding the 1914–15 Star, General Service and Victory Medals.
116, Deacon Road, Cricklewood, N.W.2   X16976.

ILES, E. A., Driver, Royal Army Service Corps.

Having volunteered in 1914, he was sent to France and served through several engagements. In 1916 he contracted a serious illness, brought on by active service, and was sent to hospital for eight months.
On leaving, he was discharged owing to ill-health, and holds the General Service and Victory Medals.
13, Furness Road, Harlesden, N.W.10   13093A.

ILES, H. V., Pte., Labour Corps.

He volunteered in December 1915, and in the following year was sent to the Western Front, where he remained for two years. During his service he was present at fighting near Hulluch, and the Retreat and Advance of 1918.
He was demobilised in September 1919, and holds the General Service and Victory Medals.
285, Chapter Road, Cricklewood, N.W.2   X17121.

ILIFF, A. A., Pte., 2nd Lancashire Fusiliers.

Volunteering in August 1914 at the outbreak of war, he was sent to France in time to take part in the retreat from Mons. Later he was present at the fighting on the Somme and at Loos, Neuve Chappelle, Armentières, Arras and the Retreat from Cambrai in 1918.
During his service he was wounded at Arras, and in 1919 was demobilised, holding the Mons Star, General Service and Victory Medals.
7, Mirabel Road, Fulham, S.W.6   X17709.

ILIFF, E. G. (Miss), Special War Worker.

Throughout the war this lady was employed in shell-filling and in the T.N.T. room at Messrs. Blake's Munition Factory, Hurlingham. Her work involved considerable risk, and she gave excellent services all the time. She received a certificate of appreciation from the firm.
7, Mirabel Road, Fulham, S.W.6   X17704.

ILIFF, H. W., Bandsman, 1st Connaught Rangers.

Volunteering in August 1914, he was sent to the Western Front, where he took part in the retreat from Mons, and the battles of Neuve Chapelle, Messines and Arras. Being wounded at La Bassée he was invalided to hospital in England, and certified unfit for further active service.
He holds the Mons Star, General Service and Victory Medals, and was still serving in 1920.
7, Mirabel Road, Fulham, S.W.6   X17705.

ILIFF, W. T., Pte., R.A.S.C.

He volunteered in August 1915, and served in the Departmental Supply Section at Hazebrouck, Calais and Havre. He was present at a serious explosion at one of the ammunition dumps when many lives were lost, but he himself escaped injury.
In December 1917 he was discharged owing to ill-health as medically unfit for further service, and holds the 1914–15 Star, General Service and Victory Medals.
7, Mirabel Road, Fulham, S.W.6   X17923A.

ILIFF, W. T., Pte., 2/23rd London Regiment.

He joined in April 1916, and served at Salonica and in Egypt and Palestine, where he took part in engagements at Jerusalem, Jericho, Jaffa and Beersheba. Later he was drafted to France, and was killed in action at Cambrai on October 14th, 1918, during the Allied Advance.
He was entitled to the General Service and Victory Medals.
7, Mirabel Road, Fulham, S.W.6   X17923B

ILIFF, F. W. (M.S.M.), Sergt., 1st Connaught Rangers and Supply and Transport Corps (Indian Army).

He volunteered in August 1914, and was sent to the Western Front, where he took part in the fighting at Mons, Messines, Neuve Chapelle, where he was wounded, and La Bassée. Later he was sent to Mesopotamia, and was in action at Kut-el-Amara and Baghdad. He was mentioned in despatches for gallantry and distinguished service in the field in preventing the capture of a convoy by Turkish cavalry. He returned to England in March 1920 and was demobilised.
He holds the Meritorious Service Medal, awarded for his consistent good work, the Mons Star, General Service and Victory Medals.
7, Mirabel Road, Walham Green, S.W.6   TX17706.

ILLINGWORTH, C. (Mrs.), Special War Worker.

During the war this lady did valuable work in connection with munitions, first in the manufacture of rifle parts at Enfield Lock, and later for two years in the dangerous T.N.T. and Cordite departments at Ponder's End Munition Factory.
98, Hartington Road, Tottenham, N.17   X19107B.

ILLINGWORTH, P. W. (M.M.), Cpl., R.G.A.

Volunteering in October 1914 he was sent to France in 1916, where he took part in engagements on the Somme and at Ypres, and was wounded. For conspicuous gallantry in the field on June 24th, 1918, he was awarded the Military Medal, and in addition holds the General Service and Victory Medals.
He was demobilised in February 1919.
98, Hartington Road, Tottenham, N.17   X19107A.

ING, A. E., Driver, Royal Field Artillery.

He volunteered in October 1915, and after his training was drafted to the Western Front, where he took part in many engagements, including the battles of Arras, Ypres and the Somme.
He was demobilised in July 1919, and holds the 1914–15 Star, General Service and Victory Medals.
91, Bounces Road, Lower Edmonton, N.9   13075.

ING, G. E., Driver, Royal Field Artillery.

Volunteering in 1915, he was sent in the same year to the Western Front, where he took part in several engagements, including those on the Somme, and at Arras and Bapaume.
He was demobilised in 1919, and holds the 1914–15 Star, General Service and Victory Medals.
101, Monmouth Road, Lower Edmonton, N.9   13021A.

ING, J. H., Pte., Duke of Cornwall's Light Infantry.

He volunteered in 1914, and after his training served at various stations on important duties with his unit. He gave valuable services, but was not successful in obtaining his transfer overseas owing to ill health, and was discharged in consequence as medically unfit for further military service in 1918.
101, Monmouth Road, Lower Edmonton, N.9   13021B.

ING, J. T., Pte., 3rd Middlesex Regiment.

Volunteering in August 1914, he was sent to France in the same year, and took part in the retreat from Mons, the battles of Ypres, La Bassée, Arras, and the Somme and was twice wounded.
He was demobilised in March 1919, holding the Mons Star, General Service and Victory Medals.
101, Monmouth Road, Lower Edmonton, N.9   13021C.

ING, W., Driver, Royal Field Artillery.

He joined in 1916, and was sent to France, where he took part in many important engagements on the Western Front, including the battles of Arras, St. Quentin, Bullecourt and the Advance of 1918.
He afterwards went to Germany with the Army of Occupation, and remained there until he returned to England for his demobilisation in April 1920.
He holds the General Service and Victory Medals.
8, Lundy Street, Fulham, S.W.6   14808.

INGHAM, A., Poineer, Royal Engineers.

He volunteered in August 1915, and was shortly afterwards drafted overseas. He served on the Western Front, and took part in many engagements, including those at Arras, Ypres, and Nieuport, where he was badly gassed.
He holds the 1914–15 Star, General Service and Victory Medals, and was demobilised in February 1919.
163, Estcourt Road, Fulham, S.W.6   T17068.

INGRAM, A., Bandsman, Royal Fusiliers.

He was serving in the Territorials at the outbreak of war, and was mobilised in August 1914. He was engaged on important duties with his unit until the following year, when he was drafted to the Dardanelles, where he took part in many engagements, and suffered from frost bite and rheumatism. Owing to this he was invalided to hospital in England, and subsequently discharged as medically unfit for further service in December 1918.
He holds the 1914–15 Star, General Service, Victory and the Territorial Efficiency Medals.
8oa, Deacon Road, Cricklewood, N.W.2   X17117B.

INGRAM, A. E., Pte., 2nd Queen's (Royal West Surrey Regiment).

He enlisted in January 1913, and at the outbreak of war was drafted overseas. He took a conspicuous part in much of the severe fighting on the Western Front, and was wounded in action three times.
After the cessation of hostilities he returned to England, and was demobilised in March, 1919. He holds the 1914–15 Star, General Service and Victory Medals.
42, Chaldon Road, Dawes Road, S.W.6   X17726.

INGRAM, E., Rifleman (1st-Class Signaller), Rifle Brigade.

He volunteered in March 1915, and in the same year was sent to France, where he took part in many engagements on the Western Front, including those at Ypres, Arras, Vimy Ridge, and the Somme, and was wounded.
He holds the 1914–15 Star, General Service and Victory Medals, and was demobilised in June 1919.
8oa, Deacon Road, Cricklewood, N.W.2   X17117A.

INGRAM, S., Cpl., Machine Gun Corps.

He enlisted in 1915 and was sent overseas the same year, where he took part in many important engagements on the Western Front. He was wounded twice, and badly gassed during his service.
He holds the 1914–15 Star, General Service and Victory Medals, and was demobilised in 1919.
8, Hartington Road, Lower Edmonton, N.9   14250B.

INGRAM, W., Gunner, Royal Horse Artillery.

He volunteered for service in August 1914, and after his training was drafted to India, where he was engaged on garrison duties with his unit. In 1915 he was sent to Mesopotamia, and was actively engaged in much of the fighting in this theatre of war. He also suffered from malaria.
He holds the 1914–15 Star, General Service and Victory Medals.
8, Hartington Road, Lower Edmonton, N.9   14250A.

INGREY, A., Sapper, Royal Engineers.

Volunteering in April 1915, he was stationed at various depots on important duties with his unit until 1917, when he was drafted to the Western Front. During his service overseas he was engaged in much important fighting, and was wounded.
He holds the General Service and Victory Medals.
20, Sebastopol Road, Lower Edmonton, N.9   14965.

INKPEN, L. E., Pte., R.A.S.C.

Joining for service in December 1917, he was sent overseas at the conclusion of his training. During his service on the Western Front he was engaged on various duties in connection with transport to the forward areas.
He holds the General Service and Victory Medals.
60, Rayleigh Road, West Kensington, W.14   12425.

INSALL, G. F., Pte., Welch Regiment.

He joined in January 1917, and was shortly afterwards drafted overseas. During his service on the Western Front he took part in the fighting at Arras, and was killed in action at the battle of Ypres.
He was entitled to the General Service and Victory Medals.
67, West Street, Lower Edmonton, N.9   14602.

12

INSKIP, A., Rifleman, 12th London Regiment (Rangers).

He volunteered in 1915, and in the same year was sent overseas, where he took part in many engagements on the Western Front, including the battles of Ypres and the Somme, and was wounded three times.
He was discharged in October 1917 as medically unfit owing to his service, and holds the 1914–15 Star, General Service and Victory Medals.
6, Denton Road, Stonebridge Park, N.W.10   14699C.

IRELAND, A., Physical Training Instructor, Royal Navy, H.M.S. " Bacchante."

Having served previously in the Benin Rising, Somaliland, Soudan, China and Crete, for which campaigns he holds medals, he was with his ship off the coast of West Africa and in Australian waters during the Great War.
After 22 years' service he was demobilised, and holds the 1914 Star, General Service and Victory Medals, in addition to those above mentioned.
7, Shakespeare Avenue, Harlesden, N.W.10   13891A.

IRELAND, A. R., Pte., The Queen's (Royal West Surrey Regiment).

He joined in 1917, and was drafted to France the same year. During his service on the Western Front he took part in several engagements, including the battle of the Somme, and remained overseas until after the Armistice.
He was then returned to England and was demobilised in May 1919, holding the General Service and Victory Medals.
12, Beaufoy Road, Tottenham, N.17   X17938A.

IRELAND, H. J., Driver, R.A.S.C. (M.T.)

He volunteered in September 1914, and was shortly afterwards sent to France. He was attached to the 3rd Cavalry Division, and was engaged on important transport duties to different parts of the Front, including the Somme and Ypres sectors.
He contracted pneumonia, and died on November 1st, 1918, and was entitled to the 1914 Star, General Service and Victory Medals.
34, Franklyn Road, Willesden, N.W.10   16319.

IRELAND, P. R., Pte., 14th London Regiment (London Scottish).

He joined in 1917, and was sent to France the same year. While in this theatre of war he took part in several engagements, and was wounded in action at Oppy Wood in March 1918 during the German offensive of that year.
He was demobilised in 1919, and holds the General Service and Victory Medals.
12, Beaufoy Road, Tottenham, N.17   17938B.

IRESON, T. W., Gunner, R.F.A.

He volunteered in December 1915, and after his training was retained on useful work at various stations with his unit until 1918, when he was sent to France. He took part in the Retreat and Advance of 1918, and was gassed during his service overseas.
He returned to England after the Armistice, and was demobilised in April 1919, holding the General Service and Victory Medals.
2, Yewfield Road, Willesden, N.W.10   16368D.

IRESON, V., Pte., 1/9th Middlesex Regiment.

He volunteered for service in September 1914, and after a short period of training was drafted to India the same year, where he was engaged at various stations on important duties with his unit until his death on August 31st, 1917.
He was entitled to the 1914–15 Star, General Service and Victory Medals.
2, Yewfield Road, Willesden, N.W.10   16368A.

IRESON, W. F., Driver, Royal Field Artillery.

He enlisted in September 1914, and on completion of his training was sent overseas, where he took part in many engagements on the Western Front, including those at Trones Wood, Longueval and Delville Wood during the battle of the Somme. During his service he was gassed.
He holds the 1914–15 Star, the General Service and Victory Medals, and was demobilised in April 1919.
2, Yewfield Road, Willesden, N.W.10   16368C.

IRESON, W. H., Pte., Royal Defence Corps.

He volunteered in the R.D.C. in February 1915, and after his training served at various stations on important duties with his unit until the cessation of hostilities.
He was unable to obtain his transfer overseas, and was demobilised in March 1919.
2, Yewfield Road, Willesden, N.W.10   16368B.

IRONS, E. (Mrs.), Special War Worker.
This lady was employed on work of national importance at Hayes' Munition Factory from November 1914 until July 1915, and afterwards at the White City, where she was engaged in the manufacture of anti-gas masks, until April 1918. She performed her duties in a satisfactory manner.
32, Rayleigh Road, Shepherd's Bush, W.12   12641A.

IRONSIDE, J., Sergt., R.A.S.C. (M.T.)
Volunteering in September 1914, he was later drafted to the Western Front, where he took part in many important operations in various sectors, being chiefly engaged in the transportation of ammunition and supplies to forward areas.
In March 1919 he was demobilised, and holds the General Service and Victory Medals.
130, Farm Lane, Walham Green, S.W.6   X19609.

ISAAC, H., Gunner, R.F.A. (35th T.M. Bty.)
He joined in January 1917, and after his training was drafted overseas. During his service on the Western Front he was severely wounded in action, and was invalided to England, where he was in hospital for 14 months.
He was discharged in consequence as medically unfit in July 1919, holding the General Service and Victory Medals.
3, West Street, Lower Edmonton, N.9   14592.

ISARD, G. A., Rifleman, 16th London Regiment (Queen's Westminster Rifles).
He volunteered in 1915, and in the same year went to France, where he took part in several engagements on the Western Front. In the following year he was drafted to Salonica, and served for about two years on the Bulgarian Front. On his return to France in 1918 he was taken ill with influenza, and died in hospital in Le Hàvre.
He was entitled to the 1914-15 Star, General Service and Victory Medals
29, Hormead Road, Maida Hill, W.9   X20123A.

ISARD, T. H., Signaller, Middlesex Regiment.
He volunteered in September 1914, and in the following June went to France, where he took part in the fighting at Albert, Hill 60, and Ypres. On September 3rd, 1916, he was killed in action at the battle of the Somme.
He was entitled to the 1914-15 Star, General Service and Victory Medals.
29, Hormead Road, Maida Hill, W.9   X20123B.

ISTED, A., Pte., Grenadier Guards.
He volunteered in August 1914, and was shortly afterwards drafted to the Western Front, where he was wounded in action at Zillebeke in September 1914. On his recovery he fought in many engagements, including the battles of the Somme, Ypres and Cambrai, and was gassed.
He returned to England after the Armistice and was demobilised in March 1919, holding the Mons Star, General Service and Victory Medals.
32, Burn's Road, Harlesden, N.W.10   13140A.

IVE, A. C., Bombardier, Royal Field Artillery.
He volunteered in August 1914, and after his training served on the Western Front, where he took part in the battles of Ypres, the Somme, and the Retreat and Advance of 1918. Later he went to Germany with the Army of Occupation, and was demobilised in April 1919.
He holds the 1914-15 Star, General Service and Victory Medals.
33, Letchford Gardens, Willesden, N.W.10   X17543A.

IVES, C., Driver, Royal Army Service Corps.
He volunteered in March 1915, and at the conclusion of his training was drafted overseas. He was engaged on various duties in connection with transport in many sectors of the Western Front.
He holds the General Service and Victory Medals, and was demobilised in March 1919.
31, Church Path, Hammersmith, W.6   15904.

IVESON, J., Pte., 1st Queen's (Royal West Surrey Regiment).
He had previously served in the Army, and being a Reservist was mobilised at the outbreak of war. He was sent to France with the 1st Division, and after taking part in the retreat from Mons and the battle of the Marne, was taken prisoner on November 29th, 1914. He suffered many privations during his four years' captivity in Germany, and after the Armistice was released.
He returned to England for demobilisation in January 1919, and holds the Mons Star, General Service and Victory Medals.
49, Gloucester Road, Upper Edmonton, N.18   X16958.

IVEY, R. E., Sergt., Royal Engineers.
He volunteered for service in February 1915, and after a short period of training was drafted to France, where he was severely wounded in action in October 1915. Upon his recovery he was engaged on various important duties in the battle areas of the Western Front.
He holds the 1914-15 Star, General Service and Victory Medals.
24a, Nursery Street, Tottenham, N.17   X18147.

J

JACK, W., Sergt., Seaforth Highlanders.
Enlisting in June 1899, he was sent to France immediately on the outbreak of hostilities. He there took part in the retreat from Mons, the first and second battles of Ypres, and many other engagements.
Later he saw much heavy fighting in the Balkans.
He was overseas for a period of five years in all, and was discharged in April 1919. He holds the Queen's and King's South African Medals, the Mons Star, General Service and Victory Medals.
55, Charlton Road, Harlesden, N.W.10   13380.

JACKS, W. C., Pte., R.A.S.C. (M.T.)
He joined in February 1916, and later in the same year was drafted to France. During his two years' service there he took part in many engagements, during which he was employed on important transport work.
In September 1919 he was demobilised, and holds the General Service and Victory Medals.
20, Wakefield Road, Upper Edmonton, N.18   15811.

JACKSON, A., Driver, R.A.S.C.
He volunteered in August 1914, and was immediately sent to the Western Front. He remained in this seat of war during the whole period of hostilities, took part in engagements at Ypres, Béthune, the Somme, Arras and Mons, and was twice wounded.
He was still serving in 1920, and holds the 1914 Star, General Service and Victory Medals.
4, Lamington Street, Hammersmith, W.6   11101.

JACKSON, A., Pte., R.A.S.C.
He volunteered in April 1915, and later in the same year was sent to France, where he was engaged on transport duties of vital importance in various sectors of the Front. While carrying out his duties he met with a serious accident which kept him in hospital for some time.
He was demobilised in 1919, and holds the 1914-15 Star, General Service and Victory Medals.
32, Furness Road, Harlesden, N.W.10   13164A.

JACKSON, A. A., Pte., 17th Royal Fusiliers.
He joined in 1916, and was sent overseas in the same year. He took part in many strenuous engagements on the Western Front, and was killed in action at the battle of Arras in April 1917.
He was entitled to the General Service and Victory Medals.
56, Sheldon Road, Upper Edmonton, N.18   X17295.

JACKSON, A. C. (M.M.), Pte., M.G.C.
He volunteered in August 1914, and on completion of his training was drafted overseas in the following January. He took part in many engagements on the Western Front, including those at Givenchy and Longueval, and was wounded three times.
He was awarded the Military Medal for conspicuous bravery and devotion to duty in the field, and also holds the 1914-15 Star, General Service and Victory Medals. He was discharged as medically unfit for further service in September 1917, owing to his wounds.
191, Winchester Road, Lower Edmonton, N.9   14887.

JACKSON, C. (Miss), Special War Worker.
Although only 15 years of age, this lady volunteered for war work, and was employed at Park Royal Small Arms Factory for three years. Her valuable services were greatly appreciated, and she carried out her duties satisfactorily.
32, Furness Road, Harlesden, N.W.10   13164B.

JACKSON, C. E., Pte., Middlesex Regiment.
He joined in June 1916, and in the same year was sent to France, where he took part in many important engagements, including those on the Somme, and at Ypres, Arras and around Armentières. During his service he was wounded and gassed, and was demobilised in March 1919.
He holds the General Service and Victory Medals.
59, Purves Road, Kensal Rise, N.W.10   X17797A.

JACKSON, C. H., Pte., Somerset Light Infantry.
Volunteering in May 1915, he was sent to the Western Front, where he took part in engagements at Ypres, the Somme, and Givenchy. Owing to a wound which he received at Mailly-Maillet, he was invalided home, remaining in hospital for some time. On his recovery he was drafted to Mesopotamia, and later to India.
In 1919 he returned to England, and in December was demobilised, holding the General Service and Victory Medals.
17, Humbolt Road, Hammersmith, W.6   15308.

JACKSON, D. (Mrs.), Special War Worker.
During the war this lady was engaged on work of an important nature at the Park Royal Small Arms Factory, where she held a responsible position as inspector of small arms ammunition. She rendered valuable service, and performed her duties in a satisfactory manner.
32, Furness Road, Harlesden, N.W.10   13164C.

JACKSON, E. R., Pte., Buffs (East Kent Regt.)
He volunteered in September 1914, and was sent overseas in the following year. He participated in many engagements on the Western Front, and was badly wounded in action. After recovery he again took part in severe fighting, and was taken prisoner. During his two years' captivity in Germany, he spent some time in hospital, and on his release was demobilised in April 1919.
He holds the 1914-15 Star, General Service and Victory Medals.
3, St. Peter's Terrace, Fulham, S.W.6   X18861.

JACKSON, E. W., Rifleman, King's Royal Rifle Corps and Pte., R.A.S.C. (M.T.)
Joining the Army in July 1918, he completed his training, and after being stationed at various places with his unit, was sent to Germany with the Army of Occupation. Later he joined the Royal Army Service Corps, and was still serving in 1920.
86, Carlyle Avenue, Willesden, N.W.10   14450.

JACKSON, G., Sapper, Royal Engineers.
Volunteering in May 1915, he was sent four months later to the Eastern Front, where he took part in the capture of Baghdad. After being transferred to the Egyptian Expeditionary Force, he served at the battle of Jaffa. In June 1918 he was invalided home, and died of pneumonia in October.
He was entitled to the 1914-15 Star, General Service and Victory Medals.
50, Hazel Road, Willesden, N.W.10   X17782.

JACKSON, G., Sapper, Royal Engineers.
He volunteered in August 1914, and was drafted overseas in the same year to the Western Front. He went later to Salonica, and was engaged on the Bulgarian Front near Lake Doiran.
He was sent home and demobilised in January 1919, and holds the 1914 Star, General Service and Victory Medals.
30, Mayo Road, Willesden, N.W.10   15605.

JACKSON, H., Gunner, Royal Field Artillery.
This gunner volunteered in April 1915, and was sent overseas later in that year. He fought in the battles of Ypres, Arras, the Somme and Cambrai, and was twice wounded.
He holds the 1914-15 Star, General Service and Victory Medals, and was demobilised in March 1919.
14, Lamington Street, Hammersmith, W.6   11098.

JACKSON, H., Cpl., 2nd Grenadier Guards.
He volunteered in August 1914, and was almost immediately sent to the Western Front, where he took part in the first important engagements of the war. In November of the same year he was severely wounded at La Bassée, and being invalided home, was in hospital for a considerable period. On recovery he returned to France and served through much of the heavy fighting until the cessation of hostilities.
He was demobilised in March 1919, and holds the 1914 Star, General Service and Victory Medals.
10, Welford Terrace, Dawes Road, S.W.6   X18065.

JACKSON, H. R., Sergt., R.E. (130th Field Coy.)
He volunteered in February 1915, and was sent to France later in the same year, where he took a prominent part in the battles of Ypres, Loos, the Somme and Arras, and in engagements around Albert and Cambrai. He was wounded in 1916 while in action near Albert, and was killed near Armentières on July 21st, 1917.
He was entitled to the 1914-15 Star, General Service and Victory Medals.
19, Shelley Road, Willesden, N.W.10   13877A.

JACKSON, J. (M.M.), Driver, R.F.A.
He volunteered in March 1915, and in the same year was sent overseas, where he took part in many important engagements on the Western Front. He was awarded the Military Medal for conspicuous gallantry and devotion to duty while in action at Poelcappelle.
In June 1920, he was demobilised, and in addition to the Military Medal, holds the 1914-15 Star, General Service and Victory Medals.
69, Kimberley Road, Upper Edmonton, N.18   16582B.

JACKSON, M., Rifleman, K.R.R.
He joined in July 1917, and on completion of his training was drafted to the Western Front, where he took part in many engagements in France and Belgium. After the signing of the Armistice he proceeded to Germany with the Army of Occupation, and remained there until he was sent home for demobilisation in January 1920.
He holds the General Service and Victory Medals.
69, Kimberley Road, Upper Edmonton, N.18   16582A.

JACKSON, M. L., Air Mechanic, R.A.F.
He joined in June 1918 on attaining military age, and on completion of his training was engaged with his unit on important duties at various stations. He gave valuable services, but owing to the cessation of hostilities was not successful in obtaining his transfer overseas before the signing of the Armistice. Later he went to Germany with the Army of Occupation, and in 1920 was still serving.
24, Denzil Road, Neasden Lane, N.W.10   16079C.

JACKSON, T. W., Sapper, R.E. (179th Coy.)
He volunteered in March 1915, and in the same year went overseas, where he was engaged on important operations in various sectors of the Western Front until the cessation of hostilities.
He was demobilised in February 1919, and holds the 1914-15 Star, General Service and Victory Medals.
31, Disraeli Road, Acton Lane, N.W.10   14149.

JACKSON, W., Driver, Royal Engineers.
He volunteered in May 1915, and on completion of his training was sent overseas. He was stationed at various depots in France, and was actively engaged in many battle areas of the Western Front until the cessation of hostilities.
He was demobilised in June 1919, and holds the General Service and Victory Medals.
37, Lintaine Grove, West Kensington, W.14   16828.

JACKSON, W., Pte., 1st Coldstream Guards.
An ex-soldier with 14 years' service, he rejoined in August 1914, and five months later was sent overseas. After seeing active service in various sectors of the Western Front, he was severely wounded at Festubert in September 1915, and was invalided home.
Owing to his wound he was discharged as unfit, and holds the 1914-15 Star, General Service and Victory Medals, in addition to the Queen's and King's South African Medals.
24, Denzil Road, Neasden Lane, N.W.10   16079A.

JACKSON, W. E. (M.M.), Driver, Royal Field Artillery.
Volunteering in November 1914, he embarked for the East shortly after. While there he took part in the severe fighting throughout the Gallipoli campaign, and on the evacuation of the Peninsula was sent to France. He fought in many engagements on the Western Front, and was awarded the Military Medal for conspicuous gallantry in the field while in action on the Somme in August 1917.
He also holds the 1914-15 Star, General Service and Victory Medals, and was demobilised in March 1920.
24, Denzil Road, Neasden Lane, N.W.10   16079B.

JACKSON, W. H., Pte., Royal Fusiliers.
He joined in August 1918 on attaining military age, and was retained with his unit on important duties at various stations. Owing to the cessation of hostilities, he was not successful in obtaining his transfer overseas, but gave valuable services until his demobilisation in November 1919.
19, Shelley Road, Willesden, N.W.10   13877B.

JACOB, D., Pte., Middlesex Regiment.
He volunteered in 1915, and was sent overseas in the same year. He took part in many engagements on the Western Front, and was killed in action during the battle of the Somme on October 1st, 1916.
He was entitled to the 1914-15 Star, General Service and Victory Medals.
17, Denton Road, Stonebridge Park, N.W.10   14706B.

JACOB, G. W., Pte., Royal Fusiliers.
He joined in July 1916, and after his training was drafted to France. During his service on the Western Front he was actively engaged in the fighting, until he was killed in action, near Ypres on July 13th, 1917.
He was entitled to the General Service and Victory Medals.
315, Chapter Road, Cricklewood, N.W.2   16721

JACOB, S. F., Pte. (Signaller), Middlesex Regt.
He joined in February 1916, and on completion of his training was sent to France, where he took part in the battles of the Somme, Arras and Cambrai, and in heavy fighting around Loos. During his service he was twice wounded and was invalided to England, where he was in hospital for some time. He was demobilised in February 1919, and holds the General Service and Victory Medals.
25, Kennet Road, Maida Hill, W.9   X19386.

JACOB, W. T., Pte., 2/4th Black Watch.
Volunteering in 1915, he completed his training and was sent overseas. While on the Western Front he took part in several engagements, including those during the Advance of 1918, and was wounded.
He holds the General Service and Victory Medals, and was demobilised in 1919.
17, Denton Road, Stonebridge Park, N.W.10   14706A.

JACOBSON, E. (D.C.M.), Pte., Monmouthshire Regt.
He volunteered in November 1914, and early in the following year was sent to France, where he took part in the battle of Loos, the engagements at La Bassée, and the Retreat and Advance of 1918. In September 1917 he was awarded the Distinguished Conduct Medal for conspicuous gallantry and devotion to duty, when, as a stretcher-bearer, he brought in several wounded men under heavy shell fire. During the Advance in July 1918 he was again recommended for bringing in a wounded officer with absolute disregard for his own personal safety during a bombardment.
He was twice wounded while overseas, and in 1919 was demobilised, holding in addition to the Distinguished Conduct Medal, the 1914–15 Star, General Service and Victory Medals.
64, Shakespeare Avenue, Willesden, N.W.10   13623.

JACQUES, E. R., Pte., Northamptonshire Regt.
He joined in March 1916, and after his training was sent to the Western Front, where he took part in many important engagements, including those at Ypres, Arras and Cambrai. During his active service he was severely gassed and was invalided home.
In January 1920 he was demobilised, and holds the General Service and Victory Medals.
62, Stanley Road, King's Road, S.W.6   X19786.

JACQUES, W., Lce.-Cpl., Middlesex Regiment.
He was mobilised in August 1914, and almost immediately embarked for India, where he was engaged on important duties at various stations for some time. He was later sent to Mesopotamia, taking part in the heavy fighting during the Advance. After the conclusion of the campaign there he again returned to India, and fought in the North-West Frontier engagements against the Afghans.
In October 1919 he was demobilised, and holds the 1914–15 Star, General Service and Victory Medals, and the Indian General Service Medal (with clasp Afghanistan N.W. Frontier, 1919). 121, Villiers Road, Cricklewood, N.W.2   16339.

JAGGS, G., Pte., Middlesex Regiment.
He volunteered in August 1914, and shortly afterwards was sent overseas, where he took part in many important engagements on the Western Front, including the retreat from Mons and the battle of the Somme.
He was twice wounded during his service, and holds the Mons Star, General Service and Victory Medals.
36, Eldon Road, Lower Edmonton, N.9   13056B.

JAMES, A., Pte., R.A.S.C. and Tank Corps.
Volunteering in 1915, he was sent to France in the same year. After being transferred to the Tank Corps he took part in the battles of the Somme, Arras, Ypres (1917), and Cambrai. During the Retreat in March 1918 he was wounded and was for some time in hospital.
He was demobilised in March 1919, and holds the 1914–15 Star, General Service and Victory Medals.
130, Shakespeare Avenue, Willesden, N.W.10   13896.

JAMES, A., Pte., Royal Army Service Corps.
He joined in 1917, and in the same year was sent overseas, where he was actively engaged in various battle areas of the Western Front. He was in hospital in France and in England with illness contracted on active service.
In May 1919 he was demobilised, and holds the General Service and Victory Medals.
47, Sherbrooke Road, Fulham, S.W.6   X18478.

JAMES, A., Rifleman, 6th London Regt. (Rifles).
He joined in 1916, and was shortly afterwards drafted overseas, where he took part in many important engagements on the Western Front, including the battle of the Somme. While in action in 1917 he was taken prisoner, and suffered many hardships in Germany. He was released at the cessation of hostilities, and returned to England for demobilisation in December 1918.
He holds the General Service and Victory Medals.
52, Rowallan Road, Munster Road, S.W.6   X19279.

JAMES, A., Pte., 7th London Regiment.
He joined in October 1916, and on completion of his training, served at various stations on important duties with his unit. He gave valuable services, but was not successful in obtaining his transfer overseas owing to his being certified as medically unfit for Foreign service, and was demobilised in March 1919.
7, Varna Road, Fulham, S.W.6   X18750.

JAMES, A. B., Pte., 7th London Regiment.
He volunteered immediately on the outbreak of war in August 1914, and was sent to France in the following March. While there he fought in the battles of Ypres, Festubert and Loos, and was twice wounded. He was in hospital in France for some time, and was then invalided home, being eventually discharged owing to wounds, as medically unfit for further service in April 1916.
He holds the 1914–15 Star, General Service and Victory Medals.
23, Kilmaine Road, Munster Road, S.W.6   TX18853.

JAMES, A. J., Gunner, Royal Field Artillery.
He volunteered in September 1914, and after his training was sent to France. While there he took part in the battle of Ypres, and during the heavy fighting round Albert was gassed and wounded. On his recovery he was drafted to Salonica, where he fought in the Balkan campaign.
In June 1919 he was demobilised, and holds the 1914–15 Star, General Service and Victory Medals.
7, Jervis Road, Fulham, S.W.6   TX17371.

JAMES, C. H., Pte., 1st Buffs (East Kent Regt.)
He had served in the Army previous to the war, but at the outbreak of hostilities was engaged on important duties in a large works. In June 1915 he rejoined the Army, and was immediately sent to France. While there he fought in the battles of Loos, the Somme and Ypres (1917), and was severely wounded in 1918. He remained for a long time in hospital, and on recovery went with the Army of Occupation to Germany.
He remained there until he returned to England for his demobilisation in March 1919, and holds the 1914–15 Star, General Service and Victory Medals.
26, Grove Street, Upper Edmonton, N.18.   X17886.

JAMES, C. H., Pte., Royal Warwickshire Regt.
He joined in September 1916, and after his training was sent overseas. After taking part in several engagements during his service on the Western Front, he was killed in action on August 25th, 1918.
He was entitled to the General Service and Victory Medals.
23, Kinnoul Road, Hammersmith, W.6   T14470C.

JAMES, E., Trooper, Royal Horse Guards.
He volunteered in August 1914, and in the following year was sent to France, where during his four years' service he was engaged on special observation duties in the battles of Ypres, Arras and Bullecourt, and in the Retreat and Advance of 1918.
He holds the 1914–15 Star, General Service and Victory Medals, and was serving in 1920.
409, Chapter Road, Cricklewood, N.W.2   16163.

JAMES, E., 1st Air Mechanic, R.A.F.
Joining in 1916 he was, on completion of his training, retained on important duties requiring a high degree of technical skill at various aerodromes. He gave valuable services, but was not successful in obtaining his transfer overseas before the cessation of hostilities.
He was demobilised in February 1919.
3, Colville Road, Lower Edmonton, N.9   11995C.

JAMES, E. G., Pte., R.A.S.C. (M.T.)
He volunteered in May 1916, and in the following year was sent to France, where he took an active part in several important engagements. He suffered from shell-shock twice during his services overseas, and was for a long period in hospital in France.
In January 1919 he was demobilised, and holds the General Service and Victory Medals.
61, St. Paul's Road, Tottenham, N.17   X18824.

JAMES, F. W., Pte., 19th Middlesex Regiment.
He volunteered in August 1915, and after his training served on the Western Front, where he took part in many important engagements, including the battle of Ypres.
In November 1919 he was demobilised, and holds the General Service and Victory Medals.
23, Kinnoul Road, Hammersmith, W.6   T14470A.

JAMES, G., Pte., 6th Middlesex Regiment.
He volunteered in December 1915, and on completion of his training was sent in the following year to France, where he took part in engagements in various battle areas of the Western Front. He was killed in action on the Somme on August 1st, 1916, and was entitled to the General Service and Victory Medals.
34, Elsdon Road, Tottenham, N.17   X18499B.

JAMES, H., Sapper, Royal Engineers.

He volunteered in September 1914, and in the following year was sent to the Western Front, where he took part in engagements at Loos, Ypres, Arras, Armentières and Amiens. He was invalided to England on account of ill-health, and on his recovery returned to France, where he took part in the Advance of 1918.
He holds the 1914–15 Star, General Service and Victory Medals, and was demobilised in April 1919.
48, Humbolt Road, Hammersmith, W.6   15296.

JAMES, H. S., 1st-Class Petty Officer, R.N.

He was mobilised on the outbreak of hostilities, and proceeded to sea immediately in August 1914. He served on board H.M.S. " Patrician " with the Grand Fleet in the North Sea, and was later engaged on important patrol duties in many dangerous waters.
He holds the 1914 Star, General Service and Victory Medals, and was serving in 1920.
21, Star Road, West Kensington, W.14   16178.

JAMES, J. E., 3rd Air Mechanic, R.A.F.

He joined in March 1917, and after his training was engaged on important duties, which called for a high degree of technical skill, with his unit on the East and South-East coasts. He gave valuable services, but was unsuccessful in obtaining his transfer overseas before the cessation of hostilities.
He was demobilised in May 1919.
3, Colville Road, Lower Edmonton, N.9   11995B.

JAMES, J. W., Pte., 9th Devonshire Regiment.

Volunteering in August 1914, he was sent to France after the completion of his training. While on this Front he took part in many important operations, and was wounded in action at Loos.
He was demobilised in February 1919, and holds the General Service and Victory Medals.
23, Kinnoul Road, Hammersmith, W.6   T14470B.

JAMES, M. E., Pte., 10th London Regiment.

He volunteered in August 1914, and in the following year was drafted with his unit to the Dardanelles, where he took part in many important engagements, and was severely wounded in August 1915. He was invalided home and discharged in the following September, as medically unfit for further service, owing to his wounds.
He holds the 1914–15 Star, General Service and Victory Medals.
3, Colville Road, Lower Edmonton, N.9   11995A.

JAMES, T., Gunner, Royal Horse Artillery.

He was serving in India when hostilities commenced, and was immediately sent to the Western Front. He fought through the retreat from Mons and took part in the battles of the Marne, the Aisne, Hill 60, Vimy Ridge, Cambrai and in other important engagements.
In March 1919 he secured his discharge, and holds the Mons Star, General Service and Victory Medals.
12, Melville Road, Stonebridge Park, N.W.10   14428.

JAMES, W., 1st-Class Stoker, Royal Navy.

He volunteered in March 1915, and during his service was on board H.M.S. " Albatross," which was engaged on the important duties of locating enemy submarines in the English Channel. He met with a serious accident whilst carrying out his duties, and was in hospital for a considerable period.
In March 1919 he was demobilised, and holds the 1914–15 Star, General Service and Victory Medals.
4, Worlidge Street, Hammersmith, W.6   12787.

JAMES, W. A., Driver, Machine Gun Corps.

Volunteering in December 1914, he was sent to the Western Front in the following year. During his 3½ years' service on this Front he was actively employed on various sectors, taking part in heavy fighting at Ypres, Passchendaele, on the Somme, St. Quentin, and in the Advance in 1918.
He holds the 1914–15 Star, General Service and Victory Medals.
25, Hazelwood Crescent, N. Kensington, W.10   16511.

JAQUES, S. T., Bugler, Oxfordshire and Buckinghamshire Light Infantry.

He joined in August 1916, and the following year was sent overseas, where he took part in many engagements on the Western Front, principally in the Cambrai sector. On the cessation of hostilities he was sent to Germany with the Army of Occupation.
He holds the General Service and Victory Medals, and was serving in 1920.
99a, Deacon Road, Cricklewood, N.W.2   16605B.

JAQUES, T., Driver, Royal Field Artillery.

Volunteering in December 1914, he proceeded in the following year to the Western Front, where he remained for two years. During that time he took part in many engagements, being in action during the battles of Loos and Arras. In 1917 he was drafted to Italy, and fought in the important operations on the Piave.
On his return from this theatre of war in February 1919 he was demobilised, and holds the 1914–15 Star, General Service and Victory Medals.
99a, Deacon Road, Cricklewood, N.W.2   16605C.

JAQUES, T. E., Pte., Bedfordshire Regiment.

He joined in April 1918, and after his training was engaged on important duties with his unit at various stations. He gave valuable services, but was unsuccessful in obtaining his transfer overseas before hostilities ceased. After the signing of the Armistice he was sent to Germany with the Army of Occupation, and remained there until his demobilisation in March 1920.
99a, Deacon Road, Cricklewood, N.W.2   16605A.

JAQUEST, H., Rifleman, K.R.R.

He volunteered in August 1914, and was sent overseas in the following June. He took part in many engagements on the Western Front, including the battles of Loos, the Somme, Arras, Messines and Ypres (1917), and was wounded.
In March 1919 he was demobilised, and holds the 1914–15 Star, General Service and Victory Medals.
15, Mordaunt Road, Willesden, N.W.10   14121.

JARMAN, A., Special War Worker.

During the war this lady was engaged on work of national importance at the Greenford Munition Works. Her duties were carried out in the dangerous T.N.T.-powder rooms, and she contracted poisoning while at work. On her recovery she went to Messrs. Waring & Gillow's Munition Factory, and again rendered valuable services.
12, Parkfield Road, South Harrow.   15116B.

JARMAN, C. E., Sergt., East Surrey Regiment.

He was mobilised in August 1914, and was later sent to France, where he took part in many important engagements. During his service he was twice wounded, and spent a considerable time in hospital in France and England. On his recovery he was discharged, but later re-enlisted for service in Russia.
He has completed 18 years' service with His Majesty's Forces, and holds the 1914–15 Star, General Service and Victory Medals. He was still serving in 1920.
85, Sherbrooke Road, Fulham, S.W.6   X18476B.

JARMAN, H. W., Pte., 22nd Manchester Regt.

He joined in May 1916, and after his training was sent to France, where he took part in many engagements, and was severely wounded. On his recovery he was drafted to Italy, and again saw much service. While there he contracted a severe illness, which kept him in hospital for a time. In March 1920 he was demobilised, and holds the General Service and Victory Medals.
85, Sherbrooke Road, Fulham, S.W.6   X18476C.

JARMAN, J. H., Cpl., R.A.S.C. (M.T.)

Volunteering in 1915, he was later sent to the Western Front, where he was engaged as corporal in charge of motor-lorries, carrying supplies and ammunition to the forward areas during many of the important engagements.
He remained in France over three years, and was eventually demobilised in July 1919, holding the 1914–15 Star, General Service and Victory Medals.
85, Sherbrooke Road, Fulham, S.W.6   X18476A.

JARVIS, C. Pte., 7th Bedford Regiment.

He volunteered in 1914, and in 1916 was sent to France, where he served for three years with distinction, taking part in the battles of the Somme, Ypres (where he was gassed), Vimy Ridge, and Albert. At the two latter places he was wounded, and was in hospital for 16 months.
He was eventually demobilised in March 1919, holding the General Service and Victory Medals.
7, Durban Road, Tottenham, N.17   X18094.

JARVIS, T. K., Sergt., Sherwood Foresters.

He rejoined the Army in August 1914, having previously served for 15 years, and during his service in France took part in the retreat from Mons and in the battles of Ypres, Loos, the Somme, and Arras. He also served throughout the Retreat and Advance in 1918, rendering valuable services as divisional bandmaster while in this theatre of war.
He holds the Mons Star, General Service and Victory Medals.
179, Portnall Road, Maida Hill, W.9   X19579.

JARVIS, W. A., Leading Seaman, Royal Navy.
Mobilised in August 1914, he served during the war in H.M.
T.B.D.'s "Landrail" and "Skilful." While with these
destroyers he took part in several engagements, and served
throughout the war.
He was demobilised in March 1919, and holds the 1914 Star,
General Service and Victory Medals.
99, Yeldham Road, Hammersmith, W.6   13238.

JASPER, J., Lce.-Cpl., Royal Naval Division (Howitzer Battery).
Joining in February 1916, he was drafted to the Western
Front later in the same year. During his 2½ years' service
in this seat of war he took part in many important engagements. He was in action during the battles of Arras, Ypres
and Passchendaele, and was wounded in 1917.
He returned to England in February 1919 for demobilisation,
and holds the General Service and Victory Medals.
80, Seymour Avenue, Tottenham, N.17   X19158B.

JASPER, J. E., 1st Air Mechanic, R.A.F.
He volunteered in July 1915, and after his training was
drafted to the Western Front later in the same year. He was
attached to the 231st Siege Battery, and was in action at the
battles of the Somme, Ypres, St. Quentin and in heavy fighting around La Bassée.
In February 1919 he secured his demobilisation, and holds
the 1914-15 Star, General Service and Victory Medals.
80, Seymour Avenue, Tottenham, N.17   X19158A.

JAY, F., Gunner, Royal Field Artillery.
This gunner volunteered in April 1915, and was retained on
important duties at various stations until January 1917,
when he was sent to France. He there took part in heavy
fighting at Ypres, Arras, Soissons and on the Somme.
He returned to England in May 1919 for demobilisation,
and holds the General Service and Victory Medals.
83, Minet Avenue, Willesden, N.W.10   13634.

JAY, O., Pte., 1st Duke of Wellington's (West Riding Regiment).
He was serving in India at the outbreak of war, having enlisted in the Army in 1907. During the war he was retained
on important duties in India, and was engaged in heavy fighting on the Frontier.
In 1919 he returned to England, and in October of the same
year was discharged, after completing 12 years with the
Colours. He holds the Delhi Durbar Medal, 1914 Star,
General Service and Victory Medals, and the Indian General
Service Medal with clasp—Afghanistan, N.W. Frontier, 1919.
18, Bertie Road, Willesden, N.W.10   X17394.

JEFCOATE, H. A., Wireless Operator (1st-Class), R.N.V.R.
He joined in May 1918, and was engaged on the important
duties of a wireless operator on H.M. mine-sweeper "John
Alfred" in the North Sea and other Home waters. During
his service his vessel was engaged on many dangerous operations.
In March 1919 he secured his demobilisation, and holds the
General Service and Victory Medals.
115, Fortune Gate Road, Harlesden, N.W.10   13468C.

JEFFCOATE, W. T., Rifleman, Royal Irish Rifles.
He volunteered in 1914, and was sent to Egypt in the same
year. From there he was drafted to the Dardanelles, and
served throughout the Gallipoli campaign. On the evacuation of the Peninsula he proceeded to the Western Front, and
was again in action in important engagements.
He secured his demobilisation in 1918, and holds the 1914-15
Star, General Service and Victory Medals.
70, Kenninghall Road, Upper Edmonton, N.18   16905.

JEFFERIES, E., Special War Worker.
During the war this lady was engaged on important work in
the tracing office of Messrs. Handley Page's aeroplane works.
Her duties required much care and skill, and her valuable
services were greatly appreciated by the authorities.
46a, Furness Road, Harlesden, N.W.10   13361A.

JEFFERIES, R., Pte., Labour Corps.
He joined in 1918, having been previously exempted from
military service owing to his low category.
He was sent overseas to the Western Front, but after a short
period there was invalided home as medically unfit for further
active service.
He rendered valuable service until his demobilisation in 1919,
and holds the General Service and Victory Medals.
46a, Furness Road, Harlesden, N.W.10   13361B

JEFFERY, F. W., Pte., Middlesex Regiment.
Volunteering in August 1914, he was drafted overseas early
in the following year. He took part in many important
engagements on the Western Front and was twice wounded.
He remained overseas until 1918, when, in August of that
year, he was discharged in consequence of his wounds as
medically unfit for further service.
He holds the 1914-15 Star, General Service and Victory
Medals.
94, King's Road, Upper Edmonton, N.18   15516.

JEFFERY, J., Pte., Middlesex Regiment.
He volunteered for service in 1915, and later in the same year
was sent to France. During his four years' service on the
Western Front he took part in many engagements, and was
severely wounded.
He returned to England for demobilisation in 1919, and
holds the General Service and Victory Medals.
78, Churchill Road, Cricklewood, N.W.2   16623A.

JEFFREY, J. H. R. A., Gunner, R.F.A.
Volunteering early in 1915, he was sent to the Dardanelles
later in the same year, and served through the latter end of
the Gallipoli campaign. On the evacuation of the Peninsula
he was drafted to France, and took part in the battles of the
Somme, Ypres (1917) and Cambrai.
He was demobilised in February 1919, holding the 1914-15
Star, General Service and Victory Medals.
45, Chamberlain Road, Lower Edmonton, N.9   14021A.

JEFFREY, W. W., Lce.-Cpl., 18th London Regt. (London Irish Rifles).
He volunteered in April 1915, and at the conclusion of his
training was drafted overseas the following year. He took
part in many engagements on the Western Front, and was
wounded.
He holds the General Service and Victory Medals.
45, Chamberlain Road, Lower Edmonton, N.9   14021B.

JENKINS, A., Pte., East Surrey Regiment.
He volunteered for service in August 1914, and was sent to
France the same year. During his service on the Western
Front he took part in much heavy fighting in the retreat from
Mons and the battles of Ypres, the Somme and Cambrai.
He was wounded during his service overseas.
He holds the Mons Star, General Service and Victory Medals.
131, Winchester Road, Lower Edmonton, N.9   14951B.

JENKINS, C. (M.S.M.), S.M., Royal Fusiliers and Royal Scots Fusiliers.
He volunteered in August 1914, and was immediately sent to
France, where he took part in the retreat from Mons, during
which he was wounded. After five months in hospital he
was sent back to France. He then served with distinction
in the battles of Hill 60, Ypres, Loos, Arras, Bullecourt and
St. Quentin, and was again wounded. On recovery he took
part in the Allied Offensive in 1918, and while in action at
Cambrai was wounded, and awarded the Meritorious Service
Medal for conspicuous bravery in the field. He was invalided
home, and was once more in hospital for a considerable
period. In February 1919 he secured his demobilisation. In
addition to the Meritorious Service Medal he holds the Mons
Star, General Service and Victory Medals.
18, Kingwood Road, Fulham, S.W.6   X19629.

JENKINS, E. C., Gunner, Royal Field Artillery.
He volunteered for service in October 1914 and was drafted
overseas the following year. He took part in many engage-
ments on the Western Front, including the battles of the
Somme (where he was wounded) and Cambrai.
He holds the 1914-15 Star, General Service and Victory
Medals, and was demobilised in April 1919.
111, Adelaide Road, Shepherd's Bush, W.12   11839.

JENKINS, F., Gunner, Royal Field Artillery.
He volunteered in August 1914, and in the same year proceeded to France, where he took part in many engagements,
and was wounded in action near Loos. He remained
in France until 1917, and was then sent to Italy, and served
in the later operations there.
He was demobilised in March 1919, and holds the 1914 Star,
General Service and Victory Medals.
48, Maldon Road, Lower Edmonton, N.9   15781.

JENKINS, G., Pte., Royal Fusiliers.
He joined early in 1916, and later in the same year was sent
to France, where he took part in the battles of the Somme,
Arras, Vimy Ridge, Ypres (where he was wounded) and
Cambrai. He also served throughout the Allied Retreat and
Advance of 1918, and was again wounded near Bapaume.
He was later drafted to the Mesopotamian Front, and holds
the General Service and Victory Medals.
40, Orbain Road, Fulham, S.W.6   X18685.

JENKINS, G., Gunner, Royal Field Artillery.
He volunteered for service in August 1914, and shortly afterwards was drafted overseas. He took part in the retreat from Mons, and in many important engagements on the Western Front. Being severely wounded during his service in France, he was discharged as medically unfit for further service in December 1916.
He holds the Mons Star, General Service and Victory Medals.
131, Winchester Road, Lower Edmonton, N.9   14951A.

JENKINS, H. G., Cpl., 5th Middlesex Regiment.
He volunteered in July 1915, and on completion of his training was sent overseas. While on the Western Front he took part in the battles of Loos, Arras and Ypres, and in many other important engagements.
He secured his demobilisation in April 1920, and holds the General Service and Victory Medals.
10, Ashwell Grove, Upper Edmonton, N.18.   X17885.

JENKINS, J., Cpl., 18th Middlesex Regiment and Royal Engineers.
He volunteered in February 1915, and went to France the same year, where he took part in the battles of Hill 60, Ypres, Loos, the Somme and Arras, and also in heavy fighting near Béthune, Armentières, St. Quentin, and in the Allied Advance of 1918. During his long service overseas he was wounded while in action at Arras.
He holds the 1914-15 Star, General Service and Victory Medals, and was demobilised in April 1919.
248, Chapter Road, Cricklewood, N.W.2   X16979B.

JENKINS, J. W., Sapper, Royal Engineers.
He joined in 1916, and on completion of his training was sent to France. While on this Front he was engaged on important engineering work on account of his special qualifications, and rendered valuable services.
He was demobilised in December 1919, and holds the General Service and Victory Medals.
307, Lillie Road, Fulham, S.W.6   X18432.

JENKINS, S., Pte., Royal Fusiliers.
He volunteered in 1915 and was retained on important duties until 1917, when he was sent overseas. While on the Western Front he took part in many important engagements, and after the signing of the Armistice went to Germany with the Army of Occupation.
He remained there until his demobilisation in October 1919, and holds the General Service and Victory Medals.
66, Montague Road, Lower Edmonton, N.9   16508.

JENKINS, S. J., Lce.-Cpl., Middlesex Regiment.
Joined in 1916, he was retained after his period of training on important duties with his unit at various stations. He rendered valuable service, but was unsuccessful in obtaining his transfer overseas before hostilities ceased. After the signing of the Armistice he was drafted to Egypt on important garrison duties.
248, Chapter Road, Cricklewood, N.W.2   X16979A.

JENNER, F., A.B., R.N.V.R.
He volunteered immediately on the outbreak of hostilities and was sent to Belgium with the Royal Naval Division. He took part in the siege of Antwerp and was taken prisoner there. He was interned in Holland from 1914 until 1918, when he was released and demobilised in December of that year.
He holds the 1914 Star, General Service and Victory Medals.
31, Brenthurst Road, Church End, N.W.10   16383.

JENNINGS, A. (Mrs.), Special War Worker.
At the outbreak of war this lady offered her services at Messrs. Beaton's Munition Factory in St. James's Square, where she was engaged on the important work of making hand-grenades. She later went to the Perivale Park Royal Factory, where she was employed on dangerous work in the T.N.T. powder room. She did excellent work.
206, King's Road, Chelsea, S.W.3   15883B.

JENNINGS, D. (Mrs.), Special War Worker.
During the war she worked first at Messrs. Beaton's Munition Factory, St. James's Square, and was employed in making hand-grenades. She afterwards went to Messrs. Blake's Works, Wood Lane, Shepherd's Bush, and in the course of her dangerous work on shell-filling in the T.N.T. room was poisoned by the explosive, and had to give up her duties for a time. She rendered valuable services to her country.
6, Fane Street, West Kensington, W.14   15888B.

JENNING, G. A., Driver, Royal Field Artillery.
He volunteered in August 1914, and after training was sent overseas in the following year. While on the Western Front he fought in the battles of Ypres, Armentières, Neuve Chapelle, Arras and Ploegsteert Wood. He also served in Salonica, taking part in heavy fighting on the Struma Front. During his overseas' service he was twice wounded and gassed, and in consequence was discharged in 1917 as medically unfit for further service.
He holds the 1914-15 Star, General Service and Victory Medals.
6, Fane Street, West Kensington, W.14   15888A.

JENNINGS, S. G., Pte., Machine Gun Corps.
Joining in December 1916 he was sent to France in the following March. On this Front he took part in many engagements and fought in the battles of the Somme, Ypres (1917), and Roye, where he was badly wounded in March 1918. He was invalided home and was in hospital until his demobilisation in February 1919.
He holds the General Service and Victory Medals.
70, Rucklidge Avenue, Harlesden, N.W.10   T12941A.

JENNINGS, T. W., Cpl., Royal Canadian Regt.
He was already serving at the outbreak of war, and from 1915 to 1918 served on the Western Front. He took part in the battles of Ypres, Arras, Cambrai, Vimy Ridge and other engagements. On August 27th, 1919, he died from the effects of gas poisoning at Ypres.
He was entitled to the General Service and Victory Medals.
4, Garnet Road, Willesden, N.W 10.   15973A.

JENNINGS, W., Cpl., Royal Fusiliers.
He volunteered for service in 1914, and was retained for some time on important duties with his regiment at various stations. Later he was sent to the Western Front, where he took part in many important engagements.
At the commencement of the German Advance in 1918 he was killed in action on March 21st.
He was entitled to the General Service and Victory Medals.
68, Ancill Street, Hammersmith, W.6   14476A.

JENNINGS, W. J., Gunner, Royal Field Artillery.
He volunteered in August 1914, and in the following year was sent to France. During his service in this theatre of war he took part in many important engagements and fought in the battles of Hill 60 and Ypres. While in action in 1915 he was badly wounded, and as a result was discharged in the same year as medically unfit for further service.
He holds the 1914-15 Star, General Service and Victory Medals.
206, King's Road, Chelsea, S.W.3   15883A.

JENNINGS, W. S., Cpl., Royal Fusiliers.
He volunteered in August 1914, and was sent overseas in the same year. During his service on the Western Front he fought in many important engagements, until on March 21st, 1918, at the beginning of the German Offensive he was killed in action.
He was entitled to the 1914 Star, General Service and Victory Medals.
68, Ancill Street, Hammersmith, W.6   13980.

JERVIS, A. H., Pte., The Queen's (Royal West Surrey Regiment).
He joined in May 1916, and on the completion of his training was sent overseas. He took part in many engagements on the Western Front, and was severely wounded in action on the Somme.
He was demobilised in December 1918 and holds the General Service and Victory Medals.
24, Herbert Road, Lower Edmonton, N.9   13035.

JEWELL, J. H., Rifleman, 19th Rifle Brigade.
Volunteering in May 1915, he was sent to the Western Front, where he fought in many important engagements. He afterwards took part in operations in the Egyptian theatre of war. He remained there for three years and eventually returned to England in April 1919 for demobilisation.
He holds the 1914-15 Star, General Service and Victory Medals.
63, Everington Street, Hammersmith, W.6   13975A.

JEWELL, S., Pte., Durham Light Infantry.
He joined in July 1916, served for a time in Ireland and afterwards in France, where he took part in many engagements. Being taken prisoner he was held in captivity in North Germany. He suffered many hardships, and died as a result in hospital in Germany on September 29th, 1918.
He was entitled to the General Service and Victory Medals.
49, Hannell Road, Munster Road, S.W.6   X18154A.

JEWITT, H. T., Pte., 21st Labour Company.

He joined in September 1918, and was immediately sent to the Western Front, where he took an active part in the final engagements of the Allied Advance. After the signing of the Armistice he remained in France, and was engaged on important duties until his demobilisation in March 1919.
He holds the General Service and Victory Medals.
58, Chaldon Road, Dawes Road, S.W.6   X17728.

JIPPS, G. A., Pte., Middlesex Regiment.

Volunteering in March 1915, he was sent overseas the following year. He took part in many engagements on the Western Front and was twice wounded in action.
He was demobilised in March 1919, and holds the General Service and Victory Medals.
85, Winchester Road, Lower Edmonton, N.9   T14988A.

JIPPS, H. C., Gunner, Royal Field Artillery.

Volunteering in February 1915, he was sent to Mesopotamia in the same year. He took part in much of the fighting in this theatre of war. On his recovery from malaria he was drafted to India. In 1918 he was sent to France, and was in action throughout the Allied Advance of that year. After the Armistice he was retained on special duties in France until the end of 1919, when he returned to England and was demobilised in February 1920.
He holds the 1914-15 Star, General Service and Victory Medals.
85, Winchester Road, Lower Edmonton, N.9   T14988B.

JOBBINS, A., Pte., Royal Defence Corps.

He volunteered in 1914, and was engaged on special garrison duties at various important places with his unit. While on duty he met with a serious accident in consequence of which he was discharged as medically unfit for further service in November 1917.
72, Fortune Gate Road, Harlesden, N.W.10   13195A.

JOHNS, L., Pte., Queen's Own (Royal West Kent Regiment).

He joined in February 1916, and in the same year was sent to France. During his service on the Western Front he took part in the battles of the Somme, Arras, Vimy Ridge, Ypres and Cambrai and the engagements during the Allied Retreat and Advance of 1918, when he was wounded
He was demobilised in March 1919, and holds the General Service and Victory Medals.
56, Deacon Road, Cricklewood, N.W.2   16737A.

JOHNS, T. F. W., Pte., 17th Royal Fusiliers.

He joined in May 1916, and after his training was sent to France during the battle of the Somme later in the same year. While in action at Beaumont Hamel in November 1916 he was severely wounded. After hospital treatment in France and England he was discharged in September 1917 as medically unfit for further service in consequence of his wounds.
He holds the General Service and Victory Medals.
45, Wilson's Road, Hammersmith, W.6   15848.

JOHNSON, A., Drummer, East Yorkshire Regt.

Having previously served in the Army, he re-joined immediately on the outbreak of war and was sent to France in 1914. While on this Front he was in action in many important engagements and was wounded.
He returned home for demobilisation in March 1919, and holds the Queen's and King's South African Medals, the 1914 Star, General Service and Victory Medals.
38, Delorme Street, Hammersmith, W.6   14082.

JOHNSON, A., Rifleman, 5th London Regiment (L.R.B.)

He joined in 1916, and after completing his training was drafted overseas later in the same year. During his three years' service on the Western Front he took part in much heavy fighting on many sectors.
He was demobilised in 1919, and holds the General Service and Victory Medals.
42, Litchfield Gardens, Willesden, N.W.10   T17352C.

JOHNSON, A. A., Rifleman, 8th London Regt. (P.O. Rifles).

He joined in August 1916, and on completion of his training was sent overseas. While on the Western Front he took part in the battles of Ypres, Arras, Messines, the Somme and in other engagements. He was demobilised in September 1919, and holds the General Service and Victory Medals.
127, Sheldon Road, Upper Edmonton, N.18   X17298.

JOHNSON, A. J., Sergt., The Rifle Brigade.

He joined in May 1916, and on completion of his training was drafted overseas. During his service in France he took part in many important engagements, and gained promotion. After the signing of the Armistice he proceeded to Germany with the Army of Occupation, and remained there until his demobilisation in September 1919.
He holds the General Service and Victory Medals.
10, Delorme Street, Hammersmith, W.6   14270B.

JOHNSON, A. R., Pte., 4th Royal Fusiliers.

He was serving in the Army at the outbreak of war and was retained at various stations on special duties until March 1915. when he was drafted to France. During his long service overseas he took part in the important fighting on many sectors of the Western Front. After the signing of the Armistice he went with the Army of Occupation to Germany, and remained there until March 1919, when he was discharged.
He holds the 1914-15 Star, General Service and Victory Medals.
43, Burrow's Road, Willesden, N.W.10   X18252.

JOHNSON, A. R., Pte., Middlesex Regiment.

He volunteered in 1914 and in the following year was sent to the Western Front. After taking part in several important engagements in many sectors, he was drafted to Salonica, where he again saw heavy fighting. During his service he was twice wounded, and in June 1919 was demobilised.
He holds the 1914-15 Star, General Service and Victory Medals.
26, Steele Road, Willesden, N.W.10   13838C.

JOHNSON, A. S., Rifleman, The Rifle Brigade.

Volunteering for service in November 1915, he completed his training on important duties at various stations with his unit. Owing to physical disability he unfortunately was prevented from proceeding overseas.
He rendered valuable services, and was discharged in November 1917 as medically unfit for further service.
5, Hartham Road, Bruce Grove, N.17   X18519A.

JOHNSON, A. S. (jun.), Cpl., Essex Yeomanry.

Volunteering in August 1914, he was sent to the Western Front in the same year. He remained in this seat of operations for five years and took part in many important engagements, including the battles of Loos and the Somme. He returned to England for demobilisation in April 1919, and holds the 1914 Star, General Service and Victory Medals.
5, Hartham Road, Bruce Grove, N.17   X18519C.

JOHNSON, A. W., Drummer, Middlesex Regt.

He volunteered in August 1914, and was soon sent to India. He remained there on important garrison duties until 1917, when he was drafted to Mesopotamia. There he took part in the advance of General Marshall's forces through Baghdad and to Mosul. He had previously served in the Territorial Forces and, in addition to the 1914 Star, General Service and Victory Medals, holds the Territorial Efficiency Medal.
He was demobilised in March 1919.
41, Essex Road, Willesden, N.W.10   15941.

JOHNSON, C. E., Pte., Royal Naval Division.

Joining in 1916, he was sent to the Western Front on completion of his training. He took part in many important operations while on this Front, including the battles of Arras and Ypres in 1917.
He remained in France until his demobilisation in 1919, and holds the General Service and Victory Medals.
42, Litchfield Gardens, Willesden, N.W.10   T17352B.

JOHNSON, C. S., Pte., Middlesex Regiment.

Volunteering in July 1915, he was sent at the end of his training to the Western Front. After taking part in several important engagements there, he was drafted to Salonica, where he again saw much severe fighting.
He holds the General Service and Victory Medals.
70, Gilpin Grove, Upper Edmonton, N.18   16795.

JOHNSON, D., Driver, Royal Engineers.

He volunteered in 1915, and later in the same year was sent to the Western Front. During his four years in this seat of war he took part in many important engagements, including the battles of the Somme and Ypres.
He holds the 1914-15 Star, General Service and Victory Medals.
42, Pretoria Road, Upper Edmonton, N.18   X17025A.

JOHNSON, E., Pte., 13th Hampshire Regiment.
He volunteered in August 1914, and on completion of his training was ordered with his unit to the Dardanelles. While on the voyage on the " Royal Edward " he was drowned when that vessel was torpedoed by an enemy submarine on August 14th, 1915. This was the first of our transports to be sunk during the war.
He was entitled to the 1914–15 Star, General Service and Victory Medals.
19, Reporton Road, Fulham, S.W.6   X18865.

JOHNSON, E. L., Gunner, R.F.A.
He volunteered in January 1915, and was drafted overseas in the following year. During his service on the Western Front he took part in the battles of the Somme and Ypres, and in other important engagements. At the beginning of the German Advance on March 21st, 1918, he was taken prisoner and interned in Germany. Upon his release he returned to England, and was demobilised in March 1919, holding the General Service and Victory Medals.
29, Cedars Road, Lower Edmonton, N.9   14032.

JOHNSON, F., Sergt., Royal Engineers.
Volunteering in 1914, he was sent overseas in the following year. During his four years' service on the Western Front he took part in the battles of Ypres, the Somme, La Bassée and Arras, and received promotion for his skill and general ability.
He was demobilised in 1919, and holds the 1914–15 Star, General Service and Victory Medals.
20, Town Road, Lower Edmonton, N.9   13568.

JOHNSON, F. L., Pte., East Surrey Regiment.
Volunteering in August 1914, he was immediately sent to France, where he took part in the retreat from Mons and in the battles of La Bassée, Ypres, Loos and the Somme. After bearing a charmed life for so long a period, he was killed in action on March 23rd, 1918, during the German Advance.
He was entitled to the Mons Star, General Service and Victory Medals. 35, Shorrolds Road, Walham Green, S.W.6 X19344.

JOHNSON, G., Lce.-Cpl., Royal Engineers.
He joined in 1915, was sent to France in the same year, and took part in the fighting on the Somme and in other engagements. He was discharged as medically unfit for further service in 1917, and holds the 1915 Star, General Service and Victory Medals.
42, Pretoria Road, Upper Edmonton, N.18   X17025B.

JOHNSON, G., Special War Worker.
Being over age for military service and desirous of helping his country, he offered his services at the Kensington Infirmary, where he released a younger man for His Majesty's Forces. He was engaged as a stoker, and carried out his arduous duties to the entire satisfaction of the authorities.
86, Chesson Road, West Kensington, W.14   TX17249.

JOHNSON, G. E., 1st-Class Stoker, Royal Navy, H.M. Submarine " K.12."
Having previously served in the Royal Navy, he was mobilised from the Reserve at the outbreak of war. He was first engaged on important duties with the Grand Fleet, and later went to the Dardanelles, where he served throughout the naval operations there. He also served with his vessel in Italian waters, and on special patrol duties in the English Channel.
He holds the 1914 Star, General Service and Victory Medals.
85, Sherbrooke Road, Fulham, S.W.6   18477.

JOHNSON, H., Pte., Machine Gun Corps.
He volunteered in December 1915, and in the following year was sent to the Western Front, where he took part in the battles of Arras, Bullecourt, Ypres and Cambrai, and in other important engagements. During his service he was severely wounded. In 1918, as a result of his wounds, he was discharged as medically unfit for further service.
He holds the General Service and Victory Medals.
4, Chapman's Cottages, High Road, Willesden, N.W.10   T17352A.

JOHNSON, H., Pte., 2nd Middlesex Regiment.
He joined in May 1916, and was drafted overseas on completion of his training. He took part in many engagements on the Western Front, including the battle of Ypres, in which action he was wounded.
He was demobilised in 1919, holding the General Service and Victory Medals.
16, Bounces Road, Lower Edmonton, N.9   13955.

JOHNSON, H., Pte., 1st Queen's Own (Royal West Kent Regiment).
He volunteered in 1914, and on completion of his training was retained on important duties at various stations with his unit. He rendered valuable service until the beginning of 1917, when he was taken ill, and died on April 7th of that year. 46, Ancill Street, Hammersmith, W.6   13983B.

JOHNSON, H. F., Driver, Royal Field Artillery.
Volunteering for service in April 1915, he was drafted to India in the following September, where he was first engaged on important garrison duties. He also took part in the North-West Frontier campaign against the Afghans, and saw much fighting.
He returned to this country in November 1919, and in January of the following year was demobilised, holding the General Service and Victory Medals, and the Indian General Service Medal, 1908, with clasp (Afghanistan, N.W. Frontier, 1919).
107a, Adelaide Road, Shepherd's Bush, W.12   11838.

JOHNSON, J., Driver, Royal Field Artillery.
He volunteered for service in 1914, and later in that year was sent overseas. During his five years' service on the Western Front this driver took part in the battles of La Bassée, Ypres, Loos and the Somme, and in other important engagements.
In 1919 he secured his demobilisation, and holds the 1914 Star, General Service and Victory Medals.
178, Brettenham Road East, Upper Edmonton, N.18 15222.

JOHNSON, J. E., Lce.-Cpl., R.A.S.C.
He joined in 1916, and on completion of his training was engaged on special duties of an important nature at various stations with his unit. He rendered excellent service, but was not successful in obtaining his transfer overseas before the cessation of hostilities. He was demobilised in 1919.
36, Ladysmith Road, Upper Edmonton, N.18   16466.

JOHNSON, J. E., Pioneer, Royal Engineers.
He volunteered in August 1915, and was shortly afterwards drafted overseas. During his service on the Western Front he was engaged on special duties of an important nature in many sectors.
He secured his demobilisation in March 1919, and holds the 1915 Star, General Service and Victory Medals.
11, Corby Road, Willesden, N.W.10   14400A.

JOHNSON, J. F. (M.M.), Lce.-Cpl., Seaforth Highlanders.
He volunteered for service in March 1915, and the following year was drafted to Mesopotamia, where he took part in very severe fighting. He was wounded in action near Kut, and was awarded the Military Medal for conspicuous bravery and devotion to duty in the field.
He also holds the General Service and Victory Medals, and was demobilised in June 1919.
59, Westminster Road, Lower Edmonton, N.9   12698.

JOHNSON, J. J., Pte., North Staffordshire Regt.
He volunteered in August 1914, and served on the Western Front. He was killed on March 20th, 1915, during the fighting near Armentières. He had volunteered to fetch water for his comrades, and was in the act of returning with it when he was killed. For his gallant conduct on this occasion he was recommended for a decoration, and was also entitled to the 1914 Star, General Service and Victory Medals.
5, Knivet Road, Walham Green, S.W.6   X19422.

JOHNSON, J. T. H., Pte., 1/4th Essex Regt.
He joined for service in August 1916, and on completion of his training went to Egypt with his regiment. He took part in various engagements in this theatre of war, and was twice wounded in action.
He was demobilised in December 1919, and holds the General Service and Victory Medals.
11, Corby Road, Willesden, N.W.10   14400B.

JOHNSON, P., Cpl., 4th Worcestershire Regt.
He joined in March 1917, and at the conclusion of his training was drafted to France. He took part in the Retreat and Advance of 1918, and was wounded in action.
He holds the General Service and Victory Medals.
43, Deacon Road, Cricklewood, N.W.2   X17210A.

JOHNSON, P. A., Pte., Seaforth Highlanders.
He volunteered for service in October 1915, and was drafted overseas at the conclusion of his training. He took part in many engagements on the Western Front, and was killed in action during the Allied Advance in September 1918.
He was entitled to the General Service and Victory Medals.
42, Beaconsfield Road, Lower Edmonton, N.9   14562.

JOHNSON, R. Pioneer, Royal Engineers.
Volunteering in August 1915, he was almost immediately sent to the Western Front. During his services there he was engaged, on account of his special qualifications, on important engineering work of a varied description in different sectors.
He was demobilised in February 1919, and holds the 1915 Star, General Service and Victory Medals.
43, Deacon Road, Cricklewood, N.W.2   17210B.

JOHNSON, R. E., Pte., 1st Queen's Own (Royal West Kent Regiment).

He volunteered in November 1915, and on completion of his training was drafted to the Western Front. He there took part in many important engagements, and was killed in action at the opening of the battle of Vimy Ridge on April 9th, 1917.
He was entitled to the General Service and Victory Medals.
46, Ancill Street, Hammersmith, W.6   13983A.

JOHNSON, R. W., Staff Sergt., R.A.O.C.

He volunteered in November 1914, and was retained on important duties requiring a high degree of technical skill until 1916. He was then drafted to Salonica, and during his three years' service on that Front was again engaged on vitally important duties.
He was demobilised in June 1919, and holds the General Service and Victory Medals.
16, Armadale Road, Walham Green, S.W.6   X19404.

JOHNSON, S. E. (M.M.), Cpl., 18th London Regiment (London Irish Rifles).

He volunteered in November 1915, and in the following June was sent to the Western Front. During his services there he took part in many important engagements, including the battle of the Somme, where he was wounded in 1916.
He was awarded the Military Medal for conspicuous bravery and devotion to duty in the field. On May 30th, 1918, he was killed in action during the heavy fighting in the Allied Retreat, and is buried in the British cemetery at Pernois.
He was also entitled to the General Service and Victory Medals.
53, Charlton Road, Harlesden, N.W.10   13105.

JOHNSON, S. J., Pte., Machine Gun Corps.

He volunteered for service in 1915, and in the following year was drafted to German East Africa, where he saw much fighting and contracted malaria. He was sent to France in 1917, and took part in several battles on the Western Front.
He holds the General Service and Victory Medals, and was demobilised in 1919.
26, Steele Road, Willesden, N.W.10   13838B.

JOHNSON, W., Pte., The Queen's (Royal West Surrey Regiment).

He joined in July 1916, and went in the same year to the Western Front. He fought in many battles, including Ypres, the Somme and Arras, and in the Retreat and Advance of 1918. Later he served with the Army of Occupation in Germany, and was demobilised in January 1919, holding the General Service and Victory Medals.
43, Ravensworth Road, College Park, N.W.10   X1761.

JOHNSON, W., Pte., R.A.S.C. and Royal Berkshire Regiment.

He volunteered in May 1915, and in the same year was sent to France. While with the R.A.S.C. he was engaged on special duties at important stations. He later transferred to the Royal Berkshire Regiment, and took part in many important engagements, including the battles of the Somme and Cambrai, and in the heavy fighting during the Allied Retreat and Advance in 1918.
He was demobilised in February 1919, and holds the General Service and Victory Medals.
22, Cooper Road, Dudden Hill, Willesden, N.W.10   16634.

JOHNSON, W. C., Pte., Royal Scots.

He volunteered for service in December 1915, and after his training was engaged on important duties at various stations with his unit. He gave valuable services, but was not successful in obtaining his transfer overseas before hostilities ceased.
He was demobilised in March 1919.
41, Studland Street, Hammersmith, W.6   12428.

JOHNSON, W. E., Pte., 2nd London Regiment (Royal Fusiliers).

He volunteered for service in June 1915, and was drafted overseas on completion of his training. He took part in many important battles on the Western Front, and died of wounds received in action in August 1917.
He was entitled to the General Service and Victory Medals.
19, Claybrook Road, Hammersmith, W.6   13679A.

JOHNSON, W. H., Pte., Lancashire Fusiliers.

He volunteered for service in November 1915, and after his training was engaged on important duties at various stations with his unit until 1917. He was then sent to France, and took part in many engagements there, including the extensive operations in the Somme area. On April 25th, 1918, at the beginning of the Allied Retreat, he was killed in action near Armentières.
He was entitled to the General Service and Victory Medals.
43, Greyhound Road, College Park, N.W.10   X17796.

JOHNSON, W. H., 1st Air Mechanic, R.A.F.

He volunteered for service in November 1915, and on completion of his training was retained on important duties at various stations with his unit until May 1917. He was then drafted to the Western Front, where he served as a wireless operator in various sectors.
In May 1919 he secured his demobilisation, and holds the General Service and Victory Medals.
10, Delorme Street, Hammersmith, W.6   14270A.

JOHNSON, W. R., Sapper, Royal Engineers.

He volunteered in June 1915, and in the same year was sent overseas. During his four years' service on the Western Front he was actively engaged in many important engagements, including those at Ypres and on the Somme. While in action at Ypres he was badly gassed. In consequence he was discharged in March 1919.
He holds the 1915 Star, General Service and Victory Medals.
5, Hartham Road, Bruce Grove, Tottenham, N.17   X18519B.

JOHNSTON, C., 7th Royal Fusiliers.

He volunteered in January 1916, and after his training was retained on important duties at various stations with his unit until 1918. He was then sent to France, and was there engaged on special guard duties until his demobilisation in October 1919.
He holds the General Service and Victory Medals.
105, Mayo Road, Willesden, N.W.10   15427

JOHNSTON, F. C., Stoker, Royal Navy, H.M.S. "Vanguard" and "Albury."

He enlisted in the Navy in 1913, and during the war served in the North Sea, taking part in the battles of Jutland and Heligoland Bight. He was also present at the attack on Zeebrugge, and was demobilised in March 1920, holding the 1914 Star, General Service and Victory Medals.
44, Carlyle Avenue, Willesden, N.W.10   14408B.

JOHNSTON, H. J., Pte., Middlesex Regiment and Machine Gun Corps.

He volunteered in September 1914, and was sent to France a year later, taking part in several engagements, including the battle of the Somme and the Retreat and Advance of 1918, and being wounded twice.
He was demobilised in January 1919, and holds the 1915 Star, General Service and Victory Medals.
44, Carlyle Avenue, Willesden, N.W.10   14408A.

JOHNSTON, L. A., Sergt., 2nd London Regiment.

Volunteering in August 1914, he was in the same year sent to France. While on this Front he fought at the battles of Hill 60, Ypres, the Somme and Arras, and in other engagements. During this period he was twice wounded. In 1917 he was drafted to West Africa, where he served with distinction with the Nigerian Regiment for 16 months.
He returned to this country for demobilisation in March 1919, and holds the 1914–15 Star, General Service and Victory Medals.
67, Shrewsbury Road, Stonebridge Park, N.W.10   13841.

JOLLEY, F. T., Pte., Suffolk Regiment.

He joined the service in 1917, and later in the same year was sent to France. While in this theatre of war he took part in many important engagements.
He remained there until his demobilisation in 1919, and holds the General Service and Victory Medals.
46, Town Road, Lower Edmonton, N.9   13569C.

JOLLEY, G. S., Sergt., Royal Field Artillery.

He volunteered in December 1914, and was sent to France in the following year. After three months' service there he was transferred to the Salonica theatre of operations. He remained on this Front for three years, and took part in many important engagements. During his service in the East he contracted malaria, and in April 1919 was discharged.
He holds the 1915 Star, General Service and Victory Medals.
43, Gloucester Road, Upper Edmonton, N.18   X17275.

JOLLEY, T. H., Flying Officer, R.A.F.

He joined as a private in January 1916, and served on the Western Front until February 1917, when he was transferred to Italy. He took part in the battle of the Piave, and in June 1919 was granted a commission.
He holds the General Service and Victory Medals.
50, Caird Street, Queen's Park Estate, W.10   X18940.

JOLLEY, W., Cpl., Middlesex Regiment.

He volunteered in August 1914, and served on the Western Front, where he took part in the retreat from Mons and the battles of Ypres, Loos, La Bassée and Arras.
He was demobilised in 1919, holding the Mons Star, General Service and Victory Medals.
46, Town Road, Lower Edmonton, N.9   13569A

JOLLY, H., A.B., R.N., H.M.S. " Warspite."
He joined in 1916, and acting as seaman-torpedoman in
H.M.S. " Warspite," saw service with the Grand Fleet in the
North Sea. He was present at the surrender of the German
High Seas Fleet at Scapa Flow in November 1918, and was
demobilised in May 1919, holding the General Service and
Victory Medals. During his service he had a nervous break-
down caused by a weak heart, as a result of which, in
February 1920, he died.
114, Deacon Road, Cricklewood, N.W.2   X16977.

JONES, A., Pte., 25th King's (Liverpool Regt.)
He joined in 1917 and was immediately sent out to Egypt,
where he was stationed throughout the war.
He holds the General Service and Victory Medals.
20, Church Road, Hammersmith, W.6   11106A.

JONES, A., Gunner, Tank Corps.
He joined in October 1915, and was sent to the Western Front
in the following February. While in France he took part in
several important engagements, and in March 1919 was
demobilised, holding the General Service and Victory Medals.
18, Claybrook Road, Hammersmith, W.6   15727A.

JONES, A., Leading Aircraftsman, R.A.F.
Volunteering in October 1915, he was retained on important
duties which required a high degree of technical skill. However, in December 1917 he was drafted to Mesopotamia,
taking part in several engagements. In the following March
he was sent home, and was still serving in 1920.
He holds the General Service and Victory Medals.
18, Claybrook Road, Hammersmith, W.6   15727C.

JONES, A., Driver, Royal Horse Artillery.
Having enlisted previously in 1905, he was sent to the Front
as soon as the war broke out, taking part in the battle of
and retreat from Mons, and the battles of Arras and the
Somme.
In 1919 he was demobilised, holding the Mons Star, General
Service and Victory Medals.
18, Chauncey Street, Lower Edmonton, N.9   14253B.

JONES, A., Pioneer, Royal Engineers.
He volunteered in January 1915, and after his training was
sent to the Western Front, where he was seriously wounded
in action in 1916. He was in consequence discharged in May
of the same year as medically unfit.
He holds the General Service and Victory Medals.
18, Chauncey Street, Lower Edmonton, N.9   14253D.

JONES, A. G., Pte., Middlesex Regiment.
He volunteered in June 1915, and in the following December
was sent to Egypt. During his 3½ years' service in this
theatre of operations he was engaged on duties of a special
nature.
He returned home for demobilisation in July 1919, and holds
the 1914-15 Star, General Service and Victory Medals.
4, Denbigh Road, Willesden, N.W.10   15097.

JONES, A. M., Bombardier, Royal Field Artillery.
Volunteering in August 1914, he was a year later sent
to the Dardanelles, where he took part in the Gallipoli
campaign. On the evacuation of the Peninsula he saw
service in Serbia, Macedonia and Bulgaria, and was wounded.
In April 1919 he was demobilised, and holds the 1914-15 Star,
General Service and Victory Medals.
5, Albert Terrace, Milton Avenue, Willesden, N.W.10.
                                              14114A.

JONES, A. V., Driver, Royal Army Service Corps.
He joined in May 1917, and after his training was engaged
on important duties with his unit at various stations. He
gave valuable services, but was unsuccessful in obtaining his
transfer overseas before hostilities ceased. After the Armistice he proceeded to Germany with the Army of Occupation,
and remained there until his return to England in February
1920 for demobilisation.
44, Herries Street, N. Kensington, W.10   X18564A.

JONES, C., Lce.-Cpl., 3rd Middlesex Regiment.
He volunteered in August 1915, and was sent to Salonica,
where he took part in several engagements. Later he was
invalided home with malaria, and was eventually demobilised
in February 1919, holding the General Service and Victory
Medals.
45, Greyhound Road, Hammersmith, W.6   15169.

JONES, C. E. (Mrs.), Special War Worker.
For a considerable period of the war this lady was engaged
on work of national importance at Stanstead House, Tottenham. Her duties, which were connected with the manufacture of military equipment, were carried out in a capable
and thorough manner, and she was highly commended for
her valuable services.
30a, Durban Road, Tottenham, N.17   X18087.

JONES, C. J., 1st-Class Petty Officer, Royal Navy.
He volunteered in August 1914 and served with his ship,
H.M.S. " Espiegle," in Eastern waters with the Fleet.
His duties were chiefly in connection with the landing of
troops at various places of importance.
He holds the 1914 Star, General Service and Victory Medals.
1, Wimborne Road, Lower Edmonton, N.9   15212.

JONES, D., Pte., 7th London Regiment.
He volunteered in December 1915, and after his training was
employed on important work with his unit at various stations.
He gave valuable services, but in September 1916 was discharged as medically unfit for further military service.
18, Claybrook Road, Hammersmith, W.6   15727D.

**JONES, E., Pte. and Rifleman, 9th Middlesex
Regiment and Rifle Brigade.**
He volunteered in October 1914, and was sent two years
later to the Western Front, where he took part in several
engagements, including the battle of Ypres. On September
16th, 1917, he was killed in action on the Somme.
He was entitled to the General Service and Victory Medals.
46a, Charlton Road, Harlesden, N.W.10   13385.

JONES, E., Driver, Royal Field Artillery.
He volunteered in October 1914, and after serving at home
for some time was sent to France in 1916, where he took part
in several engagements. He was later sent to the Balkans,
and fought in engagements on the Struma Front, where he
contracted malaria.
He was demobilised in May 1919, holding the General Service
and Victory Medals.
25, Hiley Road, Willesden, N.W.10   X18241A.

JONES, E. A., Air Mechanic (Armourer), R.A.F.
He joined in 1917, and after his training was drafted to the
Western Front in the following year. His duties called for
a high degree of technical skill, and he took part in the
Advance of 1918. He remained overseas until after the
Armistice, when he returned to England and extended his
service for a period of two years.
He holds the General Service and Victory Medals.
25, Hiley Road, Willesden, N.W.10   X18241B.

JONES, E. J., Pte., 17th Middlesex Regiment.
He volunteered in November 1914, and was sent to the
Western Front, where he served on the Somme and took
part in the battle of Ypres. Later he was sent to Salonica,
and served there until his demobilisation in April 1919.
He holds the General Service and Victory Medals.
5, Chichester Road, Lower Edmonton, N.9   15273.

**JONES, E. T., Rifleman, 6th London Regiment
(Rifles).**
He joined in November 1916, and served on many sectors
of the Western Front. Later, owing to ill health, he was
invalided to England, and was discharged in October 1918,
as medically unfit for further military duties.
He holds the General Service and Victory Medals.
36, Allestree Road, Munter Road, S.W.6   X19208.

**JONES, F. G., Q.M.S., 25th London Regiment
(Cyclist Battalion).**
He was mobilised in August 1914, and in January 1916 was
drafted to India, where he served for three years, taking part
in the Afghanistan Expedition in North West India in 1919.
He was demobilised in November 1919, and holds the India
General Service Medal (with Afghanistan N.W. Frontier,1919,
clasp), General Service and Victory Medals.
5, Minet Avenue, Willesden, N.W.10   T13914B.

JONES, G. W., Sergt., R.A.O.C.
He joined in May 1917, and was sent to the Western Front,
where he was actively engaged in operations around Ypres
and Armentières. He later took over responsible duties as
Sergeant in charge of ammunition dumps at various places
of importance.
In November 1919 he was demobilised, and holds the General
Service and Victory Medals.
168, Wandsworth Bridge Road, Fulham, S.W.6   19850A.

JONES, H. A., Gunner, Royal Garrison Artillery.
He volunteered in August 1914, and served on the Western
Front, where he took part in the battle of Ypres. Later he
was transferred to Italy, but returned to France in time to
take part in the Retreat and Advance of 1918.
During his service he was twice wounded, and was demobilised
in April 1919, holding the 1914-15 Star, General Service and
Victory Medals.
341, Chapter Road, Cricklewood, N.W.2   TX17343.

JONES, H. N., Sergt., 7th Royal Fusiliers.

He volunteered for service in September 1914, and was retained on important duties as an instructor at various training centres. He gave valuable services, but, owing to his being medically unfit for active service, was not successful in obtaining his transfer overseas.
He was demobilised in February 1919.
42, Salisbury Road, Lower Edmonton, N.9   T14025B.

JONES, H. M., Driver, Royal Engineers.

He volunteered in June 1915, and was later sent to the Western Front. During his service overseas he took part in many important engagements, and was wounded in action at Cambrai in 1918.
In the following April he was demobilised, and holds the General Service and Victory Medals.
18, Chauncey Street, Lower Edmonton, N.9   14253A.

JONES, J., Pte., 2nd Worcestershire Regiment.

He volunteered in 1915 and served on the Western Front, taking part in the battles of the Somme, Ypres, Bullecourt, Arras and many others. He was in hospital for some months as the result of an accident, and in June 1919 was demobilised, holding the 1914-15 Star, General Service and Victory Medals. 42, Durban Road, Tottenham, N.17   X18286.

JONES, J., Pte., Royal Army Medical Corps.

He volunteered in October 1915, and after his training was sent to France in the following year. He took an active part in the battle of the Somme in 1916, and was later engaged on special duties at advanced hospitals on the Western Front. He was demobilised in July 1919, and holds the General Service and Victory Medals.
42, Durban Road, Tottenham, N.17   X18285.

JONES, J. A., Bombardier, R.F.A.

He volunteered in August 1914, and was drafted to the Western Front shortly afterwards. He took part in the battle of Ypres (November 1914), where he was badly gassed, and on his recovery was again in action at St. Eloi and on the Somme. In 1916 he was sent to Salonica, and fought in various sectors of the Bulgarian Front until 1919, when he went to Russia.
In May 1919 he returned to England and was demobilised, holding the 1914 Star, General Service and Victory Medals.
153, Rucklidge Avenue, Harlesden, N.W.10   13159.

JONES, J. E., Pte., 2nd Royal Fusiliers.

He volunteered in September 1914, and in the following year was sent to the Dardanelles, where he saw heavy fighting, and was severely wounded in August. As his wound incapacitated him for further active service he was employed on special duties in England from 1915 until discharged as unfit in June 1916.
He holds the 1914-15 Star, General Service and Victory Medals. 40, Bravington Road, Maida Hill, W.9   X19192.

JONES, J. H., Driver, Royal Field Artillery.

He volunteered in 1915, and in the same year was sent to France, where he served in the ammunition column throughout his service. He was present during many engagements, and was demobilised in March 1919, holding the 1914-15 Star, the General Service and Victory Medals.
104, Ancill Street, Hammersmith, W.6   13663B.

JONES, J. H. S., Sapper, R.E. (Postal Section) and Pte., Seaforth Highlanders.

He volunteered in April 1915, and was sent overseas, where he was engaged on important duties in various sectors of the Western Front with the Postal Section of the Royal Engineers. He was later transferred to the Seaforth Highlanders, and took part in the fighting at Cambrai. He remained in France until after the cessation of hostilities, when he returned to England for demobilisation in October 1919.
He holds the General Service and Victory Medals.
30, Rednall Terrace, Hammersmith, W.6   16215

JONES, J. M., Pte., Middlesex Regiment.

He joined in March 1916, and on completion of his training was sent to France. While on the Western Front he took part in many important engagements, and was twice wounded He holds the General Service and Victory Medals, and was still serving in 1920.
14, Montpelier Road, Hammersmith, W.6   13273.

JONES, J. M., Pte., Middlesex Regiment, Border Regiment and Labour Corps.

He volunteered in September 1914, and after his training was drafted to the Dardanelles with the Middlesex Regiment in in the following June. He remained in this theatre of war until the evacuation of the Peninsula, when he was wounded. Upon his recovery he was sent to the Western Front, where he was again wounded in action. He was invalided home, and being physically unfit for further service overseas was transferred to the Labour Corps and employed on duties at various stations until his demobilisation in March 1919.
He holds the 1914-15 Star, General Service and Victory Medals. 43, West Ella Road, Willesden, N.W.10   15129.

JONES, P., Pte., Royal Defence Corps.

He volunteered in May 1915, and served throughout the war with the Royal Defence Corps on important guard duties at various places in the South of England.
He gave valuable services, and was demobilised in March 1919.
49, Station Road, Hanwell, W.7   12387.

JONES, R. C., Pte., 13th London Regiment (Kensington) and R.A.M.C.

He volunteered in March 1915, and two years later was sent to France, where he served for a year. His health, however, broke down, and he was discharged as medically unfit in August 1919, holding the General Service and Victory Medals.
92, Rosebank Road, Hanwell, W.7   11061.

JONES, S. T., A.B., Royal Navy.

He joined in January 1917, and was engaged on important duties with H.M.S. "Lord Nelson" in the Black Sea. He remained in Eastern waters throughout his active service, and was demobilised in May 1919, holding the General Service and Victory Medals.
51, Wendover Road, Harlesden, N.W.10   12549.

JONES, T. L., Pte., Lincolnshire Regiment.

He joined in July 1917, and proceeded in the same year to the Western Front, where in April 1918 he was wounded. After being in hospital in France for some time he was invalided home, and was demobilised in September 1919, holding the General Service and Victory Medals.
117, Winchester Road, Lower Edmonton, N.9   14954.

JONES, T. W., Sergt., Machine Gun Corps.

He volunteered in 1915, and on completing his training was sent to the Western Front, where he took a prominent part in many important engagements and was wounded.
After the cessation of hostilities he was drafted to India, where he was serving in 1920, and holds the General Service and Victory Medals.
51, Lintaine Grove, West Kensington, W.14   16823B.

JONES, V. H. W., A.B., Royal Naval Division.

He volunteered in June 1915, and in the same year was sent to Gallipoli. After the evacuation of the Peninsula he was transferred to the Western Front, where he took part in the battles of the Somme, Vimy Ridge, Ypres, Arras and Cambrai. During his service he was gassed and twice wounded, and was demobilised in February 1919, holding the 1914-15 Star, General Service and Victory Medals.
181, Boston Road, Hanwell, W.7   11017.

JONES, W., Pte., 3rd London Regiment (Royal Fusiliers).

He volunteered in August 1914, and in the following year was sent to Malta, where he remained for two years. In December 1916 he was transferred to France, where he took part in many engagements and was wounded.
He was demobilised in February 1919, holding the General Service and Victory Medals.
18, Claybrook Road, Hammersmith, W.6   15727B.

JONES, W. E., Pte., 17th Lancers.

He enlisted in April 1904, and at the outbreak of war in 1914 was sent to France, where he took part in the retreat from Mons and the battles of the Somme, Arras, Ypres and Cambrai.
In January 1919 he was discharged, holding the Mons Star, General Service and Victory Medals.
18, Chauncey Street, Lower Edmonton, N.9   14253C.

JONES, W. E., Lce.-Cpl., 2nd Bedfordshire Regt.

He volunteered in October 1914, and in the following year was sent to the Western Front, where he took part in several engagements, and was three times wounded.
He was demobilised in March 1919, holding the 1914-15 Star, General Service and Victory Medals.
44, Herries Street, N. Kensington, W.10   X18564B.

JONES, W. H., Air Mechanic, Royal Air Force.

Volunteering in September 1915, he was sent to the Western Front, where he took part in the battles of Arras and Ypres. Later he served with the Royal Air Force at Farnborough, on duties which required a high degree of technical skill.
He was demobilised in January 1919, and holds the General Service and Victory Medals.
38, Westoe Road, Lower Edmonton, N.9   13124.

JONES, W. H. A., Cpl., R.A.O.C.

Volunteering in October 1915, he was sent to Egypt in the following year. During his three years' service on that Front he was engaged on important duties of a special nature owing to his qualifications as a draughtsman. He remained in Egypt until after the Armistice, when he was sent home and demobilised in August 1919.
He holds the General Service and Victory Medals.
5, Minet Avenue, Harlesden, N.W.10   T13914A.

JONES, W. M., Gunner, Royal Field Artillery.

He volunteered in August 1915, and shortly afterwards was sent to the Western Front, where, during his three years' service in this theatre of war, he took part in many important engagements, and was killed in action on the Somme on September 21st, 1918.
He was entitled to the 1914-15 Star, General Service and Victory Medals.
18, Winchester Road, Lower Edmonton, N.9   14684.

JONES, W. N., Cpl., Hampshire Regiment.

He volunteered in August 1914, and shortly afterwards was sent to the Western Front, where he fought in the battle of Ypres and in engagements around Armentières. He was then sent to the Dardanelles and served through the Gallipoli campaign. On the evacuation of the Peninsula he was drafted to Salonica, where he again saw much fighting.
In 1919 he was demobilised, holding the 1914 Star, General Service and Victory Medals.
27, Crefeld Road, Hammersmith, W.6   14536.

JONES, W. R. E., Sapper, Royal Engineers.

He joined in October 1918, and served with his unit at various stations. He gave valuable services, but was not successful in obtaining his transfer overseas before the cessation of hostilities.
He was demobilised in March 1919.
66, Fairfield Road, Upper Edmonton, N.18   15613A.

JORDAN, A. E., Cpl., 2nd Middlesex Regiment.

He enlisted in November 1910, and on the outbreak of hostilities was sent to the Western Front, where he took part in many important engagements. He was for over two years in hospital suffering from shell-shock, and as he was incapacitated for further active service, was retained on important duties until his discharge in November 1919.
He holds the 1914 Star, General Service and Victory Medals.
7, Gilpin Crescent, Upper Edmonton, N.18   T16842.

JORDAN, D., Pte., Royal Army Service Corps.

He joined in 1917, and later in the same year was drafted to Salonica, where he was engaged on important duties in connection with the unloading of ammunition and stores. He remained on this Front until sent home for demobilisation in December 1919, and holds the General Service and Victory Medals.
2, Lundy Street, Hammersmith, W.6   14793B.

JORDAN, E. P., Pte., The Queen's (Royal West Surrey Regiment).

He volunteered in August 1915, and was sent to Egypt and later to Palestine. Eventually he was drafted to the Western Front, where he took part in the battle of the Somme and other engagements, and was three times wounded.
He was demobilised in March 1919, and holds the 1914-15 Star, General Service and Victory Medals.
62, Fairfield Road, Upper Edmonton, N.18   15617.

JORDAN, J., Pte., Royal Army Service Corps.

He volunteered in May 1915, and after his training was retained, owing to ill-health, on important duties with his unit at various stations. He gave valuable services, but in the following January was discharged as medically unfit for further military service.
20, Church Path, Hammersmith, W.6   16391.

JORDAN, K. (Miss), Special War Worker.

For a period of 3½ years during the war this lady gave valuable services as an electric motor driver at a large food supply depot in London, and thereby released a man for military service. She carried out her duties to the entire satisfaction of her employers, and was commended for her work.
2, Lundy Street, Hammersmith, W.6   14793A.

JORDAN, M. B., Pte., Royal Army Service Corps.

He volunteered in August 1914, and was sent to France immediately. He took part in the retreat from Mons, and in the battles of Ypres, the Somme, Arras and Cambrai. During his service he was wounded, and in February 1919 was demobilised, holding the Mons Star, General Service and Victory Medals.
83, Deacon Road, Cricklewood, N.W.2   16699.

JOSLIN, F. C., Pte., Middlesex Regiment.

Volunteering in July 1915, he was sent in the following year to the Eastern Front, where, during his 3½ years in Salonica, he took part in many important operations.
In December 1919 he was demobilised, and holds the General Service and Victory Medals.
2, Brereton Road, Tottenham, N.17   X18105.

JOSLYN, N., Pte., Suffolk Regiment.

He volunteered in September 1914, and shortly afterwards was sent to France. During his service on this Front he fought in the battle of Ypres, in heavy fighting around Armentières, and in other important engagements. He was wounded, and also suffered from trench feet, which necessitated a serious operation.
In January 1919 he was demobilised, and holds the 1914 Star, General Service and Victory Medals.
58, Felixstowe Road, Lower Edmonton, N.9   15376.

JOURDEN, C., A.B., Royal Navy, H.M.S. "Prince Rupert."

He volunteered in the Navy in August 1914, and was engaged on important duties with the Grand Fleet in the North Sea. During his service he took part in several bombardments of the Belgian coast and in the naval raid on Zeebrugge.
He holds the 1914 Star, General Service and Victory Medals.
43, St. Martin's Road, Lower Edmonton, N.9   12981B.

JOURDEN, E., A.B., Royal Navy, H.M.S. "Royal Sovereign."

He joined in November 1917, and with his ship H.M.S. "Royal Sovereign" was engaged on important duties with the Grand Fleet in the North Sea and also in Turkish waters.
He holds the General Service and Victory Medals.
43, St. Martin's Road, Lower Edmonton, N.9   12981C.

JOURDEN, G., Steward, Merchant Service.

He was serving as a steward in the "Ionic" at the outbreak of war, and was later engaged with this ship on the important duties of transporting supplies from Australia, New Zealand, and America, to England and France.
He holds the Mercantile Marine, General Service and Victory Medals.
43, St. Martin's Road, Lower Edmonton, N.9   T12981A.

JOYCE, E., Pte., 3rd Royal Fusiliers.

Having previously served for some time in the Army, he rejoined in August 1914 and was sent to the Western Front. After taking part in many important engagements he was taken prisoner at the battle of Ypres in April 1915, and was interned in Germany, where he was made to work in the coal mines and suffered many hardships.
He was released after the cessation of hostilities and returned to England for demobilisation in March 1919. He holds the 1914 Star, General Service and Victory Medals.
12, Lansfield Avenue, Upper Edmonton, N.18   15229.

JOYCE, H., Pte., Royal Army Service Corps.

He volunteered in August 1914 at the outbreak of war, and was sent to the Western Front on completion of his training. While in this seat of operations he took part in many engagements, including the battle of the Somme. He was taken ill in France and was invalided home, where he died from pneumonia on October 19th, 1918.
He was entitled to the General Service and Victory Medals.
90, Winchester Road, Lower Edmonton, N.9   14761.

JOYCE, M. A. (Miss), Special War Worker.

During the war this lady was engaged on important work at the Aylesbury Dairy Company, and thereby released a man for military service. She carried out her duties to the entire satisfaction of her employers, and rendered valuable services throughout.
13, Dieppe Street, West Kensington, W.14   16265.

JUDD, A., Pte., 21st Middlesex Regiment.

Volunteering in July 1915, he was drafted overseas in the following year. During his service he took part in many important engagements, and was wounded while in action on the Somme in 1918.
He was demobilised in 1919, and holds the General Service and Victory Medals.
11, Sebastopol Road, Lower Edmonton, N.9   14549.

JUDGE, A. R., Pte., R.A.S.C. (M.T.)

He joined in April 1916 and was drafted to France in the same year, taking part in many engagements, including the battles of the Somme, the Marne, Cambrai and Ypres. In 1918 he was sent to Germany with the Army of Occupation, where he served for twelve months, and in April 1920 was demobilised, holding the General Service and Victory Medals.
9, Oak Road, Willesden, N.W.10   15083.

JUDGE, R. M. (Mrs.), Special War Worker.

During the war this lady gave very valuable services. She was first employed at Messrs. Waring & Gillows on the manufacture of military equipment, and later went to No. 2 Filling Factory, Fulham, where she was engaged on packing grenades and sewing cordite rings. She carried out her duties in a very efficient manner and received high commendation.
31, Averill Street, Hammersmith, W.6   14169.

JUDGE, V., C.S.M., 7th Border Regiment.
Volunteering in August 1914, he was drafted after his training
to the Dardanelles and took part in some of the severe
fighting on the Peninsula. After the evacuation he was sent
to France, where he was actively engaged in various sectors of
the Western Front. He was killed in action during the
Advance of October 20th, 1918, and was entitled to the 1914–
15 Star, the General Service and Victory Medals.
8, Beaufoy Road, Tottenham, N.17.   X17937.

JULIER, F. B., 1st Air Mechanic, R.A.F.
Joining in 1916, he was retained after his training on important duties with his squadron. His work required a high
degree of technical skill and he gave valuable services, but
was unable to secure his transfer overseas before hostilities
ceased.
He was demobilised in 1919.
46, Wingmore Road, Tottenham, N.17   X17969.

JUPP, A. J., Pte., Machine Gun Corps.
He volunteered in April 1915, and was later drafted to the
Western Front, where he took part in many important
engagements.
In 1919 he returned to England and was demobilised in
August, holding the General Service and Victory Medals.
28, Eastbournia Avenue, Lower Edmonton, N.9   13580A.

JUPP, F., Lce.-Cpl., Royal Army Medical Corps.
He volunteered in September 1915, and was sent to France,
where he was in action on several occasions. Later he was
transferred to Egypt and joined the forces of General
Allenby for the Palestine campaign. He contracted a serious
illness whilst in the East and was invalided home.
After a considerable time in hospital he was demobilised in
July 1919, holding the General Service and Victory Medals.
11, Bramber Road, W. Kensington, W.14   16278.

K

KATESMARK, A. G., Pte., Devonshire Regt.
He joined in February 1917, and later in the same year was
drafted to the Western Front, where he took part in the
battles of Arras and Ypres and in other important engagements. He was invalided home and was in hospital some
time. On his recovery, being medically unfit for further
active service, he was retained on special duties on Salisbury
Plain until his demobilisation in November 1919.
He holds the General Service and Victory Medals.
7, Eustace Road, Walham Green, S.W.6   X19416.

KEAN, A., Pte., Middlesex Regiment.
He volunteered in August 1914, and in the following year
was sent to the Western Front, where he took part in the
second and third battles of Ypres, Loos, the Somme and
Cambrai. During his service overseas he was wounded.
He secured his demobilisation in February 1919, and holds
the 1915 Star, the General Service and Victory Medals.
13, St. Martin's Road, Lower Edmonton, N.18   12976.

KEARIN, W. H. G., Sapper, Royal Engineers.
He joined in June 1916, and on the completion of his training
was sent to Egypt in the same year. During his three years'
service there he was engaged on important duties in connection with the extensive operations in that theatre of war.
He holds the General Service and Victory Medals, and was
demobilised in September 1919.
4, Wingmore Road, Tottenham, N.17   X17973.

KEAT, F., Pte., Royal Army Service Corps.
He volunteered in 1915, and in the same year was sent to the
Western Front. During his four years' service he took part
in the battle of Ypres (1915) and in heavy fighting at La
Bassée and Bapaume.
He returned to England for demobilisation in May 1919, and
holds the 1914–15 Star, the General Service and Victory
Medals.
104, Lopen Road, Upper Edmonton, N.18   X17915.

KEEBLE, C. E., Cpl., South Staffordshire Regt.
He enlisted in 1906, and immediately on the outbreak of war
was sent to the Western Front, where he fought in the retreat
from Mons, the battles of the Marne, the Aisne, Ypres, the
Somme and in the closing campaign of 1918.
In April 1919 he was discharged, holding the Mons Star,
General Service and Victory Medals.
104, Carlyle Avenue, Willesden, N.W.10   14455B.

KEELER, A., Gunner, Royal Field Artillery.
He was serving when war broke out and in 1914 went to the
Western Front, where he took part in the retreat from Mons
and many other battles, including those of the Marne and
Aisne, and the Retreat and Advance in 1918.
He was demobilised in 1919, holding the Mons Star, General
Service and Victory Medals.
17. Portnall Road, Maida Hill, W.9   X19305A.

**KEELER, C. F., Pte., Queen's Own (Royal West
Kent Regiment).**
Volunteering shortly after the outbreak of hostilities, he was
sent to the Western Front. He took part in several battles
and was killed in action at Loos in September 1915, being
buried in the British cemetery near the town.
He was entitled to the 1914–15 Star, General Service and
Victory Medals.
17, Portnall Road, Maida Hill, W.9   X19305B.

KEELER, H., Pte., Bedfordshire Regiment.
He enlisted in 1902, and immediately on the outbreak of war
was sent to the Western Front, where he took part in the
retreat from Mons and in the battles of the Marne and Aisne.
He was twice wounded and was later drafted to Mesopotamia.
During his service there he was engaged on special wireless
signalling duties throughout the campaign against the Turks.
In March 1919 he secured his discharge after 17 years' service,
and holds the Mons Star, General Service and Victory Medals.
13, Portnall Road, Maida Hill, W.9   X19303.

KEEN, C., Cpl., Machine Gun Corps.
Joining in December 1917, he was later drafted to the Western
Front, where he took part in many important engagements in
the Retreat and Advance of the Allies in 1918.
In February 1919 he was demobilised, and holds the General
Service and Victory Medals.
112, Chaplin Road, Cricklewood, N.W.2   16630.

KEEN, E., Signaller, Royal Field Artillery.
He volunteered in 1915, and in the same year was sent to the
Western Front. He took part in the battles of the Somme,
Passchendaele Ridge and other important engagements
during the Allied Retreat and Advance in 1918. He was
wounded during the battle of the Somme.
In May 1919 he secured his demobilisation, and holds the
1915 Star, General Service and Victory Medals.
4, Portnall Road, Maida Hill, W.9   TX19803B.

KEEN, E. L., Sergt., 1st Wiltshire Regiment.
He volunteered for service in September 1914, and was sent
to the Western Front, where after taking part in many
engagements he was wounded and taken prisoner. After
spending 10 months in captivity he was released and demobilised in March 1919.
He holds the General Service and Victory Medals.
37, Musard Road, Hammersmith, W.6   15731.

**KEEN, H., Leading Stoker, Royal Navy, H.M.S.
" Ophelia."**
He was serving at the outbreak of war, and took part in
several naval engagements, including those of Heligoland
Bight and Jutland. Whilst on the way to Aden in 1917 his
ship was torpedoed and he was drowned.
He was entitled to the 1914 Star, General Service and
Victory Medals.
4, Portnall Road, Maida Hill, W.9   TX19803A.

KEEN, J. G., Cpl., 1st Wiltshire Regiment.
He volunteered in September 1914, and in the following year
was sent overseas. During his service on the Western Front
he took part in many important engagements and gained
promotion for consistent good work.
He was demobilised in March 1919, and holds the 1915 Star,
General Service and Victory Medals.
33, Kinnoul Road, Hammersmith, W.6   14459.

KEEN, S., Q.M.S., Royal Field Artillery.
Volunteering in 1914, he was drafted overseas in the following year. During his four years' service on the Western
Front he took part in the battles of the Somme and Ypres
and in other important engagements.
He was promoted to the rank of Quartermaster-Sergeant on
account of consistent good work in the field. He holds the
1915 Star, General Service and Victory Medals.
16, Kimberley Road, Upper Edmonton, N.18   16532B.

KEEN, S. G., Sapper, Royal Engineers.
Volunteering in 1915, he was sent on completion of his
training to the Western Front, where he took an active part
in the battles of the Somme and at Ypres (1917).
He remained in France until 1919 when he returned to this
country for demobilisation, holding the General Service and
Victory Medals.
16, Kimberley Road, Upper Edmonton, N.18   16532A.

**KEEN, W. A., Cpl., R.A.S.C. (M.T.) and West
Yorkshire Regiment.**
He volunteered in 1915, and served on the Western Front,
taking part in the battles of the Somme, Cambrai, Arras,
Ypres, Bullecourt and other engagements. In 1918 he went
with the Army of Occupation to Germany and remained there
until demobilised in January 1919, holding the General
Service and Victory Medals.
24, Purves Road, Kensal Rise, N.W.10   X18026.

KEENE, J., Sapper, Royal Engineers.
He volunteered in 1915, and in the following year was drafted overseas. During his service on the Western Front he took part in the battles of the Somme and Ypres, and in many other important engagements.
In 1919 he secured his demobilisation, and holds the General Service and Victory Medals.
10, Kimberley Road, Upper Edmonton, N.18   16457.

KEEP, S. L. T., Pte., Middlesex Regiment and Labour Battalion.
He joined in 1917, and later in the same year was sent to France, where he was engaged on important duties with a Labour battalion. He took part in heavy fighting around Bapaume during the Retreat of 1918.
He remained in France until his demobilisation in 1919, and holds the General Service and Victory Medals.
88, Kilburn Lane, North Kensington, W.10   18607.

KEEVIL, W., Pte., Devonshire Regiment.
Volunteering in June 1915, he was later in the same year sent to France, where he took part in heavy fighting at Givenchy, Festubert and in the battle of the Somme (being wounded at Fricourt in July 1916). In the September following he was wounded at Ginchy, and was invalided home. He remained in hospital three months, and on his recovery was drafted to Salonica, where he served through the latter part of the Balkan campaign. He was later at Batum, in South Russia, and while in the East contracted malaria.
In July 1919 he secured his demobilisation, and holds the 1915 Star, General Service and Victory Medals.
86, Bronsart Road, Munster Road, Fulham, S.W.6   X18890.

KELL, A., Driver, Royal Field Artillery.
He volunteered in August 1915, and later in the same year was sent to France. While there he took part in the battles of Arras, Vimy Ridge, Ypres (1917) and Cambrai, and in the Retreat and Advance of the Allies in 1918.
He was demobilised in 1919, and holds the 1915 Star, General Service and Victory Medals.
25, Melville Road, Stonebridge Park, N.W.10   14625B.

KELL, B., Pte., King's Shropshire L I.
He enlisted in 1908, and at the outbreak of war was sent to the Western Front. He took part in the retreat from Mons and in other engagements until he was drafted in 1915 to the 22nd Division, which was then stationed at Salonica.
After serving for three years at this important seat of war he was sent back to France, where he took part in the Allied Retreat and Advance in 1918. He was wounded while on active service. Upon his return to England in 1920 he was discharged, after 12 years' service with the Colours.
He holds the Mons Star, General Service and Victory Medals.
47, Mordaunt Road, Willesden, N.W.10   13860A.

KELL, F., Pte., Royal Fusiliers.
Joining in February 1916, he was soon afterwards sent to France. While on the Western Front he took part in the battles of the Somme, Arras, Ypres (1917), Cambrai, and in other important engagements.
In September 1919 he secured his demobilisation, and holds the General Service and Victory Medals.
25, Melville Road, Stonebridge Park, N.W.10   14625A.

KELL, G., Pte., Royal Army Medical Corps.
He volunteered in August 1914, and was immediately sent to the Western Front, where he served with the 52nd Field Ambulance for nearly four years. During this time he took part in several important engagements. He died on August 31st, 1918, from wounds received two days previously whilst in action at Ypres.
He was entitled to the 1914 Star, General Service and Victory Medals.
47, Mordaunt Road, Willesden, N.W.10   14094.

KELL, J. W., Bombardier, R.F.A.
He volunteered for service in January 1916, and shortly afterwards was drafted overseas. He took part in many engagements on the Western Front, including the battle of Ypres, and was killed in action at Vimy Ridge on May 7th, 1917.
He was entitled to the General Service and Victory Medals.
47, Mordaunt Road, Willesden, N.W.10   13860B.

KELL, T., Cpl., Royal Army Medical Corps.
He was mobilised from the Reserve on the outbreak of war, and immediately proceeded to the Western Front. He took part in the retreat from Mons and in the battles of Neuve Chapelle, Ypres (1915), the Somme, Cambrai, and in heavy fighting near Amiens. He remained in France until May 1919, when he returned to England for his discharge, having completed 17 years with the Colours.
He holds the Mons Star, General Service and Victory Medals.
195, Portnall Road, Maida Hill, W.9   14093.

KELLY, E. J., Lce.-Sergt., 8th East Surrey Regt.
He joined in October 1916, and on completion of his training was drafted overseas. During his service on the Western Front he took part in many important engagements, and gained promotion for consistent good work. After being both wounded and gassed, he was invalided to England.
In November 1919 he secured his demobilisation, and holds the General Service and Victory Medals.
16, Werley Avenue, Dawes Road, S.W.6   17875.

KELLY, J., Pte., Royal Army Service Corps.
He volunteered for service in August 1914, and in the following year was drafted to the Western Front, where he remained for nearly four years. During this time he did good work with the R.A.S.C. in various sectors, and was present at the battles of Ypres, the Somme, Arras and Cambrai.
He returned to England in April 1919, and was demobilised, holding the 1914-15 Star, General Service and Victory Medals. 22, Clarendon Street, Paddington, W.2   X20547.

KELLY, J., Cpl., King's Royal Rifle Corps.
Volunteering in May 1915, he was shortly afterwards sent to the Western Front, where he took part in the battles of Loos, the Somme, Arras and Messines, and also in engagements near Ypres. He was severely wounded in June 1917 during the battle of Messines, and three months later was discharged as being medically unfit for further service.
He holds the 1914-15 Star, General Service and Victory Medals. 24, Westbury Road, Willesden, N.W.10   15454.

KELLY, J. B., Pte., R.A.S.C. (Labour Coy.)
He volunteered in 1914, and during his service on the Western Front was in action on the Somme, at Loos, Arras, Neuve Chapelle, Armentières, Amiens, Ypres, Vimy Ridge and St. Quentin, and in the Allied Advance of 1918.
He was demobilised in 1919, holding the 1914 Star, General Service and Victory Medals.
5, Archel Road, West Kensington, W.14   16200.

KELLY, T., A.B., Royal Navy.
He enlisted in the Navy in 1897, and went to sea immediately on the outbreak of hostilities. He served on board H.M.S. "Agincourt" and "Castor," and took part in many important naval engagements, including the battle of Jutland. He holds the African General Service Medal (1902), the 1914 Star, General Service, Victory, Royal Humane Society and the Messina Earthquake Medals.
He was serving in 1920 in H.M.S. "Coventry," and had then completed 23 years' service in the Royal Navy.
98, Hartington Road, Tottenham, N.17   TX19109.

KELLY, W., Cpl., Royal Inniskilling Fusiliers, Royal Dublin Fusiliers and R.A.F.
He volunteered in November 1914, and was almost immediately sent to France, where he took part in much severe fighting. He was then drafted to the Dardanelles, and served throughout the Gallipoli campaign. Later he went to Serbia, and fought on the Doiran and Vardar Fronts. He took part in the final operations in Palestine in 1918.
He holds the 1914-15 Star, General Service and Victory Medals.
24, Mulgrave Road, Fulham, S.W.6   TX17065.

KEMBLE, W. H., Pte., 20th Middlesex Regiment.
He volunteered for service in 1915, and on completion of his training served at various stations on important duties with his unit until 1917, when he was drafted overseas. He took part in many engagements on the Western Front, and remained there until his demobilisation in February 1919.
He holds the General Service and Victory Medals.
23, Sunnyside Road, Lower Edmonton, N.9   14557.

KEMP, E., Cpl., R.A.S.C. (Labour Coy.)
He volunteered for service in February 1915, and in the same year was sent to the Western Front, where he was wounded, and later contracted consumption. He was discharged physically unfit for further service in February 1916, and has since died.
He was entitled to the 1914-15 Star, General Service and Victory Medals.
113, Love Lane, Tottenham, N.17   X18521B.

KEMP, E., Driver, Royal Field Artillery.
Volunteering in November 1914, he was sent overseas early in the following year. He took part in many important engagements on the Western Front, including the battles of Neuve Chapelle, Loos and Ypres, where he was wounded in 1917. He was discharged in consequence in December of the same year.
Having also served in the South African war, he holds the Queen's Medal with three clasps, the King's Medal with two clasps, in addition to the 1915 Star, General Service and Victory Medals.
1, St. Martin's Road, Lower Edmonton, N.9   12972.

KEMP, F. J., Pte., R.A.S.C. (M.T.)
He enlisted in February 1916 at the age of 51, having previously served in the R.M.L.I. and King's Liverpool Regiment. He was on duty with the supply column of the 31st Division in France until September 1916, after which he was stationed in England, being medically unfit on account of his age for further service overseas.
He was demobilised in February 1919, and holds the General Service and Victory Medals.
100, Strode Road, Willesden, N.W.10   17315B.

KEMP, H. G., Pte., 2nd Norfolk Regiment.
He joined in October 1916, and on completion of his training was sent to Mesopotamia, where he took part in many engagements, including the operations on the Dialah Front. He was afterwards sent to India, and was demobilised in March 1920, holding the General Service, Victory and India General Service Medal, 1908, with clasp—Afghanistan, N.W. Frontier, 1919.
100, Strode Road, Willesden, N.W.10   17315A.

KEMP, J., Rifleman, 21st London Regiment (1st Surrey Rifles).
He volunteered for service in February 1915, and was sent to France the same year, where he took part in many engagements on the Western Front. He was twice wounded, and was eventually taken prisoner. After eight months' captivity in Germany he was demobilised in February 1919.
He holds the 1915 Star, General Service and Victory Medals.
46, Bounces Road, Lower Edmonton, N.9   13944.

KEMP, W. A., Pte., Labour Corps.
Joining in 1916, he completed his training, and was sent to the Western Front, where he served for about three years. He rendered valuable services on various sectors of the Front until he was sent home for demobilisation in 1919.
He holds the General Service and Victory Medals.
60, Shorrolds Road, Walham Green, S.W.6   X19367.

KEMP, W. C., Special War Worker.
During the war he held a responsible position as manager of a large military canteen at Colchester. His duties were in connection with the war supply of provisions, and were satisfactorily carried out. His work was greatly appreciated by the troops.
23, Archel Road, West Kensington, W.14   16431.

KEMP, W. E., Pte., Middlesex Regiment.
He volunteered in March 1915, and in the same year was sent to Salonica, where he took part in much heavy fighting. He was later drafted to Russia, and was wounded while in action there.
In 1919 he was demobilised, but shortly after rejoined the Army. He holds the 1915 Star, General Service and Victory Medals.
113, Love Lane, Tottenham, N.17   X18521A.

KEMPSON, C., Pte., Machine Gun Corps.
He joined in February 1917, and after his training was sent to the Western Front, where he took part in many engagements. He fought at the battles of Arras and Kemmel Hill, and while in action on the Aisne, during the Allied Retreat, was killed on May 27th, 1918.
He was entitled to the General Service and Victory Medals.
35, Melville Road, Stonebridge Park, N.W.10   15662B.

KEMPSON, G. (M.M.), Pte., Bedfordshire Regt.
Enlisting in June 1914, he was sent to the Western Front in March 1916. He took part in the battles of Arras, Vimy Ridge, Ypres and Cambrai, and was wounded and gassed. In 1917 he was awarded the Military Medal for conspicuous bravery and devotion to duty in the field.
He also holds the General Service and Victory Medals, and was demobilised in March 1919.
35, Melville Road, Stonebridge Park, N.W.10   15662C.

KEMPSON, J., Pte., Attached Royal Air Force.
He joined in June 1918, and at the conclusion of his training was sent overseas. During his service on the Western Front he was engaged as a Lewis gunner with a kite-balloon section. He did consistent good work against enemy aircraft in the closing stages of the war.
In January 1919 he secured his demobilisation, and holds the General Service and Victory Medals.
35, Melville Road, Stonebridge Park, N.W.10   15662A.

KEMPSTER, A., Pte., 9th Royal Fusiliers.
He volunteered in 1914, and early in the following year was sent to France, where he took part in many important engagements, and was killed in the battle of Loos.
He was entitled to the 1915 Star, General Service and Victory Medals.
61, Barret's Green Road, Willesden, N.W.10.   13554C.

KEMPSTER, H., Pte., 3rd Middlesex Regiment.
He volunteered for service in 1915, and at the conclusion of his training was drafted to Salonica, where he saw much fighting during the campaign. He contracted malaria during his service in the Balkans.
He was demobilised in 1919, and holds the General Service and Victory Medals.
65, Barret's Green Road, Willesden, N.W.   13556A.

KEMPSTON, H. R., Bombardier, R.F.A.
Volunteering in August 1915, he was drafted overseas in the following year. While on the Western Front he took part in the battles of the Somme, Vimy Ridge, Messines and Ypres, and in other important engagements. He was wounded in action. In 1917 he was sent to Italy, and at the close of the campaign he returned in April 1919 to this country for demobilisation.
He holds the General Service and Victory Medals.
27, Sheldon Road, Upper Edmonton, N.18   X17307.

KEMSLEY, E. A. (Miss), Special War Worker.
Anxious to serve her country, this lady accepted in 1916 a post at the Park Royal Munition Factory. She was employed in applying lacquer, which was an occupation of a very injurious character. She fulfilled her responsible position to the entire satisfaction of her superiors, and received high commendation.
31, Holly Lane, Willesden, N.W.10   15575A.

KEMSLEY, E. L. (Mrs.), Special War Worker.
During the war this lady was engaged at the Park Royal Munition Factory. She was employed in filling fuses and in lacquering, and in consequence of the injurious nature of the latter her health was affected. She continued her work until 1918, giving entire satisfaction to those in authority.
31, Holly Lane, Willesden, N.W.10   15575C.

KEMSLEY, F. W., Gunner, Royal Marine Artillery.
He volunteered in 1915, and later in the same year was drafted overseas. While on the Western Front he took part in many important engagements, and in 1917 died of wounds received in action.
He was entitled to the 1914-15 Star, General Service and Victory Medals.
31, Holly Lane, Willesden, N.W.10   15575B.

KENDALL, B., Bombardier, R.F.A.
Volunteering for service in September 1914, he was drafted to the Eastern theatre of war in the following year. He took an active part in the heavy fighting on the Gallipoli Peninsula, and was killed in action there on November 15th, 1915.
He was entitled to the 1914-15 Star, General Service and Victory Medals.
4, Hazel Road, Willesden, N.W.10   X17597A.

KENDALL, E., Pte., Queen's Own (Royal West Kent Regiment).
He volunteered in September 1914, and in the following year was sent to France. During his three years' service on the Western Front he took part in the battles of Loos, the Somme, Arras, Ypres, Cambrai, Albert and Amiens.
He was demobilised in February 1919, and holds the 1914-15 Star, General Service and Victory Medals.
4, Hazel Road, Willesden, N.W.10   X17597B.

KENDLY, E. F. (Mrs.), Special War Worker.
This lady rendered valuable services in France throughout the war, where she was engaged on important work at a large aeroplane factory in Rouen. She also worked in an Army tailor's shop. She carried out her duties in a very capable manner, and received high commendation for her splendid work.
69, Humbolt Road, Hammersmith, W.6   14983B.

KENNEDY, E., Cpl., Royal Garrison Artillery.
Volunteering in August 1914, he was sent in the following year to the Western Front, where he served for nearly four years, taking part in the battles of the Somme, Arras and Ypres, and in other important engagements. During his service overseas he was wounded and gassed.
He was demobilised in February 1919, and holds the 1914-15 Star, General Service and Victory Medals.
38, Lurgan Avenue, Hammersmith, W.6   13665A.

KENNEDY, K. B. (Mrs.), Special War Worker.
During the war this lady was engaged at first at the White City, where she was an examiner. She went later to Messrs. Brice & Western's, Fulham, and was there employed as a turner.
She proved herself efficient and painstaking, and did splendid work for her country.
38, Lurgan Avenue, Hammersmith, W.6   13665B.

KENT, E. J., Cpl., Essex Regiment.

He volunteered in September 1914, and in the following year was sent to Salonica. He was drafted later to the Dardanelles, and served throughout the Gallipoli campaign. While in the East he contracted malaria, which led in June 1918 to his discharge as medically unfit for further service.
He holds the 1914-15 Star, General Service and Victory Medals.
12, Warwick Road, Upper Edmonton, N.18   X17269

KENT, H. J., Driver, Royal Engineers.

This driver volunteered in October 1915, and on completion of his training was sent overseas in the following June. He took an active part in important operations in various sectors of the Western Front, and was invalided home in 1918, suffering from trench fever.
In January 1919 he secured his demobilisation, and holds the General Service and Victory Medals.
81, Shakespeare Road, Willesden, N.W.10   13704.

KERR, R., Leading Stoker, Royal Navy.

Having previously served in the Royal Navy, he was mobilised from the Reserve at the outbreak of war, and immediately proceeded to sea.
He was engaged with the Grand Fleet in many important operations throughout the war, and served on H.M.S. submarines " K.1 " and " K.16."
In February 1919 he secured his discharge, and holds the 1914 Star, General Service and Victory Medals.
99, Yeldham Road, Hammersmith, W.6   13239.

KERRIDGE, F., Pte., Royal Fusiliers.

Joining in September 1916, he was sent to the Western Front on completion of his training. During his service there he took part in many important engagements, and was severely wounded. As a result he was invalided home, and after a long period in hospital was discharged as medically unfit for further service in January 1919.
He holds the General Service and Victory Medals.
61, Reporton Road, Munster Road, S.W.6   18912A.

KERRIDGE, J., Pte., Duke of Cornwall's L.I.

Volunteering in August 1914, he was sent on completion of his training to the Western Front. He there took part in many important engagements, and was killed in action at Vimy Ridge on October 3rd, 1916.
He was entitled to the 1914-15 Star, General Service and Victory Medals.
61, Reporton Road, Munster Road, S.W.6   X18912B.

KERRY, H., Lce.-Cpl., Middlesex Regiment.

He joined up in May 1916, and after his training served at various stations on important duties with his unit. He rendered valuable service, but was unsuccessful in obtaining his transfer overseas owing to physical disability.
He was demobilised in January 1919.
16, Bramber Road, West Kensington, W.14   16284A.

KERRY, P., Pte., Suffolk Regiment.

He enlisted in 1917, although he was below military age. Whilst serving with his unit, he made many applications to be sent overseas, but he was retained in England on account of his youth.
He rendered valuable service at Home, and was demobilised in December 1919.
16, Bramber Road, West Kensington, W.14   16284B.

KERSWELL, H., Bombardier, R.F.A.

He volunteered for duty in November 1914, and was sent to the Western Front, where he was in action until 1916, during which time he took part in several important engagements.
He was discharged in November 1916 as medically unfit for further military duties.
He holds the General Service and Victory Medals.
8, Moylan Road, Hammersmith, W.6   15288.

KESSELL, R. S., Pte., 1st Essex Regiment.

He volunteered for service in September 1914, and in the following year was drafted to Gallipoli, where in December 1915 he was badly wounded. Afterwards he was sent to Egypt, and thence to the Western Front, where he took part in many engagements. In July 1917 he was again wounded during the third battle of Ypres.
He was discharged in July 1918, owing to his wound, and holds the 1914-15 Star, General Service and Victory Medals.
34, St. Ervan's Road, North Kensington, W.10   X20385.

KETLEY, W. A., Driver, R.A.S.C. (M.T.)

Having previously served for 12 years in the Army, he re-enlisted in August 1914, and was immediately sent overseas. He took part in the retreat from Mons and in the battles of Loos and Arras. In 1916 he was invalided home with paralysis, and after a period in hospital was discharged in April of the same year as medically unfit for further service.
He holds the Mons Star, General Service and Victory Medals.
44, Walham Grove, Fulham, S.W.6   19616.

13

KEY, W. E., Pte., 20th Middlesex Regiment.

He volunteered for service in August 1915, and at the conclusion of his training was sent overseas. He took part in many important engagements on the Western Front, and was severely wounded in heavy fighting at Loos in October 1916, in consequence of which his left leg had to be amputated.
He was discharged as physically unfit for further service in September 1918, and holds the General Service and Victory Medals.
3, Ray's Road, Upper Edmonton, N.18   15351.

KEYS, T., Pte., 1st Hunts. Cyclists' Battalion.

He joined up in October 1916, and on completing his training, served on the East Coast defence, being physically unfit for service overseas. He rendered valuable service, and was discharged as medically unfit for further military duties in September 1917.
1, Gilpin Crescent, Upper Edmonton, N.18   T16843.

KIBBLE, E., S.M., 6th Buffs (East Kent Regt.)

He volunteered for service in September 1914, and was drafted to the Western Front the following year, where he took part with distinction in several engagements, and was badly gassed at the battle of Loos in October 1915.
He was demobilised in July 1919, and holds the 1915 Star, General Service and Victory Medals,
45, Disraeli Road, Acton Lane, N.W.10   14152.

KIDD, W., Pte., 17th Essex Regiment.

Joining up in May 1918, he was almost immediately sent overseas, and was engaged on important escort duties during the Allied Retreat and Advance on the Western Front.
He remained in France until his demobilisation in March 1919, and holds the General Service and Victory Medals.
2a, Dunraven Road, Shepherd's Bush, W.12   11928A.

KIDD, W. H., 1st Air Mechanic, R.N.A.S. and Royal Air Force.

Volunteering in November 1914, he was soon after drafted overseas. He was engaged on important work in connection with the repair of seaplanes operating in the Mediterranean Sea, and later served in important operations near the Suez Canal and on the Struma Front in the Balkan campaign.
He was demobilised in December 1919, and holds the 1914-15 Star, General Service and Victory Medals.
2a, Dunraven Road, Shepherd's Bush, W.12   11928A.

KIDDS, E. H., Cpl., Machine Gun Corps.

He joined in January 1916, and on completion of his training was sent to the Western Front, where he took part in the battles of the Somme, Ypres (1917), and in other important engagements. He was wounded during the Allied Advance in October 1918.
In the following year he secured his demobilisation, and holds the General Service and Victory Medals.
3, Compton Terrace, Pretoria Road, Tottenham, N.17   X17936.

KIELLOR, H., Gunner, Royal Marine Artillery.

He volunteered in 1914, and during the war served in H.M.S. " Dreadnought " with the Grand Fleet in the North Sea. He took part in the naval engagements off Heligoland and Zeebrugge, and was also engaged on important patrol duties. During his service he was twice wounded, and holds the 1914 Star, General Service and Victory Medals.
63, Barret's Green Road, Willesden, N.W.10   13555C.

KIELLOR, J., Pte., Royal Army Medical Corps.

Volunteering in 1914, he was drafted to the Dardanelles, and served throughout the Gallipoli campaign. After much service in Egypt he proceeded to the Western Front. He again saw much heavy fighting, and early in 1918 was drafted to Italy, and took part in the final engagements at that theatre of war.
In 1919 he secured his demobilisation, and holds the 1914-15 Star, General Service and Victory Medals.
63, Barret's Green Road, Willesden, N.W.10   13555B.

KIELLOR, L. (Miss), Special War Worker.

This lady's war service extended over a period of four years. She was first employed by the Westminster Engineering Company, and later by the Addressograph Company, in the manufacture of gun-sights, which work required great care and skill. Afterwards she was engaged by Messrs. Thorneycroft at Basingstoke, and remained there until 1918.
Throughout the war she did splendid work, and received high commendation.
63, Barret's Green Road, Willesden, N.W.10   13555A.

KILBOURN, A. G., Rifleman, K.R.R.

Joining up in 1916, he was later in the same year sent to the Western Front, where he took part in the battle of the Somme and other important engagements.
He remained in France until 1919, when he returned for demobilisation, holding the General Service and Victory Medals. 7, Winchester Road, Lower Edmonton, N.9   14676.

KILBOURN, E. S., Pte., The Buffs (East Kent Regiment.)
He joined in August 1916, and after his training was sent to India, where he was engaged on important duties at various stations. He was later drafted to Salonica, and after taking part in much heavy fighting there was sent to Mesopotamia. He fought throughout the latter part of the campaign in that theatre of war, and returned for demobilisation in 1919. He holds the General Service and Victory Medals.
39, Felixstowe Road, Lower Edmonton, N.9   15386.

KILBOURN, S. F., Cpl., 2/7th Middlesex Regt.
Volunteering in September 1914, he was soon after sent to Gibraltar, from where, after being engaged on important garrison duties, he was drafted to Egypt. He remained in this theatre of war for three years, and took part in many engagements. In 1918 he was sent to the Western Front, where he fought in the operations near Ypres and on the Somme during the Allied Retreat and Advance.
He was demobilised in January 1919, and holds the 1914-15 Star, General Service and Victory Medals.
53, Brettenham Road, Upper Edmonton, N.18   15235.

KILBY, A., Pte., R.A.S.C. (M.T.)
He joined in May 1917, and went overseas in the following month, where he was employed on important transport work during many engagements on the Western Front, including the battles of the Somme and Ypres.
He was demobilised in October 1919, and holds the General Service and Victory Medals.
33, Denbigh Road, Willesden, N.W.10 .   15094.

KILHAN, W., Pte., R.A.S.C. (M.T.)
He joined in May 1917, and was drafted to the Western Front in the following month. He was engaged on important duties in connection with the supply of ammunition in many engagements during the Allied Retreat and Advance. He met with a serious accident whilst on duty, and was detained in hospital for some time.
In November 1919 he secured his demobilisation, and holds the General Service and Victory Medals.
109, Roundwood Road, Willesden, N.W.10   16048.

KILLEY, C., Pte., 7th Middlesex Regiment.
Volunteering in December 1914, he was sent to the Western Front on completion of his training in the following year. During his four years' active service he took part in the battle of the Somme and other important engagements. He was wounded in action at Ypres in 1916.
He was demobilised in January 1919, holding the 1914-15 Star, General Service and Victory Medals.
15, Beaufoy Road, Tottenham, N.17   X17943.

KILLICK, T. W. (M.M.), Acting Squadron S.M., 20th Hussars.
He was serving at the outbreak of war, and was immediately sent to the Western Front. He took part in the retreat from Mons, in the battles of the Marne, Ypres, the Somme, Vimy Ridge and Cambrai. He was awarded the Military Medal for conspicuous gallantry and devotion to duty in the field, and in addition holds the Queen's South African Medal with four bars, the Mons Star, General Service and Victory Medals.
In November 1919 he was discharged after 22 years' service with the Army.
16, Bolton Road, Harlesden, N.W.10   13375.

KILLINGBACK, E. A. (Miss), Special War Worker.
During the war this lady was engaged in the danger zone at Hayes' Munition Factory. Her work was shell-filling, which was capably done. She was commended for her efforts.
30, Dieppe Street, West Kensington, W.14   16259A.

KILLINGBACK, G. E., Tpr., 4th (Royal Irish) Dragoon Guards and Pte., Dorset Regiment.
He volunteered in 1914, and served throughout the Gallipoli campaign. On the evacuation of the Peninsula he saw much fighting on the Salonica Front, and from there was drafted to France, where he fought at Ypres, Loos, Neuve Chapelle, Arras and in the Allied Retreat and Advance of 1918. He was wounded in action in the Dardanelles and was severely gassed in France.
Demobilised in 1919, he holds the 1914-15 Star, General Service and Victory Medals.
30, Dieppe Street, West Kensington, W.14   16259B.

KILLINGBACK, J. A., Pte., Middlesex Regt.
He joined in 1916, and on completion of his training was drafted to the Middle East. He took part in various engagements on the Mesopotamian Front, where he remained until his demobilisation in 1919.
He holds the General Service and Victory Medals.
9, Pretoria Road, Tottenham, N.17   X18123.

KILLINGBACK, W. J., Pte., Royal Fusiliers.
Volunteering in April 1915, he was sent in the same year to France, where he took part in many important engagements. He fought in the battles of the Somme, and was killed in action at Guillemont on August 16th, 1916.
He was entitled to the 1914-15 Star, General Service and Victory Medals.
31, Hilmer Street, West Kensington, W.14   15920.

KILLINGBACK, W. J., Pte., R.A.S.C.
He volunteered in 1914, and on completion of his training was sent to France, where he took an active part in the battles of the Somme, Arras and Ypres and in important operations around Armentières. He was later drafted to Salonica, and after taking part in engagements on that Front was sent to Russia.
He was demobilised in June 1919, and holds the General Service and Victory Medals.
30, Dieppe Street, West Kensington, W.14   16260.

KILLINGER, R. P., Lce.-Cpl., M.F.P.
Volunteering in June 1915, he was retained in England on important police duty at various stations. He also served in the Intelligence Department, but was not successful in obtaining his transfer overseas in spite of many applications. He was discharged in September 1918.
20, Lancaster Road, Upper Edmonton, N.18   X17057.

KIME, J. A. (Miss), Special War Worker.
During the war this lady held a responsible position on the clerical staff of the Army Pay Department. Her work, which required great care, was carried out with precision to the satisfaction of the authorities. She rendered very valuable services.
13, Mirabel Road, Fulham, S.W.6   X17717.

KIMPTON, A. J., Pte., The Queen's (Royal West Surrey Regiment) and Middlesex Regiment.
Joining in 1917, he was later in the same year drafted to Mesopotamia, where, after serving with a Trench Mortar Battery in many important engagements, he contracted malaria and was in hospital for a considerable period.
He was demobilised in 1920, and holds the General Service and Victory Medals.
50a, Deacon Road, Cricklewood, N.W.2   16621A.

KIMPTON, H. J., Pte., The Buffs (East Kent Regiment.)
Joining in May 1917, he was drafted to the Western Front. He fought in several engagements, including those of Passchendaele and Ypres, where he was badly wounded. After his recovery he guarded German prisoners until the signing of the Armistice, when he returned to England and was demobilised in 1919.
He holds the General Service and Victory Medals.
2, Belton Road, Cricklewood, N.W.2   16621B.

KIMPTON, J. R., Pioneer, R.E. (R.O.D.)
He joined in July 1918, and after his training served at Longmoor Camp on important duties with his unit. He gave valuable services, but in spite of many applications was not successful in obtaining his transfer overseas.
He was demobilised in February 1919.
14, Northcote Road, Willesden, N.W.10   14916.

KINCH, J. G., Sapper, Royal Engineers.
Volunteering in January 1915, he was immediately sent to France, where he took an active part in the battles of Neuve Chapelle, Ypres, Loos, the Somme, Vimy Ridge and Bulle-court, and in heavy fighting in Cambrai, St. Quentin and Amiens during the Allied Retreat and Advance in 1918.
He was demobilised in February 1919, and holds the 1914-15 Star, General Service and Victory Medals.
24, Chesson Road, West Kensington, W.14   X17164.

KING, A. C., Sapper, Royal Engineers.
He was serving at the outbreak of war and was immediately sent to the Western Front, where he took part in the retreat from Mons, the battles of Ypres, the Somme, Arras and Albert, and in important engagements during the Advance of 1918.
He was discharged in September 1919, and holds the Mons Star, General Service and Victory Medals.
15, Faroe Road, W. Kensington, W.14   T12437A.

KING, A. F., Cpl., Royal Field Artillery.
Having previously served in the South African war, he re-enlisted immediately on the outbreak of hostilities, and was sent to Egypt. After taking part in the operations in that theatre of war he was drafted to Mesopotamia, where he contracted malaria, and was invalided to India.
On recovery he returned to Mesopotamia and later saw service in Italy and France.
He holds the South African Medals, the 1914-15 Star, General Service and Victory Medals.
23, Mall Road, Hammersmith, W.6   13789.

KING, A. T., Driver, Royal Field Artillery.

He was mobilised from the Reserve and drafted to France in August 1914. During his service on the Western Front he took part in many important engagements, including the retreat from Mons. On June 4th, 1917, he was severely wounded during an enemy bombing raid, and died later at a field ambulance.
He was entitled to the Mons Star, General Service and Victory Medals.
54, Denbigh Road, Willesden, N.W.10   15538.

KING, A. W., Lce.-Cpl., 3rd Middlesex Regiment.

He enlisted in 1907, and at the outbreak of war was stationed in India. He was drafted to the Western Front in December 1914, and took part in the battles of Ypres and Hill 60. In May 1915 he was severely wounded in action, and died in England on June 12th of the same year.
He was entitled to the 1914-15 Star, General Service and Victory Medals.
52, Oldfield Road, Willesden, N.W.10   16060B.

KING, A. W., Cpl., Royal Army Service Corps.

He joined in 1916 and shortly after was sent to the Eastern theatre of war, where, while taking part in the operations on the Salonica Front, he contracted malaria and was invalided home. On his recovery he was certified medically unfit for further service overseas, and was retained on important duties with a Red Cross Ambulance.
He was demobilised in 1919, holding the General Service and Victory Medals.
9, Humbolt Mansions, Lillie Road, Fulham, S.W.6.   X18870B.

KING, B. G., Lce.-Cpl., King's Royal Rifle Corps and Seaforth Highlanders.

He volunteered in August 1914, and in the following year was sent to France, where he took part in many important engagements, including the battle of the Somme. He was severely wounded in action and as a result was discharged as medically unfit for further service in February 1917.
He holds the 1914-15 Star, General Service and Victory Medals.
36, Bounces Road, Lower Edmonton, N.9   13953.

KING, D. S., Rifleman, 9th London Regiment (Queen Victoria's Rifles).

He joined for service in November 1916, and after his training was sent to France in the following February. He took part in many engagements on the Western Front, where he remained until the cessation of hostilities.
He was demobilised in October 1919, and holds the General Service and Victory Medals.
143, Portnall Road, Maida Hill, W.9   X19575.

KING, E., Pte., 13th Royal Fusiliers.

Volunteering in September 1914, he was drafted on the completion of his training to the Western Front, where, while taking part in several engagements, he was wounded five times. After being gassed and suffering from fever he was for a considerable period in hospital.
He holds the 1914-15 Star, General Service and Victory Medals, and was demobilised in April 1919.
18, Lintaine Grove, West Kensington, W.14   TX17078B.

KING, E. A., Lce.-Cpl., 12th London Regiment (Rangers).

He volunteered in June 1915, and at the conclusion of his training was drafted overseas. He took part in many engagements on the Western Front and was wounded in action.
In January 1919 he was demobilised, and holds the General Service and Victory Medals.
15, Disbrowe Road, Hammersmith, W.6   15913.

KING, E. F., Pte., 31st Middlesex Regiment.

He joined for service in October 1916, and after his training was engaged on important duties with his unit at various stations. He gave valuable services, but was unsuccessful owing to physical disability in obtaining his transfer overseas. He was discharged as medically unfit for further military service in May 1918.
31, Lochaline Street, Hammersmith, W.6   13252.

KING, G., Pte., 3rd Middlesex Regiment.

He volunteered in April 1915, and at the conclusion of his training was drafted overseas to Salonica, where he was actively engaged in various sectors of the Balkan Front. He was later stationed at Constantinople, where he remained until sent home for demobilisation in November 1919.
He holds the General Service and Victory Medals..
50, Bath Road, Lower Edmonton, N.9   13132.

KING, H. E. (M.S.M.), Sapper, Royal Engineers.

Volunteering in November 1914, he was sent to the Eastern Front on completion of his training. While in Egypt he was engaged on special signalling duties at General Headquarters and was later sent to Palestine, where he took part in the important operations around Jerusalem. He was awarded the Meritorious Service Medal for devotion to duty, and was also mentioned in despatches for conspicuous services.
In June 1919 he was demobilised, and also holds the 1914-15 Star, General Service and Victory Medals.
15, Faroe Road, W. Kensington, W.14   T12437B.

KING, J. W., Driver, Royal Engineers.

He joined in September 1916, and on completion of his training was sent to France, where he took part in the battles of Arras, Ypres (1917) and the Somme (1918). After the signing of the Armistice he went to Germany with the Army of Occupation and remained there until his return to England for his demobilisation in August 1919.
He holds the General Service and Victory Medals.
15, Faroe Road, W. Kensington, W.14   T12437C.

KING, M., Cpl., Royal Dublin Fusiliers.

Volunteering in August 1915, he was sent in the following year to the East. During his service on the Balkan Front he took part in important engagements against the Bulgarians. He was later drafted to France, and, while in action during the Advance of 1918, was wounded.
He holds the General Service and Victory Medals, and was demobilised in December 1919.
26a, Deacon Road, Cricklewood, N.W.2   16138.

KING, R., Pte., Coldstream Guards.

He enlisted in January 1914, and at the outbreak of war was sent to France. He took part in many engagements on the Western Front, where he served until the cessation of hostilities.
He was demobilised in 1919, and holds the 1914 Star, General Service and Victory Medals.
14, Yeldham Road, Hammersmith, W.6   12959B.

KING, R., Lce.-Cpl., Labour Corps.

Having joined in July 1917, he was sent to France, where he was employed largely on important railway work. Owing to a bad accident, which he met with during the course of his duties, he was in hospital for three months.
He holds the General Service and Victory Medals, and was demobilised in November 1919.
18, Lintaine Grove, W. Kensington, W.14   TX17078A.

KING, S. C., Pte., 1st Essex Regiment.

He volunteered in July 1915, and later in the same year was drafted to France, where he took part in the battles of Loos, the Somme and Ypres (1917). While in action near Ypres he was killed on August 12th, 1917.
He was entitled to the 1914-15 Star, the General Service and Victory Medals.
52, Oldfield Road, Willesden, N.W.10   16060A.

KING, T., Pte., Middlesex Regiment.

He volunteered for service in 1915 and was drafted overseas in the same year. He took part in many important engagements on the Western Front and was wounded in action three times.
He holds the 1914-15 Star, General Service and Victory Medals, and was demobilised in 1919.
346, High Road, Willesden, N.W.10   16746C.

KING, T., Pte., Middlesex Regiment.

He volunteered in June 1915, and after his training was drafted overseas, where he took part in several engagements in various sectors of the Western Front. He suffered from shell-shock, and was in consequence discharged as medically unfit for further service in December 1917.
He holds the General Service and Victory Medals.
105, Bounces Road, Lower Edmonton, N.9   13015.

KING, T., Pte., 4th Middlesex Regiment.

He volunteered in October 1914, and in the following month was sent to France, where he took part in the battles of Neuve Chapelle, Ypres, the Somme, Arras and Cambrai, and in other important engagements. He was wounded three times during his service, and in January 1919 was demobilised.
He holds the 1914 Star, General Service and Victory Medals.
57, Brett Road, Stonebridge Park, N.W.10   14525.

KING, W., Rifleman, 2/6th London Regt. (Rifles).

He joined in 1916, and after his training was engaged on important duties at various places with his unit. He rendered valuable services during his duty as a Lewis gunner on the aerial defences of London, but was unsuccessful in obtaining a transfer overseas before the cessation of hostilities.
He was demobilised in March 1919, and holds the General Service Medal.
22, Denzil Road, Neasden Lane, N.W.10   16082A.

KING, W., Pte., East Surrey Regiment.

He volunteered for service in March 1915, and after his training was drafted overseas. After taking part in many engagements on the Western Front, he was severely wounded in action, and in consequence his right leg had to be amputated.
He was discharged as physically unfit for further service in July 1916, and holds the 1914-15 Star, General Service and Victory Medals.
80, Adeney Road, Hammersmith, W.6   14461.

KING, W. A., Sergt., 17th (Duke of Cambridge's Own) Lancers.

He enlisted in February 1905, and immediately on the outbreak of war was sent to France, where he took part in the retreat from Mons, the battle of Ypres and in many other engagements, including the Retreat and Advance of 1918. After the signing of the Armistice he went to Germany with the Army of Occupation, and remained there until his discharge in May 1919, after completing 14 years' service with the Colours.
He holds the Mons Star, General Service and Victory Medals.
77, Rayleigh Road, W. Kensington, W.14   12644.

KING, W. C., Pte., 3rd Royal Fusiliers.

He volunteered in 1914, and was shortly afterwards drafted overseas. He took part in various engagements on the Western Front, and was killed in action at Ypres on September 15th, 1915.
He was entitled to the 1914 Star, General Service and Victory Medals.
68, Kenninghall Road, Upper Edmonton, N.18   16903.

KING, W. J., Pte., 8th Essex Regiment.

He joined in September 1916, and after his training served at various stations on important duties with his unit. He gave valuable services on coastal defence, and being unsuccessful in obtaining his transfer overseas owing to ill-health, was discharged as medically unfit for further service in September 1918.
27, Melville Road, Stonebridge Park, N.W.10   14623A.

KINGDOM, A. F. W., Driver, R.A.S.C. (M.T.)

He joined for service in May 1917, and was sent overseas in the same year. He was employed on transport work in various battle areas of the Western Front, and was actively engaged in the fighting at St. Quentin.
He holds the General Service and Victory Medals, and was demobilised in April 1920.
45, Sandringham Road, Cricklewood, N.W.2   X17100.

KINGDOM, F. J., Driver, Royal Field Artillery.

He joined for service in 1916 and was sent to France during the same year. He took part in many engagements on the Western Front until 1917, when he was drafted to Salonica. While there he contracted influenza, from which he died on November 10th, 1918.
He was entitled to the General Service and Victory Medals.
15, Wingmore Road, Tottenham, N.17   17978B.

KINGDOM, J. A., Pte., Middlesex Regiment.

He volunteered in July 1915, at the early age of 15, and was sent to France shortly afterwards. After taking part in important engagements he was discharged owing to his youth in October of the same year. In 1918 he rejoined the Forces and went to Germany with the Army of Occupation.
He holds the 1914-15 Star, General Service and Victory Medals.
15, Wingmore Road, Tottenham, N.17   X17978C.

KINGHAM, F., Cpl., Royal Fusiliers.

A time-serving soldier who had previously taken part in the South African War, he was sent with the first expeditionary force to France, where he went through the retreat from Mons. Owing to wounds he was invalided to England, but on his recovery returned to the Western Front, taking part in several important engagements.
In addition to the South African Medals, he holds the Mons Star, General Service and Victory Medals, and was discharged in 1919.
86, Ancill Street, Hammersmith, W.6   13655.

KINGHAM, J. C., Pte., Durham Light Infantry and Labour Corps.

Joining in July 1916, he was drafted in the same year to Salonica, where he took part in several important engagements on the Balkan Front, and was wounded. In 1918 he was invalided home, and in October was discharged owing to ill-health.
He holds the General Service and Victory Medals.
62, Farrant Street, Queen's Park Estate, W.10   X19064B.

KINGSFORD, F. R., Pte., Machine Gun Corps.

He joined for service in December 1916, and after his training was drafted to Egypt, where he served in the Egyptian Expeditionary Force under General Allenby. He took part in many important engagements in Palestine, acting as signaller during the whole of his service.
He holds the General Service and Victory Medals, and was demobilised in December 1919.
38, Tubb's Road, Harlesden, N.W.10   12742.

KINGSNORTH, A. W., Gunner, R.F.A.

Volunteering in December 1915, he was sent in the same year to the Western Front, where he took part in the battles of the Somme, Ypres and Cambrai, and in many other important engagements. During his service he was wounded and gassed, and in February 1919 was demobilised, holding the General Service and Victory Medals.
89, Oldfield Road, Willesden, N.W.10   16064.

KINNIER, T. J., 1st-Class Stoker, Royal Navy, H.M.S. "Malaya."

He volunteered in August 1915, and after his training joined his ship and took part in many important engagements with the Grand Fleet in the North Sea, including the battle of Jutland.
He holds the General Service and Victory Medals, and was still serving in 1920.
74, Biscay Road, Hammersmith, W.6   13357.

KINSEY, J. H., Gunner, R.G.A.

He joined in June 1917, and was drafted overseas, where he took part in important engagements on the Western Front, and was wounded five times.
He was killed in action on June 3rd, 1918, and was entitled to the General Service and Victory Medals.
5, Kilmaine Road, Munster Road, Fulham, S.W.6 TX18876.

KIRBY, G. W., Pioneer, Royal Engineers.

Volunteering in April 1915, he was drafted to the Western Front in the following July. After serving there for four months he was transferred to Salonica, where he took part in several important engagements during the Balkan campaign. In 1917 he was invalided home suffering from shell-shock and heart trouble, and in September was discharged as unfit.
He holds the 1914-15 Star, General Service and Victory Medals.
73, Waldo Road, College Park, N.W.10   X17638.

KIRBY, W., Driver, Royal Field Artillery.

He joined in September 1916, and at the conclusion of his training was drafted overseas. He took part in many important engagements on the Western Front, where he remained until after the cessation of hostilities.
He was demobilised in October 1919, and holds the General Service and Victory Medals.
2, Purcell Crescent, Fulham, S.W.6   14851.

KIRKBY-SODEN, G., Rifleman, K.R.R.

He joined in August 1918, but was unable to obtain his transfer overseas before the cessation of hostilities. However, after his training he was drafted in the following April to Egypt, and later served with the Army of Occupation at Adana, in Asia Minor.
In 1920 he returned home, and in April was demobilised.
36, Drayton Road, Harlesden, N.W.10   14902.

KIRK, E. E. (Mrs.), Special War Worker.

During the war this lady gave very valuable services. She was at first engaged on work of national importance at Messrs. Edgar's, Hammersmith, in connection with the making of hand-grenades. Later, in order to release a man for military service, she acted as a guard on the Metropolitan Railway, and carried out her duties in an able manner.
52, Leamore Street, Hammersmith, W.6   12606E.

KIRK, H. G., Pte., Royal Army Medical Corps.

He volunteered in August 1914, and in the same year was sent to the Western Front, where he served in important operations until 1916. After taking part in the retreat from Mons, the battles of Hill 60 and the Somme, he was drafted to Salonica, and was engaged there on special duties during the Balkan campaign. After the signing of the Armistice he went to Germany with the Army of Occupation, and holds the Mons Star, General Service and Victory Medals.
45, Raynham Road, Hammersmith, W.6   11103.

KIRK, J. W., Cpl., 15th (The King's) Hussars.

He volunteered in August 1914, and was soon drafted to the Western Front, where he took part in the retreat from Mons. He also fought in numerous other engagements, notably those at Neuve Chapelle, Loos, Ypres, the Somme and Lille, and later served in Italy for a time.
He was discharged in October 1918 as medically unfit for further service owing to gas poisoning, and holds the Mons Star, General Service and Victory Medals.
63, Farm Lane, Walham Green, S.W.6   X19495.

KIRK, W. W., Cpl., R.A.S.C. (M.T.)

He volunteered for service in May 1915, and after his training served at various stations on important duties with his unit. He gave valuable services, but was not successful in obtaining his transfer overseas owing to physical disability. He was discharged in February 1917 as medically unfit for further service.
52, Leamore Street, Hammersmith, W.6   12606A.

KIRTON, A., Pte., Middlesex Regiment.

He joined the Army in March 1917, and was drafted to the Western Front in the following year. While on active service he took part in several engagements connected with the Retreat and Advance of 1918, and was wounded at Cambrai in September 1918.
He holds the General Service and Victory Medals, and was still serving in 1920.
28, Humbolt Road, Hammersmith, W.6   15144.

KIRTON, D. (Miss), Special War Worker.

During the war this lady was engaged on work of vital importance at the National Filling Station, in connection with the manufacture of shells. She carried out her duties in a very skilful manner, and gave every satisfaction. She did excellent work and rendered very valuable services.
28, Humbolt Road, Hammersmith, W.6   15145.

KITCHEN, A. E., Pte., Royal Marine Light Inf.

Volunteering in 1915, he was soon drafted to the Dardanelles, where he took part in much of the heavy fighting in the Gallipoli Peninsula. He was killed in action in 1915, six months after joining the Army
He was entitled to the 1914-15 Star, General Service and Victory Medals.
52, Ilex Road, Willesden, N.W.10   15958C.

KITCHEN, E. J., Pte., 1st Royal Irish Regiment.

He volunteered in August 1914, and after his training was sent in the following year to France, where he took part in many engagements, including the battle of Loos. In 1916 he was drafted to Salonica, and later to Egypt, where he was killed in action in March 1918.
He was entitled to the 1914-15 Star, General Service and Victory Medals.
52, Ilex Road, Willesden, N.W.10   15958B.

K ITCHEN, W. G., Cook, Royal Navy.

Volunteering for service in 1914, he served with the Grand Fleet in the North Sea, and later in other waters. His ship was the first to force the Narrows in Turkish waters, and was also engaged on mine-sweeping operations. During his service he was in H.M. ships " Amethyst," " Dahlia," and several others.
He holds the 1914 Star, General Service and Victory Medals, and was still serving in 1920.
52, Ilex Road, Willesden, N.W.10   15958A.

KITCHENER, C. J., Cpl., The Queen's (Royal West Surrey Regiment).

He volunteered for service in August 1915, and after his training served at various stations on important duties with his unit. He gave valuable services, but was not successful in obtaining his transfer overseas before the cessation of hostilities.
He was demobilised in August 1919.
67, Raynham Avenue, Upper Edmonton, N.18   16481A.

KITCHENER, F. D., Pte., 2nd Devonshire Regt.

He volunteered for service in February 1915, and on completion of his training was drafted overseas, where he took part in many engagements on the Western Front. He was killed in action on the Somme in July 1916, and was entitled to the General Service and Victory Medals.
67, Raynham Avenue, Upper Edmonton, N.18   16481B.

KITCHENER, S. L., Pte., R.F.C. and Middx. Regt.

He volunteered for service in November 1914, and in the following year was drafted to the Western Front, where he took part in several engagements, including the battle of the Somme.
In March 1919 he was demobilised, and holds the 1914-15 Star, General Service and Victory Medals.
41, Folkestone Road, Upper Edmonton, N.18   15373.

KLIEGL, E. W., Gunner, Royal Marine Artillery (Transport Section).

He volunteered for one year's special service from the London Omnibus Company in October 1914, and proceeded to France at once. He was engaged on important duties there until the end of his period of service, when he was discharged.
He holds the 1914 Star, General Service and Victory Medals.
16, Beaconsfield Road, Church End, Willesden, N.W.10   16326.

KLUTH, F., Pte., Royal Army Service Corps.

Joining in October 1916, he was drafted overseas on the completion of his training. During his service on the Western Front he was attached to the Duke of Cornwall's Light Infantry, with which he took part in many important engagements, including the heavy fighting on the Somme. He was demobilised in March 1919, and holds the General Service and Victory Medals.
128, Blythe Road, West Kensington, W.14   12625.

KNAPTON, B., Pte., 23rd, 17th and 2nd Middlesex Regiment and 5th Royal Fusiliers.

He joined in December 1916, and in the following year went overseas, where he took part in various engagements on the Western Front, and was wounded in action on the Somme in March 1918. In September 1919 he was drafted to Mesopotamia, and was serving there in 1920 with the 5th Royal Fusiliers.
He holds the General Service and Victory Medals.
55, St. Mark's Road, Hanwell, W.7   11071.

KNEE, E. H., Cpl., 2nd Essex Regiment.

He volunteered in 1915, and in the following year was sent to the Western Front, where he took part in the battles of Vimy Ridge and the Somme (1917), and in the heavy fighting at Contalmaison, Mametz Wood, Longueval, Ginchy, Maricourt and Albert.
During his service he was badly wounded, and was in hospital for ten months. He was demobilised in May 1919, holding the General Service and Victory Medals, but re-enlisted and was sent to Malta.
4, Lundy Street, Hammersmith, W.6   14803A.

KNEE, H., Pte., Royal Berkshire Regiment.

He volunteered for service in September 1914, and at the conclusion of his training was drafted to the Western Front, where he took part in many engagements, including the battle of the Somme. He was in hospital in Rouen for a time with dysentery, and on recovery was attached to the Graves Registration Corps, with which he remained until his demobilisation in February 1919.
He holds the General Service and Victory Medals.
4, Lundy Street, Hammersmith, W.6   14803B.

KNEE, W. H., A.B., Royal Navy, H.M.S. " Hibernia."

He enlisted in the Navy in 1900, and on the outbreak of hostilities was sent to sea with the North Sea Flotilla, with which he was engaged on important duties until February 1915. He was then discharged owing to temporary blindness, but on recovering his sight he joined the Army, and was retained on special duties for six months. He was again discharged as medically unfit for further service, and holds the 1914 Star, General Service and Victory Medals.
81, Sherbrooke Road, Fulham, S.W.6   X18469.

KNEVETT, V. G., Pte., 2nd Essex Regiment.

Volunteering in April 1915, he was drafted on completion of his training to the Western Front, where he took part in many important engagements. During his service he was twice wounded, and after being in hospital in France for some time was invalided home.
In September 1919 he was demobilised, and holds the General Service and Victory Medals.
10, Stanley Road, King's Road, S.W.6   X19869.

KNEVETT, W. C., Lce.-Cpl., 5th Middlesex Regt.

He volunteered in March 1915, and later in the same year was sent to the Western Front, where he took part in many important engagements. During his service overseas he was three times wounded, and after a time in hospital in France was invalided home, and was in hospital in Scotland for ten months.
He was demobilised in January 1919, holding the 1914-15 Star, General Service and Victory Medals.
6, Francis Street, Hammersmith, W.6   14797A.

KNIBBS, W. A., Pte., 25th Durham Light Inf.

He joined for service in July 1916, and later in the same year was sent to the Eastern theatre of war. While in Egypt he was engaged with the infantry transport in many important engagements.
He remained on that Front until he returned to England for demobilisation in July 1919, and holds the General Service and Victory Medals.
58, Shakespeare Avenue, Willesden, N.W.10   13619.

KNIGHT, A., Cpl., Labour Corps.

He volunteered for service in 1915, and after his training served at various stations on important duties with his unit. In 1918 he was drafted overseas, where he was engaged on special work during the operations on the Western Front.
He was demobilised in 1919, and holds the General Service and Victory Medals.
20, Holly Lane, Willesden, N.W.10   15583B.

KNIGHT, A., Rifleman, 2nd K.R.R.

He volunteered for service in 1914, and was shortly afterwards drafted to France, where he took part in the battle of Mons, and was taken prisoner. He endured many hardships, and was subjected to much ill-treatment during his captivity. Upon his release he was demobilised in 1919, and holds the Mons Star, General Service and Victory Medals.
20, Holly Lane, Willesden, N.W.10   15583C.

KNIGHT, A. E., Pte., 16th (Queen's) Lancers.

Having enlisted in 1907, he was recalled from the Army Reserve at the outbreak of war and drafted overseas. He took part in many engagements on the Western Front, including the battles of Mons, Ypres, Arras, the Somme and Cambrai. After being wounded at Ypres in February 1916, he was invalided home, and on recovery returned to France. He was again in action for some time, but his health broke down, and he was discharged as medically unfit for further service in January 1920.
He holds the Mons Star, General Service and Victory Medals.
64, Bramber Road, West Kensington, W.14   16224.

KNIGHT, C., Driver, Royal Field Artillery.

He volunteered for service in 1914, and was sent to France the following year. He took part in various engagements on the Western Front, including those at Hill 60, the Somme, Bullecourt, Passchendaele, Arras, Bourlon Wood and Cambrai.
He holds the 1914-15 Star, General Service and Victory Medals, and was demobilised in 1919.
20, Holly Lane, Willesden, N.W.10   15583A.

KNIGHT, D., Pte., Machine Gun Corps.

Joining the Army in March 1917, Pte. Knight was sent, after a brief training, to France in August of the same year. He served in the Ypres sector for six weeks, when he was killed in action near that town on September 22nd.
He was entitled to the General Service and Victory Medals.
132, Stephendale Road, Fulham, S.W.6   X20821.

KNIGHT, J., Lce.-Cpl., Queen's Own (Royal West Kent Regiment) and Royal Fusiliers.

He joined in 1916, and after his training served at various stations with his unit. He was drafted to the Western Front in 1918, where he took part in engagements on the Somme, Bapaume, and during the Retreat and Advance of 1918.
He holds the General Service and Victory Medals, and was demobilised in April 1919.
10, Greyhound Road, College Park, N.W.10   X17801.

KNIGHT, S., Pte., Middlesex Regiment.

He volunteered in September 1914, and at the conclusion of his training was drafted overseas, where he took part in many important engagements on the Western Front. He was later sent to Salonica, and was again in action, remaining there until after the cessation of hostilities.
He was demobilised in April 1919, and holds the General Service and Victory Medals.
8, Argyle Road, Upper Edmonton, N.18   15263A.

KNIGHTS, W., Gnr., Royal Garrison Artillery.

He joined in 1916, and later in the same year was sent to France, where he took part in the battles of the Somme, Arras and Ypres (1917), and in many important engagements during the Retreat and Advance of 1918.
In February 1919 he was demobilised, and holds the General Service and Victory Medals.
149, Fifth Avenue, Queen's Park Estate, W.10   X18736.

KNIGHTSBRIDGE, A., Pte., R.A.S.C. (M.T.)

He volunteered in April 1915, and later in the same year was drafted to France, where he was engaged on the transportation of munitions to the forward areas during important engagements at Loos, the Somme, Arras, Ypres and Cambrai.
He was demobilised in May 1919, and holds the 1914-15 Star, General Service and Victory Medals.
38, Laundry Road, Hammersmith, W.6   15051.

KNIGHTSBRIDGE, W., Pte., R.A.S.C.

Volunteering in October 1914, he was immediately sent to the Western Front, where he took an active part in the battles of Ypres, Loos, the Somme and Arras. During his service he was attached to the Royal Garrison Artillery for two years, during which period he took part in many engagements with a heavy battery.
He remained in France until his demobilisation in April 1919, and holds the 1914 Star, General Service and Victory Medals.
80, Fernhead Road, Maida Hill, W.9   TX19688.

KNOTT, A. E., Lce.-Cpl., 6th Middlesex Regt.

He volunteered in August 1914, and after a period of training was drafted overseas. During his service on the Western Front he took part in heavy fighting at Loos, Neuve Chapelle, and Cambrai, and was taken prisoner during the battle of Ypres in 1917. While in captivity at various camps in Germany he suffered many hardships, and on his release was demobilised in January 1919.
He holds the General Service and Victory Medals.
6, Halford Road, Walham Green, S.W.6   X19476A.

KNOTT, C. B., Lce.-Cpl., Hampshire Regiment.

Volunteering in August 1914, he was drafted in the following year to the Dardanelles, where he took part in much of the heavy fighting during the Gallipoli campaign, and was severely wounded in action. While being conveyed to Alexandria in August 1916 he died on board the " Gloucester Castle," and was buried at sea.
He was entitled to the 1914-15 Star, General Service and Victory Medals.
6, Halford Road, Walham Green, S.W.6   X19476B.

KOLLER, E. H. (Mrs.), Special War Worker.

This lady was engaged throughout the war at Messrs. Waring & Gillow's factory at the White City, where she was employed in the manufacture of tents, marquees, haversacks and similar articles of Army equipment. She carried out her duties in a satisfactory manner, and rendered very valuable services.
85, Greyhound Road, Hammersmith, W.6   X19410A.

KOLLER, W. D., Pte., R.A.S.C. (M.T.)

Volunteering in September 1915, he served for four years on the Eastern Front, going first to Egypt and being shortly afterwards drafted to Mesopotamia. While on the Tigris he contracted malaria, which necessitated his being sent to hospital in India. On his recovery he returned to Basra, and joined the expedition which attempted to relieve the garrison in Kut.
In 1919 he was sent back to England, and in March was demobilised, holding the 1914-15 Star, General Service and Victory Medals.
85, Greyhound Road, Hammersmith, W.6   X19410B.

KRAMER, P., Pte., 17th Royal Fusiliers.

He joined in April 1918, and after his training was engaged on important duties at various stations with his unit. He gave valuable services, but could not obtain his transfer overseas before the cessation of hostilities. However, in March 1919 he was drafted to the Army of Occupation on the Rhine, with which he remained until his demobilisation in December 1919.
21, Burrow's Road, Willesden, N.W.10   X18249.

KUHLMAN, T. W., Pte., 12th Middlesex Regt.

He volunteered in December 1915, and after completing his training was drafted to the Western Front, where he took part in the battles of the Somme, Arras, Ypres and Cambrai, and in many other important engagements. During his service overseas he was wounded, and in October 1919 was demobilised, holding the General Service and Victory Medals.
36, Brownlow Road, Willesden, N.W.10   15008B.

KUHLMAN, W. A., Rifleman, King's Royal Rifle Corps and London Regiment.

He joined in 1917, and was drafted to France immediately after the commencement of the Retreat in the following year. While on the Western Front he took part in heavy fighting at Ypres, Cambrai, St. Quentin and on the Somme, where he was wounded in October 1918.
He was demobilised in November 1919, and holds the General Service and Victory Medals.
36, Brownlow Road, Willesden, N.W.10   15008A.

KUHN, G. C. (M.M.), Lce.-Cpl., 24th Royal Fus.

Joining in April 1916, he was sent to the Western Front in the following November. He took part in many important engagements in this theatre of war, and was wounded in action near Bapaume in March 1918.
During the Advance he was awarded the Military Medal for conspicuous gallantry and devotion to duty in rallying his section under heavy shell-fire at Béhagnies on August 23rd. In addition, he holds the General Service and Victory Medals, and was demobilised in April 1919.
53, St. Margaret's Road, Willesden, N.W.10   X17821.

KYBERT, M. (Mrs.), Special War Worker.

During the war this lady was engaged on work of national importance at Woolwich Arsenal. She first worked in the fuse-making department, and later as a machine operator on the capstan lathe. Her duties were carried out in a very skilful manner, and she rendered valuable services.
13, Mirabel Road, Fulham, S.W.6   X17922A.

KYBERT, W. A., Pte., Bedfordshire Regiment.
Joining in 1916, he was retained after the completion of his
training on duties in England until 1918. He was then
drafted to the Western Front, where he took part in the
Retreat and Advance during that year. Owing to a severe
wound which he received in action, he was invalided to
England, and after spending six months in hospital, was
discharged in 1919 as unfit.
He holds the General Service and Victory Medals.
13, Mirabel Road, Fulham, S.W.6   X17922B.

L

LABAN, H. C., Pte., Middlesex Regiment.
He joined in 1916, and in the same year was drafted to India,
where he was engaged on important duties until 1918. He
was then sent to France at the beginning of the German
Offensive, and took part in many important engagements,
during which he was wounded.
He was eventually demobilised in 1919, and holds the
General Service and Victory Medals.
16, Durham Road, Lower Edmonton, N.9   14871.

**LABAN, J. G., Leading Stoker, Royal Navy,
H.M.S. " Garmus."**
Having previously served in the Royal Navy, he rejoined
in August 1914, and on board H.M.S. "Garmus," left Home
waters immediately for the East. He took part in important naval engagements in the Pacific and was twice
wounded. His vessel was also engaged on special duties
in Chinese seas.
In March 1919 he was demobilised, and holds the 1914 Star,
General Service and Victory Medals.
149, Winchester Road, Lower Edmonton, N.9   14948.

LABAN, T. H., Pte., 19th London Regiment.
He joined in May 1916, and after completing his training was
ordered to Egypt, where he took part in many engagements,
and was wounded in action in November 1917. On recovery
he saw more heavy fighting and was again wounded.
He was demobilised in January 1920, and holds the General
Service and Victory Medals.
45, Cedars Road, Lower Edmonton, N.9   13950.

LABBETT, A., Pte., 6th Bedfordshire Regiment.
Joining in 1915, he was sent on completion of his training in
the following year to the Western Front, where he took part
in many important engagements. He was killed in action
during the battle of Arras on April 10th, 1917, and was
buried near by.
He was entitled to the General Service and Victory Medals.
3, Birchington, Roundwood Road, Willesden, N.W.10.
                                                  16302.

LACEY, F., Sergt., 5th Middlesex Regiment.
He joined in August 1914, and during his service on the
Western Front took part in the battles of Hill 60 and Vimy
Ridge, and was twice wounded. In 1916 he was invalided
home, and, not again becoming fit for active service, was
retained on Home duties until his demobilisation in February
1919.
He holds the 1914–15 Star, General Service and Victory
Medals.
47, Shrewsbury Road, Stonebridge Park, N.W.10.   14126.

LACEY, J., Sapper, Royal Engineers.
He volunteered in March 1915 and in the following year was
drafted to the Western Front, where he took an active part
in many important engagements, notably those on the
Somme and at Arras. In 1917 he was sent to Italy, and
again saw much fighting. He remained on this Front until
he was sent home for demobilisation in March 1919.
He holds the General Service and Victory Medals.
1, Headcorn Road, Tottenham, N.17   X18488C.

LACEY, S., Sapper, Royal Engineers.
He volunteered in 1914, and a year later was sent to France,
where he was wounded on the Somme in 1916. He was then
transferred to Egypt and contracted malaria, which necessitated his being in hospital for some time. He was also
accidentally injured while in France.
In 1919 he was demobilised, holding the 1914–15 Star,
General Service and Victory Medals.
34, Somerset Road, Upper Edmonton, N.18   16862

LADYMAN, G. E., Rifleman, Rifle Brigade.
He joined in April 1918 as soon as he attained military age,
and after his training was engaged on important duties at
various stations with his unit. He gave valuable services,
but was unsuccessful in obtaining his transfer overseas before
hostilities ceased. After the signing of the Armistice he
went to Germany with the Army of Occupation and remained there until demobilised in January 1920.
3, Disraeli Road, Acton Lane, N.W.10   14161.

LAGDON, H. O., Rifleman, King's Royal Rifles.
He joined in July 1918, and after a short period of training
was drafted to France, where he took part in the Advance in
that year. Shortly after his arrival on this Front he was
invalided to hospital, and remained there until February 1919,
when he was discharged owing to ill-health as medically
unfit for further service.
He holds the General Service and Victory Medals.
41, Warwick Road, Upper Edmonton, N.18   X17509.

LAIN, G. C., Driver, Royal Field Artillery.
He was mobilised in August 1914, and was sent to the Western
Front on the completion of his training in 1916. He took
part in the battles of Vimy Ridge and Ypres, and was then
drafted to Italy, where he saw much heavy fighting on the
Piave. He later returned to France and served throughout
the Retreat and Advance of 1918.
During his service overseas he was wounded, and in
December 1919 was demobilised, holding the General Service
and Victory Medals.
34, Mordaunt Road, Willesden, N.W.10   13854.

LAIRD, W., Sapper, Royal Engineers.
He enlisted in June 1914, and on the outbreak of war was
sent to the Western Front, where he took part in the retreat
from Mons, in the battles of Ypres, the Somme and Vimy
Ridge (where he was wounded). After being in hospital
in France and England for some months he was discharged
owing to his wounds as medically unfit for further service in
December 1917.
He holds the Mons Star, General Service and Victory Medals.
14, Linton Road, Upper Edmonton, N.18   X17472.

**LAKE, A. D., Rifleman, 1/21st London Regt.
(1st Surrey Rifles).**
Joining in March 1917, he was drafted to the Western Front
on the completion of his training early in the following
year. He took part in many important engagements and
saw much severe fighting around Albert and Lille during
the Retreat and Advance of the Allies in 1918.
In March 1919 he was demobilised, and holds the General
Service and Victory Medals.
71, Burn's Road, Harlesden, N.W.10   14715B.

LAKE, J. H., Pte., R.A.S.C. (M.T.)
He volunteered for duty in 1915, and having received
training, served for two years in German East Africa, where
he did good work. At the end of 1917 he was drafted to the
Western Front, where he was present at numerous engagements, including the battle of the Somme, and after the
cessation of hostilities went with the Army of Occupation
to Germany.
He returned to England in 1919 and was demobilised, holding
the 1914–15 Star, General Service and Victory Medals.
24, Clarendon Street, Paddington, W.2   X20546.

LAKE, W. J., Pte., 11th Bedfordshire Regt.
He joined in October 1918, but was unable to obtain his
transfer overseas before the cessation of hostilities. He
was, however, retained on important duties with his unit
on the East coast.
He gave valuable services, and was demobilised in February
1919.
71, Burn's Road, Harlesden, N.W.10   14715A.

**LALLY, A. R., Stoker Petty Officer, Royal
Navy, H.M.S. " Sylvia."**
He enlisted in the Royal Navy in November 1910, and at
the outbreak of war immediately went to sea with the Grand
Fleet. He took part in several important naval engagements
in the North Sea, and was also engaged on special duties on
board H.M.S. " Sylvia."
In September 1919 he was discharged, and holds the 1914
Star, the General Service and Victory Medals.
3, Chaldon Road, Dawes Road, S.W.6   X17644.

**LAMACRAFT, A., Pte., The Queen's (Royal West
Surrey Regiment).**
He joined in January 1917, and later in the same year was
drafted to Mesopotamia, where he took part in many impor-
tant operations against the Turks. He remained on this
Front until his return to England for demobilisation in 1920.
He holds the General Service and Victory Medals.
1, Tilson Road, Tottenham, N.17   X19092.

LAMB, A., Pte., Royal Army Medical Corps.
He joined in January 1917, and was later sent to the Western
Front, where he acted in many important engagements as a
stretcher-bearer, and was gassed while in action. In consequence he spent some time in hospital in France. On his
recovery he remained on special duties in a field hospital
until demobilised in March 1919.
He holds the General Service and Victory Medals.
20, Lintaine Grove, W. Kensington, W.14   TX17079.

LAMB, W. F., Sapper, Royal Engineers.

Volunteering early in 1915, he was almost immediately sent to the Dardanelles, where he took an active part in the operations during the Gallipoli campaign. On the evacuation of the Peninsula he was drafted to France, and again saw much heavy fighting on various sectors of that Front. He remained in France until demobilised in 1919, and holds the 1914–15 Star, General Service and Victory Medals.
192, Brettenham Road East, Upper Edmonton, N.18　15218.

LAMBERT, A. E., Pte., 3rd Grenadier Guards.

He volunteered in 1915, and was sent to the Western Front in July of the same year, after completing his training, but was killed in action two months later on September 15th.
He was entitled to the 1914–15 Star, General Service and Victory Medals.
38, Oldfield Road, Willesden, N.W.10　15761B.

LAMBERT, F. J., Pte., 20th Hampshire Regt.

He joined in June 1917, and in the following month was drafted to the Western Front, where he took part in the battles of Ypres and Passchendaele, and in other important engagements.
He was wounded in action during the battle of Passchendaele, and holds the General Service and Victory Medals.
9, South Street Cottages, Hammersmith, W.6　12506.

LAMBERT, J. F., Pte., 23rd London Regiment.

Joining in 1917 he was sent to the Eastern Front on completion of his training. He was at first engaged on special duties in Egypt, but later proceeded to Palestine and served under General Allenby during the Advance in that theatre of war.
In 1919 he was demobilised, and holds the General Service and Victory Medals.
38, Oldfield Road, Willesden, N.W.10　15761A.

LAMBIRD, E. H., Sergt., Yorkshire Regiment.

He volunteered in November 1914, and was posted to the Yorkshire Regiment, with which he completed his training, and served at various stations. He was chiefly employed in conducting drafts to the Western Front, but was unsuccessful in obtaining a permanent transfer overseas.
He was demobilised in January 1919, holding the 1914–15 Star, General Service and Victory Medals.
119, Fortune Gate Road, Harlesden, N.W.10　13469.

LAMBIRTH, W. H., Sapper, R.E.

He joined in August 1916, and having completed his training was sent later the same year to the Western Front, where he was in action at Lens, the Somme, Ypres, Cambrai and near Lille.
He was demobilised in May 1919, and holds the General Service and Victory Medals.
25, Mozart Street, N. Kensington, W.10　X18930B.

LAMBOURNE, F. W. J., Pte., Seaforth Highlanders.

He volunteered in August 1915, and was sent to Mesopotamia, where he took part in the expedition that was sent to attempt the relief of Kut. A year later he was transferred to France, and was in action at the battle of Arras and capture of Vimy Ridge. He was taken prisoner at La Bassée in April 1918, and on his release was demobilised in April 1919.
He holds the General Service and Victory Medals.
25, Beamish Road, Lower Edmonton, N.9　T13940.

LAMBURN, T. H., Rifleman, K.R.R.

He volunteered in December 1915, and served in France. He was wounded and taken prisoner in November 1917 at Cambrai, and was in Germany for a year, where he suffered many hardships.
On his release he returned to England, and was demobilised in February 1919, holding the General Service and Victory Medals.
25, Letchford Gardens, Willesden, N.W.10　X17542.

LAMMIN, C. E., Pte., 2nd Royal Sussex Regt.

He joined in March 1918, and after his training was engaged on important duties with his unit at various stations. He gave valuable services but was not successful in obtaining his transfer overseas before hostilities ceased. In February 1919 he was sent to Germany, and remained with the Army of Occupation until his demobilisation in the following December.
10, Brownlow Road, Willesden, N.W 10　14921.

LANCASTER, T. W., Special War Worker.

During the war he was employed by the British Motor Cab Company of Grosvenor Road, S.W.1 for three years. Throughout this period he was engaged on the working of electrical machines used in the manufacture of munitions, thereby rendering valuable services. He was highly commended for his excellent work.
83, Yeldham Road, Hammersmith, W.6　13236.

LANDER, C., Pte., 7th London Regiment.

He joined in 1916, and after completing his training was drafted to the Western Front, where he took part in the battles of the Somme, Arras, Ypres and Cambrai, and in other important engagements. He was wounded and gassed and was invalided home, but on his recovery returned to France, where he remained until his demobilisation in January 1919.
He holds the General Service and Victory Medals.
55, Strode Road, Munster Road, S.W.6　15337.

LANDERS, W., Cpl., Royal Field Artillery.

Having enlisted in February 1912, he was sent on the outbreak of war to France with the expeditionary force, with which he took part in the battle of Mons, and the retreat from Mons, and the first battle of Ypres, where he was severely wounded. Later he fought at the second battle of Ypres, Loos, Arras, the Somme and Le Cateau, and while in action at Cambrai in October 1918 was gassed.
After a total active service of over four years he was discharged owing to his injuries as medically unfit in April 1919, holding the Mons Star, General Service and Victory Medals.
40, Milton Avenue, Willesden, N.W.10　14434.

LANDON, C., Pte., R.A.S.C.

He volunteered in January 1915, and after his training was drafted to the Western Front, where he took an active part in many important operations on various sectors.
He returned to this country for demobilisation in March 1920, and holds the General Service and Victory Medals.
14, Rayleigh Road, West Kensington, W.14　12421.

LANE, A. R., Pte., Durham Light Infantry.

He joined in 1916, and in the same year was sent to the Western Front, where he served for three years. During this period he took part in several engagements, and in 1919 was demobilised, holding the General Service and Victory Medals.　46, Aspenlea Road, Hammersmith, W.6　14287A.

LANE, C. E. W., Sapper, Royal Engineers.

He volunteered for service in July 1915, and was drafted overseas in the same year. He took part in many important engagements on the Western Front, including the battles of Ypres and the Somme. After serving in France for nearly four years, he returned to England and was demobilised in July 1919.
He holds the 1914–15 Star, General Service and Victory Medals.
104, Kimberley Road, Upper Edmonton, N.18　16793.

LANE, C. F., Pte., 9th Royal Fusiliers.

He joined in February 1916, and at the conclusion of his training was drafted overseas, where he was actively engaged in many sectors of the Western Front. He fought at the battles of the Somme, Vimy Ridge and Cambrai, and during his service was twice wounded.
He holds the General Service and Victory Medals, and was demobilised in October 1919.
24, Bayonne Road, Hammersmith, W.6　14506.

LANE, D., Pte., Queen's (Royal West Surrey Regt.)

He joined in July 1916, and on completion of his training was drafted to the Western Front. During his service in this theatre of war he took part in the battles of Arras, Ypres, and Cambrai, and in other important engagements.
He was demobilised in February 1920, and holds the General Service and Victory Medals.
51, Garvan Road, Hammersmith, W.6　14838.

LANE, E., Pte., 2nd Royal Inniskilling Fusiliers.

He joined in April 1916, and in the same year went to the Western Front, where he took part in the engagements at Passchendaele, Lens, and Cambrai, where he was wounded and gassed. In March 1918 he was taken prisoner at St. Quentin, and spent nearly a year in captivity.
He was demobilised in June 1919, and holds the General Service and Victory Medals.
56, Chippenham Road, Maida Hill, W.9　X20888.

LANE, H., Pte., 2/5th Gloucestershire Regt.

Volunteering in February 1915, he was drafted in the same year to the Western Front, where he took part in many engagements, including the battles of Ypres, Loos, Albert, the Somme and Arras. After his recovery from gas poisoning, he was sent in 1917 to Italy, where he remained until he returned to England for demobilisation in 1919.
He holds the 1914–15 Star, General Service and Victory Medals.　12, Clarendon Street, Paddington, W.2　X20640.

LANE, J., Pte., Royal Army Veterinary Corps.

Joining in April 1917, he was shortly afterwards sent to the Western Front, where he was engaged on special duties in connection with the transport of sick and wounded horses from the forward areas.
He returned to this country for demobilisation in June 1919, and holds the General Service and Victory Medals.
9, Farm Lane, Walham Green, S.W.6　X19494

LANE, J. W., Special War Worker.

During the war he was engaged on important work at Messrs. Furman's of Scrubb's Lane in connection with aeroplane fittings. His duties demanded a high degree of skill, and were carried out in a very efficient manner, and to the satisfaction of his employers.

32, Stracey Road, Stonebridge Park, N.W.10   15680A.

LANE, L. G., Cpl., Royal Air Force.

He joined in 1917, and after his training served at various aerodromes on important duties. He gave valuable services which called for a high degree of technical skill, but was not successful in obtaining his transfer overseas before the cessation of hostilities.

He was demobilised in March 1919.

46, Asplenea Road, Hammersmith, W.6   14287B.

LANE, R., Gunner, Royal Garrison Artillery.

He joined in July 1916, and in the following November was sent to the Western Front, where he took part in the battles of Arras, Messines and Ypres, and in many other important engagements. During his active service he was wounded, but remained in France until his demobilisation in January 1919.

He holds the General Service and Victory Medals.

41, Mayo Road, Willesden, N.W.10   15475.

LANE, T., Pte., 2/5th Hampshire Regiment.

He volunteered in 1914, and in the same year was sent to India, where he was engaged on important garrison duties until 1916. He was then drafted to Egypt, and after a short period there was discharged owing to his health as medically unfit for further service in 1917.

He holds the General Service and Victory Medals.

221, Roundwood Road, Willesden, N.W.10   16306B.

LANE, W. G., Lce.-Cpl., Machine Gun Corps.

He volunteered in May 1915, and in June of the following year was drafted to the Western Front, where he took part in engagements on the Ancre and the Somme. In December 1916 he was invalided home suffering from shell-shock, and on his recovery acted as an instructor until his demobilisation in January 1919.

He holds the General Service and Victory Medals.

5, Sandringham Road, Cricklewood, N.W.2   X17096.

LANE, W. H., Sergt., Middlesex Regiment.

He volunteered in November 1914, and in the following year was drafted to the Dardanelles, where he took part in the heavy fighting in the Gallipoli campaign. On the evacuation of the Peninsula he went to Egypt, and from there was sent to Palestine. He served with General Allenby's Force during the Advance and was wounded at the battle of Gaza. He also acted as Lewis gun instructor to the 17th Loyal Indian Regiment.

In June 1919 he returned from Palestine for demobilisation, and holds the 1914-15 Star, General Service and Victory Medals.

221, Roundwood Road, Willesden, N.W.10   16306A.

LANE, W. K. G., Gunner, R.G.A.

He volunteered in October 1915, and after completing his training was drafted to Mesopotamia, where he took part in several important engagements. He was later sent to India, and while on service there developed consumption. As a result he was discharged as medically unfit for further service in August 1918, and died from the effects of his illness on March 22nd, 1920.

He was entitled to the General Service and Victory Medals.

13, Montague Road, Lower Edmonton, N.9   13079.

LANG, W. A., Pte., 5th Middlesex Regiment.

Volunteering in June 1915, he was sent to France later in the same year, and took part in the battles of the Somme and Ypres, and in other important engagements. He was invalided home owing to wounds received in action, and was in hospital in Liverpool for some time.

In January 1919 he was demobilised, and holds the 1915 Star, General Service and Victory Medals.

111, Durban Road, Tottenham, N.17   X17958.

LANGDON, S. T., Pte., R.A.S.C.

He volunteered in August 1914, and during his service was retained on important duties, for which he had special qualifications, with his unit. He was also engaged on the transport of horses to and from France, but was not successful in obtaining a permanent transfer overseas before hostilities ceased.

In April 1919 he was demobilised, and holds the General Service and Victory Medals.

10, Somerset Place, Hammersmith, W.6   13792.

LANGDON, W. H., Sergt., 12th London Regt. (Rangers).

He was already serving in the Territorials, and at the outbreak of war was mobilised and drafted to France. He took part in many engagements on the Western Front, including the battles of Ypres, Vimy Ridge and the Somme, and was later sent to Egypt, where he was actively engaged until early in 1919, when he was discharged as medically unfit for further service.

He holds the 1914 Star, General Service and Victory Medals.

8, Holberton Gardens, Willesden, N.W.10   X17556.

LANGFORD, H. G., Driver, R.F.A.

He volunteered in August 1914, and was immediately sent to the Western Front, where he took part in the retreat from Mons, the battles of La Bassée, Ypres, Loos and Arras, and in many other important engagements.

He remained in France until his demobilisation in March 1919, and holds the Mons Star, General Service and Victory Medals.

18, Ray's Road, Upper Edmonton, N.18   15628.

LANGFORD, J., Driver, R.F.A.

He volunteered in August 1915, and on completion of his training was sent overseas. During his service on the Western Front he took part in many important engagements, and remained in France until demobilised in March 1919. Three months later he re-enlisted, and was drafted to India.

He holds the General Service and Victory Medals.

17, Lintaine Grove, W. Kensington, W.14   16770.

LANGFORD, W. S., Rifleman, 1st Royal Irish Rifles.

He joined in May 1916, and after his training was retained on important duties until December 1917, when he was drafted to the Western Front. He took part in many engagements, and at the beginning of the German Offensive in March 1918 was wounded in action near St. Quentin.

In the following January he was demobilised, and holds the General Service and Victory Medals.

99, Sixth Avenue, Queen's Park Estate, W.10   X18680.

LANGLEY, E., Lce.-Cpl., 15th London Regt. (Civil Service Rifles).

He joined in November 1916, and after his training was drafted to Egypt, where he was employed on important duties. In 1918 he was sent to France, and was actively engaged on the Western Front until the cessation of hostilities, when he went to Germany with the Army of Occupation. He remained there until his demobilisation in March 1920, and holds the General Service and Victory Medals.

19, Ancill Street, Hammersmith, W.6   13737A.

LANGLEY, E. J., Pte., R.A.V.C.

Volunteering in 1915, he was sent to France later in the same year, and was engaged on important duties in connection with sick and wounded horses.

He remained in France until his demobilisation in February 1919, and holds the 1914-15 Star, General Service and Victory Medals.

19, Ancill Street, Hammersmith, W.6   13737B.

LANGLEY, F., A.B., Royal Navy.

Volunteering for service in August 1914, he served with the Grand Fleet in the North Sea on patrol and other duties. During his service he was in H.M. ships "Verity" and "Whirlwind," and was torpedoed. He also took part in the naval raid on Zeebrugge, and holds the 1914-15 Star, General Service and Victory Medals.

29, Denton Road, Stonebridge Park, N.W.10   14702.

LANGLEY, R., Cpl., Royal Engineers.

Volunteering in August 1914, he was immediately sent to France, and took an active part in the retreat from Mons. He also fought at La Bassée and in other important engagements before being drafted to the Dardanelles. On the Peninsula he took part in much heavy fighting and was wounded. As a result he was invalided home and discharged in 1917 as medically unfit for further service.

He holds the Mons Star, General Service and Victory Medals.

31, Denton Road, Stonebridge Park, N.W.10   14701.

LANGLEY, W., Pte., The Queen's (Royal West Surrey Regiment).

He joined in 1916, and later in the same year was drafted to the Western Front, where he took part in the battle of the Somme and other important engagements. During his service on this Front he was twice wounded, and in 1918 left the Service, holding the General Service and Victory Medals.

5, Purves Road, Kensal Rise, N.W.10   X18023.

LANGLEY, W A. (M.M.), Pte., Queen's (Royal West Surrey Regiment).

He joined in 1917, and soon after was drafted to the Western Front, where he took part in heavy fighting on the Somme and at Gouzeaucourt, Epéhy, Hendecourt and Péronne. On September 21st, 1918, he was killed in action at " Devil's Post " near Villers-Guislain.

He was awarded the Military Medal for conspicuous gallantry and devotion to duty in the field, and in addition was entitled to the General Service and Victory Medals.

42, Brownlow Road, Stonebridge Park, N.W.10   15010.

LANGMEAD, W., Rifleman, 6th London Regt. (Rifles).

He volunteered for service in 1914, and after his training was drafted overseas in the following year. He took a prominent part in many important engagements on the Western Front, where he remained until the cessation of hostilities.

He was demobilised in 1919, and holds the 1914-15 Star, General Service and Victory Medals.

60, Pretoria Road, Upper Edmonton, N.18   X17027.

LANGRIDGE, A. J., A.B., Royal Navy.

He enlisted in August 1913, and at the outbreak of war proceeded to Foreign waters on board H.M.S. " Implacable." He took an active part in the naval operations during the Dardanelles campaign and was later frequently in action with enemy submarines while serving with His Majesty's " mystery " ships.

In June 1919 he secured his discharge, holding the 1914 Star, General Service and Victory Medals.

21, Delorme Street, Hammersmith, W.6   14078.

LANGRIDGE, G., Special War Worker.

During the war he gave very valuable services, being at first engaged on work of national importance at Messrs. Lyon and Wrench's at Willesden Junction, where he remained for three years. He then went to Messrs. Smith's, Cricklewood, and did useful work in the tool-making department.

417, High Road, Willesden, N.W.10   T17339B.

LANGSTON, F. (Mrs.), Special War Worker.

For a period of three years during the war this lady rendered valuable services at Messrs. Grahame White's Works, Hendon, where she was engaged on important work in connection with the construction of aeroplanes. Her duties, which required great care, were carried out in a very satisfactory manner.

36, Leopold Road, Willesden, N.W.10   14918.

LANKESTER, C. E., Pte., R.A.S.C.

He joined in 1917, and on completion of his training was drafted overseas to the Western Front, where he was engaged on important transport duties in connection with the Expeditionary Force Canteens. He remained in France until after the cessation of hostilities, and was demobilised in April 1919.

He holds the General Service and Victory Medals.

205, Chapter Road, Cricklewood, N.W.2   TX17202A.

LANKESTER, L. J., Pte., Royal Fusiliers.

He joined in 1918, and after his training was engaged on important duties at various stations with his unit. He gave valuable services, but was not successful in obtaining his transfer overseas before the Armistice.

He was demobilised in 1919.

205, Chapter Road, Cricklewood, N.W.2   TX17202C.

LANKESTER, R. W., A.B., Royal Navy.

Joining in June 1916, he served on board H.M.S. " Gloucester," which ship was engaged on special transport work between England and America, and also on important patrol duties in the North Sea.

He gave very valuable services, and was demobilised in January 1919, holding the General Service and Victory Medals.

205, Chapter Road, Cricklewood, N.W.2   TX17202B

LANSLEY, C., 2nd Air Mechanic, R.A.F.

He joined for service in April 1915, and after training was employed at various aerodromes as a fitter on aero engines. He rendered valuable services which called for a high degree of technical skill, but was not successful in obtaining his transfer overseas before the signing of the Armistice.

He was demobilised in February 1920.

34, Hazel Road, Willesden, N.W.10   X17778.

LANSLEY, T. H., Driver, R.A.S.C.

Volunteering in 1915, he was later in the same year drafted to France, where he was engaged on important duties in various sectors. He was gassed and invalided home, and on his recovery was sent to Salonica. After a period of service there he was again invalided home with malaria, and in May 1919 he was demobilised.

He holds the 1914-15 Star, General Service and Victory Medals. 51, Rowallan Road, Munster Road, S.W.6 X19264.

LANT, S., Sergt., R.A.S.C. (M.T.)

He volunteered in October 1915, and in the following month was sent to the Western Front. During his service overseas he was engaged as a sergeant fitter and turner in large workshops on various sectors of the Front. His duties called for a high degree of technical skill, and he remained in France until his demobilisation in August 1919.

He holds the 1914-15 Star, General Service and Victory Medals. 143, Hill Side, Stonebridge Park, N.W.10 15798A.

LANT, J., Artificer, Royal Navy.

He volunteered in October 1915, and during his service was engaged on important escort duties in the North Sea and the Mediterranean. While on board one of H.M. submarines the bow of the vessel was blown off, and there were several casualties, but he escaped injury.

He was demobilised in April 1919, and holds the General Service and Victory Medals.

143, Hill Side, Stonebridge Park, N.W.10   15798B.

LARCOMBE, J., Gunner, R.F.A.

Volunteering in 1915, this Gunner was sent later in the same year to the Western Front, where he took part in many important engagements. During 1918 he was severely wounded, and died in consequence in January 1919.

He was entitled to the 1914-15 Star, General Service and Victory Medals.

43, Hazel Road, Willesden, N.W.10   X17598B.

LARGE, A. E., Lce.-Cpl., R.E. (I.W.T.)

He joined in May 1917, and after his training was sent to the Western Front, where he was engaged on important duties with the Inland Water Transport. He met with a serious accident while carrying out his duties and was invalided home.

In February 1919 he secured his demobilisation, holding the General Service and Victory Medals.

75, Claxton Grove, Hammersmith, W.6   13666.

LARGE, F., Gunner, R.N., H.M.S. " Malaya."

He volunteered in August 1914, and served with the Grand Fleet during the whole of his service. He took part in the battle of Jutland, and was on board H.M.S. " Britannia " when she was torpedoed and sunk by enemy action.

He holds the 1914 Star, General Service and Victory Medals, and in 1920 was still serving in the Royal Navy.

27, Lintaine Grove, West Kensington, W.14   168 12.

LARGE, J., Pte., Royal Fusiliers.

He joined in 1916, and after his training was drafted overseas, where he took part in many engagements on the Western Front. He was taken prisoner and kept in captivity for over a year, during which time he suffered many hardships. On his release he returned to England and was demobilised in December 1918. He holds the General Service and Victory Medals.

22, Rosaline Road, Munster Road, S.W.6   X18177.

LARKE, A. A., Pte., 3rd Norfolk Regiment.

He volunteered for service in September 1914, and after his training served at various stations on important duties with his unit. He did good work, but owing to physical disability was not drafted overseas.

He was discharged as medically unfit for further service in June 1916.

34, Essex Road, Willesden, N.W.10.   15589.

LARKIN, F. E., Pte., 14th London Regiment (London Scottish).

He volunteered in March 1915, and on completion of his training was sent to France. He took part in important operations on the Western Front, and was killed in action on the Somme on July 1st, 1916.

He was entitled to the 1914-15 Star, General Service and Victory Medals.

43, Manor Park Road, Harlesden, N.W.10   13219B.

LARKIN, G. F., Pte., 5th Middlesex Regiment.

Volunteering in 1915, he was sent later in the same year to the Western Front, where he took part in the battles of the Somme, Vimy Ridge and Ypres, and in other important engagements.

He served in France until his return to England for demobilisation in February 1919. He holds the 1914-15 Star, General Service and Victory Medals.

20, Humbolt Road, Hammersmith, W.6   15147A.

LARKIN, W. J., Pte., 19th Middlesex Regiment.

He volunteered in January 1916, and was drafted overseas in the following July. He took part in many important engagements on the Western Front, and was killed in action at Arras on March 23rd, 1917.

He was entitled to the General Service and Victory Medals.

43, Manor Park Road, Harlesden, N.W.10   13219A.

LARKING, S. G., Pte., 8th Devonshire Regt.
Volunteering in November 1915, he was drafted to the
Western Front in 1917. After serving there for a brief
period he was sent to Italy, where he took part in several
engagements. He was later returned to France and demobilised from there in February 1919. During his service
in Italy he was in hospital with illness.
He holds the General Service and Victory Medals.
118, Townmead Road, Fulham, S.W.6   X21063.

LARKMAN, H., Rifleman, Rifle Brigade.
He volunteered for service in January 1915, and after his
training served at various stations on important duties with
his unit. He rendered valuable service, but was not successful in obtaining his transfer overseas before the cessation of
hostilities.
He was demobilised in January 1919.
11, Westminster Road, Lower Edmonton, N.9   12705.

LARMAN, A. L., Gunner, R.G.A.
He joined in June 1916, and was drafted overseas, where he
took an active part in many engagements in various sectors of
the Western Front, including the battle of Ypres.
He was demobilised in October 1919, holding the General
Service and Victory Medals.
9, Plevna Road, Lower Edmonton, N.9   14576.

LARRETT, A. W., Staff-Sergt., R.A.S.C. (M.T.)
He volunteered for service in August 1914, and was immediately drafted overseas. He held a responsible position with
the Mechanical Transport during his 5½ years' service on the
Western Front, and was engaged in various sectors on
important duties.
He holds the 1914 Star, General Service and Victory Medals,
and was demobilised in February 1920.
37, Disbrowe Road, Hammersmith, W.6   15911.

LASHBROOK, E. A., Sapper, R.E.
Volunteering in November 1915, he was sent to the Western
Front on completion of his training in the following year.
He took part in many important engagements and was
wounded in heavy fighting near Valenciennes in October
1918 during the Allied Advance.
He was demobilised in March 1919, and holds the General
Service and Victory Medals.
15, Maybury Gardens, Willesden, N.W.10   X17444.

LAST, F. F., Pte., Royal Army Medical Corps.
He volunteered in December 1914, and shortly after was
drafted to Malta. He remained at this important station
until he was demobilised in May 1919, and during this time
was engaged on special duties in a large military dental
hospital.
He holds the General Service and Victory Medals.
18, Lydford Road, Maida Hill, W.9   T19686.

LAUGHLIN, R. H., Q.M.S., R.A.O.C.
Volunteering for service in November 1914, he was drafted
overseas shortly afterwards. He was responsible for the
repair of guns in various sectors of the Western Front, and was
thus employed for more than four years.
He was demobilised in March 1919, and holds the 1914-15
Star, General Service and Victory Medals.
34, Lyndhurst Road, Upper Edmonton, N.18   15502.

LAVENDER, W., Rifleman, 8th London Regt. (P.O. Rifles).
He joined in July 1916, and after his training was drafted
overseas. He took part in many important engagements on
the Western Front, and was wounded in action. After the
cessation of hostilities he went to Germany with the Army
of Occupation, and remained there until his demobilisation in
April 1919.
He holds the General Service and Victory Medals.
38, Haldane Road, Walham Green, S.W.6   X17379.

LAVEY, F. T., Pte., 1/6th East Surrey Regt.
He joined in February 1916, although suffering from a
deformed foot, and after his training was engaged on important duties at various stations with his unit. He gave
valuable services, but later in the same year was discharged
as medically unfit for military duties owing to his infirmity.
28, Tasso Road, Hammersmith, W.6   14653.

LAWFORD, R. H., Pte., Middlesex Regiment.
He joined in 1916, and later in the same year was drafted to
the Western Front, where he took part in many important
engagements. While in action in 1917 he was wounded.
He remained in France until his demobilisation in 1919,
and holds the General Service and Victory Medals.
24, Kenninghall Road, Upper Edmonton, N.18   16901B.

LAWFORD, W. J., Pte., Middlesex Regiment.
Volunteering in 1914, he was sent to France in the following
year, while in this theatre of war he took part in the battles
of Ypres and the Somme, and in many other important
engagements. He was wounded three times during his
service. In 1920 he was still serving with His Majesty's
Forces.
He holds the 1914-15 Star, General Service and Victory
Medals.
24, Kenninghall Road, Upper Edmonton, N.18   16901A.

LAWLER, T. F., Lce.-Cpl., Middlesex Regiment.
He volunteered in 1914, and on completion of his training
was sent to the Western Front in the following year. He
took part in many important engagements, notably those
on the Somme, at Ypres and La Bassée.
In 1919 he returned from France for demobilisation. He
holds the 1914-15 Star, General Service and Victory Medals.
38, Kimberley Road, Upper Edmonton, N.18   16533.

LAWRANCE, A. G., Rifleman, K.R.R.
He volunteered in August 1914, and was killed in action at
Hooge on July 30th in the following year. He had previously taken part in many engagements, including the
battle of Ypres, and was entitled to the 1914-15 Star,
General Service and Victory Medals.
21, Droop Street, Queen's Park Estate, W.10   X18575B.

LAWRANCE, H. W., Pte., The Queen's (Royal West Surrey Regiment) and Labour Corps.
He volunteered for service in June 1915, and after his training
was drafted overseas. He took part in many engagements
on the Western Front, where he remained until the cessation
of hostilities.
He was demobilised in October 1919, and holds the General
Service and Victory Medals.
79, Dyson's Road, Upper Edmonton, N.18   16556.

LAWRANCE, J. M., Bombardier, R.G.A.
He volunteered in August 1914, and was shortly afterwards
drafted to the Western Front, where, after taking part in
numerous important engagements, including those of the
Marne and the Somme, he was killed in action in June 1918,
during the German Offensive of that year.
He was entitled to the 1914 Star, General Service and Victory
Medals.
21, Droop Street, Queen's Park Estate, W.10   X18575A.

LAWRANCE, W., Sergt., 17th Middlesex Regt.
He volunteered for service in August 1914, and was immediately sent to the Western Front, where he took part
in the retreat from Mons and in many other important
engagements.
He was discharged in November 1915 as medically unfit for
further service, and holds the Mons Star, General Service
and Victory Medals.
17, Ancill Street, Hammersmith, W.6   13746B.

LAWRENCE, A. F., Lce.-Cpl., 2/9th Middlesex Regiment.
He volunteered in January 1915, and saw active service
on the Western Front. After taking part in engagements
at Bapaume and on the Somme, he went to the East, took
part in the fighting at Jericho and Gaza, and with General
Allenby went through the Palestine campaign.
He was demobilised in March 1919, and holds the General
Service and Victory Medals.
101, Fortune Gate Road, Harlesden, N.W.10   13466.

LAWRENCE, C., Driver, R.F.A.
He volunteered in December 1915, and was sent to the
Western Front, where he took part in several engagements,
including those at Zillebeke and Dickebusch. In 1917 he
was drafted to Italy, and during his service there, which
lasted two years, took part in operations on the Piave.
He holds the General Service and Victory Medals, and was
demobilised in February 1919.
148, Fifth Avenue, Queen's Park Estate, W.10   X18583.

LAWRENCE, G. T., Pte., R.A.M.C.
He volunteered in October 1915, and at the conclusion of
his training was drafted overseas, where he acted as a
stretcher-bearer. He took part in important engagements
on the Western Front, and was killed in action on September
3rd, 1916.
He was entitled to the General Service and Victory Medals.
61, Elthorne Avenue, Hanwell, W.7   11063.

LAWRENCE, J., Pte., 4th Bedfordshire Regt.
He joined in May 1917, and after his training was sent overseas. He took part in many engagements on the Western
Front, including the battles of Ypres and the Somme, and
was wounded in action in August 1918 during the Allied
Advance.
He holds the General Service and Victory Medals, and was
demobilised in January 1919.
50, Eastbournia Avenue, Lower Edmonton, N.9   13573.

LAWRENCE, J., Pte., Duke of Cornwall's L.I.
At the outbreak of war he was serving in China, but was sent to France in October 1914. While on the Western Front he was for a time in hospital, and was invalided home. In 1915 he was drafted to India, where he served against the Afghans in 1919.
He was demobilised in November 1919 on his return to England, and holds the 1914 Star, General Service and Victory Medals, and the India General Service Medal (with clasp—Afghanistan, N.W. Frontier, 1919).
181, Stephendale Road, Fulham, S.W.6   X20818.

LAWRENCE, J. D., Pte., Cheshire Regiment.
He joined in November 1916, and after his training served at various stations on important duties with his unit. He rendered valuable service, but was not successful in obtaining his transfer overseas before the cessation of hostilities.
He was demobilised in January 1919.
15, Asplin Road, Tottenham, N.17   X18818.

LAWRENCE, R. J., Farrier, R.A.S.C. (H.T.)
Having previously served in the South African war, he volunteered in November 1915, and early in the following year was sent to the Balkan Front, where he was engaged on important duties during the fighting on the Doiran and Struma Fronts. He remained in this theatre of operations until August 1919, when he returned for demobilisation.
In addition to the Queen's and King's South African Medals, he holds the General Service and Victory Medals.
10, Colin Road, Dudden Hill, N.W.10   16290.

LAWRENCE, T. H. G., Pte., R.A.S.C.
He joined in May 1916, and in the same year was sent to the Western Front, where he served as driver of a "caterpillar" engine drawing heavy guns. He took an active part in the battles of the Somme and Ypres, and in heavy fighting around Armentières during the Allied Retreat and Advance of 1918. In January 1919 he returned to England for demobilisation, and holds the General Service and Victory Medals.
74, Felixstowe Road, Lower Edmonton, N.9   15378.

LAWRENCE, W. H., Pte., 4th Royal Fusiliers.
Volunteering in December 1914, he was drafted overseas in the following June. While on the Western Front he took part in the battles of Loos and the Somme, and in heavy fighting around Ypres and Dickebusch. He met with a serious accident at the end of July 1916, and in consequence was discharged in December of the same year as medically unfit for further service.
He holds the 1914-15 Star, General Service and Victory Medals.
35, Hiley Road, Willesden, N.W.10   X18239.

LAWRENCE, W. J., Cpl., Royal Fusiliers.
Volunteering in August 1914, he was immediately drafted to France, where he took part in the retreat from Mons and in the battles of Ypres, Loos and the Somme. He was severely wounded in action, and after a considerable period in hospital in France and England was discharged owing to his wounds as medically unfit for further service in September 1917.
He holds the Mons Star, General Service and Victory Medals.
1, Welford Terrace, Dawes Road, S.W.6   X18072.

LAWRENCE, W. J., Pte., R.A.S.C.
He volunteered in 1914, and on completion of his training was drafted to the Western Front, where he was engaged on the important duties of conveying ammunition to the forward areas during the battles of the Somme, Arras, Ypres, and Cambrai, and in the heavy fighting at Armentières, Amiens, St. Quentin and the Allied Advance in 1918.
He was demobilised in May 1919, and holds the General Service and Victory Medals.
89, Rayleigh Road, West Kensington, W.14   12629.

LAWS, J. J., Pte., 3rd Grenadier Guards.
He volunteered in January 1915, and was shortly afterwards drafted overseas, where he took part in important engagements on the Western Front.
He was killed in action at the battle of Loos in September 1915, and was entitled to the 1914-15 Star, General Service and Victory Medals.
10, Tilson Road, Tottenham, N.17   19090.

LAWSON, E. C., Pte., 2/10th Middlesex Regt. and Machine Gun Corps.
He volunteered in September 1914, and after his training was sent overseas in the following year to the Dardanelles, where he was actively engaged in heavy fighting on the Peninsula. He afterwards went to Egypt, and took part in the Palestine campaign. During his service he was twice wounded, and was discharged as medically unfit for further service in June 1918.
He holds the 1914-15 Star, General Service and Victory Medals. 38, Tubb's Road, Harlesden, N.W.10   12741.

LAWSON, W., Pte., 2nd Dragoons (Royal Scots Greys).
Having enlisted in 1898, he was sent in August 1914 to France, where he took part in the retreat from Mons. While in action at Kemmel he was killed on November 20th of the same year. He was awarded a Russian decoration, and having served in the South African war held the Medals for that campaign. In addition he was entitled to the Mons Star, General Service and Victory Medals.
9, Cobbold Road, Church End, N.W.10   16954D.

LAY, F. W., Pte., Royal Sussex Regiment and Machine Gun Corps.
He volunteered for service in 1915, and after his training served at various stations on important duties with his unit. He was afterwards transferred to the Machine Gun Corps, and during his training at Belton Park contracted influenza, from which he died on October 25th, 1918.
70, Milton Avenue, Willesden, N.W.10   14316.

LAYCOCK, L. S. (Mrs.), Special War Worker.
During the war this lady volunteered her services, and was engaged by the Central London Railway Company on duties of an important nature in order to release a man for military service. She did splendid work throughout, and was highly commended by her Employers.
20, Mund Street, West Kensington, W.14   16921B.

LAYCOCK, W. L., Driver, R.A.S.C.
He was called up from the Reserve in August 1914, and during his service in France was engaged in the transport of rations and ammunition. In 1918 he was drafted to Egypt, where he spent some time in hospital, having contracted malaria. He holds the 1914 Star, General Service and Victory Medals, and was demobilised in 1919.
20, Mund Street, West Kensington, W.14   16921C.

LAYTON, E. J., Driver, Royal Engineers.
He volunteered in February 1915 at the age of 16, and later in the same year was sent to France, where he took part in numerous engagements. After serving throughout the war he was killed in an explosion in Belgium on December 15th, 1918, one month after the cessation of hostilities. He was entitled to the 1914-15 Star, General Service and Victory Medals.
20, Allestree Road, Fulham, S.W.6   X19199.

LAYTON, W. J., Pte., Queen's Own (Royal West Kent Regt.)
He volunteered in June 1915, and served on the Western Front, where he took part in the battles of the Somme, Arras, Ypres and other engagements. He contracted rheumatic fever during his service overseas, and after being in hospital at Rouen, was invalided home and eventually discharged as medically unfit for further service in May 1917. He holds the 1914-15 Star, General Service and Victory Medals.
13, Brenthurst Road, Church End, N.W.10   16382.

LAZARUS, R., Pte., 2nd Lincolnshire Regiment.
He volunteered for service in August 1914, and was shortly afterwards drafted overseas, where he was in many important engagements on the Western Front. He was killed in action at the battle of the Somme on July 1st, 1916, and was entitled to the 1914 Star, General Service and Victory Medals.
16, Rayleigh Road, West Kensington, W.14   12420.

LAZELL, W. E., Gnr., Royal Garrison Artillery.
He joined in March 1917, and was drafted overseas during the same year. While on the Western Front he took part in the Retreat and Advance of 1918, and was severely wounded in action in November of that year.
He was demobilised in January 1919, and holds the General Service and Victory Medals.
81a, Deacon Road, Cricklewood, N.W.2   T17330.

LEA, T. R. H., Gunner, Royal Field Artillery.
He volunteered in November 1914, and after his training was drafted overseas in the following year. He took part in many important engagements on the Western Front, including the battle of the Somme in 1916, and the Retreat and Advance of 1918.
He holds the 1914-15 Star, General Service and Victory Medals, and was still serving in 1920.
148, Town Road, Lower Edmonton, N.9   13588.

LEACH, A. G. (Mrs.), Special War Worker.
During the war this lady was engaged on work of national importance at the Perivale Munition Factory, where she was employed as an overseer in connection with the packing of fuses. She carried out her duties in a capable manner, and received high commendation for her valuable services.
22, St. Margaret's Road, Willesden, N.W.10   X17817

LEACH, A. J., Pte., Hampshire Regiment and Royal Army Service Corps.

Joining in November 1917, he was retained after his training on important duties at various stations with his unit. Later he was transferred to the Royal Army Service Corps, and was engaged on motor repair work. He rendered valuable service, but was not successful in obtaining his transfer overseas before hostilities ceased.
He was demobilised in May 1919.
46, Gowan Road, Willesden, N.W.10   TX16955B.

LEACH, E. J., Pte., Royal Sussex Regiment.

He joined in July 1917, and was drafted to the Western Front, where he served in important engagements until the cessation of hostilities. After the Armistice he was sent with the Army of Occupation into Germany, and on returning to England he was demobilised in September 1919, and holds the General Service and Victory Medals.
60, Stanley Road, Fulham, S.W.6   X19785.

LEACH, G., Pte., Queen's Own (Royal West Kent Regiment).

He volunteered in June 1915, and at the conclusion of his training was sent to Palestine. In this theatre of war he took part in many important engagements, but was killed by a bomb during an air raid on May 8th, 1917.
He was entitled to the General Service and Victory Medals.
37, Maldon Road, Lower Edmonton, N.9   14788.

LEACH, H. W., Cpl., 2nd Middlesex Regiment.

He was serving at the outbreak of war, and was immediately sent to the Western Front, where he took part in many important engagements. He fought in the retreat from Mons and at the battles of Ypres, the Somme, Arras and Cambrai, and was killed in action during the Retreat on May 27th, 1918, having previously been twice wounded.
He was entitled to the Mons Star, General Service and Victory Medals.
46, Gowan Road, Willesden, N.W.10   TX16955A.

LEADBETTER, A. W., Cpl., R.A.S.C. (M.T.)

He volunteered for service in March 1915, and at the conclusion of his training was drafted overseas, where he took an active part in important engagements on the Western Front, and was twice wounded. After the Armistice he went with the Army of Occupation to Germany, returning to England for his demobilisation in July 1919.
He holds the 1914–15 Star, General Service and Victory Medals.
97, Adeney Road, Hammersmith, W.6   15321B.

LEADBETTER, H. J., Bombardier, R.F.A.

He volunteered in June 1915, and after his training was drafted overseas, where he took part in many engagements on the Western Front, and was wounded during his service. He holds the General Service and Victory Medals, and was demobilised in April 1919.
97, Adeney Road, Hammersmith, W.6   15321A.

LEADBETTER, J. R., Sergt., R.A.M.C.

He volunteered in August 1914, and was drafted overseas on the completion of his training. He held a responsible position in the sanitary section during his four years' service in France, and was engaged on important duties in many sectors of this theatre of war.
He holds the 1914–15 Star, General Service and Victory Medals, and was demobilised in January 1919.
49, Humbolt Road, Hammersmith, W.6   15316B.

LEADER, A. (M.M.), Sapper, Royal Engineers.

He volunteered in February 1915, and two months later was sent to France, where he was in action at Ypres, Vermelles, Arras, Armentières, Béthune, Albert, Bapaume, the Somme, Loos, Lens, Delville Wood, and Valenciennes. He was awarded the Military Medal for gallant conduct in carrying dispatches under heavy fire with disregard of personal safety.
He also holds the 1914–15 Star, General Service and Victory Medals. He was demobilised in March 1919.
20, Shelley Road, Willesden, N.W.10   13609B.

LEADER, P. (M.M.), Pte., 8th Suffolk Regiment and Cambridgeshire Regiment.

He volunteered for service in August 1914, and was sent in the following year to France, where he took part in the battles of Ypres, the Somme, Arras and many other engagements. He was awarded the Military Medal and bar for conspicuous gallantry and devotion to duty in the field. He was wounded twice during his service, the second wound, in August 1918, necessitating the amputation of his left leg.
He was discharged in September 1919, holding the 1914–15 Star, General Service and Victory Medals.
20, Shelley Road, Willesden, N.W.10   13609A.

LEADS, G., A.B., R.N., H.M.S. "Vanguard."

He volunteered in 1915, and was posted to H.M.S. "Vanguard." While on this vessel he took part in important naval operations with the Grand Fleet in the North Sea, and was engaged in the battle of Jutland. He was later transferred to the Royal Air Force, and was retained on important duties at various Home stations.
In 1919 he was demobilised, and holds the General Service and Victory Medals.
64, Bathurst Gardens, Kensal Rise, N.W.10   X18413.

LEAMAN, C. J., Sapper, Royal Engineers.

He volunteered in October 1915, and in the following year was drafted to Salonica, where he took part in important operations during three years. Whilst serving on this Front he contracted malaria, and was for some time in hospital.
In June 1919 he was demobilised, and holds the General Service and Victory Medals.
7, Yewfield Road, Willesden, N.W.10   16524.

LEARY, C. E., Pte., 7th Royal Fusiliers.

He joined in January 1917, and in April was sent to the Western Front. After taking part in many important engagements in this theatre of war he was killed in action near Bapaume on October 18th, 1918, during the Allied Advance. He was wounded previously three times, and was entitled to the General Service and Victory Medals.
30, Hazel Road, Willesden, N.W.10   X17596.

LEARY, H., Pte., Essex Regiment.

He volunteered for service in July 1915, and after his training served at various stations on important duties with his unit. He did good work, but was not successful, owing to physical disability, in obtaining his transfer overseas, and he was discharged as medically unfit for further service in 1918.
12, Ancill Street, Hammersmith, W.6   13765.

LEARY, J. W., Rifleman, Rifle Brigade.

He joined in 1916, and on completion of his training was sent to France. He took part in many important engagements on the Western Front, including the battle of the Somme, where he was badly gassed. Later he took part in the Allied Retreat and Advance, and was demobilised in January 1919. Having previously served in the South African war, he holds the Queen's and King's Medals, in addition to the General Service and Victory Medals.
78, Willow Vale, Shepherd's Bush, W.12   12055A.

LEARY, W. (Miss), Special War Worker.

This lady offered her services at the outbreak of war, and was engaged on work of national importance in the shell-packing department of Messrs. Blake's Munition Factory at Hammersmith. She carried out her duties in a very capable manner, and received high commendation for her valuable work.
12, Ancill Street, Hammersmith, W.6   13992A.

LEATHERDALE, H., Pte., R.A.O.C.

He joined in 1916, and after his training was drafted overseas to Salonica, where he was engaged on important duties with his unit in various sectors of the Balkan Front. He remained in this theatre of war until 1919, when he was demobilised, holding the General Service and Victory Medals.
7, Beamish Road, Lower Edmonton, N.9   13937.

LEATHERDALE, O., Sapper, R.E.

He joined in June 1916, and at the conclusion of his training was drafted overseas, where he took an active part in many engagements in various sectors of the Western Front. He was wounded during his service overseas.
He holds the General Service and Victory Medals, and was demobilised in January 1919,
50, Wakefield Street, Upper Edmonton, N.18   16564.

LEATT, B., Gunner, 303rd Siege Battery, R.G.A.

He volunteered for service in 1915, and was drafted overseas in the same year. He took part in many engagements on the Western Front, including the battles of the Somme, Cambrai, Ypres, Arras, Amiens and the Advance of 1918. He was wounded and gassed during his service in France. After the Armistice he went with the Army of Occupation to Germany.
He was demobilised in 1919, and holds the 1914–15 Star, General Service and Victory Medals.
17, Spezzia Road, Harlesden, N.W.10   T12951A.

LEAVER, J., Gunner, Royal Field Artillery.

Volunteering in January 1915, he was sent in the same year to the Western Front, where he took part in several engagements during his year's service there. In 1916 he was drafted to Salonica, and contracted blood-poisoning, which kept him in hospital for some time. Later he was transferred to Egypt, whence, in 1919, he was returned home, and in July was demobilised.
He holds the 1914–15 Star, General Service and Victory Medals. 118, Stephendale Road, Fulham, S.W.6   X20825.

LEE, A. W., Pte., 10th London Regiment.
He volunteered in August 1914, and after his training served at various stations on important duties with his unit. He did good work, but owing to physical disability he was not drafted overseas. He was discharged as medically unfit for further service in July 1916.
Prior to the war he served in the Territorial Force.
25, Hartham Road, Bruce Grove, N.17   X18520.

LEE, B. J., Pte., Royal Fusiliers.
He joined in August 1916, and on completion of his training was drafted to France in the following year. He took part in many engagements on the Western Front, and was gassed in June 1917. He remained overseas until the cessation of hostilities, when he returned to England and was demobilised in February 1919.
He holds the General Service and Victory Medals.
27, Linton Road, Upper Edmonton, N.18   TX17252.

LEE, C. H., Stoker, H.M. T.B.D. " Simoon."
He volunteered in 1915, and served on board his ship on important naval operations with the Grand Fleet in the North Sea. He was killed in an engagement with a German squadron off Harwich on January 23rd, 1917, and was entitled to the General Service and Victory Medals.
18, Carlyle Avenue, Willesden, N.W.10   14207.

LEE, E. E. (Mrs.), Special War Worker.
During the war this lady was engaged at Messrs. Waring & Gillow's factory in the manufacture of tents, marquees and general Army equipment. On account of her good work she was promoted to the responsible position of examiner. She rendered valuable service by her patriotic action.
19, Hartopp Avenue, Dawes Road, S.W.6   X18045.

LEE, F. W., Pte., Middlesex Regiment.
He volunteered in March 1915, and after his training was drafted overseas. He fought in many engagements on almost every sector of the British Front in France, where he remained until after the cessation of hostilities.
He was demobilised in January 1919, and holds the General Service and Victory Medals.
49, Lyndhurst Road, Lower Edmonton, N.9   15497.

LEE, G., Pioneer, Royal Engineers.
He volunteered in August 1915, and was drafted overseas the same year. He took part in many engagements in various sectors of the Western Front, where he remained on important duties long after the cessation of hostilities.
He holds the 1914–15 Star, General Service and Victory Medals, and in 1920 was still serving.
60, Hartington Road, Lower Edmonton, N.9   14059.

LEE, H., Lce. Cpl., 22nd Manchester Regiment.
He volunteered in November 1915, and was later drafted to the Western Front. After taking part in many important engagements in this seat of war, during which time he was wounded in the battle of the Somme, he was sent to Italy, and served in the operations on that Front.
He was demobilised in March 1919, and holds the General Service and Victory Medals.
10, Beaconsfield Road, Lower Edmonton, N.9   14771.

LEE, P., Driver, Royal Army Veterinary Corps.
He volunteered in August 1914, and after his training was drafted overseas to Salonica, where he served with his unit in various sectors of the Balkan Front. He returned to England in 1919, and was demobilised in August of the same year, holding the 1914–15 Star, General Service and Victory Medals.
12, Northcote Road, Willesden, N.W.10   14917.

LEE, R., Driver, Royal Engineers.
He joined in 1916, and was drafted to France, where he took part in important engagements on the Western Front, including the battles of the Somme, Arras, Armentières, Ypres, Vimy Ridge and the Advance of 1918. He returned to England after the cessation of hostilities, and was demobilised in 1919, holding the General Service and Victory Medals.
3, Shotley Street, Hammersmith, W.6   15046C.

LEE, S. J. A., A/Sergeant Major, Royal Army Medical Corps.
He volunteered in November 1914, and in the following February was sent to France, where he took part in the battles of Ypres, Loos, the Somme and Messines Ridge, and in important engagements at Givenchy and Armentières. He was killed in action on June 7th, 1917, during the battle of Messines.
He was entitled to the 1914–15 Star, General Service and Victory Medals.
6, Bathurst Gardens, Kensal Rise, N.W.10   X18414.

LEE, S. W., Pte., Middlesex Regiment.
Volunteering shortly after the outbreak of hostilities in August 1914, he was quickly drafted overseas. He took part in the fighting round Mons, and was taken prisoner during the Retreat. During his long captivity in Germany he suffered many hardships.
He holds the Mons Star, General Service and Victory Medals.
7, Monmouth Road, Lower Edmonton, N.9   12993.

LEECH, E. F. (Miss), Worker, Q.M.A.A.C.
She joined in June 1917, and went to France, where she was stationed at Calais and Abbeville on special duties with the R.A.S.C. She afterwards returned to England, and was employed as a clerk at the Regents Park Stores Depot. After giving valuable services she was demobilised in January 1920, holding the General Service and Victory Medals.
108, Portnall Road, Maida Hill, W.9   X19596.

LEEDER, A. G., Stoker, R.N., H.M.S. " Tiger."
He volunteered in 1915, and was posted to H.M.S. " Tiger." While on board this vessel he took part in important naval operations with the Grand Fleet in the North Sea, and was also engaged on special convoy duties across the Atlantic Ocean.
He was demobilised in 1920, and holds the General Service and Victory Medals.
26, Oldfield Road, Willesden, N.W.10   16110B.

LEEDER, A. H., Driver, R.F.A.
Volunteering in September 1914, he was sent to France in the following year. After taking part in many important engagements, including the battle of the Somme, he was drafted to Salonica in 1916, and served throughout the heavy fighting on the Doiran and Struma Fronts.
He holds the 1914–15 Star, General Service and Victory Medals, and was demobilised in 1919.
26, Oldfield Road, Willesden, N.W.10   16110C.

LEEDER, H., Gunner, Royal Garrison Artillery.
He volunteered in 1915, and later in the same year was drafted to the Western Front, where he took part in the battles of the Somme, Arras, Ypres, Bapaume and Cambrai, and in other engagements during the Retreat and Advance of 1918.
He was demobilised in 1919, and holds the 1914–15 Star, General Service and Victory Medals.
26, Oldfield Road, Willesden, N.W.10   16110A.

LEEDS, A., Sapper, Royal Engineers.
He joined in September 1917, and on the completion of his training served at various places, being employed in the making of roads and loading vessels with ammunition and stores for transport overseas.
After rendering valuable services he was demobilised in January 1919.
45a, Deacon Road, Cricklewood, N.W.2   X17212.

LEFEVRE, P. D., Pte., 1/8th Hampshire Regt.
He joined in November 1916, and on completion of his training was sent to France, where he took part in the battle of Arras and in important engagements on the Somme and at La Bassée and Tournai. After being wounded in action he was invalided home, and on his recovery was drafted to Egypt. He remained there until sent home for his demobilisation in April 1920.
He holds the General Service and Victory Medals.
16, Eustace Road, Walham Green, S.W.6   X19419.

LE FEVRE, G., A.B., R.N., H.M.S. " Courageous."
He joined in April 1916, and served with his ship on important operations with the Grand Fleet in the North Sea. He took part in the battle of Heligoland, and was present at the surrender of the German Fleet at Scapa Flow.
In March 1919 he was demobilised, and holds the General Service and Victory Medals.
49, Hiley Road, Willesden, N.W.10   X18167B.

LE FEVRE, T. H. W., Gunner, R.F.A.
He volunteered in November 1914 for a period of six years, and in the following July was sent to the Western Front. He took part in the battles of Loos, the Somme, Arras, Messines, Ypres, Cambrai and St. Quentin, and was wounded. In February 1919 he returned to England, and was still serving in 1920.
He holds the 1914–15 Star, General Service and Victory Medals.
49, Hiley Road, Willesden, N.W.10   X18167A.

LEFTLEY, G. M. (Mrs.), Special War Worker.
Early in the war this lady was engaged in filling fuses at the Perivale Munition Factory, Park Royal. Later she went to the British Thomson-Houston works at Willesden, where she was employed on the making of shells. She carried out her duties in an efficient and satisfactory manner.
21, Shakespeare Avenue, Willesden, N.W.10   13882B.

LEFTLEY, J. W., Cpl., 2nd Hampshire Regt.

He volunteered in August 1914, and in the following year was drafted overseas to the Western Front, where he took part in several engagements, including those on the Somme and during the Retreat of 1918. Owing to a serious wound which he received at La Bassée in April 1918, he had to have his leg amputated, and in consequence he was discharged in November 1918.
He holds the 1914–15 Star, General Service and Victory Medals.
21, Shakespeare Avenue, Willesden, N.W.10   13882A.

LEGGETT, G. W., Rifleman, 6th London Regt.

He joined in March 1916, and after his training was retained on important duties with his unit at various stations. He gave valuable services, but in the following September was discharged owing to ill-health as medically unfit for further military service.
6, Ancill Street, Hammersmith, W.6   13755A.

LEGGETTER, E. T., 2nd Cpl., R.E.

Joining in June 1915, he served for over three years on the Eastern Front, where he took part in the Advance from Egypt to Palestine, and was present at many important engagements.
He was demobilised in July 1919, and holds the General Service and Victory Medals.
4, Preston Gardens, Willesden, N.W.10   15981.

LE-GOOD, F. J., Air Mechanic, R.A.F.

He volunteered in 1915, and at the conclusion of his training was drafted overseas in the same year. During his service in France he was engaged on important work as a wireless operator, and was gassed whilst on duty. He returned to England in 1919 for demobilisation, and holds the 1914–15 Star, General Service and Victory Medals.
2, Ilex Road, Willesden, N.W.10   16096B.

LE-GOOD, H., Pte., 9th Middlesex Regiment.

He joined in 1917, and on completion of his training was drafted overseas, where he took part in many important engagements on the Western Front. While in action at Cambrai during the Advance of 1918 he was severely wounded, and in consequence was discharged as medically unfit for further service in the same year.
He holds the General Service and Victory Medals.
2, Ilex Road, Willesden, N.W.10   16096A.

LE-GOOD, H., Pte., Royal Army Medical Corps.

He joined in April 1918, and on completion of his training was retained on important duties at various stations with his unit. He gave valuable services, but was not successful in obtaining his transfer overseas before the cessation of hostilities.
He was demobilised in January 1920.
1, St. James' Place, Church Road, Tottenham, N.17
TX18541.

LE-GOOD, W. A., Pte., R.A.S.C. (M.T.)

Joining in 1917, he was immediately drafted to Mesopotamia, where he was engaged on important duties during the operations against the Turks. In 1918 he was sent to Egypt, and served under General Allenby in the advance through Palestine, during which he was wounded twice whilst in action in the Jordan valley.
In 1920 he returned to this country for demobilisation, and holds the General Service and Victory Medals.
2, Ilex Road, Willesden, N.W.10   16069C.

LEIGHS, J., Gunner, Royal Field Artillery.

He volunteered in September 1914, and in the following year was sent to France, where he fought in the battle of the Somme and in many other important engagements. He was twice wounded, and in 1916 returned home, where, owing to his wounds, he was certified unfit for further active service, but gave valuable services at various stations until his demobilisation in February 1919.
He holds the 1914–15 Star, General Service and Victory Medals.
50, Kimberley Road, Upper Edmonton, N.18   16536.

LEIGHTON, A. J., Cpl., R.F.A., R.A.S.C. and Middlesex Regiment.

He was serving at the outbreak of war, and was immediately sent to France, where he fought in the retreat from Mons and in the battles of Ypres, Loos, the Somme, Vimy Ridge and Messines. During his service he was twice wounded, and remained in France until December 1918, when he returned to England, and was discharged.
He holds the Mons Star, General Service and Victory Medals.
19, Mayo Road, Willesden, N.W.10   15124B.

LEITH, F. C., Driver, R.A.S.C.

He joined in 1917, and after training at various stations was drafted to France, where he did valuable work as a transport driver. He was severely wounded by a bomb which was dropped from a Zeppelin during a raid on Calais.
In 1919 he was demobilised, holding the General Service and Victory Medals.
7, Ilex Road, Willesden, N.W.10   16098C.

LE MAR, E. W., Pte., East Surrey Regiment.

He volunteered in 1915, and after his training was sent overseas the same year. During his service he took part in many important engagements on the Western Front, including the battles of the Somme, Ypres, and the Retreat and Advance of 1918, and was three times wounded. After his last wound in July 1918, he was invalided to hospital in England, and subsequently discharged as medically unfit for further service.
He holds the 1914–15 Star, General Service and Victory Medals.
71, Monmouth Road, Lower Edmonton, N.9   13017.

LE MARIE, J. W., Sapper, Royal Engineers.

He volunteered in 1915, and on completion of his training was drafted to Egypt. From there he was sent to Palestine, and fought with General Allenby's Forces at Gaza and Jerusalem. Being sent to France later, he took an active part in important engagements during the Retreat and Advance of 1918.
He remained in France until his demobilisation in July 1919, and holds the 1914–15 Star, General Service and Victory Medals.
32, Half-acre Road, Hanwell, W.7   12379.

LENIHAN, A. G., Pte., York and Lancaster Regt.

Volunteering in May 1915, he was sent to France later in the same year. While on the Western Front he took part in many important engagements with his unit, until the cessation of hostilities.
In January 1919 he was demobilised, and holds the 1914–15 Star, General Service and Victory Medals.
15, Marsden Road, Lower Edmonton, N.9   13064.

LENNON, J. R., Pte., 2nd Suffolk Regiment.

He volunteered in 1915, and during his service in France took part in several important engagements, and was for some time in hospital suffering from trench fever.
He was demobilised in November 1919, and holds the General Service and Victory Medals.
18, York Road, Upper Edmonton, N.18   16781.

LENNOX, W. A., Cpl., 13th Royal Fusiliers.

He volunteered in 1914, and on completion of his training, was drafted in the following year to the Western Front, where he took part in the battles of Neuve Chapelle, Loos, Somme, Arras, Vimy Ridge, Bullecourt and Ypres, and in heavy fighting around Armentières. During his service he was twice wounded, and in June 1917 was discharged as medically unfit for further service owing to his wounds.
He holds the 1914–15 Star, General Service and Victory Medals.
13, Francis Street, Hammersmith, W.6   15042.

LENTON, A. A., Pte., 22nd Royal Fusiliers.

He volunteered in October 1914, and in the following year was drafted to France, where he fought in the battles of the Somme, Arras and Ypres, and in other important engagements. He was in hospital in France for a considerable time owing to a serious injury caused by being caught in barbed wire entanglements.
Demobilised in March 1919, he holds the 1914–15 Star, General Service and Victory Medals.
21, Hilmer Street, West Kensington, W.14   T15706B.

LENTON, E. A., Pte., R.A.M.C.

Volunteering in October 1914, he was sent to France on the completion of his training in the following year. While on the Western Front he took an active part in many important engagements as a stretcher-bearer.
He remained in France until the cessation of hostilities, when he returned to England for his demobilisation in April 1919, and holds the 1914–15 Star, General Service and Victory Medals.
21, Hilmer Street, West Kensington, W.14   T15706A.

LEONARD, W. E., Pte., Queen's (Royal West Surrey Regiment).

He joined in 1916, and was drafted overseas the same year. During his service on the Western Front he took part in many important engagements, including the battles of the Somme, Arras and Cambrai. He was killed in action near Lens on October 30th during the Advance of 1918, and was buried at Burmaines.
He was entitled to the General Service and Victory Medals.
44, Greyhound Road, College Park, N.W.10   X17600A.

LEPPARD, D. P., Gunner, R.G.A.
This gunner volunteered in August 1914, and in 1916 was sent to the Western Front, where he served in various engagements on the Somme sector. As a result of ill-health contracted whilst on active service he was invalided home in 1917, and demobilised in February 1919, holding the General Service and Victory Medals.
11, De Morgan Road, Townmead Road, Fulham, S.W.6.
X20845.

LESLIE, B., Driver, Royal Field Artillery.
Volunteering in 1914, he was sent in the following year to the Salonica seat of operations, and took part in many important engagements. In 1916 he was drafted to the Western Front, and fought in the battle of the Somme and during the Retreat and Advance of 1918.
He was demobilised in 1918, and holds the 1914–15 Star and the General Service and Victory Medals.
41, Shorrolds Road, Walham Green, S.W.6   X19345B.

LESLIE, E., Gunner, Machine Gun Corps.
Volunteering in August 1914, he soon proceeded to the Western Front, where he took part in the retreat from Mons. After being in action at Ypres and Messines, and being twice wounded, he was drafted to Mesopotamia in 1915, and two years later to India, where he fought against the Afghans in 1919.
He was sent home and demobilised in February 1920, holding the Mons Star, General Service and Victory Medals, and the Indian General Service Medal (with clasp—Afghanistan, N.W. Frontier, 1919).
41, Shorrolds Road, Walham Green, S.W.6   X19345A.

LESLIE, M., Gunner, Royal Field Artillery.
He volunteered in 1915, and later in the same year was drafted to the Western Front, where he took part in the battle of Loos and other important engagements. In 1916, after being invalided home owing to ill-health, he was discharged as medically unfit for further service, and subsequently died in 1919.
He was entitled to the 1914–15 Star, General Service and Victory Medals.
41, Shorrolds Road, Walham Green, S.W.6   X19345C.

LESTER, F., Pte., Royal Army Medical Corps.
He volunteered in 1914, and was soon drafted to the Western Front, where he took part in the retreat from Mons and the battles of La Bassée, Ypres, Loos, the Somme and Arras. He remained in France until after the cessation of hostilities, when he returned to England for his demobilisation in 1919.
He holds the Mons Star, General Service and Victory Medals.
307, Brettenham Road East, Upper Edmonton, N.18
15632C.

LESTER, H., Gunner, Royal Horse Artillery.
Volunteering in 1915, he was retained on important duties at various stations until 1917 when he was drafted to France, where he took part in many engagements on the Western Front, including the battle of Cambrai.
He holds the General Service and Victory Medals, and was still serving in 1920.
307, Brettenham Road East, Upper Edmonton, N.18
15632A.

LESTER, J., Gunner, Royal Field Artillery.
He joined in February 1916, and was sent to France on completion of his training. After taking part in important engagements on the Western Front, he was drafted to Salonica, where he again saw much fighting. Later he was sent to Palestine and served with General Allenby's Forces during the Advance against the Turks, but was in hospital for a considerable time at Jerusalem, suffering from malaria. In June 1919 he was demobilised, but has since re-enlisted for a further period of two years. He holds the General Service and Victory Medals.
30, Garvan Road, Hammersmith, W.6   15061.

LESTER, P., Drummer, 1st Welch Regiment.
He volunteered in 1915, and was immediately afterwards sent to the Western Front. He was killed in action at Hill 60 on February 16th, 1915, shortly after his arrival in France.
He was entitled to the 1914–15 Star, General Service and Victory Medals.
307, Brettenham Road East, Upper Edmonton, N.18
15632B.

LESTRILLE, J., Gunner, R.G.A.
He was mobilised from the Reserve at the outbreak of war and was immediately sent to France, where he took part in the retreat from Mons, the battles of Ypres, Arras, Bullecourt and several important engagements during the Retreat and Advance of 1918. During his service he was wounded, and spent a considerable time in hospital in France.
In January 1919 he was discharged, holding the Mons Star, General Service and Victory Medals.
69, Coomer Road, Fulham, S.W.6   16444.

LETHBRIDGE, S. W., Air Mechanic, R.A.F.
He joined in 1916, and after his training served at various stations on important duties with his unit. He gave valuable services, and his duties called for a high degree of technical skill, but he was not sent overseas because he was over age for Foreign service.
He was demobilised in 1919.
55, Ilex Road, Willesden, N.W.10   16360.

LEUTY, C. G., Cpl., Royal Garrison Artillery.
Volunteering in November 1915, he was sent later in the same year to the Western Front, where he took part in the battles of the Somme and Ypres and in other important engagements.
He returned to England for demobilisation in February 1919, and holds the 1914–15 Star, General Service and Victory Medals.
70, Hawthorn Road, Upper Edmonton, N.18   X17051.

LEVERETT, E. W., Rifleman, 11th and 12th London Regiment.
He volunteered in 1915, and in November of the same year was drafted to France, where he took part in many important engagements, including the battle of the Somme. He was wounded near Gommecourt on July 1st, 1916, and on his recovery was sent to Palestine. While in this theatre of war he took part in the Advance with General Allenby's Forces, and remained there until sent to England for demobilisation in July 1919.
He holds the 1914–15 Star, General Service and Victory Medals.
59, Villiers Road, Cricklewood, N.W.2   T17324A.

LEVERETT, G. H., Special War Worker.
For a period of five years during the war he was engaged as an engineer in a large aeroplane works at Hendon. His duties called for a high degree of technical skill and were carried out in a capable and satisfactory manner. He gave valuable services throughout.
59, Villiers Road, Cricklewood, N.W.2   T17324B.

LEVETT, W. J., Pte., Middlesex Regiment.
He volunteered in November 1914, and after his training was engaged on important duties at various stations with his unit. He gave valuable services, but in 1917, owing to his suffering severely from rheumatism, he was discharged as medically unfit for further service.
11, Asplin Road, Tottenham, N.17   X18819.

LEVICK, J. H., Drummer, 1/2nd London Regt. (Royal Fusiliers).
Volunteering in June 1915, he was retained on important duties at various stations with his unit until 1917, when he was drafted to France. He took part in the battles of Arras and Cambrai, and in important engagements during the Retreat and Advance of 1918.
In the following February he was demobilised, and holds the General Service and Victory Medals.
16, Earlsmead Road, College Park, N.W.10   X18030A.

LEVICK, W. A., Pte., Suffolk Regiment and Queen's Own (Royal West Kent Regiment).
He joined in 1917, and in August of the following year was sent to France, where he took part in the final operations during the Advance of 1918.
In 1919 he was demobilised, but in July re-enlisted in the Queen's Own (Royal West Kent Regiment), and in 1920 was serving in India. He holds the General Service and Victory Medals.
16, Earlsmead Road, College Park, N.W.10   X18030B.

LEWELL, F. L., Sergt., Royal Engineers.
He volunteered in 1915, and being sent to France in the following year, took part in the fighting on the Somme, where he was wounded. He was in hospital for some months, and after returning to the Western Front was in action at Cambrai, Arras, Vimy Ridge, and during the Advance of 1918.
He was demobilised in July 1919, and holds the General Service and Victory Medals.
86, Durban Road, Tottenham, N.17   X17948.

LEWIN, W. J., Driver, Royal Field Artillery.
He volunteered in October 1914, and in the following year was sent to the Western Front. He remained in France until 1918, and during that period took part in the battles of the Somme, Arras and Ypres.
While on active service he was wounded, and in February 1919 was demobilised, holding the 1914–15 Star, General Service and Victory Medals.
35, Beaconsfield Road, Lower Edmonton, N.9   14776.

LEWINGTON, A. H., Gunner, R.H.A.

Enlisting in February 1906, he was sent to France immediately on the outbreak of hostilities, and took part in the retreat from Mons and the battles of the Marne, Aisne, Ypres, Loos and Cambrai. He was invalided home with trench fever, and after three months in hospital was discharged in January 1918 as medically unfit for further service.

He holds the Mons Star, General Service and Victory Medals.
141, Poynton Road, Tottenham, N.17   X18951.

LEWINGTON, L., Driver, R.F.A.

He volunteered in June 1915, and was later sent to France, where he took part in the battles of the Somme, Arras, Ypres, Cambrai, and the fierce fighting at Loos in 1916. Owing to a weak heart he was invalided out of the Service in March 1919, holding the General Service and Victory Medals.
18, Bayonne Road, Hammersmith, W.6   14503.

LEWIS, A. E. (Miss), Special War Worker.

For a considerable period of the war this lady was engaged at the Park Royal Munition Factory, where she rendered valuable assistance. Throughout her service she carried out her duties, which were of an arduous character, in an efficient manner, and received high commendation.
22, Steele Road, Willesden, N.W.10   13836A.

LEWIS, A. V., A.B., Royal Navy.

He volunteered in August 1914, and soon proceeded to sea, where, during his five years' service he was on board H.M. ships " Warrior " and " Cairo," taking part in many important naval engagements. While in the " Warrior " during the battle of Jutland his ship was disabled, and after many hours' fierce fighting sank in flames.
In 1919 he was demobilised, and holds the 1914 Star, General Service and Victory Medals.
76, Chesson Road, West Kensington, W.14   X17691A.

LEWIS, C., Pte., East Surrey Regiment and Royal Fusiliers.

Joining in 1916, he was sent to France on completion of his training, and fought in the battles of the Somme, Arras and Ypres, and in important engagements around Loos and Béthune. While in action he was badly gassed and was temporarily blinded.

He was demobilised in 1919, and holds the General Service and Victory Medals.
106, Holly Lane, Willesden, N.W.10 .   *15398C.

LEWIS, C. E., 1st Class Stoker, Royal Navy.

He joined in December 1917, and on board H.M.S. " Monarch " served with the Grand Fleet in the final naval engagements in the North Sea. He was present at the surrender of the German Fleet at Scapa Flow, and in 1920 was still serving.
He holds the General Service and Victory Medals.
66, Hiley Road, Willesden, N.W.10   X18655B.

LEWIS, C. H. W., Driver, R.F.A.

He volunteered in 1915, and later in the same year was sent to France. After a short time there he was drafted to Salonica, where he remained for nearly three years, during which period he took part in many important engagements in the Balkan campaign.

He returned to France and served in the final operations during the Retreat and Advance of 1918. In 1919 he was demobilised, and holds the 1914-15 Star, General Service and Victory Medals.
22, Steele Road, Willesden, N.W.10   13836C.

LEWIS, C. J., Pte., Duke of Cornwall's L.I.

He joined in March 1916, and on the completion of his training was drafted to the Western Front, where he took part in many important engagements. He returned to England in 1919, when he was demobilised, holding the General Service and Victory Medals.
194, Winchester Road, Lower Edmonton, N.9   14885.

LEWIS, E. C. (Mrs.), Special War Worker.

For a considerable period during the war this lady patriotically gave up her household duties in order to take up work of national importance at Messrs. Klinger's factory, Tottenham, where she was engaged in the manufacture of military equipment. She carried out her duties satisfactorily, and was commended for her valuable services.
58, Hartington Road, Tottenham, N.17   X19112B.

LEWIS, E. L., Pte., Durham Light Infantry.

He joined in June 1916, and after his training was retained on important duties at various stations with his unit. He gave valuable services, but owing to his being medically unfit for active service, was not successful in obtaining his transfer overseas.
He was demobilised in February 1919.
6, Fourth Avenue, Queen's Park Estate, W.10   X18668.

14

LEWIS, F., Cpl., King's Royal Rifle Corps.

He joined in 1916, and shortly afterwards was drafted to the Western Front. His service overseas lasted for three years, during which period he took part in many of the principal engagements, including the battles of Ypres and the Somme, and was twice wounded.

He returned to England in 1919 when he was demobilised, holding the General Service and Victory Medals.
1, Pretoria Road, Tottenham, N.17   X18124A.

LEWIS, F., Pte., 6th and 13th Middlesex Regt.

He volunteered in 1914, and was drafted to France in the following year. He took part in many important engagements, including those at Arras and Fricourt, and was wounded. In 1917 he was invalided home, having been badly gassed, and in consequence was discharged as medically unfit for further service in 1918.

He holds the 1914-15 Star, General Service and Victory Medals.   100, Holly Lane, Willesden, N.W.10   15398B.

LEWIS, G. F., Rifleman, Rifle Brigade.

Volunteering in February 1915, he was later in the same year sent overseas. While on the Western Front he took part in the battle of the Somme and other important engagements, and was wounded in action in 1916. He remained in France until after the cessation of hostilities, and on his return to England in 1919 was demobilised, holding the 1914-15 Star, General Service and Victory Medals.
45, Monmouth Road, Lower Edmonton, N.9   13027.

LEWIS, H., Pte., Labour Corps.

He joined in 1916, and was engaged on special duties at various stations with his unit. He gave valuable services, but was not successful in obtaining his transfer overseas before the cessation of hostilities, and in 1919 was demobilised.
58, Hartington Road, Tottenham, N.17   X19112A.

LEWIS, J. E., Pte., R.A.S.C. (M.T.)

Volunteering in August 1914, he was shortly afterwards drafted to the Western Front, where he served for nearly five years. He did useful work with the Royal Army Service Corps in various important sectors, and was present at the battles of the Marne, Ypres, Loos, the Somme, Arras and Cambrai, and in the last Retreat and Advance of 1918.
In 1919 he returned to England where he was demobilised, holding the 1914 Star, General Service and Victory Medals.
39, College Road, Willesden, N.W.10   X17816.

LEWIS, M., Pte., Connaught Rangers.

Volunteering in November 1914, he was shortly afterwards drafted to the Western Front, where he took part in much of the heavy fighting in various sectors, including Ypres, Arras and Armentières. His service in France lasted until July 1919, when he returned to England and was demobilised, holding the 1914-15 Star, General Service and Victory Medals.   7, Delorme Street, Hammersmith, W.6   T14095.

LEWIS, M. E. (Miss), Special War Worker.

For nearly four years during the war this lady was engaged on work of national importance at No. 3 Filling Factory, Park Royal.

She worked in the T.N.T. shop, and while there suffered severely from poisoning. She carried out her dangerous duties in a very capable manner, for which she received high commendation.   22, Steele Road, Willesden, N.W.10   13836B.

LEWIS, R., Air Mechanic, Royal Air Force.

He joined in 1918, and after his training was engaged on important duties at various aerodromes in Yorkshire. His work required a high degree of technical skill, and he gave valuable services, but was unable to secure his transfer overseas before hostilities ceased.
He was demobilised in 1919.
1, Pretoria Road, Tottenham, N.17   X18124B.

LEWIS, R., Driver, Royal Army Service Corps.

He joined in December 1917, and was engaged on important transport duties with his unit at various stations. He gave valuable services, but owing to ill-health was not successful in securing his transfer overseas, and in October 1918 was discharged as medically unfit for further service.
74, Brett Road, Stonebridge Park, N.W.10   14379A.

LEWIS, R. H. S., Pte., 25th London Regiment (Cyclists).

He volunteered in August 1914, and after his training was retained on important duties with his unit until 1916, when he was drafted to India. He remained there until 1919, and during that period took part in the fighting on the North-West Frontier and in quelling the Amritsar riots. While abroad he contracted malaria, and in December 1919 was demobilised.

He holds the General Service and Victory Medals, and the India General Service Medal (with clasp—Afghanistan, N.W. Frontier, 1919).
74, Brett Road, Stonebridge Park, N.W.10   14379B.

LEWIS, W. E., Pte., 18th (Queen Mary's Own) Hussars.
He joined in May 1918, and on completion of his training was engaged on important duties with his unit at various stations. He gave valuable service, but was not successful in obtaining his transfer overseas before the cessation of hostilities. In April 1919 he was drafted to Syria, and after a period of service there was sent to Egypt, where in 1920 he was still serving.
66, Hiley Road, Willesden, N.W.10   X18655A.

LEWIS, W. J., Pte., Middlesex Regiment.
Joining in February 1916, he was drafted to the Western Front in the following July. His service overseas lasted until the cessation of hostilities, and during this time he took part in several important battles, including those of the Somme, Ypres, Arras and Cambrai, and was twice wounded. He was demobilised in February 1919, holding the General Service and Victory Medals.
76, Strode Road, Willesden, N.W.10   X17095.

LEWSEY, J. S., Special War Worker.
He volunteered for military service, but on seven occasions was rejected, and afterwards obtained work of national importance, first at the British Thompson-Houston Munition Works, and later at the De Dion Bouton Co., Ltd.   For three years he was engaged on work in connection with the manufacture of shells, and throughout the war gave valuable services.
14, Drayton Road, Harlesden, N.W.10   14900.

LEYBOURNE, L. (Mrs.), Special War Worker.
During the war this lady gave up her household duties in order to undertake work of national importance. At first she was employed at Messrs. Maycock's, Willesden, where she remained for two years. Later she went to the Willesden Co-operative Society, and after a period there, was engaged on important duties for nearly a year at the Cricklewood Post Office.   She gave valuable service throughout the war.
25, Belton Road, Cricklewood, N.W.2   16593A.

LIDDARD, F. C., Pte., The Queen's (Royal West Surrey Regiment).
He volunteered in September 1914, and during his service on the Western Front took part in several engagements, including the battles of Ypres, Loos and the Somme. He was demobilised in May 1919, holding the 1914-15 Star, General Service and Victory Medals.
65, Grove Street, Upper Edmonton, N.18   X17888B.

LIDDIARD, C., Pte., 3rd Middlesex Regiment.
He volunteered in June 1915, and early in the following year was sent to the Western Front, where he took part in the battles of the Somme, Vimy Ridge and Ypres. After completing nearly three years' service overseas he returned to England, and in December 1919 was demobilised.   He holds the General Service and Victory Medals.
77, Portnall Road, Maida Hill, W.9   X19511.

LIDDIARD, C., Sapper, R.E., and Pte., Northumberland Fusiliers.
He joined in July 1916, and was drafted six months later to the Western Front, where he took part in several engagements. Owing to a wound which he received at Arras in June 1917 he was invalided to England, and was retained on special duties, being unfit for further active service. He was demobilised in May 1919, and holds the General Service and Victory Medals.
49, Carlyle Avenue, Willesden, N.W.10   14194B.

LIDDIARD, P. C., Leading Seaman, Royal Navy.
He volunteered in August 1914, and served on board H.M. " Monitor 17," with which he took part in the naval operations in the Dardanelles. He was also engaged with his ship on important duties in the Mediterranean and Russian waters, and off the coast of German East Africa. He holds the 1914 Star, General Service and Victory Medals, and in 1920 was still serving.
49, Carlyle Avenue, Willesden, N.W.10   14194A.

LIDDIARD, S. A. G., Rflmn., 5th Rifle Brigade.
Volunteering in May 1915, he was sent to France on completion of his training in the following April. While on the Western Front he took part in many important engagements, and was twice wounded whilst in action on the Somme. In February 1919 he was demobilised, holding the General Service and Victory Medals.
49, Disraeli Road, Acton Lane, N.W.10   14151.

LIFFORD, E., Sergt., 1st King's (Liverpool) Regt.
He had previously served in India for seven years and was mobilised on the outbreak of hostilities. He was soon drafted to the Western Front, where he went through the retreat from Mons and many of the important engagements which followed, including the battles of Festubert and Loos. In 1916 he received a severe wound which necessitated his return to England, and in June of the same year was invalided out of the Service.
He holds the Mons Star, General Service and Victory Medals.
7, Barclay Road, Walham Green, S.W.6   X19711.

LIGGITT, G. H., Pte., Middlesex Regiment and Lancashire Fusiliers.
Joining in September 1916, he was sent to Salonica on the completion of his training. After taking part in important operations on the Balkan Front he was drafted to France, where he took part in heavy fighting on many sectors, and in the Retreat and Advance of 1918.
He was demobilised in 1919, holding the General Service and Victory Medals.
64, Earlsmead Road, College Park, N.W.10   X17612A.

LIGGITT, G. J., Pte., East Surrey Regiment.
He joined in 1918, and after completing his training was engaged on special duties with his regiment. He gave valuable services, but was not successful in obtaining his transfer overseas before the cessation of hostilities. He was demobilised in 1919.
64, Earlsmead Road, College Park, N.W.10   X17162B.

LIGHT, A. B., Rifleman, 12th Rifle Brigade.
He joined in October 1917, and in the following April was drafted overseas. While in the Western Front he took part in many important engagements, and after the signing of the Armistice remained in Belgium until February 1920, when he returned to England and was demobilised.
He holds the General Service and Victory Medals.
145, Purves Road, Kensal Rise, N.W.10   X18410.

LIGHT, A. R., Sergt., R.A.S.C.
Volunteering in March 1915, he was soon drafted overseas, and while on the Western Front took part in many important engagements, and was wounded near Cambrai. He remained in France until March 1920, when he returned to England and was demobilised, holding the 1914-15 Star, General Service and Victory Medals.
70, Laundry Road, Hammersmith, W.6   15056.

LIGHT, E., Pte., Labour Corps.
He joined in July 1918, and after being drafted to the Western Front in the same month, served with the Labour Corps, first in Belgium and then at Cambrai, where he did much useful work during the Advance of 1918.
In March of the following year he was demobilised, holding the General Service and Victory Medals.
35, Furness Road, Fulham, S.W.6   X21136A.

LIGHT, E. L. (Mrs.), Special War Worker.
In December 1915, this lady offered her services at St. Mark's Military Hospital (2nd London General), and was employed for 2½ years as a ward maid. Throughout this period she rendered careful and willing services, which terminated in June 1918.
35, Furness Road, Fulham, S.W.6   X21136B.

LILLEY, E., Sapper, Royal Engineers.
He volunteered in September 1914, and on completion of his training was sent to France early in 1916. While on the Western Front he was engaged on special duties of an important nature, and was working at a large ammunition dump behind the line when it was blown up in May 1918.
He remained in France until February 1919, when he returned to England and was demobilised, holding the General Service and Victory Medals.
26, Cobbold Road, Church End, N.W.10   16071.

LINCOLN, F. A. W., Sergt., Royal Welch Fus.
He volunteered in November 1914, and in the following year was sent to France. After taking a prominent part in the battles of the Somme, Vimy Ridge, Bullecourt and Ypres, he was drafted to the Italian theatre of war, where he again took part in heavy fighting. During his service he was twice wounded, and was in hospital in France and England for several months.
He was demobilised in March 1919, and holds the 1914-15 Star, General Service and Victory Medals.
15, Headcorn Road, Tottenham, N.17   X18491.

LINDFIELD, A. A. E., Pte., Royal Fusiliers.
Volunteering in November 1914, he was drafted to the Western Front in the following year. He took part in several important battles, including that of Bullecourt, and whilst in action on the Somme in 1916 was seriously wounded, in consequence of which he was sent to England. After a protracted illness he was invalided out of the Service, holding the 1914-15 Star, General Service and Victory Medals.
59, Earlsmead Road, College Park, N.W.10   X17837B.

LINDFIELD, W. G. F., 2nd Air Mechanic, R.A.F.

He joined in June 1917, and on completion of his training was drafted to the Western Front, where he was engaged in the Royal Air Force workshops on special duties which demanded a high degree of technical skill. He was also present at several engagements, and later saw service in Russia. In 1919 he returned to England and was still serving in 1920.

He holds the General Service and Victory Medals.

59, Earlsmead Road, College Park, N.W.10 X17837A.

LINDSEY, E., Cpl., Oxfordshire and Buckinghamshire Light Infantry.

Called from the Reserve in August 1914, he was shortly afterwards drafted to the Western Front, where he went through the memorable retreat from Mons. He also took part in many of the engagements which followed, including the battles of Ypres and the Somme, was wounded, and also suffered from shell-shock.

He returned to England in 1919 when he was demobilised, holding the Mons Star, General Service and Victory Medals.

11, Shotley Street, Hammersmith, W.6 14796A.

LINDSEY, W., Sapper, Royal Engineers.

As he was serving in the Army at the outbreak of war, he was sent almost immediately to France, where he took part in the retreat from Mons and the battles of the Somme and Ypres. On one occasion he was seriously injured by an explosion, and was kept in hospital for some weeks.

After serving in France for nearly five years, he was demobilised in 1919, holding the Mons Star, General Service and Victory Medals.

11, Shotley Street, Hammersmith, W.6 14796B.

LINE, A. E., Pte., Northamptonshire Regiment.

He joined in March 1916, and shortly afterwards was drafted to the Western Front, where he served for three years. During this time he took part in many of the principal engagements, including the battles of Ypres, Arras and Cambrai, and in 1919 returned to England, where he was demobilised.

He holds the General Service and Victory Medals.

27, Melville Road, Stonebridge Park, N.W.10 14623B.

LINE, J. A., Pte., Middlesex Regiment.

Volunteering in February 1915, he was shortly afterwards drafted to the Western Front, where he served for nearly four years. He took part in many of the principal engagements, including those at Ypres and on the Somme, where in 1916 he saw some very heavy fighting.

He returned to England in 1919 when he was demobilised, holding the General Service and Victory Medals.

6, Lichfield Road, Lower Edmonton, N.9 14668.

LINES, A., Pte., Labour Corps.

Volunteering in January 1915, he was shortly afterwards drafted to the Western Front, where he was present at several battles, including those of Ypres and the Somme. Later he was sent to Egypt, and thence to Macedonia, where he did useful work with the Labour Corps on various Fronts.

He returned to England in 1919 when he was demobilised, holding the 1914-15 Star, General Service and Victory Medals.

3, Cornwallis Road, Lower Edmonton, N.9 13285.

LINES, A. E., Pte., 18th (Queen Mary's Own) Hussars.

He joined in February 1917, and during his service on the Western Front, took part in several engagements, including those of Arras and Cambrai. After serving overseas for about two years he was demobilised in November 1919, and holds the General Service and Victory Medals.

66, Clarendon Street, Paddington, W.2 X20357.

LINES, C. P., 1st Class Petty Officer, R.N.

He volunteered in January 1915, and after a short period of training was posted to H.M.S. "Phaeton." He was on board this vessel with the British warships, when their gunfire brought down the Zeppelin "L.7" off Schleswig, on May 4th, 1916, and also during the battle of Jutland on May 31st of the same year. He had previously taken part in naval operations at the Dardanelles, and also saw service with the Grand Fleet in the North Sea, later being transferred to H.M.S. "Calypso."

He was demobilised in 1919, holding the 1914-15 Star, General Service and Victory Medals.

97, Bravington Road, Maida Hill, W.9 X19330.

LINES, F. R., Leading Aircraftsman, R.A.F.

He volunteered in December 1915, and after his training served with his unit on important duties which called for great technical skill. He gave valuable services, but was not successful in obtaining his transfer overseas before the cessation of hostilities.

He was demobilised in March 1919.

14, Queen's Avenue, Muswell Hill, N.10 B2167.

LINES, W. S., Cpl., Royal Fusiliers.

He joined in November 1916, and having received training at various stations was drafted to the Western Front. Until the cessation of hostilities, except for a few weeks when he was confined to hospital through ill-health, he was in almost continuous action, and among the battles in which he took part are those of Ypres and the Somme.

He returned to England in 1919 and was demobilised, holding the General Service and Victory Medals.

69, Garvan Road, Hammersmith, W.6 14827.

LINES, W. S., Lce. Cpl., East Surrey Regiment

He volunteered for service in August 1914, and soon afterwards proceeded to the Western Front, where he was in action in many important engagements, including those of the Marne and the Aisne. He was severely wounded at Hill 60 in July 1916, and lost a leg in consequence.

In the following September he was discharged as medically unfit, and holds the 1914 Star, General Service and Victory Medals.

66, Clarendon Street, Paddington, W.2 X20675.

LINFORD, A., Pte., Irish Guards.

Volunteering in 1914, he received his training at various stations in England, and in the following year was drafted to Gallipoli, where during that memorable campaign, he was killed in action in August 1915.

He was entitled to the 1914-15 Star, General Service and Victory Medals.

94, Montague Road, Lower Edmonton, N.9 16878A.

LINFORD, G. H., Pte., Grenadier Guards.

He volunteered in 1915, and shortly afterwards was drafted to the Western Front, where after taking part in much of the heavy fighting in various sectors he was killed by a shell on September 16th, 1916.

He was entitled to the 1914-15 Star, General Service and Victory Medals.

94, Montague Road, Lower Edmonton, N.9 16878B.

LINFORD, T. C., Pte., R.A.S.C.

He joined in 1916, and after a short period of training was drafted to the Western Front. Whilst overseas he was present at many important engagements, including that at Ypres, where he was wounded, and the Retreat and Advance of 1918.

He was demobilised in 1919, holding the General Service and Victory Medals.

84, Willow Vale, Shepherd's Bush, W.12 12057.

LINFORD, W. G., Pte., R.A.S.C.

He joined in February 1918, and after a period of training was drafted to Salonica, where he did excellent work with the Royal Army Service Corps, and also with the Military Foot Police.

He returned to England in 1919 and was demobilised in April, holding the General Service and Victory Medals.

73, Chippenham Road, Maida Hill, W.9 X21090.

LING, A. E., Sergt., South Wales Borderers.

Volunteering in August 1914, he was shortly afterwards drafted to the Western Front, and first went into action at La Bassée in October of the same year. Afterwards he took part in many other battles, including those of Ypres, the Somme, Arras and Cambrai, and was killed in October 1918, during the last Advance.

He had been on active service for four years, and was entitled to the 1914 Star, General Service and Victory Medals.

47, Windsor Road, Cricklewood, N.W.2 X17387A.

LING, A. W., Cpl., Royal Berkshire Regiment.

He volunteered in September 1914, and after training was drafted to the Western Front, where he took part in several engagements, and was wounded in action on the Somme in July 1916.

He was demobilised in April 1919, holding the General Service and Victory Medals.

98, Felixstowe Road, Lower Edmonton, N.9 15374.

LING, W., Pte., London Regiment (Royal Fusiliers) and R.A.S.C.

He volunteered for service in February 1915, and having received training at various stations in England, was drafted to the Western Front. He took part in several engagements, including the battle of the Somme in July 1916, but in the following year was invalided home owing to ill-health. On his recovery he was transferred to the Royal Army Service Corps, and later returned to France, where he remained until the cessation of hostilities.

He was demobilised in May 1919, holding the General Service and Victory Medals.

47, Windsor Road, Cricklewood, N.W.2 17387B.

LINGWOOD, F., Sapper, Royal Engineers.

He volunteered in April 1915, and on completion of his training was drafted to the Western Front. During his service overseas he did excellent work with the Royal Engineers, and whilst in the Somme sector in July 1916 was twice severely wounded.
He was demobilised in January 1919, holding the General Service and Victory Medals.
5, Hazelbury Road, Lower Edmonton, N.9   X17496.

LINNETT, H. L. J., Pte., 6th Buffs (East Kent Regiment).

Volunteering in 1915, he was shortly afterwards drafted to the Western Front, where he died on November 21st, 1917, of wounds received in action on the previous day at Cambrai. He had taken part in many other important engagements during his service, and was entitled to the 1914-15 Star, General Service and Victory Medals.
88, Lopen Road, Upper Edmonton, N.18   X17912.

LINTORN, H., Sergt., R.A.V.C.

He volunteered in May 1915, and after training was drafted to the Western Front, where, attached to the Royal Field Artillery, he rendered valuable services in connection with the sick and wounded horses.
He was demobilised in June 1919, holding the 1914-15 Star, General Service and Victory Medals.
40, Tasso Road, Hammersmith, W.6   14652.

LINWOOD, G. W., Pte., Middlesex Regiment.

Volunteering in August 1914, he was sent on completion of his training to the Western Front, where he was wounded during the second battle of Ypres. From 1916 until 1918 he saw service in Salonica, taking part in the fighting in various sectors.
He was demobilised in February 1919, holding the 1914-15 Star, General Service and Victory Medals.
186, Brettenham Road, Upper Edmonton, N.18   15219.

LINWOOD, H. E., Pte., 1st Queen's Own (Royal West Kent Regiment).

Joining in October 1916, he completed his training in England, and a year later was drafted to India. He served for two years on garrison duty, and in 1919 he returned to England, where early in the following year he was demobilised.
He holds the General Service and Victory Medals.
13, St. Martin's Road, Lower Edmonton, N.9   12977.

LIPPIATT, F. J. O. (M.M.), Sergt., R.F.A.

Volunteering in August 1914, he was shortly afterwards drafted to the Western Front, where he took part in many important engagements.
He was awarded the Military Medal for conspicuous gallantry and devotion to duty in the field. He died from wounds received in action on April 1st, 1918, and was entitled to the 1914-15 Star, General Service and Victory Medals.
121, Greyhound Road, Hammersmith, W.6.   15020.

LIPSCOMBE, R. J., Cpl., Royal Engineers.

He volunteered for service in January 1915, and later in the same year was drafted to Gallipoli, where he took part with the 63rd Division in the memorable first landing at Suvla Bay. In 1916 he went to the Western Front, where he was engaged on bridge construction in the Passchendaele, Somme, Ypres, and Arras sectors.
He was demobilised in February 1919, holding the 1914-15 Star, General Service and Victory Medals.
51, Woodchester Street, Paddington, W.2   X20641.

LISTER, J., Pte., Coldstream Guards.

He was drafted to the Western Front in August 1914, and took part in the retreat from Mons. Owing to a wound which he received in the battle of the Marne he was invalided home, but on his recovery returned in 1915 to France, where he was in action at Ypres and Loos. Later he was again invalided to England, and was eventually discharged in April 1916, holding the Mons Star, the General Service and Victory Medals.
47, Sandilands Road, Wandsworth Bridge Road, S.W.6
                                                        X20504.

LITCHFIELD, H., Staff Sergt., R.A.S.C.

He volunteered in August 1914, and after his training was drafted to the Western Front for a year. From 1915 until 1918 he saw service in Salonica, where he did excellent work with the Royal Army Service Corps, and saw active service on various sectors. Afterwards he was sent to Russia, remaining there until 1919, when he returned to England and was demobilised.
He holds the 1914 Star, General Service and Victory Medals.
116, Church Road, Tottenham, N.17   X18141.

LITTLE, B. M. (Miss), Special War Worker.

When on the outbreak of hostilities a national call for war workers was made, this lady volunteered, and was subsequently engaged at the munition works of Messrs. Blake, Stevenage Road, Fulham. Her work, besides being very difficult, was of a dangerous character, but throughout her service she carried out her duties in a manner which won for her high commendation.
34, Ancill Street, Hammersmith, W.6   13987B.

LITTLE, E., Sapper, Royal Engineers.

He volunteered in April 1915, and in the following year was sent to Egypt, whence he was drafted shortly after to France. He took part in many of the principal engagements, including the battle of Ypres (during which he was wounded and gassed), and the Retreat and Advance of 1918. After the cessation of hostilities he went with the Army of Occupation to Germany, where he remained until 1919, when he returned to England and was demobilised.
He holds the General Service and Victory Medals.
100, Portnall Road, Maida Hill, W.9   X19537.

LITTLE, G., Lce. Cpl., 12th Middlesex Regt.

He volunteered in August 1914, and was later drafted to the Western Front, where, after taking part in many important battles, he was killed in action at Carnoy, near Albert.
He was entitled to the 1914-15 Star, General Service and Victory Medals.
47, Adeney Road, Hammersmith, W.6   14164.

LITTLE, J. T., Pte., 2nd King's Shropshire L.I.

He volunteered in August 1914, and after taking part in several battles on the Western Front, including those of Ypres, Neuve Chapelle and Hill 60, was sent to Salonica. Later he was drafted to Russia, and then returned to Salonica. He holds the 1914 Star, General Service and Victory Medals, and was demobilised in June 1919.
34, Ancill Street, Hammersmith, W.6   13987A.

LITTLE, S., Pte., East Surrey Regiment.

He volunteered in September 1914, and after training was drafted to the Western Front, where he saw much heavy fighting prior to being severely wounded on the Somme in June 1916. He returned to England, and in May 1917, owing to his wound, was invalided out of the Service.
He holds the 1914-15 Star, General Service and Victory Medals.
64, Beaconsfield Road, Lower Edmonton, N.9   14566.

LIVERMORE, A., Pte., Middlesex Regiment.

He volunteered in July 1915, and after his training was drafted to the Western Front, where he took part in several important battles, and in 1916 was seriously wounded. He was in consequence invalided home, and on being found medically unfit was discharged from the Service in March 1918. He holds the 1914-15 Star, General Service and Victory Medals. 56, Dyson's Road, Upper Edmonton, N.18   16771.

LIVERMORE, W., Cpl., 9th Middlesex Regt.

He volunteered in May 1915, and after training served with the Royal Defence Corps and the Nottinghamshire Hussars. He was engaged on work in connection with horses, and gave valuable services, but was not successful in obtaining his transfer overseas before the termination of the war.
He was demobilised in March 1919.
2, Brett Road, Stonebridge Park, N.W.10   14383.

LLOYD, F., Cpl., R.A.F. (late R.N.A.S.)

He joined in 1916, and during his service was engaged with the R.N.A.S. at Dunkirk on special duties, which demanded a high degree of technical skill.
He was demobilised in January 1919, holding the General Service and Victory Medals.
56, Roseberry Road, Lower Edmonton, N.9   14346B.

LLOYD, F. V., Pte., Royal Sussex Regiment.

He joined in May 1918, and after his training was drafted to Germany with the Army of Occupation. He was engaged on special duties whilst overseas, and returned to England in 1920, when he was demobilised.
56, Roseberry Road, Lower Edmonton, N.9   14346A.

LLOYD, H. L., Driver, Royal Army Service Corps.

Volunteering in January 1915, he was shortly afterwards drafted to the Western Front. His service overseas lasted for four years, during which time he did useful work with the 185th Tunnelling Company attached to the Royal Engineers, and in this way saw action in various sectors.
49, Denzil Road, Neasden Lane, N.W.10   16130.

LLOYD, W. J., Pte., 5th Essex Regiment.

Volunteering in June 1915, he was shortly afterwards drafted to Egypt, and took part in the fighting in Palestine. He also saw service in Mesopotamia before returning to England in 1919, when he was demobilised, holding the General Service and Victory Medals.
15, Aberdeen Road, Upper Edmonton, N.18   16590.

LOADER, E. M., Pte., 8th Middlesex Regiment.
He volunteered at the age of 16 in February 1915, and after receiving training at various stations was drafted to the Western Front. His service overseas lasted for three years, during which time he took part in the fighting in many important sectors, and also went through the Retreat of 1918, during which he was severely wounded. He returned to England, and in June 1918 was invalided out of the Service in consequence.
He holds the 1914-15 Star, General Service and Victory Medals.
116, Felix Road, West Ealing, W.13   11023C.

LOADER, J. H., Pte., 8th Middlesex Regiment.
He volunteered in February 1915, and shortly afterwards was drafted to the Western Front. Whilst overseas he took part in many of the principal engagements, but in 1918 was so seriously wounded as to necessitate his removal to a hospital in Cardiff, where, on April 28th of the same year, he died of wounds.
He was entitled to the 1914-15 Star, General Service and Victory Medals.
116, Felix Road, West Ealing, W.13   11023B.

LOADER, W. J., Sapper, Royal Engineers.
Volunteering in September 1915, he was drafted to the Western Front on completion of his training. Whilst overseas he was engaged in many important sectors, including the Ypres salient, and throughout his service did excellent work with the Royal Engineers. He returned to England and was demobilised in February 1919, holding the 1914-15 Star, General Service and Victory Medals.
11, Walbrook Road, Lower Edmonton, N.9   13084.

LOADER, W. L., Pte., 10th Middlesex Regt.
He volunteered in February 1915, and in the following year was sent to India, where he served on special garrison duty until 1919, when he returned to England and was demobilised.
He holds the General Service and Victory Medals.
116, Felix Road, West Ealing, W.13   11023A.

LOBB, W. H. J., Cpl., Royal Army Medical Corps.
Volunteering in October 1914, he was drafted in the following year to the Western Front, where he did useful work with the Royal Army Medical Corps, frequently being under fire. On May 28, 1918, when carrying out his duties as stretcher-bearer at Bapaume, he was killed. His service in France lasted for nearly three years, and he was entitled to the 1914-15 Star, General Service and Victory Medals.
37, Star Road, West Kensington, W.14   16684.

LOBBAN, J., Pte., Machine Gun Corps.
He joined in February 1917, and in October of the same year was sent to France, where he remained until September 1918. He was in action at Passchendaele, St. Quentin and Albert, and was wounded at the latter place on August 8th, 1918.
He was demobilised in February 1919, holding the General Service and Victory Medals.
8, Minet Avenue, Willesden, N.W.10   13907.

LOCK, V. N., Pte., Middlesex Regiment.
He joined in 1916, and after training was engaged on garrison and other special duties at various stations with his unit. He gave valuable services, but was not successful in securing his transfer overseas before the termination of the war.
He was demobilised in 1919.
59, Asplin Road, Tottenham, N.17   X18822.

LOCKE, W. W., Pte., 2nd Middlesex Regiment.
An ex-soldier, he volunteered for further service in August 1914, and shortly afterwards was drafted to the Western Front. He took part in the retreat from Mons and many of the battles which followed, including that of Hill 60, and was killed in action on May 11th, 1915.
He was entitled to the Mons Star, General Service and Victory Medals.
44, Gloucester Road, Upper Edmonton, N.18   X17011.

LOCKLEY, G. C., Sergt. Farrier, R.A.S.C. (H.T.)
Mobilised in August 1914, he was drafted to the Western Front in the following year, and later to Salonica. His service overseas lasted for four years, during which time he did excellent work in the capacity of farrier with the Royal Army Service Corps, and saw service in many sectors. He was wounded and gassed, and whilst in the East contracted a severe form of malaria.
In 1919 he returned to England, where he was demobilised, holding the 1914-15 Star, the General Service and Victory Medals.
9, Shotley Street, Hammersmith, W.6   14799A.

LOCKLEY, W. G., Gunner, R.F.A.
Joining in 1915, he was shortly afterwards drafted to the Western Front, where he was engaged on various special duties in connection with the horses. In 1916 he returned to England in consequence of ill-health, and after a protracted illness in hospital at Cambridge was invalided out of the Service in the following year.
He holds the 1914-15 Star, General Service and Victory Medals.   9, Shotley Street, Hammersmith, W.6   14799B.

LOCKWOOD, F. H., A.B., Royal Navy.
Volunteering in 1914, he was shortly afterwards posted to H.M.S. "Canterbury," in which he served with distinction with the Grand Fleet throughout the war.
He was demobilised in March 1919, holding the 1914-15 Star, General Service and Victory Medals.
37, Beaufoy Road, Tottenham, N.17   X18002.

LOCKWOOD, J. G., Cpl., R.A.S.C.
He volunteered in November 1914, and after his training was under orders for service at the Dardanelles. Whilst on his voyage to the East his ship, the "Royal Edward," was torpedoed in the Ægean Sea, and he was drowned on August 13th, 1915.
He was entitled to the 1914-15 Star, General Service and Victory Medals.
164, Stephendale Road, Fulham, S.W.6   X20817.

LOCKYER, J. J., Private, Royal Fusiliers.
He volunteered in August 1914, and was shortly afterwards sent to Malta, where he was engaged on special duties, which he carried out in an efficient manner. In November 1915 he was invalided out of the Service suffering from the effects of sunstroke, and now holds the General Service and Victory Medals.
48, Brett Road, Stonebridge Park, N.W.10   15688C.

LOCKYER, W. (M.M.), Pte., 9th Middlesex Regt.
Volunteering in 1915, he was shortly afterwards drafted to the Dardanelles, where he took part in the memorable first landing at Suvla Bay, and was in continuous action for nearly a year. In 1916 he was invalided home through illness, but on recovery a few months later was sent to the Western Front, where he again took part in heavy fighting. He was awarded the Military Medal for conspicuous gallantry and devotion to duty whilst in action at Messines Wood, where he was also severely wounded while acting as runner for his battalion.
He was demobilised in March 1919, holding in addition the 1914-15 Star, General Service and Victory Medals.
48, Brett Road, Stonebridge Park, N.W.10   15688A.

LODER, T. J., Sapper, Royal Engineers.
He joined in 1917, and after his training was drafted to France. Whilst overseas he served in many sectors in various capacities, and was for a time stationed at Le Havre, where he was employed as a carpenter and joiner. He returned to England in 1919 and was demobilised, holding the General Service and Victory Medals.
36, Bravington Road, Maida Hill, W.9   X19190.

LODGE, D. W., A.B. (Torpedoman), R.N.
Volunteering in 1914, he was posted to H.M.S. "Agamemnon," in which ship he took part in the naval operations at the Dardanelles, and served with the Grand Fleet throughout the war.
He holds the 1914 Star, General Service and Victory Medals.
128, Kimberley Road, Upper Edmonton, N.18   16866.

LODGE, J. J. (M.M.), Pte., Suffolk Regiment.
He volunteered in September 1915, and in the following year went to the Western Front, where he took part in engagements at Ypres, Arras, Amiens and Bullecourt. He was awarded the Military Medal for great gallantry at Wancourt, where he was wounded. He was also wounded on two other occasions, and was in hospital for some time.
He also holds the General Service and Victory Medals, and was demobilised in March 1919.
53, Clarendon Street, Paddington, W.2   X20388.

LODGE, R., Cpl., Military Police.
He was serving when war broke out, and in 1915 was drafted to the Western Front. During his service overseas, which lasted for nearly four years, he was engaged on special duties at Arras, Amiens, Cambrai and other places, and did excellent work throughout.
He returned to England for demobilisation in July 1919, and holds the 1914-15 Star, General Service and Victory Medals.
20, Melville Road, Stonebridge Park, N.W.10   14431.

LODGE, W. J., Sapper, Royal Engineers.
Joining in 1916, he was shortly afterwards drafted to the Western Front, where he remained for three years. Throughout his service he was engaged on important duties in various battle areas, and was wounded in action. He returned to England for demobilisation in 1919, and holds the General Service and Victory Medals.
78, Montague Road, Lower Edmonton, N.9   16507.

LOFTHOUSE, F., Gunner, R.F.A.
Joining at the age of 16 in March 1915, he was sent a year
later to the Western Front, where he took part in several
important engagements, including the battles of the Somme
and Ypres. Whilst on service he was gassed, and during
the Advance of 1918 he was very badly wounded on
November 2nd, dying four days later.
He was entitled to the General Service and Victory Medals.
65, Coomer Road, Fulham, S.W.6   16441B.

LOFTHOUSE, J. H., Pte., Middlesex Regiment.
Volunteering in August 1914 on the declaration of hostilities,
he was drafted a year later to the Western Front, where he
served with distinction in several engagements. Owing to
a wound that he received in the battle of the Somme in 1916,
he was invalided home to England, and discharged in 1917
as unfit for further service.
He holds the 1914–15 Star, General Service and Victory
Medals. 27, Beaufoy Road, Tottenham, N.17   X17941B.

LOFTHOUSE, J. J., Gunner, R.F.A.
Volunteering at the outbreak of war in August 1914, this
gunner was sent to France two years later, and rendered
valuable services. While on the Western Front he took part
in several engagements, and was present at the battles of the
Somme and Ypres.
He was demobilised in April 1919 after over two years'
service in action, and holds the General Service and Victory
Medals. 27, Beaufoy Road, Tottenham, N.17   X17941A.

LOFTHOUSE, J. T., Cpl., R.A.S.C. (M.T.)
Volunteering in April 1915, he was drafted in the following
year to the Western Front, where he was engaged in conveying food and ammunition supplies up to the lines. Throughout his service, which lasted for three years, he did excellent
work with his unit, and in 1919 returned to England, where
he was demobilised.
He holds the General Service and Victory Medals.
65, Coomer Road, Fulham, S.W.6   16441C.

LOFTHOUSE, W., Gunner, R.G.A.
This gunner volunteered in November 1915, and was drafted
to the Western Front, where he took part in several engagements, including the battles of the Somme and Ypres, and
was gassed. Later he served for a short period in Ireland,
and in January 1919 was demobilised, holding the General
Service and Victory Medals.
65, Coomer Road, Fulham, S.W.6   16441A.

LOGUE, H. P., Cpl., Royal Field Artillery.
Volunteering in December 1914, he was drafted to the
Western Front in the following July. He took part in many
of the principal engagements, including the battles of Ypres,
Neuve Chapelle and Cambrai, and throughout his service,
which lasted for four years, did good work with his unit.
In March 1919 he returned to England for demobilisation,
and holds the 1914–15 Star, General Service and Victory
Medals.
1, Alric Avenue, Stonebridge Park, N.W.10   14611.

**LONERGAN, T., Leading Seaman, R.N., H.M.S.
"Repulse."**
He was called up in August 1914, after having previously
served for 15 years in the Navy, and was engaged through-
out the war in the drifter section in Italian waters and off the
coast of Belgium.
He was demobilised in January 1919, and holds the South
African and China Medals, the 1914–15 Star, the Naval
General Service Medal (with Persian Gulf clasp), and the
General Service and Victory Medals.
10, Rowallan Road, Munster Road, S.W.6   TX19266.

LONG, D., Pte., Middlesex Regiment.
Joining in 1915, he was shortly afterwards drafted to the
Western Front, where he took part in the battles of Hill 60,
Ypres, the Somme and Passchendaele. His service overseas
lasted until March 1917, when he was reported missing.
He was entitled to the 1914–15 Star, General Service and
Victory Medals.
4, Garnet Road, Willesden, N.W.10   15572B.

LONG, J., Pte., Grenadier Guards.
Joining in 1917, he was soon drafted to the Western Front,
where he served until the cessation of hostilities. He was
sent with the Army of Occupation to Germany, but returned
to England for demobilisation in 1919, and holds the General
Service and Victory Medals.
4, Garnet Road, Willesden, N.W.10   15572C.

LONG, P., Rifleman, King's Royal Rifle Corps.
He joined in January 1917, and after completing his training
was drafted to the Western Front, where he played a distinguished part in engagements at Arras, Vimy Ridge, Bullecourt, Ypres, Bapaume and Cambrai. After serving in the
Army for two years, he was demobilised in January 1919,
and holds the General Service and Victory Medals.
6, Oakbury Road, Fulham, S.W.6   X20933.

LONG, R., Pte., 4th Leicestershire Regiment.
Joining in January 1916, he was drafted to France on completion of his training, and took part in many engagements,
including those on the Somme, at Arras, Cambrai and Ypres,
where he was severely wounded. On recovery he again went
into action, taking part in the Advance of 1918.
In the following year he was invalided home through illness,
and when he recovered was demobilised, holding the General
Service and Victory Medals.
52, Stanley Road, King's Road, S.W.6   X19801.

LONG, W., Sergt., Suffolk Regiment.
With a previous record of 21 years' service, he volunteered in
September 1914, and until May of the following year, when
he was drafted to France, did excellent work as a drill
instructor. Whilst overseas he was in charge of a machine-
gun section at Loos, where he was wounded, and also took
part in the trench warfare at Ploegsteert.
He holds the 1914–15 Star, General Service and Victory
Medals, and was demobilised in March 1919.
122, Fernhead Road, Maida Hill, W.9   X18831.

**LONGHURST, J. F. (M.M.), Cpl., 4th (Queen's
Own) Hussars and Royal Irish Rifles.**
He volunteered in 1914, and after being sent to the Western
Front, took part in the retreat from Mons and the battles of
the Marne, the Aisne, Ypres and Cambrai. For conspicuous gallantry in capturing an enemy machine-gun he
was awarded the Military Medal, and in addition holds the
Mons Star, General Service and Victory Medals. He was
twice wounded during his service, and was demobilised in
November 1918.
415, Chapter Road, Cricklewood, N.W.2   16161.

LONGHURST, S. A., Pte., 7th London Regt.
He joined in October 1916, and in the same year was drafted
to the Western Front. While in action on the Somme
he was wounded, and after being in hospital for some months
was discharged in September 1918 as medically unfit for
further service owing to his wound.
He holds the General Service and Victory Medals.
6, Harwood Terrace, Walham Green, S.W.6   X19860.

LONGLEY, F. C., Rifleman, 18th London Regt.
He volunteered in August 1914, and in the following year
was sent to the Western Front, where he took part in many
important engagements, including the battle of the Somme.
Later in 1916 he was drafted to Mesopotamia, but on
December 3rd, 1917, was killed in action.
He was entitled to the 1914–15 Star, General Service and
Victory Medals.
39, Brookville Road, Dawes Road, S.W.6   X20422.

LONGMAN, E., Pte., Royal Fusiliers.
Having joined in July 1916, he was sent to East Africa in the
following year, and after seeing service was drafted to
France in April 1918. He took part in various engagements
whilst on the Western Front, including the battles of the
Somme, Cambrai and the Advance of 1918. After the cessation of hostilities he was drafted to India, but was sent home
and demobilised in January 1920.
He holds the General Service and Victory Medals.
165, Rucklidge Avenue, Harlesden, N.W.10   T13734B.

LONGMAN, F., Pte., R.A.V.C.
He joined in June 1916, and in the same year was sent to
France, where he was engaged on special duties caring for
sick and wounded horses. He also served with the Army of
Occupation on the Rhine, until in April 1919 he returned to
England and was demobilised, holding the General Service
and Victory Medals.
165, Rucklidge Avenue, Harlesden, N.W.10   T13734A.

LONGMAN, S. A., Bombardier, R.F.A.
Joining in April 1915, he was shortly afterwards drafted to
the Western Front, where he took part in many engagements,
including the battles of the Somme, Messines, Ypres,
Cambrai, and the Retreat and Advance of 1918.
He holds the 1914–15 Star, General Service and Victory
Medals, and was demobilised in July 1919.
165, Rucklidge Avenue, Harlesden, N.W.10
                                          T13734C.

LONGMAN, W., Pte., 17th Royal Fusiliers.
He volunteered in June 1915, and served first on Home
defence in Scotland, and afterwards on the Western Front.
After eight months' service overseas he was invalided home
and was discharged through ill-health in February 1918.
He holds the General Service and Victory Medals.
27, Goodwin Road, Lower Edmonton, N.9   13002.

LONGSHAW, E. W., Pte., 2nd Royal Fusiliers.

He enlisted in October 1908, and in April 1915 was sent to the Dardanelles, where he was wounded in action. Later he served on the Western Front, and after being again wounded, was discharged in October 1916.
He holds the 1914–15 Star, General Service and Victory Medals.
50, St. John's Avenue, Harlesden, N.W.10   13391.

LONNON, F., Lce.-Cpl., Royal Engineers.

He volunteered in August 1914, at the outbreak of war, and during over five years' service on the Western Front took part in several engagements and was seriously wounded. After the cessation of hostilities he returned to England, and in February 1920 was demobilised, holding the 1914 Star, General Service and Victory Medals.
9, Musard Road, Hammersmith, W.6   15737.

LOONEY, G. (Mrs.), Special War Worker.

During the war this lady was engaged as an overlooker in the cartridge and shell departments at Woolwich Arsenal. Her duties were of an extremely important nature, and she was responsible for the training and work of the large number of women under her charge. She rendered valuable services throughout, for which she was highly commended.
4, Chesson Road, West Kensington, W.14   16207B.

LOONEY, W. B., Special War Worker.

During the war he was employed at Woolwich Arsenal as a driver of Red Cross ambulances. Whilst air raids were in progress he rendered invaluable services to those injured by hostile air-craft and also gave help to people who met with accidents at the Arsenal.
4, Chesson Road, West Kensington, W.14   16207A.

LOREY, G. C., Pte., Bedfordshire Regiment.

He joined in January 1916, and on completion of his training was engaged on important duties at various stations. Owing to physical unfitness he was not successful in obtaining his transfer overseas, but gave valuable services before being discharged in July 1918 as unfit.
10, Bull Lane, Upper Edmonton, N.18   X17883.

LOUCH, T. W., Pte., 1st Middlesex Regiment.

Pte Louch volunteered in July 1915, and in the following April was sent to the Western Front. After taking part in several engagements he was killed in action at the battle of the Somme on July 15th, 1916.
He was entitled to the General Service and Victory Medals.
22, Aintree Street, Dawes Road, S.W.6   TX18628.

LOVE, T. (D.C.M.), Lance-Sergt., 1st Devonshire Regiment.

He volunteered in August 1914, and quickly crossed to the Western Front, where for over two years he saw much heavy fighting. He took part in the battles of the Aisne, La Bassée, the first and second battles of Ypres, and Festubert, and was wounded at Delville Wood in July 1916, and again near Triangular Wood two months later.
He was awarded the D.C.M. for great bravery and devotion to duty, and in addition holds the 1914 Star, General Service and Victory Medals. He was discharged in October 1917.
17, Hazlebury Road, Fulham, S.W.6   X20493.

LOVEDAY, A., Lce.-Cpl., Rifle Brigade.

He was in the Army when war broke out, and shortly afterwards was drafted to the Western Front. His service overseas lasted for nearly five years, during which time he took part in many important engagements, including those in the Ypres salient.
He returned to England for demobilisation in January 1919, and holds the 1914 Star, General Service and Victory Medals.
46, Cobbold Road, Willesden, N.W.10   16133.

LOVEDAY, A. W., Gunner, R.F.A.

He joined in June 1916, and was shortly after sent to the Western Front, where he played a distinguished part on several sectors. Owing to a severe wound he was in hospital for a considerable time at Etaples and in England. Later he served in the Army of Occupation on the Rhine until May 1919, when he was demobilised
He holds the General Service and Victory Medals.
18, Rosaline Road, Munster Road, S.W.6   X18176.

LOVEGROVE, A., Sapper, Royal Engineers.

Volunteering in April 1915, this Sapper was drafted to the Western Front, and took part in several engagements, including those at Armentières, Loos, Amiens and Bullecourt. Later he saw service on the Italian Front.
In July 1919 he was sent home to England and demobilised, holding the 1914–15 Star, General Service and Victory Medals.
17, Humbolt Road, Hammersmith, W.6   15305.

LOVEGROVE, A. E., Cpl., 16th London Regt. (Queen's Westminster Rifles).

He joined the Army in November 1916, and after a brief period of training was drafted to the Western Front, where he was present at several engagements. While overseas he was seriously wounded, and in June 1918 was discharged as unfit.
He holds the General Service and Victory Medals.
47, Chaldon Road, Dawes Road, S W.6   X17652.

LOVEGROVE, H. W., Cpl., R.F.A.

Volunteering in August 1914, at the outbreak of hostilities, he was sent to the Western Front, where he took part in the retreat from Mons and the battles of Neuve Chapelle and Arras. After being wounded in February 1915, and in hospital in England for some time, he again returned to France, but was killed on July 21st, 1916, during the battle of the Somme
He was entitled to the Mons Star, General Service and Victory Medals.
93, Carlyle Avenue, Willesden, N.W.10   13816.

LOVELAND, W. G., Pte., R.A.S.C. (M.T.)

He volunteered in April 1915, and was sent out to France, where he was employed with the motor transport, conveying troops to and from the trenches.
He saw service on many sectors of the Western Front, and was demobilised in June 1919, holding the 1914–15 Star, General Service and Victory Medals.
241a, Kilburn Lane, North Kensington, N.W.10   X18742.

LOVELL, A. W. J., Sergt., 12th Middlesex Regt.

Volunteering at the outbreak of war, he was sent to the Western Front at an early date, and took part in several engagements. During the battle of the Somme he was severely wounded, and died on July 16th, 1916.
He was entitled to the General Service and Victory Medals.
31, Purcell Crescent, Fulham, S.W.6   15167.

LOVELL, J., Pte., Loyal North Lancashire Regt.

He volunteered in August 1914, and served overseas for about four years. During this period he saw fighting in France, Egypt and East Africa, and was four times wounded. In March 1919 he was demobilised, and holds the 1914–15 Star, General Service and Victory Medals.
66, Laundry Road, Hammersmith, W.6   15054.

LOVELOCK, A. J., Pte., 8th East Surrey Regt.

He joined in June 1916, and during his two years' service on the Western Front took part in the fighting at Cambrai, Albert and Arras, and in the Advance of 1918
He was demobilised in October 1919, and holds the General Service and Victory Medals.
6, Brownlow Road, Harlesden, N.W.10   14922B.

LOVELOCK, E. H., Rifleman, London Regt. (P.O. Rifles) and Pte., Grenadier Guards.

He joined in February 1918, and on completion of his training was engaged on various special duties, and also acted as a signaller. Owing to his being under age he was not successful in obtaining his transfer overseas before the cessation of hostilities, but gave valuable services before being demobilised in October 1919.
6, Brownlow Road, Willesden, N.W.10   14922A.

LOVETT, A., Pte., 26th Middlesex Regiment.

He joined in April 1916, and for over two years served in Salonica, taking part in the Balkan campaign. Afterwards he was drafted to Russia, where he remained until September 1919, when he returned to England and was demobilised.
He holds the General Service and Victory Medals.
15, Oldfield Road, Willesden, N.W.10   15753.

LOVETT, A., Pte., Royal Fusiliers.

This man volunteered in August 1914, at the outbreak of war, and was later sent to the Western Front, where he took part in several engagements, and was three times wounded.
He holds the General Service and Victory Medals, and was demobilised in March 1919.
91, Adeney Road, Hammersmith, W.6   15325B.

LOVETT, P. D., Pte., The Queen's (Royal West Surrey Regiment).

He joined in January 1918, and after his training was drafted to the Western Front, where he was killed in action on September 27th, 1918.
He was entitled to the General Service and Victory Medals.
91, Adeney Road, Hammersmith, W.6   15325A.

LOW, A. E., Pte., Machine Gun Corps.

He volunteered in August 1914, and during his service in France, which lasted from 1915 until 1918, he took part in the battles of the Somme, Arras, Lens and Cambrai, and was wounded.
He holds the 1914–15 Star, General Service and Victory Medals.   34, Westbury Road, Willesden, N.W.10   15444B

LOW, G. F., Pte., 9th Middlesex Regiment.
He volunteered in August 1914, and served on the Western Front from the following year until 1918. During this period he took part in various engagements, including the battles of the Somme, Ypres and Arras.
He holds the 1914-15 Star, General Service and Victory Medals.
34, Westbury Road, Willesden, N.W.10   15444A.

LOW, G. M. (Miss), Special War Worker.
During the war this lady was employed from November 1916 until November 1918 at a large munition works, where she performed very useful and important duties in connection with the manufacture of shells.
She rendered valuable service and received high commendation for her good work.
83, Shakespeare Avenue, Harlesden, N.W.10   13701.

LOW, W., Special War Worker.
This worker was employed from October 1914 until February 1920 at the Park Royal Munition Factory, during which time he was engaged on various duties in connection with the loading of ammunition. He did much useful work, and gave every satisfaction to his Employers.
83, Shakespeare Avenue, Harlesden, N.W.10   13699.

LOWDELL, A. E., Pte., 1st Hampshire Regt.
He joined in June 1915, and served in France for three years. He fought at Arras, La Bassée, St. Quentin and the Somme, and was three times wounded.
He holds the General Service and Victory Medals, and was demobilised in February 1919.
23, Monmouth Road, Lower Edmonton, N.9   12990A.

LOWDELL, G. S., Rifleman, 17th London Regt.
He joined in March 1917, and after his training was drafted overseas in the same year. During his service on the Western Front he took part in many engagements, and was wounded in action near St. Quentin during the advance in 1918.
He holds the General Service and Victory Medals, and was demobilised in October 1919.
23, Monmouth Road, Lower Edmonton, N.9   12990B.

LOWE, A. J., Pte., Durham Light Infantry.
Joining in 1916 he went to France in the same year, and took part in many battles, including the Somme, Ypres and Passchendaele. He was badly gassed, which necessitated his being in hospital for three months.
He holds the General Service and Victory Medals, and was demobilised in September 1919.
100, Estcourt Road, S.W.6   16689.

LOWE, B., Pte., 4th Middlesex Regiment.
Volunteering shortly after the outbreak of hostilities, he was sent to France, where he took part in the retreat from Mons, the battles of the Marne, the Aisne, Ypres, Loos and Lens and the Retreat and Advance of 1918. He was wounded at Hill 60, and on two other occasions.
He was demobilised in March 1919, holding the Mons Star, General Service and Victory Medals.
27, Cirencester Street, Paddington, W.2   X20764A.

LOWE, E. J., Pte., Royal Army Service Corps.
He joined in August 1914, and in the same year went to the Western Front, where he fought in the battles of the Marne and the Somme, and was badly gassed. After being in hospital at Rouen for some time he was invalided home and discharged in November 1916.
He holds the 1914 Star, General Service and Victory Medals.
46, Milton Avenue, Willesden, N.W.10   14322.

LOWE, G. A., Pte., 29th Middlesex Regiment.
He joined in September 1916, and after his training served at various stations. He rendered valuable service, but was unsuccessful in obtaining his transfer overseas before the cessation of hostilities, and was demobilised in July 1919.
9, Alston Road, Upper Edmonton, N.18   16553.

LOWE, S. (Mrs.), Special War Worker.
During the war this lady held an important position at Messrs. Blake's Munition Factory, Wood Lane. Her services in connection with the output of munitions proved of the utmost value, and on relinquishing her appointment she was presented with a certificate thanking her for her good work.
27, Cirencester Street, Paddington, W.2   X20764B.

LOWEN, G., Pte., The Queen's (Royal West Surrey Regiment).
Volunteering in August 1914, he was drafted to the Western Front, where he took part in many engagements. In 1917 he was sent to Italy, and in the next year, during his service in that theatre of war he was severely wounded during an air raid on the Piave Front. He was invalided to hospital in England, and on his recovery was demobilised in March 1919.
He holds the General Service and Victory Medals.
123, Winchester Road, Lower Edmonton, N.9   14953C.

LOWETH, C., Pte., 2nd London Regiment (Royal Fusiliers).
He volunteered in January 1915, and was drafted to the Western Front during the same year. He was actively engaged in much of the severe fighting in this theatre of war, and during the battle of Loos was severely wounded and buried by shell-fire. He was sent to hospital in England, and after his recovery was discharged in July 1916, being medically unfit for further service.
He holds the 1914-15 Star, General Service and Victory Medals.
75, College Road, Willesden, N.W.10   X18006A.

LOWETH, H., Sergt., 5th Wiltshire Regiment.
He volunteered in September 1914, and after completing his training was drafted to the Dardanelles in April 1915. He was severely wounded in the landing at Suvla Bay. Upon his recovery he was sent to France, and was wounded again in action on the Somme. He was later sent to Mesopotamia, and from there to India. In November 1919 he returned to England for demobilisation, and holds the 1914-15 Star, General Service and Victory Medals.
75, College Road, Willesden, N.W.10   18006B.

LOXTON, J. A., Pte., Royal Fusiliers.
He volunteered for service in January 1915, and was sent to France the same year During his service on the Western Front he took part in the battles of Ypres, Loos and the Somme. After the signing of the Armistice he returned to England, and was demobilised in 1919.
He holds the 1914-15 Star, General Service and Victory Medals.
107, Asplin Road, Tottenham, N.17   X19086.

LUCAS, A., Gunner, R.H.A. (O Battery).
He was called up at the outbreak of war, and served for four years on the Western Front, during which period he took part in several important engagements, and was wounded in action near Bapaume in August 1918.
He was demobilised in February 1919, holding the 1914 Star, General Service and Victory Medals
26, Leopold Road, Willesden, N.W.10   14913.

LUCAS, A., Pte., Suffolk Regiment.
He volunteered in April 1915, and went to France in the same year, serving there until 1916, when he was sent to Salonica. In 1917 he returned to France, and fought in the battles of Ypres, Arras, and the Advance of 1918. He was wounded and suffered from malaria during his service in the East. He holds the 1914-15 Star, General Service and Victory Medals, and was demobilised in September 1919.
23, Headcorn Road, Tottenham, N.17   X18267.

LUCAS, F. W., 1st-Class Stoker, R.N., H.M.S. "Bulwark."
He rejoined in August 1914, having previously served since 1902, and was stationed at Sheerness. He died on November 26th, 1914, in consequence of wounds received in an explosion which occurred on board H.M.S. "Bulwark."
He was entitled to the 1914 Star, General Service and Victory Medals.
20, Montagu Street, Hammersmith, W.6   16405.

LUCAS, L. F., Pte., Royal Fusiliers and The Queen's (Royal West Surrey Regiment).
He volunteered in December 1915, and after his training was drafted overseas in June of the following year. During his service on the Western Front he took part in the battles of the Somme, Ypres and Messines Ridge, and was wounded. He returned to England, and after his recovery was discharged as medically unfit for further service in January 1918.
He holds the General Service and Victory Medals.
71, West Ella Road, Willesden, N.W.10   15133.

LUCAS, S., Coach Repairer, British Red Cross Society.
He volunteered for service in February 1916, and was sent overseas to France, where he was engaged on special duties connected with the repairing of Red Cross wagons. He gave valuable services, and was discharged in May 1916, holding the General Service and Victory Medals
5, Haldane Road, Walham Green, S.W.6   X16990.

LUCAS, W. A., Pte., 1st Norfolk Regiment and Middlesex Regiment.
He volunteered in 1915, and was drafted to India later in the same year. He was engaged at various stations on important garrison duties. On account of malaria and eye trouble, he was sent to hospital in England, and in 1918 was eventually discharged as medically unfit for further service.
He holds the 1914-15 Star, General Service and Victory Medals.
51, Steele Road, Willesden, N.W.10   14369.

LUCK, C., Pte., 17th Middlesex Regiment.

He volunteered in May 1915, went to France in the same year, and took part in many battles, including those of Ypres, Arras, Cambrai, Givenchy, Albert, the Somme, the Marne, Delville Wood, and Armentières. He was wounded three times, and was demobilised in June 1919, holding the 1914–15 Star, General Service and Victory Medals.
2, Rainham Road, Kensal Rise, N.W.10   X18662.

LUCK, T. A., Lce.-Cpl., 12th Royal Lancers.

He volunteered in August 1914, and served for four years on the Western Front. He was in action on the Somme, at Cambrai, Arras and St. Quentin, and was wounded at Bourlon Wood on March 22nd, 1918. Upon his recovery he served with the Army of Occupation in Germany until his demobilisation in February 1919.
He holds the 1914–15 Star, General Service and Victory Medals.
12, Wesley Road, Harlesden, N.W.10   13876.

LUCK, T. H., Sapper, Royal Engineers.

He enlisted in August 1914, and in the following year was sent to the Dardanelles, where he took part in the landing at Suvla Bay with the 11th Division. Whilst there he suffered from dysentery and debility, and was in hospital for six months.
He was demobilised on April 23rd, 1919, holding the 1914–15 Star, General Service and Victory Medals.
34, Elsdon Road, Tottenham, N.17   X18499A.

LUCKETT, W. J., Pte., Royal Warwickshire Regt.

He volunteered in 1914, and after his training was sent to France in the following year. He took part in many engagements on the Western Front until 1918, when he was drafted to Egypt. He saw much service in this theatre of war until 1919, when he returned to England for demobilisation.
He holds the 1914–15 Star, General Service and Victory Medals.
2, Ladysmith Road, Upper Edmonton, N.18   16467.

LUCKHURST, F. A., Pte., R.A.O.C.

He joined in 1916, and was drafted overseas in the following year. After serving in various sectors of the Western Front he was sent to Egypt, where he was actively engaged until after the signing of the Armistice.
He was demobilised in 1919, and holds the General Service and Victory Medals.
13, Ray's Road, Upper Edmonton, N.18   15358.

LUMLEY, G. A., Pte., Somerset L.I.

He joined in July 1916, and at the conclusion of his training was drafted to the Western Front, where he served for nearly three years. During this time he took part in many important engagements, and was wounded in action.
He holds the General Service and Victory Medals, and was demobilised in March 1919.
23, Musard Road, Hammersmith, W.6   15735.

LUND, W., Pte., 17th Royal Fusiliers.

He joined in January 1918, and was sent to France in the same year. He took part in the battles of the Somme, Arras and Cambrai, where he was wounded on September 27th, 1918. He was demobilised in December 1919, holding the General Service and Victory Medals.
69, Leghorn Road, Harlesden, N.W.10   T12956B.

LUPTON, C. F., Pte., Middlesex Regiment.

He volunteered in November 1915, and was sent to India in the following July, where he was engaged on important duties with his unit. He was later drafted to Mesopotamia, and saw much fighting in this theatre of war.
He returned to England after the Armistice, and was demobilised in February 1919.
He holds the General Service and Victory Medals.
21, Villiers Road, Cricklewood, N.W.2   16726.

LURWAY, G., Pte., Tank Corps.

Volunteering in April 1915, he was drafted overseas the following year. He took part in many engagements on the Western Front, including the battles of Beaumont-Hamel, Arras, the Somme, Ypres and Cambrai. He served in the Royal Fusiliers before his transfer to the Tank Corps.
He holds the General Service and Victory Medals, and was demobilised in September 1919.
5, Shorrolds Road, Walham Green, S.W.6   X19431.

LURY, H., Cpl., R.A.S.C. (M.T.)

He volunteered in September 1914, and in the same year went to the Western Front, where he served throughout the remainder of the war, being chiefly engaged in driving motor lorries in various sectors.
After such lengthy service he was demobilised in February 1919, and holds the 1914–15 Star, General Service and Victory Medals.
33a, Althea Street, Townmead Road, Fulham, S.W.6   X21143.

LUSCOMBE, A. G., Gunner, R.F.A.

He joined in September 1914, and in the same year went to France, where he took part in many important battles, including those of Mons, the Marne and the Aisne. He was severely gassed in July 1917, and subsequently died from the effects.
He was entitled to the Mons Star, General Service and Victory Medals. 56, Fordingley Road, Maida Hill, W.9   X19670B.

LYNCH, J., Rifleman, King's Royal Rifle Corps.

He joined in August 1916, and after his training was drafted to North Russia, where he was engaged on various important duties and took part in the fighting on the Murmansk coast. He was demobilised in October 1919, and holds the General Service and Victory Medals.
11, Church Path, Hammersmith, W.6   15899.

LYNCH, T., Cpl., Royal Army Ordnance Corps.

He volunteered in January 1915, and was drafted to the Western Front, where for over two years he was engaged on special duties, which he carried out in an exemplary manner. Later he served for a year and a half in Egypt, Palestine and Syria. He contracted malaria, and after being for some time in hospital in the East he was invalided home, and in May 1919 was demobilised.
He holds the 1914–15 Star, General Service and Victory Medals. 29, Stanley Road, King's Road, S.W.6   X19873

LYNHAM, A. E., Sergt., The Queen's (Royal West Surrey Regiment).

He joined in 1916, and was sent to the Western Front in the following year. During his service in this theatre of war he took part in engagements on the Somme and at Ypres and Cambrai. He returned to England after the cessation of hostilities, and was demobilised in January 1919.
He holds the General Service and Victory Medals.
241, Chapter Road, Cricklewood, N.W.2   17206.

LYONS, G., Driver, Royal Field Artillery.

He volunteered in November 1915, and was drafted to the Western Front. During his service in this theatre of war he took part in many important engagements, and was wounded in action.
He holds the General Service and Victory Medals, and was demobilised in January 1919.
28, Delorme Street, Hammersmith, W.6   14087.

LYONS, H., Pte., Royal Fusiliers.

He was serving at the outbreak of war, and was immediately drafted to the Western Front. He took part in much of the early fighting, including the battles of La Bassée and Ypres. During the latter engagements he was severely wounded in action. He was invalided home and subsequently discharged in May 1915.
He holds the 1914 Star, General Service and Victory Medals.
39, Redfern Road, Willesden, N.W.10   13204A.

LYONS, W., Driver, Royal Army Service Corps.

Volunteering in November 1915, he was drafted overseas in the following February. During his three years' service on the Western Front he was engaged in important duties in connection with the transport of rations and ammunition.
He was demobilised in January 1919, and holds the General Service and Victory Medals.
27, College Road, Willesden, N.W.10   X18007.

M

MABERLY, J. G., Pte., 1/7th Middlesex Regt.

Volunteering in August 1914, he was sent to the Western Front in the following March, where, after taking part in the battle of Ypres and other important engagements, he was killed during the battle of the Somme on July 16th, 1916.
He was entitled to the 1914–15 Star, General Service and Victory Medals.
71, Brett Road, Stonebridge Park, N.W.10   14523.

MABLEY, F. J., Gunner, Royal Field Artillery.

He volunteered in February 1915, went to France the following year, and took part in many engagements, including those of Ypres, Cambrai, St. Quentin, La Bassée, and Armentières. Being badly gassed he was invalided home, and was demobilised in March 1919, holding the General Service and Victory Medals.
84, Wakeman Road, Kensal Rise, N.W.10   18657.

MACCABEE, H., Pte., Lancaster Regiment.

He volunteered in August 1914, and was sent to the Western Front, where he took part in many of the earlier engagements, including the retreat from Mons. He was badly wounded three times, and was discharged in consequence in July 1918 as medically unfit for further service.
He holds the Mons Star, General Service and Victory Medals.
1, Colville Road, Lower Edmonton, N.9   11994A.

MACCABEE, S. (M.M.), Rifleman, Royal Irish Rifles.

He volunteered in August 1914, and in the following year was sent to France. After taking part in many important engagements on this Front he was drafted to Egypt and from there went to Salonica. While in this seat of war he again saw much heavy fighting.
He was awarded the Military Medal for conspicuous gallantry in the field, and in addition holds the 1914-15 Star, General Service and Victory Medals. In June 1919 he was demobilised.
1, Colville Road, Lower Edmonton, N.9   11994B.

MACCABEE, T., Pte., Middlesex Regiment.

He volunteered in August 1914, and was speedily drafted to the Western Front, where he took part in the retreat from Mons and other important engagements. During his service there he was wounded twice and badly gassed. He was afterwards sent to Gibraltar, where he was engaged on special duties for some time.
He was demobilised in January 1919, and holds the Mons Star, General Service and Victory Medals.
1, Colville Road, Lower Edmonton, N.9   11994C.

MACDONALD, R., Cpl., R.F.A.

Volunteering in August 1914, he was sent in the following February to the Western Front, where he took part in the battles of Ypres, Loos, the Somme, Arras and other important engagements.
He holds the 1914-15 Star, General Service and Victory Medals, and was demobilised in April 1919.
12, Stanley Grove, Tottenham, N.17   X18301.

MACE, A. E., Driver, R.A.S.C. (M.T.)

He joined in May 1917, and during his service on the Western Front, was engaged on important duties, conveying troops and ammunition to and from the trenches.
He was demobilised in November 1919, and holds the General Service and Victory Medals.
7, Brownlow Road, Willesden, N.W.10   14930.

MACE, E. W., Pte., Gloucestershire Regiment.

He joined in April 1916, and after his training was retained on important duties with his regiment until 1917, when he was drafted to France.
He was killed in his first engagement at the battle of Ypres on August 10th, 1917.
He was entitled to the General Service and Victory Medals.
29, Humbolt Road, Hammersmith, W.6   15041.

MACEY, E., Pte., Royal Fusiliers.

He volunteered in August 1914, and was drafted to France, where he took part in the retreat from Mons and the battle of Ypres. He was severely wounded in the latter engagement, was invalided home and discharged owing to his wounds as unfit for further service in August 1915.
He holds the Mons Star, General Service and Victory Medals.
44, Raynham Road, Upper Edmonton, N.18   16940.

MACEY, H., Pte., Royal Fusiliers.

He volunteered in 1915, and later in the same year was drafted to the Western Front, where he took part in the battles of the Somme, Arras, Vimy Ridge, Cambrai and other important engagements. During his service he was gassed. He remained in France until his demobilisation in April 1919, and holds the 1914-15 Star, General Service and Victory Medals.
34a, Deacon Road, Cricklewood, N.W.2   X17113A.

MACKENZIE, M. F. (Miss), Special War Worker and Q.M.A.A.C.

Shortly after the outbreak of war this lady offered her services at Messrs. Beaton & Son's Munition Factory, where she was engaged on the manufacture of hand-grenades. Later she went to the Ailsa Craig Munition Works, Stroud Green, and was employed on the making of shells. She carried out these arduous duties in a very efficient manner. In June 1918 she enrolled in Queen Mary's Army Auxiliary Corps, and served until her discharge on compassionate grounds in the following February.
27, Archel Road, West Kensington, W.14   16208.

MACKIE, A. S., Cpl., 9th Black Watch (Royal Highlanders).

Volunteering in August 1914, he was sent to France on the completion of his training in the following year. While there he took part in much heavy fighting and was killed in action at Passchendaele on August 25th, 1917.
He was entitled to the 1914-15 Star, General Service and Victory Medals.
80, Lopen Road, Upper Edmonton, N.18   X17911B₁

MACKIE, J. A., Sergt., R.A.S.C. (M.T.)

He was mobilised in August 1914, and was sent to France in the same month. He took an active part in the retreat from Mons and in the battles of Ypres, the Somme, Arras and other important engagements. During his service he was attached for special duties of a responsible nature to various Cavalry brigades.
In February 1919 he was demobilised, and holds the Mons Star, General Service and Victory Medals.
88, Roundwood Road, Willesden, N.W.10   T15976.

MACKIE, W. J., Pte., 8th Royal Fusiliers.

He volunteered in September 1914, and in the following year was drafted to the Western Front, where he took part in the battles of Ypres, the Somme and other important engagements. During his service he was three times wounded, and lost a leg while in action at Cambrai in 1917. He was invalided home and discharged as medically unfit for further service in November of the same year.
He holds the 1914-15 Star, General Service and Victory Medals.
80, Lopen Road, Upper Edmonton, N.18   X17911A.

MACKLEY, H. J., Lce.-Cpl., 1/7th Middlesex Regt.

Volunteering in November 1915, he was sent to France in the following year, and fought in the battle of the Somme, Arras, Ypres, and in important engagements during the Retreat and Advance of the Allies in 1918. During his active service he was wounded.
He holds the General Service and Victory Medals, and was demobilised in June 1919.
1, Barbot Street, Lower Edmonton, N.9   14584B

MACROW, G., Gunner, R.F.A.

He volunteered in September 1914, and in the following year was sent to France, where he took part in many important engagements, including those at Ypres and on the Somme. Later he was drafted to Salonica and played a conspicuous part on the Struma during the Balkan campaign. Owing to an attack of malaria, he was sent to hospital in Malta and later to England, and was discharged in July 1918.
He holds the 1914-15 Star, General Service and Victory Medals.
11, Beethoven Street, North Kensington, W.10   TX19038.

McADAM, T., Boy, Royal Navy.

He joined the Navy as a boy in August 1918, and on completion of his training went to sea in the following year. During his service he was on board H.M. ships " Benbow" and " Cardiff," and for a time also served on a torpedo-boat destroyer.
In January 1920 he was demobilised, after rendering valuable services.
9, Tenterden Road, Tottenham, N.17   X18261C.

McADAM, W. E., Pte., Middlesex Regiment.

He joined in February 1918, and on completion of his training was engaged on important duties with his unit He rendered valuable services, but was not successful in obtaining his transfer overseas before hostilities ceased. In 1919, however, he was sent to Egypt, and remained there until he was sent home for his demobilisation in March 1920.
9, Tenterden Road, Tottenham, N.17   X18261A.

McADAM, W. W., Sapper, Royal Engineers.

He joined in 1915, and later in the same year went to the Western Front, where he served for nearly four years. He took part in several engagements, including the battles of Ypres and the Somme, and was wounded during the Advance of 1918.
He holds the 1914-15 Star, General Service and Victory Medals.
9, Tenterden Road, Tottenham, N.17   X18261B.

McCARTHY, E., Pte., 12th Hampshire Regt. and Royal Army Service Corps (M.T.)

Volunteering in 1915, he was sent to the Western Front in the same year. After taking part in the battles of Loos, the Somme and Ypres, and in other important engagements, he was drafted to Italy in 1917. While on this Front he served in much of the heavy fighting in the Doiran sector. As a result of his service he was discharged as medically unfit in 1918, and holds the 1914-15 Star, General Service and Victory Medals.
24, Cooper Road, Dudden Hill, Willesden, N.W.10   16635.

McCARTHY, J., Pte., Royal Scots Fusiliers.

Joining in May 1916, he was sent on the completion of his training in the following year to the Western Front, where he took part in several important engagements, including the battle of Cambrai, and was wounded.
In February 1920 he was demobilised, and holds the General Service and Victory Medals.
4, Eldon Road, Lower Edmonton, N.9   13130.

McCARTHY, J., Lce.-Cpl., 1/8th Middlesex Regt.
He was mobilised in 1914, and in the following year was sent to the Western Front, where he took part in the battles of Ypres (where he was gassed), Passchendaele and Cambrai. During the Advance of 1918 he was again gassed at Oppy Wood, and was in hospital for a considerable period. In March 1919 he was demobilised, and holds the 1914-15 Star, General Service and Victory Medals.
22, Tenterden Road, Tottenham, N.17   X18276.

McCARTHY, J. F., Pte., The Queen's (R.W.S.R.)
He joined in February 1917, and was sent to the Western Front in the following month. During his service overseas he was engaged in repairing roads and bridges as the troops advanced on many sectors of the Front.
He was demobilised in January 1920, and holds the General Service and Victory Medals.
13, Oldfield Road, Willesden, N.W.10   15754.

McCARTHY, W., Pte., 7th London Regiment.
Volunteering in April 1915, he was retained in the same year drafted overseas. While on the Western Front he fought in many important engagements, and was killed in action on Vimy Ridge on May 21st, 1916.
He was entitled to the 1914-15 Star, General Service and Victory Medals.
19, Ancill Street, Hammersmith, W.6   13747B.

McCLELLAN, A., Mechanical Staff Sergt., R.A.S.C. (M.T.)
He joined in 1917, and in the same year was drafted to Mesopotamia, where he played a distinguished part in the campaign. In 1918 he was transferred to India, remaining there until 1919, when he returned to England and was demobilised.
He holds the General Service and Victory Medals.
38, Seymour Avenue, Tottenham, N.17   X19166.

McCLELLAN, S. A., Pte., The Queen's (R.W.S.R.)
He volunteered in August 1914 at the outbreak of war, and was soon sent to the Western Front, where he played a conspicuous part in the fighting. In 1917 he was drafted to India, and served there for two years at several different stations. He remained in India until he was sent to England in 1919 for demobilisation, and holds the 1914 Star, General Service and Victory Medals.
36, Seymour Avenue, Tottenham, N.17   TX19164.

McCORMACK, L., Sapper, R.E.
Volunteering in August 1914, he was later in the same year drafted to the Western Front, where he took part in the battles of the Somme and in many important engagements during the Retreat and Advance of 1918. He remained in France until his demobilisation in April 1919, and holds the 1914-15 Star, General Service and Victory Medals.
20, Carlyle Road, Willesden, N.W.10   14208.

McDERMOTT, L., Driver, R.A.S.C. (H.T.)
He volunteered in November 1914, and in the following year was drafted to the Western Front, where he was employed on important transport duties in the engagements on the Somme, at Arras, Ypres, Cambrai, Bapaume and Albert, and during the Retreat and Advance of 1918.
He returned to this country for his demobilisation in February 1919, and holds the 1914-15 Star, General Service and Victory Medals.
17, Conley Road, Willesden, N.W.10   15540.

McDONALD, A., Gunner, R.F.A.
He volunteered in September 1914, and was shortly after sent to the Western Front, where he took part in several engagements. While in action in the Cambrai sector he was severely wounded by shrapnel.
He was demobilised in March 1919, and holds the 1914 Star, General Service and Victory Medals.
16, Chester Road, Lower Edmonton, N.9   12715.

McDONALD, E., Gunner, R.F.A.
Having volunteered in September 1914, he was quickly sent to France, where on several sectors he saw much desperate fighting. After a period of service on the Western Front he was drafted with his battery to Italy, and took part in several engagements against the Austrians.
He holds the 1914 Star, General Service and Victory Medals, and was demobilised in March 1919.
95, Winchester Road, Lower Edmonton, N.9   14957A.

McDONALD, T. S., 1st-Class Petty Officer, R.N.
He was serving in the merchant service at the outbreak of war, and in 1915 was transferred to the Royal Navy. He was engaged on highly important duties of a responsible nature in Scotland and at Chatham until 1916, when owing to the effects of his service he was discharged.
During the South African war he served with the 5th Northumberland Yeomanry, and holds the King's Medal for that campaign. In addition he also holds the 1914-15 Star, Mercantile Marine, General Service and Victory Medals.
77, Droop Street, Queen's Park Estate, W.10   TX18582.

McDOWELL, G., Rifleman, Royal Irish Rifles.
He joined in June 1916, but within a short time of his arrival in France was taken ill before he had seen any actual fighting. Later in 1916 he was invalided home, and after a prolonged stay in hospital was discharged as medically unfit in November 1918.
He holds the General Service and Victory Medals.
21, Shorrolds Road, Walham Green, S.W.6   X19401.

McFARLANE, W., Pte., 2nd Middlesex Regt.
Volunteering in May 1915, he was retained on important duties on completion of his training. He gave very valuable services, but in 1916 was discharged as medically unfit for further military duty, owing to defective sight.
48, Herries Street, North Kensington, W.10   X18565.

McGILL, C., Bandsman, 3rd Dorsetshire Regt.
He volunteered in May 1915, and on completing his training was retained on important duties at various stations with his unit. He was sent to Ireland and gave valuable services, but was not able to secure his transfer to the Front owing to his being under age for service overseas.
In 1920 he was still serving.
30, Milton Avenue, Willesden, N.W.10   15640B.

McGILL, H., Pte., 26th Royal Fusiliers.
Joining in November 1916, he was drafted to France in the following April. After taking part in important engagements at Delville Wood, Armentières and Ploegsteert, he was drafted in 1918 to the Italian theatre of war, where he again saw much fighting on the Asiago Plateau and on the Piave. In December 1918 he returned for demobilisation, and holds the General Service and Victory Medals.
30, Milton Avenue, Willesden, N.W.10   15640A.

McGILL, H., Bandsman, Royal Warwickshire Regt.
He was serving at the outbreak of war, and in 1915 was sent to the Western Front, where he took part in many important engagements. He was wounded three times, and in September 1917 was killed in action near Armentières.
He was entitled to the 1914-15 Star, General Service and Victory Medals.
30, Milton Avenue, Willesden, N.W.10   15640C.

McGINLEY, F. J., Cpl., Buffs (East Kent Regt.)
Volunteering in October 1914, he was retained after completing his training on important duties with his unit until January 1916, when he was sent to Mesopotamia. While in this theatre of war he played a distinguished part in many important engagements, and remained there until his demobilisation in March 1919.
He holds the General Service and Victory Medals.
26, Waldo Road, College Park, Willesden, N.W.10   X18190.

McGLASHON, A., Driver, R.F.A.
He volunteered in September 1914, and in the following year was ordered overseas. He took part in many important engagements on the Western Front, including the battles of the Somme, Arras, Ypres (where he was wounded), and Passchendaele Ridge.
In December 1919 he returned from France for demobilisation, and holds the 1914-15 Star, General Service and Victory Medals.
153, Felixstowe Road, Lower Edmonton, N.9   14544.

McGOWAN, T., Sergt., The Queen's (Royal West Surrey Regiment).
He joined in March 1917, and shortly after was drafted to the Western Front, where he took a prominent part in the battles of Arras, Vimy Ridge, Cambrai and the Somme (1918), and in heavy fighting at Lens. He was later attached to the Labour Corps, with which he served until his demobilisation in March 1919.
He holds the General Service and Victory Medals.
7, St. John's Buildings, Kilburn Lane, North Kensington, W.10   X18667.

McGRAIL, D., Pte., Royal Dublin Fusiliers.
He volunteered for service in January 1915, and later in the year was drafted to the Western Front, where he took part in many important engagements up to the date of his death in action at St. Eloi on April 1st, 1916.
He was entitled to the 1914-15 Star, General Service and Victory Medals.
55, Clarendon Street, Paddington, W.2   X20393C.

McGRAIL, J., Driver, Royal Field Artillery.
He volunteered in October 1914, and in the following year was drafted to Salonica, where he took a distinguished part in important engagements until 1916. He contracted malaria and was invalided home, but after a considerable period in hospital was sent to the Western Front, where he again saw much fighting during the Advance of 1918.
He went to the Rhine with the Army of Occupation after the signing of the Armistice, and remained there until May 1919, when he was demobilised. He holds the 1914-15 Star, General Service and Victory Medals.
32, Woodfield Place, Maida Hill, W.9   X19569.

McGRATH, J., Pte., Wiltshire Regiment.

He volunteered in 1915, and on completing his training was
sent to the Western Front, where he took part in many
important engagements, including the Retreat and Advance
of 1918.
In the following year he was demobilised, and holds the
General Service and Victory Medals.
44, Redfern Road, Willesden, N.W.10   14185.

McGUIRE, A., Rifleman, Rifle Brigade.

Volunteering in August 1914, he was sent in the following
year to France, where he took part in the battle of the Somme
and in heavy fighting near Ypres, during which he was
severely wounded. As a result he was invalided home, and
eventually discharged as medically unfit for further service
in April 1916.
He holds the 1914–15 Star, General Service and Victory
Medals. 42, Clarendon Street, Paddington, W.2   X20663.

McGUIRE, G., Pte., Middlesex Regiment.

He volunteered in August 1914, at the outbreak of hostilities,
and was shortly afterwards sent to the Western Front, where
he took part in the retreat from Mons and the battles of
Ypres, Loos, Arras and Bullecourt. During his service he
was three times wounded and was in hospital for a considerable period. He was killed in action in April 1918,
during the Retreat.
He was entitled to the Mons Star, General Service and
Victory Medals.
55, Clarendon Street, Paddington, W.2   X20393A.

McGUIRE, T., Rifleman, Rifle Brigade.

On the outbreak of war he volunteered, and a year later was
sent to the Western Front, where he played a distinguished
part in the battles of Loos, the Somme and Arras, and
was gassed Whilst in the third battle of Ypres he was
killed in October 1917 by a shell in Sanctuary Wood.
He was entitled to the 1914–15 Star, General Service and
Victory Medals.
55, Clarendon Street, Paddington, W.2   X20393B.

McINTOSH, A. W., Driver, Machine Gun Corps (34th Division).

He volunteered in November 1915, and served for three years
on the Western Front, where he was in action at Arras,
Soissons, Bapaume, Courcelles, Ypres and Armentières, and
in several other engagements.
In May 1919 he was demobilised, holding the General
Service and Victory Medals.
6, Winchelsea Road, Willesden, N.W.10   13715.

McINTOSH, W., Engine-room Artificer (Chief Petty Officer), H.M. T.B.D. " Sabrina."

He joined in May 1916, served in the North Sea and Iceland
patrol on dangerous anti-submarine duties, and was present
at the surrender of the German Fleet at Scapa Flow. He
was specially rated for the valuable services he rendered in
carrying out repairs to H.M.S. " Pellew " after she had been
seriously damaged in April 1918, when in action with four
enemy destroyers.
In February 1919 he was demobilised, holding the General
Service and Victory Medals.
43, Hawthorn Road, Willesden, N.W.10   X17221.

McINTYRE, A., Cpl., Middlesex Regiment.

He volunteered in August 1914, and after his training was
engaged on important duties at various stations with his
unit. He was eventually drafted to the Western Front,
where he took part in many engagements and saw much
severe fighting.
In March 1919 he was demobilised, holding the General
Service and Victory Medals.
91, Adeney Road, Hammersmith, W.6   15325C.

McKAY, E. A., Pte., Royal Fusiliers and Essex Regiment, and Sapper, Royal Engineers.

Volunteering in December 1914, he was later drafted to the
Western Front, where he took part in the battle of Ypres
and in other important engagements. During his service
overseas he was wounded, and in January 1917 was discharged as medically unfit for further service owing to
nervous debility.
He holds the General Service and Victory Medals.
13, Colin Road, Dudden Hill, N.W.10   16297.

McKAY, W. W., Sergt., Royal Air Force.

He volunteered in March 1915, and after his training was
retained for some time as a mechanic on duties which required a high degree of technical skill. Later he was drafted
to France and, being promoted to Sergeant, was engaged on
responsible work at a large depot in connection with the
mechanical transport.
He was demobilised in April 1919, and holds the General
Service and Victory Medals.
49, Ongar Road, Lillie Road, Fulham, S.W.6   X19626.

McKEE, A. E., A.B., Royal Navy.

He joined the Navy in June 1916, and on board the " Iron
Duke " served in important operations with the Grand
Fleet in the North Sea. He was also present at the surrender
of the German Fleet at Scapa Flow.
In March 1919 he was demobilised, and holds the General
Service and Victory Medals.
35, Maldon Road, Lower Edmonton, N.9   14787A.

McKEOWN, E. (Miss), Special War Worker.

During the war this lady was engaged by the Great
Central Railway Company, and thus released a man for
military service. She carried out her duties in a thoroughly
efficient manner, and received high commendation for her
valuable services to her country.
49, Tasso Road, Hammersmith, W.6   14635.

McKEOWN, F., Pte., 1st Connaught Rangers.

He volunteered in June 1915, and during his service on the
Western Front took part in the battles of the Somme, Arras,
Vimy Ridge, Ypres, Cambrai and St. Quentin. He was taken
prisoner at the latter place, and after 24 hours he escaped,
swam the Somme, and, mounting a riderless horse, rode to
Amiens. He served for a time as a despatch rider at General
Headquarters, and was then sent to Germany with the Army
of Occupation, where he enlisted for a further period of four
years and was sent to India.
He holds the General Service and Victory Medals.
49, Tasso Road, Hammersmith, N.W.6   14634B.

McKEOWN, M. (Mrs.), Special War Worker.

During the course of the war this lady rendered valuable
service in the packing and dispatching departments at
Messrs. Lyons & Co.'s works, Cadby Hall, where she was
chiefly concerned with food stuffs for the Army and Navy.
By acting in this capacity she released a man for military
service. 49, Tasso Road, Hammersmith, W.6   14634A.

McKIMMIE, C. E., Pte., King's Own (Royal Lancaster Regiment) and Royal Air Force.

He volunteered in 1915, and joined the Royal Lancaster
Regiment, but was afterwards transferred to the Air Force.
In 1916 he proceeded to the Western Front, and saw much
severe fighting in the battles of Messines Ridge, the Somme,
and other engagements.
He was demobilised in 1919, holding the General Service
and Victory Medals.
51, Ilex Road, Willesden, N.W.10   16359.

McKITTERICK, A. J., A.B., Royal Navy.

He joined the Royal Navy in 1916 and was posted to H.M.S.
" Marksman." During his service he took a prominent part
in the naval operations with the Grand Fleet in the North Sea,
remaining there with his ship until his demobilisation in 1919.
He holds the General Service and Victory Medals.
14, Avalon Road, New King's Road, Fulham, S.W.6
X19790.

McLAUGHLIN, G., Driver, R.F.A.

Volunteering in September 1914, he was sent a year later
to the Western Front, where he remained until November
1918. After taking part in engagements at Ypres, Loos
and the Somme, and being gassed, he was severely wounded
at Cambrai in October 1918.
He holds the 1914–15 Star, General Service and Victory
Medals, and was still serving in 1920.
13, Westbury Road, Willesden, N.W.10   15068B.

McLELLAN, A., Pte., Royal Fusiliers.

He volunteered in August 1914, and in the following March
was sent to the Western Front, where he took part in the
battle of Neuve Chapelle and was wounded. On his recovery he took part in engagements at Ypres, the Somme,
Bullecourt and Delville Wood, and during the Advance of
1918, and after being again wounded, was invalided home.
He was eventually demobilised in May 1919, and holds the
1914–15 Star, General Service and Victory Medals.
48, Brett Road, Stonebridge Park, N.W.10   15688B.

McLUCKIE, D., Rifleman, 10th Cameronians (Scottish Rifles).

Volunteering in September 1914, he was sent in the following
year to the Western Front, where, among other important
engagements, he took part in the battle of Loos in 1915.
He was invalided home and was discharged in February 1916
as medically unfit for further duties, owing to his service.
He holds the 1914–15 Star, General Service and Victory
Medals. 56, Shrubbery Road, Lower Edmonton, N.9 14098.

McMILLAN, T. W. (sen.), Special War Worker.

During the war he was engaged on important Government
work at Messrs. Garlick's Aircraft Factory. His duties,
which required much skill, were carried out in a very capable
manner, and he rendered most valuable services for over
two years.
29, Kilmaine Road, Munster Road, S.W.6   TX18880B.

McMILLAN, T. W. (jun.), Air Mechanic, R.A.F.
He volunteered in July 1915, and on the completion of his training was drafted to the Eastern Front. While in Egypt he was engaged on important duties which called for a high degree of technical skill.
He was demobilised in March 1919, and holds the General Service and Victory Medals.
29, Kilmaine Road, Munster Road, S.W.6.   TX18880A.

McMILLAN, W., Sergt., 3rd Black Watch.
He volunteered in August 1914, and was at once drafted to France, where he took part in the retreat from Mons, in the battles of Loos, Arras and Cambrai, and in other important operations. During his service he was wounded three times, and was demobilised in January 1919.
He holds the Mons Star, General Service and Victory Medals.
12, St. Martin's Road, Lower Edmonton, N.9   13037.

McNALLY, M., Pte., 4th London Regiment (R.F.).
He was serving at the outbreak of war, and was immediately sent with the 3rd Division to France, where he took part in the retreat from Mons. During the first battle of Ypres he was severely wounded in November 1914, and was invalided home. After a considerable period in hospital he was discharged in February 1917 as medically unfit for further service.
He holds the Mons Star, General Service and Victory Medals.
337, Chapter Road, Cricklewood, N.W.2   16715.

McNISH, J., Cpl., R.A.S.C.
He volunteered in October 1915, and later in the same year was drafted to the Western Front. During his service, which extended for 3½ years, he was attached to a Labour Company, and was engaged on important duties in various sectors of the Front.
He remained in France until his demobilisation in March 1919, and holds the 1914-15 Star, General Service and Victory Medals.
50, Shrewsbury Road, Stonebridge Park, N.W.10   14016.

McPHERSON, J., Bandsman, 2nd Worcestershire Regiment.
He volunteered in August 1914, and in the following February was drafted overseas. While on the Western Front he took part in many important engagements, including the battles of Ypres and Messines, where he was badly wounded. He was for a considerable period in hospital in France and England, and on his discharge from hospital was certified unfit for service overseas. He was, however, retained on important duties at home until his demobilisation in January 1919, and holds the 1914-15 Star, General Service and Victory Medals.
71, Ormiston Road, Shepherd's Bush, W.12   11919.

McQUEEN, D., Pte., 9th Middlesex Regiment and Pioneer, Royal Engineers.
He volunteered in December 1914, and after his training was retained on important duties with his unit at various stations until 1917, when he was drafted to the Western Front. While there he took part in the heavy fighting at Péronne, St. Quentin and on the Somme, and was badly gassed at Chaulnes, in consequence of which he was invalided home. After a period in hospital he was discharged as medically unfit for further service in July 1918, and holds the General Service and Victory Medals.
36, Westbury Road, Willesden, N.W.10   15447.

McRAE, W., A.B., Royal Navy, H.M.S. "Erin."
He volunteered in August 1914, and was posted to H.M.S. "Erin," with which vessel he took part in important naval operations with the Grand Fleet in the North Sea, and was present during the battle of Jutland.
In January 1919 he was demobilised, holding the 1914 Star, General Service and Victory Medals.
30, Florence Road, Upper Edmonton, N.18   16008.

McSWEENEY, D. (M.M.), Sergt., Ryl. Welch Fus.
Volunteering in August 1914, he was later in the same year drafted to the Western Front, where he took a prominent part in many important engagements, and during the British offensive on the Somme in 1917 was badly wounded. He was invalided home, and after a period in hospital was discharged as medically unfit for further service in 1917.
He was awarded the Military Medal for conspicuous bravery and devotion to duty in the field, and in addition holds the 1914 Star, General Service and Victory Medals.
73, Berry Street, Willesden, N.W.10   15415B.

McSWEENEY, J., Cpl., Suffolk Regiment.
He volunteered in August 1914, and in the following year was drafted to the Western Front, where he took part in many important engagements, including the battle of the Somme (where he was wounded) and the Retreat and Advance of 1918.
He holds the 1914-15 Star, General Service and Victory Medals, and was demobilised in February 1919.
73, Berry Street, Willesden, N.W.10   51415A.

McVICAR, J., Lce.-Cpl., Hertfordshire Regiment.
He joined in 1917, and later in the same year was sent to the Western Front, where he took part in the heavy fighting on the Somme, and in important engagements during the Retreat and Advance in the closing stages of the war.
He holds the General Service and Victory Medals, and in 1920 was still serving.
103, Kimberley Road, Upper Edmonton, N.18   16788.

MADDISON, G. W., Pte., 2nd Norfolk Regt.
In February 1917 he joined the Army, and on the completion of his training was sent to the Western Front. He took part in many engagements during the Retreat and Advance of 1918, and in March 1919 was demobilised.
He immediately re-enlisted, and was drafted to India, where he was still serving in 1920.
He holds the General Service and Victory Medals.
52, Lorenco Road, Tottenham, N.17   18389.

MADDOCK, H. J. (D.C.M.), Sergt., Duke of Cornwall's Light Infantry.
He volunteered in 1914, was sent to France early in the following year, and was in action at Ypres. He was then drafted to Salonica, took part in engagements there, and returned to the Western Front, where he was in action again at Passchendaele, Arras, the Retreat and Advance of 1918, and was wounded. He was awarded the D.C.M. for conspicuous gallantry and devotion to duty at the village of Irles, near Bapaume, in 1918. In addition holds the 1914-15 Star, General Service and Victory Medals, and was demobilised in 1919.
2, Sunnyside Road North, Lower Edmonton, N.9   14556A.

MADDOCK, J. E., Seaman Gunner, Royal Navy.
He volunteered immediately on the outbreak of war, and quickly proceeded to sea. He took part in important naval operations with the Grand Fleet in the North Sea, and was present at the battle of Jutland.
In 1920 he was still serving, and holds the 1914 Star, General Service and Victory Medals.
2, Sunnyside Road North, Lower Edmonton, N.9   14556B.

MAGNER, H. (M.M.), Trooper, 2nd Dragoon Guards.
He volunteered in August 1914, and went to the Western Front the same year. He was in action in the battles of Ypres, Arras and Cambrai, and was wounded on the Somme in March 1918. He was awarded the Military Medal for conspicuous gallantry and devotion to duty, and holds in addition the 1914 Star, General Service and Victory Medals. He was demobilised in March 1919.
6, Ray's Road, Upper Edmonton, N.18   15494.

MAGUIRE, T., Lce.-Cpl., R.A.S.C. (M.T.)
He volunteered in November 1914, and was sent to France in the following January. While overseas he was engaged on important duties with an ammunition column in various sectors, and was also employed as a fitter in workshops immediately behind the firing-line.
In April 1919 he was demobilised, and holds the 1914-15 Star, General Service and Victory Medals.
118, Villiers Road, Cricklewood, N.W.2   16154.

MAIDLOW, E. W., Pte., Royal Defence Corps.
He volunteered in October 1914, and was engaged on important duties on the railways of the country. He was also stationed at a large internment camp, where he performed special guard duties very efficiently until his demobilisation in February 1919.
27, Sandringham Road, Cricklewood, N.W.2   X17097.

MAJOR, A. J., Cpl., 1st London Regiment (Royal Fusiliers).
He volunteered in August 1914, and in the same year was sent to the Western Front, where he took part in much heavy fighting, and was killed in action near Fromelles on May 9th, 1915.
He was entitled to the 1914-15 Star, General Service and Victory Medals.
97, Churchill Road, Willesden, N.W.10.   16695A.

MAJOR, L., Pte., Royal Berkshire and Royal Warwickshire Regiments.
He volunteered in May 1915, and in the following July was drafted to the East. He took part in important operations in North-East Africa, Egypt and Mesopotamia, and remained in the Eastern seat of operations until his demobilisation in March 1919.
He holds the 1914-15 Star, General Service and Victory Medals.
13, Albert Terrace, Milton Avenue, Stonebridge Park, N.W.10   T14337.

MAJOR, L., Pte., 1/6th North Staffordshire Regt.

He joined in 1917, and on the completion of his training was drafted to France in the following year, and took part in the Allies' Advance. During his service he was gassed. After the signing of the Armistice he went to Germany with the Army of Occupation, and remained there until his demobilisation in September 1919.
He holds the General Service and Victory Medals.
30, Guinness's Buildings, Fulham Palace Road, S.W.6 14490.

MAKER, S., Pte., 4th Royal Fusiliers.

He was mobilised from the Reserve immediately on the outbreak of hostilities, and was sent to the Western Front. He took part in the retreat from Mons, and during the battle of La Bassée in October 1914 was severely wounded. As a result he was invalided home and discharged in May 1916 as medically unfit for further service.
He holds the Mons Star, General Service and Victory Medals.
156, Stephendale Road, Fulham, S.W.6   X20829.

MALCOLM, H., Pte., 6/7th Royal Warwickshire Regiment.

He volunteered in November 1914, and in the following May was sent to France, where he took part in many important operations. He was severely wounded in action at Laventie in July 1916, and was invalided home. Later in the year he was discharged as medically unfit for further service owing to shell-shock and loss of sight.
He holds the 1914–15 Star, General Service and Victory Medals.   15, Gowan Road, Willesden, N.W.10   X16969.

MALING, F. G., Pte., Bedfordshire Regiment and Machine Gun Corps.

He volunteered in September 1914, and was sent to France in the following year. While on the Western Front he served in the battles of Loos, Arras, Vimy Ridge, Passchendaele and Cambrai, and in the important operations during the Allied Retreat and Advance. He also acted as a despatch-rider, and was three times wounded. After the signing of the Armistice he went to Germany with the Army of Occupation, and remained there until demobilised in January 1919.
He holds the 1914–15 Star, General Service and Victory Medals.   76, Mayo Road, Willesden, N.W.10   15437.

MALLEN, C. (sen.), Sergt., Royal Air Force.

Volunteering in January 1915, he was sent to the Western Front in the same year. While in this seat of war he served with distinction, and was engaged on duties which called for a high degree of technical skill. He also took part in important operations, particularly in the vicinity of Béthune. In June 1919 he was demobilised, and holds the 1914–15 Star, General Service and Victory Medals.
30a, Deacon Road, Cricklewood, N.W.2   16647B.

MALLEN, C. (jun.), Cpl., 2/9th Middlesex Regt.

He volunteered in November 1914, and in 1915 was sent to the Western Front, where he took part in the battles of Ypres, the Somme, Arras, Vimy Ridge, and in other important engagements. After the Armistice he went to Germany with the Army of Occupation, and remained there until his demobilisation in June 1919.
He holds the 1914–15 Star, General Service and Victory Medals.   30a, Deacon Road, Cricklewood, N.W.2   16647A.

MALLETT, A. B., Cpl., Machine Gun Corps.

Joining in May 1916, he was retained on completion of his training at various stations with his unit. He was engaged on important duties until November 1917, when he was drafted to France. While overseas he took part in much severe fighting, and in November 1918 was wounded in action.
He was demobilised in the following March, and holds the General Service and Victory Medals.
35, Smalley Road, Stoke Newington, N.16   X18347.

MANCHESTER, A., Rifleman, 2/6th London Regt.

He joined in November 1916, and in the following February was drafted to the Western Front, where he took part in many important engagements, including the battles of Arras, Ypres and the Somme.
He remained in France until his demobilisation in November 1919, and holds the General Service and Victory Medals.
75, Sandringham Road, Cricklewood, N.W.2   X17133.

MANDER, A. J., Cpl., R.A.S.C.

Having served previously for 16 years in the 11th Hussars, he was called up in August 1914, and in the same year was sent to the Western Front, where he took part in the retreat from Mons. Whilst with the Royal Army Service Corps he was employed at various depots in France, and rendered valuable services.
In February 1919 he was demobilised, and holds the Mons Star, General Service, Victory and India General Service (with two clasps) Medals.
36, Kingwood Road, Fulham, S.W.6   TX19017.

MANGUM, A. G., Sapper, Royal Engineers.

He joined in 1916, and on the completion of his training was sent in the same year to Egypt. After being engaged on important duties in this theatre of operations, he was drafted to France, where he took part in much severe fighting during the Retreat and Advance of the Allies in 1918.
He was demobilised in 1919, and holds the General Service and Victory Medals.
26, Berry Street, Willesden, N.W.10   15425C.

MANGUM, H. J., Sergt., 22nd London Regiment.

He volunteered in September 1914, and in the following year served at the Dardanelles, where he was twice wounded. After the evacuation of the Peninsula in January 1916 he was sent to Egypt and Palestine. He took part in numerous engagements with General Allenby's Forces, including the capture of Jerusalem, and was again wounded twice.
He was demobilised in July 1919, holding the 1914–15 Star, General Service and Victory Medals.
118, Deacon Road, Cricklewood, N.W.2   X16974.

MANGUM, J. H. (sen.), Rflmn., Lon. Rifle Brigade.

Volunteering in October 1914, he was drafted to India later in the same year. He remained there until 1919, and during this time was engaged on garrison duties at Rangoon. He rendered valuable service, but was unable to secure his transfer to one of the active theatres of war.
He was demobilised in November 1919, and holds the General Service and Victory Medals.
26, Berry Street, Willesden, N.W.10   15425A.

MANGUM, J. H. (jun.), Sergt., London Regt.

He volunteered in August 1914, and was almost immediately sent to Egypt. He served with the Egyptian Expeditionary Force throughout the whole campaign, and was continually in action. He was present at the taking of both Gaza and Jerusalem, and was wounded three times. In August 1919 he returned to England for demobilisation, and holds the 1914 Star, General Service and Victory Medals
26, Berry Street, Willesden, N.W.10   15425B.

MANGUM, J. W. G., Cpl., 13th Rifle Brigade.

He joined in February 1917, and in the following year was sent to France. After a short period of active service on the Western Front he was invalided home, and was retained on important duties until his demobilisation in January 1920.
He holds the General Service and Victory Medals.
45, Oldfield Road, Willesden, N.W.10   15987A.

MANGUM, W. F., Rifleman, 18th London Regiment (London Irish Rifles).

He volunteered in March 1915, and from the following November until 1919 served in India, where he was engaged on special duties as a signaller. During his service overseas he contracted heart disease, and in consequence was discharged in April 1919.
He holds the General Service and Victory Medals.
45, Oldfield Road, Willesden, N.W.10   15987B.

MANIX, J., Chief Petty Officer, R.N., H.M.S. "Defiance."

He enlisted in the Navy in 1882, and on the outbreak of war was called up for service on H.M.S. "Defiance." Later he was engaged in connection with the anti-aircraft defences of London, and was chiefly employed in operating search-lights.
He was discharged in March 1918, and holds the General Service Medal.
28, Adeney Road, Hammersmith, W.6   14310A.

MANIX, J. A. S., Lce.-Cpl., 1st Lon. Regt. (R.F.).

He volunteered in August 1914, and was immediately sent to France, where he took part in the retreat from Mons and the battle of Ypres. While in action at Armentières he was killed on February 9th, 1915.
He was entitled to the Mons Star, General Service and Victory Medals. 23, Adeney Road, Hammersmith, S.W.6 14310B.

MANIX, W. N., Pte., 13th London Regiment (Kensingtons).

He was mobilised in August 1914, and early in the following year was drafted to France, where he was severely wounded in action at Armentières. He was in hospital in France and England for some months, and was eventually discharged in December 1915 as medically unfit for further service.
He holds the 1914–15 Star, General Service and Victory Medals. 23, Adeney Road, Hammersmith, W.6 14310C.

MANLEY, H. L., Lce.-Cpl., 3rd Hussars.

He enlisted in April 1897, and was serving at the outbreak of war. He was immediately sent to the Western Front, where he took part in the retreat from Mons, the battles of Ypres, Arras and other important engagements until the end of the war. Having previously served in the South African War, he holds the Queen's Medal with three clasps, in addition to the Mons Star, General Service and Victory Medals. He was demobilised in January 1919.
59, Hawthorn Road, Willesden, N.W.10   X17428.

MANLY, F., Pte., Royal Army Medical Corps.

Joining in April 1916, he was sent to the Western Front on completion of his training. While in this seat of war he was engaged as a stretcher-bearer, and took an active part in many important engagements. Later he served as an orderly in a large field-hospital.
He holds the General Service and Victory Medals, and was demobilised in October 1919.
28, Knivet Road, Walham Green, S.W.6   X19428C.

MANLY, J. W., Cpl., 13th London Regiment (Kensingtons).

He was mobilised in August 1914, and was quickly drafted to the Western Front, where he served until 1919. He took part in many engagements in France, including those at Mons, Loos, Arras, the Somme, Ypres and Cambrai.
He was demobilised in May 1919, and holds the Mons Star, General Service and Victory Medals.
28, Knivet Road, Walham Green, S.W.6   X19428B.

MANLY, W. G., Special War Worker.

Throughout the war he was employed at Messrs. Dunlop's factory at the White City, where he rendered valuable services in connection with the manufacture of airships. His work was carried out in a very satisfactory manner.
3, Lurgan Avenue, Hammersmith, W.6   13449.

MANN, A. W., Cpl., 5th Cavalry Reserve.

He was mobilised in August 1914, and was at once drafted to France, where he took part in the retreat from Mons and other important engagements. Being medically unfit for further active service, he returned to England in 1915, and afterwards rendered valuable service at a large veterinary hospital until March 1918, when he was discharged on account of indifferent health.
He holds the Mons Star, General Service and Victory Medals.
4a, Drayton Road, Harlesden, N.W.10   14899.

MANN, B., Pte., Royal Berkshire Regiment.

He volunteered in December 1915 at the age of 17 years, and in the next year was sent to France, where he served with a Lewis gun section at the battle of the Somme and at Ypres. He was twice wounded and gassed, and was in hospital for some months in France and England.
In March 1919 he was demobilised, and holds the General Service and Victory Medals.
117, Durban Road, Tottenham, N.17   X17957.

MANN, G. C. F., Pte., Queen's Own (Royal West Kent Regiment).

He joined in July 1918, and after his training was sent to the Western Front, where he took part in the final engagements during the Advance of the Allies. After the Armistice he went to Germany with the Army of Occupation, and in 1919 was drafted to India, where he was still serving in 1920.
He holds the General Service and Victory Medals.
27, Monmouth Road, Lower Edmonton, N.9   12985.

MANNAKEE, F., Lieut., Royal Navy.

He was mobilised at the outbreak of war, and immediately proceeded to sea. He served with the Grand Fleet on board H.M.S. "Bat," "Loyal," and "Tempest," and took part in important naval operations. Later he served on H.M.S. "Amphitrite," on dangerous mine-laying duties in the North Sea.
He holds the 1914 Star, General Service and Victory Medals, and was still serving in 1920.
64, Manor Road, Tottenham, N.17   X18801.

MANNING, R. F., Pte., 9th Essex Regiment.

He joined in June 1916, and in the following September was drafted to the Western Front. After taking part in much heavy fighting he was killed in action at Arras in December of the same year.
He was entitled to the General Service and Victory Medals.
109, Burn's Road, Harlesden, N.W.10   13454.

MANSBRIDGE, L. F., Pte., 1st Border Regiment.

He volunteered in September 1914, and on the completion of his training was drafted to Egypt. After a period of service in this seat of war he was sent to France, and took part in many important engagements.
He was killed in action on October 28th, 1917, and was entitled to the General Service and Victory Medals.
73, Beryl Road, Hammersmith, W.6   13351.

MANSELL, A., Lce.-Cpl., Norfolk Regiment.

Volunteering in November 1914, he was sent to France in the following year. While overseas he took part in much heavy fighting, and was wounded no less than four times.
In January 1919 he was demobilised, and holds the 1914-15 Star, General Service and Victory Medals.
24, Wingmore Road, Tottenham, N.17   X17981A

MANSELL, G. A., Sapper, Royal Engineers.

He volunteered in 1915, and in the same year took part in the British landing at Suvla Bay, where he was badly wounded and lay exposed for several days, during which time he suffered terribly from thirst. He also contracted dysentery, and after being invalided home was discharged as medically unfit for further service in 1917.
He holds the 1914-15 Star, General Service and Victory Medals.
90, Ilex Road, Willesden, N.W.10   15951.

MANSELL, H. G., Pioneer, Royal Engineers.

Volunteering in February 1915, he was later in the same year drafted to the Western Front, where he took an active part in the battles of Ypres, Loos, Armentières, and in other important engagements. He suffered from shell-shock and met with a serious accident whilst on duty, and in consequence was invalided home and discharged in December 1917 as medically unfit for further service.
He holds the 1914-15 Star, General Service and Victory Medals.
168, Kilburn Lane, North Kensington, W.10   X18710B.

MANSELL, R., Cpl., King's Royal Rifle Corps.

Volunteering in September 1914, he was drafted to France later in the same year. While on this Front he took part in much heavy fighting, was wounded in the battle of Loos, and died on November 20th, 1915.
He was entitled to the 1914 Star, General Service and Victory Medals.
24, Wingmore Road, Tottenham, N.17   X17981B.

MANSELL, W. J., Driver, Royal Field Artillery.

Having served for three years previous to the war, he rejoined in September 1914, and was sent overseas early in the following year. While on the Western Front he took part in much heavy fighting in France and Belgium. He was invalided home on account of a serious accident, and was in hospital for several months.
He was demobilised in February 1919, and holds the 1914-15 Star, General Service and Victory Medals.
8, Argyle Road, Upper Edmonton, N.18   15263B

MANSFIELD, G. W., Pte., 1/4th Northamptonshire Regiment.

He joined in March 1917, and after a short course of training in England was drafted to Egypt. He subsequently took part in the Palestine campaign, and was killed in action at Gaza in November 1917.
He was entitled to the General Service and Victory Medals.
16, Kemble Road, Tottenham, N.17   X19105.

MANSOR, E., Gunner, Royal Field Artillery.

Volunteering in September 1915, he was drafted overseas in the same year, and while on the Western Front took an active part in heavy fighting in various sectors.
He remained in France until his demobilisation in January, 1920, and holds the 1914-15 Star, General Service and Victory Medals.
27, Alexandra Road, West Kensington, W.14   12090B

MANTLE, J. H., Gunner, R.G.A.

He joined in June 1917, and on completion of his training was sent to the Eastern theatre of war. He saw much service in Egypt and Palestine, and during this period was chiefly engaged with the anti-aircraft section.
He holds the General Service and Victory Medals, and was demobilised in January 1920.
35, Rosaline Road, Munster Road, S.W.6   TX18694.

MANTLE, W. J., Pte., Royal Fusiliers.

Joining at the outbreak of war, he was immediately drafted to the Western Front, where he was killed in action at the battle of Mons in August 1914.
He was entitled to the Mons Star, General Service and Victory Medals.
21, Maybury Gardens, Willesden, N.W.10   X1/367C.

MANWILL, A. W., Pte., Machine Gun Corps.

He volunteered in 1914 immediately on the outbreak of hostilities, and later in the same year was drafted to the Western Front. During his service in this seat of war he took part in much severe fighting. He remained in France until his demobilisation in February 1920, and holds the 1914 Star, General Service and Victory Medals.
24, West Street, Lower Edmonton, N.9   14236A.

MANWILL, J., Pte., 53rd Royal Sussex Regt.

He joined in September 1918, on attaining military age, but owing to the early cessation of hostilities was not drafted overseas until after the Armistice. He was then sent to Germany with the Army of Occupation, and remained there until his demobilisation in March 1920.
24, West Street, Lower Edmonton, N.9   14236B

MAPPLEY, E. J. T., Sergt., 3rd Middlesex Regt.
He was serving at the outbreak of war, and was sent to France in 1915. After only two weeks' service, during which time he was in action at Ypres, he was killed on February 17th, 1915.
He was entitled to the 1914-15 Star, General Service and Victory Medals.
105, Mayo Road, Willesden, N.W.10   15429B.

MAPPLEY, W., Pte., 18th Middlesex Regiment.
He was in the Army at the outbreak of the war, and was immediately drafted to France, where he took part in the battles of Mons, the Marne, the Aisne, Ypres, the Somme, Cambrai and many other engagements. After being twice wounded he was killed in hospital on October 26th, 1918, by a shell which fell on the building.
He was entitled to the Mons Star, General Service and Victory Medals.
105, Mayo Road, Willesden, N.W.10   15429A.

MARC, E. W., Pte., Royal Air Force.
He volunteered in January 1915, and in 1916 was sent to the Western Front, where he was employed on special duties with his unit.
He was discharged as medically unfit for further service in October 1917, holding the General Service and Victory Medals. 98, Portnall Road, Maida Vale, W.9   X19538.

MARCH, W. E., Pte., 3rd Middlesex Regiment.
He volunteered in August 1914, and in the same year was sent to France, where he took part in many engagements, until he was killed in the action of Loos in October 1915.
He was entitled to the 1914-15 Star, General Service and Victory Medals.
25, Ambleside Road, Willesden, N.W.10   16934.

MARCHANT, A., Rifleman, Rifle Brigade.
He joined in March 1917, and on the completion of his training was retained with his unit on important duties. He rendered valuable services, but was not successful in obtaining his transfer overseas before the cessation of hostilities.
He was demobilised in 1919.
59, Droop Street, Queen's Park Estate, W.10   X18703.

MARCHI, A. V., Pte., 23rd Middlesex Regiment.
He joined in April 1917, and served in Italy and on the Western Front. He took part in the battles of the Somme, Ypres and Messines, where he was severely wounded and lost his left arm. He was in hospital for some months, and was discharged in May 1919, holding the General Service and Victory Medals.
18, Bridport Road, Upper Edmonton, N.18   X17898B.

MARCHI, E. (Miss), Special War Worker.
During the war this lady was employed at an important Government factory at Tottenham making military uniforms. She fell ill as a result of strain and overwork, and died on January 16th, 1917, after having performed very useful services for her country.
18, Bridport Road, Upper Edmonton, N.18   X17898A.

MARDALL, F., Driver, R.E. (91st Field Coy.)
He volunteered in 1914, and was speedily sent to France, where he took part in the retreat from Mons and in the battles of the Somme and at Ypres and other important engagements up to the close of the war.
He was demobilised in April 1919, holding the Mons Star, General Service and Victory Medals.
72, Hawthorn Road, Upper Edmonton, N.18   X17366B.

MARDELL, F., Pte., Royal West Kent Regt.
He joined in 1916, and after his training was drafted to France. While on the Western Front he took part in many engagements. Afterwards he was drafted to Italy, where he contracted malaria.
He was demobilised in 1919, holding the General Service and Victory Medals.
26, Wingmore Road, Tottenham, N.17   X17983.

MARDLE, F. J., Pte., The Queen's (Royal West Surrey Regiment).
He joined in 1918, and at the conclusion of his training served with the Army of Occupation in Germany. He was afterwards drafted to Russia, where he did much useful work, and on his return was demobilised in April 1920.
92, Bridport Road, Upper Edmonton, N.18   X17899.

MARKHAM, J. M., Gnr., Royal Garrison Artillery.
He volunteered in October 1914, and was retained with his unit on important duties until he was sent to Malta in 1917. There he remained until he was demobilised in February 1919, holding the General Service and Victory Medals.
57, Humbolt Road, Hammersmith, W.6   15312A.

MARKHAM, J. W. C., Rifleman, K.R.R.
He joined in June 1918, and after the completion of his training went to Germany with the Army of Occupation. He remained there until he was demobilised in March 1920.
57, Humbolt Road, Hammersmith, W.6   15312B.

MARKHAM, W. H., Sapper, Royal Engineers.
He volunteered in September 1915, and served on the Western Front in the battles of the Somme, Arras, Loos, Neuve Chapelle, St. Quentin, Bapaume, Ypres, Vimy Ridge and Cambrai. He was severely wounded, and in consequence was discharged in 1918, unfit for further service.
He holds the 1914-15 Star, General Service and Victory Medals.
91, Archel Road, West Kensington, W.14   16669.

MARKS, B., Pte., Royal Engineers.
He joined in July 1916, and was ordered to the Western Front, where he served with the Lewis gun section of his unit, and took part in many engagements until he was wounded and sent home.
He was discharged as medically unfit for further service in April 1918, and holds the General Service and Victory Medals.   12, Purcell Crescent, Fulham, S.W.6   14848.

MARKS, G. (sen.), Pte., R.A.S.C.
Volunteering in May 1915 he was in the same year drafted to France, and while there took an active part in important operations in various sectors. He was wounded in action, and in February 1919 was demobilised, holding the 1914-15 Star, General Service and Victory Medals.
12, Purcell Crescent, Fulham, S.W.6   14848B.

MARKS, G. (jun.), Driver, R.F.A.
He joined in July 1917, and after the completion of his training was sent to India, where he took part in the operations in Afghanistan and was wounded.
In December 1919 was demobilised, holding the General Service and Victory Medals, and the India General Service Medal, with clasp—Afghanistan N.W. Frontier, 1919.
12, Purcell Crescent, Fulham, S.W 6   14848A.

MARKS, R. G., King's Cpl., R.A.S.C. (M.T.)
He volunteered in August 1914, and saw much service on the Eastern Front, where he took an active part in the Gallipoli operations and was severely wounded. He was promoted to King's Corporal for gallant conduct and general efficiency in the field.
He was demobilised in June 1919, holding the 1914-15 Star, General Service and Victory Medals.
5, Everington Street, Hammersmith, W.6   14089.

MARKS, W. J. R., Pte., R.A.V.C.
Having previously served in the South African war, he volunteered in November 1914, and for more than two years did valuable work on the Western Front, where he tended sick and wounded horses.
He was discharged in July 1917, and holds the Queen's and King's South African Medals, the 1914-15 Star, General Service and Victory Medals.
62, Carlyle Avenue, Willesden, N.W.10   14416A.

MARR, G. B., Sergt., Royal Engineers.
He joined in April 1916, and was drafted in the following year to the Western Front, where he took part in the Retreat and Advance of 1918. He was also attached to the Headquarter Staff for special duties.
He was demobilised in February 1919, and holds the General Service and Victory Medals.
119, Drayton Road, Harlesden, N.W.10   15259.

MARRIAGE, T., Staff Sergt., R.G.A.
He was serving in August 1914, having enlisted in 1905, and was drafted to the Western Front in 1916. While there he took part in the battles of the Somme, Ypres, Arras and in the Retreat and Advance of 1918, and suffered from shell-shock.
He was demobilised in May 1919, holding the General Service and Victory Medals.
37, Chalgrave Road, Tottenham, N.7   X18972.

MARRINER, F. C., Pte., 2/25th London Regt. (Cyclists).
He joined in April 1916, served for a year on coastal defence, and in 1917 was drafted to the Western Front, where he remained until the following year. During this period he took part in numerous engagements, including those of Passchendaele, Bullecourt and Arras, and was seriously wounded. He was invalided home, and in September 1919 was discharged as unfit for further service.
He holds the General Service and Victory Medals.
147, Ashmore Road, Harrow Road, W.9   X19742.

MARRIOTT, F. G., 2nd Air Mechanic, R.A.F.
Joining in May 1916, he was retained on special duties with his unit at various important stations. He gave valuable services, which called for a high degree of technical skill, but was not successful in obtaining his transfer overseas before hostilities ceased. After the signing of the Armistice he was drafted to France, and remained there until he was demobilised in April 1919.
27, Kimberley Road, Upper Edmonton, N.18   16585.

MARSH, A. G., Pte., 7th Suffolk Regiment.

He joined in June 1916, and on completion of his training was drafted to the Western Front, where he took part in many engagements, until he was killed in action at Albert on March 26th, 1918.
He was entitled to the General Service and Victory Medals.
2, Somerset Place, Hammersmith, W.6   13793.

MARSH, E. (Mrs.), Special War Worker.

This lady was employed for nine months during the Great War inspecting small arms ammunition at Park Royal Munition Factory. She did valuable work, and was on duty during several enemy air-raids.
46, Winchelsea Road, Willesden, N.W.10   13847A.

MARSH, J., Pte., 13th London Regiment.

He volunteered in August 1914, and was sent to the Eastern Front, where he took part in many engagements in Salonica, Egypt and Palestine, including the capture of Jerusalem. He was demobilised in May 1919, after 10 years in the Army, and holds the General Service and Victory Medals.
84, Sherbrooke Road, Fulham, S.W.6   X18754.

MARSH, W., Leading Seaman, Royal Navy.

He joined the Navy in September 1896, and during the war saw much service in many vessels, including H.M.S. "Havelock," "Furious," "Excellent," "Talbot," "Albion," "Illustrious" and "Blenheim." He took part in the Dardanelles expedition of 1915, and at the expiration of his service was discharged in February 1919.
He holds the 1914–15 Star, General Service and Victory Medals
100, Third Avenue, Queen's Park Estate, W.10   X19290.

MARSHALL, A., Pte., Bedfordshire Regiment.

He joined in May 1918, proceeded to the Western Front in October, and served in the Cambrai sector until sent to Germany with the Army of Occupation.
He holds the General Service and Victory Medals, and was demobilised in March 1920.
127, Deacon Road, Cricklewood, N.W.2   16614.

MARSHALL, E. W., Cpl., R.A.S.C.

He joined in 1916, and in the same year was drafted to the Western Front, where his great skill as a smith was of the highest value to his unit, until the close of the war
He was demobilised in 1919, holding the General Service and Victory Medals.
41, Lamb Lane, Redbourne, St. Albans.   13830A.

MARSHALL, F. G., Pte., 1st Scots Guards.

Serving at the outbreak of war, he was immediately drafted to France, where he played a distinguished part in the retreat from Mons. Afterwards he fought in several engagements, but was killed near Ypres on December 24th, 1915.
He was entitled to the Mons Star, General Service and Victory Medals.
31, Cranbury Road, Fulham, S.W.6   X21061A.

MARSHALL, G. H., Rifleman, Rifle Brigade.

He volunteered in September 1914, and after the completion of his training was drafted to the Western Front, where he took part in many engagements until the close of the war, and was wounded on the Somme.
He was demobilised in May 1919, holding the 1914–15 Star, General Service and Victory Medals.
86, Ancill Street, Hammersmith, W.6   13658.

MARSHALL, G. S., Pte., 7th Middlesex Regt.

He volunteered in August 1914, and after completing his training was ordered to Gibraltar, and later to France, where he took part in many engagements, including those on the Somme.
He was demobilised in February 1919, and holds the General Service and Victory Medals.
54, Winchester Road, Lower Edmonton, N.9   14866.

MARSHALL, H., 2nd Lieut., Royal Air Force.

He volunteered in December 1915, and was soon sent to the Western Front, where he played a prominent part in the fighting on Vimy Ridge, and was wounded while in action. During his flights over the battle areas he was again wounded, and rendered valuable services in reconnaisance and other duties.
In March 1919 he was demobilised, and holds the General Service and Victory Medals.
6, Denton Road, Stonebridge Park, N.W.10   14699A.

MARSHALL, H., Gunner, R.G.A.

He volunteered in August 1915, and after the termination of his training, was retained on special duties in England until April 1917, when he was drafted to France. After taking part in several engagements on the Western Front, he was sent to Germany with the Army of Occupation, with which he remained until his demobilisation in July 1919.
He holds the General Service and Victory Medals.
10, Grove Street, Upper Edmonton, N.18   X17486

15

MARSHALL, H., Sapper, Royal Engineers.

He volunteered in March 1915, and in the following year was drafted to Egypt, where, during an engagement, he was severely wounded by shrapnel in the spine. For a long time he was in hospital, but on October 12th, 1918, he died of his wound.
He was entitled to the General Service and Victory Medals.
20, Hartington Road, Lower Edmonton, N.9   14248.

MARSHALL, H. C., Special War Worker.

Being physically unfit for military service he was engaged from 1914 to 1917 on the clerical staff at the Park Royal Munition Factory, and carried out his highly important duties with great zeal and punctuality.
93, Barret's Green Road, Willesden, N.W.10   13830B.

MARSHALL, R., Rifleman, 13th Rifle Brigade.

Joining in March 1917, he completed his training and was drafted to the Western Front, where he took part in the Advance in 1918. While in action he received a severe wound which kept him in hospital for twelve months, and eventually caused his discharge as medically unfit in 1919.
He holds the General Service and Victory Medals.
15, Tenterden Road, Tottenham, N.17   X018265.

MARSHALL, S. T., Sapper, Royal Engineers.

He joined in June 1917, and after completion of his training was drafted to France, where he took part in several engagements, and later served with the Army of Occupation in Germany.
He was demobilised in April 1919, and holds the General Service and Victory Medals.
62, St. Peter's Road, Lower Edmonton, N.9   12323.

MARSHALL, W., Pte., 13th Middlesex Regiment.

He volunteered in November, 1915, and during his service on the Western Front, which lasted three years, took part in the fighting at Vimy Ridge, Cambrai and on the Somme, and was wounded in action at Ypres.
He holds the General Service and Victory Medals, and was demobilised in February 1919.
15, Tenterden Road, Tottenham, N.17   X18263.

MARSHALL, W. D., Sergt., 14th London Regt. (London Scottish).

He was in the Territorial Forces before the war, and was mobilised at the outbreak of hostilities. Owing to his skill as a Gymnastic Instructor he was not successful in obtaining his transfer overseas, but was retained at various cadet training schools, where he did most valuable work until the close of the war.
He was demobilised in February 1919.
37, Burrow's Road, Willesden, N.W.10   X18250.

MARSHMENT, J., Pte., 13th London Regt. (Kensingtons).

He volunteered in May 1915, and proceeding to the Western Front in 1917, took part in many important engagements up to the close of the war, including those at Arras, Cambrai and the final Retreat and Advance. He was wounded twice in the course of his service.
He was demobilised in January 1919, holding the General Service and Victory Medals.
26, Aspenlea Road, Hammersmith, W.6   14292.

MART, A. P., Q.M.S., 2nd Bedfordshire Regt.

He was serving in 1914, and took part in many important engagements on the Western Front throughout the war, including the battles of Ypres and the Somme, in both of which he was wounded.
He was still serving in 1920, and holds the 1914 Star, General Service and Victory Medals.
22, Pretoria Road, Upper Edmonton, N.18   X17021B.

MART, S. H. (D.C.M.), Q.M.S., 2nd Bedfordshires.

He was serving in 1914, and was on the Western Front until 1919, taking part in the battles of Ypres, the Somme and other engagements.
He was awarded the D.C.M. and a Russian Order for devotion to duty and conspicuous gallantry in the field, and also holds the 1914 Star, General Service and Victory Medals.
22, Pretoria Road, Upper Edmonton, N.18   17021A.

MART, W. H. (D.C.M.), S.M., 2nd Bedfordshire Regiment.

He was serving in 1914, and was sent to France in the same year. He took part in many engagements and was wounded in action on the Somme in 1916.
He was awarded the D.C.M. for gallant conduct in the field, and also holds the 1914 Star, General Service and Victory Medals.
He was still serving in 1920.
22, Pretoria Road, Upper Edmonton, N.18   X17021C.

MARTIN, A., Rifleman, 5th London Regiment (London Rifle Brigade).
He joined in 1917, and at the conclusion of his training proceeded to France, where he took part in many engagements and was taken prisoner in 1918. He was released after some months' captivity in Germany.
He was still serving in 1920, and holds the General Service and Victory Medals.
16, New Holly Lane, Willesden, N.W.10   15581A.

MARTIN, A., Lce.-Cpl., R.A.S.C. (Remounts Section).
He volunteered in April 1915, and was attached to the Royal Field Artillery as a horse breaker. He volunteered for service overseas, but was retained to perform this special work, in the course of which he was injured several times.
He was demobilised in April 1919.
61, Garvan Road, Hammersmith, W.6   14836.

MARTIN, A. C., Pte., 17th Middlesex Regiment.
He volunteered in April 1915, and after the completion of his training was drafted to the Western Front, where he took part in many engagements, including the Somme (1916) and the Ancre (1917).
He was demobilised in March 1919, and holds the General Service and Victory Medals.
23, Delorme Street, Hammersmith, W.6   T13775.

MARTIN, A. G. (M.M.), Sergt., 18th London Regiment (London Irish Rifles).
He volunteered in September 1914, and after the completion of his training was drafted in 1915 to Egypt, where he served until 1916. He was then sent to France and took part in many engagements, including those on the Somme, and at Ypres.
He was awarded the Military Medal for conspicuous bravery and devotion to duty in the field, and also holds the 1914-15 Star, General Service and Victory Medals. He was demobilised in 1919.
21, Sunnyside Road North, Lower Edmonton, N.9   14558B.

MARTIN, C. H., Sapper, Royal Engineers.
Volunteering in May 1915, he was drafted to the Western Front, where he took part in many engagements. During his service he was wounded on the Somme Front in April 1916.
He holds the 1914-15 Star, General Service and Victory Medals, and was demobilised in January 1919.
8, Oxford Road, Lower Edmonton, N.9   13118.

MARTIN, C. W., Capt., R.A.S.C. and Labour Corps.
Volunteering in the ranks of the Royal Army Service Corps in 1914, he was drafted overseas the same year and was in action in many engagements on the Western Front. He was afterwards commissioned, attained the rank of Captain, and was in command of a Labour Corps Company.
He was demobilised in 1920, and holds the 1914 Star, General Service and Victory Medals.
16, Pretoria Road, Upper Edmonton, N.18   X17364.

MARTIN, E. W., Pte., Durham Light Infantry and Machine Gun Corps.
He joined in July 1916, and proceeding to the Eastern Front later in that year saw much service in the Balkan campaign until 1919. While in the East he suffered severely from malaria.
He was demobilised in March 1919, holding the General Service and Victory Medals.
49, Oldfield Road, Willesden, N.W.10   15988.

MARTIN, F., Lce.-Cpl., Royal Engineers.
He volunteered in 1915, and served in France, where he was engaged on Field Telephone work on various fronts, including the Somme and Ypres.
He was demobilised in February 1919, and holds the General Service and Victory Medals.
31, Waldo Road, College Park, N.W.10   X18194.

MARTIN, F., 2nd Cpl., Royal Engineers.
He volunteered in July 1915, and after completing his training, was drafted in the same year to France, where he took part in many engagements, including the battles of Ypres, Arras, and in the heavy fighting near Lille.
He was demobilised in March 1919, and holds the 1914-15 Star, General Service and Victory Medals.
39, Leopold Street, Willesden, N.W.10   14608.

MARTIN, F., 1st-Class Stoker, Royal Navy.
He volunteered in August 1914, and served on important duties with the Grand Fleet in the North Sea.
He holds the 1914 Star, General Service and Victory Medals.
In 1920 he was still serving.
21, Sunnyside Road North, Lower Edmonton, N.9   14558A.

MARTIN, F. G. C., Pte., R.A.S.C.
He volunteered in August 1914, and was drafted in the following year to the Western Front, where he took part in many engagements, including Ypres, the Somme and Cambrai.
He was wounded and was discharged as medically unfit for further service in June 1918, holding the 1914-15 Star, General Service and Victory Medals.
231, Shirland Road, Maida Hill, W.9   19231—16152A.

MARTIN, F. W., Pte., R.A.S.C.
He joined in May 1918 on attaining military age, and after completing his training was engaged on important duties with his unit. Later he was sent to Germany with the Army of Occupation, and remained there until he was demobilised in March 1920.
4, Maldon Road, Lower Edmonton, N.9   14242.

MARTIN, G., Pte., Northumberland Fusiliers.
He volunteered in February 1915, and after the completion of his training was retained with his unit on important duties until 1918, when he was sent to France. He took part in the engagements in the final Advance and was wounded.
He was demobilised in March 1918, and holds the General Service and Victory Medals.
138, Portnall Road, Maida Hill, W.9   X19589.

MARTIN, G. E., Lce.-Cpl., Royal Engineers.
He volunteered in August 1914, and served on the Western Front, taking part in the battles of Mons, Loos, Arras and Ypres. He was engaged as Regimental Saddler, and also assisted in laying cables.
In March 1919 he was demobilised, and holds the Mons Star, General Service and Victory Medals.
79, Bramber Road, West Kensington, W.14   15719.

MARTIN, G. W., Pte., 8th Royal Fusiliers.
He volunteered in December 1914, and in 1915 was drafted to the Western Front, where he was wounded in the battle of Ypres. He was afterwards invalided home and discharged as medically unfit for further service in July 1917.
He holds the 1914-15 Star, General Service and Victory Medals.
306, Brettenham Road, Upper Edmonton, N.18   15215.

MARTIN, J. C., Special War Worker.
Having lost the sight of an eye, he was rejected for service in the Army, and being anxious to serve his country, worked at Messrs. Well's Aviation Factory, Chelsea, from 1914 to 1918. He was there engaged in the construction of undercarriages for aeroplanes and his duties required a high degree of skill. He carried out his work in a very efficient manner, and rendered valuable services throughout.
42, Mulgrave Road, Fulham, S.W.6   16170.

MARTIN, J. E., C.S.M., 2/9th Middlesex Regt.
He volunteered in January 1915, and was retained on important duties until September of the following year, when he was drafted to France. While in England he had gained rapid promotion for consistent good work. While serving in France in November 1916 he was taken prisoner of war during heavy fighting on the Somme, and suffered many hardships during his captivity.
In December 1918 he was demobilised, and holds the General Service and Victory Medals.
51, Manor Park Road, Harlesden, N.W.10   13221.

MARTIN, J. J., Pte., 9th West Yorkshire Regt.
He volunteered in September 1914, and in the following year was sent to the Dardanelles, where he took part in the heavy fighting during the Gallipoli campaign. After the evacuation of the Peninsula he was drafted to France, and after serving in many engagements, was killed in action during the battle of the Somme on September 25th, 1916.
He was entitled to the 1914-15 Star, General Service and Victory Medals.
6, Francis Street, Hammersmith, W.6   14797B.

MARTIN, M. (Mrs.), Special War Worker.
This lady volunteered for work of national importance, with a view to relieving a man for service in the Army, and secured a position on the Central London Underground Railway. She was employed for a considerable time during the war, and her services proved very valuable.
20, Mund Street, West Kensington, W.14   16920B.

MARTIN, P. C., Pte., 14th Middlesex Regiment.
Volunteering in 1915, he was drafted to France in the following year. While overseas he was attached to the Royal Air Force, and was engaged on important duties at various aerodromes behind the firing line.
He remained in France until his demobilisation in April 1919, and holds the General Service and Victory Medals.
20, Mund Street, West Kensington, W.14   16920A.

MARTIN, S. J., Sapper, Royal Engineers.

He joined in 1917, and was ordered overseas later in the same year. While on the Western Front he took an active part in the battles of Arras and Ypres, and in other important engagements.
In 1919 he was demobilised, and holds the General Service and Victory Medals.
120, Town Road, Lower Edmonton, N.9. 13572.

MARTIN, T. E., Rifleman, Rifle Brigade.

He joined in June 1918, and after his training was engaged on duties of the greatest importance. He gave valuable services, but was not successful in obtaining his transfer overseas before the cessation of hostilities.
He was demobilised in February 1919.
76, Bramber Road, West Kensington, W.14 16218.

MARTIN, W., Sapper, Royal Engineers.

Volunteering in August 1914, he was in the same year sent to India. After a period of special duty there, he was drafted to the Western Front in 1915. He took an active part in many important engagements and was severely wounded in action.
In March 1919 he was demobilised, and holds the 1914-15 Star, General Service and Victory Medals.
35, Maldon Road, Lower Edmonton, N.9 14787B.

MARTIN, W. H., Stoker, R.N., H.M.S. "Heron."

He joined in June 1918 on attaining the age of 18, and was engaged on important duties at a large Naval Base in Scotland. He also served on board H.M.S. "Heron," and was present at the surrender of the German Fleet at Scapa Flow.
In 1920 he was still serving.
5, Milton Road, Upper Edmonton, N.18 X17283.

MARTIN, W. J., Sergt., R.A.S.C. (M.T.)

Volunteering in June 1915, he was retained on special duties at various stations with his unit. He carried out important work in the motor repair shops and gained promotion to Sergeant for consistent good work. In 1917 he was drafted to France and served on various sectors of the Front, taking part in many engagements.
He was demobilised in February 1919, and holds the General Service and Victory Medals.
170, Kilburn Lane, North Kensington, W.9 18708.

MARTIN, W. J., Pte., Labour Battalion, Royal West Surrey Regiment.

He volunteered in September 1916, and served in France, where he suffered from trench fever. He was invalided home and died after four months in hospital in Wales, on February 20th, 1919.
He was entitled to the General Service and Victory Medals.
18, Werley Avenue, Dawes Road, S.W.6 X17874.

MARTIN, W. L. (Mrs.), Special War Worker.

From August 1916 until June 1918 this lady was engaged at Cricklewood as examiner of fuses for shells, in which capacity she rendered valuable service. She was also for a time at Swindon on important work in connection with the despatch of shells to our armies in the field. She received high commendation for her good work.
231, Shirland Road, Maida Hill, W.9 16152-19231B.

MARTINA, A. C., Pte., 7th Middlesex Regiment.

He joined in 1917, and was drafted to the Western Front shortly after. While in this seat of war he took part in the battles of Ypres and Bullecourt, and in the Advance of the Allies in 1918. During his active service he was wounded and gassed. After the signing of the Armistice he went to Germany with the Army of Occupation and remained there until his demobilisation in 1919.
He holds the General Service and Victory Medals.
22, Dieppe Street, West Kensington, W.14 16257.

MARTINDALE, H. D., Pte., 18th Middlesex Regt.

He volunteered in March 1915, and in the following November was drafted to the Western Front, where he took part in the battles of the Somme, Ypres, Arras and Cambrai, and in other important engagements.
In March 1919 he was demobilised, and holds the 1914-15 Star, General Service and Victory Medals.
10, Brett Road, Stonebridge Park, N.W.10 14385.

MARTINDALE, T., Cpl., Northamptonshire Regt. and Bedford Regiment.

He joined in 1917, and was drafted to the Western Front early in the following year. He saw much severe fighting during the Retreat and Advance of the Allied Armies, and returned to England for demobilisation in January 1919.
He holds the General Service and Victory Medals.
27, Berry Street, Willesden, N.W.10 15409.

MARVEN, W. J., Pte., 1st Middlesex Regiment.

He volunteered in August 1914, and was ordered overseas in the following November. During his service on the Western Front he took part in the battles of Neuve Chapelle, the Somme and Cambrai, and in heavy fighting round Armentières. He also served throughout the Retreat and Advance of the Allies in 1918, and remained in France until his demobilisation in February 1919.
He holds the 1914-15 Star, General Service and Victory Medals.
83, Sandringham Road, Cricklewood, N.W.2 X17132.

MARVIN, A. F. (M.M.), C.Q.M.S., Somerset L.I.

He rejoined in January 1917, after having previously served in the Boer War, and was sent to the Western Front in that year. He took part in the Allied Retreat and Advance of 1918, and was awarded the Military Medal for conspicuous bravery in taking charge of the Company after all the officers had been killed
He also holds the King's and the Queen's South African, the General Service and Victory Medals, and was demobilised in January 1918.
253, Portnall Road, Maida Hill, W.9 X19767

MASEY, R. W. J., Pte., 7th Bedfordshire Regt.

He volunteered in September 1914, and after the completion of his training was retained on special duties with his unit for some time. Later he was drafted to France and took part in the heavy fighting on the Somme, during the course of which he was severely wounded in April 1917.
He was invalided home, and eventually discharged in August 1918 as medically unfit for further service, holding the General Service and Victory Medals.
23, Fourth Avenue, Queen's Park Estate, W.10 X18669B.

MASLEN, F. J., Pte., 4th Middlesex Regiment.

He volunteered in August 1914, and was sent to France later in the year. While on the Western Front he fought at Ypres, Hill 60, and the Somme, and in other important operations. During his active service he was wounded no less than four times, and was eventually demobilised in May 1919.
He holds the 1914 Star, General Service and Victory Medals.
7, Cornwallis Avenue, Lower Edmonton, N.9 13295.

MASLIN, J. C., Pte., Grenadier Guards.

Volunteering in 1915, he was drafted to the Western Front in the same year and was in action at Loos, where he was wounded. He was invalided home, but on recovery returned to France, and was again wounded during the heavy fighting on the Somme in 1916 For some months he was in a military hospital at Oxford, and when he again returned to France was killed in action at Fontaine Notre Dame on November 27th, 1917.
He was entitled to the 1914-15 Star, General Service and Victory Medals.
67, Hartington Road, Tottenham, N.17 X19146A.

MASLIN, W., Cpl., 1/7th Middlesex Regiment.

He was mobilised in August 1914, in the same year was sent to Gibraltar, and thence in 1915 to the Western Front, where he served for nearly three years. During this time he took part in many important engagements, including the battles of Ypres and the Somme, and the Allied Advance of 1918, in which he was severely wounded. He was invalided home, and after a protracted illness was demobilised, holding the 1914-15 Star, General Service and Victory Medals.
67, Hartington Road, Tottenham, N.17 X19146B.

MASON, E., Rifleman, King's Royal Rifle Corps.

He joined in June 1916, and later in the same year was drafted to the Western Front. He was in action on the Somme and other engagements, and was killed near Arras on May 12th, 1917.
He was entitled to the General Service and Victory Medals.
53, Farrant Street, Queen's Park Estate, W.10 X19050.

MASON, F., Wireless Operator, R.N., H.M.S. "Blonde" and H.M.S. "Fitzroy."

He joined in December 1916, and served with the Fleet in the North Sea, taking part in the battle of Heligoland. H.M.S. "Blonde," on which he was then serving, was one of the vessels that escorted the German Fleet to Scapa Flow. In 1920 he was serving on board H.M.S. "Fitzroy," and holds the General Service and Victory Medals.
1, Church Lane, Willesden, N.W.10 16032

MASON, H. G., Signalman, R.N., H.M.S. "Anemone."

He volunteered in August 1914, and was at first engaged on important mine-sweeping duties in the Mediterranean Sea. He took part in the naval operations during the Dardanelles campaign, and was fatally wounded by a Turkish sniper on January 28th, 1916.
He was entitled to the 1914 Star, General Service and Victory Medals.
34, Alston Road, Upper Edmonton, N.18 16501.

MASON, J., Sergt., 2nd Coldstream Guards.

He enlisted in January 1913, and on the outbreak of war was sent to the Western Front, where he served until 1918. He was in action at Mons, Loos, Ypres, the Somme, Cambrai, Arras, Bapaume, Mauberge and in the Allied Advance of 1918, and was twice wounded. After the cessation of hostilities he was sent to Germany with the Army of Occupation, and in January 1920 was discharged, holding the Mons Star, General Service and Victory Medals.

33, Droop Street, Queen's Park Estate, W.10   X18579.

MASON, W. W., Pte., Seaforth Highlanders.

Joining in August 1916, he was retained on important duties with his unit at various stations. He gave valuable services, but was not successful in obtaining his transfer overseas before the cessation of hostilities.

He was demobilised in March 1919.

53, Chauncey Street, Lower Edmonton, N.9   14268.

MASSEY, F. J., Pte., Royal Fusiliers.

He volunteered in June 1915, was sent to France in the following year, and took part in many engagements, including the battle of the Somme. He received six wounds at Ypres in June 1916, and was again wounded at the same place at a later date. He died from his wounds at Bristol Hospital on August 24th, 1917, and was entitled to the General Service and Victory Medals.

15, Westbury Road, Willesden, N.W.10   15066A.

MASSINGHAM, W. J., Mechanic, R.A.F.

Volunteering in 1915, he was sent to France later in the same year. While on the Western Front he was engaged at aeroplane workshops on duties which called for a high degree of technical skill.

He was demobilised in 1919, holding the 1914–15 Star, General Service and Victory Medals.

28, Florence Road, Upper Edmonton, N.18   16007.

MASTERS, A., Pte., Bedfordshire Regiment.

He volunteered in 1914, and after being engaged on special duties until 1916 was drafted to France. He then took part in the battles of the Somme, Arras and Ypres, and in heavy fighting during the Allied Retreat and Advance in 1918.

He holds the General Service and Victory Medals, and was demobilised in 1919.

46, Hartington Road, Tottenham, N.17   X19111.

MASTERS, A. E. (Miss), Special War Worker.

During the war this lady was engaged on a large farm in Dorsetshire, and thereby released a man for military service. Her work was carried out in a very efficient manner and earned high praise. She gave up a good situation in order to do this excellent work.

34, Dieppe Street, West Kensington, W.14   16251B.

MASTERS, F., Pte., 6th Middlesex Regiment.

He joined in September 1916, was sent to France and thence to Italy in the following year, and in 1918 returned to the Western Front. While abroad he took part in the fighting at Arras and Cambrai, was twice wounded, and suffered from shell-shock. He was invalided home, and after being in hospital in England for some time was demobilised in September 1919.

He holds the General Service and Victory Medals.

27, Durban Road, Tottenham, N.17   X18427.

MASTERS, F. H. J., Leading Seaman, R.N., H.M.S. " Temeraire."

He was in the Navy at the outbreak of war, saw much service with the Grand Fleet in the North Sea and other waters, and took part in the battle of Jutland and many engagements of a minor character.

He was discharged in October 1919, and holds the 1914 Star, General Service and Victory Medals.

18, Fordingley Road, Maida Hill, W.9   X19680.

MASTERS, G., Driver, R.A.S.C. (M.T.)

He volunteered in 1914, and immediately proceeded to the Western Front, where he took an active part in the retreat from Mons and in the battles of Ypres, Loos, the Somme and Arras. In August 1916, owing to his age, he was discharged, and immediately joined the Special Constabulary, with whom he rendered valuable service.

He holds the Mons Star, General Service and Victory Medals.

34, Dieppe Street, West Kensington, W.14   16251A.

MASTERS, H., Pte., Suffolk Regiment.

He joined in October 1916, and after his training was retained on important duties with his unit at various stations. He gave valuable services, but was unsuccessful in obtaining his transfer overseas before hostilities ceased. In 1919, however, he volunteered for Russia, and saw service with the Relief Force there until his demobilisation in the same year.

27, Durban Road, Tottenham, N.17   X18287.

MASTERS, P. G. E. (Miss), Special War Worker.

During the war this lady was engaged on important duties at Messrs. Waring & Gillow's factory, where she carried out work of national importance in connection with the manufacture of aeroplanes. She performed her duties in a capable manner, and received high commendation for her valuable services.

34, Dieppe Street, West Kensington, W.14   16251C.

MASTERS, W., Driver, Royal Engineers.

He volunteered for service in August 1914, and in the following year was drafted to Salonica, where he took part in many engagements. In 1917 he was invalided home owing to shell-shock, and on recovery he was retained on important duties until he was demobilised in March 1920.

He holds the 1914–15 Star, General Service and Victory Medals.

66, Clarendon Street, Paddington, W.2   X20669.

MASTERS, W. A., 1st Air Mechanic, R.A.F.

He volunteered in 1915, and in the following year was sent overseas. While on the Western Front he took an active part in the battles of the Somme, Arras, Ypres and Cambrai, and in other engagements.

He was demobilised in 1919, and holds the General Service and Victory Medals.

12, Kenmont Gardens, College Park, N.W.10   X17577A.

MATHER, N. E. G., Rifleman, 6th London Regt. (Rifles).

He joined in April 1918, and after his training was drafted to Russia, where he saw much severe fighting, and suffered from trench fever and malaria. He remained there until December 1919, when he returned to England and was demobilised.

He holds the General Service and Victory Medals.

22, Allestree Road, Munster Road, S.W.6   X19201.

MATHERON, W. J., Sapper, Royal Engineers.

He volunteered in 1915, and later in the same year was drafted to Egypt, where he took an active part in important operations against the Turks. He remained on that Front until his demobilisation in 1919, and holds the 1914–15 Star, General Service and Victory Medals.

68, Kimberley Road, Upper Edmonton, N.18   16540.

MATHEWS, G. H., A.B., R.N., H.M.S. " Empress of India."

He volunteered in January 1915, and was posted to H.M.S. " Empress of India." While with this ship he was engaged on important escort duties with the North Sea Patrol.

He was still serving in 1920, and holds the 1914–15 Star, General Service and Victory Medals.

21, Raynham Road, Upper Edmonton, N.18   16001A.

MATHEWS, H., Pte., 5th Middlesex Regiment.

He joined in August 1916, and served for three years on the Western Front, where he took part in the battles of Ypres, Arras, Cambrai and other important engagements.

He was demobilised in September 1919, and holds the General Service and Victory Medals.

42, Earlsmead Road, College Park, N.W.10   X18035.

MATHEWS, H., Rifleman, 16th Royal Irish Rifles.

He volunteered in August 1914, and was retained on special duties with his unit until September 1916, when he was sent to France. While on the Western Front he took part in many important engagements, including the battles of the Somme, Messines, Ypres, Cambrai and St. Quentin.

He returned from France for his demobilisation in January 1919, and holds the General Service and Victory Medals.

8, Minet Avenue, Willesden, N.W.10   13906.

MATHEWS, W., 1st Air Mechanic, R.A.F.

He joined in March 1916, and later in the same year was sent to France, where for a period of eight months he was engaged on duties which called for a high degree of technical skill. He then met with a serious accident during the landing of an airship, and was invalided home. On his recovery he was medically unfit for further duties overseas, and rendered valuable services at home until his demobilisation in February 1919.

He holds the General Service and Victory Medals.

45, Brenthurst Road, Church End, N.W.10   16380.

MATSELL, J. H., Pte., 7th London Regiment.

He volunteered for service in 1915, and was sent to the Western Front, where he fought in many engagements, and was badly wounded. After being in hospital for some time he was invalided home and discharged in January 1918 as medically unfit for further service.

He holds the 1914–15 Star, General Service and Victory Medals. 9, Rock Avenue, Fulham Road, S.W.6   X20224.

MATTEY, J., Pte., Royal Fusiliers and R.A.F.
Volunteering in August 1914, he was shortly after sent to the Western Front, where he took part in much heavy fighting. He was severely wounded and invalided home, and after a period in hospital was discharged as medically unfit for further service in December of the same year. Later on, however, he rejoined in the R.A.F., but owing to his previous wound was retained on important duties at a large aerodrome in England, where he rendered valuable services until his final demobilisation in February 1920.
He holds the 1914 Star, General Service and Victory Medals.
17, Reporton Road, Munster Road, S.W.6   X18864.

MATTHEWS, A., Pte., Duke of Cornwall's L.I.
He joined in September 1914, and served in various sectors in France until April 1917, when he was discharged on account of the loss of an eye. He was also wounded on another occasion.
He holds the General Service and Victory Medals.
38, Bath Road, Lower Edmonton, N.9   13047B.

MATTHEWS, A. E., Pte., R.A.M.C.
He joined in 1916, and was sent after his training was completed to France, where he served as an orderly in an important base hospital at Rouen. He rendered similar service elsewhere in France and at Antwerp, and was demobilised in 1920.
He holds the General Service and Victory Medals.
79, Rayleigh Road, West Kensington, W.14   12719.

MATTHEWS, C., Pte., R.A.S.C.
Joining the Army on June 7th, 1915, he was sent during the following year to France, where he was engaged on active service for three years.
He holds the General Service and Victory Medals, and was demobilised on June 13th, 1919.
97, Harley Road, Willesden, N.W.10   13174B.

MATTHEWS, C., C.S.M., Northumberland Fus.
Sergeant-Major Matthews joined shortly after the outbreak of war, and at first served on the Western Front. In 1916 he was drafted to Mesopotamia, and returned in October 1919 to England to be demobilised. His promotion resulted from his energy and technical knowledge.
He was twice wounded, and holds the 1914-15 Star, General Service and Victory Medals.
38, Bath Road, Lower Edmonton, N.9   13047A.

MATTHEWS, D., Pte., Labour Corps.
He joined in July 1917, and served on Home defence duty at West Ham. He was unsuccessful in obtaining his transfer overseas, but rendered excellent service, being demobilised in July 1919.
4, Chaldon Road, Dawes Road, S.W.6   X17719.

MATTHEWS, E., Pte., The Queen's (Royal West Surrey Regiment).
He joined in May 1917, and after his training was drafted to Italy. In this theatre of war he served until 1919, when he was transferred to India, where he was still serving in 1920. He was wounded once, and holds the General Service and Victory Medals.
38, Bath Road, Lower Edmonton, N.9   13047C.

MATTHEWS, F., Pte., Labour Corps.
Joining in March 1917, he was sent to the Western Front, being engaged there on special duties of a responsible character during the whole of his service.
He was demobilised in March 1919, and holds the General Service and Victory Medals.
105, Roundwood Road, Willesden. N.W.10   16046.

MATTHEWS, F. H., Pte., R.A.M.C.
Joining in June 1915, he was drafted after training to the Western Front. There he took part in the battles of the Somme and Ypres, and was gassed while in action.
He was demobilised in April 1919, and is entitled to the General Service and Victory Medals.
26, Bounces Road, Lower Edmonton, N.9   13945.

MATTHEWS, F. W., Rifleman, K.R.R.
He joined in September 1914, and during his long and varied service on the Western Front, took part in the battles of the Somme, Festubert, Arras, Loos, Neuve Chapelle, Ypres and Vimy Ridge. He subsequently went to Germany with the Army of Occupation, and there acted as an officer's batman. In February 1920 he was demobilised, holding the 1915 Star, General Service and Victory Medals.
24, Chesson Road, West Kensington, W.14   X17160.

MATTHEWS, G. J., Gunner, R.F.A.
He joined in January 1915, and served on both Western and Eastern Fronts. He took part in the battle of the Somme. After two months in France he was sent to Salonica, and thence to Egypt and Palestine, where he served with General Allenby at Jerusalem, Jaffa, Jericho and Beersheba. He was demobilised in July 1919, and holds the General Service and Victory Medals.
85, Archel Road, West Kensington, W.14   16661.

MATTHEWS, H. P., Pte., Royal Scots Fusiliers.
He joined in October 1915, and was sent when his training was completed, in the following year to Salonica. After three years' varied service on this Front he was demobilised in April 1919, holding the General Service and Victory Medals.
133, Drayton Road, Harlesden, N.W.10   T16516B.

MATTHEWS, J. H., Sapper, Royal Engineers.
He joined in April 1915, and served on the Western Front. While in France he suffered from rheumatic fever and ague and was sent to hospital. In response to an appeal by the G.P.O. for his services, he was discharged in September 1918.
He holds the General Service and Victory Medals.
11, Lintaine Grove, West Kensington, W.14   16818.

MATTHEWS, L. C., Lce.-Cpl., 5th London Regt. (L.R.B.)
He joined on September 14th, 1914, and was drafted to the Western Front, where he took part in several engagements, including the battle of the Somme, during which he was wounded on September 9th, 1916. After being for some time in hospital in France, he was invalided to England. After varied treatment in hospital he was discharged unfit for further service in December 1917, holding the General Service and Victory Medals.
1, Wycombe Road, Tottenham, N.17   X19073.

MATTHEWS, S. C., Cpl., Royal Engineers.
Joining in July 1915, he served on the Western Front. He took part in the battles of the Somme, Arras, Loos, Neuve Chapelle, Bullecourt, St. Quentin, Ypres, Vimy Ridge, Poperinghe and Cambrai. He was engaged in the Railway Operative Division in the conveyance of ammunition, rations and troops.
In May 1919 he was demobilised, holding the 1915 Star, General Service and Victory Medals.
24, Chesson Road, West Kensington, W.14   X17161.

MATTHEWS, S. F. P., 1st-Class Aircraftsman, Royal Air Force.
During his service, which extended from September 1917 until October 1919, he was stationed at Eastchurch and Ascot. He did not succeed in securing his transfer overseas as his duties in England were of an essential character.
He holds the General Service Medal.
133, Drayton Road, Harlesden, N.W.10   T16516A.

MATTHEWS, T. H. R., A.B., Royal Navy, H.M.S. "Phæton."
Joining in August 1917 at the age of 18, his service was of a varied and dangerous character. He first served on a mine-layer in the North Sea and later on a mine-sweeper at Scapa Flow. This vessel assisted in bringing in the German light cruisers.
He was demobilised in April 1919, being entitled to the General Service and Victory Medals.
14, Colville Road, Lower Edmonton, N.9   12005.

MATTHEWS, T. J., Pte., Essex Regiment.
He joined in 1917, and served on the Western Front, taking part in the battles of the Somme, Vimy Ridge, Arras, Bullecourt, during which he was twice wounded. Whilst he was in hospital at Etaples it was severely bombed during an air-raid.
In 1919 he was demobilised, and holds the General Service and Victory Medals.
85, Archel Road, West Kensington, W.14   16660.

MATTHEWS, W. A., Sapper, Royal Engineers.
He joined in August 1914 and went to France in the following January. He was wounded in the left leg at Passchendaele in June 1917 and was invalided to England, where he remained on Home service until February 24th, 1919, when he was demobilised.
He holds the 1914-15 Star, General Service and Victory Medals.
97, Harley Road, Willesden, N.W.10   13174A.

MATTHEWS, W. G., Sapper, Royal Engineers.
He joined in 1915, and served with the postal section in Salonica, where he contracted malaria and was for some months in hospital.
He was demobilised in March 1919, and holds the 1914-15 Star, General Service and Victory Medals.
102, Bulwer Road, Upper Edmonton, N.18   X17289A.

MATTHEWS, W. G., Sapper, Royal Engineers.
He joined in October 1914, and in the following year was sent to France, where he remained until February 1919. Here he was engaged in varied and responsible work for nearly four years.
He holds the 1915 Star, General Service and Victory Medals, and was demobilised in February 1919.
97, Harley Road, Willesden, N.W.10   13174C.

MATTHEWS, W. H. E., A.B., R.N., H.M.S. " Bayano."

He joined in March 1917 and served in the North Sea. H.M.S. " Bayano " was employed on such varied duties as convoying troopships, searching for submarines and in laying mines.
He holds the General Service and Victory Medals, and was demobilised on February 1st, 1917.
31, Warwick Road, Upper Edmonton, N.18   X17506.

MATTHEWS, W. S., Pte., Middlesex Regiment.

He joined on April 15th, 1918, at the age of 16 years, and served at various camps in England. Despite many efforts to secure his transfer overseas he was unsuccessful since he was below military age.
He was demobilised on January 10th, 1920.
102, Bulwer Road, Upper Edmonton, N.18   X17289B.

MATTHIAS, A. E., Lce.-Cpl., 2nd Essex Regt.

He joined in May 1917 and in the following year was sent to France, where he took part in the engagements near Amiens, Bapaume, Cambrai and Ypres. He was severely wounded and invalided home, and after spending some time in hospital was eventually demobilised in October 1919, holding the General Service and Victory Medals.
4, Pearscroft Road, Fulham, S.W.6   X20508B.

MATTHIAS, H. E., Pte., 2nd London Regiment (Royal Fusiliers).

He volunteered in December 1914 and was sent to the Western Front, where he took part in many engagements, including those of Vimy Ridge, the Somme, Beaumont-Hamel and Arras. He was badly wounded and invalided home, and discharged as medically unfit for further service in 1917.
He holds the General Service and Victory Medals.
4, Pearscroft Road, Fulham, S.W.6   X20508C.

MATTINGLEY, J. W., Sergt., 8th Tank Corps.

He joined in March 1916 and after his training was sent to the Western Front, where he took part in many engagements, including the Somme, Ypres and Cambrai.
He was demobilised in February 1919, holding the General Service and Victory Medals.
49, Station Road, Hanwell, W.7   12386.

MAXTED, E., Sergt., R.A.S.C. (M.T.)

He volunteered in August 1914 and was retained with his unit on important duties until he was sent to the Western Front in 1916. He took an active part in many engagements, and in 1919 was ordered to India, where he was still serving in 1920.
He holds the General Service and Victory Medals.
28, Fairlight Avenue, Willesden, N.W.10   14018.

MAXWELL, J. R., Rifleman, 15th London Regt. (Civil Service Rifles).

He volunteered in November 1915 and after his training was retained with his unit on important duties until April 1918. He was then drafted to the Western Front, where he took part in many engagements and was wounded.
He was demobilised in January 1919, holding the General Service and Victory Medals.
21, Rockley Road, West Kensington, W.14   11818.

MAY, A., Sergt., R.N.A.S. and R.A.S.C.

He volunteered in 1914 and in the following year was sent to France with the armoured cars While there he was transferred to the R.A.S.C., and acted as an ambulance driver. He was present in many important engagements, including those on the Somme, the Marne and Ypres, and was wounded in the neck.
He was discharged as medically unfit for further service in 1917, and holds the 1914-15 Star, General Service and Victory Medals.
33, Droop Street, Queen's Park, W.10   X18578A.

MAY, A., Bandsman, Northumberland Fusiliers.

He volunteered in August 1914 and was retained with his unit on important duties until drafted to the Western Front. He took part in many engagements until 1918, when he was invalided home and discharged as medically unfit for further service in October in the same year.
He holds the General Service and Victory Medals.
100, Adeney Road, Hammersmith, W.6   14280B.

MAY, E., Lce.-Cpl., 4th Middlesex Regiment.

He volunteered in August 1914 and was drafted to the Western Front, where he took part in many engagements and was taken prisoner. While in captivity in Germany for three years he suffered many privations.
He was demobilised in March 1919, holding the General Service and Victory Medals.
100, Adeney Road, Hammersmith, W.6   14280A.

MAY, E. W., Staff-Sergt., R.A.S.C.

He volunteered in 1914 and after completing his training was retained with his unit on important duties as an instructor. He gave valuable services, but was unable to obtain his transfer overseas before the cessation of hostilities.
He was demobilised in 1919.
423, High Road, Willesden, N.W.10   16620C.

MAY, F., Pte., 13th Middlesex Regiment.

He volunteered in February 1915 and after his training was drafted to the Western Front, where he took part in many important engagements, and was wounded.
He was demobilised in December 1918, holding the General Service and Victory Medals.
100, Adeney Road, Hammersmith, W.6   14280C.

MAY, J., A.B., R.N., H.M.S. " Pathfinder."

He enlisted in the Navy in February 1912, and on the declaration of war cruised in the North Sea. He was drowned in September 1914 when his vessel was sunk off St. Abb's Head. This was the first of our ships to be sunk by a German submarine.
He was entitled to the 1914 Star, General Service and Victory Medals.
33, Droop Street, Queen's Park, W.10   X18578B.

MAY, R. D., Petty Officer, R.N., H.M.S. " Renown."

During the war he served on H.M.S. " Agincourt," and took part in the battle of Jutland and other naval engagements. He was on H.M.S." Renown " at the time when H.R.H. the Prince of Wales visited the Colonies, and in 1920 was still serving.
He holds the 1914-15 Star, General Service and Victory Medals.
33, Droop Street, Queen's Park Estate, W.10   X18578C.

MAYCLEM, F., Pte., Manchester Regiment.

He volunteered in February 1915 and saw much service on the Eastern Front, where he contracted dysentery. He was invalided home in consequence and was eventually discharged as medically unfit for further service in February 1918.
He holds the 1914-15 Star, General Service and Victory Medals.
9, Lintaine Grove, West Kensington, W.14   X16998.

MAYCOCK, W. G., Rifleman, 6th London Regt. (Rifles).

Joining in August 1917 he served on the Western Front, and took part in the Allied Advance in the following year. He was wounded in action at Morlancourt, near Albert, and after the signing of the Armistice went to Germany with the Army of Occupation. He remained there until his demobilisation in October 1919, and holds the General Service and Victory Medals.
103, Roundwood Road, Willesden, N.W.10   16045.

MAYER, A., Pte., 2/4th Duke of Wellington's (West Riding Regiment).

He volunteered in March 1916 and later in the year was drafted to the Western Front, where he took part in heavy fighting in various sectors. He was terribly wounded in the face while in action at Bullecourt in September 1918, and in 1920 was still in hospital under treatment.
He holds the General Service and Victory Medals.
61, Somerset Road, Upper Edmonton, N.18   X17043.

MAYES, D., Pte., 14th London Regiment (London Scottish).

He joined in February 1916 and was later in the same year sent to the Western Front to France. While on the Western Front he fought in the battles of Arras, Ypres and Cambrai and in important engagements during the concluding stages of the war.
In November 1918 he was discharged, and holds the General Service and Victory Medals.
1, Evesham House, Stanlake Road, Shepherd's Bush, W.12   11835.

MAYHEW, G., Pte., Machine Gun Corps.

Volunteering in September 1915 he was sent to France in the following April, and took part in much heavy fighting. He was killed in action on December 3rd, 1917, at the battle of Cambrai.
He was entitled to the General Service and Victory Medals.
129, Sandringham Road, Cricklewood, N.W.2   17353B.

MAYHEW, J., Pte., 2nd Queen's (Royal West Surrey Regiment).

He volunteered in September 1915 and was drafted overseas in the following April. After only a short period on the Western Front he was killed in action at the battle of the Somme on July 1st, 1916.
He was entitled to the General Service and Victory Medals.
129, Sandringham Road, Cricklewood, N.W.2   17353A.

MAYHEW, T. C., Pte., R.N.D., and Sapper, R.E.

He volunteered in September 1914, served in the Gallipoli campaign, and in March 1916 was transferred to the Royal Engineers and drafted to the Western Front. After taking part in the battles of Arras and Vimy Ridge he was invalided home as unfit for further service overseas.

He was demobilised in February 1919, and holds the 1914–15 Star, General Service and Victory Medals.

39, Melville Road, Stonebridge Park, N.W.10   15659C.

MAYHEW, W. A., Sergt., 18th Middlesex Regt.

Volunteering in March 1915, he was sent in the same year to the Western Front, where he served with distinction during many important operations. He suffered from shell-shock and heart trouble and was invalided home, and in June 1918 he was discharged as medically unfit for further service.

He holds the 1914–15 Star, General Service and Victory Medals.

41, Melville Road, Stonebridge Park, N.W.10   15654.

MAYLED, E., Pte., R.A.V.C.

He joined in May 1916, and after a period of service on special duties in Ireland was drafted to the Western Front in the following year.

He was there engaged on important work on various sectors of the Front and remained until his demobilisation in 1919.

He holds the General Service and Victory Medals.

8, Lichfield Road, Lower Edmonton, N.9   14666.

MAYOSS, F. W., Sapper, Royal Engineers.

He joined in June 1918, and after his training gave valuable services while engaged on important duties with his unit at various stations. He was not successful in being transferred overseas before hostilities ceased, but after the Armistice went to Germany with the Army of Occupation and remained there until his demobilisation in March 1920.

59, Waldo Road, College Park, N.W.10   X17633.

MEABY, E., Pte., 11th Cambridgeshire Regiment and Suffolk Regiment.

Joining in March 1917, he was sent later in the same year to the Western Front, where he took part in several important engagements. During the Advance of 1918 he was killed in action on October 24th.

He was entitled to the General Service and Victory Medals.

34, Raynham Avenue, Upper Edmonton, N.18   16765A.

MEABY, W., Lce.-Cpl., 2nd Seaforth Highlanders.

He volunteered in November 1915, and during his four years' service in France took part in the battles of Arras, La Bassée and Cambrai, and was in hospital for six weeks suffering from wounds received in action at Ypres.

He was demobilised in August 1919, holding the 1914–15 Star, General Service and Victory Medals.

34, Raynham Avenue, Upper Edmonton, N.18   16765B.

MEAD, E. P., Sergt., Middlesex Regiment.

Volunteering in November 1915, he was sent in the same year to the Western Front, where he took part in the battles of Ypres and the Somme. Whilst in action at Arras he received a severe wound that necessitated his being invalided to England and remaining in hospital for eight months.

He was demobilised in April 1919, holding the 1914–15 Star, General Service and Victory Medals.

129, Raynham Avenue, Upper Edmonton, N.18   15834A.

MEAD, J., Pte., Middlesex Regiment.

He volunteered in 1914 shortly after the outbreak of war, and a year later was sent to Egypt. Later he was drafted to Mesopotamia, and whilst in action there was seriously wounded. On his return to Egypt at the close of the war he contracted a serious illness, from the effects of which he died in 1919.

He was entitled to the 1915 Star, General Service and Victory Medals.

22, Ambleside Road, Willesden, N.W.10   16928.

MEAD, J. L., Lce.-Cpl., R.M.L.I.

He volunteered in September 1914 and was sent with the Mediterranean Expeditionary Force to the Dardanelles, where he took part in the heavy fighting throughout that campaign and bore a distinguished part.

He was still serving in the Marines in 1920, and holds the 1914–15 Star, General Service and Victory Medals.

66, Langhedge Lane, Upper Edmonton, N.18   X17261.

MEAD, S. S., Gunner, Royal Garrison Artillery.

He joined in November 1916, and was soon drafted to Gibraltar, where he served for over two years in the capacity of a fireman.

In February 1919 he was demobilised, and holds the General Service and Victory Medals.

38, Whitehall Street, Tottenham, N.17   X18132.

MEADE, H. D., Cpl., The Queen's (Royal West Surrey Regiment).

He volunteered for service in August 1914, and was employed on the recruiting Staff until 1915, when he was sent to France. He took part in the fighting at Loos, Ypres, Arras and Cambrai, and in the engagements at Festubert and the Somme, in both of which he was gassed.

He was demobilised in February 1919, and holds the 1914–15 Star, General Service and Victory Medals.

10, Harwood Terrace, Walham Green, S.W.6   X19858.

MEAGER, W. J., Gunner, R.F.A.

Joining in August 1916, he served in Salonica, Egypt and Palestine, and later on the Western Front, where he took part in several battles as well as the Advance of 1918.

He holds the General Service and Victory Medals, and was demobilised in May 1919.

49, Mayo Road, Willesden, N.W.10   15478.

MEALE, W. J., 1st-Class Stoker, Royal Navy.

He volunteered in August 1914 at the outbreak of hostilities, and served in the North Sea with the Grand Fleet in H.M.S. "Courageous." He played an important part in the Naval engagement in the Heligoland Bight, and in January 1919 was demobilised, holding the 1914–15 Star, General Service and Victory Medals.

16, Rowallan Road, Munster Road, S.W.6   X19270.

MEARS, A., Pioneer, Royal Engineers.

Volunteering in May 1915, he completed his training and was drafted to Ireland, where he was employed on various duties, and was in hospital for some time with chest trouble. He rendered valuable services, but owing to physical unfitness was unable to obtain his transfer overseas before the cessation of hostilities.

He was demobilised in March 1919.

42, Walham Grove, Fulham Road, S.W.6   X19617.

MEARS, A., A.B., R.N., H.M.S. "Pembroke."

Joining the Navy in February 1918, he was employed for about a year in escort duties to Russia.

He was demobilised in March 1919, and holds the General Service and Victory Medals.

19, Ambleside Road, Willesden, N.W.10   16115A

MEARS, G. A., Pte., Queen's Own (Royal West Kent Regiment).

Volunteering in October 1915, he was sent to the Western Front, where he took part in several engagements, including the battles of Ypres and the Somme and the Retreat and Advance of 1918 as a Lewis gunner, and was twice wounded. After the cessation of hostilities in France he was sent to Russia, and on his return to England in August 1919 was demobilised.

He holds the 1914–15 Star, General Service and Victory Medals.

19, Ambleside Road, Willesden, N.W.10   16115B.

MEARS, I. J., Cpl., Royal Air Force.

He joined in June 1915, and during his service on the Western Front took a prominent part in several engagements, including those at Ypres and Cambrai. Later he served in the Independent Air Force and performed valuable duties which required great technical skill.

He was demobilised in February 1919, and holds the General Service and Victory Medals.

32, Walham Grove, Fulham Road, S.W.6   X19613.

MEDCALF, F. A., Pte., Middlesex Regiment.

He volunteered in 1914, and during his service on the Western Front took part in various engagements, including the battles of the Marne and the Somme. He was taken prisoner while in action, and died in captivity in 1918, having suffered many hardships.

He was entitled to the 1914 Star, General Service and Victory Medals.

37, Cooper Road, Dudden Hill, N.W.10   16295A.

MEDCALF, G. W., Pte., The London Regiment.

He volunteered in March 1915, and served on the Western Front, taking part in the battles of Ypres, Arras and Cambrai. He acted for a time as sergeant in the 30th Field Bakery, and in January 1919 was demobilised, holding the 1914–15 Star, General Service and Victory Medals

30, Talbot Road, Willesden, N.W.10   16034.

MEE, A. E., Pte., Royal Army Service Corps.

He enlisted in August 1914, a few days before the outbreak of hostilities, and was sent to France in time to take part in the retreat from Mons. During his service overseas he fought in several engagements and was wounded. He holds the Mons Star, General Service and Victory Medals, and was discharged in June 1919.

17, Alexandra Road, West Kensington, W.14   12093.

MEECH, P. H., Pte., 6th Suffolk Regiment.
Joining in March 1917 he completed his training and was employed in various places as a motor driver. He gave valuable services, but was unable to secure a transfer overseas before the end of the war, and was demobilised in April 1919.
19, St. Mary's Road, Lower Edmonton, N.9   11951.

MEEK, A. C., Pte., East Surrey Regiment.
He joined in January 1915, and fifteen months later was sent to Mesopotamia, where he saw service at Basra, Baghdad, Kut-el-Amara and Ctesiphon. He was also stationed for a short time at Alexandria and later went to India, where he was in action during the risings on the North-Western Frontier.
Whilst abroad he was wounded, and in March 1919 was demobilised, holding the General Service and Victory Medals.
18, Strode Road, Fulham, S.W.6   X19628.

MEERS, A. E., A.B., Royal Navy.
He joined the Navy in 1918 and during his service was engaged in supplying the Grand Fleet in the North Sea with oil. This was attended with great danger, as his ship had to navigate waters which were infested with hostile submarines and mines.
Through ill-health, caused by active service, he was discharged in 1919, and holds the General Service and Victory Medals.
82, Holly Lane, Willesden, N.W.10   15393—15392B.

MEERS, A. R. H., Pte., 24th Royal Fusiliers.
He joined in 1916 and in the same year was sent to France, where he took part in the fighting at Arras, the Somme, Bullecourt, Monchy and Cambrai.
He was wounded and gassed during his service, and holds the General Service and Victory Medals, being demobilised in 1920.
82, Holly Lane, Willesden, N.W.10   15393—15392C.

MELBOURNE, W. D., Rifleman, K.R.R.
He volunteered in June 1915 and in the following year was sent to the Western Front, where he took part in engagements at Vimy Ridge, Arras, Cambrai and St. Quentin.
On March 28th, 1918, during the German Offensive he was reported missing.
He was entitled to the General Service and Victory Medals.
46, Brenthurst Road, Church End, N.W.10   16146.

MELBOURNE, W. J., Pte., Middlesex Regiment.
He enlisted in August 1914 and during his service on the Western Front was severely wounded.
He was discharged as medically unfit owing to his service in December 1917, and holds the 1914 Star, General Service and Victory Medals.
52, Gilpin Grove, Upper Edmonton, N.18   16799.

MELLOR, J. H., Pte., Grenadier Guards.
He joined in October 1916 and served on the Western Front, where he took part in the battles of Arras and Cambrai. He was discharged in April 1918 owing to the effects of his service, and holds the General Service and Victory Medals.
21, Argyle Road, Upper Edmonton, N.18   15265.

MELTON, W. H., Trooper, 3rd County of London Yeomanry.
Volunteering in 1914 he served in the East, taking a distinguished part in several important engagements. Whilst overseas he suffered from malaria, and on October 29th, 1918, he was killed in action in Palestine.
He was entitled to the General Service and Victory Medals.
38, Litchfield Gardens, Willesden, N.W.10   X17448B.

MELVIN, H. W., Gunner, Royal Field Artillery.
He volunteered in May 1915 and was sent to France in the following year. Shortly after his arrival on the Western Front he was killed in action during the battle of the Somme on October 8th, 1916.
He was entitled to the General Service and Victory Medals.
168, Winchester Road, Lower Edmonton, N.9   14890B.

MELVIN, W. J., Pte., Queen's Own (Royal West Kent Regiment).
Joining in March 1918 he completed his training and was stationed with his unit at an important place for a year. He gave valuable services, but was unable to secure his transfer overseas before the cessation of hostilities, and was demobilised in 1919.
168, Winchester Road, Lower, Edmonton, N.9   14890A.

MENCE, C. M., Pte., Royal Fusiliers.
Volunteering in August 1915 he was in the same year sent to the Western Front, where he took part in the battles of the Somme, Ypres and Arras, and was twice wounded. He was in hospital for a considerable period, but returned to France in time to take part in the Advance of 1918.
He holds the 1914-15 Star, General Service and Victory Medals, and was demobilised in February 1919.
123, Manor Road, Tottenham, N.17   TX18976A.

MENCE, F. G., Sergt., 12th London Regiment (Rangers).
He volunteered in August 1915 and in the same year was sent out to Mesopotamia, where he served until 1918.
He was taken ill while abroad and was in hospital for a time, and was eventually discharged as medically unfit in February 1919.
He holds the 1914-15 Star, General Service and Victory Medals.
123, Manor Road, Tottenham, N.17   TX18976B.

MENCE, G. H., Pte., Royal Fusiliers.
He volunteered in August 1915 and later in the same year was drafted to the Western Front, where he took a prominent part in several engagements. On October 3rd, 1916, he was killed in action during the battle of the Somme.
He was entitled to the 1914-15 Star, General Service and Victory Medals.
123, Manor Road, Tottenham, N.17   TX18976C.

MERCER, A. E., Pte., R.A.M.C.
He volunteered in January 1915 and was drafted in the same year to Egypt, where he was engaged on various duties at the base hospital until his return to England for demobilisation in June 1919.
He gave valuable services, and holds the 1914-15 Star, General Service and Victory Medals.
30, Nightingale Road, Harlesden, N.W.10   12511.

MERCER, J. H., Sergt., Royal Field Artillery.
He joined in November 1914, and in the following year was sent to France, where he remained until 1919. While abroad he took part in several important engagements, including Loos, Vimy Ridge, the Somme, Ypres and Cambrai, and was wounded.
He holds the 1914-15 Star, General Service and Victory Medals, and was demobilised in February 1920.
11, Herbert Road, Lower Edmonton, N.9   12975.

MEREDITH, E. J., Pte., R.A.S.C.
He volunteered in 1915, and was sent to the Western Front, where he served in engagements on the Somme and at Arras, Loos, Neuve Chapelle, Armentières, Amiens, Bullecourt, Ypres, Vimy Ridge, Cambrai, and during the Advance of 1918. After the Armistice he went with the Army of Occupation to Germany, and returned to England for his demobilisation in 1919.
He holds the General Service and Victory Medals.
88, Chesson Road, West Kensington, W.14   X17248A.

MEREDITH, H. (Mrs.), Special War Worker.
During the war this lady was engaged on work of national importance at the Trench Warfare Munition Factory, Stevenage Road, Fulham, in connection with the sewing of cordite. She rendered valuable services, and performed her duties in a capable manner.
88, Chesson Road, West Kensington, W.14   X17248B.

MERHOFF, A. J., Pte., 18th Middlesex Regt.
He joined in July 1917, and after his training was drafted overseas. He took part in various engagements on the Western Front, and was severely wounded during the German Offensive of 1918. He subsequently died at No. 2 Canadian Casualty Clearing Station on April 14th, 1918.
He was entitled to the General Service and Victory Medals.
60, Estcourt Road, Fulham, S.W.6   T17070.

MERISON, M. J., Leading Stoker, R.N., H.M.S. "Curacoa."
He joined in June 1914, and at the outbreak of war served with the Grand Fleet in the North Sea on various duties, and was wounded.
He holds the 1914 Star, General Service and Victory Medals, and was demobilised in January 1919.
35, Beaconsfield Road, Lower Edmonton, N.9   14770.

MERRETT, A., Rifleman, Rifle Brigade.
He joined in May 1918, and after his training served at various stations on important signalling duties with his unit until after the Armistice, when he was drafted to Germany with the Army of Occupation.
He returned to England for his demobilisation in March 1919.
93a, Deacon Road, Cricklewood, N.W.2   16602.

MERRETT, J. A., Gunner, R.H.A.
He joined in April 1915, and in the following June was drafted to the Western Front, where he took part in the battle of Armentières, and was badly gassed during an engagement at Loos. He was invalided home, and in July 1916 was discharged as medically unfit for further service.
He holds the 1914-15 Star, General Service and Victory Medals.
206, Shirland Road, Maida Hill, W.9   X19603.

MERRICK, R. G., Driver, R.A.S.C. (H.T.)
He volunteered in November 1914, and went to France in the following year. He was chiefly engaged with the food transport, and throughout his service did valuable work.
He holds the 1914-15 Star, General Service and Victory Medals, and was demobilised in June 1919.
28, Crefeld Road, Hammersmith, W.6   14499.

MERRICK, T. W., Sapper, Royal Engineers.
He volunteered in June 1915, and until he was drafted to the Western Front was engaged on important duties at various stations in England. Whilst overseas he was in action in many sectors, and throughout his service did valuable work with the Royal Engineers. He was discharged in September 1918, owing to the effects of his service, and holds the General Service and Victory Medals.
85, Roundwood Road, Willesden, N.W.10   16044.

MERRY, A. T., Air Mechanic, R.A.F.
He joined in 1916, and after his training was engaged on important duties, which demanded a high degree of technical skill, with his squadron. He was not successful in obtaining his transfer overseas before the close of hostilities, but gave valuable services before being demobilised in 1919.
7, Lundy Street, Hammersmith, W.6   14893B.

MERRY, F. P., Pte., Leicestershire Regiment.
He volunteered in 1915, and during four years' service on the Western Front took part in the fighting on the Somme, at Ypres and in the Advance of 1918, when he was wounded.
He was demobilised in May 1919, holding the 1914-15 Star, General Service and Victory Medals.
7, Lundy Street, Hammersmith, W.6   14893C.

MERRY, J., Pte., Middlesex Regiment.
He joined in April 1917, but after training was unable to pass the necessary medical examination for overseas service. He was engaged on various duties at different stations, and did valuable work before being demobilised in May 1919.
84, Raynham Road, Upper Edmonton, N.18   16946.

MERRY, J., Sergt., Royal Engineers.
He volunteered in August 1915, and after his training was engaged on important duties at various stations with his unit. He was not successful in obtaining his transfer overseas before the cessation of hostilities, but gave valuable services before his demobilisation in April 1919.
83a, Deacon Road, Cricklewood, N.W.2   16700A

MERRY, W. C., Rifleman, K.R.R.
Joining in April 1917, he was drafted to the Western Front on completion of his training. After taking part in several battles, including that of Cambrai, he was killed in action at Albert on August 22nd, 1918.
He was entitled to the General Service and Victory Medals.
83a, Deacon Road, Cricklewood, N.W.2   16700B.

MERRYFIELD, G., Pte., R.A.S.C. (M.T.)
He volunteered in August 1914, and after his training served at various stations on important duties with his unit. He gave valuable services, but was not successful in being drafted overseas before the cessation of hostilities.
He was demobilised in June 1919.
43, Earlsmead Road, College Park, N.W.10   17836.

MESSENGER, A. G., Driver, R.F.A.
He volunteered in February 1915, and during his 3½ years' service on the Western Front took part in many battles, including those at Ypres, the Somme, Arras, Passchendaele and Cambrai, and was wounded.
In May 1919 he was demobilised, holding the 1914-15 Star, General Service and Victory Medals.
269, Shirland Road, Maida Hill, W.9   X19601.

MESSENGER, H., Driver, R.A.S.C. (M.T.)
Joining in March 1916, he was sent to the Western Front where he did excellent work with the ammunition and supply columns. He was in action in many important sectors, frequently being under heavy fire. In 1919 he returned to England, where he was demobilised, holding the General Service and Victory Medals.
51, Hiley Road, Willesden, N.W.10   X18234C.

MESSENGER, W., Rifleman, 15th London Regt. (Civil Service Rifles).
He volunteered in June 1915, and was drafted to France in the following year. He took part in many important engagements, including the fighting at Vimy Ridge, where he was killed in action on May 21st, 1916.
He was entitled to the General Service and Victory Medals.
19, Third Avenue, Queen's Park Estate, W.10   X18935.

METHVEN, F. W., Pte., Bedfordshire Regt.
He joined in February 1917, and on completion of his training was drafted to the Western Front. After taking part in several important battles he was killed in action during the Advance in September 1918.
He was entitled to the General Service and Victory Medals.
82, Church Road, Tottenham, N.17   X18335.

MEW, J., Lce.-Cpl., 7th Royal Berkshire Regt.
Volunteering in September 1914, he was drafted to the West ern Front, where he took part in many of the principal engagements. Later he was sent to Salonica, and during his service there, which lasted for over two years, saw some heavy fighting, and was severely wounded in action on the Doiran Front. He was in the 24th General Hospital for some time, and on his return to England in June 1918 was invalided out of the Service.
He holds the 1914-15 Star, General Service and Victory Medals.
14, Lintaine Grove, West Kensington, W.14   X17002.

MEYER, J. S., Lieut., 23rd Middlesex Regiment.
Volunteering in April 1915, he joined as a private in the 23rd Middlesex Regiment, later gaining promotion. In the following November he was drafted to the Western Front, where he took part in heavy fighting in many sectors, and was wounded in action on three occasions—at Serre, Beaumont-Hamel and Courcellette.
He was demobilised in March 1920, holding the 1914-15 Star, General Service and Victory Medals.
6, Glentham Road, Barnes, S.W.13   13797.

MEYRICK, R., Pte., R.A.S.C. (M.T.)
He joined in 1916 and did good service for three years on various battle Fronts in France and Palestine, being chiefly engaged on conveying food and stores of all kinds to the lines. He was under fire on many occasions and also suffered from malaria.
He was demobilised in June 1919, and holds the General Service and Victory Medals.
29, Fordingley Road, Maida Hill, W.9   X19726.

MIALL, A. E., Stoker, Royal Navy.
Volunteering in August 1914, he was posted to H.M.S. "Neptune," and throughout the war served with the Grand Fleet in the North Sea. He was present at several naval engagements, including the battle of Jutland on May 31st, 1916, and in February 1919 was demobilised, holding the 1914 Star, General Service and Victory Medals.
10, Cedars Road, Lower Edmonton, N.9   14360.

MICHELMORE, E. (Miss), Special War Worker.
This lady rendered excellent service for a considerable period of the war at Messrs. Dunlop's at the White City. She was engaged upon fabric work and other important duties, and carried out this very necessary work in a manner which won for her high commendation.
10, Havelock Road, West Kensington, W.14   12628A.

MICHELMORE, F. (Miss), Special War Worker.
During the war this lady rendered valuable service at Messrs. Blake's Munition Works, Wood Lane. The work upon which she was engaged was of a highly dangerous character and demanded the greatest care and accuracy. On resigning she was commended for her good work.
10, Havelock Road, West Kensington, W.14   12628B.

MIDDLEBROOK, H. S., Rifleman, K.R.R.
He volunteered in June 1915, and served on the Western Front, taking part in many engagements, including the battles of the Somme and Ypres. Whilst in action at the Menin Road he was killed in action on September 26th, 1917.
He was entitled to the 1914-15 Star, General Service and Victory Medals.
14, Bridport Road, Upper Edmonton, N.18   X17582B

MIDDLETON, G. E., Pte., Machine Gun Corps.
He volunteered for duty in August 1914, and during his service on the Eastern Front, which lasted nearly four years, saw much service in Egypt, Syria and Palestine, and was severely wounded.
He holds the 1914-15 Star, General Service and Victory Medals, and was demobilised in January 1919.
4, Sotheron Road, King's Road, S.W.6   X19878.

MIDDLETON, J. A., Pte., Middlesex Regiment.
He volunteered in 1915, and was sent to France the same year. He took part in many engagements on the Western Front, including the battles of Ypres, and was also stationed near Dunkirk.
He returned to England after the Armistice, and was demobilised in February 1919, holding the 1914-15 Star, General Service and Victory Medals.
6, Warwick Road, Upper Edmonton, N.18.   X17270.

MIDDLETON, W. C., A.B., Royal Navy.
He volunteered in August 1914 and after his training was posted to H.M.S. "New Zealand," in which ship he served with the Grand Fleet in the North Sea. He was in action at the battles of Heligoland Bight, Dogger Bank and Jutland.
He holds the 1914-15 Star, General Service and Victory Medals, and was demobilised in December 1919.
16, Ray's Road, Upper Edmonton, N.18   15490.

MIDWINTER, T., Rifleman, 16th London Regt. (Queen's Westminster Rifles).
He joined in 1917, and after his training was drafted overseas the following year. During his service on the Western Front he took part in engagements at Arras, Ypres, Cambrai and the Retreat and Advance of 1918.
He was demobilised in November 1919, and he holds the General Service and Victory Medals.
6, Victor Road, College Park, N.W.10   X17768.

MILBOURN, A. H., Pte., Buffs (East Kent Regt.)
He joined in May 1917, and after his training served at various stations with his unit.
He was later engaged on farm work in the South of England, and gave valuable services until his demobilisation in September 1919.
7, Wimborne Road, Lower Edmonton, N.9   15207.

MILES, A. J., Cpl., 1/14th London Regiment (London Scottish).
He volunteered in November 1914, and was immediately drafted to the Western Front, where he took part in the fighting around La Bassée and was severely wounded. He returned to England and on his recovery was engaged as an instructor of signalling until his demobilisation in February 1919.
He holds the 1914 Star, General Service and Victory Medals.
72, Biscay Road, Hammersmith, W.6   13229C.

MILES, B. (Mrs.), Special War Worker.
During the war this lady was engaged on work of national importance at Messrs. Blake's Munition Factory, Fulham, in connection with the manufacture of boxes for packing shells and bombs. She gave valuable services and was commended for her good work.
20, Orbain Road, Fulham, S.W.6   X18224B.

MILES, E. W., Pte., R.A.M.C.
He volunteered in 1915, and at the conclusion of his training was drafted to Salonica, where he was employed as a stretcher-bearer in many sectors of this theatre of war. He was afterwards sent to India, where he was engaged on important duties.
He holds the General Service and Victory Medals, and in 1920 was still serving.
28, Fane Place, West Kensington. W.14   15923.

MILES, F. G. (D.C.M.), Sergt., M.G.C.
He volunteered for service in September 1914, and in the following year was drafted to the Western Front, where he took part in many of the principal engagements. In May 1916 he was badly wounded at Vimy Ridge, whilst rescuing wounded men under heavy fire, and for this conspicuous act of bravery he was awarded the Distinguished Conduct Medal. In 1918 he was drafted to Italy, where he served until his demobilisation in 1919.
He holds the 1914-15 Star, General Service and Victory Medals.
21, Bradiston Road, Maida Hill, W.9   X19974.

MILES, H. L. W., Pte., Royal West Kent Regt.
He joined in 1917, was sent to France in the same year, and served on the Western Front until his demobilisation in 1919. During this period he took part in much of the heavy fighting, and was five times wounded. He was also blown up, buried by an exploding shell, and badly gassed.
He holds the General Service and Victory Medals.
151, Winchester Road, Lower Edmonton, N.9   15194.

MILES, H. T., Cpl., Royal Engineers.
He joined in August 1915, and in the same year went to the Western Front, where he took part in many engagements including those of Ypres, Cambrai and Loos, and later was invalided home.
He was demobilised in January 1919, holding the 1914-15 Star, General Service and Victory Medals.
84, Deacon Road, Cricklewood, N.W.2   X17116B.

MILES, J., Pte., 17th Middlesex Regiment.
He volunteered in March 1915, and after his training was drafted to the Western Front. He took part in many engagements in this theatre of war, and was severely wounded in action. He was invalided to hospital in England and discharged as medically unfit for further service in November 1918.
He holds the General Service and Victory Medals.
97, Sherbrooke Road, Fulham. S.W.6   X18461.

MILES, J., Special War Worker.
Being too old for military service he voluntarily gave up his civil occupation in order to perform work of national importance, and during 1917-1918 was engaged as store-keeper at the Shell Factory, Wandsworth Road.
170, Third Avenue, Queen's Park, W.10   X19441.

MILES, J., Special War Worker.
During the war he was engaged at Park Royal Munition Factory on important duties as despatch manager. His position was a very responsible one and he performed his various duties with great credit.
52a, St Mary's Road, Craven Park, N.W.10   15113A.

MILES, J., Special War Worker.
During the war he was engaged on work of military importance at Woolwich Arsenal in connection with the manufacture of shells. He also was employed as a stoker at the Ministry of Food Office. He performed his various duties with great credit.
20, Orbain Road, Fulham, S.W.6   18224A.

MILES, M., Pte., Machine Gun Corps.
He joined in 1915, and during his service on the Western Front took part in engagements at Arras, Ypres, Albert, Cambrai, Vimy Ridge, and the Retreat and Advance of 1918. He was wounded in June 1916 at Ploegsteert.
He holds the General Service and Victory Medals, and was demobilised in 1919.
20, Orbain Road, Fulham, S.W.6   X18225.

MILES, R. W., Sapper, Royal Engineers.
He joined in May 1916, and at the conclusion of his training was drafted to France, where he was engaged on important duties in many engagements, and was wounded.
He holds the General Service and Victory Medals, and was demobilised in February 1919.
35, Claybrook Road, Hammersmith, W.6   13678A.

MILES, T., Special War Worker.
Not being of military age he worked on munitions at the Park Royal Shell Filling Factory during the war. On attaining military age he joined the Royal Engineers as a sapper, and in 1920 was serving with his unit at Chatham.
20, Orbain Road, Fulham, S W.6   X18224C.

MILES, T. W., Sergt., 13th London Regiment (Kensingtons).
He volunteered in July 1915, and served on the Western Front from that year till 1917, and again in 1918. He was wounded in the battle of the Somme in 1916, and in his second period of service went through the Retreat and Advance of 1918. After the Armistice he went with the Army of Occupation into Germany.
He was demobilised in February 1919, and holds the 1914-15 Star, General Service and Victory Medals.
42, Portnall Road, Maida Hill, W.9   X19693.

MILES, W., Mechanic, Royal Air Force.
He enlisted in 1914, and served on the Western Front until 1917, taking part in the battle of Mons, and was wounded. He was afterwards sent to Toronto, where he acted as flying instructor, and was killed in 1918 in an aeroplane accident.
He was entitled to the 1914 Star, General Service and Victory Medals.
52a, St. Mary's Road, Craven Park, N.W.10   15113B.

MILES, W. A., Sergt., 11th Middlesex Regiment.
He volunteered in August 1914, and was shortly afterwards drafted overseas. He took part in much of the severe fighting on the Western Front, and was severely wounded in action at the battle of Ypres, in consequence of which he lost the sight of his left eye. He was invalided to England, and subsequently discharged as medically unfit for further service in September 1916.
He holds the 1914 Star, General Service and Victory Medals.
32, Rayleigh Road, West Kensington, W.14   12636.

MILES, W. D., Pte., 2/7th London Regiment.
He volunteered in October 1915, and after his training served at various stations with his unit on important duties until January 1917, when he was drafted to France. He took part in many important engagements on the Western Front, including the battles of Albert, St. Quentin, Arras and Bullecourt. He was wounded and gassed, and also suffered from shell-shock, and was in hospital at Rouen for some months.
He holds the General Service and Victory Medals, and was demobilised in March 1919.
20, Fane Place, West Kensington, W.14   15697.

MILFORD, G. W., Cpl., 4th Canadian Regiment.
Volunteering in August 1914, he was soon drafted to the Western Front, where he was severely wounded during the second battle of Ypres in 1915. He was invalided home, and was in hospital for some time. On recovery he returned to France, and served through the final stages of the war. He was demobilised in April 1919, holding the 1914-15 Star, General Service and Victory Medals.
25, Kilmaine Road, Munster Road, S.W.6   TX18855A.

MILLARD, H. G., Sergt., 7th London Regiment.
He volunteered in May 1915, and after his training was drafted to the Western Front. He took part in fighting at Ypres, Loos, the Somme, Arras and Cambrai, where he was twice severely wounded. For some months he was in hospital in France, and later was invalided to Liverpool, but on recovery returned to France and went through the final stages of the war.
He was demobilised in March 1919, holding the 1914–15 Star, General Service and Victory Medals.
17, Lintaine Grove, West Kensington, W.14   16769.

MILLBANK, A. G., Driver, R.F.A.
He volunteered in October 1914, and during his service in France, which lasted for three years, took part in many engagements, including those at Ypres and the Somme.
He holds the 1914-15 Star, General Service and Victory Medals, and was demobilised in April 1919.
40, Harton Road, Lower Edmonton, N.9   13340.

MILLBANK, J. C., Driver, R.F.A.
Volunteering in October 1914, he was drafted to France on completion of his training in the following year. He took part in several engagements, including those at Ypres and Loos, where he was so severely wounded and gassed as to necessitate his removal to a hospital in England. On his recovery in 1917 he returned to France, but after a further period of service lasting for five months he was discharged as physcially unfit owing to ill-health.
He holds the 1914–15 Star, General Service and Victory Medals.   14, Lydford Road, Maida Hill, W.9   TX19685.

MILLER, G. D. (Mrs.), Special War Worker.
Throughout the war this lady was engaged with Messrs. Waring & Gillows at the White City, where she rendered excellent service in the construction of bell-tents and other articles of Army equipment. She carried out her duties in a very capable manner, for which she was highly commended.
3, Humbolt Mansions, Lillie Road, Fulham, S.W.6
TX18873B.

MILLER, L. S., Sergt., British Ambulance Committee.
He joined in June 1916, and during his service on the Western Front was stationed in the Vosges sector at Fraize, Gérardmer, Nancy and Manonville, doing Red Cross work. He rendered invaluable services in tending casualties as they were brought from the front line. As an appreciation of his gallant conduct he was decorated in the Market Square at Gérardmer with the Croix de Guerre by H.R.H. Prince Arthur of Connaught. He holds in addition the General Service and Victory Medals, and was discharged in August 1918.
3, Humbolt Mansions, Lillie Road, Fulham, S.W.6
TX18873A.

MILLER, A. H., Sergt., R.G.A.
He enlisted in 1908, and in 1915 was drafted to Gallipoli, where he took part in the memorable first landing at Suvla Bay, and later contracted enteric fever. In 1918 he was sent to the Western Front, where he saw much heavy fighting during the Retreat and Advance.
He holds the 1914-15 Star, General Service and Victory Medals, and was demobilised in February 1919.
65, Fermoy Road, Maida Hill, W.9   X20007.

MILLER, A. J., Pte., Labour Corps.
Joining in June 1916, he was drafted to the Western Front on completion of his training, and did good work with the Labour Corps. He was killed in action in the vicinity of Hill 60 on October 16th, 1917, and he was entitled to the General Service and Victory Medals.
59, Gervan Road, Hammersmith, W.6   14832A.

MILLER, A. W., Gunner, R.F.A.
He volunteered in 1914, and whilst in training at Thetford, preparatory to being drafted overseas, sustained severe injuries in an accident, from which in October 1915 he died.
25, Monmouth Road, Lower Edmonton, N.9   T12989A.

MILLER, A. W. L., Gunner, R.F.A.
He joined in April 1918, and in the same year went to France. After a short time he was transferred to the Royal Defence Corps, and was employed guarding German prisoners in France and England.
He was demobilised in December 1919, and holds the General Service and Victory Medals.
25, Monmouth Road, Lower Edmonton, N.9   12989B.

MILLER, E., Pte., 2/9th Middlesex Regiment.
Volunteering in August 1914, he was sent to Manchester, where for some time he was engaged on special munition work, in which he was highly skilled. Afterwards he went into training, but was not successful in obtaining his transfer overseas before the close of hostilities.
He gave valuable services, and was demobilised in January 1919.
14, Brenthurst Road, Church End, N.W.10   T16373.

MILLER, F. A. (M.M.), Lce.-Cpl., R.E.
He volunteered in March 1915, and after his training was drafted to the Western Front, where he was engaged in many sectors. Throughout his service he did valuable work with the Royal Engineers, and was awarded the Military Medal for gallantry in the field. In addition he holds a French decoration, the 1914–15 Star, the General Service and Victory Medals, and was still serving in 1920.
56, Claybrook Road, Hammersmith, W.6   13768.

MILLER, J., Pte., 4th Middlesex Regiment.
Volunteering in August 1914, he was drafted to the Western Front, and at the end of the same month he was killed in action during the memorable retreat from Mons.
He was entitled to the Mons Star, General Service and Victory Medals.
53, Strode Road, Munster Road, S.W.6   15335B.

MILLER, J. R., Mechanic, R.A.F. (late R.F.C.)
He volunteered in September 1914, and after his training was engaged with his squadron on important duties, which demanded a high degree of technical skill. He gave valuable services, but was not successful in being posted overseas before the cessation of hostilities.
He was demobilised in January 1919.
74, Fairfield Road, Upper Edmonton, N.18   15612.

MILLER, M. J., Rifleman, King's Royal Rifles.
Joining in June 1916, he was drafted to the Western Front on completion of his training, and in February 1917 was killed whilst on patrol. He had previously taken part in several engagements, and was entitled to the General Service and Victory Medals.
48, Claybrook Road, Hammersmith, W.6   13770.

MILLER, R. E., Driver, R.F.A.
Joining in July 1915, he was first engaged on important duties in England, and afterwards was drafted to the Western Front, where he took a prominent part in the fighting in many battle areas, and on two occasions was severely wounded in action. He returned to England in April 1919, and he was demobilised, holding the 1914–15 Star, General Service and Victory Medals.
3, Kilmaine Road, Munster Road, S.W.6   XT18878.

MILLER, W. C., Pte., 1st Middlesex Regiment.
He joined in November 1916, and having received training at various stations in England, was drafted to the Western Front. He took part in heavy fighting in many sectors, and was killed in action at Passchendaele on February 26th, 1918.
He was entitled to the General Service and Victory Medals.
3, Durham Road, Lower Edmonton, N.9   14692.

MILLER, W. F., Pte., R.A.S.C. (M.T.)
Joining in June 1916, he was drafted to Salonica in the following August, and later was sent to Russia. Throughout his service overseas he did excellent work with the mechanical transport, frequently being under heavy fire.
He returned to England in 1919, and in October of the same year was demobilised, holding the General Service and Victory Medals.
167, Purves Road, Kensal Rise, N.W.10   18409.

MILLER, W. R., Gunner, R.F.A.
He volunteered in January 1915, but when it was discovered that he was only 16 years of age was discharged. Two years later he rejoined, and in May 1917, after a short period of training, was drafted to Egypt. He took part in much of the fighting in Palestine, and during his service there suffered from recurring attacks of malaria.
He left the East for England in March 1919, and in June was demobilised, holding the General Service and Victory Medals.
48, Stephendale Road, Fulham, S.W.6   X20709.

MILLINGTON, C. H., Pte., The Buffs (East Kent Regiment).
He joined in April 1918, and on the completion of his training was employed at various stations. Owing to the cessation of hostilities he was not successful in obtaining his transfer overseas, but did valuable work before being demobilised in November 1919.
56, Langhedge Lane, Upper Edmonton, N.18   17264.

MILLS, A. E., Pte., 2nd East Surrey Regiment.
Joining in April 1918, he was soon drafted to the Western Front, where he went through the final stages of the war, during which he was twice wounded. Afterwards he was sent to Egypt, and thence to Constantinople, where in 1920 he was still serving.
He holds the General Service and Victory Medals.
59, Bramber Road, West Kensington, W.14   15710.

MILLS, A. E., Pte., 2/4th Leicestershire Regt.

He joined in September 1916, and was drafted to the Western Front, where, during his service overseas, he was in almost continuous action until 1917, when he was severely gassed at Ypres, and was in consequence for some time in hospital. He was demobilised in February 1919, holding the General Service and Victory Medals.

15, Novello Street, Parson's Green, S.W.6   X19929.

MILLS, A. H., Pte., 3rd London Regiment (Royal Fusiliers).

Volunteering in 1914, he received training at various stations in England, and in the same year was drafted to Egypt. Later he took part in the Gallipoli campaign, during which he was severely wounded, and in consequence returned to England. He was invalided out of the Service in May 1916 owing to his wounds, and holds the 1914-15 Star, General Service and Victory Medals.

45, Felixstowe Road, Willesden, N.W.10   X17760.

MILLS, C., Pte., 9th Middlesex Regiment.

An ex-soldier at the age of 59, he volunteered in his old regiment for further service in April 1915. He was engaged at various stations in England on guard and other special duties, and did valuable work until February 1918, when owing to physical unfitness he was discharged.

7, Belton Road, Cricklewood, N.W.2   16597A.

MILLS, D., Pte., R.M.L.I.

He was serving when hostilities broke out, and during the war was on board H.M. ships " Shannon " and " Repulse " with the Grand Fleet in the North Sea. He took part in several engagements, including the battle of Jutland, and in March 1920 was demobilised, holding the 1914 Star, General Service and Victory Medals.

7, Belton Road, Cricklewood, N.W.2   16597B.

MILLS, D., Rifleman, Rifle Brigade.

Volunteering in November 1915, he received his training at various stations in England, and in the following year was drafted to the Western Front. He was severely wounded in action in April 1916, and was invalided to a hospital at Chatham, where he was under treatment for some time. On his discharge from hospital, being physically unfit for further active service, he was retained on important duties at home until his demobilisation in March 1919.

He holds the General Service and Victory Medals.

7, Belton Road, Cricklewood, N.W.2   16596A.

MILLS, E. (Miss), Special War Worker.

This lady rendered valuable services at the Park Royal Munition Works throughout the war. She was engaged on the examination of cartridges, which was both difficult and responsible work, and on resigning at the termination of war was commended for the efficient manner in which she had carried out these duties.

124, Shakespeare Avenue, Willesden, N.W.10   13893B.

MILLS, Ethel (Miss), Special War Worker.

During the war this lady was engaged at the Park Royal Munition Works, where she rendered valuable assistance until the cessation of hostilities. Her work, the inspection of small-arms ammunition, was of the greatest importance, and she carried out her duties in a commendable manner.

124, Shakespeare Avenue, Willesden, N.W.10   13893C.

MILLS, E. J., Sergt., R.A.S.C.

Joining in December 1917, he was drafted to Italy in the following January. During his service overseas he did valuable work with the Royal Army Service Corps, and in connection with the canteens, and in 1919 returned to England, where he was demobilised.

He holds the General Service and Victory Medals.

3, Hawthorn Road, Upper Edmonton, N.18   X17053.

MILLS, F., Gunner, R.G.A.

He joined in 1917, and in the same year went to France, where he fought in many engagements. After the Armistice he served with the Army of Occupation in Germany until 1919, when he returned to England and was demobilised. He holds the General Service and Victory Medals.

27, Beamish Road, Lower Edmonton, N.9   13941.

MILLS, F. A., Lce.-Cpl., R.M.L.I.

Although under military age, he volunteered in November 1914, and was drafted to the Dardanelles, where he took part in much heavy fighting. Later he went to France, and in June 1917 was killed in action at Arras.

He was entitled to the 1914-15 Star, General Service and Victory Medals.

2, Hartington Road, Lower Edmonton, N.9   14251B.

MILLS, F. B., Pte., 17th Middlesex Regiment.

He joined in 1917, and during his service on the Western Front, which lasted two years, took part in many battles, and was twice wounded at Bullecourt.

He was demobilised in April 1919, holding the General Service and Victory Medals.

2, Hartington Road, Lower Edmonton, N.9   14251A.

MILLS, F. E., 1st Air Mechanic, R.A.F.

He volunteered in April 1915, and served as a driver with an airship squadron in Norfolk. Later he was sent to the Western Front, where he did valuable work with No. 2 Kite Balloon Section in various sectors.

He was demobilised in March 1919, holding the 1914-15 Star, General Service and Victory Medals.

40, Carlyle Avenue, Willesden, N.W.10   14409.

MILLS, F. J., Rifleman, Rifle Brigade.

He joined in August 1918, and having completed his training, was about to proceed overseas when the Armistice was signed. He served at several places in England, and was in hospital for some time with a serious illness.

In February 1919 he was demobilised.

9, Fabian Road, Walham Green, S.W.6   X18067.

MILLS, F. P., Pte., Middlesex Regiment.

He volunteered n October 1914, and was soon sent on garrison duty to Gibraltar, whence, in the following year, he was drafted to France. Whilst on the Western Front he took part in several important engagements, and was wounded at Ypres. Owing to the seriousness of his wound he was invalided out of the Army in June 1916.

He holds the 1914-15 Star, General Service and Victory Medals.

161, Felixstowe Road, Lower Edmonton, N.9   14543.

MILLS, H., Pte., 2nd North Staffordshire Regt.

Volunteering in August 1914, he was drafted to India, where he served throughout the war, being engaged on various special duties. He also took part in operations in Afghanistan in 1919, and at the end of the same year returned to England where he was demobilised, holding the 1914-15 Star, General Service and Victory Medals, and the India General Service Medal (with clasp—Afghanistan, N.W. Frontier, 1919).

218, Winchester Road, Lower Edmonton, N.9   14882.

MILLS, H. G., Rifleman, 15th London Regiment (Civil Service Rifles).

Joining in February 1916, he was first drafted to Salonica, and thence to Palestine, where he went through the campaign with General Allenby's forces. In June 1918 he was sent to the Western Front, and after taking part in the last Advance of 1918 contracted a severe form of influenza, from which he died in February 1919.

He was entitled to the General Service and Victory Medals.

53, Burn's Road, Harlesden, N.W.10   14713.

MILLS, H. W., Gunner, Royal Field Artillery.

Volunteering in August 1914, he saw service on the Western Front, in Salonica, and in Egypt. He took part in much of the fighting on these Fronts, and whilst in the East contracted malaria. On his demobilisation in March 1919 he joined the Metropolitan Police Force, in which his military training proved of great value.

He holds the 1914-15 Star, General Service and Victory Medals.

9, Fabian Road, Walham Green, S.W.6   X18066.

MILLS, M., Pte., King's Own (Royal Lancaster Regiment).

Joining in September 1916, he was drafted to the Western Front in the following November, and after taking part in several important engagements, was taken prisoner whilst in action in the Somme sector in April 1917. He suffered great privation during his captivity in Germany, and after being released at the termination of war returned to serve with the Army of Occupation.

He holds the General Service and Victory Medals, and was still serving in 1920.

7, Belton Road, Cricklewood, N.W.2   16596B.

MILLS, M., Pte., R.M.L.I.

He volunteered for service in August 1914, but in the same year lost his life on board H.M.S. " Cressy," which was sunk by a German submarine off the Hook of Holland on September 22, 1914.

He was entitled to the 1914 Star, General Service and Victory Medals.

53a, Ormiston Road, Shepherd's Bush, W.12   11925B.

MILLS, R., Gunner, Royal Garrison Artillery.

Joining in 1917, he received his training at various stations in England, and in the following year was drafted to the Western Front. He took part in many important engagements, including the last Retreat and Advance of 1918, and after the cessation of hostilities served with the Army of Occupation in Germany.

He was demobilised in January 1920, holding the General Service and Victory Medals.

59, Field Road, Hammersmith W.6   15155.

MILLS, R. E., Gunner, Royal Field Artillery.

Volunteering in August 1915, he was soon drafted to the Western Front, and after taking part in many important battles, was killed in action in December 1917 at Havrincourt Wood.
He was entitled to the General Service and Victory Medals.
16, Chauncey Street, Lower Edmonton, N.9   14255.

MILLS, S. T., Pte., Royal Army Service Corps.

Joining in May 1917, he was engaged on important duties at various stations. He was not successful in obtaining his transfer overseas before the cessation of hostilities, but afterwards was drafted to France, where for eight months he did valuable work.
He was demobilised in February 1919.
23, Kimberley Road, Upper Edmonton, N.18   16586.

MILNE, A. B., Mechanic, Royal Air Force.

He joined in July 1916, and after his training was engaged on important duties, which demanded a high degree of technical skill. He was not successful in obtaining his transfer overseas before the termination of the war, but gave valuable services before being demobilised in 1919.
4, Yewfield Road, Willesden, N.W.10   16366A.

MILNE, A. B., Pte., 7th Middlesex Regiment.

He volunteered in November 1914, and was sent in the following March to the Western Front, where he took part in several engagements. Whilst in an advanced trench he was killed on May 7th, 1915.
He was entitled to the 1914-15 Star, General Service and Victory Medals.
4, Yewfield Road, Willesden, N.W.10   16366C.

MILNE, L., Pte., 9th Middlesex Regiment, and Sapper, R.E. (Signal Section).

Volunteering in September 1914, he received training at various stations in England, and later was drafted to the Western Front. He took part in many important engagements whilst overseas, including the Retreat and Advance of 1918, and was also engaged on important duties with the Royal Engineers.
He returned to England in 1919, when he was demobilised, holding the General Service and Victory Medals.
4, Yewfield Road, Willesden, N.W.10   16366B.

MILNER, H. E., Pte., Duke of Cornwall's L.I.

He volunteered in August 1914, and in the same year was sent to France, where he took part in many engagements, including those at Loos, Ypres and Delville Wood. In 1916 he was wounded in action on the Somme, necessitating the amputation of his right leg, and was in hospital for about two years.
He holds the 1914-15 Star, General Service and Victory Medals, and was demobilised in March 1919.
42a, Lorenco Road, Tottenham, N.17   X18391.

MILSOM, C. E., Lce.-Cpl., Duke of Cornwall's L.I.

After volunteering in September 1914 he was sent a year later to the Western Front, where he took a distinguished part in several engagements. He was killed in Sanctuary Wood on October 4th, 1917.
He was entitled to the 1914-15 Star, General Service and Victory Medals.
34, Spencer Road, Tottenham, N.17   X19089.

MILTON, A., Pte., Royal Fusiliers.

He was sent to the Western Front after he had volunteered in August 1914, and took part in several engagements. Later he was drafted to Malta on garrison duty.
In January 1917 he was demobilised, and holds the General Service and Victory Medals.
18, Herbert Road, Lower Edmonton, N.9   13033.

MILTON, A. J., Pte., 13th London Regiment (Kensingtons).

He volunteered in August 1914, and saw service in France, Egypt and Salonica, taking part in many engagements on those Fronts.
He returned to England in May 1919, when he was demobilised, holding the 1914-15 Star, General Service and Victory Medals.   4, Beryl Road, Hammersmith, W.6   13354.

MINISTER, G., Pte., Machine Gun Corps.

He joined in September 1918, and was still in training when hostilities ceased. Afterwards he was drafted to Germany with the Army of Occupation, later being sent to India, where in 1920 he was still serving.
89, Love Lane, Tottenham, N.17   18527.

MINTER, W. J., Sergt., Royal Engineers.

He volunteered in May 1915, and in the following November was drafted to the Western Front. Whilst overseas he was present at many of the principal engagements, and was wounded. Throughout his service he did valuable work with the Royal Engineers.
He was demobilised in March 1919, holding the 1914-15 Star, General Service and Victory Medals.
91, Bruce Castle Road, Tottenham, N.17   X18315.

MISKIN, J. W., Lieut., Royal Naval Reserve.

Mobilised at the outbreak of war, he was immediately sent to the North Sea, where he served on several ships, among which was H.M.S. "Marina." His duties, which consisted chiefly of salvage work, were attended by great risk and hardship.
He was discharged in 1918, and holds the 1914-15 Star, General Service and Victory Medals.
392a, High Road, Willesden, N.W.10   16744.

MISON, L. A., Cpl., West Yorkshire Regiment.

Volunteering in November 1915, he was soon drafted to the Western Front, where he played an important part in many of the principal engagements, and was wounded.
He was demobilised in April 1920, holding the General Service and Victory Medals.
40, Haldane Road, Walham Green, S.W.6   X17382.

MISSON, W., Pte., The London Regiment.

He volunteered in February 1915, and after his training was drafted to Salonica, where he took part in many important engagements, and was twice wounded. Later he saw service in Egypt, and did valuable work throughout.
He was demobilised in July 1919, holding the 1914-15 Star, General Service and Victory Medals.
67, Greyhound Road, Hammersmith, W.6   15480.

MITCHELL, C., Pte., South Wales Borderers.

He joined in April 1915, and in the same year was drafted to Gallipoli, where he was twice wounded, and later served in India, Mesopotamia and Salonica.
He holds the 1914-15 Star, General Service and Victory Medals, and was demobilised in October 1919.
10, Montgomery Street, Hammersmith, W.6   15876.

MITCHELL, E. (Mrs., née CARVEY), Special War Worker.

Early in the war this lady was employed in the Great Western Railway Goods Department, where she did important work. Later she worked in munition factories at Hayes and Park Royal, being engaged for eighteen months on the filling of fuses. Throughout her three years' services she rendered invaluable assistance.
20, Mund Street, West Kensington, W.14   16912A.

MITCHELL, H. A., Driver, R.A.S.C.

He volunteered in 1915, and served for four years in various parts of the Eastern Front. He was at Lemnos, went through the terrible landing at Suvla Bay, and took part in the Egyptian and Palestine campaign to Jerusalem and Damascus.
In 1919 he was demobilised, holding the 1914-15 Star, General Service and Victory Medals.
36, New Holly Lane, Willesden, N.W.10   15577.

MITCHELL, H. M., Cpl., R.A.S.C. (M.T.)

He volunteered for service in October 1915, and did good work with the Royal Army Service Corps in Egypt and Salonica until 1919, when he returned to England and was demobilised. He had previously served in the Army for 12 years, for seven of which he was stationed in India, and holds the 1914-15 Star, General Service and Victory Medals.
22, Shorrolds Road, Walham Green, S.W.6   X19358.

MITCHELL, H. W., Driver, R.F.A.

He volunteered in November 1914, and on completion of his training in the following year was sent to the Western Front. He took part in several important battles, including those of Neuve Chapelle and Ypres, and whilst in the Loos sector was blown up and buried by an explosion. He returned to England, and in June 1916 was invalided out of the Service suffering from shell-shock.
He holds the 1914-15 Star, General Service and Victory Medals.
20, Mund Street, West Kensington, W.14   16911.

MITCHELL, H. W., Pte., Royal West Kent Regt.

He volunteered in November 1914, and after his training was drafted to the Western Front. He took part in many important engagements, including those at Neuve Chapelle, Ypres, Loos, Armentières and Dixmude, and was wounded. In 1916 he was sent to the East, where he was killed during an attack on the Bulgarian trenches in December of the same year. He is buried in the churchyard at Barakli, and was entitled to the 1914-15 Star, General Service and Victory Medals.
27, Albert Terrace, Milton Avenue, Willesden, N.W.   1014334.

MITCHELL, J., Lce.-Cpl., 23rd Middlesex Regt.

He joined in October 1916, and in the following January was drafted to the Western Front. He took part in many important battles, and on two occasions was severely wounded near Bullecourt in March 1918, and on the Scheldt later in the same year.
He returned to England, and was demobilised in September 1919, holding the General Service and Victory Medals.
15, Denbigh Road, Willesden, N.W.10   15096A.

MITCHELL, J., Rifleman, 12th Rifle Brigade.
Joining in May 1918, he was sent to France in the following September, and took part in the last Advance.
He was demobilised in October 1919, holding the General Service and Victory Medals.
15, Denbigh Road, Willesden, N.W.10			15096B.

MITCHELL, J. F., Gunner, R.G.A.
He volunteered in 1915, and was sent in the following year to the Western Front, where he took part in engagements at Arras, Viny Ridge, the Somme, Ypres, Hill 60 and St. Quentin. After being in the Advance of 1918, he was sent to Germany with the Army of Occupation, from which, in 1919, he returned for his demobilisation.
He holds the General Service and Victory Medals.
3, Shotley Street, Hammersmith, W.6			15046D.

MITCHELL, L. M., Special War Worker.
During the war this person worked at Perivale, Park Royal, on munitions, making caps for fuses, and rendered valuable services, which were greatly appreciated.
3, Shotley Street, Hammersmith, W.6			15046A.

MITCHELL, V. L. (Miss), Special War Worker.
During the war she was employed at Messrs. Blake's Munition Factory, Crabtree Lane, Fulham, making boxes for packing bombs and shells. Her duties were of an arduous nature, and were carried out in a satisfactory manner.
3, Shotley Street, Hammersmith, W.6			15046B.

MITCHELL, W. A., Pte., 9th Middlesex Regt.
Volunteering in April 1915, he was soon sent to the Western Front, where during the battle of Loos he was severely wounded. In 1916 he was drafted to Egypt, and served there until 1919, when he was sent home and demobilised in July.
He holds the 1914-15 Star, General Service and Victory Medals
48, Essex Road, Willesden, N.W.10			15593.

MITCHELL, W. J., Sergt., R.A.S.C.
He volunteered in September 1914, and during his service in France, which commenced later in the same year, was present at many engagements. In 1917 he was drafted to Salonica, and thence to Egypt, where he was engaged throughout in conveying food and ammunition up to the lines.
He was demobilised in July 1919, holding the 1914-15 Star, General Service and Victory Medals.
20, Mund Street, West Kensington, W.14			16912B.

MITCHELL, W. P., Pte., 11th Queen's (Royal West Surrey Regiment).
He joined in July 1917, and while on the Western Front was gassed and blown up by the explosion of a shell when serving with a Labour Company.
He was demobilised in November 1919, holding the General Service and Victory Medals.
53, Bramber Road, West Kensington, W.14			15717.

MITCHENER, A. J., Pioneer, Royal Engineers.
Volunteering in January 1915, he was sent to the Western Front in the following August, and took part in many important engagements, including those of the Somme, Ypres, Arras, Passchendaele, St. Eloi, Cambrai and Loos.
He was demobilised in March 1919, holding the 1914-15 Star, General Service and Victory Medals.
33, College Road, Willesden, N.W.10			X17811B.

MITCHENER, S. A., Pte., Middlesex Regiment.
Volunteering in February 1915, he was sent to the Western Front in the following August, and took part in many engagements, including those at Loos, Lens, Cambrai, Ypres and the Somme, where he was wounded in August 1916.
He was demobilised in February 1919, and holds the 1914-15 Star, General Service and Victory Medals.
33, College Road, Willesden, N.W.10			X17811A.

MITCHINSON, G. W., Pte., Royal Irish Fusiliers.
He joined in April 1916, and was sent in the following year to Salonica, and later to Egypt and Palestine, where he took part in the capture of Jerusalem and Jericho While abroad he suffered from malaria, and on his return home was demobilised in March 1919, holding the General Service and Victory Medals.
52a, Deacon Road, Cricklewood, N.W.2			16732.

MIZON, E., Lce.-Cpl., Middlesex Regiment.
He joined in 1916, and in the same year went to France, where he fought at the battle of the Somme and was wounded. He was demobilised in January 1919, holding the General Service and Victory Medals.
236, Town Road, Lower Edmonton, N.9			13576.

MOBBS, W. C., Sergt., 1st Royal Fusiliers.
He volunteered in August 1914, and during his service on the Western Front took part in the retreat from Mons and the battles of Loos, Arras, Ypres, the Somme and Cambrai. He was wounded on the Aisne in 1914, and again at Cambrai in 1918.
He holds the Mons Star, General Service and Victory Medals, and was demobilised in October 1919, after being in hospital for a considerable period.
38, Laundry Road, Hammersmith, W.6			15052.

MOCKRIDGE, F., Pte., R.A.S.C.
Volunteering in 1915, he was sent to France in the same year and served on many sectors of the Western Front.
He was invalided home in October 1918 owing to an injury, and was discharged in 1919, holding the 1914-15 Star, General Service and Victory Medals.
24, Ladysmith Road, Upper Edmonton, N.18			16462.

MOLE, G., Rifleman, King's Royal Rifle Corps.
He had served 12 years with the Colours prior to the war and was mobilised in August 1914, when he was drafted to the Western Front. He took part in the retreat from Mons and the battles of Arras, Loos, Ypres, and the Somme, but owing to ill-health returned to England and was discharged as medically unfit for further service in December 1916.
He holds the Mons Star, General Service and Victory Medals.
82a, Lorenco Road, Tottenham, N.17			18393.

MOLINEUX, G. H., Sergt., R.A.S.C. (M.T.)
He volunteered in August 1914, and was speedily drafted overseas to France, where for more than four years he did valuable transport work in connection with many of the most important engagements, including Mons, Ypres, Neuve Chapelle, Loos, Vimy Ridge, the Somme, Bullecourt and the Retreat and Advance of 1918.
He was demobilised in February 1919, holding the Mons Star, General Service and Victory Medals.
16, Tasso Road, Hammersmith, W.6			14654.

MOLLOY, A., Stoker, Royal Navy.
He volunteered for service in October 1915, and after his training served on H.M.S. "Sarpedon," "Eclipse" and "Rose," which were engaged on convoy and patrol work in various waters. They were all torpedoed and sunk by enemy action.
He was demobilised in April 1919, and holds the General Service and Victory Medals.
15, Waldo Road, College Park, N.W.10			X17624.

MOLLOY, H., Gunner, Royal Field Artillery.
He volunteered in November 1914, and after his training served on the Western Front, where he took part in the battles of the Somme and Ypres and was wounded and gassed.
In March 1919 he was demobilised, holding the 1914-15 Star General Service and Victory Medals.
12, Raynham Road, Upper Edmonton, N.18			16003.

MONCKTON, S. E., Pte. (Signaller), 1st Duke of Wellington's (West Riding Regiment).
He enlisted in the Territorials in April 1913, and was mobilised at the outbreak of war. In October 1914 he was drafted to India, where he remained until after the cessation of hostilities, and was employed on important duties at various stations with his regiment.
He holds the General Service and Victory Medals, and was demobilised in November 1919.
20, Buckingham Road, Harlesden, N.W.10			12521.

MONEY, E. G., Pte., Machine Gun Corps.
He joined in April 1916 and was drafted to the Western Front in the same year. During his service in this theatre of war he took part in many engagements, including the battle of Ypres, where he was wounded. In 1919 he was sent to Russia with the Relief Force, and after the withdrawal of the British troops from the Murmansk Coast was drafted to India, where he was serving in 1920.
He holds the General Service and Victory Medals.
46, Alston Road, Upper Edmonton, N.18			16498.

MONEY, H. E., Pte., 7th London Regiment.
He volunteered in June 1915, and after his training was drafted overseas. He remained for two months on the Western Front and was then invalided home on account of ill-health. Upon his recovery he was engaged at various stations on important duties until his demobilisation in April 1919.
He holds the General Service and Victory Medals.
37, Kilmaine Road, Munster Road, S.W.6			X18774.

MONK, A., Gunner, Royal Field Artillery.
He volunteered in August 1914, and was shortly afterwards drafted to the Western Front. He took part in many important engagements in this theatre of war, where he remained until after the cessation of hostilities.
On his return to England he was demobilised in March 1919, and holds the 1914 Star, General Service and Victory Medals.
95, Winchester Road, Lower Edmonton, N.9			14957B.

MONK, E. F., Pte., Middlesex Regiment.
He volunteered in January 1915, and at the conclusion of his training was sent to France during the same year. During his service on the Western Front he took part in many important engagements, including the battles of Hill 60, Ypres (1915), La Bassée and Hooge, and was four times wounded. In consequence he was invalided to England, and subsequently discharged in September 1916.
He holds the 1914–15 Star, General Service and Victory Medals.
44, Cornwallis Grove, Lower Edmonton, N.9   13329.

MONK, W. J., 1st-Class Stoker, Royal Navy.
He volunteered in August 1914, and after his training was posted to H.M.S. " Indomitable," which was engaged on many important duties in various waters. He also convoyed troops to and from France until after the cessation of hostilities. In 1920 he was still serving, and holds the 1914 Star, General Service and Victory Medals.
8, Montpelier Road, Hammersmith, W.6   13274A.

MONTAGUE, T., Pte., Royal Fusiliers.
He re-enlisted in August 1914, having previously served for 10 years, and was sent to France, where he took part in the retreat from Mons and the battles of Arras, Ypres and the Somme, and was three times wounded.
He was discharged in May 1917, holding the Mons Star, General Service and Victory Medals.
17, Chamberlain Road, Lower Edmonton, N.9   14023.

MONTRIOU, E., Pte., R.A.S.C.
He joined in December 1916, and was sent overseas in the following year. During his service on the Western Front he was engaged on important duties in connection with the transport of stores to the forward areas.
He returned to England after the Armistice and was demobilised in February 1919, holding the General Service and Victory Medals.
24, Sebastopol Road, Lower Edmonton, N.9   14970.

MOODY, E., Pte., York and Lancaster Regt.
He joined in 1917, and after his training served at various stations on important duties with his unit. He gave valuable services, but was unsuccessful in obtaining his transfer overseas owing to physical unfitness, and was demobilised in 1919.
50, Elsdon Road, Tottenham, N.17   X18497A.

MOODY, E. J. (Mrs.), Special War Worker.
During the war this lady offered her services and was engaged on work of national importance at Messrs. Klingers' Munition Factory, Tottenham, in connection with the manufacture of gas masks. She gave valuable services throughout.
50, Elsdon Road, Tottenham, N.17   18496A.

MOODY, J. G., Cpl., Queen's Own (Royal West Kent Regiment).
He rejoined in January 1916, after having previously served for 21 years, during which time he took part in the South African campaign and the fighting on the Indian North West Frontier. He was drafted to the Western Front, where he took part in some of the principal engagements, and in January 1918 was discharged through ill-health. He holds the Queen's and King's South African, Indian General Service, General Service and Victory Medals.
36, Allestree Road, Munster Road, S.W.6   X19207.

MOODY, P., Pte., Durham Light Infantry.
He joined in November 1916, and after completing his training was engaged on important duties with his unit until 1918, when he was drafted to the Western Front and was actively engaged during the Retreat and Advance of 1918.
He returned to England after the Armistice, was demobilised in November 1919, and holds the General Service and Victory Medals.
50, Elsdon Road, Tottenham, N.17   X18497B

MOODY, W., Pte., 1st Norfolk Regiment.
He joined in 1918, and was sent to the Western Front, where he took part in the Advance of 1918. Previous to his enlistment he served for nearly two years in a munition factory filling bombs.
He holds the General Service and Victory Medals, and was demobilised in 1919.
50, Elsdon Road, Tottenham, N.17   X18496B.

MOON, A. C., Bombardier, R.F.A.
He enlisted in December 1912, and on the outbreak of war was sent to the Western Front, where he served for four years. During this period he took part in the fighting at Mons, Ypres, the Marne, the Aisne, Cambrai, Armentières and La Bassée. He was wounded in action on the Somme and again at Le Cateau. In 1918 he returned to England, and was discharged in the following February.
He holds the Mons Star, General Service and Victory Medals.
75, Milton Avenue, Willesden, N.W.10   14211A.

MOON, G. E., Gunner, Royal Field Artillery.
He volunteered in January 1915, and during his service on the Western Front, which lasted for nearly four years, took part in engagements at Arras, Ypres, the Somme, Armentières, Dickebusch, Estaires and Nieppe, and during the Retreat of 1918, in which he was badly wounded.
He was discharged in November 1918, and holds the 1914–15 Star, General Service and Victory Medals.
75, Milton Avenue, Willesden, N.W.10   14211B.

MOON, H., Pte., Machine Gun Corps.
He joined in December 1915, and in the following year was drafted to Egypt. The ship on which he sailed was torpedoed, but he was rescued and landed at Greece, and later was able to continue his voyage. In 1917 he was sent to the Western Front, where he took part in the fighting at Ypres, Béthune, Arras, Albert, Festubert and Givenchy. He was gassed at Nieuport, and wounded at Bucquoy and again at Epéhy. He holds the General Service and Victory Medals, and was demobilised in February 1919.
75, Milton Avenue, Willesden, N.W.10   14211C.

MOORCROFT, T. A., C.S.M., R.A.S.C.
He was serving when war broke out, and was drafted to the Western Front, where he went through the retreat from Mons and the first battle of Ypres. His service overseas lasted for nearly four years, and during this time he saw fighting in various theatres of war.
He returned to England in 1918, and in February of the following year was demobilised, holding the Mons Star, General Service and Victory Medals.
3, Edenham Street, North Kensington, W.10   X20191.

MOORE, A. L., Shoeing smith, R.F.A.
He volunteered in February 1915, and was drafted overseas in the same year. During his service on the Western Front he was engaged on important duties until after the cessation of hostilities, when he returned to England and was demobilised in March 1919.
He holds the 1914–15 Star, General Service and Victory Medals.
40, Wakefield Street, Upper Edmonton, N.18   16562B

MOORE, C. A., Cpl., R.F.A.
He enlisted in April 1915, and served in France and Belgium from 1916 until May 1917. He took part in many important engagements during that period, including the battles of Armentières and Bullecourt, where he sustained a wound which caused the loss of his left leg.
He was discharged in August 1918, and holds the General Service and Victory Medals.
13, Grove Place, Ealing, W.5   10855C.

MOORE, C. A., Pte., Royal Fusiliers.
He joined in March 1918, and after serving in France for six weeks, died of wounds received near Bapaume in the Advance of 1918.
He was entitled to the General Service and Victory Medals.
13, Grove Place, Ealing, W.5   10855B.

MOORE, C. B., Bombardier, R.G.A.
He volunteered in October 1915, and at the conclusion of his training was drafted to Salonica, where he took part in many important engagements on the Balkan Front. He remained in this theatre of war until after the Armistice, when he returned to England and was demobilised in August 1919.
He holds the General Service and Victory Medals.
22, Beaconsfield Road, Lower Edmonton, N.9   14763A.

MOORE, C. R., A.B., Royal Navy.
He volunteered in August 1915, and after his training was posted to H.M.S. " Edgar," which vessel was engaged on important mine-sweeping duties in the North Sea until after the cessation of hostilities.
He was demobilised in September 1919, and holds the General Service and Victory Medals.
22, Beaconsfield Road, Lower Edmonton, N.9   14763B.

MOORE, E. J., Lce.-Cpl., Durham L.I.
He volunteered in May 1915, and was sent to France during the same year. He took part in many important engagements on the Western Front, including the battles of Ypres, the Somme and Arras, and was badly gassed.
He holds the 1914–15 Star, General Service and Victory Medals, and was demobilised in May 1919.
141, Beaconsfield Road, Lower Edmonton, N.9   14767A.

MOORE, F. J., Pte., 7th Norfolk Regiment.
He volunteered in November 1914, and was speedily drafted to the Western Front. In 1915 he proceeded to Egypt, where he remained till 1919. He took part in General Allenby's campaign in Palestine, and was present at the capture of Jerusalem and in other engagements in that theatre of war. He also helped to quell the Egyptian riots.
He was demobilised in August 1919, and holds the 1914–15 Star, General Service and Victory Medals.
25a, Deacon Road, Cricklewood, N.W.2   TX16957.

MOORE, F. T. H., Driver, R.A.S.C.
He volunteered in January 1915, and after his training was drafted to Egypt, and later to Palestine and from there to Salonica. During his service on these Fronts he was engaged on important duties until after the cessation of hostilities.
He was demobilised in May 1919, and holds the General Service and Victory Medals.
13, Grove Place, Ealing, W.5   10855A.

MOORE, H., Driver, R.F.A.
He volunteered in December 1914, and was sent to France in the following April. Whilst overseas he took part in many engagements and was mentioned in dispatches for gallantry in the field. During his service he was severely gassed, and was invalided home and discharged in February 1919.
He died on September 2nd, 1919, and was entitled to the 1914–15 Star, General Service and Victory Medals.
17, Burnthwaite Road, Walham Green, S.W.6   X20083B.

MOORE, H. D., Pte., Royal Fusiliers.
He joined in November 1914, and served on the Western Front, taking part in the battles of Loos, Ypres, and the Somme. He was seriously wounded in action, and after being in hospital in France and England, was demobilised in March 1919.
He holds the 1914–15 Star, General Service and Victory Medals.   137, Sherbrooke Road, Fulham, S.W.6   X18621.

MOORE, L. G., Pte., Durham L.I.
He joined in April 1917, and at the conclusion of his training was drafted overseas in the following year. He took part in various engagements during the Retreat and Advance of 1918, and after the Armistice returned to England.
He was eventually demobilised in January 1920, and holds the General Service and Victory Medals.
40, Wakefield Street, Upper Edmonton, N.18   16562A.

MOORE, P. L., Gunner, R.G.A.
He joined in October 1915, and was sent to the Western Front, where he took part in many important engagements, including those at Delville Wood, Arras, Péronne, Ypres, Bullecourt, Cambrai, and during the Advance of 1918.
He was demobilised in February 1919, holding the General Service and Victory Medals.
59b, Guinness's Buildings, Hammersmith, W.6   X17702.

MOORE, W., Gunner, R.G.A.
He volunteered in August 1915, and during his service on the Western Front took part in the battles of the Somme, Vimy Ridge, Loos and Ypres. He contracted a serious illness whilst overseas, and was in hospital for some months. In April 1918 he was badly gassed, in consequence of which he was invalided home and discharged in the following May.
He holds the General Service and Victory Medals.
20, Waverley Road, Tottenham, N.17   X19068.

MOORE, W. J., Driver, R.A.S.C. (H.T.)
He volunteered in January 1915, and after his training was drafted overseas in the following year. During his service on the Western Front he was engaged on important transport duties to the front line trenches.
He was demobilised in June 1919, and holds the General Service and Victory Medals.
7, Lundy Street, Hammersmith, W.6   14893A.

MOORMAN, F. W., Driver, R.F.A.
He volunteered for duty in 1914, and was drafted in 1917 to Salonica, where during his two years' service he saw fighting on several sectors.
He was sent home and demobilised in 1919, and holds the General Service and Victory Medals.
33, Croxley Road, Maida Hill, W.9   X19970.

MORDEY, G. L., Pte., East Surrey Regiment.
He volunteered for service in July 1915, and in the same year was drafted to the Western Front, where he remained for over three years, and took part in many of the leading engagements up to the close of hostilities, including Arras, the Somme, the Marne, and Cambrai. He was wounded at Arras in 1917, and was in hospital for a time.
He was demobilised in February 1919, and holds the 1914–15 Star, General Service and Victory Medals.
34, Woodchester Street, Paddington, W.2   X20554.

MOREMENT, R. H., Pte., R.A.S.C.
He joined in August 1916, and after receiving training at various stations in England was drafted to the Western Front, where he took part in several engagements and did much good work.
He holds the General Service and Victory Medals, and was demobilised in August 1919.
20, Enbrook Street, Queen's Park Estate, W.10   X19315.

MORETON, F. A., Rifleman, K.R.R.
He joined in 1918, and after his training served at various stations on important duties with his unit until after the signing of the Armistice. He was then drafted to Germany, and joined the Army of Occupation.
In 1920 he was still serving.
87, Ancill Street, Hammersmith, W.6   14980B.

MORETON, T. G., Rifleman, 12th London Regt. (Rangers).
He volunteered in September 1914, and was drafted to the Western Front at the conclusion of his training. During his service he took part in the battle of the Somme and in other engagements. On May 3rd, 1915, he was severely wounded in action and taken prisoner, and on February 23rd, 1916, died of wounds in Germany.
He was entitled to the 1914–15 Star, General Service and Victory Medals.
87, Ancill Street, Hammersmith, W.6   14980A.

MORGAN, F., Gunner, R.F.A.
He volunteered in 1915, and was drafted overseas the same year. During his service on the Western Front he took part in many important engagements on various sectors.
He returned to England for his demobilisation in April 1919, and was entitled to the 1914–15 Star, General Service and Victory Medals.
349, Brettenham Road East, Upper Edmonton, N.18 15627A.

MORGAN, W., Pte., 7th Essex Regiment.
He volunteered in August 1914, and after his training was drafted to the Dardanelles in the following year. After the evacuation of the Peninsula he was sent to Egypt, where he took part in many engagements. Owing to ill-health he was invalided to England, and was discharged as medically unfit for further service in 1917.
He holds the General Service and Victory Medals.
349, Brettenham Road East, Upper Edmonton, N.18 15627B.

MORLEY, A., Cpl., Royal Air Force.
He volunteered in 1915, and was drafted overseas in the same year. During his service on the Western Front he was engaged at various aerodromes on important duties which called for a high degree of technical skill.
He was demobilised in January 1919, and holds the 1914–15 Star, General Service and Victory Medals.
154, Town Road, Lower Edmonton, N.9   13585B.

MORLEY, E., Driver, R.F.A.
He volunteered in November 1914, and was drafted to France in the following year on completion of his training. He took part in many important engagements in this theatre of war, including the battles of the Somme (1916), and Cambrai (1918).
He holds the 1914–15 Star, General Service and Victory Medals, and in 1920 was still serving.
154, Town Road, Lower Edmonton, N.9   13585A.

MORLEY, H. P., Bombardier, R.F.A.
Re-enlisting in August 1914, he entered upon a remarkably long and varied war service on the Western Front. He took part in the retreat from Mons and the battles of the Somme, Ypres, Arras. Bullecourt, Armentières, St. Quentin, Vimy Ridge, and the closing campaign of 1918. During this time he was gassed, and in February 1919 was demobilised.
He had previously served for seven years in India.
He holds the Mons Star, General Service and Victory Medals.
9, Bridport Road, Upper Edmonton, N.18   TX17589.

MORLEY, J. E., Driver, R.F.A.
He joined in November 1914, and was drafted to the Western Front, where he took part in the battles of the Somme, Arras, Ypres, Loos, Neuve Chapelle and many others.
In February 1919 he was demobilised, and holds the 1914–15 Star, General Service and Victory Medals.
24, Chesson Road, West Kensington, W.14   X17162A.

MORLEY, M. E. (Mrs.), Special War Worker.
During the war this lady offered her services and was engaged on important duties at a military hospital for officers in London. She rendered valuable aid and was commended for her good work.
24, Chesson Road, West Kensington, W.14   X17162B.

MORLING, A., Lce.-Cpl., 2nd Coldstream Guards.
He volunteered in August 1914, and was drafted to France, where he took part in the battles of Mons and Ypres. He was wounded in December 1914, and invalided home, where he was retained with his unit owing to his being medically unfit for service overseas.
He gave valuable services, and holds the Mons Star, General Service and Victory Medals.
He was demobilised in March 1919.
31, Siddons Road, Tottenham, N.17   X19152.

MORLING, E. F., Cpl., R.A.F.
He joined in May 1918, and after his training was ordered to the Western Front, where he was employed on important duties until December 1919.
He was then demobilised, and holds the General Service and Victory Medals.
40, Rucklidge Avenue, Harlesden, N.W.10   12919A.

MORLING, G. P., Sapper, Royal Engineers.

He joined in February 1916, and was sent to the Western Front in the following year. He took part in many engagements, including the battles of Arras, Cambrai and the Somme, and the Retreat and Advance of 1918. During his service he was wounded, and after the Armistice joined the Army of Occupation.
He holds the General Service and Victory Medals, and was demobilised in September 1919.
40, Rucklidge Avenue, Harlesden, N.W.10   12919B.

MORRIS, A., Sapper, Royal Engineers.

He volunteered in 1914, and after his training was drafted to the Western Front, where he took part in the engagements of the Somme, Ypres, Arras, and in the Retreat and Advance of 1918.
He was demobilised in 1919, and holds the 1914-15 Star, General Service and Victory Medals.
93, Durban Road, Tottenham, N.17   X17966.

MORRIS, A., Pte., 15th Middlesex Regiment.

He volunteered in June 1915, and after his training was retained with his unit on important duties until drafted to France in 1918. He took part in many engagements, and was later transferred to the Labour Corps on account of ill-health.
He was demobilised in April 1919, and holds the General Service and Victory Medals.
8, Willows Terrace, Rucklidge Avenue, Harlesden, N.W.10   13358.

MORRIS, A. H., Cpl., Royal Engineers.

He volunteered in March 1915, and after completion of his training was drafted to the Western Front, where he took part in many engagements. He was killed in action near Ypres in September 1917.
He was entitled to the General Service and Victory Medals.
1, Nursery Street, Tottenham, N.17   X18120.

MORRIS, A. H., Pte., 1/7th Middlesex Regt.

He volunteered in November 1915, and early the following year was sent out to the Western Front. He took part in the battles of the Somme, Ypres, Loos and several other engagements, and was wounded four times.
He was discharged in February 1918, being found medically unfit as the result of his wounds.
He holds the General Service and Victory Medals.
47, Hawthorn Road, Upper Edmonton, N.18   X17054C

MORRIS, F. B., Sergt., 16th Middlesex Regt.

He volunteered in August 1914, and shortly after was sent out to the Western Front. He took part in numerous engagements, and was eventually killed in action on the Somme on July 19th, 1917.
He was entitled to the 1914-15 Star, General Service and Victory Medals.
28, Delorme Street, Hammersmith, W.6   14086B.

MORRIS, H. J., Pte., Duke of Cornwall's L.I.

Volunteering in August 1914, he was engaged on important duties at various stations for some time. He was then drafted to the Western Front and took part in many important engagements. He was severely wounded on the Somme in September 1916, and a year later was discharged as medically unfit for further service.
He holds the General Service and Victory Medals.
28, Delorme Street, Hammersmith, W.6   14086C.

MORRIS, J., Pte., Machine Gun Corps.

He joined in July 1916, and in the following October was sent to France, where he saw much severe fighting on various sectors of the Western Front.
On June 3rd, 1917, he was killed in action, and was entitled to the General Service and Victory Medals.
26, Herries Street, N. Kensington, W.10   X18723.

MORRIS, J. H., Sergt., 7th Bedford Regiment.

Volunteering in September 1914, he was engaged on important duties at home for some time and was later drafted to the Western Front. He fought in many engagements in various sectors, and on March 23rd, 1918, was killed in action at the beginning of the German Offensive.
He was entitled to the General Service and Victory Medals.
28, Delorme Street, Hammersmith, W.6   14086A.

MORRIS, R. J., Rifleman, K.R.R.

He joined in August 1916, and during his service with the Colours was stationed on the East Coast, where he was on duty in connection with the Home Defences.
He gave valuable services, but was not successful in obtaining his transfer overseas before hostilities ceased, and was demobilised in June 1919
80, Ashmore Road, Harrow Road, W.9   X19845B.

MORRIS, S., Mechanic, Royal Air Force.

Joining in 1917, he was retained on important duties at large aerodromes in the South of England. His work called for a high degree of skill, and he gave valuable services, but was not able to secure his transfer overseas before the cessation of hostilities.
He was demobilised in 1919.
42, Seymour Avenue, Tottenham, N.17   X19165.

MORRIS, S. T., Pte., The Buffs (East Kent Regt.)

He joined in December 1915, and from 1917 until 1918 served in India, where he was for some time in hospital suffering from malaria.
He holds the General Service and Victory Medals, and was demobilised in December 1919.
47, Hawthorn Road, Upper Edmonton, N.18   X17054A.

MORRIS, T., Pte., Royal Fusiliers.

He volunteered for service in August 1915, and at the conclusion of his course of training was engaged on important duties with his unit at various stations on the East coast.
He did not succeed in being transferred overseas to the fighting areas, and was discharged in April 1918.
80, Ashmore Road, Harrow Road, W.9   X19845A.

MORRIS, W. A., Rifleman, 8th London Regiment (Post Office Rifles).

Joining in 1914, he went to the Western Front in the following year and was killed in action on October 29th, 1915, after taking part in much heavy fighting.
He was entitled to the 1914-15 Star, General Service and Victory Medals.
47, Hawthorn Road, Upper Edmonton, N.18   X17054B.

MORRISH, J., Leading Stoker, Royal Navy.

He volunteered in December 1914, and immediately proceeded to sea with his ship. He served on board H.M.S. " Africa " and " Pembroke," and took part in many important naval operations with the Grand Fleet. He also served in a torpedo boat destroyer for a time, and in 1920 was still in the Royal Navy.
He holds the 1914-15 Star, General Service and Victory Medals.
20, Lydford Road, Maida Hill, W.9   X19437.

MORRISH, J. M., Pte., R.A.S.C. (M.T.)

Volunteering in September 1915, he was sent to the Western Front in the same month. While in this seat of war he took an active part in the battles of the Somme, Ypres and Cambrai, and also in important engagements at Arras, Vimy Ridge and Lens. During this time he was engaged on the transport of supplies and munitions.
He holds the 1914-15 Star, General Service and Victory Medals, and was demobilised in February 1919.
63, Hiley Road, Willesden, N.W.10   X18331.

MORRISON, C. G., Sergt., 1/19th London Regt.

He volunteered in August 1914, served on the Western Front and took part in the battles of Loos, the Somme, Arras, Ypres and Cambrai. While abroad he was also employed as regimental shoemaker, and was in hospital for some time suffering from influenza.
He was demobilised in April 1919, holding the 1914-15 Star, General Service and Victory Medals.
12, Kenneth Road, W. Kensington, W.14   X17149.

MORRISON, F., Rifleman, Rifle Brigade.

He joined in 1917, and later in the same year was sent to Egypt, where he was engaged on important duties until early in 1918. He was then drafted to France and saw much severe fighting during the Advance of the Allies in the closing stages of the war.
In 1919 he was demobilised, and holds the General Service and Victory Medals.
21, Rowallan Road, Munster Road, S.W.6   X19341.

MORRISON, W. J., Pte., Essex Regiment.

He volunteered in August 1914, and in the following year was sent out to the Dardanelles, where he was wounded and invalided home. After his recovery he was sent to the Western Front, when, in 1917 at Arras, he was again wounded. After his recovery he continued to serve on the Western Front until he was demobilised in March 1919.
He holds the 1914-15 Star, General Service and Victory Medals.
327, Brettenham Road, Upper Edmonton, N.18   15641

MORSE, W. J., Cpl., 13th London Regiment.

He joined early in 1917, and was sent to the Western Front, where he took part in engagements at Vimy Ridge, Ypres, Messines, Bullecourt and Cambrai, and also in the Allied Advance of 1918. He was twice wounded at Cambrai and at Messines.
He was demobilised in 1920, holding the General Service and Victory Medals.
75, Yeldham Road, Hammersmith, W.6   13277

MORTON, E., Cpl., Royal Field Artillery.

Enlisting in 1914, he went to France in the next year after a thorough training. During two years' active service he fought in all important battles of the period and was promoted on account of his command of men and technical knowledge. He was killed in action in the battle of the Somme on September 24th, 1916.
He was entitled to the 1914–15 Star, General Service and Victory Medals.
42, Aspenlea Road, Hammersmith, W.6   14289C.

MORTON, H., Sapper, Royal Engineers.

He volunteered in May 1915, and saw active service in France, where he took part in many engagements, including the battles of Ypres, Loos and the Somme   He was severely wounded in October 1918, and was in hospital in France until March 1919, when he was invalided to England.
He holds the 1914–15 Star, General Service and Victory Medals.
27, Moselle Street, Tottenham, N.17   X18361.

MOSELEY, W. T., Pte., Essex Regiment.

He joined in 1916, and was shortly afterwards drafted to the Western Front, where he served for nearly three years During this period he was engaged for a while on special guard duties at an internment camp.   He also fought in the closing campaigns of 1918.
He was demobilised in February 1919, and holds the General Service and Victory Medals.
95, Drayton Road, Harlesden, N.W.10   15257.

MOSS, A., Pte., Buffs (East Kent Regiment).

Volunteering in October 1915, he was sent to France early in the following year.   He there took part in much severe fighting, and in August 1918 was killed while returning to his unit after having taken a wounded officer to an advanced dressing-station.
He was entitled to the General Service and Victory Medals.
9, Nelson Road, Lower Edmonton, N.9   13289.

MOSS, C. R. (Miss), Special War Worker.

During the war this lady was engaged in the clerical department at Messrs. Martin's, Ltd., Piccadilly, in connection with the distribution of tobacco and cigarettes to troops serving overseas.   She continued these duties until the cessation of hostilities and rendered valuable services which were greatly appreciated.
19, Chesson Road, West Kensington, W.14   X16978C.

MOSS, D. E. (Miss), Special War Worker.

This lady was desirous of assisting her country and volunteered for work of national importance, as the result of which she was employed in the clerical department of the Ministry of Munitions.   She continued in this capacity throughout the war, only resigning on the Armistice being signed.   During this time she rendered valuable services.
19, Chesson Road, West Kensington, W.14   16978B.

MOSS, E., Pte., Royal Fusiliers.

He joined in 1916, and later in the same year was sent to France, where he took part in the battles of the Somme and Cambrai and in the severe fighting during the Allied Retreat and Advance in 1918.
He was demobilised in September 1919, and holds the General Service and Victory Medals.
8, Ambleside Road, Willesden, N.W.10   16124.

MOSS, E. (Miss), Special War Worker.

During the war this lady voluntarily gave her services to a large depot in Belgrave Square.   She was engaged on the making of bandages, pads and others articles of hospital equipment, and did splendid work throughout.   She received high commendation for her patriotic action.
53, Dieppe Street, West Kensington, W.14   T16427A.

MOSS, E. J., Pte., Bedfordshire Regiment.

He joined in February 1918, and after his training was retained on special duties with his unit at various stations.   He gave valuable services, but was unable to secure his transfer overseas before the cessation of hostilities.
After the signing of the Armistice, however, he went to Germany with the Army of Occupation and remained there until he was demobilised in September 1919.
112, Carlyle Avenue, Willesden, N.W.10   14457B.

MOSS, G., Gunner, Royal Field Artillery.

This gunner joined in 1916, and was later drafted to the Western Front, where he took part in the battles of the Somme and in many other engagements.   He was wounded in action at Armentières and invalided home.   On his recovery he was sent across to Ireland and remained there until his demobilisation in 1919.
He holds the General Service and Victory Medals.
53, Dieppe Street, West Kensington, W.14   T16427B.

MOSS, G. A., Pte., Machine Gun Corps.

At the outbreak of war he was serving in the West Indies, and was immediately sent to France, where he took part in the retreat from Mons and the battle of Ypres.   In 1915 he was drafted to Egypt, and a year later was again sent to France. He then fought in the battles of the Somme and Vimy Ridge, and in other important engagements.
In 1919 he was demobilised, and holds the Mons Star, General Service and Victory Medals.
99, Durban Road, Tottenham, N.17   X17963.

MOSS, G. E. A., Pte., 23rd Royal Fusiliers.

Joining in August 1916, he was later drafted to the Western Front, where he took part in the battles of Ypres and Cambrai, and in other severe fighting until hostilities ceased.   During his service he was wounded, and was eventually demobilised in September 1919, holding the General Service and Victory Medals.   35, Seymour Road, Lower Edmonton, N.9   13339.

MOSS, H., Pte., Royal Army Service Corps.

He volunteered in 1915, and was sent to the Western Front, where he was engaged on important duties during the battles of Neuve Chapelle, Ypres, Loos, the Somme, Dickebusch, Arras, and Bullecourt.   He was also present at heavy fighting on Vimy Ridge, and in the Allied Retreat and Advance of 1918.
In 1919 he was demobilised, and holds the 1914–15 Star, General Service and Victory Medals.
19, Chesson Road, West Kensington, W.14   X16984.

MOSS, H., Pte., 2nd Welch Regiment.

A serving soldier, he was drafted on the outbreak of war to the Western Front, where he took part in the retreat from Mons, the battles of the Marne and the Aisne, and in other important engagements.   He was wounded at the end of 1914 and was invalided home.   Being medically unfit for further sevice overseas, he was retained on important duties at various stations until his discharge in October 1919.
He holds the Mons Star, General Service and Victory Medals.
129, Mayo Road, Willesden, N.W.10   15433B.

MOSS, H. J., Gunner, Royal Field Artillery.

Joining in 1918, he was retained after his training on impor tant duties with his unit at various stations.   He rendered valuable service, but was not able to secure his transfer overseas before the cessation of hostilities.
He was demobilised in February 1919.
112, Carlyle Avenue, Willesden, N.W.10   14457A.

MOSS, W., Pte., Suffolk Regiment and 19th London Regiment.

He joined in August 1918, and after his training was engaged on important duties with his unit.   Owing to the early cessa tion of hostilities after his joining the Army he was unable to secure his transfer to the fighting zone, but in 1919 he was sent to Egypt with the Army of Occupation and remained there until his demobilisation in February 1920.
8, Ambleside Road, Willesden, N.W.10   16123.

MOSS, W. H., Pte., R.A.S.C. (M.T.)

He joined in February 1917, and on completion of his training was drafted to the Western Front, where he took an active part in important operations in the final stages of the war. He was in hospital in France owing to an illness contracted on service, and was invalided home.
In October 1919 he was demobilised, and holds the Genera Service and Victory Medals.
207, Munster Road, Fulham, S.W.6   X18755.

MOSS, W. H., L-Cpl., Essex Regiment.

He joined in 1917, and during his service on the Western Front took part in the battles of Arras, Ypres, Amiens, Bullecourt and Cambrai, and in the Advance of the Allies in 1918.
He remained in France guarding prisoners of war until demobilised in 1919, holding the General Service and Victory Medals.
19, Chesson Road, West Kensington, W.14   X16978A.

MOSS, W. W., Rifleman, King's Royal Rifles.

He joined in 1916, and was later drafted to the Western Front After taking part in much severe fighting on various sectors, he was killed in action at Passchendaele on December 2nd, 1917.
He was entitled to the General Service and Victory Medals.
66, Bridport Road, Upper Edmonton, N.18   X17469.

MOSSOP, W. H., 1st-Class Stoker, R.N., H.M.S. " Cyclops."

Having had nine years' previous service in the Navy he rejoined in August 1914, immediately after the outbreak of hostilities.   He was posted to H.M.S. " Cyclops," and with this ship was engaged on special duties in connection with the campaign against enemy submarines.   He was also engaged on important duties at Scapa Flow.
In 1920 he was still serving, and holds the 1914 Star, General Service and Victory Medals.
14, North Avenue, Upper Edmonton, N.18   15223

MOTH, E., Pte., 5th Middlesex Regiment.

He joined in August 1917, and was sent to the Western Front before the end of the year. While in this seat of war he took part in many important engagements, including the battles of Arras and Cambrai.

He remained in France until his demobilisation in January 1919, and holds the General Service and Victory Medals.

11, Earlesmead Road, College Park, N.W.10   X18033

MOTTRAM, F. C., Sapper, Royal Engineers.

Volunteering in August 1914, he was quickly drafted to the Western Front, where, during the retreat from Mons he was severely wounded and taken prisoner. For four years and seven months he was held captive in Germany, where he suffered great privation. He was released after the Armistice and was demobilised in April 1919.

He holds the Mons Star, General Service and Victory Medals.

11, Belmont Avenue, Lower Edmonton, N.9   12291B.

MOTTRAM, T., Pte., 1/10th Middlesex Regt.

Joining in July 1916, he was sent a year later to Cape Town. Later in 1917 he was drafted to India, where he served at Bombay and Lucknow.

After a total service of more than three years he returned to England and was demobilised in November 1919, holding the General Service and Victory Medals.

17, Nelson Road, Lower Edmonton, N.9   13287.

MOTTRAM, W. R., Stoker, R.N., H.M.S. "Tiger."

Joining in February 1916, he was engaged throughout his service with the Grand Fleet in the North Sea. He took part in many important engagements, and was once torpedoed near Scapa Flow.

He was still serving in 1920, and holds the General Service and Victory Medals.

11, Belmont Avenue, Lower Edmonton, N.9   12291A.

MOULDEN, C., Sapper, Royal Engineers.

Volunteering in August 1914, he was soon drafted to the Western Front, where he remained until the cessation of hostilities. Throughout his service he did valuable work with the Royal Engineers, and fought in many important sectors, including Mons, Loos, Arras and Cambrai.

He was demobilised in July 1919, holding the Mons Star, General Service and Victory Medals.

4, Ascot Road, Upper Edmonton, N.18   15184.

MOULDER, C. H., Gunner (Signaller), R.F.A.

He volunteered in July 1915, and served on the Western Front for four years. During this time he took part in various engagements, including the battles of Ypres, Cambrai, Arras, and the Somme, where he was wounded, and in the Retreat and Advance of 1918.

He was demobilised in May 1919, and holds the 1914-15 Star, General Service and Victory Medals.

49, Heron Road, Willesden, N.W.10   15609.

MOULDER, W. A., Pte., 1st Buffs (East Kent Regiment).

Joining in 1916, he was sent to the Western Front in the same year. He took part in many important battles, including those of the Somme, Arras and Cambrai, where he was wounded, and in the last Retreat, during which he was severely gassed. He was invalided home, and after his recovery was engaged on important duties in Ireland until October 1919, when he was demobilised, holding the General Service and Victory Medals.

49, Heron Road, Willesden, N.W.10   15610.

MOULE, G. A. F., Pte., Norfolk Regiment.

He volunteered in January 1915, and in the same year was drafted to the Western Front, where he saw much service. He was wounded three times, and being taken prisoner was in captivity for 19 months. On the cessation of hostilities he was repatriated, and rejoined his regiment

He holds the 1914-15 Star, General Service and Victory Medals.

129, Bounces Road, Lower Edmonton, N.9   13078.

MOULT, J., Gunner, Royal Field Artillery.

He volunteered in August 1914, and until 1916, when he was drafted to Salonica, served on the Western Front, and took part in many important battles. Whilst in the East he contracted malaria, and was in consequence invalided home. On his recovery he was engaged on special duties at various stations until his demobilisation in August 1919.

He holds the 1914 Star, General Service and Victory Medals.

44, Hartington Road, Lower Edmonton, N.9   14056.

MOULTON, E., Pte., Royal Defence Corps.

He was an ex-soldier with 16 years' Colour service, and at the age of 67 volunteered in November 1914. He was engaged on important duties at various stations in England, and did valuable work before being discharged in September 1918.

31, Shakespeare Avenue, Willesden, N.W.10   13892.

MOWER, J., Driver, Royal Field Artillery.

Volunteering in August 1914, he was shortly afterwards sent to the Western Front. Whilst overseas he took part in many of the principal engagements, including the battles of Ypres, the Somme, Arras and Cambrai, where he was severely wounded. He also lost the sight of one eye, and was invalided home. After being for some time in hospital at Matlock and Sheffield, he was demobilised in April 1919, holding the 1914-15 Star, General Service and Victory Medals.

15, Bayonne Road, Hammersmith, W.6   14307.

MOWER, P. J., Pte., 2nd Worcestershire Regt.

He enlisted in 1916, and early in the following year was sent to the Western Front, where he took part in the second battle of Ypres, and was wounded. He was discharged as medically unfit in December 1918 as the result of his wound, and holds the General Service and Victory Medals.

37, Cooper Road, Dudden Hill, N.W.10   16295B.

MOWER, T. S., Gunner, Royal Field Artillery.

An ex-soldier, with a previous record of 12 years' service, he volunteered on the outbreak of hostilities. He was drafted to the Western Front, where he took part in the fighting at Ypres, Loos, the Somme and Lille, but in 1916, in consequence of ill-health, he returned to England. Afterwards he did valuable work with the Anti-Aircraft Section until his demobilisation in January 1919.

He holds the Queen's South African Medal with five bars, the 1914-15 Star, General Service and Victory Medals.

18, Meyrick Road, Willesden, N.W.10   16341.

MOWLEN, C. F., Pte., Middlesex Regiment.

He joined in June 1916, and after his training was drafted to Salonica, where he took part in many engagements, and was wounded.

He holds the General Service and Victory Medals, and was demobilised in November 1919.

38, Harton Road, Lower Edmonton, N.9   13341

MOYLAN, W., Pte., South African Infantry.

He volunteered in September 1914, and was drafted from South Africa to Egypt. Later he served on the Western Front, and was in action in many important sectors. In December 1916 he was severely gassed at Arras, and in April 1918 was wounded during the German attack on Kemmel Hill. He was for some time in hospital both in France and England, and in September 1919 was demobilised, holding the 1914-15 Star, General Service and Victory Medals.

38, Hilmer Street, West Kensington, W.14   16915A.

MOYNS, A., Sapper, Royal Engineers.

He volunteered in May 1915, and on completion of his training in the following year was drafted to the Western Front. Throughout his service overseas, which lasted until November 1918, he did valuable work with the Royal Engineers in many important sectors, and was severely gassed during the battle of Arras.

He was discharged as physically unfit in January 1919, and holds the General Service and Victory Medals.

52a, Lorenco Road, Tottenham, N.17   18390.

MOYSEY, P. C., Pte., R.D.C. and R.A.F.

Volunteering in 1915, he was later transferred to the Royal Air Force, and was engaged on important work with his squadron at various stations. He was not successful in being drafted overseas before the termination of war, but gave valuable services before being demobilised in February 1919.

47, Leopold Road, Willesden, N.W.10   14909.

MUDD, A., Pte., Royal Sussex Regiment.

He joined in February 1917, and served for two years on the Western Front, where he took part in many engagements, including the battles of Arras and Cambrai, and was wounded. He was demobilised in 1919, holding the General Service and Victory Medals.

13, Napier Road, Kensal Green, N.W.10   X17599

MUDGE, F. G., Staff-Sergt., R.A.M.C.

Volunteering in August 1914, he was sent to Salonica two years later. During his service in the East he did valuable work with the Royal Army Medical Corps, and whilst carrying out his duties under fire was severely wounded.

He returned to England in 1918, and in February of the following year was demobilised, holding the General Service and Victory Medals.

3, Cecil Road, Greenhill Park, N.W.10   14015.

MUDGE, W., Pte., 24th Royal Fusiliers.

He volunteered in November 1915, and after his training was drafted to the Western Front. He fought in many important sectors, including the Somme (where he was wounded), Arras and Cambrai, and was employed as regimental pioneer.

He was demobilised in April 1919, holding the General Service and Victory Medals.

40, Garvan Road, Hammersmith, W.6   15057

MUGRIDGE, A. J., Pte., Royal Fusiliers.
Volunteering in January 1915, he was drafted to the Western Front on completion of his training in the following year. Whilst overseas he took part in the fighting in many important sectors, including the Somme and Cambrai, where he was severely wounded.
He returned to England in 1919, and in March of the same year was demobilised, holding the General Service and Victory Medals
13, Herbert Road, Lower Edmonton, N.9   12974.

MUGRIDGE, T. O., Cpl., 4th Royal Fusiliers.
He volunteered in 1914, and in the same year went to the Western Front. He was reported missing after the battle of Ypres in 1915, and has not been heard of since then.
He was entitled to the 1914-15 Star, General Service and Victory Medals.
64a, St. Mary's Road, Craven Park, N.W.10   13369A.

MUIR, A., A.B., Merchant Service.
He joined in July 1918, and was engaged on the "Messacoit," an oil tank, transporting oil to the Allied countries. He did valuable work until September 1919, when he was demobilised, holding the Mercantile Marine War, General Service and Victory Medals.
60, Faroe Road, West Kensington, W.14   T12660.

MUIR, J. H., Pte., Royal Sussex Regiment, and Gunner, Royal Field Artillery.
He joined the Army in March 1916, and was sent to the Western Front, where he played a prominent part in several engagements, being generally employed as a signaller. In September 1919 he was demobilised, and holds the General Service and Victory Medals.
25, Kilmaine Road, Munster Road, S.W.6   TX18855B.

MULADY, D. E., Pte., Northamptonshire Regt.
He volunteered in September 1914, and served in France, where he took part in the first battle of Ypres. Later he was sent to the Dardanelles, and whilst in action there was wounded. He afterwards did garrison duty in Egypt and Salonica.
He was demobilised in March 1919, holding the 1914-15 Star, General Service and Victory Medals.
21, Whitehall Street, Tottenham, N.17   X18349A.

MULADY, J. J., Pte., East Surrey Regiment.
He volunteered in January 1915, was drafted to France, and after taking part in many important engagements, was killed in action on the Somme in March 1916.
He was entitled to the 1914-15 Star, General Service and Victory Medals.
21, Whitehall Street, Tottenham, N.17   X18349B.

MULADY, T., Rifleman, King's Royal Rifles.
He joined the Army in February 1917, and saw active service in France. After taking part in many battles he was taken prisoner whilst in action on the Somme in 1918.
He was released after the Armistice, and was demobilised in October 1919, holding the General Service and Victory Medals.   21, Whitehall Street, Tottenham, N.17 X18349C.

MULDOON, O., Pte., R.M.L.I. and Labour Corps.
Volunteering in March 1915, he was soon drafted to France, and was stationed at Dieppe, Dunkirk and Le Havre. Later he went into the battle areas and took part in the engagements at Ypres, Arras and Cambrai.
He returned to England in 1919, when he was demobilised, holding the 1914-15 Star, General Service and Victory Medals. 22, Fordingley Road, Maida Hill, W.9   X19676.

MULFORD, J. C., Pte., R.A.O.C.
He enlisted in August 1916, and in the same year was sent to the Western Front. He was employed at various Ordnance Workshops on this Front in the repair of damaged arms.
He holds the General Service and Victory Medals, and was demobilised in January 1919.
90, Burn's Road, Harlesden, N.W.10   13144.

MULLENGER, J., Pte., West Yorkshire Regt.
He volunteered in April 1915, and was drafted to the Western Front, where he took part in the battles of Ypres and the Somme. Later he was sent to Italy, and in October 1918 was killed during the Offensive on the Piave.
He was entitled to the 1914-15 Star, General Service and Victory Medals.
54, Chesson Road, West Kensington, W.14   16437B.

MULLINER, G. (M.M.), Cpl., 4th Royal Fus.
He volunteered in January 1915, and was sent to France in the following June. Whilst overseas he served on practically all sectors of the Front, and on three occasions was severely wounded in action. He was awarded the Military Medal in March 1918 for conspicuous gallantry on the field near Arras, and in addition holds the 1914-15 Star, General Service and Victory Medals.
He was discharged in March 1919.
27, Manor Park Road, Harlesden, N.W.10   13218.

MULLINS, C. V. (Miss), Special War Worker.
During the war this lady rendered valuable services at Messrs. Blake's, Stevenage Road, Fulham, and at Messrs. Cole's Aircraft Works, Hammersmith Road. The work upon which she was engaged was very important, and the capable manner in which she car.ied out her duties was worthy of high commendation.
49, Averill Street, Hammersmith, W.6   14172.

MULVEY, H. W., A.B., Royal Navy.
He volunteered in 1915, and after receiving training at Devonport, was posted to H.M.S. "Tring." Later he saw service on board H.M.S "Colswood," and on various mine-sweepers. He holds the General Service and Victory Medals, and in 1920 was still serving.
44, Durban Road, Tottenham, N.17   X18078

MUMFORD, A. E., Fireman, H.M.S. "Sonia."
He joined in May 1917, and saw much service on H.M.S. "Sonia," which was engaged on mine-sweeping duties in the North and Irish Seas. She was also employed on specia duties in Russian waters.
He was demobilised in November 1919, holding the Mercantile Marine, General Service and Victory Medals.
99, Berry Street, Willesden, N.W.10   15546.

MUMFORD, A. W., R.A.S.C. (M.T.)
He volunteered in April 1915, and was drafted to France three months later. During his service on the Western Front he was attached to the Artillery and was engaged on important duties in connection with the battles of Albert, Arras, Ypres and the Somme.
He holds the 1914-15 Star, General Service and Victory Medals, and was demobilised in February 1919.
19, Herries Street, North Kensington, W.10   X18730

MUMFORD, E. J., A.B., Royal Navy, H.M.S. "Yarmouth."
He joined in February 1917, and was engaged during the remainder of the war chiefly on patrol and convoy duties in the North Sea and the Atlantic. He holds the General Service and Victory Medals, and in 1920 was still serving
219, Kilburn Lane ,North Kensington, W.10   X18717

MUNDAY, G., Rifleman, King's Royal Rifles.
Although only sixteen years of age he volunteered for service early in 1916, and later was drafted to the Western Front. Up to the time of the Armistice he saw action in various sectors, and afterwards went with the Army of Occupation to Germany.
He was demobilised in January 1920, holding the General Service and Victory Medals.
24, Avalon Road, New King's Road, S.W.6   X19780.

MUNDAY, J. R., Rifleman, Rifle Brigade.
He joined in January 1917, and was sent to France at the conclusion of his training. He was in action in many engagements on the Western Front, and during the German Offensive of 1918 was taken prisoner. He was released in December 1918 and returned to England.
He was demobilised in March 1919, and holds the General Service and Victory Medals.
24, Bramber Road, West Kensington, W.14   16272.

MUNDY, H., Cpl., M.F.P. and A.P.C.
He joined in 1916, and after his training was sent overseas the same year. During his service on the Western Front he was engaged on important Police duties. He was later transferred to the A.P.C., where he was employed on clerical duties at an Army Pay Office.
He holds the General Service and Victory Medals, and in 1920 was still serving.
158, Fifth Avenue, Queen's Park Estate, W.10   X18732.

MUNFORD, A., Pte., 25th London Regiment (Cyclists), and 10th London Regiment.
He joined in December 1915, and in the following year was sent out to France, where he served until 1917, and took part in several engagements, including those of Ypres and Arras. He was severely wounded twice, losing his left foot, and was invalided to England, where he was in hospital for two years.
He was discharged in March 1920, holding the General Service and Victory Medals.
172, Third Avenue, Queen's Park Estate, W.10   X19440.

MUNN, A. W., Sapper, Royal Engineers.
He volunteered in December 1915, and after his training was engaged on important duties at various stations with his unit. He gave valuable services, but was not successful in obtaining his transfer overseas before the cessation of hostilities.
He was demobilised in January 1919.
43, Maldon Road, Lower Edmonton, N.9   14790.

MUNN, F., Gunner, Royal Field Artillery.

He was recalled from the Reserve in August 1914, and was sent to France in the same month. He took part in the battles of Mons, Ypres and the Somme, and was killed in action at Loos on June 26th, 1916. He was buried at Loos British Cemetery.

He was entitled to the Mons Star, General Service and Victory Medals.

19, Barry Road, Stonebridge Park, N.W.10   X17788B.

MUNN, W. E., Pte., 9th Lancers.

He was called up from the Reserve in August 1914, was sent to France in the same month, and took part in several engagements, including the battle of Mons. In April 1916 he was invalided home and discharged as unfit for further military service.

He holds the Mons Star, General Service and Victory Medals.

19, Barry Road, Stonebridge Park, N.W.10   14947.

MUNN, S. P., Pte., 7th London Regiment.

He volunteered in June 1915, and was sent overseas during the same year. He took part in many important engagements on the Western Front, including the battles of Ypres, Arras, Vimy Ridge, Bullecourt, Havrincourt, where he was wounded, and the Retreat of 1918, during which he was taken prisoner. He was released after the Armistice, and returned to England for demobilisation in April 1919.

He holds the 1914-15 Star, General Service and Victory Medals.

52, Chesson Road, West Kensington, W.14   16439.

MUNRO, J. H., Rifleman, 9th London Regiment (Queen Victoria's Rifles).

He volunteered in August 1914, and after his training was drafted to France in the following year. During his two years' service overseas he took part in several engagements, including the battles of Loos, Ypres and the Somme. He was invalided to England in 1917 owing to ill-health, and discharged as medically unfit for further service.

He holds the 1914-15 Star, General Service and Victory Medals. 13, Armadale Road, Walham Green, S.W.6 X19403.

MUNRO, P. E., Sergt., R.A.M.C.

He volunteered in October 1914, and after his training served at various stations on important duties with his unit. He gave valuable services, but was unsuccessful in obtaining his transfer overseas owing to ill-health.

He was discharged in June 1919 as medically unfit for further military service.

35, Somerford Grove, Stoke Newington, N.16   18701A.

MUNRO, S., Gunner, Royal Field Artillery.

He volunteered in August 1914, and was shortly afterwards drafted to the Western Front. He took part in several engagements, including the retreat from Mons and the battles of Loos and Ypres, where he was badly gassed.

He holds the Mons Star, General Service and Victory Medals, and in 1920 was still serving.

35, Somerford Grove, Stoke Newington, N.16   18701B.

MUNSON, A. E., Pte., 2nd East Surrey Regt.

He volunteered in August 1914, and after his training was sent to France in the following year, where he took part in many engagements. He died of wounds received in action on September 30th, 1915.

He was entitled to the 1914-15 Star, General Service and Victory Medals

30, Aintree Street, Dawes Road, S.W.6   T18636B

MUNSON, C. R., Pte., 5th Middlesex Regiment.

He volunteered in January 1915, and was shortly afterwards drafted overseas. He was actively engaged in the severe fighting on the Western Front until he was killed in action near Lille on April 30th, 1915.

He was entitled to the 1914-15 Star, General Service and Victory Medals.

30, Aintree Street, Dawes Road, S.W.6   TX18636A.

MUNSON, W., Pte., 17th Middlesex Regiment.

He volunteered in August 1914, and was sent overseas at the conclusion of his training. He took part in various engagements on the Western Front, including the battle of Armentières. He contracted a serious illness while in France, and was invalided home and discharged in consequence in May 1916.

He holds the 1914-15 Star, General Service and Victory Medals. 9, Welford Terrace, Dawes Road, S.W.6 X18064.

MURCUTT, H., Sapper, Royal Engineers.

He volunteered in September 1914, and in the following year was drafted to the Dardanelles, where he was engaged on important duties in connection with operations in this theatre of war. After the evacuation of the Peninsula he was sent to Egypt, and served with General Allenby in the advance through Palestine.

He was demobilised in July 1919, and holds the 1914-15 Star, General Service and Victory Medals.

91, Roundwood Road, Willesden, N.W.10   16042.

MURDOCK, D., Pte., Oxford and Bucks L.I.

He was called up from the Reserve on the outbreak of war, and in August 1914 was sent to the Western Front, where he took part in the battles of Mons, Loos, the Somme, Ypres and Neuve Chapelle. He was invalided home as the result of shell-shock in April 1916, and was discharged as unfit for further service in August 1916.

He holds the Mons Star, General Service and Victory Medals.

194, Shirland Road, Maida Hill, W.9   X19599.

MURLEY, W. G., Sergt., R.F.A.

He volunteered in August 1914, and after his training was drafted to France in the following year. He took part in many important engagements on the Western Front, including the battles of Ypres and the Somme. During the Advance of 1918 he was badly gassed and was invalided home.

He was demobilised in January 1919, and holds the 1914-15 Star, General Service and Victory Medals.

69, Humbolt Road, Hammersmith, W.6   14983A.

MURPHY, D., Sergt., R.E. (Postal Section).

He volunteered in November 1914, and after his training was drafted to France. After a few months' service overseas he returned to England. He was sent to Italy in 1918, and in the following year came back to England for his demobilisation in May. During his service he was engaged on important duties with the Postal Section of the Royal Engineers.

He holds the 1914-15 Star, General Service and Victory Medals.

65, Mirabel Road, Fulham, S.W.6   X17713.

MURPHY, E., Lce.-Cpl., Seaforth Highlanders.

He enlisted in September 1914, and early in the following year was sent to the Western Front, where he was very severely wounded at Neuve Chapelle in March 1915, as the result of which he was discharged as medically unfit in September 1916.

He holds the 1914-15 Star, General Service and Victory Medals.

55, Raynham Avenue, Upper Edmonton, N.18   T16517A.

MURPHY, E. (Mrs.), W.R.A.F.

She joined in October 1918, and after her training was engaged at various stations on important duties in connection with the fitting of aero engines. She gave valuable services and was demobilised in March 1919.

55, Raynham Avenue, Upper Edmonton, N.18   T16517B.

MURPHY, H. E. (M.M.), Sergt., R.G.A.

He volunteered in November 1915, and after completing his training was drafted to the Western Front in the following year. During his service in this theatre of war he was wounded in action at Ypres in May 1916, and at Messines Ridge in April 1917 was awarded the Military Medal for conspicuous bravery and devotion to duty in the field.

He also holds the General Service and Victory Medals.

118, Lopen Road, Upper Edmonton, N.18   X17917.

MURPHY, M., Driver, Royal Field Artillery.

He joined in August 1914, and served on the Western Front, where he took part in the battles of Mons, Loos, the Somme, Cambrai, Arras and Albert. From 1917 until his demobilisation in November 1918 he served in Salonica.

He holds the Mons Star, General Service and Victory Medals.

18, Kenmont Gardens, College Park, N.W.10   X17576.

MURPHY, W., Pte., Middlesex Regiment.

He enlisted in 1915, and was sent to the Western Front in the following year, when he took part in several important engagements previous to being taken prisoner in 1918. He was released after the Armistice, and was demobilised in 1919.

He holds the General Service and Victory Medals.

15, Durham Road, Lower Edmonton, N.9   14873.

MURPHY, W. C., Lce.-Cpl., 1st Middlesex Regt.

He enlisted in August 1914, and during his service on the Western Front took part in the severe fighting at Ypres, and was wounded in action on the Somme.

He was discharged in March 1918, and holds the 1914-15 Star, General Service and Victory Medals.

38, Gloucester Road, Upper Edmonton, N.18   X17008.

MURRAY, J., Gunner, Royal Field Artillery.

He was called up from the Special Reserve in August 1914, and went to France in the following year, where he took part in many battles, including Loos, Arras, Ypres, Armentières, Neuve Chapelle and Soissons.

He was demobilised in March 1919, hold e 1914-15 Star, General Service and Victory Medals.

74, Lorenco Road, Tottenham, N.1   X18 96B

MURRAY, M., Cpl., Royal Field Artillery.

He volunteered in August 1914, and was shortly afterwards drafted to the Western Front, where he took part in many engagements. He died of wounds received in action at the battle of Ypres on July 19th, 1917.
He was entitled to the 1914 Star, General Service and Victory Medals. 74, Lorenco Road, Tottenham, N.17   X18396A.

MURRAY, R. E. S., Pte., R.A S.C.

He volunteered in December 1915, and after his training served at various stations on important duties with his unit. He gave valuable services, but was not successful in obtaining his transfer overseas owing to ill-health. He was discharged as medically unfit for further service in May 1919.
24, Barbot Street, Lower Edmonton, N.9   14357.

MURRAY, S., Pte., Royal Fusiliers and Air Mechanic, R.A.F.

He enlisted in December 1914, went to Gallipoli in July 1915, and after the evacuation was drafted to France, where he took part in the battles of the Somme, Ypres and Arras. He was twice wounded, and was discharged in January 1919, holding the 1914-15 Star, General Service and Victory Medals.
11, Elthorne Avenue, Hanwell, W.7   11074.

MURRAY, W., Gunner, Royal Field Artillery.

He joined in February 1915, and went to France the same year, taking part in the battles at Cambrai, Ypres and the Somme. He was invalided home in 1917, and later went out to the East, where he served in Egypt, Salonica and Palestine
He was demobilised in 1919, holding the 1914-15 Star, General Service and Victory Medals.
110, Purves Road, Kensal Rise, N.W.10   X18420.

MURRAY, W. J., Sergt., 15th Royal Fusiliers.

He re-enlisted in August 1914, was quickly drafted to the Western Front and took part in the retreat from Mons. He was discharged as unfit for further service in November 1915, having completed 21 year's service.
He holds the Mons Star, General Service, Victory, and the King's and Queen's South African Medals.
12, Bramber Road, West Kensington, W.14   16283.

MURTAGH, F., Special War Worker.

This lady was engaged during the whole course of the war on work of national importance at Messrs. Beaton's factory, Holland Park. She was chiefly employed in the manufacture of hand-grenades and shell parts, and rendered valuable service throughout.
21, Archel Road, West Kensington, W.14   16194.

MURTAGH, H., Pte., South Lancashire Regt.

He was serving at the outbreak of hostilities, and proceeding to the Western Front with the First Expeditionary Force in August 1914, took part in the retreat from Mons. He also fought on the Marne and at La Bassée. He was taken prisoner n October 1914, and whilst in captivity in Germany suffered many privations.
He was demobilised in February 1920, holding the Mons Star General Service and Victory Medals.
7, Shotley Street, Hammersmith, W.6   14801B.

MURTAGH, J. E., Rifleman, Rifle Brigade.

He joined in 1916, and was sent to France in the same year. During his service on the Wetsern Front he took part in many engagements, including the battles of the Somme and Ypres. He returned to England after the Armistice, and was demobilised in February 1919, holding the General Service and Victory Medals.
7, Shotley Street, Hammersmith, W.6   14801A.

MUSCHAMP, A. E., Sergt., Machine Gun Corps.

He enlisted in 1916, and in the same year was sent to the Western Front. After a short period of active service on this Front he was transferred to Mesopotamia, where he contracted malaria fever, and was invalided home.
He was demobilised in November 1919, and holds the General Service and Victory Medals.
110, Montague Road, Lower Edmonton, N.9   16884.

MUSGRAVE, A., Pte., Middlesex Regiment and London Regiment.

He joined in 1915, and in the same year was sent to the Western Front, where he took part in many important engagements, including the battles of Messines and Ypres. He was severely wounded in the latter engagement in 1917, and as a result was discharged as medically unfit in June 1918.
He holds the 1915 Star, General Service and Victory Medals.
24, Mulgrave Road, Fulham, S.W.6   16169.

MUSGRAVE, R., Pte., Middlesex Regiment.

He joined in August 1914, and served on the Western Front, taking part in the battles of the Somme, Ypres, Loos and many other important engagements. He was both gassed and wounded during his active service, and was demobilised in 1919, holding the General Service and Victory Medals
24, Mulgrave Road, Fulham, S.W.6   16171A.

MUSKETT, R., 1st-Class Stoker, R.N., H.M.S., "Reindeer."

He enlisted in 1916, and after a period of shore training was posted to the destroyer "Reindeer," which was employed in patrol work in the Mediterranean. He served throughout the war in this zone until his demobilisation in January 1919.
He holds the General Service and Victory Medals.
32, Denzil Road, Neasden Lane, N.W.10   16080.

MUSKETT, W. H., Gunner, Royal Field Artillery.

He was already serving at the outbreak of hostilities and proceeding to the Western Front with the first Expeditionary Force, took part in the retreat from Mons. He also served in the battles of the Marne and Ypres and was wounded at the latter place in November 1914. After a short period at home, he was sent to the Dardanelles, where he was again wounded in October 1915.
He was demobilised in June 1919, holding the Mons Star, General Service and Victory Medals.
97, Manor Park Road, Harlesden, N.W.10   13227.

MUTTON, C. H., C.S.M., Machine Gun Corps.

He enlisted in November 1914, and served on the Western Front from 1915 until the cessation of hostilities. He took part in many important engagements, including the battles of Lens, Arras, the Somme and Cambrai, and was wounded.
He holds the 1914-15 Star, General Service and Victory Medals   48, St. Mark's Road, Hanwell, W.7   11032.

MYNETT, F. T. E., Lce.-Cpl., Rifle Brigade.

He joined in April 1918, and after his trainig served at various stations on important duties with his unit until the cessation of hostilities where he was drafted fo Germany in the Army of Occupation.
He returned to England in January 1920, for demobilisation.
13, Hiley Road ,Willesden, N.W.10   X18247

N

NANKIVELL, F., Sergt., R.A.S.C. (M.T.)

Volunteering in October 1914, he was soon sent out to the Western Front, where he was employed with the Ammunition and supply column on several sectors of the Western Front, more particularly those of Armentières and Ypres Owing to his service he was discharged as medically unfit in January 1918, and holds the 1914 Star, General Service and Victory Medals.
78, Strode Road, Willesden, N.W.10   X17640.

NARRAWAY, H. E., Pte., Machine Gun Corps.

He volunteered in 1916, and after taking part in engagements at Arras, Bullecourt, Cambrai and Ypres whilst on the Western Front, was taken prisoner at Bus, in March 1918 during the German Offensive. During his internment at Guissen Camp he met with a serious accident whilst working at Heredorf, and was in hospital at Limburg. On his release from captivity after the Armistice he was sent to England, where he was employed on the Education Staff at Rugeley.
In 1919 he was demobi ised, and holds the General Service and Victory Medals.
39, Bronsart Road, Munster Road, S.W.6   X19130

NASH, A., Pte., 9th Royal Fusiliers.

He joined in March 1916, and was sent to the Western Front, where he took a distinguished part in several important engagements.
He was killed in action at Arras on May 3rd, 1917, and was entitled to the General Service and Victory Medals.
67, Cassidy Road, Walham Green, S.W.6   X20213.

NASH, E., Pte., 23rd Middlesex Regiment.

He volunteered in November 1915, and after his training was sent to France, where he took part in many engagements. He was killed in action at Fleury in October 1916, and was entitled to the General Service and Victory Medals.
8, Corby Road, Willesden, N.W.10   14535B

NASH, H. A., Pte., 6th Middlesex Regiment.

He joined in 1916,and after completing his training in England was engaged on important duties with his unit. In spite of the fact that his health broke down and prevented him from being sent overseas, he rendered valuable services until in 1917 he was discharged as medically unfit for further services.
77, Ancill Street, Hammersmtih, W.6   14001—18001B.

NASH, M. (Mrs.), Special War Worker.

During the war this lady was employed on important work in the inspection department at Park Royal, working on fuses &c. She carried out her duties in a satisfactory manner, and was working during several air raids.
8, Corby Road, Willesden, N.W 10   14535A.

NASH, R., Lce.-Cpl., Machine Gun Corps.
He volunteered in August 1914, having previously served in the Territorials, and was immediately sent to the Western Front, where he took a prominent part in many engagements. He was recommended for a decoration for gallantry in the field, and was demobilised in January 1919, holding the 1914–15 Star, General Service and Victory Medals.
19, Allestree Road, Munster Road, S.W.6   X19258.

NASH, W., 2nd Cpl., Royal Engineers.
He rejoined from the Reserve in August 1914, and during his service on the Western Front took a prominent part in engagements at Arras, Cambrai and Vimy Ridge. He was for some time engaged on special work in connection with railways, and during his service was wounded.
He holds the 1914–15 Star, General Service and Victory Medals, and was demobilised in June 1919.
88a, Deacon Road, Cricklewood, N.W.10   X17111B.

NASH, W. C., Sergt., 9th Middlesex Regiment.
Having previously served in the Territorials, he was mobilised at the outbreak of war and was drafted to India. Later he was sent to join the East African Expeditionary Force, with which he gave valuable services, and took part in several engagements until he fell ill and was invalided home.
In February 1920 he was demobilised, and holds the 1914–15 Star, General Service and Victory Medals.
88a, Deacon Road, Cricklewood, N.W.2   X17111A.

NASH, W. E. L., Pte., Gordon Highlanders.
He volunteered in December 1915, and after his training served on important duties with his unit. In 1918 he went to Russia with the Relief Force, remaining there until the following year, when he returned home and was demobilised, holding the Victory Medal.
43, Broughton Road, Fulham, S.W.6   X20903.

NATION, S. F., Cpl., 2nd Royal Fusiliers.
He volunteered in August 1914, and after his training was sent to France, where he took an important part in many engagements, including the battle of the Somme, where he was killed in July 1916.
He was entitled to the 1914 Star, General Service and Victory Medals.
62, Sherbrooke Road, Fulham, S.W.6   X18767.

NAUNTON, J. R., Gunner and Signaller, R.F.A.
He was serving at the outbreak of war, and in 1914 was sent to the Western Front. He took part in the battles of Mons and Neuve Chapelle, and many other engagements, and while in action on the Somme was killed on May 28th, 1917.
He was entitled to the Mons Star, General Service and Victory Medals.
25, Woodfield Place, Maida Hill W.9   X20091—20092A.

NAUNTON, V. A., Lce.-Cpl., Suffolk Regiment, Durham Light Infantry and Military Police.
He joined in November 1916, and in the following year, was sent to the Western Front where he took part in many engagements. He was in action on the Somme, at Festubert, Ypres and Passchendaele, and was wounded.
In December 1919 he was demobilised, holding the General Service and Victory Medals.
25, Woodfield Place, Maida Hill, W.9   X20091—20092B.

NEAL, A. (D.C.M., M.M.), Sergt., R.F.A.
Volunteering in August 1914, he was soon sent to the Western Front, where he took a prominent part in the retreat from Mons and the battles of Loos, Arras, Neuve Chapelle, Ypres, the Somme, Vimy Ridge and Cambrai. For conspicuous gallantry in saving the guns he was awarded the D.C.M., and later won the M.M. for great bravery in the field. In 1918 he was seriously wounded, and after being invalided home, was discharged as unfit.
He holds the D.C.M., M.M., Mons Star, General Service and Victory Medals.
26, Hanwell Road, Munster Road, S.W.6   X18907.

NEAL, A. (Miss), Special War Worker.
During four years of the war this lady worked at the Park Royal Munition Factory, filling shells in the T.N.T. room. She carried out this dangerous work in a satisfactory manner, and rendered valuable services but suffered from the effects.
407, High Road, Willesden, N.W.10   T17342A.

NEAL, A. E., Pte., R.A.S.C. (M.T.)
He joined in December 1916, and was retained on important duties with his unit until 1918, when he was drafted to Mesopotamia. Whilst there he was employed on special work and contracted malaria.
He was sent home and demobilised in 1920, holding the General Service and Victory Medals.
40, Hawthorn Road, Upper Edmonton, N.18   X17044.

NEAL, C., Pte., Royal Fusiliers
He volunteered in 1914, and was sent to the Western Front in the same year. Whilst taking part in the retreat from Mons he was taken prisoner, and suffered many hardships in captivity.
After being finally released, he was demobilised in 1919, holding the Mons Star, General Service and Victory Medals.
32, Bronsart Road, Munster Road, S.W.6   X18904.

NEAL, C. H., Pte., 8th Essex Regiment.
Joining in 1916, he was drafted a year later to the Western Front, where he took a prominent part in the battles of Ypres, Armentières and Arras, and in the Advance of 1918. During his service he was gassed, and in October 1919 was demobilised, holding the General Service and Victory Medals.
40, Hawthorn Road, Upper Edmonton, N.18   X17047

NEAL, R. (Miss), Special War Worker.
From 1914 until the cessation of hostilities this lady was employed at the White City in the manufacture of tents and other equipment. She devoted all her energies to this long and tedious work, and gave great satisfaction.
407, High Road, Willesden, N.W.10   T17342B.

NEALE, H. W., Rifleman, 16th London Regt. (Queen's Westminster Rifles).
He joined in January 1917, and on completion of his training was drafted to the Western Front, where he took a prominent part in many engagements. He was killed in action on November 29th, 1917, and was entitled to the General Service and Victory Medals.
23, Haldane Road, Walham Green, S.W.6   X16988.

NEALE, J. J., Pte., 2nd Middlesex Regiment.
Mobilised in August 1914, he was soon drafted to France, where he played a prominent part in the retreat from Mons and the battles of the Somme and Ypres. During the Advance of 1918 he was employed on transport work, and gave very valuable services.
In December 1919 he was demobilised, and holds the Mons Star, General Service and Victory Medals.
91, Durban Road, Tottenham, N.17   X17967C.

NEALE, T., Driver, Royal Field Artillery.
He joined in November 1916, and after the completion of his training was drafted to India, where he gave valuable services in the capacity of a driver.
On his return from India he was demobilised in October 1919, holding the General Service and Victory Medals.
91, Durban Road, Tottenham, N.17   X17967B.

NEALE, W. J., Pte., 2nd Middlesex Regiment.
He volunteered in August 1914, and served for two years on the Western Front, during which time he took part in the retreat from Mons and the battles of Ypres and the Somme, where he was killed on September 16th, 1916.
He was entitled to the Mons Star, General Service and Victory Medals.
91, Durban Road, Tottenham, N.17   X17967A.

NEATE, A. F., Pte., Royal Army Service Corps.
Volunteering in November 1915, he served on the Western Front, taking part in the fighting at Ypres, the Somme, and during the Retreat and Advance of 1918. He was employed chiefly in conveying troops and ammunition to the front lines.
In May 1919 he was demobilised, and holds the 1914–15 Star, General Service and Victory Medals.
13, Maybury Gardens, Willesden, N.W.10   X17445.

NEIGHBOUR, J., Rfimn., 8th London Regiment (P.O. Rifles).
He volunteered in September 1914, and on completion of his training was retained with his unit on important duties. He contracted fever, and in consequence was discharged as medically unfit for further service in January 1915.
12, Britannia Court, Hammersmith, W.6   15875A.

NELTHORPE, C. A., Cpl., R.A.S.C. (M.T.)
He joined in 1917, and during his two years' service on the Western Front, where he was engaged on repairing motors, was gassed.
He holds the General Service and Victory Medals, and was demobilised in July 1919, after giving valuable services.
35, Elsden Road, Tottenham, N.17   X18501.

NEVILLE, J., Cpl., R.A.S.C.
Mobilised in August 1914, he was drafted in the following March to the Western Front, where for three years he served with the 47th Division, being engaged in bringing up supplies. After giving valuable services throughout the war, he was demobilised in June 1919, holding the 1914–15 Star, General Service and Victory Medals.
37, Broughton Road Fulham, S.W   X20905.

NEVILLE, J. B., Sergt., South Lancashire Regt.
He joined in September 1916, and served in Salonica, taking part in the Balkan campaign. Later he was transferred to Greece and Constantinople, and on his return to England was demobilised in November 1919.
He holds the General Service and Victory Medals.
50, Winchester Road, Lower Edmonton, N.9   14861.

NEVISON, G. R., Pte., 14th London Regiment (London Scottish).
He volunteered in December 1914, and in the same year was drafted to the Western Front, where he took a distinguished part in several engagements. On July 4th, 1916, he died of wounds received four days previously whilst in action on the Somme.
He was entitled to the 1914-15 Star, General Service and Victory Medals.
140, Portnall Road, Maida Hill, W.9   X19587.

NEW, A., Pte., King's Own (Yorkshire L.I.)
Joining in June 1916, he served on the Western Front at Ypres, Albert and several other places, and was wounded in action at Cambrai in November 1917.
He was demobilised in March 1919, holding the General Service and Victory Medals.
33, Mordaunt Road, Willesden, N.W.10   13864A.

NEW, B. R., 1st Air Mechanic, R.A.F.
He joined in February 1916, and was retained on special duties with his unit at various important stations. He gave valuable services, which called for a high degree of technical skill, but was not successful in obtaining his transfer overseas before hostilities ceased.
He was demobilised in March 1919.
263a, Kilburn Lane, N. Kensington, W.10   X18720B.

NEWBURY, H. R., Pte., 6th Middlesex Regt.
He volunteered in September 1915, and whilst stationed at Sheerness, preparatory to being drafted to France, was badly injured during a Gotha raid on the camp, which was entirely demolished. He was in hospital at Chatham for 12 months, and in December 1917 was discharged as unfit for further service.
He died in St. Mary's Hospital on September 28th, 1919, as a result of his injuries.
53, Ashmore Road, Harrow Road, W.9   X19805.

NEWELL, E. F., Sapper, Royal Engineers.
Joining in 1917, he served for two years on the Western Front, where he took a prominent part in the battles of Ypres, Arras and Cambrai Whilst overseas, he was engaged on special railway work, and was severely wounded in action.
In December 1919 he was demobilised, and holds the General Service and Victory Medals.
105, Denmark Road, Kilburn, N.W.6   X17439B.

NEWELL, H. S. T., Driver, R.M.A.
Volunteering in 1915, he was later sent to the Western Front, where he took part in the battles of Arras, Vimy Ridge, Ypres and Cambrai, and in heavy fighting near Amiens, Bullecourt, Armentières and Lille, during the Retreat and Advance of 1918. He was demobilised in 1919, and holds the General Service and Victory Medals.
25, Eustace Road, Walham Green, S.W.6   X19339.

NEWELL, R. H., Pte., 16th (The Queen's) Lancers.
He was in the Army, and when war broke out proceeded to the Western Front, where he took part in the memorable retreat from Mons. He also took part in many of the engagements which followed, including those at Ypres, Neuve Chapelle, Festubert, Vimy Ridge, Bullecourt and Arras, and was severely gassed during the Advance of 1918.
He holds the Mons Star, General Service and Victory Medals, and was discharged in April 1919, having completed 12 years' service.
1, Eustace Road, Walham Green, S.W.6   TX19336.

NEWLAND, C., Pte., R.A.S.C.
Volunteering in 1915, he was drafted in the same year to the Western Front, where he was engaged on special duties during the battles of Loos, the Somme and Ypres, and in heavy fighting on various other sectors. In 1916 he met with a serious accident whilst on duty, was invalided home, and after a protracted illness died on December 3rd, 1917.
He was entitled to the 1914-15 Star, General Service and Victory Medals.
31, Novello Street, Parson's Green, S.W.6   X20055.

NEWLAND, W. H. E., Pte., Highland L.I.
He volunteered in December 1915, and was later drafted to the Western Front, where he took a prominent part in many important engagements. Early in 1918 he was taken prisoner, and after suffering many hardships for ten months, managed to escape from Germany very shortly before the Armistice.
In December 1918 he was demobilised, and holds the General Service and Victory Medals.
45, Reporton Road, Munster Road, S.W.6   TX18849.

NEWMAN, E., Pte., 10th Middlesex Regiment and 19th London Regiment.
He joined in September 1916, and in December of the following year sailed for Palestine on board the "Aragon." This ship was torpedoed during the voyage, but he was rescued and continued his journey on board H.M.S. "Attack," which was also torpedoed and sunk. He served in Palestine from January 1918 until the following October when the Turkish Armistice was signed, and afterwards in Egypt and Syria, until December 1919.
He holds the General Service and Victory Medals, and was demobilised in January 1920.
108, Maurice Avenue, Noel Park, Wood Green, N.22 19319B.

NEWMAN, G. A. H., Mechanic, British Red Cross Society.
He volunteered in October 1915, and was sent to France, where he was engaged on important duties at a large Red Cross Depot. He gave valuable services for a period of nearly four years, and in July 1919 was demobilised.
He holds the General Service and Victory Medals.
5, Effie Place, Walham Green, S.W.6   TX19707.

NEWMAN, G. W., Driver, R.F.A.
He volunteered in September 1914, and in the following year was sent to the Western Front, where, after taking part in much severe fighting in various sectors, he met with a serious accident whilst carrying out his duties. He was invalided home, and after a long period in hospital was discharged as medically unfit for further service in 1918.
He holds the 1914-15 Star, General Service and Victory Medals.
37, Stanley Road, King's Road, S.W.6   TX19865.

NEWMAN, H. G. (D.S.M.), Chief Petty Officer, Royal Navy, H.M.S. "Agincourt."
He was in the Navy when war broke out, and until the cessation of hostilities served with the Grand Fleet on board H.M.S. "Agincourt." He took part in several naval engagements, and for his gallant work as a gunner during the battle of Jutland on May 31st, 1916, was mentioned in dispatches and awarded the Distinguished Service Medal. He also holds the Long Service and Good Conduct Medal, the 1914 Star, General Service and Victory Medals, and in March 1919 was demobilised, having completed 30 years' service.
5, Fermoy Road, Maida Hill, W.9   X20012.

NEWMAN, H. G., Pte., 1st Northants. Regt.
He volunteered in December 1914, and during his service on the Western Front took a distinguished part in several important engagements. Whilst in action in October 1915 at the battle of Loos, he was severely wounded and a year later, through his service, was discharged as medically unfit.
He holds the 1914-15 Star, General Service and Victory Medals.
45, College Road, Willesden, N.W.10   X18016.

NEWMAN, H. J., Rifleman, King's Royal Rifles.
He volunteered for service in August 1914, and in the following November was drafted to the Western Front. He first went into action at Neuve Chapelle in March 1915, and afterwards took part in the fighting at St. Eloi, Hill 60, and at Ypres, where he was severely wounded and gassed. He was sent to England, and after a protracted illness was invalided out of the service in 1916.
He holds the 1914-15 Star, General Service and Victory Medals.
54, Burnthwaite Road, Walham Green, S.W.6   X20201B.

NEWMAN, H. W., Gunner, R.F.A.
Volunteering in October 1914, he was sent to Egypt later in the same year. Whilst in this seat of war he took part in many important engagements, and later was drafted to Palestine, where he fought in the battle of Gaza and during the operations in the advance of General Allenby's Forces. He remained in the East until his demobilisation in July 1919, holding the 1914-15 Star, General Service and Victory Medals.
34, Bridge Road, Willesden, N.W.10   15462.

NEWMAN, J., Rifleman, 8th London Regiment (Post Office Rifles).
He volunteered in July 1915, and after his training was retained on important duties at various stations with his unit. In July 1916 he was discharged as medically unfit for further service owing to injuries received in an accident. During his twelve months in the Army he gave valuable services.
135, Purves Road, Kensal Rise, N.W.10   X18412.

NEWMAN, J., Pte., British Red Cross Society.
He joined in October 1918, and served on the Western Front in the final stages of the Advance, where he was engaged as a stretcher-bearer at Warneton. He returned to England in January 1919 and was demobilised, holding the General Service and Victory Medals.
41, Woodchester Street, Paddington, W   TX20653.

NEWMAN, J. J., Sergt., 26th Middlesex Regt.
He volunteered in August 1914, and during his service in Salonica, which extended from August 1916 until January 1919, took part in several engagements on the Struma and Vardar Fronts, and in the final rout of the Bulgarians. He was sent to England and demobilised in February 1919, holding the General Service and Victory Medals.
108, Maurice Avenue, Noel Park, N.22   19319A.

NEWMAN, J. J., Rifleman, 13th Rifle Brigade.
He volunteered in October 1915, and during his service on the Western Front, which lasted three years, took part in the fighting on the Somme, at Arras, and Ypres and in the Advance of 1918.
He was demobilised in March 1919, and holds the General Service and Victory Medals.
108, Maurice Avenue, Noel Park, Wood Green, N.22 19319C.

NEWMAN, R. J., Pte., Royal Inniskilling Fus.
Joining in May 1916, he was sent on completion of his training to the Western Front, where he took part in the battles of Arras and Cambrai and other important engagements. During his active service he was wounded four times, and in 1920 was still serving.
He holds the General Service and Victory Medals.
39, Seymour Road, Lower Edmonton, N.9   13343.

NEWMAN, T. W., Pte., Tank Corps.
He volunteered in May 1915, and later in the year was drafted to the Western Front, where he took part in much severe fighting, and was in action during the battles of the Somme, Arras and Vimy Ridge. As the result of an injury received while carrying out his duties he was in hospital in France and England for some time, and was demobilised in February 1919. He holds the 1914-15 Star, General Service and Victory Medals. 1, Hartopp Avenue, Dawes Road, S.W.6   X17661.

NEWMAN, W., Pte., 12th Suffolk Regiment.
He volunteered in October 1915, and shortly after was sent to the Western Front, where he took part in many important engagements, including the battles of the Somme, Ypres and Cambrai. He was badly gassed at Cambrai, and after a period of two months in hospital at Rouen, was invalided home. On his recovery he was found medically unfit for further service overseas, and was retained on important duties at his depot until demobilised in April 1919.
He holds the 1914-15 Star, General Service and Victory Medals.
44, Hilmer Street, W. Kensington, W.14   16909.

NEWMAN, W., Cpl., 2nd Middlx. Regt. and R.E.
Volunteering in December 1914, he was sent to the Western Front in the following March, and took part in many important engagements. He was wounded in action in July 1916 at the battle of the Somme and was invalided home. On his recovery he was retained on special duties, as his wound incapacitated him for further active service.
In January 1919 he was demobilised, and holds the 1914-15 Star, General Service and Victory Medals.
2, Alric Avenue, Stonebridge Park, N.W.10   14610.

NEWNHAM, A., Rifleman, King's Royal Rifles.
He joined in February 1916, and after his training was drafted to the Western Front, where he took an active part in heavy fighting on various sectors. When in France he was in hospital some time with pneumonia contracted while on duty, and was eventually invalided home.
He was demobilised in September 1919, and holds the General Service and Victory Medals.
31, Horder Road, Munster Road, S.W.6   19026A.

NEWNHAM, E. A. (Mrs.), Special War Worker.
For a considerable period during the war this lady patriotically gave up her household duties in order to do work of national importance at Messrs. Blake's Munition Factory, Fulham. She was engaged on the manufacture of hand-grenades, and carried out her work in an efficient manner, thereby rendering valuable services.
31, Horder Road, Munster Road, S.W.6   X19026B.

NEWSHAM, J., Pte., Lincolnshire Regiment.
He joined in November 1916, and in the following year was sent to France, where he was in action at Ypres, Arras, La Bassée, Bapaume and on the Somme. During his service overseas he was wounded and gassed, and in April 1919 was demobilised, holding the General Service and Victory Medals.   28, Netley Road, Brentford.   T16513A.

NEWSON, A. T., Pte., Royal Fusiliers.
He volunteered in August 1914, and was immediately sent to France, where he saw much severe fighting, and took part in the retreat from Mons and the battles of the Marne, the Aisne, Ypres, La Bassée, Neuve Chapelle, St. Eloi, Hooge and the Somme.
He was demobilised in 1919, and holds the Mons Star, General Service and Victory Medals.
20, Dieppe Street, W. Kensingto , W.14   16256A.

NEWSON, E. S. (Mrs.), Special War Worker.
During the war this lady rendered valuable services at Messrs. Blake's Munition Factory, Hurlingham, where she was engaged on the packing of shells for transport overseas. Her arduous duties were carried out in a satisfactory manner and she received high commendation for her work.
20, Dieppe Street, W. Kensington, W.14   16256B.

NEWSON, G., Sergt., R.F.A.
Volunteering in March 1915, he was retained on important duties at various stations with his unit. He gave valuable services whilst holding a responsible position, but was not successful in obtaining his transfer overseas before the cessation of hostilities.
He was demobilised in February 1919.
19, Siddons Road, Tottenham, N.17   X19155.

NEWTON, A. E., Pte., R.A.O.C.
He joined in May 1916, and in the following January was drafted to Egypt, where he remained for nearly three years. During this period he was employed in the important duties of examining bombs and grenades.
In September 1919 he returned to England and was demobilised, holding the General Service and Victory Medals.
56, Mordaunt Road, Willesden, N.W.10   13632.

NEWTON, A. J., Pte., Labour Corps.
He joined in September 1918, and was retained on important transport duties at various large camps, but owing to his being medically unfit for active service, was unable to obtain a transfer overseas.
He gave valuable services until his demobilisation in March 1919.
36, Fifth Avenue, Queen's Park Estate, W.10   X18319.

NEWTON, E. W., Sapper, R.E. (Signal Section).
He joined in 1917, and later in the same year was sent to France, where he was engaged with the signalling section of his unit. He took part in the battles of Arras, Ypres and the Somme, and in other important engagements, and during his service was gassed. After the signing of the Armistice he went to Germany with the Army of Occupation, with which he remained until his demobilisation in 1919.
He holds the General Service and Victory Medals.
59, Ilex Road, Willesden, N.W.10   16361B.

NEWTON, H., Rifleman, King's Royal Rifles.
Joining in June 1917, he was drafted to the Western Front, where he took part in many important engagements, and was wounded.
He was demobilised in December 1918, and holds the General Service and Victory Medals.
1, Ship Lane, Hammersmith, W.6   13788.

NEWTON, H., Sapper, Royal Engineers.
He volunteered in March 1915, and was later drafted to the Western Front, where he took a distinguished part in the battles of the Somme, Arras, Ypres and Cambrai, and in important engagements during the Retreat and Advance in 1918. He remained in France until his demobilisation in 1919, and holds the General Service and Victory Medals.
32, Letchford Gardens, Willesden, N.W.10   X17551.

NEWTON, T. I., Pte., Middlesex Regiment.
He volunteered in 1914, and was almost immediately sent to the Western Front, where he took part in much heavy fighting on various sectors. He was killed in action on the Somme on August 27th, 1918, and was entitled to the 1914 Star, General Service and Victory Medals.
92, Kimberley Road, Upper Edmonton, N.18   16485.

NEWTON, W. J. (M.M.), Cpl., Royal Fusiliers.
He volunteered in September 1914, and during his service in France took part in many important engagements, including those at Loos, the Somme, Hulluch, Arras and Orillers, and was three times wounded. In June 1916 he was awarded the Military Medal for conspicuous gallantry and devotion to duty in the field, and in August and again in October of the same year was mentioned in dispatches for his splendid work.
He also holds the 1914-15 Star, General Service and Victory Medals, and was demobilised in January 1919.
23, Milton Avenue, Willesden, N.W.10   15645.

NICKOLDS, H. W., Pte., Essex Regiment.
Volunteering immediately on the outbreak of hostilities, he was drafted to the Western Front, but was killed in action during the battles of Mons on August 21st, 1914.
He was entitled to the Mons Star, General Service and Victory Medals. 64, Argyle Road, Upper Edmonton, N.18   15268B.

NICKOLDS, W., Pte., Middlesex Regiment.
He joined in September 1916, and after his training was retained on important duties at various stations with his unit. He gave valuable services, but was not successful in obtaining his transfer overseas before the cessation of hostilities, and was demobilised in December 1919.
64, Argyle Road Upper Edmonton ,N.18   15268A.

NICHOLLS, A., Pte., R.A.S.C. (M.T.)

He joined in February 1916, and was sent to France later in the same year. Whilst on the Western Front he was engaged on important duties n connection with the transport of supplies and ammunition to the firing line and was wounded. In March 1920 he was demobilised, and holds the General Service and Victory Medals.
60a, Deacon Road, Cricklewood, N.W.2   17357B.

NICHOLLS, C. H., Pte., 5th Middlesex Regt. and R.A.S.C.

Volunteering in September 1914, he served for four years on the Western Front. Whilst overseas he took part in the battles of the Somme, Arras, Ypres and Cambrai, and was wounded.
He was demobilised in February 1919, and holds the 1914–15 Star, General Service and Victory Medals.
93, Mayo Road, Willesden, N.W.10   15442.

NICHOLLS, E. E., Cpl., R.A.S.C.

Volunteering in May 1915, he was drafted later in the year to the East, where he took an active part in important operations in the Egyptian and Bulgarian theatres of war. He was twice in hospital during this period with malaria, and on his return to England in April 1919 he was demobilised.
He holds the 1914–15 Star, General Service and Victory Medals.
31, Everington Street, Hammersmith, W.6   13968.

NICHOLLS, F., Driver, Royal Field Artillery.

He volunteered in January 1915, and was later sent to the Western Front, where he took part in many important engagements in various sectors.
He remained in France until his demobilisation in June 1919, and holds the General Service and Victory Medals.
127, Greyhound Road, Hammersmith, W.6   14820.

NICHOLLS, H., Special War Worker.

For a period of over three years during the war he was engaged on work of national importance at Messrs. Stillers', Fulham. He carried out his duties in a very capable manner, and rendered valuable services.
19, Ancill Street, Hammersmith, W.6   13747A.

NICHOLLS, W. A., Driver, R.E.

He volunteered in August 1914, and during his service on the Western Front took part in the battles of Arras, Cambrai, Ypres and the Somme. During his service he was badly gassed, and after nine months in hospital was discharged in June 1919 as medically unfit for further service.
He holds the 1914–15 Star, General Service and Victory Medals.
42, Earlsmead Road, College Park, N.W.10   X18036.

NICHOLS, B., Clerk, Q.M.A.A.C.

She joined in April 1917, and in June was sent to France, where she held a responsible position on the clerical staff at General Headquarters. She remained there until 1920, and during this time rendered valuable services.
In February of the same year she was demobilised, and holds the General Service and Victory Medals.
84, Montague Road, Lower Edmonton, N.9   16876A.

NICHOLS, H. A. (M.M.), Staff-Sergt., R.A.S.C. (M.T.)

He volunteered in May 1915, and was sent to France, where he was engaged on important duties with the Mechanical Transport. Later he went to the forward areas, where he took part in many engagements, and was wounded whilst conveying ammunition to the line near Albert in June 1916. He was awarded the Military Medal for conspicuous bravery and devotion to duty in the field, and in addition holds the General Service and Victory Medals.
29, Bath Road, Lower Edmonton, N.9   13305B.

NICHOLS, H. C. W., Pte., 1st Middlesex Regt.

Volunteering in November 1914 at the age of 18, he was soon sent to the Western Front, where he took part in heavy fighting at Armentières and Béthune. Whilst helping to rescue wounded at La Bassée on September 25th, 1915, he was killed in action.
He was entitled to the 1914–15 Star, General Service and Victory Medals.
29, Bath Road, Lower Edmonton, N.9   13305A.

NICHOLS, W., Pte., Irish Guards.

He volunteered in September 1914, and during his service on the Western Front, which lasted for five years, he took a distinguished part in many important engagements.
He holds the 1914 Star, General Service and Victory Medals, and was demobilised in November 1919.
52, Hannell Road, Munster Road, S.W.6   X18077

NICHOLS, W. M., Pte., 16th Middlesex Regt.

He volunteered in August 1915, and early in the following year was sent to France, where, after taking part in much severe fighting, he was mortally wounded in action on the Somme on July 1st, 1916. He died of his wounds on the following day.
He was entitled to the General Service and Victory Medals.
84, Montague Road, Lower Edmonton, N.9   16876B.

NICHOLSON, H. C., Pte., East Surrey Regiment.

He volunteered in August 1914, and after his training was engaged on important duties with his unit at various stations. He gave valuable services, but was not able to obtain his transfer overseas before the cessation of hostilities, and was demobilised in February 1919.
17, Alric Avenue, Stonebridge Park, N.W.10   14443.

NICHOLSON, J. (Mrs.), Special War Worker.

During the war this lady was engaged on work of national importance at Messrs. Blake's, Stevenage Road, Fulham. Her duties, which were in connection with the making of boxes for the transport of munitions, were carried out in a capable manner, and she received high commendation for her services.
9, Field Road, Hammersmith, W.6   15029A.

NICKERSON, C. J., Pte., 2nd Middlesex Regt.

Joining in April 1916, he was sent to France on completion of his training. After taking a prominent part in many important engagements on the Western Front, he was killed in action at Ypres on August 16th, 1917.
He was entitled to the General Service and Victory Medals.
13, Felixstowe Road, Willesden, N.W.10   X17765.

NIGG, F. V. (Mrs.), Special War Worker.

During the war this lady was employed as a 'bus conductress with the London General Omnibus Company in order to release a man for service in the Army. She gave very valuable services and carried out her work in a satisfactory manner.
23, St. Margaret's Mansions, Fulham, S.W.6   X18994A.

NIGG, F. X., Pte., Machine Gun Corps.

He joined in 1916, and during his service on the Western Front took part in many engagements, including those at Arras, Armentières, Bullecourt, Lille, the Somme, Vimy Ridge and Ypres, and in the Advance of 1918.
He was demobilised in 1919, and holds the General Service and Victory Medals.
23, St. Margaret's Mansions, Lillie Road, Fulham, S.W.6   X18994B.

NIGHTINGALE, J., Driver, R.F.A.

He volunteered in October 1914, and was drafted to Egypt in January 1916. Later he was transferred to the Western Front, where he took a distinguished part in the engagements on the Somme, at Ypres and Arras. He was invalided home and discharged as medically unfit in March 1918, holding the General Service and Victory Medals.
39, Lancefield Street, North Kensington, W.10   X18845.

NIPPER, W. H., Pte., R.A.S.C. and 7th Essex Regt.

He volunteered in September 1914, and on completion of his training in the following year was drafted to Salonica, where he saw action on the Doiran and Struma. In 1917 he was sent to Egypt, and during that year took part in the fighting in Palestine, where later he contracted fever.
He was invalided home in 1918, and in March of the following year was demobilised, holding the 1914–15 Star, General Service and Victory Medals.
102, Milton Avenue, Willesden, N.W.10   15799.

NIXSON, F. G., A.B., Royal Navy.

He volunteered in November 1915, and after his training was posted to H.M.S. "Europa," in which vessel he served in the Mediterranean and Ægean Seas on important duties until after the cessation of hostilities.
He was demobilised in February 1919, and holds the General Service and Victory Medals.
105, Harley Road, Willesden, N.W.10   13172.

NIXON, W. A., Pte., Royal Fusiliers.

He joined in January 1917, and was drafted overseas during the same year. He took part in many important engagements on the Western Front, including the battle of Ypres, and was twice wounded and gassed.
He holds the General Service and Victory Medals, and was demobilised in February 1919.
23, Cornwallis Road, Lower Edmonton, N.9   13281.

NOAD, A., Pte., 7th London Regiment.

He volunteered in May 1915, and was drafted to the Western Front on the completion of his training. During his service in this theatre of war he took part in many engagements, until he contracted a serious illness. He was invalided to hospital in England, and subsequently discharged as medically unfit for further service in November 1917.
He holds the General Service and Victory Medals.
137 Greyhound Road, Hammersmith, W.6   14824.

NOAD, H. J., Pte., R.A.S.C.
He volunteered in July 1915, and was drafted to France in the same year. He took part in many important engagements, including the battles of the Somme, Arras, Loos and Ypres, and afterwards served in Italy on the Piave. On his return to France in 1918 he was engaged on transport duties during the Advance. After the Armistice he went into Germany with the Army of Occupation.
He was demobilised in May 1919, holding the 1914-15 Star, General Service and Victory Medals.
29, Averill Street, Hammersmith, W.6   14171.

NOADES, W. R., Gunner, R.F.A.
This gunner volunteered in August 1914, and after his training served at various stations on important duties with his unit. He rendered valuable services, but was not successful in obtaining his transfer overseas owing to an accident. He was discharged in consequence in December 1917, as medically unfit for further service.
14, Lintaine Grove, West Kensington, W.14   X17001.

NOAKES, B. (Mrs.), Special War Worker.
For three years during the war this lady was at Messrs. Hooper's, Chelsea, where she was engaged on work of an important nature in connection with the manufacture of aeroplane wings. At the termination of her services she was presented with a certificate testifying to the excellence of her work.
16, Novello Street, Parson's Green, S.W.6   X19932B.

NOAKES, G., Pte., R.A.S.C.
He joined in April 1916, and was sent first to France and later to Salonica. During his 3½ years' service overseas he was engaged as a baker. Whilst in Salonica he contracted eye trouble, which necessitated the removal of his left eye. He returned to England after the Armistice, and was discharged in November 1919, holding the General Service and Victory Medals.
3, Brereton Road, Tottenham, N.17   X18103

NOBLE, J. G., Pte., Royal Berkshire Regiment.
He volunteered in September 1914, and was drafted to France. He took part in many engagements in this theatre of war, and was twice badly wounded. He also served with the 3rd Hussars and the 5th Middlesex Regiment before being demobilised in April 1919.
He holds the 1914-15 Star, General Service and Victory Medals.
16, Hartopp Avenue, Dawes Road, S.W.6   X17662.

NOBLE, J. W., Sapper, Royal Engineers.
He volunteered in August 1914, and was drafted to France the following month. He was invalided to England in 1915, and remained at home until 1917, when he was sent to Egypt, and took part in the fighting at Gaza and Jaffa. He later went to Salonica, where he took part in engagements on the Doiran Front until he contracted malaria and black-water fever. He returned to hospital in England, and was eventually demobilised in March 1919, holding the 1914 Star, General Service and Victory Medals.
30, Westbury Road, Willesden, N.W.10   15445.

NOBLE, W. S., Rifleman, 18th London Regt. (London Irish Rifles).
He joined in August 1916, and after his training was drafted to the Western Front. While in this theatre of war he took part in many of the principal engagements, until he met with a serious accident to his knee. He was invalided home to hospital in London, and was eventually demobilised in October 1919, holding the General Service and Victory Medals.
14, Colehill Lane, Fulham, S.W.6   X18924A.

NOKES, R. C., Pte., R.A.S.C. (M.T.)
He joined in October 1916, and during his service on the Western Front took part in the battles of the Somme, Arras, Bullecourt, Armentières, Ypres, Lille, St. Quentin and many other engagements. After the Armistice he went to Germany with the Army of Occupation, and returned to England for his demobilisation in April 1920, holding the General Service and Victory Medals.
1b, Eaton Chambers, Halford Road, Walham Green, S.W.6   X19851.

NOONAN, R. J., Gunner, R.F.A.
He joined in 1916, and after his training was drafted overseas. He took part in many important engagements on the Western Front, was gassed and suffered from shell-shock, and in consequence was in hospital at Rouen for a time. He returned to England, and was eventually demobilised in February 1919, holding the General Service and Victory Medals.
15, Whitehall Street, Tottenham, N.17.   X18127

NORBURY, T. W., Rifleman, K.R.R.
He joined in September 1914, and was sent in the following November to the Western Front, where he was in action at Festubert, Givenchy, La Bassée, Ypres, the Somme and in several other engagements. He was recommended for the D.C.M. for great bravery on the field, and was also mentioned in dispatches.
He was demobilised in March 1919, and holds the 1914 Star, General Service and Victory Medals. Previous to the war he had served for about 20 years in the 18th Middlesex Volunteer Corps.
74, First Avenue, Queen's Park Estate, W.10   X18938.

NORCOTT, G. H., Pte., 13th Oxford and Bucks Light Infantry.
He joined in March 1916, and at the conclusion of his training was drafted overseas. During his service on the Western Front he took part in engagements on the Somme and at Ypres and Cambrai. He was later sent to Italy, where he was killed in action on the Asiago Plateau in June 1918.
He was entitled to the General Service and Victory Medals.
27, Claxton Grove, Hammersmith, W.6   13676.

NORDEN, A. E. V., Gunner, R.G.A.
He joined in September 1916, and after his training served at various stations on important duties with his unit. He gave valuable services, but was unsuccessful in obtaining his transfer overseas before the cessation of hostilities.
He was demobilised in September 1919.
171, Bulwer Road, Upper Edmonton, N.18   X17201.

NORDEN, G. W. C., Pte., Machine Gun Corps.
He volunteered in May 1915, and was sent to the Western Front the following year. While in this theatre of war he took part in many engagements, and was killed at the battle of the Somme on July 3rd, 1916.
He was entitled to the General Service and Victory Medals.
171, Bulwer Road, Upper Edmonton, N.18   X17291.

NORDEN, H. J. P., Pte., Machine Gun Corps.
He joined in January 1916, and after his training served on the Western Front, where he took part in the battles of the Somme, Bullecourt, Messines and Ypres. He was invalided to England owing to illness contracted on active service, and was in hospital for nine months. Upon his recovery he returned to France, and was in action during the Allied Advance of 1918.
He holds the General Service and Victory Medals, and was demobilised in February 1919.
171, Bulwer Road, Upper Edmonton, N.18   X17292.

NORFIELD, J., Pte., 160th Labour Company.
He joined in February 1917, and was sent overseas during the same year. He was engaged on important duties in various sectors of the Western Front in connection with operations at Ypres, Armentières and Arras. He was demobilised in April 1920, and holds the General Service and Victory Medals.
59, Brettenham Road, Upper Edmonton, N.18   15232A.

NORMAN, E. (Miss), Special War Worker.
During the war this lady was engaged on work of national importance in connection with agriculture at various places in the South of England. She gave valuable services and enabled a man to be released for military service.
23, Half Acre Road, Hanwell, W.7   12382.

NORMAN, G., Pte., Queen's Own (R.W.K.R.)
He joined in January 1918, and shortly afterwards was sent to the Western Front, where he took part in several engagements during the Retreat and Advance of that year.
He was demobilised in July 1919, and holds the General Service and Victory Medals.
39, Nursery Street, Tottenham, N.17   X18151.

NORMAN, G., A.B., Royal Navy.
He volunteered in September 1915, and after his training was posted to H.M.S. "Gainsboro'," in which ship he was engaged on mine-sweeping duties in the North Sea until after the cessation of hostilities.
He was demobilised in April 1919, and holds the General Service and Victory Medals.
25, Somerset Road, Upper Edmonton, N.18   X17032B.

NORMAN, H., Cpl., R.A.S.C. and Royal Irish Fus.
He volunteered in November 1914, and was drafted overseas the following year. During his three years' service on the Western Front he was engaged as a baker. In July 1918 he was transferred to the Royal Irish Fusiliers, and took part in engagements near Lille during the Allied Advance.
He returned to England in 1919 and was demobilised, holding the 1914-15 Star, General Service and Victory Medals.
72, Milton Avenue, Willesden, N.W.10   14317.

NORMAN, S. E., 3rd Air Mechanic, R.A.F.

He joined in 1917, and after his training was engaged at various stations on important duties with his squadron. During his service he was badly injured in an aeroplane crash, and later met with an accident while motoring. In 1920 he was still in hospital receiving treatment for his injuries.

25, Somerset Road, Upper Edmonton, N.18   X17032A.

NORRIS, C. J. F., Rifleman, Rifle Brigade.

He joined in November 1916, and after his training was drafted overseas. He took part in many engagements on the Western Front and was wounded. He was later taken prisoner, and suffered many hardships during his captivity in Germany.

Upon his release after the Armistice he returned to England, and was demobilised in December 1919, holding the General Service and Victory Medals.

43, Beryl Road, Hammersmith, W.6   13348A.

NORRIS, G. (D.C.M.), Sergt., 4th London Regt. (Royal Fusiliers).

He volunteered in August 1914, and was drafted to Malta shortly afterwards. He later went to the Western Front and took part in numerous engagements, including the battles of Neuve Chapelle, Ypres, Passchendaele, Festubert, Lens, Lille and the Somme. He was severely wounded at Arras in 1917, and in consequence lost the sight of his left eye. At Cambrai in 1918 he was awarded the Distinguished Conduct Medal for gallant conduct in bringing in 30 German prisoners and three machine guns, and for returning to No Man's Land to fetch in the wounded.

He was demobilised in May 1919, and holds the 1914–15 Star, General Service and Victory Medals.

47, Farrant Street, Queen's Park Estate, W.10   X19051.

NORRIS, G. H., Pte., Middlesex Regiment and North Staffordshire Regiment.

He joined in November 1916, and was shortly afterwards drafted to the Western Front. During his service in this theatre of war he was wounded in action at Ypres in March 1917. On his recovery he again took part in action, and was killed at Bailleul on April 15th, 1918, during the Allied Retreat. He was buried at Steenwerck (Nord), and was entitled to the General Service and Victory Medals.

341, Chapter Road, Cricklewood, N.W.2   16714.

NORRIS, H. G. F., Pte., Royal Sussex Regiment.

He joined in August 1918, and after his training served at various stations on important duties with his regiment. He gave valuable services, but was not successful in obtaining his transfer overseas before the cessation of hostilities.

He was demobilised in February 1919.

43, Beryl Road, Hammersmith, W.6   13348B.

NORRIS, H. R., Pte., Royal Fusiliers.

He volunteered in November 1915, and in the following year was drafted to France, where he took part in many engagements. He was badly wounded in action in the Somme area, and was in consequence in hospital for seven months. Upon his recovery he was engaged at various stations on important duties, until his demobilisation in January 1919.

He holds the General Service and Victory Medals.

15a, Elsdon Road, Tottenham, N.17   X18500

NORRIS, W. H., Pte., 3rd London Regiment (Royal Fusiliers).

He volunteered in June 1915, and was drafted overseas two months later. He took part in many engagements on the Western Front, including the battles of the Somme, Ypres, Bullecourt and Cambrai, and was wounded. He returned to England after the Armistice, and was demobilised in March 1919, holding the 1914–15 Star, General Service and Victory Medals.

148, Ilbert Street, Queen's Park Estate, W.10   X18677.

NORTH, B. E. (Miss), Special War Worker.

During the war, in order to release a man for service with the Army, she acted as a van driver for Messrs. Lyons & Co., Ltd., Cadby Hall, West Kensington, and rendered valuable services in this capacity.

45, Averill Street, Hammersmith, W.6   14175.

NORTH, H. H., 2nd Cpl., Royal Engineers.

He joined in February 1916, and in the following year was drafted to the Western Front, where he took part in many engagements, including those of Arras, Cambrai, and the Retreat and Advance of 1918, and was specially employed on railway work.

He was demobilised in June 1919, holding the General Service and Victory Medals.

45, Heron Road, Willesden, N.W.10   15607.

NORTH, P., Pte., 3rd, and 4th London Regiment (Royal Fusiliers).

He volunteered in 1914, and in the following year was drafted to the Western Front, where he took part in several engagements, and was wounded. He was invalided home, but on his recovery returned to France, and served until September 1916, when he was reported missing.

He was entitled to the 1914–15 Star, General Service and Victory Medals.

20, Stracey Road, Stonebridge Park, N.W.10   15676.

NORTH, T. E., Pte., R.A.S.C. (H.T.)

He enlisted in 1901, and when war broke out in August 1914 volunteered for further service. He was immediately drafted to the Western Front, where he was present at the retreat from Mons, the battles of the Marne and the Aisne, and many of the engagements which followed, including those at Loos, the Somme, Arras and Cambrai. He was injured by a horse, and was in hospital for some time before being discharged in February 1918.

He holds the Mons Star, General Service and Victory Medals.

51, Adeney Road, Hammersmith, W.6   14312.

NORTH, W., Rifleman, 9th London Regiment (Queen Victoria's Rifles).

He volunteered in May 1915, and in the following year was sent to France, where he remained for three years. During this time he took part in many engagements, including those on the Somme, at Arras and St. Quentin, and in the Advance of 1918.

He holds the General Service and Victory Medals, and was demobilised in November 1919.

17, Woodfield Place, Maida Hill, W.9   X20173.

NORTHAM, L. G., Driver, R.F.A.

He volunteered in August 1915, and after his training was engaged at various stations on important duties with his unit until the beginning of 1918, when he was drafted to the Western Front, and was actively engaged during the Allied Retreat and Advance. After the Armistice he returned to England, and was demobilised in May 1919.

He holds the General Service and Victory Medals.

71, Burrow's Road, Willesden, N.W.10   X18254.

NORTON, J. E., Pte., 9th Middlesex Regiment.

After four years' service in the Territorial Forces, he volunteered in September 1914, and on the conclusion of his training was drafted in 1915 to the North Western Frontier of India. In 1917 he was transferred to Mesopotamia, where he took part in many engagements until the close of hostilities.

He returned to England in 1919, and was demobilised in March, holding the 1914–15 Star, General Service and Victory Medals.

80, Fortune Gate Road, Harlesden, N.W.10   13186.

NORTON, O. G., Pte., The King's Own (Royal Lancaster Regiment).

He joined in February 1916, and after a short period of training was drafted to the Western Front. He took part in many battles and was wounded, and in March 1918 was killed in action in the Arras sector.

He was entitled to the General Service and Victory Medals.

57, Netherwood Road, West Kensington, W.14   T12111.

NORVAL, J., Cpl., R.A.F. (6th Squadron).

He volunteered in September 1915, and on the conclusion of his training was sent in 1917 to the Western Front, where he served as a wireless operator until hostilities ceased.

He was demobilised in March 1919, holding the General Service and Victory Medals.

8, Tasso Road, Hammersmith, W.6   14792.

NORWOOD, G., Pte., 18th Middlesex Regiment.

Volunteering in September 1914, he was for some time engaged on special duties at various stations in England. In 1916 he was drafted to France, and after taking part in several engagements died in hospital on August 9, 1916, of wounds received during the battle of the Somme.

He was entitled to the General Service and Victory Medals.

8, Hill View, Brett Road, Stonebridge Park, N.W.10   14532.

NORWOOD, H., Pte., Middlesex and North Staffordshire Regiments.

Volunteering in August 1914, he was drafted to the Western Front in the following year. Throughout his service he did good work with his unit, and served in many sectors before returning to England for demobilisation in March 1919.

He holds the 1914–15 Star, General Service and Victory Medals.

30, Disraeli Road, Acton Lane, N.W.10   1439

NORWOOD, R. W., Sergt., 7th Norfolk Regt.
He volunteered in October 1914, and served for four years on the Western Front. He took part in many engagements, including the battles of Arras, Albert, Cambrai, Poperinghe and Lille, and was twice wounded.
In March 1919 he was demobilised, holding the 1914-15 Star, General Service and Victory Medals.
14, Brett Road, Stonebridge Park, N.W.10   14387.

NORWOOD, W. D., Pte., 4/10th Middlesex Regt.
He volunteered in September 1915, and was drafted to France in the following year. He was afterwards transferred to India, but owing to a breakdown in health, returned to England and was discharged as medically unfit for further service in August 1917.
He holds the General Service and Victory Medals.
10, Disraeli Road, Acton Lane, N.W.10   14163.

NUNAN, H., Cpl., The London Regiment (Royal Fusiliers) and Machine Gun Corps.
He volunteered in 1915, and was soon drafted to the Western Front, where he took part in fighting in many important sectors until October 1917, when he was reported missing.
He was entitled to the 1914-15 Star, General Service and Victory Medals.
37, New Holly Lane, Willesden, N.W.10   15576

NUNN, A., Pte., 4th Suffolk Regiment.
He volunteered in September 1914, and was drafted to the Western Front. While in action at Ypres in April 1915 he was severely wounded, and two months later he died.
He was entitled to the 1914-15 Star, General Service and Victory Medals.
6, Ponsard Road, College Park, N.W.10   X17751.

NUNN, A. J., Pte., Royal Army Medical Corps.
He joined in September 1917, and served with the North Russian Expeditionary Force at Archangel from July 1918 until September 1919, when he was invalided home. He remained in hospital until he was demobilised in March 1920, holding the Victory and General Service Medals and the Russian Order of St. George.
64, South Road, Lower Edmonton, N.9   12169A.

NUNN, W. C., A.B., R.N., H.M.S. " Nairana."
Joining in August 1916, he was posted to H.M.S. " Nairana," in which he saw much service in the White Sea, the Mediterranean and other waters until the close of the war.
He holds the General Service, Victory and Arctic Medals, and was still serving in 1920.
64, South Road, Lower Edmonton, N.9   12169B.

NUNNEY, H. C., Pte., 5th Middlesex Regiment.
He volunteered in September 1914, and saw much service on the Western Front, where he was wounded during the battle of Neuve Chapelle. He was in hospitals at Boulogne and Folkestone, also in Wales, before being demobilised in January 1919.
We holds the 1914-15 Star, General Service and Victory Medals.
41, Everington Street. Hammersmith, W.6   13970.

NURSE, E. G., Sergt., 3rd Queen's (R.W.S.Regt.)
He volunteered in August 1914, saw much service for two years in France, and was twice wounded. He was later stationed at Aldershot, where he acted as musketry and drill instructor.
He holds the 1914–15 Star, General Service and Victory Medals.
14, Marryat Street, Hammersmith, W.6   12498.

NUTLAND, J. F., Pte., Royal Fusiliers and Machine Gun Corps.
Joining in August 1916, he served on the Western Front from the following December until May 1918, and took part in the battles of Neuve Chapelle, Loos, Amiens and the Somme. He was three times wounded—at Gommecourt, Ypres and Arras.
He was demobilised in January 1919, and holds the General Service and Victory Medals.
36, Hazel Road, Willesden, N.W.10   X17786.

NUTLEY, F. E., Cpl., 7th London Regiment.
He joined in 1916, and after his training served at various stations on important duties. Owing to physical unfitness he was unable to obtain his transfer overseas, but gave valuable services before being discharged in 1917.
16, Kennet Road, Maida Hill, W.9   X19379A.

NUTLEY, G. (Mrs.), Special War Worker.
During the war this lady was engaged at the Park Royal Munition Works, where she rendered excellent service in the cartridge inspection department. This work was very responsible, and entailed the greatest care and accuracy. On resigning at the cessation of hostilities she was commended for her valuable assistance at the factory.
16, Kennet Road, Maida Hill, W.9   X19379B.

NUTT, A. G., Air Mechanic, Royal Air Force.
Joining in September 1916, he was sent to the Western Front in the following November. Whilst overseas he saw action in many sectors with the R.A.F., including Albert, the Somme, Arras, St. Quentin, and in the last Advance, and was engaged on special duties throughout.
He was demobilised in February 1919, holding the General Service and Victory Medals.
39. Furness Road, Fulham, S.W.6   X21137.

NUTTER, C., Driver, R.A.S.C.
He volunteered in August 1914, and was sent to the Western Front, where he saw action in many sectors with the R.A.S.C., and gave valuable services until 1917, when he returned to England and was discharged through ill-health.
He holds the 1914-15 Star, General Service and Victory Medals.
5, Cobbold Road, Church End, N.W.10   15942.

NUTTMAN, A., Sergt., Expdy. Force Canteen.
He joined in August 1916, and later in the same year was drafted to Mesopotamia, where for three years he did excellent work with the Expeditionary Force canteen.
He returned to England in 1919, when he was demobilised, holding the General Service and Victory Medals.
24, Somerset Road, Upper Edmonton, N.18   16864.

NYE, E., A.B., R.N., H.M.S. " King George V."
He volunteered in August 1914, and saw much service in many waters during the following 4½ years. On board H.M.S. " Europa " he took part in the bombardment at the Dardanelles, went through the battle of Jutland in H.M.S. " King George V.," and did much patrol duty in North Sea waters on board H.M.S. " Grafton."
He was demobilised in February 1919, and holds the 1914-15 Star, General Service and Victory Medals.
94, Shorrolds Road, Walham Green, S.W.6   X19497.

O

OAKE, A. J., Pte., R.M.L.I.
He volunteered in August 1914, and was sent to France in September, where he was engaged with the Naval Transport until the close of the war.
He gave valuable services, and was demobilised in 1919, holding the 1914 Star, General Service and Victory Medals.
70, Dyson's Road, Upper Edmonton, N.18   T16851.

OAKHAM, H., Pte., 7th Royal Fusiliers.
He joined in January 1917, and in the same year went to France, where he took part in many engagements. He was in action on the Somme and in the Advance of 1918, when he was gassed. After the Armistice he went to Egypt, and from there to Jerusalem. In January 1920 he returned to England and was demobilised.
He holds the General Service and Victory Medals.
31, Bulow Road, Fulham, S.W.6   X20915.

O'BRIEN, D., Rifleman, The Cameronians (Scottish Rifles).
He volunteered in 1914, and in the following year was sent to France, where he took part in many engagements, including the Somme. He suffered from shell-shock, was invalided home in 1917, and was discharged as medically unfit for further service in 1918.
He holds the 1914-15 Star, General Service and Victory Medals.   4, Tilson Road, Tottenham, N.17   X19091.

O'BRIEN, J., Lce.-Cpl., 1st King's Royal Rifles.
He volunteered in 1914, was sent to France in the same year, and took part in the battles of Neuve Chapelle, Ypres and the Somme, and was severely wounded.
He was discharged in 1917 as medically unfit for further service, and holds the 1914-15 Star, General Service and Victory Medals.
398a, High Road, Willesden, N.W.10   16745B

O'CONNELL, E., Pte., R.A.S.C.
He volunteered in May 1915, and served in France, where he took part in many engagements. He was invalided home, and was in hospital at Bath until discharged as medically unfit for further service in June 1918.
He holds the 1914-15 Star, General Service and Victory Medals.   2, Werley Avenue, Dawes Road, S.W.6   X17880.

O'CONNELL, T. A., Sergt., R.A.S.C.
He volunteered for service in March 1915, and in the same year went to France, where he did valuable work until 1916. In November 1918 he was discharged as medically unfit for further service, and holds the 1914-15 Star, General Service and Victory Medals.
70, St. Ervan's Road, N. Kensington, W.10   X20376

O'KEEFE, D., Pte., 4th Middlesex Regiment.
Volunteering in August 1914, he was drafted to the Western Front in the following October. He was in action in various important sectors, and after taking part in the battle of Loos in September 1915 was reported missing. In a later report he was stated to have been killed in action.
He was entitled to the 1914 Star, General Service and Victory Medals.
73, Southam Street, North Kensington, W.10   X20780.

OLANDO, G., Pte., 21st Middlesex Regiment.
He volunteered for service in August 1914, and in the same year was drafted to the Western Front, where he took part in many engagements, including those at Mons, Ypres, the Somme and Cambrai.
He was demobilised in September 1919, holding the Mons Star General Service and Victory Medals.
92, Burnthwaite Road, Walham Green, S.W.6   X20262.

OLD, A., Sapper, Royal Engineers.
He joined in August 1916, and in the following year was drafted to the Western Front, where he took part in many important engagements, including that of the Somme. In the course of his service he was wounded and gassed.
He was demobilised in May 1919, holding the General Service and Victory Medals
20, Winchelsea Road, Willesden, N.W.10   13853C.

OLD, T., Pte., 1st Middlesex Regiment.
He was serving in India at the outbreak of war, and was at once sent to France, where he took part in many engagements, including those of Mons, the Marne, Cambrai, Arras, Béthune and the Somme, and was three times wounded   He was discharged as a result of wounds, but re-joined and served until January 1919, when he was demobilised.
He holds the Mons Star, General Service and Victory Medals.
20, Winchelsea Road, Willesden, N.W.10   13853A.

OLDFIELD, G. F., Rifleman, 4th Rifle Brigade.
He volunteered in February 1915, and in May of that year was sent to the Western Front. After taking part in the battles of Ypres, Festubert, and Loos, he was sent to Salonica in November 1915. He again saw much heavy fighting on the Bulgarian Front, but contracting malaria, was invalided to Malta. Later he was sent to England and eventually discharged as medically unfit for further service in March 1919.
He holds the 1914-15 Star, General Service and Victory Medals.
39, Furness Road, Fulham, S.W.6   X21140.

O'LEARY, W., Pte., 1st Suffolk Regiment.
He joined in July 1916, and in August of the following year went to the Eastern theatre of war, where he served in the Balkan campaign on the Struma Front and took part in many engagements. After the signing of the Armistice he went with the Army of Occupation to Constantinople.
During his service he suffered from malaria, and in November 1919 was demobilised, holding the General Service and Victory Medals.
123, Deacon Road, Cricklewood, N.W.2   TX20302.

O'LEARY, W. A. (D.C.M.), C.S.M., Middlesex and Queen's (Royal West Surrey) Regts.
He enlisted in 1910, and on the outbreak of hostilities was drafted to the Western Front, where he saw much of the fighting at La Bassée, the Somme, Ypres, Neuve Eglise and in various other sectors, and was twice wounded. He was awarded the Distinguished Conduct Medal for the conspicuous gallantry and initiative displayed in taking charge of his company on the death of its commander during the Retreat in March 1918.
In 1919 he returned to England and was demobilised, holding the 1914 Star, General Service and Victory Medals.
123, Deacon Road, Cricklewood, N.W.2   X17130.

OLIVER, G. A. (sen.), Driver, R.F.A.
Having previously served in the Boer War, he volunteered in August 1914 and was immediately drafted to the Western Front. After taking part in many important engagements he died as a result of gas poisoning on December 26th, 1917.
He was entitled to the 1914 Star, General Service and Victory Medals, and in addition held the Queen's and King's South African Medals
1, St. Leonard's, Ambleside Road, Willesden, N.W.10 15556A.

OLIVER, G. A. (M.M.), Pte., 20th London Regt., and Rifleman, Rifle Brigade.
He joined in November 1917, was sent to France in the following year, and took part in the Allied Advance. He was awarded the Military Medal for conspicuous bravery in swimming the Lens Canal and capturng German machine guns, and also holds the General Service and Victory Medals.
He was demobilised in December 1919.
1, St. Leonard's, Ambleside Road, Willesden, N.W.10 15556B.

OLIVER, H., Rifleman, 15th London Regt.
He joined in June 1916, and was sent to the Western Front, where he took part in the engagements on the Somme and at Bullecourt, St. Julien, Beaumont-Hamel, Arras and St. Quentin. He was wounded at St. Julien and on one other occasion, and was invalided home
He holds the General Service and Victory Medals, and was demobilised in February 1919.
35, Sandilands Road, Wandsworth Bridge Road, S.W.6
                                              X20506.

OLIVER, W., Driver, Royal Field Artillery.
He volunteered in September 1914, and during his service took part in many engagements on the Western Front, in Salonica and in Egypt.
He was demobilised in March 1919, and holds the 1914-15 Star, General Service and Victory Medals.
88, Adeney Road, Hammersmith, W 6   14660C.

OLVER, J., Rifleman, 18th London Regiment (London Irish Rifles).
He volunteered in May 1915, and in the same year was sent to France, where he took part in the battles of Loos, the Somme, Ypres, Cambrai and Bourlon Wood (where he was badly wounded in November 1917).
In the following February he was discharged as medically unfit for further service owing to wounds, and holds the 1914-15 Star, General Service and Victory Medals.
25, Stanley Road, King's Road, S.W.6   X19864.

O'NEILL, E. C., Pte., 135th Labour Corps.
He joined in March 1917, and shortly afterwards was drafted to the Western Front, where for over two years he did good work with the Labour Corps in various sectors. In 1920 he returned to England and in March of the same year was demobilised, holding the General Service and Victory Medals.
30, St. Ervan's Road, North Kensington, W.10   X20386.

ORAM, F. J. (M.M.), Cpl., 20th London Regt.
He joined in 1916, and in the same year went to France, where he saw much heavy fighting   He was awarded the Military Medal for conspicuous bravery and devotion to duty whilst in charge of a trench mortar. In March 1918, during the Retreat he was taken prisoner, and held in captivity until after the Armistice.
In addition to the M.M., he holds the General Service and Victory Medals, and was demobilised in December 1919.
54, Tubb's Road, Harlesden, N.W.10   12561A.

ORDERS, A., Cpl., 22nd Royal Fusiliers.
He joined in April 1916, and was drafted to the Western Front in the same year. He took part in many important engagements, including that of Oppy Wood, where he was killed in action in April 1917.
He was entitled to the General Service and Victory Medals.
145, Ashmore Road, Harrow Road, W.9   X19747.

O'RERDIEN, J. W., Chief Petty Officer, R.N., H.M.S. "Commonwealth" and "Gibraltar."
He joined in April 1917, and served with the Grand Fleet in the North Sea and the English Channel, where he was engaged on important convoy duties, escorting food and troopships to and from France. He held a responsible position in the electrical department of the ship.
In January 1919 he was demobilised, and holds the General Service, Victory and the Mercantile Marine Medals.
64, Portnall Road, Maida Hill, W.9   TX19683.

O'ROURKE, D., Air Mechanic, R.A.F.
Volunteering at the outbreak of war, he was sent immediately to the Western Front, where he took part in the retreat from Mons and the battles of Ypres, Loos, Arras and the Somme. During his service he was twice wounded and suffered from shell-shock. Throughout his duties, which called for a high degree of technical skill, were performed in an excellent manner.
In December 1919 he was demohilised, holding the Mons Star General Service and Victory Medals.
8, Moselle Street, Tottenham, N17   X18365.

ORPWOOD, J., Pte., Middlesex Regiment.
He joined in December 1915, and was sent to the Western Front, where he was engaged on important duties in connection with salvage in many sectors of this theatre of war.
He was demobilised in February 1919, holding the General Service and Victory Medals.
28, Ashford Road, Tottenham, N.17   X18353A.

ORTON, R., Driver, Royal Field Artillery.
He volunteered in 1914, and was shortly afterwards drafted to the Western Front, where he served until the cessation of hostilities, taking part in many important engagements. He then went to Germany with the Army of Occupation, with which he remained until he was sent to Palestine, where in 1920 he was still serving
He holds the 1914-15 Star, General Service and Victory Medals.
24, Hartington Road, Lower Edmonton, N.9   14051B

ORTON, S., Pte., East Surrey Regiment.
He volunteered in 1915, and was sent to the Western Front in the same year. During his service he took part in many of the principal engagements before the cessation of hostilities. He was then drafted to Egypt and in 1920 he was still serving there.
He holds the 1914-15 Star, General Service and Victory Medals.
24, Hartington Road, Lower Edmonton, N.9   14051A.

OSBORN, A. J. (M.M.), Sergt., R.A.V.C.
He volunteered in January 1915, and was immediately drafted overseas, where he was engaged on special duties in connection with the doctoring of horses on the Somme and Ypres sectors of the Western Front. He was awarded the Military Medal in March 1918 for gallant conduct and devotion to duty during the German Offensive. He returned to England after the Armistice and was demobilised in April 1919.
He also holds the 1914-15 Star, General Service and Victory Medals.
43, Mordaunt Road, Willesden, N.W.10   13862A.

OSBORN, H., Pte., Royal Army Service Corps.
He volunteered in 1914, and after his training served at various stations with his unit until 1916, when he was sent to France. During his service on the Western Front he was engaged on important duties in connection with the transport of stores and ammunition to the forward areas particularly in the Somme and Ypres sectors.
He was demobilised in 1919, and holds the General Service and Victory Medals.
114, Lopen Road, Upper Edmonton, N.18   X17919.

OSBORN, W., Gunner, Royal Horse Artillery.
He volunteered in August 1914, and was shortly afterwards drafted overseas, where he played a prominent part during the retreat from Mons and the battles of Ypres, Loos, Arras and the Somme.
He holds the Mons Star, General Service and Victory Medals, and in October 1918 was discharged, owing to the effects of his service.
10, St. James's Place, Church Road, Tottenham, N.17   X18536.

OSBORN, W. W., Cpl., Lancashire Fusiliers.
He volunteered in April 1915 in the R.A.V.C., and after his training was sent to the Western Front, where he was employed on important duties in connection with sick and wounded horses. He was afterwards transferred to the Lancashire Fusiliers and drafted to Italy, where he was in action in the operations on the Piave.
He holds the General Service and Victory Medals, and was demobilised in February 1919.
43, Mordaunt Road, Willesden, N.W.10   13862B.

OSBORNE, C., Sergt., Royal Field Artillery.
He volunteered in August 1914, and after completing his training was drafted in the following year to Salonica, where he took part in many important engagements on the Balkan Front until the cessation of hostilities.
In 1920 he was still serving with his unit, and holds the 1914-15 Star, General Service and Victory Medals.
38, Bronsart Road, Munster Road, S.W.6   X18899A.

OSBORNE, E. C., Driver, R.F.A.
He volunteered in December 1915, and at the conclusion of his training was sent to France, where he took part in the battles of the Somme (1916), Vimy Ridge and Ypres (1917). He went to Italy in October 1917, and was engaged in operations on the Piave. In the following year he returned to France, and was in action during the Advance of 1918 until the cessation of hostilities.
He was demobilised in February 1919, and holds the General Service and Victory Medals
14, Colin Road, Dudden Hill, N.W.10   16294A.

OSBORNE, G. T., A.B., Royal Navy.
Volunteering in December 1914, he did patrol duty in the North, Mediterranean and Black Seas with the Fleet. In 1919 he served against the Bolshevists in the Caspian Sea, near Baku. During the war he served in H.M.S. "Arlanza" and "Lancaster," and was demobilised in 1919, holding the 1914-15 Star, General Service and Victory Medals.
20, Greyhound Road, College Park, N.W.10   TX17929A.

OSBORNE, T. J., Cpl., The Queen's (Royal West Surrey Regiment).
Volunteering in September 1914, he played a prominent part in the battles of the Somme, Cambrai, Ypres and Loos, and during the Advance of 1918. During his service on the Western Front he was wounded.
In March 1919 he was demobilised, and holds the 1914-15 Star, General Service and Victory Medals.
20, Greyhound Road, College Park, N.W.10   TX17929B.

OSBORNE, W., Driver, Royal Field Artillery.
He volunteered in November 1914, and during his service on the Western Front took part in many engagements, including those on the Somme, at Ypres, Vimy Ridge, Arras, Loos, Neuve Chapelle, Armentières, Amiens, Bullecourt and the Advance of 1918.
He was demobilised in April 1919, holding the 1914-15 Star, General Service and Victory Medals.
38, Bronsart Road, Munster Road, S.W.6   X18899B.

OSBORNE, W., Lce.-Cpl., Middlesex Regiment and Royal Army Ordnance Corps.
He volunteered in October 1914, and after his training served at various stations with his unit until December 1916, when he was sent to France He took part in the battles of Vimy Ridge and Messines, where he was badly wounded and was invalided home. On his recovery he was transferred to the R.A.O.C., with which unit he was engaged on important duties until demobilised in February 1919. Previous to the war he served for over 11 years in the R.M.L.I.
He holds the General Service and Victory Medals.
118, Roundwood Road, Willesden, N.W.10   16052.

OSBOURN, K. (Mrs.), Special War Worker.
During the war this lady volunteered for work of national importance, and was engaged by Messrs. Hooper & Co., aircraft manufacturers, Chelsea, on special duties in connection with the manufacture of aeroplane wings. She gave valuable services, and received a certificate of appreciation of her good work from her employers.
16, Novello Street, Parson's Green, S.W.6   X19932A.

OSELTON, H. G., Sapper, Royal Engineers.
He volunteered in August 1914, and after his training served on important duties in connection with searchlights in the Channel Islands and other places in England.
He gave valuable services throughout, and was demobilised in February 1919.
2, Lamington Street, Hammersmith, W.6   / 11102.

O'SHEA, W., Pte., M.G.C. (Cavalry).
He volunteered in December 1915, and at the conclusion of his training served at various stations on important duties with his unit until 1917, when he was drafted to Egypt, and later to Palestine, where he was employed as a range-finder. He suffered from malaria during his service in the East and returned to England, and was subsequently demobilised in 1919.
He holds the General Service and Victory Medals.
76, Third Avenue, Queen's Park Estate, W.10   X19297.

OSLER, H., Pioneer, R.E. and Pte., Labour Corps.
Volunteering in August 1915, he was soon drafted to the Western Front, where he remained for 3½ years. Throughout his service he did valuable work, and saw service in many important sectors, including Ypres, the Somme, Cambrai, Béthune and Armentières.
He was demobilised in 1919, holding the 1914-15 Star, General Service and Victory Medals.
6, Kenmont Gardens, College Park, N.W.10   X17578.

OSMOND, S., Pte., Middlesex Regiment.
He joined in April 1916, was sent to France in the following year, and after taking part in the battle of the Somme, was killed in action at Arras on April 28th, 1917.
He was entitled to the General Service and Victory Medals.
20, Cedars Road, Lower Edmonton, N.9   14361.

OTTARWAY, P. J., Pte., 1st Middlesex Regiment.
He volunteered in September 1914, and in the same year was sent to France. He took part in engagements at Ypres, Loos, Arras and Cambrai, where he was killed in action on April 23rd, 1917.
He was entitled to the 1914-15 Star, General Service and Victory Medals.
65, Portnall Road, Maida Hill, W.9   X19514.

OUTRAM, E. (M.M.), Sergt., 8th M.G.C.
He was in the Army when war broke out, and in August 1914 was sent to the Western Front. Throughout his service, which lasted for five years, he did splendid work with his unit, and was in action on practically all ectors.
He was awarded the Military Medal for the conspicuous bravery and contempt of danger in fighting one of our machine guns under heavy fire, and in addition holds the 1914 Star, General Service and Victory Medals. He was demobilised in November 1919.
4, Northcote Road, Willesden, N.W.10   T14907A.

OUTRAM, W., Pte., 4th Norfolk Regiment.
Volunteering in June 1915, he served in Egypt from the following year until December 1918, when he died in Cairo of a severe illness.
He was entitled to the General Service and Victory Medals.
4, Northcote Road, Willesden, N.W.10   T14907B.

OVENDEN, S., Lce.-Cpl., Royal Fusiliers.
Volunteering in June 1915, he was drafted to the Western Front, where, after taking part in many important battles, he was killed in action on July 1st, 1917.
He was entitled to the General Service and Victory Medals.
13, Gloucester Road, Upper Edmonton, N.18   X17173.

OVENS, A. W. S., Pte., Essex Regiment.
He joined in 1916, and after a short period of training was drafted to the Western Front. Throughout his service, which lasted three years, he did valuable work with his unit in many important sectors, and was severely wounded.
He returned to England, and in February 1919 was demobilised, holding the General Service and Victory Medals
152, Montague Road, Lower Edmonton, N.9   15840A.

OVENS, J., Pte., R.A.S.C. (M.T.)
He volunteered on the outbreak of hostilities, and after a short period of training was drafted to the Western Front. He saw action in many sectors whilst carrying out his duties with the Mechanical Transport, and on three occasions was severely wounded—at Neuve Chapelle, Aubers Ridge and on the Somme.
He was demobilised in January 1919, holding the Mons Star, General Service and Victory Medals
31, Nelson Road, Lower Edmonton, N.9   13581.

OVENS, R. A., Pioneer, Royal Engineers.
He volunteered in October 1915, and later in the same year was drafted to Salonica, remaining there until 1916, when he was sent to the Western Front. He saw much service on both Fronts, and whilst in the East was severely wounded and contracted malaria.
He was demobilised in April 1919, holding the 1914-15 Star, General Service and Victory Medals.
152, Montague Road, Lower Edmonton, N.18   15840B.

OVER, W., Pte., 9th East Surrey Regiment.
He volunteered in September 1914, and in September 1915 was sent overseas. He took part in heavy fighting on all sectors of the Western Front until the cessation of hostilities
He was twice wounded—at Loos and at Messines.
In February 1919 he returned to England, and was demobilised, holding the 1914-15 Star, General Service and Victory Medals.
23, Ray's Avenue, Upper Edmonton, N.18   15486.

OVER, W. J., Pte., 16th Worcestershire Regt.
He volunteered in December 1915, and after his training was engaged at various stations on special duties with his unit. He gave valuable service, but was not successful in obtaining his transfer overseas before the cessation of hostilities.
He was demobilised in April 1919.
88, Montague Road, Lower Edmonton, N.9   16875.

OVERTON, Herbert, Special Constable, " N " Division (Tottenham).
He volunteered in August 1914, and throughout the war did valuable service, including special duty during air raids. He holds the Long Service Medal and Star, and also a Silver Medal which was specially awarded for services rendered.
He was discharged in August 1919.
4, King's Road, Tottenham, N.17   X18540B.

OVERTON, Horace, Driver, R.F.A.
He volunteered in October 1914, and in the following December was sent to France, where he was on active service for six months. Later he went to Salonica, and took part in the Balkan campaign.
After four years' service overseas he was demobilised in February 1919, holding the 1914-15 Star, General Service and Victory Medals.
4, King's Road, Tottenham, N.17   X18540A.

OVERTON, J., Pte., Labour Corps.
He volunteered in 1915, and for nearly four years served with the Labour Corps in France, where he did good work in many important sectors
He returned to England in 1919, when he was demobilised, holding the 1914-15 Star, General Service and Victory Medals.
22, Kimberley Road, Upper Edmonton, N.18   16530.

OWEN, E., Pte., 1/4th Royal Sussex Regiment.
Joining in September 1917, he was shortly after drafted to Palestine, where he saw active service. Later, after he had been transferred to the Western Front, he was killed in action on June 23rd, 1918.
He was entitled to the General Service and Victory Medals.
29, Alexandra Road, West Kensington, W.14   12092

OWEN, H. (Miss), Special War Worker.
During the war this lady was engaged at the Perivale Filling Factory, Park Royal. She carried out her work, which was in connection with the T.N.T. and C.E. powders, and most dangerous, in a very capable manner, for which she was highly commended.
50, Steele Road, Willesden, N.W.10   14144A.

OWEN, J. E., Pte., R.A.S.C. (M.T.)
He volunteered in June 1915, and for three years was engaged in the transport of food and munitions on the Western Front, where he did valuable work.
He returned to England in 1918, and in December was demobilised, holding the 1914-15 Star, General Service and Victory Medals.
14, Butterswick Cottages, Hammersmith, W.6   15873.

OXLADE, J. S., Rifleman, 1st Rifle Brigade.
He joined in August 1916, and after his training was sent to the Western Front, where he was killed in action on October 23rd, 1916.
He was entitled to the General Service and Victory Medals.
43, Hartington Road, Lower Edmonton, N.9   13920.

P

PACKER, B. B., Sergt., Bedfordshire Regt.
Joining in May 1918, he was engaged on the important work of conducting drafts to the Western Front, and at the conclusion of hostilities went with the Army of Occupation to Germany. He was demobilised in April 1920, holding the General Service and Victory Medals.
29, Hawthorn Road, Willesden, N.W.10   X17219B.

PACKER, C. H., Pte., 2/20th London Regiment.
Joining in May 1916, he was sent in the following year to the Balkan Front, and later to Egypt. Whilst in the East he took a prominent part in the fighting, and was wounded. After the Armistice he was sent to Germany, where he served with the Army of Occupation till his demobilisation in August 1919. He holds the General Service and Victory Medals.
7, Bradiston Road, Maida Hill, W.9   X19976.

PACKER, E. J., Sapper, Royal Engineers.
He joined in February 1917, and in the following March was sent to the Western Front, where he did much valuable work in the engagements at Arras, Vimy Ridge, Cambrai, and during the Advance of 1918.
In October 1919 he was demobilised, holding the General Service and Victory Medals.
29, Hawthorn Road, Willesden, N.W.10   X17219A.

PACKWOOD, A. W. H., Sgt., 1st Grenadier Guards.
He volunteered in August 1914, and was sent to France, where he took part in many important engagements, and was killed in action at Cambrai in 1918. He was entitled to the 1914 Star, General Service and Victory Medals.
75, Bounces Road, Lower Edmonton, N.9   12882B.

PACKWOOD, H. L., Pte., Royal Fusiliers.
He volunteered in December 1914, and, after his training, in the following year was sent to France, where he took part in many important engagements. He was accidentally killed at Givenchy whilst throwing hand-grenades, on January 30th, 1915, and was entitled to the 1914-15 Star, General Service and Victory Medals.
75, Bounces Road, Lower Edmonton, N.9   12882A.

PACKWOOD, L. G., Pte., R.M.L.I.
Joining in July 1917, he served in H.M.S. " Britannia " off the coasts of Africa and America, and in Chinese waters. On Nov. 9th, 1918, his ship was torpedoed, but he was rescued He holds the General Service and Victory Medals, and was still serving in 1920.
75, Bounces Road, Lower Edmonton, N.9   12882C.

PADLEY, A. G., Sergt., 7th London Regiment.
He volunteered in September 1914, and in the following year was sent to France, where he took part in many important engagements. He was wounded in action on the Somme in 1916, and at Messines in 1917.
In January 1919 he was demobilised, holding the 1914-15 Star, General Service and Victory Medals.
32, Kimberley Road, Upper Edmonton, N.18   16529B.

PADLEY, G. W., Flight-Sergt., R.A.F.
He volunteered in January 1915, and on completion of his training was retained with his unit on important duties (as an instructor). Despite his efforts, he was unable to obtain his transfer overseas before the cessation of hostilities.
He was demobilised in March 1920, holding the General Service Medal.
117, Rucklidge Avenue, Harlesden, N.W.10   13156C.

PADLEY, L. H., Rifleman, 16th London Regt. (Queen's Westminster Rifles).
He joined in November 1917, and was immediately sent to the Eastern Front. While on board H.M.S. " Aragon " on his way to Egypt his vessel was torpedoed, and he was drowned on December 30th of the same year.
He was entitled to the General Service and Victory Medals.
32, Kimberley Road, Upper Edmonton, N.18   16529A.

PADLEY, P. J., Lce-Cpl., 3rd Cheshire Regt.

He volunteered in December 1915, and on completion of his training was sent to France, where he took part in many important engagements, including those at Ypres, the Somme and Bullecourt.

He was wounded and invalided home, and after a considerable time in hospital was demobilised in September 1919, holding the General Service and Victory Medals.

117, Rucklidge Avenue, Harlesden, N.W.10   13156A.

PADLEY, R. B., Sergt., 2nd Queen's (Royal West Surrey Regiment).

He volunteered in December 1915, and after the completion of his training was retained with his unit on important duties until he obtained his transfer to France in 1918. He took part in many engagements, and after the Armistice went with the Army of Occupation to Germany.

He was demobilised in June 1919, and holds the General Service and Victory Medals.

117, Rucklidge Avenue, Harlesden, N.W.10   13156B.

PADWICK, W., Pte., Middlesex Regiment.

He volunteered in November 1915, and served in India from the following year until he was sent to Salonica in 1918. He took part in various engagements whilst abroad, and contracted malaria.

He was demobilised in March 1919, and holds the General Service and Victory Medals.

105, Ashmore Road, Harrow Road, W.9   X19650.

PAGE, A., Sergt., Machine Gun Corps.

He volunteered in August 1914, and was sent to Gibraltar in the same year. In 1915 he was drafted to France, where he took part in many engagements, including those on the Somme, at Ypres and La Bassée.

He holds the 1914–15 Star, General Service and Victory Medals, and was demobilised in 1919.

13, Pretoria Road, Tottenham, N.17   X18152.

PAGE, A., Lce.-Cpl., 4th Royal Fusiliers.

Having enlisted in December 1911, he was sent to France on the outbreak of war and took part in the retreat from Mons and the battles of Ypres, the Somme, Cambrai, and in the Retreat and Advance of 1918. He also served with the Army of Occupation in Germany from 1919 until discharged in February 1920, holding the Mons Star, General Service and Victory Medals.

122, Felix Road, W. Ealing, W.13   11030A.

PAGE, A. R., Gunner, Royal Field Artillery.

He volunteered in November 1914, and proceeded in the following year to the Western Front, where he took part in the battle of Loos. He was transferred to Italy in 1916, and in the same year went to Egypt, where he served throughout the Palestine campaign.

He returned home in March 1920 to be demobilised, and holds the 1914–15 Star, General Service and Victory Medals.

19a, Althea Street, Townmead Road, S.W.6   X21149.

PAGE, C. J., Driver, Royal Field Artillery.

He volunteered in January 1915, and later in the same year was sent to France. After taking part in severe fighting on the Western Front he was drafted to Salonica, where he served in many important engagements.

In 1919 returned to England for demobilisation, and holds the 1914–15 Star, General Service and Victory Medals.

75, Winchester Road, Lower Edmonton, N.9   14756A.

PAGE, E. (Mrs.), Special War Worker.

For six months during the war this lady gave very valuable services in a large munition works at Staines, where she was employed in the brass room on caps. Throughout, her work was done in a thorough and capable manner.

99, Ashmore Road, Harrow Road, W.9   TX19654B.

PAGE, E. J., Pte., Machine Gun Corps.

He volunteered in August 1914, and served from September 1915 to March 1919 on the Western Front. He was in action on the Somme, at Ypres, Loos, and Arras, and in other engagements, and was gassed.

He was demobilised in March 1919, holding the 1914–15 Star, General Service and Victory Medals.

32, Burn's Road, Harlesden, N.W.10   13140B.

PAGE, E. R., A.B., R.N., H.M.S. "Africa."

He joined in November 1917, and during his service with the Navy, was engaged on important duties near Sierra Leone. In January 1919 he was demobilised, and holds the General Service and Victory Medals.

75, Winchester Road, Lower Edmonton, N 9   14756B.

PAGE, F. W., Rifleman, 16th Rifle Brigade.

Joining in June 1916, he was engaged on important duties at various stations on the completion of his training. He served for a time in Ireland, but was not successful in obtaining his transfer overseas to a battle zone before the signing of the Armistice.

He was demobilised in October 1919.

1, Chesson Road, W. Kensington, W.14   X16985.

17

PAGE, G., Sergt., Royal Army Service Corps.

He volunteered in March 1915, and served on the Western Front until 1919. During that time he took part in the battle of Ypres and in many engagements on the Somme Front, and was gassed.

He holds the 1914–15 Star, General Service and Victory Medals, and was demobilised in February 1919.

34, Raynham Road, Upper Edmonton, N.18   16483B.

PAGE, G., Special War Worker.

For a period of three years during the war, this worker was engaged on duties of national importance at Messrs. Petrie's Factory at West Ealing, in connection with the manufacture of aeroplanes, and gave very valuable services.

5, St. Margaret's Road, Hanwell, W.7   11054A.

PAGE, G. E., Cpl., Middlesex Regiment.

He joined in May 1916, and during his three years' service on the Western Front acted as instructor to the men in the Labour Corps who were engaged in repairing roads.

He holds the General Service and Victory Medals, and was demobilised in February 1919.

99, Ashmore Road, Harrow Road, W.9   TX19654A.

PAGE, H. L., Sapper, Royal Engineers.

Joining in May 1916, he was drafted to the Western Front on completion of his training. While in this seat of war he took part in much of the severe fighting.

In October 1919 he was demobilised, and holds the General Service and Victory Medals.

49, Musard Road, Hammersmith, W.6   15729B.

PAGE, H. O., Pte., Royal Army Service Corps.

He volunteered in April 1915, and in the same year was sent to France, where he was engaged on important duties during much heavy fighting on various sectors. He was wounded, and in March 1918 was taken prisoner during the Retreat. He remained in captivity until after the Armistice, when he returned home and was demobilised in April 1919, holding the 1914–15 Star, General Service and Victory Medals.

39, Love Lane, Tottenham, N.17   X18530.

PAGE, H. W., Cpl., 13th East Surrey Regiment.

He joined in February 1916, and on completion of his training was sent to France, where he took part in much severe fighting. He was killed in action at Mory during the Retreat on March 23rd, 1918, having been previously wounded three times.

He was entitled to the General Service and Victory Medals.

49, Musard Road, Hammersmith, W.6   15729A.

PAGE, J., Pte., 11th Royal Fusiliers.

He joined in June 1916, and served on the Western Front, taking part in the battle of Beaumont-Hamel, where he was wounded. He was then invalided home, and owing to his wounds was discharged in 1917 as medically unfit for further service.

He holds the General Service and Victory Medals.

5, St. Margaret's Road, Hanwell, W.7   11054B.

PAGE, J. W., Driver, Royal Field Artillery.

He had previously served through the South African war, and volunteered for service in October 1914. In the following year he was drafted to the Western Front, where, attached to an ammunition column, he saw fighting in various sectors, and did excellent work.

In 1916 was invalided home, and after treatment at a hospital in Leeds, was discharged as physically unfit for further service in June of the same year.

He holds the 1914–15 Star, General Service and Victory Medals, in addition to the South African Medals.

305, Shirland Road, Maida Hill, W.9   X19560.

PAGE, R. H., Stoker, Royal Navy.

Volunteering in August 1914, he was posted to H.M.S. "Natal," and was engaged on important patrol duties with the Grand Fleet in the North Sea.

He lost his life when his ship was blown up in December 1916, and was entitled to the 1914 Star, General Service and Victory Medals.

32, Burn's Road, Harlesden, N.W.10   13140C.

PAGE, T., Pte., Black Watch.

He volunteered in August 1914, and was immediately sent to France, where he took part in the retreat from Mons and the battles of the Marne, Ypres, Loos and the Somme. He was then drafted to Salonica, but later returned to France, where he served until the cessation of hostilities.

During his service he was wounded three times, and was demobilised in January 1919. In the following April he re-enlisted, in order to join the Russian Relief Force, and on his return was finally demobilised in October 1919. He holds the Mons Star, General Service and Victory Medals

60, Oldfield Road, Willesden, N.W.10   15764A.

PAGE, W., Bombardier, R.F.A.
Volunteering in January 1915, he was sent to the Western Front in the same year, and served there for four years. During this period he took part in many engagements, including those of Armentières, Arras and the Somme, and was badly gassed, as a result of which he was in hospital for three months.
He holds the 1914-15 Star, General Service and Victory Medals, and was still serving in 1920.
34 Raynham Road, Upper Edmonton, N.18   16483A.

PAGE, W. J., Gunner, Royal Field Artillery.
Volunteering in September 1914, he was drafted in the following year to the Western Front, where he took part in many battles, including those of Loos and the Somme, and was wounded in action during the Advance of 1918.
He returned to England in 1919, when he was demobilised, holding the 1914-15 Star, General Service and Victory Medals.
51, Southam Street, North Kensington, W.10   X20777.

PALFREY, B., Pte., The Queen's (Royal West Surrey Regiment) and Essex Regiment.
He volunteered in January 1916, and after his training served at various stations on important duties with his unit. He gave valuable services, but was not successful in obtaining his transfer overseas owing to being medically unfit for Foreign service, and he was demobilised in May 1919.
10, Vallier Road, College Park, N.W.10   X17679B.

PALLITT, A. J., Pte., 7th and 9th Middlesex Regt.
He volunteered in May 1915, and served for three years on the Western Front, during which time he took part in the battles of Ypres, the Somme, Arras and Cambrai, and was wounded and gassed.
He was demobilised in March 1919, and holds the General Service and Victory Medals.
183, Chapter Road, Cricklewood, N.W.2   17207B.

PALMER, A. J., Pte., Duke of Cornwall's Light Infantry and Somerset Light Infantry.
Volunteering in August 1914, he was sent to France in the same year, and took part in the retreat from Mons and the battles of Loos, La Bassée and Lille, where he was wounded, and invalided home. On his recovery he was sent to India, where he was in action and again wounded during the Afghan risings.
He was demobilised in December 1919, holding the Mons Star, General Service and Victory Medals, and the India General Service Medal (with clasp—Afghanistan, N.W. Frontier, 1919).   14, Orbain Road, Fulham, S.W.6   X18050A.

PALMER, C. (Mrs.), Special War Worker.
She was employed during the war at Messrs. Blake's Munition Factory, Fulham, filling shells and grenades. Later she worked at another branch of the same firm, and was engaged on the machines for making grenade threads. She received a certificate of commendation for her excellent and patriotic services.
14, Orbain Road, Fulham, S.W.6   X18050B.

PALMER, C., Pte., R.A.S.C. (M.T.)
He volunteered in March 1915, and was drafted to the Western Front in the same year. He took part in engagements at Loos, Arras, Ypres and the Somme on important transport duties in the forward areas.
He holds the 1914-15 Star, General Service and Victory Medals, and was demobilised in April 1920.
38, Wilson's Road, Hammersmith, W.6   15853B.

PALMER, H., Pte., 2nd Coldstream Guards.
He joined for service in May 1917, and after his training was drafted to the Western Front, where he took part in many of the principal engagements during this period.
He was demobilised in March 1919, and holds the General Service and Victory Medals.
76, Faroe Road, West Kensington, W.14   12658B.

PALMER, J., Rifleman, King's Royal Rifle Corps.
He joined in 1916, and served on the Western Front until he was invalided to hospital in England suffering from frostbite. Upon his recovery he returned to France, and was taken prisoner during the fighting in 1917. He suffered many hardships whilst in captivity, and after the Armistice was released, and returned to England for demobilisation in March 1919.
He holds the General Service and Victory Medals.
38, Wilson's Road, Hammersmith, W.6   15853C.

PALMER, J., Pte., 2nd Dorset Regiment.
He joined in 1916, and after his training was drafted to India, and later to Mesopotamia, where he suffered from malaria. He afterwards saw service in Palestine, and at the close of that campaign was sent to the Soudan.
He returned to England, and was demobilised in 1920, holding the General Service and Victory Medals.
50, Church Road, Tottenham, N.17   X18338.

PALMER, L., Rifleman, 21st London Regiment (1st Surrey Rifles).
He joined in November 1917, and at the conclusion of his training served on the Western Front, where he took part in many important engagements.
After the cessation of hostilities he returned to England, and was demobilised in September 1919, holding the General Service and Victory Medals.
76, Faroe Road, West Kensington, W.14   12658A.

PALMER, R. E., Pte., 1st Middlesex Regiment.
Volunteering in September 1914, he was sent to France in the same year, and took part in many engagements. He was in hospital for some months, suffering from the effects of being blown up by a shell.
He was demobilised in May 1919, holding the 1914 Star, General Service and Victory Medals.
5, Shotley Street, Fulham, S.W.6   14800B.

PALPHREYMAN, A. B., Lce.-Cpl., R.A.M.C.
He joined in June 1917, and after his training served at various stations on important duties with his unit. He gave valuable services, but was unsuccessful in obtaining his transfer overseas before the signing of the Armistice, and he was demobilised in February 1920.
113, Woodheyes Road, Neasden, N.W.10   15460A.

PALPHREYMAN, G. W., Pte., Training Reserve Battalion.
He joined in May 1917, and after his training served at various stations on important duties with his unit. Owing to ill-health he was prevented from going overseas, and in January 1918 he was discharged as medically unfit for further military service.
113, Woodheyes Road, Neasden, N.W.10   15460B.

PAMMENT, A. E. (Miss), Special War Worker.
For over two years during the war this lady gave valuable services in work of national importance. She was employed for 18 months in the Yellow Room at Perivale, Park Royal, and later operated the machine for making bullets. Towards the close of the war she was engaged at Hayes, Middlesex, on work connected with liquid T.N.T. Her duties were performed in a patriotic way, and she did not cease giving assistance till after the Armistice
28, Woodfield Place, Maida Hill, W.9   X19717.

PAMMENT, E. (Mrs.), Special War Worker.
For 18 months during the war this lady was employed by Messrs. Simmons Ltd. on special work in connection with Army uniforms. She rendered very valuable and patriotic services throughout.
28, Woodfield Place, Maida Hill, W.9   X19718B.

PAMMENT, H. C., A.B., Royal Navy.
He joined in December 1916, and after the conclusion of his training at Devonport in 1917 was sent to sea, where he did very valuable work on H.M. Ships "Agamemnon" and "Spiræa." In 1920 he was serving in H.M.S. "Arthur," and holds the General Service and Victory Medals.
28, Woodfield Place, Maida Hill, W.9   X19718A.

PANNALL, C. (D.S.O., M.C.), Major, Durham Light Infantry.
Called from the Reserve on the outbreak of hostilities, he was first engaged on special duties in England, and in 1915 was drafted to the Western Front. He took a prominent part in many important battles, including those of the Somme (where in July 1916 he was severely wounded), Givenchy, Festubert, Loos, the Lys and Cambrai. In 1917 he was sent to Italy, where he saw some very heavy fighting on the Piave and in other sectors. Throughout his service he did valuable work, and was awarded the Distinguished Service Order and the Military Cross for conspicuous gallantry and devotion to duty on the field.
In addition he holds the 1914-15 Star, General Service and Victory Medals, and was still serving in 1920.
18, Oakbury Road, Fulham, S.W.6   20932.

PANNEL, W. J., Sapper, Royal Engineers.
He volunteered in April 1915, and later was drafted to the Western Front. Throughout his service he did valuable work with the Royal Engineers, chiefly in connection with the light railways, and in this way saw action in many sectors.
He holds the 1914-15 Star, General Service and Victory Medals, and was demobilised in May 1919.
57, Reporton Road, Munster Road, S.W.6   X18921.

PANNELL, H., Pte., 3rd Royal Fusiliers.
Volunteering in August 1914, he was soon drafted to the Western Front, and after taking part in several important battles, was killed in action at Givenchy on October 15th, 1915.
He was entitled to the 1914 Star, General Service and Victory Medals.
124, Lopen Road, Upper Edmonton, N.18   X17918A.

PANNELL, J. E. R., Sapper, Royal Engineers.
He joined in 1917, and served for two years on the Western Front, where he did very valuable work in the Ypres and Somme sectors.
After the Armistice he returned to England, and was demobilised in 1919, holding the General Service and Victory Medals.
124, Lopen Road, Upper Edmonton, N.18   X17918B.

PANTLING, L., Sapper, Royal Engineers.
He joined in February 1915, and was drafted to the Western Front in the same year.   After serving in many engagements he was killed in action on July 12th, 1916, at the battle of the Somme.
He was entitled to the 1914-15 Star, General Service and Victory Medals.
9, Letchford Gardens, College Park, Willesden, N.W.10
X17539.

PAPWORTH, R. G. (Miss), Special War Worker.
During the war she was engaged on work of national importance at Messrs. Eley Bros. and Messrs. Klinger's Munition Factories.   Her work was of an important character, and the care and skill which she displayed won for her high praise.
64, Durban Road, Tottenham, N.17   X18648C.

PAPWORTH, R. S. (Mrs.), Special War Worker.
During the war this lady rendered valuable service in various munition factories, where she was engaged in the T.N.T. and the gun-cotton departments and also in shell-filling and pellet-making.   Her care and skill in this work of national importance won for her high commendation.
64, Durban Road, Tottenham, N.17   X18281.

PAPWORTH, T., A.B., Royal Navy.
He was in the Navy at the outbreak of hostilities and immediately went to sea.   After doing valuable patrol duties he died while on service.
He was entitled to the 1914 Star, General Service and Victory Medals.
64, Durban Road, Tottenham, N.17   X18648A.

PAPWORTH, T. W., Pte., Durham Light Infty.
He joined in 1916, and at the conclusion of his training was drafted to the Eastern Front, where he saw much active service against the Bulgarians up to the close of the war. While at Salonica he contracted malaria, and was in hospital for several months.
He was demobilised in May 1919, holding the General Service and Victory Medals.
64, Durban Road, Tottenham, N.17   X18648B.

PARADINE, A., Pte., 4/2nd Royal Fusiliers.
He volunteered in June 1915, and after his training served on important duties with his unit at various stations.   He rendered valuable services, but was unsuccessful in obtaining his transfer overseas before the close of the war.
He was demobilised in May 1919.
43, Minet Avenue, Willesden, N.W.10   13915B.

PARDINGTON, P. M., Gunner, R.F.A.
He volunteered in January 1915, and was first stationed in Ireland for 15 months.   He was then sent to France, where he saw much service at Arras, Cambrai and the Somme, and was especially employed as a cook.
He was demobilised in April 1919, and holds the General Service and Victory Medals.
32, Napier Road, College Park, Kensal Green, N.W.10
X17352B.

PARFITT, F., Bombardier, R.F.A.
He volunteered in August 1914, and served on the Western Front at Mons, Ypres, Loos and Arras andl ater in Salonica, where he contracted malaria.
He holds the Mons Star, General Service and Victory Medals, and was demobilised in January 1919.
53, Strode Road, Munster Road, S.W.6   15335A.

PARIS, J. W. S., Sergt., 23rd Royal Fusiliers.
He volunteered in March 1915, and later in the year was drafted to the Western Front, where he took part in many important engagements up to the cessation of hostilities.
In December 1918 he went with the Army of Occupation to Germany, and on his return was demobilised in April 1920, holding the 1914-15 Star, General Service and Victory Medals.
32, Hartington Road, Lower Edmonton, N.9   14053.

PARKER, A. E., Sergt., 13th London Regiment (Kensingtons).
He volunteered in January 1915, and served on the Western Front for two years.   He took part in many engagements, including the Retreat and Advance in March 1918.
He was demobilised in March 1919, holding the General Service and Victory Medals.
34, Carlyle Avenue, Willesden, N.W.10   14210.

PARKER, A. W., Pte., R.A.V.C.
He volunteered in May 1915, and proceeded to the Western Front in the following September.   He rendered valuable service overseas for three years, tending sick and wounded horses in the veterinary hospitals.
He was demobilised in October 1918, and holds the 1914-15 Star, General Service and Victory Medals.
99, Carlyle Avenue, Willesden, N.W.10   13817B.

PARKER, A. W., Sergt. Major, King's Own Scottish Borderers.
He was mobilised in August 1914, went to France at once, and took part in the retreat from Mons, the battles of the Somme and Ypres, and many others, including the final Advance in 1918.   He was wounded four times during his service.
He holds the Mons Star, General Service and Victory Medals, and was demobilised in 1919.
98, Bulwer Road, Upper Edmonton, N.18   17287C.

PARKER, C. E., 1st-Class Stoker, Royal Navy, H.M.S. "Cordelia."
He was in the Navy when war broke out, served in the North Sea and other waters, and took part in the battle of Jutland. He was on board H.M.S. "Shark" until she was sunk, and then was transferred to H.M.S. "Vanguard," and later, when that ship was blown up, to H.M.S. "Cordelia."
He has been in the Navy for eight years, and holds the 1914-15 Star, General Service and Victory Medals.
78, Bravington Road, Maida Hill, W.9   X19323.

PARKER, C. R., Signaller, Royal Navy.
He volunteered in August 1914, and during the course of the war saw much service in the North Sea and the Mediterranean on board H.M.S. "Cardiff" and H M.S. "Royal Sovereign."
He was still serving in 1920, and holds the General Service and Victory Medals.
27, Alexandra Road, West Kensington, W.14   12091B.

PARKER, D., A.B., R.N., H.M.S. "Albemarle."
Volunteering in August 1914, he saw much service during the course of the war.   He took part in many engagements in the North Sea, and also cruised off the coast of Egypt.
In 1920 he was still serving in the Navy, and holds the General Service and Victory Medals.
2, Winchester Road, Lower Edmonton, N.9   14689A.

PARKER, E. J., Pte., 23rd Middlesex Regiment.
He joined in May 1915, and at the close of his training was sent to the Western Front, where he took part in much fighting and was killed in action on the Somme on September 15th, 1916.
He was entitled to the General Service and Victory Medals.
71, Reporton Road, Munster Road, S.W.6   X18916.

PARKER, F., Cpl., 2nd London Regiment (R.F.)
He volunteered in January 1915, and was engaged at various stations until February 1917, when he was sent out to France. He took part in several engagements, and was killed near Bullecourt on June 16th, 1917.
He was entitled to the General Service and Victory Medals.
14, Bravington Road, Maida Hill, W.9   X19189.

PARKER, F. A., Pte., Royal Berkshire Regt.
He volunteered in August 1914, and proceeding at once to France, took part in the battles of Mons, the Aisne, Ypres, and many others.
In June 1916 he was discharged in consequence of wounds received in action, and holds the Mons Star, General Service and Victory Medals.
12, Essex Road, Willesden, N.W.10   15937

PARKER, G., Lce.-Cpl., Middlesex Regiment.
He joined in April 1916, and was shortly afterwards sent to Palestine, where he served for a year.   He was there severely wounded in action, and after being in hospital for a long time, was discharged in January 1918, holding the General Service and Victory Medals.
73, Love Lane, Tottenham, N.17   X18309.

PARKER, H., Gunner, Royal Field Artillery.
He rejoined in August 1914, and soon proceeded to the Western Front,where he took part in many important battles, including that of the Somme.
He holds the 1914-15 Star, General Service and Victory Medals, and was demobilised in December 1919, after having completed 18½ years' Colour service, and a year and a half in the Reserve.
26, Gordon Road, Lower Edmonton, N.9   12884.

PARKER, J., Pte., 9th East Surrey Regiment.
He joined in February 1918, and was drafted to France in the following month.   He took part in the heavy fighting that followed, and was wounded at Péronne.
He was demobilised in October 1919, holding the General Service and Victory Medals.
52, Barry Road, Stonebridge Park, N.W.10   15668.

PARKER, J. B., S.M., 7th Middlesex Regiment.
He was mobilised at the outbreak of hostilities and rendered most valuable service in the training of the troops, but did not succeed in being transferred overseas before the close of the war. He had previously fought in the Boer War, and holds the Queen's and King's South African Medals.
He was demobilised in January 1919.
98, Bulwer Road, Upper Edmonton, N.18   17287A.

PARKER, J. E. (Miss), Special War Worker.
From 1914 to 1918 this lady was engaged on work of national importance at Messrs. Sparklet's munition factory, Edmonton, where she was responsible for the machines for making bullets and cartridges. Her carefulness and skill were very marked, and won high praise.
98, Bulwer Road, Upper Edmonton, N.18   X17386.

PARKER, J. P., Pte., 1st Middlesex Regiment.
He volunteered in August 1914, and was drafted to the Western Front, where he saw much service, and was killed in action at Loos on September 25th, 1915.
He was entitled to the 1914–15 Star, General Service and Victory Medals.
59, Brettenham Road, Lower Edmonton, N.9   15232C.

PARKER, N. N., Pte., 12th Royal Fusiliers.
He volunteered in September 1914, and at the close of his training was sent to France in the following July.
He was killed in action at Loos on September 28th, 1915, and was entitled to the 1914–15 Star, General Service and Victory Medals.
81, Shakespeare Avenue, Willesden, N.W.10   13703B.

PARKER, O. J., Pte., 1/19th London Regiment.
He joined in February 1917, and at the close of his training was drafted to France, where he served in many sectors and took part in numerous engagements in the concluding stages of the war.
He was demobilised in February 1919, and holds the General Service and Victory Medals.
11, Lintaine Grove, W. Kensington, W.14   16819.

PARKER, P., Gunner, Royal Garrison Artillery.
He volunteered in 1915, and was drafted to France in the same year, where he took part in many engagements, including those of the Somme, Ypres, Cambrai and the Advance in 1918. During his service overseas he was wounded three times and gassed, and was in hospital for 11 months.
He holds the 1914–15 Star, General Service and Victory Medals, and was demobilised in December 1918.
6, Linton Road, Upper Edmonton, N.18   X17284.

PARKER, S. J. S., Pte., Middlesex Regiment.
He joined in 1916, and on the conclusion of his training was drafted to the Western Front later in the same year. He remained overseas until hostilities ceased and took part in many important engagements.
In 1919 he was demobilised, holding the General Service and Victory Medals.
30, Wingmore Road, Tottenham, N.17   X17984.

PARKER, T. A., Pte., 7th Middlesex Regiment and Royal Fusiliers.
He volunteered in 1915, and after his training was retained for important duties with his unit until July 1918, when he was drafted to France. He took part in the concluding engagements of the war, and was killed in action on October 24th, 1918.
He was entitled to the General Service and Victory Medals.
98, Bulwer Road, Upper Edmonton, N.18   17287B.

PARKER, W., Pte., South Staffordshire Regt.
He volunteered in February 1915, and was sent to France in the same year. He took part in many engagements, including that at Bullecourt, and was wounded and taken prisoner in 1917.
After his release he was demobilised in December 1919, holding the 1914–15 Star, General Service and Victory Medals.
78, Kimberley Road, Upper Edmonton, N.18   16528.

PARKER, W. F., Cpl., R.A.S.C. (M.T.)
He volunteered in October 1914, and was at once drafted to France, where he rendered valuable service on various sectors of the Front up to the cessation of hostilities.
He was demobilised in June 1919, holding the 1914 Star, General Service and Victory Medals.
46, Leamore Street, Hammersmith, W.6   12612.

PARKER, W. H., Driver, R.A.S.C.
He joined in March 1916, and after his training served at various stations on special duties, which he carried out in a commendable manner. He met with a serious accident during his service which prevented his transfer overseas before the cessation of hostilities.
He was demobilised in September 1919.
24, Avalon Road, New King's Road, S.W.6   X19778.

PARKER, W. H., Pte., Royal West Kent Regt.
He volunteered in September 1914, and saw much active service in France from 1915 until 1918. He was wounded in action on the Somme in 1916, and again at Arras in 1917. He was discharged in June 1918 in consequence of his wounds, and holds the 1914–15 Star, General Service and Victory Medals.
15, Ray's Avenue, Upper Edmonton, N.18   15488.

PARKES, O. L., Pte., Machine Gun Corps.
He joined in May 1916, and after his training served with his unit on important duties. He gave valuable services, but was not successful in securing his transfer overseas before the close of the war.
He was demobilised in February 1919.
7, Lyndhurst Road, Upper Edmonton, N.18   15514

PARKIN, E. P., Sergt., Royal Fusiliers.
He was mobilised in August 1914, and was at once drafted to the Western Front, where he took part in the Mons Retreat and the battles of Neuve Chapelle, Ypres, Festubert, Loos, Vimy Ridge, Arras and many others. He was wounded four times in the course of his service. After the Armistice he went with the Army of Occupation to Germany.
He was still serving in 1920, and holds the Mons Star, General Service and Victory Medals.
42, Dieppe Street, West Kensington, W.14   16424.

PARKIN, J., Gunner, Royal Field Artillery.
He volunteered in April 1915, and saw much service on all parts of the Western Front and also in Salonica and Mesopotamia, where he took part in many engagements and was engaged as a dispatch rider.
He was demobilised in August 1919, holding the General Service and Victory Medals.
24, Mooltan Street, W. Kensington, W.14   X17142.

PARKIN, J., Rifleman, 18th London Regiment (London Irish Rifles).
He joined in 1916, and was drafted to the Western Front, where he took part in many important engagements, including Arras, Cambrai and the Advance of 1918, and was chiefly engaged as a signaller.
He was demobilised in 1919, holding the General Service and Victory Medals.
42, Dieppe Street, W. Kensington, W.14   16426.

PARKIN, J. H., Pte., 13th Labour Company (attached to Royal Army Service Corps).
He joined in 1916, and did much valuable service on the Western Front, where he was engaged in conveying stores and materials of all kinds in the Arras, La Bassée and other sectors. He was also engaged at the base at Calais and Boulogne unloading vessels.
He was demobilised in 1919, and holds the General Service and Victory Medals.
42, Dieppe Street, W. Kensington, W.14   16452.

PARKS, J., Lce.-Cpl., Royal Engineers.
He volunteered in 1915, and was sent to the Western Front, where for four years he was employed on engineering works. After rendering valuable services, he was demobilised in December 1919, and holds the 1914–15 Star, General Service and Victory Medals.
41, Laurel Gardens, Hanwell, W.7   T12351.

PARRITT, A. A., Pte., Royal Scots Fusiliers.
He volunteered in August 1914, and during his service on the Western Front took part in the battle of the Aisne, where he was severely wounded.
He was incapacitated for further service overseas and was eventually discharged in February 1918, holding the 1914 Star, General Service and Victory Medals.
47, Berry Street, Willesden, N.W.10   14982.

PARROTT, C. D., Pte., Middlesex Regiment.
He joined in August 1917, and was sent to the Western Front, where he took a prominent part in the fighting, and was wounded and gassed. On his recovery he rejoined his unit, and was still serving in 1920.
He holds the General Service and Victory Medals.
42, Lintaine Grove, West Kensington, W.14   X16993A.

PARROTT, G. C., Pte., Middlesex Regiment.
He joined in September 1916, and was sent to the Western Front, where he took part in several engagements and rendered valuable service. Whilst overseas he was in hospital for some time owing to injuries he had received in an accident.
He was demobilised in February 1919, and holds the General Service and Victory Medals.
42, Lintaine Grove, West Kensington, W.14   X16993B.

PARRY, A., Rifleman, 21st London Regiment.
He joined in August 1916, and having completed his training at various stations in England was sent to the Western Front. Whilst overseas he took part in the fighting on the Ancre, at Lens, Arras, Messines, Ypres, the Somme, Vimy Ridge and Bullecourt, and on October 15, 1918, was killed in action at Armentières during the Advance.
He was entitled to the General Service and Victory Medals.
54, Burnthwaite Road, Walham Green, S.W.6   X20201A.

PARRY, J., Pte., Royal Defence Corps.
He volunteered in August 1914, and did work of importance in guarding prisoners at several internment camps.
After rendering valuable services during air-raids he was demobilised in 1918.
106, Ilex Road, Willesden, N.W 10   15945A.

PARRY, J. H. J., Lieut., Machine Gun Corps and Middlesex Regiment.
Volunteering in 1914, he was sent to the Western Front, where he took part in engagements on the Somme, at Hill 60, Ypres and Vimy Ridge. During his service he was badly gassed, and suffered from fever.
He holds the 1914–15 Star, General Service and Victory Medals, and was serving in 1920.
106, Ilex Road, Willesden, N.W.10   15945B.

PARRY, P., Pte., 4th Bedfordshire Regiment and 2/4th Oxfordshire and Buckinghamshire L.I.
Joining in 1917, he was sent to France in the following year, and took part in the fighting at Mailly-Maillet and on the Somme. In 1919 he was drafted to Syria, and thence to Egypt, where he remained until demobilised in 1920.
He holds the General Service and Victory Medals.
106, Ilex Road, Willesden, N.W.10   15945C.

PARSELLE, D. C. J., Sergt., Royal Engineers.
He joined in November 1915, and during his service on the Western Front, took part in many engagements, including those of the Somme, Ypres, Arras, St. Quentin, Bullecourt, Lille, Armentières, Amiens, Delville Wood and Cambrai. Later he was sent to Germany with the Army of Occupation.
He was demobilised in November 1919, holding the General Service and Victory Medals.
218, Munster Road, Fulham, S.W.6   X19253B.

PARSELLE, M. T. (Mrs.), Special War Worker.
During the war this lady voluntarily devoted a large portion of her time to the making of mufflers and other comforts for sick and wounded soldiers at the 3rd General Hospital in London. Her kindly services were greatly appreciated.
218, Munster Road, Fulham, S.W.6   X19253A.

PARSLOW, A., Pte., 7th Bedfordshire Regt.
He joined in June 1916, and during his service on the Western Front was in action at Ypres, on the Somme, at Cambrai, Arras, Armentières, and Béthune, and was wounded near St. Jean.
He was demobilised in September 1919, holding the General Service and Victory Medals.
88, Purves Road, Kensal Rise, N.W.10   X18422.

PARSONS, A., Lce.-Cpl., 13th London Regt. (Kensingtons).
Volunteering in June 1915, he was sent to the Western Front, where he took part in the battles of Arras, Ypres, the Somme, Neuve Chapelle, and Cambrai, and was three times wounded.
He was demobilised in February 1919, and holds the 1914–15 Star, General Service and Victory Medals.
30, Laundry Road, Hammersmith, W.6   15049.

PARSONS, C. H., Pte., 1st Middlesex Regiment.
He enlisted in March 1919 for 12 years' service, but unfortunately his health broke down, and he was discharged after eight months' service in November 1919.
41, Mayo Road, Willesden, N.W.10   15473A.

PARSONS, E. S., Pte., 17th Middlesex Regt.
He volunteered in December 1915, and in the following year was drafted to France. After taking part in several engagements on the Western Front, including those at Vimy Ridge, Beaumont-Hamel, Trones Wood and Delville Wood, he was sent to England and demobilised in June 1919.
He holds the General Service and Victory Medals.
41, Mayo Road, Willesden, N.W.10   15473B.

PARSONS, F. (Miss), Special War Worker.
From 1914 until 1918 this lady was engaged at the Crypto Electrical Engineering Co., Park Royal, winding wire for submarines. She then served until 1919 on very dangerous work at Perivale Munition Factory, filling shells. Throughout she rendered very valuable services.
65, Ilex Road, Willesden, N.W.10   T16362A.

PARSONS, F., Gunner, Royal Field Artillery.
Volunteering in September 1914, he was sent to the Western Front, where he played a distinguished part during several engagements. Later he was sent with his battery to render assistance to the Italians during the Austrian Offensive on the Piave.
He holds the General Service and Victory Medals, and was demobilised in March 1919.
37, Aintree Street, Dawes Road, S.W.6   X18211A.

PARSONS, H. (Mrs.), Special War Worker.
This lady was employed during the war at the Park Royal Munition Factory, where she was engaged in the very dangerous task of making 1.7 detonators. This work called for a very high degree of skill, and was done in a most satisfactory manner.
1, Hastings, Ambleside Road, Willesden, N.W.10   15555.

PARSONS, H. T. (Pte.), R.A.S.C. (Motor Transport).
Volunteering in 1915, he served in East Africa until the last of the Germans had been captured. During this campaign he saw much fighting, and suffered badly from malaria, which kept him in hospital on several occasions.
He was demobilised in March 1919, and holds the General Service and Victory Medals.
54, Laundry Road, Hammersmith, W.6   15345.

PARSONS, J. W., A.B., Royal Naval Division.
Volunteering in May 1915, he was soon drafted to the Dardanelles, where he saw heavy fighting. On the evacuation of the Peninsula he was sent to France, and whilst there took a prominent part in several engagements.
He was wounded during his service, and in January 1919 was demobilised, holding the 1914–15 Star, General Service and Victory Medals.
37, Aintree Street, Dawes Road, S.W.6   X18211B.

PARSONS, L. (M.M.), Sergt., Coldstream Guards.
He volunteered for service in July 1915, and in the following year was sent to France, where he took part in the battles of Festubert, Loos, the Somme, Arras, Passchendaele, Lens, Cambrai, Amiens and Ypres. He was mentioned in despatches for courage and skill displayed in working his Lewis gun at Fontaine in 1917, and was awarded the Military Medal for conspicuous bravery in the field. He was twice wounded, and was demobilised in February 1920, holding the General Service and Victory Medals.
77, Chippenham Road, Maida Hill, W.9   X21094.

PARSONS, W., Cpl., 11th West Yorkshire Regiment.
After volunteering in September 1914, he was sent to the Western Front, where, during the battle of the Somme, he was severely wounded. He was invalided home, and was discharged as unfit in consequence in September 1917, holding the 1914–15 Star, General Service and Victory Medals.
1, Mooltan Street, West Kensington, W.14   X17145.

PARSONS, W. F., Pte., Middlesex Regt. and Rifleman, 17th London Regiment.
He volunteered in August 1914, and whilst on the Western Front was wounded in action at Neuville St. Vaast. Later he was drafted to Salonica, where he was again wounded and taken prisoner. On August 16th, 1918, he died whilst in captivity.
He was entitled to the 1914–15 Star, General Service and Victory Medals.
41, Mayo Road, Willesden, N.W.10   15473C.

PARSONS, W. J., Gunner, 396th Battery, Royal Field Artillery.
He joined the Army in July 1916, and after completing his training in England, was employed on special duties with his battery.
He was unsuccessful in obtaining his transfer overseas before the cessation of hostilities, and after rendering valuable services was demobilised in January 1919.
32, Denbigh Road, Willesden, N.W.10   15534.

PARTRIDGE, H. W., Pte., Machine Gun Corps.
Volunteering in August 1915, he was drafted a year later to Salonica, where he played a distinguished part in the Balkan campaign. In 1918 he was transferred to the Western Front, and fought during the Advance.
After the conclusion of hostilities he was demobilised in May 1919, holding the General Service and Victory Medals, but rejoined the Army in 1920.
2, Avalon Road, New King's Road, S.W.6   X19794.

PARTT, A., Cpl., 7th London Regiment.

He volunteered in August 1914, and was soon sent to the Western Front, where, after taking a prominent part in the fighting, he was killed in action on September 25th, 1915. He was entitled to the 1914-15 Star, General Service and Victory Medals.

19, Warwick Road, Upper Edmonton, N.18　　　X17503

PASCOE, F. C., Rifleman, King's Royal Rifles.

He volunteered in March 1915, and was drafted to Salonica, where he took a prominent part in the Balkan campaign, and contracted malaria.

After being in hospital in the East and in England he was demobilised in 1919, holding the General Service and Victory Medals.

35, Rosaline Road, Munster Road, S.W.6　　　X18623.

PASLEY, G., C.Q.M.S., Machine Gun Corps.

He rejoined in August 1914, having previously enlisted in 1908, and served at the Dardanelles, where he was wounded. Later he was sent to France, and took part in the battles of Arras, Ypres and the Somme. He was demobilised in January 1919, holding the 1914-15 Star, General Service and Victory Medals.

19, Everington Street, Hammersmith, W.6　　　13966.

PATCH, J. J., Sergt., Bedfordshire Regiment.

He volunteered in October 1914, and after completing his training was employed on special duties with his unit. He gave valuable services, but was unable to obtain his transfer overseas before the termination of the war, and was demobilised in April 1919.

34, Hartington Road, Lower Edmonton, N.9　　　14055A.

PATEMAN, A. H., Cpl., 4th Middlesex Regiment.

He volunteered in August 1914, and saw much service on various sectors of the Western Front. He was wounded four times and was kept in hospital in France and England for several months.

He was demobilised in January 1919, and holds the 1914 Star, General Service and Victory Medals.

20, Goodwin Road, Lower Edmonton, N.9　　　12999.

PATEMAN, G. S., Pte., 13th Essex Regiment.

He volunteered in 1915, and a year later was sent to the Western Front, where he played a conspicuous part in the fighting at Arras, Ypres and the Somme. Whilst in action at Vimy Ridge he was wounded and taken prisoner. After being in hospital in Germany and Switzerland and receiving bad treatment at the hands of the Germans, he was released. On his arrival in England he was discharged in 1919, and holds the General Service and Victory Medals.

3, Headcorn Road, Tottenham, N.17　　　X18490.

PATES, W., Pte., Labour Corps.

He joined in June 1917, and in the following month was sent to the Western Front, where he was engaged on important work on various sectors, more particularly those of the Somme and Cambrai.

He holds the General Service and Victory Medals, and was demobilised in April 1919.

18, College Road, Willesden, N.W.10　　　X18256.

PATMAN, J., Pte., Middlesex Regiment.

He joined in 1915, and served on the Western Front, taking a prominent part in the battles of the Somme and Ypres and the Advance of 1918.

He was twice wounded, and in February 1919 was demobilised, holding the 1914-15 Star, General Service and Victory Medals.

59, Sutherland Road, Tottenham, N.17　　　X18802.

PATMORE, W., Sapper, Royal Engineers.

He volunteered in February 1915, and during his service on the Western Front played a distinguished part in several engagements.

Whilst overseas he suffered from shell-shock, and in February 1919 was demobilised, holding the 1914-15 Star, General Service and Victory Medals.

9, Nursery Street, Tottenham, N.17　　　X18144.

PATRICKSON, H., Lce.-Cpl., 13th London Regiment (Kensingtons).

He joined in 1916, and was sent to Egypt and later to Palestine. Whilst with the Expeditionary Force he took part in the advance through Palestine, fighting at Jerusalem, Jericho and Jaffa under General Allenby.

On his return home he was demobilised in 1919, holding the General Service and Victory Medals.

61, Dieppe Street, West Kensington, W.4　　　16453.

PATTEN, C., Sergt., Royal Air Force.

He volunteered in August 1914, and was soon sent to the Western Front, where he performed duties that called for a high degree of technical skill. During his service he took part in several engagements and was wounded. He holds the 1914-15 Star and the General Service and Victory Medals, and was serving in 1920.

51, Lyndhurst Road, Upper Edmonton, N.18.　　　15513.

PATTENDEN, W. T. H., Pte., Northumberland Fusiliers.

He joined in June 1917, and was sent out to France, where he took part in engagements at Cambrai, and was killed in action on May 27th, 1918. He was entitled to the General Service and Victory Medals.

13, St. Peter's Road, Lower Edmonton, N.9.　　　12320.

PATTERSON, J., Driver, Royal Field Artillery.

He volunteered in November 1914, and during his service in France took part in the battles of the Somme and Arras, and was once wounded. He was demobilised in January 1919, and holds the 1914-15 Star and the General Service and Victory Medals.

21, Harton Road, Lower Edmonton, N.9.　　　13041.

PATTERSON, W. H., Rifleman, 15th London Regiment (Civil Service Rifles).

He joined in December 1917, and was sent to the Western Front, where he took part in several engagements. After serving until 1919 he was demobilised in December, and holds the General Service and Victory Medals.

48, Bath Road, Lower Edmonton, N.9.　　　13131.

PAUL, H., Gunner, Royal Garrison Artillery.

Joining in 1917 he was sent to the Western Front, where he was wounded at the battle of Ypres, and again later. He was discharged in 1919 suffering from shell-shock, and holds the General Service and Victory Medals.

45, Crefold Road, Hammersmith, W.6.　　　14483.

PAUSEY, J. D., Rifleman, Rifle Brigade.

Volunteering in September 1914, he was drafted a year later to the Western Front, where he took a prominent part in the battles of Arras, Ypres and the Somme. During his service he was wounded, and in March 1919 was demobilised, holding the 1914-15 Star and the General Service and Victory Medals.

6, Brereton Road, Tottenham, N.17.　　　X18106.

PAUSEY, W. C., Pte., Middlesex Regiment, and Rifleman, 15th Rifle Brigade.

He volunteered in September 1914, and in the following year was drafted to India, where he took part in several engagements. After nearly five years' distinguished service he was sent home and demobilised in December 1919, holding the 1914-15 Star and the General Service and Victory Medals.

52, Asplin Road, Tottenham, N.17.　　　X18821.

PAVETT, G., Pte., Royal Marine Light Infantry.

An ex-Marine, he rejoined in August 1914 and was retained on special duties of an important nature with his unit. He gave very valuable services, but was unable to secure his transfer overseas, and was demobilised in February 1919.

131, Mirabel Road, Fulham, S.W.6.　　　X17853.

PAVEY, G. W., Sapper, R.E. (R.O.D.)

He joined the Army in August 1917, and during his service on the Western Front was engaged on special duties, which consisted of laying railway lines and working on communications. Whilst overseas he was taken seriously ill and in September 1919 was demobilised, holding the General Service and Victory Medals.

20, Winchelsea Road, Willesden, N.W.10.　　　13853B.

PAXTON, E. (M.M.), Sergt., 12th Middlesex Regt.

He volunteered in August 1914, and served on the Western Front from 1915 until 1917. He fought at Ypres, Arras, Loos, Lens, Albert and the Somme, and was killed in action in April 1917. He was awarded the Military Medal for great bravery on the field, and was also entitled to the 1914-15 Star and the General Service and Victory Medals.

18, Brownlow Road, Willesden, N.W.10.　　　15005B.

PAXTON, E. R., Gunner, Royal Field Artillery.

He volunteered in 1914, and served in France for a few months in 1916, taking part in the battles of the Somme and Ypres. He was then sent to Salonica, where he was engaged till the close of the war and saw much service of an important nature. He was demobilised in 1919, holding the General Service and Victory Medals.

70, Holly Lane, Willesden, N.W.10.　　　15400B.

PAXTON, H. H., Pte., 2nd Bedfordshire Regt.

He joined in January 1917, and later in that year was drafted to India, where he was engaged on garrison duty at Karachi for the three following years. He was demobilised in January 1920, holding the General Service and Victory Medals.

18, Brownlow Road, Willesden, N.W.10. 15005A.

PAXTON, L., Corporal, Royal Engineers.

He volunteered in 1915, and shortly afterwards was sent to France, where he took part in the battles of Loos and the Somme, and afterwards was engaged on engineering work of a most important nature. He was both gassed and wounded. He was demobilised in 1919, and holds the 1914-15 Star and the General Service and Victory Medals.

70, Holly Lane, Willesden, N.W.10. 15400A.

PAXTON, T., Pte., Royal Defence Corps.

He joined in September 1914, and rendered valuable service during the whole course of the war, being engaged on anti-aircraft work, garrison duty, and guarding prisoners. In January 1919 he was demobilised.

89, Carlyle Avenue, Willesden, N.W.10. 13815B.

PAXTON, T. E., Bombardier, Royal Field Artillery.

He volunteered in December 1914, and was drafted in the following year to the Western Front, where he took part in a large number of important engagements, until the close of the war, including Arras and the Somme, and was badly wounded at Albert in April 1917. He was demobilised in January 1919, holding the 1914-15 Star and the General Service and Victory Medals.

89, Carlyle Avenue, Willesden, N.W.10. 13815C.

PAXTON, W., Corporal, Royal Air Force.

He joined in May 1917, and at the close of his training served as an engine-fitter at various stations with his unit. He rendered valuable service, but was unsuccessful in obtaining his transfer overseas. He was still serving in 1920.

89, Carlyle Avenue, Willesden, N.W.10. 13815A.

PAXTON, W. S., Sapper, Royal Engineers.

He joined in February 1917, proceeded to the Western Front in the same year, and served through many engagements, including those of Ypres, the Somme and Armentières. He holds the General Service and Victory Medals, and was demobilised in May 1919.

13, Talbot Road, Willesden, N.W.10. 15962

PAYNE, A. C., 1st Air Mechanic, Royal Air Force.

He joined in June 1916, and whilst on the Western Front was employed at Le Havre on duties which called for a high degree of technical skill. On his return he served as a despatch rider, and in January 1919 was demobilised, holding the General Service and Victory Medals.

4, Ancill Street, Hammersmith, W.6. 13761.

PAYNE, A. C., Pte., Somerset Light Infantry.

He volunteered for service in January 1915, and in the same year was sent to France, where he served for nearly four years. During this time he fought in the battles of Ypres, Arras, Cambrai, and the Somme, and was three times wounded. He was demobilised in June 1919, holding the 1914-15 Star and the General Service and Victory Medals.

80, Clarendon Street, Paddington, W.2. X20374A.

PAYNE, A. E., Rifleman and Private, King's Royal Rifle Corps and Middlesex Regiment.

Having already served for twelve years in the K.R.R.C., he re-enlisted in September 1914 and was retained on special duties with his unit, and later with the Middlesex Regt. He gave very valuable services, but, owing to receiving severe injuries in an accident, was discharged as medically unfit. Later he died from influenza.

68, Hiley Road, Willesden, N.W.10. X18166B.

PAYNE, Annie E., Special War Worker.

For two years during the War this lady was employed at the Park Royal Filling Factory and Small Arms Factory, where she contracted C.E. powder poisoning. Throughout the whole period she rendered valuable services.

10, Steele Road, Willesden, N.W.10. 13829A.

PAYNE, A. H., Gunner, Royal Garrison Artillery.

Joining in March 1918, he was sent to France two months later and took part in various engagements, including one near Arras, where he was seriously wounded. He was demobilised in November 1919, holding the General Service and Victory Medals.

10, Steele Road, Willesden, N.W.10. 13829B.

PAYNE, A. J., Driver, Royal Field Artillery.

Volunteering in May 1915, he was sent in the following November to the Western Front, where he saw much service. After taking a distinguished part in engagements at Ypres, Arras, Vimy Ridge, Passchendaele, Messines, Cambrai, and the Somme, he was sent home and demobilised in March 1919, holding the 1914-15 Star and the General Service and Victory Medals.

68, Hiley Road, Willesden, N.W.10. X18166A.

PAYNE, A. S., Sapper, Royal Engineers.

Mobilised from the Reserve at the outbreak of War, he was sent to the Western Front, where he took part in the Retreat from Mons and engagements at Ypres, the Somme, Bullecourt, and St. Quentin, and was wounded near Arras. After four years' service overseas, he was discharged owing to his wounds, and holds the Mons Star and the General Service and Victory Medals.

20, Tasso Road, Hammersmith, W.6. 14655.

PAYNE, B. G., Driver, Royal Field Artillery.

Volunteering in August 1914, he was sent to the Western Front shortly after. He had only served in Flanders for two months when he was taken prisoner near Hill 60. After being interned in Germany for nearly three years he was sent home, and in January 1919 was demobilised. He holds the 1914-15 Star and the General Service and Victory Medals.

4, Rayleigh Road, West Kensington, W.14. 12422.

PAYNE, C. F., Driver, Royal Field Artillery.

He volunteered in April 1915, and in the following December was sent to the Western Front, where he served with the Howitzers in several engagements, including those in the Arras and Cambrai sectors. After nearly four years overseas he was demobilised in April 1919, holding the 1914-15 Star and the General Service and Victory Medals.

38, Denbigh Road, Willesden, N.W.10. 15536.

PAYNE, E., Driver, Royal Field Artillery.

He volunteered in August 1914, and during his service on the Western Front he was present during the Retreat from Mons and engagements at St. Quentin, where he was wounded in 1914, Loos, Arras, and Ypres. He also was in action in Salonika, Palestine, and the Dardanelles, and was on garrison duty in India. On his return to England, he was demobilised, and holds the Mons Star and the General Service and Victory Medals.

4, Jervis Road, Fulham, S.W.6. X17384.

PAYNE, F. C. D., Pte., Labour Corps and Middlesex Regiment.

He joined in August 1916, but during his training contracted fever and was shortly afterwards discharged as medically unfit for further service in the same year.

51, Barbot Street, Lower Edmonton, N.9. 14583.

PAYNE, G. A., Pte., Royal Sussex Regiment.

He volunteered in December 1914, and was sent to the Western Front, where he took part in several engagements. On June 17th, 1916, whilst near Messines Ridge he was killed in action, after being severely wounded and gassed. He was entitled to the General Service and Victory Medals.

63, Dieppe Street, West Kensington, W.14. 16454A.

PAYNE, G. H., Pte., 1st West Yorkshire Regt.

He volunteered in August 1914, went to France, where he took part in several engagements in the same year, and was wounded during the battle of the Somme. He was demobilised in February 1919 and holds the 1914 Star and the General Service and Victory Medals.

58, Hartington Road, Lower Edmonton, N.9. 14061.

PAYNE, H. W., Driver, Royal Field Artillery.

He enlisted in August 1914, and in the same year was sent to France, where he served until 1918, taking part in the Retreat from Mons and the battles of Ypres, the Somme, and Arras. He was demobilised in February 1919, holding the Mons Star and the General Service and Victory Medals.

16, Chauncey Street, Lower Edmonton, N.9. 14258.

PAYNE, J., Pte., 5th Middlesex Regiment.

He joined in February 1917, and after completing his training was stationed at various places on special duties. He gave very valuable services, but was unable to obtain his transfer overseas before the cessation of hostilities, and was demobilised in June 1919.

16, Napier Road, Kensal Green, N.W.10. X17774.

PAYNE, J. E., Pte., 3rd Middlesex Regiment.
Serving at the outbreak of war, he was sent in 1915 to the Western Front, where he played a prominent part in the battles of Loos, Ypres, the Somme, Arras, and Cambrai, and was wounded. After rendering valuable services, he was demobilised in 1919, and holds the 1914–15 Star and the General Service and Victory Medals.
80, Clarendon Street, Paddington, W.2.   X20374B.

PAYNE, J. W., Pte., 3rd Middlesex Regiment.
He was serving in India when war broke out, and shortly afterwards was drafted to France, where he remained for nearly five years. During this period he saw much heavy fighting in various sectors of the front, including Ypres, Arras, the Somme, Albert and La Bassée, and was for a time in hospital, suffering from malaria. He was demobilised in June 1919, holding the 1914–15 Star and the General Service and Victory Medals.
16, Clarendon Street, Paddington, W.2.   X20553.

PAYNE, L. T., Driver, R.A.S.C. and R.H.A.
Volunteering in October 1914, he served on the Western Front, and was stationed at a Remount Depot at Rouen. Later he took part in the fighting at Armentières, Béthune, Albert, and Loos, and holds the 1914 Star and the General Service and Victory Medals.
36, Shelley Road, Willesden, N.W.10.   13608.

PAYNE, R. H., Rifleman, 16th The London Regiment (Queen's Westminster Rifles).
He joined in November 1916, and during his service on the Western Front took part in engagements on the Somme at Loos, Armentières, Arras, St. Quentin, Ypres, Cambrai, and in the Advance of 1918. He was demobilised in January 1919, holding the General Service and Victory Medals.
4, Ancill Street, Hammersmith, W.6.   13763.

PAYNE, T. C., A.B., Royal Navy.
Volunteering in August 1914, he served in H.M.S. "Princess Royal" throughout the war, and took part in the battles of Dogger Bank and Jutland. He was wounded, and in 1920 was still serving. He holds the 1914 Star and the General Service and Victory Medals.
18, Barbot Street, Lower Edmonton, N.9.   14578.

PAYNE, W. E., Pte., 7th The London Regiment.
Volunteering in 1918, he completed his training and was stationed with his unit on important duties. He was unable to obtain his transfer overseas before the cessation of hostilities, and after giving valuable services was demobilised in March 1919.
4, Ancill Street, Hammersmith, W.6.   13762.

PAYNTER, R. J., Stoker, Auxiliary Patrol Service, Royal Naval Reserve.
Prior to the war he had been in the Merchant Service, and in 1915 volunteered. Throughout he was employed on patrol duties off Gibraltar, the Mediterranean, and in home waters. He was demobilised in March 1919, holding the General Service and Victory Medals.
50, Charlton Road, Harlesden, N.W.10.   13384.

PEACH, C. F., Sergt., 1st County of London Yeomanry and Army Pay Corps.
He volunteered in September 1914, and in the following April was sent to Egypt and from there to Palestine, where he took part in the offensive against the Turks. He was wounded in the engagement at Beersheba in October 1917, and after being in hospital for some time was transferred to the Army Pay Corps. Later he served in the Balkans, and in 1919 he returned to England to be demobilised in August. He holds the 1914–15 Star and the General Service and Victory Medals.
37, Waverley Road, Paddington, W.2.   TX20411.

PEACOCK, E. G., Pte., Suffolk Regiment and King's (Liverpool) Regiment.
He joined in June 1917, and served on the Western Front at the Somme, Cambrai, Ypres, and Arras. In December of the same year he was gassed, and in consequence invalided home. After his recovery he went to Ireland for three months, later returning to France, where he remained until his demobilisation in March 1919. He holds the General Service and Victory Medals.
115, Oldfield Road, Willesden, N.W.10.   16103.

PEACOCK, E. G., Pte., 6th Bedfordshire Regt.
Volunteering in August 1914, he was sent to France in the following year and taken prisoner while in action on the Somme in May 1916. He was released after suffering many hardships whilst in captivity, and in November 1919 was demobilised, holding the 1914–15 Star and the General Service and Victory Medals.
72, Hawthorn Road, Upper Edmonton, N.18.   X17366A.

PEACOCK, J., Pte., 18th Middlesex Regiment and Royal Army Service Corps.
Joining the 18th Middlesex Regiment in April 1915, he was shortly afterwards transferred to the R.A.S.C., and after his training was engaged on the important work of conveying troops and food between Southampton and Le Havre. He was demobilised in January 1919, holding the General Service and Victory Medals.
35, Southam Street, North Kensington, W.10.   X20624.

PEACOCK, L. (Miss), Special War Worker.
During the war she was engaged at Perivale Munition Factory inspecting fuses, and also at the Bowden Wire Co. Throughout she carried out her work in a capable manner and rendered valuable services.
53, Drayton Road, Harlesden, N.W.10.   14996B.

PEACOCK, L. G., Pte., Royal Fusiliers.
Joining in April 1918, he was drafted to the Western Front, where he took part in several engagements during the Advance against the Germans. After the Armistice he went with the Army of Occupation to Germany, and in 1920 was still serving. He holds the General Service and Victory Medals.
75, Yewfield Road, Willesden, N.W.10.   16369.

PEACOCK, S., Pte., Royal Fusiliers.
He joined in November 1915, and during his service on the Western Front was wounded at the battle of the Somme, and later took part in the Retreat and Advance of 1918. He was demobilised in March 1919, and holds the 1914–15 Star and the General Service and Victory Medals.
53, Drayton Road, Harlesden, N.W.10.   14996A.

PEACOCK, W., Sapper, Royal Engineers.
Volunteering in February 1915, he was first sent to France, where he took a prominent part in several of the principal engagements, and was later drafted to Salonika. After also being stationed at Malta, he was sent home, and owing to his service was discharged as medically unfit in November 1917, holding the 1914–15 Star and the General Service and Victory Medals.
198, Chapter Road, Cricklewood, N.W.2.   X17125.

PEACOCK, W., A.B., Royal Navy, H.M. Destroyer "Penn."
He joined in 1902, and during the war served in the North Sea and the Dardanelles. He holds the Queen's South African Medal and the 1914 Star, General Service and Victory Medals, and was demobilised in February 1919, after rendering valuable services.
46, Haldane Road, Walham Green, S.W.6.   X17383.

PEACOCK, W., Stoker, Royal Navy.
He was in the Navy when war broke out, and served with the Grand Fleet in the North Sea, taking part in the battle of Jutland and other engagements. He was in H.M.S. "Vanguard" when she was blown up off the north coast of Scotland on July 9th, 1916. He holds the 1914–15 Star and the General Service and Victory Medals, and was still serving in 1920.
97, Mayo Road, Willesden, N.W.10.   15428.

PEAKE, G. H., Pte., 12th Suffolk Regiment.
Volunteering in October 1915, he was shortly sent to the Western Front, where he took part in several engagements, and during the fighting at Cambrai was killed in action on May 6th, 1917. He was entitled to the General Service and Victory Medals.
5, Laundry Road, Hammersmith, W.6.   15342.

PEARCE, A. G., Pte., Royal Army Medical Corps, and 2/19th The London Regiment.
Volunteering in January 1915, he was drafted to the Egyptian Expeditionary Force, with which he took a prominent part in the Advance through Palestine. He holds the 1914–15 Star and the General Service and Victory Medals and was demobilised in June 1919.
17, Ridgeley Road, Willesden, N.W.10.   X17784.

PEARCE, A. T., Pte., Labour Corps.
He joined in 1917, and was sent to France early in the following year. He saw service on various parts of the Western Front, and took part in the Advance of 1918. He was demobilised in February 1919, and holds the General Service and Victory Medals.
27, Holly Lane, Willesden, N.W.10.   15527B.

PEARCE, E. W., Pte., 9th Middlesex Regiment.
He volunteered in August 1914, and in the same year was drafted to India, where he saw much service and took part in the Afghanistan Campaign. He was sent home in 1919, and was demobilised, holding the 1914–15 Star and the General Service and Victory Medals.
27, Holly Lane, Willesden, N.W.10.   15527A.

PEARCE, F., Rifleman, King's Royal Rifle Corps.

Volunteering in October 1914, he was sent in the following June to the Western Front, where he remained for six months. He was then drafted to Salonika, taking part in the Balkan Campaign. In 1918 he returned to France, and during his whole service took part in engagements at Ypres, Arras, Cambrai, and the Somme, and was twice wounded. In March 1919 he was demobilised, and holds the 1914-15 Star and the General Service and Victory Medals.
14, Brett Road, Stonebridge Park, N.W.10.   14528.

PEARCE, F. H., Leading Cook, Royal Navy.

Being in the Navy at the outbreak of war, he served in H.M.S. "Téméraire" with the Grand Fleet in the North Sea throughout the War. He holds the 1914 Star and the General Service and Victory Medals, and was still serving in 1920.
25, Alric Avenue, Stonebridge Park, N.W.10.   14439.

PEARCE, F. W., Sergt., Queen's Own (Royal West Kent Regiment).

Mobilised at the outbreak of war, he took part in the Retreat from Mons and several important engagements on the Western Front. After being three times wounded, he was demobilised in January 1919, holding the Mons Star and the General Service and Victory Medals.
5, New Street, Hammersmith, W.6.   13787.

PEARCE, G. H., Rifleman, King's Royal Rifle Corps.

Joining in June 1918, he was soon sent to the Western Front, where he served until the cessation of hostilities. In February 1920 he was demobilised, and holds the General Service and Victory Medals.
86, Winchester Road, Lower Edmonton, N.9.   14760A.

PEARCE, H., Pte., 8th Somerset Light Infantry.

He volunteered in September 1915, and served in France from 1916 to 1918, taking a prominent part in many engagements and being wounded in August 1918 at Ypres. He holds the General Service and Victory Medals, and was demobilised in February 1919.
5, Gowan Road, Willesden, N.W.10.   X17137.

PEARCE, H. W., Staff Sergeant, R.A.O.C.

Mobilised in August 1914, he was quickly sent to France, where he was present during the Retreat from Mons and in the battles of the Somme, Loos, Ypres, and Cambrai and the Advance of 1918. He was discharged in June 1909 holding the Mons Star and the General Service and Victory Medals.
14, Avalon Road, New King's Road, S.W.6.   X19788.

PEARCE, J., Gunner, Royal Field Artillery.

He was serving at the outbreak of hostilities, and went to the Western Front in the following March. Whilst overseas he acted as a signaller and took part in engagements at Loos, the Somme, Ypres, Vimy Ridge, and Messines Ridge, and was once wounded.. He was awarded the Military Medal for conspicuous gallantry and devotion to duty, and also holds the 1914-15 Star and the General Service and Victory Medals, being demobilised in February 1919.
7, Albert Terrace, Milton Avenue,
Stonebridge Park, N.W.   14122.

PEARCE, J., Pte., 1st Royal Scots Fusiliers.

Called from the Reserve at the declaration of war, he took part in the Retreat from Mons, but was killed in action at Ypres on November 13th, 1914. He was entitled to the Mons Star and the General Service and Victory Medals.
23, Beaconsfield Road, Church End, N.W.10.   16078.

PEARCE, J., Pte., Labour Corps.

He joined in 1917, and after completing his training was engaged on important duties with his Corps. He gave valuable services, but was unsuccessful in obtaining a transfer overseas before the cessation of hostilities, and was demobilised in 1919.
47, Crefeld Road, Hammersmith, W.6.   14481B.

PEARCE, J., Sapper, Royal Engineers.

He volunteered in 1915, and during his service on the Western Front took part in several engagements, including the battles of the Somme, Arras, and Armentières. He was invalided out of the Army in 1916 on account of ill-health, and holds the General Service and Victory Medals.
47, Crefeld Road, Hammersmith, W.6.   14481C.

PEARCE, J. V. (M.M.), Corporal, M.G.C.

Volunteering in August 1914, he was sent to the Dardanelles where he took part in the Gallipoli Campaign. Later, after being drafted to Egypt, he fought during the advance through Palestine. He was awarded the Military Medal for conspicuous gallantry, and holds the 1914-15 Star and the General Service and Victory Medals, and was demobilised in June 1919.
86, Winchester Road, Lower Edmonton, N.9.   14760B.

PEARCE, N. (Miss), Special War Worker.

She was engaged during the war in the powder shed at the Fulham Filling Factory, Stevenage Road. She performed her dangerous duties well and gave valuable services.
47, Crefeld Road, Hammersmith, W.6.   14481A.

PEARCE, T., Pte., 9th Middlesex Regiment.

He volunteered in February 1915, but on the completion of his training was unable to obtain his transfer overseas on account of his being over age. He, however, gave valuable services before being demobilised in February 1919.
111, Carlyle Avenue, Willesden, N.W.10.   13684A.

PEARCE, T. H., 1st Aircraftsman, Royal Air Force

He joined in July 1917, and completed his training in England. Owing to his high degree of technical knowledge he was unable to obtain his transfer overseas, but was employed at various aerodromes and training schools, where he rendered valuable services. He was still serving in 1920.
111, Carlyle Avenue, Willesden, N.W.10.   13684B.

PEARCE, T. H., Sergeant., 7th Rifle Brigade.

Volunteering in August 1914, he was soon sent to the Western Front where, after taking part in the Retreat from Mons and the battles of Loos, Ypres and the Somme, he was killed in action at Delville Wood on August 18th, 1916. He was entitled to the Mons Star and the General Service and Victory Medals.
42, Mulgrave Road, Fulham, S.W.6.   16190.

PEARCE, T. J., A.B., Royal Navy.

Joining in February 1916, he served in H.M. Ships "Walpole," "Nestor," and "Hornet" in the North Sea. He also took part in the Expedition to N.W. Russia, and in February 1920 was demobilised, holding the General Service and Victory Medals.
4, Meyrick Road, Willesden, N.W.10.   16343D.

PEARCE, W. J., Rifleman and Trooper, Rifle Brig. and 3rd (Prince of Wales's) Dragoon Guards.

Joining in April 1917, he completed his training in England, but being medically unfit for service overseas was stationed at various places as a signaller and Lewis gunner. He rendered very valuable services before being demobilised in September 1919.
17, Ridgeley Road, Willesden, N.W.10.   X17783.

PEARMAIN, A., Pioneer, Royal Engineers.

He volunteered in September 1915, and during his service on the Western Front, which extended from the following October until December 1917, did valuable work with the R.E.'s in many important sectors. He was afterwards invalided home and in March 1919 was demobilised, holding the 1914-15 Star and the General Service and Victory Medals.
6, Belton Road, Cricklewood, N.W.2.   16598.

PEARMAIN, J. F. G., Sapper, Royal Engineers.

Joining in January 1916, he was soon sent to the Western Front. Throughout his service overseas, which lasted for three years, he did excellent work with the Royal Engineers in many important sectors, including Ypres and Cambrai. He returned to England in 1919, and in October of the same year was demobilised, holding the General Service and Victory Medals.
103, Yeldham Road, Hammersmith, W.6.   13237B.

PEARMAN, W., Sergeant, R.A.S.C. (M.T.).

Volunteering in February 1915, he was drafted to the Western Front. Whilst there he was engaged with the Mechanical Transport in many important sectors, including Elverdinghe, Boesinghe, Neuve Chappelle, Loos, Vimy Ridge, the Somme, Poperinghe and Armentières, and throughout his service did valuable work. After the cessation of hostilities and whilst still in France, he contracted a severe illness, from which he died on February 20th, 1919. He was entitled to the 1914-15 Star and the General Service and Victory Medals.
86, Archel Road, West Kensington, W.14.   16659.

PEARSE, A. E., Rifleman, Rifle Brigade.

He volunteered in March 1915, and served for three years on the Western Front, during which time he took part in engagements at Ypres, Passchendaele, Messines, and Cambrai, and was wounded. He was demobilised in February 1919, and holds the 1914-15 Star and the General Service and Victory Medals.
89, Burn's Road, Harlesden, N.W.10.   13457B.

PEARSE, H., Rifleman, Rifle Brigade.

He volunteered in September 1914, and in the following January was drafted to the Western Front. He was wounded in action at St. Eloi, and was invalided home, but returned to France on his recovery in October 1915. Later he took part in many other engagements, but in consequence of his being again severely wounded whilst in action at Flers in September 1916, he returned to England, and in the following May was invalided out of the service. He holds the 1914-15 Star and the General Service and Victory Medals.
89, Burn's Road, Harlesden, N.W.10.   13457A.

PEARSON, A. L., A.B., Royal Navy.

He joined in 1917, and after his training was posted to H.M.S. " Caradac," on which he served with the Grand Fleet, until the cessation of hostilities. He holds the General Service and Victory Medals, and in 1920 was still serving.
28, Star Road, West Kensington, W.14.   T16683A.

PEARSON, C. B., Air Mechanic, Royal Air Force.

He joined in August 1917, and after his training was engaged on important duties, which demanded a high degree of technical skill, with his squadron. He was not successful in obtaining his transfer overseas before the cessation of hostilities, but gave valuable services before being demobilised in February 1919. He holds the General Service Medal.
59, Reporton Road, Munster Road, S.W.6.   X18919A.

PEARSON, J. D., Pte., Royal Army Medical Corps.

He joined in August 1917, was drafted to the Western Front, and whilst carrying out his duties as stretcher-bearer at Ypres, was killed in September 1918. He had previously done very valuable work with the R.A.M.C., and was entitled to the General Service and Victory Medals.
59, Reporton Road, Munster Road, S.W.6.   X18919B.

PEARSON, R., Pte., R.A.S.C. (M.T.)

He volunteered in April 1915, and later served in France, where he was engaged in conveying ammunition and rations up to the lines, and did valuable work in that capacity. He holds the 1914-15 Star and the General Service and Victory Medals, and was demobilised in April 1919.
30, Lintaine Grove, West Kensington, W.14.   X16992.

PEARSON, R.A., Pte., 12th Lancers and 23rd Royal Fusiliers.

He volunteered in September 1899, took part in the South African Campaign from 1900 to 1902, and holds the Queen's Medal with five clasps. In 1915 he was sent out to France, where he remained on active service until 1919, took part in engagements at Loos, the Somme and Cambrai, and was wounded. In addition to the South African Medal, he holds the 1914-15 Star and the General Service and Victory Medals, and was demobilised in March 1919.
35, St. Martin's Road, Lower Edmonton, N.9.   12982.

PEARSON, R. J., Pte., 3rd East Surrey Regt.

He joined in 1916, and in the same year was sent to France, where after being wounded he was taken prisoner during the battle of the Somme. He was interned at Hanover and died there on 2nd November 1918. He was entitled to the General Service and Victory Medals.
28, Star Road, West Kensington, W.14.   T16683B.

PEARSON, W., Corporal, Royal Field Artillery.

An ex-soldier, with a previous record of eighteen years' service, he re-joined in August 1915. He was drafted to the Western Front, but after taking part in several engagements returned to England suffering from shell shock, and in February 1917 was invalided out of the service. He holds the General Service and Victory Medals.
119, Felixstowe Road, Lower Edmonton, N.9.   14547.

PEARSON, W. E., Pte., 7th London Regiment.

He volunteered in 1915, and during his service on the Western Front took part in several important battles, and was twice wounded. He also gave his blood for transfusion to save the life of a comrade, and was in hospital both in France and England. He was demobilised in 1919, and holds the 1914-15 Star and the General Service and Victory Medals.
59, Reporton Road, Munster Road, S.W.6.   X18920.

PEARSON, W. T., Pte., R.A.S.C. (M.T.).

He joined in June 1916, and after his training served at various stations on important duties with his unit. He was not successful in obtaining his transfer overseas before the cessation of hostilities, but gave valuable services before being demobilised in 1919.
23, Ambleside Road, Willesden, N.W.10.   16116.

PEASLEY, A. J., Lce.-Cpl., 6th (Inniskilling) Dragoons.

Called from the Reserve at the outbreak of war, he served for nearly three years on the Western Front, where he took part in several engagements, including the Retreat from Mons and the battle of Loos. Having fought in the South African War and completed nineteen years' service he was demobilised in March 1919, and holds the Queen's South African Medal (with five clasps), the Mons Star, and the General Service and Victory Medals.
22, Albert Terrace, Milton Av., Willesden, N.W.10.   14330.

PECK, A., Bombardier, Royal Field Artillery.

He volunteered in April 1915, went to France in March 1916, and took part in the battles of Ypres, Vimy Ridge and the Somme, where he was twice wounded and gassed. He holds the General Service and Victory Medals, and was demobilised in April 1919.
63, Humbolt Road, Hammersmith, W.6.   15318A.

PECK, C., Sapper, Royal Engineers.

He joined in March 1916, and during his three years' service on the Western Front took part in several important battles and did invaluable work with the Royal Engineers. On his return to England he was demobilised in March 1919, and holds the General Service and Victory Medals.
75, Love Lane, Tottenham, N.17.   X18310.

PECK, J., Corporal, Royal Army Service Corps.

He volunteered in 1914, and in the following year was drafted to the Western Front, where he served until 1919. During his four years' service he was present at many important engagements, including those at Ypres, the Somme, and Loos. After giving very valuable services, he was demobilised in 1919, holding the 1914-15 Star and the General Service and Victory Medals.
17, Rowallan Road, Munster Road, S.W.6.   X19275.

PECK, J., Pte., Bedfordshire Regiment.

He was rejected on four occasions, but in April 1916 joined in the Bedfordshire Regiment and was soon afterwards drafted to India. For nearly two years he was engaged on guard and other important duties, but on October 27th, 1918, died in hospital as the result of a severe attack of malaria. He is buried at Karachi, and was entitled to the General Service and Victory Medals.
63, Humbolt Road, Hammersmith, W.6.   15318B.

PECK, W. G., Driver, R.A.S.C. (H.T.).

He was in the Army when war broke out, having enlisted in 1912. In 1914 he was drafted to the Western Front, where for nearly five years he served with the Horse Transport, engaged in conveying food and ammunition to the lines, and in this capacity did valuable work. He returned to England in April 1919, when he was demobilised, holding the 1914 Star and the General Service and Victory Medals.
63, Humbolt Road, Hammersmith, W.6.   15318C.

PEDLEY, A., Pte., 7th Middlesex Regiment.

He volunteered in December 1914, but after his training was pronounced physically unfit, and in February 1915 was invalided out of the service.
32, Durban Road, Tottenham, N.17.   X18083A.

PEEL, C., Pte., Coldstream Guards.

He was mobilised in August 1914, and at once crossed to France where he fought in the early engagements, and was killed in action in November 1914. He was entitled to the Mons Star and the General Service and Victory Medals.
40, Durban Road, Tottenham, N.17.   X18081B.

PEEL, R. A., 1st Class Stoker, Royal Navy.

He joined in January 1917, and after his training was posted to H.M.S. " Inflexible," later being transferred to H.M.S. " Starfish." He served with the Grand Fleet for two years, during which time he took a prominent part in several naval engagements and was wounded. He holds the General Service and Victory Medals, and was demobilised in July 1919.
40, Durban Road, Tottenham, N.17.   X18081A.

PEMBERTON, D., Corporal, Machine Gun Corps.
He volunteered in 1914, and in the following year was sent to the Western Front, where he was in action in various sectors and was wounded during the battle of the Somme. After rendering valuable services, he was demobilised in 1919, and holds the 1914-15 Star and the General Service and Victory Medals.
99, Asplin Road, Tottenham, N.17.   X19083.

PEMBLE, E. W., Gunner, Royal Field Artillery.
He joined in June 1916, and later was drafted to the Western Front where for the remainder of his service he was engaged with the R.F.A., and did valuable work in various important sectors. He was demobilised in July 1919, and holds the General Service and Victory Medals.
10, Purcell Crescent, Fulham, S.W.6.   14846.

PENDLE, A. P., Pte., R.A.M.C. attached R.A.F.
He joined in October 1916, and served at Malta and on the Western Front from the following May until December 1918. He acted as stretcher-bearer, and was also on duty in the hospitals until wounded at Ypres. He was demobilised in February 1919, and holds the General Service and Victory Medals.
76, Bravington Road, Maida Hill, W.9.   X19324.

PENDREY, A. L., 1st Class Stoker, Royal Navy.
He volunteered in August 1914, and after his training was posted to H.M.S. "Cornwallis," in which he served with the Grand Fleet throughout the war. He holds the General Service and Victory Medals, and was demobilised in June 1919.
168, Brettenham Road, Upper Edmonton, N.18.   15226.

PENFOLD, J. W., A.B., Royal Navy.
He volunteered in August 1914, and rendered valuable service until the close of hostilities. On board H.M.S. "Active" he took part in the battle of Jutland in May 1916, and he was serving in H.M.S. "Emperor of India" which escorted the German Fleet to Scapa Flow. He was still serving in 1920, and holds the 1914-15 Star and the General Service and Victory Medals.
38A, Furness Road, Fulham, S.W.6.   X21142.

PENFORD, R. A., Pte., Machine Gun Corps.
He joined in 1917, and in the same year was drafted to the Western Front where he took part in engagements on various sectors. On October 2nd, 1918, he was killed in action at Gommecourt, during the Advance, and is buried in the village of Bellenglise, near St. Quentin. He was entitled to the General Service and Victory Medals.
71, Clarendon Street, Paddington, W.2.   X20390.

PENMAN, C., Pte., Royal Army Medical Corps.
Volunteering in July 1915, he was drafted to the Western Front, where he did valuable work with the 72nd Field Ambulance until March 1918, when he was taken prisoner. He was accidentally killed whilst in an internment camp in Germany in the following June. He was entitled to the 1914-15 Star and the General Service and Victory Medals.
26, Westbury Road, Willesden, N.W.10.   15453B.

PENMAN, H., Bombardier, Royal Garrison Artillery
He volunteered in November 1915, and served on the Western Front where he took part in the fighting at Ypres, Loos, the Somme and Arras, and was badly wounded in November 1917. In January 1919 he was demobilised, holding the General Service and Victory Medals.
26, Westbury Road, Willesden, N.W.10.   15453A.

PENNY, E., Pte., The Buffs (East Kent Regt.).
He joined in August 1916, and in the following year was drafted to Salonika, where he served until January 1918. He was then drafted to the Western Front, and until the cessation of hostilities was in almost continuous action. He returned to England in November 1919, when he was demobilised, holding the General Service and Victory Medals.
45, Sandringham Road, Cricklewood, N.W.2.   X17103.

PENNY, J. G., Driver, Royal Army Service Corps.
He joined in March 1915, and served with the Egyptian Expeditionary Force until he was discharged in September 1916 on account of ill-health. He holds the General Service and Victory Medals.
64, Claybrook Road, Hammersmith, W.6.   13767B.

PENNY, W. P., Gunner, Royal Horse Artillery.
Joining in August 1918, he completed his training and was retained on important duties until August 1919, when he was drafted to Salonika where he was still serving in 1920.
64, Claybrook Road, Hammersmith, W.6.   13767C.

PEPLOW, H. T., Chief Petty Officer, Royal Navy.
He joined in April 1917, and for two years served on motor boats with the North Sea Patrol in home waters. He holds the General Service and Victory Medals, and was demobilised in 1919, after rendering very valuable services.
17, Fourth Avenue, Queen's Park Estate, W.10.   X18693.

PEPLOW, W. A., Corporal, Royal Engineers.
He joined in March 1915, went to the Western Front in the same year and took a prominent part in many engagements, including those of Ypres, Bapaume, Albert, Achiet-le-Grand, and the Retreat and Advance of 1918. He was demobilised in May 1919, holding the 1914-15 Star, General Service and Victory Medals.
50, Portnall Road, Maida Hill, W.9.   X19455.

PEPPER, W. C., Sergeant, Royal Field Artillery.
He rejoined in August 1914, having previously served in the Army, and was sent to the Western Front, where he took part in the Retreat from Mons and the battles of Loos, Ypres, Arras and the Somme, and was wounded. He holds the 1914-15 Star and the General Service and Victory Medals, and was demobilised in April 1919.
21, Bayonne Road, Hammersmith, W.6.   14308.

PEPPIATT, A. (Mrs.), Special War Worker.
During the war this lady was employed on important duties at the Fulham Military Hospital, where throughout she worked in a very thorough manner and rendered very valuable services.
6, Shotley Street, Hammersmith, W.6.   14810A.

PEPPIATT, F. C., Gunner, Royal Field Artillery.
Volunteering in October 1915, he was sent in the following February to the Western Front, where he took part in engagements at Ypres, Hill 60 and during the Advance of 1918, and was wounded. After giving valuable services, he was demobilised in February 1919, and holds the General Service and Victory Medals.
46, St. Margaret's Road, Willesden, N.W.10.   X17825.

PEPPIATT, T. W., Driver, Royal Field Artillery.
Volunteering in 1914, he was sent to the Western Front, where he took part in engagements at Neuve Chapelle, Loos, Ypres, Hill 60, the Somme, and Lille. Later he was drafted to the Egyptian Expeditionary Force, with which he served in the Advance against the Turks. During this period overseas he was twice wounded, and holds the 1914-15 Star and the General Service and Victory Medals. He was demobilised in 1919.
6, Shotley Street, Hammersmith, W.6.   14810B.

PEPPIN, J. A., Corporal, Royal Garrison Artillery.
He joined in September 1916, and during his service on the Western Front, which lasted three years, acted as wireless telegraphy instructor. He also performed the duties of wireless operator in the battle of Armentières and the Retreat and Advance of 1918. He holds the General Service and Victory Medals and was demobilised in January 1919.
127, Portnall Road, Maida Hill, W.9.   X19535.

PERCIVAL, A. H., Pte., Royal Army Medical Corps.
He volunteered in September 1914, and during the war served on board the hospital ship "Kanowna" in the North Sea and at the Dardanelles. His ship was twice torpedoed by enemy submarines. He was awarded the General Service and Victory Medals, and was still serving in 1920.
52, Gloucester Road, Upper Edmonton, N.18.   X17006.

PERCIVAL, E. J., Pte., 9th Middlesex Regiment.
He volunteered in February 1915, and in the following year was drafted to the Western Front, where he was severely wounded whilst in action at Arras. Owing to his wound he was invalided home and discharged in November 1917, holding the General Service and Victory Medals.
210, Kilburn Lane, N. Kensington, W.10.   X18711B.

PERCIVAL, R. W., Pte., 3rd Coldstream Guards.
He joined in 1917, and served on the Western Front for two and a half years. During this period he took a prominent part in engagements at Ypres, the Somme, Arras, Loos and Cambrai, and in November 1917 was gassed at Bourlon Wood. He was wounded at Merville in April 1918, and was demobilised in March 1919, holding the General Service and Victory Medals.
23, Fourth Avenue, Queen's Park Estate, W.10.   X18669A.

PERCIVAL, W. W., 2nd Lieut., Middlesex Regt.
Joining in February 1916, he was drafted shortly after to the Western Front, where he played a distinguished part in several engagements, including that at Arras. After giving valuable services he was demobilised in June 1919, and holds the General Service and Victory Medals.
210, Kilburn Lane, N. Kensington, W.10.   X18711A.

PERCY, A. G., Pte., 5th Middlesex Regiment.

Volunteering in October 1914, he was sent to the Western Front in May 1917. After taking part in several important engagements, including those near Givenchy, Loos and Armentières, he was sent home and demobilised in February 1919. He holds the General Service and Victory Medals.
18, Brett Road, Stonebridge Park, N.W.10.   15686.

PERCY, H. E., Pte., Royal Army Medical Corps.

Volunteering in August 1914, he was drafted to the Western Front, where he was attached to the 30th C.C.S at Arras, and also for a while to a General Hospital. During the Advance he was stationed at Cambrai in the 4th Canadian C.C.S., and gave valuable services throughout. He holds the 1914-15 Star and the General Service and Victory Medals, and was demobilised in November 1919.
10, Goodhall Street, Harlesden, N.W.10.   12723A.

PERCY, H. J. A., Pte., 6th Queen's Own (Royal West Kent Regiment).

He joined in 1916, and during nearly three years' service on the Western Front was employed at Etaples in the officers' mess, and later at Cambrai. In 1919 he returned to England, and was demobilised in December, holding the General Service and Victory Medals.
10, Goodhall Street, Harlesden, N.W.10.   12723B.

PERKINS, A. G., Staff Sergt., 5th Middlesex Regt.

He volunteered in 1915, and was retained on special duties as a drill instructor at various stations. While holding this responsible position he gave valuable services, but was not successful in obtaining his transfer overseas before the cessation of hostilities. He was demobilised in 1919.
21, Florence Road, Upper Edmonton, N.18.   16016.

PERKINS, E., Pte., Royal Fusiliers.

He volunteered in August 1914, and during his service on the Western Front was wounded at the battle of Ypres in October 1914. After being in hospital for some time, he was discharged in April 1917 as medically unfit for further service owing to wounds. He holds the 1914 Star, General Service and Victory Medals.
14, Stanley Grove, Tottenham, N.17.   X18299.

PERKINS, G., Pte., Royal Fusiliers.

Volunteering in September 1914, he was sent to the Western Front on completion of his training. During his three years active service he took a prominent part in the battles of the Somme, Arras, Ypres and Cambrai, and in other severe fighting. In January 1919 he was demobilised, and holds the General Service and Victory Medals.
44, Greyhound Road, College Park, N.W.10.   X17600B.

PERKINS, G., Pte., R.A.S.C. (M.T.).

He joined in May 1916, and in the same year was drafted to France, where he served until 1919. During this time he was engaged in conveying troops and ammunition to the lines, and was present during engagements on the Somme, at Ypres, and in the Retreat and Advance of 1918. He was demobilised in September 1919, and holds the General Service and Victory Medals.
49, Woodchester Street, Paddington, W.2.   X20656.

PERKINS, J., Pte., 13th Royal Fusiliers.

Volunteering in September 1914, he was sent to France in the following year. During his service on the Western Front he saw much heavy fighting until 1917, when he contracted a serious illness, and was invalided home. He was discharged as medically unfit for further service in October 1917, and holds the 1914-15 Star and the General Service and Victory Medals.
74, Church Road, Tottenham, N.17.   X18336.

PERKINS, J., Rifleman, King's Royal Rifle Corps.

Volunteering in August 1914, he was later in the same year sent to the Eastern Front. While in this seat of war he took part in important operations on the Salonika Front, and was wounded in action. He also contracted malaria, and in 1917 was invalided home. In 1920 he was still serving, and holds the 1914-15 Star and the General Service and Victory Medals.
48, Cedars Road, Lower Edmonton, N.9.   14219.

PERKINS, J., Pte., Leicestershire Regiment.

He volunteered in 1914, and in the following year was sent to the Western Front, where, during his four years' service, he took a distinguished part in the battles of Ypres, the Somme and Arras. After the signing of the Armistice he joined the Army of Occupation and went to Germany. He was demobilised in June 1919, and holds the 1914-15 Star and the General Service and Victory Medals.
20, Clarendon Street, Paddington, W.2.   X20550.

PERKS, A., 1st Air Mechanic, Royal Air Force.

He volunteered in 1915, and in the following year was sent to Egypt. After a period of service in this seat of war he was drafted to Greece and carried out important duties which called for a high degree of technical skill. In 1919 he was demobilised, and holds the General Service and Victory Medals.
56, Somerset Road, Upper Edmonton, N.18.   16860A.

PERKS, C., Sapper, Royal Engineers.

He volunteered in September 1914, and during his service on the Western Front, to which he was sent in the following year, was wounded by the explosion of a mine in the Somme sector in 1916. In 1917 he was drafted to Mesopotamia, and thence to India, where he remained until his demobilisation in September 1919. He holds the 1914-15 Star and the General Service and Victory medals.
56, Somerset Road, Upper Edmonton, N.18.   16860A.

PERRETT, A., Trooper, Westmoreland and Cumberland Yeomanry.

He joined in August 1916, and after his training was engaged in important garrison duties in Ireland with his unit. He gave valuable services but, owing to defective eyesight, was not successful in obtaining his transfer to a fighting area before the signing of the Armistice. In January 1919 he was demobilised.
22, College Road, Willesden, N.W.10.   X18183A.

PERRIN, T., Driver, Royal Field Artillery.

He volunteered in July 1915, and was sent to the Western Front, where he saw much severe fighting on various sectors, and was for some time in hospital. He was later drafted to the Italian seat of war, and played a prominent part in important operations whilst there. In May 1919 he was demobilised, holding the General Service and Victory Medals.
15, Cambrai Street, Fulham, S.W.6.   X19881.

PEERING, A. C., Pte., 1st Welch Regiment.

Having served for a period of eight years previous to the war, he was mobilised from the Reserve immediately on the outbreak of hostilities, and was drafted to France, where he took part in much severe fighting. On June 25th, 1915, he died in hospital from wounds received in action, and was entitled to the 1914-15 Star and the General Service and Victory Medals.
64, Oxford Road, Lower Edmonton, N.9.   12962A.

PERRING, J., Pte., Royal Army Medical Corps.

He volunteered in March 1915, and in the following year was drafted to France, where he was engaged on important duties at a Base Hospital. In April 1916 he was discharged as medically unfit for further service, as the result of a severe illness. He holds the General Service and Victory Medals.
64, Oxford Road, Lower Edmonton, N.9.   12962B.

PERRY, A. E., Sergeant, Middlesex Regiment.

Being in the Army at the outbreak of war, he was sent in 1914 to France, where he took part in many engagements, including the Retreat from Mons and the battles of the Marne, the Somme, and Ypres, and was wounded. Whilst he was on board the "Cameronian," bound for Mesopotamia, his ship was torpedoed, but he was rescued by another vessel after having been adrift for several hours, and was shipwrecked again during his voyage. He holds the Mons Star, General Service, and Victory Medals, and was discharged in February 1919.
24, Letchford Gardens, College Road, Willesden, N.W.10.   X17545B / 17546

PERRY, A. R., Bombardier, R.G.A.

He volunteered in February 1915, and was later drafted to France. After taking part in important operations on the Western Front, he was sent to the Eastern Theatre of war. He saw much fighting in Salonika, Egypt, and Italy, and was for a time in hospital in Salonika with malaria. He was also stationed at Malta and in 1920 was still serving and holds the General Service and Victory Medals.
1, Kelmaine Road, Munster Road, S.W.6.   TX18858A.

PERRY, E., Pte., Essex Regiment.

He joined in February 1916, and served on the Western Front, where he took a prominent part in many engagements, including the Somme, Arras, Ypres, the Retreat and Advance of 1918, and was wounded. He holds the General Service and Victory Medals, and was demobilised in March 1919.
24, Letchford Gardens, Willesden, N.W.10.   X17545C / 17546

PERRY, E. F., Pte., Essex Regiment.
He joined in April 1916, and served for three years on the Western Front, taking part in the battles of Arras, Ypres, St. Quentin and Amiens. He was wounded three times, and in November 1919 was demobilised, holding the General Service and Victory Medals.
19, Ridgeley Road, Willesden, N.W.10. X18242.

PERRY, F., A.B., R.N., H.M.S. "Stonehenge."
He joined in 1917, and was engaged on board his ship with the Grand Fleet in important operations. He served in the Mediterranean and Baltic, and was present in Flensburg during the plebiscite. In 1920 he will still serving, and holds the General Service and Victory Medals.
89, Drayton Road, Harlesden, N.W.10. 15255.

PERRY, F., A.B., Mercantile Marine.
During the war he was engaged with his ship on work of vital importance in connection with the supply of oil to vessels of the Grand Fleet. He was also engaged on hazardous patrol duties in the North Sea, and holds the Mercantile Marine and the General Service and Victory Medals.
24, Letchford Gardens, Willesden, N.W.10. X$^{17545}_{17546}$A.

PERRY, F. E., Mechanic, Royal Air Force.
He volunteered in May 1915, and after his training was engaged on duties which called for a high degree of technical skill. He gave valuable services in Ireland and at other important stations, but was not successful in obtaining his transfer overseas before hostilities ceased. He was demobilised in March 1919.
21, Hannell Road, Munster Road, S.W.6. X18159.

PERRY, G., Pte., R.A.S.C. (M.T.).
He volunteered in August 1914, and served in France, where he took part in many engagements, including the Retreat from Mons and the battles of Ypres and the Somme and the Retreat and Advance of 1918. He was mentioned in despatches for conspicuous bravery in carrying gun cotton to the troops whilst under heavy fire. He holds the Mons Star and the General Service and Victory Medals, and was demobilised in January 1919.
24, Letchford Gardens, Willesden, N.W.10. X$^{17545}_{17546}$D.

PERRY, G. W., Pte., R.A.S.C. (M.T.).
Joining in 1916, he was engaged on important transport duties and ambulance work at various stations with his unit. He gave valuable services, but was not successful in obtaining his transfer overseas before the cessation of hostilities, and was demobilised in 1919.
97, Churchill Road, Cricklewood, N.W.2. 16995B.

PERRY, H. (M.M.), Lce.-Cpl., 12th Middlesex Regiment.
He volunteered in August 1914, and later in the same year was drafted to France. While on the Western Front he took a prominent part in the battles of the Somme and Arras, where he was wounded in May 1917. He was awarded the Military Medal for conspicuous bravery and devotion to duty at the taking of Thiepval in September 1916, and in addition holds the 1914-15 Star and the General Service and Victory Medals. He remained in France until his demobilisation in July 1919.
5, Kenninghall Road, Upper Edmonton, N.18. 16893.

PERRY, J., Sergeant, Norfolk Regiment.
He volunteered in August 1914, and was quickly drafted to the Western Front, where he took part in the Retreat from Mons and the battles of the Marne, the Aisne and Ypres. In 1915 he was sent to Egypt and later to Palestine, where he served in the advance with General Allenby's forces. He was demobilised in February 1919, and holds the Mons Star and the General Service and Victory Medals.
156, Portnall Road, Maida Hill, W.9. X19663.

PERRY, J. A., Sergeant, Middlesex Regiment.
He rejoined in August 1914, having previously served for seven years, and was sent to the Western Front, where, after taking part in several important engagements, including the Retreat from Mons, he was killed in action on October 30th, 1916. He was entitled to the Mons Star and the General Service and Victory Medals.
86, Dyson's Road, Upper Edmonton, N.18. T16841.

PERRY, J. P., Pte., Royal Fusiliers.
He volunteered in August 1914, was immediately sent to the Western Front, and took part in the Retreat from Mons and the battles of Ypres and the Somme, where he was taken prisoner, having been fired at and wounded for refusing to surrender. He had previously been wounded and gassed in action. Whilst in captivity he suffered many hardships, and after his release was in hospital for over 12 months and underwent an operation as a result of the wound he had sustained. He was demobilised in January 1919, and holds the Mons Star and the General Service and Victory Medals.
11, Headcorn Road, Tottenham, N.17. X18493A.

PERRY, P. H., Petty Officer, Royal Navy.
He was serving in 1914, and during the war was in H.M.S. "Warrior" with the Grand Fleet in the North Sea. He took a prominent part in many important naval operations, including the Battle of Jutland, and was also at Scapa Flow when the German Fleet was surrendered. In 1920 he was serving in the Black Sea on H.M.S. "Resolution" and has completed ten years' service in all. He holds the 1914 Star and the General Service and Victory Medals.
1, Kilmaine Road, Munster Road, S.W.6. TX18858B.

PERRY, S., Pte., Royal Fusiliers.
Volunteering in 1914, he was sent in the same year to the Western Front, where he played a conspicuous part in the fighting, and was killed in action on September 9th, 1915. He was entitled to the 1914 Star and the General Service and Victory Medals.
11, Headcorn Road, Tottenham, N.17. X18493B.

PERRY, T. J., Rifleman, King's Royal Rifle Corps.
He joined in 1916, and on completion of his training was drafted to France. After taking part in much heavy fighting on the Western Front, he was killed in action near Ypres on December 24th, 1917. He was entitled to the General Service and Victory Medals
24, Letchford Gardens, Willesden, N.W.10 X$^{17545}_{17546}$B

PERRY, W., Pte., Queen's (Royal West Surrey Regiment).
He joined in 1916, and was sent to the Western Front. After serving in several engagements, he was taken prisoner on March 21st, 1918, during the German offensive, and suffered ill-treatment at the hands of the enemy. On his release he was demobilised in September 1919, and holds the General Service and Victory Medals.
84, Carlyle Avenue, Willesden, N.W.10. 14449.

PERRYMAN, Pte., R.E. (Signal Section).
Volunteering in September 1914, he was drafted to France in the following August. While on the Western Front he carried out important signalling duties at the battles of the Somme, Arras, and Cambrai, and in heavy fighting during the Advance of 1918. He was demobilised in May 1919, and holds the 1914-15 Star and the General Service and Victory Medals.
1, North Avenue, Upper Edmonton, N.18. 15227.

PETCHEY, A., Pte., 1st Tank Corps.
Joining in February 1916, he was sent to France in the same year and took part in engagements at Arras, Cambrai, Bullecourt, Neuve Chapelle, the Marne, the Somme, and Grandcourt, and was wounded. He holds the General Service and Victory Medals, and was demobilised in February 1919.
87, Tubb's Road, Harlesden, N.W.10. 12878B.

PETCHEY, S. F., Pte., Middlesex Regiment.
He joined in May 1918, and after his training was sent to France, where he carried out important duties with the regimental transport during the concluding stages of the war. He was demobilised in 1919, and holds the General Service and Victory Medals.
87, Tubb's Road, Harlesden, N.W.10. 12878A.

PETCHEY, S. T., Sapper, Royal Engineers.
He volunteered in September 1914, and was sent to the Western Front, where he took part in the fighting at Ypres, Vimy Ridge, Loos and the Somme, and was wounded. He was discharged in 1916 owing to wounds as medically unfit for further service, and holds the 1914-15 Star and the General Service and Victory Medals.
87, Tubb's Road, Harlesden, N.W.10. 12878C.

PETERS, C., Pte., Royal Army Medical Corps.

Volunteering in August 1915, he was sent overseas in the following year. Whilst on the Western Front he carried out the important duties of a stretcher-bearer in many important engagements, and took part in the battles of the Somme, Arras, Vimy Ridge and Cambrai, and was gassed. He was demobilised in June 1919, and holds the General Service and Victory Medals.

8, Rainham Road, Kensal Rise, N.W.10.   X18660A.

PETERS, C. E. (M.M.), Sergt., East Surrey Regt.

Volunteering in September 1914, he was later in the year sent to the Western Front, where he took part in the battle of the Somme and in the Retreat and Advance of 1918. During his service he was wounded five times, and was awarded the Military Medal for conspicuous bravery and devotion to duty in the field. In February 1919 he was demobilised, and holds, in addition to the Military Medal, the 1914-15 Star and the General Service and Victory Medals.

303, Chapter Road, Cricklewood, N.W.2.   X17118.

PETERS, G. E., Pte., 7th The London Regiment.

He joined the Army in April 1917, and in the following July was drafted to the Western Front. After taking a conspicuous part in engagements at Arras, Ypres, Passchendaele, Poelcappelle, Albert, Villers-Bretonneux and Bray, he was wounded in the Advance in August 1918. Fourteen months later he was demobilised, and holds the General Service and Victory Medals.

29, Chesson Road, West Kensington, W.14.   TX17064.

PETERS, J., Pte., 9th Middlesex Regiment.

He volunteered in 1915, and was sent to the Eastern Front, where he took part in heavy fighting at the Dardanelles. On the evacuation of the Gallipoli Peninsula he was drafted to Egypt and served in the important operations in that theatre of war, but contracted malaria. He was in hospital for some time, and was eventually demobilised in 1919. He holds the 1914-15 Star and the General Service and Victory Medals.

42A, St. Mary's Road, Craven Park, N.W.10.   15121.

PETERS, S. J., Pte., 8th Middlesex Regiment.

He volunteered in April 1915, and was drafted to Salonika in the following December. During his service on the Balkan Front he took part in many important engagements and was in hospital three times with malaria. He holds the 1914-15 Star, and the General Service and Victory Medals, and was demobilised in April 1919.

113, Carlyle Avenue, Willesden, N.W.10.   13685.

PETERS, T. J., Pte., Royal Fusiliers.

He volunteered in August 1914, and in the following year was sent to the Western Front, where he took a conspicuous part in several engagements, including those at Loos, Albert, La Bassée, Vimy Ridge, and the Somme, and was three times wounded. In June 1919 he was demobilised, holding the 1914-15 Star and the General Service and Victory Medals, but rejoined for four years in March 1920 in the R.A.S.C. (M.T.) for service with the Army of Occupation.

8, Rainham Road, Kensal Rise, N.W.10.   X18660B.

PETERS, W. J., A.B., Royal Navy.

Volunteering in November 1915, he served in the North Sea, being engaged in mine-sweeping and submarine-chasing. He was in H.M.S. "Alyssum" when she was blown up and sunk off the Irish Coast in March 1917. He was demobilised in September 1919, and holds the General Service and Victory Medals.

13, Montague Street, Hammersmith, W.6.   16409.

PETT, A. A., Sapper, Royal Engineers.

He volunteered in August 1915, and in the same year was sent to the Balkan Front, where he served throughout the remainder of the war. He was largely employed in the Postal Section and during his service suffered frequently from malaria. In June 1919 he returned home and was demobilised, holding the 1914-15 Star and the General Service and Victory Medals.

90, Chippenham Road, Maida Hill, W.9.   TX20768.

PETT, C. J., Sergt., 1/25th London Regiment.

Volunteering in November 1914, he was quickly sent to India, where he played a prominent part in the fighting on the North-West Frontier. In 1919 he was sent home, and in December was demobilised, holding the General Service and Victory Medals.

45, Chaldon Road, Dawes Road, S.W.6.   X17650.

PETT, J. H., Lce.-Cpl., 12th Rifle Brigade.

He joined in 1916 and during his service on the Western Front took part with distinction in the battles of Arras, Ypres and Vimy Ridge. On March 23rd, 1918, in the German offensive, he was killed in the vicinity of Cambrai. He was entitled to the General Service and Victory Medals.

31, Earlsmead Road, College Park, N.W.10.   X17832.

PETTAFOR, O., Pte., Machine Gun Corps.

He joined in 1916, and in the same year was sent to France where he took a prominent part in the battle of the Somme and the Advance of 1918, and was wounded. He was demobilised in 1918, and holds the Victory and General Service Medals.

25, Tenterden Road, Tottenham, N.17.   X18278B.

PETTIGREW, T. C., Pte., 16th Middlesex Regt.

After volunteering in December 1915, he was drafted in the following year to the Western Front, where he served for nearly three years. Whilst overseas he took part in engagements at Ypres, Cambrai, Bullecourt, Arras and St. Quentin and the Advance of 1918, and was wounded three times. He holds the General Service and Victory Medals, and was demobilised in February 1919.

11, Guinness's Buildings, W.6.   14493.

PETTITT, A. J., Corporal., 1st Suffolk Regiment.

Having previously served for nearly fourteen years in the Army, he was mobilised on the outbreak of war and was quickly sent to France, where he took part in the Retreat from Mons and the battles of Ypres and Loos, and was wounded. Later he served in Egypt and Salonika, but returned to France in time to be present at the fighting at Kemmel Hill, Dickebusch and Cambrai during the Advance of 1918. After a total service of eighteen years, over four of which were in the Great War, he was discharged in January 1919, holding the Mons Star and the General Service and Victory Medals.

3, Shelley Road, Willesden, N.W.10.   13879.

PETTITT, D. (Miss), Special War Worker.

From the commencement of the war until after the cessation of hostilities, this lady gave splendid services at Messrs. Eley Brothers' Munition Works, where she was engaged on highly important duties.

33, Hartington Road, Tottenham, N.17.   X19139B.

PETTITT, H. H., Assistant Steward, H.M.S. "Merionethshire."

Volunteering in 1915, he was largely employed in conveying New Zealand troops to England, and gave valuable services. Whilst in the "Merionethshire" in 1918, his ship was torpedoed. He was still serving in 1920, and holds the 1914-15 Star and the General Service and Victory Medals.

17, Wingmore Road, Tottenham, N.17.   X17989.

PETTITT, T., Leading Aircraftsman, R.A.F.

He joined in February 1917, and in the same year was drafted to France, where he served for nearly two years. His duties, which required a high degree of technical skill, were connected with the repair of aeroplane engines. He holds the General Service and Victory Medals, and was still serving in 1920.

33, Hartington Road, Tottenham, N.17.   X19139A.

PETTITT, W. A., Pte., Queen's Own (Royal West Kent Regiment).

He joined in December 1916, and in the following June was sent to the Western Front, where he took part in the battles of Ypres, Cambrai, and Arras, and was wounded. Later he was sent to Cologne with the Army of Occupation. He holds the General Service and Victory Medals, and was demobilised in October 1919.

46, Charlton Road, Harlesden, N.W.10.   13387.

PETZING, A., A.B., Royal Navy.

Volunteering in 1915, he was engaged on guard duties in the Mediterranean Sea and the Indian and Pacific Oceans. He saw service in several vessels, among which was H.M.S. "Sapphire," and also suffered from malaria. He was demobilised in April 1919, holding the General Service and Victory Medals.

24, Mund Street, W. Kensington, W.14.   16913A.

PETZING, C. H. J., Pte., The Queen's (Royal West Surrey Regiment).

Joining in 1917, he was sent to the Western Front in the same year and was killed during the Retreat of 1918, having previously taken part in the battle of the Somme. He was entitled to the General Service and Victory Medals.

23, Ilex Road, Willesden, N.W.10.   16101.

PETZING, H., Lce.-Cpl., 12th Middlesex Regt.
Volunteering in August 1914, he was sent to France the following year, and took part in the battles of the Somme and Ypres. Later he was transferred to the Military Mounted Police, with which he served until his demobilisation in January 1918. He holds the 1914-15 Star and the General Service and Victory Medals.
24, Mund Street, W. Kensington. W.14.   16913B.

PEVERETT, F., Chief Petty Officer, Royal Navy.
He volunteered in August 1914, and served in H.M.S. "Cyclops" on patrol and convoy duties in the North Sea. Whilst in H.M.S. "Edinburgh Castle" he took part in the effort to catch German vessels before reaching Turkish waters, and was later sent to the East Coast of Africa. He was demobilised in February 1919, and holds the 1914-15 Star and the General Service and Victory Medals.
87, Chesson Road, West Kensington, W.14.   X17685.

PEYTON, G. H., Driver, Royal Field Artillery.
He volunteered in 1914, and served on the Western Front, taking a prominent part in engagements at Loos, Neuve Chapelle, Arras, Ypres, Vimy Ridge, St. Quentin, Bullecourt, Festubert, Cambrai and the Retreat and Advance of 1918. He holds the 1914-15 Star and the General Service and Victory Medals, and was demobilised in 1919.
36, Chesson Road, West Kensington, W.14.   X17237.

PEZET, A., Pte., 5th East Surrey Regiment.
Joining in June 1916, he completed his training, and was employed at various places with his unit. Owing to physical unfitness he was unable to secure his transfer overseas, but gave valuable services before he was discharged in October 1918, owing to his ill-health.
74, Sherbrooke Road, Fulham, S.W.6.   X18751.

PHAFF, C. E., Sapper, Royal Engineers.
Joining in 1917, he was sent to the Western Front, where he took part in the Retreat and Advance of 1918, and was later sent with the Army of Occupation to Germany. He holds the General Service and Victory Medals, and was demobilised in October 1919.
51, Ranelagh Road, Harlesden, N.W.10.   12558.

PHEBY, J. G., Sapper, Royal Engineers.
He joined in August 1915, and served on the Western Front, taking a conspicuous part in several engagements, including that at Arras. He holds the General Service and Victory Medals, and was demobilised in February 1919.
15, Kenneth Road, West Kensington, W.14.   TX17372.

PHELPS, E., Pte., 2nd Leicestershire Regiment.
Volunteering for service in September 1914, he was sent two years later to Mesopotamia, and later to Egypt. He served under General Allenby in the capture of Jerusalem and the advance through Palestine, and after the conclusion of the campaign was sent to England for demobilisation in May 1919. He holds the General Service and Victory Medals.
17, Burnthwaite Road, Walham Green, S.W.6.   X20083C.

PHILIP, E. (Mrs.), Special War Worker.
During the war this lady was engaged for three years at Park Royal Munition Factory inspecting small arms ammunition. Her duties required great skill, and were carried out to the entire satisfaction of her employers.
40, Winchelsea Road, Willesden, N.W.10.   13849A.

PHILIP, R. Pte., 14th London Regiment (London Scottish), and R.A.S.C.
He joined in 1917, and served in France. After taking part in several engagements on the Western Front, he was wounded near Ypres in August of the same year. Later he was transferred to the Royal Army Service Corps, in which he remained until his demobilisation in 1919. He holds the General Service and Victory Medals.
40, Winchelsea Road, Willesden, N.W.10.   13849B.

PHILLIPS, A., Driver, Royal Field Artillery.
He volunteered in August 1914, and was sent to the Western Front, where he was in action in the Retreat from Mons and at Loos. In 1915 he was drafted to Mesopotamia, and served for a year. He was then re-drafted to France, where he took part in the Advance during August 1918, and was gassed. He was demobilised in January 1919, after over 4½ years' service, and holds the Mons Star and the General Service and Victory Medals.
32, Waldo Road, Willesden, N.W.10.   X17566A.

PHILLIPS, A., Pte., 13th The London Regiment (Kensingtons).
He volunteered in August 1915, and in the same year was sent to France, where he took part in many important engagements, and was wounded three times. After the signing of the Armistice, he went to Germany with the Army of Occupation. He was still serving in 1920, and holds the 1914-15 Star, and the General Service and Victory Medals.
1, St. Peter's Terrace, Kilmaine Road,
Munster Road, S.W.6.   X18866A.

PHILLIPS, A. E., Corporal, Duke of Cornwall's Light Infantry.
He volunteered in August 1914, and was drafted to the Western Front, where he took part in many important engagements, including the actions on the Somme, and at Arras, Ypres, Armentières, and in the Advance of 1918 and was wounded twice. He was demobilised in 1919, holding the 1914-15 Star, and the General Service and Victory Medals.
13, Lurgan Avenue, Hammersmith, W.6.   13450A.

PHILLIPS, A. E., Special War Worker.
During the war he was employed on work of national importance in making military equipment, at Messrs. Prussia's factory. He rendered valuable services, and gave great satisfaction by his care and skill.
13, Lurgan Avenue, Hammersmith, W.6.   13450B.

PHILLIPS, A. G., Pte., 23rd Middlesex Regiment.
He volunteered in 1915, was sent to the Western Front in the same year, and took part in the fighting on the Somme and at Arras, Armentières, Ypres, Bullecourt, Vimy Ridge, St. Quentin, Cambrai and the Advance in 1918. He was also for a time in Italy. In 1920 he was still serving, and holds the 1914-15 Star and the General Service and Victory Medals.
67, Ongar Road, Lillie Road, S.W.6.   X19624.

PHILLIPS, A. W., Pte., Middlesex Regiment, East Surrey Regiment.
He joined in February 1916, and after his training was sent to France, where he took part in many engagements on the Ypres Front, and was wounded twice. He was afterwards drafted to Italy, and was wounded in action on the Piave. In consequence of his wounds he was discharged in July 1918 as unfit for further service, and holds the General Service and Victory Medals.
32, Waldo Road, College Park, N.W.10.   X17567.

PHILLIPS, C., Pte., Royal Army Service Corps.
He volunteered in December 1915, and served in Salonika from that year until 1919, when he was sent to Constantinople. He rendered valuable service as a workshop storekeeper, and was demobilised in March 1920, holding the 1914-15 Star and the General Service and Victory Medals.
65, Cobbold Road, Church End, Willesden, N.W.10. 16074.

PHILLIPS, C. J., Pioneer, R.E. (R.O.D.).
He joined in June 1918, and in October of the same year was sent to Italy, where he was engaged on railway work, chiefly repairs. After much valuable service there he was demobilised in January 1920, after 15 months' service, holding the General Service and Victory Medals.
32, Waldo Road, Willesden, N.W.10.   X17566B.

PHILLIPS, F., Rifleman, 17th King's Royal Rifle Corps.
He volunteered in June 1915, and after his training was drafted in 1916 to the Western Front, where he took part in the battles of the Somme, Loos, Arras and Ypres, and other important engagements until the close of hostilities. He was demobilised in March 1919, holding the General Service and Victory Medals.
23, Lyndhurst Road, Upper Edmonton, N.18.   15509.

PHILLIPS, F. G., Sapper, Royal Engineers.
He volunteered in 1915, was sent to the Western Front in the following year, and took part in many important engagements, including those of Arras, Cambrai, the Somme, and Delville Wood. During his three years' service in France he was engaged chiefly on bridge building and other engineering work. He was demobilised in April 1919, and holds the General Service and Victory Medals.
49, Earlsmead Road, College Park, N.W.10.   X17842.

PHILLIPS, F. S., Pte., 2nd Norfolk Regiment.
He volunteered in December 1915, and on the completion of his training was drafted to Mesopotamia, where he saw much service and took part in many important engagements. He was demobilised in September 1919, and holds the General Service and Victory Medals.
16, Enbrook Street, Queen's Park, W.10.   X19318.

PHILLIPS, F. T., Gunner, Royal Field Artillery.
He volunteered in 1915, and was sent to France, where he took part in many engagements, including the actions on the Somme, and was badly gassed. He afterwards saw valuable service in Italy, until he was demobilised in 1919. He holds the 1914-15 Star and the General Service and Victory Medals.
3, Bramber Road, West Kensington, W.14.   16279.

PHILLIPS, G. F., Gunner, Royal Field Artillery.
He volunteered in October 1914, and in November 1915 was sent to the Western Front, where he took part in many engagements, including those at the Somme and near Amiens. Later he was transferred to the Eastern theatre of war, and fought on the Doiran Front. He was demobilised in March 1919, and holds the 1914-15 Star and the General Service and Victory Medals.
54, Bravington Road, Maida Hill, W.9.   X19196.

PHILLIPS, H.G., Gunner, Royal Garrison Artillery.
He joined in June 1916, and on the completion of his training was retained with his unit on most important duties. He gave valuable services, but was not successful in obtaining his transfer overseas before hostilities ceased. He was demobilised in February 1920.
14, Folkstone Road, Upper Edmonton, N.18.   15364.

PHILLIPS, W., Pte., 2nd Middlesex Regiment.
He joined in December 1916, and after the completion of his training was drafted to France, where he took part in many engagements, and remained until hostilities ceased. During his service he was wounded. He was demobilised in November 1919, holding the General Service and Victory Medals.
1, St. Peter's Terrace, Kilmaine Road,
Munster Road, S.W.6.   X18866B.

PHILLIPS, W., Sapper, Royal Engineers.
He volunteered in August 1914, and was speedily drafted to the Western Front, where he remained until hostilities ceased. He rendered valuable services throughout and took part in numerous important engagements, including those of Loos, Ypres and the Somme. He was demobilised in November 1918, and holds the 1914-15 Star and the General Service and Victory Medals.
72, Beaconsfield Road, Lower Edmonton, N.9.   14568.

PHILLPOT, C., Pte., Middlesex Regiment.
He volunteered in October 1915, and after completing his training served in France, where he took part in many engagements, including the Somme and Ypres, and was wounded. He holds the General Service and Victory Medals, and was demobilised in April 1919.
7, Gloucester Road, Upper Edmonton, N.18.   X17273.

PHILP, F. L., Pte., 16th Royal Fusiliers.
He joined in June 1916, and on the completion of his training was sent to France, where he took part in many important engagements until he was killed in action near Oppy Wood on April 30th, 1917. He was entitled to the General Service and Victory Medals.
8, Buckingham Road, Harlesden, N.W.10.   12522.

PHILPOT, H. J., Rifleman, 15th The London Regiment (Civil Service Rifles).
He volunteered in November 1915, and served on the Western Front, in Salonika and Egypt. He took part in many engagements with General Allenby's forces in Palestine, and also in the Retreat and Advance of 1918. In February 1919 he was demobilised, holding the 1914-15 Star and the General Service and Victory Medals.
29, Drayton Road, Harlesden, N.W.10.   14991.

PHILPOT, R. A., Pte., Essex Regiment and Gloucestershire Regiment.
He volunteered in January 1916, proceeded to the Western Front in the following June, and took part in the battles of the Somme, Cambrai, Arras, Bapaume and Albert, and was wounded. In 1917 he went to Italy and served there until the war ended. He was demobilised in October 1919, holding the General Service and Victory Medals.
5, Colin Road, Duddin Hill, N.W.10.   16292.

PHIPPS, H. R., Pte., Royal Army Service Corps.
He volunteered in January 1915, and in February was sent to France, where he was engaged on special duties with the M.T. Supply Section during the fighting at Béthune, the Somme and other engagements. He was demobilised in May 1919, and holds the 1914-15 Star and the General Service and Victory Medals.
102, Felix Road, West Ealing, W.13.   11020.

PIBWORTH, A. S., Gunner, Royal Field Artillery.
He volunteered in August 1914, and was immediately sent to the Western Front, where he took part in the fighting of the Aisne, the Marne and Ypres. In April 1915 he was discharged as medically unfit for further service through deafness caused by gun-fire. In October 1919 he rejoined and served until his demobilisation in January 1920. He holds the 1914-15 Star and the General Service and Victory Medals.
2, Hartopp Avenue, Dawes Road, S.W.6.   X17738.

PICKERING, W. H., Pte., Middlesex Regiment.
He volunteered in June 1915, and in the same year was sent to France, where he served until the close of the war and took part in many engagements, especially those on the Somme front. During his service overseas he suffered from shell shock. He holds the 1914-15 Star and the General Service and Victory Medals, and was demobilised in February 1919.
13, Heckfield Place, Fulham Road, S.W.6.   X20245.

PICKETT, F. W., Pte., 18th Middlesex Regiment.
He volunteered in April 1915, and went to the Western Front in November of the same year. He took part in many important engagements, including those of the Somme and La Bassée, and was severely wounded at Ypres in September 1917. He was unfit for further service in consequence of his wounds, and was discharged in July 1918 holding the 1914-15 Star and the General Service and Victory Medals.
24, Oldfield Road, Willesden, N.W.10.   15749.

PIDGEON, T., Pte., Middlesex Regiment.
He joined in August 1916, and after his training did valuable service with his unit. Owing to medical unfitness he was not successful in securing his transfer to the fighting areas, and was discharged in July 1917.
18, Moselle Street, Tottenham, N.17.   X18370.

PIDGEON, W., Stoker, R.N., H.M.S. " Cunico."
He volunteered in January 1916, and until the cessation of hostilities rendered valuable service with the Grand Fleet in the North Sea and other waters. He was demobilised in January 1919, and holds the General Service and Victory Medals.
83, Wakefield Street, Upper Edmonton, N.18.   16755

PIGHTLING, E. W., Pte., Royal Fusiliers.
He volunteered in February 1915, and on completing his training was drafted in the same year to the Western Front, where he was in action on many sectors, and remained until hostilities ceased. He was demobilised in 1919, and holds the 1914-15 Star and the General Service and Victory Medals.
37, Monmouth Road, Lower Edmonton, N.9.   13026.

PIKE, A. (M.M.), Sapper, Royal Engineers.
He volunteered in April 1915, and saw service in the same year in the Dardanelles and Mesopotamia. In 1917 he was drafted to France, and was wounded at Ypres, at Cambrai, and a third time in the Advance of 1918. He was awarded the Military Medal for conspicuous bravery in the field, and holds in addition the 1914-15 Star and the General Service and Victory Medals. In 1920 he was still serving.
28, Stanley Road, King's Road, S.W.6.   X19799.

PIKE, D. V., Lce.-Cpl., 51st Bedfordshire Regt.
He joined in July 1918, and rendered valuable service with his unit, but was not successful in securing his transfer overseas before the cessation of hostilities. After the Armistice, however, he was drafted to Germany in the Army of Occupation, and was demobilised in January 1920.
33, Felixstowe Road, Lower Edmonton, N.9.   X17757.

PIKE, W. T., Rifleman, Royal Irish Rifles.
He joined in April 1916, and at the close of his training in the same year was drafted to the Western Front. He took part in many important engagements, was severely wounded at Cambrai in 1918, and was in consequence discharged in August of that year as unfit for further service. He holds the General Service and Victory Medals.
83, Winchester Road, Lower Edmonton, N.9.   14750.

PIKETT, A., Sapper, Royal Engineers.
He volunteered in April 1915, and from that year until 1917 rendered valuable service on the Western Front, where he was wounded at Givenchy in September 1916. He was afterwards drafted to Italy, and remained there until hostilities ceased. He was demobilised in March 1919, holding the 1914-15 Star and the General Service and Victory Medals.
24, Oxford Road, Lower Edmonton, N.9.   13123A.

PINNELL, F. G., Pte., The Queen's (Royal West Surrey Regiment).
He joined in April 1917, and later in the same year was drafted to France, where he took part in many engagements, including Loos and Cambrai, and was wounded. He also acted for a period as a stretcher-bearer. He was demobilised in October 1919, holding the General Service and Victory Medals.
72, Cobbold Road, Church End, N.W.10. 16075C.

PINNELL, S. C., Pte., 9th Middlesex Regiment.
He volunteered in August 1914, and rendered valuable service with his unit, but owing to ill-health was unsuccessful in securing his transfer overseas. He was discharged in May 1915 as medically unfit for further military duty.
72, Cobbold Road, Church End, N.W.10. 16075A.

PINNELL, S. C., Pte., 9th Middlesex Regiment.
He volunteered in December 1914, and at the conclusion of his training was drafted to the Western Front in 1915. He rendered valuable service there until 1919, and was frequently engaged in convoying German prisoners to the Base. He was demobilised in April 1919, holding the 1914-15 Star, and the General Service and Victory Medals.
72, Cobbold Road, Church End, N.W.10. 16075B.

PINNOCK, H., Gunner, Royal Field Artillery.
He volunteered in July 1915, and in the same year was sent to France, where he fought in numerous engagements, including those at Ypres, Arras and Cambrai. He was twice wounded and gassed, and during the battle of the Somme was buried by a shell explosion. Later he went to Germany with the Army of Occupation. He returned to England and was demobilised in May 1919, holding the 1914-15 Star, and the General Service and Victory Medals.
40, Clarendon Street, Paddington, W.2. X20529.

PIPER, A. F., Sergeant, 12th The London Regiment (Rangers).
He volunteered in August 1914, and was shortly afterwards drafted to the Western Front. During his service in this theatre of war he took part in many important engagements, including the Retreat from Mons and the battles of Ypres and Neuve Chapelle, and was wounded four times. He holds the Mons Star and the General Service and Victory Medals, and was demobilised in March 1919.
49, Greyhound Road, Hammersmith, W.6. 15017.

PIPER, B. F. J., Gunner, Royal Garrison Artillery.
He volunteered in December 1915, and at the conclusion of his training was drafted overseas. He took part in many important engagements on many sectors of the Western Front, where he remained until after the cessation of hostilities. He was demobilised in May 1919, and holds the General Service and Victory Medals.
22, Colehill Lane, Fulham, S.W.6. X18911B.

PIPER, H. J., Staff Q.M.S., Royal Army Pay Corps.
He was serving at the outbreak of the war and was drafted to the Western Front, where he remained for three years. While in this theatre of operations he was engaged on important duties with his unit. He returned to England in 1917, and served at various stations. He holds the 1914-15 Star and the General Service and Victory Medals. In 1920 he was still serving.
13, Osborne Road, Cricklewood, N.W.2. X17405.

PIPER, P. E. G., Gunner, Royal Garrison Artillery.
He volunteered in August 1914, and after his training was drafted to German East Africa, where he remained for the whole period of his overseas service. He took part in many important engagements on this front, and suffered from malaria. He was invalided to hospital in London, and eventually demobilised in January 1919. He holds the 1914-15 Star and the General Service and Victory Medals.
22, Colehill Lane, Fulham, S.W.6. X18911A.

PIPER, W. F., Pte., Gloucestershire Regiment.
He volunteered in 1915, and in the same year was drafted to the Western Front, where he saw much heavy fighting. In 1916 he was seriously wounded in action on the Somme and in consequence was invalided home. The following year, after a protracted illness, he was discharged, and holds the 1914-15 Star and the General Service and Victory Medals.
3, Sotheron Road, King's Road, S.W.6. X19868.

PITCHER, W. A., Corpl., Royal Sussex Regt.
He joined in October 1916, and served on the Western Front during 1917 and 1918. He took part in several engagements, including the battles of the Somme and Cambrai, and was twice wounded. He was demobilised in June 1919, and holds the General Service and Victory Medals.
84A, St. Margaret's Road, Hanwell, W.7. 11060.

PITHER, F., A.B., Royal Navy.
He volunteered in 1916, and was posted to the "Giaki" when that vessel was taken over by the Admiralty. He was engaged on important duties in various waters until the cessation of hostilities. He holds the General Service and Victory and the Mercantile Marine Medals, and in 1920 was still serving.
5, Hilmer Street, West Kensington, W.14. 15921.

PITHER, J., Pte., Loyal North Lancashire Regt.
He joined in December 1916, and in the following year proceeded to France, where he took part in several important engagements, and was wounded at Passchendaele. After considerable hospital treatment he was discharged in February 1918 as medically unfit for further service. He holds the General Service and Victory Medals.
5, Hilmer Street, West Kensington, W.14. 15708.

PITHER, W. J., Leading Stoker, Royal Navy, H.M.S. "St. George."
He volunteered in August 1914, and served with H.M.S. "Intrepid" in the North Sea on mine-laying duties. Afterwards he was on H.M.S. "Magnolia" mine-sweeping in the Mediterranean, and later on H.M.S. "Mimosa" on patrol and convoy duties. He holds the 1914-15 Star and the General Service and Victory Medals, and was demobilised in August 1919.
44, Burnthwaite Road, Walham Green, S.W.6. X20207.

PITMAN, A.W., Driver, Royal Army Service Corps.
He volunteered in September 1915, and after his training served at various stations on important duties until 1917, when he was drafted to the Western Front. He was engaged on transport work in many sectors of this theatre of war until the Armistice. He was demobilised in September 1919, and holds the General Service and Victory Medals.
14, Church Road, Tottenham, N.17. X18343.

PITT, H. W., Sapper, Royal Engineers.
He joined in June 1916, and after his training rendered much valuable service on the Western Front, where he was severely wounded in action at Vimy Ridge. He was in consequence discharged in August 1917 as medically unfit for further service, and holds the General Service and Victory Medals.
111, Sherbrooke Road, Fulham, S.W.6. X18618.

PITT, M., Rifleman, King's Royal Rifle Corps and 17th London Regiment (Rifles).
He joined in November 1917, and was drafted to the Western Front, where he took part in many engagements, and was badly wounded. After being for some time in hospitals in France and England he was discharged, and was demobilised in February 1919, holding the General Service and Victory Medals.
5, Chancellor's Road, Hammersmith, W.6. 12814.

PITFIELD, W., Pte., 7th Middlesex Regiment.
He volunteered in November 1915, and served from 1917 to 1919 in France, where he took part in many engagements, including the battles of Ypres, Arras, Festubert and the Somme. He holds the General Service and Victory Medals, and was demobilised in February 1919.
89, Sandringham Road, Cricklewood, N.W.2. X17134.

PITT, W. O., Leading Seaman, Royal Navy, H.M.S. "Tempest."
He volunteered in August 1914, and served with his ship in the North Sea, where he took part in the sinking of a German destroyer in October 1914, and later was in action off Zeebrugge. He holds the 1914-15 Star and the General Service and Victory Medals, and was demobilised in March 1919.
24, Hannell Road, Munster Road, S.W.6. X17865.

PITTS, E. (Mrs.), Special War Worker.
From February 1915 until after the Armistice this lady was engaged on work of national importance at the Park Royal Munition Factory, Willesden, in connection with the manufacture of shells and cartridges. She was highly commended for her valuable services.
49, Denbigh Road, Willesden, N.W.10. 15089A.

PITTS, H. J., Gunner, Royal Field Artillery.
He volunteered in October 1915, and after two years' active service in Mesopotamia, where he took part in many engagements, was drafted to India and remained for six months. He was demobilised in October 1919, and holds the General Service and Victory Medals.
7, Willows Terrace, Rucklidge Avenue, Harlesden, N.W.10. 13503.

PITTS, W. R., Special War Worker.
During the war this worker was engaged on work of
national importance with Messrs. Willetts, of Ruislip, in
connection with the construction of hangers for aeroplanes
and buildings for stores and barracks. He performed
his various duties to the complete satisfaction of his
employers.
49, Denbigh Road, Willesden, N.W.10.   15089B.

PITTUCK, A. E., Gunner, Royal Garrison Artillery.
He volunteered in August 1914, and after his training was
drafted to France, where he took part in many important
engagements, including the battles of the Somme, Ypres,
Neuve Chapelle, Arras, Armentieres, St. Quentin and
Ploegsteert. He was invalided home owing to ill-health,
and subsequently demobilised in March 1919, holding the
General Service and Victory Medals.
24, Averill Street, Hammersmith, W.6.   13988.

**PIZZIE, K. J., Lance-Corporal, 2nd Royal
Berkshire Regiment.**
He volunteered in August 1914, and was at once sent to
France, where he took part in the battles of Mons, Loos,
Arras, Ypres, the Somme, and many others. He was
wounded three times—at Ypres in August 1915, at Delville
Wood in September 1916, and at the second battle of
Ypres. He was demobilised in August 1919, holding
the Mons Star and the General Service and Victory Medals.
19, Love Lane, Tottenham, N.17.   X18293.

PIZZIE, P., Pte., East Yorkshire Regiment.
He was in the Reserve, and being mobilised at the outbreak of hostilities proceeded to the Western Front,
where he took part in the Retreat from Mons and other
important engagements, and was wounded. He holds
the Mons Star, General Service and Victory Medals, and
was demobilised in March 1919.
45, Love Lane, Tottenham, N.17.   X18529.

PLANT, H. E., Sergeant, Royal Marines.
He was called up from the Reserve on the outbreak of
war, having previously served for seventeen years, and
was engaged in his ship off the East and West Coasts of
Africa, and in the North Sea on important duties until
the cessation of hostilities. He was discharged in January
1919, holding the 1914-15 Star and the General Service
and Victory Medals.
71, Manor Park Road, Harlesden, N.W.10.   13223.

PLATT, W. G., Sergt., Royal West Kent Regt.
He was already serving at the outbreak of war, and was
drafted to Mesopotamia, where he was actively engaged in
much of the severe fighting on this front, and suffered from
malaria. He was later sent to India, and was employed
on important duties there until his return to England for
his discharge in April 1920. He holds the 1914-15 Star
and the General Service and Victory Medals.
29, Barry Road, Stonebridge Park, N.W.10.   14937A.

PLATTEN, C., Lce.-Corpl., Royal Defence Corps.
Being unfitted for service with the colours, he joined the
R.D.C. in October 1914, and after his training served at
various stations on important guard duties, and was also
engaged for over two years with an anti-aircraft gun
battery. He was demobilised in January 1919, after giving
valuable services.
16, College Road, Willesden, N.W.10.   X18005.

**PLAW, H. W., Sergt., 2nd Middlesex Regiment,
transf. 4/5 Welch Regiment.**
He volunteered in June 1915, and was sent to the Eastern
Front in the following month, where he served for nearly
four years. He took part in the Dardanelles operations,
in the Canal Defence, and in the campaigns in Palestine and
Egypt. He was demobilised in April 1919, and holds the
1914-15 Star and the General Service and Victory Medals.
4A, Allington Road, North Kensington, W.10.   X18609.

PLAYER, E. C., Pte., Royal Army Service Corps.
He joined in February 1917, and was drafted to the East.
He saw much service on the Bulgarian Front and at
Salonika, and was employed on transport work to and from
the lines and other special duties. He rendered much
valuable service, and was demobilised in June 1919,
holding the General Service and Victory Medals.
56, Litchfield Gardens, Willesden, N.W.10.   X17434.

PLAYLE, W. H., Corpl. (Shoeing Smith), R.A.S.C.
He volunteered in November 1914, and after his training
was drafted to the Western Front, where he was engaged
on important duties in various sectors of this theatre of
war. He returned to England after the Armistice, and was
demobilised in April 1919, holding the 1914-15 Star and the
General Service and Victory Medals.
74, Adeney Road, Hammersmith, W.6.   14662.

PLEDGER, C. E., Rifleman, Rifle Brigade.
He volunteered in January 1915, and was sent overseas
the same year. During his service on the Western Front,
he was in action at Loos where he was wounded, Passchendaele, and Cambrai, and was taken prisoner. He was
released from captivity after the Armistice, and returned
to England for his demobilisation in March 1919. He
holds the 1914-15 Star and the General Service and Victory
Medals.
34, Charlton Road, Harlesden, N.W.10.   13111.

PLUME, G. T., Air Mechanic, Royal Air Force.
He joined in December 1916, and after his training served
at various stations on important duties as a cook with
his unit. He gave valuable services, but was not successful
in obtaining his transfer overseas before the cessation of
hostilities. He was demobilised in February 1919.
7, Ray's Road, Upper Edmonton, N.18.   15353.

PLUMERIDGE, A. M. (Mrs.), Special War Worker.
This lady was engaged throughout the war on work of
national importance, making tents, marquees, haversacks
gas-bags and other articles of Army equipment at Messrs.
Waring & Gillow's Factory, The White City. She gave
valuable services throughout, which were highly appreciated.
25A, Guinness's Buildings,
Fulham Palace Road, Hammersmith, W.6.   14475A.

**PLUMERIDGE, C. F., Corporal, 11th, 13th and
10th Hussars.**
He volunteered in August 1914, and during his long service
on the Western Front took part in the battles of the Somme,
Neuve Chapelle, Armentieres, Amiens, Ypres and Vimy
Ridge. He was severely gassed twice, wounded at Arras
and Albert, and buried alive through a shell explosion at
Guillemont. He was discharged in February 1919, holding
the 1914-15 Star and the General Service and Victory
Medals.
25A, Guinness's Buildings,
Fulham Palace Road, Hammersmith, W.6.   14475B.

PLUMMER, S. H., Sapper, Royal Engineers.
He joined in 1917, and after his training served at various
stations on important duties with his unit. He gave
valuable services, but was not successful in obtaining his
transfer overseas before the cessation of hostilities, and
was demobilised in 1919.
45, Bronsart Road, Munster Road, S.W.6.   X19007.

PLUMMER, W., Mechanic, R.A.F. & Tank Corps.
He volunteered in October 1915, and was drafted to France
in the following year. He took part in many battles,
including Arras, Ypres, Croiselles, Bapaume, Loos, Lens,
Albert, Malincourt and Grandcourt, and was wounded
and gassed. He was demobilised in February 1919, holding the General Service and Victory Medals.
74, Brownlow Road, Willesden, N.W.10.   14717.

PLUMRIDGE, A. D. (Mrs.), Special War Worker.
From the beginning of the war until the cessation of
hostilities this lady was engaged on work of national
importance at Hayes and Park Royal Munition Factories
in connection with shell-filling. She gave valuable services
and was commended for her good work.
34, Furness Road, Harlesden, N.W.10.   13097A.

PLUMRIDGE, J. (Mrs.), Special War Worker.
This lady was engaged for two years on work of great
importance in the shell-making departments at Ponders
End Factory, and afterwards was employed in shell filling
at the Banbury National Filling Factory. Her services
in this responsible work were of the greatest value.
41, Chalgrove Road, Tottenham, N.17.   X18975.

POCOCK, B., A.B., Royal Navy.
He volunteered in August 1914, and after his training
served in various ships with the Grand Fleet in the North
Sea, on duties of an important nature, until after the
cessation of hostilities. In 1920 he was still serving, and
holds the General Service and Victory Medals.
5, Beamish Road, Lower Edmonton, N.9.   13936.

POCOCK, C., Pte., Royal Fusiliers.
He volunteered in August 1914, and was drafted to the
Dardanelles the following year. He was actively engaged
in much of the severe fighting on the Peninsula and was
wounded. Upon his recovery he was sent to German
East Africa and took part in many engagements in this
theatre of war. He was demobilised in 1919, holding the
1914-15 Star and the General Service and Victory Medals.
5, Beamish Road, Lower Edmonton, N.9.   13935.

POCOCK, T., Pte., Royal Army Medical Corps.

He volunteered in October 1915, and after his training served at a large military hospital on important duties. Owing to ill-health he was not successful in obtaining his transfer overseas, and he was discharged as medically unfit for further service in October 1916.
64, Burn's Road, Harlesden, N.W.10. 13464.

POCOCK, W. T., Pte., Royal Army Medical Corps.

He joined in 1917, and in the course of his service in the Army Medical Corps was engaged as orderly at various large hospitals. He rendered much valuable service, but was not successful in securing his transfer overseas before the close of hostilities. He was demobilised in August 1919.
4, Kennet Road, Maida Hill, W.9. X19377.

POCKETT, A. W., Gunner, Royal Field Artillery.

He joined in December 1916, and after his training was engaged on important duties with his unit at various stations. He rendered valuable services, but owing to medical unfitness was unable to secure his transfer overseas to a fighting area. He was demobilised in November 1919.
62, Hartington Road, Tottenham, N.17. X19106.

POLDEN, F. H., Rifleman, 16th Rifle Brigade.

He joined in November 1916, and served on the Western Front. He took part in the battles of the Somme, Ypres, St. Quentin, Bullecourt, Monchy, Cambrai and many others, and was three times wounded in action. He was discharged in February 1919, holding the General Service and Victory Medals.
41, Crefeld Road, Hammersmith, W.6. 14486.

POLE, T. H., Pte., Royal Army Service Corps.

He volunteered in January 1915, and in the same year was drafted to Salonika, where he served on the Struma and Doiran Fronts in many engagements, and contracted malaria. He was later sent to North Russia, and employed on special duties until his return to England for demobilisation in June 1919. He holds the 1914-15 Star and the General Service and Victory Medals.
28, Meyrick Road, Willesden, N.W.10. 16342.

POLLARD, A. E., Special War Worker.

Throughout the war this worker was engaged on duties of national importance at Messrs. Hooper's Aircraft Works, King's Road, Chelsea, in connection with machinery in the engineering department, and throughout gave valuable services, which were highly appreciated.
91, Mirabel Road, Fulham, S.W.6. 17856B.

POLLARD, A. G., Corpl., 7th London Regiment.

He joined in June 1915, and after his training served in France, taking part in many important engagements, including the battles of the Somme, Ypres and Cambrai. He holds the General Service and Victory Medals, and was demobilised in February 1919.
36, Church Road, Hammersmith, W.6. 11105A.

POLLARD, F. W., A.B., Royal Navy.

He was already serving at the outbreak of war, and was engaged on important duties in submarines in various waters until the cessation of hostilities. He holds the 1914-15 Star and the General Service and Victory Medals, and in 1920 was still serving.
36, Church Road, Hammersmith, W.6. 11105C.

POLLARD, S. H., A.B., Royal Navy.

He joined in July 1917, and from that date until the cessation of hostilities saw much sea service in the light battle cruisers. He was on board the "Conquest" when she was blown up by a mine, but he was saved. He was demobilised in February 1919, holding the General Service and Victory Medals.
36, Church Road, Hammersmith, W.6. 11105B.

POLLARD, W. E., Pte., 13th The London Regiment (Kensingtons).

He enlisted in August 1914, and during his service on the Western Front acted as a dispatch rider and took part in the fighting at Mons, Neuve Chapelle, Loos, Armentieres and in other engagements. He was killed in action at Aubers Ridge on May 9th, 1915, and was entitled to the 1914 Star and the General Service and Victory Medals.
91, Mirabel Road, Fulham, S.W.6. X17856A.

POLLARD, W. G. A., Pte., Labour Corps (259 A.E. Coy.).

He joined in June 1917, and three months later was sent to the Western Front, where he was engaged on special duties in connection with important operations in this theatre of war until October 1919, when he returned to England and was demobilised. He holds the General Service and Victory Medals.
123, Roundwood Road, Willesden, N.W.10. 16041.

POLTOCK, T. C., Pte., Labour Corps.

He joined in January 1917, and after his training at various stations in England was drafted to the Western Front in March 1918. Whilst overseas he was present at several engagements, and did good work with the Labour Corps, attached to the Royal Engineers. He returned to England in January 1919, and was demobilised, holding the General Service and Victory Medals.
65, Portnall Road, Maida Hill, W.9. X19516.

POLTON, O., Corporal, Royal Air Force.

He volunteered in July 1915, and at the close of his training served with the R.A.F. at various stations on responsible duties that required a high degree of technical skill. He rendered valuable services, but was unsuccessful in obtaining his transfer overseas before hostilities ceased. He was demobilised in March 1919.
89, Raynham Avenue, Upper Edmonton, N.18. 15826A.

POLTON, P., Pte., Seaforth Highlanders.

He volunteered in November 1915, and after serving for twelve months in England, was sent to France, where he took part in the fighting on the Somme and other fronts, and was wounded. He was demobilised in March 1919, and holds the General Service and Victory Medals.
89, Raynham Avenue, Upper Edmonton, N.18. 15826B.

POMFRETT, A., Special War Worker.

Throughout the war he rendered valuable services as canteen manager at Folkstone Camp, under the Army and Navy Canteen Board. His duties were discharged in a thorough manner throughout.
114, Bronsart Road, Munster Road, S.W.6. X19003A.

POMFRETT, H. A. (Mrs.), Special War Worker.

During the war she did valuable work as manageress of the Café at the Belgian Refugee Camp in Earl's Court, and discharged her duties with tact and efficiency.
114, Bronsart Road, Munster Road, S.W.6. X19003B.

POOLE, A., Corporal, Royal Sussex Regiment.

After rendering valuable service in the early part of the war at the Park Royal Munition Works, he volunteered for military duty in January 1915. On the conclusion of his training he was drafted to Ireland during the Sinn Fein Rising, and remained there until 1919, doing much valuable work as a Lewis-gun instructor. He was unsuccessful, however, in securing his transfer to the Western Front before the war closed, and was demobilised in February 1919.
257, Portnall Road, Maida Hill, W.9. X19768A.

POOLE, F. C., Stoker, Royal Navy.

He volunteered for duty in August 1914, and after his training was posted to the "Brunswick," which vessel served on important duties in the North Sea and off the coasts of Zanzibar, China, and America, until after the cessation of hostilities. He holds the 1914-15 Star and the General Service and Victory and the Mercantile Marine Medals, and was demobilised in 1918.
11, Portnall Road, Maida Hill, W.9. X19302.

POOLE, J. E., Gunner, Royal Field Artillery.

He volunteered in August 1914, and in the following year was drafted to the Western Front, where he took part in many important engagements up to the time of his death in action on the Somme on November 11th, 1917. He lies buried in the St. Julien British Cemetery near Ypres, and was entitled to the 1914-15 Star and the General Service and Victory Medals.
257, Portnall Road, Maida Hill, W.9. X19768B.

POOLE, S., Bombardier, Royal Field Artillery.

He volunteered in August 1915, and on the close of his training was drafted in 1916 to France, where he took part in numerous engagements and was gassed in the Arras sector in 1917, and at Cambrai in 1918. He returned from overseas in February 1919, and was then demobilised, holding the General Service and Victory Medals.
52, Maldon Road, Lower Edmonton, N.9. 15789.

POOLE, S. A., Pte., 4/2nd Royal Fusiliers.

He volunteered in May 1915, and after his training was drafted to Egypt. Later he was transferred to the Western Front, where he saw much service, and was wounded in action. He was discharged as medically unfit for further military duties in April 1917, and holds the General Service and Victory Medals.
14, Purcell Crescent, Fulham, S.W.6. 15166.

POOLE, W., Pte., Royal Army Service Corps.
He volunteered in May 1915, and in the same year was sent to France, where he was engaged on special duty conveying stores and ammunition to the firing line in various sectors. In 1916 he was transferred to Italy, and there served for nearly three years on various duties. He was demobilised in September 1919, holding the 1914-15 Star and the General Service and Victory Medals.
7, Shrewsbury Road, Stonebridge Park, N.W.10.   14133.

POOLE, W. J., Pte., Royal Army Medical Corps.
He volunteered in January 1916, and in the following year was sent to France where he served as a stretcher-bearer, and was present at the engagements on the Somme front and at Ypres, Loos and Béthune. He holds the General Service and Victory Medals and was demobilised in August 1919.
45, Broughton Road, Fulham, S.W.6.   X20920.

POOLEY, A., Air Mechanic, Royal Air Force.
He joined in August 1916, and at the close of his training was drafted to the Western Front, where he rendered valuable services with his unit in various fighting areas until the cessation of hostilities. He was demobilised in January 1919, holding the General Service and Victory Medals.
52, Lyndhurst Road, Upper Edmonton, N.18.   15506.

POOLEY, A. E., Corporal, The Queen's (Royal West Surrey Regiment).
He joined in 1917, and after his training served at various stations on important duties, but was not successful in securing his transfer overseas before the cessation of hostilities. After the Armistice he went to Germany with the Army of Occupation. He was demobilised in 1920.
24, May Street, West Kensington, W.14.   15894C.

POOLEY, G., Driver, Royal Field Artillery.
He volunteered in July 1915, and was drafted to France in the following February. He took part in many engagements, including the battles of Vermelles, Arras, Armentieres and Cambrai. Later he served with the Army of Occupation in Germany until demobilised in March 1919. He holds the General Service and Victory Medals.
39, Carlyle Avenue, Willesden, N.W.10.   14193.

POOLEY, S., Pte., 10th Hampshire Regiment.
He volunteered in January 1915, and after his training served on the Western Front, where he took part in many engagements, and was killed in action on the Somme Front on July 1st, 1917. He was entitled to the General Service and Victory Medals.
24, May Street, West Kensington, W.14.   15894B.

POOLEY, W. F., Pte., Royal Army Medical Corps.
He volunteered in 1915, and was drafted to Egypt, where he performed valuable ambulance and sanitary work until discharged through ill-health in 1917. He holds the General Service and Victory Medals.
24, May Street, West Kensington, W.14.   15894A.

POORE, H. J., Petty Officer, Royal Navy, Royal Naval Division (Armoured Cars).
He volunteered in November 1914, and was soon afterwards drafted to the Western Front, where he remained until the close of hostilities, and rendered valuable services in various battle areas. He was demobilised in February 1919, and holds the 1914-15 Star and the General Service and Victory Medals.
63, Musard Road, Hammersmith, W.6.   15331.

POPE, A., Pte. (Signaller), 4th Hussars.
He volunteered in February 1916, and after rendering valuable service at various stations, was engaged on the Western Front, from August 1918 until the close of the war, taking part in many engagements in the last Advance. He afterwards served with the Army of Occupation in Germany. He holds the General Service and Victory Medals, and was demobilised in March 1919.
79, Mayo Road, Willesden, N.W.10.   15469.

POPE, A. E., Driver, British Red Cross Society.
He joined in January 1915, and rendered valuable service for four years on the Western Front and in Salonika as an ambulance driver. He was demobilised in 1919, and holds the 1914-15 Star and the General Service and Victory Medals.
12, Kenmont Gardens, College Park, N.W.10.   X17577B.

POPE, E. (Miss), Special War Worker.
During 1917 and 1918 this lady was engaged on work of national importance in the wire-making department at the British Lucksford Co., Harlesden, and performed her important duties with great care and skill.
99, Barrets Green Road, Willesden, N.W.10.   13826B.

POPE, F. G., Pte., The Buffs (East Kent Regt.).
He was mobilised on the outbreak of hostilities, and was drafted to the Western Front, where he took part in the Retreat from Mons and in many of the engagements which followed, including those at Albert, Ypres and Arras. His service overseas lasted until 1919, when he returned to England and was demobilised, holding the Mons Star and the General Service and Victory Medals.
77, Southam Street, North Kensington, W.10.   X20782A.

POPE, S. G., Pte., 2nd Middlesex Regiment.
He joined in April 1916, and at the end of the same year was drafted to the Western Front, where he took part in many of the principal engagements up to the cessation of hostilities. His service overseas lasted until 1919, when returned to England and was demobilised in April, holding the General Service and Victory Medals.
77, Southam Street, North Kensington, W.10.   X20782B.

POPE, W. H. C., Corporal, 3rd King's Royal Rifle Corps.
He joined in 1916, and in the same year was drafted to the Western Front, where he took part in many important engagements up to the cessation of hostilities, and was wounded in action at Guillemont. He was still serving in 1920, and holds the General Service and Victory Medals.
21, Florence Road, Upper Edmonton, N.18.   16017.

POPLE, C. W. (Senior), Pte., Durham Light Inf.
He volunteered for duty in August 1915, and in the same year was drafted to Salonika, where he saw much service for three and a half years, and suffered from malaria. He was demobilised in February 1919, holding the 1914-15 Star and the General Service and Victory Medals.
14, Walham Avenue, Fulham Road, S.W.6.   X20233A.

POPLE, C. W. (Junior), Corporal, 17th Middlesex Regiment.
He volunteered at the outbreak of war and, being quickly drafted to France, took part in the Retreat from Mons. He also served at Loos, where he was wounded and taken prisoner in 1915. He was released after three years' captivity, and was demobilised in January 1919, holding the Mons Star and the General Service and Victory Medals.
14, Walham Avenue, Fulham Road, S.W.6.   X20233B.

POPLE, H. J., Pte., The Queen's (Royal West Surrey Regiment).
He joined in July 1916, and in the same year went to Egypt and Palestine, where he took part in many engagements. He was killed in action on December 23rd, 1917, and was buried in a military cemetery in Palestine. He was entitled to the General Service and Victory Medals.
14, Walham Avenue, Fulham Road, S.W.6.   X20233C.

PORRETT, W. E. J., Pte., 7th London Regiment.
He volunteered in July 1915, and during his two years service on the Western Front took part in the engagements of Ypres, Arras, Messines, and the Somme. In April 1918 he was gassed at Cambrai, and after receiving treatment in the 26th General Hospital, was invalided home. He was discharged in September 1918 as medically unfit for further service, and holds the General Service and Victory Medals.
33, Ancill Street, Hammersmith, W.6.   13745.

PORTER, B. (Miss), Special War Worker.
During the war this lady held a responsible post at Park Royal Munition Factory, where she was engaged on very dangerous and important work, filling shells and fuses in the T.N.T. shop. She also worked in the explosive magazine. Throughout she proved herself efficient in the duties she had undertaken.
53, Orbain Road, Fulham, S.W.6.   X18260B.

PORTER, E. W., Corporal, Royal Engineers.
He joined in 1916, and on the conclusion of his training went to the Western Front, where he took part in numerous important engagements, including those of Ypres, Arras, Armentieres, Vimy Ridge and Cambrai. He was demobilised in 1919, and holds the General Service and Victory Medals.
5, Eustace Road, Walham Green, S.W.6.   X19333.

PORTER, F. E., Gunner, Royal Field Artillery.
Volunteering in May 1915, he was drafted later in that year to the Western Front, where he took an active part in many important engagements in various battle areas. Owing to exposure he suffered from ill-health, and was for some time in hospital overseas. He was demobilised in May 1919, holding the 1914-15 Star and the General Service and Victory Medals.
39, Horder Road, Munster Road, S.W.6.   TX19024.

PORTER, J., Rifleman, 17th London Regiment.
He volunteered in January 1915, and in 1917 was sent to the Western Front. After three months' active service abroad, he was invalided home suffering from shell-shock in October 1917, and in the same month was discharged as medically unfit for further duty. He holds the General Service and Victory Medals.
1, Oldfield Road, Willesden, N.W.10.   15760.

PORTER, R., Pte., 13th Hussars.
He was mobilised in August 1914, having previously served in the Army, proceeded at once to the Western Front, and took part in the Retreat from Mons and the battle of Loos and other engagements. In 1916 he was drafted to Mesopotamia, where he saw much service until he was demobilised in March 1919, holding the Mons Star and the General Service and Victory Medals.
15, Halford Road, Walham Green, S.W.6.   X19636.

PORTER, W. C., Pte., The Queen's (Royal West Surrey Regiment) and Royal Air Force.
He joined in September 1916, served on the Western Front from June until November 1917, and took part in the battle of Ypres, where he was severely wounded. On his recovery he was transferred to the R.A.F., and served in England, being medically unfit for duty overseas. He was demobilised in January 1919, and holds the General Service and Victory Medals.
74, Bravington Road, Maida Hill, W.9.   X19325.

PORTER, W. J., Pte., The King's Own (Royal Lancaster Regiment).
He volunteered in 1914, and after completing his training was engaged on important duties at various stations, but was not successful in obtaining his transfer overseas. He did much good work with his unit until January 1918, when he was accidentally drowned.
1, Hartington Road, Lower Edmonton, N.9.   14247B.

PORTSMOUTH, G., Driver, R.A.S.C. (M.T.).
He joined immediately on attaining military age in May 1918, and was at once drafted to the Western Front, where he did much good work as a driver in various sectors. In 1919 he returned to England, and in June of that year was demobilised, holding the General Service and Victory Medals.
7, The Grove, Hammersmith, W.6.   14489.

POTTER, C. A., Pte., R.A.S.C. (M.T.).
He joined in June 1916, and in the following month was sent to France, where he was employed with the field ambulance until the war ended. He was in many engagements and was twice wounded. He was demobilised in July 1919, holding the General Service and Victory Medals.
243, Kilburn Lane, N. Kensington, W.10.   X18743.

POTTER, F. W., Sergeant, Middlesex Regiment.
He volunteered in October 1914, and in the same year was drafted to France, where he took part in many engagements, including those of Arras, Ypres, Cambrai, Loos, Vimy Ridge, and the Somme, and was wounded at Loos. He was demobilised in April 1919, holding the 1914 Star and the General Service and Victory Medals.
59, Brenthurst Road, Church End, N.W.10.   16374.

POTTER, G. F., Corporal, R.H.A. and R.F.A.
He volunteered in September 1914, and in the same year was drafted to the Western Front, where he remained for over four years. During this time he took part in many engagements, including those of Ypres, the Somme and Cambrai, and was wounded seven times. In 1919 he returned to England and was demobilised in April holding the 1914 Star and the General Service and Victory Medals.
12, Brett Road, Stonebridge Park, N.W.10.   14386.

POTTER, J. H., Sapper, Royal Engineers.
He volunteered in April 1915, and in the same year was sent to France, where he did good service in many important sectors of the Front, especially around Ypres and the Somme, until the close of hostilities. He was discharged in May 1919, holding the 1914-15 Star, the General Service and Victory Medals.
2, De Morgan Road, Townmead Road, S.W.6.   X21053.

POTTER, W., A.B., Royal Navy.
He joined in August 1917, and saw much service in the Mediterranean until 1919, on board H.M.S. "Valhalla," "Ark Royal" and "Europa." On one occasion his ship was torpedoed, but he escaped injury. He was demobilised in May 1919, holding the General Service and Victory Medals.
54, Scotland Green, Tottenham, N.17.   X19136.

POTTINGER, W. G., Gunner, R.F.A.
He volunteered in August 1914, and in the following year was sent to France, where he remained for four years, During this time he took part in many engagements, including those of Ypres, Arras, Cambrai, the Somme, Loos, Vimy Ridge, and the Retreat and Advance of 1918, in which he was wounded. He was demobilised in June 1919, holding the 1915 Star, and the General Service and Victory Medals.
36, Clarendon Street, Paddington, W.2.   X20534.

POTTS, A., Driver, Royal Field Artillery.
Volunteering in January 1915, he was drafted to France in the same year. While on the Western Front, he was in action in the battles of Loos, Ypres, Cambrai, and the Retreat and Advance of 1918, in which he was wounded. He was demobilised in July 1919, holding the 1914-15 Star and the General Service and Victory Medals.
80, Carlyle Avenue, Willesden, N.W.10.   14447.

POUILLON, E. M., Driver, R.A.S.C. (M.T.).
He volunteered in June 1915, and later in the same year was drafted to the Western Front. During his service, which lasted four years, he was engaged in conveying food and ammunition to the various sectors, and fought at Ypres, the Somme and in the last Advance. He holds the 1914-15 Star and the General Service and Victory Medals, and was demobilised in May 1919.
149, Ashmore Road, Harrow Road, W.9.   X19746A.

POUILLON, W. A. R. (Mrs.), Special War Worker.
For over three years during the war this lady rendered excellent service as a clerk in the Army Pay Office, Regent Street, at Regent's Park and at the War Pensions Office in Baker Street, where her work was very highly valued.
149, Ashmore Road, Harrow Road, W.9.   X19746B.

POULDEN, Arthur, Pte., 3rd Leicestershire Regt.
He joined in March 1916, and went to France in the same year. He took part in many important engagements, and was badly wounded in action. He was in hospital on the Western Front, and in Hull for four months previous to being discharged medically unfit for further service in February 1918. He holds the General Service and Victory Medals.
90, Langhedge Lane, Upper Edmonton, N.18.   TX17092A.

POULDEN, A., Pte., Middlesex Regiment.
He joined in April 1916, and after his training served at various stations on important duties with his unit. He gave valuable services, but was not successful in obtaining his transfer overseas before the cessation of hostilities. He was discharged in March 1918, as he was medically unfit for further military duty.
90, Langhedge Lane, Upper Edmonton, N.18.   TX17092B.

POULDEN, F., Pte., 7th London Regiment.
He joined in November 1917, served on the Western Front, and after taking part in many engagements was killed in action in August 1918, during the last Advance. He was entitled to the General Service and Victory Medals.
90, Langhedge Lane, Upper Edmonton, N.18.   X17091A.

POULDEN, W., Corporal, Royal Air Force.
He joined in August 1916, and served as a 1st Air Mechanic at various stations, where he was engaged throughout his service on important duties that called for a high degree of technical skill. He did valuable work with the R.A.F. until January 1919, when he was demobilised.
90, Langhedge Lane, Upper Edmonton, N.18.   X17091B.

POULSON, A. S., Driver, Royal Field Artillery.
He volunteered for service in October 1914, and in the following year was drafted to the Western Front, where he remained for four years. He took part in many of the principal engagements whilst overseas, and with his unit did some fine work during the operations on the Somme. In June 1919 he was demobilised, holding the 1914-15 Star and the General Service and Victory Medals.
55, Heckfield Place, Fulham Road, S.W.6.   X20348.

POULSON, O. F. (D.C.M., M.M.), Gnr., Tank Corps.
He joined in April 1917, served on the Western Front during 1918 and 1919, and was wounded in action in the last Advance. He was awarded the Military Medal and the D.C.M. for conspicuous gallantry and devotion to duty on the field, and holds also the General Service and Victory Medals. He was demobilised in January 1919.
30, Star Road, West Kensington, W.14.   16680.

POULTER, C., Sapper, Royal Engineers.
He volunteered in January 1915, and in the same year was sent to France where he fought at the battles of Ypres, Arras, Cambrai, the Somme and the Marne. He was recommended for the Military Medal for conspicuous gallantry during the German Offensive in the Spring of 1918, and was twice mentioned in dispatches. He holds the 1914–15 Star, and the General Service and Victory Medals, and was demobilised in April 1919.
117, Fernhead Road, Maida Hill, W.9.   X19994.

POULTER, H. W., Lce.-Corpl., Royal Fusiliers.
He volunteered in August 1914, and served first in Salonika and Gallipoli, where he was wounded in action. He was then sent to France, and was again badly wounded. He was in hospital on the Western Front, and in Yorkshire before being demobilised in February 1919, and holds the 1914–15 Star and the General Service and Victory Medals.
24, Montagu Street, Hammersmith, W.6.   16406.

POULTER, W. H., Lce.-Corpl., R.A.M.C.
He volunteered in October 1914, and in the same year was sent to the Western Front, where he remained for nearly five years. During this time he was present at many engagements on various sectors of the Front, acting as a stretcher-bearer. He was demobilised in June 1919, holding the 1914–15 Star and the General Service and Victory Medals.
49, Stephendale Road, Fulham, S.W.6.   X21032.

POULTNEY, J. G., Driver, R.A.S.C.
He volunteered in July 1915, and saw much service on all parts of the Eastern Front. While there he contracted malaria, and was in consequence invalided home, and after being for some time in hospital at Brighton was discharged in March 1918 as unfit for further duty. He holds the General Service and Victory Medals.
7, Kilmaine Road, Munster Road, S.W.6.   TX18859B.

POULTON, T. W., A.B., Royal Navy, H.M.S. "Shrewsbury."
He joined in September 1917, and during his service was chiefly engaged on mine-sweeping duties in home waters. He also took part in the famous engagement at Zeebrugge. He was demobilised in October 1919, and holds the General Service and Victory Medals.
54, Langhedge Lane, Upper Edmonton, N.18.   X17262.

POULTON, W. E., Corporal, Labour Corps.
He joined in February 1916, rendered much valuable service on the Western Front from that year until 1919, and was wounded twice, first at Hill 60 and again at Ypres. He was demobilised in December 1919, holding the General Service and Victory Medals.
28, Raynham Road, Upper Edmonton, N.18.   16490.

POUT, A., Lce.-Corpl., 2nd West Yorkshire Regt.
He volunteered in October 1914, and during his service in France from December of the same year until he was taken prisoner early in 1918 took part in several important engagements, and was twice wounded. He was released after the Armistice, and was demobilised in January 1920, holding the 1914–15 Star and the General Service and Victory Medals.
29, St. John's Avenue, Harlesden, N.W.10.   14745.

POUT, J. J., Shoeing Smith, Royal Field Artillery.
He volunteered in August 1914, and after his training was sent to France in the following year, where he took part in the battles of Arras, Loos, Armentieres and the Somme, and was wounded. He was demobilised in April 1919, holding the 1914–15 Star and the General Service and Victory Medals.
17, Earlsmead Road, College Park, N.W.10.   X17829.

POWELL, A. W., Sapper, Royal Engineers.
He volunteered in February 1915, and in the following year was sent to the Western Front, where he rendered valuable service on many sectors as a linesman in the field until 1919. In March of that year he was demobilised, holding the General Service and Victory Medals.
15, Tenterden Road, Tottenham, N.17.   X18264.

POWELL, E., Pte., 4th Middlesex Regiment.
He joined in March 1917, and until 1919 served on the Western Front, where he took part in many engagements and was wounded in action at Albert and again during the Advance of 1918. He holds the General Service and Victory Medals.
359, Chapter Road, Cricklewood, N.W.2   16716C.

POWELL, G., Pte., Royal Army Service Corps.
He joined in April 1917, and in the following month was drafted to France. During his service overseas, which lasted for two years, he was stationed at Calais, Le Havre and various other places, and did excellent work with his unit. He was demobilised in October 1919, holding the General Service and Victory Medals.
18, Southam Street, North Kensington, W.10.   X20567.

POWELL, J. W., Pte., Gordon Highlanders.
He volunteered in June 1915, and from 1916 until 1919 served on the Western Front, taking part in the battles of the Somme, Arras, Ypres, Albert, Passchendaele Ridge and Vimy Ridge. He was wounded in action during the Advance of October 1918. He holds the General Service and Victory Medals, and was demobilised in February 1919.
359, Chapter Road, Cricklewood, N.W.2.   16716B.

POWELL, L. C. A., Pte., 3rd Middlesex Regiment.
He volunteered in 1915, and in the following year was drafted to France, where he saw much service and was wounded in action, and severely gassed and burnt by the explosion of a mustard gas shell. He was afterwards sent into Germany, where he served with the Army of Occupation during 1920. He holds the General Service and Victory Medals.
44, Alston Road, Upper Edmonton, N.18.   16500.

POWELL, P. H., Pte., Middlesex Regiment.
He joined in 1917, and was drafted to Italy, where he took part in numerous engagements during the Retreat on that Front. He was also in action in many engagements in France during the Retreat and Advance of 1918, and soon after the close of hostilities returned to England, and was demobilised in February 1919. He holds the General Service and Victory Medals.
14, Denton Road, Stonebridge Park, N.W.10.   14696B.

POWELL, T. W. (D.C.M.), 2nd Lieut., Middlesex Regiment.
He enlisted in 1908, and on the outbreak of war was sent to the Western Front. In 1915 he served in Gallipoli and, after taking part in many engagements there, returned to France. Here, in November 1917, he was awarded the D.C.M. and promoted to commissioned rank for gallantry and devotion to duty on the field. He was four times wounded during his service abroad, and was killed while on patrol duty during the Retreat of April 1918. He was entitled to the 1914–15 Star and the General Service and Victory Medals.
14, Denton Road, Stonebridge Park, N.W.10.   14696A.

POWELL, W., Corporal, Royal Field Artillery.
He volunteered in August 1914, and during his service on the Western Front, took part in many battles, including those of Ypres, Arras, Loos and the Somme. In July 1918 he was severely wounded and lost his right arm. He was discharged in April 1919, and holds the 1914–15 Star and the General Service and Victory Medals.
1, Bayonne Road, Hammersmith, W.6.   14300.

POWELL, W. A., Rifleman, 18th The London Regiment (London Irish Rifles).
He volunteered in February 1915, was sent to France in March 1916, took part in the battles of the Somme and Ypres. He also served in Palestine and Macedonia, was in action in the engagements at Gaza, Beersheba, Jerusalem and Jericho, and also took part in the advance from Jaffa to Aleppo. He was demobilised in March 1919, and holds the General Service and Victory Medals.
33, Biscay Road, Hammersmith, W.6.   T13044.

POWER, W. M., Lieut. Col. (T.F.), The Queen's (Royal West Surrey Regiment), Labour Corps and R.N.V.R.
In March 1878, at the age of 18, he joined the Volunteers, and continued in this Force with hardly a break until it was disbanded in 1906. Subsequently he served in the Territorials, and was the first attested member. In 1911 he organised the Volunteer Civil Force, which in succeeding years proved of the greatest value in protecting Free Labour and in assisting the authorities to maintain law and order, particularly during the great Dock Strike of 1912. On the outbreak of war in 1914 the Force under his command immediately supplied over one thousand men to act as Special Constables for immediate service. He was also intensely interested in recruiting and in the training of recruits, particularly in musketry, and for this purpose established the Westminster Rifle Ranges. His patriotic efforts in these directions were recognised by the Army Council, who warmly thanked him for his services. In 1917 he offered himself for a command in the Labour

POWER, W. M., Lieut. Col. (T.F.)—_contd._
Corps that was then being formed, and received a commission in The Queen's (Royal West Surrey Regiment). The corps under his command was almost immediately transferred to the Western Front, and its valuable work obtained special commendation in regimental orders. In the following year he was appointed a King's Messenger (with a commission as lieutenant in the R.N.V.R.) to convey dispatches between the Admiralty and units of the Grand Fleet wherever situated. He was demobilised in 1919, when all danger of hostilities being renewed had finally passed. He holds the Volunteer Long Service Medal, the Special Constabulary Medal, and the General Service and Victory Medals.
Artillery Mansions, Westminster, S.W. X20901.

POWIS, H. J., Sergeant, Royal Horse Artillery.
He volunteered for service in August 1914, and in the same year was drafted to the Western Front, where he remained until 1918. During this period he took part in many of the principal engagements, including the battles of the Marne, the Aisne, Ypres, the Somme, Arras and the Retreat and Advance of 1918, and was gassed. He holds the 1914 Star and the General Service and Victory Medals, and was still serving in 1920.
126, Portnall Road, Maida Hill, W.9. TX19719A.
TX19660

PRATT, E. J., Pte., 4th East Surrey Regiment.
He joined in June 1918 on reaching military age, and was sent to France in September of the same year. He was in action in several engagements on the Western Front, and after the Armistice went with the Army of Occupation to the Rhine. He holds the General Service and Victory Medals, and in 1920 was still serving.
24, Holberton Gardens, Willesden, N.W.10. X17559.

PRATT, F., Pte., 1st Middlesex Regiment.
He volunteered in 1915, proceeded to France in the following year, and took part in many battles, including those of the Somme, Ypres, Bullecourt, Arras, and the final Advance of 1918. He was gassed at Cambrai, and was in consequence in hospital for two months. He holds the General Service and Victory Medals, and was demobilised in 1919.
58, Durban Road, Tottenham, N.17. X17945.

PRATT, H., Sergeant, 5th Middlesex Regiment.
He served through the Boer War, and re-enlisted in August 1914. In the following year he went out to the Western Front, and while overseas took part in several battles, including those of Loos, Guillemont and the Somme. He was afterwards engaged on special duties at important home stations. He holds the Queen's and King's South African Medals, 1914–15 Star, General Service and Victory Medals, and also the Royal Humane Society's Medal, awarded for saving life when he was in China. He was demobilised in June 1919.
172, Portnall Road, Maida Hill, W.9. X19668B.

PRATT, P. T., Sergeant, 8th Leicestershire Regt.
He volunteered in August 1914, and in the following year was sent to the Western Front, where he took part in several engagements, was wounded three times, and on October 1st, 1917, he was killed in action at Polygon Wood. He was entitled to the 1914–15 Star and the General Service and Victory Medals.
17, Ancill Street, Hammersmith, W.6. 13746A.

PRATT, T. H., Pte., 1/7th Middlesex Regiment.
He joined in February 1917, was sent to the Western Front, and during his service abroad took part in the Retreat and Advance of 1918. He was wounded in action and was in the hospital at Etaples which was blown up during the Air Raid in May 1918. He holds the General Service and Victory Medals, and was demobilised in January 1919.
172, Portnall Road, Maida Hill, W.9. X19668A.

PRATT, W. E., Pte., 7th London Regiment.
He joined in July 1916, and after his training saw service on many sectors of the Western Front, where he took part in several of the most important battles up to the end of the war. On his return to England he was demobilised in April 1919. He holds the General Service and Victory Medals.
73, Musard Road, Hammersmith, W.6. 15329.

PRATT, W. F., Sapper, Royal Engineers.
He volunteered in January 1915, and saw four and a half years' service in France and Italy. He was present in numerous important engagements on both these Fronts, including those at Arras, Ypres and Cambrai. He holds the 1914–15 Star and the General Service and Victory Medals, and was demobilised in June 1919.
203, Kilburn Lane, North Kensington, W.10. X18720A.

PRATT, W. F., Pte., 3rd The London Regiment (Royal Fusiliers).
He volunteered for duty in October 1915, and during his service on the Western Front was in action on the Somme and at Arras, Ypres and Cambrai. After being severely wounded three times he was invalided home, and in December 1917 was discharged as medically unfit for further duty. He holds the General Service and Victory Medals.
77, Bramber Road, West Kensington, W.14. 15718.

PREECE, G. I., Pte., 13th Middlesex Regiment.
He volunteered in September 1915, and in the following year was sent to the Western Front, where he saw much service and was in hospital for a time. On returning to his battalion he took part in the fighting on the Somme, and while in action at Trones Wood in the summer of 1916 sustained a wound which necessitated the amputation of his left arm. He was discharged as physically unfit for further service in February 1917, and holds the General Service and Victory Medals.
67, Earlsmead Road, College Park, N.W.10. X18000.

PREEDY, F. G., Driver, Royal Field Artillery.
He volunteered for service in August 1915, and in the same year was drafted to the Western Front, where he took part in the battles of Loos and the Somme. In 1916 he went to Italy, but later returned to France, and saw action at Arras, Ypres, and in the Advance of 1918. He was demobilised in December of the same year, holding the 1914–15 Star and the General Service and Victory Medals.
8, Windsor Place, Maida Hill, W.9. X20398.

PREIST, F. C. H., Pte., 9th Royal Fusiliers.
He joined in March 1917, and in the following November was drafted to the Western Front, where he was severely wounded and taken prisoner at Albert in March 1918. After suffering much through privation whilst in captivity he was released in December of the same year. He holds the General Service and Victory Medals, and in February 1919 was demobilised.
6, Minet Gardens, Willesden, N.W.10. 13904.

PRENTICE, T., Pte., Suffolk Regiment.
He volunteered in 1915, and during his service on the Western Front took part in many battles, including those of Neuve Chapelle, Ypres, Loos, Armentieres, the Somme, Vimy Ridge, and Cambrai, where he was taken prisoner, in March 1918. He was kept in captivity in Germany until 1919, when he returned to England and was demobilised, holding the 1914–15 Star and the General Service and Victory Medals.
100, Chesson Road, West Kensington, W.14. X17241.

PRENTICE, W., Pte., West Yorkshire Regiment.
Joining in June 1916, he was drafted to Malta, where he was engaged on important defence duties throughout his service. He did much valuable work there with his unit, and in January 1920 was demobilised, holding the General Service and Victory Medals.
35, Lintaine Grove, West Kensington, W.14. 16827.

PRESS, E. H., Pte., R.A.S.C. (M.T.).
He volunteered in October 1914, went to the Western Front in the same year, and was present at many important engagements, including those on the Somme, at Ypres, Arras, Loos, Cambrai and Lille. He was demobilised in March 1919, holding the 1914 Star and the General Service and Victory Medals.
21, College Road, Willesden, N.W.10. X17812.

PRESTAGE, A. J., Pte., Middlesex Regiment.
He joined in June 1916, and after his training was engaged on important duties at various stations with his unit. He gave valuable services, but was not successful in obtaining his transfer overseas to a battle area before he was discharged in April 1918 as unfit for further military duty.
5, Newlyn Road, Tottenham, N.17. X18516.

PRESTON, A. H., Pte., 6th Queen's Own (Royal West Kent Regiment).
He joined in June 1916, and served on the Western Front, taking part in the engagements at Arras, Cambrai, Albert, Passchendaele and many other places. During this period he was gassed and twice wounded. In May 1919 he was demobilised, holding the General Service and Victory Medals.
14, Brett Road, Stonebridge Park, N.W.10. 14388

PRESTON, E., Pte., Queen's Own (Royal West Kent Regiment).

Volunteering in August 1915, he was sent to France in October of the same year. While on the Western Front he took part in many important engagements, and was wounded in action at Arras in April 1916. During the Battle of Cambrai in 1917 he was taken prisoner, and suffered many hardships while in captivity. He was released after the signing of the Armistice, and was demobilised in November 1919, holding the 1914–15 Star and the General Service and Victory Medals.
56, St. Margaret's Road, Willesden, N.W.10.   X17824.

PRESTON, E. J., Driver, Royal Field Artillery.

He volunteered in December 1914, and was later drafted to France. After taking part in much severe fighting, including the battles of Ypres and the Somme, he was killed in action during the Battle of Cambrai on December 12th, 1917. He was entitled to the 1914–15 Star and the General Service and Victory Medals.
116, St. Mary's Road, Lower Edmonton, N.9.   11981.

PRESTON, F. J., Special War Worker.

During the war he was engaged on work of vital importance in connection with the manufacture of magnetos for aeroplanes at the North London Engineering Co., Willesden. He held the responsible position of foreman, and carried out his duties in a capable manner, thereby rendering valuable services to his country.
417, High Road, Willesden, N.W.10.   T17337.

PRESTON, J. P., Pte., 2nd Royal Fusiliers.

He was called up from the Reserve in August 1914, and proceeded to France in the following month. He served in important engagements on the Western Front for a time, and was then drafted to Gallipoli, where he took part in many operations, and was twice wounded. In the succeeding year he returned to France, where he served till the cessation of hostilities, and during this period was three times wounded in action. He was demobilised in March 1919, and holds the 1914 Star and the General Service and Victory Medals.
83, Southam Street, North Kensington, W.10.   X20784.

PRETLOVE, R. A., Air Mechanic, Royal Air Force (late Royal Flying Corps).

He joined in October 1916, and apart from his ordinary duties, which called for a high degree of skill, was engaged in ambulance work during enemy air raids. He gave valuable services, but was not successful in obtaining his transfer overseas before hostilities ceased. He was demobilised in February 1919.
203 Bounces Road, Lower Edmonton, N.9.   13086.

PRETTY, A. H., Gunner, Royal Field Artillery.

He volunteered in August 1914, and served for eighteen months on the Western Front, during which time he took part in several engagements, including the Retreat from Mons. He holds the Mons Star and the General Service and Victory Medals, and in consequence of recurring attacks of malaria, was discharged as medically unfit for further service in April 1916.
90, Raynham Road, Upper Edmonton, N.18.   16948.

PRETTY, F. H., 1st Air Mechanic, R.A.F.

He joined in March 1916, and in the following year was drafted to France, where he was engaged on duties which called for a high degree of technical skill. Owing to a serious accident whilst flying, he became deaf, but continued to serve on the Western Front until his demobilisation in March 1920. He holds the General Service and Victory Medals.
21, Leeds Street, Upper Edmonton, N.18.   16873.

PRICE, A., Pte., 9th Middlesex Regiment.

He volunteered in June 1915, and on completion of his training was drafted to India, where he remained on important duties until 1917. He was then sent to Mesopotamia, and took part in severe fighting in that seat of war. In September 1918 he returned to England, and was engaged on special duties on the East Coast until his demobilisation in February 1919. He holds the General Service and Victory Medals.
78, Oldfield Road, Willesden, N.W.10.   15541.

PRICE, A. L., Bombardier, Royal Field Artillery.

Volunteering in August 1914, he was drafted to the Western Front, and took part in much heavy fighting. He served in the battles of Loos, the Somme, Arras and Cambrai, and in engagements around Mons during the Advance of 1918. He was wounded and gassed during his service, and was demobilised in February 1919, holding the 1914–15 Star and the General Service and Victory Medals.
7, Bayonne Road, Hammersmith, W.6.   14303.

PRICE, A. T., Pte., Labour Corps.

He volunteered in May 1915, and was drafted to the Western Front, where he was engaged on important duties with the Labour Corps on various sectors. After the signing of the Armistice, he went to Germany with the Army of Occupation, and remained there until his demobilisation in September 1919. He holds the General Service and Victory Medals.
116, Queen Street, Hammersmith, W.6.   13799.

PRICE, F., Corporal, Royal Field Artillery.

He volunteered in August 1914, and was immediately sent to France, where he took an active part in the Retreat from Mons, the battles of Ypres, Loos and the Somme, and in many other engagements. He remained on the Western Front until 1919. He was still serving in 1920, and holds the Mons Star and the General Service and Victory Medals.
45, Ladysmith Road, Upper Edmonton, N.18   16459.

PRICE, F. R., Pte., Devonshire Regiment.

Volunteering in 1915, he was drafted to Salonika in the following year. During his service in this theatre of war, he was engaged on important duties with the Pioneers until April 1919, when he returned to England for demobilisation. He holds the General Service and Victory Medals.
16, Fane Place, West Kensington, W.14.   15698.

PRICE, G., Pte., Royal Inniskilling Fusiliers.

He joined in June 1916, was sent to France in the following March, and took part in the battles of Arras and Ypres. During the latter engagement he was blown up and seriously wounded. He was invalided home and, after a long period in hospital, was discharged in March 1918 as medically unfit for further service. He holds the General Service and Victory Medals.
141, Harley Road, Willesden, N.W.10.   13169.

PRICE, G., Sapper, Royal Engineers.

He volunteered in May 1915, and shortly afterwards was sent to the Western Front, where he took an active part in the battles of Loos, Arras and Ypres, and in heavy fighting around Armentieres. In April 1919 he was demobilised, and holds the 1914-15 Star and the General Service and Victory Medals.
55, Delorme Street, Hammersmith, W.6.   T13778.

PRICE, H., Gunner, Royal Garrison Artillery.

He joined in November 1916, and after his training served in many important engagements on the Western Front, where he was wounded in action near Albert in April 1918. He holds the General Service and Victory Medals, and was demobilised in February 1919.
64, Laundry Road, Hammersmith, W.6.   15053.

PRICE, H. A., Gunner, Royal Field Artillery.

Volunteering in September 1914, he was later drafted to the Western Front, where he took part in the battles of Loos, the Somme and Arras, and in heavy fighting in other important engagements. He was wounded in action at Ypres in August 1917, and was invalided home. After a considerable period in hospital he was discharged in May 1919 as medically unfit for further service owing to wounds. He holds the 1914–15 Star and the General Service and Victory Medals.
44, Raynham Avenue, Upper Edmonton, N.18.   16767.

PRICE, H. E., Pte., 24th London Regiment.

He joined in March 1916, and was drafted to Salonika. After taking part in much heavy fighting on the Balkan Front, he was sent to Palestine, where he served with General Allenby's Forces. In June 1918 he was drafted to France, took part in important engagements, and was wounded in action at Arras in the following October. He was demobilised in July 1919, and holds the General Service and Victory Medals.
49, Burn's Road, Harlesden, N.W.10.   14714.

PRICE, J., Driver, Royal Horse Artillery.

He volunteered in August 1914, and was immediately drafted to the Western Front, where he fought in the Retreat from Mons and the Battle of Loos. He was badly gassed during the latter engagement, was invalided home and eventually discharged in June 1917 as medically unfit for further service. He holds the Mons Star and the General Service and Victory Medals.
29, Elric Street, Hammersmith, W.6.   15865.

PRICE, J., Battery Q.M.S., Royal Field Artillery.

He volunteered in October 1914, and was sent to the Western Front in the following year. He served with distinction in the battles of Loos, the Somme, Arras, Ypres and Cambrai, and in other important engagements, and during his service overseas was wounded. In December 1919 he was demobilised, and holds the 1914–15 Star and the General Service and Victory Medals.
3, Wilson's Road, Hammersmith, W.6.   16419.

PRICE, J. T., Pte., Machine Gun Corps.
He volunteered in August 1914, immediately on the outbreak of hostilities, and after his training was drafted to India. He remained there until October 1919, and during that period was engaged on important duties at various stations with his unit. In 1920 he was still serving, and holds the General Service and Victory Medals.
8, Somerset Place, Hammersmith, W.6.   13791.

PRICE, J. W., Sapper, Royal Engineers.
He volunteered in November 1915, and in the following year was drafted to the Western Front. During his three years' service in this theatre of war he took an active part in important operations on various sectors, and remained there until his demobilisation in January 1919. He holds the General Service and Victory Medals.
46, York Road, Upper Edmonton, N.18.   16541.

PRICE, W. G., Pte., 23rd Middlesex Regiment.
He joined in August 1916, and early in the following year was drafted to France. After a short period of service there he was sent to Italy, where he saw much heavy fighting. Later he returned to the Western Front, took part in severe fighting at Ypres, Zonnebeke, Bray and Albert, and was wounded in action near Bapaume in March 1918. He was also gassed, and on being invalided home in August 1918, was discharged as medically unfit for further service. He holds the General Service and Victory Medals.
100, Fortune Gate Road, Harlesden, N.W.10.   13192.

PRICE, W. H., Staff Sergeant, R.F.A.
He volunteered in August 1914, and during his service on the Western Front took a prominent part in the battles of Mons and Loos. In September 1915 he was drafted to Salonika, and after taking part in several engagements was invalided home in April 1918 with malaria. He holds the Mons Star and the General Service and Victory Medals, and in 1920 was still serving.
91, Burn's Road, Harlesden, N.W.10.   13456.

PRIDDLE, S. C., Rifleman, Rifle Brigade.
He was mobilised from the Reserve immediately on the outbreak of war, and was drafted to France early in 1915. After a short period on the Western Front he was sent to Salonika later in the same year. While in this theatre of war he took part in much severe fighting on the Balkan Front, and returned to this country in January 1919, when he was discharged. He holds the 1914–15 Star and the General Service and Victory Medals.
2, Walham Avenue, Fulham Road, S.W.6.   X20234.

PRIDMAN, H. J., Pte., Leicestershire Regiment.
Volunteering in September 1915, he was almost immediately drafted to the Western Front, where he took part in severe fighting at Bullecourt, Bapaume, St. Quentin and Ypres. He was badly wounded at Ypres, and was invalided home. On his recovery he went with the Relief Force to Russia, and remained there until his demobilisation in August 1919. He holds the 1914–15 Star and the General Service and Victory Medals.
44, Orbain Road, Fulham, S.W.6.   X18215.

PRIGMORE, E. W., Pte., 2/4th The London Regiment.
He joined in 1917, and on completion of his training was drafted to the Western Front. During his service in this theatre of war he took part in many important engagements, and was wounded in action. He returned for demobilisation in January 1919, and holds the General Service and Victory Medals.
28, Oxford Road, Lower Edmonton, N.9.   12960.

PRINCE, C. J., Pte., Royal Army Service Corps.
Joining in March 1917, he was sent to France later in the same year. While on the Western Front he was engaged on important duties with his unit, and after the signing of the Armistice went to Germany with the Army of Occupation. He returned for demobilisation in May 1919, and holds the General Service and Victory Medals.
46, Somerset Road, Upper Edmonton, N.18.   16861.

PRINCE, F., Driver, Royal Field Artillery.
He volunteered in October 1915, and on completion of his training was sent to France. During his service on the Western Front he took part in numerous important engagements on various sectors, and was wounded in action. He was demobilised in April 1919, and holds the General Service and Victory Medals.
35, Claybrook Road, Hammersmith, W.6.   13678B.

PRINCE, H., Lce-Corpl., Royal Engineers.
He was mobilised from the Reserve at the outbreak of hostilities, and was immediately drafted to France, where he took an active part in the Retreat from Mons, in the battles of Ypres, Arras and Cambrai, and in other important engagements. During his service he was wounded, and after a period of four years on the Western Front, was discharged in November 1918. He holds the Mons Star and the General Service and Victory Medals.
76, Clarendon Street, Paddington, W.2.   X20360A.

PRINCE, V., Sergt., Bedfordshire Regiment.
He volunteered in 1914, and in the following year was sent to France. After taking part in important engagements on the Western Front, he was drafted to Egypt, where he served with distinction until 1919. He then returned to this country for demobilisation, and holds the 1914–15 Star and the General Service and Victory Medals.
62, Kimberley Road, Upper Edmonton, N.18.   16538.

PRINCE, W., Pte., Essex Regiment.
He joined in February 1916, and after his training served at various stations on special duties with his unit. He also did good work in Ireland, but was not successful in being drafted overseas before the cessation of hostilities. He was demobilised in March 1919.
76, Clarendon Street, Paddington, W.2.   X20360B.

PRIOR, A. M., Pte., Middlesex Regiment.
He joined in January 1916, and embarked for France later in the same year. He saw much heavy fighting on various parts of the Western Front until April 1918, when he was killed in action at Vimy Ridge. He was entitled to the General Service and Victory Medals.
66, Fairfield Road, Upper Edmonton, N.18.   15613B.

PRIOR, B. (Mrs.), Special War Worker.
During the war this lady gave up her domestic duties in order to do work of national importance as a munition worker, and was engaged at the Park Royal Munition Factory, where she carried out duties of a very arduous nature. She received high commendation for her valuable services to her Country.
60, Holly Lane, Willesden, N.W.10.   15401A.

PRIOR, E. E., Special War Worker.
During the war he was engaged on work of national importance at Messrs. Smith's Munition Factory, Cricklewood, in connection with the manufacture of shells and fuses. His duties, which were of an arduous nature, were carried out in an efficient manner, to the entire satisfaction of his employers.
60, Holly Lane, Willesden, N.W.10.   15401D.

PRIOR, E. M. (Mrs.), Special War Worker.
During the war this lady undertook work of national importance at the Glendower Aircraft Co., Ltd., South Kensington, where she was engaged on the manufacture of aeroplane parts. Her duties, which required great care, were carried out in a very capable manner.
28, Chesson Road, West Kensington, W.14.   X17168.

PRIOR, H., Special War Worker.
For a period of nearly four years during the war he carried out work of national importance at Messrs. Smith's Munition Factory, Cricklewood. He was engaged in the manufacture of heavy shells and fuses, and rendered valuable services to his Country.
60, Holly Lane, Willesden, N.W.10.   15401C.

PRIOR, W., Pte., Royal Defence Corps.
He volunteered in 1915, and was engaged on important work at Alexandra Park, where he served as a guard at a German internment camp. He fell dead while carrying out his duties in 1918.
60, Holly Lane, Willesden, N.W.10.   15401B.

PRIOR, W., Staff Sergeant, R.A.S.C.
He volunteered in 1915, and in the same year was drafted to the Western Front, where he was engaged on important transport duties. He was also in charge of the repair section of his unit, and did consistent good work. He was demobilised in 1918, and holds the 1914–15 Star and the General Service and Victory Medals.
74, Ilex Road, Willesden, N.W.10.   15954.

PRIOR, W., Pte., Royal Army Medical Corps.
He volunteered in November 1914, and after his training was engaged on important duties on the South East Coast. He gave valuable services, but owing to a severe injury, was not successful in obtaining his transfer overseas. In April 1916, he was discharged as medically unfit for further service.
42, Cornwallis Grove, Lower Edmonton, N.9.   13324.

PRIOR, W. J., Pte., 7th Middlesex Regiment.
He volunteered in August 1914, was sent to France in the
same year, and after taking part in much severe fighting
was killed in action at Loos on October 16th, 1915. He
was entitled to the 1914-15 Star and the General Service
and Victory Medals.
8, Plevna Road, Lower Edmonton, N.9.   14574.

**PRITCHARD, E. C., Rifleman, Royal Irish Rifles
and 1/11th London Regiment.**
He joined in March 1917, went to the Western Front, and
was wounded during his first engagement at Ypres, and
was invalided to Ireland. After his recovery he was
drafted to Egypt, and on the voyage out his troopship,
"Aragon," was torpedoed. He was rescued, and later
was able to continue his journey. During his service in
Palestine he contracted malaria, and after being for some
time in hospital, was sent to Turkey. He holds the
General Service and Victory Medals, and was demobilised
in 1919.
66, Humbolt Road, Hammersmith, W.6.   15885.

PRITCHARD, E. R., Sergeant, R.A.S.C. (M.T.).
He volunteered in October 1915, and in the same year
was sent to France, where he was engaged on responsible
duties in the fitting shops near Arras. After the signing
of the Armistice he went to Germany with the Army of
Occupation, and remained there until he was demobilised
in August 1919. He holds the 1914-15 Star and the
General Service and Victory Medals.
53, Earlsmead Road, College Park, N.W.10.   X17839.

PRITCHARD, H. C., Sapper, Royal Engineers.
He volunteered in May 1915, and served for nearly four
years on the Western Front, where he was in action at
the Somme, Arras, Bullecourt, Vimy Ridge, Cambrai, and
many other engagements, and was severely wounded. He
was demobilised in May 1919, and holds the 1914-15 Star
and the General Service and Victory Medals.
311, Shirland Road, Maida Hill, W.9.   X19566.

PRITCHARD, T. E., Lce. Cpl., Military Foot Police.
He volunteered in August 1914, and was immediately sent
to France, where he took part in the Retreat from Mons.
After serving in many important engagements with a line
regiment, he was transferred to the Military Foot Police
and carried out special duties with this unit. On August
3rd, 1919, he died from the effects of shell-shock. He
was entitled to the Mons Star and the General Service and
Victory Medals.
60, Bruce Castle Road, Tottenham, N.17.   X18548A.

**PROCTOR, F. J., Lce.-Sergt., 2/19th The London
Regiment.**
Volunteering in October 1914, he was retained for a period
in England on important duties at various stations with
his unit. In June 1916 he was drafted to the Western
Front, and was killed in action on July 25th, 1916, at Mont
St. Eloi. He was buried in the Military Cemetery at
Ecoivres. He was entitled to the General Service and
Victory Medals.
34, Bolton Road, Harlesden, N.W.10.   13379.

PROCTOR, W., 1st Air Mechanic, R.A.F.
He joined in November 1917, and after qualifying as a
mechanic was drafted to France. During his service there
he was engaged on important duties, which called for a
high degree of technical skill, at large repair shops behind
the line. He was demobilised in April 1919 on his return
from the Western Front, and holds the General Service
and Victory Medals.
6, Nutbourne Street, Queen's Park Estate,W.10. X18704.

PROSSER, E., Pte., Middlesex Regiment.
He volunteered in September 1914, served in France from
1915 until demobilised in March 1919, and took part in
many important engagements including the battles of
Ypres, Arras, Cambrai and St. Quentin. He holds the
1914-15 Star and the General Service and Victory Medals.
68, Mordaunt Road, Willesden, N.W.10.   14113A.

PROSSER, H., Rifleman, King's Royal Rifle Corps.
He joined in 1916, and at the close of his training was
drafted to Salonika. After taking part in important
operations in this theatre of war, he contracted malaria
and was invalided home. On his recovery he was sent to
France, and served throughout the Advance in 1918. He
holds the General Service and Victory Medals, and was
demobilised in 1919.
45, Chesson Road, West Kensington, W.14.   X17155A.

PROSSER, R. (Mrs.), Special War Worker.
During the war this lady undertook arduous work with
the London Electric Railway. She held a responsible
position, and carried out her duties in a thoroughly capable
manner. By doing this work she released a man for
military service, and thereby rendered valuable help to
her country.
45, Chesson Road, West Kensington, W.14.   X17155B.

PROUSE, F., Pte., 4th London Regiment.
He volunteered in December 1914, and after his training
was retained on important duties with his unit until
June 1916. He was then drafted to France, fought in the
Battle of the Somme, and was killed in action in September
of the same year. He was entitled to the General Service
and Victory Medals.
6A, Drayton Road, Harlesden, N.W.10.   14897.

PROUT, R. A., 1st Air Mechanic, R.A.F.
He volunteered in November 1915, and served at various
stations with his squadron, and was engaged on duties
which called for a high degree of technical skill. Later he
was drafted to Russia, where he served in the Armoured
Car Division. On his return he was demobilised in
January 1919. He holds the General Service and Victory
Medals.
85, Manor Road, Tottenham, N.17.   X18800.

PROWSE, R. M., Pte., Northamptonshire Regt.
He volunteered in June 1915, and after completing his
training was drafted to the Western Front, where he took
part in many important operations until his discharge in
July 1917. He holds the General Service and Victory
Medals.
52, Claybrook Road, Hammersmith, W.6.   13771.

PRYOR, A. J., Pte., 4th Royal Fusiliers.
He joined in 1916, and was later drafted to the Western
Front. While in this seat of war he took part in many
important engagements, including the Battles of the
Somme and Cambrai. He was killed in action during the
latter engagement, on December 16th, 1917, and was
entitled to the General Service and Victory Medals.
10, Linton Cottages, Linton Road,
Upper Edmonton, N.18.   X17471B.

PRYOR, E. T., Pte., 1/5th Hampshire Regiment.
Volunteering in September 1915, he was drafted to India
in the following year. He remained there until his demobilisation in November 1919, and during this period
was engaged on duties of an important nature at various
stations with his unit. He holds the General Service and
Victory Medals.
19, Linton Cottages, Linton Road,
Upper Edmonton, N.18.   X17471A.

PRYOR, H. H., Pte., Middlesex Regiment.
He volunteered in January 1915, and was almost immediately drafted to France, where he took part in the battles
of Ypres and Kemmel. He was twice wounded, was
invalided home, and in November of the same year was
discharged, owing to his wounds, as medically unfit for
further service. He holds the 1914-15 Star and the
General Service and Victory Medals.
51, Westminster Road, Lower Edmonton, N.9.   12699.

PRYOR, T. W., Gunner, Royal Garrison Artillery.
He joined in April 1916, and later in the same year was
drafted to France. While on the Western Front he took
part in the Battle of Ypres and other important engagements, and suffered from trench fever. He was demobilised in March 1919, but has since re-enlisted, and in 1920
was serving in India. He holds the General Service and
Victory Medals.
64, Felixstowe Road, Lower Edmonton, N.9.   15375.

PULLEN, D. J., Pte., Labour Corps.
He joined in April 1916, and was afterwards sent to the
Western Front, where he was engaged on important duties
with the Labour Corps in France and Belgium. He gave
valuable services until his demobilisation in October 1919,
and holds the General Service and Victory Medals.
94, Winchester Road, Lower Edmonton, N.9.   14758.

PUNTER, A. H., Rifleman, 14th Rifle Brigade.
He volunteered in June 1915, and was drafted to France
in the following August. He took part in many important
engagements, and was wounded in September 1915 at the
Battle of Loos, and again in September 1916, during the
Battle of the Somme. He was invalided home, and after
a considerable period in hospital was discharged in August
1917 as medically unfit for further service owing to his
wounds. He holds the 1914-15 Star and the General
Service and Victory Medals.
42, Ponsard Road, College Park, N.W.10.   X17749A.

PUNTER, W., Pte., R.A.S.C. (M.T.).
Joining in June 1915, he was sent to the Western Front in the following month. While in this seat of war he was engaged on important transport duties in many engagements, including the Battle of Ypres. In 1917 he was invalided home, and in August of that year was discharged as medically unfit for further service through ill-health caused by exposure. He holds the 1914-15 Star and the General Service and Victory Medals.
36, Franklyn Road, Willesden, N.W.10.   16524.

PUNTER, W. J., Rifleman, 14th Rifle Brigade.
He volunteered in June 1915, and on completion of his training was sent to the Western Front in the following August. At the Battle of Loos in September 1915, he was wounded, and was invalided home. After a long period in hospital he was discharged in April 1916, as medically unfit for further service owing to his wound, and holds the 1914-15 Star and the General Service and Victory Medals.
42, Ponsard Road, College Park, N.W.10.   X17749B.

PURCELL, J. H., Corporal, 3rd Middlesex Regt.
He enlisted in April 1903, and at the outbreak of war was stationed at Cawnpore, in India. He was drafted to France early in 1915, and among other important engagements fought at the battles of Ypres, Neuve Chapelle and Armentieres. During his service on the Western Front he was wounded and gassed. He also took part in important operations in Salonika, and in February 1919 was discharged, holding the 1914-15 Star and the General Service and Victory Medals.
70A, Sandringham Road, Cricklewood, N.W.2.   T17548.

PURDY, A., Rifleman, The London Regiment.
He joined in March 1917, and on completion of his training was drafted to the Western Front, where he took part in the heavy fighting around Albert, the Somme and the Retreat and Advance of 1918. He was demobilised in March 1919, and holds the General Service and Victory Medals.
14, Felixstowe Road, Lower Edmonton, N.9.   15171A.

PURDY, T., Rifleman, 1st King's Royal Rifle Corps.
Volunteering in December 1915, he was drafted to the Western Front on completion of his training. During his service in this theatre of war he took part in many important engagements, including the battles of the Vimy Ridge and Delville Wood. He was wounded in the last-named battle, was invalided home, and was eventually discharged as medically unfit for further service in March 1917. He holds the General Service and Victory Medals.
14, Felixstowe Road, Lower Edmonton, N.9.   15171B.

PURDY, W. A., Pte., East Surrey Regiment.
He volunteered in 1915, and in the following year was drafted to Salonika. During his service in this theatre of war, which lasted until his demobilisation in May 1919, he took part in many important operations. He holds the General Service and Victory Medals.
18, Crefeld Road, Hammersmith, W.6.   14500B.

PURDY, W. L., Stoker, Royal Navy, H.M.S. "Champion."
He joined in April 1917, and whilst on board H.M.S. "Champion" took part in important naval operations with the Grand Fleet in Home waters. He was also engaged on special duties at Scapa Flow, and in April 1919, was demobilised. He holds the General Service and Victory Medals.
6, Waverley Road, Tottenham, N.17.   X18967.

PURE, W., Driver, Royal Field Artillery.
He volunteered for service in August 1914, and after his training at various stations in England was drafted to France in the following year. His service overseas lasted for three years, during which time he took part in several important battles, including those of Ypres, the Somme, Arras, St. Quentin and Cambrai. In 1918 he returned to England and was demobilised. He holds the 1914-15 Star and the General Service and Victory Medals.
90, Clarendon Street, Paddington, W.2.   X20369.

PURKIS, W. H., Pte., Loyal North Lancashire Regiment.
He volunteered in June 1915, and was drafted to the Western Front in the following November. After a period of four months in this theatre of war, during which time he took part in heavy fighting and was wounded, he was invalided home and discharged in March 1916, as medically unfit for further service. He holds the 1914-15 Star and the General Service and Victory Medals.
32, Brereton Road, Tottenham, N.17.   X18116.

PURNELL, R. A., Driver, R.A.S.C.
He joined in 1916, and later in the year was drafted to the Western Front. After taking part in important operations in this theatre of war he was sent to Salonika in 1917, where he was engaged on special duties during the fighting in the Balkan Campaign. He was demobilised in 1919, and holds the General Service and Victory Medals.
34, Roseberry Road, Lower Edmonton, N.9.   14067.

PURVIS, W., Driver, Royal Field Artillery.
He volunteered in August 1914, and in the following year took part in the heavy fighting at the Dardanelles. On the evacuation of the Gallipoli Peninsula he was drafted to Salonika, and served in important operations on the Doiran Front and in Serbia. From there he was sent to Italy, and saw further fighting on the Piave, and was finally drafted to the Western Front, where he took part in engagements on the Somme sector. During his service overseas he suffered from malaria and shell-shock. He returned to England in June 1919 for demobilisation, and holds the 1914-15 Star and the General Service and Victory Medals.
33, Brownlow Road, Willesden, N.W.10.   14492.

PUSEY, F. W., Corporal, Labour Corps.
Joining in 1917, he was sent to the Western Front almost immediately, and was engaged on special guard duties at a large internment camp. During his service overseas he met with a serious accident and severely injured his leg. He was demobilised in 1919, and holds the General Service and Victory Medals.
10, Corby Road, Willesden, N.W.10.   14363.

PUSEY, J. C., Pte., 7th Royal Fusiliers.
He joined in 1916, and in the following year was sent to East Africa, where he took part in many skirmishes and contracted malaria, enteric and pneumonia. In 1918 he was sent to France, where he fought on the Somme and at Cambrai, and was twice wounded. He was demobilised in 1920, holding the General Service and Victory Medals.
10, Corby Road, Willesden, N.W.10.   14364.

PUSEY, W. E., Pte., Royal Marine Light Infantry.
He volunteered in October 1914, and in the following May was sent to the Dardanelles, where he took part in the heavy fighting during the Gallipoli Campaign. After the evacuation of the Peninsula he served on the Western Front, and was in action on the Somme, at Arras, Delville Wood, Ypres, Bullecourt, Armentieres and Cambrai, and in the 1918 Advance. He was demobilised in March 1919, and holds the 1914-15 Star and the General Service and Victory Medals.
71, Shorrold's Road, Walham Green, S.W.6.   X19500.

PUTTOCK, A. A. J., Electrician, R.N., H.M.S. "Victory."
He volunteered in 1915, and was posted to H.M.S. "Victory," with which ship he took part in important naval operations with the Grand Fleet in Italian waters. He was demobilised in April 1919, and holds the General Service and the Victory Medals.
106, Shakespeare Avenue, Willesden, N.W.10.   13899A.

PYLE, F., Corporal, 3rd Bedfordshire Regiment.
He volunteered in October 1914, and after completing his training was engaged on important duties at various stations with his unit. He gave valuable services and gained promotion for consistent good work, but was not successful in obtaining his transfer overseas before hostilities ceased. He was demobilised in January 1919.
76, Shrewsbury Road, Stonebridge Park, N.W.10.   13637.

PYMM, F. A., Pte., 13th London Regiment.
Volunteering in September 1914, he was drafted to the Western Front in 1916, after having been engaged on important duties at various home stations. Later in the same year he was sent to Egypt, and served with General Allenby's Forces in the Advance through Palestine. He was twice wounded during his service overseas, and in August 1919 he returned to England for demobilisation. He holds the General Service and Victory Medals.
35, College Road, Willesden, N.W.10.   X17809.

PYMM, S. A., Pte., 6th Royal Fusiliers.
He joined in October 1916, and after his training was engaged on important duties at various stations with his unit until August 1918. He was then drafted to France, and saw much fighting around Armentieres, Lille and Tournai during the Advance in the concluding stages of the war. He returned to England for demobilisation in October 1919, and holds the General Service and Victory Medals.
35, College Road, Willesden, N.W.10.   X17810.

QUELCH, W. L., Pte., Middlesex Regiment.
Volunteering in 1914, he was sent to the Western Front,
where he took part in the battles of Loos, Arras, the
Somme and Hill 60, and was seriously wounded and
gassed. In consequence he was discharged as medically
unfit in 1917, holding the 1914–15 Star and the General
Service and Victory Medals.
78, Churchill Road, Cricklewood, N.W.2.　　16624A.

**QUESNEL, E. A., Pte., 2nd North Staffordshire
Regiment.**
He volunteered in November 1915, and shortly afterwards
embarked for India. During nearly four years' service in
the East he was engaged on important duties on the
North West Frontier, and rendered valuable services. In
1919 he returned to England, and in December was
demobilised, holding the General Service and Victory
Medals, and the Indian General Service Medal (with clasp
Afghanistan, N.W. Frontier 1919).
6, Effie Place, Walham Green, S.W.6.　　TX19706.

QUICK, C. R., Gunner, Royal Garrison Artillery.
He joined in 1916, and served as a Signaller on the Western
Front, where he took part in many engagements, including
those of the Somme, Arras, Messines, St. Quentin, Armentieres, Lille and during the Retreat and Advance of 1918.
He was demobilised in 1919, holding the General Service
and Victory Medals.
45, Bronsart Road, Munster Road, S.W.6.　　X19006.

QUICK, F. A., Rifleman, Rifle Brigade.
He joined in 1916, and after the completion of his training
was drafted to the Western Front, where he took part in
many engagements. He was sent home for demobilisation
in 1920, and holds the General Service and Victory Medals.
75, Garvan Road, Hammersmith, W.6.　　14828B.

QUILTER, R. C., Stoker, Royal Navy.
He joined in January 1918, and was posted to H.M.S.
"Carnarvon" and with this vessel was engaged on convoy
duties in the Atlantic. He holds the General Service
and Victory Medals, and in 1920 was still serving.
190, Kilburn Lane, North Kensington, W.10.　　X18706A.

QUINLAND, E. L., Pte., 8th East Surrey Regt.
He volunteered in September 1914, and served in France,
where during the battle of the Somme in 1916 he was
wounded at Delville Wood. Subsequently he took part
in the battles of Ypres, Cambrai, Arras and Bapaume,
and during the German Offensive was reported missing
and believed killed on March 23rd, 1918. He was entitled
to the 1914–15 Star and the General Service and Victory
Medals.
36, Dudden Hill Lane, Willesden, N.W.10.　　X17392.

**QUINN, C. H., Pte., Middlesex Regiment and
Machine Gun Corps.**
Joining in 1916, he was sent to Salonika in the same year
and took part in the fighting on the Struma and Doiran
Fronts and at Bukoba. In 1918 he went to Russia and
thence to Constantinople. He was demobilised in December 1919, holding the General Service and Victory Medals.
68, Brownlow Road, Willesden, N.W.10.　　14718.

RABSON, F. J., Sapper, Royal Engineers.
He volunteered in May 1915, and in the same year was
drafted to the Western Front, where he was wounded.
On recovery he was sent to Salonika in the following
December, and took part in the Serbian Retreat, during
which he was again wounded and contracted malaria.
He also served for a time in Roumania, and was demobilised
in April 1919, holding the 1914–15 Star and the General
Service and Victory Medals.
20, Strode Road, Munster Road, S.W.6.　　X19854.

RABSON, M. (Miss), Special War Worker.
During the war this lady was engaged on very useful and
important work in the telegraph department of the South
Western District Post Office, Westminster, and discharged
all her duties, which previously had been performed by a
man, with care and punctuality.
20, Strode Road, Munster Road, S.W.6.　　X19411.

RADBAND, A., Driver, R.A.S.C. (M.T.).
He volunteered in October 1915, and in the same year was
drafted to France, where he took part in many engagements,
transporting ammunition and stores to the forward area.
During his service he was gassed, and the lorry he was
driving was hit by a shell, but he escaped unhurt. He
was demobilised in June 1919, and holds the 1914–15
Star and the General Service and Victory Medals.
25, Hazlebury Road, Fulham, S.W.6.　　X20492.

RADCLIFFE, C. F., Pte., 7th Middlesex Regiment.
He volunteered in May 1915, and was drafted to Eygpt
in the same year. After a period of service there he was
sent in 1916 to France, where he took part in many engagements, until he was wounded in action at Delville Wood
in August 1916. He was invalided home, and after being in
hospital for some time was discharged as medically unfit
for further service in April 1917. He holds the 1914–15
Star and the General Service and Victory Medals.
9, Ray's Road, Upper Edmonton, N.18.　　15354.

**RADFORD, A. G., Rifleman, 3rd Canadian
Mounted Rifles.**
He volunteered in January 1915, and was sent to France
in the following June. During his service he took part in
several engagements, including those of Ypres, Vimy Ridge
and the Somme, where he was wounded. He holds the
1914–15 Star and the General Service and Victory Medals,
and was demobilised in November 1919.
48, Hiley Road, Willesden, N.W.10.　　X18172A.

RADFORD, C. C., Pte., 9th Royal Sussex Regt.
Previous to volunteering in 1914, he was taken prisoner
by the German cruiser "Karlsbuke" in September 1914,
and was released on its surrender to the British in November 1914. He took part in many engagements on the
Western Front, and was killed in action on March 21st,
1918. He was entitled to the General Service and Victory
Medals.
27, Church Path, Hammersmith, W.6.　　15903A.

RADFORD, D. J., Driver, Royal Field Artillery.
He volunteered in August 1914, and a year later was drafted
to the Western Front, where he took part in numerous
engagements, including those of Ypres, Cambrai, Arras,
Vimy Ridge, Messines, Amiens, and the Somme. He holds
the 1914–15 Star and the General Service and Victory
Medals, and was demobilised in January 1919.
48, Hiley Road, Willesden, N.W.10.　　X18172B.

RADFORD, W. J., Sergeant, 1/2 Royal Fusiliers.
He volunteered in September 1914, and was sent to Malta
in the same month. In the following January he was
drafted to the Western Front, where he took part in several
engagements, including those of Ypres and the Somme, and
on May 3rd, 1917, was killed in action at Arras, having
previously been gassed. He was entitled to the 1914–15
Star and the General Service and Victory Medals.
48, Hiley Road, Willesden, N.W.10.　　X18172C.

RADFORD, W., Pte , Royal Army Service Corps.
He volunteered in July 1915, and after completion of his
training was drafted to the Western Front, where he took
part in many engagements until he fell ill and was invalided
home. After some time in hospital he was discharged as
medically unfit for further service in April 1918, and holds
the General Service and Victory Medals.
27, Church Path, Hammersmith, W.6.　　15903B.

RAINFORTH, H. T., Bombardier, R.G.A.
Joining in 1916, he was drafted in the same year to Salonika
and later to Egypt, where he joined the Expeditionary
Force under General Allenby. He served throughout
the Palestine Campaign, and was present at the fall of
Jerusalem. On his return to England he was demobilised
in 1919, and holds the General Service and Victory Medals.
5, Maybury Gardens, Willesden, N.W.10.　　X17442.

RAKE, F. (M.M.), Pte., 11th Royal Fusiliers.
He volunteered in September 1914, and was drafted to the
Western Front, where he took part in many engagements,
including those at Ypres, Combles, Arras and during the
Retreat and Advance of 1918. He was awarded the
Military Medal for conspicuous bravery in the field, and
during his service was wounded five times. He also holds
the 1914–15 Star and the General Service and Victory
Medals, and was demobilised in February 1919.
104, Shakespeare Avenue, Willesden, N.W.10.　　13626.

**RAMAGE, F. C., Corporal, 3rd The London
Regiment (Royal Fusiliers).**
Volunteering in August 1914, he was shortly afterwards
sent to the Western Front, where he played a distinguished
part in engagements at Neuve Chapelle, Loos, the Somme,
Arras, Ypres and Cambrai. After being wounded and taken
prisoner at St. Quentin, he had his right leg amputated
in hospital in Germany. On his release he was sent
to England and invalided out of the service as medically
unfit in December 1918. He holds the 1914–15 Star
and the General Service and Victory Medals.
62, Fernhead Road, Maida Hill, W.9.　　X19461

RAMSEY, G., Pioneer Corporal, Rifle Brigade and East Kent Regiment.
He joined in September 1917 and after his training was retained with his unit on important duties. His ill-health prevented him from going overseas before the end of the war, but he gave valuable services before he was demobilised in November 1919.
52, Bravington Road, Maida Hill, W.9.   X19187.

RAMSEY, H. E., Pte., Suffolk Regiment.
He joined in 1916, and was sent to France, where he took part in many engagements, and whilst in action near Ypres was wounded. He was demobilised in 1919, holding the General Service and Victory Medals.
9, Winchester Road, Lower Edmonton, N.9.   14677.

RAMSEY, S. W., Pte., R.A.S.C. (M.T.).
He joined in November 1916, and was sent in the same year to France, where he was employed on the ammunition and supply column in the Ypres, Armentieres, Soissons, Cambrai, Albert, Arras, and Bapaume sectors. He was demobilised in November 1919, and holds the General Service and Victory Medals.
52, Bravington Road, Maida Hill, W.9.   X19186.

RANCE, H., Pte., Queen's (Royal West Surrey Regiment).
Volunteering in November 1915, he was sent to France in the following year, and remained in that theatre of war for three years. During this time he saw much severe fighting on various sectors. He holds the General Service and Victory Medals, and was demobilised in February 1919.
55, Oxford Road, Lower Edmonton, N.9.   12964.

RANDALL, A., Driver, Royal Engineers.
He volunteered in August 1914, and later in the year was drafted to the Western Front, where he took part in important operations in various sectors. He was present at the battles of the Somme and St. Quentin, and in heavy fighting around Armentieres. Whilst on active service he suffered severely from concussion, and is now totally deaf in one ear. He was demobilised in February 1919, and holds the 1914 Star and the General Service and Victory Medals.
15, Cornwallis Grove, Lower Edmonton, N.9.   13522.

RANDALL, F. J. (M.M.), Lce.-Corpl., Wiltshire Regiment.
He joined in October 1916 and in the following January was drafted to the Western Front, where he took part in the battles of Vimy Ridge, Ypres and Cambrai, and in heavy fighting during the Advance in 1918. He was awarded the Military Medal for conspicuous bravery and devotion to duty in the field, and in addition holds the General Service and Victory Medals. He was demobilised in March 1919.
45, Melville Road, Stonebridge Park, N.W.10.   15652A.

RANDALL, G. (Miss), Special War Worker.
For a period of three years during the war this lady was engaged on work of national importance at the Park Royal Munition Factory. She held a responsible position as an examiner in the bomb-making department, and rendered valuable services throughout.
39, Melville Road, Stonebridge Park, N.W.10.   15661B.

RANDALL, H., Pte., 1st Essex Regiment.
He joined in 1917, and on completion of his training was drafted to Russia, where he underwent trying experiences and saw much severe fighting. In 1919 he returned to this country and was sent to Ireland, where he was still serving in 1920. He holds the General Service and Victory Medals.
36, Chesson Road, West Kensington, W.14.   X17236.

RANDALL, H. E. (Mrs.), Special War Worker.
During the war this lady was engaged at the Park Royal Munition Factory, where she held a responsible position in the Fuse and Small Arms Inspection Departments. She carried out her duties in a very efficient manner and received high commendation for her valuable services.
45, Melville Road, Stonebridge Park, N.W.10.   15652B.

RANDALL, T., Pte., Suffolk Regiment.
Volunteering in 1915, he was sent in the following year to Egypt. While in this seat of operations he took part in many important engagements against the Turks and was in hospital for a considerable time with malaria. In 1919 he returned to this country for demobilisation, and holds the General Service and Victory Medals.
24, Brenthurst Road, Church End, N.W.10.   16385A.

RANFORD, G. H., Sapper, Royal Engineers.
He volunteered in December 1915, and on completion of his training was drafted to the Western Front, in the following September. He took part in many important engagements, including the battles of the Somme and Ypres, and was severely wounded near Cambrai in March 1918. On April 9th of the same year he died in hospital from the effects of his wounds, and was entitled to the General Service and Victory Medals.
26, Fifth Avenue, Queen's Park Estate, W.10.   X18325.

RANGER, C., Corporal, Royal Army Medical Corps.
He enlisted in 1903, and was sent to France immediately on the outbreak of hostilities. He took part in the Retreat from Mons and was later engaged on important duties as ward master on a hospital-ship crossing to and from France. He also served in Egypt, Syria and Palestine, where he again saw much fighting. In March 1919 he was discharged after 16 years' service, and holds the Mons Star and the General Service and Victory Medals.
19, Ravensworth Road, College Park, N.W.10.   X17617.

RANSCOMBE, T. (M.M.), Pte., Royal Berkshire Regiment.
He was serving at the outbreak of war and was immediately sent to the Western Front, where he took a prominent part in the retreat from Mons and the battles of the Marne, the Aisne, Ypres, Neuve Chapelle, Festubert, Loos, the Somme and Cambrai. He was wounded in March 1918, and was awarded the Military Medal for conspicuous bravery and devotion to duty in the field. In addition he also holds two Divisional Parchment Certificates, the Mons Star, and the General Service and Victory Medals. He was discharged in October 1918 as medically unfit for further service owing to wounds.
20, Farrant Street, Queen's Park Estate, W.10.   X19312.

RANSOM, H. H., Pte., R.A.V.C.
He joined in September 1916, and on completion of his training was sent to the Western Front in the following year. He remained in this seat of war until 1919, and during this time was engaged on important duties with his unit on various sectors of the Front. He holds the General Service and Victory medals, and was demobilised in April 1919.
111, Harley Road, Willesden, N.W.10.   13183.

RANTELL, A. T., Pte. and Rifleman, 10th and 8th London Regiment.
He joined in June 1916, and in the following December was sent to the Western Front, where he took part in many important engagements, including the battle of Cambrai. During his service he was wounded three times, and in November 1917 was invalided home. On discharge from hospital he was medically unfit for further service overseas, and was retained on special duties until his demobilisation in September 1919. He holds the General Service and Victory Medals.
206, Shirland Road, Maida Hill, W.9.   X19606.

RATCLIFF, H. C., Pte., 2nd Manchester Regiment.
Joining in June 1916, he was sent to France later in the same year, and took part in many important engagements in various sectors. During his service overseas he was wounded. On his return to this country he was demobilised in November 1919, and holds the General Service and Victory Medals.
38, Lion Road, Lower Edmonton, N.9.   15193B.

RATCLIFF, W., Sergeant, Royal Field Artillery.
Volunteering in June 1915, he was drafted to the Western Front, and took a prominent part in the battles of the Somme, Ypres, Arras and Cambrai and was wounded. In March 1919 he returned to England for demobilisation, and holds the General Service and Victory Medals.
57, Garvan Road, Hammersmith, W.6.   14840.

RATCLIFF, W. A. J., Rifleman, 5th The London Regiment (L.R.B.).
He joined in January 1916, and on completion of his training was drafted to the Western Front, where, after taking part in severe fighting, he was killed in action at Loos on September 9th of the same year. He was entitled to the General Service and Victory Medals.
38, Lion Road, Lower Edmonton, N.9.   15193A.

RATCLIFFE, W. A., Rifleman, 12th The London Regiment (Rangers).
He volunteered in 1915, and was drafted to the Western Front, where he took part in the heavy fighting at the battles of Ypres (where he was wounded) and during the Retreat and Advance of 1918. He was demobilised in February 1919, and holds the General Service and Victory Medals.
104, Carlyle Avenue, Willesden, N.W.10.   14455A.

RATTY, F., Bombardier, Royal Field Artillery.
He volunteered in November 1914, and after his training
was drafted to the Western Front, where he took part in
the battles of Hill 60 and Loos. He was wounded in the
latter engagement, and was invalided home. After a
long time in hospital he was discharged, owing to his
wounds, as medically unfit for further service, in September
1916. He holds the 1914–15 Star and the General Service
and Victory Medals.
47, Cornwallis Road, Lower Edmonton, N.9.   13403.

RAVEN, A., Sapper, Royal Engineers.
He joined in 1916, and served in France for three years,
during which time he took part in many important engagements. He was demobilised in April 1919, holding the
General Service and Victory Medals.
49, Humbolt Road, Hammersmith, W.6.   15316A.

RAVEN, C. S., Driver, R.A.S.C. (M.T.).
Joining in April 1916, he was sent to France in the following
month. Whilst on the Western Front he was engaged on
important duties with his unit on various sectors, and
remained in this seat of war until December 1918. He was
demobilised in January 1919, and holds the General
Service and Victory Medals.
41, Wendover Road, Harlesden, N.W.10.   12551.

RAVEN, H. A., Corpl., 12th Middlesex Regiment.
He volunteered in September 1914, at the age of forty,
and was drafted to the Western Front, where he
took part in many important engagements, and during
heavy fighting was wounded in action at Albert. In
November 1918 he was demobilised, and holds the 1914–15
Star and the General Service and Victory Medals and the
King's Certificate.
143, Estcourt Road, Fulham, S.W.6.   16238.

**RAVEN, H. J., Lce.-Corpl., 2/5th Durham Light
Infantry.**
He joined in July 1916, and in the same year was sent
to Salonika, where he took part in important operations until
1918, when he was then sent into Bulgaria and Serbia.
In January 1919 he was sent home and demobilised,
holding the General Service and Victory Medals.
141, Croyland Road, Lower Edmonton, N.9.   13926.

**RAWDEN, G., Corporal, 18th The London
Regiment (London Irish Rifles).**
Volunteering in August 1914, he was sent to France in the
following January, and took part in the battle of Neuve
Chapelle and in heavy fighting at Givenchy and Loos,
when he was wounded in action at Loos. He was invalided
home in August 1915, and after being in hospital for some
time was discharged in December 1916 as medically unfit
for further service. He holds the 1914–15 Star and the
General Service and Victory Medals.
1, Woodheyes Road, Neasden, N.W.10.   15586B.

**RAWDON, K. A., Rifleman and Pte., King's
Royal Rifle Corps, and Black Watch.**
He volunteered in July 1915, and in the following January
was drafted to the Western Front, where he took part in
heavy fighting at Ypres. In April 1916 he returned home,
and was engaged on important duties at various stations
until August, 1918, when he was again sent to France.
He took part in engagements during the concluding stages
of the war, and was eventually demobilised in February
1920, holding the General Service and Victory Medals.
1, Woodheyes Road, Neasden, N.W.10.   15586A.

**RAWLINGS, E., Corporal, The Queen's (Royal
West Surrey Regiment).**
He was mobilised early in August 1914, and in the same year
was drafted to the Western Front, where he took part in
the Retreat from Mons, the battles of Ypres, Loos, and the
Somme, and for a time acted as bodyguard to Sir Douglas
Haig. From 1916 until 1918 he served in Egypt, and was
wounded three times. He holds the Mons Star and the
General Service and Victory Medals, and was discharged in
March 1918 as medically unfit for further service.
28, Woodfield Place, Maida Hill, W.9.   X19716A.

RAWLINGS, H., Driver, Royal Field Artillery.
He joined in 1917, and on completion of his training was
sent to Mesopotamia, where he took part in many important
operations. In 1920 he was still serving in the East, and
holds the General Service and Victory Medals.
43, Lurgan Avenue, Hammersmith, W.6.   13785.

RAWLINGS, J. E., Gunner, Royal Field Artillery.
He joined in January 1916, and was later drafted to the
Western Front, where he took part in the battles of Arras
and Cambrai and in heavy fighting on the Marne in the
Advance of 1918. During his service overseas he was
twice wounded, and in October 1919 was demobilised,
holding the General Service and Victory Medals.
37, Raynham Avenue, Upper Edmonton, N.18.   15822.

RAWLINGS, L. E. (Mrs.), Special War Worker.
This lady was engaged on very necessary work throughout
the war, making military uniforms for a firm of Army
contractors in Regent Street, W. Her valuable services
were very highly appreciated, and she received high commendation for her work.
28, Woodfield Place, Maida Hill, W.9.   X19716B.

RAWLINSON, E., Pte., Middlesex Regiment.
He joined in March 1916, and was almost immediately
sent to the Western Front, where he took part in heavy
fighting until July of the same year, when he was wounded
in action at Delville Wood and invalided home. On his
recovery he was incapacitated for further active service,
and was sent to Ireland. He remained there on important
duties until his demobilisation in August 1919, and holds
the General Service and Victory Medals.
16, Shakespeare Road, Upper Edmonton, N.18. X17180.

RAWLINSON, H., Pte., Royal Army Service Corps.
Volunteering in May 1915, he served in France for nearly
four years. During this period he was engaged on important transport duties, and took a prominent part in many
engagements. He holds the 1914–15 Star and the General
Service and Victory Medals, and was demobilised in
March 1919.
89, Love Lane, Tottenham, N.17.   X18528.

RAWLINSON, J. J. E., Pte., 20th Royal Fusiliers.
He volunteered in November 1914, and was sent to the
Western Front in the following February. He took part
in much heavy fighting until June 28th, 1916, when he was
killed in action at Carnoy, near Albert. He had been
previously wounded, and was entitled to the 1914–15
Star and the General Service and Victory Medals.
3, Kenmont Gardens, College Park, N.W.10.   X17449B.

RAWLINSON, W. O., Pte., 2nd Middlesex Regt.
Joining in November 1917, he was sent to France almost
immediately, and took part in much severe fighting on
various sectors. In 1919 he was drafted to Egypt, and
was engaged on important duties there. He was still
serving in the East in 1920, and holds the General Service
and Victory Medals.
95, Asplin Road, Tottenham, N.17.   X19082.

RAXWORTHY, E. G., Pte., Royal Sussex Regt.
He joined in March 1916, and was drafted to France in
the following year. He remained on the Western Front
for nearly three years, and during this period saw much
severe fighting on various sectors. He holds the General
Service and Victory Medals, and was demobilised in
September 1919.
143, Winchester Road, Lower Edmonton, N.9.   14950B.

RAXWORTHY, G. W., Mechanic, Royal Air Force.
He joined in September 1916, and on completion of his
training was drafted to France in the same year. He
carried out important duties with his squadron until 1917,
when he returned to England. He was then engaged on
work which called for a high degree of skill, until his
demobilisation in March 1919, and holds the General
Service and Victory Medals.
143, Winchester Road, Lower Edmonton, N.9.   14950A.

RAY, T., Rifleman, King's Royal Rifle Corps.
He joined in March 1917, and after his training was drafted
to the Western Front, where he took part in the battles of
Ypres and Cambrai, and in other important engagements,
and was severely wounded in action. After spending a
considerable period in hospital in France, he was invalided
to England, and on his recovery was retained on special
duties until his demobilisation in May 1920. He holds the
General Service and Victory Medals.
56, Rosaline Road, Munster Road, S.W.6.   X18181.

**RAYMENT, S. E., Pte., The Queen's (Royal
West Surrey Regiment).**
Volunteering in April 1915, he was retained for some time
on special duties in England. Early in 1918, however, he
was drafted to France, and after taking a prominent
part in severe fighting, died in April from wounds received
in action. He was entitled to the General Service and
Victory Medals.
15, Brereton Road, Tottenham, N.17.   X18382.

RAYMOND, F., Pte., Royal Fusiliers.

He volunteered in 1915, and in the same year was sent to the Western Front, where he fought in many important engagements, including the Retreat and Advance of 1918, and was wounded in action. He holds the 1914–15 Star and the General Service and Victory Medals, and was demobilised in February 1919.

37, Redfern Road, Willesden, N.W.10.　　13204B.

RAYMOND, J. F., Pte., R.A.S.C. (M.T.).

He volunteered in August 1914, and was sent to France shortly after the outbreak of hostilities. Whilst on the Western Front, he was engaged on important transport duties at the battles of Ypres and the Somme, and in heavy fighting in the Retreat and Advance of 1918. He was wounded during his service overseas, and in May 1919 was demobilised, holding the 1914 Star and the General Service and Victory Medals.

35, Redfern Road, Willesden, N.W.10.　　13206C.

RAYMOND, W. H., Sergt., Royal Defence Corps.

Volunteering in October 1914, he was drafted to the Western Front, where he was engaged on responsible work with the Chinese Labour Corps and gave valuable services. After the signing of the Armistice, he was employed on special duties, convoying the Chinese back to their own country. He holds the General Service and Victory Medals.

35, Redfern Road, Willesden, N.W.10.　　13206A.

RAYNER, A., Saddler, Royal Field Artillery.

He volunteered in August 1914, and in the following year was drafted to Egypt, where he remained for three months. He was then sent to Salonika and saw service there until 1917, during which time he took part in severe fighting, and served throughout the Retreat from Serbia. In March 1919, he was demobilised, and holds the 1914–15 Star and the General Service and Victory Medals.

119, Victor Road, College Park, N.W.10.　　X17530.

RAYNER, F., Pte., Royal Fusiliers and Bedfordshire Regiment.

He joined in 1917, and after his training was engaged on important duties at various stations with his unit. He gave valuable services, but was not successful in obtaining his transfer overseas before the cessation of hostilities. He was demobilised in September 1919.

8, Oak Road, Willesden, N.W.10.　　15082.

RAYNER, W., 1st Class Stoker, R.N., H.M.S. "Osea."

Volunteering in August 1914, he was posted to H.M.S. "Osea," and during his service took part in important naval operations with the Grand Fleet in the North Sea. He remained at sea until his demobilisation in April 1919, and holds the 1914–15 Star and the General Service and Victory Medals.

21, Victor Road, College Park, N.W.10.　　X17538.

RAYNER, W., Pte., Royal Defence Corps.

He volunteered in September 1914, and, after the completion of his training, was employed on special duties at various stations. He gave valuable services, but not being successful in obtaining his transfer overseas, was demobilised in March 1919.

6, Bridge Road, Willesden, N.W.10.　　15465B.

RAYNOR, W. H., Sapper, Royal Engineers.

He volunteered in November 1914, and was shortly after sent to France, where he was employed on important duties during operations in various sectors. He was demobilised in February 1920, and holds the 1914–15 Star and the General Service and Victory Medals.

28, Selwyn Road, Willesden, N.W.10.　　14609.

READ, A. E., Pte., Royal Army Veterinary Corps.

Joining in April 1917, he was drafted to the Western Front, where, with the Royal Army Veterinary Corps, he did valuable work in connection with the transporting and tending of horses. He returned to England in 1919, when he was demobilised, holding the General Service and Victory Medals.

12, Mooltan Street, West Kensington, W.14.　　X17148.

READ, B. (Mrs.), Special War Worker.

During the war this lady was engaged at the Perivale and Park Royal Munition Factories. She worked as a packer in the fuse section, and also in other departments, and throughout her service carried out her duties in a commendable manner.

14, Winchelsea Road, Willesden, N.W.10.　　13719A.

READ, C., Pte., Machine Gun Corps.

Volunteering in October 1914, he was drafted to the Western Front, where he took part in the battles of Ypres, Neuve Chapelle, Vimy Ridge, the Somme, Hill 60, Loos, Festubert, Bullecourt, Lille and the last Advance. He returned to England in April 1919, when he was demobilised, holding the 1914–15 Star and the General Service and Victory Medals.

230, Munster Road, Fulham, S.W.6.　　X19252.

READ, C., Pte., Queen's (Royal West Surrey Regt.).

He volunteered in June 1915, and served for a time on the Western Front. Later he was sent to Mesopotamia, and thence to Egypt and Palestine, where he took a conspicuous part in engagements at Haifa and in other sectors with General Allenby's forces. He was demobilised in April 1919, and holds the 1914–15 Star and the General Service and Victory Medals.

2, Salcombe Road, Stoke Newington, N.16.　　X18900.

READ, E. (Miss), Special War Worker.

This lady was engaged during the war first in making hand grenades at Messrs. Vandervell's Munition Factory, Acton, and afterwards on difficult and responsible work at the Glendover Aircraft Factory at South Kensington, where she was employed in making parts of aeroplane engines, and in this capacity rendered valuable service.

230, Munster Road, Fulham, S.W.6.　　X19245.

READ, E. H., Gunner, Royal Field Artillery.

He volunteered in October 1914 and in the following year was drafted to the Western Front. He took part in the battles of Loos and the Somme, and was also in action at St. Julien. In 1917 he was severely wounded, losing a leg, in consequence of which he was invalided home; and in March of the same year was discharged, physically unfit for further service. He holds the 1914–15 Star and the General Service and Victory Medals.

43, Brookville Road, Dawes Road, S.W.6.　　X20423A.

READ, F., Air Mechanic, Royal Air Force.

When war broke out he was serving in the Middlesex Regiment, and was afterwards transferred to the Royal Air Force. He was drafted to the Western Front in 1914, and during his service overseas, which lasted five years, saw fighting in many important sectors, including Ypres, the Somme, Arras and Cambrai, and on two occasions was severely wounded. He also went through the final Retreat and Advance, and in 1919 returned to England, where he was demobilised. He holds the Territorial Efficiency Medal, the 1914–15 Star and the General Service and Victory Medals.

14, Winchelsea Road, Willesden, N.W.10.　　13719B.

READ, F. J., Gunner, Royal Field Artillery.

He volunteered in March 1915, and, after his training was drafted to Salonika, where he took part in engagements on various sectors, and did good work with his unit. Later he contracted a severe form of malaria as the result of which he was invalided home, and in 1919 he was demobilised, holding the General Service and Victory Medals.

230, Munster Road, Fulham, S.W.6.　　X19244.

READ, G., Tpr., 1st (King's) Dragoon Guards.

He was serving at the outbreak of war, and in August 1914 was sent out to France. Whilst overseas he took a prominent part in many engagements, including those of Ypres, Festubert, and Arras. In December 1919 he was demobilised, holding the 1914 Star and the General Service and Victory Medals.

77, Southam Street, N. Kensington, W.10.　　X20781.

READ, G., Sergeant, Wiltshire Regiment.

He volunteered in October 1915, having previously served for over twelve years, and was on the secret service train ferry from England to France. He was demobilised in February 1919, and holds the General Service and Victory Medals.

11, Bull Lane, Upper Edmonton, N.18.　　X17884.

READ, G. H., Gunner, Royal Field Artillery.

Volunteering in 1914, he received his training at various stations in England, and later was drafted to Salonika. He saw fighting on several sectors with his unit, and was severely wounded, and later, having contracted malaria, was invalided home. On recovery he was certified unfit for further foreign service, and sent to Stock, in Essex, where, until his demobilisation in 1919, he did valuable work with the anti-aircraft guns. He holds the 1914–15 Star and the General Service and Victory Medals.

13, Orbain Road, Fulham, S.W.6.　　X18216.

READ, H., Driver, Royal Army Service Corps.

He was in the Army when war broke out, and was drafted to the Western Front where, with the ammunition columns, he went through the memorable Retreat from Mons. In 1915 he returned to England, and in December of the same year, owing to his service, was discharged as unfit. He holds the Mons Star and the General Service and Victory Medals.

54, Huddlestone Road, Cricklewood, N.W.2. X17412.

READ, M. (Miss), Special War Worker.

This lady was employed on important and responsible work at Messrs. Du Cros' Munition Factory, Acton, where she was engaged on shell making. Afterwards she went to the Glendover Aircraft Factory, South Kensington, as a metal worker, for aeroplane engines, and rendered valuable service in this capacity.

230, Munster Road, Fulham, S.W.6. X19251.

READ, S., Pte., Labour Corps.

He joined in March 1917, and after his training served at various stations engaged on hut building and other special duties. He did good work with his unit, but was not successful in being transferred overseas before the cessation of hostilities. He was demobilised in November 1919.

43, Brookville Road, Dawes Road, S.W.6. X20423B.

READ, T., Corporal, 3rd Royal Fusiliers.

He volunteered in February 1915, and at the conclusion of his training was engaged at various stations for coastal defence and similar useful military purposes. He was not successful in obtaining his transfer overseas before the cessation of hostilities, but did valuable work before being demobilised in February 1919.

5, Fordingley Road, Maida Hill, W.9. X19700.

READ, V. A., 1st Class Stoker, Royal Navy.

He was called up on the outbreak of war in 1914, and was posted to H.M.S. "Cressy," later being transferred, first to H.M.S. "Cornwallis" and then to H.M.S. "Marshal Ney." He was present at many naval engagements during his service, including the bombardment of the Dardanelles, and the battles of Jutland and Heligoland Bight, and on two occasions his ship was torpedoed. He also met with a serious accident, in which he sustained severe injuries, and in August 1919, after five years' active service, was demobilised. He holds the 1914 Star and the General Service and Victory Medals.

58, Musard Road, Hammersmith, W.6. 15320.

READ, W., Corporal, Royal Fusiliers.

Mobilised in August 1914, he was sent a year later to Salonika, where he served for two years. In 1917 he was transferred to the Western Front, and played a distinguished part in the fighting, but during the Advance was killed in action on October 4th, 1918. He was entitled to the 1914-15 Star and the General Service and Victory Medals.

32, Althea Street, Townmead Road, S.W.6. X21155B.

READ, W., 1st Air Mechanic, Royal Air Force.

He joined in 1916 and after his training was drafted to the Western Front, where he was employed on the repair of aeroplane engines, which work required high technical skill. After rendering valuable services, he was demobilised in December 1918, holding the General Service and Victory Medals.

80, Bridport Road, Upper Edmonton, N.18. X17475.

READ, W. D., Sergeant, Royal Munster Fusiliers.

He had previously enlisted in 1898, and volunteered for further service on the outbreak of hostilities in 1914. Later he was sent to Gallipoli, and took part in the memorable first landing at Suvla Bay, during which he was severely wounded. With the 10th Division he went to Salonika and thence to Egypt, where he was again in action, and afterwards saw service in Russia with the Royal Fusiliers. He holds the 1914-15 Star and the General Service and Victory Medals, and was demobilised in December 1919.

73, Bramber Road, West Kensington, W.14. 15726.

READ, W. G., Sergeant, Middlesex Regiment.

He volunteered in November 1915, and in the following year was drafted to France, where he remained for three years. He took a prominent part in many important battles, and whilst in action on the Somme in 1916, when there was some particularly heavy fighting, was severely gassed. In 1919 he returned to England, and in May was demobilised, holding the General Service and Victory Medals.

18, Brereton Road, Tottenham, N.17. 18107.

READER, A. R., 1st Class Petty Officer, Royal Navy, H.M.S. "Diadem."

He volunteered in August 1914, saw service in Russian waters and in the North Sea, and lost his life on April 25th, 1917, when the hospital ship on which he was then serving was torpedoed. He was entitled to the 1914 Star and the General Service and Victory Medals.

89, Rayleigh Road, West Kensington, W.14. 12631.

READING, D. M. (Miss), Special War Worker.

From January 1915 until June 1918 this lady was employed at Messrs. Sparklet's on the manufacture of cartridges. Whilst engaged on this important work she was injured in an accident, and suffered the loss of two of her fingers. On resigning she was commended for her valuable services.

25, Balfour Road, Lower Edmonton, N.9. 14043.

READING, T., Pte., 2nd East Surrey Regiment.

Having previously been engaged on work of national importance, he volunteered for military service in December 1915, and in the following year was drafted to Salonika. He took part in the Balkan campaign, and did valuable work with his unit until July 1919, when he returned to England and was demobilised. He holds the General Service and Victory Medals.

419, Chapter Road, Cricklewood, N.W.10. 16160.

READY, W. J., Driver, R.A.S.C. (H.T.).

Volunteering in August 1914, he was drafted to Egypt in the following year. Afterwards he was sent to Mesopotamia, and thence to the Western Front, where he remained for nearly four years. Throughout his service he did valuable work with the Horse Transport, and saw service in many important sectors, including St. Eloi, Ypres, Passchendaele, Loos, the Somme and Arras, and also went through the Advance of 1918. He returned to England in 1919, and was demobilised, holding the 1914-15 Star and the General Service and Victory Medals.

16, Woodchester Street, Paddington, W.2. X20688.

REAMS, A., Pte., 2nd Royal Sussex Regiment.

Joining in January 1916, he was drafted to the Western Front, where during his three years service he took part in many battles, including those of Ypres and the Somme, and was twice wounded. He holds the General Service and Victory Medals, and was demobilised in January 1919.

136, Bounces Road, Lower Edmonton, N.9. 13010A.

REARDON, F. J., Pte., Motor Machine Gun Corps.

He joined in March 1917, and in the same year was sent to France, where he gave valuable services and remained until the cessation of hostilities. He holds the General Service and Victory Medals, and in 1920 was still serving.

19, Folkstone Road, Upper Edmonton, N.18. 15567.

REASON, J. W., Rifleman, 15th The London Regiment (Civil Service Rifles).

He joined in 1918 and after his training served at various stations on important duties with his unit. He was not successful in obtaining his transfer overseas before the cessation of hostilities, but gave valuable services before being demobilised in 1919.

20, Steele Road, Willesden, N.W.10. 13835C.

REASON, W., Pte., Royal Defence Corps.

He volunteered in September 1914, and was engaged on the important duties of guarding prisoners of war at various stations. He was also employed as a guard over munition stores. He was unsuccessful in obtaining his transfer overseas and, after giving valuable services, was demobilised in January 1919.

12, Ambleside Road, Willesden, N.W.10. 16126.

REBBECK, A. J., Pte., 22nd The London Regiment (Queen's).

He volunteered in July 1915, and after his training was drafted to the East. He went through the Palestine campaign with General Allenby's forces, and was present at the entry into Jerusalem, besides taking part in various engagements in Egypt. In 1919 he returned to England, and in July was demobilised, holding the 1914-15 Star and the General Service and Victory Medals.

9, Brenthurst Road, Church End, N.W.10. 16381B.

REBBECK, R. S., Pte., Royal Sussex Regiment.

Joining in January 1916, he was drafted to Egypt on completion of his training in the following year. He took part in the Palestine campaign with General Allenby's forces and was so severely wounded during some heavy fighting as to necessitate his return to England. For some time he was under treatment in hospital and in March 1918 was invalided out of the service. He holds the General Service and Victory Medals.

9, Brenthurst Road, Church End, N.W.10. 16381A.

REBBECK, W. G., Pte., 19th The London Regt.
Volunteering in September 1914, he received his training at various stations in England. In 1915 he was drafted to Egypt, and after taking part in various engagements there, was sent to Palestine, where with General Allenby's forces he again saw heavy fighting, and was present at the entry into Jerusalem. He returned to England in 1919, and was demobilised in March, holding the 1914-15 Star and the General Service and Victory Medals.
9, Brenthurst Road, Church End, N.W.10.   16381C.

RECORD, C. H., Pte., The London Regiment.
He joined in June 1917, and served on the Western Front, where he took part in fighting on the Somme, at Lille and in the Retreat and Advance. He was demobilised in October 1919, and holds the General Service and Victory Medals.
53, Felixstowe Road, Lower Edmonton, N.9.   15385.

REDDICK, J., Pte., 8th East Surrey Regiment.
He volunteered in May 1915 and after being sent to France in 1917, took part in engagements at Cambrai, Hill 60, Bullecourt and Armentieres. In September 1918 he was severely wounded in action and died on the following day. He was entitled to the General Service and Victory Medals.
33, Winchelsea Road, Willesden, N.W.10.   13708B.

REDDING, W., Pte., 19th Middlesex Regiment.
He volunteered in February 1915, and during his service in France, which lasted for three years, took an important part in many engagements, and was gassed. He was demobilised in December 1918, and holds the General Service and Victory Medals.
28, Somerford Grove, Tottenham, N.17.   X18809.

REDELSPERGER, P., 4th Zouaves, French Army.
On the outbreak of War he was residing in England, and immediately proceeded to France to join his regiment (The Zouaves). He fought side by side with the British Army at Mons, and was also engaged at Ypres, Arras, the Battle of the Somme, Cambrai, and numerous other places. He was wounded, and was then transferred to the Artillery. For bravery in the field he was awarded the Croix de Guerre, and the French Government Certificate acknowledging his valour and services, and he is also in possession of official notification that he is entitled to the Mons Star, the General Service and Victory Medals. He was demobilised in November 1919, after over five years' continuous service at the Front.
43, Minet Avenue, Willesden, N.W.10.   13915A.

REDHEAD, W. R., Gunner, Royal Field Artillery.
He volunteered in November 1914, and served for four years on the Western Front, during which time he was in action in many sectors, including the Somme, Arras, and Cambrai. He was demobilised in January 1919, and holds the 1914-15 Star and the General Service and Victory Medals.
51, King's Road, Upper Edmonton, N.18.   [15520.

REDMAN, G., Driver, Royal Army Service Corps.
He volunteered in October 1915, and after his training was sent to German East Africa, where he served with the R.A.S.C. under General Smuts. On his return to England he was demobilised in November 1919, holding the General Service and Victory Medals.
21, Moylan Road, Hammersmith, W.6.   15291.

REDPATH, C. O., Sergeant, Royal Engineers.
Volunteering in March 1915, he received his training at various stations in England, and afterwards was drafted to the Western Front. Throughout his service he did valuable work with the Royal Engineers in many important sectors, and was severely gassed in June 1918. He returned to England in 1919, when he was demobilised, holding the General Service and Victory Medals.
84, Mordaunt Road, Willesden, N.W.10.   13855.

REECE, A., Special War Worker.
He was employed from 1915 until 1918 in the Cartridge Inspection Department of Park Royal Munition Factory, where his services, which were of great value, were much appreciated.
13, St. Mary's Mansions, St. Mary's Road,
Craven Park, N.W.10.   15120A.

REECE, A., Special War Worker.
During the war he served at the Fairlop Aerodrome, where besides being engaged on work which demanded a high degree of technical skill, he helped in the erection of hangars. Throughout his service proved valuable, and he was highly commended when, at the cessation of hostilities, he resigned.
13, St. Mary's Mansions, St. Mary's Road,
Craven Park, N.W.10.   15120B.

REED, A. V., Pte., Middlesex Regiment.
Joining in November 1916, he was sent to the Western Front on completion of his training. He took a prominent part in several important battles, and in December 1917 was killed in action in the Cambrai sector. He was entitled to the General Service and Victory Medals.
45, College Road, Willesden, N.W.10.   X18014B.

REED, C., Driver, R.A.S.C. (M.T.).
He joined in October 1916, and saw three years' service in France, where he was engaged in conveying food and ammunition to the lines. He holds the General Service and Victory Medals, and was demobilised in July 1919.
20, Church Road, Hammersmith, W.6.   11106B.

REED, E. G. W., Pte., Royal Army Medical Corps.
He joined in June 1916, and after his training, being physically unfit for foreign service, served at various important duties with his unit. He did valuable work, but in April 1918 was invalided out of the service.
12, Bramber Road, West Kensington, W.14.   16282.

REED, F., Sergeant, Royal Army Medical Corps.
Volunteering in 1914, he received his training at various stations, and in the following year was sent to the Western Front. Throughout his service overseas, which lasted four years, he did valuable work with the R.A.M.C., and was present at many important engagements, including those at Ypres and the Somme. He returned to England in 1919, and in April of the following year was demobilised, holding the 1914-15 Star and the General Service and Victory Medals.
9, Rowallan Road, Munster Road, S.W.6.   X19281.

REEDMAN, W., Sapper, Royal Engineers.
He joined in February 1916, and after a short period of training was drafted to the Western Front. His service overseas lasted for three years, during which time he did excellent work with the Royal Engineers in various sectors including Ypres, the Somme, Arras and Cambrai. He returned to England in 1919, when he was demobilised, holding the General Service and Victory Medals.
80, Chippenham Road, Maida Hill, W.9.   X20761.

REEGAM, J., Pte., R.A.S.C. (M.T.).
He joined in February 1916, and after his training was drafted to the Western Front. For two years he served with the Mechanical Transport in various important sectors, and was present during the battles of Vimy Ridge, Arras and Cambrai. He was demobilised in June 1919, and holds the General Service and Victory Medals.
92A, Deacon Road, Cricklewood, N.W.10.   X17311.

REESE, E. W., Lce.-Corpl., 3rd Middlesex Regt.
Joining in January 1918, he received his training at various stations in England, and was also engaged on special duties. He was not successful in obtaining his transfer overseas before the cessation of hostilities, but afterwards was drafted to the Army of Occupation in Germany, where in 1920 he was still serving.
6, Selwyn Road, Willesden, N.W.10.   14613B.

REESE, W. H., Pte., Royal Army Service Corps.
He volunteered in July 1915, and for three years served in France, where he did valuable work with the Labour Corps. He was afterwards stationed in Ireland until May 1918, when he was discharged, holding the 1914-15 Star and the General Service and Victory Medals.
6, Selwyn Road, Willesden, N.W.10.   14613A.

REEVE, A., Pte., 7th Suffolk Regiment.
He joined in October 1916, and served for eight months on the Western Front, during which time he took part in many engagements, including the battle of the Somme. He holds the General Service and Victory Medals, and was demobilised in May 1919.
16, Chelmsford Street, Hammersmith, W.6.   15733.

REEVE, F., Pte., 16th Royal Sussex Regiment.
Joining in October 1916, he received his training at various stations, and in the following year was sent to Egypt, where he served until 1918. He was then drafted to the Western Front, and after taking part in several important battles was severely wounded in action at Cambrai. He returned to England, and in February 1919 was demobilised, holding the General Service and Victory Medals.
27, York Road, Upper Edmonton, N.18.   16545.

20

REEVE, F. J., Corporal, 17th Tank Corps.

Joining in August 1916, he served in various sectors of the Western Front, where throughout his service he did valuable work with the Tank Corps. He returned to England on the termination of the war, and in 1920 was stationed in Limerick. He holds the General Service and Victory Medals.
93, Manor Park Road, Harlesden, N.W.10.   13225.

REEVE, J., Pte., 23rd Middlesex Regiment.

He volunteered in November 1915, and during his service on the Western Front took part in several engagements, and was wounded three times. He was demobilised in February 1919, and holds the General Service and Victory Medals.
42, Hannell Road, Munster Road, S.W.6.   18074B.

REEVE, J. W., Gunner, R.G.A. (217th Siege Bty.).

Joining in February 1916, he was drafted to the Western Front in the following year. Whilst overseas he acted as signaller and took part in many important engagements, but in March 1917 was severely wounded in action at Arras. After being sent home to England, he was invalided out of the Service in May 1918, and holds the General Service and Victory Medals.
3, Napier Road, Kensal Green, N.W.10.   X17771.

REEVE, J. W., Corporal, 2nd Middlesex Regt.

He was in the Army when war broke out, having enlisted in 1910, and in 1914 was sent to the Western Front. He served through the memorable Retreat from Mons, and also took part in many of the engagements which followed, including those of Neuve Chapelle and Ypres. Whilst in action at Sailly in 1915 he was seriously wounded, and in consequence returned to England, being invalided out of the Service in April of the following year. He holds the Mons Star and the General Service and Victory Medals.
45, Milton Avenue, Willesden, N.W.10.   14320.

REEVE, W. G., Pte., 1/8th Warwickshire Regt.

He joined in March 1916, and was soon sent to the Western Front, where, after taking part in several engagements, he was killed on November 14th, 1916. He was entitled to the General Service and Victory Medals.
16, Hilmer Street, West Kensington, W.14.   16263.

REEVES, A. A., Gunner, Royal Garrison Artillery.

He volunteered in November 1915, and for two years served on the Western Front. During this time he took part in many important battles, including those of Ypres, Bullecourt and Cambrai, and in consequence of ill-health was for some weeks in hospital in France. He returned to England in 1919, and in April was demobilised, holding the General Service and Victory Medals.
77, Coomer Road, Fulham, S.W.6.   16446.

REEVES, A. E., Pte., The Buffs (East Kent Regt.).

Joining in August 1916, he was soon drafted to the Western Front. After taking part in several important battles he was so seriously wounded as to necessitate his removal to England, and in September 1917, he was invalided out of the Service. He holds the General Service and Victory Medals.
27, Haldane Road, Walham Green, S.W.6.   X16989.

REEVES, E. A. W., Rifleman, Rifle Brigade.

He had previously volunteered, but was exempted, owing to the importance of the work upon which he was engaged with the Metropolitan Railway Co. He, however, joined in August 1918, and served with the Rifle Brigade at various stations, but was not successful in obtaining his transfer overseas before the termination of war, and in February 1919, was demobilised. In the following August he rejoined in the Royal Air Force, and was drafted to Egypt, where in 1920 he was still serving.
61, Star Road, West Kensington, W.14.   16451.

REEVES, H., Pte., Royal Fusiliers and Labour Corps.

He volunteered in 1915, and after his training was drafted to the Western Front. He took part in many important engagements, including those at Ypres, Neuve Chapelle, Loos, the Somme, St. Quentin and Armentieres, and also did good work with the Labour Corps. In 1919 he returned to England, where he was demobilised, holding the 1914-15 Star and the General Service and Victory Medals.
65, Orbain Road, Fulham, S.W.6.   X18646A.

REEVES, W. G., Sapper, Royal Engineers.

Volunteering in 1915, he was drafted to the Western Front, where, with the Royal Engineers, he did good work in many important sectors, including Ypres, Loos, Vimy Ridge, and the Somme. Later, in consequence of ill-health, he was invalided home, but on recovery returned to France, and was for a time in charge of German prisoners engaged on construction work. In 1917 he was again invalided home, and in the same year was discharged as physically unfit. He holds the 1914-15 Star and the General Service and Victory Medals.
65, Orbain Road, Fulham, S.W.6.   X18646B.

REGNIER, F., Cpl., Royal Army Ordnance Corps.

He volunteered in November 1915, and during his service in France did valuable work in the Ordnance repair shops. He was also present during the Retreat and Advance of 1918, and remained on the Western Front until 1919, when he returned to England and was demobilised. He holds the 1914-15 Star and the General Service and Victory Medals.
97, Drayton Road, Harlesden, N.W.10.   15258A.

REGNIER, L. G., Gunner, Royal Field Artillery.

He joined in 1916, and after his training was engaged on various important duties with his unit. He was not successful in obtaining his transfer overseas before the cessation of hostilities, but did valuable work until his death, which occurred on July 14th, 1919, as the result of injuries received in an accident, whilst on duty.
97, Drayton Road, Harlesden, N.W.10.   15258B.

REGNIER, W. J., Pte., Royal Army Service Corps.

He volunteered in April 1915, and saw service on the Western Front, and in Salonika, where he was engaged on special duties with the field bakery. He holds the General Service and Victory Medals, and was demobilised in February 1919.
97, Drayton Road, Harlesden, N.W.10.   15258C

REID, C. E., Pte., 9th Middlesex Regiment.

He volunteered in August 1914, and in the following year took part in the Gallipoli campaign, remaining until the evacuation in 1916. He was then sent to India, where he was engaged on important duties, and during 1918 served in Mesopotamia. Whilst overseas he was on two occasions severely wounded, and in 1918 returned to England. He was demobilised in April 1919, holding the 1914-15 Star and the General Service and Victory Medals.
10, Burn's Road, Harlesden, N.W.10.   13139.

REID, R., Pte., Royal Fusiliers and M.G.C.

Volunteering in March 1915, he received his training and was afterwards engaged on special duties on the East Coast. He was not successful in obtaining his transfer overseas before the cessation of hostilities, but did valuable work before his demobilisation in June 1919. He holds the General Service Medal.
1, Fordingley Road, Maida Hill, W.9.   X19699.

REIDY, J. J., Special Constable (Metropolitan Special Constabulary, Civil Service Section).

He joined in January 1916, and during his service was engaged on special guard duties in connection with the Ministry of Munitions. He did valuable work, and holds a letter of commendation from the Chief Commissioner. He also holds the Long Service Medal and Star, and was demobilised in March 1919.
20, Lydford Road, Maida Hill, W.9.   X19438.

REILLY, W., Pte., 3rd The London Regiment (Royal Fusiliers).

He volunteered in August 1914, was first drafted to Malta and thence to the Western Front. Whilst overseas he took part in many important engagements, including those at Ypres, Neuve Chapelle, the Somme and Cambrai, and was severely wounded. He was invalided home in September 1917, and on his recovery, being physically unfit for further foreign service, was retained on important duties until his demobilisation in February 1919. He holds the 1914-15 Star and the General Service and Victory Medals.
14, Bravington Road, Maida Hill, W.9.   X19188.

RELF, H., Pte., East Surrey Regiment.

He volunteered in 1915, and was drafted to Mesopotamia, where he took a prominent part in the expedition which attempted to relieve Kut, and in engagements in the vicinity of Baghdad. Later he was sent to Egypt, where he joined the Expeditionary Force, and saw much fighting under General Allenby's command in Palestine, taking part in the capture of Jerusalem. He was sent home and demobilised in 1919, holding the 1914-15 Star and the General Service and Victory Medals.
63, Orbain Road, Fulham, S.W.6.   TX18647A.

RELF, E., Pte., Tank Corps.
Joining in 1916, he was drafted to the Western Front, where he took part in many important battles, including those of Vimy Ridge, the Somme, Ypres, Loos, Bullecourt and Cambrai. He also took part in the Advance of 1918, during which he was serving with the Whippet Tanks. In 1919 he returned to England, where he was demobilised, holding the General Service and Victory Medals.
63, Orbain Road, Fulham, S.W.6. TX18647B.

RELF, E. (Mrs.), Special War Worker.
During the course of the war this lady was engaged in very responsible and dangerous work in the T.N.T. and yellow-powder shops at Messrs. Blake's Munition Factory, Hurlingham Road, where she rendered valuable service.
63, Orbain Road, Fulham, S.W.6. TX18647C.

RELF, W. T., Driver, Royal Engineers.
Volunteering in April 1915, he was drafted to Mesopotamia on completion of his training, and throughout his service did valuable work with the Royal Engineers, being present at many important engagements. Whilst in the East he contracted malaria, and was in consequence for some time in hospital. He holds the 1914-15 Star and the General Service and Victory Medals, and was demobilised in May 1919.
51, Rowallan Road, Munster Road, S.W.6. X19263.

REMMERS, E., Pte., Royal Army Service Corps.
Volunteering in August 1914, he was drafted to the Western Front after a short period of training. During his service overseas, which lasted for nearly five years, he did valuable work with the R.A.S.C. in many important sectors, including Mons, Le Cateau, Ypres, Albert, Bullecourt, Vimy Ridge and Verdun. He returned to England in 1919, when he was demobilised, holding the Mons Star and the General Service and Victory Medals.
346, High Road, Willesden, N.W.10. 16746B.

REMMERS, N. A., Corporal, R.A.S.C. (M.T.).
He joined in 1917, and for a year served on the Eastern and Western Fronts, where he did valuable work with the Mechanical Transport. Afterwards he returned to England and until his demobilisation in April 1919 was engaged on important duties as Instructor of driving to the R.A.S.C. at Norwood. He holds the General Service and Victory Medals.
281, Chapter Road, Cricklewood, N.W.2. X17123.

RENDALL, A., Pte., 1st Royal Fusiliers.
He joined in February 1916, and for three years served on the Western Front, where he took part in many important battles, and was severely wounded in action at Bullecourt. He returned to England in 1919, when he was demobilised, holding the General Service and Victory Medals.
24, Felixstowe Road, Lower Edmonton, N.9. 15278.

RENSHAW, C. R., Pte., East Surrey Regiment.
He volunteered in 1914, and during his training rescued a comrade from drowning, for which act of bravery he was awarded a special certificate. Afterwards he was drafted to the Western Front, where he took part in many important battles, and sustained a serious wound whilst in action at Loos. He was demobilised in 1919, holding the 1914 Star and the General Service and Victory Medals.
101, Barrets Green Road, Willesden, N.W.10. 13825A.

RENSHAW, T., Special War Worker.
This worker was engaged at the Park Royal Munition Factory, and for five years was employed on important and dangerous duties in the T.N.T. shop, rendering valuable services throughout the war.
101, Barrets Green Road, Willesden, N.W.10. 13825B.

RENSHAW, H. J., Sapper, Royal Engineers.
Joining in 1916, he was drafted to France in the same year, and throughout his service did valuable work in connection with the construction of railways. He was demobilised in January 1920, holding the General Service and Victory Medals.
101, Barrets Green Road, Willesden, N.W.10. 13825C.

REYLAND, W. T., (M.M.), Pte., Royal Sussex Regt.
Volunteering in April 1915, he was sent later in the same year to the Western Front, where he played a distinguished part in the fighting. For conspicuous bravery and devotion to duty during the Battle of the Somme in 1916, he was awarded the Military Medal, and in addition holds the 1914-15 Star and the General Service and Victory Medals. After three years overseas he was demobilised in November 1918.
70A, Lorenco Road, Tottenham, N.17. X18388.

REYNOLDS, A. H., A.B., Royal Navy.
He joined in April 1916, and was posted to H.M.S. "Stoke," in which he served with the Grand Fleet in the North Sea for three years. He was demobilised in December 1919, holding the General Service and Victory Medals.
63, St. Dunstan's Road, Hanwell, W.7. 11000B.

REYNOLDS, E. W., Lieutenant, Royal Air Force.
Joining in January 1915, he was drafted to Egypt on completion of his training. His service in the East lasted four years, during which time he did valuable work as a pilot and later, as an observer, in Egypt, Palestine and Mesopotamia. He returned to England in November 1919, when he was demobilised, holding the 1914-15 Star and the General Service and Victory Medals.
3, Burn's Road, Harlesden, N.W.10. 14710.

REYNOLDS, F., Lce.-Corpl., 9th East Surrey Regt.
He volunteered in August 1915, but when it was discovered in October 1917 that he was not of age he was discharged. Rejoining in February of the following year, he was drafted to the Western Front, where he took part in the fighting in several sectors. He returned to England in 1919, when he was demobilised, holding the General Service and Victory Medals.
17, Colehill Lane, Fulham, S.W.6. X18922.

REYNOLDS, G., Pte., 2nd Oxfordshire and Buckinghamshire Light Infantry.
Called from the Reserve on the outbreak of war, he was drafted to France, where he took part in many important battles, including that of Mons. In 1915 he returned to England, and was discharged in February of the same year, on completion of his service. He was again called up in April 1918, returned to the Western Front, and in the following August was so seriously wounded as to necessitate his being invalided to England. He holds the Mons Star and the General Service and Victory Medals, and in 1920 was still in hospital under treatment.
36, Denbigh Road, Willesden, N.W.10. 15535B.

REYNOLDS, H., Pte., 27th Royal Fusiliers.
Joining in June 1916, he was drafted to the Western Front in the following year, where he took part in many important engagements during his service, and did good work with his unit throughout. After the cessation of hostilities he returned to England, and in July 1919 was demobilised, holding the General Service and Victory Medals.
34, Beaconsfield Road, Lower Edmonton, N.9. 14766.

REYNOLDS, L., Driver, Royal Army Service Corps.
Mobilised on the outbreak of war, he was drafted to the Western Front, where he went through the memorable Retreat from Mons. He was also present at many of the engagements which followed, and throughout his service, which lasted for nearly five years, did valuable work with the R.A.S.C. He returned to England in 1919, when he was demobilised, holding the Mons Star and the General Service and Victory Medals.
36, Denbigh Road, Willesden, N.W.10. 15535A.

REYNOLDS, P. C., A.B., Royal Navy.
Joining in July 1917, he was posted to H.M.S. "Bayano," and during his service was engaged in the North Sea and the Atlantic. He holds the General Service and Victory Medals, and was demobilised in December 1918.
63, St. Dunstan's Road, Hanwell, W.7. 11000A.

REYNOLDS, T., Pte., 2nd Middlesex Regiment.
He volunteered in January 1915, and was drafted to the Western Front, where he took part in many important battles, including those at Loos, the Somme, Arras and Cambrai. He was severely wounded in action at Ypres, and in consequence was invalided home. On recovery he returned to France, and in 1920 was serving in Belgium. He holds the 1914-15 Star and the General Service and Victory Medals.
5, Bayonne Road, Hammersmith, W.6. 14302.

REYNOLDS, T. W. (Sen.), Pte., Middlesex Regt.
He volunteered in August 1915, and after training served at various stations on important duties with his regiment. He was not successful in obtaining his transfer overseas before the termination of war, but gave valuable services before his demobilisation in June 1919.
27, Clarendon Street, Paddington, W.2. X20658B.

REYNOLDS, T. W. (Jun.), (M.M.), Corporal, Royal Fusiliers.
He volunteered in August 1914, and in the following year was drafted to France, where he served for four years. During this period he took part in the battles of Ypres, the Somme, Arras and Cambrai, was in action throughout the Retreat and Advance of 1918, and was twice wounded. He won the Military Medal on April 26th, 1918, for distinguished conduct on the field, and in addition holds the 1914-15 Star and the General Service and Victory Medals. After the cessation of hostilities he was drafted to India, where in 1920 he was still serving.
27, Clarendon Street, Paddington, W.2. X20658C.

REYNOLDS, W. J., Pte., Middlesex Regiment.
Joining in May 1916, he was drafted to the Western Front, where he took part in many important battles, including that of the Somme, and was wounded. He returned to England, and in October 1919 was demobilised, holding the General Service and Victory Medals.
38, Wakefield Street, Upper Edmonton, N.18.   16561.

REYNOLDS, W. T., Pte., Bedfordshire Regiment.
He joined in May 1918, and after his service was engaged at various stations on important duties with his unit. He was not successful in obtaining his transfer overseas before the cessation of hostilities, but gave valuable services before being demobilised in November 1919.
27, Clarendon Street, Paddington, W.2.   X20658A.

RHODES, C. F., Pte., Lancashire Fusiliers.
Volunteering in 1915, he was first drafted to France, and thence to Italy. He took part in important engagements on both Fronts, and on two occasions was wounded and gassed. In 1918 he returned to the Western Front, where he served until the termination of war. He was demobilised in 1919, holding the General Service and Victory Medals.
12, Steele Road, Willesden, N.W.10.   13831.

RIBBONS, S. H., Gunner, Royal Field Artillery.
Volunteering in December 1915, he was drafted to France in 1917, and after the signing of the Armistice was sent with the Army of Occupation to Cologne. Whilst training, previous to his service in France, he was thrown from his horse, and as a result has since had to undergo an operation. He was demobilised in September 1919, holding the General Service and Victory Medals.
128, Montague Road, Lower Edmonton, N.9.   15849.

RIBCHESTER, L. (Miss), Special War Worker.
During the war this lady did valuable work in munition factories. For eighteen months she was engaged by Messrs. Vickers on work in connection with the output of shells. Afterwards she was employed for six months by Messrs. Beardmore as a fuse-packer, and was injured by an accident that occurred whilst she was in their employ. Throughout she gave very valuable services.
54, Third Avenue, Queen's Park Estate, W.10.   X19298.

RICE, A. J., Sapper, Royal Engineers.
He volunteered in May 1915, and served on the Western Front, where he took part in many engagements. He was invalided home suffering from rheumatism, and was in hospital at Chelsea for some time. In May 1916 he was discharged as medically unfit for further service, and now holds the General Service and Victory Medals.
30, Lintaine Grove, West Kensington, W.14.   16991A.

RICE, D. A. (Mrs.), Member W.R.A.F.
She joined in July 1917, and served as a storekeeper at No. 5 Depot, Earl's Court, until she was demobilised in February 1919. Throughout she rendered valuable services, and holds a certificate of commendation for her good work and conduct.
30, Lintaine Grove, W. Kensington, W.14.   X16991B.

RICE, E. R. (Mrs.), Special War Worker.
During the course of the war this lady was engaged in very responsible work as an examiner of small arms at the Park Royal Munition Works. Her service, alternately by day and by night, lasted from 1915 to 1919, and was continued during the frequent and alarming air-raids then occurring.
1, Napier Road, Kensal Green, N.W.10.   TX17776B.

RICE, F. R., Sapper, R.E. (Signal Section).
Volunteering in February 1915, he was drafted to the Western Front on completion of his training. Whilst overseas he did valuable work with the Royal Engineers in many important sectors, including Ypres, the Somme and Cambrai, and during the Retreat and Advance of 1918 was engaged on special duties in connection with the light railways and wireless. He holds the General Service and Victory Medals, and was demobilised in October 1919.
1, Napier Road, Kensal Green, N.W.10.   TX17776A.

RICE, G. E., Gunner, Royal Garrison Artillery.
Volunteering in December 1914, he was drafted in February 1916 to the Western Front, where he took part in several important engagements. After being overseas for three years, he was sent home and demobilised in February 1919, holding the General Service and Victory Medals.
9, Gilpin Crescent, Upper Edmonton, N.18.   16858.

RICE, S. A., Bombardier, Royal Garrison Artillery.
He enlisted in 1916, and during his training passed as a first-class signaller at Dover Castle. He proceeded to the Western Front in 1917, and fought through the Retreat and Advance, during which he was wounded at Péronne. He was demobilised in February 1919, and holds the General Service and Victory Medals.
265, Portnall Road, Maida Hill, W.9.   X19759.

RICE, T., Pte., Lincolnshire Regiment.
Joining in 1917, he was drafted to the Western Front, where he took part in many engagements, including that of Lens, and in September 1918 was severely wounded. He returned to England in 1919, when he was demobilised, holding the General Service and Victory Medals.
243, Brettenham Road East,
Upper Edmonton, N.18.   15630.

RICHARDS, E. E., Driver, Royal Field Artillery.
Joining in April 1916, he was drafted to the Western Front, where for two years he was in almost continuous action. He took part in the third Battle of Ypres and in the Advance and Retreat of 1918, and throughout his service did valuable work with the R.F.A. After the cessation of hostilities he returned to England, and in February 1919 was demobilised, holding the General Service and Victory Medals.
30, Bath Road, Lower Edmonton, N.9.   13048.

RICHARDS, J. A., Rifleman, 12th K.R.R.
Joining in October 1916, he was sent to the Western Front on completion of his training the following April. After taking part in many important engagements, including the fighting on the Somme, he was seriously wounded, and on August 18th, 1917, died. He was entitled to the General Service and Victory Medals.
13, West Ella Road, Willesden, N.W.10.   T15127.

RICHARDS, L. F., Pte., Queen's (Royal West Surrey Regt.) and Buffs (East Kent Regt.).
Joining in July 1916, he was soon sent to the Western Front, where he took a prominent part in the heavy fighting, and later was drafted to Italy. Whilst on this front he was taken prisoner in March 1918, and was interned for seven months. After his release he was demobilised in June 1919, and holds the General Service and Victory Medals.
26, Knivet Road, Walham Green, S.W.6.   X19427.

RICHARDS, P. L., Sergeant, 1st London Regiment (Royal Fusiliers).
He volunteered in January 1915 and, after being sent to the Western Front in the same year, took a distinguished part in the heavy fighting. During his service he was severely wounded, and in February 1920 was demobilised, holding the 1914-15 Star and the General Service and Victory Medals.
46, Church Road, Tottenham, N.17.   X18340.

RICHARDSON, C. H., Rifleman, 12th King's Royal Rifle Corps.
Volunteering in November 1915, he was drafted to the Western Front, where, after taking a conspicuous part in several engagements, he was killed in action on November 20th, 1917. He was entitled to the General Service and Victory Medals.
131, Sherbrooke Road, Fulham, S.W.6.   X18620.

RICHARDSON, F. S., Pte., Labour Corps.
He joined in 1917, and during his service on the Western Front was employed on important duties in several parts of the line, more particularly in the vicinity of Arras. After rendering valuable services he was demobilised in February 1919, and holds the General Service and Victory Medals.
42, Fermoy Road, Maida Hill, W.9.   X19581.

RICHARDSON, S., Pte., Labour Corps.
He joined in June 1916, and having received training at various stations in England, was drafted to the Western Front. Throughout his service he was engaged on road repairs, and did valuable work with the Labour Corps in many important sectors. He returned to England in 1919, when he was demobilised, holding the General Service and Victory Medals.
58, Woodchester Street, Paddington, W.2.   X20791.

RICHARDSON, T. J., Pte., 5th Royal Fusiliers.
Joining in June 1916, he was drafted to France, where he took part in several important engagements. After the cessation of hostilities he was sent with the Army of Occupation to Germany, remaining there until March 1919, when he returned to England, and was demobilised, holding the General Service and Victory Medals.
34, Langhedge Lane, Upper Edmonton, N.18.   X17260.

RICHES, H., Pte., 11th Middlesex Regiment.
Having volunteered in August 1914, he was sent in the following year to the Western Front, where he took part in several engagements, including the Battle of Ypres, and was wounded. In 1918 he was drafted to Malta, and served there on garrison duty until early in the following year, when he was sent home and demobilised. He holds the 1914–15 Star and the General Service and Victory Medals.
65, Woodheyes Road, Neasden, N.W.10. 15463.

RICHES, L. (Mrs.), Special War Worker.
This lady rendered valuable service during the war in the Inspection Department at the Park Royal Munition Factory. Her work demanded the greatest care and accuracy, and throughout her service she carried out her duties in an efficient and capable manner.
64, New Holly Lane, Willesden, N.W.10. 15399B.

RICHES, W. A., Corporal, Royal Engineers.
He volunteered in 1915, and after being drafted in the following year to Egypt, was sent to France. He was present at the battles of Arras, the Somme, Bullecourt, Neuve Chapelle, Ypres, and Cambrai, and during his service was gassed. He was demobilised in 1919, holding the General Service and Victory Medals.
64, New Holly Lane, Willesden, N.W.10. 15399A.

RICKETTS, H., Pte., Labour Corps and Middlesex Regiment.
Being in the Army when war broke out, he was soon drafted to the Western Front, where he took part in the Retreat from Mons and the battles of Ypres and the Somme, and was wounded on three occasions. In 1918 he returned to England, and in February of the following year was demobilised, holding the Mons Star and the General Service and Victory Medals.
29, Ambleside Road, Willesden, N.W.10. 16120.

RICKMAN, A., Rifleman, King's Royal Rifle Corps.
He volunteered in August 1914, and was sent in the same year to France, where he took part in the battles of Mons, the Somme and Ypres, and was wounded. After being in hospital for some months he was discharged as physically unfit in 1916. He holds the Mons Star and the General Service and Victory Medals.
8, Francis Street, Hammersmith, W.6. 15151B.

RICKMAN, A., Special War Worker.
During the war he was engaged on important work at Uxbridge, in connection with the construction of aerodromes. The services which he rendered proved of the utmost value.
18, Francis Street, Hammersmith, W.6. 15036B.

RICKMAN, A., Corporal, East Surrey Regiment and Military Mounted Police
He volunteered in August 1914, and was sent to the Western Front in the same year. He served through the Mons Retreat, and took part in the battles of Neuve Chapelle, Loos, Ypres, and Vimy Ridge and in the Advance of 1918. During his service he was three times wounded. On the conclusion of hostilities he went with the Army of Occupation to Germany. He holds the Mons Star and the General Service and Victory Medals, and was demobilised in 1919.
18, Francis Street, Hammersmith, W.6. 15036C.

RICKMAN, A. F. (Mrs.), Special War Worker.
This lady was engaged on important work in connection with the output of munitions at Messrs. Blake's, Fulham. She held a responsible position, and carried out the duties assigned to her in a highly efficient manner.
8, Francis Street, Hammersmith, W.6. 15151A.

RICKMAN, H. J., Bombardier, Royal Field Artillery
Volunteering in August 1914, he was shortly afterwards drafted to the Western Front, where he took part in the battles of Ypres, Loos, and the Somme, and was severely wounded. He was invalided home, and seven months later returned to France, and served through the Advance of 1918. He was demobilised in June 1919, holding the 1914–15 Star and the General Service and Victory Medals.
126, Farm Lane, Walham Green, S.W.6. X19639B.

RICKMAN, S. (Mrs.), Special War Worker.
During the war this lady was engaged on work of national importance at Fulham, thus enabling a man to be released for service in the Army. She carried out her duties in a highly commendable manner.
18, Francis Street, Hammersmith, W.6. 15036A.

RICKMAN, S. C., Pte., 1st Border Regiment.
He volunteered for service in January 1915, and shortly afterwards was sent to Gallipoli, where he was in almost continuous action until the evacuation in January 1916. He was then sent to the Western Front, where he was killed during the heavy fighting on the Somme on July 1st of the same year. He was entitled to the 1914–15 Star and the General Service and Victory Medals.
126, Farm Lane, Walham Green, S.W.6. X19639A.

RICKMAN, W. E., Rifleman, 5th London Regiment (London Rifle Brigade).
Volunteering in March 1915, he was drafted to France in the same year. He took part in several engagements, and was severely wounded. He was invalided home in consequence, and after being in hospital for eighteen months was discharged as medically unfit for further service in December 1918. He holds the 1914–15 Star and the General Service and Victory Medals.
44, Dyson's Road, Upper Edmonton, N.18. 16773.

RIDLEY, J. H., Pte., 5th West Riding Regiment.
He volunteered in April 1915, and was shortly afterwards drafted to the Western Front. He took part in numerous important engagements, and was killed in action on March 27th, 1918. He was entitled to the 1914–15 Star and the General Service and Victory Medals.
30, Bayonne Road, Hammersmith, W.6. 14508.

RIDLEY, J. W., Pte., Machine Gun Corps.
Joining in August 1916, he was sent to the Western Front, where he was in action in numerous engagements. Later he was transferred to Italy, and took part in the campaign which ended in the débâcle of the Austrian Army. He returned to England, and was demobilised in February 1919. He holds the General Service and Victory Medals.
132, Shakespeare Avenue, Willesden, N.W.10. 13895A.

RIGELSFORD, F. W., Pte., Royal Army Service Corps and Labour Corps.
He volunteered in August 1915, and in the same year was drafted to the Western Front, where he was engaged on important duties with his unit. He was invalided home and discharged in April 1916. He holds the 1914–15 Star and the General Service and Victory Medals.
65A, Drayton Road, Harlesden, N.W.10. 15001B.

RIGELSFORD, L. W. H., Pte., Royal Sussex Regt.
He volunteered in August 1915, and was sent to the Western Front. Whilst overseas he took part in the engagements at Ypres, Mount Kemmel and the Menin Road, and served through the Retreat and Advance of 1918. He holds the General Service and Victory Medals, and is now demobilised.
65a, Drayton Road, Harlesden, N.W.10. 15001A.

RIGELSFORD, S. T., Corporal, R.A.S.C. (M.T.).
Volunteering in June 1915, he was sent to the Western Front after his training, and whilst overseas served at St. Eloi, the Somme, Arras, Lens, St. Quentin and Cambrai. After nearly four years' active service he was demobilised in June 1919. He holds the 1914–15 Star and the General Service and Victory Medals.
65a, Drayton Road, Harlesden, N.W.10. 15000.

RIGLIN, R., Pte., Machine Gun Corps.
He joined in December 1917, and was drafted to the Western Front, where he took part in the engagements at Ypres and Cambrai, and was wounded. He was invalided home to hospital, and after his recovery was demobilised in February 1919. He holds the General Service and Victory Medals.
52, Great Church Lane, Hammersmith, W.6. 16212.

RILEY, E. (Mrs.), Special War Worker.
During the war this lady was engaged on work of great national importance, and held an important position at the Park Royal Munition Factory, where her great care and skill led to her being appointed to the responsible post of inspector of fuses.
57, Manor Park Road, Harlesden, N.W.10. 13222B.

RILEY, E. E. (Mrs.), Special War Worker.
During the war this lady took over her brother's work on a farm at Newmarket in order to release him for service in the Army, and carried out her strenuous duties in a highly commendable manner.
145, St. Olaf's Road, Munster Road, S.W.6. 18632A.

RILEY, J., Special War Worker.
Being unsuccessful in his efforts to join His Majesty's Forces, owing to medical unfitness, he accepted an important position at Messrs. Fellow's Works, Willesden, and here rendered most valuable services in connection with the manufacture of magnetos for aircraft engines.
57, Manor Park Road, Harlesden, N.W.10. 13222A.

RILEY, M. A. (Mrs.), Special War Worker.
For nearly three years during the war this lady held an
important position at the Hayes Munition Factory, where
she was engaged on responsible work in the Fuse, Gaines
and Cylinder Departments.
25, Farrant Street, Queen's Park, W.10.   19099.

RILEY, P. E., Corporal, Royal Engineers.
He volunteered in April 1915, and after his training was
sent out to Mesopotamia, where he contracted malaria.
He also saw active service in India, where he helped to
quell the Afghan risings. He was demobilised in October
1919, and holds the General Service and Victory Medals
and the India General Service Medal with Afghan Clasp.
145, St. Olaf's Road, Munster Road, S.W.6.   X18632B.

RIMELL, E., Driver, Royal Army Service Corps.
He joined in June 1916, and in the following year was
drafted to the Western Front, where he rendered much
valuable service on various sectors until the conclusion of
hostilities. He then went with the Army of Occupation
to Germany. On his return to England was demobilised
in July 1919. He holds the General Service and Victory
Medals.
153, Winchester Road, Lower Edmonton, N.9.   T15195B.

RIMELL, E. G., Pte., 2nd Hertfordshire Regiment.
Volunteering in 1915, he was drafted to France in 1917,
and in the same year was wounded at Armentières. Later
he was gassed at Albert, and also suffered from shell-shock.
He returned to England, and was demobilised in January
1919, holding the General Service and Victory Medals.
153, Winchester Road, Lower Edmonton, N.9.   T15195C.

**RIMELL, S. W., Pte., The Queen's (Royal West
Surrey Regiment).**
Volunteering in November 1915, when he was only fifteen
years of age, he was retained on home service until 1919,
when as soon as he became of age for service overseas he
was drafted to Germany for duty with the Army of
Occupation. He was demobilised in September 1919.
153, Winchester Road, Lower Edmonton, N.9.   T15195A.

RIMMELL, H. H., Rifleman, 1st Rifle Brigade.
He volunteered in August 1914, and later in the same year
was sent to France, where he took part in several important
engagements. After seeing much service he was demobilised in June 1919, and holds the 1914 Star and the
General Service and Victory Medals.
182, Montague Road, Lower Edmonton, N.9.   15845.

RING, C. J., Bombardier, Royal Field Artillery.
He volunteered in August 1914, and in the same year was
sent to the Western Front. After taking part in many
important engagements, he was killed in action on April
7th, 1917. He was entitled to the 1914 Star and the
General Service and Victory Medals.
144, Town Road, Lower Edmonton, N.9.   13592B.

**RING, H. E., Pte., 21st (Empress of India's)
Lancers.**
Volunteering at the outbreak of war, he was early sent to
India, where he remained on garrison duty throughout
the war. He returned home in 1919, and in October was
demobilised, holding the General Service and Victory
Medals.
144, Town Road, Lower Edmonton, N.9.   13592A.

RINGWOOD, C., Corporal, Royal Air Force.
He joined in January 1916, and after completing his
training, was employed as a carpenter, and on special
duties which demanded a high degree of technical skill.
After rendering valuable services at various stations, he
was discharged on account of his health in April 1918.
22, Lion Road, Lower Edmonton, N.9.   15186.

RINGWOOD, R., Driver, Royal Army Service Corps.
Joining in February 1916, he was drafted to the Western
Front, where he served during several important operations. After three years overseas, he was discharged in
November 1919, owing to his suffering from shell-shock,
and holds the General Service and Victory Medals.
22, Lion Road, Lower Edmonton, N.9.   15187.

RISBY, A. J., Driver, Royal Field Artillery.
He volunteered in August 1914, and in the following year
was sent to the Western Front, where he took a prominent
part in engagements at Ypres, Arras, Cambrai, Albert and
La Bassée, and was gassed. He holds the 1914-15 Star
and the General Service and Victory Medals, and was
demobilised in February 1919.
72, Clarendon Street, Paddington, W.2.   X20528.

RISBY, W., Bombardier, Royal Field Artillery.
He volunteered in October 1914, and in the following year
was sent to the Western Front, where he served in numerous
engagements, including those at Ypres, Loos, Arras, Albert
and Cambrai, and in the Retreat and Advance of 1918.
In April 1919 he was demobilised, holding the 1914-15
Star and the General Service and Victory Medals.
32, Clarendon Street, Paddington, W.2.   TX20532A.

RISEAM, E., Pte., Royal Army Medical Corps.
He joined in August 1915, and served on the Western
Front, taking a prominent part in various engagements,
including the battles of Ypres, Arras and Cambrai. During
this time he was gassed, and in February 1919 was demobilised, holding the 1914-15 Star, the General Service and
Victory Medals.
1, Earlsmead Road, College Park, N.W.10.   X18032.

RISLEY, W. C., Driver, Royal Engineers.
He joined in May 1916, and served in France, where he
took an important part in engagements at Arras, Ypres,
La Bassée and the Somme. He was wounded, and was in
hospital at Boulogne for several weeks. He was demobilised in March 1919, and holds the General Service and
Victory Medals.
23, Park Lane, Tottenham, N.17.   X18813

RITCHINGS, C. H., Pte., R.A.S.C. (M.T.).
Volunteering in 1915, he served in France, taking part in
several engagements, and was wounded in action. After
being in hospital in France and England, he was sent, on
his recovery, to Ireland, where he was still serving in 1920.
He holds the General Service and Victory Medals.
9, Horder Road, Munster Road, S.W.6.   X19027.

RIVENELL, J. J., Sapper, Royal Engineers.
He joined in 1916, and during his service on the Western
Front took part in many engagements, including the
battles of Hill 60, the Somme and Ypres. He also fought
during the Advance of 1918. In September 1919 he was
demobilised, holding the General Service and Victory
Medals.
54, Chesson Road, West Kensington, W.14.   16437A.

RIVERS, H. J., Corporal, Royal Engineers.
He joined in 1917, and was sent to France, where he took
part in several important operations. After two years
service overseas he was demobilised in 1919, and holds the
General Service and Victory Medals.
37, Maldon Road, Lower Edmonton, N.9.   16134.

RIX, F. A., Pte., The Buffs (East Kent Regt.).
He volunteered in September 1914, and served on the
Western Front, taking a distinguished part in the battles
of Ypres and Passchendaele, where he was wounded in
October 1917. In 1918 he was drafted to Salonika, where
he served until his demobilisation in April 1919. He holds
the 1914-15 Star, and the General Service and Victory
Medals.
18, Waverley Road, Tottenham, N.17.   X19066.

RIXON, A. A., Pte., 3rd Lancashire Fusiliers.
Joining in 1917, he was drafted a year later to the Western
Front, where, during his eight weeks overseas, he was
severely wounded. After being invalided home, he was
demobilised in the following year, and holds the General
Service and Victory Medals.
48, Ilex Road, Willesden, N.W.10.   15959A.

RIXON, F., Pte., 19th Middlesex Regiment.
He volunteered in 1915, and during his service on the
Western Front, where he acted as a signaller, was in action
on the Somme, at Ypres and Cambrai, and was gassed.
Later he was sent to Cologne with the Army of Occupation,
but in 1919 was demobilised, holding the General Service
and Victory Medals.
48, Ilex Road, Willesden, N.W.10.   15959B.

**RIXON, J. W. H., Rifleman, 21st London
Regiment (1st Surrey Rifles).**
He joined in November 1917, and in the following May
was drafted to France, where he played a distinguished
part in the fighting. In August he was taken prisoner at
Bray, but died whilst in captivity, on September 3rd, 1918.
He was entitled to the General Service and Victory Medals.
40, Hiley Road, Willesden, N.W.10.   X18162.

ROACH, W., Sapper, Royal Engineers.
He joined in August 1917, and after completing his training
was employed on important duties with his company. He
was unsuccessful in obtaining his transfer overseas before
the cessation of hostilities, and after giving valuable
services was discharged owing to ill-health in November
1918.
86, Warwick Road, Upper Edmonton, N.18.   X17903.

ROAF, F. H. R., Pte., Royal Fusiliers.
An ex-soldier with sixteen years' service, he rejoined in October 1914, and was sent to France in the following June. Whilst overseas he took part in several important engagements, including those at Ypres, the Somme, Messines Ridge and Arras, and was twice wounded. In December 1917 he was taken prisoner, and was not released until after the cessation of hostilities. On his return to England he was demobilised in March 1919, and holds the Queen's and King's South African Medals (with seven clasps), the 1914-15 Star and the General Service and Victory Medals.
96, Milton Avenue, Willesden, N.W.10. 15646.

ROBBINS, C., Sapper, Royal Engineers.
Joining in October 1917, he served on the Western Front from the following February, taking part in the fighting in the Cambrai sector and on the Somme, and accompanied the victorious armies into Belgium. He was afterwards sent with the Army of Occupation to the Rhine, and was demobilised in October 1919, holding the General Service and Victory Medals.
1, Elmtree Villas, Brett Road,
Stonebridge Park, N.W.10. 14378A.

ROBBINS, F., Air Mechanic, Royal Air Force.
Having made seven previous attempts to join the Forces, he was eventually accepted in May 1917, and served with the R.A.F. on various duties with his unit. He was retained on medical grounds and on account of his technical knowledge, and remained with his unit until November 1919, when he was demobilised.
1, Elmtree Villas, Brett Road,
Stonebridge Park, N.W.10. 14378B.

ROBBINS, J. F., Corporal, R.A.S.C. (M.T.).
He volunteered in January 1915, and during his three years' service on the Western Front was engaged as a transport driver. In 1919 he was discharged as medically unfit for further service owing to illness contracted abroad. He holds the 1914-15 Star and the General Service and Victory Medals.
152, Third Avenue,
Queen's Park Estate, W.10. X19383B.

ROBBINS, T., Pte., 5th Middlesex Regiment.
He volunteered in August 1915, at the age of seventeen years, and was employed on various duties with his unit until discharged in 1917. He was not able to secure a transfer overseas, but performed his duties at home in a conscientious and painstaking manner.
13, Bruce Castle Road, Tottenham, N.17. X18546.

ROBBINS, W., Pte., 12th Middlesex Regiment.
He volunteered in November 1914, and served on the Western Front from 1915 as a motor transport driver. After being injured whilst on active service, he was invalided home, and on his recovery returned to France to resume his former duties. In January 1919 he was demobilised, holding the 1914-15 Star, the General Service and Victory Medals.
3, Raynham Road, Upper Edmonton, N.18. 16005.

ROBBINS, W. J., Rifleman, 8th London Regiment (P.O. Rifles).
Volunteering in 1915, he was sent in the same year to the Western Front, and after taking a prominent part in the fighting, was severely wounded near Loos. He was invalided to England, and on his recovery was drafted to Salonika, where he served in several engagements until 1919, when he was sent home and demobilised. He holds the 1914-15 Star and the General Service and Victory Medals.
152, Third Avenue,
Queen's Park Estate, W.10. X19383A.

ROBERT, W., Pte., Royal Fusiliers.
He volunteered in October 1914, and at the close of his training was drafted to the Western Front. After taking a prominent part in numerous important engagements, he was killed in action in May 1917. He was entitled to the General Service and Victory Medals.
44, Enbrook Street,
Queen's Park Estate, W.10. X19316B.

ROBERTS, A., Pte., 11th King's Own (Royal Lancaster Regiment.).
Volunteering in January 1915, he served for over three years on the Western Front, where he took part in the battles of Cambrai and the Somme. He was demobilised in August 1919, and holds the General Service and Victory Medals.
63, Charlton Road, Harlesden, N.W.10. 13383B.

ROBERTS, A. C., Pte., Middlesex Regiment.
Volunteering for service in November 1914, he was sent to the Western Front, where for four months he was in the vicinity of Neuve Chapelle. Later he served for over three years in Egypt, and on his return to England was demobilised in July 1919, holding the 1914-15 Star and the General Service and Victory Medals.
7, Lyndhurst Road, Upper Edmonton, N.18. 15361C.

ROBERTS, A. S., 1st Class Stoker, Royal Navy.
He volunteered in May 1915, and saw much service on minelayers in various waters. He was demobilised in April 1919, and holds the 1914-15 Star and the General Service and Victory Medals.
87, Monmouth Road, Lower Edmonton, N.9. 13020B.

ROBERTS, C. E., Driver, Royal Field Artillery.
He volunteered in January 1915, and later in the same year was sent to the Western Front, where during his three years' service he took part in several engagements, including the Battle of Ypres. After being transferred to Italy for a year, he was sent home and demobilised in February 1919, holding the 1914-15 Star and the General Service and Victory Medals.
11, Whitehall Street, Tottenham, N.17. X18128A.

ROBERTS, C. M., Pte., R.A.S.C. (M.T.).
Volunteering in April 1915, he was sent to France in the same month, and was present at the battles of Arras, Ypres, the Somme and Cambrai. He was demobilised in April 1919, holding the 1914-15 Star and the General Service and Victory Medals.
18, Eccleston Road, West Ealing, W.13. 11019.

ROBERTS, C. W., Air Mechanic, Royal Air Force.
He joined in January 1917, and during his service with the Royal Air Force was on duty at various stations as mechanical transport and aero-engine fitter. He had passed several examinations, and was regarded as indispensable in this branch of the service in which he was highly proficient. He was demobilised in February 1919.
26, Kennet Road, Maida Hill, W.9. X19572.

ROBERTS, E., Gunner, Royal Field Artillery.
He volunteered in September 1914, and served on the Western Front, taking part in the battles of Loos, Arras, Ypres, the Somme and Cambrai. For nine months he served with the Army of Occupation in Germany, and in July 1919 was demobilised. He holds the 1914-15 Star, General Service and Victory Medals.
19, Montagu Street, Hammersmith, W.6. 16403.

ROBERTS, E. R., Pte., Royal Fusiliers.
He volunteered in January 1915, and was sent to the Western Front, where he was taken prisoner during the battle of Loos in the same year. He was finally released and in January 1919 was demobilised, holding the 1914-15 Star and the General Service and Victory Medals.
51A, Deacon Road, Cricklewood, N.W.2. X17213.

ROBERTS, F. J., Pte., East Surrey Regiment and Middlesex Regiment.
He volunteered in August 1915, and during his service on the Western Front took part in several important engagements, including those of La Bassée, Oppy Wood, Neuve Chapelle and Vimy Ridge. He was twice wounded whilst abroad, and holds the General Service and Victory Medals, being demobilised in May 1919.
23, Albert Terrace, Milton Avenue,
Willesden, N.W.10. 15636.

ROBERTS, G. W., Sapper, Royal Engineers.
He volunteered in March 1915, and was sent to France, where he was engaged on important duties on many sectors of the Front. He was discharged owing to his service in December 1917, and holds the General Service and Victory Medals.
15, Gastein Road, Hammersmith, W.6. 14815.

ROBERTS, H., Gunner, Royal Field Artillery.
He had been serving for three years when war broke out, and in August 1914 was sent to France, where he took part in the battles of Mons, La Bassée, Vimy Ridge, and Cambrai and was twice wounded. He holds the Mons Star and the General Service and Victory Medals, and was demobilised in February 1919.
63, Charlton Road, Harlesden, N.W.10. 13383A.

ROBERTS, H. G., Sapper, Royal Engineers.
He volunteered in February 1915, and in the following September was drafted to the Western Front. He was transferred in the same year to Salonika, where he was engaged on important duties and saw fighting at various places. He was demobilised in March 1919, and holds the 1914-15 Star and the General Service and Victory Medals.
72, Roseberry Road, Lower Edmonton, N.9. 14071.

ROBERTS, H. G., Gunner, Royal Field Artillery.

He volunteered in August 1914, and served for four years on the Western Front, taking part in the battles of Loos, the Somme, Arras, Messines, Ypres and Passchendaele. He was gassed whilst in France, and in September 1919 was demobilised, holding the 1914–15 Star and the General Service and Victory Medals.
9, Earlsmead Road, College Park, N.W.10.   X18028.

ROBERTS, J., Corporal, Royal Army Service Corps.

Volunteering in 1914, he was sent to the Western Front, where he took part in several important engagements, and in the Retreat and Advance of 1918. Whilst overseas he was wounded, and in February 1919 was demobilised, holding the General Service and Victory Medals.
78, Shakespeare Avenue, Harlesden, N.W.10.   13623.

ROBERTS, J., Driver, Royal Army Service Corps.

He joined in 1916, and after completing his training was stationed at various depots engaged on duties of a highly important nature. He was not successful in obtaining his transfer overseas, but did splendid work throughout his service. He contracted consumption through exposure, and in 1917 died in consequence.
47, Steele Road, Willesden, N.W.10.   14533.

ROBERTS, J. (Miss), Special War Worker.

During the war this lady volunteered her services and was offered a responsible post at Messrs. Berrick's, Park Royal, where she was engaged in inspecting bullets and fuses. The important duties she had undertaken demanded great exactness and skill, and the efficiency and quickness she showed in her work proved her worthy of the highest commendation.
28, Ponsard Road, College Park, N.W.10.   X17748.

ROBERTS, S. S., Corporal, 3rd Lincolnshire Regt.

After joining in March 1916, he was sent to France in the same year, and was severely wounded whilst in action on the Somme. He was in hospital for some time, in France and England, and was demobilised in October 1919, holding the General Service and Victory Medals.
121, Raynham Avenue, Upper Edmonton, N.18.   15831.

ROBERTS, T. C., 1st Class Stoker, Royal Navy.

He volunteered in May 1915, and throughout served with the Grand Fleet in the North Sea. He was engaged on various important duties with his ship until March 1919, when he was demobilised. He holds the 1914–15 Star and the General Service and Victory Medals.
87, Monmouth Road, Lower Edmonton, N.9.   13020C.

ROBERTS, T. G., Pte., Manchester Regiment.

He joined in March 1917, and was immediately sent to the Western Front, where in the following May he was reported missing. He is believed to have been killed in action, and was entitled to the General Service and Victory Medals.
7, Lyndhurst Road, Upper Edmonton, N.18.   15361A.

ROBERTS, T. J., Driver, Royal Field Artillery.

He volunteered for duty in September 1915, and during his service on the Western Front saw fighting on various sectors, and was severely gassed in 1916. His eyesight has in consequence become impaired. He was demobilised in April 1919, and holds the General Service and Victory Medals.
39, Hartington Road, Lower Edmonton, N.9.   13918.

ROBERTS, W., A.B., Royal Navy.

He joined in August 1917, and served with the Grand Fleet in the North Sea, where his ship was engaged on various important duties throughout. He was demobilised in October 1919, and holds the General Service and Victory Medals.
87, Monmouth Road, Lower Edmonton, N.9.   13020A.

ROBERTS, W., Rifleman, 17th London Regiment.

He volunteered for duty in April 1915, and after completing his training was sent to the Western Front in the following year. He had been on active service in France for only three weeks when, on October 3rd, 1916, he was killed in action at Ypres. He was entitled to the General Service and Victory Medals.
78, Mayo Road, Willesden, N.W.10.   15436.

ROBERTS, W., Bombardier, Royal Field Artillery.

He volunteered in October 1915, and served for nearly three years in Salonika, where he saw much of the heavy fighting. He was demobilised in May 1919, on his return to England, and holds the General Service and Victory Medals.
7, Lyndhurst Road, Upper Edmonton, N.18.   15361B.

ROBERTS, W., Pte., Labour Corps.

He volunteered in August 1915, and in the following year was drafted to France. For two years he was engaged on special duties with the Labour Corps in various sectors of the front, and as a result of his being continually under fire suffered from shell shock. He was discharged physically unfit for further service in March 1918, and holds the General Service and Victory Medals.
55, Clarendon Street, Paddington, W.2.   X20394.

ROBERTS, W. C., Driver, Royal Field Artillery.

He volunteered for duty in November 1914, and in the following September was drafted to the Western Front, where he saw service on various sectors, and was severely gassed. He was demobilised in August 1919, and holds the 1914–15 Star and the General Service and Victory Medals
12, Disraeli Road, Acton Lane, N.W.10.   14006.

ROBERTS, W. C. S., Lance-Corporal, 2/18th London Regiment (London Irish Rifles).

He volunteered in September 1914, and was sent in June 1916 to the Western Front, where he took part in several engagements, including a night-raid near Neuville St. Vaast in October. In November 1916 he was drafted to Salonika and was promoted to his present rank. Eight months later he was transferred to Egypt and, whilst taking part in the advance through Palestine, lost his leg owing to a wound. He was sent to England, and in November 1918 was discharged as unfit, holding the General Service and Victory Medals.
274, Uxbridge Road, West Ealing, W.13.   9751. 9752.

ROBERTS, W. G., Corporal, Royal Engineers.

Volunteering in September 1914, he proceeded to France in 1915, and was in action on the Somme, at Arras and Passchendaele, and was wounded. He holds the 1914–15 Star and the General Service and Victory Medals, and was demobilised in March 1919.
60, Sebastopol Road, Lower Edmonton, N.9.   14972.

ROBERTS, W.J., Pte., Royal Army Ordnance Corps.

He volunteered in September 1915, and after completing his training, was sent to France in the following January. He was engaged on important gun repair duties on the Somme sector, but later served in the line at Cambrai. He returned to England in 1919, and in May was demobilised, holding the General Service and Victory Medals.
55, Oldfield Road, Willesden, N.W.10.   15990.

ROBERTS, W. E., Pte., Middlesex Regiment and Royal Army Service Corps.

He joined in April 1916, and in the same year was drafted to the Western Front, where he was in action at Ypres and other engagements, and was wounded in 1917. He was demobilised in May 1919, and holds the General Service and Victory Medals.
11, Whitehall Street, Tottenham, N.17.   X18128B.

ROBERTSON, H. (M.M.), Pte., Royal Fusiliers.

He joined in June 1917, and served on the Western Front, where he took part in many engagements, and was awarded the M.M. for conspicuous bravery on the field. After serving with distinction, he was killed in action at Cambrai on March 21st, 1918. He was entitled to the General Service and Victory Medals.
240, Lillie Road, Fulham, S.W.6.   15905.

ROBINI, W., Pte., Royal Army Service Corps.

He volunteered in 1915, and was soon sent to the Western Front, where he took part in the battles of Loos, Arras, Ypres and the Somme. After serving with distinction he was invalided home in 1918 with illness, and in February 1919 was demobilised, holding the 1914–15 Star and the General Service and Victory Medals.
40, Droop Street, Queen's Park Estate, W.10.   X18435B.

ROBINS, A. J., Lce.-Corpl., R.A.S.C. (M.T.).

He volunteered in August 1914, and whilst serving on the Western Front, was in action at Mons, Ypres, on the Somme, at Armentieres, Loos, Rheims, Noyon and Cambrai, and in the Advance of 1918. He was then sent to Cologne with the Army of Occupation, and in February 1919 was demobilised, holding the Mons Star and the General Service and Victory Medals.
23, Letterstone Road, Fulham, S.W.6.   X18444.

ROBINS, A. W., Pte., 3rd Royal Fusiliers.

He volunteered in January 1915, and in the following year was drafted to the Western Front, where he was in action on the Somme, and was wounded at Gommecourt in May. He was invalided home, and in January 1919 was discharged as medically unfit. He holds the General Service and Victory Medals.
40, Droop Street, Queen's Park, W.10.   18435A.

ROBINS, D. E. (Mrs.), Special War Worker.
This lady was engaged for two years during the war at the Hayes Munition Factory, where she was employed in filling shells. She also served at the Grahame-White Factory, Hendon, and proved a most efficient worker in the trimming and doping of aeroplane wings. In 1918 she was transferred to Messrs. Unities, Ltd., Edgware Road, a firm of naval contractors, with whom she also did good work.
138, Third Avenue, Queen's Park, W.10. X19381B.

ROBINS, G. M., Driver, R.A.S.C. (M.T.).
He volunteered in March 1915, and during his service in France served with the Ammunition Column. In the following year he was drafted to Salonika, where he was again in action. On his return to England he was demobilised, holding the 1914–15 Star and the General Service and Victory Medals.
27, Percy Road, Shepherd's Bush, W.12. 17928A.

ROBINS, J. H., Rifleman, 2/18th London Regiment (Royal Irish Rifles).
He joined in August 1916, and after serving for a time in France was drafted to Salonika, where he was injured during an advance. In 1917 he was sent to Egypt, and took part in the Palestine campaign, during which he was present at the capture of Jerusalem. Whilst in the East he contracted malaria, and for some months lay dangerously ill in hospital at Cairo and Alexandria, and afterwards was invalided home. He holds the General Service and Victory Medals, and was demobilised in January 1919.
138, Third Avenue, Queen's Park, W.10. X19381A.

ROBINS, N. H. J., Pte., Royal Fusiliers.
Joining in March 1916, he was sent in the following January to the Western Front, where, after taking part in the heavy fighting, he was killed at Arras on May 17th, 1917. He was entitled to the General Service and Victory Medals.
27, Percy Road, Shepherd's Bush, W.12. 17928B.

ROBINS, S. W., Pte., Middlesex Regiment.
Volunteering in August 1914, he was sent to the Dardanelles, where he was wounded at Suvla Bay. On the evacuation of the Peninsula, he was transferred to Egypt, and whilst in action there was twice wounded. He holds the 1914–15 Star and the General Service and Victory Medals, and was demobilised in March 1919.
27, Percy Road, Shepherd's Bush, W.12. 17928C.

ROBINSON, A. (M.M.), Pte., 1/4th Royal Fusiliers.
He volunteered in June 1915, and until 1919 served on the Western Front. He was awarded the M.M. for conspicuous bravery in the field at Cambrai in 1916, and was in action in many other engagements, including those of Ypres, Arras, and Vimy Ridge. He was demobilised in February 1919, and holds the 1914–15 Star and the General Service and Victory Medals.
23, Fordingley Road, Maida Hill, W.9. X19725.

ROBINSON, A., Leading Seaman, Royal Navy.
Having previously served for four years, he rejoined at the outbreak of war, and was employed in the convoying of foodships. In June 1915 he was in H.M.S. "Roxburgh," when she was torpedoed. He holds the 1914–15 Star and the General Service and Victory Medals.
115, Winchester Road, Lower Edmonton, N.4. 14956.

ROBINSON, A. G., Sergt., Royal Garrison Artillery.
He volunteered in August 1914, and was drafted to the Western Front, where he took a prominent part in several engagements, including that of the Somme. For two months he was in hospital at the Base, having been badly gassed at Havrincourt Wood, and later went to Germany with the Army of Occupation. He holds the General Service and Victory Medals, and was demobilised in April 1919.
50, Wycombe Road, Tottenham, N.17. X19071.

ROBINSON, A. G., Pte., King's Own Scottish Borderers.
He joined in October 1916, and during his service on the Western Front took part in engagements at Meteren and Ypres. After serving for over three years with distinction, he was demobilised in November 1919, holding the General Service and Victory Medals.
41, Kilmaine Road, Munster Road, S.W.6. TX18857C.

ROBINSON, B. (Miss), Special War Worker.
This lady was engaged during the war on responsible work of national importance, in connection with making life-belts and filling them with kapok. The valuable services which she rendered merited the highest commendation, and were greatly appreciated by the firm with which she was engaged.
59, Tasso Road, Hammersmith, W.6. 14632B.

ROBINSON, C., Corporal, Royal Fusiliers and Royal Army Medical Corps.
He volunteered in February 1915, and served for six months on the Western Front, taking part in the fighting at Arras, Vimy Ridge and Richebourg St. Vaast. Later he was sent to Malta and Egypt, and in 1917 to India, where he took part in the fighting on the North West Frontier. On his return to England he was demobilised in July, 1919, holding the 1914–15 Star and the General Service and Victory Medals, and the India General Service Medal 1908 (with clasp, Afghanistan, N.W. Frontier, 1919).
62, Mayo Road, Willesden, N.W.10. 14630A.

ROBINSON, C. G., Pte., 24th London Regiment (The Queen's).
He joined in October 1916, and was sent to the Western Front, where he took part in many battles, including those of Arras, Lille, Vimy Ridge and the Advance of 1918. He was demobilised in January 1919, holding the General Service and Victory Medals.
55, Tasso Road, Hammersmith, S.W.6. 14630B.

ROBINSON, C. V. (D.F.M.), Sergt.-Observer, R.A.F.
Volunteering in February 1915, he was sent in November 1916 to the Western Front, where he took a prominent part in engagements at Nieuport and on the Somme. For bombing raids, a great number of which were successful, he was awarded the Distinguished Flying Medal. In May 1918 he dropped a 102lb. bomb on Chaulnes railway station, and a day later his formation was attacked by seven enemy scouts, which were repulsed. In November 1918 he was demobilised, and holds the D.F.M. and the General Service and Victory Medals.
48, First Avenue, Queen's Park Estate, W.10. X18847.

ROBINSON, E., Pte., Bedfordshire Regiment and Royal Army Service Corps.
He joined in June 1917, and did much valuable service in France, Italy, Salonika, at the Dardanelles, and in Constantinople, engaged on important duties. He was demobilised in December 1919, and holds the General Service and Victory Medals.
19, Albert Terrace, Milton Avenue, Willesden, N.W.10. 14329.

ROBINSON, G. J., Sergt., Royal Army Pay Corps.
He volunteered in June 1915, and was engaged on important duties at various stations during the war, but was unable to obtain his transfer overseas on medical grounds. He did much valuable work with his unit, and later, re-engaging for three years, was drafted to Mesopotamia in January 1920.
61, Villiers Road, Cricklewood, N.W.2. T17324C.

ROBINSON, H., Pte., Royal Fusiliers.
He joined in February 1916, and during his service in France was wounded in action at Messines in June 1917. He was in hospital until March 1918 and was discharged in June, holding the General Service and Victory Medals.
180, Victoria Road, Lower Edmonton, N.9. 14590.

ROBINSON, H. G., Driver, Royal Field Artillery.
He volunteered in May 1915, and after his training was drafted to the Western Front, where he took an active part in many engagements on various sectors. He was in hospital for some time owing to serious injury to his wrist. He was demobilised in May 1919, holding the General Service and Victory Medals.
41, Kilmaine Road, Munster Road, S.W.6. TX18857B.

ROBINSON, M. (Mrs.), Special War Worker.
During the war this lady held a responsible post at Messrs. Roe & Co.'s Factory, West Kensington, where she was engaged on important work in connection with the making of life-belts and Army shirts. Her quickness and efficiency in the duties she had undertaken proved of immense value.
59, Tasso Road, Hammersmith, W.6. 14632A.

ROBINSON, W. J., Rifleman, 8th London Regiment (Post Office Rifles).
He joined in December 1916, and proceeding to France, took part in many important engagements. He was wounded and taken prisoner in the battle of Cambrai in March 1918, and was in hospital during his captivity in Germany. On his return to England he was demobilised in September 1919, holding the General Service and Victory Medals.
41, Kilmaine Road, Munster Road, S.W.6. TX18857A.

ROBSON, A., Pte., 29th London Regiment.
He joined in May 1917, and after his training served at various stations on important duties with his unit. He gave valuable services, but was not successful in obtaining his transfer overseas before the cessation of hostilities. He was demobilised in February 1919.
53, Hawthorn Road, Upper Edmonton, N.18. 17055.

ROBSON, J., Leading Aircraftsman, R.A.F.

He joined in June 1916, and after his training was drafted to France where he served for six months. In 1917 he was sent back to England on special engineering duties, which demanded a high degree of technical skill. He was demobilised in March 1920, holding the General Service and Victory Medals.
50, Rayleigh Road, West Kensington, W.14.   12424.

ROBSON, M. J. (Mrs.), Special War Worker.

During the war this lady was engaged at Messrs. Blake's Munition Factory on work of the utmost importance in the T.N.T. shop, filling shells. She gave valuable services, for which she received a certificate of appreciation from her employers.
78, Ancill Street, Hammersmith, W.6.   13653A.

ROBSON, S., Pte., South Wales Borderers.

He was called up from the Reserve when war broke out, and was at once drafted to the Western Front. While in France he took part in the battle of Mons, where he was seriously wounded. He was afterwards invalided home, and was discharged as medically unfit for further service in 1915. He holds the Mons Star and the General Service and Victory Medals.
78, Ancill Street, Hammersmith, W.6.   13653B.

ROBSON, W. E., Pte., Seaforth Highlanders.

Joining in May 1916, he was drafted to the Western Front in the following year. While in France he took part in the battles of Ypres and Arras, and on the cessation of hostilities went into Germany with the Army of Occupation. He was demobilised in August 1919, holding the General Service and Victory Medals.
36, Gowan Road, Willesden, N.W.10.   X16960.

ROCHE, J.(M.M.),Pte., Royal Army Medical Corps.

He was mobilised in August 1914, and was drafted to the Western Front, where he rendered valuable service throughout the war in many important engagements and in hospital at St. Omer. He was awarded the Military Medal for great gallantry and devotion to duty in the field and was also mentioned in dispatches. In February 1919, after the completion of fifteen years' service, he was demobilised, holding the 1914-15 Star and the General Service and Victory Medals.
13, Lintaine Grove Flats, West Kensington, W.14.   16999.

ROCHE, J. H., Corporal, Royal Engineers.

He volunteered in August 1914, and after his training served at various stations on special duties as a wireless and cable operator. He gave valuable services but was not successful in obtaining his transfer overseas before the cessation of hostilities. He was demobilised in March 1919.
76, Rucklidge Avenue, Harlesden, N.W.10.   12935.

RODWAY, A. E., Pte., 1st Essex Regiment.

He volunteered for duty in February 1915, and after his training was drafted to France, where he saw much active service. Whilst taking part in an engagement at Albert he was killed on April 8th, 1918. He was entitled to the General Service and Victory Medals.
50, Cornwallis Grove, Lower Edmonton, N.9.   13327B.

RODWAY, W. C., Pte., Royal Army Service Corps.

He volunteered in August 1914, and after his training was drafted to France, where he was injured whilst on duty. Later he was sent to Salonika, and took an active part in many important operations. He was demobilised in April 1919, holding the General Service and Victory Medals.
50, Cornwallis Grove, Lower Edmonton, N.9.   13327A.

RODWELL, A., Sergeant, 23rd Royal Fusiliers.

He volunteered in October 1914, served on the Western Front from September 1915 to September 1916, and took part in numerous engagements. He was discharged as physically unfit for further service in April 1917, and holds the 1914-15 Star and the General Service and Victory Medals.
110, Burn's Road, Harlesden, N.W.10.   13135.

RODWELL, G. S., Pte., Middlesex Regiment.

He volunteered in April 1915 and in the same year was sent to France, where he took part in many engagements, including those at Ypres, Vimy Ridge and Arras. After serving also in the Retreat and Advance of 1918, he was demobilised in November 1919, holding the 1914-15 Star and the General Service and Victory Medals.
63, Woodchester Street, Paddington, W.2.   X20750.

ROGERS, C., Sergeant, South Wales Borderers.

He volunteered in 1914, and in that year saw much service in France, where he fought at Mons and on the Marne and Aisne. In 1915 he went to the Dardanelles, and took part in the landing at Suvla Bay. From 1916 to 1919 he was again in France, and went through much heavy fighting up to the end of the war. He was demobilised in 1920, and holds the 1914 Star and the General Service and Victory Medals.
22, New Holly Lane, Willesden, N.W.10.   15570B.

ROGERS, C., Driver, Royal Army Service Corps.

He was in His Majesty's forces at the outbreak of war, and from August 1914 to 1919 saw active service on the Western Front. He was present during the battles of the Somme, Ypres, Arras, Cambrai, and other engagements, and was wounded. He was demobilised in August 1919, holding the 1914-15 Star and the General Service and Victory Medals.
4, Alric Avenue, Stonebridge Park, N.W.10.   14614.

ROGERS, E., Driver, Royal Field Artillery.

He volunteered in November 1914, and in the following year was drafted to France, where he remained for three years. During this period he took part in the battles of Cambrai, Arras, Vimy Ridge, Ypres, the Somme and in several other engagements, and was twice wounded in action. He was demobilised in February 1919, and holds the 1914-15 Star and the General Service and Victory Medals.
23, Rucklidge Avenue, Harlesden, N.W.10.   12918.

ROGERS, E., Pte., Labour Corps.

He volunteered for service in September 1914, and was drafted to the Western Front, where he was present in the battle of Ypres and was wounded. He was afterwards transferred to Salonika, where he contracted malaria, and died on January 9th, 1919. He held the King's and Queen's South African Medals, and was also entitled to the 1914-15 Star and the General Service and Victory Medals.
124, Shakespeare Road, Willesden, N.W.10.   13893A.

ROGERS, E., Pte., Machine Gun Corps.

Volunteering in August 1914, he was shortly afterwards drafted to the Western Front, where he went through the Retreat from Mons. He also took part in many of the engagements which followed, including the battles of the Aisne, Ypres, Neuve Chapelle, Loos, Albert and Cambrai, and was wounded in action on the Somme. During his service overseas, which lasted for nearly five years, he acted as 1st Class Machine Gunner, and in this capacity did excellent work. He was demobilised in August 1919, holding the Mons Star and the General Service and Victory Medals.
76, Burnthwaite Road, Walham Green, S.W.6.   X20260A

ROGERS, E. (Mrs.), Special War Worker.

During the war this lady was engaged on work of national importance at Messrs. Waring & Gillow's Army Equipment Factory, The White City, and carried out her duties in a highly creditable manner. She was afterwards engaged as a conductress by the General Omnibus Company, and by so doing released a man for military duty.
73, Orbain Road, Fulham, S.W.6.   TX18641A.

ROGERS, E. E. (Mrs.), Special War Worker.

From 1916 until 1918 this lady served as an overlooker at Park Royal Inspection Factory on very responsible and tedious work connected with the examination of cartridges and fuses. She was also engaged at the Admiralty Munition Works, Cricklewood, on duties entailing great strain. Her duties throughout were discharged in a highly creditable manner.   16742C
389, High Road, Willesden, N.W.10.   16743

ROGERS, F. A. J., Pte. and Rifleman, Middlesex Regiment and King's Royal Rifle Corps.

He volunteered in September 1915, and in the following year was drafted to the Western Front, where he took part in many engagements, including the Somme and Ypres, and was severely gassed. He was invalided home in 1917, and was eventually demobilised in September 1919, holding the General Service and Victory Medals.
35, Droop Street, Queen's Park, W.10.   X18436.

ROGERS, F. C. (M.M.), Sergeant, Royal Garrison Artillery and Tank Corps.

He volunteered in August 1914, and served for nearly four years on the Western Front, where he took part in many engagements of importance. On the introduction of the tanks in 1916 he joined that corps and rendered most valuable services, especially on the Somme Front. He was awarded the Military Medal for conspicuous bravery in the field, and also holds the 1914-15 Star and the General Service and Victory Medals. He was demobilised in 1918.
92, Winchester Road, Lower Edmonton, N.9   14762C

ROGERS, F. C., Stoker, Royal Navy, H.M.S. "Challenger."

He joined in February 1917, and rendered much valuable service in H.M.S. "Challenger" cruising off the coast of South Africa, until the close of hostilities. He was demobilised in March 1919, holding the General Service and Victory Medals.

94, Winchester Road, Lower Edmonton, N.9. 14754.

ROGERS, H., Pte., 2nd & 11th Middlesex Regt.

He volunteered in 1914 and in the following year was sent to France, where he took part in the battles of Neuve Chapelle and the Somme, and sustained a wound which caused his permanent disablement. He was discharged as unfit for further service in 1917, and holds the 1914–15 Star and the General Service and Victory Medals.

589, High Road, Willesden, N.W.10. 16742
16743D

ROGERS, H., Sergeant, Royal Air Force.

He volunteered in January 1915, and during the first part of his service did valuable work with his unit at various stations. In 1917 he was drafted to the Western Front, where he took part in many important operations up to the cessation of hostilities. He was demobilised in January 1919, holding the General Service and Victory Medals.

33, Rowallan Road, Munster Road, S.W.6. X19276.

ROGERS, H. E., Armourer, R.A.N., H.M.A.S. "Australia."

He volunteered in January 1915, and did valuable service on board H.M.A.S. "Australia," which was engaged on important duties in the North Sea. In February 1919 he was demobilised, holding the General Service and Victory Medals.

27, Alexandra Road, West Kensington, W.14. 12091A.

ROGERS, H. L., Sergeant, 25th Canadian Regt.

He volunteered in September 1914, and during his service on the Western Front took part in many engagements, including those of the Somme, Kemmel, Arras, Ypres, Loos and Neuve Chapelle. He was wounded three times, and gassed. He was recommended for the D.C.M. for bringing in the wounded under shell-fire, and was also mentioned in dispatches in 1916. He holds the 1914–15 Star, and the General Service and Victory Medals, and was demobilised in August 1919.

73, Orbain Road, Fulham, S.W.6. TX18641B.

ROGERS, J., Pte., 20th London Regiment and Queen's Own (Royal West Kent Regt).

He joined in April 1918, and served at various stations with his unit. He gave valuable services, but was unsuccessful in securing his transfer to a fighting area before the close of hostilities. He was demobilised in February 1919.

102, Brett Road, Stonebridge Park, N.W.10. 14380.

ROGERS, J. T., Pte., 13th Royal Fusiliers.

He volunteered in September 1914, and was soon sent to the Western Front, where he took part in several engagements. While serving in the Ypres salient he was killed on March 18th, 1918. He was entitled to the 1914–15 Star and the General Service and Victory Medals.

76, Burnthwaite Road, Walham Green, S.W.6. X20260B.

ROGERS, R., Pte., 12th London Regiment.

He joined in September 1916, and at the close of his training was drafted to the Western Front, where he saw considerable service, and was killed in action at Guemappe, near Arras, on May 5th, 1917. He was entitled to the General Service and Victory Medals.

42, Kingwood Road, Fulham, S.W.6. TX19032.

ROGERS, R. J., Driver, Royal Army Service Corps.

He volunteered in August 1914, and was speedily drafted to France, where he took part in the battle of Mons and many later engagements, and was wounded. He was returning to England on board the hospital ship "Anglia" when she was torpedoed, on November 17th, 1915, with great loss of life. After considerable hospital treatment at home he was discharged in August 1916 as unfit for further military service. He holds the Mons Star and the General Service and Victory Medals.

77, Rayleigh Road, West Kensington, W.14. 12643.

ROGERS, W., Driver, Royal Field Artillery.

He joined in November 1916, and served on important duties with his unit during his training. He was unsuccessful in obtaining his transfer overseas, and was discharged in 1917, as physically unfit for further duties owing to illness contracted during his service.

34, Gloucester Road, Upper Edmonton, N.18. X17010.

ROKE, A., Pte., The Queen's (Royal West Surrey Regiment).

He joined in June 1917, and at the close of his training served for nearly two years on the Western Front, where he took part in many engagements. He also served with the Army of Occupation in Germany for a short period before being demobilised in November 1919. He holds the General Service and Victory Medals.

3, Raynham Road, Upper Edmonton, N.18. 16186A.

ROLFE, A., Sapper, Royal Engineers.

He volunteered in September 1914, and was sent to the Western Front in the following year. He was actively engaged in many operations in this theatre of war, and was killed in action during the battle of the Somme, on July 15th, 1916. He was entitled to the 1914–15 Star and the General Service and Victory Medals.

8, First Avenue, Queen's Park Estate, W.10. X18842B.

ROLFE, F., Gunner, Royal Field Artillery.

He joined in January 1915, and was sent to the Western Front in December of the same year. After serving in France for two months he was transferred to Salonika. He took part in the Balkan Campaign and served on the Struma Front until the end of the war. He was demobilised in May 1919, and holds the 1914–15 Star and the General Service and Victory Medals.

8, First Avenue, Queen's Park Estate, W.10. X18842C.

ROLFE, G., Pte., Royal Army Medical Corps (6th Australian Field Ambulance).

He came over from Australia to join His Majesty's Army in 1916, and after his training was sent to the Western Front the same year. He was employed on important duties in connection with engagements at Ypres and the Somme. He met with a serious accident during his service overseas, which rendered his right hand useless, and he was discharged as medically unfit for further service in consequence. He died at Plymouth just before returning to Australia in November 1918, and was buried at Aston Clinton. He was entitled to the General Service and Victory Medals.

8, First Avenue, Queen's Park Estate, W.10. 18842A.

ROLFE, L. H., Gunner, Royal Field Artillery.

He volunteered in February 1915, and after his training served at various stations on important duties until 1917, when he was sent to the Western Front. During his service overseas he took part in engagements at Arras, Ypres, Cambrai, and was wounded and gassed. He holds the General Service and Victory Medals, and was demobilised in June 1919.

158, Kilburn Lane, North Kensington, W.10. X18602

ROLFE, S. J., Sapper, Royal Engineers.

He volunteered in January 1915, and was drafted to the Western Front the following August, where he was engaged on important duties in connection with railways and defence works in many sectors. He was later sent to Salonika, and was there employed on similar work. While on the Balkan Front he contracted malaria and returned to England. He was demobilised in January 1919, holding the 1914–15 Star and the General Service and Victory Medals.

71, Villiers Road, Cricklewood N.W.2. T17327.

ROLLS, A. E., Pte., 1st Hampshire Regiment.

He volunteered in August 1914, and was shortly afterwards sent to the Western Front. He was engaged in much of the severe fighting in this theatre of war, and was severely wounded in action at the Battle of the Somme in July 1916. He was invalided to hospital in England, and discharged as medically unfit for further military service in December 1916. He holds the Mons Star and the General Service and Victory Medals.

109, Hazelbury Road, Upper Edmonton, N.18. X17501.

RONAN, J., Rifleman, Rifle Brigade.

He volunteered in 1915, but owing to ill-health was discharged as medically unfit for further service the same year. He rejoined, however, in 1918, and after his training served at various stations on important duties with his unit. He gave valuable services, but was not successful in obtaining his transfer overseas, and was demobilised in September 1919.

5 Avalon Road, New King's Road, S.W.6. 19798B.

RONAN, W., Driver, Royal Field Artillery.

He volunteered in February 1915, and during the same year was drafted to Salonika, where he was actively engaged in much of the heavy fighting in various sectors of the Balkan Front. He returned to England after the Armistice, and was demobilised in May 1919, and holds the 1914–15 Star and the General Service and Victory Medals.

5, Avalon Road, New King's Road, S.W.6. 19798A.

ROOKE, H., Pte., Royal Fusiliers.

He volunteered for service in August 1915, and later in the same year was drafted to the Western Front. After taking part in several battles, including those of Ypres, the Somme and Arras, he was severely wounded at Neuve Chapelle, in consequence of which he was for some time in hospital. On recovery he again went into action, and later, having been wounded a second time and thus rendered unfit for further fighting, was transferred to the Labour Corps. In April 1919 he returned to England, and was demobilised, but in the same year rejoined and returned to France, where he was on garrison duty. He was finally discharged in May 1920, holding the 1914–15 Star and the General Service and Victory Medals.
65, Clarendon Street, Paddington, W.2.   X20401.

ROSE, Pioneer, Royal Engineers.

Volunteering for service in September 1915, he was shortly afterwards drafted to the Western Front, where he was engaged on various special duties with the Royal Engineers. In consequence of ill-health he returned to England, and in November 1916 was invalided out of the service. He holds the 1914–15 Star and the General Service and Victory Medals.
38, Woodchester Street, Paddington, W.2.   X20794.

ROSE, G. A., Rifleman, 9th London Regiment (Queen Victoria's Rifles).

He volunteered in August 1915, and proceeded in 1916 to the Western Front. After about four months' service there, in which he fought in many engagements, he was killed in action on October 1st, near Combles. He was entitled to the General Service and Victory Medals.
126, Ashmore Road, Harrow Road, W.9.   X19737A.

ROSE, W., Corporal, Royal Air Force.

He joined in October 1916, and in the same year was drafted to the Western Front, where he served as a wireless operator and was engaged on other special duties, which called for a high degree of technical skill. Whilst in action he was wounded, and in April 1919 was demobilised, holding the General Service and Victory Medals.
126, Ashmore Road, Harrow Road, W.9.   X19737B.

ROSE, W. E., Pte., Royal Fusiliers.

He volunteered in December 1915, and in the following year was sent to France, where he took a prominent part in engagements near Ypres, Armentieres and Cassel. He was demobilised in March 1919, holding the General Service and Victory Medals.
54, Bulow Road, Fulham, S.W.6.   X20730B.

ROSS, G., C.S.M., 8th Middlesex Regiment.

He was already serving at the outbreak of war, and owing to special qualifications he was engaged on important staff duties at an Infantry Record Office in the South of England. He gave very valuable services, and in 1920 was still serving. He is the holder of four medals awarded during his service prior to the Great War.
38, Litchfield Gardens, Willesden, N.W.10.   X17436.

ROSS, W., Sapper, Royal Engineers.

He joined in June 1916, and after his training served at various stations on important duties with his unit. He gave valuable services, but was not successful in obtaining his transfer overseas before the cessation of hostilities. He was demobilised in 1919.
78, Hazlebury Road, Fulham, S.W.6.   X20525.

ROUSE, W. G., Pte., R.A.S.C. (M.T.).

He volunteered in June 1915, and was soon sent to the Western Front, where he played a prominent part in the battles of Loos, St. Eloi, Vimy Ridge, Messines, Bapaume and during several engagements in the battles of the Somme and Cambrai. During his service he was largely employed on the transport of food and ammunition, and in 1918 was discharged owing to ill-health. He holds the 1914–15 Star and the General Service and Victory Medals.
46, Burnthwaite Road, Walham Green, S.W.6.   X20205.

ROWE, A., Pte., Royal Army Service Corps.

He volunteered for service in August 1914, and in the same year was sent to France, where he played a conspicuous part at the Retreat from Mons and the battles of the Marne, Aisne, Ypres, Festubert, Loos, Albert, Vimy Ridge, Messines, Lens, Passchendaele and the Somme. He was mentioned in dispatches for excellent work, and holds the Mons Star and the General Service and Victory Medals. He was demobilised in May 1919.
73, Chippenham Road, Maida Hill, W.9.   X21091.

ROWLAND, J. S., Sergeant, Royal Irish Rifles.

He volunteered in August 1914, and after his training served with his unit in Ireland as band-sergeant. He did excellent work in this capacity, but owing to his being medically unfit was unsuccessful in obtaining his transfer overseas. He was demobilised in February 1919.
53, Brookville Road, Dawes Road, S.W.6.   X20425.

RUDGE, P. W., Pte., Royal Army Medical Corps.

Joining in 1914, he did valuable work on the Western Front as a qualified male nurse, but his health broke down and he was discharged in 1916 as medically unfit for further service. He holds the 1914–15 Star and the General Service and Victory Medals.
130, Third Avenue, Queen's Park Estate, W.10.   X19385.

RUDKINS, J. J., Pte., Queen's Own (Royal West Kent Regiment).

Volunteering in December 1915, he took part in several engagements in France, including the battles of the Somme and Arras, acting as a company runner. After being twice wounded, he was taken prisoner at Cambrai on November 30th, 1917, and during his captivity in Germany was made to do very heavy work. On his release he was demobilised in July 1919, and is still suffering from the effects of his ill-treatment. He holds the General Service and Victory Medals.
82, Hartington Road, Tottenham, N.17.   X19118.

RUFF, H. E., Special War Worker.

During the war this lady was engaged in a coal merchant's office on important work in order to release a man for military service. She gave valuable services, and performed her duties in a satisfactory manner.
12, Field Road, Hammersmith, W.6.   15037A.

RUFF, S. G., Special War Worker.

During the war this lady was engaged on work of national importance at the factory of Messrs. Roe, Norman Road, Fulham, in connection with the manufacture of life-saving jackets and life-belts. She rendered valuable services, and was commended for her good work.
12, Field Road, Hammersmith, W.6.   15037B.

RULE, B. A., Pte., 4th Middlesex Regiment.

Volunteering in November 1915, he was drafted to France in the following year, and was in action during many important engagements on the Western Front, including the Battle of the Somme. Whilst overseas he was wounded and suffered from ill-health. He was demobilised in March 1919, and holds the General Service and Victory Medals.
61, Gloucester Road, Upper Edmonton, N.18.   X17272.

RULE, F. G., Pte., Middlesex Regiment.

He volunteered in February 1915, and was sent to Salonika seven months later. While in this theatre of war he took a prominent part in several engagements before the signing of the Armistice, when he returned to England, and was demobilised in August 1919. He holds the 1914–15 Star and the General Service and Victory Medals.
20, Grove Street, Upper Edmonton, N.18.   X17887.

RULE, W., Pte., Queen's (Royal West Surrey Regt.)

He joined in March 1917, and after his training was drafted overseas. He took part in many important engagements on the Western Front, where he remained until after the cessation of hostilities. On his return to England he was demobilised in November 1919, and holds the General Service and Victory Medals.
3, Somerset Road, Upper Edmonton, N.18.   X17035.

RUMSEY, A. E., Stoker, Royal Navy.

He joined in 1916, and at the conclusion of his training was posted to H.M.S. "Pegasus," which vessel was engaged on important duties convoying and transporting R.A.F. men and seaplanes across the North Sea. This ship was also used as a decoy for enemy aircraft. He was demobilised in 1919, and holds the General Service and Victory Medals.
72, Bronsart Road, Fulham, S.W.6.   X18896.

RUMSEY, C. J., Pte., Royal Naval Division.

He joined in 1916, and in June of the same year was sent to the Western Front. He took part in the engagements at Arras and Amiens, and was severely gassed during the heavy fighting on the Somme. He was invalided home and discharged in 1918. He holds the General Service and Victory Medals.
8, Cambridge Road, Hammersmith, W.6.   12622A.

RUMSEY, J. A., Pte., Royal Army Medical Corps.

He joined in 1916, and was drafted to Malta, where he was for some time engaged as an orderly in the operating theatre. Later he was sent to Palestine, and remained there until January 1919, when he was transferred to France. In October 1919 he returned to England and was demobilised. He holds the General Service and Victory Medals.
8, Cambridge Road, Hammersmith, W.6.   12622B.

RUNECKLES, G. H., Pte., R.A.O.C.

He joined in 1917, and after his training was drafted to Salonika, where he took part in many important engagements and contracted malaria. He returned home on the conclusion of hostilities, and was demobilised in 1919, holding the General Service and Victory Medals.
5, Eustace Road, Walham Green, S.W.6. X19332.

RUSH, J., Gunner, Royal Horse Artillery.

He volunteered in August 1914, and in the same year was sent to the Western Front, where he was in action on the Marne, the Aisne, the Somme, Ypres and many other engagements down to the Retreat and Advance of 1918. On two occasions his horse was killed under him, and in 1917 he was wounded. He holds the 1914 Star and the General Service and Victory Medals. TX19719B.
126, Portnall Road, Maida Hill, W.9. TX19660

RUSSELL, A., Pte., East Surrey Regiment and Labour Corps.

He volunteered in 1915, and in the following year went to France, where he took part in the Battle of the Somme, and was severely wounded. He was invalided home, and after his recovery was transferred to a Labour Battalion, in which he served until his demobilisation in 1919. He holds the General Service and Victory Medals.
2, Hazlebury Road, Fulham, S.W.6. X20511.

RUSSELL, A. R. (Mrs.), Special War Worker.

For three years of the war this lady was engaged on important work at the Fulham Filling Factory, where the efficiency and skill which she displayed in her responsible duties proved of the greatest value.
39, Leamore Street, Hammersmith, W.6. 12610A.

RUSSELL, C.A., Bombardier, Royal Field Artillery.

He volunteered in January 1915, and after his training rendered valuable services with his unit. In February 1917 he was drafted to the Western Front, and took part in several engagements, but later in the same year he fell ill and was invalided to England. In May 1918 he was discharged as medically unfit for further military service holding the General Service and Victory Medals.
26, Siddons Road, Tottenham, N.17. X19147.

RUSSELL, G. A. V., Gunner, Royal Field Artillery.

He joined in February 1916, and in the following year was sent to the Western Front, where he was in action at Ypres and many other important engagements. After the Armistice he served with the Army of Occupation in Germany. He holds the General Service and Victory Medals, and was demobilised in November 1919.
245, Shirland Road, Maida Hill, W.9. X19529A.

RUSSELL, H., Pte., 24th Royal Fusiliers.

He volunteered for service on the outbreak of war, and in 1915 went to France, where he took part in many engagements, including those of Loos, Ypres and the Somme. After the Armistice he was drafted to Germany with the Army of Occupation, and was demobilised in April 1919. He holds the 1914-15 Star and the General Service and Victory Medals.
76, St. Ervan's Road, North Kensington, W.10. X20377.

RUSSELL, H. H., Corporal, Duke of Cornwall's Light Infantry.

He volunteered for service in January 1915, and in the same year was drafted to the Western Front. Up to the time of his death in action on the Somme in August 1916, he took part in much of the heavy fighting in that sector. He was entitled to the 1914-15 Star and the General Service and Victory Medals.
39, Stanley Road, King's Road, S.W.6. X19866.

RUSSELL, M. V. (Mrs.), Special War Worker.

From May 1917 until September 1919 this lady was engaged on work of national importance, and held an important position in the Ministry of Munitions, where she rendered valuable service in the Accountant's Department at the National Gallery.
245, Shirland Road, Maida Hill, W.9. X19529B.

RUSSELL, W. J., (M.M.), C.S.M., Royal Engineers.

He volunteered in October 1914, served on the Western Front from the following year until 1918, and took part in the battles of Loos, the Somme, Ypres and Arras. In 1916 he was mentioned in dispatches, and was awarded the Military Medal for devotion to duty and conspicuous gallantry while in action on the Somme. He was demobilised in February 1919, and holds the 1914-15 Star and the General Service and Victory Medals.
145, Sheldon Road, Upper Edmonton, N.18. X17299.

RUSSELL, W. J., Driver, Royal Field Artillery.

He joined in January 1916, and after his training served at various stations on important duties with his unit. He gave valuable services, but was not successful in obtaining his transfer overseas before the cessation of hostilities. He was demobilised in 1919.
39, Leamore Street, Hammersmith, W.6. 12610B.

RUSSILL, H. E., Pte., Middlesex Regiment.

He volunteered in 1915, and on the conclusion of his training was drafted to Egypt, where he was on service until transferred in 1917 to the Western Front. He took part in many engagements in both these theatres of war, and was demobilised in 1919, holding the 1914-15 Star and the General Service and Victory Medals.
28, Pretoria Road, Upper Edmonton, N.18. X17022.

RUST, L. W. C., Pte., The Yorkshire Regiment.

He volunteered in August 1914, and in the same year was drafted to France, where he took part in many important engagements until he was killed in action on the Cambrai Front on November 21st, 1917. He was entitled to the 1914 Star and the General Service and Victory Medals.
76, Raynham Road, Upper Edmonton, N.18. 16944B.

RYALL, A. G., Driver, R.A.S.C. (M.T.).

Volunteering in August 1914, he was drafted to the Western Front in the same year. While in this theatre of war he was present at many important engagements, including those of Mons, Loos, Neuve Chapelle, the Somme, Armentieres, Arras, Ypres, Vimy Ridge, Lille and Cambrai, during which he was engaged on responsible transport duties. He was demobilised in March 1919, holding the Mons Star and the General Service and Victory Medals.
39, Ongar Road, Lillie Road, S.W.6. X19630.

RYALL, A. G., Rifleman, 9th London Regiment (Queen Victoria's Rifles).

He volunteered in April 1915, and in the following year was drafted to the Western Front, where he took part in many engagements. In August 1918 he was reported missing, and afterwards killed. He was entitled to the General Service and Victory Medals.
104, Claxton Grove, Hammersmith, W.6. 13873C.

RYALL, F., Pte., 13th London Regiment (Kensington Battalion).

He volunteered in December 1915, and in the following year was sent to France, where he was in action on the Somme. Later he was drafted to Salonika, and took part in the heavy fighting on the Doiran Front. In 1917 he was transferred to Palestine, and saw service at Beersheba, Julis and Tel-el-Sheria, where he was wounded. On his recovery he returned to the Western Front, and took part in the Advance of 1918. He was demobilised in March 1919, and holds the General Service and Victory Medals.
104, Claxton Grove, Hammersmith, W.6. 13873A.

RYALL, H., Pte., 7th London Regiment.

He volunteered in 1915, and after his training served on important duties with his unit. He gave valuable services, but was unable to secure his transfer to a fighting area before hostilities ceased. He was discharged in March 1916 as medically unfit for further military duty.
104, Claxton Grove, Hammersmith, W.6. 13873B.

RYALL, T., Gunner, Royal Garrison Artillery.

He volunteered for duty in August 1914, and in the following year was sent to the Western Front, and later to Italy. He took part in much of the heavy fighting on both Fronts up to the Armistice, and on two occasions was wounded in action. Afterwards he went to Germany with the Army of Occupation, and in October 1919 was demobilised, holding the 1914-15 Star and the General Service and Victory Medals.
15, Ancill Street, Hammersmith, W.6. 13872C.

RYAN, F. G., Pte., 1st Queen's Own (Royal West Kent Regiment).

He volunteered in October 1914, and was sent to the Western Front, where he took part in the fighting at Ypres, Loos and in many other engagements, and was killed in action during the Battle of the Somme on July 20th, 1916. He was entitled to the General Service and Victory Medals.
41, Moselle Street, Tottenham, N.17. X18362.

RYAN, H., Sergeant, Scots Guards.

He was in the Army when war broke out, and during his service discharged very important duties as musketry instructor with his unit, and as Acting Quartermaster-Sergeant. He was unsuccessful in obtaining his transfer overseas to a fighting area, and was discharged in June 1916.
60, Deacon Road, Cricklewood, N.W.2. 17357A.

RYAN, G. (Senior), Driver, Royal Engineers.
He volunteered in September 1914, and in the following year went to the Western Front, where he was engaged on special duties in laying cables. Later in the same year he was drafted to Salonika, and served throughout the Balkan Campaign, taking part in numerous engagements. In April 1919 he was demobilised, and holds the 1914-15 Star and the General Service and Victory Medals.
59, Cirencester Street, Paddington, W.2.   X20874A.

RYAN, G. (Junior), (M.M.), Pte., Middlesex Regt.
Joining in March 1916, he was soon sent to the Western Front, and took a conspicuous part in several important engagements. Whilst at the Battle of Cambrai he was severely wounded, and was awarded the Military Medal for gallantry and devotion to duty. He also holds the General Service and Victory Medals, and was demobilised in May 1919.
59, Cirencester Street, Paddington, W.2.   X20874B.

RYAN, P. J., Pte., 2nd London Regiment (Royal Fusiliers).
He volunteered in September 1914, and after three months service at Malta was drafted to the Western Front in January 1915, where he was killed by a shell at Ypres on August 23rd of the same year. He was entitled to the 1914-15 Star and the General Service and Victory Medals.
34, Disbrowe Road, Hammersmith, W.6.   15909B.

RYMELL, T., Pte., 17th Royal Fusiliers.
Volunteering in February 1915, he was drafted to France a few months later, and took an active part in many engagements of importance up to the close of the war, including Ypres, Arras, Cambrai and the Retreat and Advance of 1918. During his service he was wounded and gassed. He was demobilised in June 1919, holding the 1914-15 Star and the General Service and Victory Medals.
4, Earlsmead Road, College Park, N.W.10.   X17835.

SABINI, H., Pte., Oxfordshire and Buckinghamshire Light Infantry.
He volunteered for service in November 1915, and in the following May was drafted to Mesopotamia, where he took a prominent part in many engagements, including those at Kut, Ramadieh and Khan Baghdadi. He was afterwards transferred to Afghanistan, and assisted in suppressing the risings there. On his return he was demobilised in November 1919, and holds the General Service and Victory Medals and Indian General Service Medal (with clasp, Afghanistan, N.W. Frontier, 1919).
27, Mozart Street, North Kensington, W.10.   X19182.

SABINI, V., Rifleman, 18th London Regiment (London Irish Rifles).
He joined in August 1916, and during his service on the Western Front saw heavy fighting in the neighbourhood of Hill 60 and Hooge. Owing to his service he was discharged in June 1918, holding the General Service and Victory Medals.
27, Mozart Street, Queen's Park Estate, W.10.   X18932.

SACH, W. E., Rifleman and Pte., 8th London Regiment (Post Office Rifles) and 22nd London Regiment (Queen's).
He joined in August 1916, and in the following December was drafted to the Western Front, where he took a prominent part in the fighting, including the battles of Ypres and Cambrai, and was wounded. In March 1919 he was demobilised, and holds the General Service and Victory Medals.
60, Stephendale Road, Fulham, S.W.6.   X20707.

SACK, C. E., Corporal, Middlesex Regiment.
Volunteering at the outbreak of war, he was sent in 1915 to the Western Front, where he took part in the Battle of the Somme and the fighting at Ypres, and was wounded. He holds the 1914-15 Star and the General Service and Victory Medals, and was demobilised in 1919.
5, Sunnyside Road South, Lower Edmonton, N.9.   14554A.

SACK, G., Pte., York and Lancaster Regiment.
He joined in 1917, and whilst on the Western Front took part in several engagements, including the Battle of the Somme in 1918. After two years' service overseas he was demobilised in November 1919, and holds the General Service and Victory Medals.
5, Sunnyside Road South, Lower Edmonton, N.9.   14554B

SADD, G. T., Petty Officer, Royal Navy, H.M.S. "Hibernia."
At the outbreak of war he was already serving in the Navy, and during the war was with his ship in the Mediterranean and patrolling the North Sea. He also took part in the campaign at the Dardanelles. In 1920 he was still serving in the Royal Navy, and holds the 1914 Star and the General Service and Victory Medals.
40, Western Road, Ealing, W.5.   10853.

SADLER, C., Sergeant, The Queen's (Royal West Surrey Regiment) and Royal Engineers.
Joining in February 1916, he was drafted in the same year to the Western Front, where he played a distinguished part in the battles of Arras, Vimy Ridge, Cambrai and the Somme. Later he was transferred to the R.E., and in March 1919 was demobilised, holding the General Service and Victory Medals.
34, Napier Road, Kensal Green, N.W.10.   X17527A.

SADLER, D. (Mrs.), Special War Worker.
This lady offered her services and was employed at No. 3 Filling Factory, Park Royal, from October 1916 to December 1918. She served alternately on day and night shifts during the period of her engagement at the factory, and did much valuable work in spite of several air-raids. She was commended for her services.
34, Napier Road, Kensal Green, N.W.10.   X17527B

SADLER, F. G., Pte., Royal Army Service Corps.
He volunteered in September 1915, and after a period of training was engaged on important duties in connection with the transportation of supplies. He gave valuable services, but was not successful in obtaining his transfer overseas before the cessation of hostilities, and was demobilised in February 1919.
3, Oldfield Road, Willesden, N.W.10.   15759B.

SADLER, F. W., A.B., Royal Navy.
He volunteered in August 1915, and saw service off the coast of German East Africa on board H.M.S. "Princess." When that ship was destroyed he was transferred to H.M.S. "Macedonia," and served on dangerous submarine patrol duties with that vessel. He holds the 1914-15 Star and the General Service and Victory Medals, and was still serving in 1920.
3, Oldfield Road, Willesden, N.W.10.   15759A.

SADLER, G., Pte., Middlesex Regiment.
He joined in March 1916, and in the following July was drafted to the Western Front. After taking part in the heavy fighting and being wounded three times, he was killed in action on October 23rd, 1918. He was entitled to the General Service and Victory Medals.
28, Mordaunt Road, Willesden, N.W.10.   13731B.

SADLER, T., Pte., Royal Fusiliers and 2/20th London Regiment.
Joining in February 1916, he served on both Western and Eastern Fronts, and took part in the offensive in July 1916, during which he was wounded. He also fought in several operations in Salonika, and was reported missing and believed killed on April 25th, 1917. He was entitled to the General Service and Victory Medals.
28, Mordaunt Road, Willesden, N.W.10.   13731A.

SAGE, A. E., Pte., Bedfordshire Regiment.
He joined in 1917, and on the completion of his training was retained on important duties with his unit. Being unable to obtain his transfer overseas before the cessation of hostilities, he was demobilised in 1919, after rendering very valuable services on the East Coast.
90a, Deacon Road, Cricklewood, N.W.2.   X17109A.

SAGE, C. G., Special War Worker.
This lady was engaged for four years by Messrs Lebus on work of national importance at their munition works at Tottenham, where she made ammunition boxes and parts of aeroplanes. She carried out her work in an excellent way, and gave entire satisfaction.
58, Hartington Road, Tottenham, N.17.   X19113.

SAGE, P., Corpl., 1/8th Middlesex Regiment.
Volunteering in February 1915, he was drafted to France in the following year and took a prominent part in many engagements, including those at Arras, Cambrai, Ypres, and La Bassée. He was demobilised in June 1919, and holds the General Service and Victory Medals.
90A, Deacon Road, Cricklewood, N.W.2.   X17109B

SAGE, R., Pte., 9th Middlesex Regiment.
He joined in March 1916, and after serving in India for a year, was sent to Mesopotamia, where he took part in many engagements. He was sent home and demobilised in October 1919, holding the General Service and Victory Medals.
296, Chapter Road, Cricklewood, N.W.2. 16728.

SAICH, F., Pte., 9th Middlesex Regiment.
He volunteered in February 1915, but whilst undergoing his training was discharged as medically unfit for further service in the same month, after a patriotic attempt to serve.
30, Ambleside Road, Willesden, N.W.10. 16932A.

SAICH, T. E., Gunner, Royal Field Artillery.
He volunteered in August 1914, and served as a signaller with his unit in France, where he took part in the Retreat from Mons and the battles of the Somme, Ypres, Delville Wood, and in the Retreat and Advance of 1918. He was wounded three times, and holds the Mons Star and the General Service and Victory Medals, and in 1920 was still serving.
30, Ambleside Road, Willesden, N.W.10. 16932B.

SALISBURY, T. J., Sergeant, 6th East Lancashire Regiment.
He volunteered in September 1914, and in the following year was sent to the Dardanelles, where he took a prominent part in the heavy fighting. He also served in Mesopotamia and India, and holds the 1914-15 Star and the General Service and Victory Medals. On his return to England he was demobilised in February 1919.
40, Herries Street, North Kensington, W.10. X18728.

SALTER, E., Lce.-Corpl., R.A.S.C. (M.T.).
He joined in July 1916, and in the same year was sent to the Western Front, where until 1919 he served with the ammunition column on the Arras and Ypres sectors. He holds the General Service and Victory Medals, and was demobilised in March 1920.
265, Shirland Road, Maida Hill, W.9. X19531.

SALTMARSH, W. G., Pte., Northumberland Fus.
He volunteered in August 1914, and was sent in the same year to France, where he took part in the Retreat from Mons, and the battles of the Somme, Ypres and La Bassée. He was invalided home in 1918, suffering from the effects of being buried alive, and was discharged as medically unfit for further service in the same year. He holds the Mons Star and the General Service and Victory Medals.
11, Milton Road, Stoke Newington, N.16. X19162.

SALTWELL, H. A., Air Mechanic, R.A.F.
He joined in August 1917, and having completed his training, was retained on special duties in connection with Coast Defence, where his technical skill proved of the greatest value. After rendering valuable services he was demobilised in September 1919, holding the General Service Medal.
47, Lancefield Street, North Kensington, W.10. X18844.

SAMBROOK, J., Pte., 3rd Royal Fusiliers.
He volunteered in November 1914, and was sent overseas early in the following May. Whilst in France he saw much active service, and was reported missing, but was later found killed on May 24th, 1915. He was entitled to the 1914-15 Star and the General Service and Victory Medals.
12, Moselle Street, Tottenham, N.17. X18364.

SAMUEL, A. C., Staff Sergeant, Suffolk Regiment.
He joined in February 1917, and in the same year was drafted to the Western Front, where he took part in severe fighting on various sectors. In 1918 he returned to England, and was retained on important duties until his demobilisation in November 1919. He holds the General Service and Victory Medals.
11, Plevna Road, Lower Edmonton, N.9. 14575B.

SAMUEL, R. G., Gunner, Royal Field Artillery.
He volunteered in July 1915, and on completing his training was sent to France. After a period of service there, during which he saw much heavy fighting, he was drafted to Egypt. He took part in many operations on the Eastern Front, and was twice wounded. In July 1919 he was demobilised, and holds the General Service and Victory Medals.
11, Plevna Road, Lower Edmonton, N.9. 14575A.

SAMUELS, A., Sapper, Royal Engineers.
He volunteered in July 1915, and was sent to the Western Front, where he took part in many engagements, including the fighting on the Somme, at Cambrai, Lille and on the Marne. He was demobilised in December 1918, and holds the 1914-15 Star and the General Service and Victory Medals.
22, Brownlow Road, Willesden, N.W.10. 15006B.

SAMUELS, A., Pte.,2nd Royal Berkshire Regiment.
Serving in India at the outbreak of war, he was sent three months later to the Western Front, where, after taking a conspicuous part in the fighting, he was killed at La Bassée on November 18th, 1914. He was entitled to the 1914 Star and the General Service and Victory Medals.
19, Fourth Avenue, Queen's Park Estate, W.10.
TX18670A.

SAMUELS, G., Rifleman, 5th London Regiment. (London Rifle Brigade).
Volunteering in 1915, he completed his training and was drafted to Salonika in the following January. Whilst in the Balkans he took a prominent part in the fighting, but in April 1916 was killed in action. He was entitled to the General Service and Victory Medals.
19, Fourth Avenue, Queen's Park Estate, W.10.
TX18670B.

SAMUELS, J., Sergeant, 2nd Rifle Brigade.
He enlisted in 1908, and at the outbreak of hostilities was serving in India. In 1914 he was drafted to the Western Front, where he took a distinguished part in many of the principal engagements, including those of Ypres, Neuve Chapelle, Cambrai, Arras, Loos, the Somme and the Advance of 1918. He holds the 1914 Star and the General Service and Victory Medals, and was discharged in February 1919.
19, Fourth Avenue, Queen's Park Estate, W.10.
TX18670C.

SANDERS, C., Rifleman, 12th London Regiment (Rangers).
Volunteering in February 1915, he was drafted to the Western Front in the following year, and was in action at the battles of Arras, Ypres and Cambrai and in other important engagements. He also served for a time with the Mechanical Transport, and remained in France until his demobilisation in March 1919. He holds the General Service and Victory Medals.
36, Napier Road, Kensal Green, N.W.10. X17529.

SANDERS, C. G., Pte., 1/19th London Regiment.
He volunteered in 1915, and was drafted to the Western Front, where he took part in much severe fighting. He was wounded in action at Passchendaele, and on his recovery was ordered to Egypt. Whilst on his way to the East he was drowned when the transport on which he was sailing was torpedoed on December 30th, 1917. He was entitled to the General Service and Victory Medals.
82, Yeldham Road, Hammersmith, W.6. 13280B.

SANDERS, C. R., Special War Worker.
For a considerable period during the war he was engaged as a mechanic at Messrs. Bowden's Wire Works, Acton, on work in connection with the manufacture of aircraft. His duties called for a high degree of skill, and he gave valuable services throughout.
42, Steele Road, Willesden, N.W.10. 14142A.

SANDERS, E. (Mrs.), Special War Worker.
During the war this lady patriotically undertook work of national importance at the Park Royal Munition Factory, where she held a responsible position as an examiner in the cartridge-making department. She carried out her duties in an efficient manner, and rendered valuable services.
42, Steele Road, Willesden, N.W.10. 14142B

SANDERS, E. B., Rifleman, K.R.R.
He joined in May 1917, and in the same year was sent to France, where he took part in many engagements, including those at Arras, Corbie and Hangard Wood, where he was severely wounded. He was discharged in November 1918 owing to his wound, holding the General Service and Victory Medals.
49, Cranbury Road, Fulham, S.W.6. X21059.

SANDERS, F. G., Q.M.S., Middlesex Regiment.
Serving at the outbreak of war, he was sent to France with the Expeditionary Force, and played a distinguished part in the Retreat from Mons and several important engagements. Whilst at the battle of Neuve Chapelle he was badly gassed, and in September, from causes due to his service, he was discharged. He holds the Mons Star and the General Service and Victory Medals.
59, Warlock Road, Maida Hill, W.9. X19826.

SANDERS, W., Gunner and Pte., Royal Field Artillery and Bedfordshire Regiment.

He volunteered in February 1915, and after his training was engaged on important guard duties on the East Coast Defences. He gave valuable services, but was not successful in obtaining his transfer overseas before hostilities ceased, and in March 1919 was demobilised.
106, Burn's Road, Harlesden, N.W.10.   13143B.

SANDERS, W. H., Special War Worker.

During the war this worker was engaged on important duties at the Gothic Works, Edmonton, on the manufacture of munitions, and gave valuable services throughout.
55, King's Road, Upper Edmonton, N.18.   15519B.

SANDERS, W. J., Stoker, R.N., H.M.S. " Garry."

He volunteered in August 1914, and was posted to H.M.S. "Garry." While on this ship he took part in important naval operations with the Grand Fleet in the North Sea, and was also engaged in chasing enemy submarines. In 1920 he was still serving in the Royal Navy, and holds the 1914 Star and the General Service and Victory Medals.
55, King's Road, Upper Edmonton, N.18.   15519A.

SANDERSON, H. D., Sergeant, 18th Rifle Brigade.

He volunteered in October 1914, and in the following year was sent to India, where he remained for four years and gave distinguished services. Whilst in the East he contracted malaria and suffered from it a great deal. He holds the General Service and Victory Medals, and was demobilised in December 1919 on his return to England.
73, Somerset Road, Upper Edmonton, N.18.   X17041A.

SANDERSON, H. M., A.B., Royal Navy.

Called up from the Reserve in August 1914, he soon went to sea, and during his service in the North Sea, which extended until 1919, played a prominent part in the battles of Jutland and Heligoland Bight. During the war he was in H.M.S. "Liberty," and in 1920 was serving in the submarine "K.12." He holds the 1914–15 Star and the General Service and Victory Medals.
60, Third Avenue, Queen's Park Estate, W.10.   X19285.

SANDFORD, A., Sergeant, Royal Irish Rifles.

Volunteering in February 1915, he was sent in the following year to the Western Front, where he saw much heavy fighting, and was wounded at Ypres and Cambrai. He was invalided home, and after being in hospital for several weeks was drafted again to France. He suffered from illness, and was again invalided home. On his recovery he was once more sent to the Western Front, saw further severe fighting, and was again twice wounded. In February 1919 he was demobilised, and holds the General Service and Victory Medals
29, Eli Street, West Kensington, W.14.   16916B.

SANDFORD, G., Sergeant, Royal Horse Artillery.

He was in the Army at the outbreak of war, and in 1914 was sent to France, where he took part in the Retreat from Mons and the battles of the Marne, the Aisne, Ypres, Arras, and the Somme. In April 1919 he was demobilised, holding the Mons Star and the General Service and Victory Medals.
128, Ashmore Road, Harrow Road, W.9.   X19736.

SANDWELL, H. W., Pte., East Lancashire Regt.

He joined in June 1916, and in the following year was sent to the Western Front. He took part in many engagements, including those at Messines and Cambrai, where he was wounded. In April 1919 he was demobilised, and holds the General Service and Victory Medals.
3, Heckfield Place, Fulham Road, S.W.6.   X20248.

SANSOM, H. H., Pte., 2/6th South Staffordshire Regiment.

He volunteered in September 1915, and in the following year was sent to Ireland, where he served during the Rebellion. Later he was transferred to France, and after serving in the firing line for some time contracted blood-poisoning and was invalided to hospital. On his recovery he was attached to the R.A.O.C. and afterwards to the R.E., with whom he served until his demobilisation in January 1919. He holds the General Service and Victory Medals.
8, Byam Street, Townmead Road, S.W.6.   X21313.

SAPCOTE, A., Pte., Royal Army Service Corps.

He joined in April 1917, and in the following year was sent to the Eastern Front, where he served as a driver in Egypt. He took a prominent part in many engagements, was very severely wounded, and discharged as medically unfit for further service in March 1919. He holds the General Service and Victory Medals.
149, Stephendale Road, Fulham, S.W.6.   X20957.

SAPSFORD, E., Pte., Queen's (Royal West Surrey Regiment).

He volunteered in August 1914, and was later drafted to France. During his service on the Western Front he was in action at the battles of Loos, the Somme, Arras and Ypres, and in many other engagements. In December 1919 he was demobilised, and holds the 1914–15 Star and the General Service and Victory Medals.
11A, Lorenco Road, Tottenham, N.17.   X17992.

SATCHELL, W., Pte., Middlesex Regiment.

He volunteered in March 1915, and during his service on the Western Front, took part in many important engagements, and was badly gassed while in action at Loos. He was invalided home, and after a considerable period in hospital, was discharged as medically unfit for further service in October 1917. He holds the General Service and Victory Medals.
1, Burlington Road, Tottenham, N.17.   X19119.

SAUNDERS, A. L., Wireless Officer, Mercantile Marine, H.M.S. " Hunsbridge."

He joined in December 1916, and whilst carrying out important duties in H.M.S. " Hunsbridge," this ship was torpedoed. He was rescued by a Spanish fisherman and taken to Cadiz. Later he joined H.M.S. " Finland," and this boat sank after a collision off the Orkney Islands in 1917. He was again rescued, and saw further service. He was demobilised in November 1919, and holds the Mercantile Marine and the General Service and Victory Medals.
120, Sheldon Road, Upper Edmonton, N.18.   X17453B.

SAUNDERS, A. R., Pte., Royal Army Service Corps.

He volunteered in August 1914, and was immediately sent to the Western Front, where he took a prominent part in the Retreat from Mons. Later he was engaged on important duties during the battles of Ypres, Loos, the Somme and Arras and other heavy fighting. He was demobilised in May 1919, and holds the Mons Star and the General Service and Victory Medals.
120, Sheldon Road, Upper Edmonton, N.18.   X17453A.

SAUNDERS, D. W. (Miss), Special War Worker.

For a considerable period during the war this lady patriotically offered her services at Messrs. Waring and Gillows, where she was engaged on the manufacture of military equipment. She carried out her important duties with great care and efficiency, and received high commendation for her excellent work.
18, Humbolt Road, Hammersmith, W.6.   T15770C.

SAUNDERS, E. M. (Miss), Special War Worker.

During the war this lady gave valuable services at the Air Ministry, where she held a responsible position in the clerical department. She carried out her duties in a very able manner, and received high commendation for her work.
18, Humbolt Road, Hammersmith, W.6.   T15770D.

SAUNDERS, F., Gunner, Royal Field Artillery.

He volunteered for service in August 1915, and in the same year was sent to France, where he took a prominent part in engagements on the Somme, at Ypres and La Bassée, and was twice wounded. He was invalided home, but later returned to France, and was in action during the Advance of 1918, in which he was severely gassed. He was demobilised in April 1919, holding the 1914–15 Star and the General Service and Victory Medals.
32, Bulow Road, Fulham, S.W.6.   X20725.

SAUNDERS, F. B. (Miss), Special War Worker.

During the war this lady undertook work of national importance at Messrs. Waring and Gillow's, where she was engaged on the manufacture of military equipment. She carried out her work in an efficient manner, and gave valuable services throughout.
18, Humbolt Road, Hammersmith, W.6.   T15770B.

SAUNDERS, H. G., Pte., The London Regiment.

He volunteered in August 1914, and was drafted to the Western Front, where he took part in many engagements. He was discharged as medically unfit for further service through wounds received in action in June 1917, and holds the 1914–15 Star and the General Service and Victory Medals.
108, Church Road, Tottenham, N.17.   X18140B.

SAUNDERS, J. W., Special War Worker.

During the war he undertook work of national importance at a large factory in Pimlico, where he held a responsible position as an inspector of military equipment. He carried out his duties in a very satisfactory manner, and gave valuable services.
81, Humbolt Road, Hammersmith, W.6.   T15770A.

SAUNDERS, L. F., Pte., Royal Fusiliers.
He volunteered in March 1915, and on completion of his training was drafted to France, where, after taking a prominent part in important engagements, he was killed in action on August 12th, 1919. He was entitled to the 1914-15 Star and the General Service and Victory Medals.
108, Church Road, Tottenham, N.17.   X18140A.

SAVAGE, C., Trooper, 2nd Life Guards, Cavalry Machine Gun Corps.
He volunteered in August 1914, after having previously served in the Army for eighteen years, and taken part in the South African War. He was drafted to the Western Front, where he saw much of the heavy fighting throughout the war, and was killed in action on September 24th, 1918. He was entitled to the 1914-15 Star and the General Service and Victory Medals, and also held the Queen's and King's South African Medals.
45, Reporton Road, Munster Road, S.W.6.   TX18850.

SAVAGE, E. C., Sergt., 17th West Yorkshire Regt.
He volunteered in April 1915, and after rendering valuable service with his unit at various stations, was drafted to the Western Front in March 1917. He took part in much heavy fighting that ensued, and was killed in action at Ypres on July 14th, 1917. He was entitled to the General Service and Victory Medals.
42, Huddlestone Road, Cricklewood, N.W.2.   X17411C.

SAVAGE, G. E., Lce.-Corpl., 1st Highland Light Infantry.
He volunteered for duty in April 1915, and in the following year was drafted to Mesopotamia, where he remained until 1919 and took part in the Baghdad Campaign. He was demobilised in October 1919, and holds the General Service and Victory Medals.
42, Huddlestone Road, Cricklewood, N.W.2.   X17411A.

SAVAGE, H. G., Captain, 15th Hampshire Regt.
He volunteered for duty in September 1914, and was sent to the Western Front in the following year. After taking part in much heavy fighting on various sectors for two years he was killed near Ypres on September 20th, 1917. He was entitled to the 1914-15 Star and the General Service and Victory Medals.
42, Huddlestone Road, Cricklewood, N.W.2.   X17411B.

SAVAGE, J., Pte., 22nd London Regiment and The Queen's (Royal West Surrey Regt.).
He joined in August 1916, and in the following January was drafted to the Eastern Front. He took part in the fighting in the Balkans and in the Advance through Egypt to Palestine, where he was present at the fall of Jerusalem. He also saw service in France, where he fought in the Offensive of 1918. In May 1919 he returned to England for demobilisation, and holds the General Service and Victory Medals.
21, Caird Street, Queen's Park, W.10.   X18949.

SAVILL, F. R., Corporal, 4th Middlesex Regiment.
Volunteering in August 1914, he was drafted to the Western Front in the following year, and took part in numerous engagements of importance until the close of hostilities. He was in action on various sectors and was wounded twice. He was demobilised in August 1919, holding the 1914-15 Star and the General Service and Victory Medals.
35, Warwick Avenue, Upper Edmonton, N.18.   X17502.

SAVILLE, W., Pte., R.A.S.C. (M.T.).
He joined in June 1916, and in the following month was sent to France, where he was engaged till the war ended on important duties on many sectors of the Front. After the cessation of hostilities he went into Germany with the Army of Occupation, and in July 1919 was demobilised, holding the General Service and Victory Medals.
25, York Avenue, Hanwell, W.7.   12390B.

SAVILLE, W. W., Signalman, Royal Navy, H.M.S. "Petard."
He volunteered in June 1915, and served till the end of the war with the Grand Fleet on important duties in the North Sea. He was one of the survivors of the crew of H.M.S. "Otway," which was torpedoed off the coast of Scotland on 22nd July, 1917. He was demobilised in March 1919, and holds the General Service and Victory Medals.
25, York Avenue, Hanwell, W.7.   12390A.

SAWKINS, G., Pte., Machine Gun Corps.
He volunteered in 1915, and later in the year was drafted to France, where he rendered much excellent service. He was afterwards transferred to Salonika and Egypt, and there took part in many important engagements. In the course of his service he was twice wounded. He was demobilised in April 1919, and holds the 1914-15 Star and the General Service and Victory Medals.
1, Ray's Avenue, Upper Edmonton, N.18.   15496B.

SAWKINS, G. J., Pte., 11th The Queen's (Royal West Surrey Regiment).
He joined in March 1917, and in the same year was drafted to the Western Front, where he took part in much of the heavy fighting that followed, and was twice wounded in October 1918, at Menin Road and Ypres. In January 1919 he returned to England and was demobilised, holding the General Service and Victory Medals.
1, Ray's Avenue, Upper Edmonton, N.18.   15496A.

SAWYER, G., Corporal, R.A.S.C. (M.T.).
He volunteered in March 1915, and immediately proceeded to the Western Front, where he rendered valuable services on many sectors up to the cessation of hostilities. He then went to Germany with the Army of Occupation, and was demobilised in March 1919, holding the 1914-15 Star and the General Service and Victory Medals.
70, Stephendale Road, Fulham, S.W.6.   X20705.

SAXTON, F. R., Pte., 16th Worcestershire Regt.
He joined in April 1916, and on the completion of his training was engaged at various stations on important duties with his unit. He rendered valuable services, but was unsuccessful in obtaining his transfer overseas. He was demobilised in November 1919.
34, Orbain Road, Fulham, S.W.6.   X18218.

SAXTON, G. F., 1st Air Mechanic, Royal Air Force.
He volunteered in August 1914, and was immediately drafted to France, where he rendered valuable services which required a high degree of technical skill. He was present at many important engagements till the end of the war, and was wounded at Guillemont in October 1916. He holds the 1914 Star and the General Service and Victory Medals, and was demobilised in 1919.
87, Somerset Road, Upper Edmonton, N.18.   X17037.

SAYLES, V. J., Sergeant, Royal Field Artillery.
He volunteered in September 1914, and after his training was drafted first to France and afterwards to Salonika and Egypt. He rendered valuable service in all these theatres of war up to the close of hostilities. He took part in many important engagements. He was demobilised in June 1919, holding the General Service and Victory Medals.
29, Chaldon Road, Dawes Road, S.W.6.   X17699.

SCALES, F. G., Mechanic, Royal Air Force.
Joining in August 1918, he was soon drafted to the Western Front. Whilst overseas he was engaged on important duties in the Independent Air Force aerodromes, and did valuable work until 1919, when he returned to England and was demobilised in April. He holds the General Service and Victory Medals.
43, Hampden Street, Paddington, W.2.   X21266.

SCAMMELL, E., Pte., 9th Middlesex Regiment.
Volunteering in August 1914, he served for three years in India, and in 1917 was drafted to Mesopotamia, where he took part in heavy fighting and suffered from malaria. He was demobilised in May 1919, after being sent home, and holds the General Service and Victory Medals.
9, Oldfield Road, Willesden, N.W.10.   15756B.

SCAPLEHORN, C., Driver, R.A.S.C. (M.T.).
He volunteered in August 1914, and in the same year was sent to the Western Front, where he was engaged in valuable work in connection with the repair of engines and conveying food and ammunition to the lines. Whilst overseas he was taken seriously ill, and died on April 6th, 1915, being buried at Bailleul. He was entitled to the 1914 Star and the General Service and Victory Medals.
99, Third Avenue, Queen's Park Estate, W.10.   X19444.

SCAPLEHORN, H. (Miss), Special War Worker.
During the war this lady was engaged on important work at Park Royal Filling Factory, where she performed responsible duties in a very satisfactory manner throughout.
52, Winchelsea Road, Willesden, N.W.10.   T13870.

SCARFF, H., Pte., Queen's Own (Royal West Kent Regiment).
He volunteered in October 1915 at the age of fourteen, and in the same year was sent to France, where he was wounded. He was discharged in 1916 on account of his age, and holds the 1914-15 Star, the General Service and Victory Medals.
79, Winchester Road, Lower Edmonton, N.9.   T14987.

SCARLET, W. E., Pte., 1st Middlesex Regiment.
He joined in November 1916, and served in France until 1919. During this time he took part in much severe fighting, and was in action at the battles of Arras (where he was wounded), Messines and Ypres. He holds the General Service and Victory Medals, and was demobilised in December 1919.
2, Sandringham Road, Cricklewood, N.W.2.   16713A

21

SCHAFER, J., Pte., Royal Scots Fusiliers.
Having previously served during the Boer War, he volunteered immediately on the outbreak of hostilities, and was retained on special duties with his unit at various stations. He gave valuable services, but was not able to obtain his transfer to a fighting area before the cessation of hostilities. He was demobilised in March 1919, and holds the Medals for the South African campaign.
103, Sherbrooke Road, Fulham, S.W.6.   X18472A.

SCHAFFER, T. F., Gunner, Royal Field Artillery.
He volunteered in September 1914, and the following year was drafted to the Western Front, where he took a prominent part in the battle of the Somme and in several other important engagements. He remained in France until his demobilisation in October 1919, and holds the 1914-15 Star and the General Service and Victory Medals.
28, Warwick Road, Upper Edmonton, N.18.   X17268.

SCHUMACHER, H. R., Gunner, R.F.A.
He volunteered in September 1914, and on completion of his training was drafted to the Western Front, where he took a distinguished part in many of the principal engagements, including those at Arras, Ypres, and Cambrai. He was for some time in hospital in France with pneumonia. Later he was sent to Italy, and again saw much fighting, and in May 1919 was demobilised, holding the General Service and Victory Medals.
1, Horder Road, Munster Road, S.W.6   X19031.

SCHWARZ, J., Sergt. Major, Northumberland Fusiliers.
Mobilised at the outbreak of hostilities, he was drafted to the Western Front, where he played a conspicuous part during the Retreat from Mons and the battles of Loos, the Somme, Ypres and Arras. Later, whilst fighting during the Advance of 1918, he was severely wounded and was invalided home. After being in hospital for some time, he was demobilised in December 1919, and holds the Mons Star and the General Service and Victory Medals.
309, Shirland Road, Maida Hill, W.9.   X19573.

SCOLTOCK, W. J., Pte., R.A.S.C. (M.T.).
Volunteering in August 1914, he was drafted in the same year to the Western Front, where he took a prominent part in engagements at Ypres, St. Eloi and Loos, and was wounded near Kemmel. In 1915 he was transferred to Salonika, and whilst serving there displayed great bravery during the great fire that broke out. For this courage he was awarded by the Greek Government the Order of St. George (1st Class). He also holds the 1914-15 Star and the General Service and Victory Medals, and was demobilised in May 1919.
79, Stephendale Road, Fulham, S.W.6.   TX21028

SCORAH, W. T., Sapper, Royal Engineers.
Volunteering in February 1915, he was sent to Egypt in the following November, and served there for seven months. He was then drafted to France, where he took a prominent part in the battles of the Somme, Ypres, Arras and Bapaume, and was gassed. In March 1919 he was demobilised, holding the 1914-15 Star and the General Service and Victory Medals.
31, Third Avenue, Queen's Park Estate, W.10.   X18937.

SCOTT, A. W., Pte., Northumberland Fusiliers.
He joined in August 1916, and was drafted to Egypt in the following January. He took part in important operations in this theatre of war and also served in the Soudan. During his service in the East he was in hospital three times suffering from malaria. In January 1920 he returned home for demobilisation, and holds the General Service and Victory Medals.
88, Durban Road, Tottenham, N.17.   X17947.

SCOTT, F., Sapper, Royal Engineers.
He volunteered in 1915, and during his four years' service on the Western Front took a prominent part in the fighting at Loos, the Somme and Ypres. He holds the 1914-15 Star and the General Service and Victory Medals, and was demobilised in 1919.
12, Cranbrook Road, Tottenham, N.17.   X18560B.

SCOTT, H. J., Pte., Middlesex Regt. and M.G.C.
He volunteered in the Middlesex Regiment in February 1915, was transferred to the Machine Gun Corps and sent to France in the following August. He took part in the battles of the Somme, Arras, Ypres and Albert, and in heavy fighting around Armentieres, and in July 1916 was wounded during the Somme battle. He holds the 1914-15 Star and the General Service and Victory Medals and was demobilised in February 1919.
28, Netley Road, Brentford.   T16513B.

SCOTT, J., Pte., Royal Naval Division.
He joined in 1916, and during his service on the Western Front, which lasted for nearly two years, took part in the Retreat and Advance of 1918, and was three times wounded. He holds the General Service and Victory Medals, and was demobilised in January 1919.
16, Carlyle Avenue, Willesden, N.W.10.   14206A.

SCOTT, J., Driver, Royal Field Artillery.
Volunteering in August 1915, he was sent to France on completing his training and took part in the battles of the Somme, Bullecourt and Ypres, and in heavy fighting at Vermelles and Loos. Later he was drafted to Italy and fought on the Asiago and Piave Fronts. He was demobilised in August 1919, and holds the General Service and Victory Medals.
26, Raynham Avenue, Upper Edmonton, N.18   16764B.

SCOTT, J. P., Sergeant, Rifle Brigade.
He joined in August 1917, and on completion of his training was drafted to the Western Front in the following April. He took part in the Retreat of 1918, and was severely wounded. On his recovery he went to Germany with the Army of Occupation, and remained there until his demobilisation in December 1919. He holds the General Service and Victory Medals.
357, Chapter Road, Cricklewood, N.W.2.   T17321.

SCOTT, M., Sergt. Major, Scots Guards & R.A.F.
He volunteered in August 1914, and was immediately drafted to the Western Front, where he served with distinction in the Retreat from Mons and in the battles of the Marne and La Bassée. He was taken prisoner at the first battle of Ypres, but at the end of nine months was able to escape from the internment camp, and evading his pursuers reached the British lines in safety. He was then transferred to the R.A.F., with which unit he rendered valuable services. In 1920 he was still serving, and holds the Mons Star and the General Service and Victory Medals.
46, Burthwaite Road, Walham Green, S.W.6.   X20203.

SCOTT, P. A., Sergeant, R.A.S.C. (M.T.).
He was serving at the outbreak of war, and was immediately drafted to the Western Front, where he took part in the Retreat from Mons. He was also present at many of the important engagements which followed, including those on the Marne and at Ypres, Passchendaele, St. Quentin and Albert, and was wounded in action at Neuve Eglise. At the end of 1915 he returned to England, and in September of the following year was invalided out of the service, owing to pneumonia contracted whilst overseas. He holds the Mons Star and the General Service and Victory Medals.
56, Farrant Street, Queen's Park Estate, W.10.   X19067.

SCOTT, S., Stoker, Royal Navy.
He joined in August 1918, and immediately proceeded to sea on board H.M. T.B.D. " Sea Fire." During his service he was engaged in important operations with the North Sea Patrol and in the Baltic. He was demobilised in September 1919, and holds the General Service and Victory Medals.
47, Graham Road, Lower Edmonton, N.9.   T12870A.

SCOTT, T. J., Pte., 25th London Regiment (Cyclist Battalion)
He volunteered for service in November 1915, and at the close of his training went to Salonika, where he contracted malaria. From there he was sent to India, where he did duty at Simla and other stations, and also took part in quelling the Afghan risings. He was demobilised in December 1919, and holds the General Service and Victory Medals, and the India General Service Medal (with Clasp, Afghanistan, N.W. Frontier 1919).
34, Strode Road, Fulham, S.W.6.   X19847.

SCOTT, W., Pte., Coldstream Guards.
He volunteered in 1915, and in the following year was drafted to France, where he took part in much heavy fighting, and was in action during the battles of the Somme, Ypres, and Cambrai. During his service on the Western Front he was wounded. In January 1919 he was demobilised, and holds the General Service and Victory Medals.
47, Graham Road, Lower Edmonton, N.9.   T12870B.

SCOTT, W. E., Rifleman, 2nd Rifle Brigade.
He joined in June 1917, and on completion of his training was sent to France in the following year. He served as a signaller during the Retreat of 1918, and was taken prisoner on the Aisne in May. After his release in 1919 he was sent to Egypt, and remained there until his demobilisation in April 1920. He holds the General Service and Victory Medals.
16, St. Ervan's Road, N. Kensington, W.10.   X20678.

SCOTT, W. J., Pte., Middlesex Regiment.

He joined in April 1916, and was later drafted to India. After doing important duties there he was drafted to Mesopotamia, where he took part in much fighting. He was demobilised in April 1919, and holds the General Service and Victory Medals.

26, Raynham Avenue, Upper Edmonton, N.18.　16764A.

SCOVELL, L. D., Pte., Middlesex Regiment.

He volunteered in January 1915, and served in France, taking a prominent part in many important engagements, including those on the Somme and during the Retreat of 1918, where he was wounded. He holds the General Service and Victory Medals, and was demobilised in May 1919.

43, Letchford Gardens, Willesden, N.W.10.　X17698

SCRATCHLEY, E. C., Sapper, Canadian Engnrs.

He joined in 1916, and was drafted to the Western Front, where he took a prominent part in many engagements, including those of Vimy Ridge, Arras, and Passchendaele. He was demobilised in 1919 and holds the General Service and Victory Medals.

44, Purves Road, Kensal Rise, N.W.10.　X18025A.

SCRIPPS, F., Pte., Royal Dublin Fusiliers.

He joined in June 1916, and whilst in Salonika, where he was sent five months later, took part in the heavy fighting and contracted malaria. In 1918 he was drafted to the Western Front, and served there until his demobilisation in March 1919. He holds the General Service and Victory Medals.

2, Marsden Road, Lower Edmonton, N.9.　13067C.

SCRIVEN, F., Rifleman and Private, 18th London Regiment (London Irish Rifles) and The Queen's (Royal West Surrey Regiment).

He joined in July 1916, and in the following year was drafted to the Western Front, where, among other engagements, he took a prominent part in the Retreat and Advance of 1918. He was demobilised in February 1919, and holds the General Service and Victory Medals.

48, Shorrolds Road, Walham Green, S.W.6.　TX19364.

SCRIVENER, J. S., Lieut., R.N.R., H.M.S. "P40."

Volunteering originally in January 1915, he served throughout the operations in the Dardanelles with the New Zealand Contingent, and during heavy fighting at Gallipoli was wounded in September 1915. After the evacuation of the Peninsula he remained on the Eastern Front until August 1916, when he was granted a commission in the Royal Naval Reserve, and did important patrol and escort duty on board H.M.S. "P40." In June 1919 he was demobilised, and holds the 1914-15 Star and the General Service and Victory Medals.

51, Second Avenue, Queen's Park Estate, W.10.　X19049B.

SCUDDER, A., Pte., Middlesex Regt. and R.E.

Volunteering in August 1914, he was sent to France in the following year and took part in many important engagements. He was severely wounded in action, and as a result he had to have his right leg amputated. In January 1917 he was discharged as medically unfit for further service, and holds the 1914-15 Star and the General Service and Victory Medals.

54, Wakefield Street, Upper Edmonton, N.18.　16566.

SCUDDER, A., Pioneer, Royal Engineers.

He volunteered in September 1914, and in the following July was sent to France, taking part in heavy fighting at Loos, Arras and on the Somme. He was severely wounded in action in August 1916 at Guillemont and lost his right eye and his right leg. He was discharged as medically unfit for further service in December 1917, and holds the 1914-15 Star and the General Service and Victory Medals.

2, Belton Road, Cricklewood, N.W.2.　16601.

SEABROOK, J. C., Corporal, R.A.S.C. (M.T.).

He joined in September 1916, and in the same year was drafted to France, where he took part in many engagements. He was severely wounded in action at Nieuport in November 1917, and was discharged as medically unfit for further service owing to his wound in January 1918, holding the General Service and Victory Medals.

53, St. John's Avenue, Harlesden, N.W.10.　14747A.

SEABROOK, W., Rifleman, 2/17th London Regt.

He volunteered in September 1914, and after his training was drafted to the Western Front, where he took part in many engagements, including those on the Somme. Later he served in Salonika, Egypt and Palestine. He was demobilised in March 1920, and holds the General Service and Victory Medals.

53, St. John's Avenue, Harlesden, N.W.10.　14747B

SEALES, B. T., Pte., Royal Fusiliers.

He volunteered in September 1914, and in the following year was sent to France, where he took a prominent part in many engagements, including that at Ypres. He was severely wounded, invalided home, and was afterwards discharged as medically unfit for further service in June 1916. He holds the 1914-15 Star and the General Service and Victory Medals.

1, Headcorn Road, Tottenham, N.17.　X18488A.

SEALES, H. A., 1st Air Mechanic, Royal Air Force.

He volunteered in April 1915, and served with his unit on important duties which required a high degree of technical skill in Egypt and Gibraltar. He was demobilised in March 1919, and holds the General Service and Victory Medals.

15, Gloucester Road, Upper Edmonton, N.18.　X17174.

SEALES, S. F., Corporal, Royal Fusiliers.

He joined in March 1916 and in the same year was drafted to France. Whilst serving overseas he contracted a serious illness and was invalided home and discharged as medically unfit for further service in February 1918. He holds the General Service and Victory Medals.

1, Headcorn Road, Tottenham, N.17.　X18488B.

SEALEY, W. G., Pte., Middlesex Regiment.

Having enlisted in 1912, he was sent to France with the Expeditionary Force, and took part in the Retreat from Mons and engagements at Loos, Arras and Dickebusch. Later he fought through the Retreat and Advance of 1918, and was wounded four times during his service. He holds the Mons Star and the General Service and Victory Medals, and was discharged in 1920.

20, Berry Street, Willesden, N.W.10.　15547.

SEARLE, J. H. A., Sergeant, Royal Fusiliers and Machine Gun Corps.

He joined in June 1916 and served on the Western Front, taking part in engagements at Ypres and Meteren. Later he served with the Army of Occupation in Germany. He holds the General Service and Victory Medals, and was demobilised in February 1919.

6, Hill View, Brett Road, ¦
Stonebridge Park, N.W.10.　14530.

SEARLE, R. A., Sergeant, Middlesex Regiment.

He volunteered in August 1914, and was retained with his unit on most important duties on coastal defence. Later he was drafted with the Army of Occupation to Germany, where he was severely injured in a railway accident, and in 1920 he was still in hospital.

6, Hill View, Brett Rd.,
Stonebridge Park, N.W.10.　T14531.

SEARLES, S., Pte., Royal Army Veterinary Corps.

He volunteered in June 1915, and was soon after sent to the Eastern Front. He carried out important duties at Salonika for some time, and was then drafted to France. On the Western Front, he was stationed at a large veterinary hospital, and rendered valuable services in connection with the treatment of sick and wounded horses. He was demobilised in December 1919, holding the 1914-15 Star and the General Service and Victory Medals.

78, Bronsart Road, Munster Road, S.W.6.　X18906.

SEARS, R. L., Gunner, Royal Field Artillery.

Volunteering in April 1915, he served on the Western Front, where he took part in many important engagements and was badly wounded and gassed. He holds the 1914-15 Star and the General Service and Victory Medals, and was demobilised in February 1919.

32, Bruce Castle Road, Tottenham, N.7.　18551.

SEARS, W., Lce.-Corp., East Surrey Regiment.

Volunteering in August 1914, he was sent to the Western Front, where he was wounded at Hill 60. After being invalided home he returned to France, but was again wounded and taken prisoner. He spent more than three years in an internment camp in Germany, where he suffered many privations, and on his release rejoined his regiment, with which he was still serving in 1920. He holds the 1914 Star and the General Service and Victory Medals.

30, Moylan Road, Hammersmith, W.6.　15285.

SEARSON, A. J. (M.M.), Sapper, R.E. (Signal Sec.).

He volunteered in August 1914, and later was drafted to the Western Front. After taking part in heavy fighting in this theatre of war, he was drafted to Russia and served with General Jackson's Archangel Expedition. He was awarded the Military Medal for conspicuous bravery and devotion to duty in the field and in addition holds the 1914-15 Star, the General Service and Victory Medals, and a Russian decoration. In 1920 he was still serving.

141, Estcourt Road, Fulham, S.W.6.　16526.

SEARSON, E., Pte., Royal Fusiliers.
Joining in December 1916, he was sent to the Western
Front after his course of training and took part in very
heavy fighting, particularly in the vicinity of Ypres and
Noyon. He was twice wounded during his service abroad,
and in March 1919 was demobilised, holding the General
Service and Victory Medals.
145, Estcourt Road, Fulham, S.W.6.   16239.

SEARSON, K. (Miss), Special War Worker.
In October 1914 this lady volunteered and throughout the
war rendered valuable services as a postwoman at Walham
Green. She carried out her fatiguing duties of letter and
parcel delivery with efficiency and unfailing regularity,
and devoted her spare time to entertaining the wounded
at St. Mark's Hospital, Chelsea. Her patriotic efforts
were most commendable and were highly appreciated by
all concerned.
28, Kilkie Street, Fulham, S.W.6.   X21481.

SEATHARD, G., Pte., Middlesex Regiment.
In November 1915 he volunteered for duty, and was
drafted to the Western Front in the following year. During
his service in this seat of war he fought in several important
engagements, and was wounded in action at Passchendaele.
He was also gassed at a later date. In May 1919 he was
demobilised, holding the General Service and Victory
Medals.
18, Brereton Road, Tottenham, N.17.   X18108.

SEAWARD, B. D., Lieutenant, H.A.C.
He was granted a commission in 1915, and after his course
of instruction, was drafted to France in the following year.
Whilst on the Western Front he took a prominent part in
much heavy fighting, and was wounded in action at
Beaumont Hamel in 1917. He remained in France until
his demobilisation in 1919, and holds the General Service
and Victory Medals.
150, Lansdowne Road, Tottenham, N.17.   X19163.

SEBBAGE, E. W., Pte., Northamptonshire Regt.
Volunteering in March 1916, he was drafted to the Western
Front on finishing his period of training, and played a
prominent part in several important engagements, and
was wounded in action. In 1920 he was still serving, and
holds the General Service and Victory Medals.
13, Kenneth Road, West Kensington, W.14.   TX17373.

SECKER, R., Pte., Royal Irish Regiment.
He joined in July 1916, and was later sent to the Western
Front. After taking part in much heavy fighting, including the Battle of Arras he was drafted to the East. He
served in important operations in Salonika and Palestine
and returned to England for demobilisation in April
1919, holding the General Service and Victory Medals.
21, Seymour Road, Lower Edmonton, N.9.   13336.

SEED, A. G., A.B., Royal Navy.
He joined in July 1917, and during his service took part
in important naval operations with the Grand Fleet in
the North Sea. He was demobilised in January 1919, and
holds the General Service and Victory Medals.
64, Balfour Road, Lower Edmonton, N.9.   14047.

SEEX, S. E., Gunner, Royal Garrison Artillery.
Volunteering in December 1915, he was retained on important duties with his unit at various stations. He gave
valuable services, but was not successful in obtaining his
transfer overseas before the cessation of hostilities. He
was demobilised in March 1919.
15, Ancill Street, Hammersmith, W.6.   13872A.

SELFE, A. E., Pte., 6th Middlesex Regiment.
He volunteered in August 1915 and was sent to France,
where he took part in heavy fighting on various sectors.
He fought in the battles of Arras and Ypres, and in important engagements around Mons in the 1918 Advance.
During his service on the Western Front he was twice
wounded. In February 1919 he was demobilised, and
holds the General Service and Victory Medals.
38, Goodwin Road, Lower Edmonton, N.9.   13000.

SELLICK, W. H., Pte., 1st Middlesex Regiment.
He volunteered in February 1915, and on completion of
his training was retained on special duties with his unit
until 1918. He was then drafted to France, and during
the Advance was severely wounded. As a result he had
his left leg amputated, and after a considerable period in
hospital was invalided out of the service in February 1920.
He holds the General Service and Victory Medals.
4, Tenterden Road, Tottenham, N.17.   X18272.

SELLIS, W. G., Pte., R.A.S.C. (M.T.).
He joined in February 1916, and was later drafted to the
Western Front, where he was engaged on important
transport duties during the battles of Arras, Ypres and
Cambrai. He holds the General Service and Victory
Medals, and was demobilised in April 1919.
40, Wilson's Road, Hammersmith, W.6.   15852.

SELLWOOD, A., Pte., 2/5th Norfolk Regiment.
He joined in March 1916, and after his training was
engaged on important duties with his unit at various
stations. He was then discharged owing to ill-health as
medically unfit for further military service in the following
June.
81, Shakespeare Avenue, Willesden, N.W.10.   13703A.

SELMAN, A. E. J., Bombardier, R.F.A.
He volunteered in January 1915, and was sent to France
soon afterwards. He took a prominent part in many
important engagements on the Western Front, and was
taken prisoner during the Retreat in April 1918. After a
period of nine months' captivity in Germany he was
released, and was demobilised in March 1919. He holds
the 1914-15 Star and the General Service and Victory
Medals.
48, Stanley Road, King's Road, S.W.6.   X19784.

**SELMAN, S. J., Lce.-Corpl., Royal Berkshire
Regiment (Cycle Corps).**
He joined in May 1917, and in the same year was sent to
France, where he served in many engagements before the
cessation of hostilities. After the signing of the Armistice
he went to Germany with the Army of Occupation, and
remained there until his demobilisation in November 1919.
He holds the General Service and Victory Medals.
186, Town Road, Lower Edmonton, N.9.   13506.

SELMES, A. J., Driver, Royal Army Service Corps.
He joined in July 1918, and having completed his training,
was about to proceed overseas when he was prevented by
the precarious state of his son's health. He gave valuable
services, and was demobilised in January 1919.
33, Everington Street, Hammersmith, W.6.   13969A.

SELMES, H. R., Gunner, Royal Field Artillery.
He joined in November 1917, and after his training was
engaged on important duties with his unit at various
stations. After giving valuable services, he was sent to
hospital at Norwich for some time, and was operated on
for appendicitis. This illness prevented his transfer overseas, and he was discharged as a result in March 1919.
33, Everington Street, Hammersmith, W.6.   13969B.

SELWAY, F. (M.M.), Pte., 7th Canadian Regt.
He joined in 1917, and was drafted to the Western Front
where he took part in heavy fighting during the Retreat
and Advance in 1918, and was wounded. He was awarded
the Military Medal for conspicuous bravery and devotion
to duty under heavy shell-fire, and in addition holds the
General Service and Victory Medals. He was demobilised
in 1919.   14001C.
77, Ancill Street, Hammersmith, W.6.   18001

SELWOOD, J., Sergeant, 18th Royal Irish Regt.
Volunteering in 1914, he was sent to France later in the
same year. Whilst on the Western Front he was engaged
on responsible duties as a dispatch rider, and saw much
severe fighting. After being seriously wounded on the
Somme, he was invalided home, and after a considerable
period in hospital was discharged in 1917 as medically
unfit for further service owing to his wound. He holds
the 1914-15 Star and the General Service and Victory
Medals.
4, Steele Road, Willesden, N.W.10.   13828.

SENHENN, E. A., Pte., 1/23rd The London Regt.
Volunteering in 1915, he was drafted to France on the
completion of his training. After taking a prominent part
in much heavy fighting on the Western Front, including
the Battle of the Somme, he was killed in action at Loos
on April 23rd, 1917. He was entitled to the General
Service and Victory Medals.
44, Purves Road, Kensal Rise, N.W.10.   X18025C.

SENIOR, S. G., Q.M.S., 1st Dorsetshire Regt.
He volunteered in August 1914, and in the following year
saw much severe fighting in Gallipoli. After the evacuation of the Peninsula he was drafted to France, and there
took part in many important engagements. In 1920 he
was still serving, and holds the 1914-15 Star and the
General Service and Victory Medals.
84, Montague Road, Lower Edmonton, N.9.   16877.

SERVAT, R. H., Corporal, 194th Siege Battery, Royal Garrison Artillery.

Joining in June 1916, he was sent to France in the following January, and took a prominent part in several important engagements. On May 27th, 1918, he was severely wounded, and died two days later at Berry-au-Bac. He was entitled to the General Service and Victory Medals.
139, Purves Road, Kensal Rise, N.W.10.   X18411.

SETCHFIELD, T., Pte., 17th Essex Regiment.

He joined in August 1918, and after his training was engaged on important duties with his unit at various stations. Owing to the early cessation of hostilities after the completion of his training, he was not successful in obtaining his transfer overseas. He gave valuable services until his demobilisation in December 1919.
134, Estcourt Road, Fulham, S.W.6.   16232.

SETTERS, F., Staff Sergeant, R.A.M.C.

He volunteered in January 1915, and in the following year was drafted to France, where he took part in the fighting on the Somme, Hill 60 and Ypres. During his service he contracted ague, and was discharged as medically unfit for further service in 1916. He holds the General Service and Victory Medals.
77, Barret's Green Road, Willesden, N.W.10.   13557B.

SETTERS, M. (Miss), Special War Worker.

Although only seventeen years of age, this lady undertook work of national importance at the Park Royal Filling Factory, where she was engaged in the T.N.T. and fuse-making departments. She carried out these dangerous duties in a very able manner, and rendered valuable services.
77, Barret's Green Road, Willesden, N.W.10.   13557A.

SEWARD, A., Rifleman, 6th London Regiment.

Volunteering in October 1915, he was sent to the Western Front on completion of his training. Whilst overseas he took part in many important engagements, including those of Ypres, Vimy Ridge, Arras and Cambrai, and throughout his service did valuable work with his unit. Later he fell ill, and after being for some time in hospital in France, was invalided home. He was demobilised in March 1919, holding the General Service and Victory Medals.
35, Garvan Road, Hammersmith, W.6.   14834B.

SEWARD, A. J., Pte., Royal Berkshire Regiment.

He joined in June 1917, and after his training was sent to Salonika. Throughout his service he did valuable work with his unit, and took part in much of the heavy fighting. He returned to England in August 1919 and was demobilised, holding the General Service and Victory Medals.
39, Musard Road, Hammersmith, W.6.   15332C.

SEWARD, C. E., Corpl., The King's (Liverpool Regiment).

Joining in November 1916, he received his training at various stations in England, and later was drafted to the Western Front. Throughout his service he did valuable work with his unit, and whilst in France served in many important sectors. He returned to England in 1919, and was demobilised in November holding the General Service and Victory Medals.
59, Musard Road, Hammersmith, W.6.   15332A.

SEWARDS, H. G., (M.M.), Pte., 1st Royal Fusiliers.

Volunteering at the outbreak of hostilities, he was drafted to the Dardanelles and served through the Gallipoli Campaign. On being transferred to the Western Front he served with distinction on many sectors, and was awarded the Military Medal for gallant conduct in the field. In the course of his many engagements in this theatre of war he was wounded. He was demobilised in February 1919, and holds, in addition to the M.M., the 1914-15 Star and the General Service and Victory Medals.
71, Denzil Road, Neasden Lane, N.W.10.   15931.

SEWELL, C., Pte., 1st Gloucestershire Regiment.

Volunteering in October 1915, he received his training at various stations in England and in the following year was drafted to the Western Front. During his service he took part in engagements on the Somme and at Ypres, Passchendaele and Arras, and was killed in action during the Retreat in April 1918. He was entitled to the General Service and Victory Medals.
52, Woodchester Street, Paddington, W.2.   X20789.

SEWELL, R., Pte., The King's (Liverpool Regt. and Tank Corps.

Volunteering in 1914, he was speedily drafted to India, and was engaged there on important duties until 1915, when he contracted a severe form of malaria, and was invalided home and discharged. In 1917 he rejoined in the Tank Corps, and was engaged on experimental work stationed at Wareham and Cricklewood. He holds the 1914-15 Star and the General Service and Victory Medals, and in 1920 was still serving.
45, Ilex Road, Willesden, N.W.10.   16356.

SEWELL, T. H., Pte., 9th Middlesex Regiment.

Joining in April 1916 he was drafted to France later in the year, and took part in numerous engagements, including the first battle of the Somme, up to April 1917, when he was killed at Vimy Ridge. He was entitled to the General Service and Victory Medals.
103, Oldfield Road, Willesden, N.W.10.   16059B.

SEXTON, G. W., Pte., Royal Army Medical Corps.

Joining in August 1914, he was soon drafted to the Western Front, where he went through the Retreat from Mons. Throughout his service he acted as stretcher-bearer, and in this capacity did valuable work with the R.A.M.C. in many important engagements, including Vimy Ridge, Loos, Arras and Cambrai. He returned to England in 1919 when he was demobilised, holding the Mons Star and the General Service and Victory Medals.
17, Winchelsea Road, Willesden, N.W.10.   13711.

SEYMOUR, F., Pte., Somerset Light Infantry.

Volunteering in August 1914, he was immediately sent to the Western Front, where he took part in the Retreat from Mons and the Battle of Ypres, in which he was severely wounded. From 1915 until 1917 he served in Mesopotamia, and again sustained serious wounds, in consequence of which he was invalided home. In May 1917 he was discharged as physically unfit. He holds the Mons Star and the General Service and Victory Medals.
47, Felixstowe Road, Willesden, N.W.10.   X17761.

SEYMOUR, G., Sergeant, Royal Engineers.

He was serving in West Africa when war broke out, and remained there until 1915, when he was discharged. Later in the same year, however, he rejoined, but owing to physical unfitness was not successful in obtaining his transfer to a battle area. In 1917 he was invalided out of the Service, and holds the General Service and Victory Medals.
2, St. John's Buildings, Kilburn Lane,
North Kensington, W.10.   X18666.

SEYMOUR, H., Stoker, Royal Navy.

Joining in September 1917, he was posted to H.M.S. "Marlborough," and during his service was engaged on highly important duties with the Grand Fleet in the North Sea and off the Coast of Scotland. He was demobilised in April 1919, holding the General Service and Victory Medals.
3, Avalon Road, New King's Road, S.W.6.   X19797.

SEYMOUR, S. H., Sapper, Royal Engineers.

He joined in June 1915, and after his training was engaged on important duties at various stations with his unit. Owing to physical unfitness he was not successful in obtaining his transfer overseas, but did valuable work before being discharged in March 1917.
20, Gloucester Road, Upper Edmonton, N.18.   X17015.

SHAFE, E., Pte., Bedfordshire Regiment.

He joined in May 1918, and after his training was engaged on important duties at various stations with his unit. He rendered valuable services, but was not successful in obtaining his transfer overseas before the cessation of hostilities. He was, however, afterwards sent to Germany with the Army of Occupation, and returned to England in March 1920, when he was demobilised.
33, Monmouth Road, Lower Edmonton, N.9.   13025.

SHAILER, W. A., Rifleman, Rifle Brigade.

Volunteering in 1914, he was sent to the Western Front in the following year. His service overseas lasted for four years, and during this time he took part in many important engagements, including those at Ypres, the Somme, Arras and Cambrai, and was twice wounded. He returned to England in 1919, and was demobilised in May, holding the 1914-15 Star and the General Service and Victory Medals.
20, Clarendon Street, Paddington, W.2.   X20551

SHALLIS, F. E., Rifleman, 5th Rifle Brigade.
He joined in May 1918, and after his training was engaged on important duties at various stations with his unit. He was not successful in obtaining his transfer overseas before the cessation of hostilities, but gave valuable services before being demobilised in September 1919.
39, Chichester Road, Lower Edmonton, N.9.   14856A.

SHALLIS, G. E., Pte., Essex Regiment.
He volunteered in August 1915, and after his training served at various stations, engaged on special duties with his unit. Owing to physical unfitness he was not successful in being drafted overseas, but did valuable work before being demobilised in March 1919.
33, Raynham Road, Upper Edmonton, N.18.   15999.

SHAMBROOK, J. A., Pte., Middlesex Regiment.
Volunteering in September 1915, he was drafted to the Western Front on completion of his training in the following year. He took part in many important engagements, and in 1916 was taken prisoner during the Battle of Loos. After the signing of the Armistice he was released, and in December 1918 was demobilised, holding the General Service and Victory Medals.
65, Earlsmead Road, College Park, N.W.10.   X18029.

SHANNON, R. J., Pte., Royal Army Service Corps.
Volunteering in March 1915, he was sent to France in the following year, to Italy in 1917, and in 1918 to Salonika. He was present at many important engagements while overseas, and in Salonika contracted malaria, from which he suffered for many months. He was demobilised in June 1919, and holds the General Service and Victory Medals.
6, Rainham Road, Kensal Rise, N.W.10.   X18661.

SHARKEY, T., Lieut., Durham Light Infantry.
He volunteered in August 1914, and saw much service in many important engagements on the Western Front, where his admirable qualities as a leader won for him his commission. He was killed on the Somme on March 26th, 1918, while leading his men into action, and was entitled to the General Service and Victory Medals.
63B, Guinness's Buildings, Hammersmith, W.6.   X17700B

SHARMAN, W., Corpl., Royal Naval Division.
Volunteering in September 1914, he was drafted to Gallipoli, and took part in the memorable first landing at Suvla Bay. Later he was invalided home suffering from fever, and on his recovery was for a time engaged on special duties. In 1917 he was sent to the Western Front, where he went through the Retreat and Advance of 1918. He returned to England in 1919, and in May of the same year was demobilised, holding the 1914-15 Star and the General Service and Victory Medals.
75, Waldo Road, College Park, N.W.10.   X17639.

SHARP A., Sergeant, Royal Fusiliers.
Volunteering in August 1914, he was drafted to the Dardanelles in the following year, and was severely wounded during the first landing at Suvla Bay. He was invalided to a hospital in Egypt, and on his recovery was sent to NorthEast Africa. Later he saw service in France with the Royal Engineers, and was engaged on important duties in connection with the railway transport. He returned to England in 1919, and in May of the same year was demobilised, holding the 1914-15 Star and the General Service and Victory Medals.
28, Fifth Avenue, Queen's Park, N.W.10.   X18324.

SHARP, A. P., Gunner, Royal Garrison Artillery.
Joining in June 1916, he was drafted to the Western Front on completion of his training. Throughout his service overseas he acted as a dispatch rider in many sectors, and whilst carrying out these duties near Arras was severely wounded in April 1918. He returned to England, and in June of the following year was demobilised, holding the General Service and Victory Medals.
201, Portnall Road, Maida Hill, W.9.   X19657.

SHARP, H., Lce. Corpl., 8th Middlesex Regiment.
Volunteering in August 1914, he was first drafted to France, where he took part in the fighting in many important sectors, and he afterwards saw service with the Egyptian Expeditionary Force until the close of hostilities. He holds the 1914-15 Star and the General Service and Victory Medals, and was demobilised in February 1919.
135, Sherbrooke Road, Fulham, S.W.6.   X18683A.

SHARP, H., Pte., Royal Dublin Fusiliers.
Volunteering in 1915, he was drafted to the Western Front on completion of his training. Whilst overseas he took part in many important engagements, including those at Ypres, the Somme, Arras, Bullecourt, Armentieres and the Advance of 1918, during which he was twice severely wounded. He was demobilised in 1919, and holds the 1914-15 Star and the General Service and Victory Medals.
79, Archel Road, West Kensington, W.14.   16666.

SHARP, H. G. A., Corporal, 13th K.R.R.
He joined in June 1918, and rendered valuable service at various stations with his unit, but was not successful in obtaining his transfer overseas until the cessation of hostilities, when he was drafted with the Army of Occupation to Germany. He returned to England in 1920, and in February of the same year was demobilised.
177, Framfield Road, Hanwell, W.7.   10535B.

SHARP, L. A. (Miss), Special War Worker.
This lady was engaged on work of national importance as an inspector of ammunition at the Hayes Munition Factory, Middlesex, where for three years she rendered valuable service. In 1918 she joined the Women's Royal Air Force and did excellent work as a clerk until 1919, when she was demobilised.
177, Framfield Road, Hanwell, W.7.   10535A.

SHARP, R., Pte., 12th Somerset Light Infantry.
He volunteered in April 1915, and after his training was sent to the Western Front, where he took part in many important engagements. Later he was drafted to the East and saw service in Palestine until the close of the war, when he returned to England and in April 1919 was demobilised, holding the 1914-15 Star and the General Service and Victory Medals.
135, Sherbrooke Road, Fulham, S.W.6.   X18683B

SHARP, S. T., Corporal, Royal Air Force.
Joining in August 1916, he was drafted to the Western Front on completion of his training. Whilst overseas, he was present at many important engagements, and was severely wounded at Ypres in 1917. He was invalided home, and on his recovery was stationed at Denham, in Buckinghamshire, where he was engaged as wireless instructor until his demobilisation in January 1919. He holds the General Service and Victory Medals.
60, Portnall Road, Maida Hill, W.9.   X19450.

SHARP, W. T., Sergt., Royal Engineers (R.O.D.)
He joined in March 1917, and in the same year crossed to the Western Front, where he remained until 1919. During his service overseas he did excellent work with the Railway Operation Department of the R.E. on various sectors. He was demobilised in October 1919, and holds the General Service and Victory Medals.
20, Bolton Road, Harlesden, N.W.10.   13376.

SHARPE, H. W., Pte., Royal Fusiliers.
Joining in December 1917, he was drafted to the Western Front, where he took part in many important engagements and was wounded. In September 1918 he was reported missing, but a later report stated that he was killed in action. He was entitled to the General Service and Victory Medals.
20, Brereton Road, Tottenham, N.17.   X18109A.

SHARPE, S. H., Air Mechanic, R.A.F. (late R.N.A.S.).
Joining in 1915, he was drafted to the Western Front, and was for some time stationed at Dunkirk and Nieuport. Throughout his service overseas, which lasted three years, he did good work with the R.A.F., and in 1919 returned to England. He was demobilised in March 1919, and holds the General Service and Victory Medals.
16, Hamilton Road, Highbury Park, N.5.   16286.

SHARPE, W. D., Pte., M.G.C.
Volunteering in August 1914, he was drafted to the Western Front, where he served for three years. Whilst overseas he took part in the fighting on the Somme, at Ypres, Cambrai and in the Retreat and Advance of 1918, and was wounded and gassed. He was demobilised in March 1919 holding the General Service and Victory Medals.
20, Brereton Road, Tottenham, N.17.   X18109B .

SHARPE, W.W., Gunner, Royal Marine Artillery.
He volunteered in August 1914, and after his training was engaged on special duties with his unit. He was not successful in being drafted overseas before the cessation of hostilities, but gave valuable services before being demobilised in January 1919.
55, Guilsborough Road, Willesden, N.W.10.   15251.

SHARPIN, H. R., 2nd Corpl., Royal Engineers.
He joined in May 1917, and served on the Western Front for two years, during which time he did valuable work with the Royal Engineers, in many important sectors. He was demobilised in October 1919, and holds the General Service and Victory Medals.
92, Barry Road, Stonebridge Park, N.W.10.   15665.

SHAW, A. E., 1st Air Mechanic, R.A.F. (late R.N.A.S.).
Volunteering in January 1916, he quickly crossed to the Western Front, where he was engaged at various aerodromes and did much excellent work which called for a high degree of technical skill. He was demobilised in February 1919, holding the General Service and Victory Medals.
29, Aspenlea Road, Hammersmith, W.6.   14294.

SHAW, C. D., Pte., 25th Canadian Regiment.
Volunteering in 1915, he was drafted to the Western Front on completion of his training. After taking part in several important engagements he was killed in the vicinity of Kemmel Hill on February 6th, 1916. He was entitled to the General Service and Victory Medals.
22, Kenninghall Road, Upper Edmonton, N.9.   16902A ·

SHAW, C. J., Pte., Royal Army Service Corps.
Volunteering in August 1914, he was drafted to the Wester Front in the following year. For four years he did valuable work with the R.A.S.C. in many important sectors, including La Bassée, Ypres, Loos and the Somme. He returned to England in 1919, and in March of the same year was demobilised, holding the 1914-15 Star and the General Service and Victory Medals.
51, Shorrolds Road, Walham Green, S.W.6. |X19350B.

SHAW, C. W., Pte., R.A.S.C. (M.T.).
Joining in May 1917, he was drafted to Mesopotamia, where he was engaged in driving an armoured car. In the following year he was sent to Russia, and later saw service in Persia in a similar capacity. He returned to England in 1920, and was demobilised in April, holding the General Service and Victory Medals.
27, Hazlebury Road, Fulham, S.W.6.   X20491

SHAW, F. C., Pte., Royal Marine Light Infantry.
Volunteering in August 1914, he was posted to H.M.S. "Royal Oak." He served throughout with the Grand Fleet, and was present at the Battle of Jutland on May 31st, 1916, and at the surrender of the German Fleet at Scapa Flow. He was demobilised in March 1919, holding the 1914-15 Star and the General Service and Victory Medals.
136, Bounces Road, Lower Edmonton, N.9.   13010B.

SHAW, G., Driver, R.A.S.C. (Horse Transport).
He joined in 1901, and went to France in June 1915. After taking part in the battles of Ypres, Loos, Lens, Albert, Cambrai and the Somme, he returned to England in consequence of serious wounds in September 1916. In December of the following year he went to Egypt and thence to Palestine, where he was present at the Capture of Jerusalem. In 1918 he was again sent to France, remaining there until 1919. He holds the 1914-15 Star and the General Service and Victory Medals, and in 1920 was still serving.
34, Shelley Road, Willesden, N.W.10.   13649.

SHAW, H. J., Pte., 1st Grenadier Guards.
He was recalled to the colours in August 1914, and served on the Western Front from that month until April 1916, during which period he went through the heavy fighting at Mons and Ypres, and was wounded at Neuve Chapelle. In consequence he was shortly afterwards discharged as medically unfit for further service. He holds the Mons Star and the General Service and Victory Medals.
25, Charlton Road, Harlesden, N.W.10.   13103

SHAW, J., Sergeant, Seaforth Highlanders.
He joined in January 1916, and during his service on the Western Front took part in many important engagements, and was wounded in action at Mametz Wood in July 1916. He was demobilised in February 1919, and holds the General Service and Victory Medals.
34, Walham Grove, Fulham, S.W.6.   X19614.

SHAW, J. J., Corpl., The Buffs (East Kent Regt.).
Volunteering in August 1914, he was at once drafted to the Western Front, where he went through the Retreat from Mons. He also took part in many of the engagements which followed, including those at Ypres and Cambrai, and was on two occasions severely wounded. He holds the Mons Star and the General Service and Victory Medals, and was demobilised in 1919.
20, Monmouth Road, Lower Edmonton, N.9.   13317.

SHAW, T., Pte., Labour Corps.
Volunteering in October 1915, he was first drafted to the Western, and then to the Eastern Front. Throughout his service he was engaged on special duties, and was for a time attached to the R.A.S.C. He was demobilised in February 1919, holding the General Service and Victory Medals.
58, Shakespeare Avenue, Willesden, N.W.10.   13618B.

SHAW, W., Pte., Wiltshire Regiment.
Joining in 1916, he was drafted to the Western Front, where in September of the following year he was severely wounded in action at Ypres, and lost a leg. He returned to England, and in January 1918 was invalided out of the Service. He holds the General Service and Victory Medals.
58, Shakespeare Avenue, Willesden, N.W.10.   13618A.

SHAW, W. D., Corporal, Machine Gun Corps.
He joined in July 1916, and saw much valuable service in France, where he took part in the battles of the Somme, Ypres and Cambrai, and other engagements. He was demobilised in January 1919, holding the General Service and Victory Medals.
23, Harton Road, Lower Edmonton, N.9.   13040.

SHEAD, J., Lce.-Corpl. R.A.S.C. (M.T.), and Tank Corps.
Volunteering in August 1914, he was speedily drafted to the Western Front. He took part in the Retreat from Mons and the battles of Ypres, Loos, Lens, the Somme, Arras and Cambrai, and was recommended for a decoration for the conspicuous bravery and devotion to duty he displayed during the Advance of 1918. His service overseas lasted for four and a half years, and in March 1919 he returned to England and was demobilised. He holds the Mons Star and the General Service and Victory Medals.
13, Purves Road, Kensal Rise, N.W.10.   X18019.

SHEAHAN, J. W., Pte., Royal Dublin Fusiliers.
Volunteering in 1914, he was drafted to the Western Front, where he took part in several battles and was gassed. In 1915 he was sent to the East, and was killed in action at Gallipoli. He was entitled to the 1914-15 Star and the General Service and Victory Medals.
48, Winchester Road, Lower Edmonton, N.9.   15201.

SHEARING, H. J., Driver, R.A.S.C. (M.T.).
He joined in May 1916, and after a short period of training was drafted to the Western Front. His service overseas lasted for three years, during which time he did excellent work with the ammunition and supply columns in various sectors, including the Somme, and was frequently under shell-fire. In 1919 he was invalided home suffering from shell-shock and after being some months in hospital, was demobilised in September of the same year. He holds the General Service and Victory Medals.
300, Shirland Road, Maida Hill, W.9.   X19559

SHEARING, L. (Miss), Special War Worker.
This lady was engaged for three years at the Park Royal Munition Factory, Willesden. Her work was of an extremely dangerous character, and the capable manner in which she carried out her duties was greatly appreciated.
101, Carlyle Avenue, Willesden, N.W.10.   13683A.

SHEARING, W., Gnr., Royal Field Artillery.
Volunteering in September 1914, he was soon drafted to the Western Front, where he took part in important engagements, and in June 1915 he was killed near Armentieres. He was entitled to the 1914-15 Star and the General Service and Victory Medals.
101, Carlyle Avenue, Willesden, N.W.10.   13683B.

SHEARS, G. F., Rifleman, Rifle Brigade.
He volunteered in September 1914, and in the following year was sent to France, where he remained for four years. During that time he took part in many engagements, including those at Ypres, where he was three times wounded, Arras, the Somme, Hill 60, Messines Ridge and the Advance of 1918. He was demobilised in February 1919, and holds the 1914-15 Star and the General Service and Victory Medals.
67, Bulow Road, Fulham, S.W.6.   X20807.

SHEARWOOD, J., Pte., East Surrey Regiment.
He volunteered in August 1914, and during his five years' service on the Western Front took part in many engagements, including the Battle of the Somme, and was twice wounded. In 1919 he was demobilised, holding the 1914-15 Star and the General Service and Victory Medals.
89, Lopen Road, Upper Edmonton, N.18.   X17916

SHEED, W. F., Pte., R.A.S.C. (M.T.).

He volunteered in November 1915, and after his training was drafted to France, where throughout his service he did valuable work with the Mechanical Transport in many important sectors. He was demobilised in 1919, holding the 1914-15 Star and the General Service and Victory Medals.

46, Alston Road, Upper Edmonton, N.18.   16499.

SHEEHAN, C., 2nd Lieut., Royal Flying Corps.

Volunteering in August 1914, he was drafted to Salonika on the completion of his training. He did valuable work with the Royal Flying Corps, and in August 1917 was killed whilst flying, through using a faulty machine. He was entitled to the 1914-15 Star and the General Service and Victory Medals, and his relatives hold a letter of condolence from His Majesty the King.

179, Estcourt Road, Fulham, S.W.6.   16242.

SHEEN, F. W., (M.M.)., Sergt., 2nd Royal Scots Fusiliers.

Volunteering in August 1914, he was at once drafted to the Western Front. After taking a prominent part in many important engagements from the opening of the war, including the Battle of Mons and the Somme, he was killed near Albert, on August 7th, 1916. He was awarded the Military Medal for conspicuous bravery and devotion to duty, and was also entitled to the Mons Star and the General Service and Victory Medals.

25, Church Path, Hammersmith, W.6.   15916.

SHELDON, G. E., Pte., Middlesex Regiment.

Joining in May 1916, he was drafted to the Western Front, where he took part in many important battles, and was wounded and gassed. For some time he was in hospital, and after the cessation of hostilities, was sent with the Army of Occupation to Germany. He returned to England in September 1919, when he was demobilised, holding the General Service and Victory Medals.

66, Bramber Road, West Kensington, W.14.   16226.

SHELDON, T., Trooper, 7th (Princess Royal's) Dragoon Guards.

He volunteered in September 1914, and after his training served at various stations on important duties with his unit. He gave valuable services, but was not successful in obtaining his transfer overseas owing to ill-health. He was discharged in September 1917.

4, Pearscroft Road, Fulham, S.W.6.   X20508A.

SHELLEY, A. E. (M.M.), Lce.-Corpl., 13th Durham Light Infantry.

He enlisted in 1916, and went to the Western Front in June 1917. In the following October he was transferred to Italy, where he saw much fighting. In 1918 he returned to France, and was killed in a bombing raid on October 23rd, 1918. He was awarded the Military Medal for conspicuous gallantry, and was also entitled to the General Service and Victory Medals.

15, Farrant Street, Queen's Park Estate, W.10.   X19060.

SHENTON, F.(M.M.), Sergt.,1st Grenadier Guards.

He joined the Army in October 1901, and during the recent war saw active service on the Western Front. He took a prominent part in many important engagements, including those at Ypres, the Somme and Festubert, and was awarded the Military Medal for conspicuous bravery on the field. In addition he holds the 1914 Star and the General Service and Victory Medals, and was demobilised in January 1919.

43, Mordaunt Road, Willesden, N.W.10.   13861.

SHEPHARD, A., Pte., 2/9th Middlesex Regiment.

Volunteering in March 1915, he received his training at various stations, and was afterwards engaged on important guard duties. He was not successful in obtaining his transfer overseas owing to physical unfitness, and in August 1916 was invalided out of the Service.

121, Claxton Grove, Hammersmith, W.6.   13671.

SHEPHERD, A. E. F., Special War Worker.

During the war he was engaged at Messrs. Vickers' factory on work of national importance in connection with the construction of aeroplane sheds and hangars of all kinds for the Government, and his skilled services proved of the greatest value.

86, Portnall Road, Maida Hill, W.9.   TX19541A.

SHEPHERD, B. F., Sergt., 2/7th Middlesex Regt.

Volunteering in September 1914, he was sent to Egypt in the following year. Having been transferred to France in 1916, he was taken prisoner on July 13th, 1916, during the Battle of the Somme. He was discharged in March 1919, after two years and eight months' captivity in Germany. He holds the 1914-15 Star and the General Service and Victory Medals.

72, Chester Road, Lower Edmonton, N.9.   12288.

SHEPHERD, E. A., Gunner, R.F.A.

He volunteered for service in September 1914, and served with the Royal Field Artillery at various stations. Whilst on duty during Zeppelin raids he was seriously injured, and was for some months in hospital. In July 1917 he was discharged as unfit for further service. Afterwards he was engaged on work of national importance at the Park Royal Munition Works, where he rendered valuable service which was greatly appreciated. He holds the General Service Medal.

305, Shirland Road, Maida Hill, W.9.   X19561A.

SHEPHERD, E. R., Rifleman, 1st Rifle Brigade.

He joined in April 1918, and after serving at various stations in England was drafted to Mesopotamia, where he was in charge of Turkish prisoners. In 1920 he was still serving in the East, and holds the General Service and Victory Medals.

305, Shirland Road, Maida Hill, W.9.   X19561B.

SHEPHERD, F. B. (Miss), Special War Worker.

During the war this lady rendered valuable service at Messrs. Blake's Factory, Sudbury, and at the Perivale Filling Factory, Park Royal. Whilst in the latter post she was engaged upon work of an extremely dangerous character in the T.N.T. shop, and was for some months ill with poisoning contracted in the course of her duty. Her efficient work was greatly appreciated.

305, Shirland Road, Maida Hill, W.9.   X19561C.

SHEPHERD, F. C., Pte., R.A.S.C. (M.T.).

He volunteered in June 1915, and was engaged on various important duties on the Western Front throughout his service. He was engaged on many sectors, and was present at the Battle of Ypres, where, acting as a dispatch rider, he ran many risks in order to deliver safely the messages entrusted to him. He finally returned to England after much good work in France, and in December 1918 was demobilised. He holds the General Service and Victory Medals.

158, Bounces Road, Lower Edmonton, N.9.   13007.

SHEPHERD, F. R., Pte., 3rd Royal Fusiliers (City of London Regiment).

He volunteered for duty in September 1914, and after completing his training was drafted to the Dardanelles. He served through the campaign in Gallipoli until October 1915, when he was wounded in action at Suvla Bay. He was invalided home, and in May 1916 was discharged as medically unfit. He holds the 1914-15 Star and the General Service and Victory Medals.

78, Burn's Road, Harlesden, N.W.10.   13461.

SHEPHERD, G., Pte., Royal Fusiliers.

Volunteering in January 1915, he was sent to the Western Front in the same year, and took part in many engagements, including those of Arras, Cambrai, Loos and the Somme. He was in action through the German Offensive of March 1918, and in the later British Advance. He was subsequently transferred to a Labour Battalion on account of his health. He was demobilised in March 1919 holding the 1914-15 Star and the General Service and Victory Medals.

55, Earlsmead Road, College Park, N.W.10.   X17840B.

SHEPHERD, J. E. (Mrs.), Storewoman, W.R.A.F.

This lady was engaged for some time during the war at Messrs. Blake's Munition Factory, Wood Lane, where she loaded 18-lb. shells and charges for shipment to Russia. In January 1918 she joined the Woman's Royal Air Force, and until her demobilisation in November 1918 did excellent work as storewoman at the R.A.F. Aeroplane Components Stores, Edgware Road.

86, Portnall Road, Maida Hill, W.9.   TX19541B.

SHEPHERD, W., Gnr., Royal Garrison Artillery.

Volunteering on the outbreak of war, this gunner was quickly sent to the Western Front. He took part in the memorable Retreat from Mons, and was also in action at Ypres and Cambrai and in many other important engagements. After fighting with distinction in France for over four years, he went to Germany with the Army of Occupation. He was demobilised on his return to England in February 1919, and holds the Mons Star and the General Service and Victory Medals.

29, St. John's Avenue, Harlesden, N.W.10.   14744.

SHEPHERD, W., Pte., 3rd Grenadier Guards.

He volunteered in August 1914, and having completed his training was drafted to the Western Front in the same year. He saw service in various important engagements on many sectors, and took part in the battles of La Bassée, Vimy Ridge and Ypres. In 1917 he was invalided home suffering from shell-shock, and in November of that year was discharged as medically unfit. He holds the 1914-15 Star and the General Service and Victory Medals.

55, Earlsmead Road, College Park, N.W.10.   X17840A.

SHEPPARD, A. (Mrs.), Special War Worker.
This lady was engaged first at Messrs. Blake's Munition Works on fuse binding, and afterwards at Messrs. Davison's Aircraft Factory, doping aeroplanes. She rendered valuable service throughout the war, and was commended for her excellent work.
14, Francis Street, Hammersmith, W.6. |15032A.

SHEPPARD, A. (Miss), Special War Worker.
During the war this lady was engaged at Messrs. Brown's Aircraft Works, Hammersmith, on work in connection with the construction of aeroplanes. She carried out her duties in an efficient manner and was worthy of high commendation.
14, Francis Street, Hammersmith, W.6. 15044.

SHEPPARD, C., Corpl., Royal Horse Artillery.
A serving soldier, he was drafted to the Western Front on the outbreak of war. He took part in many important engagements, including the memorable Retreat from Mons and the battles of the Aisne and the Somme, and in November 1916 he was discharged. He holds the Mons Star and the General Service and Victory Medals.
7, Essex Road, Willesden, N.W.10. |15935.

SHEPPARD, F. G. C., Pte., 3rd London Regiment (Royal Fusiliers).
He was mobilised in August 1914, but after five months' valuable service in guarding railways was discharged through medical unfitness. He then undertook munition work, first at Park Royal Munition Factory and later at the aircraft works at College Park, where he was engaged in making aeroplane parts until 1919.
60, Third Avenue, Queen's Park Estate, W.10. |X19293.

SHEPPARD, J. (Miss), Special War Worker.
During the war this lady was engaged on work of an important nature at Messrs. Brown's Factory, Hammersmith, where she rendered valuable services in connection with the construction of aircraft. Her ability, and the quickness and skill she showed in the responsible duties allotted to her, quickly won her the appreciation and commendation of the firm.
14, Francis Street, Hammersmith, W.6. |15030.

SHEPPARD, J., Special War Worker.
He was engaged throughout the war in constructing tents, marquees and other articles for military purposes at Messrs. Waring & Gillow's Factory, The White City. He rendered valuable services, which were greatly appreciated.
14, Francis Street, Hammersmith, W.6. 15032B.

SHEPPARD, J. (M.M.), Bombardier, R.F.A.
Having previously served for five years, he was drafted to the Western Front immediately on the outbreak of war. Here he fought at Mons, Loos and in the battle of the Somme. He was awarded the Military Medal for conspicuous gallantry in the field. After serving with distinction in France for nearly two years, he was killed in action at Fricourt on July 14th, 1916. He was also entitled to the Mons Star and the General Service and Victory Medals.
24, Fernhead Road, Maida Hill, W.9. | X19389B.

SHEPPERD, J., Special War Worker.
Being unsuccessful in his efforts to join the Army, and desiring to serve his Country, he accepted an important post at Messrs. W. & G. Du Cros' Factory at Acton. Here he held the responsible post of a charge hand, controlling a section employed in the making of shells. The able and conscientious way in which he performed his work was of the utmost value to his Country.
48, Bronsart Road, Munster Road, S.W.6. 18888.

SHEPPERSON, D. (Mrs.), Special War Worker.
Throughout the period of the war this lady rendered valuable services of national importance. She was first engaged as a fuse examiner at the Park Royal Factory, where she merited high commendation. She resigned her post, however, to take up work at the National Filling Station, Fulham, where, in spite of the dangerous nature of her duties, she continued until the end of the war.
63, Orbain Road, Fulham, S.W.6. ||X18640B.

SHEPPERSON, C., Gunner, Royal Field Artillery.
He joined in January 1916, and after his training was sent to the Western Front, where he took part in many engagements, including those of the Somme, Ypres, Arras, Loos, Neuve Chapelle, Armentieres, Bullecourt and St. Quentin. He was wounded at Festubert, and also at Cambrai during the final Advance. He was invalided home, and was demobilised, after his recovery, in June 1919. He holds the General Service and Victory Medals.
63, Orbain Road, Fulham, S.W.6. |X18640A.

SHERIDAN, T., Pte., Royal Dublin Fusiliers.
Volunteering in November 1914, he was drafted to the Western Front immediately on completing his training. He took part in the engagements on the Somme and at Arras, Loos, Armentieres, Neuve Chapelle and Givenchy, and was gassed while fighting at Mt. Kemmel. After being severely wounded in action at Ypres, he was invalided home, and, being medically unfit for further military duties, was discharged in January 1918. He holds the 1914-15 Star and the General Service and Victory Medals.
22, Archel Road, West Kensington, W.14. 16195.

SHERING, A., Leading Aircraftsman, R.A.F.
Joining in June 1916, he was engaged until the close of hostilities on important duties that called for a high degree of technical knowledge and skill. He served on various sectors on the Western Front, and was demobilised on his return to England in March 1919. He holds the General Service and Victory Medals.
43, Moselle Street, Tottenham, N.17. |18398.

SHERMAN, M., Pte., 19th City of London Vltrs.
Having been exempted on compassionate grounds from joining the Regular Army, he became a member of the County of London Volunteers in July 1916, and rendered valuable services in trench digging and in guarding railways. Later he was engaged on important Government work in connection with military tailoring. He was discharged in July 1918, and holds the King's Certificate.
21, Farrant Street, Queen's Park Estate, W.10. TX19057.

SHERRAT, T. W., Corpl., Cheshire Regiment.
He was serving in India at the outbreak of war, and in January 1915 was drafted to the Western Front. Here he took part in the battles of Ypres and St. Eloi, and in various other important engagements. In May 1915 he was gassed and wounded in action. He was demobilised in October 1919, holding the 1914-15 Star and the General Service and Victory Medals.
59, Love Lane, Tottenham, N.17. X18307.

SHERRATT, J., Driver, Royal Field Artillery.
Having joined the Army before the outbreak of war, he was drafted to the Western Front in August 1914. He took part in the memorable Retreat from Mons, and also fought on the Somme, the Aisne and at Arras. Later he was engaged in guarding prisoners of war at Havrincourt Wood. After being severely wounded at the battle of Ypres, he was invalided home and discharged as medically unfit in July 1918. He holds the Mons Star and the General Service and Victory Medals.
23, Letchford Gardens, Willesden, N.W.10. X17541.

SHERRIFF, F. M., 1st Air Mechanic, 1st London Regiment (Royal Fusiliers).
He was mobilised on the outbreak of war, and in March 1915 was sent to the Western Front. He took part in much heavy fighting in France, and was in action at the battles of Loos, Aubers Ridge, and with reinforcements at Neuve Chapelle. Later he was transferred to the R.A.F., and was engaged on important duties as a 1st Air Mechanic, until his demobilisation in January 1919. He holds the 1914-15 Star and the General Service and Victory Medals.
1, Ashburnham Road, Willesden, N.W.10. 18656.

SHERVILL, G. W., Pte., Royal Welch Fusiliers.
He volunteered in January 1915, and in the same year was sent to France. He served on many sectors of the Western Front. After fighting with distinction in the trenches for nearly four years, he returned to England for demobilisation in January 1919. He holds the 1914-15 Star and the General Service and Victory Medals.
19, Ray's Avenue, Upper Edmonton, N.18. 15487.

SHERWOOD, F.W., Pte., Royal Sussex Regiment and Bedfordshire Regiment.
Volunteering in November 1915, he went to India in March of the following year, and served there until November 1919, during which period, in addition to other duties, he helped to quell the riots at Delhi. He holds the General Service Medals, and was demobilised in December 1919, on his return to England.
2, Ashmore Road, Maida Hill, W.9. X19465.

SHEW, S. V., Flight Sergeant, Royal Air Force.
He volunteered in February 1915, and in the same year was drafted out to France. While abroad he served in numerous engagements, including those of Loos, Albert and the Somme, and also took part in several bombing raids and acted as an observer. He was demobilised in June 1919, holding the 1914-15 Star and the General Service and Victory Medals.
28, Goldney Road, Maida Hill, W.9. X21275.

HEWRY, E., Pte., 7th Wiltshire Regiment.
He volunteered for duty in February 1915, and on completing his training was sent to Salonika, where he saw much fighting up to November 1917, when he was wounded in action on the Doiran Front. On recovery he was transferred to France, where he served with distinction until after the cessation of hostilities. He returned to England for demobilisation in January 1919, and now holds the 1914–15 Star and the General Service and Victory Medals.
18, Oxford Road, Lower Edmonton, N.9.   13120.

SHILHAM, A. J., Pte., 2/4th Leicestershire Regt.
Volunteering in March 1915, he was drafted to France early in the next year. He fought on many sectors of the front, and took part with distinction in the battles of Arras, Ypres, and Péronne. He returned home in 1919, and in October of that year was demobilised, holding the General Service and Victory Medals.
106, Churchill Road, Cricklewood, N.W.2.   16709.

SHILLINGFORD, W., Pte., West Yorkshire Regt.
Joining in June 1916, he was drafted to the Western Front in the same year upon the completion of his training. He took part in much heavy fighting, and on two occasions was wounded in action. He was subsequently taken prisoner, and was held in captivity in Germany for nine months. He was demobilised in October 1919, and holds the General Service and Victory Medals.
168, Bounces Road, Lower Edmonton, N.9.   13013.

SHINGLES, J., Rifleman, King's Royal Rifle Corps.
He joined in 1916, and after completing his training was drafted to the Western Front. Here he saw fighting on many sectors. He was wounded in action, and was twice gassed. He went later with the Army of Occupation to Germany, and remained there until 1919, when he returned to England to be demobilised. He holds the General Service and Victory Medals.
103, Sherbrooke Road, Fulham, S.W.6.   X18472C.

SHINGLES, T. A., Pte., Royal Fusiliers.
He volunteered in April 1915, and during a long service on the Western Front acted as 1st class signaller. He spent some time in hospital suffering from wounds received in action. Later he served with the Army of Occupation in Germany until his return to England for demobilisation in 1919. He holds the 1914–15 Star and the General Service and Victory Medals.
103, Sherbrooke Road, Fulham, S.W.6.   X18472B.

SHIP, C. J., Pte., Norfolk Regiment.
He volunteered in December 1914, and was sent to the Western Front in the following June. He was in action at the battle of Ploegsteert Wood, near Ypres, in September 1915, when he was severely wounded. He was invalided home, and after treatment in hospital was discharged in July 1916 as medically unfit for further service. He holds the 1914–15 Star and the General Service and Victory Medals.
22, Allington Road, North Kensington, W.10.   X18610.

SHIPLEY, J., Driver, Royal Field Artillery.
He volunteered in September 1915, and immediately on the completion of his training was sent to the Western Front, where he saw action on many sectors. He remained in France throughout his service and took part with distinction in various engagements up to the date of the Armistice. On his return to England he was demobilised in March 1919. He holds the General Service and Victory Medals.
16, Kilmaine Road, Munster Road, S.W.6.   X18780A.

SHIPLEY, J., Pte., 2nd East Surrey Regiment.
Volunteering in August 1915, he was drafted to the Western Front on completing his training. He saw much active service in various parts of the Western Front, and fought in many important engagements until June 1st, 1918, when he was killed in action. He was entitled to the General Service and Victory Medals.
16, Kilmaine Road, Munster Road, S.W.6.   X18780B.

SHIPP, A., Pte., Durham Light Infantry.
Volunteering in December 1915, he was drafted to the Western Front. After taking part with distinction in the fighting on various sectors he was invalided home on account of trench feet, and ultimately discharged in November 1917. He holds the General Service and Victory Medals.
22, Raynham Road, Upper Edmonton, N.18.   16488.

SHIPP, J. W., Pte., Royal Welch Fusiliers.
He volunteered in August 1914, and was engaged on important duties at various stations until September 1917, when he was discharged. He was not successful in obtaining his transfer overseas, but did splendid work with his unit throughout his service.
8, Ascot Road, Upper Edmonton, N.18.   15183.

SHIPTON, A., Sergt., 2/17th London Regiment.
A time-serving soldier at the outbreak of war, he was sent in 1916 to the Eastern Front. He fought at Salonika, and was later transferred to Egypt. He subsequently took part in General Allenby's Advance in Palestine, and was present at the capture of Jerusalem. He was also engaged in the Offensive of 1918, when he was wounded in action. Returning to England in February 1919, he was demobilised, and holds the General Service and Victory Medals.
359, Chapter Road, Cricklewood, N.W.2.   16716A.

SHIPTON, G., Lce.-Corpl., 7th London Regiment.
He volunteered for duty in August 1914, and was drafted to the Western Front on the completion of his training. He saw much service until September 15th, 1916, when he was killed in action on the Somme. He was entitled to the 1914–15 Star and the General Service and Victory Medals.
38, Garvan Road, Hammersmith, W.6.   15059.

SHIRE, W. J., Pte., Oxford and Bucks Light Inf.
He volunteered in August 1914, and in the following year was drafted to Mesopotamia, and afterwards to India. Here he was invalided to hospital on account of sunstroke. He remained in India until his return to England for demobilisation in March 1919. He holds the 1914–15 Star and the General Service and Victory Medals.
187, Stephendale Road, Fulham, S.W.6.   X20816

SHORE, W. E., A.B., R.N., H.M.S. "Agamemnon."
Volunteering in September 1914, he was present in all important engagements in the Dardanelles whilst serving in his ship, which subsequently cruised in Eastern waters. He was demobilised in April 1919, and holds the 1914 Star and the General Service and Victory Medals.
18, Barbot Street, Lower Edmonton, N.9.   14585.

SHORT, A., Corpl., Royal Army Service Corps.
Having previously served with the Territorials, he was mobilised at the outbreak of hostilities, and for nearly three years was stationed at St. Albans doing clerical work. In 1917 he was drafted to France, and in the same capacity served at a supply depôt. He was demobilised in July 1919, holding the General Service and Victory Medals.
303, Shirland Road, Maida Hill, W.9.   X19558A.

SHORT, H., Lce.-Corpl., Queen's Own (Royal West Kent Regiment).
He joined in December 1917, and after serving at various places in England was drafted to the Western Front. During the 1918 campaign he was taken prisoner, and whilst in captivity in Germany was very badly treated. After the signing of the Armistice he was released and in December 1918 was demobilised, holding the General Service and Victory Medals.
303, Shirland Road, Maida Hill, W.9.   X19558B.

SHORT, H. (M.M.), Lce.-Corpl., 1st Middlesex Regt.
He volunteered in October 1915, and was almost immediately drafted to France. From there he was sent to Russia, where he took part in many engagements and was wounded. He was awarded the Military Medal for conspicuous bravery on the field, and also holds the General Service and Victory Medals.
12, Chauncey Street, Lower Edmonton, N.9.   14254B.

SHORT, J. D., Signalman, Royal Navy.
He volunteered for duty in October 1915, and saw much service in the North Sea and off the coasts of China and Italy. He holds the General Service and Victory Medals, and was still serving in 1920.
12, Chauncey Street, Lower Edmonton, N.9.   14254A.

SHORT, W. R., Lce.-Corpl., 2/6 Norfolk Regt.
He joined in September 1916, and after his training served at various stations on important duties with his unit. He gave valuable services, but was medically unfit for service overseas, and was demobilised in August 1919.
24, Purcell Crescent, Fulham, S.W.6.   14841

SHORTLAND, E. A., Corporal, 24th London Regt.
He enlisted in April 1909, and during the war was engaged on special duties with his unit. He rendered valuable services as range-keeper, but was not successful in obtaining his transfer to the Front. In March 1916 he was discharged as medically unfit for further military duty.
26, Lancefield Street, North Kensington, W.10.   X19914.

SHOWELL, B. H., Pte., Middlesex Regiment and Manchester Regiment.

He volunteered in August 1914, and in the same year was drafted to France, where he remained for three years. During this time he took part in much of the heavy fighting on the Somme, and was wounded at Armentieres. Later he was transferred to the Manchester Regiment, and in 1917 was wounded at Passchendaele, and invalided home. He was discharged owing to wounds in June 1918, and holds the 1914–15 Star and the General Service and Victory Medals.

12, Heron Road, Willesden, N.W.10. 15563.

SHOWELL, S. H., Pte., Duke of Wellington's (West Riding Regiment).

Mobilised from the Reserve in August 1914, he served at various stations on important duties with his unit. On September 29th, 1919, he died from paralysis caused by a serious accident. Throughout he gave very valuable services before his death.

48, Oakbury Road, Fulham, S.W.6. X20924.

SHRIMPTON, A., Driver, Royal Field Artillery.

Volunteering in December 1914, he was sent to France early in the following year and took part in the battles of Ypres and Vimy Ridge. Later he was transferred to Salonika, where he was in action and suffered from shell-shock. On recovery he returned to France and was seriously wounded and invalided home. He was discharged owing to his wound in June 1918, and holds the 1914–15 Star, the General Service and Victory Medals.

46, Crefeld Road, Hammersmith, W.6 14495

SHRIMPTON, C. R., Driver and Pioneer, R.F.A. and R.E.

Volunteering in October 1914, he was soon drafted to the Western Front, where he took part in the battles of Ypres, Vimy Ridge, Neuve Chapelle, Loos and the Advance of 1918. During his service he was twice wounded, and also gassed. In February 1919 he was demobilised, and holds the 1914 Star and the General Service and Victory Medals.

46, Crefeld Road, Hammersmith, W.6. 14496.

SHRIMPTON, H., Sapper, Royal Engineers.

He volunteered in March 1915, and in the same year was sent to France where he was employed with the Royal Engineers near Albert in making fortifications and lines of communication. Later he was drafted to Salonika, and served there on similar work until the cessation of hostilities, when he returned home and was demobilised in April 1919. He holds the 1914–15 Star and the General Service and Victory Medals.

61A, Drayton Road, Harlesden, N.W.10. 15015.

SHULVER, F. E., Pte., Queen's Own (Royal West Kent Regiment) and Labour Corps.

He joined in September 1916, and after his training served at various stations on important duties with his unit. He gave valuable services, but was not successful in obtaining his transfer overseas, being medically unfit. He was discharged in February 1919.

31, Shelley Road, Willesden, N.W.10. 13781A.

SIBLEY, F., Corpl., 2/2 London Regiment (Royal Fusiliers).

He volunteered in September 1914, and in the same year was sent to France, from where he was soon after transferred to the Dardanelles. Whilst on the Eastern Front he took part in the heavy fighting in Gallipoli. In 1916 he returned to France, and was in action at Bourlon Wood and Gommecourt Wood, where he was wounded. He was demobilised in February 1919, holding the 1914–15 Star and the General Service and Victory Medals.

31, Albert Terrace, Milton Avenue,
Stonebridge Park, N.W.10. 14335.

SIBLEY, F. G., Pte., Machine Gun Corps.

Having joined the Army previous to the outbreak of war, he was immediately drafted to the Western Front, where he remained until December 1918. He took part in the memorable Retreat from Mons and in the battles of Loos, Ypres, Neuve Chapelle, Cambrai, and the Somme. During his distinguished service he was wounded on three occasions, and after the signing of the Armistice was engaged on various important duties up to the date of his demobilisation in January 1920. He holds the Mons Star and the General Service and Victory Medals.

34, Hiley Road, Willesden, N.W.10. X18426B

SIBLEY, G. W., 2nd Air Mechanic, R.A.F.

Joining in September 1917, he took part in several engagements on the Western Front, but was later employed on the air defences of London, where he rendered invaluable services with the guns. He holds the General Service and Victory Medals.

8, Cranbrook Road, Tottenham, N.17. X18378.

SIBLEY, W., Rifleman, Rifle Brigade.

Volunteering in May 1915, he was drafted to the Western Front. Being over age for the trenches, he gave valuable services in France, where he was in charge of German prisoners. He was demobilised in February 1919, holding the General Service and Victory Medals.

24, Cornwallis Grove, Lower Edmonton, N.9. 13323.

SIDEBOTHAM, N. W., Corporal, R.A.M.C.

Having enlisted in October 1905, he was sent to France a the outbreak of war. Early in 1915 he served on the hospital ships "Aquitania" and "Britannic" as they were conveying the wounded from Lemnos to Southampton, and later served for three years in Mesopotamia and India. He was mentioned in dispatches in June 1919 for devotion to duty whilst bringing wounded from Mesopotamia. He was demobilised in September 1919, holding the 1914 Star and the General Service and Victory Medals.

32, Shakespeare Avenue, Willesden, N.W.10. 13610.

SILCOX, G. B. E., Pte., 12th Cheshire Regiment.

He joined in March 1917, and in the following year was sent to France, where he took a prominent part in the battles of the Somme, Passchendaele, and Achiet-le-Grand and many others. He remained on the Western Front until he was demobilised in 1919, and holds the General Service and Victory Medals.

8, Windsor Gardens, Maida Hill, W.9. X20176B.

SILCOX, J. O. G., Pte., Duke of Cornwall's L.I.

He volunteered in May 1915, and in the same year was sent to France, where he remained on active service for four years. During this time he took part in engagements on the Somme, at Arras, Ypres, St. Quentin, Delville Wood and Passchendaele, and was wounded. He was demobilised in May 1919, and holds the 1914–15 Star and the General Service and Victory Medals.

8, Windsor Gardens, Maida Hill, W.9. X20176A.

SILLITON, F. C., Pte., Canadian Expeditionary Force.

He volunteered in 1915, went to the Western Front in the same year, and took a prominent part in the battles of Loos, Ypres and the Somme. He was severely gassed whilst in action at Arras, and died from the effects on October 29th, 1918. He was entitled to the 1914–15 Star and the General Service and Victory Medals.

52, Farm Lane, Walham Green, S.W.6. X19478A.

SILLITON, W., Pte., 7th London Regiment.

Joining in April 1918, he was sent to the Western Front and took part in the Advance. After the cessation of hostilities he was transferred to Gibraltar. He holds the General Service and Victory Medals.

52, Farm Lane, Walham Green, S.W.6. X19478B.

SILLS, A. D., Pte., 1st East Surrey Regiment.

He volunteered in August 1914, proceeded to the Western Front, and in the same month was taken prisoner during the Retreat from Mons. He was interned in Germany until December 1918, when he was released and demobilised. He holds the Mons Star and the General Service and Victory Medals.

20, Laundry Road, Hammersmith, W.6. 15346B.

SILLS, G., Pte., 1st Staffordshire Regiment.

He joined in March 1916, and in the following year was drafted to the Western Front, where he was reported missing on October 26th, 1917. He was entitled to the General Service and Victory Medals.

47, Woodheyes Road, Neasden, N.W.10. 15592.

SILLS, G., A.B., Royal Navy.

He volunteered in August 1914, and until 1915 served on H.M. Trawler "Manor" on patrol duties. He was then sent to Egypt on H.M.S. "Jupiter" and remained in the East until December 1916. In the following May he was posted to H.M.S. "Monas Isle," and was engaged on various important duties until November 1918, when he was demobilised. He holds the 1914 Star and the General Service and Victory Medals.

8, Monmouth Road, Lower Edmonton, N.9. 3318

SILVESTER, H. C. H., Pte., 13th Royal Fusiliers.

He joined in July 1916, and during his service on the Western Front took part in the battles of Ypres and the Somme, where he was wounded. On his return to England he was demobilised in January 1919, and holds the General Service and Victory Medals.

17, Yeldham Road, Hammersmith, W.6.   T13045A.

SILVESTER, P. J., Pte., Royal Fusiliers and 13th London Regiment (Kensington).

Volunteering in June 1915, he took part in the battles of the Somme and Cambrai on the Western Front, and was twice wounded. He was demobilised in April 1919, and holds the 1914-15 Star and the General Service and Victory Medals.

17, Yeldham Road, Hammersmith, W.6.   T13045C.

SILVESTER, T. W., Pte., Norfolk Regiment.

Volunteering in August 1914, he served for four years on the Western Front, where he was fighting on the Somme, at Ypres and Arras, and during the Retreat of 1918. During his service he was five times wounded, and was demobilised in February 1919, holding the 1914-15 Star and the General Service and Victory Medals.

17, Yeldham Road, Hammersmith, W.6.   T13045B.

SILVESTER, W., Pte., 7th The London Regt.

He volunteered in 1915, and after his training was drafted to the Western Front. While in France he served with distinction in numerous engagements, and was severely wounded. After being invalided home he was discharged in 1918, and holds the General Service and Victory Medals.

8, Rosaline Road, Munster Road, S.W.6.   X18175.

SILVESTER, W. E., Pte., 19th Queen's (Royal West Surrey Regiment).

He joined in November 1916, and after his training served at various stations on important duties. He gave valuable services as clerk to the medical officer of his unit, but was not successful in obtaining his transfer overseas before the cessation of hostilities. He was demobilised in 1919.

28, Fairlight Avenue, Willesden, N.W.10.   14017.

SIMCO, J. G., Pte., Royal Fusiliers.

He joined in 1916, and in the same year was drafted to the Western Front, where he took a prominent part in several engagements. He was killed in action during the battle of Arras on May 1st, 1917, and was entitled to the General Service and Victory Medals.

74, Bruce Castle Road, Tottenham, N.17.   X18544.

SIMKINS, G. J., Corporal, 23rd Royal Fusiliers.

He joined in 1917, and in the same year was drafted to France, where he remained until 1919. During this time he saw much of the heavy fighting, and took a distinguished part in many engagements, including those at Arras, Cambrai and in the Advance of 1918. He was gassed on two occasions, and, in consequence, was in hospital for several weeks. He holds the General Service and Victory Medals, and was demobilised in October 1919, after his return to England.

115, Manor Road, Tottenham, N.17.   TX18977A.

SIMKINS, H. E., Pte., 24th Canadian Regiment.

He volunteered in January 1915, and was sent to France in the same year. Whilst on the Western Front he took a prominent part in many engagements, and was seriously wounded at Ypres in April 1916. He died from the effects four days later. He was entitled to the 1914-15 Star and the General Service and Victory Medals.

115, Manor Road, Tottenham, N.17.   X18977B.

SIMMONDS, A. (Mrs.), Special War Worker.

From 1916 until 1918 this lady was engaged on work of national importance at No. 3 Filling Factory, Perivale, Park Royal. Her duties, which were in connection with filling " T " tubes, were of a difficult and arduous nature. During her service she was chosen as a representative to march before their Majesties the King and Queen, from whom she received praise for her good work.

45, Leopold Road, Willesden. N.W.10.   14908.

SIMMONDS, C., Gunner, Royal Field Artillery.

He volunteered for duty in August 1914, and was sent to France immediately on completing his training in the same year. He saw service on various sectors of the Front, and took part in the battles of the Somme, Cambrai, Ypres, Vimy Ridge and Neuve Chapelle. In 1919 he returned to England, and in May was demobilised, holding the 1914-15 Star and the General Service and Victory Medals.

87, Woodheyes Road, Neasden, N.W.10.   15459A.

SIMMONDS, D., 1st Class Stoker, Royal Navy.

Serving at the outbreak of war in the Navy, he was employed in H.M.S. " Stuart " in the North Sea and Mediterranean on mine-sweeping and secret service duties, in which he rendered valuable assistance. He holds the 1914 Star and the General Service and Victory Medals, and in 1920 was still serving, having been in the Navy for twelve years.

36, St. Margaret's Road, Willesden, N.W.10.   X17826.

SIMMONDS, H. E., Gnr., Royal Field Artillery.

Joining in February 1916, he was drafted to the Western Front, where he took part in the battles of Ypres, Arras, Vimy Ridge and Cambrai. After also fighting through the Retreat and Advance of 1918, he was demobilised in March 1919, holding the General Service and Victory Medals.

41, Heron Road, Willesden, N.W.10.   15606.

SIMMONS, E., Pte., Lancashire Fusiliers.

Joining in January 1916, he was drafted to the Western Front in June of the following year. He took part in much of the heavy fighting on various sectors and was severely wounded in action. After over a year's service in France, he was killed in action in November 1918. He was entitled to the General Service and Victory Medals.

45, Mayo Road, Willesden, N.W.10.   15476.

SIMMONS, E., 3rd Air Mechanic, R.A.F. (late R.F.C.).

He volunteered in August 1915, and after completing his training was sent to the Western Front, where he saw service on all sectors and throughout was engaged on duties of a highly technical nature. He was demobilised in April 1919, on his return to England, and holds the General Service and Victory Medals.

112, Queen Street, Hammersmith, W.6.   13786A.

SIMMONS, F., Pte., 7th London Regiment and Royal Army Service Corps.

He volunteered in April 1915, and during his service on the Western Front was engaged on important motor repair and other duties at Dunkirk and Rouen. He returned to England after doing much valuable work in France, and in 1919 was demobilised. He holds the General Service and Victory Medals.

93, Yeldham Road, Hammersmith, W.6.   13276B.

SIMMONS, G., Pte., Royal Army Service Corps.

Volunteering in April 1915, he was sent to the Western Front on the completion of his training, and was engaged throughout his service on transport and other important duties at Calais and elsewhere. He was invalided home owing to ill-health, and in January 1916 was discharged as medically unfit. He holds the 1914-15 Star and the General Service and Victory Medals.

93, Yeldham Road, Hammersmith, W.6.   13276A.

SIMMONS, J. W., Pte., Royal Army Service Corps.

He joined in July 1916, and in the same year was sent to the Western Front, where he took a prominent part in the battles of the Somme, Arras, and Cambrai. In July 1919 he was demobilised, holding the General Service and Victory Medals.

48, Novello Street, Parson's Green, S.W.6.   X19934.

SIMMONS, P. L., Pte., Middlesex Regiment.

Joining in 1916, he was sent to the Western Front in the following year. He saw fighting on various sectors, and took part in many important engagements up to September 28th, 1918, when he was killed in action at Eagle Farm, near Poperinghe. He was entitled to the General Service and Victory Medals.

6, Cooper Road, Dudden Hill, N.W.10.   16698.

SIMMONS, W., Pte., Hampshire Regiment.

He volunteered for duty in August 1914, and in the following year was drafted to the Dardanelles. After taking part in the operations in Gallipoli, where he saw much fighting, he was transferred to Salonika. In January 1919, after his return to England, he was demobilised, and holds the 1914-15 Star and the General Service and Victory Medals.

112, Queen Street, Hammersmith, W.6.   13786B.

SIMMS, G. L., Pte., R.A.S.C. (M.T.).

He volunteered in November 1915, and whilst on the Western Front served in numerous engagements, including those of the Somme, Ypres, Armentieres, Amiens, Bullecourt, St. Quentin, Arras and Lille, and the 1918 Advance at Cambrai. He was demobilised in August 1919, holding the General Service and Victory Medals.

106, Burnthwaite Road, Walham Green, S.W.6.   X20105.

SIMMS, H. T., 2nd Lieut., Royal Field Artillery.
He volunteered in June 1915, and in the same year was sent to France, where he took part in engagements at Ypres, the Somme, Passchendaele, Arras, and many other places, and was wounded. Later he was transferred to Egypt, and remained there until he was demobilised in 1919. He joined as a private and was promoted thro' the ranks by reason of his general efficiency. He holds the 1914–15 Star and the General Service and Victory Medals.
8, Edenvale Street, Fulham, S.W.6.   X20949.

SIMMS, T. A., Lce.-Corpl., R.A.S.C. (M.T.).
Volunteering in 1915, he was engaged on the Western Front for four years in conveying ammunition to the lines. He saw service in various sectors, and was badly gassed. In September 1919 he was demobilised, and holds the 1914–15 Star and the General Service and Victory Medals.
11, Ancill Street, Hammersmith, W.6.   13748.

SIMPKINS, G. A., Lce.-Corpl., Middlesex Regt.
He volunteered in August 1914, and after his training was drafted overseas. He took part in many important engagements on the Western Front, including the battles of Loos, Ypres and the Somme, and was wounded three times. After so long a period of service he was demobilised in January 1919, and holds the 1914–15 Star and the General Service and Victory Medals.
21, Forest Road, Lower Edmonton, N.9.   11955.

SIMPSON, A., Pte., East Surrey Regiment.
Joining in March 1918, he was sent to France shortly afterwards. He took part in several engagements in the final Advance, and was reported missing at Cambrai, where it was subsequently stated that he was killed. He was entitled to the General Service and Victory Medals.
162, Winchester Road, Lower Edmonton, N.9.   14892.

SIMPSON, E. W., Pte., 15th Essex Regiment.
He joined in June 1916, and after his training served at various stations on important duties with his unit until 1918, when he was drafted to the Western Front. There he took part in the fighting during the Retreat and Advance of the Allies. He was invalided to hospital on account of trench fever. He was demobilised in February 1919, and holds the General Service and Victory Medals.
43, Denny Road, Lower Edmonton, N.9.   12004.

SIMPSON, F. A., Bombardier, R.F.A.
He volunteered in January 1915, and was sent overseas in the same year. During his service he took part in the battles of Arras, La Bassée, Ypres, Armentieres, Lens, Cambrai and the Retreat and Advance of 1918. He returned to England after the Armistice, and was demobilised in February 1919, holding the 1914–15 Star and the General Service and Victory Medals.
32, Melville Road, Stonebridge Park, N.W.10.   14422.

SIMPSON, F. J., Lce.-Corpl., 1st Royal Dublin Fusiliers.
Volunteering in January 1915, he was sent to France, and was wounded during a bombing raid on the Somme in June 1916. He was invalided home, and, being physically unfit for further service overseas, he was sent to Cork, where he was still serving in 1920 with the Military Police. He holds the 1914–15 Star and the General Service and Victory Medals.
64, Ancill Street, Hammersmith, W.6.   13979.

SIMPSON, F. S. (Mrs.), Special War Worker.
During her war service, which extended over a period exceeding two years, this lady was employed by the British Oxygen Co. as an examiner of tubes. She also operated a lathe in making spindles for fixing valves. Her work was of great importance, and called for care and accuracy. She was highly commended for her services.
168, Third Avenue, Queen's Park Estate, W.10. X19443B.

SIMPSON, H. A., Pte., 1st Duke of Cornwall's Light Infantry.
He was called up from the Army Reserve at the outbreak of war, and was sent to France in the following November. After taking part in the first battle of Ypres, he was subsequently killed in action on February 24th, 1915, and was buried near Wulverghem. He was entitled to the 1914 Star and the General Service and Victory Medals.
10, Glynfield Road, Willesden, N.W.10.   14732.

SIMPSON, J. A., Pte., Royal Fusiliers.
He volunteered in August 1914, and was drafted to the Western Front shortly afterwards. During the Retreat from Mons he was wounded, and taken prisoner. He suffered many hardships during his captivity, which was partly spent at Holzminden and Hameln. He returned to England and was demobilised in March 1919, holding the Mons Star and the General Service and Victory Medals.
58, Aspenlea Road, Hammersmith, W.6.   14285.

SIMPSON, J. J., Sergeant, K.R.R.
He rejoined in June 1916, went to France in December of the same year, and took part in many battles including those of Ypres, the Somme, and the Retreat and Advance of 1918, during which he was wounded. He had previously served for thirteen years in the R.M.L.I., and was awarded the Messina Medal for assisting in rescuing people during the earthquake. He also holds the General Service and Victory Medals, and was demobilised in February 1919.
75, Portnall Road, Maida Hill, W.9.   TX19508.

SIMPSON, P., Sergeant, East Surrey Regiment.
He was mobilised in August 1914, and was drafted to the Western Front, where he took part in the Retreat from Mons and in the fighting at Le Cateau, where he was wounded. He was invalided home, and on recovery was stationed for a time at Dover. In 1917 he returned to France, and on being transferred to the Labour Corps, acted as instructor to troops on road repairing, and was also engaged as guard to German prisoners. He holds the Mons Star and the General Service and Victory Medals, and was demobilised in February 1919.
168, Third Avenue, Queen's Park Estate, W.10. X19443A

SIMPSON, R., Pte., 5th Middlesex Regiment.
He volunteered in August 1914, and after his training served at various stations on important duties with his unit. He rendered valuable service, but owing to ill health he was not drafted overseas, and he died of double pneumonia, whilst still in the service.
2, Marsden Road, Lower Edmonton, N.9.   13067A.

SIMPSON, T. J., Driver, Royal Field Artillery.
He volunteered in August 1914, and was shortly afterwards sent to France where he took part in the early fighting in this theatre of war. He was later sent to Egypt and Gallipoli, where he was wounded. He was demobilised in February 1919, and holds the Mons Star and the General Service and Victory Medals.
2, Marsden Road, Lower Edmonton, N.9.   13067B.

SIMS, C. W., Sapper, Royal Engineers.
He joined in September 1917, and at the conclusion of his training was engaged on important duties with the Royal Engineers in England. He did not succeed in obtaining his transfer overseas, being medically unfit for foreign service. He was demobilised in December 1919.
103, Love Lane, Tottenham, N.17.   X18524.

SIMS, D. H., Artificer, Royal Artillery.
He volunteered in August 1914, and after his period of training was sent to the Western Front in the following year. He took part in many engagements in this theatre of war, including the battles of Ypres, the Somme and Cambrai. He holds the 1914–15 Star and the General Service and Victory Medals, and was demobilised in January 1919.
52, Burn's Road, Harlesden, N.W.10.   13465B.

SIMS, F. E. (Miss), O.B.E., Special War Worker.
During the war this lady was employed at the National Filling Factory, Park Royal. She was awarded the O.B.E. for great courage and resource which she exhibited during an explosion which occurred while she was on duty, and in which her hand was severely injured and mutilated.
3, Westgate, Roundwood Road,
Willesden, N.W.10.   16301B.

SIMS, F. G., 1st Air Mechanic, R.A.F. (late R.N.A.S.).
He volunteered in November 1914, and at the termination of his training was employed with his squadron on important duties which called for a high degree of technical skill. In July 1916 he was sent to the Western Front, and in the following January was accidentally killed by a bomb whilst examining an aeroplane which had just returned from a raid. He was entitled to the General Service and Victory Medals.
52, Burn's Road, Harlesden, N.W.10.   13465A.

SIMS, L., Sapper, Royal Engineers.
He volunteered in January 1915, and was drafted overseas on completion of his training. He was engaged on important duties in connection with the battles of the Somme, Loos and Gommecourt Wood. Owing to ill-health he returned to England and was discharged as unfit for further service in January 1917, and he holds the 1914–15 Star and the General Service and Victory Medals.
4, Cannon Terrace, Ship Lane, Hammersmith, W.6. 13798.

SIMS, R. J., Pte., East Surrey Regiment,
Joining in 1917, he was sent in the following year to the Western Front, where, after taking part in the Allied Advance, he died in hospital at Rouen as a result of wounds received in action on the Somme. He was buried in the Military Cemetery near the town. He was entitled to the General Service and Victory Medals.
52, Milton Avenue, Willesden, N.W.10.   14325.

SIMSON, C. M. (Miss), Special War Worker.
For a period of nearly four years this lady was engaged on work of national importance at the Perivale Munition Factory. She was occupied in inspection of fuses and shells, and her services were much appreciated by the authorities.
407, High Road, Willesden, N.W.10.   16739B.

SIMSON, H. C., Pte. (Signaller), 1/8th and 3/10th Middlesex Regiment.
He volunteered in April 1915, and served on the Western Front for four years. During this period he took part in many battles, including those of Delville Wood, Ypres, Arras, and the Somme, and whilst proceeding to Poelcappelle was wounded at Langemarck. He was demobilised in March 1919, holding the 1914-15 Star and the General Service and Victory Medals.
407, High Road, Willesden, N.W.10.   T16739A.

SINFIELD, H.J., C.Q.M.S., 29th London Regt.
He joined in May 1915, but being unfit for active service, was, to his regret, retained at Headquarters at Colchester and other stations, on the clerical staff. So valuable were his services he soon rose to a position of responsibility and won for himself the commendation of his superiors. He was demobilised in May 1919.
79, Barnsdale Road, Maida Hill, W.9.   X19547.

SKEET, A. E., Trooper, 6th Dragoon Guards.
He was serving at the outbreak of the war, and was sent to the Western Front with the first overseas contingent, and took part in the Battle and Retreat from Mons. He was killed in action at Ypres on October 13th, 1914, and was entitled to the Mons Star and the General Service and Victory Medals.
13, Charlton Road, Harlesden, N.W.10.   13100B.

SKEET, W. O., C.S.M., Lancashire Fusiliers.
He joined in 1905, and served in India until 1914, when he returned to England. In 1915 he went to the Dardanelles and was wounded at the landing. After being in hospital at Malta he was invalided home. In 1918 he went to France, where he remained until 1919. He was discharged in June 1919 as being medically unfit for further service, and holds the 1914-15 Star and the General Service and Victory Medals.
45, Brownlow Road, Willesden, N.W.10.   15013.

SKELCHER, H., Special War Worker.
Being ineligible to join his Majesty's Army, he volunteered his services in March 1916 for work of national importance. He was sent to France, where he was engaged on building operations in co-operation with the Royal Engineers, until July 1918, when he returned home.
33, Oldfield Road, Willesden, N.W.10.   15747.

SKELTON, H. W., Leading Telegraphist, R.N., H.M.S. "Pembroke."
He joined the Navy in February 1914, and during the war served in Home waters, in the Mediterranean, and the Dardanelles. His ship was engaged in submarine chasing and patrol duties, and also took part in the naval actions at the Dardanelles. He was discharged in September 1919, and holds the 1914-15 Star and the General Service and Victory Medals.
92, Warwick Road, Edmonton, N.18.   TX17587.

SKENNERTON, T. (M.M.), Pte., 3rd Grenadier Guards.
Volunteering in August 1915, he was sent in the following year to the Western Front, where he fought at Ypres, Arras and Cambrai. He was wounded in action in May 1918, and again in the fierce fighting during the Great Offensive in July of the same year. He was awarded the Military Medal for conspicuous bravery in the field, and also holds the General Service and Victory Medals. He was demobilised in May 1919.
87, Southam Street, North Kensington, W.10.   X20785.

SKINGSLEY, G. S., Pte., 1st London Regiment (Royal Fusiliers).
He volunteered in 1915, and the following year was drafted overseas. During the next two years he took part in much of the heavy fighting on the Western Front, and was killed in action in March 1917. He was entitled to the General Service and Victory Medals.
19, Linton Road, Upper Edmonton, N.18.   X17477.

SKINNER, A. E., Pte., Royal Fusiliers.
He joined in February 1918, and was shortly afterwards drafted to the Western Front. He fought in several engagements during the Retreat and Advance of the Allies, and he was killed in action on August 20th, 1918. He was entitled to the General Service and Victory Medals.
4, Knivet Road, Walham Green, S.W.6.   X19394B.

SKINNER, B. S., Pte., Royal Fusiliers.
He joined in January 1916, and was sent to France in the following year. He took part in many engagements on the Western Front, and was reported missing and subsequently killed in action on June 16th, 1917. He was entitled to the General Service and Victory Medals.
13, Beethoven Street, Queen's Park Estate, W.10. X18747.

SKINNER, C. R., A.B., Royal Navy, H.M.S. "Champion."
He joined in June 1916, and served in the North Sea and in Russian waters. Amongst many varied duties his ship took part in escorting the German Fleet to Scapa Flow. He holds the General Service and Victory Medals, and was still serving in 1920.
67, Dieppe Street, West Kensington, W.14.   16423C.

SKINNER, E. A. (Mrs.), Special War Worker.
For a period exceeding three years this lady was employed at Park Royal Munition Factory in the inspection section of small arms ammunition. Her duties, which were of an important character, necessitated her working on alternate day and night shifts, when she was occasionally exposed to the dangers of air raids. Her services were greatly appreciated by the Authorities.
43, Melville Road, Stonebridge Park, N.W.10.   15653B.

SKINNER, J. E., Air Mechanic, Royal Air Force.
He joined in August 1918, having previously been rejected five times. Although most anxious to serve overseas he was retained for home duties owing to his ill-health, and was stationed in Scotland. He was demobilised in April 1919.
52, Lintaine Grove, W. Kensington, W.14.   X16997

SKINNER, W. F., Pte., Royal Army Service Corps.
He volunteered in 1914, and in the same year went to the Western Front, where he served at Mons, Ypres, Loos, La Bassée, the Somme, and in the Advance of 1918. He holds the Mons Star and the General Service and Victory Medals, and was demobilised in April 1919.
4, Knivet Road, Walham Green, S.W.6.   X19394A.

SKINNER, W. H., Pte., Northumberland Fusiliers.
Volunteering in December 1915, he was engaged on completion of his training on important duties at various stations with his unit. He rendered valuable services, but was not successful in obtaining his transfer overseas. He was demobilised in March 1919.
37, Halford Road, Walham Green, S.W.6.   X19506.

SKINNER, W. J., Gunner, Royal Horse Artillery.
He joined in July 1915, and was drafted to France in the same year. During his service on the Western Front he took part in many important battles, including those of Ypres, Arras, Cambrai, the Somme, and the Retreat and Advance of 1918. He holds the 1914-15 Star and the General Service and Victory Medals, and was demobilised in June 1919.
43, Melville Road, Stonebridge Park, N.W.10.   15653A

SKIPPER, R. L., Pte., R.M.L.I.
Volunteering in August 1914, he was present at the siege of Antwerp and later fought at Ypres and elsewhere in France. After being drafted to Egypt, he was sent to Salonika, where he was actively engaged for a time. From there he was sent to France and afterwards to England. In 1920 he was serving with his unit at Mudros. He holds the 1914 Star and the General Service and Victory Medals.
25A, Cooper Road, Dudden Hill, N.W.10.   16636.

SKULL, G. H., Rifleman and Pte., 5th London Regt. (London Rifle Brigade), and R.A.O.C.

He joined in April 1918, and at the conclusion of his training served at various stations on important duties with his unit. He gave valuable services, and was transferred to the R.A.O.C. and went to Germany with the Army of Occupation, where he was engaged on special work. He returned to England for his demobilisation in April 1920.
59, Fernhead Road, Maida Hill, W.9.　　　X19459.

SKULL, J. J., Rifleman, 51st Rifle Brigade.

He joined in August 1918, on attaining military age, and at the conclusion of his training was sent to Germany with the Army of Occupation the following March. He remained overseas a year and then returned to England, and was demobilised in March 1920.
37, Marsden Road, Lower Edmonton, N.9.　　　T13061.

SKUSE, G. L., Rifleman, 9th London Regiment (Queen Victoria's Rifles).

He volunteered in March 1915, and in the following year was drafted overseas. He was in action during much of the heavy fighting on the Western Front, including the battles of Ypres, Cambrai, Vimy Ridge and Messines Ridge, where he was wounded by an explosion. He holds the General Service and Victory Medals, and was demobilised in February 1919.
194, Kilburn Lane, N. Kensington, W.10.　　　X18712.

SLACK, E., Pte. and 1st Air Mechanic, Royal Fusiliers and Royal Air Force.

He volunteered in February 1915, and in 1917 was sent to the Western Front, where he was wounded in action during the battle of Passchendaele. On his recovery, he was transferred to the R.A.F., and after his training as a wireless operator was drafted to Russia, where he remained until he was demobilised in September 1919. He holds the General Service and Victory Medals.
9, Hampden Street, Paddington, W.2.　　　X21267.

SLADE, A., Rifleman, 16th Rifle Brigade.

He volunteered in September 1914, and served on the Western Front from August 1916 until March 1918. He took part in the fighting on the Somme, at Ypres, Passchendaele, Messines, and in the Retreat of 1918, when he was severely wounded. He was discharged in consequence as unfit for further service in September 1918. He was twice mentioned in dispatches for great bravery and devotion to duty while under heavy fire, and holds the General Service and Victory Medals.
75, Hawthorn Road, Willesden, N.W.10.　　　X17427.

SLADE, H., Pte., Machine Gun Corps.

He joined in April 1916, and was sent to France in the same year. During three years' varied service in this theatre of war he was in action on the Somme and at Ypres. He subsequently suffered from shell-shock. He was demobilised in February 1919, and holds the General Service and Victory Medals.
22, Whitehall Street, Tottenham, N.17.　　　X18257.

SLATER, S. C., Pte., Middlesex Regiment.

He was serving on the outbreak of war, and was immediately sent to the Western Front, where he took part in engagements at Mons, the Marne, the Aisne, Ypres, Neuve Chapelle, and the Somme, and was wounded and invalided home. On his recovery he was drafted to Salonika, and was in action during the Balkan campaign on the Struma, Doiran and Vardar Fronts. He contracted malaria whilst in the East. He was demobilised in March 1919, holding the Mons Star and the General Service and Victory Medals.
33, Hampden Street, Paddington, W.2.　　　X21263.

SLATTER, C. H., Pte., Royal Fusiliers.

He joined in 1914, and was sent to the Western Front. He took part in many important engagements, including the battles of the Somme, Vimy Ridge, Neuve Chapelle, Ypres, Bullecourt and Cambrai. He was invalided home on account of ill-health, and was discharged in 1918, as medically unfit for further service. He holds the General Service and Victory Medals.
21, Lillie Mansions, Lillie Road, Fulham, S.W.　　X18787B.

SLATTER, H., Gunner, Royal Field Artillery.

He volunteered for service on attaining military age in August 1918, and on the completion of his training was drafted to India, where he was engaged on important garrison duties with his unit. He was still serving in India in 1920. He is entitled to the General Service and Victory Medals.
17, Brereton Road, Tottenham, N.17.　　　18383.

SLATTER, M. (Mrs.), Special War Worker.

This lady was engaged upon work of national importance at Messrs. Darracq's Aircraft Factory, Walham Green. She was chiefly occupied in assembling the parts of aeroplanes. She rendered valuable service for which she was highly complimented.
21, Lillie Mansions, Lillie Road, Fulham, S.W.6.　　X18787A.

SLAUGHTER, H., Special War Worker.

This worker was engaged throughout the war on work of national importance at Woolwich Arsenal in making and filling shells in the danger zone. These duties, which were of a very dangerous nature, were performed with much energy and skill.
15, Lanfrey Place, West Kensington, W.14.　　　15881.

SLAUGHTER, H., Pte., 6th Labour Corps.

He joined in March 1917, and at the conclusion of his training was drafted overseas. He was engaged in various sectors of the Western Front on important duties. He returned to England after the Armistice, and was demobilised in March 1919, holding the General Service and Victory Medals.
104, Claxton Grove, Hammersmith, W.6.　　　13438.

SLAYMAKER, J. T., Lce.-Corpl., 6th Hampshire Regiment and M.F.P.

He was called up in August 1914, and in the same year was drafted to India, where he rendered valuable service until 1919. Whilst overseas he was transferred to the Military Police. He returned to England and was demobilised in October 1919, holding the 1914-15 Star and the General Service and Victory Medals.
36, Althea Street, Townmead Road,
Fulham, S.W.6.　　　X21154.

SLEE, J., Pte., Royal Army Medical Corps.

He joined in October 1915, and during his service on the Western Front saw action in many sectors, including the battle of the Somme. He was wounded in 1917, as a result of which he was in hospital for six weeks. He was demobilised on March 30th, 1919, and holds the General Service and Victory Medals.
53, Lancaster Road, Upper Edmonton, N.18.　　X17085.

SLEET, A. F., 1st Air Mechanic, Royal Air Force.

He volunteered in May 1915, and after his training was drafted overseas to the Western Front. He was engaged at many aerodromes on important duties, which called for a high degree of technical skill. During his service he was wounded. He holds the General Service and Victory Medals, and was demobilised in December 1919.
184, Dyson's Road, Upper Edmonton, N.18.　　16558.

SLEVIN, F., Special Constable, Hammersmith "T." Division.

During a long period of service, which lasted from July 1916 to June 1919, he rendered very varied help. He was constantly on duty during air raids and, in addition, gave assistance while Sunday munition work continued at the White City. He holds the Long Service Medal and also a special medal for drill.
168, The Grove, Hammersmith, W.6.　　　11097.

SLOGGETT, J. W., Rifleman, K.R.R.

He volunteered in September 1914, and on completion of his training served at various stations on important duties with his unit. He rendered valuable services, but was not successful in obtaining his transfer overseas owing to medical unfitness and he was discharged in consequence, in May 1915.
111, Victor Road, College Park, N.W.10.　　　X17532.

SMALL, G., Pte., 9th Royal Fusiliers.

Volunteering in 1914, he was quickly sent overseas. He took part in the Retreat from Mons, and subsequently fought at Ypres and in the Battle of the Somme. He was severely wounded in the head, and gassed. He was demobilised in 1919, and holds the 1914 Star and the Victory and General Service Medals.
38, Steele Road, Willesden, N.W.10.　　　14140B.

SMALL, J. A., Pte., The Queen's (Royal West Surrey Regiment).

He joined in May 1916, in the same year was sent to the Western Front, and later was invalided home suffering from wounds received in action. In 1917 he returned to France, and after taking part in some important engagements was drafted to Italy. In 1918 he again returned to France, and while taking part in the Advance of the Allies, was reported missing, but was later believed to have been killed in action. He was entitled to the General Service and Victory Medals.
29, Eli Street, W. Kensington, W.14.　　　16916A.

SMALL, J. J., Pte., Essex and Northamptonshire Regiments.

He joined in 1916, and in the following year was sent to France where he took part in the battles of Ypres and the Somme, and was twice wounded. He was discharged unfit for further service in 1918, and holds the General Service and Victory Medals.

13, Oak Road, Willesden, N.W.10.   15034.

SMALL, L. (Mrs.), Special War Worker.

From 1917 until 1919 this lady was engaged at the Park Royal Box Factory upon work of military importance in connection with the making of boxes for shells and ammunition. Her various duties were performed in a highly satisfactory manner.

38, Steele Road, Willesden, N.W.10.   14140A.

SMART, A., Trooper, 1st County of London Yeomanry.

Volunteering in August 1914, he was sent to the Eastern Front in the following April, and took part in the second landing and the evacuation of the Dardanelles. He also served in Palestine, and took part in the engagements at Damascus and elsewhere. He was demobilised in February 1919, and holds the 1914-15 Star, and the General Service and Victory Medals.

76, First Avenue, Queen's Park Estate, W.10.   X18947B.

SMART, H. (M.M.)., Rifleman, K.R.R.

He joined in June 1916, and was sent shortly afterwards to the Western Front, where he took part in many important engagements. He distinguished himself in carrying dispatches under heavy artillery fire near Nieuport Bains, and for this act of gallantry he was awarded the Military Medal. He was killed in action on May 22nd, 1918, during the German Offensive. He was also entitled to the General Service and Victory Medals.

76, First Avenue, Queen's Park Estate, W.10.   X18947A.

SMEE, E. H., Gunner, Royal Field Artillery.

He joined in September 1916, and at the conclusion of his training was engaged on important duties with his unit until 1918, when he was sent overseas to the Western Front, where he took part in the Retreat and Advance of the Allies. After the Armistice he returned to England and was demobilised in October 1919, holding the General Service and Victory Medals.

102, Church Road, Tottenham, N.17.   X18138.

SMITH, A., Corporal, Royal Defence Corps.

He volunteered in January 1915, having previously served in the Bedfordshire Regiment for eighteen years. After his training he served with his unit on important duties in Ireland. He rendered valuable services, but was not successful in obtaining his transfer to the Front, and was demobilised in March 1919.

27, St. Ervan's Road, North Kensington, W.10.   X20692.

SMITH, A., Pte., 24th Middlesex Regiment.

He joined in May 1916, and served on the Western Front until 1919, during which time he took a prominent part in the battles of the Somme and Ypres, and in other important engagements. He holds the General Service and Victory Medals, and was demobilised in April 1919.

49, Lorenco Road, Tottenham, N.17.   X17987.

SMITH, A., Pte., 3/13 London Regiment (Kensington).

He volunteered in January 1915, and after his training was retained on important duties with his unit at various stations. He gave valuable services for some time, but was then invalided to hospital. After long treatment he was discharged in 1916 as medically unfit for further service.

52, Aspenlea Road, Hammersmith, W.6.   14297A.

SMITH, A., Corporal, 1/9th Middlesex Regiment.

Volunteering in August 1914, he was drafted to the East in the following December, and for nearly five years was engaged on important garrison duties in India. During this period he gave valuable services, and returned to England for demobilisation in September 1919, holding the 1914-15 Star, General Service and Victory Medals.

96, Barry Road, Stonebridge Park, N.W.10.   15667B

SMITH, A. C., Pte., 1/7th Middlesex Regiment.

He volunteered in August 1914, and later in the same year was drafted to the Western Front. After taking part in much severe fighting on various sectors, he was killed in action on August 18th, 1916, while rescuing a wounded comrade. He was entitled to the 1914 Star and the General Service and Victory Medals.

39, Salisbury Road, Lower Edmonton, N.9.   13957B.

SMITH, A. E., Pte., R.A.S.C. (Remounts).

He volunteered in April 1915, and after his training was engaged on important duties with the Remounts Section. He rendered valuable service, but was unable to obtain his transfer to the Front before the cessation of hostilities. He was demobilised in June 1919.

34, Ashmore Road, Harrow Road, W.9.   X19895A.

SMITH, A. E., Sergeant, Middlesex Regiment.

He volunteered in May 1915, and after his training served with his unit on important duties. He rendered valuable services, but was unsuccessful in procuring his transfer overseas prior to the cessation of hostilities. He was demobilised in February 1920, after nearly five years' service.

30, Clarendon Street, Paddington, W.2.   X20539A.

SMITH, A. E., Corporal, Royal Field Artillery.

Volunteering in November 1914, he was sent to the Western Front a year later and took a prominent part in engagements at Ypres, the Somme, the Ancre, Arras and during the Retreat and Advance of 1918. After the Armistice he was sent with the Army of Occupation to Germany, where he remained until March 1919, when he was demobilised. He was wounded during his service, and holds the 1914-15 Star and the General Service and Victory Medals.

14, Greyhound Road, College Park, N.W.10.   X17803B.

SMITH, A. E. (Mrs.), Special War Worker.

For a period of more than four years during the war, this lady, in spite of domestic responsibilities, patriotically undertook work of national importance at the Park Royal Filling Factory. She carried out her duties in an efficient manner, and was promoted to a responsible position in the Cartridge Inspection Department. She gave valuable services throughout.

61, Barret's Green Road, Willesden, N.W.10.   13552A.

SMITH, A. G., Pte., 13th London Regiment (Kensington).

He volunteered for service in May 1915, and later in that year was drafted to the Western Front, where, after taking part in many engagements, he was killed in action in the first battle of the Somme, on July 1st, 1916. He was entitled to the 1914-15 Star, General Service and Victory Medals.

24, Hampden Street, Paddington, W.2.   X20900

SMITH, A. J., Bugler, 28th London Regiment (Artists' Rifles).

Previous to his joining in November 1916, he had been rejected for service several times. He was drafted to France in the following January, and saw much fighting until November 1917, when he was invalided home. In January 1918 he was discharged as medically unfit for further service, and holds the General Service and Victory Medals.

13, Denzil Road, Neasden Lane, N.W.10.   15929B.

SMITH, C., Air Mechanic and Driver, R.N.A.S. and Tank Corps.

He volunteered in July 1915, and served in Egypt and Mudros from the following year until 1919. He was first engaged on duties which called for a high degree of technical skill with the Royal Naval Air Service, but later was transferred to the Tank Corps, and took part in important engagements. He was demobilised in February 1919, and holds the General Service and Victory Medals.

67A, Deacon Road, Cricklewood, N.W.2.   17361.

SMITH, C., Pte., Northamptonshire Regiment.

He joined in 1916, and was soon drafted to the Western Front, where he took part in the battles of the Somme, Arras, Ypres and Cambrai, and in heavy fighting near St. Quentin and Dickebusch. He was later invalided home owing to ill-health, and was in hospital at Sandgate for some time. In 1919 he was demobilised, and holds the General Service and Victory Medals.

49, Gayford Road, Shepherd's Bush, W.12.   X18219A.

SMITH, C. A., Gunner, Royal Field Artillery.

He joined in January 1917 and was sent in the same year to the Western Front, where he served until 1920. He took a prominent part in many engagements, including the Battle of Ypres, and was wounded at Bullecourt in January 1918. He holds the General Service and Victory Medals, and was demobilised in February 1920.

25, Tilson Road, Tottenham, N.17.   X19076

SMITH, C. C., Pte., 6th Suffolk Regiment.
He joined in April 1918, and whilst training met with a serious injury which afterwards prevented him from being transferred to a fighting Front. He was therefore retained on important duties at various stations, and gave valuable services until his demobilisation in February 1919.
26, College Road, Willesden, N.W.10.　　X18184.

SMITH, C. E., Pte., 5th Royal Fusiliers.
He joined in 1918, and after training was retained on important duties with his unit on the South East Coast. He gave valuable services, but was not successful in obtaining his transfer overseas before hostilities ceased. He was demobilised in 1919.
37, Barret's Green Road, Willesden, N.W.10.　　13548.

SMITH, C. E., Pte., Northamptonshire Regiment.
He joined in 1916, and during his service on the Western Front acted as stretcher-bearer at Ypres, Dickebusch and in many other sectors, and also worked on an ammunition dump on the Belgian coast. He was demobilised in 1919, and holds the General Service and Victory Medals.
37, Lurgan Avenue, Hammersmith, W.6.　　13446.

SMITH, C. F., Driver, R.F.A. and R.H.A.
He joined in August 1916, and having received training at various stations in England, was drafted to the Western Front. His service overseas lasted for two years, and during this time he took part in many important battles, including those of Lens, Bullecourt and the Somme, and in the Retreat and Advance of 1918. He returned to England in 1919, and was demobilised in February, holding the General Service and Victory Medals.
20, Hampden Street, Paddington, W.2.　　X20898A.

SMITH, C. F., Corporal, 13th London Regiment (Kensington).
Volunteering in May 1915, he was drafted to the Western Front before the end of the year. While in this theatre of war he took part in many important engagements, and was severely wounded in action. He was invalided home, and after a considerable time in hospital at Fulham, was demobilised in 1919. He holds the 1914–15 Star and the General Service and Victory Medals.
56, Sherbrooke Road, Fulham, S.W.6.　　X18753B.

SMITH, C. G., Pte., R.A.S.C. (Labour Corps).
He volunteered in October 1915, and was shortly after drafted to France, where he was engaged on important duties on various sectors. He was wounded during his service, and later met with a serious accident whilst on duty. He was invalided home, and spent some time in hospital, but on his recovery he again went to France, and remained there until his demobilisation in April 1919. He holds the 1914–15 Star and the General Service and Victory Medals.
7, Lintaine Grove, West Kensington, W.14.　　16817.

SMITH, C. N., Gunner, Royal Field Artillery.
Volunteering in 1914, he was sent to France in the following year, and took a prominent part in many engagements, including those of the Somme, Arras, Ypres and the Advance in 1918. He was in hospital for some weeks whilst abroad, and was demobilised in May 1919, holding the 1914–15 Star and the General Service and Victory Medals.
30, Chalgrove Road, Tottenham, N.17.　　X18959.

SMITH, C. S., Mechanic, R.A.F. (late R.N.A.S.).
He joined in January 1917, and after his training was engaged on important experimental work. His duties called for a high degree of technical skill, and he gave valuable services, but was not successful in obtaining his transfer overseas before the cessation of hostilities. He was demobilised in February 1919.
12, Burn's Road, Harlesden, N.W.10.　　13228.

SMITH, D., Pte., 7th Hussars.
He volunteered in August 1914, and in the following year was drafted to the East. After a period of service in India, he was sent to Mesopotamia, where he took a distinguished part in important engagements. On October 13th, 1918, he died of cholera, and was entitled to the 1914–15 Star and the General Service and Victory Medals.
105, Sherbrooke Road, Fulham, S.W.6.　　X18334.

SMITH, D. O., Pte., Durham Light Infantry.
Joining in June 1916, he was sent to France on the completion of his training, and whilst on the Western Front saw much severe fighting. He was wounded in action at Kemmel Hill during the advance in 1918. He holds the General Service and Victory Medals, and was demobilised in May 1919.
132, Blythe Road, West Kensington, W.14.　　12495.

SMITH, E. (Mrs.), Special War Worker.
During the war this lady rendered valuable services at Hayes Munition Works, in Middlesex, where she was engaged on the filling and stamping of shells. She carried out her arduous duties in a very efficient manner, and thereby rendered very valuable services.
21, Belton Road, Cricklewood, N.W.2.　　16594.

SMITH, E., Driver, Royal Field Artillery.
He was mobilised in 1914, immediately on the outbreak of hostilities, and was drafted to the Western Front in 1915. During his service in this seat of war he was in action in many important engagements, and was twice wounded. In March 1919 he was demobilised, and holds the 1914–15 Star, the General Service and Victory Medals, and the Territorial Efficiency Medal.
13, Delorme Street, Hammersmith, W.6.　　14080A.

SMITH, E. (Mrs.), Special War Worker.
During the war this lady gave valuable services. At first she was engaged on work of national importance at Woolwich Arsenal, where she held a responsible position as an examiner of fuses. Later she undertook work as a motor driver at Messrs. Derry and Toms, Kensington, in order to release a man for military service. She did splendid work, and received high commendation.
56, Chesson Road, West Kensington, W.14.　　X17235.

SMITH, E. (Mrs.), Special War Worker.
For two years during the war this lady held a responsible position as examiner in the fuse inspection room of Messrs. Smith and Son's munition works at Cricklewood. She was forced to resign owing to ill-health brought about by the continuous strain of her work, and underwent an operation. She had rendered valuable services throughout.
99, Ashmore Road, Harrow Road, W.9.　　X19653A.

SMITH, E. J., Corpl., 26th Middlesex Regiment.
He volunteered in January 1916, and in the same year was sent to Salonika, where he took a distinguished part in many engagements. He was gassed in action, and was also in hospital on several occasions suffering from malaria. In 1918 he was drafted to Russia, where he was engaged on responsible clerical work. He was demobilised in July 1919, and holds the General Service and Victory Medals.
99, Ashmore Road, Harrow Road, W.9.　　X19653B.

SMITH, F., Pte., 5th Essex Regiment.
He volunteered in August 1914, and after his training was retained with his unit on important duties. In June 1917, however, was drafted to France, where he took part in many engagements but was discharged as medically unfit for further service in December 1918, through wounds received in action in the previous May. He holds the General Service and Victory Medals.
13, Denzil Road, Neasden Lane, N.W.10.　　15929A.

SMITH, F., Driver, Royal Field Artillery.
He volunteered in August 1914, and in the following year was drafted to the Western Front, where he took a prominent part in engagements at Loos, the Somme, Arras and Albert, and was wounded in action near Ypres in 1917. In June 1918 he was discharged as medically unfit owing to his service, and holds the 1914–15 Star and the General Service and Victory Medals.
16, Clarendon Street, Paddington, W.2.　　TX20552.

SMITH, F. (Miss), Special War Worker.
For nearly two years during the war, this lady was engaged on most important work, in making boxes for transporting shells. at the Metropolitan Joinery Works, Walham Green. She carried out her work to the entire satisfaction of her employers.
39, Ancill Road, Hammersmith, W.6.　　13868A.

SMITH, F., Gunner, Royal Garrison Artillery.
He volunteered in November 1915, and in the following year was sent to France, where he took part in important engagements on the Somme in 1916, and at Ypres. He was demobilised in March 1919, and holds the General Service and Victory Medals.
25, Tilson Road, Tottenham, N.17.　　X19077

SMITH, F. C., Sapper, Royal Engineers.
Joining in January 1916, he was drafted a year later to the Western Front, where he was chiefly engaged on railway work but took a prominent part in engagements at Ypres and Arras. He was demobilised in June 1919, and holds the General Service and Victory Medals.
32, Napier Road, Kensal Green, N.W.10.　　X17523A.

22

SMITH, F. C. T., Rifleman, 6th London Regiment (Rifles).

He joined in November 1916, and after being sent to the Western Front took a distinguished part in the battles of Ypres, Arras and Cambrai, and the Retreat and Advance of 1918. He holds the General Service and Victory Medals, and was demobilised in February 1919.
4, Kennet Road, Maida Hill, W.9.   X19375.

SMITH, F. E., Pte., 13th London Regiment (Kensington).

He volunteered in August 1914, and in the following year was sent to the Western Front, where he took a conspicuous part in the battles of Ypres, Arras, Cambrai and the Somme. He holds the 1914-15 Star and the General Service and Victory Medals, and was demobilised in May 1919.
34, Ashmore Road, Harrow Road, W.9.   X19895B

SMITH, F. J. G., Sergeant, R.E.

He volunteered in 1915, and in the same year was sent to France, where he took a prominent part in many important engagements, and was gassed. He remained in France until his demobilisation in 1919, and holds the 1914-15 Star and the General Service and Victory Medals.
24, Nursery Street, Tottenham, N.17.   X18146.

SMITH, G., Pte., 1st Dorsetshire Regiment.

He volunteered in May 1914, and in the following year took part in the Dardanelles Campaign. Afterwards he was drafted to the Western Front, where he served in the battles of Hill 60, Ypres, Loos and Arras, and was so severely wounded in the arm, in action on the Somme, as to necessitate its amputation. He was discharged in February 1917, and holds the 1914-15 Star and the General Service and Victory Medals.
81, Portnall Road, Maida Hill, W.9.   X19510.

SMITH, G., Pte., Royal Fusiliers.

Volunteering in August 1914, he was drafted very quickly to the Western Front, and remained on service there until the war ended. He took an active part in many notable engagements, including the Retreat from Mons, the battles of Ypres and the Somme, and the Advance of 1918. He was demobilised in 1919, holding the Mons Star and the General Service and Victory Medals.
24, Durban Road, Tottenham, N.17.   X18090.

SMITH, G., Sergeant, Royal Engineers.

He volunteered in March 1915, and was drafted to the Western Front in the following month, where he was engaged on important duties in connection with operations in this theatre of war, and was wounded in action. Being invalided home he was subsequently discharged as medically unfit for further service in October 1916. He holds the 1914-15 Star and the General Service and Victory Medals.
30, Bertie Road, Willesden, N.W.10.   X17396.

SMITH, G., Pte., 7th London Regiment.

He volunteered in November 1915, and was drafted to the Western Front on completion of his training. He took part in much of the severe fighting in this battle area, where he remained until after the cessation of hostilities. He holds the General Service and Victory Medals, and in 1920 was still serving.
23, Haldane Road, Walham Green, S.W.6.   X17375.

SMITH, G. A., Pte., 2nd Essex Regiment.

He volunteered in August 1915 and was shortly afterwards drafted to the Western Front where he took part in many engagements including the battles of the Somme, Hill 60, Cambrai and Arras. During his service he was twice wounded and gassed, and was invalided to hospital in England. He holds the 1914-15 Star and the General Service and Victory Medals, and in 1920 was serving in Malta.
39, Ancill Road, Hammersmith, W.6.   13868B.

SMITH, G. C., Pte., Royal Army Ordnance Corps.

He joined in June 1917, and in the following month was sent out to France, where he was engaged on important duties with his unit until his death on December 24th, 1918, at Le Havre. He was entitled to the General Service and Victory Medals.
13, Woodfield Gardens, Maida Hill, W.9. X20134.

SMITH, G. E., Pte., Royal Fusiliers.

He joined in December 1915, and in the following year proceeded to the Western Front, where he fought in the Battle of the Somme, and was taken prisoner. During his captivity in Germany he was made to work in the mines until his release after the Armistice. He was demobilised in April 1919, holding the General Service and Victory Medals.
3, Avalon Road, New King's Road, S.W.6. X19796.

SMITH, G. H., Rifleman, Royal Irish Rifles.

He volunteered for service in June 1915, and in the same year went to France, where he remained for three years. During this period he took part in many engagements, including those of Ypres, Arras, Cambrai and the Somme, and was twice severely wounded and gassed. He was discharged as medically unfit in April 1918, and holds the 1914-15 Star and the General Service and Victory Medals.
30, Clarendon Street, Paddington, W.2.   X20539B.

SMITH, G. W., Gunner, R.H.A. and R.F.A.

He volunteered in August 1914, and was at once drafted to France, where he took part in the Retreat from Mons. Throughout the war he was frequently in action, and the Battles of Ypres, Arras, Bullecourt, the Somme and the Retreat and Advance of 1918, are among the numerous engagements in which he took part. He holds the Mons Star and the General Service and Victory Medals, and was demobilised in 1919. Previous to the war he had served in the Royal Navy for four years.
138, Third Avenue, Queen's Park Estate, W.10. X19381C.

SMITH, H., Corpl., 7th Bedfordshire Regiment.

He volunteered in September 1914, and in 1915 was drafted to France, where he took part in many engagements. In the Battle of Arras in 1917 he was severely wounded, and was, in consequence, invalided home. After his recovery he acted as a physical training instructor at Norwich. He was demobilised in March 1919, and holds the 1914-15 Star and the General Service and Victory Medals.
220, Portnall Road, Maida Hill, W.9.   X19831B.

SMITH, H., Pte., 10th Middlesex Regiment.

He volunteered in July 1915, and at the conclusion of his training was drafted to the Egyptian Front. He was actively engaged in the severe fighting in this theatre of war, and on April 19th, 1917, was killed in action at Gaza. He was entitled to the General Service and Victory Medals.
96, Barry Road, Stonebridge Park, N.W.10.   15667C.

SMITH, H., A.B., Royal Navy, H.M.S. "Africa."

He volunteered in May 1915, and served with the Grand Fleet in the North Sea. Later he was transferred to the West African Station, and was engaged in patrolling the coast, and in convoying food and troop ships. In August 1918 he returned from Africa, and was posted to H.M.S. "Dreadnought," with which vessel he served off the coast of Scotland. He was demobilised in February 1920, and holds the 1914-15 Star and the General Service and Victory Medals.
11, Pearscroft Road, Fulham, S.W.6.   X20702.

SMITH, H. A., Pte., Machine Gun Corps.

He joined in July 1917, and in the following May was sent to France, where he took part in engagements at Arras and Cambrai. Later he was transferred to Egypt and stationed at Alexandria and Cairo. He returned to England and was demobilised in April 1920, holding the General Service and Victory Medals.
21, Edenham Street, North Kensington, W.10. X20129.

SMITH, H. C., 2nd Lieut., 3rd South Lancashire Regt.

He joined in April 1916, and in the same year was drafted to the Western Front, where he took a distinguished part in many important engagements, including the Battles of the Somme, Bapaume, Ypres and the Retreat and Advance of 1918. He returned to England after rendering valuable services overseas, and was demobilised in May 1919, holding the General Service and Victory Medals.
120, Bulwer Road, Upper Edmonton, N.18.   X17196.

SMITH, H. E., Sapper, Royal Engineers.

Volunteering in December 1915, he was sent to the Western Front the following February, where he was engaged, during the whole period of his service overseas, on special duties with the carrier pigeon service. He was demobilised in May 1919, and holds the General Service and Victory Medals.
237, Shirland Road, Maida Hill, W.9.   X19527.

SMITH, H. G., Pte., 1/4th Suffolk Regiment.

He joined in July 1916, and crossed to the Western Front later in the same year. He was in action in numerous engagements in the Somme area and the offensive of 1918, and was once badly gassed. In March 1919 he was demobilised, holding the General Service and Victory Medals.
21, Novello Street, Parson's Green, S.W.6.   X19952.

SMITH, H. G., Driver, Royal Field Artillery.

Volunteering in December 1914, he proceeded to Salonika in the following June, and saw active service there until 1916, when he was invalided home with enteric fever. On his recovery he was drafted to France, where he served until 1919, and took part in many important engagements on the Somme and Cambrai Fronts. He was demobilised in May 1919, holding the 1914–15 Star and the General Service and Victory Medals.

129, Deacon Road, Cricklewood, N.W.2. 16314A.

SMITH, H. G., Sergeant, Rifle Brigade.

He enlisted in August 1905, and at the outbreak of war was drafted to the Western Front, where he was engaged in the early fighting in this theatre of war, and was wounded in action at the Battle of Ypres. Upon his recovery he again saw much fighting until the cessation of hostilities. He was discharged in January 1919, holding the 1914 Star and the General Service and Victory Medals.

100, Adeney Road, Hammersmith, W.6. 14279A.

SMITH, H. P. W., Pte. and Air Mechanic, Middlesex Regiment and Royal Air Force.

He volunteered in 1915, and was sent to France in the following year. During his service on the Western Front he was in action during much heavy fighting, and was severely wounded. He was invalided home, and on his recovery was transferred to the R.A.F., with which unit he served at various aerodromes on important duties until his demobilisation in March 1919. He holds the General Service and Victory Medals.

36A, Westbury Road, Willesden, N.W.10. 15449.

SMITH, H. R., Pte., 11th Royal Fusiliers.

He volunteered in September 1914, and during his service on the Western Front took part in heavy fighting at Ypres, Loos, Lens, Cambrai and the Somme. During the German offensive of 1918 he was reported missing, but as no further news of him has been heard, it is presumed that he was killed on March 22nd. He was entitled to the 1914–15 Star and the General Service and Victory Medals.

46, Hampden Street, Paddington, W.2. X20971.

SMITH, J., Sapper, Royal Engineers.

He volunteered in May 1915, and three months later was sent to France, where he was actively engaged on important duties until December, when he was drafted to Egypt. He remained in this theatre of war until the Armistice, when he returned to England, and was demobilised in February 1919. He holds the General Service and Victory Medals.

96, Barry Road, Stonebridge Park, N.W.10. 15667A.

SMITH, J., Lce.-Corpl., Duke of Wellington's (West Riding Regiment).

He volunteered in March 1915, and later in the year, at the conclusion of his training, was drafted to the Western Front, where he took part in many important engagements, especially those on the Somme Front, up to the close of the war. He was demobilised in January 1919, holding the 1914–15 Star and the General Service and Victory Medals.

15, De Morgan Road, Townmead Road, S.W.6. X21005.

SMITH, J., Pte., King's Own (Royal Lancaster Regiment).

Volunteering in 1914, he served on the Western Front, and took part in many important engagements. He was wounded during his service, and in September 1917 was discharged as medically unfit for further service, owing to shell-shock. He holds the 1914–15 Star and the General Service and Victory Medals.

103, Cassidy Road, Walham Green, S.W.6. X20216.

SMITH, J. A., Pte., 1st East Surrey Regiment.

He volunteered in August 1914, and shortly afterwards sent to the Western Front, where he took part in the Retreat from Mons and the battles of Ypres and Loos, and was wounded. He was later drafted to Egypt, and from there to Salonika, and was in action on the Balkan Front. He was still serving in 1920, and holds the Mons Star and the General Service and Victory Medals.

75, Garvan Road, Hammersmith, W.6. 14828A.

SMITH, J. E., 1st Class Petty Officer, Royal Navy, H.M.S. "Glory."

He was mobilised on the outbreak of hostilities, and during 1914 served as convoy to the Canadians. In 1915 he went to the Dardanelles, and took part in the bombardment of Suvla Bay. Later, owing to ill-health, he was invalided home, and after his recovery was on duty off the coast of Scotland, until his demobilisation in February 1919. He holds the 1914–15 Star and the General Service and Victory Medals.

114, Ashmore Road, Harrow Road, W.9. X19835

SMITH, J. E., Corporal, Royal Engineers.

He volunteered in November 1915, and was drafted to Salonika in the following year. During his service in this theatre of war he contracted malaria, and was in hospital at Corfu for a time. On his recovery he was sent to Italy, where he was engaged on important duties in connection with operations on the Piave. He was demobilised in March 1919, and holds the General Service and Victory Medals.

80, Chesson Road, West Kensington, W.14. X17695.

SMITH, J. S., Corporal, 5th Royal Fusiliers.

He volunteered in June 1915, and after his training served at various stations on important duties with his unit. He gave valuable services, but was not successful in obtaining his transfer overseas before the cessation of hostilities. He was demobilised in February 1919.

6, Pretoria Road, Upper Edmonton, N.18. X17017.

SMITH, J. W., Driver, R.A.S.C. and Labour Corps.

He joined in 1918, and after his training served with his unit at various stations. He rendered valuable services, but was not successful in being transferred to a fighting Front prior to the close of the war. He was demobilised in 1919.

14, Steele Road, Willesden, N.W.10. 13839B.

SMITH, J. W., Sergeant, Middlesex Regiment.

He had previously served in the South African War, and rejoined in 1915. He rendered valuable services as a drill instructor at various stations, but was unable to obtain his transfer to the Front. He was demobilised in August 1919, and holds the Queen's and King's South African Medals.

24, Headcorn Road, Tottenham, N.17. X18269.

SMITH, J. W., Pte., Royal Fusiliers.

He joined in February 1916, and after a short period of training was drafted to the Western Front. While overseas he was frequently in action, but in consequence of a serious wound received in the Battle of Ypres, returned to England, and was invalided out of the Service in February 1917. He holds the General Service and Victory Medals.

20, Hampden Street, Paddington, W.2. X20898B.

SMITH, L. (Mrs.), Special War Worker.

This lady was engaged during the whole of the war on work of national importance at Messrs. Waring and Gillow's factory, The White City, making army equipment of various kinds. Owing to the excellent quality of her work she was promoted by the firm to be a supervisor in the tent department.

49, Gayford Road, Shepherd's Bush, W.12. X18219B.

SMITH, L. P., Pte., 10th Durham Light Infantry.

He joined in June 1916, and in the same year was sent to France, where he took part in many engagements, including the Battle of Ypres, where he was killed in action in August 1917. He was entitled to the General Service and Victory Medals.

68, Hazlebury Road, Fulham, S.W.6. X20524.

SMITH, Mary, Special War Worker.

From 1916 onwards this lady was engaged on most important and dangerous work in the T.N.T. filling shops at the Park Royal Munition Factory. She carried out the arduous duties assigned to her in a highly commendable manner.

14, Steele Road, Harlesden, N.W.10. 13839A.

SMITH, M. (Miss), Special War Worker.

During the war this lady was engaged on work of national importance at Messrs. Klingers, Tottenham, in connection with the manufacture of gas-masks. Her valuable services were greatly appreciated by the authorities.

30, Durban Road, Tottenham, N.17. X18086.

SMITH, P., Rifleman, 3rd Rifle Brigade.

Joining in 1917, he was drafted in the same year to the Western Front, where he took part in many engagements, including those of Vimy Ridge, Messines and Cambrai, and was wounded. He was demobilised in 1919, holding the General Service and Victory Medals.

61, Barret's Green Road, Willesden, N.W.10. 13552B.

SMITH, P., Petty Officer, R.N.A.S.

He volunteered in August 1914, and was sent to the Western Front in the same year. He fought for two years in France, and was then drafted to Russia, where he was killed near the Roumanian frontier on April 26th, 1917, whilst in charge of an armoured car serving with the Russian Forces. He was entitled to the 1914–15 Star, General Service and Victory Medals, and was also awarded the Russian Order of St. George for gallantry and devotion to duty.

25, Mozart Street, North Kensington, W.10. X18930A.

SMITH, R., Pte., Training Reserve.
He joined the Army in August 1916, and began his training in England. However, in the following December he was discharged as medically unfit for further service on account of ill-health.
40, Herries Street, North Kensington, W.10.   X18727.

SMITH, R., Pte., Royal Marine Light Infantry.
Volunteering in 1915, he was sent to France later in the same year, and was engaged on important duties on the North West Coast. He was killed during an air raid on Boulogne on June 30th, 1918, and was entitled to the 1914–15 Star and the General Service and Victory Medals.
77, Ancill Street, Hammersmith, W.6.   14001A.
18001

SMITH, R. F., Pte., Duke of Cornwall's Light Infantry.
He volunteered for duty in August 1915, and during his service on the Western Front saw much heavy fighting, and was severely wounded. He was invalided home and discharged as medically unfit for further military service owing to his wound in August 1916. He holds the 1914–15 Star and the General Service and Victory Medals.
109, Cassidy Road, Walham Green, S.W.6.   X20211.

SMITH, R. W., Pte., 3rd Norfolk Regiment.
He volunteered in August 1914, and in the following January was sent to the Western Front. Whilst overseas he took part in engagements at Loos, Ypres and the Somme. He was twice wounded at Arras, and was invalided home, and finally discharged as unfit for further military duties in October 1916. He holds the 1914–15 Star and the General Service and Victory Medals.
30, Glenrosa Street, Townmead Road, S.W.6.   X21341.

SMITH, S., Driver, R.A.S.C. (M.T.).
He volunteered in September 1914, and was retained on special duties at various stations until 1917, when he was drafted to Salonika. Whilst in this seat of war, he was engaged on important transport work on the Doiran and Struma Fronts, and in 1918 was sent to France. He remained on the Western Front until his demobilisation in February 1919, and holds the General Service and Victory Medals.
64, Milton Avenue, Willesden, N.W.10.   14315A.

SMITH, S., Sapper, Royal Engineers.
He volunteered in April 1915, and in the same year was sent to France, where he carried out important duties, and took part in several engagements until his demobilisation in December 1918. He holds the 1914–15 Star and the General Service and Victory Medals.
13, Delorme Street, Hammersmith, W.6.   14080B.

SMITH, S. A., Mechanic, Royal Air Force.
Joining in February 1916, he was sent to the Western Front soon afterwards. After a short period in France he was sent home, and gave valuable services, which called for a high degree of skill, at various aerodromes on the East Coast. He was demobilised in June 1919, holding the General Service and Victory Medals.
190, Kilburn Lane, North Kensington, W.10.   18706B.

SMITH, S. C., Pte., Royal Fusiliers and M.G.C.
He joined in 1916, and in the same year was sent to the Western Front, where he remained until October 1917, and took part in many engagements, including the battles of the Somme, Albert and Ypres. He then went to German East Africa, where he served for eight months, and was afterwards transferred again to France, where he was killed in action at Ovillers on October 29th, 1918. He was entitled to the General Service and Victory Medals.
44, Milton Avenue, Willesden, N.W.10.   14321.

SMITH, S. R. J., Pte., Royal Sussex Regiment.
He volunteered in January 1915, and in the same year was sent out to Egypt, where he remained until 1918, and took part in the engagements at Gaza. In 1918 he was transferred to France, and on September 22nd was taken prisoner. He remained in Germany until November 1918, when he was released and demobilised. He holds the 1914-15 Star, General Service and Victory Medals.
87, Hazlebury Road, Fulham, S.W.6.   X20587.

SMITH, S. S., Rifleman, Rifle Brigade.   .
He joined in March 1917, and during his service in France was severely wounded in action and taken prisoner. His left leg was amputated while he was in captivity, and six months later he was released. In October 1919 he was discharged as physically unfit for further service, holding the General Service and Victory Medals.
56, Sherbrooke Road, Fulham, S.W.6.   X18753C.

SMITH, T., Leading Stoker, Royal Navy.
He volunteered in August 1914, and served in the North Sea on board H.M.S. "Antrim." He took a prominent part in many naval engagements, including the Battle of Jutland and the bombardment of Zeebrugge, and later was transferred to H.M.S. "Dragon." He holds the 1914 Star and the General Service and Victory Medals, and was still serving in 1920.
65, Burnthwaite Road, Walham Green, S.W.6.   TX20098.

SMITH, T., Pte., The Queen's (Royal West Surrey Regiment).
He volunteered in 1914, and in the same year was sent to the Western Front, where he was taken prisoner. During his captivity he was badly treated, but after four years in Germany was released. He returned to England, and in 1919 was demobilised, holding the 1914–15 Star and the General Service and Victory Medals.
61, Barret's Green Road, Willesden, N.W.10.   13552C.

SMITH, W. (M.M.), Corporal, 18th M.G.C.
He volunteered in 1915, and served on the Western Front, taking part in the battles of the Somme, Givenchy and Vimy Ridge. He was awarded the Military Medal for conspicuous bravery in carrying in the wounded under shell-fire on the Somme, and was demobilised in 1919, holding, in addition, the 1914–15 Star and the General Service and Victory Medals.
171, Bulwer Road, Upper Edmonton, N.18.   X17290.

SMITH, W., Pte., 1st Bedfordshire Regiment.
He was serving at the outbreak of war, and was immediately sent to the Western Front, where he was severely wounded during the Retreat from Mons. He died from his wounds on September 14th, 1914, and was entitled to the Mons Star and the General Service and Victory Medals. He had completed seven years' service in the Army.
38, Hartopp Avenue, Dawes Road, S.W.6.   X17742.

SMITH, W., Pte., Loyal North Lancashire Regt.
He joined in February 1916, and in the same year was sent to France, where he remained until 1919. During this period he took a prominent part in the battles of Ypres, Arras, Cambrai, Vimy Ridge and the Somme. He was demobilised in April 1919, holding the General Service and Victory Medals.
36, Clarendon Street, Paddington, W.2.   X20536

SMITH, W. C., Driver, Royal Field Artillery.
He volunteered in October 1914, was sent to the Western Front in the following September, and fought in the Battle of Loos. He was then drafted to Salonika, where he took part in much of the heavy fighting during the Balkan Campaign, and suffered from malaria. In March 1919 he was demobilised, and holds the 1914–15 Star and the General Service and Victory Medals.
129, Deacon Road, Cricklewood, N.W.2.   16314B.

SMITH, W. C., A.B., Royal Navy.
Volunteering in August 1914, he was posted to H.M.S. "Mars," and served with the Grand Fleet in the North Sea. He also took part in several naval engagements, including the bombardment of the Dardanelles, and was wounded. He was discharged in May 1919, holding the 1914 Star and the General Service and Victory Medals.
8, Breer Street, Fulham, S.W.6.   X21671

SMITH, W. E., Rifleman, K.R.R. attd. R.A.P.C.
He joined in September 1918, and after his training carried out responsible duties with the Army Pay Corps. He gave valuable services, but was not successful in obtaining his transfer overseas before the cessation of hostilities. In March 1920 he was demobilised.
39, Ancill Road, Hammersmith, W.6.   13868C.

SMITH, W. G., Rifleman, 18th London Regiment (London Irish Rifles).
He volunteered in August 1914, and during his service on the Western Front, played a prominent part in the fighting at Ypres, Armentieres, Bullecourt, St. Quentin, Passchendaele, Cambrai and the Advance of 1918. He was demobilised in 1919, and holds the General Service and Victory Medals.
19, Letterstone Road, Fulham, S.W.6.   X18445A

SMITH, W. G., Lce.-Corpl., 2nd West Yorkshire Regiment.
Volunteering in August 1914, he was later sent to the Western Front, where, after playing a distinguished part in the fighting, he was killed in action on the Somme in July 1915. He was entitled to the 1914–15 Star and the General Service and Victory Medals.
36, Hartopp Avenue, Dawes Road, S.W.6.   X17741B.

SMITH, W. G., Rifleman, King's Royal Rifle Corps.

He volunteered in May 1915 and in the following year was sent to the Western Front, where he took a prominent part in several engagements, including the Battle of Ypres. He was invalided home and discharged through illness as medically unfit for further service in September 1917. He holds the General Service and Victory Medals.
53, Woodchester Street, Paddington, W.2.   X20748.

SMITH, W. G. (Mrs.) (née Clements), Special War Worker.

For a period of fourteen months during the war this lady was employed at Victoria Post Office as a sorter, thereby releasing a man for military service. Throughout she worked in a thorough and satisfactory manner and rendered valuable services.
52, Aspenlea Road, Hammersmith, W.6.   14297B.

SMITH, W. H., Gunner, Royal Field Artillery.

He joined in 1916, and, after serving at various stations in England, was in 1917 drafted to the Western Front. For nearly two years he was engaged in various parts of the Somme sector, where he saw much heavy fighting. He was demobilised in November 1919, holding the General Service and Victory Medals.
46, Southam Street, North Kensington, W.10.   X20565.

SMITH, W. H., Gunner, Royal Field Artillery.

Volunteering in September 1915, he served with distinction on several sectors of the Western Front. Owing to a severe injury he was invalided home, and spent some time in hospital. In April 1917 he was demobilised, and holds the General Service and Victory Medals.
56, Sherbrooke Road, Fulham, S.W.6.   X18753A.

SMITH, W. J., Corporal, Royal Engineers.

He joined in November 1916 and in the following year was drafted to France, where he took a prominent part in many important engagements, including those on the Somme. He was demobilised in January 1919, and holds the General Service and Victory Medals.
15, Bradiston Road, Maida Hill, W.9.   X19975.

SMITH, W. J., Pte., 36th Machine Gun Corps.

He volunteered in 1915 and after his training was retained with his unit on important duties. In 1918, however, he was drafted to France and took part in the fighting at Ypres, and other important engagements. He was demobilised in 1919, and holds the General Service and Victory Medals.
29, Leghorn Road, Harlesden, N.W.10.   13363A.

SMITH, W. J., Gunner, Royal Field Artillery.

He volunteered in September 1915, and was sent in the same year to the Dardanelles, where he saw heavy fighting. In 1916 he was drafted to France, and took a prominent part in many engagements, including those at Ypres, Bullecourt, the Somme, Arras and during the Retreat and Advance of 1918. He holds the 1914-15 Star and the General Service and Victory Medals, and was demobilised in 1918.
14, Denmark Street, Tottenham, N.17.   X18799.

SMITH, W. J., Pte., 2nd Essex Regiment.

He volunteered in November 1915, and after his training was drafted to France, where he saw much fighting. He was killed in action on July 1st, 1916, and was entitled to the General Service and Victory Medals.
39, Salisbury Road, Lower Edmonton, N.9.   13957C.

SMITH, W. J., Pte., R.A.S.C. (M.T.).

Volunteering in March 1915, he was shortly afterwards drafted to the Western Front, where he was generally employed in conveying ammunition and rations to the lines. He rendered valuable services during the battles of Loos, Arras, Ypres and the Somme, and was demobilised in January 1919, holding the 1914-15 Star and the General Service and Victory Medals.
18, Lintaine Grove, West Kensington, W.14.   X17082.

SMITH, W. J., Corporal, Royal Field Artillery.

He volunteered in January 1915, and in the following June was sent to the Western Front, where he took part in many engagements, including those on the Somme, at Ypres and Cambrai. During his service he was wounded three times and gassed. He was demobilised in March 1919 and holds the 1914-15 Star and the General Service and Victory Medals.
44, Mordaunt Road, Willesden, N.W.10.   13727B.

SMITH, W. P., Pte., R.A.S.C. (M.T.).

He volunteered in 1915 and in the same year was sent to France, where he took part in the battles of Ypres and Arras, and the Retreat and Advance of 1918. He was demobilised in June 1919, holding the 1914-15 Star and the General Service and Victory Medals.
110, Shakespeare Avenue, Willesden, N.W.10.   14203A.

SMITHSON, J. P., Pte., Middlesex Regiment.

He volunteered in May 1915 and in the same year was drafted to France, where he fought in the battle of Loos and other important engagements. He was later sent to Salonika, and took part in the operations during the offensive on the Bulgarian Front in 1918. In March 1919, he was demobilised and holds the 1914-15 Star and the General Service and Victory Medals.
7, Durham Road, Lower Edmonton, N.9.   14690B.

SMITHSON, J. W., Sapper, Royal Engineers.

Volunteering in March 1915, he was drafted to France in the same year, and during his service in this seat of war took an active part in much heavy fighting. He was wounded in action during the battle of the Somme in 1916. In November 1918 he was demobilised, and holds the 1914-15 Star and the General Service and Victory Medals.
7, Durham Road, Lower Edmonton, N.9.   14690A.

SNAPS, J., Pte., Royal Munster Fusiliers.

He volunteered in 1915 and in the same year was sent to the Western Front, where, after taking a prominent part in several engagements, he was seriously wounded. In consequence, he was invalided home and discharged in May 1917, holding the 1914-15 Star and the General Service and Victory Medals.
8, Ashmore Road, Harrow Road, W.9.   X19905.

SNELL, G. C., Rifleman, King's Royal Rifle Corps.

Volunteering in August 1914, he was sent to the Western Front in April of the following year, on completion of his training. After taking part in heavy fighting during this month, he was killed in action at Hill 60 on May 4th, 1915. He was entitled to the 1914-15 Star and the General Service and Victory Medals.
75, Melville Road, Stonebridge Park, N.W.10.   15656.

SNELL, H., Pte., R.A.S.C. (Expeditionary Force Canteens).

After having been rejected on medical grounds on four previous attempts to join the Army, he succeeded in joining the R.A.S.C. in August 1917, and was sent to France. He rendered valuable services at various canteens until his demobilisation in November 1919, and holds the General Service and Victory Medals.
119, Ashmore Road, Harrow Road, W.9.   X19754.

SNELLING, E. C., Pte., Royal Defence Corps.

He volunteered in 1915, and during his service was engaged on special guard duties at various stations on the South East coast. He rendered valuable services until 1918, when he was discharged as medically unfit for further service owing to indifferent health.
54, Ancill Street, Hammersmith, W.6.   13981B.

SNELLING, E. W. (Miss), Special War Worker.

During the war this lady was engaged at Messrs. Llewellyn and Dent's Munition Factory, in connection with the manufacture of bombs and mines. She carried out her dangerous duties in an efficient manner, and rendered valuable services throughout.
54, Ancill Street, Hammersmith, W.6.   13981A.

SNELLING, H., Sergeant, Grenadier Guards.

He volunteered in August 1914, and was immediately drafted to the Western Front, where he was severely wounded in the Battle of Mons. He was invalided home and was under treatment in hospital for several months. On his recovery he was medically unfit for further service overseas, and was therefore retained on important duties at various stations. In 1920 he was still serving, and holds the Mons Star and the General Service and Victory Medals.
6, Orbain Road, Fulham, S.W.6.   X18051

SNELLING, W., Special War Worker.

During the War he was engaged on work of national importance at the Park Royal Electric Light Factory, where he held a responsible position. He carried out his duties in an efficient manner, and gave valuable services to his Country.
6, Orbain Road, Fulham, S.W.6.   X18054.

SNELLING, W. T. (M.M.), Corpl., Essex Regt.

He volunteered in March 1915, and during his service on the Western Front took part in the battles of the Somme, Arras, Ypres, Bullecourt and Albert, and in heavy fighting at Neuve Chapelle, Loos and Hill 60. He was twice wounded and also suffered from shell-shock. He was awarded the Military Medal for conspicuous bravery and devotion to duty in bringing in wounded under heavy fire, and in addition holds the General Service and Victory Medals. He was demobilised in 1919.
6, Orbain Road, Fulham, S.W.6.   X18055.

SNOW, E., Rifleman, King's Royal Rifle Corps.

He joined in 1916, was drafted to the Western Front at the end of December, and was killed in action at Combles five weeks later in January 1917. He was entitled to the General Service and Victory Medals.
50, Shorrolds Road, Walham Green, S.W.6.   X19365.

SOLE, A. T., Pte., Royal Fusiliers.

Having previously served with the Army in India, he was mobilised immediately on the outbreak of hostilities, and was drafted to France. He took part in much severe fighting, and was killed in action at the Battle of Hill 60, on April 26th, 1915. He was entitled to the 1914-15 Star and the General Service and Victory Medals.
22, Hartopp Avenue, Fulham, S.W.6.   X17666A.

SOLE, E. E., Lce.-Corporal, R.A.S.C.

Having previously served in the Army, he rejoined immediately on the outbreak of hostilities, and was soon drafted to the Western Front. He took part in many important operations in this theatre of war, and was badly wounded. In May 1919 he was demobilised, but again enlisted in July and in 1920 was still serving. He holds the 1914-15 Star and the General Service and Victory Medals.
22, Hartopp Avenue, Fulham, S.W.6.   X17666B.

SOLE, W. T., Sergt., Royal Marine Light Infantry.

He volunteered in August 1914, and during his service took part in many important operations. While on board H.M.S. "Irresistible" he fought at the Dardanelles, and was on this ship when she was torpedoed and sunk in March 1915. He was rescued by H.M.S. "Queen Elizabeth," and afterwards served at Malta. He holds the 1914-15 Star and the General Service and Victory Medals, and in 1920 was still serving.
22, Hartopp Avenue, Fulham, S.W.6.   X17666C.

SOMERVILLE, J. C., Aircraftsman, R.A.F.

He joined in August 1918, and in the same year was drafted to France, where on account of his great technical skill he was employed at the R.A.F. Motor Transport Depot at St. Omer, and also at Arques. After the Armistice he was sent to Germany with the Army of Occupation, and remained there until his demobilisation in February 1920. He holds the General Service and Victory Medals.
17, De Morgan Road, Fulham, S.W.6.   X20843.

SOTHERAN, G. F., Tpr., 2nd Dragoon Guards.

He had been serving since 1906, and in 1914 was drafted to the Western Front, where he took part in many early important operations, and was twice wounded. He was invalided home, and after treatment in hospital at Norwich was discharged in July 1915 as medically unfit for further service owing to shell-shock. In May 1920 he re-enlisted in the Territorial Forces. He holds the 1914 Star and the General Service and Victory Medals.
77, Reporton Road, Munster Road, S.W.6.   X18918.

SOUSTER, I. (Miss), Special War Worker.

During the war this lady undertook work of national importance at the Park Royal Munition Factory, where she was first engaged on dangerous duties in the T.N.T. powder room. Later she worked in the shell and fuse filling departments and rendered valuable services. She received high commendation for her splendid work.
53, Orbain Road, Fulham, S.W.6.   X18260A.

SOUTER, E., Driver, Royal Field Artillery.

He volunteered for service in August 1914, and in the following year was sent out to the East, where he took part in the operations against the Bulgarians on the Salonika Front. Later he served with General Allenby in Palestine, and was present at the capture of Jerusalem. He was demobilised in June 1919, and holds the 1914-15 Star and the General Service and Victory Medals.
84, Ashmore Road, Harrow Road, W.9.   X19844.

SOUTER, H., Pte., Royal Marine Light Infantry.

He volunteered in 1914, and immediately proceeded to sea with H.M.S. "Formidable." While on board this ship he took part in important naval operations, and was drowned when she was torpedoed in the English Channel on January 1st, 1915. He was entitled to the 1914 Star and the General Service and Victory Medals.
36, Steele Road, Willesden, N.W.10.   14139B.

SOUTER, J., Pte., Northumberland Fusiliers.

He volunteered in 1914, and was drafted to the Western Front later in the same year. After taking part in much severe fighting during the early vital operations, he was killed in action in January 1915. He was entitled to the 1914 Star and the General Service and Victory Medals.
36, Steele Road, Willesden, N.W.10.   14139A.

SOUTHGATE, C., Bombardier, R.F.A.

He volunteered in August 1914, and was drafted to Mesopotamia, where, after taking part in many engagements, he was taken prisoner when General Townshend's forces surrendered at Kut in 1916. He suffered terrible hardships while in captivity, and died from starvation. He was entitled to the 1914-15 Star and the General Service and Victory Medals.
83, Somerset Road, Upper Edmonton, N.18.   X17038A.

SOUTHGATE, W., Stoker, Royal Navy, H.M.S. "Indomitable."

He volunteered in August 1914, and was posted to the "Indomitable," with which ship he saw service in important naval operations with the Grand Fleet in the North Sea. He took part in the sinking of the "Blücher" at the battle of Dogger Bank in January 1915. In 1920 he was still serving, and holds the 1914-15 Star and the General Service and Victory Medals.
83, Somerset Road, Upper Edmonton, N.18.   X17038B.

SOUTHWARD, J., Pte., Middlesex Regiment and Sherwood Foresters.

He joined in May 1916, and having received training at various stations in England was sent to the Western Front in February of the following year. He took part in numerous engagements whilst overseas, and was wounded and taken prisoner at Bullecourt. For many months he suffered great privation in an internment camp in Germany, and in December 1918 was released. He was demobilised in August 1919, holding the General Service and Victory Medals.
41, Victor Road, College Park, N.W.10.   X19047.

SOWDEN, C. H., Corpl., West Yorkshire Regt.

Volunteering in December 1914, he was drafted to the Western Front in the following year. He took part in the battles of Loos (where he was wounded), the Somme and Ypres, and in important engagements during the 1918 Advance. He was also gassed during his service abroad and was in hospital in France for some time. In January 1919 he was demobilised, holding the 1914-15 Star and the General Service and Victory Medals, but has since rejoined.
6, Eli Road, W. Kensington, W.14.   16917B.

SOWDEN, R. (Mrs.), Special War Worker.

For a period of over three years during the war, this lady rendered valuable services on the District Railway and released a man for military service. She carried out her duties in a very capable manner, and did excellent work for her country.
6, Eli Street, W. Kensington, W.14.   16917A.

SPARK, J. E., Sapper, Royal Engineers.

He volunteered in 1914, and was immediately sent to the Western Front, where he took part in the Retreat from Mons and in the battles of Ypres, Loos, the Somme and Arras. He was then drafted to Salonika, and again saw much heavy fighting. In 1919 he returned to this country for demobilisation, holding the Mons Star and the General Service and Victory Medals.
26A, Furness Road, Harlesden, N.W.10.   13165A.

SPARK, J. S., Pte., 3rd Devonshire Regt. and Lancashire Fusiliers.

He volunteered in April 1915 at the early age of sixteen, and after his training was retained on important duties until 1918. He was then drafted to France, where he took part in much severe fighting, including the second Battle of Arras, and was wounded. In January 1919 he was demobilised, and holds the General Service and Victory Medals.
26A, Furness Road, Harlesden, N.W.10.   13165B.

SPARKS, F., Pte., The Queen's (Royal West Surrey Regiment).

He volunteered in January 1916, and later in the same year was drafted to Salonika, where he took part in much heavy fighting until August 1918. He was then invalided home and discharged as medically unfit for further service, and on May 11th, 1919, died from the effects of illness contracted whilst in the Army. He was entitled to the General Service and Victory Medals.
65, Lopen Road, Upper Edmonton, N.18.   TX17584/ 17585.

SPAUL, E. J., Air Mechanic, Royal Air Force.

He joined in December 1917, and in the following year was drafted to France, where he took part in the 1918 Retreat and Advance. In 1919 he went to Egypt where he served until 1920, when he returned to England and was demobilised. He holds the General Service and Victory Medals.
51, Brookville Road, Dawes Road, S.W.6. X20424.

SPEARING, C., Pte., R.A.V.C.

He volunteered for duty in February 1915, and during his service on the Western Front, which lasted for four years, was engaged in tending sick and wounded horses in various sectors. He returned to England in 1919, and was demobilised, holding the 1914-15 Star and the General Service and Victory Medals.
30, Clarendon Street, Paddington, W.2. X20540.

SPEARING, F., Gunner, Royal Field Artillery.

He volunteered in September 1914, and in the same year was sent to France, when he took an important part in various engagements, including that at Neuve Chapelle. In 1916 he was drafted to the Eastern Front, and served for nearly three years in operations against the Bulgarians. During this period he contracted malaria from which he suffered intermittently, and on his return home was demobilised in March 1919, holding the 1914-15 Star and the General Service and Victory Medals.
112, Chippenham Road, Maida Hill, W.9. X20774.

SPEARING, I., Driver, Royal Field Artillery.

He volunteered in November 1914, and was sent to the Western Front in the following August. He took part in many important engagements, including Neuve Chapelle, Ypres, the Somme, Arras, St. Quentin and Cambrai, and also fought in Italy on the Piave. He was demobilised in May 1919, and holds the 1914-15 Star and the General Service and Victory Medals.
7, Ashmore Road, Harrow Road, W.9. TX19696.

SPEARING, R. F., Driver, R.A.S.C. (H.T.).

He volunteered in August 1914, and was drafted to the Western Front where he was engaged in conveying troops, ammunition and food supplies to the various sectors. He served at Mons, Loos, Ypres, the Somme, Arras, Bullecourt and many other places, and was also present during the Retreat and Advance of 1918, in which he was severely wounded. He was demobilised in February 1919, holding the Mons Star and the General Service and Victory Medals.
77, Clarendon Street, Paddington, W.2. X20395.

SPEED, A. P., Rifleman, 8th London Regiment (Post Office Rifles).

He joined in April 1917, and in the following July went to the Western Front, where he took part in many engagements, and was severely wounded. He was invalided home and spent some time in hospital. He holds the General Service and Victory Medals, and was demobilised in 1919, but has since re-enlisted in the Duke of Cornwall's Light Infantry, and in 1920 was serving in India.
59, Allestree Road, Munster Road, S.W.6. TX19262B.

SPEED, C. R., Gunner, Royal Field Artillery.

Volunteering in September 1914, he was drafted in the following March to the Western Front, where he took part in many important engagements, including those at Ypres, the Somme, Vimy Ridge, Arras and Albert. On account of wounds received in action he was invalided home, and on his recovery proceeded to Salonika in 1918. He was demobilised in May 1919, holding the 1914-15 Star and the General Service and Victory Medals.
59, Allestree Road, Munster Road, S.W.6. TX19262A

SPELLER, A., Pte., 19th London Regiment and Middlesex Regiment.

He volunteered in August 1914, in the 19th Battalion The London Regiment, and gave valuable services at various stations until November 1915, when he was discharged as being under military age. In April 1918 he rejoined in the Middlesex Regiment and after the signing of the Armistice, went to Germany with the Army of Occupation. He remained there until November 1919, when he was demobilised.
20, Albert Terrace, Milton Avenue,
Willesden, N.W.10. 14326C.

SPELLER, G. H. H. (M.S.M.), Driver, R.F.A. and R.A.S.C., and Pte., 16th Lancers.

He was mobilised from the Reserve immediately on the outbreak of hostilities, and was sent to the Western Front. He took part in the Battle and Retreat from Mons, the battles of Ypres (1914, 1915 and 1917), Arras, Bullecourt, Passchendaele, and St. Quentin, and other important engagements, and was wounded. He was awarded the Meritorious Service Medal for great gallantry and devotion to duty in the field. In addition, he holds the Mons Star and the General Service and Victory Medals and was discharged in March 1919.
20, Albert Terrace, Milton Avenue,
Willesden, N.W.10. 14326B.

SPELLER, H. A., Pte., Bedfordshire Regiment and King's Own Scottish Borderers.

He joined in June 1914, and proceeded to the Western Front, where he took part in the engagements at Hill 60 and Passchendaele and other operations, and was twice wounded. He afterwards saw much service in Gallipoli, Egypt and Italy. He holds the 1914-15 Star and the General Service and Victory Medals, and in 1920 was serving in India.
20, Albert Terrace, Milton Avenue,
Willesden, N.W.10. 14326A.

SPELLER, P. W., Bombardier, R.F.A.

Volunteering in October 1914, he was drafted to the Western Front early in the following year. After taking part in much severe fighting, he was killed in action near Ypres on December 10th, 1915, and was buried in the Ypres Military Cemetery. He was entitled to the 1914-15 Star, and the General Service and Victory Medals.
50, Carlyle Avenue, Willesden, N.W.10. 14404A.

SPENCE, P., A.B., R.N., H.M.S. "Calliope."

He volunteered in August 1914, and during his service on board H.M.S. "Calliope" took part in important naval operations with the North Sea Patrol. He was also in action at the Battle of Jutland, where his ship caught fire and the crew suffered heavy casualties. He was demobilised in January 1919, holding the 1914 Star and the General Service and Victory Medals.
99, Victor Road, College Park, N.W.10. X17537.

SPENCELEY, G. A., Driver, Royal Field Artillery.

He volunteered in November 1914, and was drafted to the Western Front in the following year. During his service in this seat of war, he took part in the battles of the Somme and Ypres, and in heavy fighting during the Retreat and Advance in 1918. In the course of his service he was gassed. In July 1919 he was demobilised, holding the 1914-15 Star and the General Service and Victory Medals.
32, Linton Road, Upper Edmonton, N.18. X17901

SPENCER, H., Pte., Middlesex Regiment.

He volunteered in August 1914, after seventeen years' previous service, during which he had served in India and in South Africa. He was drafted to the Western Front, and took part in many important engagements in various sectors. In consequence of wounds he was in hospital for a considerable time and on his recovery proceeded to Mesopotamia, where he rendered valuable service. In 1919 he was demobilised, holding the 1914-15 Star and the General Service and Victory Medals, in addition to the King's and Queen's South African Medals.
107, Sherbrooke Road, Fulham, S.W.6. X18616.

SPENCER, H. J., Driver, R.A.S.C. (M.T.).

He was called up from the Reserve in August 1914, and was drafted to the Western Front, where he was engaged on important transport work. He took an active part in many engagements, including the Retreat from Mons and the battles of Ypres and St. Quentin. He was gassed during his service, and on his recovery was sent to Italy, where he saw much service. He was discharged in February 1919, and holds the Mons Star and the General Service and Victory Medals.
133, Ashmore Road, Harrow Road, W.9. X19741.

SPENCER, W., Pte., 1/2nd Middlesex Regiment.

He volunteered in May 1915, and was sent to the Western Front, where he took part in many engagements including those at Ypres, the Somme, Arras and Cambrai. During his service he was twice wounded and gassed, and was invalided home. He was demobilised in February 1919, and holds the 1914-15 Star and the General Service and Victory Medals.
38, Hartopp Avenue, Fulham, S.W.6. X17793.

SPENCER, W. H., Sergt., Somerset Light Infantry.

He volunteered in November 1914, and served at various stations on important duties with his unit. He was chiefly engaged as sergeant-instructor, and during his service was attached to the Royal Air Force for a time. He did valuable work, but was not successful in obtaining his transfer overseas before the termination of hostilities. He was demobilised in February 1919.
114, Townmead Road, Fulham, S.W.6. X20959.

SPICE, A. C., Gunner, Royal Garrison Artillery.

He volunteered in 1915, and was sent to the Western Front, where he took part in the heavy fighting at Neuve Chapelle, Loos, Armentières, St. Quentin, and in the Retreat and Advance of 1918. He was demobilised in 1919, and holds the 1914-15 Star, and the General Service and Victory Medals.
71, Yeldham Road, Hammersmith, W.6. 14166B

SPICE, N. (Mrs.), Special War Worker.
During the war this lady was engaged at the Park Royal Munition Factory where her exceptional abilities led to her being appointed to the important position of examiner in the shell-making department. The services which she rendered proved of the utmost value.
71, Yeldham Road, Hammersmith, W.6.　　14166A.

SPICER, E. M., Special War Worker.
During the war this lady was engaged in the clerical department of Messrs. Carter, Paterson & Co., Hurlingham Road, and thus released a man for military service. She did valuable service and gave complete satisfaction to her employers.
10, Bronsart Road, Munster Road,
Fulham, S.W.6.　　TX18988.

SPILLER, G.F., Driver, Royal Army Service Corps.
He volunteered in August 1914, and was sent to France, where he took an active part in many engagements. He was severely wounded in April 1918, and invalided home, and afterwards was discharged as medically unfit for further service. He holds the 1914–15 Star and the General Service and Victory Medals.
14, Lintaine Grove, W. Kensington, W.14.　　X17000.

SPILLETT, H. A., Gunner, Royal Field Artillery.
He volunteered in January 1915, and on completion of his training was drafted to the Western Front, where he took part in many engagements, including those at Ypres and the Somme, and was gassed. He was demobilised in April 1919, and holds the 1914–15 Star and the General Service and Victory Medals.
7, Cornwallis Road, Lower Edmonton, N.9.　　13284.

SPINDLER, L. H. H., Corpl., Royal Field Artillery.
He was serving at the outbreak of war, and went at once to France, where he took part in the Retreat from Mons, the battles of the Marne, the Aisne, Ypres, and Menin Road, and the Retreat and Advance in 1918, and was wounded twice. Later he served in India. He was discharged in May 1919, and holds the Mons Star and the General Service and Victory Medals.
54, Tubb's Road, Harlesden, N.W.10.　　12561B.

SPITTELS, A. W., Pte., 24th Royal Fusiliers.
He joined in March 1916, and in the following November was drafted to France. After taking part in many important engagements in the Ypres sector, he was killed in action near Arras on May 1st, 1917. He was entitled to the General Service and Victory Medals.
34A, Deacon Road, Cricklewood, N.W.2.　　X17113B.

SPITTLE, J. W., 1st Air Mechanic, R.A.F.
He joined in May 1916, and on completion of his training was retained at the Central Flying Schools on important duties, which called for a high degree of technical skill. During his service he met with a serious accident, and in 1920 he was still in hospital.
22, Fifth Avenue, Queen's Park Estate, W.10.　　X18327.

SPOONER, F., Bombardier, Royal Field Artillery.
Volunteering in August 1914, he was immediately drafted to France, where he took part in the Retreat from Mons and in other important engagements, and was badly gassed. In 1916 he was sent to Salonika, saw much heavy fighting during the operations on the Balkan Front, and suffered from malaria. In April 1919 he was demobilised, and holds the Mons Star and the General Service and Victory Medals.
21, Bruce Castle Road, Tottenham, N.17.　　X18547.

SPORLE, J., Seaman Gunner, Royal Navy, H.M.S. "Warspite."
He volunteered in September 1915. He saw much service with the Grand Fleet in the North Sea, and took part in the battles of Jutland and Heligoland. Later, he went on active service in Russian waters and suffered severely from frost-bite. He returned to England and was demobilised in June 1919. He holds the 1914–15 Star and the General Service and Victory Medals.
13, Heckfield Place, Fulham, S.W.6.　　X20246.

SPRATT, S., Pte., Royal Fusiliers.
He joined in July 1917, and shortly afterwards was drafted to the Western Front, where he took part in several engagements, and was wounded. As a result of his wounds he was invalided home, and remained in hospital for some time, being subsequently demobilised in August 1919. He holds the General Service and Victory Medals.
49, Aintree Street, Dawes Road, S.W.6.　　X18214.

SPRINGETT, C. H., Corporal, R.A.F., and R.E.
He joined the Royal Air Force in June 1916, and after training served at various stations on important duties with his squadron. He was afterwards transferred to the Royal Engineers and sent to France, where he was engaged on special duties, and in 1920 was still serving.
34, Novello Street, Parson's Green, S.W.6.　　TX20015

SPRY, F., Pte., Royal Fusiliers.
Joining in March 1917, he was later drafted to the Western Front, where he took part in several engagements, including the Retreat and Advance of 1918, and was gassed. He holds the General Service and Victory Medals, and was demobilised in January 1920.
129A, Deacon Road, Cricklewood, N.W.2.　　16315B

SPRY, F. J., Pte., 13th Middlesex Regiment.
He volunteered in August 1914, was sent to the Western Front in the following year, and took part in many engagements, including Ypres, Loos, Vimy Ridge and the Somme. He was discharged in December 1917, and holds the 1914–15 Star and the General Service and Victory Medals.
129A, Deacon Road, Cricklewood, N.W.2.　　16315A.

SQUIBB, E. (Mrs.), Special War Worker.
This lady was engaged during the war, at the Neasden Munition Factory, where her duties, although of a dangerous and very strenuous nature, were carried out in a manner worthy of high commendation.
40, New Holly Lane, Willesden, N.W.10.　　15578B

SQUIBB, F. H., Pte., Tank Corps.
Volunteering in 1915, he was drafted to the Western Front on completion of his training. His service overseas lasted for three years, during which time he took part in many important engagements, including those of Ypres, the Somme and Cambrai. Whilst overseas he suffered from shell-shock. He returned to England, and was demobilised in 1919, and holds the General Service and Victory Medals.
40, New Holly Lane, Willesden, N.W.10.　　15578A.

SQUIBB, H. F., Special War Worker.
Being under age for military service, and desirous of helping his country during a time of great need, he obtained work of national importance at an aircraft factory. He was engaged as a mechanic, and in this capacity did much valuable work throughout the war.
40, New Holly Lane, Willesden, N.W.10.　　15578C.

STACEY, B. (Mrs.), Special War Worker.
During the war this lady was engaged at Messrs. Smith's Munition Works, Cricklewood, and was employed in the making of shell-cases and fuses. Her work was of a dangerous and extremely arduous nature, and in spite of air raids she carried out her duties in a most efficient manner, for which she was commended.
5, Chapman's Cottages,
High Road, Willesden, N.W.10.　　16615A.

STACEY, F. W., Pte., Bedfordshire Regiment.
He joined in May 1918, and after his training was drafted to Germany, where he served with the Army of Occupation until January 1920, when he returned to England and was demobilised.
15, Dartington Terrace, Paddington, W.2.　　X21685A.

STACEY, H. J., Corpl., Royal Garrison Artillery.
Volunteering in September 1914, he was drafted to the Western Front later in the same year. Until the cessation of hostilities, he was in almost continuous action, taking part in the battles of La Bassee, Ypres and Loos. He returned to England in 1919, and in March of the same year was demobilised, holding the 1914–15 Star and the General Service and Victory Medals.
28, Whitehall Road, Tottenham, N.17.　　X18131

STACEY, J., Pte., Royal Defence Corps.
He volunteered in 1914, and served at various stations on important duties, and was also employed guarding German prisoners. He rendered valuable services in England and Ireland throughout the whole period of the war, and was demobilised in January 1919.
5, Chapman's Cottages,
High Road, Willesden, N.W.10.　　16615B

STACEY, R. W., Driver, Royal Field Artillery.
Volunteering in January 1915, he was drafted in the following year to the Western Front, where he took a prominent part in numerous engagements, including those of Loos, Arras, Vimy Ridge and the Battle of the Somme. He also served in the Retreat and Advance of 1918, and was demobilised in February 1919, holding the General Service and Victory Medals.
15, Dartington Terrace, Paddington, W.2.　　X21685B

STACK, J., Pte., Middlesex Regiment.
Volunteering in August 1914, he was drafted to the Western Front. His service overseas lasted for nearly five years, during which time he took part in the Retreat from Mons, the battles of the Marne, the Aisne, Ypres, Arras and Cambrai, and was severely gassed. In 1919 he returned to England, and in June of the same year was demobilised, holding the Mons Star and the General Service and Victory Medals.
39, Clarendon Street, Paddington, W.2.   X20637.

STAFFORD, F. W., Corporal, Royal Sussex Regt.
Joining in September 1918, he was not successful in obtaining his transfer overseas before the cessation of hostilities. Afterwards, however, he was sent with the Army of Occupation to Germany, where he served until 1920, when he returned to England, and was demobilised.
26, Sherbrooke Road, Fulham, S.W.6.   X18769A.

STAFFORD, J., Pte., Royal Army Medical Corps.
Volunteering in September 1914, he received his training at various stations in England, and later served with the Egyptian Expeditionary Force. He was afterwards drafted to Salonika, and throughout his service, which lasted for five years, did valuable work with the R.A.M.C. He holds the General Service and Victory Medals, and was demobilised in July 1919.
26, Sherbrooke Road, Fulham, S.W.6.   X18769B.

STAFFORD, J. W., Sapper, Royal Engineers.
He volunteered in March 1915, and served on the Western Front, where he took part in many important battles, and was severely wounded. He was discharged in June 1917, and holds the 1914–15 Star, and the General Service and Victory Medals.
26, Sherbrooke Road, Fulham, S.W.6.   X18769C

STAFFORD, W. A., Corporal, R.A.M.C.
He volunteered in 1914, and after a short period of training was sent to the Western Front. His service overseas lasted for nearly five years, and during this time he did good work with the R.A.M.C. in practically all sectors, and was wounded. He returned to England in 1919, and in April of the same year was demobilised, holding the 1914 Star and the General Service and Victory Medals.
2, Holberton Gardens, Willesden, N.W.10.   X17560.

STAGG, G. F., Pte., Royal Army Medical Corps.
He volunteered in 1915, and after a short period of training was drafted to the Western Front. During his service overseas, which lasted for four years, he was in practically every sector of the Front, including Ypres, the Somme, Arras and Cambrai, and in the capacity of stretcher-bearer did valuable work. He returned to England in 1919, when he was demobilised, holding the 1914–15 Star and the General Service and Victory Medals.
11, St. John's Buildings, Kilburn Lane,
North Kensington, W.10.   X18430A.

STAGG, T., Pte., 9th Middlesex Regiment.
He volunteered in August 1914, and after his training was engaged on special guard and other duties. Owing to physical unfitness at that time, he was not successful in obtaining his transfer overseas, and in December 1915 was invalided out of the service.
51, Milton Avenue, Willesden, N.W.10.   X18430B.

STAINES, F., Sapper, Royal Engineers.
Having previously served through the South African Campaign, he rejoined in August 1918. For some time he was stationed at Longmoor Camp, and later was drafted to Russia, where he did valuable work with the Royal Engineers. He was demobilised in September 1919, and holds the Queen's South African Medal with four Bars.
6, Hazelbury Road, Lower Edmonton, N.9.   X17498.

STAINES, F. E., Seaman-Gunner, Royal Navy.
Volunteering in 1914, he was posted to H.M.S. " Edgar," which struck a mine in the North Sea and was disabled in November of the same year. He was then transferred to " Monitor 21," and served on this ship until October 20th, 1918, when she was sunk. He served in the North Sea, took part in the bombardment of the Dardanelles, the raid on Zeebrugge, and several other naval engagements. He was demobilised in 1919, holding the 1914 Star and the General Service and Victory Medals.
60, Yeldham Road, Hammersmith, W.6.   12829A.

STAINES, J. M., R.S.M., Rifle Brigade.
He had served for twelve years in India before the outbreak of war, and on his return to England acted as an instructor before proceeding to France in May 1915. After taking part in many important engagements there, he was killed in action at Delville Wood on August 21st, 1916. He held the Indian Medal and Clasp (Punjaub), and the Long Service and Good Conduct Medals, and was entitled to the 1914–15 Star and the General Service and Victory Medals.
184, Kilburn Lane, North Kensington, W.10.   X18709.

STAINES, L. R. (Mrs.), Special War Worker.
This lady held an important post as manageress for Messrs. Waring and Gillow's, at the White City, during the war. She superintended the making of various articles of army equipment, including gas masks, haversacks, tents and hospital marquees. Throughout her service she did valuable work, and was worthy of high commendation.
60, Yeldham Road, Hammersmith, W.6.   12829B.

STAINES, R. (Mrs.), Special War Worker.
During the war this lady held the important post of supervisor at Messrs. Waring and Gillow's at the White City. She was responsible for the training and work of a large number of employees who were engaged in making gas masks, haversacks, and other articles of soldiers' equipment, and throughout her service did valuable work.
60, Yeldham Road, Hammersmith, W.6.   13168A.

STAINES, R., Stoker, Royal Navy.
Volunteering in 1915, he was posted to H.M.S. " Erebus." On board this ship he served in the North Sea and the English Channel, and also took part in various engagements, including the bombardment of Zeebrugge. He was demobilised in 1919, holding the 1914–15 Star and the General Service and Victory Medals.
60, Yeldham Road, Hammersmith, W.6.   13168B.

STAMP, F., Rifleman, 18th London Regiment (Irish Rifles).
He volunteered for service in May 1915, and in the same year was drafted to the Western Front, where he was wounded in action at Loos. He was invalided to a hospital, and on his recovery in 1917 returned to France, where he remained until his demobilisation in December 1919. He holds the 1914–15 Star and the General Service and Victory Medals.
35, Novello Street, Parson's Green, S.W.6.   X20053B.

STAMP, W. G., Pte., 13th Hussars.
He was serving when war broke out, and was drafted to the Western Front, where he saw action on the Somme, at Ypres and in various other sectors. Later he went to the East, and took part in much of the heavy fighting during the Palestine Campaign and in Mesopotamia. He holds the General Service and Victory Medals, and was demobilised in May 1919, at the conclusion of nine years' service.
35, Novello Street, Parson's Green, S.W.6.   X20053A.

STANBOROUGH, H. E., Pte., 2nd Welch Regt.
He volunteered in April 1915, having previously served for twelve years, and was immediately drafted to the Western Front. He was in action at Loos, Arras, Ypres and on the Somme, and in September 1917 was invalided home and discharged owing to ill-health as medically unfit for further military duties. He holds the 1914–15 Star and the General Service and Victory Medals.
16, Glenrosa Street, Townmead Road, S.W.6.   X21339.

STANBRIDGE, E. B., Pte., R.A.S.C.
He joined in March 1917, and served at various stations on important duties with his unit. Being retained on duties in England, he was not successful in obtaining his transfer overseas before the cessation of hostilities. He secured his demobilisation in April 1920.
79, Barnsdale Road, Maida Hill, W.9.   X19546.

STANDING, C., Pte., Queen's Own (Royal West Kent Regiment).
Joining in July 1916, he was drafted to the Western Front. His service overseas lasted for three years, during which time he was engaged with the Labour Corps, and did valuable work in many important sectors. He returned to England in 1919, when he was demobilised, holding the General Service and Victory Medals.
32, Chalgrove Road, Tottenham, N.17.   X18961A.

STANDING, R., Pte., 17th Gloucestershire Regt.
He joined in September 1916, and after his training was engaged on special duties at various stations with his unit. He was not successful in obtaining his transfer overseas before the cessation of hostilities, but did valuable work before being demobilised in April 1919.
32, Chalgrove Road, Tottenham, N.17.   X18961B.

STANDISH, W. J., Leading Stoker, Royal Navy.
Volunteering in August 1914, he was posted to H.M.S. " Cornwallis," in which he served with the Grand Fleet until she was torpedoed and sunk on January 11th, 1917. He was then transferred to the " Royal Oak," in which he was serving in 1920. He holds the 1914 Star and the General Service and Victory Medals.
147, Poynton Road, Tottenham, N.17.   X18953.

STANFORD, E. S. J., Pte., 3rd London Regiment.

Volunteering in September 1914, he was first sent to Malta. In the following year he was drafted to Egypt, and thence to Gallipoli, where he was killed in action in November 1916. He was entitled to the 1914-15 Star and the General Service and Victory Medals.

125A, Hill Side, Stonebridge Park, N.W.10.   15804.
15805.

STANLEY, A., Sergeant, Rifle Brigade.

He volunteered in August 1914, and was drafted to the Western Front, where he took part in many engagements, including those at Ypres and the Somme. He served on many sectors throughout the war, and was wounded in action on three occasions. He holds the 1914 Star and the General Service and Victory Medals, and was still serving in 1920.

10, Montpelier Road, Hammersmith, W.6.   13266.

STANLEY, J., Pte., 14th Queen's (Royal West Surrey Regiment).

He volunteered in July 1915, and in the same year was drafted to Salonika, where he was engaged on important duties with his unit. After the cessation of hostilities he returned home, and was demobilised in August 1919, holding the 1914-15 Star and the General Service and Victory Medals.

4, Dieppe Street, West Kensington, W.14.   15701.

STANLEY, J., Pte., Middlesex Regiment.

He volunteered in May 1915, and served with distinction with the Middlesex Regiment at various stations. He was not successful in obtaining his transfer overseas, but was engaged on important duties with his unit until he was discharged in February 1919.

1B, Eaton Chambers, Halford Road,
Walham Green, S.W.6.   X19852.

STANLEY, J. P., A.B., Royal Navy.

Volunteering in June 1915, he served with the Grand Fleet in the North Sea and off the Belgian coast, where he played a prominent part in the bombardment of Zeebrugge. Whilst in H.M. Ships " Tiger," " Norseman," " Laurel " and " Dido," he was in several naval engagements. He holds the General Service and Victory Medals, and was demobilised in March 1920.

37, Rock Avenue, Fulham Road, S.W.6.   TX20078.

STANMORE, F., Leading Signalman, R.N.

He volunteered in January 1915, and after being stationed for nearly three years at Harwich, served in the North Sea, where he took part in the Battle of Heligoland Bight and other actions. He was demobilised in January 1919, and holds the General Service and Victory Medals.

7, Osman Road, Lower Edmonton, N.9.   14539B.

STANMORE, S., Pte., 1/7th Middlesex Regiment, and R.A.S.C.

He volunteered in August 1914, and after his training was sent to France, where he was wounded in action in June 1915. On recovery he was transferred to the R.A.S.C., and during several important engagements he was employed on transport duties. He was demobilised in February 1919, holding the 1914-15 Star and the General Service and Victory Medals.

7, Osman Road, Lower Edmonton, N.9.   14539A.

STANNARD, A. C., Pte., 3rd Leicestershire Regt.

In 1916 he came home from Colombo to join up, and in the same year was drafted to the Western Front, where he saw service on many sectors and took part in the battles of Béthune and La Bassée. He also fought in the Retreat and Advance of 1918, and was wounded. On his return to England in 1920 he was demobilised, and holds the General Service and Victory Medals.

10, Portnall Road, Maida Hill, W.9.   X19370B.

STANNARD, L. (Mrs.), (née Streams), Special War Worker.

This lady was engaged at Messrs. Blake's, Shepherd's Bush, on work of national importance, for two years, making pellets and filling shells, and afterwards went to the Hayes Munition Factory, Middlesex, where she cleaned and painted shells. Whilst working at the latter place she met with an accident, as a result of which she had to undergo an operation, and was in hospital for some time.

76, Ancill Street, Hammersmith, W.6.   14003B.

STANNARD, S. R., Lieut., 3rd Essex Regiment.

He joined in 1916, and served with distinction in many engagements on the Western Front, where he was wounded during the last offensive. During part of his service he acted as Lewis-gun instructor at Hythe. He was demobilised in 1919, and holds the General Service and Victory Medals.

10, Portnall Road, Maida Hill, W.9.   X19370A.

STANNARD, W. A., Pte., Royal Fusiliers.

He joined in 1916, and after his training served at various stations on important duties with his unit. He was unable to obtain a transfer overseas, and after rendering valuable services was discharged in 1917 medically unfit.

76, Ancill Street, Hammersmith, W.6.   14003A.

STANNARD, W. E., Sergt., 1st Border Regiment.

Being in the Army, he was sent at the outbreak of war to the Western Front, where he took part in all the earlier engagements, and was wounded on the Somme. Later he was drafted to the Dardanelles, and whilst in the heavy fighting was again wounded. He holds the Mons Star and the General Service and Victory Medals, and was still serving in 1920.

29, Disraeli Road, Acton Lane, N.W.10.   14156.

STANNERS, A. E., Pte., 2/5 Manchester Regt.

Joining in 1916, he was drafted to the Western Front in the following year. Whilst abroad he was engaged in many of the important battles, including those of Passchendaele, Bullecourt, Ypres and the Somme, and was wounded on three occasions. After the cessation of hostilities he returned to England, and was demobilised in January 1919, holding the General Service and Victory Medals.

59, Deacon Road, Cricklewood, N.W.2.   17360A.

STANNERS, F. W., Bombardier, R.F.A.

He volunteered in September 1914, and in the same year was sent to France, where he took part in many important engagements. In 1916 he was drafted to Salonika, and was in action during the Balkan Campaign, and suffered from malaria. On recovery he returned to France, and fought in the Retreat and Advance of 1918 on the Cambrai Front. He was demobilised in June 1919, holding the 1914 Star and the General Service and Victory Medals.

59, Deacon Road, Cricklewood, N.W.2.   17360B.

STANSBY, A. J., Pte., Essex Regiment.

He joined in 1916, and after a year's training was drafted to the Western Front. After taking part in several engagements he was killed in action on September 26th, 1917. He was entitled to the General Service and Victory Medals.

1, Abbotsbury, Ambleside Road,
Willesden, N.W.10.   16122C.

STANSBY, C. S., Pte., Royal Fusiliers.

He volunteered in 1915, and in the following year was sent to France, where he took part in many engagements, and was wounded on two occasions. He also fought in the Retreat and Advance of 1918, and after the signing of the Armistice was engaged on important duties until he returned home and was demobilised in 1919. He holds the General Service and Victory Medals.

1, Abbotsbury, Ambleside Road,
Willesden, N.W.10.   16122A.

STANSBY, W. J., Corporal, Sherwood Foresters.

He was in the Army at the outbreak of war, and in 1914 was drafted to France, where he remained for a year. Whilst overseas he was in action on many occasions, and in March 1915 was killed during the Battle of Neuve Chapelle. He was entitled to the 1914 Star and the General Service and Victory Medals.

1, Abbotsbury, Ambleside Road,
Willesden, N.W.10.   16122B.

STANTON, A., Pte., Middlesex Regiment.

He volunteered in June 1915, and after his training was sent to the Western Front. He took part in much of the heavy fighting on the Somme sector, and on two occasions was wounded. Later he was drafted to Russia, where he was also in action. He was still serving in 1920, and holds the General Service and Victory Medals.

17, Harton Road, Lower Edmonton, N.9.   13029.

STANTON, E., Pte., 10th Queen's Own (Royal West Kent Regiment).

He joined in December 1917, and in the following year was sent to France, where he was in action at Cambrai during the Retreat and Advance of 1918. After the Armistice he went into Germany with the Army of Occupation. He returned to England for demobilisation in November 1919, and holds the General Service and Victory Medals.

51, Carlyle Avenue, Willesden, N.W.10.   14196.

STANTON, S. J. H., Gnr., Royal Horse Artillery.

He joined in May 1916, and in the same year was sent to the Western Front, where he took a prominent part as a signaller in the battles of Arras, Passchendaele, St. Quentin and Péronne. He was demobilised in February 1919, and holds the General Service and Victory Medals.

32, Windermere Avenue, Queen's Park, N.W.6.   X20676.

STANTON, W. E., Sapper, R.E. (R.O.D.).
He joined in 1917, and in the same year was sent to France, where he was engaged on various duties in connection with railway transport. During his two years' service he was employed on many sectors of the Western Front, and was also present during the battles of the Somme, Cambrai, Bapaume, Arras and Ypres. He was demobilised in 1919, holding the General Service and Victory Medals.
3, Kenmont Gardens, College Park, N.W.10.   X17449A.

STAPLES, H. H., Corpl., 1st Buffs (East Kent Regiment).
Having joined the Army in June 1912, he was drafted to France on the outbreak of war. Whilst on the Western Front he took part in the memorable Retreat from Mons, the first and second battles of Ypres, the battles of the Somme, Cambrai, the Aisne, the Marne and St. Quentin, and was wounded on two occasions. He holds the Mons Star and the General Service and Victory Medals, and was still serving in 1920.
31, Rucklidge Avenue, Harlesden, N.W.10.   T12756B.

STAPLES, T. H.V., Gnr., Royal Garrison Artillery.
He volunteered in November 1914, and during his service in France took part in the battles of Arras and the Somme. In 1917 he was invalided home, owing to ill-health, and served on special duties until his demobilisation in June 1919. He holds the 1914–15 Star and the General Service and Victory Medals.
11, Shrewsbury Road, Harlesden, N.W.10.   14130.

STAWELL, J. S., Pte., 8th Devonshire Regiment.
He joined in March 1916, and served on the Western Front, where he took a prominent part in many engagements and was severely wounded on the Somme in July 1917. He was in hospital in France and Scotland, where his right arm was amputated, and as a result he was discharged as unfit for further service in December 1918. He holds the General Service and Victory Medals.
30, Kingwood Road, Fulham, S.W.6.   X19019.

STEAN, J., Sergeant, Scots Guards.
Having enlisted in June 1901, he was sent at the outbreak of war to the Western Front, where he served with distinction in the battles of Neuve Chapelle, Ypres, Loos, the Somme, Arras, Vimy Ridge and Cambrai, and several minor operations. He was still serving in 1920, and holds the 1914 Star and the General Service and Victory Medals.
188, Shirland Road, Maida Hill, W.9.   X19598.

STEBBINGS, H. L., Pte., The Queen's (Royal West Surrey Regiment).
He volunteered in March 1915, and after his training was sent to the Western Front. Whilst in France he took part in the heavy fighting on the Somme sector, and in the battles of Ypres and Cambrai. He was killed in action at High Wood on July 21st, 1916, and was entitled to the General Service and Victory Medals.
35, Claxton Grove, Hammersmith, W.6.   13673.

STEED, E. (Mrs.), (O.B.E.), Special War Worker.
For three years during the war this lady was employed on important work at Messrs. Sparklet's Munition Factory in connection with the making of bullets. She was presented with the insignia of the O.B.E. by the Duke of Bedford at the Guildhall, in recognition of her valuable services.
180, Dyson's Road, Upper Edmonton, N.18.   16555.

STEED, E. G., Pte., Royal Army Service Corps.
He joined in January 1918, immediately on attaining military age, and was engaged on important transport duties. He did much valuable work during his service, but was not able to obtain his transfer overseas, and was demobilised in February 1919.
44, Bloemfontein Road, Shepherd's Bush, W.12.   12053.

STEEL, E. J., Pte., Royal Army Service Corps.
Volunteering in March 1915, he was soon sent to the Western Front, where he gave valuable services during the remainder of the war. He holds the 1914–15 Star and the General Service and Victory Medals, and was demobilised in January 1919.
120, Townmead Road, Fulham, S.W.6.   X21098.

STEEL, E. W. J., Gunner, Royal Marine Artillery.
He joined in August 1918, and after his training served at various stations with his unit. He gave valuable services, but was not successful in obtaining his transfer overseas before the cessation of hostilities. He was still serving in 1920.
120, Townmead Road, Fulham, S.W.6.   X21102.

STEEL, G. A., Pte., Royal Army Service Corps.
He volunteered in March 1915, and in the same year was sent to the Western Front, where for the first two years of his service he was engaged on transport work. Later he was transferred to the R.G.A. and served as a gunner. He was in action at Neuve Chapelle, Hill 60, Festubert, Loos, the Somme, Vimy Ridge and during the Advance of 1918, and was wounded. He holds the 1914–15 Star and the General Service and Victory Medals, and was demobilised in March 1919.
62, Langford Road, Fulham, S.W.6.   X21279.

STEEL, K. F. (Miss), Special War Worker.
During the war this lady offered her services at the Gas Light and Coke Company, Nine Elms Lane, where she was employed on yard work and delivering coke, thus releasing a man for military duties. She gave valuable assistance for over two years, and carried out her work in a satisfactory manner.
62, Langford Road, Fulham, S.W.6.   X21466A.

STEEL, W. A., Special War Worker.
During the war he was engaged on work of national importance at Messrs. Crossley's, Imperial Road, Fulham, where he rendered valuable services in the forging of shoes for Army horses. He carried out his duties in a most satisfactory manner.
62, Langford Road, Fulham, S.W.6.   X21466B.

STEEL, W. S., Corporal, Royal Marines.
He volunteered for service in March 1915, and in the same year was sent to France, where he was engaged on important dockyard work. After nearly four years' service abroad he was demobilised in March 1919, holding the 1914–15 Star and the General Service and Victory Medals.
54, Townmead Road, Fulham, S.W.6.   X21099.

STEELE, A. G., Lce.-Corpl., East Surrey Regt.
He joined in April 1917, and during his service on the Western Front took part in the battles of Arras and Cambrai. Whilst in action at Ypres he was severely wounded, and invalided home. On his recovery he was retained as a musketry instructor until his demobilisation in February 1919. He holds the General Service and Victory Medals.
28, Deacon Road, Cricklewood, N.W.2.   16136.

STEELE, J. A., C.Q.M.S., The Queen's (Royal West Surrey Regiment).
He joined in November 1916, and in the following year was sent to the Western Front, where he took part in the Retreat and Advance, and was wounded and gassed at Beaumont Hamel. He holds the General Service and Victory Medals, and was demobilised in November 1919.
90, Lancefield Street, North Kensington, W.10.   X19984.

STENNING, H., Pte., Leinster Regiment.
Being already in the Army in August 1914, he served first at the Dardanelles and later in France, where he took part in the battles of Ypres, Arras and the Somme. In December 1917 he was killed in action, after more than ten years' service. He was entitled to the 1914–15 Star and the General Service and Victory Medals.
24, Mulgrave Road, Fulham, S.W.6.   16171B.

STENT, W., Driver, Royal Field Artillery.
He volunteered in August 1914, and in the same year was drafted to the Eastern Front. During his service in Mesopotamia he took part in the fighting on the Tigris, and was in action in many engagements. He was also stationed for a time in Egypt, before he returned to England, and was discharged in September 1919 as medically unfit owing to heart trouble. He holds the 1914–15 Star and the General Service and Victory Medals.
71, Raynham Road, Upper Edmonton, N.18.   16952.

STEPHENS, H. J., Rifleman, 6th London Regt. (Rifles).
He volunteered in June 1915, and served on the Western Front, where he took part in much of the heavy fighting up to November 1917, when he was wounded in action and taken prisoner at Cambrai. He was held captive by the enemy for six months, when, after suffering much ill-treatment, he was exchanged. He was discharged in September 1918 as medically unfit for further military duties, and holds the General Service and Victory Medals.
56, West Street, Lower Edmonton, N.9.   T14596.

STEPHENS, W. T., Pte., Machine Gun Corps.
Joining in September 1916, he was quickly sent to the Western Front, where he took part in several engagements. After being severely wounded at Arras, he was discharged as unfit in October 1918, holding the General Service and Victory Medals.
13, Alexandra Road, West Kensington, W.14.   12094.

STEPNEY, J. H., Sergeant, 1/28th London Regt. (Artists' Rifles).

He joined in August 1916, and after his training was sent to the Western Front. After taking part in many important engagements he was seriously wounded, and died from the effects in France on August 22nd, 1918. He was entitled to the General Service and Victory Medals.

37, Purcell Crescent, Fulham, S.W.6.   15168A

STEPTO, J. R., Rifleman, 5th London Regiment (London Rifle Brigade).

He volunteered for duty in August 1914, and after completing his training served on the Western Front, where he saw much fighting on the Somme. He was invalided home suffering from shell-shock, and later was drafted to Egypt. In April 1917 he was discharged as medically unfit owing to shell-shock, and holds the General Service and Victory Medals

46, Winchester Road, Lower Edmonton, N.9.   14860.

STEPTOE, F. T., Pte., 16th Essex Regiment.

He joined in February 1916, and was drafted five months later to the Western Front, where he took part in several engagements, including those at Cambrai. He was demobilised in October 1919 on his return to England, and holds the General Service and Victory Medals.

1, Norfolk Road, Willesden, N.W.10.   14928.

STEVENS, A. T., Pte., 13th London Regiment (Kensington).

Volunteering in September 1914, he was drafted to the Western Front immediately on the completion of his training. He fought with distinction on various sectors, and was severely wounded in an engagement at Vimy Ridge in July 1917. After being for a time in hospital in England he was demobilised in April 1919, and holds the 1914–15 Star and the General Service and Victory Medals.

42, Wilson's Road, Hammersmith, W.6.   15857.

STEVENS, A. W., Gunner, Machine Gun Corps.

He volunteered in August 1914, and was engaged on important duties as a machine-gun instructor at various stations. He did excellent work throughout his service, although he was unable to obtain his transfer overseas, and was eventually demobilised in November 1919.

132, Shakespeare Avenue, Willesden, N.W.10.   13895B.

STEVENS, B., Pte., 13th Middlesex Regiment.

Volunteering in April 1915, he was sent to the Western Front in November. After taking part in many important engagements and fighting on various sectors, he was killed in action on the Somme on December 1st, 1916. He was entitled to the 1914–15 Star and the General Service and Victory Medals.

69A, Deacon Road, Cricklewood, N.W.2.   17363B.

STEVENS, E. A., Pte., R.A.S.C. (M.T.).

He joined in May 1917, and was sent to France in the following month. He was engaged on important duties with the Mechanical Transport on many sectors of the Front, and served on the Somme, and at Ypres, Arras, Amiens and Albert. In 1919 he returned to England, and in October of that year was demobilised, holding the General Service and Victory Medals.

6, Belton Road, Cricklewood, N.W.2.   16599.

STEVENS, E. T. J., Driver, R.A.S.C.

He joined in 1918, and during his service in France was attached to the First Cavalry Division, following behind the line on transport duties. After taking part in the Advance of 1918, he was sent to Cologne with the Army of Occupation. He was demobilised in 1919, and holds the General Service and Victory Medals.

18, May Street, West Kensington, W.14.   15891.

STEVENS, F., Pioneer, R.E. (R.O.D.).

He joined on attaining military age in July 1918, and was immediately sent to the Western Front, where he was engaged on various important duties with the Railway Operative Department until the cessation of hostilities. He then went into Germany with the Army of Occupation, with which he served until his return to England in 1919. In May he was demobilised, holding the General Service and Victory Medals.

56, Fordingley Road, Maida Hill, W.9.   TX19671.

STEVENS, G., Corporal, Royal Irish Rifles.

He volunteered for duty in September 1914, and was drafted to the Western Front on completing his training. After seeing much fighting in various engagements he was killed in action at Hooge on September 25th, 1915. He was entitled to the 1914–15 Star and the General Service and Victory Medals.

35, Garvan Road, Hammersmith, W.6.   14834A.

STEVENS, G., Pte., Queen's Own (Royal West Kent Regiment).

He joined in July 1916, and in the following November was sent to the Western Front. There he saw fighting on many sectors, and took part in the battles of the Somme, Arras and Cambrai. He was demobilised on his return to England in February 1919, and holds the General Service and Victory Medals.

79, Minet Avenue, Willesden, N.W.10.   13643.

STEVENS, G. S., Pte., 6th Northamptonshire Regt.

Joining in February 1917, he was drafted to the Western Front, but in March 1918 he was taken prisoner on the Somme. After twelve months internment in Germany he was released, and in September 1919 was demobilised, holding the General Service and Victory Medals.

25, Farm Lane, Walham Green, S.W.6.   X19492.

STEVENS, H., Shoeing Smith, R.F.A.

He volunteered in July 1915, and during his service on the Western Front saw much service on various sectors. He took part in the engagements at the Somme, Arras, Ypres, St. Quentin, Armentieres, Bullecourt, Monchy, Givenchy and Cambrai, and also fought in the Retreat and Advance of 1918. He was demobilised in 1919, and holds the 1914–15 Star and the General Service and Victory Medals.

22, Archel Road, West Kensington, W.14.   16204.

STEVENS, J. E., Pte., 13th Middlesex Regiment.

He volunteered in September 1914, and was sent to France in the following year. After taking a prominent part in the fighting on many sectors, he was so severely wounded whilst in action at Kemmel Hill, that it necessitated the amputation of both legs. He was consequently discharged as physically unfit in May 1917. He holds the 1914–15 Star and the General Service and Victory Medals.

37, Nursery Street, Tottenham, N.17.   X18149.

STEVENS, S. E., Corpl., Royal Garrison Artillery.

Volunteering in October 1915, he was drafted to Salonika in the following year on the completion of his training. He took part in various engagements during the Balkan Campaign, but later was invalided home suffering from a severe form of malaria. He was demobilised in February 1919, and holds the General Service and Victory Medals.

12, Bruce Castle Road, Tottenham, N.17.   18553.

STEVENS, W., Pte., Royal Army Service Corps.

He volunteered in April 1915, and in the following August was sent to France, where he was engaged on important duties with the Remount Section on many sectors of the Front. He served at Ypres, Arras and on the Somme before the cessation of hostilities, and then went with the Army of Occupation into Germany. He returned to England and was demobilised in May 1919, and holds the 1914–15 Star and the General Service and Victory Medals.

29, Hiley Road, Willesden, N.W.10.   X18240A.

STEVENS, W. H., 1st Class Stoker, Royal Navy, H.M.S. " Skirmisher."

He joined in February 1918, and served with the North Russian Expeditionary Force. He was also stationed for a time in Turkey, where he was engaged on important duties at Constantinople. He was demobilised in May 1919, on his return to England, and holds the General Service and Victory Medals.

29, Hiley Road, Willesden, N.W.10.   X18240B.

STEVENS, W. M., Pte., Tank Corps.

He joined up on attaining military age in August 1918, but was unsuccessful in obtaining his transfer overseas before the signing of the Armistice. On the completion of his training, however, he was drafted to the Western Front, where he was engaged on various important duties for a time. He was still serving in the Army in 1920.

69A, Deacon Road, Cricklewood, N.W.2.   17363A.

STEVENSON, E., Sergeant, Machine Gun Corps.

He volunteered for duty in August 1914, and after completing his training was sent to the Western Front, where he took part in most of the principal engagements on the Somme sector. He fought with distinction in France up to the date of the Armistice, after which he went into Germany with the Army of Occupation. He was still with his unit in 1920, and holds the General Service and Victory Medals.

29, Barbot Street, Lower Edmonton, N.9.   14588.

STEVENSON, F. W., Mechanic, R.A.F. (late Royal Flying Corps.)
He volunteered in 1915, and was sent in the same year to the Western Front, where he took part in engagements at Ypres, Arras and the Somme. During his service he performed duties of a highly technical nature, but suffered from exposure. He was demobilised in 1919, and holds the 1914-15 Star, General Service and Victory Medals.
15A, Furness Road, Harlesden, N.W.10. 13095.

STEVENSON, P., Pte., Middlesex Regiment.
He joined in June 1916, and in the following February was sent out to France. He took part in many important engagements during his service on the Western Front, and was wounded in action. After much valuable service he returned to England, and was demobilised in September 1919, holding the General Service and Victory Medals.
145, Park Terrace, Stonebridge, N.W.10. 15802C.

STEVENSON, R., Rifleman, K.R.R.
He joined in April 1916, and was sent to France, where he was retained on important duties at Havre owing to his being physically unfit for service in the firing-line. He holds the General Service and Victory Medals, and was demobilised in March 1919.
15, New King's Road, Fulham, S.W.6. X19938.

STEVENSON, S., Pte., Royal Fusiliers.
He volunteered in May 1915, and in the same year went to the Western Front, where he saw much service. He took part in the battles of Neuve Chapelle, Ypres, St. Eloi, the Somme and Arras, and was three times wounded and twice gassed. He was invalided to hospital at Boulogne, and thence home, and was demobilised in February 1919, holding the 1914-15 Star and the General Service and Victory Medals.
8, Hampden Street, Paddington, W.2. X21605.

STEWART, A. G., Pte., 23rd Middlesex Regiment, and Sapper, Royal Engineers.
He volunteered in April 1915, and was immediately drafted to the Western Front, where he took part in the fighting on various sectors. He was in action at Ypres, Armentieres, Neuve Chapelle, Lille, Vimy Ridge and St. Quentin, and was severely wounded at Ypres. He was also wounded and buried alive by an explosion on two occasions, at Delville Wood and Bullecourt. He was demobilised in July 1919, and holds the 1914-15 Star and the General Service and Victory Medals.
24, Montgomery Street, Hammersmith, W.6. 15879A.

STEWART, E. A. (Mrs.), Special War Worker.
During the war this lady was engaged on work of great national importance. She first held a responsible post at Messrs. Blake's Factory, Fulham, where she rendered valuable services on important duties in connection with the output of shells. She resigned in order to take up work at Messrs. Du Cros', Acton, where she was engaged on similar duties, and by her good work proved herself worthy of high commendation. Her right hand was severely injured in an accident in which it was crushed between two shells, and the amputation of her finger was rendered necessary.
24, Montgomery Street, Hammersmith, W.6. 15879B.

STEWART, G. J., Corporal, Royal Engineers.
He joined in July 1917, and after his training served at various stations on important clerical duties. He gave valuable services, but was not successful in obtaining his transfer overseas before the cessation of hostilities. He was demobilised in December 1919.
18A, Furness Road, Fulham, S.W.6. X21428.

STEWART, S., 1st Air Mechanic, Royal Air Force.
He joined in January 1916, and in the following year was sent to France, where he served at Dunkirk and was engaged on important and skilful work connected with the construction of aeroplanes. He was demobilised in March 1919, holding the General Service and Victory Medals.
18, Furness Road, Fulham, S.W.6. X21427.

STICKLER, C. W., Pte., Royal Fusiliers.
Volunteering at the outbreak of war, he served in turn in Malta, Egypt, the Dardanelles, Salonika and the Western Front. Whilst in France he played a prominent part at Ypres, Albert, Cambrai and in the second battle of the Marne. After fighting through the Advance of 1918, he was sent home, and in January 1919 was demobilised, holding the 1914-15 Star and the General Service and Victory Medals.
17, Senior Street, Paddington, W.2. Xa1896.

STICKLEY, W., Rifleman, Rifle Brigade.
He joined in June 1916, and in the same year was drafted to France, where he took a prominent part in the Battle of Loos and was severely wounded. He was invalided home and on his recovery was sent to Ireland. After serving there for a short time, he returned to England and was discharged as physically unfit for further military service in September 1918. He holds the General Service and Victory Medals.
38, Senior Street, Paddington, W.2. X21559.

STIDWORTHY, H. L. (M.M.), Sergt., 1st Royal Fusiliers.
He volunteered in August 1914, and in the same year was sent to Egypt and later to Salonika, where he took part in many engagements. He was awarded the Military Medal for conspicuous bravery in the field, and during his service was wounded in action. He holds the 1914-15 Star and the Victory and General Service Medals, and was demobilised in October 1919.
3, Gloucester Road, Upper Edmonton, N.18. X17277

STILL, C. P., Gunner, Royal Field Artillery.
He volunteered in 1915, and during his service on the Western Front took a prominent part in several engagements, including those at Loos, Ypres and Neuve Chapelle. Later he was sent to the Balkans, and was in action on the Doiran and Struma sectors. After his return to England he was demobilised in February 1919, and holds the 1914-15 Star and the General Service and Victory Medals.
27, Hiley Road, Willesden, N.W.10. X18245.

STILLMAN, C. B., Pte., Bedfordshire Regiment.
He joined in April 1917, and after completing his training was engaged on important duties at various stations, not being able to obtain his transfer overseas until after the signing of the Armistice. He was then sent to Germany where he served with the Army of Occupation until his return to England for demobilisation in November 1919.
77, Lorenco Road, Tottenham, N.17. 18397A.

STILLMAN, H., Rifleman, 1/5th London Regiment (London Rifle Brigade).
He was mobilised in August 1914, and on the completion of his training was sent to the Western Front in the following year. After taking part in many important engagements he was reported missing and finally as killed in action on the Somme in September 1916. He was entitled to the 1914-15 Star and the General Service and Victory Medals.
77, Lorenco Road, Tottenham, N.17. 18397B.

STILLWELL, G., Sapper, Royal Engineers.
He joined in May 1916, and in the same year was sent to the Western Front. He served with distinction in the battles of the Somme, Ypres and Arras, and was wounded and suffered from shell-shock. In 1919 he returned to England and was demobilised holding the General Service and Victory Medals.
2A, Hazlebury Road, Fulham, S.W.6. X20512.

STILWELL, F., Corpl., 10th Middlesex Regiment.
He volunteered for duty in November 1914, and after his training served on the Eastern Front. He was first sent to Egypt, and was later transferred to Gallipoli, where he took part in much of the fighting until invalided home with dysentery. Later he was engaged on important duties at various stations and in 1919 was demobilised, holding the 1914-15 Star and the General Service and Victory Medals.
19, Letterstone Road, Fulham, S.W.6. 18445B.

STIMPSON, J., Pte., Machine Gun Corps.
He joined the East Surrey Regiment in August 1914 and was later transferred to the Machine Gun Corps. During his four years' service on the Western Front he took part in many engagements, including those of Ypres, Bullecourt, Albert, St. Quentin, Bourlon Wood, Arras, Valenciennes, and the Somme, and was wounded four times and gassed. He holds the 1914-15 Star and the General Service and Victory Medals, and was demobilised on April 1st, 1919.
21, Field Road, Hammersmith, W.6. 15772.

STIMPSON, J. S., Sergt., Royal Garrison Artillery.
He joined in August 1914, and was sent to France, where he took part in engagements on the Somme, at Arras, Ypres, Passchendaele and Vimy Ridge, and was wounded at Cambrai in December 1917. He holds the 1914-15 Star and the General Service and Victory Medals, and was discharged in August 1918 through ill-health.
77, Archel Road, West Kensington, W.14. 16655.

STINTON, W., Sapper, Royal Engineers.
He joined in February 1917, and after his training was drafted to the Western Front, where he was engaged on special duties during operations at Ypres, Cambrai and the Somme and was wounded. He holds the General Service and Victory Medals, and was demobilised in December 1919.
105, Denmark Road, Kilburn, N.W.6.   X17439A.

STOCK, N., Leading Seaman, Royal Navy.
He enlisted in the Royal Navy four years before the outbreak of war, and was sent with his ship, H.M.S. "Barham," to the North Sea with the Grand Fleet, where he was engaged on important duties. His ship also took part in the Battle of Jutland, and he was severely wounded and invalided to hospital in England. He holds the 1914 Star and the General Service and Victory Medals, and in 1920 was still serving.
31, Argyle Road, Upper Edmonton, N.18.   15267.

STOCKER, F. C., Pte., Machine Gun Corps.
He volunteered in March 1915, and in the same year was sent to the Western Front, where he saw much heavy fighting. He took part in the battles of the Somme, Ypres and Loos, and was wounded. In February 1919 he was demobilised, and holds the 1914–15 Star and the General Service and Victory Medals.
18, Lodge Avenue, Fulham Road, S.W.6.   X20108.

STOCKER, G., Pte., 9th South Staffordshire Regt.
He joined in 1916, and after his training was drafted to France, where he served until 1917. He was then sent to Italy and for two years acted as cook, in which capacity he proved invaluable. He returned to England in 1919, when he was demobilised, holding the General Service and Victory Medals.
71, Hartington Road, Tottenham, N.17.   X19145.

STOCKFORD, J. E., Leading Seaman, Royal Navy.
He joined in February 1916, and served in various seas. Whilst in the Mediterranean he was in H.M.S. "Sarnia," when she was torpedoed and sunk in September 1918, but after being in the water for over forty-eight hours he was rescued. In January 1919 he was demobilised, and holds the General Service and Victory Medals.
131, Rucklidge Avenue, Harlesden, N.W.10.   13158B.

STOCKFORD, J. W., Physical Training Instructor, Royal Navy.
He joined in January 1918, and after his training served at the Crystal Palace. Owing to his special qualifications he was retained as a physical training instructor until hostilities ceased. He gave valuable services, and was demobilised in January 1919.
131, Rucklidge Avenue, Harlesden, N.W.10.   13158C.

STOCKFORD, W. J., Pte., 9th Royal Sussex Regt.
He volunteered in August 1914, and was sent to the Western Front in the following year. After taking part in several important engagements, including the Battle of Ypres, he was killed in action on the Somme on August 18th, 1916. He was entitled to the 1914–15 Star and the General Service and Victory Medals.
131, Rucklidge Avenue, Harlesden, N.W.10.   13158A.

STOCKWELL, C., Sapper, Royal Engineers.
He volunteered in 1915, and after taking part in the battles of the Somme, Arras, Loos, Ypres and Cambrai on the Western Front, was killed near Dickebusch on April 20th, 1918. He was entitled to the 1914–15 Star and the General Service and Victory Medals.
60, Oldfield Road, Willesden, N.W.10.   15764B.

STODDART, E., Pte., 5th East Surrey Regiment.
He joined in January 1916, and in the same year proceeded to France, where he saw active service at Cambrai and St. Quentin. He was demobilised in February 1920, holding the General Service and Victory Medals.
152, Town Road, Lower Edmonton, N.9.   13586.

STOKES, A. J., Pte., Royal Army Medical Corps.
He volunteered in January 1915, and was drafted to Egypt in the same year. During his service in this theatre of war he was engaged on important duties in connection with dentistry in various hospitals. He returned to England after the Armistice, and was demobilised in April 1920, holding the 1914–15 Star and the General Service and Victory Medals.
36, Waldo Road, College Park, N.W.10.   X17563.

STOKES, E. C., Rifleman, K.R.R.
Volunteering for duty in August 1914, he took a prominent part in the fighting on the Western Front, being present at the Retreat from Mons and the battles of the Marne, Somme, Ypres and Arras. He was taken prisoner in 1916, and after his release was demobilised in December 1919, holding the Mons Star and the General Service and Victory Medals.
2, Windsor Gardens, Maida Hill, W.9.   X21392.

STOKES, F., Gunner, Royal Garrison Artillery.
He volunteered in October 1914, and after his training served at various stations on important duties with his unit. He gave valuable services, but was not successful in obtaining his transfer overseas before the cessation of hostilities, and was demobilised in February 1919.
54, Bulow Road, Fulham, S.W.6.   X20730A.

STOKES, W. F., Pte. and Driver, 4th East Surrey Regiment and R.A.S.C. (M.T.).
Volunteering in September 1914, he was sent in the following year to France, where he saw fighting at Loos. Later he was drafted to Salonika, but on contracting malaria there was invalided home. In 1917 he was transferred to the R.A.S.C. as a lorry driver, and sent again to the Western Front. After taking part in engagements on the Somme, at Arras and during the Advance of 1918, he served in Germany with the Army of Occupation until March 1919, when he was demobilised, holding the 1914–15 Star and the General Service and Victory Medals.
71, Mayo Road, Willesden, N.W.10.   15557.

STONE, A. V., Pte., 1st Wiltshire Regiment.
Volunteering in August 1914, he proceeded to the Western Front at the conclusion of his training, and was in action in many of the important engagements in this theatre of war before the cessation of hostilities. He was wounded twice, and in July 1919 was demobilised, holding the 1914–15 Star and the General Service and Victory Medals.
42, Delorme Street, Hammersmith, W.6.   14085.

STONE, C. J., Pte., Royal Army Service Corps.
He joined in November 1916, and was drafted overseas in the following year. He was engaged on important duties in connection with the transport of ammunition and supplies to the forward areas of the Western Front, and was in action at Ypres (1917) and Cambrai (1918). He was demobilised in March 1920, and holds the General Service and Victory Medals.
232, Town Road, Lower Edmonton, N.9.   13577A.

STONE, E. (Mrs.), Special War Worker.
From February 1916 until the conclusion of hostilities this lady was engaged on important work at Fulham in connection with the manufacture of aircraft. She carried out the responsible duties assigned to her in a highly commendable manner.
38, Edbrooke Road, Maida Hill, W.9.   X21548.

STONE, E. R., Stoker, Royal Navy.
He joined the Navy in November 1916, and served on special duties with his ship in the North Sea. In December 1916 the vessel struck a mine, and sank with all hands. He was entitled to the General Service and Victory Medals.
232, Town Road, Lower Edmonton, N.9.   13577B.

STONE, F., Pte., Bedfordshire Regiment.
He volunteered in August 1915, and at the conclusion of his training served at various stations on important duties until 1917, when he proceeded to Palestine, and was present at many important engagements, including the capture of Jerusalem. Suffering from malaria, he returned to England, and was eventually demobilised in February 1919, holding the General Service and Victory Medals.
5, Litchfield Gardens, Willesden, N.W.10.   X17430.

STONE, G., Steward, Royal Navy.
He joined in 1917, and after his training served with his ship, which was engaged on important duties in the North Sea with the Grand Fleet until after the cessation of hostilities. He holds the General Service and Victory Medals, and in 1920 was still serving.
232, Town Road, Lower Edmonton, N.9.   13577D.

STONE, H. C., Lce.-Corpl., 1st Royal Irish Fus.
He joined in April 1916, and in the following year proceeded to the Western Front, where, after taking part in many of the principal engagements, he was killed in action at Cambrai on October 1st, 1918. He was entitled to the General Service and Victory Medals.
53, Southerton Road, Hammersmith, W.6.   11147.

STONE, H. E., Pte., Royal Irish Fusiliers.
He enlisted in December 1914, and began his service in France in February 1916. He took part in many engagements, and was severely wounded in action at Arras in March 1918. In the following month he died in hospital in England from the effects of his wounds. He was entitled to the General Service and Victory Medals.
15, Dyson's Road, Upper Edmonton, N.18.   T16854C.

STONE, J., Pte., Royal Army Service Corps.
He joined in August 1914, and in that year crossed to France, where he served during the Retreat from Mons and in other important engagements, and was wounded. He was discharged in May 1917 owing to ill-health, and holds the Mons Star, and the General Service and Victory Medals.
108, Farm Lane, Walham Green, S.W.6.　　　X19633.

STONE, J. D., Rifleman, 8th London Regiment (P.O. Rifles).
He joined in November 1917, and on completion of his training was sent overseas. During his service on the Western Front he was in action in much of the heavy fighting, and was wounded. He holds the General Service and Victory Medals, and was demobilised in February 1919.
10, Chancellor's Street, Hammersmith, W.6.　　　13264.

STONE, J. H., Pte., Bedfordshire Regiment.
He joined in June 1918, and after his training served at various stations with his unit until March 1919, when he was sent to Germany with the Army of Occupation. He returned to England in July 1919, and was demobilised.
42, Delorme Street, Hammersmith, W.6.　　　14091.

STONE, P. J., Pte., 2/7th Middlesex Regiment.
He volunteered in September 1914, and in the following year proceeded to Egypt. He was in action during much of the fighting in this theatre of war, and was later drafted to France, where he was taken prisoner. He remained in captivity until the Armistice, and then returned to England and was demobilised in December 1918, holding the 1914-15 Star and the General Service and Victory Medals.
19, Gloucester Road, Upper Edmonton, N.18.　　　X17175.

STONE, W. A., Pte., Royal Fusiliers.
He volunteered in September 1914, and in the following year was drafted to France. During his service on the Western Front he was in action at the battles of Ypres, the Somme and Cambrai, and was wounded three times. He holds the 1914-15 Star and the General Service and Victory Medals, and was demobilised in January 1919.
232, Town Road, Lower Edmonton, N.9.　　　13577C.

STONELAKE, H., Driver, L Battery, R.H.A.
He was serving at the outbreak of war, and was speedily drafted to the Western Front in August 1914. He took part in the Retreat from Mons, the battles of the Somme, Ypres and Cambrai, and in many important engagements throughout the duration of the war, and was wounded in November 1916 on the Ancre Front. In May 1919 he was demobilised, and holds the Mons Star and the General Service and Victory Medals.
20, Swinbrook Road, North Kensington, W.10.　　　X21231.

STONEMAN, F., Driver, Royal Field Artillery.
He joined in April 1915, and was sent to the Western Front in the following December. After taking part in several engagements, he was killed in action at Ypres on September 18th, 1917. He was entitled to the 1914-15 Star and the General Service and Victory Medals.
119, Shakespeare Avenue, Willesden, N.W.10.　　　13695B.

STONEMAN, J., Driver, Royal Field Artillery.
Volunteering in August 1914, he was sent to France in the following May, and took part in several engagements, including the battles of Arras, the Somme and Ypres. He was demobilised in July 1919, and holds the 1914-15 Star and the General Service and Victory Medals.
119, Shakespeare Avenue, Willesden, N.W.10.　　　13695A.

STONEMAN, L., Pte., 1st Queen's Own (Royal West Kent Regiment).
He joined in April 1917, and after completing his training was drafted overseas in the following year. He served in many engagements during the Retreat and Advance of 1918, and after the Armistice was sent to India, where, in 1920, he was still serving. He holds the General Service and Victory Medals.
119, Shakespeare Avenue, Willesden, N.W.10.　　　13696.

STONER, C. R., Pte., Royal Fusiliers.
He volunteered in April 1915, and in the same year proceeded to France, where he took part in several engagements, including those at Loos, the Somme, Ypres and Cambrai, and was wounded. In February 1919 he was demobilised, holding the 1914-15 Star and the General Service and Victory Medals.
27, Burnthwaite Road, Walham Green, S.W.6.　　　X20084A.

STONER, W. J., Pte., 30th London Regiment.
He joined in June 1918, and after his training served at various stations with his battalion on special duties. He rendered valuable services, but was unsuccessful in obtaining his transfer overseas. He was demobilised in February 1919.
27, Burnthwaite Road, Walham Green, S.W.6.　　　X20084B.

STOPES, A. F., Pte., Queen's Own (Royal West Kent Regiment).
He joined in 1917, and was sent to France the same year. After being in action in several engagements on this Front, he was drafted in 1918 to Egypt, where he took part in much of the fighting before the cessation of hostilities. He returned to England in 1919, and was demobilised, holding the General Service and Victory Medals.
4, Wimborne Road, Lower Edmonton, N.9.　　　15209.

STOREY, A., Pte., Bedfordshire Regiment.
He joined, before attaining military age, in July 1918, and after his training served at various stations on important duties with his unit until the cessation of hostilities, when he was drafted to Germany with the Army of Occupation. He returned to England, and was demobilised in November 1919.
3, Worlidge Street, Hammersmith, W.6.　　　12584.

STOREY, A., Pte., Royal Army Service Corps.
He volunteered in March 1915, and served in France, taking part in engagements on the Somme, at Arras and Armentieres. He was afterwards invalided home, and was in hospital for two months before being discharged as medically unfit, owing to ill-health, in 1916. He holds the 1914-15 Star and the General Service and Victory Medals.
23, Wescombe Cottages, King Street,
Hammersmith, W.6.　　　TX18874A.

STOREY, H. E., Sapper, 136th Company, R.E.
He volunteered in April 1915, and a few months later was sent to Egypt, where he was engaged on important work. Later he was drafted to the Western Front, and after taking part in several engagements, was demobilised in February 1919. He holds the 1914-15 Star and the General Service and Victory Medals.
51, Manor Park Road, Harlesden, N.W.10.　　　13220.

STOREY, M. A. (Mrs.), Special War Worker.
During the war this lady was employed by Messrs. Davidson, at their munition factory at Hammersmith, where she was engaged in the manufacture of boxes for packing shells and bombs. Throughout she rendered valuable services, and gave great assistance in this important work.
23, Wescombe Cottages, Hammersmith, W.6. TX18874B.

STOREY, R. L., Corpl., 5th Hampshire Regiment.
Having originally enlisted in 1908, he was mobilised at the declaration of war but, being medically unfit for foreign service, was retained on important duties in the Channel Islands. He was discharged in March 1919, but re-enlisted shortly after in the London Irish Rifles, with which he was serving in 1920.
14, Hartopp Avenue, Dawes Road, S.W.6.　　　X17684B.

STOW, A. H., 1st Air Mechanic, R.A.F. (late R.N.A.S.).
He joined in March 1917, and after his training served at various stations on important duties in connection with the transport of ammunition and supplies. He gave valuable services, but was not successful in securing his transfer overseas before the cessation of hostilities, and was demobilised in June 1919.
63, Fabian Road, Walham Green, S.W.6.　　　X18048.

STOWE, C., Rifleman, King's Royal Rifle Corps.
Volunteering in August 1914, he was sent to the Western Front, where he played a prominent part in the fighting. During his service he was three times wounded, and after being invalided home, was discharged as unfit in December 1918. He holds the 1914-15 Star and the General Service and Victory Medals.
12, Welford Terrace, Dawes Road, S.W.6.　　　X18056.

STOWE, E. (Mrs.), Special War Worker.
For a considerable period of the war this lady was engaged at Messrs. Blake's, Wood Lane, where she rendered valuable service. Her work, in the T.N.T. shop, was of an extremely dangerous nature, and owing to the fumes from the powder she suffered from poisoning. On resigning she was very highly commended for her good work.
47, Clarendon Street, Paddington, W.2.　　　X20405A.

STOWE, H., Pte., The Queen's (Royal West Surrey Regiment).
He joined in July 1918, and in the same year was drafted to the Western Front, where he took a prominent part in the Advance. He was demobilised in January 1919, holding the General Service and Victory Medals.
47, Clarendon Street, Paddington, W.2.　　　X20405B.

STRACHAN, W., Driver, R.A.S.C.
He joined in November 1916, went to the Western Front in the following year, and took part in many engagements, including those of the Somme, Ypres, Cambrai, and the Retreat and Advance of 1918. He was demobilised in June 1919, holding the General Service and Victory Medals.
21, Waldo Road, Willesden, N.W.10. X17626.

STRADLING, W., Stoker, Royal Navy, H.M.S. "Sir John Moore."
He joined the Navy in 1916, and served with the Grand Fleet in the North Sea, taking a prominent part in several engagements, including the raid on Zeebrugge. After three years' service he was demobilised in January 1919, holding the General Service and Victory Medals.
10, Cassidy Road, Walham Green, S.W.6. X20291.

STRANG, J., Driver, R.A.S.C. (H.T.).
He joined in 1914, and was engaged in transport work for three years in Samaria, Baghdad and other places in Palestine and Mesopotamia. In June 1919 he was demobilised, and holds the General Service and Victory Medals.
28, Cooper Road, Dudden Hill, Willesden, N.W.10. 16640.

STRATH, A. H., Leading Seaman, Royal Navy.
He volunteered in August 1914, and served on H.M.S. "Indefatigable" in the Mediterranean and elsewhere. In the fighting at the Dardanelles he was severely wounded, necessitating the amputation of his right hand. He was discharged in consequence in 1915, being incapacitated for further naval service. He holds the 1914-15 Star and the General Service and Victory Medals.
123, Moore Park Road, Fulham, S.W.6. X19702.

STRAUSS, W. E., Pte., 13th Wiltshire Regiment.
He volunteered in August 1914, and saw much service overseas on the Eastern Front, where he took part in the Gallipoli expedition of 1915. On the evacuation of the Peninsula he proceeded to Egypt, and afterwards to Mesopotamia. At the close of hostilities against the Turks he was drafted to India, where he was stationed at Karachi and other places. In 1919 he returned home, and was demobilised, holding the General Service and Victory Medals.
63, Acklan Road, North Kensington, W.10. X21520.

STRAW, L. H., Corpl., King's Royal Rifle Corps.
He joined in August 1915, and in the following year was sent to France, where he remained until 1919, taking part in many engagements, including those of Ypres, Arras and Cambrai. Later he went to Germany with the Army of Occupation. He holds the General Service and Victory Medals, and was demobilised in June 1919.
56, Fordingley Road, Maida Hill, W.9. X19670A.

STREAMES, E. M., Special War Worker.
This lady was employed during the war on the manufacture of soldiers' equipment, and in particular tarring of tents and ground-sheets for use at the Front. She carried out her duties with care and diligence.
68, Ancill Street, Hammersmith, W.6. 14476B.

STREAMES, J., Special War Worker.
He was employed during the war as tool-grinder at the Townmead Engineering Co., and also worked on munitions at Messrs. Pearson & Knowles Munition Factory in Lancashire, in connection with the manufacture of wire for submarines. He remained at his post throughout the duration of the war.
68, Ancill Street, Hammersmith, W.6. 14476C.

STREET, A. J., Gunner, Royal Field Artillery.
He enlisted in November 1914, was sent to France in the following year, and took part in the battles of Ypres (Hill 60), Loos, Cambrai, and in the Retreat and Advance of 1918. He was once gassed. He was demobilised in March 1919, holding the 1914-15 Star, General Service and Victory Medals.
71, Melville Road, Willesden, N.W.10. 14430.

STREETER, E. A., Pte., 3rd London Regiment.
He volunteered in 1915, and during his service on the Western Front took part in operations on practically all sectors. He was killed in action during the final Advance in September 1918, and was buried in the British Cemetery at Epéhy. He was acting as stretcher-bearer at the time. Entitled to the General Service and Victory Medals.
29, Portnall Road, Maida Hill, W.9. X19309.

STREETER, G., Pte., Royal Fusiliers.
He joined in July 1916, was subsequently drafted to the Western Front, and took part in operations there. He was very seriously wounded in action, and died of his wounds in March 1918. He was entitled to the General Service and Victory Medals.
12, Plevna Road, Edmonton, N.18. 14573.

STREETER, P., Pte., Middlesex Regiment.
He joined in June 1915, went to France in the same year, and served there until 1918, taking part in many operations during that period. He holds the 1914-15 Star and the General Service and Victory Medals, and was demobilised in November 1919.
54, Beaconsfield Road, Lower Edmonton, N.9. 14565.

STREVENS, G. A., Lce.-Corpl., Royal Fusiliers.
He enlisted in October 1914, and served on the Western Front from the following year until demobilised in April 1919. During that period he took part in the fighting on practically all sectors, fortunately escaping unhurt. He holds the 1914-15 Star, General Service and Victory Medals.
91, Raynham Avenue, Edmonton, N.18. 15827.

STRIDE, F. G., Pte., Royal Fusiliers and R.E.
Volunteering in November 1915, he was sent to France in the following May. While on the Western Front he took part in the Battle of the Somme and other heavy fighting. In 1917 he was sent to Egypt, where he was engaged on important railway work with the Royal Engineers. He holds the General Service and Victory Medals, and in 1920 was still serving in the East.
5, Mordaunt Road, Willesden, N.W.10. 14111B.

STRIDE, H. H. F., Pte., Royal Fusiliers.
He volunteered in February 1915, and during his three years' service in France, where he was attached to the Machine Gun Corps as signaller, took part in engagements at Ypres, Loos, Cambrai, Arras and Armentieres, and was wounded. He holds the General Service and Victory Medals, and was demobilised in April 1919.
47, Brenthurst Road, Church End, N.W.10. 16377.

STRIDE, P., Pte., 19th Hampshire Regiment.
He joined in October 1917, and served on the Western Front from the following April until November 1919, when he was demobilised. During this period he was engaged on special duties in the Ypres, Valenciennes and Douai sectors. He holds the General Service and Victory Medals.
5, Mordaunt Road, Willesden, N.W.10. 14111A.

STRIDE-AGER, J., A.B., Royal Navy, H.M.S. "Aquarius."
Volunteering in April 1915, he proceeded with his ship to the Dardanelles, and took part in naval operations during the Gallipoli Campaign. On the evacuation of the Peninsula he went to Corfu, and later was engaged on important duties with the Dover Patrol. He was demobilised in February 1919, holding the 1914-15 Star and the General Service and Victory Medals.
10, Hiley Road, Willesden, N.W.10. X18329.

STRINGER, G. E., Pte., Coldstream Guards.
He volunteered in 1915, and in the following year was drafted to the Western Front, where, after taking part in many important engagements, he was killed in action at Arras on February 28th, 1917. He was entitled to the General Service and Victory Medals.
102, Ancill Street, Hammersmith, W.6. 13662.

STRINGER, L. J., Sergt., 15th London Regiment (Civil Service Rifles).
He volunteered in September 1915, and was drafted to the Western Front, where he took part in the battles of the Somme, Ypres, Passchendaele and Cambrai, and in other important engagements. During his service in France he was wounded. He holds the General Service and Victory Medals, and was demobilised in 1919.
42, Porten Road, West Kensington, W.14. 12564.

STRONG, H., Pte., Manchester Regiment.
Volunteering in September 1914, he was retained until 1918 on special Government engineering work, which called for a high degree of technical skill. He was then sent to France, took part in important engagements during the Retreat and Advance of the Allies, and was badly wounded and gassed. In January 1919 he was demobilised, holding the General Service and Victory Medals.
38, Rucklidge Avenue, Harlesden, N.W.10. 13148.

STROUD, A. G., Driver, Royal Engineers.
He volunteered in December 1914 and in the following year was drafted to the Dardanelles, where he took a distinguished part in the landing and the evacuation of Gallipoli. Later he served under General Allenby in the Advance through Egypt and Palestine, and was amongst the first to enter Jerusalem. In 1918 he was sent to France, and was in action at Messines during the Advance. He was demobilised in January 1919, holding the 1914-15 Star and the General Service and Victory Medals.
60, Torquay Street, Paddington, W.2. X21610.

STROUD, E. H., 2nd Air Mechanic, Royal Air Force.

He joined in November 1917, and after his training was engaged on important duties with his squadron. He gave valuable services which called for a high degree of technical skill, but was unsuccessful in obtaining his transfer overseas before the termination of hostilities. In 1920 he was still serving.

33, Wendover Road, Harlesden, N.W.10. 12546B.

STROUD, G. W., Boatswain's Mate, Royal Navy.

He volunteered in August 1914, and was posted to H.M.S. "Valorous." He saw much service on board a Mystery Ship at the Dardanelles, and with the Grand Fleet in many operations in the North Sea. He holds the 1914 Star and the General Service and Victory Medals, and was still serving in 1920.

5, Compton Terrace, Pretoria Road,
Tottenham, N.17. X17934C.

STROUD, J., Pte., R.A.S.C. (M.T.).

He volunteered in April 1915, and on the completion of his training was drafted to France, where he took an active part in many important operations in various sectors, until the close of the war. He was demobilised in May 1919, and holds the 1914-15 Star and the General Service and Victory Medals.

22, Denzil Road, Neasden Lane, N.W.10. 16082B.

STROUD, S. C., Pte., The Buffs (East Kent Regt.).

He joined in 1916 and served for three years in Mesopotamia where he took part in many engagements. He remained on the Eastern Front until he was demobilised in 1919, holding the General Service and Victory Medals.

5, Compton Terrace, Pretoria Road,
Tottenham, N.17. X17934A.

STROUD, T. E., Pte., 3/9th Middlesex Regiment.

He volunteered in September 1915, and in the following year was drafted to India. During his service there he was engaged on important duties at various stations, and in 1920 was still serving. He holds the General Service and Victory Medals.

33, Wendover Road, Harlesden, N.W.10. 12546A.

STROUD, W. C., Lce.-Corpl., Middlesex Regiment and M.F.P.

He volunteered in 1915, and on the completion of his training was transferred to the Military Foot Police, in which he rendered valuable service for two years. He was unsuccessful in obtaining his transfer overseas before the cessation of hostilities, and was demobilised in 1919.

5, Compton Terrace, Pretoria Road,
Tottenham, N.17. X17934B.

STRUDWICK, A., Bandsman, Royal Fusiliers.

He enlisted in 1899, and immediately on the outbreak of the war was drafted to France, where he fought in the Retreat from Mons and the Battle of the Marne. In the following year he served at the Dardanelles, and after a period in hospital in England was again sent to France, where he took part in many important engagements, including that at Arras, up to the close of hostilities. In the course of his service overseas he was wounded three times. He was discharged in July 1919, holding the Mons Star and the General Service, Victory and Long Service Medals.

40, St. Margaret's Road, Hanwell, W.7. 11062.

STRUDWICK, H. C., Sapper, Royal Engineers.

He joined in March 1916, and during his service on the Western Front was wounded in action at Vimy Ridge. From 1917 until his demobilisation in February 1919 he served at home, being unfit as a result of his wound for further duty overseas. He holds the General Service and Victory Medals.

3, Norfolk Road, Willesden, N.W.10. 14924.

STUBBERFIELD, W. H., Sapper, Royal Engineers.

He volunteered in October 1914 and served on the Western Front from the following year until 1919. During his service he was in action on the Somme, and at Ypres, Cambrai, and the Retreat and Advance of 1918. He was demobilised in June 1919, holding the 1914-15 Star and the General Service and Victory Medals.

22, Brereton Road, Tottenham, N.17. X18110.

STUBBINGS, S. C., Corpl., 2/9th Middlesex Regt.

He volunteered in August 1914, served on the Western Front, later in the same year, until 1919, took part in the Retreat from Mons, the battle of Cambrai and other engagements, and in the Retreat and Advance of 1918. He was three times wounded, once during the fighting at Cambrai, and holds the Mons Star and the General Service and Victory Medals. He was demobilised in 1920.

26, Denton Road, Harlesden, N.W.10. 14700.

STUBBINS, A. H., Bombardier, R.G.A.

He volunteered in November 1915, served on the Western Front from that year until 1918, and took part in various engagements on all sectors. He was demobilised in May 1919, holding the 1914-15 Star and the General Service and Victory Medals.

1, Wimborne Road, Lower Edmonton, N.9. T15211B.

STUBBINS, W. T., Trooper, 6th Dragoon Guards.

He enlisted in August 1913, and served in France from 1914 to 1918. He took part in various engagements, including the Retreat from Mons, La Bassee, and the Somme. He was still serving in 1920, and holds the Mons Star and the General Service and Victory Medals.

1, Wimborne Road, Lower Edmonton, N.9. T15211A.

STUBBS, J., Pte., 2nd Scots Guards.

He was in the Army at the outbreak of war, and went to France in August 1914, taking part in the Retreat from Mons, and many other engagements. In September 1917 he was invalided home as unfit for further service overseas, and was discharged in July 1919 as medically unfit after completing 19 years' continuous service. He had previously served in the South African War and holds the King's and Queen's South African Medals with three bars, the Mons Star, the General Service and Victory and Good Conduct Medals.

54, Hiley Road, Willesden, N.W.10. X18401.

STUCHBURY, C. A., Pte., 18th Middlesex Regt.

He volunteered in May 1915, went to the Western Front in the following year, and took part in many important battles, including those of the Somme, Ypres, Cambrai, and Arras. He also served with the Royal Engineers for a period. He was demobilised in May 1919, holding the General Service and Victory Medals.

21, Oldfield Road, Willesden, N.W.10. 15751.

STUCKEY, G., Pte., 1st London Regiment (Royal Fusiliers).

He joined in June 1918, and in the following October was sent to the Western Front, where he played a prominent part in the concluding stages of the Advance, and was gassed. After being invalided home, he was demobilised in August 1919, and holds the General Service and Victory Medals.

30, Fifth Avenue, Queen's Park Estate, W.10. X18322.

STURDY, J. T., Driver, Royal Engineers.

Volunteering in 1914, he was sent in the following year to Gallipoli where he took part in important operations and remained until the evacuation in January 1916. He then went to Egypt and later was drafted to France. In France he was actively engaged in the Battle of the Somme and in many other sectors. He holds the 1914-15 Star and the General Service and Victory Medals, and was demobilised in 1919.

56, St. Paul's Road, Tottenham, N.17. X18826.

STURLEY, J., 1st Class Stoker, Royal Navy, H.M. Submarine "R2."

Having joined the Navy in 1912, he was serving at the outbreak of war and took part in the initial encounters with the enemy in the North Sea, being engaged at the sinking of the "Königin-Luise" and the Battle of Heligoland Bight in August 1914, as at that time he was serving on H.M.S. "La Forcy." In January of the following year he was at the sinking of the German battle-cruiser "Blücher," and later served in Italian waters. In October 1919, having completed his term of service, he was discharged, and holds the 1914 Star and the General Service and Victory Medals.

12, Goodson Road, Willesden, N.W.10. 14927B.

STURMAN, H., Gnr., 82nd Battery R.H.A.

He joined in 1914, and the same year saw active service in France, where he took part in important engagements. Later he served with General Townshend at Kut, where he was taken prisoner, and endured considerable hardships. Whilst overseas he was twice wounded and contracted malaria. He holds the 1914 Star and the General Service and Victory Medals, and was demobilised in 1919.

50, Steele Road, Willesden, N.W.10. 14144B.

STURMEY, C. T., 1st Class Stoker, Royal Navy.

He joined the Navy in 1912, and during the war served on board H.M.S. "Bat" and other vessels. After taking part in several naval engagements, he was killed on December 30th, 1915, when his ship, H.M.S. "Natal," was blown up. He was entitled to the 1914 Star and the General Service and Victory Medals.

34, Chalgrove Road, Tottenham, N.17. X18957A.

STURMEY, T., 1st Class Stoker, Royal Navy.

He joined the Navy in July 1914, and throughout the war saw active service at sea. He took part in the Battle of Jutland, and later was engaged on mine-sweeping duties on board H.M.S. "Widnes." He also served on H.M. ships "Yarmouth," "St. George," and "Vulcan," and for a time suffered from shell-shock. He was still with his ship in 1920, and holds the 1914 Star and the General Service and Victory Medals.

34, Chalgrove Road, Tottenham, N.17.   X18957B.

STYANTS, C. W., Gunner, Royal Marine Artillery.

He was called up from the Reserve at the outbreak of war, and served with the Grand Fleet on H.M.S. "Thunderer" and other vessels in the North Sea, taking part in many engagements. In 1917 he volunteered for duty with the armed merchantmen, and was on service with them until the conclusion of hostilities. He was demobilised in November 1919, and holds the 1914 Star and the General Service and Victory Medals.

2, Windsor Place, Maida Hill, W.9.   X20687A.

STYANTS, P., Pte., Cambridgeshire Regiment and Suffolk Regiment.

He volunteered in January 1915, and in the same year was sent to France, where he remained until 1918. During this time he took part in many important engagements, including those at Arras, Albert and St. Quentin, and was wounded. On March 21st, 1918, he was taken prisoner and interned in Germany until November, when he was repatriated and demobilised. He holds the 1914-15 Star and the General Service and Victory Medals.

2, Windsor Place, Maida Hill, W.9.   X20687B.

STYLES, A. C., Sergt., 1st Middlesex Regiment.

He was in the Army when war broke out, and shortly afterwards proceeded to the Western Front, where he served for nearly five years. During this time he took part in many of the principal engagements, and was severely wounded in the heavy fighting on the Somme in July 1916. For his consistent good work on the field he was recommended for the Meritorious Service Medal. He was demobilised in November 1919, holding the 1914 Star and the General Service and Victory Medals.

31, Edenham Street, North Kensington, W.10.   X20187.

STYLES, A. J., Sapper, Royal Engineers.

He volunteered in 1915, and later proceeded to the Western Front, where he served on many sectors. He was in action at Arras, Loos, Neuve Chapelle, the Somme and Armentieres, and took part in the Retreat and Advance of 1918. On his return to England he was demobilised in 1919, and holds the General Service and Victory Medals.

12, Archel Road, West Kensington, W.14.   16429.

STYLES, C. S., Pte., 1st South Lancashire Regt.

Having enlisted in 1907, he was drafted to India in 1910, and was still serving there at the outbreak of hostilities. Throughout the war he was stationed on the North West Frontier, and was frequently in action against the Afghans. He was still in the Army in 1920, and holds the 1914-15 Star and the General Service and Victory Medals.

15, Durban Road, Tottenham, N.17.   X18289A.

STYLES, F. J., Lce.-Corpl. R.E. (Mounted).

Volunteering in 1915, he was shortly afterwards drafted to the Western Front, where, after being in action on the Somme and at Amiens, Ypres, Vimy Ridge and St. Quentin, he was severely wounded in August 1917. As a result he was discharged in the following year as medically unfit for further military duties. He holds the 1914-15 Star and the General Service and Victory Medals.

12, Archel Road, West Kensington, W.14.   16430.

STYNES, J., Pte., Royal Marine Light Infantry.

He volunteered in August 1914, and throughout served on the North Sea Station. His ship was torpedoed in the early days of the war, but fortunately he was among the survivors. He took part in the raid on Zeebrugge, and was also in many other naval engagements. He was still in the Royal Marines in 1920, and holds the 1914-1915 Star, General Service and Victory Medals.

35, Raynham Road, Upper Edmonton, N.18.   15998.

SUCH, J. B., Driver, Royal Field Artillery.

He volunteered in September 1914, and on the completion of his training was sent to India, where he remained for three years engaged on many important duties. He was demobilised in June 1919, after his return to England, and holds the 1914-15 Star and the General Service and Victory Medals.

27, Leeds Street, Upper Edmonton, N.18.   15816.

SUCKLING, W., Staff Sergt. Major, R.A.S.C.

Volunteering in December 1914, he was sent to the Western Front in the following November. He was engaged on important transport duties in France up to the date of the Armistice, and then went with the Army of Occupation into Germany, where he was stationed at Cologne. He returned to England in April 1919, and was demobilised in the same month. He holds the 1914-15 Star and the General Service and Victory Medals.

60, Litchfield Gardens, Willesden, N.W.10.   X17433.

SULLIVAN, A., Pte., 5th Essex Regiment and Labour Corps.

Volunteering in May 1915, he was retained on special agricultural work and rendered valuable services. He was not successful in obtaining his transfer to the Front owing to his being medically unfit for active service, and was demobilised in October 1919.

74, Hampden Street, Paddington, W.2.   X21065.

SULLIVAN, C. F., Driver, Royal Field Artillery.

He volunteered in August 1914, and was sent to the Western Front, where he took a prominent part in engagements at Ypres and Armentieres and on the Somme. During his service he was wounded and gassed and was demobilised in January 1919, holding the General Service and Victory Medals.

29, Heckfield Place, Walham Green, S.W.6.   X20253.

SULLIVAN, J. A., Sergt., Royal Field Artillery.

He volunteered in August 1914, and shortly after went to France where he saw fighting on many sectors of the Front. After serving abroad with distinction for nearly two years, he was killed in action at Ypres on July 27th, 1916. He was entitled to the 1914 Star and the General Service and Victory Medals.

30, Ashford Road, Tottenham, N.17.   X18357.

SULLIVAN, M., Sergt., 8th Yorkshire Regiment and Royal Marine Labour Corps.

He volunteered in September 1914, and was drafted to France in 1916. He took part in the battle of the Somme and other engagements, and was afterwards transferred to Italy. Whilst serving in the campaign against the Austrians he was in action on the Piave and at various other places. On the conclusion of hostilities he returned to England and was demobilised in January 1919. He holds the General Service and Victory Medals.

29, Wendover Road, Harlesden, N.W.10.   T12543.

SULLIVAN, T. E., Leading Stoker, Royal Navy.

He volunteered in August 1914, and, during his service in the North Sea, was in H.M.S. "Forward," engaged in submarine chasing. He also took part in the bombardment of Zeebrugge, and served off Salonika, and was demobilised in November 1918, holding the 1914 Star and the General Service and Victory Medals.

6, Denton Road, Stonebridge Park, N.W.10.   14699B.

SUMMERFIELD, F. C., Pte., 7th Middlesex Regt.

He joined in March 1917, and during his service on the Western Front took a prominent part in several engagements, including that of Arras, in which he was severely wounded in June 1918. He holds the General Service and Victory Medals, and was demobilised in February 1919.

2, Sotheron Road, King's Road, S.W.6.   X19879.

SUMPTER, G. C., Sergt., 6th London Regiment (Rangers).

He volunteered in May 1915, and was sent to France in January 1917. During his service he took part in the Battle of Bullecourt and the Offensive in 1917, when he was wounded. He holds the General Service and Victory Medals, and was demobilised in January 1919.

112, Villiers Road, Cricklewood, N.W.2.   16155.

SUMPTION, G., 1st Air Mechanic, R.A.F., 102nd Squadron.

He joined in June 1917, and in September was drafted to the Western Front, where he served on various sectors. He was engaged on important duties, demanding the utmost skill and technical knowledge, whilst in France, and was stationed at Havre, Cambrai, Arras, Dunkirk and many other places. He holds the General Service and Victory Medals, and was demobilised in February 1919.

22, Bertie Road, Willesden, N.W.10.   X17579B.

SUMPTION, J., Pte., Royal Fusiliers.

He volunteered in November 1915, and throughout his service was engaged on important coastal defence duties at different stations. He was unsuccessful in his efforts to obtain his transfer to the Front, but nevertheless did splendid work with his unit up to the date of his demobilisation in February 1919.

22, Bertie Road, Willesden, N.W.10.   X17579A.

SUSSEMS, R. C., Pte., 7th London Regiment.
He joined in 1916, and served in Egypt and Palestine, where he took part in the capture of Jerusalem. He was in hospital in Egypt for some time suffering from malaria. He was demobilised in March 1919 on his return to England, and holds the General Service and Victory Medals.
29A, Lintaine Grove, West Kensington, W.14. 16654.

SUTCLIFFE, A., Pte., Queen's Own (Royal West Kent Regiment).
He volunteered in September 1914, and a year later was sent to the Western Front, where he served for three years. During this period he was almost continuously in action, and took part in many engagements, including those at Loos, Ypres, St. Eloi, the Bluff, Hooge, Ploegsteert, Delville Wood, Souchez and Hulluch. He was demobilised in March 1919, and holds the 1914-15 Star and the General Service and Victory Medals.
4A, Kilkie Street, Fulham, S.W.6. X21351.

SUTCLIFFE, F. W., Pte., 13th Middlesex Regt.
He joined in March 1917, and in the following year was drafted to France, where he took part in numerous engagements, including the capture of Lens. During his service overseas he was twice wounded, and in October 1918 was invalided home. In the following February he was demobilised, and holds the General Service and Victory Medals.
36, De Morgan Road, Townmead Road, S.W.6. X21524.

SUTER, A. J., 1st Class Stoker, Royal Navy.
He joined in 1916, and for three years served in many waters on board H.M. Ships " Donegal " and " Vivid." He took part in several naval engagements during his service, and was employed on various duties. He was demobilised in 1919, and holds the General Service and Victory Medals.
20, Linton Road, Upper Edmonton, N.18. X17468.

SUTHERLAND, B. T., Corporal, Seaforth Highlanders.
He joined in November 1916, and served with distinction on the Western Front until July 1918, when he was severely wounded during the Advance. He was invalided home and was demobilised in January 1919, holding the General Service and Victory Medals.
87, Hawthorn Road, Willesden, N.W.10. X17423.

SUTTON, J. W., Pte., Royal Marine Engineers.
He joined in April 1917, and was employed on important coast defence work until the cessation of hostilities. He was unable to obtain his transfer overseas, but gave valuable services until demobilised in August 1919.
8, Winchester Road, Lower Edmonton, N.9. 14687.

SUTTON, T. H., Corpl., 18th London Regiment (London Irish Rifles).
He volunteered in December 1915, and a year later was sent to the Western Front. Whilst there he took part in many engagements, and fought in the battles of Messines, Bourlon Wood, Vimy Ridge and Cambrai, where he was taken prisoner in March 1918. After suffering much from privation during his captivity he was released, and in December 1918 was demobilised. He holds the General Service and Victory Medals.
55, Hawthorn Road, Willesden, N.W.10. 17220.

SUTTON, W., Pte., Middlesex Regiment.
Joining in 1916, he was sent to France in the same year, and took a prominent part in many engagements, including the Battle of Ypres, and was twice wounded during his two and a half years' service abroad. He was demobilised in 1919, and holds the General Service and Victory Medals.
28, Kenmont Gardens, College Park, N.W.10. X17573.

SUTTON, W. G. (M.M.), Corpl., 12th London Regiment (Rangers).
He volunteered in February 1915, and in 1917 was sent to France, where he took part in the battles of Ypres and Arras. He was awarded the M.M. for conspicuous bravery and devotion to duty in the field, but after much distinguished service was killed in action at Cachy on April 26th, 1918. He was entitled to the General Service and Victory Medals.
44, Winchester Road, Lower Edmonton, N.9. 14859.

SWAIN, C., Corporal, Middlesex Regiment.
Volunteering in February 1915, he was soon afterwards drafted to the Western Front. Whilst overseas he saw much heavy fighting up to May 1916, when he was severely wounded in action at Loos. After over four years' exemplary service he was demobilised in September 1919, holding the 1914-15 Star and the General Service and Victory Medals.
15, Tilson Road, Tottenham, N.17. X19078.

SWAIN, G. W. P., Stoker Petty Officer, R.N.
He volunteered in August 1914, and served in the North Sea on board H.M.S. " Leandros " until she was mined in August 1915. Afterwards he was transferred to H.M.S. " Harmatton," and on board this ship was present during the bombardment of Zeebrugge and in other naval engagements. He holds the 1914 Star and the General Service and Victory Medals, and was demobilised in October 1919.
46, Burnthwaite Road, Walham Green, S.W.6. X20204.

SWAIN, T., Pte., 1/8th Middlesex Regiment.
He volunteered in November 1915, and in the following July was drafted to France. He took part in the Battle of the Somme, and was wounded, and on September 15th, 1916, was reported missing. He was entitled to the General Service and Victory Medals.
39, Dymock Street, Fulham, S.W.6. X21664.

SWAINSBURY, L. J., Pte., 3rd Middlesex Regt.
He volunteered in August 1914, and was sent to France in the same year. After taking part in the battles of Loos, Arras, the Somme and Neuve Chapelle, he was severely wounded, and was discharged unfit for further service in May 1916. He holds the 1914 Star and the General Service and Victory Medals.
39, Steele Road, Willesden, N.W.10. 14377.

SWAINSTON, W., Leading Seaman, Royal Navy.
He joined the Navy in August 1904, and during the whole of the Great War did valuable sea service on various vessels of His Majesty's Fleet, among them being H.M. Ships " Wallflower," " Minerva," " Royal Arthur," " Grafton," " Formidable," " Excellent," " Illustrious," " St. Vincent " and " Victory." One of his vessels was blown up by a mine, but he escaped uninjured. He was demobilised in April 1920, and holds the 1914-15 Star and the General Service and Victory Medals.
100, Third Avenue, Queen's Park Estate, W.10. X19294.

SWAIT, G. E., Lce.-Corpl., 9th Middlesex Regt.
He enlisted in February 1912, and was drafted in October 1914 to India, where he was engaged on garrison duties at various stations. He also took part in the Afghanistan Campaign in 1919. He was demobilised in January 1920, and holds the 1914-15 Star and the General Service and Victory Medals, also the India General Service Medal (with Clasp Afghanistan N.W. Frontier 1919).
31, Fortune Gate Road, Harlesden, N.W.10. 14735.

SWALLOW, T., Staff Sergt., R.A.S.C.
He volunteered in August 1914, and proceeded to the Western Front on the conclusion of his training. He was engaged on important duties in connection with the transport of ammunition and supplies during operations in this theatre of war, and was wounded. He was demobilised in February 1919, and holds the 1914-15 Star and the General Service and Victory Medals.
43, Westminster Road, Lower Edmonton, N.9. 12704B.

SWALLOW, W. I. (M.M.), Pte., Royal Sussex Regt.
He volunteered in September 1914, and after his training was drafted overseas. During his service on the Western Front he was in action in much of the severe fighting, and was awarded the Military Medal for conspicuous bravery and devotion to duty in the field at Sanctuary Wood in January 1918. He was wounded three times, the last wound necessitating the amputation of his right leg, and was invalided to England. He was ultimately discharged as medically unfit for further service in October 1919, and holds the 1914-15 Star and the General Service and Victory Medals.
43, Westminster Road, Lower Edmonton, N.9. 12704A.

SWAN, G. F., Pte., Royal Irish Fusiliers.
He joined in April 1915, and served on the Western Front for three months, during which time he took part in engagements at Hulluch, Vermelles, La Bassée and Loos. In May 1916 he was badly wounded, and after being for a time in hospital at Rouen, was invalided home, and ultimately discharged in November of the same year. He holds the General Service and Victory Medals.
54, Winchelsea Road, Willesden, N.W.10. 13844.

SWANN, S., Rifleman, Rifle Brigade.
He joined in September 1917, and went to France in the following January. He took part in our Retreat in March 1918, and was killed in action near St. Quentin on March 21st. He was entitled to the General Service and Victory Medals.
126, Roundwood Road, Willesden, N.W.10. 16051.

SWASH, J., Pte., Machine Gun Corps.
He enlisted in October 1911, and was drafted to the Western Front at the outbreak of war. Whilst overseas he took a distinguished part in much of the severe fighting, including the Retreat from Mons, the battles of Ypres, Loos, Arras and the Somme, and was wounded five times. He holds the Mons Star and the General Service and Victory Medals, and was demobilised in March 1919.
39, Lorenco Road, Tottenham, N.17.　　　X17985.

SWEENEY, D., Pte., Duke of Cornwall's L.I.
He volunteered in September 1914, at the age of seventeen, and was drafted to the Western Front. He took part in several engagements in this theatre of war, and was killed in action at the Battle of Arras on April 29th, 1916. He was entitled to the General Service and Victory Medals.
28, Hartopp Avenue, Dawes Road, S.W.6.　　X17663A.

SWEENEY, P., Pte., Royal Fusiliers.
He volunteered in August 1914, and during his service on the Western Front took a conspicuous part in many engagements, and was five times wounded. He was discharged medically unfit for further service in consequence of his wounds in December 1918, and holds the 1914-15 Star and the General Service and Victory Medals.
28, Hartopp Avenue, Dawes Road, S.W.6.　　X17663B.

SWEETMAN, A., Pte., Royal West Kent Regt.
He volunteered in 1915, and proceeded to the Western Front during the same year. Whilst in this theatre of war he was in action in many of the principal engagements, and was killed at Loos on October 13th, 1916. He was entitled to the 1914-15 Star and the General Service and Victory Medals.
72, Felixstowe Road, Lower Edmonton, N.9.　　15377.

SWEETMAN, A. H. S., Petty Officer, Royal Navy.
He was serving at the outbreak of war, and served with his ship, H.M.S. "Iron Duke," on important duties with the Grand Fleet in the North Sea, off the coast of Belgium, and in the Mediterranean Sea. He holds the 1914 Star and the General Service and Victory Medals, and in 1920 he was serving at Constantinople.
9, Bridge Road, Willesden, N.W.10.　　15467B.

SWEETMAN, E. (Mrs.), Special War Worker.
During the war, in order to release a man for military service, she acted as a conductress on the Metropolitan Electric Trams in the Harlesden district. She was the first lady in her locality to take up this work, and rendered valuable services.
92, Burn's Road, Harlesden, N.W.10.　　13142B.

SWEETMAN, G. J., Driver, Royal Field Artillery.
He volunteered in January 1915, and from June 1915 served on the Western Front, where he took part in engagements at Delville Wood, Lille and Cambrai. He was demobilised in February 1919, holding the 1914-15 Star and the General Service and Victory Medals.
92, Burn's Road, Harlesden, N.W.10.　　13142A.

SWEETMAN, J. R., Pte., 20th London Regiment.
He joined in June 1918, and after his period of training served at various stations on important duties with his unit until February 1919, when he was sent to Germany with the Army of Occupation. He returned to England and was demobilised in April 1920.
9, Bridge Road, Willesden, N.W.10.　　15467A.

SWETMAN, A. E., Pte., 14th London Regiment. (London Scottish).
He joined in February 1916, and at the conclusion of his training was drafted to the Western Front. During his service in this theatre of war he was engaged in several important battles, including those of the Somme and Ypres. He holds the General Service and Victory Medals, and was demobilised in January 1919.
65, Lyndhurst Road, Upper Edmonton, N.18.　　15511.

SWIFT, C. E., Telegraphist, Royal Navy.
He volunteered in January 1916, and after his training was posted to the "Aries II," which was engaged on minesweeping duties in the English Channel. He was later transferred to H.M.S. "Holderness," in which ship he went to Russia. In 1920 he was still serving, and holds the General Service and Victory Medals.
59, Oldfield Road, Willesden, N.W.10.　　15991B.

SWIFT, R. C., Corporal, Machine Gun Corps.
He volunteered in June 1915, and after his training served with his unit on important duties until June 1917, when he was drafted to the Western Front. He took part in many engagements, and was wounded in action in June 1917, and later in October 1918. He was invalided to England, and ultimately demobilised in February 1919. He holds the General Service and Victory Medals.
113, Ilbert Street, Queen's Park Estate, W.10.　　X18678.

SWIFT, W. J., Leading Seaman Gunner, R.N., H.M.S. "Superb."
He joined in September 1914, and saw service at the Dardanelles and the Battle of Jutland. Later he was attached to the Merchant Service, and on three occasions his ship was torpedoed. He holds the 1914-15 Star and the General Service and Victory Medals, and was demobilised in February 1919.
59, Oldfield Road, Willesden, N.W.10.　　15991A.

SWINDIN, F. W., Gunner (Signaller), R.F.A.
He joined in March 1916, and served from 1917 to 1919 with General Allenby through the Palestine Campaign. He took part in many engagements, and was present at the fall of Jerusalem. He holds the General Service and Victory Medals, and was demobilised in December 1919.
6, Deacon Road, Cricklewood, N.W.2.　　16141.

SYCAMORE, A., Pte., Royal Army Medical Corps.
He volunteered in 1915, and during his four years' service on the Western Front was present at the battles of Loos, the Somme, Ypres and La Bassée, and in the Advance of 1918. He was demobilised in March 1919, and holds the 1914-15 Star and the General Service and Victory Medals.
33, Shorrolds Road, Walham Green, S.W.6.　　X19353B.

SYCAMORE, W., Rifleman, King's Royal Rifle Corps.
He joined in 1916, and was sent in the same year to Salonika, where he served for three years, and took a prominent part in many of the principal engagements in this theatre of war. He returned to England after the Armistice, and was demobilised in March 1919, holding the General Service and Victory Medals.
33, Shorrolds Road, Walham Green, S.W.6.　　X19353A.

SYKES, D. (Mrs.), Special War Worker.
During the war this lady offered her services, and rendered valuable assistance at the Morecambe Bay Shell Filling Factory, where she was engaged on important duties in connection with the filling of shells.
18, Mund Street, West Kensington, W.14.　　16906B.

SYKES, E. C., Pte., 3rd London Regiment (Royal Fusiliers).
He joined in December 1917, and was drafted to France in the following year. Whilst overseas he was actively engaged in much of the fighting during the Retreat and Advance of 1918. He holds the General Service and Victory Medals, and was demobilised in January 1920.
50, Kenninghall Road, Upper Edmonton, N.18.　　16897.

SYKES, G. W., Lce.-Corpl., 3rd Duke of Wellington's (West Riding Regiment).
He volunteered in August 1914, and served on the Western Front for five years. During this period he took part in many engagements, including those of Mons and the Somme, was badly gassed during the Advance of 1918, and in consequence was for some weeks in hospital. He holds the 1914 Star and the General Service and Victory Medals, and was demobilised in 1919.
18, Mund Street, West Kensington, W.14.　　16906A.

SYKES, H., 2nd Air Mechanic, Royal Air Force.
He joined in August 1918, and owing to special qualifications was engaged on the important duties of a mechanic of aero-engines, travelling between this country and France. His duties called for a high degree of technical skill, and he gave valuable services until his demobilisation in March 1919. He holds the General Service and Victory Medals.
2, Westgate, Roundwood Road, Willesden, N.W.10.　　16300.

SYKES, J., Pte., 4th Middlesex Regiment.
He volunteered in August 1914, and during his service in France was wounded and captured. For over four years he was a prisoner in Germany and suffered many hardships, but was released after the Armistice. On his return home he was demobilised in May 1919, and holds the 1914 Star and the General Service and Victory Medals.
7, Bucklers Place, North End Road, S.W.6.　　X17229.

SYMES, E. (D.C.M.), Sergt., Machine Gun Corps.
He volunteered in August 1914, and was drafted to France in the following year. He was in action during much of the severe fighting on the Western Front, including the battles of Ypres, Arras, the Somme and Neuve Chapelle, and was wounded three times. He was mentioned in dispatches and awarded the Distinguished Conduct Medal for gallant conduct and devotion to duty in the field. He also holds the 1914-15 Star and the General Service and Victory Medals, and was demobilised in February 1919.
47, Felixstowe Road, Willesden, N.W.10.　　X17762.

SYMES, F., Rifleman, Rifle Brigade.
Joining in 1916, he was drafted after his period of training to Salonika, and was in action in engagements in this theatre of war. He later went to Russia and then to Mesopotamia, where he was actively engaged until the cessation of hostilities. He holds the General Service and Victory Medals, and was demobilised in 1919.
79, Ancill Street, Hammersmith, W.6.　　　13803B.

SYMES, J., Gunner, Royal Field Artillery.
He joined in 1915, and saw service in India, Mesopotamia and on the Western Front, where he took part in the battles of Arras, Loos, Neuve Chapelle, and Ypres. Later he went with the Army of Occupation to Germany. He was demobilised in 1919, and holds the General Service and Victory Medals.
79, Ancill Street, Hammersmith, W.6.　　　13803A.

SYMES, L. E. (Miss), Special War Worker.
During the war this lady was employed at Messrs. Waring and Gillow's Factory, White City, in making Army equipment. Her duties, which were of an arduous nature, were performed with much care and skill.
79, Ancill Street, Hammersmith, W.6.　　　13803C.

SYMONDS, A., Lce.-Corpl., Machine Gun Corps.
He joined in 1916, served in France in the same year, and was then sent to Mesopotamia, where he took part in various engagements. He was invalided home in 1919 suffering from typhoid fever and dysentery, and was discharged in April, holding the General Service and Victory Medals.
110, Lopen Road, Upper Edmonton, N.18.　　X17910.

SYMONDS, E. G., Pte. (Signaller), 1/7th Gordon Highlanders.
He volunteered in July 1915, and on completion of his training was drafted to the Western Front. During his service in this theatre of war he was in action in many engagements, including those of the Somme, Ypres and Cambrai. He holds the General Service and Victory Medals, and was demobilised in February 1919.
105, Deacon Road, Cricklewood, N.W.2.　　16608C.

SYMONDS, G., Pte., R.A.S.C. (M.T.).
He volunteered in October 1914, and was shortly afterwards drafted to the Western Front, where he was engaged on important duties in connection with the transport of ammunition and supplies during the battles of Ypres and Neuve Chapelle. He later acted as motor driver to Generals Robinson and Whitehead, and was in action during the Retreat and Advance of 1918. After hostilities ceased he went to Germany with the Army of Occupation. He holds the 1914 Star and the General Service and Victory Medals, and was demobilised in April 1919.
33, Redfern Road, Willesden, N.W.10.　　13207.

SYMONDS, H. W., Pte. and Driver, 2/10th Middlesex Regiment and R.F.A.
He volunteered in September 1914, and proceeded to Gallipoli in the following year, and was wounded at the landing at Suvla Bay. Upon his recovery he was sent to Palestine, and served with General Allenby's forces until the signing of the Armistice. He holds the 1914-15 Star and the General Service and Victory Medals, and was demobilised in June 1919.
105, Deacon Road, Cricklewood, N.W.2.　　16608A.

SYMONDS, T. H. (D.C.M.), Sergeant, R.E.
He volunteered in September 1914, and served for nearly three years on the Eastern Front. He took part in the Dardanelles operations, and was awarded the Distinguished Conduct Medal for gallantry in the field in keeping the communication open between Suvla Bay and other landing stations during the evacuation in December 1915. He was twice mentioned in dispatches during his service in Egypt and Palestine, and was demobilised in March 1919. He had previously served with the R.E. during the Boer War, and holds the Queen's and King's South African Medals (with six bars), the 1914-15 Star and the General Service and Victory Medals.
61, West Ella Road, Willesden, N.W.10.　　15130.

SYMONDS, W. J., Lce.-Corpl., 1st Middlesex Regt.
Volunteering in August 1914, he was first sent to Egypt and in 1916 to France, where he took part in many engagements, including those of Ypres and the Somme, and was twice wounded. He was demobilised in 1919, holding the 1914-15 Star and the General Service and Victory Medals.
105, Deacon Road, Cricklewood, N.W.2.　　16608B.

SYMONS, E., Special War Worker.
During the war this lady volunteered her services, and was engaged at the office of the Euston War Pensions Committee on duties of an important nature. She gave most valuable services, and received commendation from the authorities.
134, Bulwer Road, Upper Edmonton, N.18.　　X17197.

SYRETT, E. G., A.B., Royal Navy.
He joined in December 1916, and after his training served in his ship with the Mediterranean Fleet in Eastern waters on various important duties in that theatre of war. He was demobilised in May 1919, and holds the General Service and Victory Medals.
5A, Sunnyside Road South,
Lower Edmonton, N.9.　　14342B.

T

TABRAHAM, E., Pte., Middlesex Regiment.
He volunteered in July 1915, and on completion of his training was drafted to the Western Front, where he took part in many important engagements. He was severely wounded in action, and invalided to England. On his recovery he was retained with his unit until he was demobilised in February 1919. He holds the General Service and Victory Medals.
36, Cornwall Street, Fulham, S.W.6.　　X19882.

TACK, J. W., Pte., Royal Army Service Corps.
He volunteered in March 1915, and as he was too old for service overseas was posted to the Remount Department of his unit, where he rendered valuable services. He was demobilised in February 1919.
100, Roundwood Road, Willesden, N.W.10.　　15975A.

TACK, J. W. E., Gunner, Royal Field Artillery.
He was serving at the outbreak of hostilities, and was drafted to France, where he took part in the Retreat from Mons, the action at Ypres, Festubert, Loos, the Somme, and the Retreat and Advance of 1918. During his service he was twice wounded and gassed. He was awarded a certificate for great gallantry in the field, and holds the Mons Star and the General Service and Victory Medals. He was discharged in 1919.
100, Roundwood Road, Willesden, N.W.10.　　15975B.

TADGELL, S. W., Pte., The Queen's (Royal West Surrey Regiment).
He joined in June 1916, and on the completion of his training was drafted to France, where he was employed as a signaller, and took an active part in the engagements on the Somme and near Lille, and was gassed. He served with the Army of Occupation in Germany until he was demobilised in September 1919, and holds the General Service and Victory Medals.
59, Barbot Street, Lower Edmonton, N.9.　　14582.

TAFT, J., Pte., Highland Light Infantry.
He volunteered in August 1914, and during his training contracted septic poisoning, and died on October 14th, 1914.
27, Church Path, Hammersmith, W.6.　　15917B.

TAFT, J. W., Pte., Royal Marine Light Infantry.
He joined in September 1917, and on the completion of his training was drafted to Russia, where he saw much fighting. In 1920 he was still in the forces, and holds the General Service and Victory Medals.
27, Church Path, Hammersmith, W.6.　　15917A.

TAGG, A. F., Pte., The Prince of Wales's Own (West Yorkshire Regiment).
He joined in 1917, and served on the Western Front. He took part in the battles of Ypres and Cambrai, and was severely wounded. In 1919 he was demobilised, holding the General Service and Victory Medals.
39, Holly Lane, Willesden, N.W.10.　　15633B.

TAGG, A. J., Corporal, Royal Engineers.
He volunteered in 1915, and served on the Western Front for four years, where he was engaged on bridge-building and other important work. He was demobilised in 1919, and holds the 1914-15 Star and the General Service and Victory Medals.
39, Holly Lane, Willesden, N.W.10.　　15633A.

TALBOT, A. G., Rifleman, 17th K.R.R.
He joined in June 1916, and after his training was sent to the Western Front, where he took part in many important engagements, including that of Ypres, in which he was killed on October 3rd, 1917. He was entitled to the General Service and Victory Medals.
18, Ellerslie Road, Shepherd's Bush, W.12.　　11932B

TALBOT, A. J., Lce.-Corpl., 15th Welch Regt.

He volunteered in May 1915, and served with the Royal Army Pay Corps until 1916. In 1917 he went with the 15th Welch Regiment to the Western Front, and there took part in many important actions, including those of Ypres, Albert and Armentieres, and was wounded. He was demobilised in December 1919, and holds the General Service and Victory Medals.

18, Ellerslie Road, Shepherd's Bush, W.12.   11932A.

TALBOT, G. W., Pte., Royal Fusiliers.

He volunteered in November 1914, and during his service in France, which lasted nearly three years, took part in several engagements, including those of the Somme, Ypres, Bapaume, Cambrai and Arras, and was twice wounded and gassed. After being in hospital in France, he was invalided to England, and was ultimately discharged as medically unfit for further service in October 1918. He holds the 1914-15 Star and the General Service and Victory Medals.

38, Hilmer Street, West Kensington, W.14.   16908.

TALBOT, H., Corpl., Royal Army Medical Corps.

He had previously served in the Boer War, and on re-enlisting in 1914 was at once sent to France, where he took part in the battles of Mons, the Marne, the Aisne, Loos and Ypres, and the Retreat and Advance of 1918. He was demobilised in April 1919, holding the Queen's and King's South African Medals, the Mons Star, and the General Service and Victory Medals.

34, Berry Street, Willesden, N.W.10.   15413.

TALBOT, P., Sergeant, Royal Air Force.

He volunteered in October 1914, and in the following year was sent to France, where he took an active part in many engagements. In 1916 he met with a serious accident, from the effects of which he still suffers. He was demobilised in February 1919, and holds the 1914-15 Star and the General Service and Victory Medals.

77, Somerset Road, Upper Edmonton, N.18.   X17029.

TAMS, H., Rifleman, Royal Irish Rifles.

He volunteered in November 1915, and in the following year proceeded to France, where he took part in many engagements, including the battles of Passchendaele and Cambrai, and was wounded near Messines in February 1917. He was demobilised in January 1919, holding the General Service and Victory Medals.

39, Burnthwaite Road, Walham Green, S.W.6.   X20085.

TANNER, A. J., 1st Air Mechanic, R.A.F.

He joined in July 1917, and on completion of his training was retained with his unit on important duties. He gave valuable services, which called for high degree of technical skill, but was not successful in obtaining his transfer overseas. He was demobilised in February 1919.

47, Warwick Road, Upper Edmonton, N.18.   X17510.

TANNER, F., Gunner, R.G.A. (139 Heavy Battery, R.G.A.)

He joined in 1916, and was drafted to France, where he took part in many important engagements, including the heavy fighting at Vimy Ridge, the Somme, Arras, Bulle-court, Passchendaele, Cambrai, Havrincourt and Ypres. During his service he was wounded. He holds the General Service and Victory Medals, and was demobilised in March 1919.

6, Porten Road, West Kensington, W.14.   T12180.

TANNER, H., Driver, Royal Field Artillery.

He joined in November 1916, and after his training was drafted to Mesopotamia, where he took part in many engagements. He was demobilised in April 1919, and holds the General Service and Victory Medals.

170, Hazelbury Road, Edmonton, N.18.   TX17586.

TANNER, J., Pioneer, Royal Engineers.

He joined in 1916, and on the completion of his training was drafted to Italy, where he rendered valuable service in many engagements. He was demobilised in September 1919, and holds the General Service and Victory Medals.

33, Croxley Road, Maida Hill, W.9.   X19971.

TANNER, S., Pte., 1st Middlesex Regiment.

He volunteered in August 1914, and served on the Western Front for four years. During this period he was in action at Ypres, Loos, Armentieres, the Somme, the Marne and Bethune, was wounded and gassed. He was recommended for a decoration for conspicuous gallantry on the field, holds the 1914-15 Star and the General Service and Victory Medals. He was demobilised in February 1919.

131, Hill Side, Stonebridge Park, Willesden, N.W.10.   15796B.

TANNER, W., Pte., Royal Sussex Regiment and Tank Corps.

Volunteering in 1915, he was sent to France in the same year, and took part in the battles of the Somme, Ypres, Arras, Bapaume and Cambrai. He was wounded three times during his service, and was killed in action near Ypres, on September 25th, 1917. He was entitled to the 1914-15 Star and the General Service and Victory Medals.

131, Hill Side, Stonebridge Park, Willesden, N.W.10.   15796A.

TAPNER, B., Rifleman, Rifle Brigade.

He first joined the Forces in 1886, but rejoined in August 1914, and went to France, where he took part in the Retreat from Mons and the battles of Loos, Arras and Ypres. He was wounded four times, and lost his leg in the Battle of the Somme in September 1916. He was discharged in August 1918 as medically unfit for further service, and holds the Mons Star and the General Service and Victory Medals.

13, Musgrave Crescent, Walham Green, S.W.6.   X19701.

TAPPENDEN, E. (Miss), Special War Worker.

During the war this lady was employed on munition work at Messrs. Pomeroy's Factory, Edmonton, where her duties required great skill. She carried out her responsible duties to the entire satisfaction of her employers.

30A, Durban Road, Tottenham, N.9.   X18085.

TAPPIN, B., Signalman, Royal Navy.

He joined in July 1916, and during his service was engaged in dangerous mine-sweeping duties in the Eastern waters. In 1920 he was still serving, and holds the General Service and Victory Medals.

25, Oldfield Road, Willesden, N.W.10.   16024C.

TAPPIN, F. C., Corpl., 4th Middlesex Regiment.

He volunteered in August 1914, and in the same year was drafted to France, where he took a prominent part in the engagements at Ypres, the Somme, Arras and Cambrai. During his service he was wounded, and in January 1919 was demobilised, holding the 1914-15 Star and the General Service and Victory Medals.

55, Sandringham Road, Cricklewood, N.W.2.   X17104.

TAPPIN, H., Leading Seaman, Royal Navy.

He volunteered in 1914, and was posted to H.M.S. "Radiant." Whilst on board this vessel he was engaged on important patrol and escort duty in the North Sea. In 1920 he was still serving, and holds the 1914 Star and the General Service and Victory Medals.

25, Oldfield Road, Willesden, N.W.10.   16024B.

TAPPIN, H. W., Driver, R.A.S.C. (M.T.).

He volunteered in September 1914, and in the same year was drafted to France, where he took an active part in several important engagements. He was employed largely in driving a field ambulance, and during his service was in hospital with fever. He was demobilised in November 1919, and holds the 1914 Star and the General Service and Victory Medals.

81, Rayleigh Road, West Kensington, W.14.   12646.

TAPPING, V. R., Pte., 17th Middlesex Regiment.

Volunteering in February 1915, he was in the same year drafted to the Western Front, where, after taking part in many engagements, he was killed in action at the Battle of the Somme on August 8th, 1916. He was entitled to the 1914-15 Star and the General Service and Victory Medals.

30, Humbolt Road, Hammersmith, W.6.   15143

TATMAN, G. H., Driver, Royal Army Service Corps.

He joined in July 1916, and during his service on the Western Front played a conspicuous part in the fighting. On one occasion he was badly thrown from his horse, which was startled by the bursting of a shell, and was in hospital for some time, suffering from his injuries. On the conclusion of hostilities he was sent to Germany with the Army of Occupation, but returned for his demobilisation in October 1919. He holds the General Service and Victory Medals.

25, Wingmore Road, Tottenham, N.17.   X17982.

TATTLE, G. C., Seaman-Gunner, Royal Navy.

Volunteering in August 1914, he was engaged throughout the war on important naval operations with the Grand Fleet in the North Sea. In 1920 he was still serving, and holds the 1914 Star and the General Service and Victory Medals.

45, Church Lane, Lower Edmonton, N.9.   15206C.

TAYLOR, A. (Miss), Special War Worker.
For a considerable period during the war this lady undertook work of national importance. She was first engaged at Messrs. Blake's Munition Factory, Stevenage Road, Fulham, in connection with the arduous duties of bomb-making. Later she went to their factory at Hurlingham, and worked in the cylinder-checking department. Her duties were always carried out in an efficient manner, and she rendered valuable services.
298, Lillie Road, Fulham, S.W.6.　　X19133.

TAYLOR, A. C. J., Driver, R.A.S.C. (M.T.).
He joined in January 1917, and after his training was engaged on important transport duties at various stations. He was not successful in obtaining his transfer overseas before the signing of the Armistice, but in July 1919 was sent to Russia, where he was still serving in 1920. He holds the Victory Medal.
12, Chaldon Road, Dawes Road, S.W.6.　　X17721.

TAYLOR, A. E., Driver, R.A.S.C.
He volunteered in August 1914, and was immediately sent to France, where he took a prominent part in the Retreat from Mons. He was also engaged on important duties during the battles of Ypres and the Somme, and in many other engagements. In June 1919 he was demobilised, holding the Mons Star and the General Service and Victory Medals.
38, Sheldon Road, Upper Edmonton, N.18.　　X17455.

TAYLOR, A. J., 1st Class Steward, Royal Navy.
He volunteered in June 1915, and saw service until 1917 on board H.M.S. "Godetia" and other vessels which were engaged in the hazardous task of mine-sweeping in the North Sea and the Baltic. He was demobilised in August 1919, and holds the 1914-15 Star and the General Service and Victory Medals.
14, Farrant Street, Queen's Park Estate, W.10.　　X19178.

TAYLOR, C. J., Pte., R.A.S.C. (M.T.).
Joining in November 1916, he was sent to the Western Front in the following August. After serving overseas for some months on important transport work, he was found to be physically unfit for duty abroad, and was invalided home. He was demobilised in November 1919, and holds the General Service and Victory Medals.
34M, Langford Road, Fulham, S.W.6.　　X21469.

TAYLOR, E., Pte., 7th London Regiment.
Volunteering in January 1915, he was sent four months later to the Western Front, where he took a prominent part in the fighting, and was wounded at Hill 60. After nearly four years' service in France he was demobilised in June 1919, and holds the 1914-15 Star and the General Service and Victory Medals.
43, Southam Street, North Kensington, W.10.　　X20628.

TAYLOR, E., Pte., 3rd East Surrey Regiment.
He volunteered in November 1915, and after his training was drafted to the Western Front. After taking part in much heavy fighting in this seat of war, he was killed in action on May 3rd, 1917, and was entitled to the General Service and Victory Medals.
14, Colehill Lane, Fulham, S.W.6.　　X18924B.

TAYLOR, E. (Miss), Special War Worker.
For a considerable period during the war this lady undertook work of national importance at Messrs. Blake's Munition Factory, Fulham, where she was engaged on the manufacture of bombs. Her duties were of an arduous nature, and she rendered very valuable services.
298, Lillie Road, Fulham, S.W.6.　　X19132.

TAYLOR, E. (Miss), Special War Worker.
During the war this lady was engaged as a van-driver at Messrs. Lyons, a large firm of food suppliers, and thereby released a man for military service. She carried out her duties to the entire satisfaction of her employers, and did splendid work for her Country.
7, Mablethorpe Road, Munster Road, S.W.6.　　X19120.

TAYLOR, E. H., A.B., Royal Naval Division.
He joined in October 1916, and in the following January was drafted to France, where he took part in the battles of Arras and Albert, and in heavy fighting near Béthune. Whilst in action he received a severe wound, which necessitated the amputation of his leg, and after long treatment in hospital he was discharged in June 1918 as medically unfit for further service. He holds the General Service and Victory Medals.
133, Sandringham Road, Cricklewood, N.W.2.　　T17316.

TAYLOR, E. W., Driver, Royal Field Artillery.
He joined in May 1916, and served on the Western Front, where he took a prominent part in the battles of the Somme, Arras, Ypres, Cambrai and St. Quentin, and in heavy fighting at Neuve Chapelle, Loos, Hill 60, Armentieres and Albert. He was also in Italy for a time, and after the signing of the Armistice went to the Rhine with the Army of Occupation, where he remained until his demobilisation in 1919. He holds the General Service and Victory Medals.
7, Mablethorpe Road, Munster Road, S.W.6.　　X19127

TAYLOR, F. (Miss), Special War Worker.
From October 1917 until the conclusion of hostilities this lady held an important position at the United Small Arms Factory, Fulham, and was engaged in the grooving of rifles. The manner in which she carried out her very responsible duties was highly commended.
1, Langford Road, Fulham, S.W.6.　　X21465.

TAYLOR, G., Pte., 8th Lincolnshire Regiment.
Joining in March 1916, he was drafted to France in the same year. While overseas he was in action on the Somme, at Arras, Messines, Lens, the third battle of Ypres, Cambrai, and the Retreat and Advance of 1918, and was wounded. After three years' service abroad he was demobilised in June 1919, holding the General Service and Victory Medals.
26, Brindley Street, Paddington, W.9.　　X21801.

TAYLOR, G. V., Rifleman, K.R.R.
Volunteering in November 1915, he was drafted early in 1917 to the Western Front, where he played a conspicuous part in the battles of Arras, the Somme, the Ancre and Cambrai. During the German offensive in March 1918 he was severely wounded, and in August 1919 was demobilised, holding the General Service and Victory Medals.
15, Portnall Road, Maida Hill, W.9.　　X19304.

TAYLOR, H., A.B., R.N., H.M.S. "Lawford."
He volunteered in November 1915, and after serving for a short time with the Grand Fleet in the North Sea was transferred to the East African Station. He took part in the bombardments of Lindi and Kilwakiswani in 1917. He holds the General Service and Victory Medals, and was still serving in 1920.
26, Oakbury Road, Fulham, S.W.6.　　X20928.

TAYLOR, H., Gunner, Royal Field Artillery.
Volunteering in February 1914, he was sent to France in the following March, and took a prominent part in the Battle of Ypres and in several important engagements. In November 1915 he was drafted to Salonika, and saw much heavy fighting on the Balkan Front. He returned to England in 1918, and was demobilised in November, holding the 1914-15 Star and the General Service and Victory Medals.
4, Linton Road, Upper Edmonton, N.18.　　TX17282B.

TAYLOR, H. A., Rifleman, 9th London Regiment (Queen Victoria's Rifles).
He volunteered in November 1914, and in the following February was sent to the Western Front. After taking part in many important engagements, he was reported missing, believed killed, on June 1st, 1916. He was entitled to the 1914-15 Star and the General Service and Victory Medals.
81, Vicarage Road, Neasden Lane, N.W.10.　　15743B.

TAYLOR, H. C. H., Rifleman, 1/17th London Regiment.
He joined in June 1917, and on completion of his training was drafted to the Western Front, where he took part in many important engagements, including the Battle of the Somme in 1918. During his service abroad he was twice wounded, and was also gassed. In January 1919 he was demobilised, and holds the General Service and Victory Medals.
21, Rectory Road, Parson's Green, S.W.6.　　X20013.

TAYLOR, H. G., Gunner, Royal Field Artillery.
He was mobilised with the Territorials immediately on the outbreak of hostilities, and was sent to France in the following February. Whilst on the Western Front he took part in the battles of Ypres and Loos, and in other important engagements. He holds the 1914-15 Star and the General Service and Victory Medals, and was demobilised in April 1919.
81, Vicarage Road, Neasden Lane, N.W.10.　　15743C.

TAYLOR, J., Stoker, Royal Navy.

Volunteering in August 1914, he was engaged on important and dangerous mine-sweeping and patrol duties in the North Sea for a period of nearly five years. After giving valuable services he was demobilised in January 1919, and holds the 1914 Star and the General Service and Victory Medals.

35, Waldo Road, College Park, N.W.10.   X17628.

TAYLOR, J. J., Driver, Royal Field Artillery.

Having previously served in the South African War with the Imperial Yeomanry, he volunteered in October 1914, and was sent to France in the following month. Whilst on the Western Front he took a conspicuous part in the battles of Ypres and Loos, and other important engagements, but in February 1916, owing to his services, he was discharged. In addition to the Queen's South African Medal (with 5 Clasps), he holds the 1914 Star and the General Service and Victory Medals.

54, Hazel Road, Willesden, N.W.10.   X17779.

TAYLOR, R. (Mrs.), Special War Worker.

During the war this lady was engaged on important duties at the Pimlico Wheel Works, Fulham, where she was employed painting gun carriages and artillery wheels. Later she worked at Messrs. Waring and Gillow's factory, White City, on Army equipment of various kinds. She gave valuable services, and received high commendation for her splendid work.

4, Mablethorpe Road, Munster Road, S.W.6.   X19334B.

TAYLOR, R. H., Sergeant, Seaforth Highlanders.

Volunteering in 1914, he was drafted to the Western Front and served with distinction at the battles of Neuve Chapelle, Loos and the Somme, and in heavy fighting near Armentieres, Amiens and Albert, where he was severely wounded. Later he was sent to India, and took part in the campaign on the North-West Frontier. He holds the 1914-15 Star and the General Service and Victory Medals and the Indian General Service Medal (with Clasp Afghanistan, N.W. Frontier 1919), and was demobilised in 1919.

7, Mablethorpe Road, Munster Road, S.W.6.   X19128.

TAYLOR, R. J., Rifleman, 21st London Regt. (1st Surrey Rifles).

He joined in 1917, and during his service on the Western Front, played a prominent part in engagements at Loos, Armentieres, St. Quentin, Bullecourt, Lille, Cambrai and in the Advance of 1918. He was demobilised in 1919, and holds the General Service and Victory Medals.

4, Mablethorpe Road, Munster Road, S.W.6.   X19334A.

TAYLOR, S. B., Pte., Royal Army Medical Corps.

He volunteered in October 1915, and in the following February was drafted to Egypt, where he was engaged on important duties at various places. He remained on the Eastern Front until his demobilisation in May 1919, and holds the General Service and Victory Medals.

81, Vicarage Road, Neasden Lane, N.W.10.   15743A.

TAYLOR, T. F., Pte., Middlesex Regiment.

He joined in 1917 and, after his training, was engaged on special duties at various stations with his unit. He gave valuable services, but was unsuccessful in obtaining his transfer overseas before the termination of hostilities. He was demobilised in 1919.

7, Mablethorpe Road, Munster Road, S.W.6.   X19129.

TAYLOR, W., 1st Class Petty Officer, Royal Navy.

He was in the Navy at the outbreak of war, and was posted to the Grand Fleet for duty in the North Sea. On 15th October, 1914, whilst in H.M.S. "Hawke," his ship was torpedoed and sunk, but he was one of the few to be rescued, after being on a raft for twenty-four hours. Later he was transferred to the South Atlantic Station. He returned to England, and was demobilised in August 1919, after twenty-seven years' service. He holds the 1914 Star and the General Service and Victory Medals.

1, St. Margaret's Road, Willesden, N.W.10.   X17752.

TAYLOR, W., Pte., Royal Fusiliers.

Volunteering in August 1914, he was drafted to the Western Front in 1915 and was in action at Vimy Ridge, Cambrai, Ypres, the Somme and other engagements. Whilst serving overseas he was twice wounded. After the signing of the Armistice he went with the Army of Occupation to Germany. He returned to England and was demobilised in June 1919, and holds the 1914-15 Star and the General Service and Victory Medals.

2, Lichfield Gardens, Willesden, N.W.10.   X17440.

TAYLOR, W., Pte., 13th Middlesex Regiment.

He volunteered in 1915 and was drafted to the Western Front later in the same year. During his service overseas he played a prominent part in the fighting and was severely wounded on the Somme in August 1916. He holds the 1914-15 Star and the General Service and Victory Medals, and was demobilised in 1919.

22, Southam Street, N. Kensington, W.10.   X20568.

TAYLOR, W. A., Corporal, R.A.S.C. (M.T.).

Joining in May 1917, he was drafted in the same year to Mesopotamia, where he served for three years. He rendered valuable services in connection with the Expeditionary Force Canteens and was also employed on transport duties. On his return to England he was demobilised in 1920, and holds the General Service and Victory Medals.

7, Maybury Gardens, Willesden, N.W.10.   X17441.

TAYLOR, W. E. S., Pte., 20th London Regiment.

He joined in September 1917, and in the same year was sent to the Western Front, where he took part in numerous engagements. On 18th July, 1918, he was seriously wounded and was invalided home to hospital. On his recovery he was demobilised in March 1919, and holds the General Service and Victory Medals.

18, Argyle Road, Upper Edmonton, N.18.   15261B.

TAYLOR, W. J., Pte., Royal Army Service Corps.

He joined in May 1917, and was engaged on special duties in the Remount Section of the R.A.S.C. He frequently crossed the Channel to and from France in charge of horses, and was once injured in the course of his duties. He was demobilised in March 1919, and holds the General Service and Victory Medals.

125, Portnall Road, Maida Hill, W.9.   X19534.

TAYLOR, W. W., Lce.-Corpl., Middlesex Regt.

He volunteered in 1915, and during his service took a conspicuous part in the battles of the Somme, Loos, Arras, Neuve Chapelle, Ypres and Vimy Ridge. After also fighting in the Advance of 1918, and being twice wounded, he was demobilised in 1919, and holds the 1914-15 Star and the General Service and Victory Medals.

7, Mablethorpe Road, Munster Road, S.W.6.   X19228.

TEARLE, J. H., Rifleman, Rifle Brigade.

Joining in 1916, he was drafted to the Western Front on completion of his training. After taking part in several important battles, he was killed in action on the Somme on March 16th, 1917. He is buried near Guillemont, and was entitled to the General Service and Victory Medals.

45, Letchford Gardens, Willesden, N.W.10.   X17697.

TEARLE, S. T., Pte., R.A.S.C. (M.T.).

He joined in November 1917, and in the same year was sent to the Western Front, where he was engaged in conveying food and ammunition to the lines in the Arras, Cambrai, Vimy Ridge, and other sectors. He was demobilised in March 1920, and holds the General Service and Victory Medals.

120, Ashmore Road, Harrow Road, W.9.   X19739.

TEDMAN, H., Corporal, R.E. and Tank Corps.

Joining in January 1917, he trained with the Royal Engineers, and proceeded to France three months later. He was transferred to the Tank Corps, and did excellent service at Vimy Ridge, Cambrai and other engagements up to the cessation of hostilities. He was demobilised in February 1919, holding the General Service and Victory Medals.

19, Althea Street, Townmead Road, S.W.6.   X21148.

TEMPERTON, T. R., 2nd Corporal, R.E.

He joined in June 1917, and after his training served at various stations on important duties with his unit. He gave valuable services, but owing to defective eyesight was unable to obtain his transfer overseas. He was demobilised in March 1920.

26, St. Ervan's Road, North Kensington, W.10.   X20682.

TEMPLE, G., Driver, Royal Field Artillery.

He was serving at the outbreak of war, and was at once sent to France, where he took part in the battles of Mons, the Marne, the Aisne, Ypres, Neuve Chapelle, St. Eloi, Loos, Vimy Ridge, the Somme, Messines and Cambrai, and was wounded and gassed. He was invalided home, and discharged in December 1918, holding the Mons Star and the General Service and Victory Medals.

23, Chippenham Road, Maida Hill, W.9.   X21097.

TEMPLER, A. H., Special War Worker.

Being physically unfit for military service, he performed work of national importance, first at No. 31 Store, Neasden, and afterwards at the Park Royal Munition Works, where he was engaged in sorting and packing shells for transport overseas.

5, Albert Terrace, Stonebridge Park, Willesden, N.W.10.   14114B.

TEMPLER, H., Special War Worker.
Being over age for military service, he was employed in responsible work in connection with shells at No. 31 Store, Neasden, where throughout the war he rendered valuable services.
5, Albert Terrace, Stonebridge Park, Willesden, N.W.10.   14114C.

TENCH, A., Rifleman, King's Royal Rifle Corps.
He joined in June 1916, and after his training proceeded to the Western Front, where he was killed in action in the first Battle of the Somme on October 6th, 1916. He was entitled to the General Service and Victory Medals.
19, Everington Street, Hammersmith, W.6.   13965A.

TERRY, A., Special War Worker.
In spite of his efforts to enlist at the outbreak of war, he was finally rejected owing to physical unfitness, and afterwards obtained work of national importance at Messrs. Lillshore's, Paddington. He was engaged in various capacities in connection with the transport of munitions, and his service, which lasted until 1919, proved to be of the greatest value.
309, Shirland Road, Maida Hill, W.9.   X19565.

TEW, W. A., 1st Air Mechanic, R.A.F.
He joined in May 1916, and during his service in France, which began a little later and lasted till 1919, carried out important duties that called for a high degree of technical skill. He was present at the battles of the Somme and Ypres and other important engagements. In March 1919 he was demobilised, holding the General Service and Victory Medals.
34, Gloucester Road, Upper Edmonton, N.18.   X17009.

THACKERAY, R., Pte., London Regiment (Royal Fusiliers).
He volunteered in August 1915, and after his training was stationed at various places on important guard duties. He gave valuable services, but owing to ill-health was not transferred overseas, and was ultimately discharged as medically unfit in May 1917.
126, Clarendon Street, Paddington, W.2.   X20165.

THAIN, A. E., Lce.-Corpl., 7th London Regiment.
Volunteering in 1915, he was drafted to the Western Front, and after taking part in several engagements was killed in action on May 20th, 1916, at Vimy Ridge. He was entitled to the General Service and Victory Medals.
38, Ancill Street, Hammersmith, W.6.   13986B.

THAME, A. E., Lce.-Corpl., 1st London Regiment.
He was mobilised in August 1914, and in the following year embarked for the Dardanelles. He took part in several operations of importance there, and later was drafted to Egypt and afterwards to France, where he saw much heavy fighting. In January 1917 he was discharged as medically unfit for further service, and holds the 1914-15 Star and the General Service and Victory Medals.
6, St. Ervan's Road, North Kensington, W.10. X20680.

THATCHER, G. F. C., Pte., Machine Gun Corps.
He joined in June 1916, and at the close of his training was drafted to France, where he served for twelve months. He took part in many important engagements in 1917, and was killed at the Battle of Cambrai in December of that year. He was entitled to the General Service and Victory Medals.
1, Hartington Road, Tottenham, N.17.   X19103.

THEARLE, C. W., Pte., Labour Corps.
He volunteered in November 1914, and after his training served at various stations on special duties with his unit. He was not successful in obtaining his transfer overseas before the cessation of hostilities, but gave valuable services before being demobilised in February 1920.
43, Pellant Road, Fulham, S.W.6.   X17844.

THEARLE, F. E., Pte., Royal Army Service Corps.
He joined in June 1916, and in the following July went to France, where he was engaged in the Supply Column attached to the 11th Division, with which he served on special duties until the termination of the war. He was demobilised in October 1919, and holds the General Service and Victory Medals.
54, Cranbury Road, Fulham, S.W.6.   X21161.

THEOBALD, A. E., Sergeant, Middlesex Regt. and R.A.P.C.
Joining in February 1916, his special capabilities soon won for him promotion. He was engaged on important duties at various stations, but was not successful in obtaining his transfer overseas before the cessation of hostilities. He gave valuable services, however, before his demobilisation, which occurred in April 1920.
129, Mayo Road, Willesden, N.W.10.   15433A.

THICK, C. W., Gunner, Royal Garrison Artillery.
He joined in October 1916, and during his service on the Western Front was in action at Givenchy and other important engagements up to April 26th, 1918, when he was killed in action at Bethune. He was entitled to the General Service and Victory Medals.
21, Inglethorpe Street, Fulham Palace Road, S.W.6.   TX19709.

THILTHORPE, H. J., Gunner, R.F.A.
He was mobilised in August 1914, and was speedily drafted to the Western Front, where he took part in the battles of Mons, Ypres, the Somme and other important engagements. He was afterwards drafted to Salonika, and served on various fronts in that theatre of war. During his service he was wounded three times. In June 1919 he was discharged, holding the Mons Star and the General Service and Victory Medals.
361, Essex Road, Islington, N.1.   X17470.

THOMAS, A., Pte., East Surrey Regiment and 113th Labour Coy.
He enlisted in 1916, and in 1917-18 served in France, where he took part in many engagements, including those of the Somme, Arras, and Ypres. He holds the General Service and Victory Medals, and was discharged as medically unfit for further service in March 1918.
21, Greyhound Road, College Park, N.W.10.   X17610.

THOMAS, C. A., Pte., R.A.S.C. (Labour Corps).
He volunteered in February 1915, and was sent to the Western Front almost immediately. He was engaged on important duties on the Somme and at Arras, Armentieres and Vimy Ridge, and was buried by shell-fire at Ypres in 1917, but fortunately was rescued. He returned to England and was demobilised in February 1919, but still attends hospital owing to heart trouble contracted during the war. He holds the 1914-15 Star and the General Service and Victory Medals.
28, Jews' Row, Wandsworth, S.W.18.   X21767.

THOMAS, C. E., 1st Air Mechanic, R.A.F.
He joined in June 1916, and was drafted to the Western Front, where for the remainder of his service he did valuable work of a technical nature with the R.A.F. He was demobilised in January 1919, holding the General Service and Victory Medals.
43, Chaldon Road, Dawes Road, S.W.6.   X17649.

THOMAS, E. A. F., Sergeant, Royal Fusiliers.
He rejoined in August 1914 and was drafted to the Western Front, where he took part in many important engagements. Later he served in Salonika. Whilst overseas he was wounded three times, and in December 1918 was discharged as medically unfit for further duty, having completed nineteen years' service. He holds the King's and the Queen's South African Medals, the 1914-15 Star and the General Service and Victory Medals.
32, Allestree Road, Fulham, S.W.6.   X19204.

THOMAS, G. E., Pte., Royal Fusiliers.
Joining in 1917 he was sent to France in the following year. He took a prominent part in numerous engagements, and was wounded during the heavy fighting at Cambrai in 1918. He holds the General Service and Victory Medals, and was still serving in 1920.
36, Eldon Road, Lower Edmonton, N.9.   13056A.

THOMAS, H. A. J., Sapper, Royal Engineers.
He joined in September 1918, and after his training served on important duties at various stations. He was principally engaged on special work connected with searchlights, and gave valuable services in this capacity. He was demobilised in April 1919.
14, Althea Street, Townmead Road, S.W.6.   X21197.

THOMAS, H. G., Pte., The Queen's (Royal West Surrey Regiment).
Joining in 1917, he was drafted to France in the same year. He was in action at Ypres, La Bassée and the Somme, and was three times gassed. In 1919 he returned to England, and was demobilised. He holds the General Service and Victory Medals.
7, Newlyn Road, Tottenham, N.17.   X18515.

THOMAS, H. P. (M.M.), Sergt., 8th East Surrey Regiment.
He volunteered in March 1915, was drafted in the same year to France, and took part in the battles of the Somme, Arras, and in other engagements including the Advance of 1918, in which he was wounded. He won the Military Medal for distinguished gallantry and devotion to duty on September 18th, 1918, and also holds the 1914-15 Star and the General Service and Victory Medals. He was demobilised in 1919.
38, Burnthwaite Road, Walham Green, S.W.6.   X20209

THOMAS, L. J., 1st Class Stoker, R.N., H.M.S. "Hydra."

He was in the Navy at the outbreak of war, and served for nearly four years in the North Sea. He was present at the battles of Heligoland and Jutland, took part in the Zeebrugge bombardment, and was also engaged in cruising off the Belgian Coast and chasing enemy submarines. He holds the 1914 Star and the General Service and Victory Medals, and was discharged in May 1918.
48, Portnall Road, Maida Hill, W.9.   X19454.

THOMAS, R. A. T., A.B., R.N., H.M.S. "New Zealand."

He volunteered in August 1914, and during the course of the war saw much service of an important character in home waters near Gibraltar, and along the coast of Spain. He also took an active part in the Battle of Jutland in May 1916. He holds the 1914-15 Star and the General Service and Victory Medals, and in 1920 was still serving.
19, Park Lane, Tottenham, N.17.   X18810.

THOMAS, W. C., Air Mechanic, R.A.F. (late R.N.A.S.).

He volunteered in August 1914, and was drafted in 1916 to the Western Front, where he did most important work until the end of the war in testing aeroplanes before flight. He was demobilised in February 1919, and holds the General Service and Victory Medals.
51, Shorrold's Road, Walham Green, S.W.6.   X19350A.

THOMPSON, A., Special War Worker.

During the war he held an important position at Messrs. Vanden Plas's Aircraft Works, Fulham, where he was engaged on responsible work in connection with the manufacture of aeroplanes. His special qualifications proved of the utmost value to the firm.
25, Mablethorpe Road, Munster Road, S.W.6.   X19221.

THOMPSON, E. W., Pte., R.A.S.C.

He volunteered in August 1914, and in the same year was drafted to France, where he remained until 1916. Whilst overseas he served as a baker at Le Havre and other places. In 1916 he was invalided home, and was discharged as unfit for further service abroad. He holds the 1914 Star and the General Service and Victory Medals.
72, St. Ervan's Road, North Kensington, W.10.   X20939.

THOMPSON, F., Pte., Machine Gun Corps.

He volunteered in December 1915, and went to France, where he took part in several engagements, including that of Ypres. Later he was sent to the East, and served under General Allenby, in Egypt and Palestine, at Gaza, Beersheba, Jerusalem, Jericho and elsewhere. He was demobilised in February 1919, holding the General Service and Victory Medals.
36, Bronsart Road, Munster Road, S.W.6.   X18903.

THOMPSON, G. H., Gunner, R.G.A.

He volunteered in August 1914, and went to the Western Front in March 1916. He fought in many engagements, including Ypres, the Somme, Cambrai and Arras, and also took part in the Advance of 1918. He was demobilised in February 1919, and holds the General Service and Victory Medals.
51, Second Avenue, Queen's Park, W.10.   X19049A.

THOMPSON, H., Corporal, Royal Field Artillery.

He volunteered in September 1914, and in the following year was sent to the Western Front, where he served in numerous engagements. He took part in the battles of Ypres, Festubert, Loos, St. Eloi, Albert, Arras, Vimy Ridge, Messines, Lens and Cambrai, and the Retreat and Advance of 1918, and was wounded. He was demobilised in January 1919, and died in the London Hospital on January 14th, 1920. He was entitled to the 1914-15 Star and the General Service and Victory Medals.
6, Goldney Road, Maida Hill, W.9.   X21371A.

THOMPSON, H., Corporal, R.A.S.C. (H.T.).

He volunteered in August 1914, and was sent to the Western Front, where he was engaged throughout his service in transporting food and ammunition to the fighting lines. He was wounded on the Somme, and was also gassed in action. He was discharged in November 1917, holding the 1914 Star and the General Service and Victory Medals.
32, Durban Road, Tottenham, N.17.   X18083C.

THOMPSON, H., Stoker, Royal Navy, H.M.S. "Glowworm."

He joined in June 1916, and was posted for service with the Fleet in the Baltic Sea. After taking a prominent part in the operations in that seat of war, he returned to England and was demobilised in November 1919. He holds the General Service and Victory Medals.
125, Sherbrooke Road, Fulham, S.W.6.   X18681C.

THOMPSON, H., Corporal, R.A.O.C.

He volunteered in October 1914, and after his training served at various stations on important duties. He was not successful in obtaining his transfer to a theatre of war, but rendered valuable services until hostilities ceased. He was demobilised in June, 1919.
106, Seymour Avenue, Tottenham, N.17.   X19159.

THOMPSON, H. W., Special War Worker.

During the war he was sent out to France on important work in connection with the construction of hospitals and other buildings. Whilst thus engaged he was attached to the Royal Engineers and met with a serious accident. After being in hospital for some time he was invalided home having rendered most valuable service.
59, Orbain Road, Fulham, S.W.6.   X18258

THOMPSON, J., Pte., 22nd Royal Fusiliers.

He joined in March 1917, and in the same year was sent to the Western Front, where he was severely gassed and rendered unfit for further active service. He was then sent to Normandy on special duties at the prisoners of war camp. He returned to England and was demobilised in February 1919. He holds the General Service and Victory Medals.
22, Oakbury Road, Fulham, S.W.6.   X20931.

THOMPSON, J., Driver, Royal Field Artillery.

Volunteering in August 1915, he was sent after a short period of training to the Western Front, where he took part in several battles, including those of Ypres, St. Eloi, Passchendaele, Arras, and Albert. In 1917 he was drafted to Egypt, and later saw service with General Allenby's Forces in Palestine. At the end of the same year he returned to France, and took part in the various engagements which led to victory in November 1918. He was demobilised in January of the following year, holding the 1914-15 Star and the General Service and Victory Medals.
64, Woodchester Street, Paddington, W.2.   X20793.

THOMPSON, J. H., Pte., 8th Hampshire Regt.

Volunteering in August 1914, he was drafted to Mesopotamia, where he took a prominent part in numerous engagements. Later he was transferred to Salonika, and served in the Balkan Campaign. Afterwards he was sent to Egypt, but contracted malarial fever, and was invalided home. On his recovery he was demobilised in March 1919, holding the 1914-15 Star and the General Service and Victory Medals.
52, Lintaine Grove, West Kensington, W.14.   X16996.

THOMPSON, P. N., Pte., Northamptonshire Regt.

He volunteered in February 1915, and in the same year went to the Eastern Front, where he served at Salonika and on various sectors of the Macedonian Front. He took part in the general Offensive on the Doiran, in the engagements on the Vardar, and was present at the recapture of Monastir. In 1917 he was drafted to the Western Front, and served at Arras, Messines, Ypres, Lens and Cambrai, and also fought through the Advance and Retreat of 1918. Whilst serving overseas he was wounded. After the Armistice he went to Germany, where he served with the Army of Occupation until May 1919, when he returned home and was demobilised. He holds the 1914-15 Star and the General Service and Victory Medals.
6, Goldney Road, Maida Hill, W.9.   X21371B.

THOMPSON, R., Gunner, Royal Marine Artillery.

Volunteering in August 1914, he served with the contingent which was landed at Ostend in the early days of the war. Later he was posted to the Mediterranean Station, and afterwards to the Pacific. He holds the 1914 Star and the General Service and Victory Medals, and was demobilised in February 1919.
63, Dieppe Street, West Kensington, W.14.   16454B.

THOMPSON, V., Special War Worker.

From 1917 until the end of the war this lady was engaged on work of a very important nature at Messrs. Luxford's, Willesden, in connection with the manufacture of wire entanglements. She carried out her arduous duties in a most praiseworthy manner.
2, Steele Road, Willesden, N.W.10.   13827A.

THORN, A., Pte., R.A.S.C. (M.T.).

He volunteered in October 1914, and was sent to the Western Front in the same year. While in France he took an active part in many important operations, including those of Ypres, Armentieres, the Somme, Cambrai, Arras, and Bapaume, during which he was engaged on transport duties. After the Armistice, he served in Germany with the Army of Occupation on the Rhine. He returned to England and was demobilised in May 1919, holding the 1914-15 Star and the General Service and Victory Medals.
1, Dudden Hill Lane, N.W.10.   T17336.

THORN, J. H., Petty Officer, Royal Navy, H.M.S. "Bedford."

He was in the Navy at the outbreak of war, and served until 1916 in the North Sea, where he took part in the Battle of Heligoland, and was wounded. Later his ship cruised in other waters, and was in action many times. He was demobilised in February 1919, holding the 1914 Star and the General Service and Victory Medals.
3, Maybury Gardens, Willesden, N.W.10. X17443.

THORNBOROUGH, B., Driver, R.A.S.C.

He joined in September 1916, and in the following month went to the Western Front, where he served in many sectors including those of the Somme and Cambrai. He was demobilised in August 1919, and holds the General Service and Victory Medals.
39, Southam Street, N. Kensington, W.10. X20626.

THORNE, G. F., Lce.-Corpl., 2nd Berkshire Regt.

He enlisted in August 1914, went to France in the same year, and after fighting in several important engagements was reported missing, and later killed in action. He was entitled to the 1914 Star and the General Service and Victory Medals.
34, Hartington Road, Lower Edmonton, N.9. 14055B.

THORNTON, C., Lce.-Corpl., Royal Berkshire Regt.

He volunteered in 1914, was sent to the Western Front in the following year, and served in many engagements, including those of Loos in 1915 and the Somme in 1916. He was also in action at Cambrai, Béthune, Armentieres and on various other fronts, and was wounded. He was demobilised in March 1919, after four years' service, holding the 1914-15 Star and the General Service and Victory Medals.
10, Greyhound Road, College Park, N.W.10. X17802A.

THORNTON, G. G., Rifleman, K.R.R.

He joined in July 1916, and in the same year was sent out to the Western Front, where he remained on active service until 1919. He took a distinguished part in engagements at Ypres, the Somme and Cambrai, and was present at the Retreat and Advance of 1918. He holds the Victory and General Service Medals, and was demobilised in February 1919.
26, Fifth Avenue, Queen's Park Estate, W.10. X18326.

THOROGOOD, G. J., Pioneer, Royal Engineers.

He volunteered for duty in April 1915, and in the following year was drafted to the Western Front, where he remained until 1919. During this period he took a prominent part in many engagements, including those at Ypres, Arras, Albert, Lens, Bapaume, Peronne, St. Eloi, St. Quentin and the Advance of 1918, and was severely gassed. He was demobilised in February 1919, and holds the General Service and Victory Medals.
22, Hampden Street, Paddington, W.2. X20899.

THRAVES, W. H., Corporal, Staffordshire Regt.

He joined in November 1917, and after his training served at various stations on important duties with his unit. In 1919 he was sent to France, where he remained until November of the same year, when he returned to England and was demobilised.
3A, Orchard Place, Tottenham, N.17. X18534.

THURLOW, W., Pte., Royal Army Service Corps.

He joined in January 1917, and in the same year was sent to France. Afterwards he was drafted to Egypt, where he was engaged on important work in the Remount Department. He returned to England and was demobilised in March 1920, holding the General Service and Victory Medals.
9, Heckfield Place, Walham Green, S.W.6. X20247.

THURSTON, W. J. W., Rifleman, K.R.R.

He joined in March 1917, and in the same year was drafted to the Western Front, where he played a distinguished part in several of the important engagements, particularly the Battle of Ypres. After nearly two years' service in France he was demobilised in January 1919, and holds the General Service and Victory Medals.
5, De Morgan Road, Townmead Road, S.W.6. X20850.

TIBBLES, H. D., Pte., 1st Norfolk Regiment.

He joined in June 1916, and early in the following year was drafted to India, where he remained until his demobilisation in November 1919. During this time he was engaged on important garrison duties at various stations. He holds the General Service and Victory Medals.
117, Sandringham Road, Cricklewood, N.W.2. T17319.

TIBBY, T., Pte., 4th Middlesex Regiment.

He enlisted in July 1913, and at the outbreak of war was sent to the Western Front. During the Battle of Mons he was wounded and taken prisoner, but in 1915 was released. He was discharged in November of the same year as medically unfit for further service, owing to his wounds, and holds the Mons Star and the General Service and Victory Medals.
231, Portnall Road, Maida Hill, W.9. X19764.

TIDY, F., Pte., Royal Fusiliers and 30th London Regiment.

He volunteered in February 1915, and after his training was engaged on important duties with his unit. He was medically unfit for transfer overseas, but gave valuable services at various stations until his demobilisation in February 1919. Previous to the war he had served in the 24th Middlesex Volunteers for six years.
28, Caird Street, Queen's Park Estate, W.10. X18945.

TILL, H. V., Pte., Grenadier Guards.

He volunteered in August 1914, and was sent to the Western Front in the following year. During his service in this seat of war, he took part in the heavy fighting at Ypres (Hill 60) and around Arras. In May 1915 he was killed in action, and was entitled to the 1914-15 Star and the General Service and Victory Medals.
102, Kilburn Lane, N. Kensington, W.10. X18600.

TILLEY, A. E., Sapper, Royal Engineers.

He joined in 1916, and later in the same year was drafted to the Western Front, where he remained until his demobilisation in 1919. During this time he was engaged on important duties in many of the principal engagements. He holds the General Service and Victory Medals.
168, Winchester Road, Lower Edmonton, N.9. 14890C.

TILTMAN, J. W. C., Driver, R.F.A. (T.F.).

He was mobilised immediately on the outbreak of hostilities, and was drafted to France early in 1915. During his service on the Western Front he took part in many important engagements, and was in hospital in France with a serious breakdown. He was demobilised in June 1919, holding the 1914-15 Star and the General Service and Victory Medals.
44, Kingwood Road, Fulham, S.W.6. TX19033.

TIMMS, E. E., Pte., 2nd Dorset Regiment.

He volunteered in April 1915, and in the same year was sent to Mesopotamia, where he took part in many engagements. In 1919 he was transferred to Egypt, and in July of that year was demobilised. He holds the 1914-15 Star and the General Service and Victory Medals.
30, Rowallan Road, Munster Road, S.W.6. X19269.

TINDALL, C., Sergeant, The Queen's 2nd (Royal West Surrey Regiment).

He volunteered in September 1914, having previously served in the South African War, and was sent to the Western Front. Whilst overseas he served with distinction at Neuve Chapelle, Delville Wood, and Festubert, taking a prominent part in many engagements. He returned home after more than four years' service overseas, and was demobilised in January 1919. He holds the 1914 Star and the General Service and Victory Medals.
12, Dudley Street, Paddington, W.2. X21930.

TINDALL, C. W., Corporal, Royal Field Artillery.

Volunteering in August 1914, he was drafted to France in the following year. Whilst overseas he took part in numerous engagements, including the battle of Ypres, and in February 1916 was wounded during the engagement at St. Eloi. After four years' service overseas he returned to England, and was demobilised in June 1919. He holds the 1914-15 Star and the General Service and Victory Medals.
24, North Wharf Road, Paddington, W.2. X22003.

TINK, R. D., Driver, R.A.S.C. (M.T.).

He volunteered in August 1914, and was drafted to the Western Front, where he was present at the Retreat from Mons, the Battle of Ypres and many other engagements. Throughout his service in France he did excellent work with the Royal Army Service Corps and was frequently under fire. As a result of severe wounds received on the Somme, he was invalided home, and on his recovery, being physically unfit for further active service, was stationed at various places in England. He was demobilised in June 1919, holding the Mons Star and the General Service and Victory Medals.
303, Shirland Road, Maida Hill, W.9. X19561.

TIPPER, H. J., Pte., 1st Norfolk Regiment.
In March 1915 he volunteered for service, and was drafted to the Western Front later in the same year. He took part in much heavy fighting, including the Battle of the Somme, where he was severely wounded. After being in hospital in France for three months, he was invalided home, and again underwent long treatment. He was demobilised in January 1919, holding the 1914–15 Star and the General Service and Victory Medals.
97, Third Avenue, Queen's Park Estate, W.10. X19445.

TISBURY, C. A., Rifleman, Rifle Brigade.
He was mobilised from the Reserve in August 1914, and was sent to France immediately. During his service on the Western Front he took part in the Battle and Retreat from Mons, the battles of Ypres, Loos and the Somme, and in important engagements in the Advance of 1918. He was wounded three times and gassed while in action. In February 1919 he secured his demobilisation, holding the Mons Star and the General Service and Victory Medals.
32, Durban Road, Tottenham, N.17. X18084.

TITCHENER, E E., Fte., Northumberland Fusiliers.
He volunteered in September 1914, and was immediately sent to France, where he took part in the heavy fighting during the Retreat of that year, and later in important engagements in various sectors. He was killed in action at the Battle of Arras on April 17th, 1917, and was entitled to the 1914 Star and the General Service and Victory Medals. Prior to the war he had served in the Metropolitan Police for 10 years.
19, Mayo Road, Willesden, N.W.10. 15124A.

TODD, A. J., 1st Writer, R.N., H.M.S. " Canada."
He volunteered in August 1914, and during his service with the Grand Fleet took part in the battles of Jutland, Dogger Bank and Zeebrugge, and helped to escort the German Fleet into Scapa Flow. He was demobilised in July 1919, and holds the 1914 Star and the General Service and Victory Medals.
8, Bruce Castle Road, Tottenham, N.17. X18554B.

TODD, C. W., Corporal, King's Royal Rifle Corps.
He joined in May 1916, and was drafted to the Western Front, where he took part in heavy fighting, including the battles of Arras and Vimy Ridge, before being taken prisoner on June 9th, 1917. While in captivity he suffered terrible hardships. After his release he was demobilised in March 1919, holding the General Service and Victory Medals.
36, Chesson Road, W. Kensington, W.14. X17233.

TODD, G. A., Pte., 8th Queen's Own (Royal West Kent Regiment).
Joining in January 1917, he was sent within a short time to the Western Front. After taking part in much heavy fighting during his brief service in Belgium, he was killed in action during the Battle of Ypres on August 8th, 1917. He was buried at Voormezeele Cemetery, near the Tower. He was entitled to the General Service and Victory Medals.
31, Sheeley Road, Willesden, N.W.10. 13781C.

TODD, R. C., 1st Writer, R.N., H.M.S. "Angora."
He volunteered in September 1914, and was posted to H.M.S. "Angora," in which ship he took part in important naval operations with the Grand Fleet in the North Sea. In 1920 he was still serving in the Royal Navy, and holds the 1914 Star and the General Service and Victory Medals.
8, Bruce Castle Road, Tottenham, N.17. X18554A.

TODD, T. H., Pte., 4th Middlesex Regiment.
He volunteered in August 1914, and was drafted to France in the following March. While on the Western Front, he took part in many important engagements, including the battles of Ypres (1915 and 1917), Loos, Albert and the Somme, and also in heavy fighting near Lens and Peronne. He was killed in action during the third battle of Ypres on October 15th, 1917, and was entitled to the 1914–1915 Star and the General Service and Victory Medals.
31, Shelley Road, Willesden, N.W.10. 13781B.

TOLFTS, C. J., A.B., R.N., H.M.S. "Morning Star."
He volunteered in April 1915, and saw much service with the Grand Fleet in the North Sea and Russian waters, where he took part in important Naval operations. He holds the 1914–15 Star and the General Service and Victory Medals, and was demobilised in February 1919.
68, Church Road, Tottenham, N.17. X18337.

TOMES, A., Pte., Royal Army Service Corps.
Joining in March 1916, he was drafted to Salonika, and, during his three years' service there, was engaged on important duties in the Balkan Campaign. During this period he suffered from malaria and rheumatism. In April 1919 he returned home for demobilisation, holding the General Service and Victory Medals.
95, Love Lane, Tottenham, N.17. X18526

TOMES, A. C., Pte., 1st Middlesex Regiment.
He volunteered immediately on the outbreak of hostilities, and was sent to France in 1915. During his service on the Western Front, he took part in many important engagements, and was badly wounded in action at Armentieres. He was invalided home, and was in hospital for some time. In April 1919 he secured his demobilisation and holds the 1914–15 Star and the General Service and Victory Medals.
7, Hartopp Avenue, Dawes Road, S.W.6. X17656.

TOMLIN, A. D., Pte., Manchester Regiment.
He joined in November 1916, and was drafted to France twelve months later. While on the Western Front he took part in heavy fighting until March 1918, when he was taken prisoner at the beginning of the German Advance. He was interned in Germany until after the Armistice was signed. He holds the General Service and Victory Medals, and was still serving in 1920.
129, Raynham Avenue, Upper Edmonton, N.18. 15834B.

TOMLIN, W. G., Gunner, Royal Field Artillery.
He volunteered in September 1914, and was sent soon after to the Western Front, where he took part in the battles of Ypres, the Somme, Arras and Bullecourt, and in the Advance of 1918. During his service in France he was wounded in action, and in 1919 was demobilised. He holds the 1914 Star and the General Service and Victory Medals.
92, Bridport Road, Upper Edmonton, N.18. X17900.

TOMLINSON, H. J., Pte., Tank Corps.
He joined in 1917, was drafted to the Western Front in 1918, and took an active part in the operations at the second Battle of the Somme. He was demobilised in 1919, and holds the General Service and Victory Medals.
86, Lopen Road, Upper Edmonton, N.18. X17913.

TOMLINSON, W., Rifleman, 4th Rifle Brigade.
He joined in 1918, and after completing his training was retained with his unit on important duties. He was not successful in being transferred overseas until 1919, when he was drafted to India, and served on garrison duty at Quetta. He was still serving in 1920.
10, Greyhound Road, College Park, N.W.10. X17802B.

TOMPKINS, A., Pte., 1st North Staffordshire Regt.
He joined in November 1917, completed his training, and remained on important duties with his unit in Ireland and elsewhere, his ill-health preventing his being drafted overseas. He gave valuable services and was demobilised in August 1919.
96, Bravington Road, Maida Hill, W.9. TX19690.

TOMPKINS, A. C., Lce.-Corpl., R.A.S.C., and Somerset Light Infantry.
He joined in January 1917, and was drafted to the Western Front in the same year, where he took an active part in many engagements on the Somme, at Cambrai and during the Retreat and Advance of 1918. He was demobilised in January 1919, and holds the General Service and Victory Medals.
6, Greyhound Road, College Park, N.W.10. X17604.

TONKIN, H. C., Sergeant, R.A.S.C.
He was mobilised on the declaration of war, and was sent in August 1914 to the Western Front. He took part in numerous important engagements, and was in action in the Retreat from Mons, at Loos, Neuve Chapelle, Armentieres, on the Somme, at Vimy Ridge, Ypres, Villers Bretonneux and Jeancourt. He was transferred for a short time to the Eastern front, but was again in France during the Retreat from Cambrai, and was also in action in the Advance of 1918. He was discharged in May 1919, and holds the Mons Star and the General Service and Victory Medals.
80, Chesson Road, West Kensington, W.14. X17694.

TOTHAM, H. J., Pte., Middlesex Regiment and Driver, R.A.S.C.
He volunteered in August 1914, and after his training was retained with his unit on important duties until 1916. He then served with the R.A.S.C. on the transportation of horses to and from France. He was demobilised in February 1919, and holds the General Service and Victory Medals.
39, College Road, Willesden, N.W.10. X18318.

TOTT, A., Sapper, Royal Engineers.
He volunteered in 1915, and served on the Western Front, taking part in the battles of the Somme, Ypres, Bullecourt, and other engagements. He was wounded during his service. In February 1919 he was demobilised, holding the 1915 Star and the General Service and Victory Medals.
78, Bridport Road, Upper Edmonton, N.18. X17467.

TOVEY, W. H., Pte., East Surrey Regiment.

He was mobilised from the Reserve in August 1914, and drafted to the Western Front, where he took part in the Retreat from Mons. He was severely wounded in action, and invalided home. In February 1915 he was discharged as medically unfit for further service, and holds the Mons Star and the General Service and Victory Medals.
3A, Althea Street, Fulham, S.W.6. X21153.

TOWEY, J. W., Sergeant, Royal Fusiliers and Royal Air Force.

He volunteered in August 1914, and the same year was sent out to France, where he remained until 1919. He took part in engagements at Mons, the Marne, the Aisne, Ypres and the Advance in 1918, when he was mentioned in dispatches for conspicuous bravery and devotion to duty. He was wounded. At the close of hostilities he was transferred to the R.A.F., and was demobilised in June 1919, holding the Mons Star and the General Service and Victory Medals.
202, Kilburn Lane, North Kensington, W.10. X18713.

TOWNLEY, W. J., Rifleman, 5th London Regt. (L.R.B.).

He volunteered in December 1915, served with the Labour Corps at Sheerness and in the Isle of Sheppey, was transferred to the London Rifle Brigade, and later was sent to France with the 8th Battalion The London Regiment. He was invalided home in December 1918, and in the following September was demobilised, holding the General Service and Victory Medals.
25, Bramber Road, W. Kensington, W.14. T16276.

TOWNSEND, A., Pte., 9th West Yorkshire Regt.

He volunteered in September 1914, and later was sent to the Western Front, where he saw considerable fighting, and was wounded during the Battle of the Somme. On June 14th, 1917, he was killed in action. He was entitled to the 1914-15 Star and the General Service and Victory Medals.
2, Werley Avenue, Dawes Road, S.W.6. X17881A.

TOWNSEND, E. G., Rifleman, K.R.R.

He joined in September 1916, and served in France, where he took part in many engagements and was severely wounded. He was in hospital in France and London, and was demobilised in January 1919. He holds the General Service and Victory Medals.
2, Werley Avenue, Dawes Road, S.W.6. X17881B.

TOWNSEND, F. W. (M.M.), Pte., Royal Dublin Fusiliers.

He joined in 1916, and in the same year went to France, where he was engaged as a signaller, and took part in several engagements, including those of the Somme and Ypres. He was awarded the Military Medal for gallantry in carrying an important message under heavy fire. While so doing he was severely wounded. He also holds the General Service and Victory Medals, and was demobilised in February 1919.
95, Third Avenue, Queen's Park Estate, W.10. X19442C.

TOWNSEND, G., Gunner, Royal Field Artillery.

Volunteering in January 1915, he was sent in 1917 to France, where he was in action on Vimy Ridge. Later in the same year he was sent to Salonika, and from there to Egypt. During his two years' service in that seat of operations he spent four months in hospital. He was demobilised in July 1919, and holds the General Service and Victory Medals.
95, Third Avenue, Queen's Park Estate, W.10. X19442A.

TOWNSEND, J. A., Pte., Machine Gun Corps.

Enlisting in September 1914, he was drafted to the Western Front in the following year, and took part in the fighting at Loos, the Somme, Ypres, La Bassée and in other sectors. He was demobilised in 1919, and holds the 1914-15 Star and the General Service and Victory Medals.
45, Shorrolds Road, Walham Green, S.W.6. X19347B.

TOWNSEND, W. F., Driver, Royal Engineers.

He volunteered in November 1914, and in the following year was sent to Gallipoli, where he was present during the evacuation of the Peninsula. He was subsequently drafted to France where he served until 1919, taking part in the battles of Ypres, the Somme, Bullecourt and Arras, and in the Retreat and Advance of 1918. He holds the 1915 Star and the General Service and Victory Medals, and was demobilised in March 1919.
95, Third Avenue, Queen's Park Estate, W.10. X19442B.

TOWNSEND, W. H., Corporal, Royal Fusiliers and Army Pay Corps.

Joining in 1915, he was sent to France, and in the following year was severely wounded in action on the Somme. He afterwards served in the Army Pay Corps. In 1919 he returned to England and was demobilised, holding the General Service and Victory Medals.
45, Shorrolds Road, Walham Green, S.W.6. X19347A.

TOWNSHEND, S. G., Special War Worker.

During the war he was engaged on work of a very dangerous nature at Messrs. Rushmore's Munition Factory, Parson's Green Lane, Fulham, where he was employed in making high explosive. His duties were performed with great care and thoroughness.
5, Eustace Road, Walham Green, S.W.6. X19335.

TOWNSON, A., Pte., and Gunner, Royal Fusiliers and R.F.A.

He joined in 1917, and during his service on the Western Front took part in many engagements, and was twice wounded in action. He was in hospital for a time at Abbeville. After the cessation of hostilities he went into Germany with the Army of Occupation, and later was drafted to India, where he was still serving with the R.F.A. in 1920. He holds the General Service and Victory Medals.
26, Kilmaine Road, Munster Road, S.W.6. X18764C.

TOWNSON, H. S., Pte., R.A.S.C. (M.T.).

He volunteered in November 1914, and was soon after drafted to the Western Front. He saw action on many sectors and during his service abroad was engaged as Regimental Dispatch Rider. After being for some time in hospital on account of injuries received in France, he was demobilised in September 1919. He holds the 1914-15 Star and the General Service and Victory Medals.
26, Kilmaine Road, Munster Road, S.W.6. X18764A.

TOWNSON, W. F., Driver, Royal Field Artillery.

Volunteering in August 1914, he was sent to France on the completion of his training. There he took part in various engagements until 1915, when he was invalided home suffering from gas-poisoning. On recovery he returned to the Western Front, but was again invalided to England. He was still in the Army in 1920, and holds the 1914-15 Star and the General Service and Victory Medals.
26, Kilmaine Road, Munster Road, S.W.6. X18764B.

TOYE, A. C., Driver, Royal Field Artillery.

Volunteering in September 1914, he was sent to France in the following year. There he took part in the fighting on the Somme and at Ypres, Loos and many other places, and was gassed. In 1918 he was transferred to Italy, and on his return to England was demobilised in January 1919. He holds the 1914-15 Star and the General Service and Victory Medals.
64, Manor Road, Tottenham, N.17. X18848.

TOYER, W. C., Pte., 1/13th London Regiment.

He volunteered for duty in November 1914, and soon afterwards proceeded to the Western Front. He saw much of the heavy fighting in France, and took part in the battles of Loos, the Somme and Arras, and while in action at Ypres in 1916 he was severely wounded. He returned to England in 1919, and in March of that year was demobilised, holding the 1914-15 Star and the General Service and Victory Medals.
143, Hazlebury Road, Fulham, S.W.6. X20497.

TRAVIS, A., Corpl., 13th and 11th Rifle Brigade.

Volunteering in September 1914, he was shortly afterwards sent to the Western Front. He took part in the fighting at Armentières, the Somme, Loos, Neuve Chapelle, Lens and Cambrai, and in April 1917 was wounded in action at Gavrelle on the Arras sector. He was transferred to the 11th Battn. The Rifle Brigade in April 1918, and in March 1919, after his return to England, was demobilised. He was mentioned in dispatches for his admirable services while overseas, and holds the 1914-15 Star and the General Service and Victory Medals.
13, Strode Road, Willesden, N.W.10. X17594.

TREADWELL, H. J., Gnr., Royal Field Artillery.

He volunteered in January 1915, and served on the Western Front for three years. During this period he took part in many engagements, including those of the Somme, Loos, Ypres, Vimy Ridge, Festubert, Albert and Messines. He was gassed during his service in France, and in 1918 was invalided home. He holds the 1914-15 Star and the General Service and Victory Medals, and was demobilised in January 1919.
301, Shirland Road, Maida Hill, W.9. X19556.

TREAGUS, A. J., Pte., Royal Scots Fusiliers.
He was mobilised in August 1914, after having previously served for twelve years in the Army, and shortly afterwards proceeded to the Western Front, where he saw much service on many sectors up to the close of the war. He was in hospital in France for a time suffering from shell-shock. He was demobilised in March 1919, after his return to England, and holds the 1914-15 Star and the General Service and Victory Medals.
52, Kilmaine Road, Munster Road, S.W.6.   X18758A.

TREAGUS, H. J., Pte., Royal Sussex Regiment.
Immediately on attaining military age, he joined in April 1918. He served on the Western Front, and saw much heavy fighting up to the date of the Armistice, when he was sent into Germany with the Army of Occupation. On his return to England he was demobilised in April 1920, holding the General Service and Victory Medals.
52, Kilmaine Road, Munster Road, S.W.6.   X18758C.

TREAGUS, J., Lce.-Corpl., Royal Scots Fusiliers.
Volunteering in August 1914, he was immediately drafted to the Western Front, where he took part in the Battle of Mons, and was wounded severely. He was invalided home, and in March 1915 was discharged as medically unfit for further military service. He holds the Mons Star and the General Service and Victory Medals.
52, Kilmaine Road, Munster Road, S.W.6.   X18758B.

TREBLE, C., Corporal, Royal Engineers.
Volunteering in March 1915, he was drafted to the Western Front in the same year. He was in action in many engagements, including those of Loos, Arras, Ypres and the Somme, and served through the Retreat and Advance of 1918. He was demobilised in March 1919, holding the 1914-15 Star and the General Service and Victory Medals.
19, Ballantine Street, Wandsworth, S.W.18.   X21869.

TREE, S. W., Pte., 13th East Surrey Regiment.
He volunteered in August 1915, and during his service on the Western Front was in action on many sectors. He took part in various battles, and was wounded and severely gassed. He also served with the Devonshire Regiment, the Royal Fusiliers, and the anti-aircraft section prior to his demobilisation in February 1919. He holds the General Service and Victory Medals.
12, Werley Avenue, Dawes Road, S.W.6.   X17878.

TRELEAVEN, A., Sapper, Royal Engineers.
He volunteered in November 1914, and in the following year was drafted to France, where he took part in many heavy engagements up to the close of the war, including those of the Somme, the Aisne, Marne and the Advance at Cambrai in 1918. He was wounded during his service. He holds the 1914-15 Star and the General Service and Victory Medals, and was demobilised in February 1919.
74, Torquay Street, Paddington, W.2.   X21509.

TRENDLE, F. W., Pte., The Buffs (East Kent Regt.)
He volunteered in November 1915, and in the following April went to France, where he was wounded at the Battle of the Somme on July 3rd, 1916. In 1917 he was transferred to Egypt, but after a short time returned to the Western Front, and was again wounded near Peronne, in September 1917. He was discharged in March 1918, as medically unfit for further duty, and holds the General Service and Victory Medals.
6, Tebworth Road, Tottenham, N.17.   TX18118C.

TRENDLE, G., Driver, Royal Field Artillery.
He volunteered in 1915, and was sent to France on the completion of his training. He was in action on many sectors, and took an active part in various important battles, until his return to England. In July 1918 he was discharged as medically unfit for further duty, owing to heart trouble brought about by exposure. He holds the 1914-15 Star and the General Service and Victory Medals.
6, Tebworth Road, Tottenham, N.17.   TX18118B.

TRENDLE, S., Pte., 1st Middlesex Regiment.
Joining in January 1915, he was drafted to the Western Front in the same year. He took part in many important engagements, and saw much of the heavy fighting up to July 17th, 1918, when he was killed in action. He was entitled to the 1914-15 Star and the General Service and Victory Medals.
6, Tebworth Road, Tottenham, N.17.   TX18118A.

TREVATT, F., Bombardier, R.G.A.
He joined in December 1916, and was immediately drafted to the Western Front. He saw much service up to the date of the Armistice, and fought in the battles of the Somme, Arras, Ypres, Armentieres, Vimy Ridge, Passchendaele, Bapaume, Cambrai and the Advance of 1918. He holds the General Service and Victory Medals, and in 1920 was still in the Army.
44, Burnthwaite Road, Walham Green, S.W.6.   X20206.

TREVERTON, W., Lce.-Corpl., The Buffs (East Kent Regiment).
He joined in 1917, and soon afterwards was sent to the Western Front. He took part in the fighting on many sectors, and as the result of a wound received at Vimy Ridge lost his eye. He was invalided home, and in 1918 was discharged as medically unfit for further military service. He holds the General Service and Victory Medals.
26, Richmond Avenue, Willesden, N.W.10.   T17930.

TREVILLION, G., Rifleman, K.R.R.
Joining in June 1917, he went to France in the same year. He was engaged on various sectors of the Front during his two years' service abroad, and fought at Lens, Passchendaele and Kemmel Hill. Whilst in action at Ypres he was severely wounded. He returned to England in 1919, and in November of that year was demobilised, holding the General Service and Victory Medals.
109, Love Lane, Tottenham, N.17.   X18522.

TRIGGLE, G., Pte., 2nd Middlesex Regiment.
Having previously served in the South African War, he re-enlisted in September 1914, and was almost immediately drafted to France. While on the Western Front he took part in many engagements, including the Battle of Neuve Chapelle. Later he was sent to India, but was invalided home owing to ill-health. He was demobilised in March 1919, holding the Queen's South African Medal, the 1914 Star, and the General Service and Victory Medals.
105, Cassidy Road, Walham Green, S.W.6.   X20218.

TRIM, C. G., Pte., Middlesex Regiment.
He volunteered in June 1915, and in the same year was sent to the Western Front, where he remained until 1918, taking part in many engagements during that period, and was wounded in action. He was eventually sent home and demobilised in February 1919. He holds the 1914-15 Star and the General Service and Victory Medals.
61, Wakefield Street, Upper Edmonton, N.18.   X16567.

TRITTON, A. T., Pioneer, Royal Engineers.
He volunteered in 1915, and in the same year was sent to France, where he was engaged on bridge-building and other important duties. On October 20th, 1917, he died of pneumonia contracted during his service. He was entitled to the 1914-15 Star and the General Service and Victory Medals.
46, Carlyle Avenue, Willesden, N.W.10.   14405B.

TROLLOPE, C. M., Wireless Operator, R.A.F.
Joining in 1916, he was sent to France in the same year. While on the Western Front he was engaged on important duties, demanding a high degree of technical skill. He gave valuable services up to the cessation of hostilities, when he returned home. He was demobilised in February 1919, holding the General Service and Victory Medals.
31, Hazelbury Road, Upper Edmonton, N.18.   X17493.

TROMAN, H., Sergeant, R.F.A. (40th Division).
He volunteered for service in August 1914, and in December of that year was drafted to France. Here he took part in many important engagements, including those of Loos, Lille, Ypres, the Somme, Arras, Amiens, Albert and Cambrai. He was demobilised in January 1919, holding the 1914-15 Star and the General Service and Victory Medals.
23, Hiley Road, Willesden, N.W.10.   X18233.

TROTMAN, A. L., Rifleman, Rifle Brigade.
He joined in 1917, and was sent to the Western Front, where he took part in the battles of St. Quentin, Ypres, Arras and Cambrai. He was wounded on three occasions, invalided home, and demobilised in February 1919. He holds the General Service and the Victory Medals.
8, Musgrave Crescent, Walham Green, S.W.6.   X19710.

TROWBRIDGE, F., Sergeant, 3rd Royal Fusiliers.
He volunteered in November 1914, and in the following year was sent to the Western Front, where he took part in the battles of Loos and Ypres. In November 1915 he was drafted to Salonika, and was in action during much of the heavy fighting in the Balkan Campaign. He returned to France in 1918, and served there until he was demobilised in February 1919. He was awarded a Serbian Order, and holds the 1914-15 Star and the General Service and Victory Medals.
7, Sandringham Road, Cricklewood, N.W.2.   X17098.

TRUELOVE, R. H., Flight-Sergeant, R.A.F.
He volunteered in August 1914, and was soon drafted to France. He was engaged on various important duties in many sectors of the front, and performed his work, which demanded a high degree of technical knowledge, in a conscientious and energetic manner. He was demobilised in March 1919, holding the 1914-15 Star and the General Service and Victory Medals.
7, Pellant Road, Fulham, S.W.6.   X17847.

TUBB, J., Corporal, Royal Berkshire Regiment.
He joined the Army in 1902, and on the outbreak of hostilities was drafted to France. While on the Western Front he took a prominent part in many engagements, including the battles of Mons, Ypres, Cambrai, Loos, Arras, Albert and the Somme, and was wounded on two occasions. He returned home for demobilisation in May 1919, and holds the Mons Star and the General Service and Victory Medals.
60, Milton Avenue, Willesden, N.W.10.   14314A.

TUCKER, A. H., Pte., Royal Marine Light Infy.
He had served early in 1914 on H.M.S. "Lancaster" during the Mexican Rising, and on the outbreak of war was sent on H.M.S. "Chester" to the North Sea. He took part in the engagements of Heligoland Bight and the Falkland Islands, and was in action at the Dardanelles. On the conclusion of that campaign he returned to the North Sea, and was in action with his ship in the Battle of Jutland, where he was killed on May 31st, 1916. He was entitled to the 1914-15 Star and the General Service and Victory Medals.
19, Senior Street, Paddington, W.2.   X21551A.

TUCKER, F. P., Corporal, 9th Royal Sussex Regt.
He enlisted in March 1917, and was sent to France in the following year. Whilst overseas he took a prominent part in the engagement at Loos in August 1918, and was wounded. He returned to England and was demobilised in September 1919, holding the General Service and Victory Medals.
62, Hugon Road, Fulham, S.W.6.   X21620.

TUME, G., Lce.-Corpl., The Queen's 2nd (Royal West Surrey) Regiment.
Having previously served in the South African War, he volunteered in August 1914, and was drafted to France the same year. He took part in the Battle of Ypres, where he was seriously wounded, and invalided home. He was discharged as medically unfit in January 1915, and holds the 1914 Star and the General Service and Victory Medals. He also has the King's and Queen's South African Medals.
6, Wingmore Road, Tottenham, N.17.   X17974.

TUNKS, A., Sergeant, The Queen's (Royal West Surrey Regiment).
He joined in 1916, and in the same year was drafted to the Western Front, where, after some time, he was attached to the Labour Corps. He gave valuable services, whilst engaged on various strenuous duties during his three years overseas. He was demobilised in 1919, holding the General Service and Victory Medals.
41, Steele Road, Willesden, N.W.10.   14534D.

TUNKS, D. (Mrs.), Special War Worker.
During the war this lady was engaged on work of national importance at Park Royal Munition Factory. She carried out her heavy and arduous duties in a highly commendable way, and proved herself to be of great value to the country.
41, Steele Road, Willesden, N.W.10.   14534C.

TURL, F. C., Special War Worker.
During the war he was engaged on work of national importance at Messrs. Darracq's Aircraft Works. He gave valuable service in connection with the construction of aeroplanes, and showed a high degree of technical skill.
39, Archel Road, West Kensington, W.14.   16201B.

TURL, M. M. (Mrs.), Special War Worker.
During the war this lady held an important position in the Civil Service, where she rendered valuable assistance, thus releasing a man for overseas. She showed great efficiency, and rendered very valuable services.
39, Archel Road, West Kensington, W.14.   16201A.

TURNER, A., Pte., R.A.S.C. (M.T.).
He volunteered in April 1915, and later in the same year was drafted to the Western Front, where he remained for nearly four years. During this time he was attached to the supply column, and saw service in various sectors, including Arras, Cambrai, Albert and the Somme. He was demobilised in April 1919, holding the 1914-15 Star and the General Service and Victory Medals.
17, Clarendon Street, Paddington, W.2.   X20631.

TURNER, A. J., Driver, Royal Field Artillery.
He volunteered in January 1915, and was sent out to Gallipoli, where he was in the fighting at Suvla Bay. Later he was sent to Mesopotamia, and served under General Townshend at Kut. Whilst abroad he suffered from malaria. He returned to England and was demobilised in January 1919, holding the 1914-15 Star and the General Service and Victory Medals.
10, Pearscroft Road, Fulham, S.W.6.   X20503.

TURNER, E. M. (Miss), Special War Worker.
During the war this lady offered her services, and was engaged on important duties at the Park Royal Munition Factory, in connection with the examination of fuses and cartridges. She gave valuable services, and performed her duties in a very capable manner.
19, Winchelsea Road, Willesden, N.W.10.   13720A.

TURNER, E. W., Pte., 1st Middlesex Regiment.
He volunteered in August 1914, and was almost immediately drafted to the Western Front, where he took part in the Retreat from Mons and other early engagements. He was killed in action during the first Battle of Ypres, on October 26th, 1914. He was entitled to the Mons Star and the General Service and Victory Medals.
19, Winchelsea Road, Willesden, N.W.10.   13721B.

TURNER, G. C., Pte., 12th Middlesex Regiment.
He joined in 1916, and was sent to France after his period of training. During his service on the Western Front he took a prominent part in many important engagements, and was reported missing after the Battle of Arras, on May 3rd, 1917, but was subsequently found to have been killed in action on that date. He was entitled to the General Service and Victory Medals.
115, Durban Road, Tottenham, N.17.   X17954.

TURNER, H. D., Special War Worker.
In April 1915 he volunteered his services, and was engaged on important duties in the stores of the New Engine Co., Willesden Green, where he had charge of aero engines and other machine parts. He gave valuable services, and in 1920 he was still in the employ of this Engineering Co.
105, Sandringham Road, Cricklewood, N.W.2.   X17139.

TURNER, H. E., Rifleman, 16th London Regiment (Queen's Westminster Rifles).
He joined in May 1917, and was sent out to Egypt. On the voyage his ship, H.M.S. "Aragon," was torpedoed, and about four hundred and fifty lives were lost, but he was, fortunately, among the rescued. On reaching Egypt he was drafted to Palestine, and served with the 60th Division under General Allenby at Jericho and Jaffa, and was present at the entry into Jerusalem. He was later sent to France, and took part in the Advance of 1918. He was demobilised in November 1919, and holds the General Service and Victory Medals.
10, Pearscroft Road, Fulham, S.W.6.   X20501.

TURNER, H. G., Pte., 15th (The King's) Hussars.
He joined in May 1917, and after his training served at various stations on important duties with his unit. He gave valuable services, but was unsuccessful in obtaining his transfer overseas owing to ill-health, and he was discharged in consequence in December 1918.
3, Horder Road, Munster Road, S.W.6.   X19028.

TURNER, J., Pte., Northamptonshire Regiment.
He joined in November 1916, and served on the Western Front, where he took a prominent part in the engagements at Arras, Vimy Ridge, Bullecourt and Messines, and in the Advance of 1918. During his service he was in hospital at Etaples for a time, and was present during the air raid on that town. He holds the General Service and Victory Medals, and was demobilised in November 1919.
10, Pearscroft Road, Fulham, S.W.6.   X20502.

TURNER, J., Corpl., Royal Garrison Artillery.
He volunteered in December 1915, and served on the Western Front for over two years. He took part in the battles of Ypres, Passchendaele, Cambrai, Bourlon Wood, Bapaume, Albert and Kemmel Hill, and was gassed at Senlis. He was demobilised in October 1919, holding the General Service and Victory Medals.
69, Bulwer Road, Upper Edmonton, N.18.   X17891.

TURNER, J., Pte., Norfolk Regiment.
He volunteered in December 1915, and in the following year was drafted to the Western Front, where he took part in many engagements, including those on the Somme, at Ypres, La Bassée, Arras and Cambrai. He was demobilised in November 1919, and holds the General Service and Victory Medals.
12, Novello Street, Parson's Green, S.W.6.   X19953.

TURNER, J., Pte. and Sapper, R.A.S.C. (MT.) and Royal Engineers.
He joined in August 1916, and at the conclusion of his training was drafted to France, where he was engaged on transport duties during several operations on the Western Front. In February 1918 he was transferred to the Royal Engineers, and was sent to Italy, being employed on important duties on the Asiago and Piave Fronts. He was demobilised in March 1919, and holds the General Service and Victory Medals.
60, Victor Road, College Park, N.W.10.   X18688.

TURNER, J. H., Driver, Royal Field Artillery.
He volunteered in January 1915, and was sent to France in the same year. He was engaged on many important duties whilst on the Western Front, and took part in several engagements. He was later sent to Mesopotamia, and from there to India, where he was in action during the campaign on the Afghan Frontier. He was demobilised in December 1919, and holds the 1914–15 Star and the General Service and Victory Medals, and the India General Service Medal (with Clasp Afghanistan N.W. Frontier 1919).
19, Winchelsea Road, Willesden, N.W.10.　　13720B.

TURNER, J. H., Pte., R.A.S.C. (M.T.).
He volunteered in December 1915, and served in France. He was present at many engagements on the Western Front, including the battles of Arras, Ypres and the Somme. He was demobilised in October 1919, and holds the General Service and Victory Medals.
116, Paxton Road, Tottenham, N.17.　　X18811.

TURNER, P. A., Stoker, H.M.S. " Bacchante."
He joined in August 1914, and saw much service in the North Sea, and took a prominent part in all engagements at the Dardanelles. He was also engaged on torpedo boats chasing submarines. He holds the 1914–15 Star and the General Service and Victory Medals, and was demobilised in August 1919.
51, Love Lane, Tottenham, N.17.　　X18306.

TURNER, R., Lce.-Corpl., 16th Rifle Brigade.
He was mobilised in August 1914, and almost immediately drafted out to the Western Front, where he served until 1919. While overseas he served in numerous engagements, including the Retreat from Mons, and the battles of Ypres, Hill 60, Neuve Chapelle, Arras, Albert and the Advance in 1918, and was wounded. He was highly commended, and mentioned in a report by his commanding officer for his distinguished bravery on the field in carrying a wounded soldier to safety under heavy shell fire. He holds the Mons Star and the General Service and Victory Medals, and was demobilised in September 1919.
36, Torquay Street, Paddington, W.2.　　X21775.

TURNER, R., Pte., 6th & 12th Middlesex Regt.
He volunteered in August 1914, and in the same year was sent to the Western Front, where he saw much active service. He took part in numerous important engagements, including those on the Somme, at Ypres, Loos, Albert, Arras, Vimy Ridge and Cambrai, and was three times wounded. He was demobilised in June 1919, and holds the 1914–15 Star and the General Service and Victory Medals.
17, Clarendon Street, Paddington, W.2.　　X20630.

TURNER, W. J., Special War Worker.
During the war he offered his services to the British Caudron Aeroplane Factory, Cricklewood Broadway, and was engaged by them on important work in connection with the manufacture of aeroplane parts. He gave valuable services, and in 1920 was still working with this firm.
19, Winchelsea Road, Willesden, N.W.10.　　13721A.

TURNER, W. P., Pte., 7th Royal Fusiliers.
He joined in November 1916, and on completion of his training was sent overseas the following March. He was in action during much of the heavy fighting on the Western Front, and was killed at the Battle of Arras on August 22nd, 1917. He was entitled to the General Service and Victory Medals.
6, First Avenue, Queen's Park Estate, W.10.　　X18843.

TURNER, W. T., Driver, R.F.A.
He was mobilised in August 1914, and in the same year was sent to France, where he took a prominent part in engagements at Ypres, Arras, Cambrai, the Somme and Hill 60. He was discharged in June 1919, holding the 1914 Star and the General Service and Victory Medals.
50, Clarendon Street, Paddington, W.2.　　X20667.

TURNER, W. W., Pte., 9th Middlesex Regiment.
He volunteered in September 1914, and in the following year was drafted to India, where he remained for four years. Whilst there he was engaged on important garrison duties at various stations with his regiment until sent home to be demobilised in December 1919. He holds the 1914–15 Star and the General Service and Victory Medals.
201, Chapter Road, Cricklewood, N.W.2.　　X17203.

TUSTAIN, A. H., Pte., Oxfordshire and Buckinghamshire Light Infantry.
Volunteering in April 1915, he was drafted in the following July to the Western Front, where he was badly wounded at Ypres in September. He was invalided home, and after having several operations and being in hospital for a considerable period, was discharged in August 1916. He holds the 1914–15 Star and the General Service and Victory Medals.
164, Third Avenue, Queen's Park Estate, W.10.　　X19468.

TUSTAIN, H. (M.M.), Sergt., Machine Gun Corps.
He volunteered for service in March 1915, and in the following year was sent to France, where he took a prominent part in engagements at St. Julien, Ypres, the Marne and Arras, and was wounded. He was awarded the Military Medal in 1918 for conspicuous bravery and devotion to duty in the field near Cambrai. He was demobilised in May 1919, holding the General Service and Victory Medals.
76, Hazlebury Road, Fulham, S.W.6.　　X20522.

TUTT, F. C., Pte., The Queen's (Royal West Surrey Regiment).
He joined in March 1916, and was drafted to the Western Front in the following June. After taking part in several engagements and being wounded on the Somme in October 1916 and at Arras in April 1917, he was invalided home, and retained on important duties. He was demobilised in January 1919, and holds the General Service and Victory Medals.
36, Bolton Road, Harlesden, N.W.10.　　T13378A.

TUTT, H. C., Pte., Royal Army Service Corps.
He volunteered in October 1915, and was shortly afterwards drafted to Salonika, where he was engaged on important duties with his unit. Owing to ill-health he was invalided home and subsequently discharged as medically unfit for further service in May 1918. He holds the 1914–15 Star and the General Service and Victory Medals.
36, Bolton Road, Harlesden, N.W.10.　　T13378B.

TWEED, C., Driver, Royal Field Artillery.
He volunteered in 1915, and a year later he was drafted to Egypt, where he was employed on important duties. In the following year, however, he was sent to the Western Front, and took part in the battles of Arras, the Somme, Vimy Ridge and Cambrai. Whilst overseas he was badly gassed, and in 1919 was demobilised, holding the General Service and Victory Medals.
22, New Holly Lane, Willesden, N.W.10.　　15570A.

TWINING, F., Pte. Rifleman, Middlesex Regt. and 18th London Regt. (London Irish Rifles).
He volunteered in August 1914, and shortly afterwards was drafted to the Western Front, where he went through the memorable Retreat from Mons and the Battle of the Marne. He also took part in many of the engagements which followed, and was in almost continuous action until 1918, when he was invalided home in consequence of ill-health. He was demobilised in January 1919, holding the Mons Star and the General Service and Victory Medals.
46, Woodchester Street, Paddington, W.2.　　X20610.

TWINING, W., Pte., R.A.S.C. (H.T.).
He joined in November 1916, and a year later was drafted to the Western Front. Whilst overseas he played a prominent part in engagements at Arras, Albert, Passchendaele, the Somme and during the Advance of 1918. Later he went to Germany with the Army of Occupation, and remained there until his return to England for his demobilisation in March 1919. He holds the General Service and Victory Medals.
16, Woodchester Street, Paddington, W.2.　　X21268.

TWYDELL, R. G. (Miss), Special War Worker.
For two years during the war this lady was engaged on work of national importance at Messrs. Lebus, Tottenham, making ammunition boxes. Afterwards she went to Enfield Munition Factory, where she was employed as machinist for six months. She carried out her various duties with great care and skill.
149, Poynton Road, Tottenham, N.17.　　X18952B.

TWYDELL, W. J., Sapper, Royal Engineers.
He volunteered in 1915, and in the same year was drafted to the Western Front. He was present during many engagements in this theatre of war, including the battles of the Somme, Ypres, Arras (where he was wounded), Vimy Ridge and the Retreat and Advance of 1918, and returned to England at the cessation of hostilities. He was demobilised in 1919, holding the 1914–15 Star and the General Service and Victory Medals.
149, Poynton Road, Tottenham, N.17.　　X18952A.

TWYDELL, W. J. (Junior), Special War Worker.
During the war he was engaged for two years on work of national importance in connection with the manufacture of mines for the Admiralty, at Messrs. Trollopp and Co.'s factory. He performed his onerous duties in a very satisfactory and painstaking manner.
149, Poynton Road, Tottenham, N.17.　　X18952C.

TYLER, A., Sergeant, Rifle Brigade.

He joined in May 1916, and was drafted to the Western Front in the same year. During his service in France he took a prominent part in many important engagements, including the battles of Arras and Ypres, and was wounded twice. He returned to England in 1917, and was eventually demobilised in 1919, holding the General Service and Victory Medals.

28, Maybury Gardens, Willesden, N.W.10. X17224.

TYLER, F., Corpl., Royal Army Service Corps.

He volunteered for service in April 1915, and later in the same year was drafted to the Western Front, where he remained for four years. During this time he did excellent work with the R.A.S.C. in various sectors, and was severely wounded whilst carrying out his duties under heavy fire. He holds the 1914–15 Star and the General Service and Victory Medals, and was demobilised in April 1919.

39, Heckfield Place, Fulham Road, S.W.6. X20346.

TYSON, A., Corporal, R.F.A. and R.G.A.

He volunteered in September 1914, and during his service on the Western Front took a distinguished part in the battles of the Somme, Arras, Loos, Neuve Chapelle, Vimy Ridge, St. Quentin, Hill 60, Bullecourt, Cambrai and Ypres, and was wounded. He was demobilised in 1919, holding the 1914–15 Star and the General Service and Victory Medals.

2, Lillie Mansions, Lillie Road, Fulham, S.W.6. X18452A.

TYSON, E., Pte., R.N.D. (M.T.).

He volunteered, with many other members of the London General Omnibus Co.'s staff, for special service in October 1914. He was sent overseas and landed at Antwerp, being present during the siege of that city. In September 1915 he was discharged as his services were no longer required, and he holds the 1914 Star and the General Service and Victory medals.

16, Hazlebury Road, Fulham, S.W.6. TX20516.

TYSON, G. H., Corporal, R.A.S.C. (M.T.).

He joined in 1916, and during his service on the Western Front was present at engagements at Arras, Armentières, St. Quentin, Lille, Neuve Chapelle and Ypres, where he was wounded. He was invalided home, and after being in hospital for six months was discharged in 1919 as unfit for further service. He holds the General Service and Victory Medals.

8, Lillie Mansions, Lillie Road, Fulham, S.W.6. X18454.

TYSON, J. H., Rifleman, Rifle Brigade.

He joined in 1918, and after his period of training served at various stations on important duties with his unit. He gave valuable services, but was not successful in obtaining his transfer overseas before the signing of the Armistice, and was demobilised in 1919.

5, Lillie Mansions, Lillie Road, Fulham, S.W.6. X18453.

TYSON, N. (Mrs.), Special War Worker.

During the war this lady volunteered her services, and was engaged on work of national importance at Hayes No. 7 Filling Factory, Harlington, Middlesex, in connection with the filling of eighteen-pounder shells. She carried out her onerous duties with great care and skill.

2, Lillie Mansions, Lillie Road, Fulham S.W.6. X18452B.

TYTE, F. G., Pte., 5th Middlesex Regiment.

He joined in April 1917, and during his service in France, which lasted for over a year, took part in several important battles, and was wounded. He holds the General Service and Victory Medals, and was demobilised in January 1919.

10, Shrewsbury Road, Stonebridge Park, N.W.10 14012B.

UDALL, W. J., Sapper, Royal Engineers.

Volunteering in November 1915, he was drafted to the Western Front on completion of his training. Whilst overseas he did valuable work with the Royal Engineers in many important sectors, and was wounded. He was demobilised in March 1919, holding the General Service and Victory Medals.

72, Bramber Road, West Kensington, W.14. 16222.

ULRICK, G., Pte., R.A.S.C. and 2nd Suffolk Regt.

In 1915 he volunteered in the R.A.S.C., and during the course of his training in England was transferred to the Suffolk Regiment. He was drafted to the Western Front, where he took part in much of the fighting at Ypres, the Somme, Bullecourt, Arras, Dickebusch, Monchy and Cambrai, and was wounded on three occasions. He was demobilised in March 1919, and holds the General Service and Victory Medals.

14, Colin Road, Dudden Hill, N.W.10. 16294B.

ULRICH, H., Pte., Middlesex Regiment.

Joining in March 1917, he was drafted to the Western Front, where he was principally engaged on road repairing with the Labour Corps. He was demobilised in April 1919, holding the General Service and Victory Medals.

11, Bayonne Road, Hammersmith, W.6. 14305.

UNDERWOOD, W. A., Rifleman, K.R.R.

Joining in June 1916, he was drafted to the Western Front on the completion of his training. Whilst overseas he took part in the fighting at Ypres, Kemmel Hill, Passchendaele, St. Quentin, St. Eloi, and was severely wounded during the Advance at Menin Ridge in 1918. He returned to England, and in June 1919 was demobilised, holding the General Service and Victory Medals.

40, Mozart Street, North Kensington, W.10. X18832.

UNDERWOOD, W. J., Pte., 3rd Essex Regiment.

Volunteering in September 1914, he was soon drafted to the Western Front, but after taking a prominent part in many important battles, was killed in action at Ypres on May 24th, 1915. He was entitled to the 1914 Star and the General Service and Victory Medals.

71, Durban Road, Tottenham, N.17. X18291B.

UPTON, A. F. G., 1st Class Stoker, Royal Navy.

Volunteering in October 1914, he was posted to H.M.S. "Britannia," in which he served with distinction with the Grand Fleet until November 9th, 1918, when she was torpedoed. He was demobilised in October 1919, holding the 1914 Star and the General Service and Victory Medals.

68, Sheldon Road, Upper Edmonton, N.18. X17458.

URSELL, A. W., Pte., 20th Machine Gun Corps.

Joining in July 1917, he was drafted to the Western Front. Whilst overseas he took part in many important battles, including those of Vimy Ridge, Lens, Bapaume, Valenciennes and Cambrai, and in the last Retreat and Advance. He returned to England in November 1919, when he was demobilised, holding the General Service and Victory Medals.

26, Walham Grove, Fulham Road, S.W.6. X19642.

USHER, W., Pte., R.A.S.C. (M.T.).

He volunteered in March 1915, and during his service on the Western Front was attached to the R.A.F. He was engaged in conveying guns to the lines, and did other special duties for the aircraft gun section. He was demobilised in June 1919, holding the 1914–15 Star and the General Service and Victory Medals.

33, Fordingley Road, Maida Hill, W.9. X19729.

VALENTINE, A. D., Lce.-Corpl., 1/5th London Regiment.

Volunteering in September 1914, he was drafted to the Western Front. After taking a prominent part in many important engagements, he was killed in action on November 8th, 1918. He was entitled to the 1914–15 Star and the General Service and Victory Medals.

59, Gloucester Road, Upper Edmonton, N.18. X17273B.

VALENTINE, E. C., Pte., 1/7th Middlesex Regt.

He volunteered in August 1914, and was drafted to France with the First Division. He took a conspicuous part in many of the principal engagements, and was in almost continuous action until his death, which occurred in action in August 1917. He was entitled to the 1914 Star and the General Service and Victory Medals.

59, Gloucester Road, Upper Edmonton, N.18. X17273A.

VANDEPEER, A., Pte., 7th Middlesex Regiment.

He joined in November 1916, and was drafted to France, where he took a prominent part in many engagements, including those at Loos, Arras and Monchy. He was demobilised in November 1919, holding the General Service and Victory Medals.

16, Shakespeare Road, Upper Edmonton, N.18. X17181.

VANGO, J. W., Sergeant, Machine Gun Corps.

He volunteered in June 1915, having previously served in the Navy for fifteen years, and was sent out to France on active service. He played a distinguished part in the Battle of the Somme and the fighting at Messines Ridge, and in 1917 he was invalided home suffering from shell-shock. He was discharged in March 1918, holding the General Service and Victory Medals.

30, Harwood Terrace, Walham Green, S.W.6. X20731.

VANGO, J. W., Pte., 7th London Regiment.

He volunteered in May 1915, and served in France, where he fought in many engagements and was twice wounded. He also suffered from shell-shock. He holds the General Service and Victory Medals, and was demobilised in March 1919.

29, Rosaline Road, Munster Road, S.W.6. TX18624B.

VANGO, T. L., Pte., Royal Fusiliers.
He volunteered in September 1914, and served on the Western Front, where, after taking a prominent part in several engagements, he died on December 25th, 1915, of wounds received in action. He was entitled to the 1914–15 Star and the General Service and Victory Medals.
29, Rosaline Road, Munster Road, S.W.6.   TX18624A.

VARDY, W. G., Sapper, Royal Engineers.
He volunteered in April 1915, and, after being sent to France in the same year, took a conspicuous part in many important engagements. He was demobilised in April 1919, holding the 1914–15 Star, General Service and Victory Medals.
42, Gloucester Road, Upper Edmonton, N.18.   X17012.

VERNON, N. W., Pte., Northumberland Fus.
He was serving at the outbreak of war, and in 1914 was sent to the Western Front, where he was killed in action during the battle of the Aisne, in September of the same year. He is buried at Vailly, and was entitled to the 1914 Star and the General Service and Victory Medals.
26, Ambleside Road, Willesden, N.W.10.   16493A.

VESEY, E., Corporal, 3rd Rifle Brigade.
Volunteering in August 1914, he was drafted to the Western Front on completion of his training. He took part in the fighting on the Somme and at Passchendaele, was wounded in action at Hooge and a second time at Cambrai. In 1919 he returned to England, and in February was demobilised, holding the 1914–15 Star and the General Service and Victory Medals.
115, Hazelbury Road, Fulham, S.W.6.   X20500.

VIDLER, A. J., Pte., 1/2nd Royal Fusiliers.
Volunteering in September 1914, he was sent to Gallipoli in the following year, and served there until the evacuation in December 1915. He was then drafted to the Western Front, where he took part in many important engagements, including those on the Somme, at Ypres and Neuve Chapelle, and was severely wounded in action at Croiselles in May 1918. He returned to England, and in May 1919 was demobilised, holding the 1914–15 Star and the General Service and Victory Medals.
33, Villiers Road, Cricklewood, N.W.2.   16730A.

VIDLER, F. J., Pte., 9th Middlesex Regiment.
Volunteering in June 1915, he was drafted to the Western Front, where he took part in the battles of Ypres and the Somme. In October 1918 he was severely wounded in action at High Wood, and was in consequence invalided home. He holds the General Service and Victory Medals and was demobilised in May 1919.
33, Villiers Road, Cricklewood, N.W.2.   16731B.

VILLIERS, G., Pte., Royal Fusiliers.
He joined in 1917, and in the same year went out to France, where he served until 1919. Whilst overseas he took a prominent part in many engagements, including those at Ypres and on the Somme. He holds the General Service and Victory Medals, and was demobilised in 1919.
11, Rowallan Road, Munster Road, S.W.6.   X19273B.

VINCE, O., Pte., Seaforth Highlanders.
He joined in May 1916, and in the following year was drafted to the Western Front, where he took a prominent part in engagements at Ypres, Albert and Cambrai. He was wounded in the Retreat of 1918, and in September of the succeeding year was demobilised, holding the General Service and Victory Medals.
46, Portnall Road, Maida Hill, W.9.   TX19692.

VINCENT, F. C., Driver, R.A.S.C. (M.T.).
Joining in June 1916, he was drafted to the Western Front, where he played a distinguished part in several of the important engagements, and did excellent work. Later he joined the Army of Occupation on the Rhine until his demobilisation in August 1919. He holds the General Service and Victory Medals.
111, Sherbrooke Road, Fulham, S.W.6.   X18617.

VINCENT, J., Gunner, Royal Field Artillery.
He volunteered in January 1915, and during his service in France, which lasted for four years, took part in several engagements, including those at Ypres, the Somme, Arras and Cambrai, and the Retreat and Advance of 1918.
In 1919 he returned to England and was demobilised, holding the 1914–15 Star, General Service and Victory Medals.
86, Clarendon Street, Paddington, W.2.   X20371.

VINCENT, J., Pte., R.A.S.C.
Volunteering in June 1915, he was sent to the Western Front, where he was employed on transport duties, and was wounded. Whilst overseas he received a letter from his Commanding Officer congratulating him on his gallant behaviour during an explosion at Rouen.
He holds the 1914–15 Star, General Service and Victory Medals, and was demobilised in February 1919.
6, Hartopp Avenue, Dawes Road, S.W.6   X17664.

VINCENT, J. W., Bombardier, R.F.A.
He volunteered at the outbreak of hostilities, and was immediately drafted to the Western Front. Whilst in this theatre of war he was in action at the retreat from Mons, and the battles of Neuve Chapelle, Hill 60, La Bassée, Ypres, Loos, Vermelles, Vimy Ridge, the Somme, the Ancre, Messines, Cambrai, Lens and Passchendaele.
He returned to England, and in January 1919 was demobilised, holding the Mons Star, General Service and Victory Medals.
33, Waverley Road, Paddington, W.2   X21902.

VINE, T. W. (jun.), Pte., Coldstream Guards.
He volunteered in 1915, and in the same year was drafted to the Western Front, where, after taking part in several engagements, he was killed in action near Givenchy in September 1916.
He was entitled to the 1914–15 Star, General Service and Victory Medals.
14, Yeldham Road, Hammersmith, W.6   12959A.

VINE, T. W., Pte., Middlesex and Essex Regts.
He volunteered in 1915, but owing to ill-health was invalided out of the Service before the completion of his training. Shortly after his discharge he contracted an illness which resulted in his death on February 18th, 1917.
He is buried at the Kensal Green Cemetery.
14, Yeldham Road, Hammersmith, W.6   12959C.

VINER, A. V. G., Pte., East Surrey Regiment.
Volunteering in October 1914, he was drafted to the Western Front on completion of his training. After taking part in many important engagements, he was reported missing in August 1916, but is believed to have been killed in action at Guillemont.
He was entitled to the 1914–15 Star, General Service and Victory Medals.
77a, Oldfield Road, Willesden, N.W.10   16027B.

VINER, N. C. E., Pte., East Surrey Regiment.
Volunteering in October 1915, he was drafted to Salonica in the following year, and served throughout the Balkan campaign. He was wounded whilst in the East, and in 1919 returned to England for demobilisation.
He holds the General Service and Victory Medals.
77a, Oldfield Road, Willesden, N.W.10   16027A.

VINTON, J., Pte., Manchester Regiment.
An ex-soldier, he volunteered for further service in August 1914. He was first drafted to Egypt, where he took a prominent part in several engagements, and was severely wounded and also suffered from sunstroke. Afterwards he was sent to India, and in 1919 returned to England for his demobilisation in September.
He holds the General Service and Victory Medals.
11, Lorenco Road, Tottenham, N.17   X17993.

VOAK, C. F., A.B., Royal Navy.
He volunteered in August 1914, and after receiving training at Chatham, was posted to H.M.S. " Hawkins " in the North Sea. During his service he took a distinguished part in several naval engagements, and was on one occasion wounded in action.
He was demobilised in November 1919, holding the 1914–15 Star, General Service and Victory Medals.
32, Warwick Road, Upper Edmonton, N.18   X17267.

VOGAN, M. L. (Mrs.), Special War Worker.
This lady was engaged during the war at Messrs. Wells' Aircraft Factory, where she operated a machine in the engineering department. She carried out these duties in a capable and efficient manner, and was worthy of high commendation.
91, Mirabel Road, Fulham, S.W.6   X17856C.

VOLLER, E., Pte., 3rd East Surrey Regiment.
Volunteering in August 1914, he was drafted to the Western Front, where he went through the retreat from Mons. He also took a conspicuous part in many of the engagements which followed, including those on the Marne, the Aisne, at Ypres, Hill 60 and the Somme, and was wounded four times. He returned to England, and in March 1919 was invalided out of the Service owing to wounds, holding the Mons Star, General Service and Victory Medals.
25, Reporton Road, Munster Road, S.W.6   X18070.

VOLLER, J., Pte., 11th Worcestershire Regt.

He volunteered in August 1914, and served on the Western and Eastern Fronts. He took part in many engagements in France and was wounded, and also took part in fighting in Bulgaria and Egypt.

He holds the 1914–15 Star, General Service and Victory Medals, and was demobilised in April 1919.

16, Welford Terrace, Dawes Road, S.W.6   X18071.

VOOGHT, H., Pte., 1/5th King's Own (Royal Lancaster Regiment).

Joining in 1916, he was drafted to the Western Front on completion of his training. His service overseas lasted three years, and during that time he took part in many important engagements, including those at Ypres, Passchendaele, the Somme, Grandcourt, Bullecourt and Cambrai.

He returned to England in 1919, when he was demobilised, holding the General Service and Victory Medals.

6, Ilex Road, Willesden, N.W.10   16095A.

VOOGHT, H., Pte., Machine Gun Corps.

He volunteered in 1915, and served for three years on the Western Front, taking part in the battles of Loos, the Somme and Bourlon Wood.

In 1919 he was demobilised, holding the General Service and Victory Medals.

6, Ilex Road, Willesden, N.W.10   16095B.

VOST, F., Pte., Middlesex Regiment.

He was serving in the Regulars when war broke out and was at once drafted to France. He took a prominent part in many of the most important engagements up to 1916, including Mons, Ypres, Loos and the Somme, where he was severely wounded.

After protracted hospital treatment he was demobilised in November 1919, holding the Mons Star, General Service and Victory Medals.

47, Clarendon Street, Paddington, W.2   X20406A.

VOST, W., Pte., 1st Middlesex Regiment.

Joining in May 1916, he was drafted to the Western Front. After taking a distinguished part in many important engagements, he was killed in action at Polygon Wood on September 26th, 1917, having been in almost continuous action.

He was entitled to the General Service and Victory Medals.

47, Clarendon Street, Paddington, W.2   X20406B.

VOYCE, A., Pte., Royal Army Veterinary Corps.

Volunteering in 1915, he was drafted to the Western Front, and, after being stationed at Boulogne for some time, saw active service at Neuve Chapelle. In 1917 he was drafted to Italy, and served with the R.A.V.C. in many important sectors until 1919, when he returned to England for demobilisation.

He holds the General Service and Victory Medals.

62, Brownlow Road, Willesden, N.W.10   14716B.

VOYCE, A. J., 2nd Aircraftsman, R.A.F.

He joined in 1917, and after his training was engaged on duties demanding a high degree of technical skill. He was not successful, however, in obtaining his transfer overseas before the cessation of hostilities, but afterwards served for six months with the Army of Occupation in Germany.

He was serving in Kent in 1920.

66, Brownlow Road, Willesden, N.W.10   14716A.

VOYCE, W. A., Rifleman, 2nd Cameronians (Scottish Rifles).

Volunteering in March 1915, he served for two years on special guard duties in Ireland. In March 1918 he was drafted to the Western Front, where he took part in many important engagements, including those at Arras, Lens and Cambria, and was severely gassed.

He returned to England in 1919, when he was demobilised, holding the General Service and Victory Medals.

62, Brownlow Road, Willesden, N W.10   14716C.

W

WADE, W. J., Pte., 12th Middlesex Regiment.

He volunteered for service in August 1914, and went to France with the first Expeditionary Force. He served through the Mons Retreat and also took part in engagements at Ypres and on the Somme. He was with the Division which entered Mons at dawn on Armistice Day.

He holds the Mons Star, General Service and Victory Medals, and was demobilised in February 1919.

17, Burnthwaite Road, Walham Green, S.W.6   X20083A.

WAITE, G. F., Pte., R.A.S.C. (H.T.)

He volunteered for service in October 1915, and in the same year was drafted to Salonica, where he remained for two years. During this time he was engaged in conveying ammunition and supplies to the front lines. He suffered from malaria while abroad, and was invalided home and discharged in December 1917.

He holds the 1914–15 Star, General Service and Victory Medals.

7, Woodfield Place, Maida Hill, W.9   X20175.

WAITE, P. E., Gunner, Royal Field Artillery.

He joined in April 1916, and saw service on the Western Front. He fought with distinction on the Somme and on many other sectors up to the date of the signing of the Armistice. Later he went with the Army of Occupation to Germany, where he remained until he returned to England for demobilisation in 1919.

He holds the General Service and Victory Medals.

57, Sheldon Road, Upper Edmonton, N.18   X17302B.

WAITE, W., Pte., Middlesex Regiment.

Volunteering in January 1915, he was drafted to the Western Front in the same year, and while in this theatre of war took part in many engagements. He served at Ypres, Neuve Chapelle, Hill 60, Festubert and was severely wounded, and lost an eye in the heavy fighting during the Retreat of 1918.

He was demobilised, but re-enlisted, and went again to France, where in 1920 he was still serving.

He holds the 1914–15 Star, General Service and Victory Medals.

19, Senior Street, Paddington, W.2   X21551B.

WAITE, W. A., Driver, R.F.A.

Volunteering in November 1915, he was sent out to Egypt in the following year. In 1917 he was transferred to the Western Front, where he was in action on the Somme, and took a prominent part in many other important battles.

He returned to England for demobilisation in 1919, and holds the General Service and Victory Medals.

57, Sheldon Road, Upper Edmonton, N.18   X17302A.

WAITE, W. J., Gunner, Royal Garrison Artillery.

Joining in December 1916, he went out to France in the following September. He saw much fighting while abroad, and took part in numerous important battles up to November 4th, 1917, when he died of wounds received in action at Ypres.

He was entitled to the General Service and Victory Medals.

12, Denholme Road, Maida Hill, W.9   X20138.

WAKEFIELD, E. N., Gunner, R.F.A.

He joined in April 1916, and in September of the same year was drafted to the Western Front. Whilst overseas he took part in important engagements, and in June 1917 was so seriously wounded in action near Messines Ridge that he was still in hospital in 1920.

He holds the General Service and Victory Medals.

7, Bradiston Road, Maida Hill, W.9   X19977.

WAKEFIELD, G. F., Special Constable, Metropolitan Special Constabulary.

He volunteered in August 1914, and was engaged on various important duties throughout the war. He was called up in all air-raids and also did night duty, guarding munition factories, gas works and other buildings. In addition he undertook work at Messrs. Blake's Munition Factory, and was engaged in transporting munitions to the docks for shipment to the troops overseas.

272, Munster Road, S.W.6   X19331.

WAKEFORD, L. S., Pte., East Surrey Regiment.

Volunteering in November 1914, he was sent out to France on the completion of his training. He took part in the engagements on the Somme, and at Ypres, Albert, Dickebusch, and many other places. He was severely wounded in action at Poelcappelle, and in March 1918 was taken prisoner on the Cambrai sector. He was released after the cessation of hostilities, and in February 1919 was demobilised.

He holds the General Service and Victory Medals.

25, Mablethorpe Road, Munster Road, S.W.6   X19226A.

WAKEFORD, R. H., Cpl., Duke of Cornwall's Light Infantry.

He volunteered for duty in 1914, and took part in much of the heavy fighting on the Western Front. After serving with distinction in many important engagements he was killed in action during the battle of the Somme on July 26th, 1916.

He was entitled to the 1914-15 Star, General Service and Victory Medals.

25, Mablethorpe Road, Munster Road, S.W.6   X19226B.

WAKEFORD, W. A., Cpl., Royal Field Artillery.

He volunteered for duty in November 1914, and in July of the following year was sent to the Western Front. He took part in operations on various sectors and fought at Ypres, Passchendaele, Arras and in many other important engagements. In April 1918 he was invalided home suffering from shell-shock, and in the following February was demobilised. He holds the 1914–15 Star, General Service and Victory Medals.

6, Bertie Road, Willesden, N.W.10   X17401.

WAKEHAM, J. W., Pte., R.A.S.C.

He volunteered in April 1915, and in the same year was sent to France, where he was present at many engagements, including those of Loos, Armentières, Ypres, and the Somme. He was invalided home and discharged as medically unfit in June 1917.

He holds the 1914–15 Star, General Service and Victory Medals.

20, De Morgan Road, Townmead Road, S.W.6   X21050.

WAKELING, A., Gunner, R.F.A.

Volunteering in October 1914, he was drafted to the Western Front, where as a signaller he took a prominent part in the battles of Loos and the Somme, and in heavy fighting at Arras and Ypres. In August 1916 he was wounded at Thiepval during the battle of the Somme, and was in hospital at Rouen for two months. He was then invalided home, and was under hospital treatment for a considerable period. He holds the 1914–15 Star, General Service and Victory Medals, and was discharged in July 1917 as medically unfit for further service owing to wounds.

18, Waverley Road, Tottenham, N.17   X18965A.

WAKELING, S., Pte., Middlesex Regiment, and Driver, Royal Field Artillery.

He joined in March 1916 in the Middlesex Regiment, and was shortly after sent to France, where he was wounded in action at Beaumont-Hamel during the battle of the Somme in July 1916. He was in hospital for some time at Boulogne, and on his recovery was transferred to the R.F.A. He again took a conspicuous part in heavy fighting at Arras and Cambrai, where he was wounded.

In December 1919 he secured his demobilisation, holding the General Service and Victory Medals.

18, Waverley Road, Tottenham, N.17   X18965B.

WAKENELL, A., Driver, R.F.A.

He was in the Army at the outbreak of war, and was sent to the Western Front in 1914. He remained on active service in France until 1917, when he was killed at Miraumont by a bomb dropped from an aeroplane.

He was entitled to the 1914 Star, General Service and Victory Medals.

65, Cirencester Street, Paddington, W.2   X20871.

WAKNELL, A. V., Pte., Royal Fusiliers.

He volunteered in September 1914, and was sent to France. After taking a prominent part in many engagements he was killed in action between Ypres and Hill 60 on May 2nd, 1915. He was entitled to the 1914–15 Star, General Service and Victory Medals.

17a, Lorenco Road, Tottenham, N.17   X17990A.

WALDEN, G., Pte., 2nd Middlesex Regiment.

He volunteered in August 1914, and was drafted to the Western Front on completion of his training. During his service in this seat of war he took part in many important operations and was wounded in action.

He holds the 1914–15 Star, General Service and Victory Medals, and was demobilised in February 1919.

88, Adeney Road, Hammersmith, W.6   14660B.

WALDEN, P. J., Cpl., R.A.M.C.

He joined in December 1916, and after his training served in various hospitals as assistant steward. He gave valuable services, but was not successful in obtaining his transfer overseas before the cessation of hostilities.

He was demobilised in August 1919.

43, Broughton Road, Fulham, S.W.6   X20922.

WALDEN, W. J., Driver, R.A.S.C. (M.T.)

Volunteering in September 1914, he was drafted to France soon after, and was engaged on important transport duties in various sectors.

He was demobilised in June 1919, and holds the 1914–15 Star, General Service and Victory Medals.

88, Adeney Road, Hammersmith, W.6   14660A.

WALDIE, W. H., Mechanic, R.A.F. (R.N.A.S.)

He joined in 1917, and after his training was engaged on important duties as a telephone operator at the Admiralty. He gave valuable services, but was not successful in obtaining his transfer overseas before the termination of hostilities.

He was demobilised in 1919.

20, Sheldon Road, Upper Edmonton, N.18   X17308.

WALDOCK, F., Mechanic, Royal Air Force.

Volunteering in July 1915, he was sent to the Western Front in the same year, and played a prominent part in the battles of the Somme and Ypres.

After displaying a highly technical knowledge he was demobilised in March 1919, holding the 1914–15 Star, General Service and Victory Medals.

13, Beaufoy Road, Tottenham, N.17   X17944.

WALKER, A. W., Sergt., Middlesex Regiment.

He volunteered in March 1915, and was soon drafted to France, where he took a prominent part in the battles of Loos, Arras and Ypres, and in other important engagements. He was badly wounded in action, and was in hospital in France and England for some time. On his recovery he was engaged on important duties in England, owing to his being unfit for further service overseas.

In August 1919 he was demobilised, holding the 1914–15 Star, General Service and Victory Medals.

14, Shakespeare Road, Upper Edmonton, N.18   X17182.

WALKER, C. E., Pte., Middlesex Regiment.

Volunteering in March 1915, he was retained on important duties at various stations until 1917. He was then drafted to France, where he took part in heavy fighting at Arras and Albert, and during the Retreat and Advance of 1918, and was twice wounded.

He holds the General Service and Victory Medals, and was demobilised in March 1919.

34, Meyrick Road, Willesden, N.W.10   16340B.

WALKER, C. H. E., Pte., 1st Middlesex Regt.

Volunteering in February 1915, he was soon drafted to the Western Front, and played a conspicuous part in the battles of Loos, Arras, Ypres, the Somme and Cambrai. Whilst overseas he was twice wounded and gassed, and after being in hospital for some time in France was invalided to England. He was demobilised in March 1919, and holds the 1914–15 Star, General Service and Victory Medals.

67, Reporton Road, Munster Road, S.W.6   X18915.

WALKER, E., Pte., Labour Corps.

He joined in 1916, and in the following year was drafted to the Western Front, where he was engaged on duties of an important nature in various sectors.

In 1919, he returned to England for demobilisation, and holds the General Service and Victory Medals.

43, Roseberry Road, Lower Edmonton, N.9   14069A.

WALKER, E. E., A.B., Royal Navy.

He volunteered in 1914, and on board H.M.S. "Warspite" took a prominent part in important naval operations with the Grand Fleet in the North Sea. He was present when his ship played a gallant part at the battle of Jutland, and also carried out important duties off Scotland.

In February 1919 he was demobilised, holding the 1914–15 Star, General Service and Victory Medals.

21, Allestree Road, Munster Road, S.W.6   X19259.

WALKER, E., Cpl., Middlesex Regiment.

He joined in March 1917, and being medically unfit for service overseas was engaged on duties of importance as a writer in the pay office until his demobilisation in March 1920. During this time he gave very valuable services.

51, Deacon Road, Cricklewood, N.W.2   X17209A.

WALKER, F. F., Pte., Middlesex Regiment.

Joining in July 1917, he was drafted to the Western Front in the following year. After taking part in severe fighting in this theatre of war he was killed in action on August 18th, 1918.

He was entitled to the General Service and Victory Medals.

96, Third Avenue, Queen's Park Estate, W.10   X19283.

WALKER, F. W., Lce.-Cpl., 2nd Middlesex Regt.

He volunteered in October 1914, and on completion of his training was drafted to the Western Front in the following January. After taking a prominent part in much heavy fighting, he was killed in action at the battle of Neuve Chapelle on March 10th, 1915.

He was entitled to the 1914–15 Star, General Service and Victory Medals.

18, Waldo Road, College Park, N.W.10   X17565.

WALKER, G. E., Pte., Machine Gun Corps.

In August 1914 he volunteered for service and was drafted to the Western Front, where he took part in much severe fighting. Later he was sent to India, and during his 2½ years' service there was engaged on important duties at various stations.

He returned for his demobilisation in June 1919, and holds the 1914–15 Star, General Service and Victory Medals.

21, Allestree Road, Munster Road, S.W.6   X19260.

WALKER, J., Cpl., 9th Middlesex Regiment.

He volunteered in August 1914 at the age of 16, and after his training was engaged on important duties at various stations.

He gave valuable services and gained promotion for consistent good work, but on June 23rd, 1916, died after a severe illness.

51, Deacon Road, Cricklewood, N.W.2   X17209B.

WALKER, J., Pte., 3rd York and Lancaster Regt.

He joined in September 1917, immediately he attained military age, and was sent to France at the end of the same year. Whilst overseas he took part in numerous engagements, including the battle of Cambrai.

He holds the General Service and Victory Medals, and in 1920 was still serving.

48, Wornington Road, N. Kensington, W.10   X20944B.

WALKER, J. E. W., Pte., R.A.S.C. (M.T.)

Joining in June 1917, he was sent to France in the following month, and whilst on the Western Front was engaged on important transport duties in various sectors. In 1919 he joined the Army of Occupation on the Rhine, and there carried out special duties with a Head-quarters' Staff.

He was demobilised in November 1919, holding the General Service and Victory Medals.

31, Barry Road, Stonebridge Park, N.W.10   14942A.

WALKER, J. H., 1st Air Mechanic, R.A.F. (late R.N.A.S.)

He joined in September 1917, and was drafted to Italy, where he carried out important work which called for a high degree of technical skill. Later he was engaged on special duties with his squadron, and was in hospital in Malta for some time.

He was demobilised in December 1918, holding the General Service and Victory Medals.

24, Sherbrooke Road, Fulham, S.W.6   X18470.

WALKER, J. W., Pte., Middlesex Regiment and Royal Army Ordnance Corps.

He volunteered in August 1914, and in the same month was sent to France, where he took part in the retreat from Mons, the battles of Loos, the Somme and Arras. He was then transferred to the R.A.O.C., owing to his being over age for further service in the fighting line, and did valuable work in the gun repair shops until his demobilisation in February 1919.

He holds the Mons Star, General Service and Victory Medals.

51, Deacon Road, Cricklewood, N.W.2   17209C.

WALKER, J. W., Sergt., Middlesex Regiment.

He volunteered in August 1915, and served on the Western Front. After being wounded he returned to England on an ammunition ship which was torpedoed. He was among the survivors, and was taken to Manchester Infirmary, suffering from exposure and cancer, of which he died in February 1917, within three weeks of the disaster.

He was entitled to the 1914-15 Star, General Service and Victory Medals.

31, Barry Road, Stonebridge Park, N.W.10   14942B.

WALKER, S., Cpl., 1st Middlesex Regiment.

He was in the Army at the outbreak of the war, having previously served in India, and was immediately sent to the Western Front, where he took part in the retreat from Mons. On October 20th, 1914, he was killed in action.

He was entitled to the Mons Star, General Service and Victory Medals.

85, Drayton Road, Harlesden, N.W.10   15252C.

WALKER, T. C., Rifleman, King's Royal Rifles.

He re-enlisted in August 1914, having previously served for 25 years, and in 1915 was sent to France, where he took a prominent part in many engagements, including those of Ypres, Loos, Armentières and the Somme, and after being wounded was invalided home.

He was demobilised in March 1919, and holds the 1914-15 Star, General Service and Victory Medals.

44, Clarendon Street, Paddington, W.2   X20664.

WALKER, W., Gunner, 177th Battery, R.F.A.

He joined in February 1916, and in the following August was drafted to the Western Front, where he played a prominent part in the battles of Arras, Bullecourt and the Somme. In February 1919 he was demobilised, and holds the General Service and Victory Medals.

48, Wornington Road, W. Kensington, W.10   X20944A.

WALL, A., Sergt., 12th Middlesex Regiment.

He volunteered in October 1914, and in the same year went to the Western Front, where he took part in many battles, including those of La Bassèe, Ypres and Cambrai. After recovery from an operation which had been found necessary, as the result of an illness contracted in France, he was transferred to the Labour Corps.

He holds the 1914 Star, General Service and Victory Medals, and was demobilised in March 1919.

86a, Deacon Road, Cricklewood, N.W.2   X17114A.

WALL, J. (M.S.M.), Staff Sergt., R.A.S.C. (M.T.)

He volunteered in August 1914, and was drafted to the Western Front, where he was engaged on important duties of a responsible nature in charge of workshops. He met with a serious accident and was in hospital in France and England. On his recovery he was sent to Mesopotamia, and again carried out special duties. He was awarded the Meritorious Service Medal for devotion to duty and consistent good work, and in addition holds the 1914-15 Star, General Service and Victory Medals.

He was demobilised in July 1919.

24, Rosaline Road, Munster Road, S.W.6   X18178.

WALL, J. W., Staff Sergeant Major, 6th (Inniskilling) Dragoons.

He joined the Army in 1894, and was in India when war broke out. On his return he saw service on the Western Front from 1915 to 1917 and fought at Ypres and the Somme. For the two succeeding years he was in England acting as an instructor, and was discharged in March 1919. However, he rejoined the following August and went to China for six months.

He was demobilised in March 1920, and holds the Queen's South African Medal, 1914 Star, General Service and Victory Medals.

76, Droop Street, Queen's Park Estate, W.10   X18702.

WALL, S. G., Pte., The Queen's (Royal West Surrey Regiment).

He volunteered in 1915, and in the following year was sent to the Western Front, where he was engaged as a signaller, and took part in many engagements, including those at Arras, Cambrai and in the Retreat and Advance of 1918.

He was demobilised in 1919, holding the General Service and Victory Medals.

86, Deacon Road, Cricklewood, N.W.2   X17114B.

WALLACE, D., Bombardier, R.F.A.

He volunteered in September 1915, and served on the Western Front, taking a prominent part in many engagements. Later he was sent to Germany with the Army of Occupation, and remained there until he was demobilised in July 1919, holding the General Service and Victory Medals.

10, Milton Road, Upper Edmonton, N.18   X17259.

WALLACE, G. S., Rifleman, 18th London Regt. (London Irish Rifles).

After previous service, he rejoined in 1914, and was drafted to the Western Front, where he took part in many engagements. Later he went to Salonica, and thence to Egypt, and again saw heavy fighting, and was twice wounded.

He holds the 1914-15 Star, General Service and Victory Medals, and was demobilised in July 1919.

36, Avalon Road, New King's Road, S.W.6   X19771.

WALLER, F. E., Bombardier, R.F.A.

Volunteering in November 1915, he saw service in North West India, and took part in the suppression of the Afghan rising.

He holds the General Service and Victory Medals and Indian General Service Medal, 1908, with clasp—Afghanistan, N.W. Frontier, 1919. He was still serving in 1920.

12, North Road, Lower Edmonton, N.9   11958B

WALLER, L. W., Leading Telegraphist, R.N.

Volunteering in 1914, he was engaged in the North Sea on patrol duty in H.M.S. "Agincourt," and took part in the battles of Jutland and Dogger Bank.

He holds the 1914-15 Star, General Service and Victory Medals, and was still serving in 1920.

72a, St. Mary's Road, Craven Park, N.W.10   13365B.

WALLIS, E. W., Special War Worker.

During the war he gave valuable services in the clerical department of the Navy and Army Canteen Board at the head office at Knightsbridge. Throughout he held a responsible position, and performed his duties in a very satisfactory manner.

49, Bronsart Road, Munster Road, S.W.6   X19010.

WALLIS, H., Pte., Seaforth Highlanders.

He joined in 1916, and during his service in France took part in several important engagements, including those of Arras, the Somme, Vimy Ridge and Albert, and was gassed. Later he served with the Army of Occupation until his demobilisation in 1919.

He holds the General Service and Victory Medals.

380, High Road, Willesden, N.W.10   16621C.

WALLIS, R. E., Chief Petty Officer, Royal Navy.

Volunteering in August 1914, he served in H.M.S. "Africa" in the North Sea and off the coast of West Africa. During his service he also took a distinguished part in the battle of Jutland, and was stationed at Scapa Flow.
He was demobilised in January 1920, and holds the 1914–15 Star, General Service and Victory Medals.
49, Bronsart Road, Munster Road, S.W.6   X19009.

WALLIS, W. S., C.S.M., Royal Engineers.

Volunteering in March 1915, he was later in the year sent to Egypt, where he joined the Expeditionary Force and played a conspicuous part in the advance through Palestine. He saw service on both sides of the Jordan, and fought in several engagements.
He holds the 1914–15 Star, General Service and Victory Medals, and was still serving in Egypt in 1920.
19, Ashburnham Road, Willesden, N.W.10   X18332.

WALSH, J., A.B., Royal Navy.

He volunteered in August 1914, and served in the North Sea and Scapa Flow with the Grand Fleet in H.M.S. "Victorious." He was employed also on laying and sweeping mines, and has had 30 years' service in the Navy.
He was demobilised in February 1919, holding the 1914–15 Star, General Service and Victory Medals.
38, Wilson's Road, Hammersmith, W.6   15853A.

WALTER, A. G., Rifleman, King's Royal Rifles.

He joined in August 1918, and after the completion of his training was sent to join the Army of Occupation in Germany, where he rendered valuable services.
On his return to England in 1920 he was demobilised.
6, Vallier Road, College Park, Willesden, N.W.10   X17680C.

WALTER, A., Pte., Royal Fusiliers.

He volunteered in December 1915, and in the following year went to the Western Front, where he took a prominent part in many battles, including those of the Somme and Arras. In April 1917 he was taken prisoner, and during his captivity, which lasted until the following year, suffered great privations.
He was demobilised on his release in January 1919, holding the General Service and Victory Medals.
6, Vallier Road, College Park, Willesden, N.W.10   X17680A.

WALTER, P., Driver, R.A.S.C.

He volunteered in February 1915, and served on the Western Front, where he was employed with the supply columns, and also attached to the R.A.M.C. as stretcher-bearer. He was in France from August 1915 until he was demobilised in April 1919, and holds the 1914–15 Star, General Service and Victory Medals.
6, Vallier Road, College Park, Willesden, N.W.10   X17680B.

WALTERS, F. L., Cpl., 3rd London Regiment (Royal Fusiliers).

He was serving in the Territorials, and was mobilised at the outbreak of war. In 1914 he was sent to Malta, and stationed there on important duties until 1918.
He was demobilised in March 1919, and holds the 1914–15 Star, General Service and Victory Medals.
1, Holberton Gardens, Willesden, N.W.10   X17557.

WALTON, H. J., Pte., 21st Middlesex Regiment.

Volunteering in November 1915, he was sent to France in the following year, and took part in various engagements, including the battles of Hill 60 and the Somme, where he was killed in action on October 4th, 1916.
He was entitled to the General Service and Victory Medals.
51, Earlsmead, Road, College Park, N.W.10   X17841A.

WALTON, W. J., Pte., 12th Royal Fusiliers.

He volunteered in September 1914, and in the following year was sent to the Western Front. He took part in the engagements at Loos and Ypres, and on June 8th, 1916, died of wounds received in action.
He was entitled to the 1914–15 Star, General Service and Victory Medals.
51, Earlsmead Road, College Park, N.W.10   X17841B.

WANNERTON, A. (Miss), Special War Worker.

For three years during the war this lady was engaged on important work at the Munitions Factory, Park Royal. Her exceptional ability led to her being appointed to the responsible position of inspector of fuzes.
78, Churchill Road, Cricklewood, N.W.2   16623B.

WANNERTON, M. (Miss), Special War Worker.

From 1915 until 1918 this lady was engaged at Park Royal on work of a most intricate nature in connection with the manufacture of fuzes and mines, and performed her duties in a most zealous manner.
78, Churchill Road, Cricklewood, N.W.2   16624B.

WARD, A., Pte., Royal Army Medical Corps.

Joining in July 1916, he served with his unit at various stations on important duties. He gave valuable services, but owing to physical weakness was not successful in obtaining his transfer to a theatre of war prior to the cessation of hostilities.
He was demobilised in February 1919.
4, Bridport Road, Upper Edmonton, N.18   X17895.

WARD, A., Sapper, Royal Engineers.

He volunteered in August 1915, and shortly afterwards was drafted to France, where he remained for over three years. While overseas he took part in many engagements, including those of Ypres, Arras and Cambrai, and after the Armistice proceeded to Germany with the Army of Occupation.
He was demobilised in February 1919, holding the 1914–15 Star, General Service and Victory Medals.
93, Southam Street, N. Kensington, W.10   X20786.

WARD, A. H., Lce. Cpl., Middlesex Regiment.

He volunteered in February 1915, and in the following year went to the Western Front, where he saw much active service. He took part in the engagements at Ypres, Loos, Albert, Vimy Ridge and the Somme, where he was twice wounded. He was invalided home, and on his recovery was redrafted to France and served at Cambrai in the last great Advance of 1918.
He was demobilised in February 1919, and holds the General Service and Victory Medals.
35, Furness Road, Fulham, S.W.6   X21139A.

WARD, C. C., Sergt., Royal Field Artillery.

He volunteered in July 1915, and the excellent service which he rendered in connection with the canteens and messes rapidly won him promotion to the rank of sergeant. His work was of the greatest value, but he was not successful in being drafted abroad prior to the signing of the Armistice.
He was demobilised in January 1919.
37, Reporton Road, Munster Road, S.W.6   X18867.

WARD, E., Pte., 1st Devonshire Regiment.

He volunteered in February 1915, and in the same year was drafted to Mesopotamia, were he took part in several engagements. Later, with General Allenby—for whom he acted as bodyguard—he went through the Palestine campaign, and was present at the entry into Jerusalem. During his service in the East he was wounded.
He was demobilised in 1919, holding the 1914–15 Star, General Service and Victory Medals.
38, Clarendon Street, Paddington, W.2   X20530A.

WARD, E. A. (Miss), W.R.A.F.

She joined in April 1915, and was stationed at the Wormwood Scrubbs and Regent's Park centres, where she rendered valuable service as a shorthand typist. She was demobilised in September 1919, and was awarded a certificate of merit in recognition of her most useful work.
68, Shorrolds Road, Walham Green, S.W.6   X19499.

WARD, E. J., Pte., The Queen's (Royal West Surrey Regiment).

He joined in February 1917, and in the same year was sent to France, where he remained until 1919. During this time he took part in many engagements, including those of Arras, Loos, Cambrai, the Somme and the Retreat and Advance of 1918, in which he was wounded.
He was demobilised in March 1919, holding the General Service and Victory Medals.
38, Clarendon Street, Paddington, W.2   X20530B.

WARD, F. (Mrs.), Special War Worker.

During the war this lady rendered valuable services for a time as assistant cook at Messrs. Blake's Munition Factory, Hurlingham Road, Fulham, but was obliged to resign owing to ill-health.
35, Furness Road, Fulham, S.W.6   X21139B.

WARD, F. A., Sapper, Royal Engineers.

Volunteering for duty in August 1915, he was sent to France the next year, and while in this theatre of war took part in many important engagements, including the battle on the Somme. In 1917 he was transferred to Salonica, and was in action on the Vardar and Doiran Fronts. In 1918 he was drafted to Palestine, and was in General Allenby's Forces during the campaign up to the victorious entry into Jerusalem and Jericho.
He was demobilised in June 1919, holding the General Service and Victory Medals.
43, Edbrooke Road, Maida Hill, W.9   X21382.

WARD, F. J., Driver, Royal Field Artillery.

Volunteering for duty in September 1914, he was sent to France in the following year and served on that Front until 1919. During this time he was in action at Ypres and Hill 60, and was badly gassed on the Somme Front.
He was demobilised in February 1919, holding the 1914–15 Star, General Service and Victory Medals.
44, De Morgan Road, Townmead Road, S.W.6   X21674.

WARD, F. W. L., A.B., Royal Navy, H.M.S. "Queen Elizabeth."

Volunteering in August 1915, he was on escort duty in the Atlantic Ocean up to the close of the war, convoying troopships from Canada and the United States. During his service he became a qualified signaller.
He holds the General Service and Victory Medals, and was demobilised in April 1920.
12, Rowallan Road, Munster Road, S.W.6   X19268.

WARD, J. W., Trooper, 4th (Royal Irish) Dragoon Guards.

He was in the Army at the outbreak of hostilities, and was sent to France in 1914. During his service overseas he took part in numerous important engagements, including those of Mons, the Marne, the Aisne, Ypres, Loos and Cambrai, and was badly wounded and gassed. He returned to England and was demobilised in November 1919.
He holds the Mons Star, General Service and Victory Medals.
9, Napier Rd., College Park, Kensal Green, N.W.10   X17772.

WARDEN, C., Special War Worker.

During the war he was engaged on important military work at Messrs. Allen and Ensor's, Kilburn, where he held a very responsible position. He carried out his arduous duties in a manner worthy of the highest commendation.
13, Chapman's Cottages, High Road, Willesden, N.W.10
16625A.

WARDEN, N. (Mrs.), Special War Worker.

During the war this lady held a responsible post at the Park Royal Munition Factory. The work on which she was engaged, besides being extremely dangerous, demanded great care and accuracy, and was entrusted only to the most efficient workers. On resigning she was highly commended for her valuable services.
101, Ashmore Road, Harrow Road, W.9   X19751A.

WARDEN, R. E., Sergt., 1st Middlesex Regiment.

He volunteered in July 1915, and was sent to France in the same year. He took part in the battles of Béthune, Loos, the Somme and Arras, and was killed in action near Ypres in 1917.
He was entitled to the 1914–15 Star, General Service and Victory Medals.
116, Holly Lane, Willesden, N.W.10   15398A.

WARDEN, W., Pte., R.A.S.C. (M.T.)

He joined in March 1916, and later in that year was drafted to the Western Front, where for three years he did valuable service as a motor-mechanic, repairing all types of cars. His work frequently took him into the danger zone, but he escaped uninjured.
He was demobilised in June 1919, holding the General Service and Victory Medals.
101, Ashmore Road, Harrow Road, W.9   X19751B.

WARING, A. W., Pte., The Queen's (Royal West Surrey Regiment).

He joined in February 1916 in the hope of proceeding overseas. During his training, however, he was found to be physically unfit for service, and was discharged in June 1916.
64, First Avenue, Queen's Park, W.10   X18839A.

WARING, F. G., Pte. (1st-Class Signaller), 1st London Regiment (Royal Fusiliers).

He volunteered in September 1914, and was drafted to the East in the following February. He took part in the Dardanelles campaign until the evacuation of the Peninsula, when he was transferred to the Western Front. During his service in France and Belgium he was in action on the Somme and at Arras, Cambrai, Ypres and Valenciennes.
He was demobilised in March 1919, after four and a half years' service, and holds the 1914–15 Star, General Service and Victory Medals.
64, First Avenue, Queen's Park, W.10   X18839B.

WARING, W. J., Gunner, R.G.A.

He joined in April 1916, and after his training served with his unit on the Coastal Defence Batteries. He gave valuable service, but owing to being physically unfit was not successful in obtaining his transfer to the Front.
He was demobilised in August 1919.
64, First Avenue, Queen's Park, W.10   X18839C.

WARMAN, J., Gunner, R.F.A.

He volunteered in 1914, and in the following year was drafted to Salonica, where he served in the Balkan campaign. Whilst overseas he contracted malaria and was invalided home. After being in hospital for some time he was discharged in 1917 as medically unfit for further service.
He holds the 1914–15 Star, General Service and Victory Medals.
54, Hartington Road, Tottenham, N.17   X19110.

WARNE, G. H., Driver, R.A.S.C.

He attested in December 1915, but was not called up until February 1918, as he was engaged on work of national importance. He was sent to France shortly afterwards, where he was engaged on important duties during the Retreat and Advance of 1918. After the Armistice he went to Germany with the Army of Occupation, and remained there until his return to England for demobilisation in April 1920.
63, Burrow's Road, Willesden, N.W.10   X18253.

WARNE, J., Pte., R.A.S.C. (M.T.)

He volunteered for service in 1915, and on the completion of his training was drafted to the Western Front, where he was engaged on special duties in connection with the transport of ammunition and stores during operations at Cambrai, Arras, Ypres and the Somme.
He was demobilised in 1919, and holds the General Service and Victory Medals.
69, Purves Road, Kensal Rise, N.W.10   X17800.

WARNEFORD, W., Pte., 7th Bedfordshire Regt.

He volunteered for duty in September 1914, and served on the Western Front from the following year until October 22nd, 1916, when he was killed in action on the Somme. He was buried at the British Cemetery, Courcelette.
He was entitled to the 1914–15 Star, General Service and Victory Medals.
220, Portnall Road, Maida Hill, W.9   X19831A.

WARNELL, E. J., Driver, R.F.A.

He volunteered in February 1915, and during his service in France took part in many battles, including those of Loos, Arras, Ypres and Cambrai, where he was badly wounded. He was invalided to hospital in England, remaining there for some months.
He was eventually demobilised in March 1919, and holds the 1914–15 Star, General Service and Victory Medals.
17, Hartington Road, Tottenham, N.17   X19102.

WARNER, F. B., Cpl., 8th London Regiment (Post Office Rifles).

He joined in October 1916, and in the same year was drafted to the Western Front, where he took part in many important engagements. He served in the Somme sector and at Bullecourt, and was wounded.
He was demobilised in March 1919, and holds the General Service and Victory Medals.
9, De Morgan Road, Townmead Road, Fulham, S.W.6
X20847.

WARNER, T. G., Pte., 13th London Regiment (Kensingtons).

He volunteered in February 1915, and was sent to France in the same year. He was in action on the Somme and at Arras and Amiens, and was wounded.
He holds the 1914–15 Star, General Service and Victory Medals, and was demobilised in March 1919.
13, Novello Street, Parson's Green, S.W.6   X19954.

WARR, H., Pte., 3rd (King's Own) Hussars.

He volunteered in April 1915, and was drafted overseas in the same year. During his service on the Western Front he was actively engaged in much of the heavy fighting in the Somme, Ypres and Cambrai sectors.
He was demobilised in January 1919, and holds the 1914–15 Star, General Service and Victory Medals.
37, Waldo Road, College Park, N.W.10   X17629.

WARR, H., Sapper, Royal Engineers.

He volunteered in November 1914, and after his period of training served with the Royal Engineers on important duties in connection with the railways at various depots. Owing to his special qualifications he was not sent overseas, and after rendering valuable services was demobilised in March 1919.
33, St. John's Avenue, Harlesden, N.W.10   14748.

WARR, R. J., Pte., The Queen's (Royal West Surrey Regiment).

He volunteered for service in 1914, and later was drafted to the Western Front. Whilst overseas he took part in numerous engagements, including the battles of Ypres, Loos, the Somme and Arras, and was seriously wounded. He returned to England, and in April 1918 was invalided out of the Service.
He holds the 1914–15 Star, General Service and Victory Medals.   8, Cassidy Road, Walham Green, S.W.6 X20300.

WARREN, A., Pte., Middlesex Regiment.

He volunteered in 1914, and was drafted overseas in the same year. While on the Western Front he was in action during many important engagements, including the battles of the Somme and La Bassée, and was wounded and three times gassed.
He was demobilised in 1919, and holds the 1914 Star, General Service and Victory Medals.
79, Asplin Road, Tottenham, N.17   X19080B.

WARREN, C., Pte., East Surrey Regiment.

He volunteered in August 1915, at the age of 15 years, and served on the Western Front, taking part in the battles of Loos, Arras, Ypres and on the Somme. He also served in the King's Own Scottish Borderers, the Scottish Rifles and the Royal Scots.
He was demobilised in December 1918, and holds the 1914-15 Star, General Service and Victory Medals.
10, Hartopp Avenue, Dawes Road, Fulham, S.W.6 X17739.

WARREN, C. R., Lce.-Cpl., 1st Middlesex Regt.

He volunteered in August 1914, and was drafted to the Western Front shortly afterwards. During his service in this theatre of war he saw much fighting, and was in action at the battles of the Somme, Loos, Ypres, and La Bassée, and was wounded.
He holds the 1914 Star, General Service and Victory Medals, and was demobilised in March 1920.
79, Asplin Road, Tottenham, N.17   X19080A.

WARREN, E. R., Chief Petty Officer, R.N., H.M.S. " Swiftsure."

He rejoined in August 1914, and served in various waters, conveying Indian troops to France, and chasing the "Emden." He died on November 23rd, 1914, at Alexandria Hospital, and was buried at Port Said Cemetery.
He held the Long Service, Somaliland and Persian Gulf Medals, and was entitled to the 1914 Star, General Service and Victory Medals.
34, Disbrowe Road, Hammersmith, W.6   15909A

WARREN, F., Air Mechanic, Royal Air Force.

He joined in August 1916, and after his period of training served at various aerodromes on important duties with his squadron. He gave valuable services, and his duties called for a high degree of technical skill, but he was not successful in being transferred overseas.
He was demobilised in January 1919.
32, Siddons Road, Tottenham, N.17   X19148.

WARREN, G. L. (M.M.), Lce.-Cpl., 1/1st London Regiment (Royal Fusiliers).

He volunteered in August 1914, and in the following March was sent to the Western Front. He took part in numerous engagements and was awarded the Military Medal for conspicuous gallantry. On September 18th, 1918, he was killed in action at Epéhy.
He was entitled to the 1914-15 Star, General Service and Victory Medals.
56, St. Ervan's Road, N. Kensington, W.10   X20378B.

WARREN, G. V., Pte. (Signaller), Queen's Own (Royal West Kent Regiment).

He joined in March 1916, and after his period of training was engaged on special duties with his regiment until 1918, when he was drafted to France. He was in action during much of the heavy fighting in the Retreat and Advance, and was slightly gassed. He afterwards went to Germany with the Army of Occupation and returned to England for his demobilisation in October 1919.
He holds the General Service and Victory Medals.
45, Somerset Road, Upper Edmonton, N.18   X17033.

WARREN, W., Pte., 9th East Surrey Regiment.

He joined in July 1918, and was shortly afterwards sent to France, where he served until the cessation of hostilities. He took part in several engagements during the Allies' Advance, and later sent to Germany with the Army of Occupation.
He holds the General Service and Victory Medals, and was demobilised in March 1920.
1a, Orchard Place, Tottenham, N.17   X18535.

WARREN, W. J., Bandsman, 3rd (Prince of Wales') Dragoon Guards.

He joined in October 1917, and in January of the following year went to France, where he served till December. During his service he was wounded on the Belgian Frontier in October 1918 by the explosion of a shell.
He holds the General Service and Victory Medals, and in 1920 was serving with his regiment in India.
56, St. Ervan's Road, N. Kensington, W.10   X20378A.

WARREN, W. J., Pte., 2/3rd Royal Fusiliers and Machine Gun Corps.

He volunteered in September 1914, and was sent to the Eastern Front in February 1915, where he took part in the Dardanelles operations. He was next transferred to the Western Front, was in action at Ypres, Arras, and Cambrai, and was wounded at Gommecourt in 1917. He afterwards joined the North Russian Expeditionary Force, and later served in India.
He holds the 1914-15 Star, General Service and Victory Medals.
42, First Avenue, Queen's Park Estate, W.10   X18838.

WARRICK, H. T. (M.M.), Pte., Middlesex Regt.

He volunteered in November 1915, and served on the Western Front for three years. He took a distinguished part in the battle of the Somme and many other engagements, and was twice wounded. In 1916 he was awarded the Military Medal for conspicuous bravery, and in addition holds the General Service and Victory Medals.
He was demobilised in March 1919.
28, Ashford Road, Tottenham, N.17   X18353B.

WARTERS, S. A., Pte., East Surrey Regiment.

He volunteered in May 1916, and was sent overseas in the same year. He was in action at the battle of the Somme and was wounded there in 1916. Upon his recovery he again took part in much of the fighting on the Western Front, and was wounded a second time in 1918.
He holds the General Service and Victory Medals, and was demobilised in January 1919.
38, St. Paul's Road, Tottenham, N.17   X18828.

WARWICK, A. H., Pte., East Surrey Regiment.

He volunteered in 1915, and in the following year was sent overseas. He took part in many engagements on the Western Front, including the battles of the Somme and Ypres, and was gassed in action in Belgium. He afterwards fought in the Advance of 1918, and, returning to England when hostilities ceased, was demobilised in March 1919.
He holds the General Service and Victory Medals.
22, Star Road, West Kensington, W.14   16681C.

WARWICK, F. J., Gunner, Royal Field Artillery.

Volunteering in August 1914, he was sent to France in 1915, and took part in engagements at Arras, the Somme and La Bassée. In 1916 he proceeded to Egypt and Palestine, where he was in action at Gaza, and afterwards went to Salonica. After being in hospital for six months with malaria, he was discharged as medically unfit for service in May 1919. He holds the 1914-15 Star, General Service and Victory Medals.
22, Star Road, West Kensington, W.14   16681D.

WARWICK, G. A., Pte., Machine Gun Corps.

He volunteered in August 1915, and after his period of training was sent overseas. He took part in numerous important engagements on the Western Front, and was severely gassed and invalided to hospital in England, and upon his recovery in 1920 was still serving.
He holds the General Service and Victory Medals.
16, Werley Avenue, Dawes Road, S.W.6   X17876C.

WARWICK, H. G., 1st Air Mechanic, R.A.F.

He joined in May 1918, and was shortly afterwards sent to the Western Front. He was engaged on important duties which called for a high degree of technical skill at various aerodromes in this theatre of war until the cessation of hostilities.
He was demobilised in February 1919, and holds the General Service and Victory Medals.
16, Werley Avenue, Dawes Road, S.W.6   X17876A.

WARWICK, J., Pte., R.A.S.C. (H.T.)

He volunteered in November 1914, and after his training served with his unit at various depots on important duties in connection with the transport of ammunition and supplies. He did valuable work, but owing to ill-health was unfit for service overseas, and was discharged from further military service in July 1915.
22, Star Road, West Kensington, W.14   16681B.

WARWICK, T. W., Pte., 7th London Regiment.

He volunteered in August 1914, and in the following year was drafted overseas. During his service on the Western Front he took part in many important engagements until the cessation of hostilities, and was wounded.
He holds the 1914-15 Star, General Service and Victory Medals, and was demobilised in January 1919.
15, Folkestone Road, Upper Edmonton, N.18   15370B.

WARWICK, W. E., Pte., 7th East Surrey Regt.

He volunteered in August 1915, and at the conclusion of his training was drafted to the Western Front. During his service he was actively engaged in much of the heavy fighting in this theatre of war, and was wounded. Upon his recovery he was again in action and was killed on January 17th, 1918. He was entitled to the General Service and Victory Medals.
16, Werley Avenue, Dawes Road, S.W.6   X17876B.

WASHINGTON, C. G., Sapper, Royal Engineers.

He volunteered in 1915, and at the conclusion of his training was engaged on important duties as a dispatch-rider and in charge of field telephones at various stations. He gave valuable services, and owing to a serious injury which he received whilst on duty he was discharged as medically unfit for further military service in November 1917.
95, Berry Street, Willesden, N.W 10   15545A.

WASLEY, F. R. (Miss), Special War Worker.

During the war this lady offered her services to the Post Office authorities, and was employed on important duties at the Earl's Court and Victoria Post Offices in order to release her brother for military service. She discharged her duties with great efficiency.
7, Chesson Road, West Kensington, W.14   X16986.

WASLEY, W. G., Rifleman, 8th London Regt. (Post Office Rifles).

He volunteered in September 1914, and on completion of his training was sent to the Western Front. He took part in much of the heavy fighting in this theatre of war, including the battles of Givenchy, Arras, Amiens and Festubert, where he was wounded.
He was invalided to hospital in England and subsequently demobilised in 1919, holding the 1914-15 Star, General Service and Victory Medals.
7, Chesson Road, West Kensington, W.14   X16987

WASS, J., Pte., 1st Coldstream Guards.

He joined in March 1917, and on the conclusion of his training was sent to France in the same year. During his service on the Western Front he took part in much heavy fighting, including the battles of Ypres, Arras, and the Retreat and Advance of 1918. He was invalided to England, and was ultimately discharged as medically unfit for further service in February 1919.
He holds the General Service and Victory Medals.
14, Tenterden Road, Tottenham, N.17   X18262.

WATERFIELD, H. G., Pte., Machine Gun Corps.

He joined in 1918, and after his period of training served at various stations on important duties with his unit. He gave valuable services, but was not successful in obtaining his transfer overseas before the signing of the Armistice.
He was demobilised in 1919.
17, Mirabel Road, Fulham, S W.6   X17716.

WATERHOUSE, A., Driver, R.F.A.

He volunteered in September 1915, and in the following year was drafted to the Western Front, where he remained until 1919. During this time he took part in many important engagements, including those of Ypres, the Somme, Arras, Passchendaele, St. Quentin, Béthune, Vimy Ridge, and the Advance of 1918, and afterwards was sent to Germany with the Army of Occupation.
He was demobilised in May 1919, holding the General Service and Victory Medals.
14, Hampden Street, Paddington, W.2   X20895.

WATERMAN, H., Pte., Machine Gun Corps.

He joined in November 1916, and in the following year was drafted to the Western Front. While in this theatre of war he was actively engaged in much severe fighting, including the battles of the Somme, Cambrai, Ypres and Arras, and was wounded. After hostilities ceased he went to Germany with the Army of Occupation, and returned to England for demobilisation in November 1919.
He holds the General Service and Victory Medals.
36, Greyhound Road, College Park, N.W.10   X17602.

WATERS, C., Cpl., Royal Engineers.

He joined in 1917, and was drafted to the Western Front in the same year. During his service in this theatre of war he took part in numerous engagements, including those on the Somme and the Retreat and Advance of 1918.
He returned to England after the Armistice, and was demobilised in 1919, holding the General Service and Victory Medals.
39, Rowallan Road, Munster Road, S.W.6   X19278.

WATERS, D. J., Pte., R.A.S.C. (M.T.)

He joined in April 1917, and after his training was sent overseas. He was engaged on important duties in connection with the transport of ammunition and supplies to the forward areas during operations on the Western Front, and was wounded.
He was demobilised in October 1919, and holds the General Service and Victory Medals.
34, Allestree Road, Munster Road, S.W.6   X19206A.

WATERS, E. W., Pte., R.A.S.C. (M.T.)

Joining in 1916, he served until 1918 on many of the chief battle fronts of France, and was wounded twice. After considerable hospital treatment, both abroad and in England, he was discharged in August 1918 as medically unfit for further military service.
He holds the General Service and Victory Medals.
34, Allestree Road, Munster Road, S.W.6   X19206B.

WATERS, W. J. (M.M.), Bombardier, R.F.A.

Volunteering in August 1914, he went to the Western Front the following year, and took part in many engagements, including those of Ypres, Loos, Festubert, the Somme, Cambrai, Arras, Albert and Armentières, and was gassed. He was awarded the Military Medal for conspicuous bravery in the field, and also holds the 1914-15 Star, General Service, Victory, and Territorial Long Service Medals.
He was demobilised in February 1919.
2, Fourth Avenue, Queen's Park Estate, W.10   X18402A.

WATKINS, G., Cpl., R.A.M.C.

He joined in March 1916, and after a short period of training was drafted to Egypt. His service in the East lasted for two years, during which time he did splendid work with the Royal Army Medical Corps attached to General Allenby's forces in Palestine.
He returned to England in 1918, and in November of the same year was demobilised, holding the General Service and Victory Medals.
52, Woodchester Street, Paddington, W.2   X20790A.

WATKINS, A. E. C., Pte., 1/5th Buffs (East Kent Regiment).

Joining in April 1916, he was drafted to France in the same year. After taking part in several engagements, he was invalided home suffering from shell-shock. On his recovery he was sent out to Mesopotamia, where he was on active service and contracted malaria. In 1918 he was transferred to Salonica, and was in action on the Macedonian Front. He returned to England and was demobilised in April 1919, holding the General Service and Victory Medals.
11, Oakbury Road, Fulham, S.W.6   X20937.

WATKINS, E., Pte., Royal Defence Corps.

He volunteered in December 1914, and after his training was engaged on important guard duties for three years at various stations in England. He was then transferred to Ireland, where he again performed valuable services until his demobilisation in March 1919, after 4½ years' continuous service.
32, Greyhound Road, College Park, N.W.10   X17795A.

WATKINS, S., Rifleman, Rifle Brigade.

He was in the Army when war broke out, and was drafted to the Western Front, where he went through the retreat from Mons and the battle of the Marne. He also took part in many of the engagements which followed, including the battle of the Somme, and was on three occasions severely wounded, and suffered from frost-bite.
He returned to England in 1917, and holds the Mons Star, General Service and Victory Medals, and was still serving in 1920.
52, Woodchester Street, Paddington, W.2   X20790B.

WATKINS, S. C., Rifleman, Rifle Brigade.

He was in the Army on the outbreak of war, and in 1914 was drafted to France, where he remained for three years. During this time he took part in the battles of Mons, the Marne, the Aisne, the Somme, Ypres, Arras and Passchendaele, and was wounded three times and gassed. He was returned to England in 1917 and transferred to the Royal Engineers, with whom he was still serving in 1920.
He was latterly trained as a signaller, and holds the Mons Star, General Service and Victory Medals.
23, Hampden Street, Paddington, W.2   X21388.

WATKINS, S. J., Lce.-Cpl., Royal Fusiliers.

He was called up from the Reserve in August 1914, and served for nearly two years on the Western Front, being in action at Mons, Ypres and on the Somme, where he was wounded, losing his thumb and two fingers. He was also gassed while abroad, and in March 1916 was discharged as medically unfit for further service.
He holds the 1914 Star, General Service and Victory Medals.
1, Hilmer Street, West Kensington, W.14   15922.

WATKINS, W., Sapper, Royal Engineers (R.O.D.)

He joined in 1918, and was almost immediately drafted to the Western Front, where he carried out important duties on lines of communication in various sectors.
He holds the General Service and Victory Medals, and was demobilised in 1920 on returning from France.
32, Greyhound Road, College Park, N.W.10   X17795B.

WATLING, F., Rifleman, 2nd Royal Irish Rifles.
He volunteered for duty in 1915, and was almost immediately drafted to the Western Front, where, after taking part in much heavy fighting, he was killed in action on June 16th, 1915.
He was entitled to the 1914–15 Star, General Service and Victory Medals.
149, Framfield Road, Hanwell, W.7   10883A.

WATLING, G. J., Sergt., Royal Field Artillery.
Volunteering in 1914, he was immediately drafted to France, took part in the battles of Mons, the Marne, Ypres, Loos, the Somme, Bullecourt and Cambrai, and was wounded and gassed.
He was demobilised in 1919, holding the Mons Star, General Service and Victory Medals.
149, Framfield Road, Hanwell, W.7   10883B.

WATLING, W. J., Driver, R.F.A.
He volunteered in 1914, was drafted to France in the same year and took part in the battles of Mons, the Marne, Ypres, Loos, and the Somme.
He was demobilised in 1919, holding the Mons Star, General Service and Victory Medals.
149, Framfield Road, Hanwell, W.7   10883C.

WATSON, A. (Miss), Sergt., W.A.A.C.
This lady joined the Women's Legion in 1916, and was afterwards transferred to the Army Canteens, with which she was engaged as a charge hand. She then joined the Women's Auxiliary Army Corps, and rendered valuable services whilst attached to the Royal Engineers at Chatham and was recommended for the O.B.E. for her excellent work and splendid record.
She was demobilised in September 1919.
53, Cornwallis Road, Lower Edmonton, N.9   13406.

WATSON, A. (Miss), Special War Worker.
During the war this lady carried out work of national importance at No. 7 National Filling Factory, where she was engaged on the making of hand-grenades and shell-filling. Her duties were of a dangerous and arduous nature, and were performed in a capable and painstaking manner. She gave valuable services to her Country.
3, Field Road, Hammersmith, W.6   14807A.

WATSON, A. G., Driver, R.H.A.
He joined in September 1916, and was drafted to Egypt, and from there to Salonica. During his service in this seat of war he took part in important operations on the Balkan Front, and suffered from malaria.
In February 1920 he returned to England for demobilisation, holding the General Service and Victory Medals.
42, Raynham Road, Upper Edmonton, N.18   16943.

WATSON, C., Rifleman, Royal Irish Rifles.
Enlisting in 1916, he was drafted overseas on completion of his training. After taking part in much severe fighting on the Western Front, he was killed in action during the third battle of Ypres on August 2nd, 1917.
He was entitled to the General Service and Victory Medals.
3, Field Road, Hammersmith, W.6   14807B.

WATSON, F. C., Pte., 24th Training Reserve.
He joined in April 1918, on attaining military age, and underwent training at Aldershot and Hastings. He failed to secure a transfer overseas on account of the cessation of hostilities in the same year, and was demobilised a month after the Armistice.
19, Shorrolds Road, Walham Green, S.W.6   X19432B.

WATSON, G. W., Rifleman, The Cameronians (Scottish Rifles).
Joining in January 1917, he was drafted to the Western Front early in the following year. While in this theatre of war he took part in many important engagements, including the Retreat and Advance of 1918, and was wounded in action. He holds the General Service and Victory Medals, and was demobilised in 1919.
15, Denton Road, Stonebridge Park, N.W.10   14707.

WATSON, H. (Miss), Special War Worker.
For a considerable period of the war this lady was engaged on work of national importance at Messrs. Blakes' Munition Factory, Fulham, where she worked on the manufacture of shell-boxes. She carried out her arduous duties in a very efficient manner, and received high commendation for her valuable services.
3, Field Road, Hammersmith, W.6   14805A.

WATSON, H., Pte., Royal Warwickshire Regt.
He volunteered in 1915, and was drafted to the Dardanelles, took part in heavy fighting in the Gallipoli campaign and was twice wounded. After the evacuation of the Peninsula he was drafted to India, where he was engaged on important duties until his demobilisation in 1919.
He holds the 1914–15 Star, General Service and Victory Medals.   3, Field Road, Hammersmith, W.6   14805B.

WATSON, J. J., Cpl., Royal Garrison Artillery.
He volunteered in June 1915, went to the Western Front in the following year, and in 1917 was wounded in action at Loos, having previously taken part in other engagements. After being for some time in hospital at Chatham, he was sent to a convalescent home at Shoreham, where he stayed for some months.
He holds the General Service and Victory Medals, and was demobilised in August 1919.
145, Bulwer Road, Upper Edmonton, N.18   X17200.

WATSON, M. (Mrs.), Special War Worker.
During the war this lady rendered very valuable services. She was first engaged on important work in connection with the output of aeroplanes at Messrs. Handley Page's, Cricklewood. Later she assisted at the Y.W.C.A. Canteen in Queen's Gate, Kensington, and was highly commended for her valuable assistance.
102, Yeldham Road, Hammersmith, W.6   13278B.

WATSON, W. J., Driver, R.A.S.C.
He was mobilised in August 1914, and served on the Western Front for 4½ years, during which he was engaged on important transport duties in various sectors.
He was demobilised in May 1919, and holds the 1914–15 Star, General Service and Victory Medals.
19, Shorrolds Road, Walham Green, S.W.6   X19432A.

WATTERS, G. W., Pte., Machine Gun Corps.
He joined in May 1916, and in the same year was sent to Salonica, where he served for two years. During this time he saw much severe fighting on the Balkan Front.
In 1918 he was drafted to Russia, where he suffered many hardships, and in September 1919 was demobilised, holding the General Service and Victory Medals.
10, Parkfield Road, Willesden, N.W.10   X17413.

WATTS, A. H. (M.M.), Pte., Middlesex Regiment.
He volunteered for duty in August 1914, and during this service in France took part in the battles of Mons and the Somme, and was wounded three times. He was awarded the Military Medal for conspicuous bravery during the Somme operations, and was demobilised in February 1919, holding in addition the 1914–15 Star, General Service and Victory Medals.
52, Winchester Road, Lower Edmonton, N.9   14862.

WATTS, A. V., Gunner, Royal Garrison Artillery.
He volunteered in October 1915, and served for three years in Salonica, taking part in many engagements during the Balkan campaign.
In June 1919 he was demobilised, holding the General Service and Victory Medals.
4, Ashford Road, Tottenham, N.17   X18356.

WATTS, B., Pte., 3rd Royal Fusiliers.
He volunteered in August 1914, and was sent to France on completion of his training. While on the Western Front he took part in the battles of the Somme, Arras, Ypres and Albert.
Later he saw much severe fighting in Salonica, and was eventually demobilised in 1919, holding the 1914–15 Star, General Service and Victory Medals.
3, Winchelsea Road, Willesden, N.W.10   15553B.

WATTS, G. A., Pte., 3rd Royal Fusiliers.
He volunteered in August 1914, and was drafted to the Western Front. After taking part in much heavy fighting, he was killed in action between Hill 60 and Ypres, on May 3rd, 1915.
He was entitled to the 1914–15 Star, General Service and Victory Medals.
3, Winchelsea Road, Willesden, N.W.10   15553A.

WATTS, H. F., Pte., R.A.M.C.
He volunteered in November 1914, went to France the following year, and served with the Field Ambulance on many sectors of the Western Front. In 1916 he was sent to Salonica, where he served in the hospitals at Aleppo, tending Turkish prisoners.
He holds the 1914–15 Star, General Service and Victory Medals, and was demobilised in June 1919.
56, Drayton Road, Harlesden, N.W.10   14981A.

WATTS, W. C., Cpl., Royal Air Force.
He joined in February 1917, went to the Western Front in March of the following year, served as a writer in many places and gave very valuable services.
He holds the General Service and Victory Medals, and was demobilised in March 1919.
56, Drayton Road, Harlesden, N.W.10   14981B.

WATTS, J., Pte., 17th Royal Fusiliers (City of London Regiment).

He volunteered in June 1915, and before the end of the same year was drafted to the Western Front. He took part in many important engagements, and was twice wounded. After a period in hospital in France he was invalided to England for further treatment.
He holds the 1914-15 Star, General Service and Victory Medals, and was demobilised in April 1919.
1, Hannell Road, Munster Road, S.W.6   X17864.

WATTS, F. (Mrs.), Special War Worker.

This lady was employed for 2½ years during the war keeping accounts and checking in the clerical section of Park Royal Munition Factory. She carried out her responsible duties in a very efficient manner, and gave valuable services.
16, Deacon Road, Cricklewood, N.W.2   16137B.

WATTS, P. W., Cpl., Royal Engineers.

He joined in February 1916, served on the Western Front until 1919, and was present at many engagements, including the battles of Ypres and the Somme. He was engaged principally on the railways, and was gassed.
In June 1919 he was demobilised, holding the General Service and Victory Medals.
16, Deacon Road, Cricklewood, N.W.2   16137A.

WAY, C., Pte., Machine Gun Corps.

He volunteered in July 1915, served on the Western Front and took part in the battles of the Somme and Ypres, during which he was gassed.
He was demobilised in May 1919, and holds the General Service and Victory Medals.
12, Church Path, Hammersmith, W.6   15906.

WAY, C., Pte., Machine Gun Corps.

He volunteered in August 1914, and for some time was engaged on important duties at various stations. Eventually he was drafted to France, and took part in many engagements. After the signing of the Armistice he went to Germany with the Army of Occupation, remaining there until he was demobilised at the end of 1918.
He holds the General Service and Victory Medals.
12, Church Path, Hammersmith, W.6   16386.

WAY, E., Pte., R.A.S.C. (M.T.)

He volunteered in January 1915, and in the same year was drafted to the Western Front, where he served for four years. During this period he was present at various engagements, including those at Arras, Cambrai, Ypres and the Somme, and was engaged on special transport duties, carrying food supplies to the advance depots.
He was demobilised in March 1919, holding the 1914-15 Star, General Service and Victory Medals.
62, Clarendon Street, Paddington, W.2   X20672.

WAY, F. C., Pte., 13th London Regiment (Kensington Battalion).

He volunteered in November 1914, and while serving on the Western Front took part in numerous engagements, and was for a time in hospital at Rouen owing to a severe accident. He was demobilised in January 1919, holding the General Service and Victory Medals.
28, Knivet Road, Walham Green, S.W.6   X19428A.

WAYMAN, G. W., Cpl., Royal Fusiliers.

He volunteered in August 1914, and left for India the same year. In 1915 he was drafted to the Dardanelles, and in 1916 went to the Western Front. He was wounded in action at the Dardanelles, and was demobilised in 1919, holding the 1914-15 Star, General Service and Victory Medals.
69, Roseberry Road, Lower Edmonton, N.9   14074

WAYMAN, W. S., Sergt., 1st East Surrey Regt.

He volunteered in August 1914, and in the same year was sent to the Western Front, where he was in action during many engagements.
He was still serving in 1920, and holds the 1914-15 Star, General Service and Victory Medals.
71, Roseberry Road, Lower Edmonton, N.9   14072.

WEAIT, R. H., Pte., Sherwood Foresters and Royal Army Ordnance Corps.

He volunteered in April 1915, and during his service on the Western Front took part in many engagements. He was wounded in action in June 1917, and was for a time in hospital in France. He also served in the R.A.O.C.
In February 1919 he was demobilised, holding the 1914-15 Star, General Service and Victory Medals.
100, Farm Lane, Walham Green, S.W.6   X19611.

WEATHERLEY, W., Pte., Royal Sussex Regt.

He volunteered for service in 1915, and in the same year was sent to the Western Front, where he took part in many engagements.
He was killed in action at the battle of Arras in July 1917, and was entitled to the 1914-15 Star, General Service and Victory Medals.
146, Winchester Road, Lower Edmonton, N.9   14780.

WEATHERSTONE, E., Lce.-Cpl., M.M.P.

He was mobilised in August 1914, after previous service in the Army, and went out to the Western Front, where he remained on duty until after the Armistice. In the course of his long service he was wounded, and in consequence had to lose one of his fingers.
He was demobilised in 1918, and holds the General Service and Victory Medals.
3, William Street, White Hart Lane, Tottenham, N.17   X18298.

WEAVER, C. A., Pte., 2nd Loyal North Lancashire Regiment.

He volunteered for duty in 1914, served in East Africa, and was killed at Tanga on November 5th of the same year. He was entitled to the 1914-15 Star, General Service and Victory Medals.
57, Averill Street, Hammersmith, W.6   14181A.

WEAVER, G., Pte., Loyal North Lancashire Regt.

He volunteered in August 1914, and in the same year was sent to East Africa. Later he served on the Western Front, where he was gassed while in action at Arras, and in March 1919 was demobilised, holding the 1914 Star, General Service and Victory Medals.
84, Warwick Road, Upper Edmonton, N.18   X17904.

WEAVER, H. W., Gunner, R.F.A.

He volunteered in 1915, and during his service on the Western Front took part in many engagements and was wounded.
He was demobilised in 1919, holding the General Service and Victory Medals.
44, Bruce Castle Road, Tottenham, N.17   X18550.

WEAVER, J. H., Pte., 20th Middlesex Regiment.

He joined in June 1916, served on the Western Front, and took part in the fighting on the Somme, Arras, Cambrai, Bullecourt and other important engagements.
He holds the General Service and Victory Medals, and was demobilised in September 1919.
34, Averill Street, Hammersmith, W.6   14181B.

WEAVER, W. F., Pte., R.A.P.C.

He joined in 1916, and served on important duties with the Royal Army Pay Corps at various stations. He was unable to obtain his transfer overseas before the cessation of hostilities. He gave valuable services, and was demobilised in 1919.
57, Averill Street, Hammersmith, W.6   14487.

WEBB, A., Cpl., Royal Engineers.

He volunteered in August 1914, and served in France, where he was injured during the retreat from Mons and invalided home. Later he was night supervisor of the telephone exchange at Aldershot.
He holds the Mons Star, General Service and Victory Medals, and was demobilised in February 1919.
33, Parkfield Road, Willesden, N.W.10   X17418.

WEBB, A. E., Pte., Royal Army Medical Corps.

He joined in 1917, and on completion of his training was retained with his unit on important duties. He gave valuable services, but was unable to obtain his transfer overseas before the cessation of hostilities.
9, Lillie Mansions, Lillie Road, Fulham, S.W.6   X18457.

WEBB, A. R., Sergt., R.A.M.C.

Volunteering in November 1915, he was drafted to the Western Front, where he served for three years. During this time he took a prominent part in many severe actions, and was eventually demobilised in February 1919.
He holds the General Service and Victory Medals.
9, Monmouth Road, Lower Edmonton, N.9   12995B.

WEBB, C., Driver, Royal Field Artillery.

He volunteered in September 1914, and in the following March was sent to the Western Front, where he fought on the Somme and at Arras. During his service he was gassed.
He holds the 1914-15 Star, General Service and Victory Medals, and was demobilised in April 1919.
74, Roseberry Road, Lower Edmonton, N.9   T14070.

WEBB, D. J., Pte., 1/4th Leicestershire Regt.

He joined in October 1916, and during his service on the Western Front took part in several engagements, including those of the Somme, Lille, Hill 60, Armentières, Ypres, St. Quentin and Bullecourt.
He holds the General Service and Victory Medals, and was demobilised in April 1919, having previously been for three months in hospital in Devonshire.
6, Bronsart Road, Munster Rd., Fulham, S.W.6   TX18985B.

WEBB, G. W., Pte., Royal Army Service Corps.

He volunteered in March 1915, and in the same year was drafted to France, where he was engaged on important duties in connection with the supply of ammunition. In December 1917 he was discharged owing to indifferent health, and holds the 1914-15 Star, General Service and Victory Medals.
4, Linton Road, Upper Edmonton, N.18   TX17282A.

WEBB, F. A. (M.M.), Pte., 1st Middlesex Regiment.

He volunteered for duty in August 1914, and in the following year was sent to France. While on the Western Front he took part in many important engagements, and was killed in action at Zonnebeke on December 6th, 1917, having been previously twice wounded.
He was awarded the Military Medal for conspicuous bravery and devotion to duty, and was also entitled to the 1914-15 Star, General Service and Victory Medals.
9, Monmouth Road, Lower Edmonton, N.9   12995A.

WEBB, G. W., Sergt., Royal Field Artillery.

He volunteered in 1914, and was retained on special duties at various depots with his unit. He gave valuable services, and gained promotion for consistent good work, but was not successful in obtaining his transfer overseas.
He was demobilised in 1919.
10, May Street, W. Kensington, W.14   15890B.

WEBB, I. (Miss), Special War Worker.

During the war this lady, desirous of helping her Country, undertook special work in connection with Queen Mary's Guild. She was engaged on the making of comforts for the soldiers, and her work was very highly appreciated. She received a special badge as a reward for her valuable services.
10, May Street, W. Kensington, W.14   15890A.

WEBB, J. E., Pte., Royal Berkshire Regiment.

He volunteered for duty in August 1914, served in France from 1915 until 1917, took part in the battles of the Somme, Ypres and Neuve Chapelle, and was killed in action at Arras on May 2nd, 1917.
He was entitled to the 1914-15 Star, General Service and Victory Medals.
2, Sandringham Road, Cricklewood, N.W.2   16713B.

WEBB, L. F. (Mrs.), Special War Worker.

During the war this lady did useful work at Walham Green Post Office as a post woman, thus releasing a man for military service. She carried out her arduous duties in a very satisfactory manner, and gave valuable services to her Country.
6, Bronsart Road, Munster Road, S.W.6   TX18985A.

WEBB, S. (M.M.), Reg. Sergt. Major, R.E.

He volunteered for duty in September 1914, and in the following year went to the Western Front, where he remained until 1919, during which time he took part in many battles, including those of Arras, Ypres and the Somme. He was mentioned in dispatches twice, and awarded the Military Medal for conspicuous bravery and devotion to duty on the Somme battlefield.
He also holds the 1914-15 Star, General Service and Victory Medals, and was demobilised in May 1919.
38, Rucklidge Avenue, Harlesden, N.W.10   13147.

WEBB, V. (Miss), Special War Worker.

During the war this lady made comforts for the soldiers at the Front, in connection with Queen Mary's Guild. Her work was very highly appreciated by our men, and she received high commendation for her splendid services.
10, May Street, West Kensington, W.14   15887B.

WEBB, W., Special War Worker.

He worked on munitions for the duration of the war, and was engaged first at Messrs Vandervell's, Acton, in making bombs and parts of aeroplanes. Later he went to Messrs. Gwynne's Factory, where he was employed as an engineer in the machine department, making mines. He rendered valuable services to his Country during this period.
12, Mirabel Road, Fulham, S.W.6   X17860.

WEBB, W. J., Sergt., Royal Air Force.

He joined in March 1916, and served at various aerodromes on special duties with the Royal Air Force until he was demobilised in February 1919.
During this time his work called for a high degree of technical skill, and he gave valuable services, but was not successful in obtaining his transfer overseas before the termination of hostilities.   8, Bull Lane, Upper Edmonton, N.18   X17882.

WEBBER, S. T., Sapper, Royal Engineers.

He volunteered in May 1915, and in the following September went to the Western Front, where he served for over three years. He was in action in many important engagements, including those at Ypres, the Somme, Arras and Cambrai, and was gassed at Laventie.
He was demobilised in May 1919, and holds the 1914-15 Star, General Service and Victory Medals.
220, Shirland Road, Maida Hill, W.9   X19597.

WEBSTER, F. W., Rifleman, K.R.R.

He joined in March 1917, and after completing his training served at various stations on important duties with his unit. He was unable to obtain his transfer overseas before the cessation of hostilities, but later went with the Army of Occupation into Germany, where he served at Cologne.
He was afterwards transferred to Mesopotamia, where he was still serving in 1920.
32, Burnthwaite Road, Walham Green, S.W.6   X20200C.

WEBSTER, H. W., Pte., 7th London Regiment.

He volunteered in 1915, and after a short period of training was drafted to the Western Front. Whilst overseas he took a prominent part in several engagements, including those of Loos, Albert, Vimy Ridge, Hamel, Arras, Messines, Passchendaele, Lens, the Somme, Bapaume and the Retreat and Advance of 1918.
He was demobilised in December 1919, holding the 1914-15 Star, General Service and Victory Medals.
32, Burnthwaite Road, Walham Green, S.W.6   X20200A.

WEBSTER, H. W., Pte., Scots Guards.

He volunteered in August 1914, and shortly afterwards was drafted to the Western Front, where he took a distinguished part in the retreat from Mons. He also fought in the battles of the Marne, La Bassée, Ypres, Neuve Chapelle, Loos, Armentières, Albert, Vimy Ridge and Arras. In 1917 he returned to England, and owing to ill-health was invalided out of the Service.
He holds the Mons Star, General Service and Victory Medals.
32, Burnthwaite Road, Walham Green, S.W.6   X20200B.

WEEDON, J. E., Pte., East Surrey Regiment.

He joined in June 1916, and in the same year went to the Western Front, where he served for two years, and was frequently in action. He was wounded three times, at the battle of the Somme in 1916, at Arras in 1917, and at Cambrai in the following year, and was invalided home to hospital and after his recovery served at various stations until March 1919, when he was demobilised.
He holds the General Service and Victory Medals.
39, Broughton Road, Fulham, S.W.6   X20904.

WEEKS, H., Rifleman, King's Royal Rifles.

He enlisted in February 1916, and in the same year was sent to the Western Front, where he served in various engagements. He was in action on the Somme, at Loos, Arras, Albert, Ypres, Messines and Passchendaele, and was wounded.
He died on July 8th, 1918, in France of acute pneumonia.
He was entitled to the General Service and Victory Medals.
52, Chippenham Road, Maida Hill, W.9   X20887.

WEIR, A. V., Driver, Royal Engineers.

He volunteered in February 1915, and after a period of training proceeded to the Western Front. After seeing much fighting in France he was transferred to the East, where he served in Salonica and Egypt. He also took a prominent part in the Advance through Palestine, and on October 13th, 1918, died in hospital at Damascus.
He was entitled to the General Service and Victory Medals.
32, Shorrolds Road, Walham Green, S.W.6   X19361B.

WEIR, W. T., Cpl., King's Royal Rifles.

He volunteered in September 1914, and for over four years served on the Western Front, where he took part in many important engagements. He was in hospital in France and England with enteric fever for six months.
He was demobilised in March 1919, and holds the 1914-15 Star, General Service and Victory Medals.
34, Walham Grove, Fulham, S.W.6   X19615.

WEIR, W. T., Acting Lce.-Cpl., K.R.R.

He volunteered in September 1914, and during his service on the Western Front, took a prominent part in many engagements. He was invalided home through illness contracted abroad, and on his recovery served in France with the Labour Corps until demobilised in March 1919.
He holds the 1914-15 Star, General Service and Victory Medals. 32, Shorrolds Rd., Walham Green, S.W.6   X19361A.

WELCH, G. (Miss), Special War Worker.

This lady was engaged from March 1916 until 1919 as a gate-keeper on the Underground Railway, thus releasing a man for the Army. She received a certificate of appreciation on the termination of her services, thanking her for the valuable work she had done during the war.
69, Leghorn Road, Harlesden, N.W.10   T12956A.

WELCH, G. H., Pte., 8th East Surrey Regiment.
Volunteering in July 1915, he was sent out to France in the same year. After a year's valuable service on many sectors of the Front, where he saw much fighting, he was invalided home, and in July 1916 was discharged as medically unfit.
He holds the 1914–15 Star, General Service and Victory Medals.
30, Mozart Street, North Kensington, W.10   X19313.

WELCH, R., Pte., Labour Corps.
He joined in January 1917, and after his training served at various stations on important duties with his unit. Later he was drafted to Germany, where he was engaged on special work with the Army of Occupation at Cologne.
He was demobilised in February 1920.
11, Dartington Terrace, Paddington, W.2   X21562A.

WELCH, S., Rifleman, 6th London Regiment (Rifles).
He volunteered in June 1915, and in the same year was drafted to the Western Front, where he took a distinguished part in the battles of Ypres, Hill 60 and Loos. He was wounded on the Somme and again in action at Arras. He was invalided home in 1917, and died in hospital on November 6th.
He was entitled to the 1914–15 Star, General Servce and Victory Medals.
11, Dartington Terrace, Paddington, W.2   X21562B.

WELCH, T. E., Pte., 2nd Royal Fusiliers.
Volunteering in June 1915, he was drafted to the Western Front on the completion of his training, and served on various sectors, taking part in many important engagements. He was wounded during his service in France, and in December 1918, on his return to England, was demobilised.
He holds the General Service and Victory Medals.
19, Claybrook Road, Hammersmith, W.6   13679B.

WELHAM, T., Pte., Hampshire Regiment.
He joined in June 1916, and in the same year went out to Salonica. He saw much fighting on the Macedonian Front, and after good service in the firing line was admitted to hospital suffering from malaria. He died six weeks later on September 6th, 1917.
He was entitled to the General Service and Victory Medals.
66, Manor Road, Tottenham, N.17   X18970.

WELLARD, G. G., Trooper, 2nd London Yeomanry (Westminster Dragoons).
He volunteered in November 1915, and in the following April was sent to the Western Front, where he took a prominent part in the fighting up to August 1917. In November of that year he was drafted to Italy, and saw much service, being on one occasion severely gassed.
He returned to England for demobilisation in March 1919, and holds the General Service and Victory Medals.
130, Stephendale Road, Fulham, S.W.6   X20826.

WELLER, A. F. (M.M.), Bombardier, R.F.A.
He volunteered in August 1914, and went to the Western Front in September 1915. He took a prominent part in many engagements, including those of Loos, the Somme, and Cambrai, and was awarded the Military Medal for conspicuous gallantry at Epéhy Forest in 1916. He was severely gassed, and after being in hospital for some time was discharged in April 1919.
In addition to the Military Medal, he holds the 1914–15 Star, General Service and Victory Medals.
19, Rosaline Road, Munster Road, S.W.6   TX18626.

WELLER, E. R., Lce.-Cpl., Royal Engineers.
He volunteered in 1914, and was drafted to France, where he took part in many engagements, including those of the Somme, Arras, Ypres, Loos, Neuve Chapelle, Armentières, St. Quentin, Bullecourt and Festubert, He also fought in the Retreat and Advance of 1918, and was wounded in action. He holds the 1914–15 Star, General Service and Victory Medals, and was demobilised in 1919.
83, Orbain Road, Fulham, S.W.6   X18686.

WELLS, A., Pte., Middlesex Regiment and Queen's Own (Royal West Kent Regiment).
He volunteered in January 1915, and after much valuable service in England was drafted out to France. He took an active part in the fighting in the Advance of 1918, and on two occasions was severely wounded. In October 1918 he was invalided home, and in the following June was demobilised. He holds the General Service and Victory Medals.
24, Hiley Road, Willesden, N.W.10   X18696.

WELLS, A. T., Pte., 3rd Middlesex Regiment.
He volunteered in 1914, and was immediately sent out to France, taking part in the retreat from Mons, where he was severely wounded. He was invalided home, but on recovery returned to the Western Front, and fought in many important engagements up to the date of the Armistice.
He was demobilised in 1919, and holds the Mons Star, General Service and Victory Medals.
65, Barret's Green Road, Willesden, N.W.10   13556B.

WELLS, A. T., Sapper, Royal Engineers.
Volunteering in 1915, he was sent out to Egypt in the following year. He saw much active service in the East until 1918, when he was transferred to the Western Front. He was engaged on various important duties in France up to the date of the Armistice, and whilst abroad suffered from sunstroke.
He was demobilised in 1919, and holds the General Service and Victory Medals.
65, Barret's Green Road, Willesden, N.W.10   13556C.

WELLS, C. H., Cpl., R.A.S.C. (M.T.)
He joined in May 1916, and in the same year went out to Egypt. Whilst abroad he was engaged in overhauling cars and on other important duties He returned to England in 1919, and in November was demobilised.
He holds the General Service and Victory Medals.
30, Aspenlea Road, Hammersmith, W 6   14291A.

WELLS, G., Gunner, Royal Field Artillery.
He joined in September 1916, and during his 2½ years' service on the Western Front took part as a signaller in many engagements, including the battles of Arras, Messines and Vimy Ridge. He was wounded at Ypres, and in October 1919 was demobilised, after over three years' exemplary service.
He holds the General Service and Victory Medals.
24, Hiley Road, Willesden, N.W.10   X18612.

WELLS, G., Pte., 1/9th Middlesex Regiment.
Volunteering in 1915, he soon afterwards proceeded to the East. He was in action on the Macedonian Front in the Balkan campaign until drafted to Mesopotamia. There he did excellent work until 1919, when he was returned to England and demobilised in September, holding the 1914–15 Star, General Service and Victory Medals.
95a, Deacon Road, Cricklewood, N.W.2   16604B.

WELLS, H. W., 1st Air Mechanic, R.A.F.
He joined in December 1916, and on completing his training in the following year was sent out to France. He was engaged on duties of a highly technical character on many sectors of the Front, and saw service up to the date of the Armistice. He then returned to England, and in October 1919 was demobilised, holding the General Service and Victory Medals.
126, Church Road, Tottenham, N.17   X18135.

WENLOCK, J., Cpl., R.A.S.C.
He volunteered in August 1914, and was drafted to the Western Front, where he remained for nearly five years. Whilst overseas he did much excellent work with the Royal Army Service Corps, and was present during many of the principal engagements, including those of Arras and Cambrai.
He was demobilised in June 1919, holding the 1914 Star, General Service and Victory Medals.
80, Ashmore Road, Harrow Road, W.9   X19845C.

WERRELL, A. S., Stoker, R.N., H.M.S. " Test."
He was in the Navy at the outbreak of hostilities, and served with the Dover Patrol. Throughout the war he was engaged with his ship on the important work of escorting merchant vessels and troopships through the danger zone
He holds the 1914 Star, General Service and Victory Medals, and was demobilised in February 1919.
46, Wornington Road, North Kensington, W.10   X20864.

WERRELL, A. V., A.B., R.N., H.M.S. " Test."
He was serving at the outbreak of hostilities, and during the course of the war was engaged on escorting troops to and from France and in convoying American troopships. He also took part in several engagements in the North Sea.
He holds the 1914 Star, General Service and Victory Medals, and was demobilised in February 1919.
3, Portnall Road, Maida Hill, W.9   TX19300.

WEST, A., Gunner, Royal Field Artillery.
He volunteered in May 1915, and whilst on the Western Front was in action on the Somme, at Ypres, Loos, Arras, Bullecourt, Vimy Ridge, St. Quentin, Hill 60, Cambrai, and in the Advance of 1918.
He was wounded whilst abroad, and was demobilised in July 1919, holding the General Service and Victory Medals.
13, Mablethorpe Road, Munster Road, Fulham, S.W.6   X19125B.

WEST, A. (Mrs.), Special War Worker.
This lady was engaged on work of great importance during
the war at Messrs. Waring & Gillow's Army Equipment
Factory at the White City. She rendered valuable services
and carried out her duties in a way worthy of high praise.
13, Mablethorpe Road, Munster Road, Fulham, S.W.6
　　　　　　　　　　　　　　　　　　　　　　X19125A.

WEST, A. E., Pte., 1/5th East Lancashire Regt.
He volunteered in December 1915, and in March 1916 pro-
ceeded to the Western Front. He took part in much heavy
fighting at Bullecourt, where he was wounded, and at Ypres,
Cambrai and the Somme.
He was demobilised in February 1919, and holds the General
Service and Victory Medals.
60, St. Ervan's Road, North Kensington, W.10　X20380.

WEST, A. E., Driver, Royal Field Artillery.
He volunteered in April 1915, and after training was sent to
the Western Front, where he took part in the battle of Ypres
and at Kemmel Hill.
He was demobilised in June 1919, holding the General Service
and Victory Medals, but rejoined in the same month, and was
drafted to India, where he was still serving in 1920.
17, Kilkie Street, Fulham, S.W.6　　　　　X21347A.

WEST, F., Sapper, Royal Engineers.
He volunteered in November 1914, and in the following year
was drafted to the Western Front, where he served with the
Royal Engineers on various important duties. He met with
an accident whilst carrying out some work on a motor-lorry,
and was invalided home. He was discharged in consequence
in April 1918, and holds the 1914–15 Star, General Service
and Victory Medals.
9, Brereton Road, Tottenham, N.17　　　　X18380.

WEST, G. A., 1st-Class Stoker, Royal Navy.
He joined in 1916, and served on H.M.S. " Hydrangea " on
various seas, where he saw much fighting. He gave valuable
services up to his demobilisation in October 1919, and holds
the General Service and Victory Medals.
41, Elsdon Road, Tottenham, N.17　　　　X18502.

WEST, H., Gunner, Royal Field Artillery.
He joined in 1916, and after his training was drafted to India.
Whilst abroad he saw much active service on the North-
Western Frontier during the Afghan risings. After fighting
with distinction throughout his service overseas he returned
home after the cessation of hostilities, and was demobilised in
1919.
He holds the General Service and Victory Medals.
83, Mirabel Road, Fulham, S.W.6　　　　X17863A.

WEST, J. W., Pte., East Surrey Regiment.
He volunteered in September 1914, and in the following June
was sent to the Western Front, where, after taking part in
various engagements, he was killed in the heavy fighting on
the Somme on July 1st, 1916.
He was entitled to the 1914–15 Star, General Service and
Victory Medals.
17, Kilkie Street, Fulham, S.W.6　　　　X21347B.

WEST, P., Sapper, Royal Engineers.
He volunteered in April 1915, and after his training served at
various stations on important duties with his unit. He gave
valuable services, but was not successful in obtaining his
transfer overseas, being medically unfit. He was discharged
in December 1915.
32, Lion Road, Lower Edmonton, N.9　　　15192A.

WEST, R. G., Pte., Devonshire Regiment.
He volunteered in May 1915, and later in the same year was
drafted to France. During his service overseas he took
part in numerous engagements, being in almost continuous
action until the end of 1916, when he was invalided home and
discharged on medical grounds.
He holds the 1914–15 Star, General Service and Victory
Medals. 37, Heckfield Place, Fulham Road, S.W.6 X20345.

WESTACOTT, C., Sapper, Royal Engineers.
He joined in November 1916, and in the following year went
to France, where he took part in the battle of the Somme and
was wounded at Givenchy in September 1918. After being
in hospital for some months he was discharged owing to
wounds in August 1919, holding the General Service and
Victory Medals.
16, Tilson Road, Tottenham, N.17　　　　TX19095.

WESTCOTT, H., Driver, R.A.S.C.
He volunteered in March 1915, and in the following year
was drafted to the Western Front, where he remained for
three years. He did very valuable work whilst engaged on
various duties on many sectors of the front and was present
during the battle of the Somme.
He was demobilised in 1919, holding the General Service and
Victory Medals.
19, Wornington Road, North Kensington, W.10　X20938.

WESTERN, H., Pte., 4th Lincolnshire Regiment.
He joined in June 1916, and after his training served at
various stations on important duties with his unit.
He gave valuable services, but was medically unfit for duty
overseas, and was discharged in July 1918.
5, St. Margaret's Road, Willesden, N.W.10　　X17753.

WESTERN, R., Pte., 22nd Middlesex Regiment.
He volunteered in November 1915, and in the following year
was sent to the Western Front. During his service in France
he took part in many engagements, including the battles of
Ypres, Arras and Cambrai, and was wounded on two
occasions. He also served in Italy for a time, and later
went to Germany with the Army of Occupation.
He was demobilised in March 1919, holding the General
Service and Victory Medals.
33, Fordingley Road, Maida Hill, W.9　　　X19728.

WESTLAKE, A. M. (Miss), Special War Worker.
Throughout the war this lady was engaged on work of great
national importance at various munition factories. She was
engaged first at Messrs. Blakes' of Fulham, where she
rendered valuable services in the construction of hand-
grenades. From there she went to Messrs. Edgar's Engine
Works, Hammersmith, and later to Messrs. Waring and
Gillow's, the White City, at which place she did splendid
work on the manufacture of Army equipment, and by her
skill and efficiency proved herself a great asset to the firms.
4, Strode Road, Munster Road, S.W.6　　　X19407.

WESTLAKE, G. F. C., Stoker, Royal Navy.
He volunteered in August 1914, and after a short period of
training was posted to H.M.S. " Osiris," in which he served
in the North Sea, and took part in the battle of Jutland.
Later his ship was torpedoed, but after drifting for some time
on a raft he was rescued and taken to Gosport, where he
was in hospital suffering from shock and loss of memory. On
recovery he was sent to H.M.S. " Pembroke," at Chatham,
and afterwards again served at sea in various ships with the
Grand Fleet, taking part in the raids on Ostend and Zeebrugge, and the battle of Heligoland.
He was demobilised in 1919, holding the 1914–15 Star,
General Service and Victory Medals.
4, Strode Road, Munster Road, S.W.6　　　X19409.

WESTLAKE, H. B., Pte., Middlesex Regiment.
He volunteered in August 1915, and in the same year was
sent to Salonica, where he took part in the Balkan campaign.
Later he fought in the General Allied Offensive on the Doiran
Front and in the advance across the Struma. During his
service he was wounded and also suffered very severely
from malaria.
He was discharged in October 1918, and holds the 1914–15
Star, General Service and Victory Medals.
11, Senior Street, Paddington, W.2　　　　X21400A.

**WESTLAKE, F. G., Pte., Middlesex Regiment
and Royal Fusiliers.**
He joined in June 1916, and in the same year was sent to the
Western Front, where he played a prominent part in the
battles of Loos, Arras, Cambrai and Bourlon Wood, and was
present at the capture of Béhagnies and Dernancourt. He
also fought in the Retreat and Advance of 1918, and was
wounded.
In consequence he was invalided home and was discharged
in November 1918, holding the General Service and Victory
Medals.　11, Senior Street, Paddington, W.2　X21400B.

WESTLAKE, W. H. E., Sapper, R.E.
He volunteered in August 1915, and served on the Western
Front in many important engagements, including those at
Dickebusch, Ypres, Armentières, Givenchy, Bullecourt and
Monchy. In 1918 he was invalided home and discharged
owing to ill-health.
He holds the 1914–15 Star, General Service and Victory
Medals. 4, Strode Road, Munster Road, S.W.6　X19408.

WESTON, A., Pte., York and Lancaster Regt.
Volunteering in August 1914, he was drafted to the Western
Front on completion of his training. He took part in many
of the principal engagements and was twice wounded, and on
July 1st, 1916, was killed in action on the Somme.
He was entitled to the 1914–15 Star, General Service and
Victory Medals.
41, Haldane Road, Walham Green, S.W.6　TX17076B.

WESTON, T. H., A.B., R.N., H.M.S. " Blanche."
He was in the Navy when war broke out, and from that time
served with the Grand Fleet in the North Sea. He took part
in the battle of Jutland on May 31st, 1916, and was on board
H.M.S. " Speedy," a torpedo gun-boat, when she was mined
off the Humber on September 3rd, 1914. In April 1915 he was
seriously wounded by gun explosion during firing practice,
and in December of the following year was discharged.
He holds the 1914 Star, General Service and Victory Medals.
7, Edenham Street, North Kensington, W.10　X20196.

WEYMOUTH, A. P., Pioneer, Royal Engineers.
He joined in May 1917, and after his training was engaged on important duties with his unit.
Owing to ill-health he was not successful in obtaining his transfer overseas, and in June 1918 was invalided out of the Service. 38, Fordingley Road, Maida Hill, W.9 X19674.

WEYMOUTH, J. C., Sapper, Royal Engineers.
Joining in November 1916, he was drafted to France on completion of his training. For two years he was engaged as a signaller on the Lens and Arras Fronts, and did valuable work with the Royal Engineers in many important sectors. He was demobilised in November 1919, holding the General Service and Victory Medals.
67, College Road, Willesden, N.W.10 X18010.

WHALE, G., Pte., R.A.S.C. (M.T.)
Joining in June 1916, he was drafted to German East Africa, where for a year he did valuable work in the R.A.S.C. motor repair shops. During his service abroad he contracted malaria, and was in consequence in hospital for a time.
He was demobilised in September 1919, holding the General Service and Victory Medals.
6, Hawthorn Road, Upper Edmonton, N.18 X17045.

WHALER, A. H., Pte., 12th Suffolk Regiment.
Volunteering in September 1915, he was drafted to the Western Front, where he remained for more than three years. During this time he took part in many engagements, including those at Ypres, the Somme, Bullecourt, Arras and the last Retreat and Advance, and on three occasions was severely wounded.
He was demobilised in February 1919, holding the 1914-15 Star, General Service and Victory Medals.
254, Shirland Road, Maida Hill, W.9 X19571.

WHARTON, C., Pioneer, Royal Engineers.
He joined in September 1916, and on completion of his training was drafted to the Western Front. Whilst overseas he saw service in many important sectors, including the Somme, Arras, Lille and Cambrai, and did valuable work throughout. He returned to England in 1919, when he was demobilised, holding the General Service and Victory Medals.
44, Herries Street, North Kensington, W.10 X18729.

WHEATLEY, W. S., Sapper, R.E.
Volunteering in September 1914, he took part in the Gallipoli campaign in the following year. Afterwards he was sent to Egypt, and with General Allenby's forces saw service in Palestine at Jaffa, Jericho, Beersheba, the Jordan, Gaza and Jerusalem.
He was demobilised in June 1919, holding the 1914-15 Star, General Service and Victory Medals.
75, Alsen Road, Holloway, N.7 X18901.

WHEELDON, A., Special War Worker.
Throughout the war he served at Messrs. Handley Page's Aircraft Works, Cricklewood. His work, which demanded a high degree of technical skill, was of great national importance, and he rendered valuable services until 1918, when, owing to the cessation of hostilities, he resigned.
50a, St. Mary's Road, Craven Park, N.W.10 15116A.

WHEELDON, O., Special War Worker.
This lady was engaged at Park Royal Munition Factory on important work in the inspection department. During her service, which lasted from 1916 until 1919, she fulfilled her duties to the entire satisfaction of her employers.
50a, St. Mary's Road, Craven Park, N.W.10 15116C.

WHEELER, A. H., Pte., 1st West Yorkshire Regt.
Called from the Reserve on the outbreak of hostilities, he was drafted to the Western Front, where he fought through the retreat from Mons and the succeeding engagements up to October 13th, when he was killed in action.
He was entitled to the Mons Star, General Service and Victory Medals. 1, Mirabel Road, Fulham, S.W.6 X17708C.

WHEELER, F., Sergt., R.A.S.C. (M.T.)
Volunteering in January 1915, he proceeded to the Western Front in the same year, and was engaged until the close of the war in carrying men and munitions to various parts of the fighting lines. He was absent from duty for some weeks owing to an accident.
He holds the 1914-15 Star, General Service and Victory Medals, and was demobilised in 1920.
111, Ashmore Road, Harrow Road, Maida Hill, W.9 X19749.

WHEELER, F. J., Saddler, R.F.A.
Volunteering in August 1915, he served for three years in Mesopotamia, first as a gunner and afterwards as a saddler. In 1918, when he was proceeding to France, his ship was torpedoed in the Mediterranean, but he was rescued. After taking part in engagements in various sectors of the Western Front, he was killed in action on October 16th, 1918.
He was entitled to the 1914-15 Star, General Service and Victory Medals.
92, Clarendon Street, Paddington, W.2 X20367.

WHEELER, G., Air Mechanic, Royal Air Force.
He joined in May 1917, and during his training served in many valuable capacities at various aerodromes. Owing to ill-health he was unsuccessful in securing his transfer to a fighting area, and in November 1917 was discharged as medically unfit for military service.
14, Fifth Avenue, Queen's Park Estate, W.10 X18328.

WHEELER, J., Pte., Royal Fusiliers.
He volunteered in August 1914, and in the following year was drafted to the Western Front, where he took part in the battles of Neuve Chapelle, Ypres and Loos. He was wounded and taken prisoner in 1916, and was held in captivity for two years. He was released on the cessation of hostilities, when he returned to England, and in February 1919 was demobilised.
He holds the 1914-15 Star, General Service and Victory Medals.
6, Dartington Terrace, Paddington, W.2 X21560.

WHEELER, W. A., Stoker, Royal Navy.
Volunteering in October 1914, he was posted to the battle-cruiser H.M.S. "Tiger." Whilst on board this ship he served in the North Sea, and took part in several naval engagements, including the battles of the Dogger Bank and Jutland. Afterwards he was transferred to H.M.S. "Highflyer," and for the remainder of his service was engaged in convoying merchant ships between Britain and the United States.
He holds the 1914-15 Star, General Service and Victory Medals, and was demobilised in 1919.
1, Mirabel Road, Fulham, S.W.6 X17708B.

WHEELER, W. J., Driver, R.A.S.C.
He joined in 1917, and after his training was engaged on duties of great importance at various stations. He was not successful in obtaining his transfer overseas before the cessation of hostilities, but did valuable work with the R.A.S.C. before his demobilisation, which took place in 1920.
1, Mirabel Road, Fulham, S.W.6 X17708A.

WHELAN, W. P., Pte., 34th Middlesex Regt.
He volunteered in August 1914, and was sent to France, where he took part in engagements at Mons, Arras, Ypres and on the Somme. He suffered from blood poisoning, was invalided home in November 1915, and was in hospital for three months at Winchester. Later he went to Ireland, and thence to Park Royal and Didcot, where he was stationed until demobilised in 1919, holding the Mons Star, General Service and Victory Medals.
19, Park Lane, Tottenham, N.17 X18875.

WHICHELD, A. E., Pte., R.A.S.C.
He joined in March 1916, and in the same year was ordered to the Western Front. For some time he was engaged on important duties at Remount depots, but later took an active part in engagements on various sectors.
In June 1919 he was demobilised, holding the General Service and Victory Medals.
58, Deacon Road, Cricklewood, N.W.2 17356A.

WHISTLER, A., Pte., 1st Cheshire Regiment.
He volunteered in August 1914, and after a short period of training was drafted to France, where he took part in the memorable retreat from Mons, but was taken prisoner whilst in action on the Marne. For nearly five years he was held captive, during which time he suffered untold hardships, and after the signing of the Armistice was released, and in January 1919 was demobilised, holding the Mons Star, General Service and Victory Medals.
76, Clarendon Street, Paddington, W.2 X20361.

WHITAKER, G. N., Pte., R.A.S.C. (M.T.)
He volunteered in December 1914, and at the end of the same month was drafted to the Western Front. Whilst overseas he did splendid work with the Mechanical Transport Section of the R.A.S.C. in various important sectors, but in consequence of ill-health returned to England in 1916, when he was invalided out of the Service.
He holds the 1914 Star and General Service and Victory Medals.
33, Edenham Street, North Kensington, W.10 X20186.

WHITBY, R., Pte., 19th Middlesex Regiment.
In May 1915 he volunteered for service, and on completion of his training was drafted to the Western Front, where he took part in the battles of the Somme, Arras, Vimy Ridge, Ypres and St. Quentin and in heavy fighting around Loos, Neuve Chapelle and Armentières. He also served in Italy, but returned to France in time for the 1918 Advance.
After the signing of the Armistice he went to Germany with the Army of Occupation, and remained there until he was demobilised in 1919, holding the General Service and Victory Medals.
12, Mirabel Road, Fulham, S.W.6 X17854.

WHITE, A., Bombardier, R.G.A.
Joining in April 1916, he was drafted to the Western Front later in that year, and took part in many important engagements. He was in action at the battle of Ypres, and in the Retreat of 1918, when he was badly wounded and gassed. He was invalided home suffering from shell-shock and was in hospital for many months, being eventually demobilised in January 1919.
He holds the General Service and Victory Medals.
97, Ashmore Road, Harrow Road, W.9   X19656.

WHITE, C. G. L., Pte., Royal Munster Fusiliers.
He joined in 1918, and after his training served at various stations on important duties with his unit. He gave valuable services, but was not successful in obtaining his transfer overseas until after the termination of hostilities. He was then drafted to Egypt, where he was still serving in 1920.
91, Chesson Road, W. Kensington, W.14   X17926A.

WHITE, C. J., Sergt., Northumberland Fusiliers.
He joined in September 1916, and after acting for a time as musketry and bombing instructor, proceeded to the Western Front, where he took a prominent part in the battles of the Somme and the Aisne in the Retreat of 1918, and suffered from gas poisoning.
He was demobilised in November 1919, holding the General Service and Victory Medals.
144, Portnall Road, Maida Hill, W.9   X19658.

WHITE, D. E. M. (Mrs.), Special War Worker.
During the war this lady was engaged at the Munition Factory, Perivale, on work of a very dangerous nature, in the high explosives department. On relinquishing her position she received a letter of thanks for the valuable services which she had rendered.
79, Clarendon Street, Paddington, W.2   TX20397A.

WHITE, E. (Miss), Special War Worker.
This lady was engaged for nine months on work of great importance in the cordite department of the Waltham Abbey Munition Works. She also served in the Land Army for 12 months, and on her discharge in August 1919 was presented with a certificate of appreciation for her valuable services.
18, Tenterden Road, Tottenham, N.17   X18266A.

WHITE, E. T., Pte., Middlesex Regiment.
He volunteered in 1915, and served on the Western Front, where he took part in the battles of the Somme, Arras, Vimy Ridge, Ypres, Cambrai and St. Quentin, and in heavy fighting at Loos, Armentières and Neuve Chapelle.
He holds the General Service and Victory Medals, and was demobilised in 1919.
70c, Lintaine Grove, W Kensington, W.14   X17926B.

WHITE, G. A., Pte., 1st Royal Fusiliers.
He volunteered in September 1915, and was drafted to the Western Front, where he took part in the battles of the Somme, Ypres and Cambrai, and in the heavy fighting near Béthune, Loos and Hill 60. During the Advance in 1918 he was wounded and was invalided home.
In May 1919 he was discharged as medically unfit for further service, holding the General Service and Victory Medals.
29, Droop Street, Queen's Park Estate, W.10   X18577A.

WHITE, H., Driver, R.A.S.C. (H.T.)
He volunteered in August 1914, and in the following May was sent to the Western Front, where he was engaged in transporting food and munitions to the lines, and took part in the battle of Ypres. Later he served with the ambulance column. In 1918 he was transferred to Italy, where he was attached to the Mule Transport section. During his service he was gassed and suffered from shell-shock.
He returned to England and was demobilised in April 1919, holding the 1914-15 Star, General Service and Victory Medals.
79, Clarendon Street, Paddington, W.2   TX20397B.

WHITE, J., Sergt., R.A.S.C.
He volunteered in September 1914, and during his service in France, which lasted until the cessation of hostilities, took an active part in many engagements, and was wounded He holds the 1914-15 Star, General Service and Victory Medals, and was demobilised in February 1919.
3, Sherbrooke Road, Fulham, S.W.6   X18465.

WHITE, J., Pte., Labour Corps.
He joined in August 1918, and during his service in France was engaged on important duties during the Advance of that year. He was badly gassed and invalided home, and was discharged early in November 1918 as medically unfit for further service.
He holds the General Service and Victory Medals.
51, Ravensworth Road, College Park, N.W.10   X17602.

WHITE, J. G., Pte., 1st Middlesex Regiment.
He joined in June 1918, and after a short period of intensive training was drafted to France, where he took a prominent part in the Advance of that year.
He holds the General Service and Victory Medals, and in November 1919 returned to England for demobilisation.
7, Sheldon Road, Upper Edmonton, N.18   X17305.

WHITE, J. J., Special War Worker.
He was engaged on dangerous work at Waltham Abbey Powder Factory for three years, at the end of which he left to go to the Small Arms Factory at Enfield, where he served for six months on duties of an important and responsible nature He carried out his duties in a capable manner and rendered valuable services to his country.
18, Tenterden Road, Tottenham, N.17   X18266B.

WHITE, L. (Mrs.), Special War Worker.
For a considerable period of the war this lady rendered very valuable services as a post woman in the Willesden district. She gave every satisfaction and performed her duties in a commendable manner.
21, Ridgeley Road, Willesden, N.W.10   X17670B.

WHITE, R., Pte., 3rd Middlesex Regiment.
He volunteered for service in April 1915, and after his training was drafted to Salonica. He saw fighting on the Struma Front, where he did excellent work with his unit, but in May 1916 contracted a severe form of typhoid fever, in consequence of which he returned to England.
He was invalided out of the Service in March of the following year, and holds the General Service and Victory Medals.
21, Ridgeley Road, Willesden, N.W.10   X17670A.

WHITE, T., Pte., 1 /3rd London Regiment.
He was mobilised in August 1914, and in the same year went to Malta. Later he served on the Western Front, where he took part in engagements at Ypres, Festubert, Neuve Chapelle and Vimy Ridge.
He was killed in action at Arras on April 17th, 1917, and was entitled to the 1914-15 Star, General Service and Victory Medals.
79, Barnsdale Road, Maida Hill, W.9   X19545.

WHITE, W., Pte., Royal Field Artillery.
He joined in April 1917, and was drafted to France in April 1918, and took part in the Retreat and Advance. He was sent to Germany with the Army of Occupation on the signing of the Armistice, and remained there until demobilised in October 1919.
He holds the General Service and Victory Medals.
13, Westbury Road, Willesden, N.W.10   15068A.

WHITE, W., Pte., Middlesex Regiment, Northumberland Fusiliers and North Staffordshire Regiment.
He volunteered in August 1914, and in the following year was sent to France, where he took part in the battles of Loos, St. Eloi and Vermelles. Later he was transferred to the Northumberland Fusiliers, and drafted to Italy, where, after many engagements, he contracted fever. He was invalided home, and on recovery returned to France, and served with the Military Police. Before the cessation of hostilities he was transferred to the North Staffordshire Regiment, with which he remained until his demobilisation in March 1919.
He holds the 1914-15 Star, General Service and Victory Medals.
3, Hampden Street, Paddington, W.2   X21385.

WHITEHEAD, A., Cpl., Royal Field Artillery.
He was mobilised in August 1914, and crossing at once to France was killed on the 27th of the same month in action during the memorable retreat from Mons.
He was entitled to the Mons Star, General Service and Victory Medals.
30, Bruce Castle Road, Tottenham, N.17   X18552B.

WHITEHEAD, A. R., Pte., R.A.S.C.
He joined in June 1917, and after his training did important work at various stations with his unit. He was not successful in obtaining his transfer overseas before the cessation of hostilities, but rendered valuable services before his demobilisation in May 1919.
19, Balfour Road, Lower Edmonton, N.9   X14039.

WHITEHEAD, J. J., Sapper, Royal Engineers.
Volunteering in 1915, he was in the same year drafted to the Western Front, where he saw service in many important sectors, and was wounded on two occasions.
He was demobilised in 1919, holding the 1914-15 Star, General Service and Victory Medals.
30, Bruce Castle Road, Tottenham, N.17   X18552A.

WHITEHOUSE, T., Gunner, R.F.A.
He volunteered for service in August 1915, and having received training at various stations in England, was drafted to the Western Front in the following year. He took part in numerous important engagements, including the battle of the Somme, and in 1918 was sent to Italy, where he saw action on the Piave. After the cessation of hostilities he served with the Army of Occupation in Germany until 1919, when he returned to England and was demobilised.
He holds the General Service and Victory Medals.
92, Farm Lane, Walham Green, S.W.6   X19640.

WHITFIELD, T. S., Sergt., 1st Dorsetshire Regt.
He volunteered in September 1914, and on completion of his training was drafted to the Western Front. Whilst overseas he took a prominent part in many important engagements, including those at Neuve Chapelle, Ypres, Vimy Ridge, Bullecourt, Loos, St. Quentin and Armentières, and later, in consequence of ill-health, was invalided home. On his recovery he was first transferred to the Middlesex Regiment and then to the 12th Battalion " Queen's," and returned with them to France, where he was in charge of a Chinese Labour Battalion. He holds the 1914 Star, General Service and Victory Medals, and was demobilised in 1919.
38, Orbain Road, Fulham, S.W.6   X18228.

WHITING, C., Pte., 13th The Queen's (Royal West Surrey Regiment).
He joined in July 1916, and was drafted to the Western Front, where he took part in the battles of Ypres, Messines, the Somme, and the Retreat and Advance of 1918. His service overseas lasted for three years, and on one occasion whilst in action he was severely gassed.
He returned to England in 1919, and in March of the same year was demobilised, holding the General Service and Victory Medals.
34, Durban Road, Tottenham, N.17   X18082.

WHITING, E., Cpl., Royal Marine Artillery.
He was called from the Reserve in August 1914, and in the same year was drafted to France, where he served until 1919. During this period he took part in the battles of Mons, the Marne, the Aisne, Ypres, Arras and Cambrai.
He was demobilised in March 1919, and holds the Mons Star, General Service and Victory Medals.
17, Fordingley Road, Maida Hill, W.9   X19723.

WHITING, R. A., Pte., Northamptonshire Regt.
Joining in August 1916, he was sent to the Western Front in the following year. He took part in several engagements, including those at Ypres, Armentières, Passchendaele and the Somme, and was twice wounded and gassed. In 1918 he was taken prisoner, and during his captivity, which lasted until December of the same year, suffered great privation. After his release he was drafted to Egypt, where he served until 1920, when he returned to England and was demobilised.
He holds the General Service and Victory Medals.
26, Durban Road, Tottenham, N.17   X18089

WHITING, W. S., 1st Air Mechanic, R.A.F.
He volunteered in January 1915, and during his service on the Western Front, where he did valuable work with the Royal Air Force, was severely gassed.
He holds the 1914-15 Star, General Service and Victory Medals, and was demobilised in March 1919.
10, Rock Avenue, Fulham Road, S.W.6   X20226.

WHITLING, H., Pte., Duke of Wellington's (West Riding Regiment).
He volunteered in August 1914, and was soon drafted to the Western Front, where, during the retreat from Mons, he was taken prisoner. During his long captivity in Germany he was very badly treated, and was set to work on printing.
He holds the Mons Star, General Service and Victory Medals, and was demobilised on his release in December 1918.
119, Ashmore Road, Harrow Road, W.9   X19753.

WHITTAKER, R., Lce.-Cpl., 9th Royal Sussex Regiment and Royal Engineers.
An ex-Service man, he volunteered in November 1914, and was drafted to the Western Front, where he remained for over four years. During this time he took part in many important engagements, including those at La Bassée, Ypres and Vermelles. In 1916 he was invalided home through ill-health, but in 1917 he returned to France, and remained until the cessation of hostilities.
He was demobilised in February 1919, holding the Queen's and King's South African Medals, the 1914 Star, General Service and Victory Medals.
20, Shelley Road, Willesden, N.W.10   13645B.
25

WHITTICK, R., Cpl., R.G.A.
Volunteering in 1915, he served for 12 months in France and for 18 months in Egypt and Palestine. On each of these Fronts he took part in many important engagements, and in August 1916 was severely wounded in action at Delville Wood.
He was demobilised in March 1919, holding the 1914-15 Star, General Service and Victory Medals.
27, Wycombe Road, Tottenham, N.17   X19075.

WHITTINGTON, A., Driver, R.F.A.
He joined in March 1916, and in the following June was drafted to the Western Front. Whilst overseas he took part in several engagements, including the battles of Vimy Ridge, Arras and La Bassée. In June 1917, owing to ill-health, he returned to England, and in February of the following year was invalided out of the Service.
He holds the General Service and Victory Medals.
42, St. Ervan's Road, North Kensington, W.10   X20384.

WHITTY, J., Rifleman, 13th King's Royal Rifles.
He joined in 1918 on attaining military age, and on completion of his training was sent with the Army of Occupation to Germany, where he remained until February 1920, when he returned to England, and was demobilised.
101, Osterley Park View Road, Hanwell, W.7   12346C.

WICHALL, A., Pte., 2/13th London Regiment (Kensingtons).
Volunteering in November 1914, he was stationed for a time in Ireland, and in June 1916 was drafted to France. Later he saw much service in Salonica, Egypt and Palestine.
He holds the General Service and Victory Medals, and was demobilised in April 1919.
58, Herries Street, N. Kensington, W.10   X18566.

WICKS, H., Pte., R.A.V.C.
He joined in 1917, and after his training served at various stations in Ireland on important duties with his unit.
He gave valuable services, but was unsuccessful in obtaining his transfer overseas before the cessation of hostilities.
He was demobilised in June 1919.
31, Ancill Street, Hammersmith, W 6   13744B.

WIGGINS, T., Pte., 2nd Dublin Fusiliers.
He joined in July 1916, and was sent to the Western Front, where he took part in engagements at Messines Ridge, Ypres, Arras, the Somme and Péronne. Later he served with the Army of Occupation on the Rhine.
He was demobilised in January 1919, holding the General Service and Victory Medals.
86, Stephendale Road, Fulham, S.W.6   X20716.

WIGGINS, W. C., Pte., Royal Fusiliers.
He joined in May 1916, and took part in many actions from 1916 to 1918 on the Eastern Front in Bulgaria and Salonica. In 1918 he was transferred to the Western Front, where he went through the final stages of the war, and later went into Germany with the Army of Occupation.
He was demobilised in August 1919, and holds the General Service and Victory Medals.
229a, Kilburn Lane, North Kensington, W.10   X18718.

WIGMORE, R., Special War Worker.
Although 72 years of age he performed work of national importance at the Hayes Munition Factory. He was engaged in the T.N.T powder shops on work of a very dangerous character, and his service, which lasted three years, proved invaluable throughout.
34, Furness Road, Harlesden, N.W.10   13097B

WIGMORE, R. H., Rifleman, New Zealand Rifle Brigade.
Volunteering in 1914, he was first drafted to Egypt, and thence to the Western Front. He took part in many important engagements, including the battles of the Somme and Armentières, and whilst in action in 1916 was seriously wounded. He returned to England, and after protracted hospital treatment was invalided out of the Service in 1917.
He holds the 1914-15 Star, General Service and Victory Medals.
34, Furness Road, Harlesden, N.W.10   13097C

WILCOCK, E., Pte., R.A.M.C.
He volunteered in August 1914, and was sent to the Western Front in the same year. Whilst overseas, he was present at many important engagements, including the retreat from Mons and in the battles of the Marne and the Aisne. He was also at Ypres, Loos, Arras and Cambrai, and afterwards was drafted to Italy, where he remained for about a year.
He holds the Mons Star, General Service and Victory Medals, and was demobilised in June 1919.
32, Chippenham Road, Maida Hill, W.9   X20882.

WILCOX, F., Special War Worker.
Owing to the great value of his services he was exempted from military duties, and throughout the war was engaged on work of national importance at Messrs. Pinks' Factory, where he fulfilled his responsible duties in a highly commendable manner.
35, Hartington Road, Tottenham, N.17   X19141A.

WILCOX, F. M. (Mrs.), Special War Worker.
During the war this lady was engaged at Wear Hall Works, Edmonton, on work of a delicate and dangerous nature in connection with live charges. She was also at Messrs. Klingers', making gas-masks. During her service, which lasted for about three years, she carried out her duties in a manner worthy of the highest praise.
35, Hartington Road, Tottenham, N.17   X19141B.

WILDEY, E., Pte., 4th Bedfordshire Regiment.
He joined in January 1915,and was sent to the Western Front in the following year. He served for three years in France and fought in several important engagements, among which were Arras, Cambrai and the Somme battles
He was demobilised in February 1919, and holds the General Service and Victory Medals.
48, Napier Road, Kensal Green. N.W.10   X17524.

WILKES, A. D., Gunner, R.F.A.
He was recalled from the Army Reserve in August 1914, and served for nearly five years on the Western Front. He took part in the battles of Mons, the Marne, the Aisne, Ypres, Loos, Vimy Ridge, the Somme, Messines, Arras and several other engagements, and was wounded three times. He was mentioned in dispatches for gallantry, and after the Armistice served with the Army of Occupation in Germany.
In April 1919 he was demobilised, holding the Mons Star, General Service and Victory Medals.
35, Mayo Road, Willesden, N.W.10   15122

WILKINSON, G., Rifleman, King's Royal Rifles.
He joined in 1916, and was sent to the Western Front, where he took part in numerous engagements, including the battle of the Somme. During his service overseas he was twice wounded. On the cessation of hostilities he returned to England, and was demobilised in 1919.
He holds the General Service and Victory Medals.
92, Willow Vale Road, Shepherd's Bush, W.12   12392A.

WILKINSON, H., Pte., East Surrey Regiment.
He volunteered in August 1914, and in the same year was sent to the Western Front. He took part in many engagements, and was killed in action at Hill 6o.
He was entitled to the 1914 Star, General Service and Victory Medals.
92, Willow Vale Road, Shepherd's Bush, W.12   12392B.

WILKINSON, J. E., Driver, R.F.A.
He volunteered in March 1915, and was drafted to France in the same year. Later he was sent to Egypt, where he served until the cessation of hostilities, when he returned to England, and was demobilised in July 1919.
He holds the 1914-15 Star, General Service and Victory Medals.   162, Church Road, Tottenham, N.17   X18134.

WILKINSON, J. W., Staff Sergt., R.E.
Volunteering in 1915, he was drafted to the Western Front. He took part in many important engagements, including the battles of Ypres and the Somme, until his death, which occurred near Arras on December 22nd, 1917.
He was entitled to the 1914-15 Star, General Service and Victory Medals.
59, Durban Road, Tottenham, N.17   X17964.

WILKINSON, L. M. (Miss), Special War Worker.
During the war this lady held an important post at Messrs. Waring and Gillow's Factory at the White City. Throughout her service she carried out her work in an efficient manner, and was worthy of high commendation.
88, Rayleigh Road, West Kensington, W.14   12633B.

WILKINSON, T. W., Rifleman, K.R.R.
He volunteered in 1915, and in the same year was drafted to the Western Front, where he served until 1919. During this time he took part in many important engagements, including those at Ypres, Arras, Albert, St. Quentin, Cambrai, the Somme and the last Advance in 1918.
He was demobilised in May 1919, holding the 1914-15 Star, General Service and Victory Medals.
23, Hiley Road, Willesden, N.W.10   X18171A.

WILLCOX, A., Tpr., 2/1st County of London Yeomanry.
He joined in December 1916, and after his training served at various stations on important duties with his unit. He gave valuable services, but was not successful in obtaining his transfer overseas, before the cessation of hostilities.
He was demobilised in June 1919.
52, Edbrooke Road, Maida Hill, W.9   X21542

WILLCOX, W. A., Rifleman, King's Royal Rifle Corps, and Sapper, Royal Engineers.
He joined in October 1916, and was drafted to the Western Front in January 1917. He took part in much severe fighting in this theatre of war, and during an attack in the Ypres sector was severely injured. He was invalided home, transferred to the Royal Engineers and engaged on important duties until his demobilisation in September 1919.
He holds the General Service and Victory Medals.
89, Fifth Avenue, Queen's Park Estate, W.10   X18737.

WILLER, F. (Mrs.), Special War Worker.
This lady was engaged at Messrs. Blakes' Factory, Hurlingham, on work of a dangerous and delicate nature in connection with shell-filling. During her service she fulfilled her responsible duties in a highly commendable manner.
32, Bronsart Road, Munster Road, S.W.6   X18905.

WILLERTON, A., Pte., 13th Middlesex Regt.
He volunteered in September 1914, and in the following year was sent out to France, where he remained on active service for over four years, and took part in engagements on the Somme and at Loos and Ypres
He was demobilised in February 1919, holding the 1914-15 Star, General Service and Victory Medals.
30, Cranbrook Road, Tottenham, N.17   X18562.

WILLIAMS, A. J., Pte., Labour Corps.
He joined in November 1916, and was engaged on many important duties at various stations throughout his service. He was unsuccessful in obtaining his transfer overseas on medical grounds, but nevertheless did splendid work with his unit until his demobilisation in April 1919.
30, Vallier Road, College Park, N.W.10   X17677.

WILLIAMS, A.M.M. (Mrs.), Special War Worker.
This lady held an important position at Messrs. Blake's Munition Factory, Stevenage Road, Fulham, in the department responsible for the making of shell-boxes. She did excellent work throughout the war, and the manner in which she fulfilled her duties gave entire satisfaction to the firm.
38, Ancill Street, Hammersmith, W.6   13986C.

WILLIAMS, A. W., Pte., 2nd Royal Fusiliers, and Sapper, Royal Engineers.
Volunteering in November 1915, he was sent to the Western Front after the completion of his training. He saw much service with the 550th Field Company, Royal Engineers, in the Kemmel sector and also at many other places.
He returned to England for demobilisation in January 1919, and holds the General Service and Victory Medals.
6, Bravington Road, Maida Hill, W.9   TX19195.

WILLIAMS, E., Pte., The Queen's Own (R.W.K.R.).
He volunteered in June 1915 at the age of sixteen, and having received training at various stations was drafted to the Western Front, where he remained for nearly three years, taking part in many engagements. In 1919 he went with the Expeditionary Force to Russia,where'he was attached to the Oxfordshire and Buckinghamshire Light Infantry.
He holds the General Service and Victory Medals, and was still serving in 1920.
11, Windsor Gardens, Maida Hill, W.9   X20413B.

WILLIAMS, G., Pte., The King's Own (Royal Lancaster Regiment).
He volunteered in 1914, and in the following year was sent out to France, where he was shortly afterwards transferred to Salonica. He saw much fighting on the Doiran Front, and also fought in Serbia in the Balkan campaign.
He was demobilised in March 1919 after his return to England, and holds the 1914-15 Star, General Service and Victory Medals.   61, Purves Road, Kensal Rise, N.W.10   X17797C.

WILLIAMS, S. G., Pte., The Queen's (Royal West Surrey Regiment) and 129th Labour Coy.
Joining in August 1916, he was drafted to the Western Front on completion of his training in February 1917. He served on all sectors, engaged on various important duties such as trench digging and road making.
After two years' of excellent work in France he returned to England for demobilisation in January 1919, and holds the General Service and Victory Medals.
38, Parkfield Road, Willesden, N.W.10   X1741

WILLIAMS, H. C., Cpl., Bedfordshire and Hertfordshire Regiments.
He volunteered for service in October 1915, and was engaged on special duties with his unit until February 1917, when he was drafted to India. During the Afghan campaign of 1919, he was sent up to Rawal Pindi, where he remained until November of the same year, when he returned to England and was demobilised.
He holds the General Service and Victory Medals and the Indian General Service Medal (with clasp—Afghanistan, N.W. Frontier, 1919).
11, Windsor Gardens, Maida Hill, W.9   X20413A.

WILLIAMS, J. E., Sergt., Royal Air Force.
Volunteering in 1914, he was sent out to the Dardanelles in the following year. After much fighting in Gallipoli, he was transferred to Salonica, where he took part in many of the engagements on the Macedonian Front. In 1918, after two years in the Balkans, he was drafted to the Western Front, where he was in action up to the date of the Armistice.
He was demobilised in November 1919, and holds the 1914-15 Star, General Service and Victory Medals.
12, The Ravencroft, Scrubs Lane, Willesden, N.W.10 X17571.

WILLIAMS, L. (Miss), Special War Worker.
This lady was engaged on work of national importance at Messrs. Grahame White's Aircraft Factory on various duties During her service, which lasted for three years, she performed her work in a highly commendable manner. She also did good work on the railways for a time in order to release her brother for military service.
84, Church Road, Willesden, N.W.10   15391B.

WILLIAMS, L., Rifleman, 16th Rifle Brigade.
He volunteered in June 1915, and during his service in France was in action on many sectors of the Front. He saw much fighting on the Somme, and was severely wounded in an engagement at Guillemont in 1916. After being invalided home he was in the following year discharged as unfit.
He holds the General Service and Victory Medals.
63, Purves Road, Kensal Rise, N.W.10   X17798.

WILLIAMS, S., Sergt., 1st (King's) Dragoon Grds.
He volunteered in August 1914, and during his service with the Dragoon Guards did splendid work as an instructor at various depots. He was discharged as medically unfit in December 1915, and in May 1918 died from an illness contracted during his service.
He held the Queen's and King's South African Medals (with five clasps).
72, Fortune Gate Road, Harlesden, N.W.10   13195B.

WILLIAMS, W., Driver, R.A.S.C.
Volunteering in August 1914, he was drafted to the Eastern Front on the completion of his training He saw much fighting in Mesopotamia, and after being wounded in action was transferred to India.
He was discharged on account of ill-health in 1915, and holds the 1914-15 Star, General Service and Victory Medals.
38, Ancill Street, Hammersmith, W.6   13986A.

WILLIAMSON, A., Pte., The Queen's (Royal West Surrey Regiment).
He joined in August 1917, and during his service on the Western Front saw much of the heavy fighting. After taking a prominent part in many important engagements he was wounded in action.
He was invalided home, and for a time was in hospital in England, but was demobilised in September 1919, holding the General Service and Victory Medals.
18, Lintaine Grove, West Kensington, W.14   X17083.

WILLINGALE, W., Pte., Royal Berkshire Regt.
He volunteered in August 1914, and in the same year was sent to the Western Front, where he served in the retreat from Mons. Later he was drafted to Salonica, where he took part in the fighting on the Macedonian Front, and was wounded twice.
He was demobilised in May 1919, and holds the Mons Star, General Service and Victory Medals.
63, Woodchester Street, Paddington, W 2   X20749.

WILLIS, A. (Miss), Special War Worker.
During the war this lady gave valuable services on work of national importance at Messrs. Blake's, Stevenage Road, Fulham. She was engaged on responsible duties, demanding great efficiency and endurance, and by her excellent work proved herself of high value to the firm.
12, Ancill Street, Hammersmith, W.6   13992B.

WILLIS, F. A. (M.M.), Driver, R.F.A.
He volunteered in August 1914, and shortly afterwards was drafted to the Western Front, where he served for nearly five years. During this time he took part in several battles, including those of Ypres, Albert, Vimy Ridge and the Somme, and was severely gassed. He was awarded the Military Medal for the conspicuous bravery he displayed whilst in action at Cambrai in 1918, and after the cessation of hostilities was sent to Germany with the Army of Occupation.
He returned to England in 1919, when he was demobilised, holding the 1914-15 Star, General Service and Victory Medals, in addition to the Military Medal above mentioned.
108, Chippenham Road, Maida Hill, W.9   X20771.

WILLIS, G., Pte., 3rd Middlesex Regiment.
He joined in January 1917, and shortly after proceeded to the Western Front. He saw much fighting up to the cessation of hostilities, and took a prominent part in the battles of Arras, Cambrai and Ypres. Later he went with the Army of Occupation into Germany, where he was still stationed in 1920.
He holds the General Service and Victory Medals.
44, Bathurst Gardens, Kensal R se, N.W.10   X18417A.

WILLIS, G. H., A.B., R.N., H.M.S. " Benbow."
He was in the Navy previous to the opening of hostilities, and during the war served with the Grand Fleet in the North Sea. He was present at the Jutland battle and other important engagements in H.M.S. " Temeraire," and later was sent to Russian waters, where he was serving in 1920.
He holds the 1914-15 Star, General Service and Victory Medals.
168, Kilburn Lane, North Kensington, W 10   X18710A.

WILLIS, S. S., Cpl., Royal Air Force.
He joined in August 1916, and on the completion of his training was sent out to the Western Front. After fighting with distinction at various places he was severely wounded during an air-raid. He was invalided to St. John's Hospital, and was again wounded when it was bombed by the enemy in May 1918.
He was demobilised in April 1919, after his return to England, and holds the General Service and Victory Medals.
65, Warwick Road, Upper Edmonton, N.18   X17513.

WILLIS, T. H., Pte., Bedfordshire Regiment, and Rifleman, Rifle Brigade.
He was in the Army when war broke out, and served on the Western Front for over four years He took part in various engagements, including the battles of Mons, the Marne, the Aisne, Arras, Cambrai and Ypres. He was four times wounded, and suffered from shell-shock whilst abroad.
On his return to England he was demobilised in February 1919, holding the Mons Star, General Service and Victory Medals.
44, Bathurst Gardens, Kensal Rise, N.W.10   X18417B.

WILLS, A., Pte., Royal Sussex Regiment.
He joined in May 1918, and on attaining military age was drafted to France and thence to Germany, where he served on guard duty with the Army of Occupation.
He was demobilised in April 1920, after two years' exemplary service. 85, Ashmore Road, Harrow Road, W.9 X19809.

WILLS, G., Pte., Middlesex Regiment.
He volunteered in August 1914, and served for three years on the Western Front. He fought with distinction on the Somme and Arras sectors and saw much action until 1918. He was then released from the Army in order to go back to his work in the mines.
He holds the 1914-15 Star, General Service and Victory Medals. 8, Waldo Road, College Park, N.W.10 X18189.

WILLS, S. A., Pte., 1st East Surrey Regiment.
He volunteered in 1914, and was immediately sent to the Western Front. He took part in several engagements, was severely wounded in the battle of the Aisne, and died as a result in November 1914.
He was entitled to the 1914 Star, General Service and Victory Medals.
64a, St. Mary's Road, Craven Park, N.W.10   13369B.

WILLSON, W. J., A.B., R.N.R., H.M. Monitor 17.
He was called up from the Reserve in August 1914, and later was sent to the Dardanelles, where he was on active service until the conclusion of hostilities. He returned to England and was demobilised in January 1919, after 19 years' service.
He holds the 1914 Star, General Service and Victory Medals.
82, Stanley Road, King's Road, S.W.6   TY19875.

WILSHER, J. H., Stoker, Royal Navy, H.M.S. " Birmingham."
He volunteerd in August 1914, and served on H.M.S. " Birmingham " in the North Sea. He gave valuable services, taking part in many engagements, and was still in the Navy in 1920.
He holds the 1914-15 Star, General Service and Victory Medals.
63, Warwick Road, Upper Edmonton, N.18   X17512.

WILSON, A., Pte., 1/28th London Regiment (Artists' Rifles).
He volunteered in September 1915, and in the following year was drafted to the Western Front. He saw much of the heavy fighting on the Somme and at the battles of Arras and Albert, and later was transferred to Italy, where he took an active part in many engagements. In 1918 he returned to France, where he served until the cessation of hostilities.
He was demobilised in June 1919, holding the General Service and Victory Medals.
10, Ashford Road, Tottenham, N 17   X18360.

WILSON, E. S., Special War Worker.
During the war he held a responsible position at Messrs. Du Cros', Acton Vale. He showed great efficiency and skill in the performance of his duties, and proved his service of great value to the firm.
92, Willow Vale, Shepherd's Bush, W.12   12392C.

WILSON, G., Cpl., King's Royal Rifles.
He volunteered in September 1914, and during his service on the Western Front took part in many battles, including those of the Somme, Ypres, Albert and Cambrai.
He also fought in the final Retreat and Advance of 1918, and was demobilised in February 1919, holding the 1914–15 Star, General Service and Victory Medals.
9, Mortimer Road, Kensal Rise, N.W.10   X17814.

WILSON, J. (M.M.), Pte., 5th Middlesex Regiment.
He volunteered for service in August 1914, and in the same year went to France, where he took part in many battles, including those of the Somme and Passchendaele, and was wounded four times.
He was awarded the Military Medal for conspicuous gallantry on the field in 1918, holds the Mons Star, General Service and Victory Medals, and was demobilised in March 1919.
76, Raynham Road, Upper Edmonton, N.18   16944A.

WILSON, R. W., Pte., 1st South Staffordshire Regt.
He joined in March 1917, and was almost immediately drafted to France. He took part in the battle of Passchendaele, where he was severely wounded and reported missing. He was presumed killed on October 4th, 1917, and was entitled to the General Service and Victory Medals
11, Newlyn Road, Tottenham, N.17   X18513.

WILSON, T. W., Pte., 2nd Royal Fusiliers.
Volunteering in September 1914, he was drafted almost immediately to Malta. Later he was transferred to the Western Front, and took a prominent part in many important engagements, and was seriously wounded. In 1916 he was invalided home, and discharged in March 1919 medically unfit for further service.
He holds the 1914 Star, General Service and Victory Medals.
5, Armadale Road, Walham Green, S.W 6   X19420.

WILSON, W. H., A.B., Royal Navy.
He volunteered in August 1914, and served on H.M. Ships " Cæsar " and " Gorgan." During the war he was engaged on special patrol duties, and gave valuable services until his demobilisation in February 1919.
He holds the 1914 Star, General Service and Victory Medals.
1, Linton Road, Upper Edmonton, N.18   TX17278.

WILSON, W. J., Private, 15th (The King's) Hussars.
He joined in February 1917, and after serving at Aldershot for nine months, proceeded to Egypt and served with distinction throughout the Palestine and Syrian campaigns.
He holds the General Service and Victory Medals, and was demobilised in April 1920 on his return to England.
33, Siddons Road, Tottenham, N.17   X19151.

WILSON, W. W., Sergt., York and Lancaster Regt.
He volunteered in September 1914, and during his service on the Western Front was engaged on various important duties. He was also on the responsible work of escort duty with the prisoners of war, and was demobilised in March 1919, holding the General Service and Victory Medals.
41, Haldane Road, Walham Green, S.W.6   TX17076A.

WILSON, W. W., Sapper, Royal Engineers.
He joined in January 1917, and after his training was sent to the Western Front, where he took a prominent part in many engagements, including the Battles of Arras, Ypres and the Somme. After the signing of the Armistice he did excellent work with his regiment until he returned home, and was demobilised in April 1919.
He holds the General Service and Victory Medals.
18, Wycombe Road, Tottenham, N.17   X19072.

WILTON, A. E., Pte., 3/9th Middlesex Regiment.
He volunteered in March 1915, and in the following year was drafted to the Eastern Front. He took part in the memorable landing at Gallipoli, and was in other engagements at that period. Later he was transferred to Egypt, and was killed in action during the battle of Gaza on March 26th, 1917. He was entitled to the General Service and Victory Medals.
2, West Block, Garnet Mansions, Garnet Road, Willesden, N W.10   15967C.

WILTSHER, W. H., A.B., R.N., H.M.S. " Venus."
He was in the Navy at the outbreak of hostilities, and in 1914 served in the North Sea. During the war his ship was engaged on patrol duties cruising in many waters. He touched many countries, and saw service off the coasts of China, Egypt Australia, the East Indies, and the Dardanelles.
He was demobilised in February 1919, holding the 1914 Star, General Service and Victory Medals.
48 ,Maybury Gardens, Willesden, N.W.10   X17222.

WILTSHIRE, C. E., Lce.-Cpl., 9th Middlesex Regt.
He volunteered in September 1914, and served on the Western Front, taking part in the battles of the Somme, Cambrai, Neuve Chapelle, Ypres, Loos and Arras. During his service he was wounded, and in April 1919 was demobilised, holding the General Service and Victory Medals.
19, Cooper Road, Dudden Hill, N.W.10   16643A.

WILTSHIRE, G., Pte., The Queen's (Royal West Surrey Regiment).
He volunteered for duty in February 1915, and in the same year proceeded to France, where he took a prominent part in several engagements, including that of Loos, where he was severely gassed.
He was demobilised in November 1919, and holds the 1914–15 Star, General Service and Victory Medals.
43, Heckfield Place, Fulham Road, S.W.6   X20347.

WINDSOR, W. H., Gunner, R.F.A.
He volunteered in February 1915, and in the same year was drafted to Egypt, where he remained doing valuable work, until he was demobilised in 1919.
He holds the 1914–15 Star, General Service and Victory Medals.
35, Holberton Gardens, Willesden, N.W.10   X17550.

WINFIELD, A., C.S.M., Royal Engineers.
He volunteered in August 1914, and served on the Western Front for four years, during which period he took part in many important engagements, including those of Festubert, Givenchy and Loos.
He was twice wounded, and in April 1919 was demobilised, holding the 1914–15 Star, General Service and Victory Medals.
24, Fernhead Road, Maida Hill, W.9   X19389A.

WINGFIELD, F., Pte., R.A.S.C. (M.T.)
He joined in July 1916, and in the following year was drafted to the Western Front. Later he was transferred to Italy, where he was engaged on transporting rations and ammunition to the front lines, and served in the battle of the Piave. He returned to England, and was demobilised in April 1919.
He holds the General Service and Victory Medals.
59, College Road, Willesden, N.W.10   X18013.

WINTERS, S., Sapper, No. 230 Army Troop Coy., Royal Engineers.
He volunteered in June 1915, and went to France, where he served with distinction through several engagements, including those at Arras, Ypres, the Somme and Armentières.
He was demobilised in January 1919, after nearly four years' service, and holds the General Service and Victory Medals.
13, Stanley Grove, White Hart Lane, Tottenham, N.17   X18300.

WISBY, A., Cpl., Royal Army Service Corps.
Having enlisted in October 1900, he was mobilised in 1914, and sent to France, where he took a prominent part in the retreat from Mons and the battles of the Aisne, Ypres, the Somme and Arras. In 1916 he was drafted to Salonica and served there until sent home for demobilisation in April 1919
He holds the Mons Star, General Service and Victory Medals.
1, Buckler's Place, North End Road, Fulham, S.W.6   X17140.

WITHERDEN, C. B. A., Rifleman, 8th London Regiment (Post Office Rifles).
He joined in March 1917, and in the following year was drafted to the Western Front, where he took part in engagements at St. Quentin, La Fère, Amiens and Barisis. He was gassed at Villers-Bretonneux and was wounded in March 1918.
At the conclusion of hostilities he returned to England and was demobilised in September 1919.
163, Kilburn Lane, North Kensington, W.10   X18567.

WITHERDEN, S., Pte., Northumberland Fus.
He volunteered in November 1915, and in the following year was drafted to India. In 1917 he was transferred to Mesopotamia, where he served with distinction in the victorious campaign against the Turks.
At the conclusion of hostilities he returned to England and was demobilised in October 1919, holding the General Service and Victory Medals.
154, Third Avenue, Queen's Park, W.10   X19378.

WITHERS, E. (Mrs.), Special War Worker.
From 1916 until 1918 this lady devoted her time to work of national importance at the Munitions Factory, Neasden. At first she was engaged on shell cleaning, but her exceptional ability soon led to her being appointed to the responsible position of examiner. The manner in which she carried out her arduous duties was worthy of great aise.
16, Holly Lane, Willesden, N.W.10   15581C.

WITHERS, W., Sergt., R.E. (Signals).

Volunteering in 1914, he was sent to the Western Front in the same year. He served in the retreat from Mons and the battle of Ypres, and in 1915 was transferred to Egypt. Whilst in the East he took part in General Allenby's Advance to Palestine, being present at the capture of Jerusalem. In 1919 he returned to England and was demobilised, holding the Mons Star, General Service and Victory Medals.
16, Holly Lane, Willesden, N.W 10   15581B

WOLSTENHOLME, E., Air Mechanic, R.A.F. (late R.N.A.S.)

He joined in May 1916, and served with his unit at various stations on important duties. His work was of a highly technical nature, and he gave valuable services, but was not successful in obtaining his transfer overseas.
He was demobilised in 1919.
134, Bronsart Road, Munster Road, S.W.6   X18993A.

WOLSTENHOLME, E. H. (Mrs.), Nurse, V.A.D.

Throughout the war she served at the Kensington Infirmary tending the wounded. She was also on duty at various processions with the St John's Ambulance, rendering first aid. During her service she carried out her duties in a highly commendable manner.
134, Bronsart Road, Munster Road, S.W.6   X18993B.

WOND, A. E. (Mrs.), Special War Worker.

This lady was engaged at Messrs. Du Cros' Munition Factory, Acton, on shell work in the inspection department, where she rendered very valuable assistance in the output of munitions.
100, Chesson Road, West Kensington, W 14   X17246B.

WOND, H. J., Driver, R.H.A. (Ammunition Col.)

He volunteered in January 1915, and in the same year went to the Western Front, where he served in various engagements, and took part in the battles of the Somme, Loos, Ypres and Cambrai.
In March 1919 he was demobilised, and holds the 1914–15 Star, General Service and Victory Medals.
54, Allestree Road, Munster Road, Fulham, S.W. 6TX19213.

WOND, H. J., Gunner, R.F.A.

He volunteered in August 1914, and was sent to the Western Front, where he took part in many engagements, and was present at the battles of Arras, Loos, Neuve Chapelle, Armentières, Ypres, Vimy Ridge, Bullecourt, and St. Quentin. He was also in the Retreat and Advance of 1918.
He was demobilised in 1919, holding the 1914–15 Star, General Service and Victory Medals.
100, Chesson Road, West Kensington, W.14   X17246A.

WOOD, A., Pte., 1st Queen's Own (Royal West Kent Regiment).

Volunteering in 1915, he was sent in the same year to France, where he played a conspicuous part in the fighting and was gassed and wounded. He was reported missing after the fighting in Trones Wood on July 15th, 1916, and later killed in action.
He was entitled to the 1914–15 Star, General Service and Victory Medals.
67, Bulwer Road, Upper Edmonton, N.18   X17892.

WOOD, A. J., Driver, Royal Engineers.

He volunteered in April 1915, and in August was sent to the Western Front, where he took part in several engagements, including those of the Somme, Ypres and Armentières. In 1917 he was drafted to Italy, and served there for two years. He returned to England and was demobilised in February 1919, holding the 1914–15 Star, General Service and Victory Medals.
38, Wornington Road, N. Kensington, W.10   X20862

WOOD, C. W., Driver, R.A.S.C.

He joined in 1917, and in the same year was sent to France. Whilst overseas he played an important part in numerous engagements, including the battle of the Somme. At the conclusion of hostilities he returned to England and was demobilised in 1919.
He holds the General Service and Victory Medals.
16, Sheldon Road, Upper Edmonton, N.18   X17303.

WOOD, H. J., Pte., Royal Army Medical Corps.

He was called up from the Reserve in August 1914 and was drafted to the Western Front, where he served in the retreat from Mons. He was also present at the battles of the Aisne, the Marne, the Somme, Ypres, Neuve Chapelle, and was engaged in attending to the wounded on the field of action, and was himself wounded. Later he was transferred to the hospital ships voyaging to and from Egypt, and did duty on H.M.S. "St. Denis" and "Wandiller."
He was demobilised in February 1919, and holds the Mons Star, General Service and Victory Medals.
5, Senior Street, Paddington, W.2   X21407.

WOODBRIDGE, F., Pte., 11th Middlesex Regt.

He volunteered in November 1914, and served in France for four years, during which time he took part in many important engagements, including those of Cambrai and Loos.
He was demobilised in February 1919, holding the 1914–15 Star, General Service and Victory Medals.
2, Seymour Avenue, Tottenham, N.17   X19167.

WOODBRIDGE, S., Pte. (Rough Rider), R.A.S.C.

He volunteered in 1914, and served at Rouen, where he was engaged in breaking-in horses. The continual riding produced heart strain, and he was for three months in a military hospital at Whitchurch, after which he was discharged in 1915 as physically unfit for further service.
He holds the 1914 Star, General Service and Victory Medals.
3, Mablethorpe Road, Munster Road, S.W.6   X19124.

WOODBRIDGE, W., Pte., East Surrey Regt.

He volunteered in August 1914, was sent to France in the same year and took part in the battles of Mons, Loos, the Somme and Ypres.
He holds the Mons Star, General Service and Victory Medals, and was still serving in 1920.
35, Aspenlea Road, Hammersmith. W.6   14295A.

WOODMAN, S., Pioneer, Royal Engineers.

He joined in August 1916, and in the same year was sent out to Salonica, where he served until 1919. He was in action at Monastir and on the Vardar and the Doiran Fronts.
He returned to England and was demobilised in May 1919, holding the General Service and Victory Medals.
10b, Marine Field Road, Fulham, S.W.6   X21490.

WOODROFF, C., Sergt., Royal Fusiliers.

He volunteered in August 1914, and was sent to the Dardanelles. Later he was drafted to France, where he took a distinguished part in engagements on the Somme, at Arras, Armentières, Amiens, St. Quentin and the Advance of 1918. During his service he was wounded.
He holds the 1914–15 Star, General Service and Victory Medals.
32, Orbain Road, Fulham, S.W.6   X18226A.

WOODROFF, M. (Mrs.), Special War Worker.

Being anxious to serve her Country, this lady accepted a position at Messrs. Blake's Munition Factory, and was engaged on work of a most important nature. Her services proved of great value to the firm, and she was worthy of high praise.
32, Orbain Road, Fulham, S.W.6   X18226B.

WOODS, A., Pte., Machine Gun Corps.

Volunteering in August 1914, he was sent in 1917 to the Western Front, where he took part in the battles of Ypres and the Somme, and was wounded. He also served with the Middlesex and the London Regiments and the R.F.A., and was demobilised in August 1919, holding the General Service and Victory Medals.
18, Holly Lane, Willesden, N.W.10   T15580A.

WOODS, A. G., Pte., 3rd Royal Fusiliers.

Volunteering in July 1915, he was sent to the Dardanelles, and was actively engaged in this theatre of war until the evacuation of the Peninsula. He was drafted to France in July 1916, and took part in the battle of the Somme, where he was severely wounded. In consequence he was invalided to England and subsequently discharged as medically unfit for further service in October 1916.
He holds the 1914–15 Star, General Service and Victory Medals.
47, Hiley Road, Willesden, N.W.10   X18235.

WOODS, C. H., Sergt., Royal Fusiliers.

He joined in August 1917, and after his training served on the Western Front. During his service in this theatre of war he was in action in many important engagements and in the Retreat and Advance of 1918, and was wounded in August.
He was demobilised in February 1920, and holds the General Service and Victory Medals.
28, Berry Street, Willesden, N.W.10   15414A.

WOODS, S. (Mrs.), Special War Worker.

During the war this lady offered her services and was engaged by the Park Royal Munition Factory Authorities on work of national importance in connection with the making of boxes for shells. Her onerous duties were carried out in a highly satisfactory manner.
18, Holly Lane, Willesden, N.W.10   15580C.

WOOLFORD, F. L., Pte., Grenadier Guards.

He joined in February 1918, and served at various stations on important duties with his unit. He gave valuable services, but was not successful in obtaining his transfer overseas before the cessation of hostilities.
He was demobilised in September 1919.
4, Windsor Gardens, Maida Hill, W.9   X20410.

WOOLLETT, H., Pte., 23rd Middlesex Regiment.
He joined in June 1916, and was drafted to France in the same year. Whilst on the Western Front he was actively engaged in much of the severe fighting until he was killed in action on the Somme on September 22nd, 1917.
He was entitled to the General Service and Victory Medals.
10, Swan Terrace, Pretoria Road, Tottenham, N.17 X17935.

WOOLLEY, L., S.M., R.A.O.C.
Volunteering at the outbreak of war he took a distinguished part in the retreat from Mons and the battles of the Somme, Arras, Ypres and Neuve Chapelle, and the Advance of 1918. After over four years' service he was demobilised in April 1919, and holds the Mons Star, General Service and Victory Medals.
39, Mirabel Road, Fulham, S.W.6 X17715A.

WOOLLEY, R. (Mrs.), Special War Worker.
During the war this lady was engaged at Messrs. Blake's Munition Works, Stevenage Road, Fulham, on responsible duties as an inspector in the department for making hand-grenades. She rendered very valuable services throughout.
39, Mirabel Road, Fulham, S.W.6 X17715B.

WOOLLEY, W. C., Pte., 22nd Royal Fusiliers.
He volunteered in May 1915, and served on the Western Front for three years, during which time he took part in the battles of Ypres, Bourlon Wood, Vimy Ridge, the Somme and Cambrai, and was twice wounded.
In February 1919 he was demobilised, holding the 1914–15 Star, General Service and Victory Medals
204, Shirland Road, Maida Hill, W.9 X19602.

WOOLMER, A. E. (Mrs.), Special War Worker.
During the war this lady was engaged at Messrs. Blake's Munition Works, Stevenage Road, Fulham, and held a responsible position in the box shop, where she rendered very valuable services.
11, Aintree Street, Dawes Road, S.W.6 15029B.

WOOLMER, R., Rifleman, 21st London Regt. (1st Surrey Rifles).
He joined in 1916, and served on the Western Front, where he took part in the battles of the Somme and High Wood. After undergoing an operation at No. 7 General Hospital, France, he was invalided home and finally discharged unfit for further service in 1918.
He holds the General Service and Victory Medals.
11, Aintree Street, Dawes Road, S.W.6 15029C.

WOOTTON, C. R., Pte., Lancashire Fusiliers.
He was serving at the outbreak of war, and in August 1914 was sent to the Western Front, where he took part in the retreat from Mons and the battles of the Marne and the Aisne. He was severely wounded in the Cambrai sector towards the end of 1914, and taken prisoner. He remained in captivity until after the Armistice, when he returned to England for demobilisation in March 1919.
He holds the Mons Star, General Service and Victory Medals.
86, Wakeman Road, Kensal Rise, N.W.10 X18658A.

WOOTTON, D. E. H., Pte., 2/19th London Regt.
He volunteered in February 1915, and being sent to the Western Front in June 1917, was in action at Ypres, Arras and Cambrai. In the following year he went to Egypt, where he took part in the Palestine campaign, and was present at the capture of Jerusalem.
He suffered from malaria whilst abroad, and in March 1919 was sent home and demobilised, holding the General Service and Victory Medals.
86, Wakeman Road, Kensal Rise, N.W.10 X18658B.

WOOTTON, H. C. F., Cpl., 9th London Regiment (Queen Victoria's Rifles).
He joined in March 1916, and at the conclusion of his training was drafted to the Western Front. During his service in this theatre of war he was engaged in much of the heavy fighting and was wounded in the Somme sector in 1917.
He holds the General Service and Victory Medals, and was demobilised in March 1919.
12, Hazelbury Road, Lower Edmonton, N.9 X17497.

WOOTTEN, J. W., Sergt., Royal Engineers.
Volunteering in 1914, he was drafted to the Western Front, where he played a prominent part in the battles of the Somme, Arras and Ypres and the Advance of 1918, and was wounded. Later he served with the Army of Occupation in Germany until he was demobilised in 1919.
He holds the 1914–15 Star, General Service and Victory Medals.
53, Chesson Road, W. Kensington, W.14 X17153.

WORLEY, F. G., Q.M.S., R.A.S.C.
He was serving at the outbreak of war, and proceeding to the Western Front with the first Expeditonary Force, was engaged on important duties in connection with the supplies of ammunition and stores to the forward areas. In 1915 he was sent to Salonica, where he gave valuable services, and later he went to Turkey.
He returned to England in February 1920, and was discharged, holding the 1914 Star, General Service and Victory Medals.
1, Letchford Gardens, Willesden, N.W.10 X17540.

WORSLEY, J., Driver, Royal Engineers.
He volunteered in June 1915, and on completion of his training served at various stations with his unit until 1917, when he was drafted to Egypt. He was in General Allenby's Forces, and was engaged on important transport duties during the advance through Palestine.
He holds the General Service and Victory Medals, and was demobilised in August 1919.
166, Fifth Avenue, Queen's Park Estate, W.10 X18731.

WOULFE, P., Pte., 2nd Royal Munster Fusiliers.
He was mobilised in August 1914, and quickly proceeded to the Western Front, where he took part in the battle of Mons and was wounded and taken prisoner. Whilst in captivity in Germany he was forced to work in the iron pits and in a munition factory, and suffered much from ill-treatment. He was in hospital for some months and was imprisoned for a time for taking the part of a British officer who was being insulted by his captors.
In April 1919 he was demobilised, holding the Mons Star, General Service and Victory Medals
81, Barnsdale Road, Maida Hill, W.9 X19548.

WREN, C., Cpl., Royal Fusiliers.
He volunteered in 1914, and on completing his training was drafted to the Dardanelles in the following year. He was in action in the heavy fighting in this theatre of war, and after the evacuation of the Peninsula was sent to France, where he was taken prisoner in 1917. He remained in captivity until 1918, when he was released.
He returned to England and was discharged, holding the 1914–15 Star, General Service and Victory Medals
12, Tilson Road, Tottenham, N.17 X19093.

WRIGHT, A., Cpl., R.A.V.C.
Volunteering in 1915, he was later in the same year sent to France, where he was engaged on important duties tending sick and wounded horses. He was in hospital whilst overseas owing to a severe kick from a horse.
In 1919 he was demobilised, holding the 1914–15 Star, General Service and Victory Medals.
19, Wingmore Road, Tottenham, N.17 X17980D.

WRIGHT, A., Mechanic, R.A.S.C. (M.T.)
He volunteered in 1915, and after his training served at many stations on important duties with his unit. He was discharged later in the same year as medically unfit for further military duties, after giving valuable services.
19, Wingmore Road, Tottenham, N.17 X17980B.

WRIGHT, A. G. D., Driver, R.A.S.C. (M.T.)
He volunteered in February 1915, and was sent to France in the same year. Whilst overseas he was engaged in conveying food and ammunition to the lines in various sectors, and also acted as a dispatch rider.
He was demobilised in 1919, and holds the 1914–15 Star, General Service and Victory Medals.
54, Third Avenue, Queen's Park Estate, W.10 X19287B.

WRIGHT, A. J., Sergt., 13th London Regiment (Kensington).
He volunteered in October 1914, and in July 1915 was sent to the Dardanelles, where he took part in the landing at Suvla Bay. On the evacuation of the Peninsula he was sent to Egypt and Palestine, where he fought in the capture of Jerusalem.
He was demobilised in July 1919, and holds the 1914–15 Star, General Service and Victory Medals.
52, Distillery Road, Brentford. 9734—9735A.

WRIGHT, C., 1st Cl. Petty Officer, Royal Navy (Chatham Division).
He enlisted in May 1906, and in 1910 took part in the Somali-land and Persian Gulf expeditions. In August 1914 he was drafted to the Western Front, where he took part in the defence of and retreat from Antwerp, and in the following year was sent to the Dardanelles. He was present at the first landing at Suvla Bay, and also during the evacuation of Gallipoli, after which he was promoted to first-class petty officer. Later he was on escort duty to the American Army when crossing the Atlantic and the Channel.
He was demobilised in February 1919, holding the Naval General Service Medal (with the Persian Gulf clasp), the Africa General Service Medal, the 1914 Star, General Service and Victory Medals.
4, Ridgeley Road, Willesden, N.W.10 X17781.

WRIGHT, E., Lce.-Cpl., 1st Hampshire Regt.

He volunteered for duty in May 1915, and was sent to the Western Front, where he took part in many important engagements, including those of Ypres, Arras and the Somme. He was badly wounded in May 1917, and discharged in November of the following year as medically unfit for further service.
He holds the General Service and Victory Medals.
35, Burrow's Road, Willesden, N.W.10   X18251.

WRIGHT, E., Pte., South Wales Borderers.

He joined in 1916, and after his training was sent to the Western Front. Whilst in this theatre of war he took part in much heavy fighting, and was killed in action at Delville Wood on December 17th, 1917.
He was entitled to the General Service and Victory Medals.
347, North End Road, Fulham, S.W.6   15146A.

WRIGHT, F. E., 1st-Class Gunner, R.N., H.M.S. "Ark Royal."

He volunteered in August 1914, and almost immediately proceeded to sea. He took a prominent part in the naval operations at the Dardanelles, during which his ship was torpedoed, and he was badly injured. On the evacuation of the Gallipoli Peninsula he served with the Grand Fleet in the North Sea.
He holds the 1914 Star, General Service and Victory Medals, and in 1920 was still serving.
19, Wingmore Road, Tottenham, N.17   17980A.

WRIGHT, F. W., Pte., Royal Army Service Corps.

He volunteered in August 1914, and in the following year went to the Dardanelles, where he was present at the first landing in Gallipoli in April 1915. After serving on the Eastern Front he was drafted to France, where he was engaged with the R.A.S.C. in the Somme sector and at Arras until the cessation of hostilities.
He was demobilised in May 1919, and holds the 1914-15 Star, General Service and Victory Medals.
106, Clarendon Street, Paddington, W.2   X20156.

WRIGHT, H., Mechanic, Royal Air Force.

He joined in March 1917, and after his training served at various stations on important duties, which called for a high degree of skill, with the Royal Air Force.
He was medically unfit for military duties abroad, but rendered valuable services with his unit until he was demobilised in May 1919.
128, Church Road, Tottenham, N.17   X18139.

WRIGHT, M. C., Sapper, R.E. (Mounted).

Volunteering in 1915, he was sent to France in the same year and took part in many important operations whilst on the Western Front. After the signing of the Armistice he went to Germany with the Army of Occupation, remaining there until he was demobilised in 1919.
He holds the 1914-15 Star, General Service and Victory Medals.
19, Wingmore Road, Tottenham, N.17   X17980C.

WRIGHT, R., Pte., 4th Middlesex Regiment.

He volunteered in August 1914, and in December of that year went to the Western Front, where he took part in many engagements, and was wounded. Owing to ill-health he was discharged in February 1915 as medically unfit for further military duties.
He holds the 1914-15 Star, General Service and Victory Medals.
309, Shirland Road, Maida Hill, W.9   X19563.

WRIGHT, R. P. (Mrs.), Special War Worker.

During the war this lady rendered valuable services to her country. She was first engaged as a ticket collector on the London and North-Western Railway at Willesden, and thereby released a man for military duty. Later she held a responsible position in the inspection department of the Rotax Munition Factory, where she remained for several months. She received high commendation for her work.
54, Third Avenue, Queen's Park Estate, W.10   X19287A.

WRIGHT, S. J., Special Constable, Brentford Div.

At the outbreak of hostilities he was a member of St. John's Ambulance Brigade and was on duty during air-raids, assisting and transporting the wounded. In September 1914 he joined the Special Constabulary and was engaged on important guard duties at Ealing. In June 1916 he became a member of the 31st Middlesex Voluntary Aid Detachment and carried out duties at a large military hospital when not engaged as a special constable. He gave very valuable services throughout.
52, Distillery Road, Brentford.   9734—9735B.

WRIGHT, S. W., Pte., 4th Royal Fusiliers.

He was mobilised from the Reserve immediately on the outbreak of hostilities, and was sent to France in August 1914. Whilst on the Western Front he took part in the retreat from Mons and in heavy fighting at Bailleul and Kemmel, where he was wounded in December of the same year. He was invalided home, and on his recovery was engaged on important duties until April 1916.
He was then discharged as medically unfit for further service owing to his wounds, holding the Mons Star, General Service and Victory Medals.
He has completed nearly 14 years' service with the Colours and the Reserve.
54, Beethoven Street, N. Kensington, W.10   X18741.

WRIGHT, W., Pte., Royal Fusiliers.

He volunteered in August 1914, and in the same year went to Malta, where he was engaged on important police duty and as a warder in charge of German prisoners.
He holds the General Service and Victory Medals, and was demobilised in February 1919.
4, Portnall Road, Maida Hill, W.9   X19371.

WRIGHT, W. J., Pte., R.A.S.C. (M.T.)

He volunteered in August 1914, and in the following year went to France, where he was engaged on important duties in the work-shops, repairing motor lorries.
He was demobilised in May 1919, holding the 1914-15 Star, General Service and Victory Medals.
18, Gilstead Road, Fulham, S.W.6   X21523.

WROOT, A. G., Pte., 16th (The Queen's) Lancers.

He enlisted in 1909, and in 1916 was sent to the Western Front, where he took part in engagements on the Somme and at Merville and Béthune. During his service overseas he was severely gassed.
He holds the General Service and Victory Medals, and was demobilised in January 1919.
53, Shorrolds Road, Walham Green, S.W.6   TX19351.

WYBOURNE, F. F. C., Pte., 4th Hampshire Regt.

He volunteered in August 1914, and was immediately sent to the Western Front, where he took part in the retreat from Mons and the battles of the Marne, Ypres and Hill 60. He was wounded in action at Ypres and Kemmel, and in 1916 was drafted to Mesopotamia. While in this theatre of war he again saw much fighting, and in 1918 went to India. He contracted dysentery, and was invalided out of the Service in July 1919 on that account.
He holds the Mons Star, General Service and Victory Medals.
39, Winchelsea Road, Willesden, N.W.10   13723.

WYBREW, W. S., Rifleman, 9th London Regt. (Queen Victoria's Rifles).

Volunteering in 1914, he was drafted to France in the following year, and took part in the battles of St. Eloi, Hill 60, and Ypres, and in heavy fighting at Arras. He was wounded and gassed during his service and was discharged, but re-enlisted after a short period. In 1916, however, he was finally discharged as medically unfit for further service, having lost the use of one lung as the result of gas poisoning.
He holds the 1914-15 Star, General Service and Victory Medals.
94, Holly Lane, Willesden, N.W.10   15394A.

WYKES, W., Pte., Royal Army Service Corps.

He volunteered in January 1915, and was later drafted to the Western Front, where he was engaged on important transport duties. After a period of service in this theatre of war he was sent to Italy, and was in hospital some time there owing to a serious illness.
He holds the General Service and Victory Medals, and was demobilised in May 1919.
28, Kilmaine Road, Munster Road, S.W.6   X18760

WYNESS, W., Lce.-Cpl., Scots Guards and M.F.P

Volunteering in December 1914, he was drafted to the Western Front in the following June. Whilst in this seat of war he took a prominent part in heavy fighting at Ypres and in the battle of Loos, where he was wounded in September 1915. He was invalided home, and on his recovery transferred to the Military Foot Police, with which unit he rendered valuable services until his demobilisation in November 1918.
He holds the 1914-15 Star, General Service and Victory Medals.
106, Chippenham Road, Maida Hill, W.9   X20770.

YATES, J., Pte., 7th London Regiment.

He volunteered in April 1915, and during his service on the Western Front took part in many of the principal engagements and was badly wounded.
In September 1916 he was discharged as unfit for further service, and holds the 1915 Star, General Service and Victory Medals.
9, Allestree Road, Munster Road, S.W.6   TX19257.

YATES, W., Private, York and Lancaster Regiment.

He was mobilised in August 1914, having previously served in the Army for nine years, and was almost immediately drafted to France. He took part in numerous engagements and was severely wounded and invalided home. After some months in hospital, he was discharged in March 1916 as physically unfit for further military service.
He holds the 1914 Star, General Service and Victory Medals.
35, Grove Street, Upper Edmonton, N.18   X17487.

YATES, W. G., Sapper, Royal Engineers.

Volunteering in October 1915, he went to France in 1917, and took part in many battles, including those of Ypres, the Somme, and the Retreat and Advance of 1918, when he was wounded.
He holds the General Service and Victory Medals, and was demobilised in February 1919.
26, Lydford Road, Maida Hill, W.9   TX19687.

YEXLEY, C. W., Sapper, Royal Engineers.

He volunteered in 1915, and after his training was employed on important duties with the Inland Water Transport. He gave valuable service, but was not successful in procuring his transfer to a theatre of war prior to the cessation of hostilities.
He was demobilised in 1919.
119, Mirabel Road, Fulham, S.W.6   X17859.

YEXLEY, E. A., Special War Worker.

During the war he held a responsible position at the Vacuum Cleaner Co.'s Works, Fulham, where he was engaged on important work in connection with the manufacture of petrol tanks for Handley Page aeroplanes. His exceptional knowledge of this work proved of the greatest value to the firm.
119, Mirabel Road, Fulham, S.W.6   X17855.

YOUNG, A. J., Engine Room Artificer, Royal Navy, H.M.S. "Curacoa."

He joined in May 1918, and served on patrol duty in the North Sea, and off the coasts of Sweden and Holland, until demobilised in January 1919.
He holds the General Service and Victory Medals.
13, Lopen Road, Upper Edmonton, N.18   XT17931.

YOUNG, C. A., Sergt., Middlesex Regiment.

He volunteered in August 1914, and in the same year was sent to the Western Front. He served through the Mons Retreat, and was in action at Ypres and the Somme, where he was wounded, and other important engagements.
He was demobilised in July 1919, holding the Mons Star, General Service and Victory Medals.
172, Brettenham Road, Upper Edmonton, N.18   15225B.

YOUNG, F. H., Pte., 19th Durham Light Infantry.

He joined in July 1916, and in the following December was drafted to France, where he remained for two years. During this period he took part in engagements at Ypres, Albert and the Somme, and was severely wounded at Aveluy Wood in June 1918.
He was invalided home and discharged in October 1918, and holds the General Service and Victory Medals.
69, Stephendale Road, Fulham, S.W.6   X21029.

YOUNG, G. W., Gunner, Royal Field Artillery.

He joined in July 1916, and rendered valuable service at various stations until February 1918, when he was drafted to France and took part in many of the principal engagements in the Retreat and Advance of 1918.
He was demobilised in April 1919, holding the General Service and Victory Medals.
63, St. Margaret's Road, Willesden, N.W.10   X17823.

YOUNG, H. J., Pte., Royal Marine Light Infantry.

He volunteered in 1915, and after his training was posted to H.M.S. "Champion" for service with the Grand Fleet in the North Sea. At the conclusion of hostilities he returned to his base, and was demobilised in 1919, holding the General Service and Victory Medals.
172, Brettenham Road, Upper Edmonton, N.18   15225A.

YOUNG, R. J., Pte., 1st Queen's (Royal West Surrey Regiment) and Royal Air Force.

He volunteered in November 1914, and during his service on the Western Front took part in the battles of the Somme, Ypres, Arras, and Cambrai. He was twice wounded, and was in hospital in France and England for a long time.
He also served in the R.A.F. prior to his demobilisation in April 1919, holding the 1914–15 Star, General Service and Victory Medals.
22, Pellant Road, Fulham, S.W.6   X17730.

Printed in the United Kingdom
by Lightning Source UK Ltd.
127370UK00003B/41-100/A